REDFERN AND HUNTER
ON INTERNATIONAL ARBITRATION

REDFERN AND HUNTER ON INTERNATIONAL ARBITRATION

SIXTH EDITION

NIGEL BLACKABY
CONSTANTINE PARTASIDES QC
WITH
ALAN REDFERN
MARTIN HUNTER

UNIVERSITY PRESS

Great Clarendon Street, Oxford, OX2 6DP,
United Kingdom

Oxford University Press is a department of the University of Oxford.
It furthers the University's objective of excellence in research, scholarship,
and education by publishing worldwide. Oxford is a registered trade mark of
Oxford University Press in the UK and in certain other countries

© Nigel Blackaby, Constantine Partasides, Alan Redfern, Martin Hunter, 2015

The moral rights of the authors have been asserted

Fifth Edition published in 2009
Sixth Edition published in 2015

Impression: 6

All rights reserved. No part of this publication may be reproduced, stored in
a retrieval system, or transmitted, in any form or by any means, without the
prior permission in writing of Oxford University Press, or as expressly permitted
by law, by licence or under terms agreed with the appropriate reprographics
rights organization. Enquiries concerning reproduction outside the scope of the
above should be sent to the Rights Department, Oxford University Press, at the
address above

You must not circulate this work in any other form
and you must impose this same condition on any acquirer

Crown copyright material is reproduced under Class Licence
Number C01P0000148 with the permission of OPSI
and the Queen's Printer for Scotland

Published in the United States of America by Oxford University Press
198 Madison Avenue, New York, NY 10016, United States of America

British Library Cataloguing in Publication Data
Data available

Library of Congress Control Number: 2015945725

ISBN 978–0–19–871425–5 (Pbk.)

Printed and bound by CPI Group (UK) Ltd, Croydon, CR0 4YY

Links to third party websites are provided by Oxford in good faith and
for information only. Oxford disclaims any responsibility for the materials
contained in any third party website referenced in this work.

PREFACE

It is difficult to believe that over a decade has passed since we first sat down over dinner in Paris with our friends and mentors, Alan Redfern and Martin Hunter, to begin a generational transfer of their seminal work on international arbitration. Our excitement at holding the reins of parts of the work from which we learned our trade was soon accompanied by author's block. How could we honour the tradition of a work known for its style and synthesis without extending its length in a world where arbitration was in a process of normalisation and relevant sources, jurisdictions, and laws were multiplying by the day. That challenge was all the greater as we were tasked with making the work even more international. But as students of the book ourselves, we understood that the genius of *Redfern and Hunter* was its status as an elegantly written, easily comprehensible synthesis of arbitration law and practice. It was not intended to be an exhaustive encyclopaedia of arbitral sources or precedents. And the heart of the arbitral process, despite many attacks, remains as true today as it was in 1986 when the first edition was published: an independent dispute resolution process to assist international business (and states) in which private individuals selected by the parties would hear their disputes and render a binding decision enforceable throughout the world. So whilst we take care to address the proliferating novelties in the arbitration world—whether the ever stronger influence of investment arbitration, the arrival of the emergency arbitrator, the development of soft law on conflicts, ethics, and evidence, or the growing jurisprudence on arbitrator challenges, we have sought to ensure that these novelties do not overshadow the essence of the arbitral process. This in turn has allowed us to keep our promise of a single volume work.

The product of our approach will be immediately recognisable to those of you familiar with earlier editions. Our structure remains untouched. It follows an international arbitration chronologically through its life with a brief parenthesis to look at the influence of arbitration pursuant to investment treaties. As befits a work whose authors learned their trade as advocates and arbitrators, it has a strong practical focus. For this, it draws on the authors' cumulative century of experience in international arbitration.

This edition embraces the many changes that have taken place since the publication of the fifth edition in October 2009. Indeed, we delayed publication by a year to ensure we had fully integrated all of the major new rules and guidelines that have been refreshed in recent years. It therefore addresses the changes of the 2010 UNCITRAL Rules, the 2011 French Arbitration Law, the 2012 ICC Rules, and the changes to the ICDR and LCIA Rules in 2014. We also analyse the evolution of soft law such as the revised IBA Guidelines on Conflict of Interest and Party Representation. It expands references to international sources and the many developments in investment arbitration. It draws more deeply from key jurisprudence emanating from the United States, as well as arbitration's new venues: from China to Brazil, from Russia to Venezuela, and from the Middle East to Sub-Saharan Africa.

Finding the time for a work of this scope is a challenging task for busy practitioners. We have been delighted that Alan and Martin have continued to play an extremely active role, maintaining the lead pen on two key chapters and reviewing our work with an eagle eye for inconsistencies and inelegance of expression. Indeed, one of the greatest pleasures of this exercise is the excuse to retain frequent contact with two of the modern founders of international arbitration who combine insight and experience with humour and humility in equal doses. We hope that this generational collaboration will continue because we are the richer for it.

Of course, we thank our families for their unfailing support. This book is not written in place of our professional demands but in hours stolen from other parts of our lives. Without the support of Maria and Patricia, we wouldn't have advanced beyond our first edition and yet we are now proud to have completed our third edition as a team.

Our ability to ensure we were fully briefed on developments before putting pen to paper is due to the assistance of many talented international arbitration practitioners we have come to know and respect throughout the world in addition to a pool of young and talented lawyers who gave us a great deal of their free time to participate with enthusiasm for this project. There are too many names to mention but they include Chido Dunn and Caroline Richard (who led the research efforts from London and Washington respectively) and Pat Allan (who has provided indefatigable assistance to Alan). We also thank Luiz Aboim, Alipak Banerjee, Abinash Barik, Georges Chalfoun, Ricardo Chirinos, Jeffery Commission, Simon Consedine, Ella Davies, Yann Dehaudt-Delville, Francisco Franco, Lauren Friedman, Monika Hlavkova, Maanas Jain, Ashley Jones, Sofia Klot, Oliver Marsden, Penny Martin, Jenny Merrick, Claire Pauly, Sam Prevatt, Evgeniya Rubinina, Gustavo Topalian, and Tomas Vail.

Internationally, we would like to mention the following for their insights into developments in their home jurisdictions: Francisco González de Cossío, Maxim Kulkov, Gisela Mation, Javier Robalino, Diego Romero, Pedro Saghy, Sebastián Yanine, and Vladislav Zaitsev.

And finally we are grateful to the institutions who have kindly given us permission to publish their rules and guidelines, including the IBA, the ICC, the ICDR, ICSID, and the LCIA.

A traditional book format relies on a production process that is less immediate than we have come to expect in an internet world. As a consequence, we had to put pens down by a certain date. The date in this instance is May 2015.

Nigel Blackaby and Constantine Partasides
August 2015

SUMMARY CONTENTS

Table of Cases   xxi
Table of Legislation   xxxvii
Table of Arbitration Awards   lv
List of Abbreviations   lxv

1. An Overview of International Arbitration   1
2. Agreement to Arbitrate   71
3. Applicable Laws   155
4. Establishment and Organisation of an Arbitral Tribunal   229
5. Powers, Duties, and Jurisdiction of an Arbitral Tribunal   305
6. Conduct of the Proceedings   353
7. Role of National Courts during the Proceedings   415
8. Arbitration under Investment Treaties   441
9. Award   501
10. Challenge of Arbitral Awards   569
11. Recognition and Enforcement of Arbitral Awards   605

Index   661

CONTENTS

Table of Cases   xxi
Table of Legislation   xxxvii
Table of Arbitration Awards   lv
List of Abbreviations   lxv

1. An Overview of International Arbitration

   A. Introduction   1.01
      (a) Dispute resolution—worldwide   1.01
      (b) What is arbitration?   1.04
      (c) Conduct of an arbitration   1.06
      (d) A brief historical note   1.13
      (e) International rules, treaties, and conventions   1.18
      (f) Meaning of 'international'   1.19
      (g) The meaning of 'commercial'   1.35
      (h) Key elements of an international arbitration   1.39
      (i) Agreement to arbitrate   1.40
      (j) Need for a dispute   1.60
      (k) Commencement of an arbitration   1.66
      (l) Arbitral proceedings   1.77
      (m) Decision of the tribunal   1.80
      (n) Enforcement of the award   1.87
      (o) Summary   1.92

   B. Why Arbitrate?   1.94
      (a) Introduction   1.94
      (b) Main reasons   1.97
      (c) Additional reasons   1.103
      (d) Is arbitration perfect?   1.108
      (e) Summary   1.128

   C. Alternative Dispute Resolution   1.135
      (a) What is meant by alternative dispute resolution?   1.137
      (b) *Amiables compositeurs*, equity clauses, and decisions *ex aequo et bono*   1.139

   D. What Kind of Arbitration?   1.140
      (a) Introduction   1.140
      (b) Ad hoc arbitration   1.141
      (c) Ad hoc arbitration—advantages and disadvantages   1.143
      (d) Institutional arbitration   1.146

	(e)	Institutional arbitration—advantages and disadvantages	1.149
	(f)	Arbitral institutions	1.157
	(g)	Arbitrations involving a state	1.182
E.	Sovereign States, Claims Commissions, and Tribunals		1.191
F.	Regulation of International Arbitration		1.197
	(a)	Introduction	1.197
	(b)	Role of national systems of law	1.199
	(c)	State participation in the arbitral process	1.202
	(d)	Role of international conventions and the Model Law	1.206
	(e)	Practice of international arbitration	1.224
G.	Summary		1.239

2. Agreement to Arbitrate

A.	Overview		2.01
	(a)	Introduction	2.01
	(b)	Categories of arbitration agreement	2.02
	(c)	International conventions	2.06
	(d)	International standards	2.09
B.	Validity of an Arbitration Agreement		2.13
	(a)	Formal validity—need for writing	2.13
	(b)	A defined legal relationship	2.25
	(c)	A subject matter capable of settlement by arbitration	2.29
C.	Parties to an Arbitration Agreement		2.31
	(a)	Capacity	2.31
	(b)	Third parties to the arbitration agreement	2.42
	(c)	Joinder and intervention	2.59
D.	Analysis of an Arbitration Agreement		2.63
	(a)	Scope	2.63
	(b)	Basic elements	2.71
	(c)	Separability	2.101
	(d)	Summary	2.114
E.	Submission Agreements		2.119
F.	Arbitrability		2.124
	(a)	Introduction	2.124
	(b)	Categories of dispute for which questions of arbitrability arise	2.131
	(c)	Conclusion	2.160
G.	Confidentiality		2.161
	(a)	Privacy and confidentiality	2.163
	(b)	Confidentiality—classical position	2.165
	(c)	Confidentiality—the current trend	2.170
	(d)	Award	2.177
	(e)	Confidentiality in investor–state arbitrations	2.183

	(f)	Revisions to rules of arbitration	2.190
	(g)	Conclusion	2.196
H.	Defective Arbitration Clauses		2.197
	(a)	Inconsistency	2.198
	(b)	Uncertainty	2.199
	(c)	Inoperability	2.202
I.	Waiver of the Right to Arbitrate		2.204
J.	Multiparty Arbitrations		2.212
	(a)	Introduction	2.212
	(b)	Class arbitrations	2.224
	(c)	Concurrent hearings	2.236
	(d)	Court-ordered consolidation	2.238
	(e)	Consolidation by consent	2.243

3. Applicable Laws

A.	Overview		3.01
	(a)	Introduction	3.01
	(b)	No legal vacuum	3.03
	(c)	A complex interaction of laws	3.07
B.	Law Governing the Agreement to Arbitrate		3.09
	(a)	Law of the contract	3.12
	(b)	Law of the seat of the arbitration	3.15
	(c)	Parties' common intention—a French 'third way'	3.33
	(d)	Combining several approaches—a Swiss model	3.36
C.	Law Governing the Arbitration		3.37
	(a)	Introduction	3.37
	(b)	What is the *lex arbitri*?	3.42
	(c)	The content of the *lex arbitri*	3.43
	(d)	Procedural rules and the *lex arbitri*	3.48
	(e)	Seat theory	3.53
	(f)	Is the *lex arbitri* a procedural law?	3.62
	(g)	Choice of another procedural law	3.65
	(h)	Where an award is made	3.69
	(i)	Delocalisation	3.73
	(j)	Seat theory and the *lex arbitri*	3.84
D.	Law Applicable to the Substance		3.91
	(a)	Introduction	3.91
	(b)	Autonomy of the parties	3.97
	(c)	National law	3.111
	(d)	Mandatory law	3.128
	(e)	Public international law and general principles of law	3.131
	(f)	Concurrent laws, combined laws, and the *tronc commun* doctrine	3.136

	(g)	Transnational law (including the *lex mercatoria*, the UNIDROIT Principles, trade usages, and Shari'ah)	3.156
	(h)	Equity and good conscience	3.192
E.	Conflict Rules and the Search for the Applicable Law		3.198
	(a)	Introduction	3.198
	(b)	Implied or tacit choice	3.201
	(c)	Choice of forum as choice of law	3.205
	(d)	Conflict rules	3.208
	(e)	Does an international arbitral tribunal have a *lex fori*?	3.211
	(f)	International conventions, rules of arbitration, and national laws	3.214
	(g)	Conclusion	3.218
F.	Other Applicable Rules and Guidelines		3.221
	(a)	Ethical rules	3.221
	(b)	Guidelines	3.229

4. Establishment and Organisation of an Arbitral Tribunal

A.	Background		4.01
	(a)	Introduction	4.01
	(b)	Commencement of an arbitration	4.04
	(c)	Commencement of an arbitration under institutional rules	4.08
	(d)	Commencement of an ad hoc arbitration under the applicable law	4.11
	(e)	Selecting an arbitral tribunal	4.13
	(f)	Emergency arbitrators	4.17
	(g)	Sole arbitrators and multi-arbitrator tribunals	4.22
B.	Appointment of Arbitrators		4.33
	(a)	Introduction	4.33
C.	Qualities Required in International Arbitrators		4.49
	(a)	Introduction	4.49
	(b)	Restrictions imposed by the contract	4.50
	(c)	Restrictions imposed by the applicable law	4.52
	(d)	Professional qualifications	4.53
	(e)	Language	4.58
	(f)	Experience and outlook	4.59
	(g)	Availability	4.60
	(h)	Nationality	4.61
	(i)	Education and training	4.68
	(j)	Interviewing prospective arbitrators	4.72
D.	Independence and Impartiality of Arbitrators		4.75
	(a)	Introduction	4.75
	(b)	Disclosure	4.79
E.	Challenge and Replacement of Arbitrators		4.89
	(a)	Introduction	4.89
	(b)	Grounds for challenge	4.92
	(c)	Procedure for challenge	4.106

(d)	Principal bases for challenge	4.118
(e)	Waiver	4.143
(f)	Conclusion on challenges	4.150
(g)	Filling a vacancy	4.152
(h)	Truncated tribunals	4.154
(i)	Procedure following the filling of a vacancy	4.162
(j)	Insuring against a vacancy	4.167

F. Organisation of the Arbitral Tribunal — 4.169
- (a) Introduction — 4.169
- (b) Meetings and hearings — 4.170
- (c) Administrative aspects — 4.177
- (d) Role of an arbitral secretary — 4.192

G. Fees and Expenses of the Arbitral Tribunal — 4.202
- (a) Introduction — 4.202
- (b) Who fixes fees? — 4.203
- (c) Methods of assessing fees — 4.204
- (d) Negotiating arbitrators' fees — 4.210
- (e) Commitment or cancellation fees — 4.212
- (f) Expenses of the arbitral tribunal — 4.215
- (g) Securing payment of the fees and expenses of the arbitral tribunal — 4.220

5. Powers, Duties, and Jurisdiction of an Arbitral Tribunal

A. Background — 5.01
- (a) Introduction — 5.01
- (b) Practical considerations — 5.03

B. Powers of Arbitrators — 5.06
- (a) Introduction — 5.06
- (b) Sources of arbitrators' powers — 5.08
- (c) Common powers of arbitral tribunals — 5.15
- (d) Supporting powers of the courts — 5.41

C. Duties of Arbitrators — 5.43
- (a) Introduction — 5.43
- (b) Duties imposed by the parties — 5.44
- (c) Duties imposed by law — 5.47
- (d) Ethical duties — 5.79

D. Jurisdiction — 5.91
- (a) Introduction — 5.91
- (b) Challenges to jurisdiction — 5.92
- (c) Autonomy (or separability) of the arbitration clause — 5.100
- (d) Court control — 5.112
- (e) Procedural aspects of resolving issues of jurisdiction — 5.118
- (f) Options open to the respondent — 5.119
- (g) International agreements on the jurisdiction of national courts — 5.128

6. Conduct of the Proceedings

A. Overview — 6.01
- (a) Introduction — 6.01
- (b) Party autonomy — 6.07
- (c) Limitations on party autonomy — 6.09
- (d) International practice — 6.19
- (e) Procedural structure of a typical international arbitration — 6.22

B. Expedited Procedures — 6.26
- (a) Introduction — 6.26
- (b) Expedited formation — 6.28
- (c) Fast-track procedures — 6.32
- (d) Early, or summary, determinations — 6.38

C. Preliminary Steps — 6.41
- (a) Introduction — 6.41
- (b) Preliminary issues — 6.53

D. Written Submissions — 6.65
- (a) Introduction — 6.65
- (b) Terminology — 6.71
- (c) Time and length limits — 6.73

E. Collecting Evidence — 6.75
- (a) Introduction — 6.75
- (b) Categories of evidence — 6.89
- (c) Documentary evidence — 6.92
- (d) Fact witness evidence — 6.120
- (e) Experts — 6.133
- (f) Inspection of the subject matter of the dispute — 6.146

F. Hearings — 6.155
- (a) Introduction — 6.155
- (b) Organisation of hearings — 6.158
- (c) Procedure at hearings — 6.168
- (d) Default hearings — 6.191

G. Proceedings after the Hearing — 6.200
- (a) Introduction — 6.200
- (b) Post-hearing briefs — 6.201
- (c) Introduction of new evidence — 6.203

7. Role of National Courts during the Proceedings

A. Introduction — 7.01
- (a) Increasing independence of arbitration — 7.04
- (b) Limitations on independence — 7.06
- (c) 'A relay race' — 7.07

B. At the Beginning of the Arbitration — 7.09
- (a) Enforcing the arbitration agreement — 7.10

(b) Establishing the arbitral tribunal		7.11
(c) Challenges to jurisdiction		7.12

C. During the Arbitral Proceedings 7.13
    (a) Interim measures—powers of the arbitral tribunal 7.14
    (b) Interim measures—powers of the competent court 7.22
    (c) Measures relating to the attendance of witnesses 7.32
    (d) Measures related to the preservation of evidence 7.37
    (e) Measures related to documentary disclosure 7.39
    (f) Measures aimed at preserving the status quo 7.45
    (g) Interim relief in respect of parallel proceedings 7.51

D. At the End of the Arbitration 7.62
    (a) Judicial control of the proceedings and the award 7.62

E. Conclusion 7.63

8. Arbitration under Investment Treaties

A. Introduction 8.01

B. Jurisdictional Issues 8.14
    (a) Existence of an applicable treaty 8.14
    (b) Protected investors 8.17
    (c) Protected investments 8.28
    (d) Consent and conditions to access investment treaty arbitration 8.45
    (e) Bilateral investment treaties and contractual dispute resolution clauses 8.54
    (f) Parallel claims before local courts 8.57

C. Law Applicable to the Substance of the Dispute 8.62

D. Merits of the Dispute 8.78
    (a) No expropriation without prompt, adequate, and effective compensation 8.79
    (b) 'Fair and equitable treatment' and the international minimum standard 8.96
    (c) Full protection and security 8.113
    (d) No arbitrary or discriminatory measures impairing the investment 8.118
    (e) National and 'most favoured nation' treatment 8.124
    (f) Free transfer of funds related to investments 8.129
    (g) Observance of specific investment undertakings 8.134

E. Measures of Compensation under Bilateral Investment Treaties 8.141
    (a) Expropriation remedies 8.146
    (b) Compensation for other treaty breaches 8.159
    (c) Moral damages 8.164
    (d) Interest 8.166
    (e) Costs and attorneys' fees 8.168

9. Award

A. Introduction — 9.01
- (a) Destination of an international arbitration—the award — 9.01
- (b) Definition of an award — 9.05
- (c) Which rulings/orders have the status of an award? — 9.09
- (d) Rendering an internationally enforceable award — 9.14

B. Categories of Award — 9.18
- (a) Partial awards — 9.19
- (b) Foreign and domestic awards — 9.29
- (c) Default awards — 9.30
- (d) Additional awards — 9.33
- (e) Consent awards and termination of proceedings without an award — 9.34

C. Remedies — 9.40
- (a) Monetary compensation — 9.41
- (b) Punitive damages and other penalties — 9.44
- (c) Specific performance — 9.52
- (d) Restitution — 9.53
- (e) Injunctions — 9.59
- (f) Declaratory relief — 9.60
- (g) Rectification — 9.63
- (h) Filling gaps and adaptation of contracts — 9.65
- (i) Interest — 9.72
- (j) Costs — 9.85
- (k) Requirements imposed by national law — 9.99

D. Deliberations and Decisions of the Tribunal — 9.100
- (a) Introduction — 9.100
- (b) Tribunal psychology — 9.113
- (c) Bargaining process — 9.117
- (d) Majority voting — 9.119
- (e) Concurring and dissenting opinions — 9.128

E. Form and Content of Awards — 9.139
- (a) Generally — 9.139
- (b) Form of the award — 9.142
- (c) Contents of the award — 9.151
- (d) Time limits — 9.162
- (e) Notification of awards — 9.169
- (f) Registration or deposit of awards — 9.171

F. Effect of Awards — 9.173
- (a) *Res judicata* — 9.173
- (b) Existing disputes — 9.177
- (c) Subsequent disputes — 9.179
- (d) Effect of award on third parties — 9.182

G. Proceedings after the Award — 9.186
- (a) Under national law — 9.188

	(b)	Under rules of arbitration	9.190
	(c)	Review procedures other than by national courts	9.195
	(d)	Review of the award by way of settlement	9.198
	(e)	Publication of awards	9.199

10. Challenge of Arbitral Awards

A.	Introduction	10.01
	(a)	Purpose of challenge	10.06
	(b)	Preconditions to challenge	10.07
	(c)	Time limits for challenge	10.10
B.	Methods of Challenge	10.11
	(a)	Internal challenge	10.12
	(b)	Correction and interpretation of awards; additional awards; remission of awards	10.17
	(c)	Recourse to the courts	10.24
C.	Grounds for Challenge	10.34
	(a)	Grounds under the Model Law	10.38
	(b)	Adjudicability	10.42
	(c)	Procedural grounds	10.52
	(d)	Substantive grounds	10.64
D.	Effects of Challenge	10.89
E.	State Responsibility for Wrongful Setting Aside	10.93

11. Recognition and Enforcement of Arbitral Awards

A.	Background	11.01
	(a)	Introduction	11.01
	(b)	Performance of awards	11.07
	(c)	General principles governing recognition and enforcement	11.17
	(d)	Difference between recognition and enforcement	11.19
	(e)	Place of recognition and enforcement	11.24
	(f)	Methods of recognition and enforcement	11.30
	(g)	Time limits	11.33
	(h)	Consequences of refusal of recognition or enforcement	11.34
	(i)	Role of the international conventions	11.35
B.	Enforcement under the New York Convention	11.40
	(a)	Introduction	11.40
	(b)	Refusal of recognition and enforcement	11.55
	(c)	Grounds for refusal	11.63
	(d)	First ground for refusal—incapacity; invalid arbitration agreement	11.66
	(e)	Second ground—no proper notice of appointment of arbitrator or of the proceedings; lack of due process	11.71
	(f)	Third ground—jurisdictional issues	11.78

(g) Fourth ground—composition of tribunal or procedure not in accordance with arbitration agreement or the relevant law		11.82
(h) Fifth ground—award suspended, or set aside		11.87
(i) Arbitrability		11.101
(j) Public policy		11.105
(k) Other grounds		11.123
C. Enforcement under the ICSID Convention		11.125
D. Enforcement under Regional Conventions		11.131
(a) Moscow Convention		11.131
(b) Panama Convention		11.134
(c) Middle Eastern and North African Conventions		11.138
(d) Other regional conventions		11.140
E. Defence of State Immunity		11.141
(a) Jurisdictional immunity		11.144
(b) Immunity from execution		11.146

Index 661

TABLE OF CASES

A v B and X [2011] EWHC 2345 (Comm). 4.103
A Rahman Golshani v Iran Revue de l'arbitrage (2005) 993; Global Arbitration
    Review (2008) 42 . . . . 10.30
AAY and others v AAZ (AAY) [2011] 1 SLR 1093. . . . . 2.169
ABB AG v Hochtief Airport GmbH [2006] EWHC 388 (Comm); [2006] ArbLR 33 . . . . . 5.74
Abnaa Al-Khalaf Co e al v Sayed Aghajaved Raza, Qatari Court of Cassation,
    Challenge No. 64 (2012). 10.82
Abu Dhabi Gas Liquefaction Co Ltd v Eastern Bechtel Corp [1982] 2 Lloyd's
    Rep 425, CA. 2.219, 2.220, 2.221, 2.236, 2.240
ACD Tridon Inc v Tridon Australia Pty Ltd [2002] NSWSC 896. . . . . 2.207
Adesa Corp v Bob Dickenson Auction Service Ltd, 73 OR (3d) 787 (2 December 2004). . . . 2.172
Addis v Gramophone Co Ltd [1909] AC 488. . . . . 9.45
Aegis v European Re [2003] 1 WLR 1041 . . . . 2.236
AEK v National Basket Association [2002] 1 All ER (Comm) 70 . . . . 10.75
AI Trade Finance Inc v Bulgarian Foreign Trade Bank Ltd, Supreme Court of Sweden,
    27 October 2000. . . . . 2.176
AIG Capital Partners Inc v Kazakhstan [2005] App LR 10/20 . . . . 11.154
Airbus SAS v Aviation Partners Inc, United States District Court, Western District of
    Washington, No C12-1228JLR (25 October 2012) 2.210
Aita v Ojjeh (1986) Revue de l'Arbitrage 583. . . . . 2.182
Albon v Naza Motor Trading Sdn Bhd [2007] EWHC 665 (Ch) 2.202
Alcom Ltd v Republic of Colombia [1984] AC 580 . . . . 11.152
Ali Shipping Corporation v 'Shipyard Trogir' [1998] 1 Lloyd's Rep 643 . . . . 2.166
Alliance Healthcare Servs, Inc v Argonaut Private Equity, LLC, 804 F Supp 2d 808,
    811 (ND Ill 2011) 7.35
Allianz SpA, and another, v West Tankers Inc Case C-185/07 10 February 2009. . . . 5.132, 5.133,
    5.134, 5.135, 5.136
Almare Prima, The [1989] 2 Lloyd's Rep 376. . . . . 2.70
Aloe Vera of America, Inc (US) v Asianic Food (S) Pte Ltd (Singapore) and Another,
    (2007) XXXII Ybk Comm Arb 489. . . . . 11.80, 11.104
Ambassade de la Féderation de Russie en France v Compagnie NOGA d'Importation
    et d'Exportation SA, Cour d'Appel de Paris (1 Ch A) 10 August 2000, (2001)
    1 Revue de l'Arbitrage 114 . . . . 11.155
American Bureau of Shipping v Société Jet Flint SA, 170 F 3d 349 (2nd Cir 1999). 2.53
American Bureau of Shipping v Tencara SpA, Italian Corte di Cassazione, Plenary
    Session, 26 June 2001, No 8744; (2002) XXVII Ybk Comm Arb 509. . . . . 2.27
American Central Eastern Texas Gas Co v Union Pacific Resources Group, 2004 US
    App LEXIS 1216. . . . . 2.138
American Express Co v Italian Colors Restaurant, Supreme Court of the
    United States, No 12-133 (20 June 2013) 2.234, 3.32
American Safety Equipment Corp v JP Maguire Co, 391 F 2d 821(2nd Cir 1968) 2.135
Amparo Directo 465/2005, Tercer Tribunal Colegiado en Materia Civil del Primer
    Circuito, Servicios Administrativos de Emergencia (2 September 2005) 2.203
Amparo Directo en Revisión No. 8/2011 (Mexican Supreme Court). 10.25
Angelic Grace, The [1995] 1 Lloyd's Rep 87 (CA) 2.68, 2.69

Table of Cases

Antilles Cement Corporation (Puerto Rico) v Transficem (Spain) (2006) XXXI Ybk
  Comm Arb, 846 .... 11.87
Apelação 0177130-22.2010.8.26.0100, 3 December 2012 .... 10.10
Applied Industrial Materials Corp v Ovalar Makine Ticaret Ve Sanayi, AS, 492
  F 3d 132, 139 (2d Cir. 2007) 4.75
Application of Caratube Int'l Oil Co., LLP, In re 730 F Supp 2d 101 (DDC 2010) 7.44
Application of Chevron Corp. (Berlinger), In re 709 F Supp 2d 283
  (SDNY 2010) 6.131, 7.43
Application of Mesa Power Grp, In re LLC, No 2:11–mc–270–ES, 2013 WL 1890222
  (DNJ Apr. 19, 2013) 7.43
Application of the Republic of Ecuador, In re 2011 WL 4434816 (ND Cal, 2011) 7.43
Arab African Energy Corp Ltd v Olieprodukten Nederland BV [1983]
  2 Lloyd's Rep 419 .... 1.49, 2.18
Arab National Bank v El Sharif Saoud Bin Masoud Bin Haza'a El-Abdali
  [2004] EWHC 2381 .... 10.44
Arab Republic of Egypt v Southern Pacific Properties, Cour d'Appel de Paris,
  12 July 1984, (1984) 23 ILM 1048 .... 11.78
Arbitration between International Bechtel Company Limited v Department of
  Civil Aviation of the Government of Dubai, In re 300 F Supp 2d 112 (2005) 5.21
Arenson v Arenson [1977] AC 405; [1976] 1 Lloyd's Rep 179, HL 5.48
Arret du 17 Fevrier 2015, no 77 (13/13278) (Cour d'Appel de Paris) 1.25
Asghar v Legal Services Commission [2004] EWHC 1803; [2004] Arb LR 43 .... 2.93
Assicurazioni Generali SpA v Tassinari, Corte di Cassazione, Judgment No 2384
  of 18 March 1997 .... 2.53
Associated Electric and Gas Insurance Services Ltd v European Reinsurance Co
  of Zurich UKPC 11, [2003] 1 WLR 1041 .... 2.181, 9.180
Astengo v Comune di Genova, Corte di Cassazione, Judgment No 2096 of
  22 October 1970 .... 2.96
Astra Oil Co, Inc v Rover Navigation, Ltd, 344 F 3d 276 (2nd Cir 2003) 2.53
Asturcom Telecomunicaciones SL v Cristina Rodriguez Nogueira, Case C-40/80,
  [2009] ECR I-9579 .... 10.86
AT&S Transportation LLC v Odyssey Logistics & Technology Corp 803 NYS 2d 118
  (24 October 2005) 2.58
AT&T Mobility LLC v Concepcion, Supreme Court of the United States,
  (27 April 2011) 2.234
AT&T Mobility LLC v Concepcion, 131 S. Ct. 1740, 1753, (2011) 3.31
Attorney-General v Mobil Oil NZ Ltd, High Court, Wellington (1 July 1987) 2.138
Avila Group Inc v Norma J of California, 426 F Supp 537 (DCNY 1977) 2.53

Baiti Real Estate Development v Dynasty Zarooni Inc, Dubai Court of Cassation,
  Petition No 14 of 2012 .... 11.114
Baker Marine (Nig) Ltd v Chevron (Nig) Ltd 191 F 3d 194 (2nd Cir 1999) 11.97
Bank Mellat v GAA Development Construction Co [1988] 2 Lloyd's Rep 44 .... 9.132
Bank Mellat v Helliniki Techniki SA [1984] QB 291; [1983] 3 All ER 428 (CA) 3.84
Banque de Paris v Amoco Oil, 573 F Supp 1465 at 1472 (SDNY 1983) 2.55
Banque du Proche-Orient v Société Fougerolle, Cass Civ 2e, 9 December 1981
  (2nd decision); Cass Civ 1ère, 22 October 1991 (Austrian Supreme Court,
  18 November 1982); (1984) IX Ybk Comm Arb 161 .... 3.176
Banque populaire Loire et Iyonnais v Société Sangar, Cour de cassation (1re Ch civ),
  11 July 2006 .... 2.53
Bautista v Star Cruises 396 F 3d 1289 (11th Cir 2005) 11.50
Baxter Int'l Inc v Abbott Labs, 315 F 3d 829 (7th Cir, 2003) 10.74, 11.122
Baxter Int v Abbott Laboratories, 315 F 3d 163 (2nd Cir 2004) 2.136
Bay Hotel and Resort Ltd, The v Cavalier Construction Co Ltd (Turks and
  Caicos Islands) [2001] UKPC 34 .... 2.59

Table of Cases

Beijing Jianlong Heavy Industry Group v Golden Ocean Group Limited
[2013] EWHC 1063 (Comm).. 2.112
Beximco Pharmaceuticals Ltd and others v Shamil Bank of Bahrain EC [2004]
EWCA Civ 19... 3.187
BG Group PLC v Republic of Argentina, No 12-138, 572 US (March 5, 2014) 5.127, 10.47
Bharat Aluminium Co v Kaiser Aluminum Technical Service, Inc (Civil Appeal
No 7019 of 2005. Decision of 6 September 2012, given at New Delhi) 11.99
Bharat Aluminium Co v Kaiser Aluminium Technical Services Inc 2012 (9) SCC 552..... 9.59
Bharat Aluminium Co (BALCO) v Kaiser Aluminium Technical Services Civil
Appeal No. 7019 of 2005 (Sept 6, 2012)................................. 10.26
Bhatia International v Bulk Trading 2002 (4) SCC 105........................ 9.59, 10.26
Bilta (UK) Ltd (In Liquidation) v Nazir [2010] EWHC 1086 (Ch)................... 2.206
Birmingham Associates Ltd v Abbott Labatories 547 F Supp 2d 295; 2008 US Dist
LEXIS 30321 .... 2.53
BJ Export & Chemical Processing Co v Kaduna Refining and Petrochemical Co
(2003) 24 WRN 74 (31 October 2002) 2.154
BKMI and Siemens v Dutco French Cass Civ 1ere, 7 January 1992 Bull Civ 1..... 1.111, 2.214
Black Clawson International Ltd v Papierwerke Waldhof-Aschaffenburg AG
[1982] 2 Lloyd's Rep 446 .... 3.22
Boraks v AAA 517 NW2d 771 (Mich App 1994) 5.64
Borst v Allstate Insurance Company 717 NW 2d 42, 48 (Wis, 2006)................ 4.75
Bothell Bothell v Hitachi Zosen Corp 97 F Supp 2d 1048 (2000)................... 2.23
Bowen v Amoco Pipeline Co, 254 F 3d 925 (10th Cir 2001)...................... 10.80
Braes of Doune Wind Farm v Alfred McAlpine [2008] EWHC 426 (TCC)........ 2.198, 3.63
Brandon v MedPartners Inc 203 FRD 677 at 686 (SD Fla 2001) 9.52
Braspetro Oil Services Co v The Management and Implementation Authority of the
Great Man-Made River Project, Paris Cour d'Appel (1 July 1999); (1999) 14
Mealey's Intl Arb Rep 8; (1999) XXIVa Ybk Comm Arb, 297 .... 9.10, 9.11
Bratex Dominicana, C por A v Vanity Fair Inc, Supreme Court of Justice of the
Dominican Republic (31 May 2005) 2.108
Bremen, The v Zapata Off-Shore Co, 407 US 1 (1972) 11.110
Bridas SAPIC, Bridas Energy International Ltd et al v Government of Turkmenistan
and Turkmennneft, 345 F 3d 347 (5th Circuit 2006) 2.52
British Airways Board v Laker Airways Ltd [1985] AC 58 (HL).................... 9.45
Buckeye Check Cashing Inc v John Cardegna et al, 126 S Ct 1204 (2006)............. 2.107
Bulgarian Foreign Trade Bank Ltd v Al Trade Finance Inc (2001) XXVI Ybk Comm
Arb 291, Swedish Supreme Court, 27 October 2000, Case No T1881–99........... 3.25
Bundesgerichtshof, 22 February 2001, XXIX Yearbook Commercial Arbitration
(2004) 724 .... 11.97
Bundesgerichtshof 53 NJW 2346 (2000).. 2.55
Bundesgerichtshof decision (1978) 71 BGHZ 162 .... 2.55
Bundesgerichtshof (Neue Juristische Wochenschrift, 1992), 3096 et seq............... 9.49
Bunge Agribuss v Guangdong Fengyuan [2006] Min Si Ta Zi No. 41 .... 11.86
Buques Centroamericanos SA v Refinadora Costarricense de Petroleos SA, 1989
US Dist LEXIS 5429 (SDNY 1989)....................................... 2.39
Burkinabe des Ciments et Matérieux (CIMAT) v Société des Ciments d'Abidjan
(SCA) (2001) Revue de l'Arbitrage 165................................... 10.55
BVerfG, Beschluß vom 24.01.2007 - 2 BvR 1133/04............................. 9.49
BVerfG, Beschluß vom 14.06.2007 - 2 BvR 2247/06............................. 9.49

C v D [2007] EWCA Civ 1282; [2008] 1 All ER (Comm) 1001 .... 3.23
Cable & Wireless v IBM United Kingdom [2002] EWHC 2059 (Comm) 2.90, 2.91
Cambodia v Thailand [1962] ICJ Rep 6.. 9.54
Capital Trust Investments Ltd v Radio Design TJ AB [2002] EWCA Civ 135 .... 2.207
Cargill Int'l SA v M/T Pavel Dybenko, 991 F 2d 1012 (2nd Cir 1993) 2.53

xxiii

Table of Cases

Case No 4A_376/2008 of 5 December 2008 (Swiss Federal Tribunal) 2.198
Case No. I CSK 312/11 9 March 2012 (Polish Supreme Court). 10.63
Cass Civ 1, 10 October 2012 Tecso, no 11-20.299 . . . . 4.125
CE Int'l Res. Holdings, LLC v SA Minerals Ltd. P'ship, et al, No 12–CV–08087
    (CM)(SN), 2013 WL 2661037 (SDNY Jun 12, 2013) 7.44
Central Meat Products Ltd v JV McDaniel Ltd [1952] 1 Lloyd's Rep 562 . . . . 2.198
Cetelem SA v Roust Holdings Ltd [2005] EWCA Civ 618 . . . . 7.38
Champ v Siegel Trading Co, 55 F 3d 269 (7th Cir 1995). 2.212
Channel Tunnel Group Ltd v Balfour Beatty Construction Ltd [1993] AC 334 . . . . . 3.22, 7.25,
                                                                                                     7.46, 7.47, 7.58, 7.49
Channel Tunnel Group Ltd v Balfour Beatty Construction Ltd [1992] 1 QB 656. . . . . . . .3.150,
                                                                                                               3.152, 3.176
Chantiers de l'Atlantique SA v Gaztransport & Technigaz SAS [2011] EWHC 3383 . . . . . 10.62
Chaval v Liebherr, Recurso Especial No 653.733, Superior Court of Justice
    (3 August 2006) 2.49
Chevron USA, Inc, In re No. 08-08-00082-CV, 2010 Tex App LEXIS 459 . . . . 9.24
Chevron Corp v Berlinger, 629 F 3d 297 (2d Cir 2011) 6.131
Chevron Corp v Republic of Ecuador 2013 WL 2449172 (DDC 2013) 11.145
China Agribusiness Development Corp v Balli Trading [1998] 2 Lloyd's Rep 76 . . . . 11.59
China Nanhai Oil Joint Service Cpn v Gee Tai Holdings Co Ltd (1995) XX Ybk
    Comm Arb 671. . . . . .11.83, 11.84, 11.85
Chloe Z Fishing Co Inc v Odyssey Re (London) Ltd 109 F Supp 2d 1048 (2000) 2.23
Chloro Controls (I) P Ltd v Severn Trent Water Purification Inc and others, Supreme
    Court of India (28 September 2012). 2.49
Chromalloy Aeroservices v Arab Republic of Egypt, 939 F Supp 907 (DDC 1996) 3.89,
                                                                                                10.06, 11.59, 11.95, 11.97
Chun Wo Building Construction v China Merchants Tower Co [2000] 2 HKC 255 . . . . . 2.239
Citibank NA v Stok & Associates PA, No 09-13556 (11th Cir July 20, 2010) 2.210
Citigroup Global Mkts v Bacon, 562 F 3d 349 (5th Cir, 2009) 10.74
City of London v Sancheti [2008] EWCA Civ 1283 . . . . 2.45
City of Moscow v International Industrial Bank [2004] 2 Lloyd's Rep 179 . . . . 2.178
Cogecot Cotton Company c/ Marlan's Cotton Industries MCI, Gazette du Palais
    (2005) 118. . . . . 10.30
Collective Fishing Farm Krasnoye Znamya v White Arctic Marine Resources Ltd.,
    Case No. A05-4274/2007. . . . . 11.99
Commercial Caribbean Niquel v Societe Overseas Mining Investments Limited,
    Paris Court of Appeal, No. 08/23901 (Mar 25, 2010) 10.85
Commonwealth Coatings Corp v Continental Casualty Co, 393 US 145 (1968) 4.104
Commonwealth of Australia v Cockatoo Dockyard Pty Ltd [1995]
    36 NSWLR 662 . . . . .2.172, 2.183
Compagnie Tunisienne de Navigation SA v Compagnie d'Armament Maritime
    SA [1971] AC 572 . . . . 3.38, 3.63, 3.93
Companhia Estadual de Energia Eléctrica ('CEEE') v AES, Recurso Especial
    No. 612.439-RS, Superior Court of Justice (14 September 2006) 2.37
Companhia do Metropolitano de São Paolo. 10.10
Companhia Paranaense de Gas ('Compagás') v Carioca Passarelli Consortium
    ('Consortium'), Appeal No 247.646-0, Paraná Court of Appeals
    (11 February 2004) 2.37
COMSAT Corp v NSF, 190 F 3d 269, 276 (4th Cir 1999) 7.36
Consorcio Ecuatoriano de Telecomuniciaciones SA, In re v JAS Forwarding, Inc,
    685 F 3d 987 (11th Cir 2012). 7.43
Copel v Energetica Rio Pedrinho SA, Agravo de Instrumento No 174.874-9, Paraná
    Court of Appeals (11 May 2005). 2.37
Coppée Levalin NV v Ken-Ren Fertilisers and Chemicals [1994] 2 Lloyd's Rep 109 (HL) 7.01
Corcoran v Ardra Insurance Company Ltd 842 F 2d 31 (2nd Cir 1988) 2.202

Table of Cases

Corey v New York Stock Exchange 691 F 2d 1205 (6th Cir 1982) at 1209 .... 5.54, 5.55
Corporación Mexicana de Mantenimiento Integral, S de RL de CV v
    PEMEX-Exploración y Producción, No 10 Civ 206 (AKH) 2013 WL 4517225
    (SDNY, August 27, 2013) 3.89, 10.06, 11.96, 11.97
Cort v AAA, 795 F Supp 970 (NDCa 1992) 5.56, 5.57
County of Nassau v Chase, 402 Fed Appx 540 (2d Cir 2010) 3.32
Creighton Ltd (Cayman Islands) v Minister of Finance and Minister of Internal Affairs
    and Agriculture of the Government of the State of Qatar (2000) XXV Ybk Comm
    Arb 458 .... 11.148, 11.149, 11.150
Cubic Defence Systems v Chambre de Commerce International (1999) Revue
    de l'Arbitrage 103 .... 10.58
Czech Republic v CME Czech Republic BV, Svea Court of Appeal,
    Case No T 8735–01, IIC 63 (2003) 9.107

Dadourian Group International Inc v Simms and others 13 May 2004 .... 9.185
Dallah Real Estate and Tourism Holding Co v the Ministry of Religious Affairs,
    Government of Pakistan [2010] UKSC 46, [2011] 1 All ER 485 .... 3.35, 3.77, 5.111,
                                                               10.44, 11.68, 11.69, 11.80
Dallal v Bank Mellat [1986] QB 441 .... 11.19
Decision of 28 April 1992 of the Tribunal Fédéral, [1992] A SA Bull 368 .... 2.134
Decision of February 17, 1995, of the District Court of Rotterdam NIPR 1996 .... 9.49
Decision of 18 September 1997 of the regional court of Hamburg, (2000) XXV Ybk
    Comm Arb 710 .... 11.79
Decision of 11 December 1997 of the Cour de Justice of Geneva, (1998) XXIII Ybk
    Comm Arb 764 .... 11.105
Decision of 30 July 1998 of the Court of Appeal of Hamburg, (2000) XXV Ybk
    Comm Arb 714 .... 11.79
Decision of 16 August 1999 (Halogaland Court of Appeal (Norway)), (2002) XXVII
    Ybk Comm Arb 519 .... 2.23
Decision of 30 September 1999 of Bremen Court of Appeal, [2001] 4 Intl ALR N-26 .... 11.76
Decision of February 1, 2001, (2001) No1 R.P.S (German Federal Supreme Court) 10.85
Decision of 7 January 2004, 4P196/2003, ASA Bull 3/2004 (Swiss Federal Tribunal) 10.53
Decision of 1 July 2004, 4P 93/2004, ASA Bull, 1/2005 (Swiss Federal Tribunal) 10.53
Decision of 18 October 2004, District Court of The Hague, civil law section; provisional
    measures judge, challenge no 13/2004, Petition No HA/RK2004/667 .... 4.134, 4.135
Decision No 4A_294/2008 (28 October 2000) (Swiss Federal Supreme Court) 6.33
Decision No 506/2010 (10 February 2010) (Greek Supreme Court) 2.27
Decision No 4A_103/2011 (20 September 2011) (Swiss Federal Tribunal) 2.66
Decision No 4A_50/2012 (16 October 2012) (Swiss Federal Tribunal) 2.144
Decision No 4 Ob 80/08f (26 August 2008) (Supreme Court (Oberster Gerichtshof))
    No 4 Ob 80/08f (26 August 2008) 2.64
Del Monte Corp v Sunkist Growers 10 F 3d 753, 760 (11th Cir, 1993) 4.75
Desputeaux v Éditions Chouette (1987) Inc [2003] 1 SCR 178 .... 2.132
Deutsche Schachtbau und Tiefbohrgesellschaft GmbH (F/Germ) v R'as Al Khaimah
    National Oil Co (R'as Al Khaimah, UAE) Shell International Petroleum Co Ltd
    (UK) [1987] 3 WLR 1023 .... 3.176
DiMercurio v Sphere Drake Insurance plc, 202 F 3d 71 (1st Cir 2000) 2.96
Discover Bank v Superior Court, 36 Cal 4th 148 (2005) 2.229
Discovery Geo Corporation v STP Energy Pte Ltd, High Court of New Zealand,
    19 December 2013 .... 7.50
Dolling-Baker v Merrett [1991] 2 All ER 890 .... 2.165
Downing v Al Tameer Establishment [2002] EWCA Civ 721 .... 2.202
Dubai Court of Cassation, Petition No 156/2009 .... 9.148
Dubey, In re 2013 US Dist LEXIS 83972, at *7-15 (CD Cal June 7, 2013) 7.43
Dynegy Midstream Servs v Trammochem, 451 F 3d 89, 96 (2d Cir 2006) 7.35

Table of Cases

Eagle Star Insurance Co v Yuval Insurance Co [1978] 1 Lloyd's Rep 357 . . . . 2.206
Ecuador, et al v Stratus Consulting, Inc, No 13–cv–01112–REB–KLM, 2013
  WL 2352425 (D Colo May 29, 2013). 7.43
Eco Swiss China Time Ltd v Benetton International NV Case C–126/97 (1999)
  XXIV Ybk Comm Arb 629. . . . . 2.137, 2.138, 3.105, 3.131, 11.120
EDF Internacional SA v Endesa Internacional SA and YPF SA, 8 September 2011, 5(3)
  Arbitraje: Revista de Arbitraje Comercial y de Inversiones (2012) 915 . . . . 11.97
Edman Controls, Inc, 712 F 3d 1021. . . . . 10.77
Eisenwerk Hensel Bayreuth GmbH v Australian Granites Ltd [2001] 1 QDR 461 . . . . 2.208
EJR Lovelock Ltd v Exportles [1968] 1 Lloyd's Rep 163 . . . . 2.198
El Nasharty v J Sainsbury plc [2007] EWHC 2618 (Comm). 2.203
El Paso Corp v La Comision Ejecutiva Hidroelectrica Del Rio Lempa, 341
  Fed.Appx. 31 (5th Cir 2009). 7.43
Elektrim SA v Vivendi [2007] EWHC 11 (Comm) 1.238
Emirates Trading Agency LLC v Prime Mineral Exports Private Ltd [2014]
  EWHC 2104. . . . . 2.91
Emmott v Michael Wilson & Partners Ltd [2008] EWCA CW 184 . . . . 9.199
Encyclopaedia Universalis SA (Luxembourg) v Encyclopaedia Britannica Inc (US)
  (2005) XXX Ybk Comm Arb, 1136 . . . . 11.86
ENRC Marketing AG and others v OJSC 'Magnitogorsk Metallurgical Kombinat',
  Federal Court of Australia, Case No. NSD 2110 of 2011, 25 November 2011 . . . . 7.50
Esso Australia Resources Ltd and others v The Honourable Sidney James Plowman
  and others (1995) 193 CLR 10 . . . . 2.170, 2.171
Estado Nacional—Procuración del Tesoro de la Nación c/ Cámara de Comercio
  Internacional, 3 July 2007 and 17 July 2008 (not published) 4.110
ET Plus SA v Jean Paul Welter & The Channel Tunnel Group [2005]
  EWHC 2115 (Comm). 2.134
Etat Libanais v Societe FTML (Cellis) SAL, Conseil D'etat Libanais, 17 July 2001 . . . . 2.37
Exodis c/ Ricoh France, Revue de l'arbitrage (2004) 683. . . . . 10.30

F Ltd v M Ltd [2009] EWHC 275. . . . . 10.55
F & G Sykes (Wessex) Ltd v Fine Fare Ltd [1967] 1 Lloyd's Rep 53. . . . . 2.68, 9.65
Fairchild & Co, Inc v Richmond F & PR Co, 516 F Supp 1305, 1313 (DDC 1981). 4.140
Ferguson v Corinthian Colleges, Inc, 733 F 3d 928, 936 (9th Cir 2013). 3.31
Fédération de Russie v BNP Paribas (Suisse) SA Compagnie NOGA d'Importation
  et d'Exportation SA 5A_618/2007 (10 January 2008) (Federal Supreme Court
  of Switzerland) 11.155
Fédération de Russie v BNP Paribas (Suisse) SA Compagnie NOGA d'Importation
  et d'Exportation SA 4A_403/2008 (9 December 2008) (Federal Supreme Court
  of Switzerland) 11.155
Figueiredo Ferraz E Engenharia de Projeto Ltda v Republic of Peru 663 F 4d 384
  (2nd Cir 2011). 11.124
Fiona Trust and Holding Corp v Privalov [2007] UKHL 40; [2007]
  EWCA Civ 20. . . . . 2.28, 2.66, 2.69, 2.112, 2.151, 5.102
Fisher v General Steel Domestic Sales, LLC, slip copy, No. 10-cv-0109-WYD-BNB,
  2011 WL 524362 (D. Colo. Oct. 31, 2011). 10.23
Fisichella Motor Sport International SpA v Héctor, Audencia Provincial, Barcelona,
  4 March 2010 . . . . 7.50
Fletamentos Maritimos SA v Effjohn International BV [1996] 2 Lloyd's Rep 304. . . . . 2.69
Fontaine Pajot Cour de cassation, l re chambre civile, 1 December 2010, Bulletin
  2010, I, no 248 . . . . 10.84
Fortress Value Recovery Fund I LLC v Blue Skye Special Opportunities Fund LP
  [2013] EWCA Civ 367 . . . . 2.52
Fougerolle v Procofrance (1992) JDI 974 . . . . 10.20

Table of Cases

Fougerolle SA (France) v Ministry of Defence of the Syrian Arab Republic (1990)
   XV Ybk Comm Arb, 515 .... 11.67
Francelino da Silva Matuzalem v Fédération Internationale de Football Association
   (FIFA), Decision of the Swiss Supreme Court 4A_558/2011 of 27 March 2012...... 10.83
Fulham Football Club (1987) Ltd v Sir David Richards [2011] EWCA Civ 855 .... 2.159
Fyrnetics Ltd v Quantum Group Inc 293 F 3d 1023 (7th Cir 2002) 2.58

Ganz v Nationale des Chemins de Fer Tunisiens (SNCFT) (1991) Revue
   de l'Arbitrage 478 .... 10.51
Garrity v Lyle Stuart Inc, 40 NY 2d 354; 353 NE 2d 793 (1976) 9.47
Gateway Tech Inc v MCI Telecomms Corp, 64 F 3d 993 (5th Cir 1995) 10.80
Gatoil Int'l Inc v Nat'l Iranian Oil Co, High Court of Justice, Queen's Bench Division
   (1988) XVII Ybk Comm Arb 587.................... 2.39
Ghirardosi v Minister of Highways (BC) (1996) 56 DLR (2d) 469 .... 4.146
Giacobassi Grandi Vini SpA v Renfield Corp (1987) US Dist, LEXIS 1783 .... 2.173
Glaser v Legg, No. 12-cv-00805, 2013 WL 870382 (DDC Mar 11, 2013) 10.10
Glencore Ltd v Degussa Engineered Carbons LP 848 F Supp. 2d 410 (2012) 2.23
Glencore Ltd v Schnitzer Steel Products, 189 F 3d 264, 265–266 (2nd Cir 1999)........ 2.212
GMAC Commer Credit LLC v Springs Indus 171 F Supp 2d 209; 2001 US Dist
   LEXIS 5152; 44 UCC Rep Serv 2d.................... 2.55
Gold Coast Ltd v Naval Gijon SA [2006] EWHC 1044 (Comm); [2006] Arb LR 381.... 9.188
Goldman Sachs Execution & Clearing v Off'l Unsecured Creditors Committee of
   Bayou Group, 491 Fed Appx. 201, 2012 US App LEXIS 13531, 3-4 (2012)........ 10.74
Gosset Cass Civ Lere, 7 May 1963....................2.106
Gouvernement de la République arage d'Egypte c/ société Malicorp Ltd, Cour de
   cassation, 1ère chamber civile, 23 June 2010, Rev Arb 2011, 446 .... 10.55
Gouvernement du Pakistan v Société Dallah Real Estate and Tourism Holding Co,
   Cour d'Appel de Paris, 17 February 2011, (2012) Revue de l'Arbitrage 369 .... 11.69
Grand Pacific Holdings Ltd v Pacific China Holdings Ltd, CACV 136/2011,
   19 February 2013 .... 10.54
Great Offshore Ltd v Iranian Offshore Engineering and Construction Co (2008)
   14 SCC 240.................... 2.19
Great Western Mortgage Corp v Peacock, 110 F 3d 222 (3rd Cir 1997) 2.210
Greek Paper Holdings v Greece, Areios Pagos (Supreme Court of Greece),
   No. 102/2012.................... 10.46
Green Tree Financial Corp v Bazzle 539 US 444 (2003) 2.226, 2.227, 2.228, 2.229
Groenselect Management NV v Van der Boogaard, Dutch Supreme Court, NJ 2007,
   561 (10 November 2006) 2.157
Gruntal & Co, Inc v Ronald Steinberg, et al, 854 F Supp 324 (DNJ 1994).............. 2.55
Guignier v HRA Europe (2001) Revue de l'Arbitrage 199 .... 10.55
Gulf Guar. Life Ins Co v Conn Gen Life Ins Co, 304 F 3d 476, 490 (5th Cir 2002) 4.108

Habas Sinai Ve Tibbi Gazlar Istihsal Endustrisi AS v VSC Steel Company Ltd [2013]
   EWHC 4071 (Comm) 2.84
Hall Steel Co v Metalloyd Ltd, 492 F Supp. 2d 215 (ED Mich 2007).................. 7.19
Hall Street Associates, LLC v Mattel, Inc, 552 US 576 (2008)........... 9.198, 10.74, 10.80
Halpern v Halpern [2006] EWHC 603 (Comm), [2007] EWCA Civ 291 ....3.85, 3.189
Hart Surgical, Inc v Ultracision Inc, 244 F 3d 231 (1st Cir 2001) 9.24
Hassneh Insurance Co of Israel v Mew [1993] 2 Lloyd's Rep 243 ....2.165, 2.178
Harbour Assurance Co Ltd v Kansa General International Insurance Co Ltd [1993]
   1 Lloyd's Rep 455.................... 2.112
Hartford Accident and Indemnity Company v Swiss Reinsurance America Corporation,
   87 F Supp 2d 300 (SDNY 2000) 2.220
Hay Group, Inc v EBS Acquisition Corp, 360 F 3d 404, 410 (3d Cir 2004) 7.36

Table of Cases

Heifer International Inc v Christiansen [2007] EWHC 3015 (TCC) 2.21
Heisei 21 (Chu) No. 6, Tokyo District Court (June 13, 2011) 10.63
Hewlett-Packard, Inc v Berg, 867 F Supp 1126 . . . . 11.53
Heyman v Darwins Ltd [1942] AC 356 . . . . 2.102
Hilmarton I, Cour de Cassation, 1ère civ, Mar 23, 1994, Rev Arb 1994 437 Bull civ I 10.06
Hilmarton Ltd v Omnium de Traitement et de Valorisation (OTV) (1994) Revue
 de l'Arbitrage 327 . . . . 11.94, 11.97
Himpurna California Energy Ltd v Republic of Indonesia, XXV YBCA (2000), 11–432 . . . 3.90
HKL Group Co Ltd v Rizq International Holdings Pte Ltd [2013] SGHC 5 . . . . . . 1.144, 2.199
Hooper Bailie Associated v Natcon Group Pty (1992) 28 NSWLR 206 . . . . 2.92
Howard University v Metropolitan Campus Police Officer's Union, 519 F Supp 2d 27,
 35 (DDC 2007) 10.31
Howsam v Dean Witter Reynolds Inc 537 US 79, 123 S Ct 588 . . . . 1.65, 5.126
HSN Capital LLC (US) v Productora y Comercializador de Television, SA de CV
 (Mexico) (2007) XXXII Ybk Comm Arb 774 . . . . 11.86

Indian Organic Chemical Ltd v Subsidiary 1 (US) Subsidiary 2 (US) and Chemtex
 Fibres Inc (Parent Company) (US) (1979) IV Ybk Comm Arb 271 . . . . 11.47, 11.48
Industrie Technofrigo Dell'Orto SpA (Italy) v PS Profil Epitoipari Kereskedelmi
 SS Szolgatato KFT (Hungary) (2007) XXXII Ybk Comm Arb, 406 . . . . 11.77
Industrotech Constructors Inc v Duke University (1984) 67 NC App 741, 314 S E 2d 272 . . . . 2.173
Inland Revenue Commissioners v Rossminster [1980] AC 952 . . . . 1.85
INSERM v Fondation F. Saugstad, Paris Court of Appeal (Nov. 13, 2008) 2.37, 10.25
Insigma Technology Co Ltd v Alstom Technology Ltd [2008] SGHC 134 . . . . 1.59, 1.144
Intel Corp v Advanced Micro Devices, Inc 542 US 241, 124 S Ct 2466,
 159 L Ed 2d 355 (2004) 7.40, 7.42
International Electric Corp v Bridas Sociedad Anonima Petrolera, Industrial y
 Comercial, 745 F Supp. 172, 178 (SDNY 1990) 10.26
International Research Corp Plc v Lufthansa Systems Asia Pacific Pte Ltd
 [2012] SGHC 226 . . . . 2.92
International Standard Electric Corp (US) v Bridas Sociedad Anonima Petrolera
 (Argentina) (1992) VII Ybk Comm Arb 639 . . . . 11.98
Iran Aircraft Ind v Avco Corp 980 F 2d 141 (2nd Cir 1992) 11.75

Jain v de Méré 51 F 3d (7th Cir 1995), 686 . . . . 3.58
Jean Lion et Compagnie v International Company for Commercial Exchanges
 (INCOME), French Supreme Court (Civ 1), No 08-10.281 (May 6, 2009) 10.85
Jiangsu Materials Group Light Industry and Weaving Co v Hong Kong Top-Capital
 Holdings Ltd (Canada) & Prince Development Ltd ('Yuyi'), Supreme People's
 Court (1998) 2.108
Jianlong v Golden Ocean [2013] EWHC 1063 . . . . 10.44
Jianxi Provincial Metal and Minerals Import and Export Corporation v
 Sulanser Co Ltd [1996] ADRLJ 249 . . . . 2.18
Jivraj v Hashwani [2011] 1 WLR 1872, [2011] UKSC 40 . . . . 4.62, 5.50
John Forster Emmott v Michael Wilson & Partners Limited [2008]
 EWCA Civ 184 . . . . 2.167, 2.168
Jorf Lafar Energy Company SCA (Morocco) v AMCI Export Corporation (US)
 (2007) XXXII Ybk Comm Arb, 713 . . . . 11.77
JSC Surtneftegat v President & Fellows of Harvard College SDNY 04 Civ 6069,
 11 October 2007 . . . . 2.231

Kahler v Midland Bank Ltd [1950] AC 24 . . . . 3.94
Kahn Lucas Lancaster Inc v Lark International Ltd 186 F 3d 210 (1999) 2.23, 2.26
Kanematsu USA Inc v ATS - Advanced Telecommunications Systems do Brasil Ltda,
 SEC 885 (18 April 2012) 2.15

Table of Cases

Kanoria v Guinness [2006] EWCA Civ 222; [2006] Arb LR 513 . . . . 11.59, 11.75
Karaha Bodas Co v Perusahaan Pertambangan Minyak, 364 F 3d 274
　(5th Cir 2004). 2.240
Karaha Bodas Company LLC (Cayman Islands) v Perusahaan Pertambangan
　Minyak Dan Gas Bumi Negara aka Pertamina (Indonesia), United States
　District Court, Southern District of Texas, Houston Division, 17 April 2003,
　XXVIII Ybk Comm Arb 908 . . . . 11.99
Khatib Petroleum Services International Co v Care Construction Co and Care
　Service Co, Court of Cassation, Case No 4729 of the Judicial Year 72
　(June 2004). 2.49
Kaverit Steel Crane Ltd v Kone Corporation 87 DLR 4th 129; (1994) XVII Ybk
　Comm Arb 346. . . . . 2.26, 2.27
Kazakhstan v Biedermann International, 168 F 3d 880 (5th Cir 1999). 7.40
Kin-Stib & Majić v Serbia, Eur Ct HR, No 12312.05 (Apr. 20, 2010) 10.95
Koehler v Bank of Bermuda Ltd 12 NY 3d 533 (2009) 11.29
K/S Norjarl A/S v Hyundai Heavy Industries Co Ltd [1991] 1 Lloyd's Rep 260;
　appeal dismissed [1992] QB 863; [1991] 1 Lloyd's Rep 524 . . . . .4.213, 5.50
Kvaerner Cementation India Ltd v Bajranglal Aggaral (2012) 5 SCC 214 . . . . 5.108
Kyocera Corp v Prudential-Bache Trade Services Inc, 341 F 3d 987 (9th Cir 2003) 10.79

La Donna Pty Ltd v Wolford AG [2005] VSC 359. . . . . .2.207
La Générale des Carrières et des Mines v FG Hemisphere Associates LLC
　[2012] UKPC 27. . . . . 11.143
Lachmar v Trunkline LNG Co, 753 F 2d 8 (2nd Cir 1985). 2.55
Lady Muriel, The [1995] 2 HKC 320 (CA). 3.46
Lampart Vegypary Gepgyar (Hungary) v srl Campomarzio Impianti (Italy) (1999)
　XXIVa Ybk Comm Arb 699. . . . . 11.52
LaPine Technology Corporation v Kyocera Corporation (LaPine I) 130 F 3d 884
　(9th Cir 1997). 10.78, 10.79
LaPine Technology Corporation v Kyocera Corporation (LaPine II)
　909 F Supp 697 (1995) 10.79
Landesgericht Hamburg, Judgment 19 December, 1967 [1968] Arbitrale
　Rechtspraak 138 . . . . 2.57
Larsen Oil and Gas Pte Ltd v Petroprod Ltd [2011] SGCA 21. 2.142
Law Debenture Trust Corporation plc v Elektrim Finance BV [2005] EWHC 1412 (Ch). . . .2.95
Lesotho Highlands Development Authority v Impregilo SpA and others [2005]
　UKHL 43; [2006] 1 AC 221. . . . . 2.112, 9.42, 9.43, 10.29, 10.53, 10.75
Liberian Eastern Timber Company v Government of the Republic of Liberia,
　650 F Supp 73 (SDNY 1986); 659 F Supp 606 (DDC 1987) 11.153
Libyan American Oil Company (Liamco) v Libyan Arab Republic, 20 ILM 1 (1981) 11.145
Libyan American Oil Company (Liamco) v Socialist Peoples Libyan Arab Yamahyria,
　formerly Libyan Arab Republic (1982) VII Ybk Comm Arb, 382. . . . . 11.79
Life Receivables Trust v Syndicate 102 at Lloyd's of London, 549 F 3d 210, 216-217
　(2d Cir 2008) 7.36
Lipcon v Underwriters at Lloyd's, 148 F 3d 1285 (5 August 1998) 2.139
Leibinger v Stryker Trauma GmbH [2005] EWHC 690 (Comm). 3.22
L'Italia SpA v Milani, Corte de Cassazione, Judgment No 3207 of 1 April 1994. . . . . 2.53
Liv Hidravlika v Diebolt, Paris Cour d'Appel, No 05-10577 (28 February 2008) 2.131
Liversidge v Anderson [1941] 3 All ER 336 . . . . 1.85
Lloyd v Horensce LLC 369 F 3d 263 . . . . 1.55
LNC Investments Inc v Republic of Nicaragua, 115 F Supp 2d 358 (SDNY 2000). 11.154
Louisiana Stadium & Exposition District, State of Louisiana v Merrill Lynch,
　No 10-889-CV (2nd Cir November 22, 2010). 2.210
Luis Alberto Duran Valencia v Bancolombia of 24 April 2003 . . . . 2.235
Lundgren v Freeman 307 F.2d 104 (9th Cir 1962). 5.54

Table of Cases

LV Finance Group Ltd v IPOC International Growth Fund Ltd (Bermuda) 4P 102
(2006) (1st Div SFT) 10.72

Macron et IDD c/ SCAP (2003) Revue de l'arbitrage 177 .... 10.51
Mamidoil-Jetoil Greek Petroleum Company SA v Okta Crude Oil Refinery AD
[2001] 2 All ER (Comm) 193 .... 9.66
Mangistaumunaigoz Oil v United World Trade Inc [1995] 1 Lloyd's Rep 617 .... 2.198
Marc Rich Co AG v Societa Italiana Impianti PA (The Atlantic Emperor) [1989]
1 Lloyd's Rep 548 (CA) 5.129, 5.134
Marketing Displays International Inc v VR Van Raalte Reclame BV, 29
(Judgment of 24 March 2005, Case No 04/694 and 04/695) 3.105, 11.121
Matermaco SA v PPM Cranes Inc (2000) XXV Ybk Comm Arb, 20 September 1999,
Tribunal de Commerce, Brussels 3.26
Mauritius Commercial Bank v Hestia Holdings Ltd [2013] EWHC 1328 (Comm) 2.98
Maximov v Novolipetsky Metallurgicheskiy Kombinat Ruling of the Supreme
Arbitrazh Court, VAS-15384/11 (30 January 2012) 2.158, 11.103
Meadows Indemnity Co Ltd v Nutmeg Insurance Co, 157 FRD 42 (MD Tenn 1994) 7.36
Metallgesellschaft AG v M/V Capitan Constante and Yacimientos Petroliferos Fiscales,
790 F 2d 280 (2nd Cir 1986) 9.24
Metrô v Consórcio Via Amarela 10.10
Milsom v Ablyazov [2011] EWHC 955 (Ch) 2.169
Minmetals Germany v Ferco Steel (1999) XXIV Ybk Comm Arb 739 .... 11.76
Miserecchi v Agnesi, Corte di Cassazione, 13 Dec 1971, No 3620 .... 2.15
Mitsubishi Motors Corp v Soler Chrysler Plymouth Inc, 473 US 614,
105 S Ct 3346 (1985) 2.127, 2.135, 2.136, 2.139, 3.130, 9.47, 10.51, 11.110, 11.122
Mobil Cerro Negro Limited v Petroleos De Venezuela SA, High Court of Justice,
Queen's Bench Division (Commercial Court), 2008 Folio 61, 18 March 2008 .... 7.50
Monegasque de Reassurance SAM (Monde Re) v NAK Naftogart of Ukraine and
State of Ukraine 311 F 3d 488 (2002) 11.123, 11.124
Montpelier Reinsurance Ltd v Manufacturers Property & Casualty Ltd,
Supreme Court, Bermuda, 24 April 2008 .... 7.06
Morelite Construction Corp v New York City District Carpenters Benefit Funds
748 F 2d 79 (1984) 4.108
Mors/Labinal Cour d'Appel de Paris of 19 May 1993 [1993] Rev Arb 645;
Cour de Cassation of 5 January 1999 .... 2.134
Mousaka v Golden Seagull Maritime [2001] 2 Lloyd's Rep 657 .... 10.58
MRI Trading v Erdenet Mining [2013] EWCA 156 .... 10.75
Ms Emja Braack Shiffahrts KG v Wärtsilä Diesel AB Supreme Court of Sweden,
15 October 1997, [1998] Revue de l'Arbitrage 431 .... 2.55
Multistar Leasing Ltd v Twinstar Leasing Ltd, US District Court, Eastern District of
Louisiana, August 281998, Civil Action Case No 98–1330; (2000) XXV Ybk
Comm Arb 871 .... 2.27
Municipalité de Khoms El Mergeb c/ Sté Dalico, Cass Civ 1ère, 20 December 1993,
Rev Arb, 1994, 116 .... 3.34
Musawi v R E International (UK) Ltd & Others [2007] EWHC 2981 .... 3.187
Myanma Taung Chi Oo Co Ltd v Win Win Nu [2003] 2 SLR 945 .... 2.169
Mylcrist Builders Ltd v Buck [2008] EWHC 2172 (TCC) 2.127

N Radakrishnan v Maestro Engineers (2010) 1 SCC 72 .... 2.154
Nafimco, Paris Cour d'Appel, 22 January 2004 .... 2.182
Naresh Kumar Lamba v Ashok Kumar Lamba and others, High Court of Delhi
at New Delhi, 2 May, 2013 .... 7.06
Nat'l Iranian Oil Co v Ashland Oil, Inc, 817 F 2d 326 (5th Cir 1987) 3.58
National Broadcasting Co, Inc v Bear Stearns & Co, Inc, 165 F 3d 184 (2d Cir 1999) 7.40

Table of Cases

National Electricity Company AD (Bulgaria) v ECONBERG Ltd (Croatia) in
 (2000) XXV Ybk Comm Arb 678 .... 11.52
National Grid v Argentina Decision of the Fourth Chamber of the Camara
 Contencioso-Administrativo Federal, 2 July 2007 .... 7.60
National Power Corporation (Philippines) v Westinghouse (USA), Tribunal Fédéral,
 2 September 1993, ATF 119 II 380.. 2.151
National Thermal Power Corporation v The Singer Corp et al 1992 (3) 7 Judgements
 Today SC 198 .... 10.26
Naviera Amazonia Peruana SA v Compania Internacional de Seguros de Peru [1988]
 1 Lloyd's Rep 116 .... 3.68
NB Three Shipping Ltd v Harebell Shipping Ltd [2005] 1 Lloyd's Rep 205 .... 2.95
NCC International AB v Alliance Concrete Singapore Pte Ltd, Singapore Court of
 Appeal, CA 47/2007, 26 February 2008.. 7.50
New Regency Productions, Inc v Nippon Herald Films, Inc, United States Court of
 Appeals, Ninth Circuit, 05-55224, 4 September 2007 .... 4.75
Nisshin Shipping Co Ltd v Cleaves & Co Ltd [2003] EWHC 2602 (Comm)............ 2.52
Nokia Maillefer SA v Mosser, Tribunal Cantonal (Court of Appeal) 30 March 1993
 (1996) XXI Ybk Comm Arb 681 .... 2.198
Norfolk Southern Corp v Gen Sec Ins Co, 626 F Supp 2d 882 (ND Ill 2009) 7.43

O Ltd (Hong Kong) v S GmbH (Austria) (1997) XXXII Ybk Comm Arb, 254 .... 11.70
OAO Northern Shipping Company v Remolcadores De Marin SL (Remmar)
 [2007] EWHC 1821 .... 5.74
OAO Stoilensky GOK v Mabetex Project Engineering SA, et al and Interconstruction
 Project Management SA v OAO Stoilensky GOK, Case no A08-7941/02-18........ 11.99
Obergericht of Basle, June 3, 1971 (1979) IV Ybk Comm Arb 309 .... 2.15
Oberlandesgericht, Frankfurt, 24 September 1985, (1990) XV Ybk Comm Arb 666 ...... 2.69
OG 6 June 2006, 9 Ob 207/06v (Austrian Supreme Court) 5.52
Oil & Natural Gas Commission v Western Company of North America (1987)
 All Indian Reports SC 674 .... 10.26
OLG Oldenburg [2006] Schieds VZ 223... 2.199
OLG Stuttgart [2006] OLG Report Stuttgart 685................................... 2.199
Onex Corp v Ball Corp (1995) XX Ybk Comm Arb 275............................ 2.69
ONGC v Saw Pipes Ltd (2003) 5 SCC 705 .... 10.84
Operadora DB Mex, SA, In re 2009 US Dist LEXIS 68091, at *18-20
 (MD Fla Aug 1, 2009) 7.43
Orascom Telecom Holding SAE v Republic of Chad and another [2008]
 2 Lloyd's Rep 396 .... 11.152
Orion Compania Espanola de Seguros v Belfort Maatschappij Voor Algemene
 Verzekgringeen [1962] 2 Lloyd's Rep 257...................................... 3.133
Oxford Health Plans LLC v Sutter 133 S Ct 2064 (2013) 2.233
Oxus Gold plc, No Misc 06-82-GEB, 2007 US Dist LEXIS 24061
 (DNJ April 2, 2007), In re 7.43

Panevezys-Saldutiskis Railway (Estonia v Lithuania) (1939) PCIJ Reports Series A/B 76,
 ICGJ 328 (PCIJ 1939) 8.05
Paris Lapeyre v Sauvage (2001) Revue de l'Arbitrage 806 .... 10.46
Parklane Hoisery Co v Shore, 439 US 322 (1979) 9.185
Parsons Whittemore Overseas Co Inc v Société Générale de l'Industrie du Papier,
 508 F 2d 969 (2nd Cir 1974); (1976) I Ybk Comm Arb 205 .... 10.03, 10.55, 11.61,
  11.73, 11.79, 11.107, 11.111
Patel v Patel [2000] QB 551 .... 2.206
Pedcor Mgt Co Inc Welfare Benefit Plan v N Am Indemnity, 343 F 3d 355
 (5th Cir 2003)... 3.30

xxxi

Table of Cases

Pennzoil Exploration and Production Co v Ramco Energy Ltd, Case 96–20497,
   Fifth Circuit Court of Appeals on 13 May 1998. . . . . 2.69
Peterson Farms Inc v C & M Farming Ltd [2004] EWHC 121. . . . . 1.115, 2.45
Petition No 353 of 2011, Abu Dhabi Court of Cassation (24 August 2011). 2.108
Petrobras v Tractebel Energia & MSGAS, Superior Court of Justice of Brazil,
   Case No. AgRg MC 19.226 – MS (2012/0080171-0), 29 June 2012 . . . . 7.50
PPG Inc v Pilkington Plc (1995) XX Ybk Comm Arb 885. . . . . 9.45
Philippine Republic (1977) B Verf GE 342 . . . . 11.152
Pickens v Templeton [1994] 2 NZLR 718 . . . . 5.54
PK Time Group, LLC v Robert, No 12 Civ 8200 (PAC), 2013 WL 3833084
   (SDNY Jul 13, 2013). 5.77
PMT Partners Pty Ltd v Australian National Parks & Wildlife Service (1995)
   184 CLR 302 . . . . 2.96
Positive Software Solutions, Inc v New Century Fin Corp, 476 F 3d 278 (5th Cir 2007) . . . 4.104
Prest v Petrodel [2013] UKSC 34. . . . . 2.51
Preston v Ferrer 552 US 346 (2008). 2.107
Prima Paint Corp v Flood Conklin Mfg Co 388 US 395; 87 S Ct 1801;
   18 LEd2d 1270 (1967) 2.68, 2.107
Prime Therapeutics LLC v Omnicare, Inc, 555 F Supp 2d 993, 999 (D Minn 2008) 10.74
Protech Projects Construction (Pty) Ltd v Al-Kharafi & Sons [2005] EWHC
   2165 (Comm) 10.84
PT Garuda Indonesia v Birgen Air [2002] 1 SLR 393 (CA). 3.59
PT Putrabali Adyamulia v Rena Holdings, Cour de Cassation, 1ère civ, June 29, 2007 . . . 10.06
PT Thiess Contractors Indonesia v PT Kaltim Prima Coal and another [2011]
   EWHC 1842 (Comm) 2.66
PT Tugu Pratama Indonesia v Magma Nusantara Ltd, Singapore High Court, CLOUT
   Case No. 56710 September 2003 . . . . 7.06
Publicis Communications and Publicis SA v True North Communications Inc
   (2000) XXV Ybk Comm Arb 1152. . . . . 9.12, 9.13
Publicis Communication v True North Communications Inc, 206 F 3d 725, 727
   (7th Cir 2000). 9.24

R v Momdou and others [2005] EWCA Crim 177. . . . . 3.221
R SA v A Ltd (2001) XXVI Ybk Comm Arb 863. . . . . 11.52
Radio Corporation of America v China (1941) 8 ILR 26 . . . . 1.189
Rahimtoola v The Nizam of Hyderabad [1958] AC 379. . . . . 1.184
Regent Company v Ukraine, Eur Ct HR, No 773/03 (3 April, 2008) 10.95
Rena K, The [1979] QB 377. . . . . 2.203
Renusagar Power Co Ltd v General Electric Co (1995) XX Ybk Comm Arb 681 . . . . 11.56,
                                                                                        11.109, 11.112
Republic of Argentina v BG Group PLC, 665 F 3d 1363 (DC Cir 2012) 10.47
Republic of Ecuador, In re No. C-10, ND Calif; 2010 US Dist LEXIS 132045 . . . . 7.44
Republic of Ecuador v Bjorkman, 801 F Supp 2d 1121 (D Col 2011) 7.43
Republic of Kazakhstan v Istil Group Inc [2004] Eng Comm QBD 579. . . . . 10.44
Republic of Latvia v Latvijas Gaze, Svea Court of Appeal (4 May 2005) 2.138
Rhone Mediterranee v Achille Lauro 712 F 2d 50 (6 July 1983) 2.202
Richardson v Mellish (1824) 2 Bing. 229; [1824–34] All ER 25 . . . . 10.87, 11.105
Riverstone Ins Ltd v Liquidators of ICD, Paris Cour d'Appel, Case No 08/12816
   (5 November 2009). 2.240
RM Investment & Trading Company v Boeing Company, 1994 (4) SCC 541, (1997)
   XXII Ybk Comm Arb 711 . . . . 9.29, 11.49
Rocco Giuseppe e Fli v Federal Commerce and Navigation Ltd (1985) 10 Ybk
   Comm Arb 464. . . . . 2.57
Rookes v Barnard [1964] AC 1129; [1967] 1 Lloyd's Rep 28 (HL). 9.45
Roz Trading Ltd, In re 469 F Supp 2d 1221 (ND Ga 2006) 7.40, 7.41, 7.42, 7.43, 7.44

Rubenstein v Otterbourg 357 N.Y.S. 2d 62 (N.Y. Misc. 1973) 5.64
Russian Federation v Franz J Sedelmayer, Case No ö 170-10, 1 July 2011
 (Swedish Supreme Court) 11.152
Russian Telephone Company v Sony Ericsson Mobile Communications Rus,
 Case No A40-49223/11-112-401 (19 June 2012) 2.97

SA Caisse Fédérale de Crédit Mutuel du Nord de la France v Banque Delubac et
 Compagnie (2001) Revue de l'Arbitrage 918 .... 10.30
SA Clinique de Champagne v Enrico Ambrosini, 3 July 2012 (Cour d'Appel de Reims
 (First Civil Chamber)) (2012) Revue de l'Arbitrage 681 .... 7.26
SA Compagnie commercial André v SA Tradigrain France (2001) Revue de l'Arbitrage 773 ... 11.119
SA Elf Aquitaine and Total v Mattei, Lai Kamara and Reiner, Paris Court of
 First Instance, 6 January 2010 .... 7.51
SA Laboratoires Eurosilicone v Société Bez Medizintechnik GmbH (2004) Revue
 de l'Arbitrage 133 .... 11.113
Sanghi Polyesters Ltd (India) v The International Investor KCFC (Kuwait) [2000]
 1 Lloyd's Rep 480 .... 3.186, 9.72, 10.75
Santos v GE Co, No. 10 Civ 6948, 2011 US Dist LEXIS 131925 .... 9.19
Scherk v Alberto-Culver, 417 US 506 (1974) 2.139, 11.110
Secretary of State for the Home Department v Rehman [2002] 1 All ER 122 .... 6.87
Security Life Ins Co of America, 228 F 3d 865, 872 (2000) 7.35
Seidel v Telus Communications Inc [2011] 1 SCR 531 .... 2.202
SerVaas Incorporated v Rafidain Bank & Republic of Iraq and others [2012] UKSC 40 ... 11.152
Shaanxi Provincial Medical Health Products I/E Corporation v Olpesa, SA, Tribunal
 Supremo, 112/2002, 7 October 2003 in (2005) Ybk Comm Arb XXX 617 .... 11.53
Shanghai Foodstuffs Import & Export Corp v International Chemical, Inc
 No 99 CV 3320, 2004 US Dist LEXIS 1423 (SDNY Feb 4, 2004) 10.74
Shearson v McMahon, 482 US 220, 107 S Ct 2332 (1987) 2.139
Skype Technologies SA v Joltid Ltd [2009] EWHC 2783 (Ch) 2.69
Smith Ltd v H International [1991] 2 Lloyd's Rep 127 .... 3.42
SNF SAS v Chambre de Commerce International, Cour d'Appel de Paris, 1 ère
 Chambre, Section C, 22 janvier 2009 .... 1.166, 5.63, 5.64
SNF SAS (France) v Cytec Industries BV (Holland), Cass 1, 4 June 2008 ..... 2.138, 10.84, 11.121
Snyder v Smith 736 F 2d 409 (7th Cir 1984), cert denied, 469 US 1037 (1984) 3.58
Sociedad de Inversiones Inmobiliarias Del Puerto SA v Constructora Iberoamericana
 SA, Court of Appeals on Commercial Matters, Division D, 7 February 2011
 (Argentina Court of Appeals on Commercial Matters) 10.28
Société Cubic Défense Système v Chambre de Commerce Internationale (1997)
 Revue de l'Arbitrage 417 .... 5.65, 5.66
Société d'Investissement Kal (Tunisia) v Taieb Haddad (Tunisia) and Hans Barrett
 (1998) XXIII Ybk Comm Arb 770 .... 11.50
Societe Empresa de Telecomunicaciones de Cuba SA v Telefonica Antillana SA and
 SNC Banco Nacional de Comercio Exterior. Cour d'Appel de Paris, 1ere
 Chambre – Section C. Decision of 16 November 2006 .... 5.95
Société Fashion Box Group SPA v Société AJ Heelstone LLC (2006)
 Revue de l'Arbitrage 857 .... 10.55
Société Générate de Surveillance SA (SGS) v Islamic Republic of Pakistan, Pakistan
 Supreme Court, July 3, 2002 .... 7.60
Société Isover-Saint-Gobain v Société Dow Chemical France (Cour d'Appel, Paris,
 22 October, 1983) [1984] Revue de l'Arbitrage 98 .... 2.46, 2.48
Société Leng d'or v Société Pavan SPA (2007) Revue de l'Arbitrage 933 .... 10.55
Société Orthopaedic Hellas v Société Amplitude, Cass civ 1, No 11-25.891
 (7 November 2012) 2.49
Société Overseas Mining Investments Ltd v Société Commercial Caribbean Niquel,
 Cour de Cassation of Paris (CA Paris, 1ère Ch., 25 March 2010, No 08-23901) 11.75

Table of Cases

Société PT Putrabali Adyamulia v Société Rena Holding et Société Mnugotia
  Est Epices (2007) Revue de l'Arbitrage 507 ....3.76, 11.96, 11.97
Société Sardisud, March 25, 1994 (Cour d'Appel de Paris (First Civil Chamber))
  (1994) Revue de l'Arbitrage 391 .... 7.19
Soleimany v Soleimany [1999] QB 785.....................................3.105, 11.106
Sonatrach (Algeria) v Distrigas Corp (US District Court) Massachusetts (1995)
  XX Ybk Comm Arb 795..2.142, 11.110
Sonatrach Petroleum Corp v Ferrell International Ltd [2002] 1 All ER
  (Comm) 627 .... 3.22, 3.207
Sovereign Participations International SA v Chadmore Developments Ltd (2001)
  XXVI Ybk Comm Arb 299 .... 10.20
Sperry Int'l Trade, Inc v Gov't of Israel, 532 F Supp 901 (SDNY 1982)................. 9.19
Sponsor AB v Lestrade, Court of Appeal of Pau [1988] Revue de l'Arbitrage 153 .... 2.49
Sport Maska Inc v Zittrerm [1988] 1 SCR 564 .... 5.54
Spring Hope Rockwool v Industrial Clean Air Inc, 504 F Supp 1385 (1981)............. 3.58
Standard Bent Glass Corp v Glassrobots Oy, 333 F 3d 440, 449 (3d Cir 2003) 2.23
Stanton v Paine Webber Jackson Curtis Inc, 685 F Supp 1241 (SD Fla 1988)............ 7.36
Star Shipping AS v China National Foreign Trade Transportation Corp [1993]
  2 Lloyd's Rep 445 (CA)... 2.198
Starlight Shipping Co v Allianz Marine & Aviation Versicherungs AG [2011]
  EWHC 3381 (Comm) 2.69
State of New York Department of Taxation and Finance v Valenti 57 AD 2d 174 and
  393 NYS 2d 797 .... 9.164
Sté Alcatel Business Systems et Alcatel Micro Electronics c/ v and others, Cass. Civ.
  1ere 27 March 2007, Bull Civ I, No 129; JDI No 3 July 2007, comm 18............. 2.55
Stolt-Nielsen SA v Animal Feeds Intern Corp, 2008 WL 4779582 (2nd Cir,
  4 November 2008) 2.212, 2.231, 2.232
Stolt-Nielsen SA v Animal Feeds Int'l Corp, 130 S. Ct. 1758, 1768 (2010) 10.74
Stolt-Nielson SA v Celanese AG, 430 F.3d 567 (2nd Cir 2005) 5.19
Stran Greek Refineries & Stratis Andreadis v Greece, Eur Ct HR, No 13427/87
  (Dec. 9, 1994)... 10.95
Sudarshan Chopra and others v Company Law Board and others (2004) 2 Arb LR 241 .... 2.65
Sulamérica CIA Nacional de Seguros SA v Enesa Engenharia SA [2012]
  EWCA Civ 638............ 2.84, 3.12, 3.16, 3.17, 3.18, 3.19, 3.20, 3.21, 3.22, 3.23, 3.24
Sumitomo Heavy Industries Ltd v Oil & Natural Gas Commission [1994]
  1 Lloyd's Rep 45 .... 3.22
Sutcliffe v Thackrah [1974] AC 727; [1974] 1 Lloyd's Rep 312 (HL) 5.48, 5.54
Suzhou Canadian Solar v LDK Solar (unpublished)................................. 1.160
Svenska Petroleum Exploration AB v Government of the Republic of Lithuania (No 2)
  [2006] EWCA Civ 1529 .... 11.145
Syrian Petroleum Company v GTM-Entrepose SA, Swiss Federal Court decision of
  July 16, 1990, Proc No 58/1990 (unpublished)................................. 9.196

T Co Metals, LLC v Dempsey Pipe & Supply, Inc, 592 F 3d 329, 339-40 (2d Cir 2010)....10.74
Tang Chung Wah v Grant Thornton International Ltd [2013] All ER (Comm) 1226...... 2.91
teleMates Pty Ltd v Standard SoftTel Solutions Pvt Ltd [2011] NSWSC 1365
  (November 11, 2011).. 10.30
Telenor Mobile Communications AS v Storm LLC 584 F 3d 396 (2d Cir 2009) 11.79
Temple of Preah-Vihear case, The (1962) ICJ 6 .... 11.13
Tensacciai SpA v Freyssinet Terra Armata Srl, Swiss Federal Tribunal, Case
  No 4P 278/2005 (8 March 2006).......................................2.139, 11.121
TermoRio SA ESP v Electranta SP, 487 F 3d 928 (DC Cir 2007)..................... 10.06
TermoRio SA ESP v Electrificadora Del Atlantico SA ESP 421 F Supp 2d 87
  (DDC 2006) 11.97
Terna Bahrain v Bin Kamil [2012] EWHC 3283.................................... 10.10

Table of Cases

Thai-Lao Lignite (Thailand) Co, Ltd, et al v Laos, 2012 WL 966042 (SDNY, 2012) 7.44
Thai-Lao Lignite & Hongsa Lignite v Laos, Malaysian High Court, oral decision
    27 December, 2012 .... 10.46
Thalès Air Défence v Euromissile, Case No 2002/60932 (18 November 2004)
    (Paris Cour d'Appel) 2.138, 11.121
Thibodeau v Comcast Corp, 2006 Pa Super. 306 (2006) 2.229
Thyssen Canada Ltd v Mariana Maritime SA and another [2005] EWHC 219 .... 10.30
Titan Corporation v Alcatel CIT SA (Svea Court of Appeal, RH 2005:1) (T 1038-05),
    YCA XXX (2005), 139 .... 3.61, 6.162
Tongyuan International Trading Group v Uni-Clan [2001] 4 Intl ALR N-31 .... 11.83
Total v Achille Lauro Corte di Cassazione, Judgment No 361/1977, (1977) 17 Rassegna
    dell'Arbitrato 94 .... 2.57
Toyo Tire Holdings of Americas, Inc v Continental Tire North America, Inc and others,
    United States Court of Appeals for the Ninth Circuit, 10-55145, 17 June 2010 .... 7.50
Trelleborg do Brasil Ltda v Anel Empreendimentos Participações e Agropecuária Ltda,
    Apelação Cível No 267.450.4/6-00, 7th Private Chamber of São Paulo Court of
    Appeals (24 May 2004) 2.49

Uni-Kod c/ Sté Ouralkali, 30 March 2004, Cass. Civ. 1ère, Revue de l'Arbitrage,
2005, 959 .... 3.34
Union of India and others v Lief Hoegh Co (Norway) (1984) IX Ybk Comm Arb 405.... 11.48
Union of India v McDonnell Douglas Corp [1993] 2 Lloyd's Rep 48 .... 3.56
United Group Rail Services v Rail Corp New South Wales [2002] CLC 1324 .... 2.92
United Indus Workers v Gov't of the VI, 987 F 2d 162 .... 10.31
United Mexican States v Marvin Roy Feldman Karpa, File No 03-CV-23500,
    Ontario Superior Court of Justice, December 3, 2003 .... 10.83
United States Lines, Inc et al (US) v American Steamship Owners Mutual Protection
    and Indemnity Association, Inc et al (US), XXV YBCA 1057 (2000) (2nd Cir,
    1 Nov 1999) 2.142

Van Uden Maritime v Deco-Line Case C-391/95 [1999] 2 WLR 118 .... 5.130, 5.131
Vee Networks Ltd v Econet Wireless International Ltd [2005] 1 Lloyd's Rep 192.... 5.74, 5.109
Venture Global Engineering v Satyam Computer Services, 233 Fed Appx 517
    (CA 6 (Mich)) 11.99
Venture Global Engineering v Satyam Computer Services Ltd and another, (Supreme
    Court of India, Civil Appeal No 309 of 2008) [2008] INSC 40 .... 9.59, 10.26, 11.99
Vynior's Case (1609) 8 Co Rep 80a 1.16

Walford v Miles [1992] 2 WLR 174 .... 2.90
Walter Rau Neusser Oel Und Fett Ag v Cross Pacific Trading Ltd [2005] FCA 1102 ...... 2.27
Warnes SA v Harvic International Ltd 2.66
Weinburg v Silber, 140 F Supp 2d 712 (ND Tex 2001) 10.23
Wellington Associates Ltd v Mr Kirit Mehta (2000) 4 SCC 272 .... 2.65
West Tankers Inc v RAS Riunione Adriatica di Sicurta SpA (The Front Comor)
    [2005] 2 All ER (Comm) 240 .... 2.55
Westacre Investments Inc v Jugoimport-SPDR Holding Co Ltd [1999] 2 Lloyd's
    Rep 65 (CA) 11.107
Western Oil Sands Inc v Allianz Insurance Company of Canada, Alberta Court of
    Queen's Bench [2004] ABQB 79 .... 2.239
Westminster Securities Corp v Petrocom Energy, 456 Fed Appx 42, US App
    LEXIS 1069 (2012) 10.74
Westwood Shipping Lines Inc v Universal Schiffahrtsgesellschaft mbH
    [2012] EWHC 3837 (Comm) 2.169
Willoughby Roofing Supply Co v Kajima International Inc, 776 F 2d 269
    (11th Cir 1985) 9.47

Wm Passalacqua Builders v Resnick Developers 933 F2d 131 (2nd Cir 1991) 2.51
Woolf v Collis Removal Service [1948] 1 KB 11. . . . . 2.68
World Trade Corporation Ltd v Czarnikow Sugar Ltd [2004] EWHC 2332. . . . . 10.53
WSG Nimbus Pte Ltd v Board of Control For Cricket in Sri Lanka, Singapore High
 Court, No 601627 (13 May 2002) 2.96

X v 1. Union Cycliste Internationale (UCI), 2. Fédération Z, Federal Supreme Court of
 Switzerland, 1st Civil Law Chamber, Decision 4A_110/2012, 9 October 2012 . . . . 5.75
X v Banque Privée Edmond de Rothschild Europe (Rothschild), Cour de Cassation
 (26 September 2012). 2.98
X GmbH v Y Sàrl, Decision No 4A_46/2011 (16 May 2011). 2.91
X SE & Y GmbH v Z BV, First Civil Law Court (Switzerland), 4A_407/2012
 (Feb. 20, 2013) 10.33
XL Insurance Ltd v Owens Corning [2001] All ER (Comm) 530 . . . . 3.23

Yugoslavia v SEEE, 6 July 1970, France, Tribunal de Grande Instance; 65 ILR 47;
 Court of Appeal Paris, 21 April 1982; JDI (1983) 145 . . . . 11.148
Yugraneft Corporation v Rexx Management Corporation [2010] SCC 19 (Canada). 11.33
Yukos Capital SARL v OJSC Oil Company Rosneft [2014] EWHC 2188 . . . . 11.96

Zeiler v Deitsch, 500 F 3d 157, 168 (2d Cir 2007). 9.24
Zimmerman v Continental Airlines, Inc, 712 F 2d 55 (3d Cir 1983). 2.142

TABLE OF LEGISLATION

TABLE OF STATUTES

Arbitration Act 1698. . . . . 1.16
Arbitration Act 1950. . . . . 2.206, 2.211
Arbitration Act 1975
   s 1(i) 1.61
Arbitration Act 1996. . . . . 1.22, 1.61,
       1.106, 2.146, 2.206, 2.211, 3.64, 3.74,
       3.191, 4.103, 5.12, 7.48, 9.123, 11.59
   s 2 . . . . 3.55
   s 2(3) 7.33
   s 3 . . . . 3.55, 3.72
   s 4(1) 5.72
   s 5(5) 2.21
   s 5(43) 2.21
   s 7 . . . . .1.54, 2.109, 2.112, 5.101, 5.109
   s 8(1) 2.58
   s 9 . . . . .1.61, 2.52
   s 9(1) 2.127
   s 9(3) 2.206
   s 9(4) 2.206
   s 12 . . . . 5.14
   s 14 . . . . 4.13
   s 18 . . . . 4.45, 4.153
   s 18(3) 4.42
   s 20(3)–(4) 9.123
   s 24 . . . . 4.107, 5.71, 5.76
   s 24(1) 4.103, 5.04
   s 24(2) 5.67
   s 24(3) 4.107
   s 27 . . . . 2.82
   s 28 . . . . 4.220
   s 29 . . . . 5.55, 5.78
   s 30 . . . . 5.109
   s 31 . . . . 10.30
   s 31(1) 5.118
   s 32 . . . . 5.113
   s 33 . . . . 5.72
   s 33(1)(a) 1.82, 5.47
   s 33(1)(b) 5.67
   s 34 . . . . 5.12, 5.47
   s 35 . . . . 2.242
   s 38(3) 5.12
   s 38(5) 5.12, 5.21
   s 39 . . . . 9.03
   s 41(3) 2.211
   s 41(6) 5.12

   s 42 . . . . 5.42
   s 43 . . . . 5.42, 6.111, 7.33
   s 43(2) 5.42
   s 44 . . . . 5.42, 6.131, 7.27
   s 44(1) 3.46, 7.33
   s 44(2) 3.46
   s 44(2)(c) 5.42
   s 44(2)(e) 7.50
   s 44(3) 5.43, 7.38
   s 46 . . . . 1.139, 3.190
   s 46(1) 3.97
   s 46(1)(b) 3.190
   s 47 . . . . 9.22
   s 48 . . . . 9.42
   s 48(3) 9.60
   s 48(5)(b) 9.52, 9.53
   s 48(5)(c) 9.64
   s 49 . . . . 9.73, 9.76
   s 49(3) 9.74, 9.84
   s 52 . . . . 9.146
   s 52(5) 3.55, 3.70
   s 55 . . . . 3.70
   s 55(2) 9.170
   s 57 . . . . 10.07, 10.09, 10.19
   s 57(1)–(3) 9.188
   s 57(3) 9.188
   s 57(3)(b) 9.33
   s 66 . . . . 11.14
   s 67 . . . . 5.113
   s 68 . . . . 2.178, 5.67, 5.74, 10.62
   s 68(1) 10.53
   s 68(2) 10.53
   s 68(2)(a) 5.72
   s 68(2)(b) 9.43
   s 68(2)(d) 10.19
   s 68(3) 10.22, 10.53
   s 69 . . . . 9.43, 10.29
   s 69(1) 10.75
   s 69(2) 10.75
   s 69(3)(c)(ii) 10.77
   s 69(7) 10.76
   s 70(2) 10.07, 10.09
   s 70(3) 9.170
   s 73 . . . . 10.30
   s 74 . . . . 5.55
   s 82(1) 10.75

Arbitration Act 1996 (*cont.*):
   s 101(1) 11.19, 11.23
   s 101(2) 11.19
   s 107 . . . . 2.146
   Sch 1 . . . . 5.72
Arbitration (Scotland) Act 2010
   s 4 . . . . 2.22
Contracts (Rights of Third Parties)
   Act 1999 . . . . 2.52
   s 1 . . . . 2.52
   s 8 . . . . 2.52
Courts and Legal Services Act 1990 . . . . 2.211
Debt Relief (Developing Countries)
   Act 2010 . . . . 11.143
Proceeds of Crime Act 2002 . . . . 5.83
Insolvency Act 1986 . . . . 2.146
   s 349A 2.146
Limitation Act 1980
   s 7 . . . . 11.33
State Immunity Act 1978 . . . . 11.145,
                          11.152, 11.154
   s 9 . . . . 11.145
   s 13(5) 11.152
   s 14(4) 11.154

TABLE OF STATUTORY INSTRUMENTS

Civil Procedure Rules
   Pt 19 . . . . 2.225
Civil Procedure Rules 1998 . . . . 6.169
Money Laundering Regulations 2003 . . . 5.83
Money Laundering Regulations 2007 . . . 5.83
Unfair Terms in Consumer Contracts
   Regulations 1999 . . . . 2.127

OTHER LEGISLATION

Argentina
Code of Civil Procedure
   Art 737 . . . . 1.35
   Art 753 . . . . 7.16
National Code of Civil Procedure
   Art 760 . . . . 5.67
   Art 771 . . . . 5.67
National Code of Civil and Commercial
   Procedure (Further Articles)
   Art 518 . . . . 11.14

Australia
International Arbitration Act 1974
   s 28 . . . . 5.55
   s 28(1) 5.78
International Arbitration Act 1974 (Cth)
   Act No 136 of 1974, as amended
   s 35(2) 11.14

International Arbitration Acts 1974–1989
   s 25(1) 9.74
   s 26 . . . . 9.74

Austria
Code of Civil Procedure
   Art 594(4) 5.52
   Art 595 . . . . 5.52
Civil Code
   s 1008 . . . . 2.57

Belgium
Arbitration Act 1996
   Art 2 . . . . 3.97
Arbitration Law (2013)
   Art 1676 § 5 . . . . 10.50
Code Judiciaire 2.22
   Art 1676(3) 2.37
   Art 1704(5) 10.30
   Art 1717 . . . . 3.83
   Art 1718 . . . . 10.28
Law of May 19, 1998
   Art 1717.4 . . . . 10.69

Brazil
Arbitration Act
   Art 1 . . . . 2.125
   Art 8 . . . . 2.109
Arbitration Law 1996
   Art 8 . . . . 5.109
   Art 21(2) 5.72
   Art 22 . . . . 5.14
Law No 9.307 of 23 September 1996
   Art 19 . . . . 4.13

Canada
British Columbia International
   Commercial Arbitration Act 1996
   s 27(2) 3.46
   s 31(6) 9.23
Ontario International Commercial
   Arbitration Act 1990
   Art 6 . . . . 3.216

Chile
Judicial Code
   Art 235 . . . . 3.197

China
Arbitration Law of the People's Republic
   of China
   Art 19 . . . . 2.112
   Art 26 . . . . 2.209
   Art 38 . . . . 5.53

Civil Procedure Rules............10.81
New Interpretation
  Art 16.........................3.97

Ecuador

Arbitration and Mediation Law 2006
  Art 9..........................5.11
  Art 25.........................5.67
Law of Arbitration (145/1997)
  Art 3.........................3.197

Egypt

Arbitration Law (no 27 of 1994)
  Art 47........................11.14

Ethiopia

Civil Code................7.56, 7.57

France

Arbitration Law (2011)...........10.70
  Art 1520......................10.28
  Art 1522......................10.28
Civil Code............... 2.201, 9.109
  Art 1166......................2.55
  Art 1275......................2.55
  Art 1479.....................9.106
  Art 1493......................2.71
  Art 1985......................2.57
  Art 1989......................2.57
  Art 2059.....................2.125
  Art 2060............... 2.37, 2.125
Code de Commerce
  Art L1103 (formerly 109).......2.57
Code of Civil Procedure 1806......1.16
Code of Civil Procedure
  Art 1448......................3.05
  Art 1464(4)..................2.182
  Art 1505 2°, 3° and 4°........4.43
  Art 1506....................2.182
  Art 1509......................3.65
  Art 1511 .... 3.94, 3.216
  Art 1514 (as amended in 2011)..10.84
  Art 1518.....................10.70
  Art 1520.............. 10.70, 10.84
  Art 1522.....................10.71
  Art 1526.....................11.93
  Book IV, Title V—International
    Arbitration.................3.44
Code of Civil Procedure, Decree
  No 81–500 of May 12, 1981
  Art 1511....................3.190
Code of Civil Procedure Decree
  No 2011-48 of 13 January 2011,
  Book IV, Title II............2.182

Art 1504........................1.28
Art 1507........................2.22
Code of Civil Procedure, Decree Law
  No 2011–48 of 13 January 2011
  Art 1452......................4.45
  Art 1456(2).................4.105
  Art 1487.....................11.14
Code of Civil Procedure (as amended
  in 2011)
  Art 1457......................5.91
  Art 1463(2)...................5.67
  Art 1467.............. 5.18, 5.21
  Art 1520......................5.96
CPC
  Art 1456(3).................4.147
Décret n° 2011-48 du 13 janvier 2011
  portant réforme de l'arbitrage
  Art 1502....................10.20
Edict August 1560...............1.16
Law No 30 of 1999 Concerning
  Arbitration and Alternative
  Dispute Resolution
  Art 66(d)...................11.14
Nouveau Code de Procédure Civile
  Art 1476....................9.177
  Art 1500....................9.177

Germany

Code of Civil Procedure
  s 1030(1)–(2)...............2.125
Commercial Code
  s 75h(2).....................2.57
Securities Trading Act (WpHG)
  s 37h......................2.140
ZPO 1998
  Art 1051(10).................3.97
  Art 1054(1)..................5.47
  Art 1054(2)..................5.47

Hong Kong

Arbitration Ordinance
  s 59.......................2.211
Arbitration Ordinance 1997
  Ch 341......................9.74
  s 2GH.......................9.74
  s 2GI.......................9.74
Arbitration Ordinance 2003
  s 22A.......................7.17
  s 22B.......................7.17
Arbitration Ordinance 2011 (Cap 609)
  Sch 2, s 2.................2.239

India

Arbitration and Conciliation Act 1996...9.163
  Pt I........................9.59

Arbitration and Conciliation Act 1996 (cont.):
  s 2(i)(f) 1.35
  s 7 .... 2.19
  s 9 .... 9.59
  s 16 .... 2.109, 5.108
  s 31(7)(a)–(b) 9.74
  s 34 .... 9.59
  Art 28(1)(b)(iii) 3.216
  s 28(10)(b) 3.97
Foreign Awards (Recognition &
  Enforcement) Act, 1961
  s 2 .... 9.29
Limitation Act 1963
  Sch 1, Art 101 .... 11.33

Iran

Constitution
  Art 139 .... 2.37

Ireland

Arbitration Act 2010 .... 1.22
  s 22(1) 5.55
Arbitration (International) Commercial
  Act 1998
  s 10(2) 9.74

Israel

Arbitration Law (1968)
  s 1 .... 7.20

Italy

Code of Procedure of 1865 .... 1.121
Code of Civil Procedure
  Art 807 .... 1.47
Code of Civil Procedure as amended
  in 2006
  Art 813 .... 5.67
  Art 820 .... 5.67
Code of Civil Procedure (Book Four,
  Title VIII, Arbitration – as amended
  by Legislative Decree No 40, 2
  February 2006)
  Art 825 .... 11.14

Kenya

Arbitration Act 1995
  Art 29(3) 3.216
Arbitration (Amendment) Act No 11 2009
  s 16B(1) 5.55

Lebanon

Law No 40 .... 2.37

Malaysia

Arbitration Act (2005)
  s 2 .... 7.20
  s 37 .... 10.46

Malta

Arbitration Act 1996
  s 63(1) 9.74
  s 64 .... 9.74

Mexico

Commercial Code
  Art 1434 .... 5.72
  Art 1448 .... 5.48

Netherlands

Arbitration Act 1986 .... 2.238, 9.131
  Art 1021 .... 2.19
  Art 1022(2) 3.46
  Art 1034 .... 4.107
  Art 1035 .... 4.107
  Art 1037(1) 3.70
  Art 1037(3) 3.58
  Art 1046 .... 3.46
  Art 1049 .... 9.02
  Art 1053 .... 2.109
  Art 1054(3) 3.216
  Art 1054(4) 3.182
  Art 1065 .... 10.49
  Art 1065(6) 10.49
Code of Civil Procedure 1986
  Art 1027 .... 10.30
  Art 1046 .... 2.238
National Code of Civil and
  Commercial Procedure
  Art 745 .... 5.53

New Zealand

Arbitration Act 1908 .... 5.54
Arbitration Act 1996
  s 7(1) 2.22
  s 12 .... 5.14
  s 13 .... 5.55, 5.78
  Sch 1, Art 17L 7.20

Norway

Arbitration Act 2004
  s 5 .... 2.176

Portugal

Code of Civil Procedure (1986)
  Art 1096(F) 10.85

Table of Legislation

Russia

Arbitrazh Procedural Code
    Art 33 .... 2.158
    Art 225(1) 2.158, 11.103
Federation CCI
    s 26(1) 3.100
International Arbitration Law 1993
    Art 28 .... 3.97

Saudi Arabia

Law of Arbitration (Royal Decree
    No. M/34 of 16 April 2012) 4.52
    Art 10 .... 2.37

Singapore

International Arbitration Act
    Art 2A 2.17
International Arbitration Act (Ch 143A) 2002
    s 12(5)(b) 9.74
    s 20 .... 9.74
International Arbitration Act (Ch 143A)
    of 1994, as amended in 2002
    s 19 .... 11.14
International Arbitration Act (2012) 4.21

Spain

Arbitration Act 2003 .... 1.34
    Art 7 .... 3.05
    Art 13 .... 4.52
Arbitration Act 11/2011
    Art 3 .... 1.34

Sweden

Arbitration Act 1999 .... 1.22, 3.61
    s 4 .... 3.05
    s 5 .... 3.05
    s 6 .... 3.05, 3.43
    s 37 .... 3.43
    s 41 .... 3.43
    s 48 .... 3.25, 3.41

Switzerland

Code of Civil Procedure
    Part III, Art 384 .... 9.146
Federal Code on Private International
    Law of December 1987
    Art 135(2) 9.45
    Art 186(3) 9.02
    Ch 12 .... 9.02
    Ch 12, Art 189 .... 9.123, 9.146
International Arbitration Law
    Art 186.2 .... 5.118

Private International Law Act 1987
    (Swiss PIL) 1.30, 2.40, 3.44
    Art 7 .... 3.05
    Art 177(2) 2.39
    Art 178(1) 1.47
    Art 178(2) 3.36
    Art 178(3) 2.107
    Art 183 .... 5.14
    Art 184(2) 5.20, 7.33
    Art 187 .... 3.216
    Art 187(1) 3.97
    Ch 12 .... 10.72
    Ch 12, s 176(1) 3.55
    Ch 12, s 178(3) 5.109
    Ch 12, s 179 .... 4.45
    Ch 12, s 180 .... 4.107
    Ch 12, s 180(2) 4.147
    Ch 12, s 181 .... 4.12
    Ch 12, s 182 .... 3.65
    Ch 12, s 182(3) 3.66
    Ch 12, s 183 .... 3.46, 7.14
    Ch 12, s 183(1) 7.26
    Ch 12, s 183(2) 7.26
    Ch 12, s 187 .... 3.190
    Ch 12, s 189(2) 9.148
    Ch 12, s 190 .... 10.53, 10.72
    Ch 12, s 191 .... 10.25, 10.72
    Ch 12, s 192 .... 10.28
    Ch 12, s 192(1) 10.72
    Ch 12, s 193 .... 10.14

United Arab Emirates

Civil Procedure Code
    Art (211).1 .... 5.21

United States

Arbitration Fairness Act 2013 .... 2.107
California Code of Civil Procedure
    s 1297.272 .... 2.239
Federal Arbitration Act, 9 U.S. Code
    ss 1 et seq 10.73
    s 10(a) 10.25
Federal Arbitration Act 1925 (FAA) 3.28,
                  3.29, 3.31, 4.108, 5.19,
                      6.111, 9.52
    s 7 .... 3.67, 6.17, 6.111, 7.34, 7.36
    s 10 .... 10.73
    s 10(a) 4.104
    s 10(b)(5) 10.73
    s 11 .... 9.189
    s 11(c) 9.189
Federal Arbitration Act 1990 .... 1.47,
                      2.173, 2.228

Table of Legislation

Federal Rules of Civil Procedure
   r 23 . . . . .2.230
   r 26(c) 2.175
   r 45(b)(2) 7.35
Foreign Sovereign Immunities Act 1976,
   Title 28, US Code
   s 1605(a)(1) 11.145
   s 1605(a)(6) 11.145
   s 1611(b)(1) 11.154
Racketeer Influenced and Corrupt
   Organizations Act (18 USCS)
   (RICO) 9.45
Securities Exchange Act 1933 . . . . 2.68, 2.139
Shearman Act 2.133
Uniform Arbitration Act 2.73
   s 21 . . . . 9.52
Uniform Commercial Code (UCC)
   Art 9 . . . . 2.55
US Code, Title 9 (Arbitration)
   s 202 . . . . 1.30
28 U.S.C.
   s 1782 . . . . 6.131, 7.40

Venezuela

Civil Code 2.201
Commercial Arbitration Act
   Art 4 . . . . 2.37
Law on Commercial Arbitration 1998
   Art 25 . . . . 5.118

EUROPEAN DIRECTIVES

Directive 2001/97/EC dated
   December 4, 2001 . . . . 5.83, 5.84
Directive 2005/60/EC dated
   26 October 2005 . . . . 5.83, 5.84
Directive 2009/101/EC of the European
   Parliament and of the Council of
   16 September 2009 . . . . .2.35

EUROPEAN REGULATIONS

Council Regulation No 1/2003 . . . . . . .2.133
EC Council Regulation 1346/2000 . . . .2.143
European Council Regulation No 44/2001
   (formerly the Brussels and Lugano
   Conventions) in relation to judgments
   made in the Member States of the
   European Union and Switzerland
   [2001] OJ No L12/1 . . . . 1.102, 2.98,
                 5.133, 5.134, 5.135, 11.30
   Art 1(2) 5.128
   Art 1(2)(d) 5.128, 5.129, 5.134
   Art 2 . . . . 5.128
   Arts 21–23 . . . . 5.131
   Art 31 . . . . 5.130

Regulation (EC) No 593/2008 on the law
   applicable to contractual obligations
   (Rome I)
   Art 13 . . . . .2.34
Regulation 1215/2012 [2012] OJ
   No L35/1 . . . . 5.137
   Art 1(2)(d) 5.137
   Art 73(2) 5.137
   Art 75 . . . . 5.137
   Art 76 . . . . 5.137
   Recital 12 . . . . 5.137

INTERNATIONAL INSTRUMENTS

AAA Commercial Arbitration Rules
   R-21 . . . . .6.42
   R-31 . . . . 6.191
   R-32(a) 6.11
   R-32(b) 6.63
   R-33 . . . . .6.39
   R-36 . . . . 6.152
   Sections E-1–E-10 . . . . .6.33
   Sections P-1 and P-2 . . . . .6.42
AAA Rules
   Art 27(4) 2.177
AAA ICDR
   Art 25 . . . . 10.30
   Art 28(1) 3.100
   r 38 . . . . 5.66
AAA International Arbitration Rules 1991
   Art 11 . . . . 4.156
ACICA Rules 4.19
Agreement between the Government
   of Canada and the Government of
   the Republic of Argentina for the
   Protection and Promotion of
   Investments, signed on 5 November
   1991, entered into force on
   29 April 1993
   Art 1(a) 8.36
Agreement between the Government
   of Canada and the Government of
   the Republic of Venezuela for
   the Promotion and Protection of
   Investments, signed on 1 July 1996,
   entered into force on
   28 January 1998
   Art I(g) 8.19
Agreement between the Government of
   Denmark and the Government of
   the Republic of Indonesia Concerning
   the Encouragement and the Reciprocal
   Protection of Investments, signed on
   30 January 1968, entered into force
   on 10 March 1970
   Art 1 . . . . 8.18

Table of Legislation

Agreement between the Government of Lithuania and the Government of Ukraine Concerning the Protection and Promotion of Investment, signed on 8 February 1994, entered into force on 6 March 1995 ....8.22

Agreement between the Government of the French Republic and the Government of the Republic of Argentina on the Encouragement and the Reciprocal Protection of Investments, signed on 3 July 1991, entered into force on 3 March 1993
  Art 1(2)(c) 8.26

Agreement between the Government of the Republic of Peru and the Government of the People's Republic of China Concerning the Encouragement and Reciprocal Protection of Investments, signed on 9 June 1994, entered into force on 1 February 1995 ....8.32

Agreement between the Government of the Swiss Confederation and the Government of the Democratic Socialist Republic of Sri Lanka for the Reciprocal Promotion and Protection of Investments signed on 23 September 1981, entered into force on 12 February 1982 ....8.08

Agreement between the Government of the Union of Soviet Socialist Republics and the Government of the United Kingdom of Great Britain and Northern Ireland for the Promotion and Reciprocal Protection of Investments, signed on 6 April 1989, entered into force on 3 July 1991
  Art 1(a) 8.28

Agreement between the Government of the UK of Great Britain and Northern Ireland and the Government of the Republic of Argentina for the Promotion and Protection of Investments, signed on 11 December 1990, entered into force on 19 February 1993
  Art 8 ....8.62

Agreement between the Government of the United Kingdom of Great Britain and Northern Ireland and the Government of Chile for the Promotion and Protection of Investments, signed on 8 January 1996, entered into force on 21 April 1997
  Art 1(a) 8.28

Agreement between the Government of the United Kingdom of Great Britain and Northern Ireland and the Government of Sri Lanka for the Promotion and Protection of Investments, signed on 13 February 1980, entered into force on 18 December 1980............8.65

Agreement between the Republic of Chile and the Kingdom of Spain concerning the Reciprocal Encouragement and Protection of Investments, signed on 2 October 1991, entered into force on 29 March 1994 ....8.52
  Art 16.4........................8.55

Agreement between the Republic of Colombia and the Swiss Confederation on the Promotion and Reciprocal Protection of Investments, signed on 17 May 2006, entered into force on 6 October 2009
  Art 11(4) 8.57

Agreement between the Swiss Confederation and the Islamic Republic of Pakistan concerning the Reciprocal Promotion and Protection of Investments, signed on 11 July 1995, entered into force on 6 May 1996
  Art 1 ....8.17

Agreement between the Swiss Confederation and the Republic of the Philippines on the Promotion and Reciprocal Protection of Investments, signed on 23 August 1991, entered into force on 23 April 1999
  Art X(2) 8.138

Agreement for Promotion, Protection and Guarantee of Investments (the OIC Agreement) 11.139
  Art 17(d) 11.139

Agreement on Encouragement and Reciprocal Protection of Investments between the Kingdom of the Netherlands and the Argentine Republic, signed on 20 October 1992, entered into force on 1 October 1994.................8.22
  Art 1(b).........................8.20

Agreement on Encouragement and Reciprocal Protection of Investments between the Kingdom of the Netherlands and the Republic of Venezuela, signed on 22 October 1991, entered into force 1 November 1993
  Art 14 ....8.16

xliii

Table of Legislation

Agreement on the Execution of Rulings, Requests of Legal Assistance and Judicial Notices (the GCC Convention) 11.138
Arbitration Rules of the Chambre Arbitral Maritime de Paris of 2007 .... 10.12
Arbitration Rules of the European Court of Arbitration
    Art 23.12...................... 10.12
    Art 28......................... 10.12
Arbitration Rules of the Grain and Feed Trade Association ('GAFTA') 2007 .... 10.12
Arbitration Rules of the Netherlands Arbitration Institute
    Art 42(f) 7.17
Argentina–France BIT
    Art 1(2)(c) 8.26
ARIAS Arbitration Rules 3.16
ASEAN Comprehensive Investment Agreement, signed on 26 February 2009, entered into force on 29 March 2012 .... 8.11
Brussels Convention
    Art 24......................... 5.130
Bustamante Code of 1928 .... 2.06
Canada Model BIT (2004)
    Art 1.......................... 8.44
Canada–Panama Free Trade Agreement, signed on 14 May 2010, entered into force on 1 April 2013......... 8.11
CEPANI Rules
    Art 13......................... 2.246
Convention for the Execution of Foreign Arbitral Awards *see* Geneva Convention of 1927
Convention for the Pacific Settlement of International Disputes (concluded at The Hague in 1899 and revised in 1907)................ 1.189, 8.04
    Art 15......................... 4.16
    Art 37......................... 4.16
Convention on Choice of Court Agreements (not yet in force) 1.102
Convention on the Peaceful Resolution of International Disputes 1907 *see* Convention for the Pacific Settlement of International Disputes (concluded at The Hague in 1899 and revised in 1907)
Convention on the Recognition and Enforcement of Foreign Arbitral Awards *see* New York Convention 1958
Convention on the Settlement of Civil Law Disputes Resulting from Economic, Scientific and Technological Cooperation *see* Panama Convention
Criminal Law Convention on Corruption (CETS No. 191) Additional Protocol. 5.88
DIS rules
    Art 2(2)........................ 4.50
Dominican Republic–Central America–United States Free Trade Agreement, Chapter 10: Investment, signed on 5 August 2004, entered into force between 2006 and 2009..................... 8.11
Draft Articles on Responsibility of States for Internationally Wrongful Acts, adopted by the International Law Commission ('ILC') (2001).... 9.77
    Art 3.......................... 8.66
    Art 38................... 8.167, 9.79
Dubai International Arbitration Centre DIAC Rules
    Art 12......................... 6.31
    Art 17.2.................. 6.11, 6.16
    Art 22......................... 6.42
    Art 17.4....................... 6.152
    Art 34......................... 6.200
Energy Charter Treaty, signed on 17 December 1994, entered into force on 16 April 1998... 8.11, 8.75
    Art 1(6)........................ 8.28
EU Treaty
    Art 81 .... 3.105, 11.120, 11.121
European Convention for the Protection of Human Rights and Fundamental Freedoms (Rome, November 4, 1950) (as amended), (1955) (ECHR)
    Art 6 .... 10.58, 10.59, 10.95
    Art 6(1)....................... 10.57
    Additional Protocol 1, Article 1 (P1-1) 10.95
European Convention on International Commercial Arbitration 1961 ... 2.06, 2.09, 2.39, 11.92
    Art I.1(a)...................... 1.29
    Art II.1 .... 2.39
    Art II.2 .... 2.39
    Art VII 3.215
    Art VIII 9.160
European Convention on State Immunity (Basle, 16 May 1972, Cmnd 54081) 11.145
European Convention providing a Uniform Law on Arbitration (Strasbourg Uniform Law)
    Annex I, Art 22.3 .... 9.117

Table of Legislation

European Free Trade Association–Mexico
 FTA, signed 27 November 2000,
 entered into force on 1 July 2001
 Art 45 . . . . 8.44
FCN Treaty between Italy and
 Colombia of 1894
 Art 21 . . . . 8.03
GAFTA Form 125, Arbitration Rules
 (effective for contracts dated from
 1 July 2007 onwards)
 Art 22.1 . . . . 11.09
General Treaty of Friendship, Commerce
 and Navigation *see* Jay Treaty
Geneva Protocol of 1923 (1923 Geneva
 Protocol) 1.18, 1.36, 1.38, 1.57,
 1.62, 1.207, 1.208–1.209, 1.212,
 1.213, 2.06, 3.53, 11.40, 11.42
 Art 1 . . . . 1.37
 Art 2 . . . . 3.53, 6.07
Geneva Convention of 1927 (1927
 Geneva Convention) 1.18, 1.210,
 1.212, 2.06, 10.48, 10.49,
 11.40, 11.58, 11.82, 11.87
Hague Convention on Choice of Court
 Agreements of 30 June 2005 . . . . . . 11.30
Hague Convention on the Taking
 of Evidence Abroad in Civil or
 Commercial Matters 1970 . . . . 6.131
Hague Peace Conventions of 1899
 and 1907 . . . . 1.193
IBA 'Rules on the Taking of Evidence
 in International Arbitration' 3.52,
 6.95–6.103, 6.109, 6.114,
 10.56, App J
 Art 2.1 . . . . 6.103
 Art 2.2(c) 6.103
 Art 3 . . . . 1.238, 6.96, 6.99
 Art 3.3(a)(ii) 6.110
 Art 3(3)(c)(i) 6.103
 Art 3.5 . . . . 6.102
 Art 3.6 . . . . 6.103
 Art 3.9 . . . . 6.131
 Art 3.10 . . . . .6.122
 Art 3.12(a) 6.118
 Art 3.12(d) 6.119
 Art 4 . . . . 6.121
 Art 4.2 . . . . 6.126
 Art 4(3) 1.236, 6.124
 Art 5.1 . . . . 6.140
 Art 5.2 . . . . 6.141
 Art 5.4 . . . . 6.184
 Art 5.5 . . . . 6.142
 Art 5.6 . . . . 6.142
 Art 6 . . . . 5.23, 5.26
 Art 6.1 . . . . 6.137
 Art 6.2 . . . . 6.137
 Art 6.3 . . . . 6.147
 Art 6.5 . . . . 6.137, 6.147
 Art 6.6 . . . . 6.137
 Art 6.7 . . . . 6.136
 Art 7 . . . . 5.22, 6.147
 Art 8 . . . . 6.175
 Art 8.1 . . . . 6.121, 6.142
 Art 8.2 . . . . 6.178
 Art 8.3(f) 6.185
 Art 8.5 . . . . 6.122
 Art 9.1 . . . . 6.124, 6.128
 Art 9.2 . . . . .6.99
 Art 9.4 . . . . 6.132
 Art 9.5 . . . . 6.113, 6.132
 Art 9.6 . . . . 6.113
ICC
Rules
 Art 1(1) 1.28
 Art 24 . . . . 11.150
ICC Rules 1998
 Art 29 . . . . 10.09
ICC Rules 2008 . . . . 5.107
ICC Arbitration Rules 2012 . . . . . . 1.22, 1.28,
 1.78, 1.177, 1.185, 2.18,
 2.192, 2.199, 2.214, 3.186,
 4.19, 5.64, 5.95, 9.132, 9.197,
 11.37, App F
 Art 2(v) 9.21
 Art 4(1) 1.69
 Art 4.2 . . . . 4.08
 Art 6.3 . . . . 5.107
 Art 6(9) 2.105
 Art 6.9 . . . . 5.101, 5.106
 Art 7 . . . . 1.113, 2.61
 Art 7(1) 2.60
 Art 7.2 . . . . 4.82
 Art 8 . . . . 1.113
 Art 8(1) 1.113
 Art 10 . . . . 1.113, 2.245
 Art 11(2) 1.127
 Art 11.2 . . . . 4.83, 5.46
 Art 11(4) 4.111
 Art 12 (ex Art 8.4) 2.215
 Art 12.2 . . . . 4.23, 4.35
 Art 12.3 . . . . 1.71
 Art 12.4 . . . . 4.36
 Art 12.5 . . . . 1.71, 4.36
 Art 12(6) 1.111, 2.215
 Art 12(8) 2.215
 Art 13(3) 4.02
 Art 13(4) 4.02
 Art 13.5 . . . . 4.64
 Art 14(1) 4.75, 4.96, 4.99
 Art 14.2–14.3 . . . . 4.109

ICC Arbitration Rules 2012 (cont.):
  Art 14(2) 7.56
  Art 15 . . . . 2.82
  Art 15(2) 5.04
  Art 15.2 . . . . 5.76
  Art 15(4) 4.165
  Art 15(5) 4.158
  Art 18 . . . . 3.57
  Art 18.1 . . . . 3.40, 5.10
  Art 18(2) 6.162
  Art 19 . . . . 6.08
  Art 20 . . . . 2.86
  Art 21 . . . . 3.190
  Art 21.1 . . . . 3.100
  Art 21(1) 3.191, 3.216
  Art 21.2 . . . . 3.165, 3.182
  Art 22 . . . . 1.127, 6.21
  Art 22(2) 5.69
  Art 22(3) 2.179
  Art 22.4 . . . . 5.71
  Art 22(4) 6.11, 6.16
  Art 23 . . . . 5.91
  Art 23.1 . . . . 5.46
  Art 23(4) 1.113, 5.94
  Art 24 . . . . 6.42
  Art 25(4) 6.136
  Art 25.6 . . . . 1.07
  Art 26 . . . . 2.163
  Art 26.2 . . . . 1.150
  Art 26.3 . . . . 4.188
  Art 27 . . . . 5.69, 6.200
  Art 27 . . . . 5.69
  Art 28 . . . . 5.27, 7.14, 9.59
  Art 28(1) 5.28
  Art 28(2) 4.03, 7.24, 7.28
  Art 29 . . . . 1.177, 4.03, 4.17, 4.20, 5.27,
                                          6.28, 7.17, 9.190
  Art 29(1) 4.20
  Art 29(2) 4.21
  Art 29.3 . . . . 1.177
  Art 29(6) 4.20
  Art 29(7) 7.24
  Art 29.6(b) 1.177
  Art 30(1) 1.127
  Art 30.1 . . . . 5.46, 5.67
  Art 30.2 . . . . 5.46, 5.67
  Art 31(1) 9.123, 9.149
  Art 31.3 . . . . 3.70
  Art 32 . . . . 9.37
  Art 33 . . . 5.46, 7.20, 9.15, 9.133, 9.195, 10.66
  Art 34 . . . . 5.55
  Art 34(1) 9.169
  Art 34.6 . . . . 1.88, 9.01, 10.29, 10.75
  Art 34(6) 10.03, 11.150
  Art 35 . . . . 7.58, 9.33, 9.139, 10.17
  Art 35(1) 9.190, 10.09
  Art 35(2) 10.09
  Art 35(4) 10.22
  Art 37 . . . . 9.152
  Art 37.1 . . . . 9.87
  Art 37(1) 9.93
  Art 37.3 . . . . 9.95
  Art 37.3 . . . . 9.15
  Art 37(5) 3.226
  Art 38 . . . . 4.99
  Art 39 . . . . 4.99, 10.30
  Art 40 . . . . 5.55, 5.66
  Art 41 . . . . 2.153, 9.04, 9.14, 11.11
  Art 117(4) 4.111
  Appendix III . . . . 4.215, App F
  Art 2(2) 4.205
  Appendix IV 1.235, 6.42, 6.63
  para (d)(v) 6.103
  para (g) 6.167
  Appendix V 1.177, 4.03, 4.17, 4.20,
                                                6.28, 7.17f
  Art 1.2 . . . . 5.27
  Art 1(3) 4.20
  Art 1(6) 4.20
  Appendix VI 5.69
ICC 'Rules for the Adaptation of
  Contracts' 1978 . . . . 9.69
ICDR International Arbitration
  Rules . . . . 9.132, 9.199, App G
  Art 2 . . . . 6.68
  Art 3 . . . . 6.68
  Art 5 . . . . 4.24
  Art 6 . . . . 4.36, 5.27, 7.17
  Art 6(3) 1.126
  Art 6.4 . . . . 4.65
  Art 8(1) 4.75, 4.97
  Art 11.2 . . . . 4.166
  Art 16.1 . . . . 6.11, 6.21
  r 16.1 . . . . 9.125
  Art 16.2 . . . . 6.21, 6.42
  Art 16.3 . . . . 6.63
  Art 17.1 . . . . 6.68
  Art 19 . . . . 5.101
  Art 21 . . . . 5.28
  Art 22 . . . . 6.136
  Art 22.2 . . . . 6.152
  Art 23 . . . . 6.191
  Art 24.3 . . . . 7.24
  Art 27(4) 2.180
  Art 30(1) 10.03
  Art 34 . . . . 9.87
  Art 37 . . . . 4.17, 6.28
  Art 37.3 . . . . 4.03

Table of Legislation

ICSID Convention of 1965 ...... 1.18, 1.91,
    1.226, 2.01, 2.09, 3.138, 3.145, 3.156,
    8.08, 8.12, 8.43, 11.36, 11.38, 11.39,
    11.125, 11.126, 11.128, 11.147, App C
  Art 14 .... 4.100
  Art 20 .... 5.66
  Art 25 .... 8.38
  Art 25(2)(a) 8.19
  Art 25(2)(b) 8.26
  Art 25(4) 8.44, 8.45
  Art 37(2) 4.02
  Art 42 .... 3.100, 3.156, 3.189, 8.63
  Art 42(1) 3.214, 8.69
  Art 42(2) 9.122, 9.125
  Art 47 .... 5.29
  Art 48 .... 4.119
  Art 48(1) 9.125
  Art 48(3) 5.113
  Art 48.3 .... 9.159
  Art 48(4) 9.132
  Art 52 .... 10.15
  Art 52(1) 11.127
  Art 52(1)(a) 10.13, 11.127
  Art 52(1)(b) 10.13, 11.127
  Art 52(1)(c) 10.13
  Art 52(1)(d) 10.13
  Art 52(1)(e) 10.13
  Art 53 .... 11.147
  Art 53(1) 11.127
  Art 54 .... 11.38, 11.125, 11.129
  Art 54(1) 11.127
  Art 55 .... 11.147
  Art 57 .... 4.98, 4.100
  Art 58 .... 4.119
  Art 62 .... 3.56
ICSID Additional Facility Rules 11.37
  Art 7(1) 10.17
  Art 28 .... 2.185
  Art 44(2) 2.186
ICSID Arbitration (Additional Facility)
  Rules, April 2006
  r 41 .... 8.12
ICSID Rules for the Institution of
  Conciliation and Arbitration
  Proceedings .... App E
  r 6(2) 4.09
ICSID Rules
  r 2 .... 4.02
  r 48(4) 2.177
ICSID Rules 2006 .... 2.188
ICSID Arbitration Rules 9.106, 9.109,
                            App E
  r 6(2) 4.83, 5.46
  r 8, n C 4.99

r 9(1) 4.115
r 9(3) 4.116
r 9(4)–(5) 4.117
r 9(6) 4.117
r 13(1) 5.46
r 13(3) 4.170
r 13(4) 4.172
r 15.1 .... 5.46
r 16.1 .... 5.46
r 20 .... 6.42
r 20(1) 6.08
r 21 .... 6.165
r 24(2)(b) 6.153
r 27 .... 4.144, 10.30
r 28(1) 8.169
r 31(1) 6.69
r 31(2) 6.69
r 31(3) 6.69
r 34(3) 6.153
r 34(4) 6.153
r 37 .... 8.12
r 38(5) 5.21
r 39 .... 5.28, 5.29
r 41(5) 6.39
r 41(6) 6.39
r 42 .... 5.71, 6.191
r 42(4) 9.32
Art 42(4) 9.27
r 46 .... 9.136
r 47 .... 9.144
r 47(1)(i) 5.46, 9.152
r 47(3) 9.132
r 48(1) 9.169
Art 49.2 .... 9.33
rr 50–52 .... 9.194
r 51(3) 9.194
r 52 .... 10.14
r 55 .... 10.14
IDR Rules 4.19
Inter-American Convention on
  International Commercial
  Arbitration 1975 (Panama
  Convention) 11.96, 11.134,
                          11.135, 11.137
  Art 1 .... 2.08, 11.135
  Art IV 11.124
  Art 5 .... 11.135
  Art 5.2 .... 11.135
  Art 6 .... 11.136
International Bar Association (IBA) Rules
  on the Taking of Evidence in
  International Arbitration *see* IBA
  'Rules on the Taking of Evidence in
  International Arbitration'

Table of Legislation

International Dispute Resolution Procedures (International Arbitration)
　Art 30 . . . . 9.33
International Institute for the Unification of Private Law (UNIDROIT), Principles of International Commercial Contracts (2004) (UNIDROIT Principles of 2004)
　Art 6.2.2 . . . . 9.69
　Art 6.2.3 . . . . 9.69
Jay Treaty 1794 . . . . 1.191
Model Law on International Commercial Arbitration see UNCITRAL Model Law
Montevideo Convention see Treaty concerning the Union of South American States in respect of Procedural Law, signed at Montevideo, 11 January 1889
Moscow Convention of 1972 . . . 2.01, 11.131, 11.132, 11.133
　Art IV.1 . . . . 11.133
　Art IV.2 . . . . 11.133
　Art V.1 . . . . 11.133
Netherlands Arbitration Institute (NAI) Arbitration Rules
　Art 42 . . . . 4.03
　Art 42k 4.03
　Art 66 . . . . 5.66
New York Convention 1958 . . . . 1.03, 1.04, 1.18, 1.35, 1.38, 1.45, 1.57, 1.61, 1.64, 1.87, 1.91, 1.138, 1.205, 1.211–1.214, 1.220, 1.225, 2.06, 2.11, 2.16, 2.25, 2.34, 2.82, 3.47, 4.21, 5.131, 5.137, 7.19, 7.58, 9.03, 9.35, 9.171, 10.04, 10.32, 10.48, 10.55, 10.68, 11.27, 11.29, 11.33, 11.36, 11.37, 11.38, 11.39, 11.40, 11.41, 11.44, 11.47, 11.52, 11.55, 11.56, 11.57, 11.59, 11.60, 11.61, 11.62, 11.63, 11.65, 11.85, 11.89, 11.90, 11.92, 11.102, 11.107, 11.133, 11.141, App B
　Art I 11.19
　Art I(1) 1.31, 11.19, 11.42
　Art I(2) 9.05
　Art I(3) 1.37, 11.42, 11.46
　Art II 11.53
　Art II.1 . . . . 1.44, 1.212, 7.10
　Art II.2 . . . . 1.44
　Art II(1) 1.62, 2.07, 2.12, 2.29, 2.125
　Art II(2) 1.48, 2.12, 2.14, 2.16, 2.23
　Art II(3) 1.213, 2.07, 2.12, 2.32, 2.197, 2.202, 5.135, 7.11
　Art III 11.51, 11.124
　Art IV 1.44, 1.48, 11.19
　Art IV(2) 9.150, 11.54
　Art IV(1)(b) 1.212
　Art V 1.40, 1.121, 10.05, 10.06, 10.38, 11.19, 11.58, 11.62, 11.93, 11.95, 11.123
　Art V(1)(a) . . . 1.40, 1.48, 1.212, 2.12, 2.32, 3.14, 3.54, 3.69, 3.81, 5.111, 11.66
　Art V(1)(b) 6.09, 11.34
　Art V(1)(c) 2.63, 5.96, 11.78
　Art V(1)(d) 2.216, 2.240, 3.54, 4.51, 5.72, 6.02, 6.07, 11.82
　Art V(1)(e) 3.54, 3.69, 3.81, 11.87, 11.98
　Art V.1(b) 11.71
　Art V.1(e) 10.03, 10.06, 10.26, 10.49
　Art V(1) 11.59, 11.136
　Art V(2) 11.58, 11.59, 11.64, 11.109, 11.135
　Art V(2)(a) 2.29, 2.125, 11.101
　Art V(2)(b) 5.72, 9.16, 11.105
　Art VI 11.87
　Art VI(b) 2.247
　Art VII 11.95
　Art VII(1) 2.12, 11.93
　Art VII(2) 1.212, 2.07, 3.54, 11.40
North American Free Trade Agreement 2.185, 4.22, 8.126, 9.78
　ch 11 . . . . 8.11
　Art 1102(1) 8.126
　Art 1135 . . . . 9.57
　Art 1134 . . . . 2.185
PCA Arbitration Rules
　Art 27(3) 5.22
Revisions to the Model Law (the Revised Model Law) adopted in December 2006 . . . . 1.18
　Art 7, Option I 1.48, 2.13, 2.17, 2.18
　Art 7, Option II 1.48
Riyadh Arab Agreement on Judicial Cooperation 1985 (the Riyadh Convention) 11.138
Rome Convention on the Law Applicable to Contractual Obligations [1980] OJ L266/1 . . . . 3.98
　Art 1(2)(d) 3.210
　Art 3 . . . . 3.103
　Art 3(1) 3.98, 3.202
　Art 3(3) 3.128
　Art 4 . . . . 3.203
　Art 4(1) 3.210
　Art 4(2) 3.210
Rules of Arbitration of the International Chamber of Commerce see ICC Rules
Rules of the China International Economic and Trade Arbitration Commission (CIETAC Rules) 1.162, 1.168, 2.163
　Art 5(4) 2.112

Art 23	4.36
Art 28	4.66
Art 29(2)	4.75
Art 33(3)	5.15
Art 33(5)	6.167
Art 41	6.152
Art 42(1)	5.23
Art 42(2)	6.152
Ch IV	6.33

Rules of International Arbitration 2012 (Swiss Rules) 1.146, 1.157, 1.162, 2.61, 4.19, 9.123

Art 1(1)	1.10
Art 4(1)	2.246
Art 4(2)	2.61
Art 6(4)	6.33
Art 15(1)	6.11, 6.16, 6.21
Art 15(3)	6.16
Art 15(7)	6.21
Art 18(3)	6.68
Art 19(2)	6.68
Art 24(2)	6.128
Art 25(2)	6.124, 6.139
Art 25(4)	6.139
Art 26(3)	4.19, 6.28
Art 26.3	5.33
Art 27	6.136
Art 27.2	6.152
Art 28	6.191
Art 31.1	9.123
Art 32	9.143
Art 32(4)	9.148
Art 33(1)	1.10
Art 33(2)	1.10
Art 34	6.203
Art 42	6.33
Art 42(1)(c)	1.07
Art 43	4.17, 6.28
Art 44	2.192

Rules of the Hong Kong International Arbitration Centre (HKIAC Rules) 1.162, 2.61

Art 8.2	2.216
Art 11.2	4.64
Art 11(4)	4.75
Art 11.6	4.97
Art 13.1	6.11, 6.16, 6.21
Art 22.1	6.128
Art 23.1	7.17
Art 23.9	7.24
Art 25	6.136
Art 25.2	6.152
Art 26	6.191
Art 27	2.61
Art 27.6	2.61
Art 33(1)	6.16
Art 41	6.33
Art 42	2.192
Sch 4	4.17, 6.28
Art 1	7.17

Rules of the LCIA (1 January 1998 revised with effect 1 October 2014) (LCIA Rules). 1.147, 1.172, 1.174, 1.229, 2.163, 4.19, 4.166, 9.123, 9.132, 11.37

Art 1	1.70, 1.173
Art 2	1.173
Art 4	1.173
Art 5.4	1.127, 1.174, 4.36, 4.60, 4.83
Art 5.7	4.02
Art 5.8	4.23
Art 6.1	4.64
Art 7.2	4.35
Art 8.1	1.111, 2.216
Art 8.2	1.111, 2.216
Art 9	4.03
Art 9A	4.03, 4.17, 6.29
Art 9B	1.177, 4.17, 5.27, 6.28, 7.17
Art 9.11	1.177
s 9.12	7.26
Art 9.14	1.177
Art 10	2.82
Art 10(1)	4.75
Art 10(3)	4.75
Art 10.3–10.6	4.112
Art 10.6	4.112
Art 10.3	4.97
Art 11	2.82
Art 13.2	6.42
Art 14.1	1.174
Art 14.2	1.174, 6.08
Art 14.4	6.21
Art 14.4(i)	5.71, 6.11, 6.18
Art 14.4(ii)	1.174
Art 14.5	6.21
Art 15.1	6.67
Art 16	3.58, 4.170
Art 16.3	3.58, 4.172, 6.162
Art 16.4	3.15
Art 18	1.178, 3.227, 4.131
Art 18.5	1.179, 5.40
Art 18(5)	3.227
Art 18.6	5.40
Art 18(6)	3.227
Art 19.1	6.157
Art 19.2	6.63
Art 20	6.121, 6.139
Art 20.5	6.124
Art 21	6.136
Art 21.3	6.152

Table of Legislation

Rules of the LCIA (1 January 1998 revised with effect 1 October 2014) (LCIA Rules) (*cont.*):
Art 22.1(iv) 5.22, 6.152
Art 22(1)(vii) 6.128
Art 22(1)(viii) 1.113, 2.60
Art 22.1(g) 9.64
Art 22(3) 3.100, 3.216
Art 23 .... 5.101
Art 23.2 .... 2.105
Art 25 .... 5.28, 7.14
Art 25.1(i) 2.100
Art 25(2) 5.37
Art 26.3 .... 9.123, 9.124
Art 26(4) 9.149
Art 26.6 .... 9.72
Art 26(7) 9.21
Art 26(8) 10.03
Art 27 .... 9.33, 9.190
Art 27.1 .... 10.17
Art 28.1 .... 9.87
Art 28(2) 9.152
Art 28(3) 2.164
Art 28.4 .... 1.175, 9.93
Art 26.4 .... 1.106
Art 30 .... 2.178, 2.191
Art 31(1) 5.55
Art 32.1 .... 10.30
Art 32.2 .... 2.153, 11.11
Annex 5.40
Rules of the London Maritime Arbitrators Association 2.242
Art 14(b) 2.237
Rules of the Singapore International Arbitration Centre (SIAC Rules) ... 1.162, 1.169, 4.19
Art 3 .... 1.70
r 5 .... 6.33
Art 9 .... 2.216
r 11.1 .... 4.75
Art 11.1 .... 4.97
r 16.1 .... 6.21
r 16.3 .... 6.42
r 16.4 .... 6.63
r 22 .... 6.121
r 22.5 .... 6.124
r 23 .... 6.136
r 23.1(b) 6.152
r 24(e) 6.152
Art 24.1(b) 2.61
r 26.2 .... 5.27, 7.17
r 26.3 .... 7.24
r 28.1 .... 6.200, 6.203
Art 28.10 .... 2.180
Art 31.1 .... 9.87

Art 31.2 .... 9.87
r 34(1) 5.66
Art 35 .... 2.192
Sch 1 .... 4.17, 6.28, 7.17
Rules of the Stockholm Chamber of Commerce
Art 2 .... 1.70
Art 42 .... 9.33
Rules of the Vienna International Arbitration Centre 1.162
SCC Rules 4.19
Art 13(4) 2.216
Art 13(6) 2.216
Art 15(1) 4.97
Art 19(2) 6.16, 6.21
Art 20(2) 6.162
Art 22(1) 3.216
Art 26(1) 6.128
Art 28 .... 6.139
Art 29 .... 6.136
Art 32(4) 5.27, 7.17
Art 32(5) 7.24
Art 23 .... 6.42
Art 41(1) 9.191
Art 43 .... 9.87
Art 43.4 .... 9.95
Art 44 .... 9.87
App II 4.17, 6.28, 7.17
Art 3 .... 5.27
SCC Rules for Expedited Arbitrations ... 6.33
Statute of the International Court of Justice
Art 38 .... 3.134
Art 38(1) 1.195
Art 57 .... 9.128
Statutes of the International Court of Arbitration
Art 6 .... 2.192
Stockholm Institute Arbitration Rules
Art 21.1 .... 3.100
Art 24(1) 3.180
Treaty between the Federal Republic of Germany and the State of Israel concerning the Encouragement and the Reciprocal Protection of Investments, signed on 24 June 1976, not yet entered into force
Art 1(3)(b) 8.18
Treaty Between the United States and the Argentine Republic Concerning the Reciprocal Encouragement and Protection of Investment, signed on 14 November 1991, entered into force on 20 October 1994
Art I(1)(a) 8.28

l

Table of Legislation

Art 2(2) 8.134
Art II(2)(a) 8.96
Art 3(1) 8.79
Art XIV(1) 8.15
Treaty between the Government of the United States of America and the Government of the Republic of Bolivia Concerning the Encouragement and Reciprocal Protection of Investment
Art XII 8.25
Treaty between the United States of America and the Republic of Ecuador Concerning the Encouragement and Reciprocal Protection of Investment, signed on 27 August 1993, entered into force on 11 May 1997 . . . . 8.130
Art II(3)(b) 8.118
Art IV 8.129
Treaty between the United States of America and the Arab Republic of Egypt Concerning the Reciprocal Encouragement and Protection of Investments, 29 September 1982
Protocol, para 10 . . . . 8.131
Treaty between the United States of America and the Arab Republic of Egypt Concerning the Reciprocal Encouragement and Protection of Investments, signed on 29 September 1982, entered into force on 27 June 1992
Art 3(1) 8.124
Treaty concerning the Union of South American States in respect of Procedural Law 1889 (Montevideo Convention) 1.207
Treaty of Canterbury between the United Kingdom and France dated 12 February 1986
Art 19 . . . . 4.22
Treaty of Washington 8 May 1871
Art I 9.129
Treaty on the Functioning of the European Union (TFEU)
Art 101 . . . . 2.133, 2.137, 2.138, 11.120
Art 101(2) 2.133
Art 101(3) 2.133
Art 102 . . . . 2.133
UN Convention on Jurisdictional Immunities of States and their Property
Art 17 . . . . 11.145
UN/ECE Arbitration Rules for Certain Categories of Perishable Agricultural Products
Art 29 . . . . 9.150

UNCITRAL Arbitration Rules 1976
Art 33(1) 8.63
UNCITRAL Arbitration Rules (UNCITRAL Rules) adopted by resolution of the General Assembly of the United Nations in December 1976 and revised in 2010 . . . . . 1.18, 1.50, 1.145, 1.150, 1.157, 1.162, 1.190, 1.196, 1.229, 2.99, 2.117, 2.152, 2.245, 3.51, 3.96, 7.11, 7.52, 7.54, 7.60, 9.93, 9.122, 11.37, App D
Art 3 . . . . 1.68
Art 3(1) 1.67
Art 3(2) 1.76
Art 4 . . . . 1.68
Art 5 . . . . 4.193
Art 6.2 . . . . 4.46
Art 6.7 . . . . 4.63
Art 7(1) 4.27
Art 8.2 . . . . 4.39
Art 8.1 . . . . 4.47
Art 9.3 . . . . 4.39
Art 10 . . . . 2.216
Art 11 . . . . 7.11, 9.115
Art 12 . . . . 4.75
Art 12.1 . . . . 4.94
Art 12.2 . . . . 4.94
Art 13 . . . . 4.114
Art 15 . . . . 4.165
Art 16 . . . . 4.193
Art 17 . . . . 5.71
Art 17B 5.34
Art 17C(4) 5.34
Art 17C(5) 5.34
Art 17(1)–(3) 1.78
Art 17.1 . . . . 5.15, 6.11, 6.16, 6.21
Art 17.2 . . . . 6.42
Art 17.3 . . . . 6.16
Art 18 . . . . 9.120
Art 18(1) 3.40
Art 18.1 . . . . 5.16
Art 18.2 . . . . 4.170, 4.172, 6.162
Art 19.1 . . . . 5.17
Art 20 . . . . 6.16
Art 21 . . . . 6.16
Art 22 . . . . 6.74
Art 23 . . . . 1.54, 5.101
Art 23.1 . . . . 2.104, 2.110, 5.105
Art 23.2 . . . . 5.118
Art 23(2) 10.30
Art 23.3 . . . . 5.118
Art 26 . . . . 5.27, 5.28, 7.14, 9.20, 9.59
Art 26.3 . . . . 9.59
Art 26.9 . . . . 1.176, 7.24

Table of Legislation

UNCITRAL Arbitration Rules
(UNCITRAL Rules) adopted by
resolution of the General Assembly
of the United Nations in December
1976 and revised in 2010 (*cont.*):
Art 27.1 .... 6.84
Art 27.2 .... 6.139
Art 27.4 .... 6.128
Art 28 .... 3.90
Art 29 .... 6.136
Art 29.1 .... 5.23
Art 29.3 .... 6.152
Art 29.5 .... 6.16
Art 30 .... 2.85, 6.191
Art 31.2 .... 6.203
Art 32 .... 10.30
Art 33 .... 2.99
Art 33(1) 9.119
Art 33(2) 9.119
Art 35(1) 8.63
Art 34 .... 9.143, 9.192
Art 34(2) 9.01, 11.01, 11.87
Art 34.2 .... 9.18
Art 34.3 .... 1.93
Art 34(3) 9.152, 9.159
Art 34(6) 9.169
Art 35 .... 3.216, 9.70
Art 35.1 .... 5.16
Art 35.1 .... 3.100
Art 35.3 .... 3.165, 3.182
Art 36.1 .... 1.80
Art 36(1) 9.37
Art 37 .... 10.09, 10.10
Art 37(1) 9.192
Art 37(2) 9.192
Art 38 .... 10.09, 10.10, 10.17, 10.19
Art 38(2) 9.192
Art 39 .... 9.33, 10.09, 10.10
Art 39(1) 9.192
Art 40 ... 4.193, 4.208, 9.15, 9.92, 9.95, 9.152
Art 40.1 .... 9.87
Art 40.2 .... 9.87
Art 41.3-41.4 .... 9.89
Art 42 .... 8.169
Art 43 .... 4.221
UNCITRAL Conciliation Rules
Art. 7.1 .... 1.138
UNCITRAL Model Law
(adopted June 1985) 1.02, 1.18,
1.31–1.35, 1.205, 1.206, 1.218–1.223,
1.227, 1.228, 2.07, 2.10, 2.25,
2.34, 2.239, 2.245, 3.45, 3.74, 3.96,
3.191, 4.52, 5.109, 6.19, 6.20, 6.132,
6.199, 7.06, 9.05, 9.06, 9.24, 9.99,
10.38, 10.39, 10.65, 10.81, 11.56,
11.57, 11.58, 11.59, 11.60, 11.62,
11.70, 11.137, 11.141, App A
Art 1(1) 1.24
Art 1(2) 3.54, 10.38
Art 1.3 .... 1.32
Art 1(3)(a) 1.33
Art 1(3)(b)(i)–(ii) 1.33
Art 1(3)(c) 1.33
Art 4 .... 5.124
Art 5 .... 3.05, 7.06, 10.67
Art 6 .... 3.84, 7.06, 10.24, 10.38
Art 7 .... 2.17
Art 7(1) 1.46, 2.12
Art 7(2) 1.46, 2.12
Art 8 .... 3.54, 7.10
Art 8(1) 2.32, 2.197, 2.202, 2.205
Art 9 .... 3.46, 3.54
Art 10(2) 4.27
Art 11 .... 7.06
Art 11(1) 4.61
Art 13 .... 2.92, 4.107, 7.06
Art 13(2) 4.145
Art 13(3) 7.12
Art 14 .... 5.67
Art 16 .... 1.54, 5.108, 5.114, 7.06
Art 16(1) 2.104, 5.101
Art 16(2) 5.118
Art 16(3) 5.117, 7.12, 9.06, 10.42
Art 17 .... 7.14
Art 17B(1) 7.21
Art 17(2) 7.18
Art 18 .... 1.78, 1.82, 1.140, 6.10
Art 19 .... 3.45
Art 19(1) 5.12, 6.07
Art 20(2) 3.58, 6.162
Art 21 .... 4.11
Art 25 .... 6.199
Art 27 .... 3.67, 6.132, 7.06, 7.32
Art 28(2) 3.190, 3.216
Art 28(3) 1.139
Art 28(4) 3.182
Art 29 .... 9.122
Art 30 .... 9.37
Art 31(3) 3.70
Art 32(1) 9.23
Art 33 .... 10.19, 10.39
Art 33.1(b) 9.33
Art 33(1)(b) 9.188
Art 33(3) 10.49
Art 34 .... 7.06, 10.24, 10.38, 10.70,
11.64, 11.90
Art 34(2) 10.38
Art 34(2)(i) 10.42
Art 34(2)(iii) 10.42
Art 34(2)(a) 2.12, 3.14

lii

Table of Legislation

Art 34(2)(a)(i) 5.111
Art 34(2)(a)(iii) 10.45
Art 34(2)(a)(iv) 6.02, 10.60
Art 34(2)(b) 2.12
Art 34(2)(b)(i) 2.29, 2.125, 10.50
Art 34(2)(b)(ii) 10.81
Art 34(2)(c)(ii)................... 10.52
Art 34(2)(iii)..................... 2.63
Art 34(3)........................ 10.39
Art 34(4)................. 10.23, 10.40
Art 35 .... 3.54, 7.06, 11.45, 11.55
Art 36 .... 1.121, 3.54, 7.06, 11.45,
                11.55, 11.64, 11.66
Art 36(1)(a)(i) 3.69
Art 36(1)(a)(ii)................... 2.247
Art 36(1)(a)(iii) 2.63
Art 36(1)(a)(iv) 2.216, 6.02
Art 36(1)(a)(v) 3.69, 10.03, 10.06
Art 35 .... 1.40
Art 36(1)(a)..................... 2.32
Art 36(1)(a)(i) 1.40, 2.12, 3.81
Art 36(1)(a)(ii).................. 11.34
Art 36(1)(a)(v).................... 3.81
Art 36(1)(b)(i) 2.125
Art 36(2)(b)(i).............. 2.12, 2.29
Ch IV A 9.23
Option I, Art 7 .... 1.48, 2.13, 2.17,
                          2.18, 2.20
Option 1, Art 7(3)................. 2.17
Option 1, Art 7(4)................. 2.17
Option 1, Art 7(5)................. 2.17
Option 1, Art 7(6)................. 2.17
Option 2........................ 2.22
UNCITRAL Model Law
   (2006 amendment)
   Art 17 .... 5.28
UNCITRAL Rules on Transparency in
   Treaty-based Investor-State
   Arbitration 2.189, 8.12
Unified Agreement for the Investment
   of Arab Capital in the Arab States
   (the Arab League Investment
   Agreement) 11.139
Art 34(3)...................... 11.139
United States–Chile Free Trade
   Agreement, signed on 6 June 2003,
   entered into force on
   1 January 2004 .... 8.11
United States Model BIT (2012)
   Annex B 8.67
   Art 1 .... 8.44
VIAC Rules
   Art 28(1) 6.16
   Art 32 .... 6.203
Vienna Convention on the Law
   of Treaties 5.127
   Art 2(1)(a) 8.64
   Art 22.3 .... 11.155
   Art 25 .... 11.155
   Art 27 .... 8.69
   Art 31(3)(c) 8.64
   Art 1155 .... 8.64
WIPO Arbitration Rules
   Art 19 .... 4.36
   Art 34 .... 4.165
   Art 38(b)...................... 6.11
   Art 47 .... 6.167
   Art 49 .... 6.154
   Art 50 .... 6.152
   Art 51 .... 6.154
   Art 52 .... 2.193
   r 52(c)....................... 2.194
   r 52(d)....................... 2.194
   r 53(e)....................... 2.194
   Art 59(1) 3.216
   Art 63(e) 11.11
   Art 73 .... 2.195
   Art 74 .... 2.195
   Art 75 .... 2.195
   Art 76 .... 2.195
WIPO Expedited Arbitration
   Rules......................... 6.33

TABLE OF ARBITRATION AWARDS

AAA Case No 13T1810031097 . . . . 6.202
Abaclat and others v Argentine Republic (ICSID case) 4.89
Abaclat and others v The Argentine Republic, Decision on Jurisdiction and
 Admissibility, ICSID Case No ARB/07/5 (2011), IIC 504 (2011) 8.35, 8.47
Abaclat and others v Argentine Republic, ICSID Case No. ARB/07/05, Recommendation
 on Proposal for Disqualification of Prof. Pierre Tercier and Prof. Albert Jan
 van den Berg, 19 December 2011 . . . . 4.100
ABI Group Contractors Pty v Transfield Pty Ltd, Mealey's Intl Arb Rep (1999),
 Vol 14, No 1 . . . . 2.27
Accession Mezzanine Capital LP v Hungary, Decision on Respondent's Objection under
 Arbitration Rule 41(5), ICSID Case No ARB/12/3, IIC 577 (2013). 8.67
Achmea BV (formerly known as Eureko BV) v The Slovak Republic, Award on Jurisdiction,
 Arbitrability and Suspension, UNCITRAL, PCA Case No 2008-13 (2010),
 IIC 46 (2010) 8.74
ADC Affiliate Limited and ADC & ADMC Management Limited v The Republic of
 Hungary, Award, ICSID Case No ARB/03/16, IIC 1 (2006). 8.92, 8.156, 8.158, 9.78
AES Summit Generation Limited and AES-Tisza Erömü Kft v Republic of Hungary,
 Decision of the Ad Hoc Committee on the Application for Annulment,
 ICSID Case No ARB/07/22, IIC 592 (2012) 8.75, 8.117
Aguas del Tunari SA v Republic of Bolivia, Decision on Respondent's Objections to
 Jurisdiction, ICSID Case No ARB/02/3, IIC 8 (2005). 8.23
Alabama Claims. 1.192, 9.129
Alpha Projektholding GmbH v Ukraine, Award, ICSID Case No ARB/07/16,
 IIC 464 (2010) 8.167
Alps Finance and Trade AG v Slovak Republic, Award, UNCITRAL, IIC 489 (2011) 8.47
Ambiente Ufficio SPA and others v The Argentine Republic, Decision on Jurisdiction
 and Admissibility, ICSID Case No ARB/08/9, IIC 576 (2013) 8.35
Amco v The Republic of Indonesia Decision on Request for Provisional Measures, (1983)
 1 ICSID Reports 410, 9 December 1983 . . . . 2.184, 2.185
Amco Asia Corporation v the Republic of Indonesia, ICSID 16 May 1986. . . . . 3.138
Amco Asia Corp v Indonesia (Resubmission: Jurisdiction), ICSID, 89 ILR 552 . . . . 9.173
American Independent Oil Company Inc (Aminoil) v Government of the State
 of Kuwait [1982] 21 ILM 976. . . . . 3.121
American Manufacturing and Trading Inc v Republic of Zaire, Award, ICSID
 Case No ARB/93/1, IIC 14 (1997) 8.30, 8.116
Aminoil v Government of Kuwait (1982) XXI ILM 976 . . . . 2.202, 3.121,
 3.142, 3.143, 3.144, 6.45
Antoine Goetz and others v République du Burundi, Award, ICSID Case
 No ARB/95/3, IIC 16 (1999) 8.117, 8.123
Applied Industrial Materials Corp v Ovalar Makne Ticaret Ve Sanayi AS, No 05
 Civ 10540, 2006 WL 1816383 (SDNY 28 June 2006). 2.122
Aramco v Government of Saudi Arabia (1963) 27 Int L Rep 117 . . . . 3.187
Asian Agricultural Products Ltd (AAPL) v Republic of Sri Lanka, Final Award, ICSID
 Case No ARB/87/3, IIC 18 (1990) 8.09, 8.64, 8.65, 8.114, 8.153
Autopista Concessionada de Venezuela CA v Bolivarian Republic of Venezuela, Award,
 ICSID Case No ARB/00/5, IIC 20 (2003). 8.69

Table of Arbitration Awards

Award of 1982, Company Z and others (Republic of Xandu) v State Organisation
  ABC (Republic of Utopia), ICCA YB Awards, 93. . . . . 2.156
Award in ICC Case No. 4381, 113 JDI 1102 (1986) 2.39
Award in ICC Case No. 6223 (1991) 8(2) ICC Bulletin 69 . . . . 2.58
AWG Group v Argentine Republic (Challenge Decision of 22 October 2007) 4.114
AWG Group Ltd v The Argentine Republic, Decision on Liability, UNCITRAL,
  IIC 443 (2010) 8.117
Azinian and others v Mexico, Award on Jurisdiction and Merits, ICSID
  Case No ARB(AF)/97/2, IIC 22 (1999) 8.104
Azurix v Argentina I Annulment Decision of 1 September 2009. . . . . 4.117
Azurix Corp v The Argentine Republic 8.91, 8.98, 8.117,
  8.121, 8.161, 8.162
Azurix Corporation v The Argentine Republic, Award, ICSID Case No ARB/01/12;
  IIC 24 (2006) 9.78

Benteler v State of Belgium, Ad Hoc Award (18 November 1983) 2.39
Benteler v Belgium (1985) 8 European Commercial Cases 101 . . . . 7.55
Bernardus Henricus Funnekotter and others v Republic of Zimbabwe, Award,
  ICSID Case No ARB/05/6, IIC 370 (2009). 8.81, 8.159
BG Group PLC v Argentine Republic (ICSID case). 4.89
BG Group PLC v Republic of Argentina, Final Award, UNCITRAL,
  IIC 321 (2007) 8.49, 8.106
Biwater Gauff (Tanzania) Ltd v United Republic of Tanzania, Award, ICSID
  Case No ARB/05/22, IIC 330 (2008). 8.48, 8.73, 8.91, 8.95, 8.143
Biwater Gauff (Tanzania) Ltd v United Republic of Tanzania, ICSID Case
  No ARB/05/22, Procedural Order No. 3 (29 September 2006) 2.188
Blue Bank International & Trust (Barbados) Ltd v Bolivarian Republic of Venezuela
  (ICSID Case No. ARB/12/20) 4.136
Bosh International, Inc and B&P Ltd Foreign Investments Enterprise v Ukraine,
  Award, ICSID Case No ARB/08/11, IIC 565 (2012) 8.140
BP (1981) VI Ybk Comm Arb 89. . . . . 3.141, 6.193
Brescla Calcio SpA v West Ham United FC Plc, 2012 ISLR, Issue 3 . . . . 4.129
British Petroleum Company (Libya) Ltd v The Government of the
  Libyan Arab Republic (1979) 53 ILR 297. . . . . 9.55
Bureau Veritas, Inspection, Valuation, Assessment and Control, BIVAC BV v Republic
  of Paraguay, Decision on Objections to Jurisdiction, ICSID Case No ARB/07/9,
  IIC 428 (2009) 8.76, 8.140
Burlington Resources Inc v Ecuador, ICSID Case No. ARB 08/5. 5.93
Burlington Resources Inc v Republic of Ecuador, Decision on Jurisdiction,
  ICSID Case No ARB/08/5, IIC 436 (2010) 8.46, 8.50
Burlington Resources Inc v Republic of Ecuador, Decision on Liability,
  ICSID Case No ARB/08/5, IIC 568 (2012) 8.86

Camuzzi International SA v Argentine Republic (ICSID case) 4.89
Camuzzi International SA v Argentine Republic, Decision on Objections to
  Jurisdiction, ICSID Case No ARB/03/2, IIC 41 (2005). 8.56
Case Concerning Elettronica Sicula SpA (ELSI) (United States of America v Italy),
  Judgment, 15 ICJ Reports 76 (1999), ICGJ 95 (ICJ 1989),. 8.119
Case Concerning the Factory at Chorzów (Claim for Indemnity) (Germany v Poland)
  [1928] PCIJ, Series A, No 17.1, 47 . . . . 8.157, 8.159, 8.160, 8.161, 8.162, 9.54
Cementownia 'Nowa Huta' SA v Republic of Turkey, Award, ICSID Case
  No ARB(AF)/06/2, IIC 390 (2009) 8.36
Ceskoslovenska Obchodni Banka AS v The Slovak Republic, Decision on Objections
  to Jurisdiction, ICSID Case No ARB/97/4, IIC 49 (1999). 8.35
Challenge Decision of 11 January 1995, (1997) XXII YCA 227 . . . . 4.95

Table of Arbitration Awards

Channel Tunnel Group Limited and France-Manche SA v United Kingdom and
 France, Partial Award, PCA-UNCITRAL Rules, IIC 58 (2007) 4.22
City Oriente v Republic of Ecuador and Petroecuador, Decision on Interim Measures,
 ICSID Case No ARB/06/21, IIC 309 (2007) 5.30
CME Czech Republic BV v The Czech Republic, Final Award and Separate Opinion,
 Ad hoc-UNCITRAL Rules; IIC 62 (2003). 9.78
CME Czech Republic BV (The Netherlands) v The Czech Republic, Final Award,
 UNCITRAL, IIC 62 (2003). 8.167
CME Czech Republic BV (The Netherlands) v The Czech Republic, Partial Award,
 UNCITRAL, IIC 61 (2001) 8.76, 8.89, 8.99, 8.102, 8.117
CMS Gas Transmission Co v The Republic of Argentina, Decision on Objections
 to Jurisdiction, ICSID Case No. ARB/01/8, IIC 64 (2003) 5.93, 8.30, 8.59,
  8.102, 8.112, 8.162
CMS Gas Transmission Company v The Argentine Republic, ICSID Case
 No ARB/01/08; IIC 65 (2005), signed 12 May 2005 .... 9.58
Commerce Group Corp & San Sebastian Gold Mines, Inc v Republic of El Salvador
 (ICSID Case No ARB/09/17), Annulment Proceeding, Decision on El Salvador's
 Application for Security for Costs, 20 September 2012 .... 5.38
Compañía de Aguas del Aconquija SA and Vivendi Universal SA v Argentine Republic,
 Decision on Annulment, ICSID Case No ARB/97/3, IIC 307 (2007)..... 8.46, 8.55, 8.65,
  8.66, 8.91, 8.93, 8.109, 8.110, 8.112, 8.158, 8.167
Compañía de Aguas del Aconquija SA and Vivendi Universal (formerly Compagnie
 Générale des Eaux) v Argentine Republic, ICSID Case No ARB/97/3, Decision
 on Annulment, 3 July 2002 .... 11.127
Compañia Aguas del Aconquija SA and Vivendi Universal v Argentine Republic,
 Decision on the Argentine Republic's Request for a Continued Stay of Enforcement
 of the Award rendered on 20 August 2007, dated 4 November 2008 .... 11.129
Compañía de Aguas del Aconquija SA and Vivendi Universal v Argentine Republic
 ICSID Case No ARB/97/3; IIC 69 (2001); 17 ICSID Rev—Foreign Investment
 L J 168 (2002); 6 ICSID Rep 330 (2004); 125 ILR 46 (2004) 4.101, 4.123
Compañia del Desarollo de Santa Elena SA v Republic of Costa Rica (2000) 39 ILM 1317...... 9.78
Compañía del Desarrollo de Santa Elena SA v The Republic of Costa Rica,
 Final Award, ICSID Caso No ARB/96/1, IIC 73 (2000) 8.69, 8.93, 8.94
ConocoPhillips Petrozuata BV and others v Bolivarian Republic of Venezuela,
 Decision on Jurisdiction and the Merits, ICSID Case No ARB/07/30,
 IIC 605 (2013) 8.158
ConocoPhillips Company et al. v Bolivarian Republic of Venezuela, ICSID
 Case No ARB/07/30, Decision on the Proposal to Disqualify L Yves Fortier, QC,
 Arbitrator, 27 February 2012 .... 4.100, 4.117
Continental Casualty Company v Argentine Republic, Award, ICSID Case
 No ARB/03/9, IIC 336 (2008) 8.132
Corfu Channel case, Judgment of April 9th 1949, ICJ Reports 1949. .... 6.135

Daimler Financial Services v Argentina 8.53
Decision on the Challenge in the Arbitration National Grid Plc v The Republic
 of Argentina (LCIA Case No UN7949) dated 3 December 2007. .... 4.110
Desert Line Projects LLC v The Republic of Yemen, Award, ICSID Case
 No ARB/05/17, IIC 319 (2008). 8.37, 8.164, 8.165
Deutsche Bank AG v Democratic Socialist Republic of Sri Lanka, Award, ICSID
 Case No ARB/09/2, IIC 578 (2012) 8.144
Dow Chemical case (Chemical France et al v Isover Saint Gobain IX YBCA 131
 (1984) et seq). 1.115
Dow Chemical France v ISOVER Saint Gobain (France) (1983) 110 J du Droit
 Intl 899, n Derains, (ICC 4131/1982 (Interim Award)) (1984) IX Ybk
 Comm Arb 131 .... 2.45, 2.46, 2.47, 2.48, 2.50

Table of Arbitration Awards

Eastern Sugar BV v The Czech Republic, Partial Award, SCC Case No 088/2004,
IIC 310 (2007) 8.103
Economy Forms Corporation v The Islamic Republic of Iran 9.114
EDF International and others v Argentine Republic, Award, ICSID Case
No ARB/03/23, IIC 556 (2012) 8.127, 8.140
EDF International SA v Argentina, Challenge Decision of 25 June 2008 .... 4.101
El Paso Energy International Company v The Argentine Republic, Award, ICSID
Case No ARB/03/15, IIC 519 (2011)... 8.122
Electrabel SA v The Republic of Hungary, Decision on Jurisdiction, Applicable Law
and Liability, ICSID Case No ARB/07/19, IIC 567 (2012) 8.75
Emilio Agustín Maffezini v The Kingdom of Spain, Award on Jurisdiction, ICSID
Case No ARB/97/7, IIC 85 (2000)..8.52, 8.53
Emilio Agustín Maffezini v The Kingdom of Spain, Award, ICSID Case No ARB/97/7,
IIC 86 (2000) 8.102
Emilio Agustín Maffezini v Kingdom of Spain, Decision on Request for Provisional
Measures ICSID Case No. ARB/97/7, IIC 85 (2000); 16 ICSID Review—Foreign
Investment Law Journal 212 (2001) 5.30
Empresas Lucchetti, SA and Lucchetti Peru, SA v Republic of Peru, Award, ICSID
Case No ARB/03/4, IIC 88 (2005)... 8.15
Encana Corporation v Republic of Ecuador, Award, LCIA Case No UN3481,
IIC 91 (2006) 8.102
Enron Corporation and Ponderosa Assets LP v Argentine Republic, Decision on
Jurisdiction, ICSID Case No ARB/01/3, IIC 92 (2004)...............8.50, 8.69, 8.98,
8.109, 8.112
Enron Creditors Recovery Corporation (formerly Enron Corporation) and Ponderosa
Assets, LP v Argentine Republic, ICSID Case No. ARB/01/3, Decision on the Application
for Annulment of the Argentine Republic, 30 July 2010. .... 11.127
Enron Corporation Ponderosa Assets, LP v Argentine Republic, Decision on the
Argentine Republic's Request for a Continued Stay of Enforcement of the Award,
dated 7 October 2008... 11.129
Enron Creditors Recovery Corp v Argentina, ICSID Case No. ARB/01/3, Decision
on Annulment, 30 July 2010.. 10.15
Enron Creditors Recovery Corporation (formerly Enron Corporation) and Ponderosa
Assets LP v The Argentine Republic, Decision on Application for Annulment,
ICSID Case No ARB/01/3, IIC 441 (2010) 8.77, 8.162
Eureko BV v Republic of Poland, Partial Award of the Ad Hoc Committee,
UNCITRAL, IIC 98 (2005).. 8.92

Fedax NV v Bolivarian Republic of Venezuela, Decision on Objections to Jurisdiction,
ICSID Case No ARB/96/3, IIC 101 (1997) 8.34, 8.39
Fireman's Fund Insurance Company v The United Mexican States, Award, ICSID
Case No. ARB(AF)/02/01, IIC 291 (2006).................................... 8.92
Fougerolle (ICC tribunal)... 2.154
Franck Charles Arif, Mr v Republic of Moldova, Award, ICSID Case
No ARB/11/23, IIC 585 (2013) 8.163, 8.165
Fraport AG Frankfurt Airport Serv Worldwide v Republic of the Philippines, ICSID
Case No. ARB/03/25, Decision on Annulment, 23 December 2010 .... 10.15
French-Mexican Claims Commission cases 4.159

Gami Investments Inc v The Government of the United Mexican States, Award,
UNCITRAL, IIC 109 (2004)... 8.126
Gas Natural SDG, SA v Argentine Republic, Decision on Jurisdiction, ICSID
Case No ARB/03/10, IIC 115 (2005) 8.53
GEA Group Aktiengesellschaft v Ukraine, Award, ICSID Case No ARB/05/18,
IIC 487 (2011) 8.43

Table of Arbitration Awards

Gemplus SA and others v The United Mexican States, Award, ICSID Case
   No. ARB(AF)/04/3, IIC 488 (2010) 8.167
Generation Ukraine Inc v Ukraine, Award, ICSID Case No ARB/00/9, IIC 116 (2003) . . . 8.67
Genin and others v Republic of Estonia, Award, ICSID Case No ARB/99/2,
   IIC 10 (2001) 8.61
Grainger Associates v The Islamic Republic of Iran (1987) 16 Iran–US CTR 317 . . . . 9.134
Guaracachi America Inc and Rurelec Plc v The Plurinational State of Bolivia, Award,
   PCA Case No 2011-1717 IIC 628 (2014) 5.90, 8.25, 8.38, 8.42, 8.50
Guaracachi America, Inc. and Rurelec plc v Plurinational State of Bolivia, PCA
   Case no 2011-17, Procedural Order No. 14, 11 March 2013 . . . . 5.37, 5.38
Gustav F W Hamester GmbH & Co KG v Republic of Ghana, Award, ICSID
   Case No ARB/07/24, IIC 456 (2010) 8.36, 8.140

Himpurna California Energy Ltd v PT (Persero) Perusahaan Listruik Negara,
   Final Award dated 4 May 1999 . . . . 2.152
Himpurna California Energy Ltd v PT PLN, UNCITRAL (1999) XXV Ybk
   Comm Arb 13 . . . . 8.154
Himpurna California Energy Ltd v Republic of Indonesia (2000) XXV Ybk
   Comm Arb 186 . . . . 4.159
Hrvatska Elektroprivreda, dd v Republic of Slovenia, ICSID Case No. ARB/05/24,
   Tribunal's Ruling on the Participation of Counsel (6 May 2008) 4.128, 4.130

ICC Case No 3383 . . . . 1.154, 9.177
ICC Case No 5051 . . . . 9.168
ICC Case No 5103/1988 . . . . 2.49
ICC Case No 5832/1988, (1988) 115 J du Droit Intl 1198 . . . . 2.56
ICC Case No 5946, (1991) XVI Ybk Comm Arb 9 . . . . 9.45
ICC Case No 10189 . . . . 10.18
ICC Case No 10211 . . . . 6.34
ICC Case No 10623 . . . . 3.90
ICC Case No 11681 . . . . 7.30
ICC Case No 16553/GZ 4.129
ICS v Argentina, UNCITRAL, PCA Case No. 2010-9, Challenge Decision
   (17 Dec. 2009) 4.136
ICS Inspection and Control Services Limited (United Kingdom) v The Republic of
   Argentina, Award on Jurisdiction, UNCITRAL, IIC 528 (2012) 8.168
ICS Inspection and Control Services Limited v Argentine Republic, Challenge Decision
   of 17 December 2009 . . . . 4.95
Inceysa Vallisoletana SL v Republic of El Salvador, ICSID Case No ARB/03/26,
   Award (2006) 5.90
Inceysa Vallisoletana SL v Republic of El Salvador, Decision on Jurisdiction, ICSID
   Case No ARB/03/26, IIC 134 (2006) 8.36
Interim Award in ICC Case No. 7337 (1999) 24 Ybk Comm Arb 149 . . . . 2.58
International Thunderbird Gaming Corporation v The United Mexican States, Award,
   UNCITRAL, IIC 136 (2006) 8.104, 8.111
Interpretation of Peace Treaties with Bulgaria, Hungary and Romania 4.159
Ioan Micula and others v Romania, Decision on Jurisdiction and Admissibility, ICSID
   Case No ARB/05/20, IIC 339 (2008) 8.19
Iranian Assets Litigation Reporter 10860 at 10863; 8 Iran–US CTR 329 . . . . 9.97
Ireland v United Kingdom (Mox Plant) 4.22

Joint Venture Yashlar and Bridas SAPIC v Government of Turkmenistan ICC Case
   No 9151, Interim Award of 8 June 1999 . . . . 2.51
Joseph Charles Lemire v Ukraine, Decision on Jurisdiction and Liability, ICSID Case
   No ARB/06/18, IIC 424 (2010) 8.105, 8.120, 8.144, 8.159, 8.165

lix

Table of Arbitration Awards

Joy Mining Machinery Limited v Arab Republic of Egypt, Award on Jurisdiction,
    ICSID Case No ARB/03/11, IIC 147 (2004) 8.43

Karaha Bodas Company LLC v Perusahaan Pertambangan Minyak Dan Gasi Bumi
    Nehara, Award, UNCITRAL (2000) 8.154
Klöckner Industrie-Anlagen v Republic of Cameroon, ICSID Case No. ARB/81/2,
    03 May 1995 .... 3.138

Lagergren Award, ICC Case 1110 .... 5.89
Lanco International Inc v Argentine Republic, Award, ICSID Case No. ARB/97/6 .... 8.54
LESI SpA and ASTALDI SpA v People's Democratic Republic of Algeria, Award,
    ICSID Case No ARB/05/3, IIC 354 (2008) 8.40
Letco v Liberia March 31, 1986, 2 ICSID Reports 356 .... 5.120
LG&E Energy Corp and others v Argentine Republic, Decision on Liability, ICSID
    Case No ARB/02/1, IIC 152 (2006) 8.69, 8.85, 8.92, 8.98, 8.101, 8.123
LG&E Energy Corp, LG&E Capital Corp, and LG&E International Inc v
    The Argentine Republic, Award, ICSID Case No ARB/02/1; IIC 295 (2007) 9.78
Liamco arbitration (1981) VI Ybk Comm Arb 89 .... 3.121, 3.141, 6.193
Liamco v Libya (1982) 62 ILR 140 .... 3.141
Libananco Holdings v Republic of Turkey (ICSID Case No. ARB 06/8) Decision on
    Preliminary Issues of June 23, 2008 .... 5.37
Liberian Eastern Timber Corporation v The Government of the Republic of Liberia
    26 ILM 647 (1987) 9.27
Libyan American Oil Company (Liamco) v Government of the Libyan Arab Republic
    (1982) 62 ILR 140 .... 11.142
Loewen Group Inc, The and Raymond L Loewen v United States of America,
    Award, ICSID Case No ARB(AF)/98/3, IIC 254 (2003) 8.104, 8.123

Malaysian Historical Salvors, SDN, BHD v Malaysia, Decision on Jurisdiction,
    ICSID Case No ARB/05/10, IIC 289 (2007) 8.41
Malicorp Limited v Arab Republic of Egypt, ICSID Case No. ARB/08/18, Decision
    on Annulment, 3 July 2013 .... 11.127
Marion Unglaube and Reinhard Unglaube v Republic of Costa Rica, Award,
    ICSID Case Nos ARB/08/1 and ARB/09/20, IIC 554 (2012) 8.117, 8.123, 8.159
Metalclad Corporation v United Mexican States, Award, ICSID Case
    No ARB(AF)/97/1, IIC 161 (2000) 8.161
Metalclad Corporation v United Mexican States, Award, Ad hoc—ICSID Additional
    Facility Rules; ICSID Case No ARB(AF)/97/1; IIC 161 (2000) 2.185
Metalpar SA and Buen Aire SA v Argentine Republic, Award, ICSID Case
    No ARB/03/5, IIC 326 (2008) 8.132
Methanex Corporation v United States of America, Final Award on Jurisdiction and
    Merits, UNCITRAL, IIC 167 (2005) 8.90
Mexico v USA (Cross-Border Trucking) (USA-98–2008–01, 6 February 2001) 4.22
Middle East Cement Shipping and Handling Co SA v Arab Republic of Egypt,
    Award, ICSID Case No ARB/99/6, IIC 169 (2002) 8.64, 9.78
Mihaly International Corporation v Democratic Socialist Republic of Sri Lanka,
    Award, ICSID Case No ARB/00/2, IIC 170 (2002) 8.43
Millicom International Operations BV & Sentel GSM SA v The Republic of Senegal,
    Decision on Jurisdiction, ICSID Case No ARB/08/20, IIC 450 (2010) 8.26
Mobil Corporation Venezuela Holdings BV and others v Bolivarian Republic of Venezuela,
    Decision on Jurisdiction, ICSID Case No ARB/07/27, IIC 435 (2010) 8.21, 8.24, 8.33
Mondev International Ltd v United States of America, Final Award, ICSID
    Case No. ARB(AF)/99/2, IIC 173 (2002) 8.111
Mr Saba Fakes v Republic of Turkey, Award, ICSID Case No ARB/07/20,
    IIC 439 (2010) 8.40

Table of Arbitration Awards

MTD Equity Sdn Bhd & MTD Chile SA v Republic of Chile, Decision on
  Annulment, ICSID Case No. ARB/01/17, IIC 77 (2007).......... 8.72, 8.98, 8.101, 8.161
Murphy Exploration and Production Company International v Republic of Ecuador,
  Award on Jurisdiction, ICSID Case No ARB/08/4, 15 December 2010............. 8.46
Myers Inc v Government of Canada, Final Award on the Merits, UNCITRAL,
  IIC 249 (2000).. 8.161

National Grid Group plc v Argentine Republic (ICSID case)........................ 4.89
National Grid Plc v Argentine Republic, Award, UNCITRAL, IIC 361 (2008).... 8.117, 8.118
National Grid PLC v The Republic of Argentina, LCIA Case No UN7949, decision
  on the challenge dated 3 December 2007...................................... 4.138
Neer v Mexico, Opinion, United States–Mexico General Claims Commission, (1927)
  21 AJIL 555... 8.106
Nordzucker AG v The Republic of Poland, Third Partial and Final Award,
  UNCITRAL (2009)... 8.159
Nykomb Synergetics Technology Holding AB v The Republic of Latvia, Award,
  Stockholm Rules, IIC 182 (2003)... 8.123

Occidental Petroleum Corporation and Occidental Exploration and Production
  Company v Republic of Ecuador, Decision on Interim Measures, ICSID Case
  No. ARB/06/11, IIC 305 (2007), signed 17 August 2007........................ 5.31
Occidental Petroleum Corporation and others v The Republic of Ecuador, Award,
  ICSID Case No ARB/06/11, IIC 561 (2012).................................... 8.155
Occidental Petroleum Corporation and Occidental Exploration and Production Company v
  Ecuador Decision on Provisional Measures, ICSID Case No ARB/06/11, IIC 305 (2007);
  17 August 2007... 9.58
Occidental Petroleum Corporation and others v The Republic of Ecuador, Final Award,
  LCIA Case No UN 3467, IIC 202 (2004)....................................... 8.102

Pac Rim Cayman LLC v The Republic of El Salvador, Decision on the Respondent's
  Jurisdictional Objections, ICSID Case No ARB/09/12, IIC 543 (2012)............ 8.14
Pantechniki SA Contractors & Engineers (Greece) v The Republic of Albania, Award,
  ICSID Case No ARB/07/21, IIC 383 (2009)............................. 8.60, 8.115
Parker (1926) 4 Rep Intl Arb Awards 25... 6.85
Parkerings-Compagniet AS v Republic of Lithuania, Award, ICSID Case
  No. ARB/05/8.. 8.91, 8.101, 8.102, 8.126
Patrick Mitchell v Democratic Republic of the Congo, Decision on the Application
  for Annulment of the Award, ICSID Case No ARB/99/7, IIC 172 (2006).......... 8.41
Patrick Mitchell v Democratic Republic of Congo, ICSID Case No ARB/99/7,
  1 November 2006.. 11.127
Perenco Ecuador Ltd v the Republic of Ecuador and Empresa Estatal Petróleos
  del Ecuador (Petroecuador), ICSID Case No. ARB/08/6, Decision on Provisional
  Measures (2009)... 5.30
Perenco Ecuador Limited v The Republic of Ecuador & Empresa Estatal Petroleos
  del Ecuador (ICSID Case No. ARB/08/6), Decision on Challenge to Arbitrator,
  8 December 2009, (PCA Case No IR-2009/1)................................... 4.142
Petrobart Limited v The Kyrgyz Republic, Award, SCC Arbitration Arb No 126/2003,
  IIC 184 (2005).. 8.161
Phelps Dodge Corp v Iran, (1986) 10 Iran–United States CTR 121.................. 8.153
Philippe Gruslin v Malaysia, Award, ICSID Case No ARB/99/3, IIC 129 (2000);
  5 ICSID Reports 492... 8.37
Phillips Petroleum Co Iran v Islamic Republic of Iran, (1989) 21 Iran–United States
  CTR 79.. 8.93, 8.149
Phoenix Action Ltd v The Czech Republic, Award, ICSID Case No ARB/06/5,
  IIC 367 (2009).. 8.15, 8.36

lxi

Plama Consortium Limited v Republic of Bulgaria, Decision on Jurisdiction, ICSID
 Case No ARB/03/24, IIC 189 (2005).................................... 8.25
Pope & Talbot Inc v Government of Canada, Award on Damages, UNCITRAL,
 IIC 195 (2002) 8.85, 8.111, 9.78
PSEG Global, Inc., The North American Coal Corporation, and Konya Ingin
 Electrik Üretim ve Ticaret Limited Şirketi v Republic of Turkey, Award, ICSID
 Case No ARB/02/5, IIC 198 (2007)...................................8.85, 8.102
Pyramids arbitration... 9.177

R Loewen and Loewen Corporation v United States of America, Decision on Hearing
 of Respondent's Objection to Competence and Jurisdiction, ICSID Case
 No ARB(AF)/98/3; IIC 253 (2001); 7 ICSID Rep 425; 128 ILR 339 ....2.186, 2.187
Republic of Colombia v Cauca Company.................................... 4.159
Resort Condominiums Inc v Bolwell, (1995) Volume XX Yearbook of Commercial
 Arbitration 628... 7.19
Riv di Dir Internaz, Priv e Proc, 1972, p 563; also reported in (1976) I Ybk
 Comm Arb 190... 2.15
Romak SA (Switzerland) v The Republic of Uzbekistan, Award, UNCITRAL,
 PCA Case No AA280, IIC 400 (2009)................................. 8.38, 8.42
Rompetrol Group NV v Romania, Award, ICSID Case No ARB/06/3, IIC 591 (2013) ... 8.159
Rompetrol Group NV, The v Romania, Decision on Preliminary Objections, ICSID
 Case No ARB/06/3, IIC 322 (2008)..................................... 8.22
Ronald S Lauder v The Czech Republic, Final Award, UNCITRAL,
 IIC 205 (2001) 8.47, 8.76, 8.82
RSM Production, Inc. v Saint Lucia (ICSID Case No. ARB 12/10), Decision on
 Saint Lucia's Request for Security for Costs, 12 August 2014...................... 5.39
Ruler of Qatar v International Marine Oil Company Ltd (1956) 20 Int L Rep 534....... 3.187
Rumeli Telekom AS and Telsim Mobil Telekomunikasyon Hizmetleri AS v Republic
 of Kazakhstan, Award, ICSID Case No ARB/05/16, IIC 344 (2008) ... 8.114, 8.117, 8.142
Rurelec v Bolivia see Guaracachi America Inc and Rurelec Plc v The Plurinational State
 of Bolivia, Award, PCA Case No 2011-1717 IIC 628 (2014)

Sabotage cases... 4.159
Saint-Gobain Performance Plastics Europe v Bolivarian Republic of Venezuela, ICSID Case
 No. ARB/12/13, Decision on Claimant Proposal to Disqualify Mr. Gabriel Bottini from
 the Tribunal under Article 57 of the ICSID Convention, 27 February 2013 .... 4.117
Saipem S.p.A v The People's Republic of Bangladesh, ICSID Case No ARB/05/07,
 Award (Jun. 30, 2009) 10.94
Salini Construttori Spa v The Federal Democratic Republic of Ethiopia, Addis Ababa
 Water and Sewerage Authority, ICC Case No 10623, 7 December 2001 .... 7.58
Salini Costruttori SpA and Italstrade SpA v Morocco, Decision on Jurisdiction,
 ICSID Case No ARB/00/4, IIC 207 (2004)........................ 8.39, 8.40, 8.41
Saluka Investments BV v Czech Republic, Partial Award, UNCITRAL, ICGJ 368
 (PCA 2006) 8.98, 8.99, 8.102, 8.112, 8.123
Sapphire International Petroleum Ltd v The National Iranian Oil Company
 (1964) 13 ICLQ 1011 .... 3.118, 3.147, 3.148, 3.149, 3.213
Saudi Arabia v Arabian American Oil Company (Aramco) (1963) 27 ILR 117 ....9.56, 9.61
SD Myers Inc v Government of Canada, Second Partial Award, Ad hoc
 UNCITRAL; IIC 250 (2002)... 9.78
Sedco Inc v National Iranian Oil Co, Case No 129 Iran–US CTR 34 .... 4.156
Sempra Energy International v Argentine Republic, Decision on Annulment,
 ICSID Case No ARB/02/16, IIC 438 (2010) 8.77, 8.85
Sempra Energy International v Republic of Argentina, Award, ICSID Case
 No ARB/02/16; IIC 304 (2007), signed 18 September 2007, despatched
 28 September 2007... 3.138

Table of Arbitration Awards

Sempra Energy Int'l v Argentina, ICSID Case No. ARB/02/16, Decision on
　Annulment, 29 June 2010 .... 10.15
Sempra Energy International v Argentine Republic and Camuzzi International SA v
　Argentine Republic (ICSID case) 4.89
SGS Société Générale de Surveillance SA v Islamic Republic of Pakistan, Decision
　on Jurisdiction, ICSID Case No ARB/01/13, IIC 223 (2003) 8.136, 8.137, 8.139
SGS Société Générale de Surveillance SA v Republic of Paraguay, Decision on
　Jurisdiction, ICSID Case No ARB/07/29, IIC 525 (2010) 8.39, 8.76, 8.140
SGS Société Générale de Surveillance SA v Republic of the Philippines, Decision on
　Jurisdiction, ICSID Case No ARB/02/6, IIC 224 (2004) 8.76, 8.138, 8.139
Sheikh Abu Dhabi v Petroleum Development Ltd (1952) ICLQ 247 .... 3.187
Siemens AG v The Argentine Republic, Award, ICSID Case No ARB/02/8,
　IIC 227 (2007) 8.73, 8.91, 8.95, 9.78
Sr Tza Yap Shum v Republic of Peru, Decision on Jurisdiction and Competence,
　ICSID Case No ARB/07/6, IIC 382 (2009) 8.67, 8.165
Standard Chartered Bank v United Republic of Tanzania, Award, ICSID Case
　No ARB/10/12, IIC 581 (2012) 8.33
Starrett Housing Corporation v Iran, Iran–US CTR 122, 269 (1983) 9.79
Starrett Housing Corp v The Government of the Islamic Republic of Iran (1987)
　16 Iran–US CTR 112, Award No 314-21-1 .... 6.135
Starrett Housing Corp, et al. v Iran (Iran-US Claims Tribunal) Award No. 314-24-1,
　14 August 1987 .... 8.148
Suez and others v Argentine Republic (ICSID case) 4.89
Suez and others v Republic of Argentina, Disqualification Decision, ICSID Case
　No ARB/03/17; IIC 312 (2007) 4.100, 4.115
Suez, Sociedad General de Aguas de Barcelona SA and InterAguas Servicios Integrales
　del Agua SA v The Argentine Republic, Decision on Jurisdiction, ICSID Case
　No ARB/03/17, IIC 236 (2006) 8.30, 8.53, 8.76, 8.91
Suez, Sociedad General de Aguas de Barcelona SA v Argentine Republic
　(Decision on Second Proposal for Disqualification) ICSID Cases Nos ARB/03/17
　and ARB/03/19 .... 4.101
Suez, Sociedad General de Aguas de Barcelona SA, and InterAguas Servicios Integrales
　del Agua SA v The Argentine Republic and Suez, Sociedad General de Aguas de
　Barcelona SA, and Vivendi Universal SA v The Argentine Republic, ICSID Case
　No. ARB/03/17, ICSID Case No. ARB/03/19, Decision on a Second Proposal for the
　Disqualification of a Member of the Arbitral Tribunal, 12 May 2008 .... 4.120

Talsud SA v The United Mexican States, Award, ICSID Case No. ARB(AF)04/4,
　IIC 488 (2010), Part XVI 8.167
TECO Guatemala Holdings LLC v The Republic of Guatemala, Award, ICSID Case
　No ARB/10/17, IIC 623 (2013) 8.168
Técnicas Medioambientales Tecmed SA v The United Mexican States, Award,
　ICSID Case No ARB(AF)/00/02, IIC 247 (2003) 8.15, 8.100
Teinver SA, Transportes de Cercanias SA, Audobuses Urbanos del Sur SA v
　Argentine Republic, Decision on Jurisdiction, ICSID Case No ARB/09/1,
　IIC 570 (2012) 8.47
Telekom Malaysia 4.133
Texaco (1981) VI Ybk Comm Arb 89 .... 3.120, 3.141, 6.193
Texas Overseas Petroleum Company and California Asiatic Oil Company (Texaco) v
　The Government of the Libyan Arab Republic (1978) 17 ILM 3 .... 9.55
Tidewater Incorporated and others v The Bolivarian Republic of Venezuela, Decision
　on Jurisdiction, ICSID Case No ARB/10/5, IIC 573 (2013) 8.24
Tokios Tokeles v Ukraine, ICSID Case No ARB/02/18 .... 9.122
Tokios Tokelés v Ukraine, Decision on Jurisdiction, ICSID Case No ARB/02/18,
　IIC 258 (2004) 8.22, 8.34

Table of Arbitration Awards

Total SA v The Argentine Republic, Decision on Liability, ICSID Case
No ARB/04/01, IIC 484 (2010) 8.58, 8.84
Toto Construzioni Generali Spa v Republic of Lebanon, Decision on Jurisdiction,
ICSID Case No ARB/07/12, IIC 391 (2009) 8.58
TSA Spectrum de Argentina SA v Argentine Republic, Award, ICSID Case
No ARB/05/5, IIC 358 (2008) 8.22
Tulip Real Estate Investment and Development Netherlands BV v Republic of
Turkey, Decision on Bifurcated Jurisdictional Issue, ICSID Case No ARB/11/28,
IIC 583 (2013) 8.46, 8.50

Uiterwiyk Corp v Islamic Republic of Iran, Award No 375–381–1 (6 July 1988),
19 Iran–US CTR 107 .... 4.156
Ulysseas Inc v The Republic of Ecuador, Interim Award, UNCITRAL (2010) 8.25
United Parcel Service of America Inc v Government of Canada, Award, UNCITRAL,
IIC 306 (2007) 8.126
Universal Compression International Holdings, SLU v Bolivian Republic of
Venezuela, ICSID Case No. ARB/10/9, Decision on the Proposal to Disqualify
Professor Brigitte Stern and Professor Guido Santiago Tawil, Arbitrators,
20 May 2011 .... 4.100, 4.126
Urbaser SA & others v The Argentine Republic, (ICSID Case No ARB/07/26),
Decision on Claimants' Proposal to Disqualify Professor Campbell McLachlan,
Arbitrator, 12 August 2010 .... 4.141

Vito G. Gallo v Canada, Decision on the Challenge to an Arbitrator, IIC 404
(2009) October 14 2009 .... 4.132

Waguih Elie George Siag and Clorinda Vecchi v The Arab Republic of Egypt, Award,
ICSID Case No ARB/05/15, IIC 374 (2009) 8.117, 8.159
Waguih Elie George Siag and Clorinda Vecchi v The Arab Republic of Egypt, Decision
on Jurisdiction, ICSID Case No ARB/05/15, IIC 288 (2007) 8.19
Walter Bau AG v The Kingdom of Thailand, Award, UNCITRAL, IIC 429 (2009) 8.95
Waste Management Inc v United Mexican States, Award, ICSID Case
No ARB(AF)/00/3, IIC 270 (2004) 8.91, 8.104
Wena Hotels Limited v Egypt, Award, ICSID Case No ARB/98/4; IIC 273 (2000);
41 ILM 896 (2002) 9.78
Wena Hotels Limited v Arab Republic of Egypt, Decision on annulment application,
ICSID Case No. ARB/98/4; IIC 274 (2002); (2002) 41 ILM 933; (2004) 6 ICSID
Rep 129; (2003) 130 Journal du Droit International Clunet 167 .... 3.138, 8.68
White Industries Australia Ltd v The Republic of India, UNCITRAL, Final Award
(Nov. 30, 2011) 10.94
White Industries Australia Limited v The Republic of India, Final Award, UNCITRAL,
IIC 529 (2011) 8.133
Wintershall Aktiengesellschaft v Argentine Republic, Award, ICSID Case
No ARB/04/14, IIC 357 (2008) 8.53
World Duty Free Company Ltd v The Republic of Kenya, Award, ICSID Case
No. ARB/00/7, IIC 277 (2006), 4 October 2006 .... 5.90

Yukos Universal Limited (Isle of Man) v The Russian Federation, UNCITRAL, PCA
Case No. AA 227 (2014) 9.98
Yukos Universal Limited (Isle of Man) v The Russian Federation, Interim Award on
Jurisdiction and Admissibility, UNCITRAL, PCA Case No AA 228, IIC 416 (2009) ... 8.21

Zhinvali Development Ltd v Republic of Georgia, ICSID Case No ARB/00/1, Decision
on Respondent's Proposal to Disqualify Arbitrator, (19 January 2001), unpublished 4.122

LIST OF ABBREVIATIONS

AAA	American Arbitration Association, New York (Established 1926)
ABA	American Bar Association, Chicago (Established 1878)
ABQB	Alberta Court of Queen's Bench (Canada)
AC	*Law Reports Appeal Cases*, published by the Incorporated Council of Law Reporting for England and Wales
ACICA	Australian Centre for International Commercial Arbitration, Sydney (Established 1985)
AD	*New York Supreme Court Appellate Division Reports*
ADR	alternative dispute resolution
ADRLJ	*Arbitration and Dispute Resolution Law Journal*, published by Sweet & Maxwell
ALI	American Law Institute, Philadelphia, PA (Established 1923)
All ER	*All England Law Reports*, published by LexisNexis
Am J Comp L	*American Journal of Comparative Law*, published by University of Michigan Law School
Am Rev Intl Arb	*American Review of International Arbitration*, published by Juris
Arab League Investment Agreement	Unified Agreement for the Investment of Arab Capital in the Arab States, Arab League
Arb Intl	*Arbitration International*, published by the LCIA
Arb LM	*Arbitration Law Monthly*, published by Sweet & Maxwell
Arb LR	*Arbitration Law Reports and Review*, published by Oxford University Press
ARIAS	Aida Reinsurance and Insurance Arbitration Society, Mount Vernon, NY (Established 1994)
art./Art.	article (domestic)/Article (supranational)
ASA	Association Suisse de l'Arbitrage [Swiss Arbitration Association], Basel (Established 1974)
ASA Bulletin	*Bulletin of the Swiss Arbitration Association*, published by Kluwer Law International
ASEAN	Association of Southeast Asian Nations, Bangkok (Established 1967)
Asian Intl Arb J	*Asian International Arbitration Journal*, published by Kluwer Law International
BGHZ	*Entscheidungen des Bundesgerichtshofes in Zivilsachen*, published by Carl Heymanns Verlag

List of Abbreviations

Bing	*Bingham's Common Pleas Reports*, published in English Reports
BIT	bilateral investment treaty
BJIL	*Berkeley Journal of International Law*, published by University of California, Berkeley, School of Law
BR	*Bankruptcy Reporter* (US), published by West Publishing
Brussels Convention	Brussels Convention on Jurisdiction and the Enforcement of Judgments in Civil and Commercial Matters 1968
Brussels Regulation	Council Regulation (EC) No. 44/2001 on Jurisdiction and the Enforcement of Judgments in Civil and Commercial disputes
Bus L Intl	*Business Law International*, published by the IBA
BVerfGE	*Entscheidungen des Bundesverfassungsgerichts*, published by Mohr Siebeck
BYIL	*British Yearbook of International Law*, published by Oxford University Press
CA	Court of Appeal
Cal.	California
CANACO	Cámara Nacional de Comercio de la Ciudad de México [Mexican National Chamber of Commerce], Mexico City (Established 1874)
CAS	Court of Arbitration for Sport (of ICAS)
Cass. Civ.	Cour de Cassation (Chambre Civil) [Supreme Court, Civil Chamber], Paris
CCA	College of Commercial Arbitrators (US), Austin, TX (Established 2001)
CCBE	Conseil des Barreaux de la Communauté Européene [Council of Bars and Law Societies of Europe], Brussels (Established 1960)
CEDR	Centre for Effective Dispute Resolution, London (Established 1990)
CEPANI	Belgian Centre for Arbitration and Mediation, Brussels (Established 1969)
ch./Ch.	chapter (bibliographical); Chapter (legislative)
CIArb	Chartered Institute of Arbitrators (UK), London (Established 1915)
CIETAC	China International Economic and Trade Arbitration Commission, Beijing (Established 1956)
CIETAC Rules	CIETAC Arbitration Rules, revised 2014, in force 2015
Cir.	Circuit (US Federal)
CJEU	Court of Justice of the European Union, Luxembourg (Established 1952); formerly (and still informally) known as the ECJ
CLR	*Commonwealth Law Reports*, published by Lawbook Company
CMEA	Council for Mutual Economic Assistance (Comecon), dissolved 1991
Co Rep	*Correspondents' Reports*

List of Abbreviations

CPR	Center for Public Resources, New York (Established 1979)
CRCICA	Cairo Regional Centre for International Commercial Arbitration, Cairo (Established 1979)
DAC	Departmental Advisory Committee
DCF	discounted cash flow
Delvolvé Report	Commission on International Arbitration, *Final Report on Multi-Party Arbitrations* (ICC, 1994)
DIAC	Dubai International Arbitration Centre, Dubai (Established 1995)
DIS	*Deutsche Institution für Scheidsgerichtsbarkeit* [German Arbitration Institute], Cologne (Established 1920)
Disp Res Intl	*Dispute Resolution International*, published by the IBA
Disp Res J	*Dispute Resolution Journal*, published by the AAA
DLR	*Dominion Law Reports*, published by Canada Law Book
DNJ	District Court of New Jersey
DR-CAFTA	Dominican Republic and Central America–United States Free Trade Agreement, signed 5 August 2004
DS	*Recueil Dalloz et Sirey*, published by Editions Dalloz
ECHR	Convention for the Protection of Human Rights and Fundamental Freedoms (European Convention on Human Rights), signed 4 November 1950
ECJ	(formerly and informally) European Court of Justice, Luxembourg (Established 1952); now CJEU
ECR	*European Court Reports*, published by Court of Justice of the European Union
ECT	Energy Charter Treaty 1994
ECtHR	European Court of Human Rights, Strasbourg (Established 1959)
EDI	electronic data interchange
edn	edition
EFTA	European Free Trade PLC (Established 1960)
ESI	electronically stored information
European Convention of 1961	European Convention on International Commercial Arbitration, signed 21 April 1961
EWCA	Court of Appeal (England and Wales)
EWHC	High Court (England and Wales)
F, F.2d, F.3d	*Federal Reporter* (US) 1st, 2nd, and 3rd Series, published by West Publishing
FAA	US Federal Arbitration Act of 1925
FCA	Federal Court of Australia
FCN treaty	treaty of friendship, commerce and navigation
Fed. Appx	*Federal Appendix*, published by West Publishing
FET	fair and equitable treatment
FIA	Fédération Internationale de l'Automobile [International Automobile Federation], Paris (Established 1904)

lxvii

FIDIC	Fédération Internationale des Ingénieurs-Conseils [International Federation of Consulting Engineers], Geneva (Established 1913)
FRCP	US Federal Rules of Civil Procedure
FRD	*Federal Rules Decisions*, published by West Publishing
FTA	free trade agreement
GAFTA	Grain and Feed Trade Association, London (Established 1878)
GCC Convention	1995 Agreement on the Execution of Rulings, Requests of Legal Assistance and Judicial Notices, Gulf Co-operation Council
Geneva Convention	Geneva Convention for the Execution of Foreign Arbitral Awards, signed 26 September 1927
Geneva Protocol	Geneva Protocol on Arbitration Clauses of 1923, signed 24 September 1923
Global Arb Rev	*Global Arbitration Review*, published by Law Business Research Ltd
Hague Convention 1899	Hague Convention for the Pacific Settlement of International Disputes of 1899
Hague Convention 1907	Hague Convention for the Pacific Settlement of International Disputes
Hague Convention 1970	Hague Convention on the Taking of Evidence Abroad in Civil or Commercial Matters
Hague Convention 2005	Hague Convention on Choice of Court Agreements, signed 30 June 2005
Harv L Rev	*Harvard Law Review*, published by the Harvard Law Review Association
Harv Negotiation L Rev	*Harvard Negotiation Law Review*, published by the Harvard Law Review Association
HIPCs	heavily indebted poor countries
HKC	*Hong Kong Cases*, published by Butterworths Asia
HKIAC	Hong Kong International Arbitration Centre, Hong Kong (Established 1985)
HL	House of Lords
HMSO	Her Majesty's Stationery Office (UK)
Holocaust Tribunals	Claims Resolution Tribunal for Dormant Accounts in Switzerland
IACAC	Inter-American Commercial Arbitration Commission (Established 1934); Inter-American Convention against Corruption, signed 29 March 1996
IBA	International Bar Association, London (Established 1947)
IBA Rules	IBA Rules on the Taking of Evidence in International Commercial Arbitration, adopted 1 June 1999
ICANN	Internet Corporation for Assigned Names and Numbers, Los Angeles, CA (Established 1998)

List of Abbreviations

ICAS	International Council of Arbitration for Sport, Lausanne
ICC	International Chamber of Commerce, Paris (Established 1919)
ICC Court	International Court of Arbitration of the ICC, Paris (Established 1923)
ICC Rules	ICC Rules of Arbitration, revised in and in force 2012
ICCA	International Council for Commercial Arbitration, The Hague (Established 2014)
ICDR	International Centre for Dispute Resolution, London (Established 1996)
ICDR Rules	ICDR International Dispute Resolution Procedures, revised and in force 2014
ICJ	International Court of Justice, The Hague (Established 1945)
ICLQ	*International and Comparative Law Quarterly*, published by Cambridge University Press
ICSID	International Centre for the Settlement of Investment Disputes, Washington DC (Established 1965)
ICSID Rev—Foreign Investment LJ	*ICSID Review—Foreign Investment Law Journal*, published by the ICSID
ICSID Rules	ICSID Rules of Procedure for Arbitration Proceedings, 2006
IELTR	*International Energy Law and Taxation Review*, published by Sweet and Maxwell
IIC	*International Review of Intellectual Property and Competition Law*, published by Max Planck Institute for Intellectual Property, Competition and Tax Law
ILA	International Law Association, Brussels (Established 1873)
ILM	*International Legal Materials*, published by American Society of International Law
ILO	International Labour Organization, Geneva (Established 1919)
ILR	*International Law Reports*, published by Cambridge University Press
IMF	International Monetary Fund, Washington DC (Established 1944)
Incoterms	ICC International Rules for the Interpretation of Trade Terms
Int ALR	*International Arbitration Law Review*, published by Sweet & Maxwell
Intl Arb L Rev	*International Arbitration Law Review*, published by Sweet & Maxwell
Intl Construction L Rev	*International Construction Law Review*, published by Informa
Intl News	*International News*
Iran–US CTR	*Iran–United States Claims Tribunal Reports*, published by Grotius
ISDA	International Swaps and Derivatives Association, Inc., New York (Established 1985)
J CIArb	*Journal of the Chartered Institute of Arbitrators*, published by CIArb

J du Droit Intl	*Journal du Droit International* ('Clunet'), published by JurisClasseur
J Intl Arb	*Journal of International Arbitration*, published by Kluwer
J Intl Disp Settlement	*Journal of International Dispute Settlement*, published by Oxford University Press
J Priv Intl L	*Journal of Private International Law*, published by Hart
J World Energy L & Bus	*Journal of World Energy Law and Business*, published by Oxford University Press
Jay Treaty	General Treaty of Friendship, Commerce and Navigation, 1794
JBL	*Journal of Business Law*, published by Sweet and Maxwell
JCAA	Japanese Commercial Arbitration Association, Tokyo (Established 1950)
JWIT	*Journal of World Investment & Trade*, published by Brill
KLRCA	Kuala Lumpur Regional Centre for Arbitration, Kuala Lumpur (Established 1978)
L.Ed.	*United States Supreme Court Reports*, Lawyers' Edition, published by LexisNexis
Lando Principles	1998 Principles of European Contract Law
LCIA	London Court of International Arbitration, London (Established 1892)
LCIA Rules	LCIA Arbitration Rules, revised and in force 2014
LMAA	London Maritime Arbitration Association, London (Established 1960)
LNG	liquefied natural gas
LQR	*Law Quarterly Review*, published by Sweet & Maxwell
MAT	Muslim Arbitration Tribunals (England & Wales)
MD Tenn.	US District Court for the Middle District of Tennessee
Mealey's Intl Arb Rep	*Mealey's International Arbitration Report*, published by LexisNexis
med/arb	mediation/arbitration
Mercosur	Mercado Común del Sur [Common Market of the South]
MFN	most-favoured nation
Model Law	Model Law on International Commercial Arbitration, adopted 21 June 1985
Montevideo Convention	Treaty concerning the Union of South American States in respect of Procedural Law, signed 11 January 1889
Moscow Convention of 1972	Convention on the Settlement of Arbitration of Civil Law Disputes Arising from Relations of Economic, Scientific and Technical Co-operation, signed May 1972
MST	minimum standard of treatment
NAFTA	North American Free Trade Agreement, signed 17 December 1992
NAI	Netherlands Arbitration Institute, Rotterdam (Established 1949)

List of Abbreviations

NC App.	*North Carolina Appellate Reporter*
NE	*North Eastern Reporter*, published by West Publishing
NED	non-executive director
New York Convention	Convention on the Recognition and Enforcement of Foreign Arbitral Awards, signed 10 June 1958
New York LJ	*New York Law Journal*, published by the Journal
NILR	*Netherlands International Law Review*, published by Cambridge University Press
NIPR	*Nederlands Internationaal Privaatrecht* [*Netherlands International Private Law*], published by TMC Asser
NJW	*Neue Juristische Wochenschrift*, published by C.H. Beck Verlag
n.p.	no pinpoint (page/paragraph) available
NPV	net present value
NSWLR	*New South Wales Law Reports*, published by Lexis Nexis
NTIR	*Nordisk Tidsskrift for International Ret* [*Nordic Journal of International Law*], published by Martinus Nijhoff
NW	*North Western Reporter*, published by West Publishing
NY	*New York Reports*, published by West Publishing
NYL Sch J Intl Comp L	*New York Law School Journal of International and Comparative Law*, published by New York Law School
NYS	*New York Supplement*, published by West Publishing
OECD	Organisation for Economic Co-operation and Development, Paris (Established 1961)
OGEL	*Oil, Gas, & Energy Law*, published online at https://www.ogel.org/
OGEMID	Oil Gas Energy Mining Infrastructure Dispute Management email list
OGLTR	*Oil and Gas Law and Taxation Review*, published by Sweet and Maxwell
OIC Agreement	Agreement for Promotion, Protection and Guarantee of Investments, Organisation of Islamic Cooperation
OJ L	*Official Journal of the European Union*, L Series
p.	page
Panama Convention of 1975	Inter-American Convention on International Commercial Arbitration, signed 30 January 1975
para.	paragraph
PCA	Permanent Court of Arbitration, The Hague (Established 1899)
PCIJ	(former) Permanent Court of International Justice; now the ICJ
PRC	People's Republic of China
QB	*Law Reports, Queen's Bench*, published by the Incorporated Council of Law Reporting for England and Wales
QDR	*Queensland Reports*, published by Supreme Court of Queensland

r.	rule
RDAI	*Revue de Droit des Affaires Internationales*, published by Thomson Reuters/Sweet & Maxwell
Rev Arb	*Revue de l'Arbitrage* [*Arbitration Review*], published by Kluwer
revised Model Law	Model Law, as amended 2006
RF CCI	Chamber of Commerce and Industry (Russian Federation), Moscow (Established 1993)
RICO	Racketeer Influenced and Corrupt Organizations Act of 1970 (US)
Riv di Dir Internaz, Priv e Proc	*Rivista di Diritto Internazionale Privato e Processuale* [*Journal of Private International Law and Procedure*], published by CEDAM
Riyadh Convention	Riyadh Arab Agreement on Judicial Cooperation, entered into force in 1985
Rome Convention	1980 Rome Convention on the Law Applicable to Contractual Obligations
Rome I	2008 Rome Regulation on the Law Applicable to Contractual Obligations
s.	section
SCC	Stockholm Chamber of Commerce, Stockholm (Established 1917); *Supreme Court Cases* (India), published by Eastern Book Co.
SCC Rules	SCC Arbitration Rules, revised and in force 2010
SchiedsVZ	*Zeitschrift für Schiedsverfahren* [*German Arbitration Journal*], published by Verlag CH Beck
SCR	*Supreme Court Reports*, published by Canadian Government
S.Ct.	*Supreme Court Reporter*, published by West Publishing
SD	Southern District
SDNY	Southern District of New York (US District Court)
SEC	Securities and Exchange Commission (US), Washington, DC (Established 1934)
Sedona Principles	*Best Practices, Recommendations and Principles for Addressing Electronic Document Production* (2nd edn, 2007)
SGHC	Singapore High Court
SIAC	Singapore International Arbitration Centre, Singapore (Established 1991)
SIAR	*Stockholm International Arbitration Review*, published by SCC
SJIL	*Stanford Journal of International Law*, published by Stanford Law School
SLR	*Singapore Law Reports*, published by Justis
Spain Arb Rev	*Spain Arbitration Review*, published by Kluwer Arbitration
SPC	Supreme People's Court (China)
Strasbourg Uniform Law	European Convention providing a Uniform Law on Arbitration, signed 20 January 1966
Swiss PIL	Swiss Private International Law Act 1987

List of Abbreviations

Swiss Rules	Swiss Rules of International Arbitration, revised and in force 2012
TCC	Technology and Construction Court (England and Wales)
TDM	*Trade Dispute Management*, published by MARIS
Tex Intl LJ	*Texas International Law Journal*, published by University of Texas School of Law
TFEU	Treaty on the Functioning of the European Union
U Penn JIL	*University of Pennsylvania Journal of International Law*, published by the University of Pennsylvania
UAA	Uniform Arbitration Act of 2000 (US)
UAE	United Arab Emirates
UCC	Uniform Commercial Code (US)
UCC Rep Serv	*Uniform Commercial Code Reporting Service* (US), published by West Publishing
UCP	ICC Uniform Customs and Practice for Documentary Credits
UKHL	House of Lords (United Kingdom)
UKPC	Privy Council (United Kingdom)
UKSC	Supreme Court (United Kingdom)
UNCC	United Nations Compensation Commission, Geneva (Established 1991)
UNCITRAL	United Nations Commission on International Trade Law, Vienna (Established 1996)
UNCITRAL Model Law	*See* Model Law; revised Model Law
UNCITRAL Notes	UNCITRAL Notes on Organizing Arbitral Proceedings
UNCITRAL Rules	UNCITRAL Arbitration Rules, revised and in force 2010
UNCLOS	1982 United Nations Convention on the Law of the Sea
UNCTAD	United Nations Conference on Trade and Development, Geneva (Established 1964)
UNECE	United Nations Economic Commission for Europe, Geneva (Established 1947)
UNESCO	United Nations Educational, Scientific and Cultural Organization, Geneva (Established 1945)
UNIDROIT Principles	UNIDROIT Principles of International Commercial Contracts, revised and in force 2010
US	*United States Supreme Court Reports*, published by LexisNexis
Vanderbilt J Transl L	*Vanderbilt Journal of Transnational Law*, published by Vanderbilt University Law School, Nashville, TN
VIAC	Vienna International Arbitration Centre, Vienna (Established 1975)
Vienna Sales Convention	United Nations Convention on Contracts for the International Sale of Goods 1980
VJIL	*Virginia Journal of International Law*, published by University of Virginia School of Law
VSC	Supreme Court of Victoria (Australia)

List of Abbreviations

WIPO	World Intellectual Property Organization, Geneva (Established 1967)
WIPO Rules	WIPO Arbitration Rules, revised and in force 2014
WLR	*Weekly Law Reports*, published by Justis
World Arb & Med Rev	*World Arbitration and Mediation Review*, published by Juris
World Court	*See* ICJ
YBCA	*Yearbook of Commercial Arbitration*, published by ICCA
ZPO	*Zivilprozessordnung* [German Code of Civil Procedure]

1

AN OVERVIEW OF INTERNATIONAL ARBITRATION

A.	Introduction	1.01	E.	Sovereign States, Claims Commissions, and Tribunals	1.191
B.	Why Arbitrate?	1.94			
C.	Alternative Dispute Resolution	1.135	F.	Regulation of International Arbitration	1.197
D.	What Kind of Arbitration?	1.140			
			G.	Summary	1.239

A. Introduction

(a) Dispute resolution—worldwide

Arbitration is now the principal method of resolving international disputes involving states, individuals, and corporations. This is one of the consequences of the increased globalisation of world trade and investment. It has resulted in increasingly harmonised arbitration practices by specialised international arbitration practitioners who speak a common procedural language, whether they practise in England, Switzerland, Nigeria, Singapore, or Brazil. **1.01**

These harmonised practices rest on sophisticated rules of arbitration, which are administered by institutions ranging from the International Chamber of Commerce (ICC), the American Arbitration Association (AAA), and the London Court of International Arbitration (LCIA), to a host of more recently established regional arbitration centres located in Europe, Asia, the Middle East, and elsewhere.[1] The sophisticated rules themselves are supported by enlightened national arbitration laws inspired by the United Nations Commission on International Trade Law (UNCITRAL) Model Law. The aim is to maximise the effectiveness of the arbitral process, whilst minimising judicial intervention, other than when it is needed to support arbitration agreements and awards. **1.02**

---

[1] These different arbitral institutions are described in more detail later in this chapter.

1.03 The result is an impressive edifice of laws and procedures, supported by treaties such as the New York Convention of 1958, which impose an obligation on national courts around the world to recognise and enforce both arbitration agreements and arbitration awards.[2]

(b) What is arbitration?

1.04 Arbitration is essentially a very simple method of resolving disputes. Disputants agree to submit their disputes to an individual whose judgment they are prepared to trust. Each puts its case to this decision maker, this private individual—in a word, this 'arbitrator'. He or she listens to the parties, considers the facts and the arguments, and makes a decision. That decision is final and binding on the parties—and it is final and binding because the parties have agreed that it should be, rather than because of the coercive power of any state.[3] Arbitration, in short, is an effective way of obtaining a final and binding decision on a dispute, or series of disputes, without reference to a court of law (although, because of national laws and international treaties such as the New York Convention, that decision will generally be enforceable by a court of law if the losing party fails to implement voluntarily).

1.05 It is hardly surprising that such an informal and essentially *private and consensual* system of dispute resolution came to be adopted by a local tribe or community—or even by a group of dealers or merchants trading within a particular area or market, or attached to a particular chamber of commerce.[4] It is rather more surprising that such a simple system of resolving disputes has come to be accepted worldwide (and not merely by individuals, but by major corporations and states) as the established method of resolving disputes in which millions, or even hundreds of millions, of dollars are at stake. The way in which this has happened is one of the major themes of this book.

(c) Conduct of an arbitration

1.06 Arbitral proceedings take place in many different countries, with parties, counsel, and arbitrators of many different nationalities, who mix together freely during breaks in the proceedings. There is a striking lack of formality. An arbitral hearing is

---

[2] International treaties and conventions are described in more detail later in this book, as is the UNCITRAL Model Law.
[3] The limited circumstances in which national courts may set aside, or refuse to recognise and enforce, an arbitral award are discussed in Chapter 11.
[4] Many chambers of commerce adopted their own rules of arbitration for the settlement of disputes between their members as an alternative to proceedings in the courts of law. The leading example of this is, of course, the ICC, which is based in Paris and which, in 1923, established its International Court of Arbitration to provide for the resolution by arbitration of 'business disputes of an international character', in accordance with its Rules of Arbitration: see Art. 1(1) of the 1998 ICC Rules.

A. Introduction

not like proceedings in a court of law. There are no ushers, wigs, or gowns; no judge or judges sitting in solemn robes upon a dais; no outward symbols of authority—no flags, maces, orbs, or sceptres. There is simply a group of people seated around a row of tables, in a room hired or provided for the occasion. If it were not for the law books, the stacked piles of lever-arch files, and the transcript writers, with their microphones and stenotype machines, it would look to an outsider as though a conference or a business meeting were in progress. It would not look very much like a legal proceeding at all.

However, the appearance conceals the reality. It is true that the parties themselves choose to arbitrate, as an alternative to litigation or other methods of dispute resolution. It is also true that, to a large extent, arbitrators and parties may choose for themselves the procedures to be followed. If they want a 'fast-track' arbitration, they may have one[5] (although if it is to take place, for instance, under the Swiss Rules of International Arbitration, it will be known by the more dignified title of an 'expedited procedure'). If the parties wish to dispense with the disclosure of documents or with the evidence of witnesses, they may do so. Indeed, they may even dispense with the hearing itself if they so wish.[6] 1.07

Such emphasis on the 'autonomy of the parties' might suggest that parties and arbitrators inhabit a private universe of their own. But this is not so. In reality, the practice of resolving disputes by the essentially private process of international arbitration works effectively only because it is supported by a complex public system of national laws and international treaties. Even a comparatively simple international arbitration may require reference to at least four different national systems of law, which in turn may be derived from an international treaty or convention—or indeed from the UNCITRAL Model Law itself. 1.08

Amongst these different national systems or rules of law is, first, the law that governs the international recognition and enforcement of the agreement to arbitrate. There is then the law—the so-called *lex arbitri*—that governs the actual arbitration proceedings themselves. Next—and generally most importantly—there is the law or the set of rules that the arbitral tribunal is required to apply to the substantive matters in dispute. Finally, there is the law that governs the international recognition and enforcement of the award of the arbitral tribunal. 1.09

These laws may well be the same. The *lex arbitri*, which governs the arbitral proceedings themselves and which will almost always be the national law of the place 1.10

---

[5] Fast-track (or expedited) arbitration is discussed in Chapter 6.
[6] The 2012 version of the ICC Rules provides, in Art. 25(6), that the arbitral tribunal may make a decision based only on documents 'unless any of the parties requests a hearing'. Other institutions have similar rules: see, e.g., Art. 42(1)(c) of the Swiss Rules of International Arbitration 2012 (the 'Swiss Rules'), which states: 'Unless the parties agree that the dispute shall be decided on the basis of documentary evidence only, the arbitral tribunal shall hold a single hearing for the examination of the witnesses and expert witnesses, as well as for oral argument.'

of arbitration, may also govern the substantive matters in issue. But this is not necessarily so. The law that governs the substantive matters in issue (and which goes by a variety of names, including the 'applicable law', the 'governing law', or sometimes the 'proper law') may be a different system of law altogether. For example, an arbitral tribunal sitting in Switzerland, governed (or regulated) by Swiss law as the law of the place of arbitration, may well be required to apply the law of New York as the applicable or substantive law of the contract.[7] This 'applicable', or 'substantive', law will generally be a designated national system of law, chosen by the parties in their contract. But this is not necessarily so. The parties or, in default, the arbitral tribunal on behalf of the parties may choose other systems of law, for example a blend of national law and public international law, or a collection of rules known as 'international trade law', 'transnational law', the 'modern law merchant' (the so-called *lex mercatoria*), or by some other title.[8] Indeed, if so permitted by the agreement of the parties and the *lex arbitri*, the arbitral tribunal may determine the dispute on the basis of what it considers to be fair and equitable.[9]

1.11 Finally, because international arbitrations generally take place in a 'neutral' country—that is, a country that is not the country of residence or business of the parties—the system of law that governs the international recognition and enforcement of the award of the arbitral tribunal will almost always be different from that which governs the arbitral proceedings themselves.

1.12 The dependence of the international arbitral process upon different (and occasionally conflicting) rules of national and international law is another major theme of this book.

(d) A brief historical note

1.13 In its early days, arbitration would have been a simple and relatively informal process. Two merchants, in dispute over the price or quality of goods delivered, would turn to a third whom they knew and trusted, and they would agree to abide by his decision—and they would do this not because of any legal sanction, but because this was what was expected of them in the community within which they carried on their business.[10]

---

[7] In June 2012, the six leading chambers of commerce in Switzerland adopted an updated version of the Swiss Rules. Article 1(1) of these Rules states that they will govern the conduct of the arbitration—together with any mandatory rules of Swiss law (although the latter is not expressly stated). Article 33(1) provides that the arbitral tribunal shall decide the case in accordance with the rules of law agreed by the parties or, in the absence of choice, by the rules of law with which the dispute has the closest connection. Article 33(2) provides that the arbitral tribunal may decide according to equity, if expressly authorised by the parties to do so.

[8] The different systems or rules of law that may constitute the substantive law of an international commercial contract are discussed in Chapter 3.

[9] An agreement that the arbitral tribunal may decide *ex aequo et bono* is not unknown, but is comparatively rare in modern practice.

[10] After referring to 'the dispute resolution mechanisms of the post-classical mercantile world' that were adopted in particular trades or trading centres, Lord Mustill comments: 'Within such

A. Introduction

In theory, such a localised system of 'private justice' might have continued without any supervision or intervention by the courts of law—in much the same way as the law does not generally concern itself with supervising the conduct of a private members' club or intervening in its rules unless public policy requires it to do so. 1.14

However, no modern state can afford to stand back and allow a system of private justice—depending essentially on the integrity of the arbitrators and the goodwill of the participants—to be the only method of regulating commercial activities. Arbitration may well have been 'a system of justice, born of merchants',[11] but just as war is too important to be left to the generals,[12] so is arbitration too important to be left to private provision. 1.15

National regulation of arbitration came first[13]—but international arbitration does not stay within national borders; on the contrary, it crosses them again and again. A corporation based in the United States might contract with another corporation based in France, for the construction of a power plant in Indonesia, with an agreement that any disputes should be resolved by arbitration in London. Where is such an arbitration agreement to be enforced if a dispute arises and one of the parties refuses to arbitrate? Which court will have jurisdiction? And if there is an arbitration that leads to an award of damages and costs, how is that award to be 1.16

---

communities, external sanctions would have been largely redundant, even if a legal framework had been available to bring them into play, which in the main it was not.' See Mustill, 'Is it a bird...', in Reymond (ed.) *Liber Amicorum* (Litec, 2004), p. 209. See also Mustill, 'The history of international commercial arbitration: A sketch', in Newman and Hill (eds) *The Leading Arbitrators' Guide to International Arbitration* (2nd edn, JurisNet, 2008), p. 1. To similar effect, see Paulsson, *The Idea of Arbitration* (Oxford University Press, 2013), p. 1, where he says: 'The idea of arbitration is that of the binding resolution of disputes accepted with serenity by those who bear its consequences because of their special trust in chosen decision-makers.'

[11] Serge Lazareff used this illuminating phrase, which describes how arbitration was seen as a way of settling disputes by reconciling legal principle with equity. He describes it as (in the authors' translation) 'this system of justice, born of merchants, which brings together law and respect for trade usage and knows how to reconcile the approach of Antigone with that of Creon'. (In Greek mythology, Antigone pleaded with Creon for the burial of the body of her brother Eteocle within the city walls.) See Lazareff, 'L'arbitre singe ou comment assassiner l'arbitrage', in Aksen (ed.) *Global Reflections in International Law, Commerce and Dispute Resolution: Liber Amicorum in Honour of Robert Briner* (ICC, 2005), p. 478.

[12] Attributed to both Georges Clémenceau, French prime minister 1917–20, and Talleyrand (1754–1838), the French statesman.

[13] In France, an edict of Francis II promulgated in August 1560 made arbitration compulsory for all merchants in disputes arising from their commercial activity. Later, this edict came to be ignored. During the French Revolution, arbitration came back into favour as 'the most reasonable device for the termination of disputes arising between citizens' and, in 1791, judges were abolished and replaced by 'public arbitrators'. However, this proved to be a step too far and in 1806 the French Code of Civil Procedure effectively turned arbitration into the first stage of a procedure that would lead to the judgment of a court. See David, *Arbitration in International Trade* (Economica, 1984), pp. 89–90. The first English statute was the Arbitration Act 1698, although in *Vynior's Case* (1609) 8 Co Rep 80a, at 81b, the court ordered the defendant to pay the agreed penalty for refusing to submit to arbitration as he had agreed to do. For more information on the history of arbitration, see the various studies by Derek Roebuck, including Roebuck, 'Sources for the history of arbitration' (1998) 14 Arb Intl 237.

enforced against the losing party if the losing party refuses to implement the award voluntarily? Again, which court has jurisdiction?

1.17 The national law of one state alone is not adequate to deal with problems of this kind, since the jurisdiction of any given state is generally limited to its own territory. What is needed is an international treaty or convention, linking national laws together and providing (as far as possible) a system of worldwide enforcement, both of arbitration agreements and of arbitral awards. Such treaties and conventions, and other major international instruments, will be discussed in more detail towards the end of this chapter. For now, it is useful simply to list them: they are all significant 'landmarks' in the development of a modern law and practice of international arbitration—and they are landmarks to which, in practice, reference is continually made.

(e) **International rules, treaties, and conventions**

1.18 The most important 'landmarks' are:

- the Geneva Protocol of 1923 (the '1923 Geneva Protocol');[14]
- the Geneva Convention of 1927 (the '1927 Geneva Convention');[15]
- the New York Convention of 1958 (the 'New York Convention');[16]
- the International Centre for Settlement of Investment Disputes (ICSID) Convention of 1965 (the 'ICSID Convention');[17]
- the UNCITRAL Arbitration Rules (the 'UNCITRAL Rules'), adopted in 1976[18] and revised in 2010;
- the UNCITRAL Model Law (the 'Model Law'), adopted in 1985;[19] and
- revisions to the Model Law (the 'Revised Model Law'), adopted in 2006.[20]

These landmarks will be considered in more detail later in this chapter.

---

[14] The Geneva Protocol on Arbitration Clauses of 1923 was drawn up on the initiative of the ICC and under the auspices of the League of Nations, and signed at Geneva on 24 September 1923.

[15] This Convention for the Execution of Foreign Arbitral Awards followed on from the Geneva Protocol and was signed at Geneva on 26 September 1927: League of Nations Treaty Series (1929–30), Vol. XCII, p. 302.

[16] The Convention on the Recognition and Enforcement of Foreign Arbitral Awards, signed in New York on 10 June 1958: United Nations Treaty Series (1959), Vol. 330, p. 38, No. 4739. The text of the Convention is set out in Appendix B.

[17] The ICSID Convention on the Settlement of Investment Disputes between States and Nationals of Other States, signed in Washington DC on 18 March 1965: United Nations Treaty Series (1966), Vol. 575, p. 160, No. 8359. For a more detailed review of ICSID arbitrations, see Chapter 8.

[18] Adopted by Resolution 31/98 of the General Assembly of the United Nations on 15 December 1976, these Rules are set out in Appendix D. At its Thirty-ninth Session (New York, 17–28 June 2002), UNCITRAL agreed that revision of the UNCITRAL Rules should be given priority, and that such revision 'should not alter the structure of the text, its spirit, its drafting style, and should respect the flexibility of the text rather than add to its complexity': see UNCITRAL, *Report of Working Group II (Arbitration and Conciliation) on the Work of its Forty-ninth Session*, Vienna, 15–19 September 2008, Doc. No. A/CN.9/665, para. 3.

[19] The Model Law on International Commercial Arbitration, adopted by the United Nations Commission on International Trade Law on 21 June 1985. The text of this is set out in Appendix A.

[20] The Revised Model Law was approved by the United Nations in December 2006. Its text is shown in Appendix A.

A. Introduction

(f) Meaning of 'international'

(i) International and domestic arbitrations contrasted

1.19 The term 'international' is used to mark the difference between arbitrations that are purely 'national' or 'domestic' and those that in some way transcend national boundaries, hence are 'international' or (in the terminology adopted by Judge Jessup) 'transnational'.[21]

1.20 It may be said that every arbitration is a 'national' arbitration, since it must be held at a given place and is accordingly subject to the national law of that place.[22] In a narrow sense, this is correct. If an international arbitration is held in London, the place, or 'seat', of the arbitration will be London, the mandatory provisions of English law will apply to the proceedings and the tribunal's award will be an 'English' award. However, in practice, it is usual to distinguish between arbitrations that are purely 'national' or 'domestic' and those that are 'international'. There are sound legal and practical reasons for this.

1.21 First, to the extent that the procedure in any arbitration is regulated by law, that law is normally the law of the place of arbitration—that is, the law of the 'seat' of the arbitration. In an international arbitration (unlike its 'national' or 'domestic' counterpart), the parties usually have no connection with the seat of the arbitration. Indeed, the seat will generally have been chosen by the parties, or by an arbitral institution, *precisely because* it is a place with which the parties have no connection. It will be a truly *neutral* seat.

1.22 Secondly, the parties to an international arbitration are generally (but not always) business or financial corporations, states, or state entities, whilst the parties to a domestic arbitration will more usually be private individuals. This means that an element of consumer protection will almost certainly form part of the law governing domestic arbitrations.[23]

1.23 Thirdly, the sums involved in international arbitrations are generally considerably greater than those involved in domestic arbitrations, which may (for example) concern a comparatively small dispute between a customer and an agent over a faulty

---

[21] Judge Jessup used this term to describe rules of law that govern cross-border relationships and transactions: see Jessup, *Transnational Law* (Yale University Press, 1956).

[22] See, e.g., Mann, 'Lex facit arbitrum' (1986) 2 Arb Intl 241, at 244; however, as discussed later in this chapter, this statement is not true in respect of ICSID arbitrations.

[23] Many years ago, the English appellate court proclaimed that there would be 'no Alsatia in England where the King's Writ does not run'. Its concern was that powerful trade associations would otherwise impose their own 'law' on traders and citizens less powerful than they. For this reason, some control (and even 'supervision') of the arbitral process by the local courts was considered desirable. The same concern for consumer protection is to be seen in the modern laws of those states that have chosen, rightly or wrongly, to deal with both national and international arbitrations in the same legislative Act: see, e.g., the English Arbitration Act 1996, the Irish Arbitration Act 2010, and the Swedish Arbitration Act 1999.

motor car or a package holiday that failed (perhaps predictably) to live up to its advance publicity.

1.24 Fourthly, many states have chosen to adopt a separate legal regime to govern international arbitrations taking place on their territory, recognising that the considerations that apply to such arbitrations are different from those that apply to purely national (or 'domestic' arbitrations). In recognising such differences, the states concerned—which include important centres of arbitration such as France, Switzerland, and Singapore—have adopted the same approach as that adopted by the Model Law, which is expressly stated to be a law designed for *international* commercial arbitrations.[24]

1.25 To these four reasons might be added a fifth—namely, that, in some states, the state itself (or one of its entities) is permitted to enter into arbitration agreements only in respect of *international* transactions.[25]

1.26 It might be thought, given its importance, that there would be general agreement on what is meant by 'international arbitration'. But this is not so. 'When I use a word,' said Humpty Dumpty, 'it means just what I choose it to mean—neither more nor less.'[26] In accordance with this relaxed approach, the word 'international' has at least three different meanings when it comes to international arbitration: the first depends on the nature of the dispute; the second, on the nationality of the parties; and the third approach, which is that of the Model Law, depends on a blending of the first two, plus a reference to the chosen place of arbitration.

(ii) International nature of the dispute

1.27 The ICC, as already mentioned, established its Court of Arbitration in Paris in 1923[27] to provide for the settlement by arbitration of what were described as 'business disputes of an international character'.[28] Thus the ICC adopted the *nature* of the dispute as its criterion for deciding whether or not an arbitration was an 'international

---

[24] Model Law, Art. 1(1).

[25] The 'Tapie Affair' gave rise to a wave of criticism in France when it emerged that the French government had agreed that what was effectively a dispute between a major French bank and a former French minister, Bernard Tapie, should be dealt with by an arbitral tribunal of three French lawyers rather than by the French courts. One of the many criticisms made in the French media was that a case of such political significance had been referred to arbitration, a private process of dispute resolution, rather than left with the French courts. On 17 February 2015, the award of the arbitral tribunal was set aside by the Paris Cour d'Appel: Arret du 17 Fevrier 2015, No. 77 (13/13278). As at July 2015, an appeal against this decision is pending.

[26] Attributed to Humpty Dumpty in Lewis Carroll's *Alice through the Looking Glass* (1871).

[27] The court is now known as the International Court of Arbitration of the ICC. It is not a court in the generally accepted sense; rather, it is a council that, inter alia, oversees the work of arbitral tribunals constituted under the ICC Rules and approves the draft awards of those tribunals, whilst leaving the tribunals themselves in full charge of the cases before them.

[28] 1998 ICC Rules, Art. 1(1). These Rules were replaced by new Rules effective from January 2012.

A. Introduction

arbitration'. At first, the ICC considered business disputes to be 'international' only if they involved nationals of different countries, but it altered its Rules in 1927 to cover disputes that contained a 'foreign element', even if the parties were nationals of the same country. An explanatory booklet issued by the ICC used to state:

> [T]he international nature of the arbitration does not mean that the parties must necessarily be of different nationalities. By virtue of its object, the contract can nevertheless extend beyond national borders, when for example a contract is concluded between two nationals of the same State for performance in another country, or when it is concluded between a State and a subsidiary of a foreign company doing business in that State.[29]

French law, which has undoubtedly influenced the ICC Rules on this issue, considers an arbitration to be 'international' if the nature of the business (for instance the movement of goods or money) is itself 'international', even if the parties concerned are based in the same country or are of the same nationality.[30] **1.28**

(iii) Nationality of the parties

The second approach is to focus attention not on the *nature* of the dispute, but on the *parties to it*. This involves reviewing the nationality, place of residence, or place of business of the parties to the arbitration agreement. It is an approach that was adopted in the European Convention of 1961,[31] which, although little used, contains several useful definitions, including a definition of the agreements to which it applies as 'arbitration agreements concluded for the purpose of settling disputes arising from international trade between physical or legal persons having, when concluding the agreement, *their habitual place of residence or their seat in different Contracting States...*'.[32] **1.29**

Switzerland is one of the states in which the nationality of the parties determines whether or not an arbitration is 'international'. In Swiss law, an arbitration is 'international' if, at the time when the arbitration agreement was concluded, at least one of the parties was not domiciled or habitually resident in Switzerland.[33] The **1.30**

---

[29] ICC, *The International Solution to International Business Disputes: ICC Arbitration*, ICC Publication No. 301 (ICC, 1977), p. 19. (This useful booklet is no longer in print.)

[30] Decree No. 2011-48 of 13 January 2011, Bk IV, Title II, art. 1504; see also Conducci, 'The arbitration reform in France: Domestic and international arbitration law' (2012) 28 Arb Intl 125. The current ICC Rules cover 'all business disputes, whether or not of an international character', which suggests a readiness to administer purely 'domestic' disputes, if appropriate.

[31] European Convention on International Commercial Arbitration, signed at Geneva on 21 April 1961: United Nations Treaty Series (1963–64), Vol. 484, p. 364, No. 7041.

[32] European Convention of 1961, Art. I(1)(a) (emphasis added).

[33] For a commentary on Switzerland's law on international arbitration—that is, Ch. 12 of the Swiss Private International Law Act 1987 ('Swiss PIL')—see, e.g., Bucher and Tschanz, *International Arbitration in Switzerland* (Helbing & Lichtenhahn, 1989); Reymond, 'La nouvelle Loi Suisse et le droit d'arbitrage international: Réflexions de droit comparé' (1989) 3 Rev Arb 385; Lalive, 'The new Swiss Law on International Arbitration' (1998) 4 Arb Intl 2; Geisinger and Voser, *International Arbitration in Switzerland: A Handbook for Practitioners* (2nd edn, Kluwer Law International, 2013).

'nationality' test is also used by the United States for the purposes of the New York Convention—but arbitration agreements between US citizens or corporations are excluded from the scope of the Convention unless their relationship 'involves property located abroad, envisages performance or enforcement abroad or has some reasonable relation with one or more foreign states'.[34]

(iv) Model Law

1.31 Problems may arise as a result of the lack of an internationally agreed definition of 'international'. Each state has its own test for determining whether an arbitration award is 'international' or, in the language of the New York Convention, 'foreign'. The Convention defines 'foreign awards' as awards that are made in the territory of a state *other* than that in which recognition and enforcement are sought—but it adds to this definition awards that are 'not considered as domestic awards' by the enforcement state.[35] In consequence, while one state may consider an award to be 'domestic' (because it involves parties who are nationals of that state), the enforcement state might well consider it *not* to be domestic (because it involves the interests of international trade).

1.32 The Model Law was specifically designed to apply to *international* commercial arbitration. Accordingly, some definition of the term 'international' was essential. The Model Law states, in Article 1(3):

> (3) An arbitration is international if:
> (a) the parties to an arbitration agreement have, at the time of the conclusion of that agreement, their places of business in different States; or
> (b) one of the following places is situated outside the State in which the parties have their places of business:
>   (i) the place of arbitration if determined in, or pursuant to, the arbitration agreement;
>   (ii) any place where a substantial part of the obligations of the commercial relationship is to be performed or the place with which the subject-matter of the dispute is most closely connected; or
> (c) the parties have expressly agreed that the subject matter of the arbitration agreement relates to more than one country.

1.33 This definition combines the two criteria mentioned earlier and, for good measure, adds another:

- the internationality of the *dispute* is recognised in Article 1(3)(b)(i) and (ii);
- the internationality of the *parties* is recognised in Article 1(3)(a); and
- Article 1(3)(c) grants the parties liberty to agree amongst themselves that the subject matter of the arbitration agreement is 'international'.

---

[34] US Code, Title 9 ('Arbitration'), § 202.
[35] New York Convention, Art. 1(1).

A. Introduction

For the purposes of this volume, the authors adopt a wide definition. An arbitration is considered to be 'international' if (in the sense of the Model Law) it involves parties of different nationalities, or it takes place in a country that is 'foreign' to the parties, or it involves an international dispute.[36] Nonetheless, a caveat must be entered to the effect that such arbitrations will not necessarily be universally regarded as international. If a question arises as to whether or not a particular arbitration is 'international', the answer will depend upon the provisions of the relevant national law.

1.34

(g) The meaning of 'commercial'

It was once customary to refer to the 'commercial' character of arbitrations such as those to which much of this volume is devoted. This reflects the distinction made in some countries between contracts that are 'commercial' and those that are not. This distinction was important at one time because there were (and still are) countries in which only disputes arising out of 'commercial' contracts may be submitted to arbitration[37] (thus it might be permissible to hold an arbitration between two merchants over a contract made in the course of their business, but not, for example, in respect of a contract for the allocation of property on the marriage of their children).

1.35

The first of the important modern treaties on international arbitration was the 1923 Geneva Protocol. This distinguished, in Article 1, between 'commercial matters' and 'any other matters capable of settlement by arbitration'. The distinction carried with it the implication that 'commercial matters' would *necessarily* be capable of being settled (or resolved) by arbitration under the law of the state concerned (because that state would allow such matters to be resolved by arbitration), whilst it might not allow 'non-commercial' matters to be resolved in that manner.

1.36

Further emphasis was added to the distinction between 'commercial matters' and 'any other matters' by the stipulation in the Geneva Protocol that each contracting state was free to limit its obligations 'to contracts that are considered as commercial under its national law'.[38] This is the so-called commercial reservation, and it remains important since it appears again in the New York Convention.[39]

1.37

---

[36] Spain is one of the countries that has adopted this wide definition in the Spanish Arbitration Act 2003, as amended by the Arbitration Amendment Act 2011, s. 3.
[37] For instance, art. 737 of Argentina's Code of Civil Procedure states that only matters relating to commercial transactions can be validly submitted to arbitration. China is one major state that adopted the 'commercial reservation' when it ratified the New York Convention in 1987, and in India, for instance, an 'international commercial arbitration' is defined to mean an arbitration relating to legal relationships that are considered to be commercial under the law in force in India: Indian Arbitration and Conciliation Act 1996, s. 2(i)(f).
[38] Geneva Protocol of 1923, Art. 1.
[39] New York Convention, Art. I(3). It may be important to know whether the legal relationship out of which the arbitration arose was or was not a commercial relationship. If, e.g., it becomes necessary to seek recognition or enforcement of a foreign arbitral award in a state that has adhered

1.38 The draftsmen of the Model Law considered defining the word 'commercial',[40] but gave up the attempt. Instead, they stated as follows in a footnote:

> The term 'commercial' should be given a wide interpretation so as to cover matters arising from all relationships of a commercial nature, whether contractual or not. Relationships of a commercial nature include, but are not limited to, the following transactions: any trade transaction for the supply or exchange of goods or services; distribution agreement; commercial representation or agency; factoring; leasing; construction of works; consulting; engineering; licensing; investment; financing; banking; insurance; exploitation agreement or concession; joint venture and other forms of industrial or business co-operation; carriage of goods or passengers by air, sea, rail or road.[41]

The first four editions of this book dealt with 'commercial' arbitrations, using 'commercial' in the wide sense used in the Model Law. However, given the increased number and importance of investment disputes, the authors decided to delete the reference to 'commercial' in subsequent editions of this book.

(h) Key elements of an international arbitration

1.39 As readers will either know or discover, many elements go to make up an international arbitration—but the key elements are as follows:

- the agreement to arbitrate;
- the need for a dispute;
- the commencement of an arbitration;
- the arbitral proceedings;
- the decision of the tribunal; and
- the enforcement of the award.

(i) Agreement to arbitrate

1.40 The foundation stone of modern international arbitration is (and remains) an agreement by the parties to submit any disputes or differences between them to arbitration.[42] Before there can be a valid arbitration, there must first be a valid agreement to arbitrate. This is recognised both by national laws and by

---

to the New York Convention, but has entered the commercial reservation, it will be necessary to look at the law of the state concerned to see what definition it adopts of the term 'commercial'.

[40] Which neither the Geneva Protocol nor the New York Convention had done.

[41] The definition appears as a footnote to Art. 1(1), which states that the Model Law applies to 'international commercial arbitration'. It is interesting to see that the Model Law includes 'investment' within the definition of the term 'commercial', since in practice a separate regime for investment disputes has tended to develop, particularly where a state or state entity is concerned. See Chapter 8 for more on investor–state disputes.

[42] Once there is a valid agreement to arbitrate, the scope of any resulting arbitration may be enlarged, e.g. to cover so-called non-signatories, whose consent to arbitrate is a 'deemed' or 'implied' consent, rather than a real agreement. The issues of non-signatories, consolidation of arbitrations, and third-party involvement (where any 'consent' may be largely fictional) are touched upon later in this chapter, but discussed in more detail in Chapter 2.

A. Introduction

international treaties. Under both the New York Convention[43] and the Model Law,[44] recognition and enforcement of an arbitral award may be refused if the parties to the arbitration agreement were under some incapacity or if the agreement was not valid under its own governing law.[45]

1.41 An 'agreement to arbitrate' is usually expressed in an *arbitration clause* in a contract. Arbitration clauses are discussed in more detail later, but what they do is to make it clear that the parties have agreed as part of their contract that any dispute that arises out of, or in connection with, the contract will be referred to arbitration and not to the courts. Arbitration clauses are drawn up and agreed as part of the contract *before* any dispute has arisen, and so they necessarily look to the future. The parties naturally hope that no dispute will arise, but agree that if it does, it will be resolved by arbitration, and not by the courts of law.

1.42 There is a second, less common, type of agreement to arbitrate, which is made *once* a dispute has arisen. Such an agreement is generally known as a 'submission agreement'. It is generally much more complex than an arbitration clause—because, once a dispute has arisen, it is possible to nominate a tribunal, and to spell out what the dispute is and how the parties propose to deal with it.

1.43 These two types of arbitration agreement have been joined by a third—namely, an 'agreement to arbitrate', which is deemed to arise under international instruments, such as a bilateral investment treaty (BIT) entered into by one state with another. A feature of such treaties is that each state party to the treaty agrees to submit to international arbitration any dispute that *might* arise in the future between itself and an 'investor'.[46] This 'investor' is *not* a party to the treaty. Indeed, the investor's identity will be unknown at the time when the treaty is made. Hence this 'agreement to arbitrate' in effect constitutes a 'standing offer' by the state concerned to resolve any 'investment' disputes by arbitration. It is an offer of which many 'investors' have been quick to take advantage.[47]

1.44 The New York Convention, which provides for the international recognition and enforcement of arbitration agreements,[48] insists that arbitration agreements should be 'in writing'. Indeed, references to the need for 'writing' occur throughout the New York Convention. Article II(1) requires each state party to the Convention to recognise 'an agreement in writing' under which the parties have undertaken to submit to arbitration disputes that are capable of being settled by arbitration. Article II(2) defines an 'agreement in writing' to include arbitration clauses and submission agreements; Article IV states that to obtain enforcement of an arbitral

---

[43] New York Convention, Art. V.
[44] Model Law, Art. 35.
[45] New York Convention, Art. V(1)(a); Model Law, Art. 36(1)(a)(i).
[46] Investor–state arbitrations are discussed further in Chapter 8.
[47] See Chapter 8.
[48] As well as of arbitration awards.

An Overview of International Arbitration

award the winning party must produce the written agreement to arbitrate or a duly certified copy.

1.45 When the New York Convention was drawn up, the position was relatively simple: arbitration, for the purposes of the Convention, was to be based either on a written arbitration clause in a contract or on a signed submission agreement. This is how things were done when the Convention was concluded in 1958. But much has changed since then. First, modern methods of communication have moved beyond the 'letters and telegrams' to which the Convention refers. Secondly, the Convention assumes that *only* parties to the agreement to arbitrate will become parties to any resulting arbitration. However, the increased complexity of international trade means that states, corporations, and individuals who are *not* parties to the arbitration agreement might wish to become parties[49]—or, indeed, might find that they have been joined as parties, irrespective of their wishes. The idea that arbitration involves only two parties—one as claimant and the other as respondent—is no longer valid.

1.46 The Model Law, which came into force many years after the New York Convention, also envisages arbitration as taking place *only* between parties who are parties to a written arbitration agreement. Article 7(1) states that an arbitration agreement:

> ...is an agreement *by the parties* to submit to arbitration all or certain disputes which have arisen or which may arise between them in respect of a defined legal relationship, whether contractual or not. An arbitration agreement may be in the form of an arbitration clause in a contract or in the form of a separate agreement.[50]

However, the Model Law did move beyond 'letters' and 'telegrams' by extending the definition of 'in writing' to include 'an exchange of letters, telex, telegrams or other means of telecommunication which provide a record of the agreement'.[51]

1.47 Parties who agree to arbitration give up their right of recourse to the courts of law. It is not unreasonable to require written evidence that they have, in fact, agreed to do this. Many laws of arbitration insist on such evidence. In Swiss law, for example, an arbitration agreement has to be made 'in writing, by telegram, telex, telecopier or any other means of communication *which permits it to be evidenced by a text*'.[52]

---

[49] What is described here is the problem of 'non-signatories', which is considered in more detail in Chapter 2. The word 'non-signatories' is not particularly accurate, since anyone in the world who has not signed the arbitration agreement might correctly be described as such. Nevertheless, it has become a convenient way of describing those who may become a party to the arbitration despite not having signed the relevant agreement to arbitrate or a document containing an arbitration clause.

[50] Emphasis added.

[51] Model Law, Art. 7(2).

[52] Swiss PIL, s. 178(1) (emphasis added). See also, e.g., the Italian Code of Civil Procedure (art. 807), which states that 'the submission to arbitration shall, under penalty of nullity, be made in writing and shall indicate the subject matter of the dispute'. Arbitration clauses must also be in

A. Introduction

However, in modern business dealings, contracts may be made orally, for instance at a meeting or by a conversation over the telephone. In the same way, an 'agreement to arbitrate' may be made orally—and this was recognised in the deliberations that led eventually to the Revised Model Law. States that adopt this revised law are given two options. The first is to adhere to the writing requirement, but with the definition of 'writing' extended to include electronic communications of all types.[53] The second option is to dispense altogether with the requirement that an agreement to arbitrate should be in writing.[54] **1.48**

(i) Arbitration clauses

An arbitration clause (or *clause compromissoire*, as it is known in the civil law) will generally be short and to the point. An agreement that 'any dispute is to be settled by arbitration in London' would constitute a valid arbitration agreement—although in practice so terse a form is not to be recommended.[55] **1.49**

Institutions such as the ICC and the LCIA have their own recommended forms of arbitration clause, set out in their books of rules. The UNCITRAL Rules offer a simple 'Model Arbitration Clause', which states that: 'Any dispute, controversy or claim arising out of or relating to this contract, or the breach, termination or invalidity thereof, shall be settled by arbitration in accordance with the UNCITRAL Arbitration Rules.'[56] **1.50**

(ii) Submission agreements

An arbitration agreement that is drawn up to deal with disputes that have *already* arisen between the parties is generally known as a 'submission agreement', a *compromis*, or a *compromiso*. The parties may wish to choose institutional arbitration, or they may prefer to proceed ad hoc, in which case the submission agreement will **1.51**

---

writing. And, under the US Federal Arbitration Act of 1990, the minimum requirements are that the arbitration agreement be in writing and agreed to by the parties.

[53] Revised Model Law, Art. 7, Option I.

[54] Revised Model Law, Art. 7, Option II. The 'writing requirement' is discussed in more detail in Chapter 2. In states that adopt the second option of the Revised Model Law, an oral agreement to arbitrate will be sufficient and there will be no requirement to produce a written agreement to arbitrate when seeking enforcement of an award. However, Arts II(2), IV, and V(l)(a) of the New York Convention still require a written agreement in a defined form. This means that there is a risk that an arbitral award made pursuant to an oral agreement may be refused recognition and enforcement under the New York Convention, in which event the time, money, and effort expended in obtaining the award will have been wasted.

[55] For a similar short form of arbitration clause, see, e.g., *Arab African Energy Corporation Ltd v Olieprodukten Nederland BV* [1983] 2 Lloyd's Rep 419; more generally, see the discussion in Chapter 2.

[56] The current UNCITRAL Arbitration Rules are the revised 2010 edition. A note to the recommended arbitration clause, which appears in the Annex to these Rules, states that the parties may wish to add: (a) the name of the party that will appoint arbitrators ('the appointing authority') in default of any appointment by the parties or the co-arbitrators themselves; (b) the number of arbitrators (one or three); (c) the place of arbitration (town and country); and (d) the language to be used in the arbitral proceedings.

usually be a fairly detailed document, dealing with the constitution of the arbitral tribunal, the procedure to be followed, the issues to be decided, the substantive law, and other matters. At one time, it was the *only* type of arbitration agreement that the law of many states recognised,[57] since recourse to arbitration was permitted only in respect of *existing* disputes. In some states, this is still the position.[58]

1.52 However, most states now recognise the validity of arbitration clauses that relate to future disputes—and almost all commercial arbitrations now take place pursuant to an arbitration clause (which is frequently a 'standard clause' in standard forms of contract that are internationally accepted for activities as diverse as shipping, insurance, commodity trading, and civil engineering.)

(iii) Importance of the arbitration agreement

1.53 The most important function of an agreement to arbitrate, in the present context, is that of making it plain that the parties have indeed consented to resolve their disputes by arbitration. This consent is essential: without it, there can be no valid arbitration.[59] The fact that international arbitration rests on the agreement of the parties is given particular importance by some continental jurists. The arbitral proceedings are seen as an expression of the will of the parties and, on the basis of party autonomy (*l'autonomie de la volonté*), it is sometimes argued that international arbitration should be freed from the constraints of national law and treated as 'denationalised' or 'delocalised'.[60]

1.54 Once parties have validly given their consent to arbitration, that consent cannot be unilaterally withdrawn. Even if the agreement to arbitrate forms part of the original contract between the parties and that contract comes to an end, the obligation to arbitrate survives. It is an independent obligation separable[61] from the rest of the contract. Even if the validity of the contract that contained the arbitration clause is challenged, the agreement to arbitrate remains in being.[62]

---

[57] This point, and in particular the distinction between existing and future disputes, is discussed later in this chapter.

[58] For instance, a submission agreement for domestic disputes is still required (whether or not a valid arbitration agreement already exists) in Argentina and Uruguay.

[59] There are circumstances under which arbitration may be a compulsory method of resolving disputes, e.g. in domestic law, arbitrations may take place compulsorily under legislation governing agricultural disputes or labour relations. The growth of court-annexed arbitration may perhaps be said to constitute a form of compulsory arbitration. And, as previously mentioned, where the scope of arbitral proceedings is widened to include 'non-signatories', or where there is compulsory consolidation of arbitrations or joinder of third parties, the element of consent is less real.

[60] An early mention of this theory appears in Fouchard, *L'Arbitrage Commercial International* (Litec, 1965), although the presence of serious obstacles to the theory is noted; see also Gaillard, *Legal Theory of International Arbitration* (Martinus Nijhoff, 2010). The theory is discussed in more detail in Chapter 3.

[61] The doctrine of separability is discussed in more detail in Chapter 2.

[62] The concept of the 'autonomy' of an arbitration clause, although not immune from criticism, is now well established: see, e.g., Model Law, Art. 16. By way of example, see also UNCITRAL Rules 2010, Art. 23; English Arbitration Act 1996, s. 7 ('Separability of arbitration agreement').

A. Introduction

This allows a claimant to begin arbitration proceedings, based on the survival of the agreement to arbitrate as a separate agreement, independent of the contract of which it formed part. It also allows an arbitral tribunal that is appointed pursuant to that arbitration agreement to decide on its own jurisdiction—including any objections with respect to the existence or validity of the arbitration agreement itself. The tribunal, in other words, is competent to judge its own competence.

(iv) Enforcement of the arbitration agreement

1.55 An agreement to arbitrate, like any other agreement, must be capable of being enforced at law; otherwise, it would simply be a statement of intention, which, whilst morally binding, would be of no legal effect. But an agreement to arbitrate is a contract of imperfect obligation. If it is broken, an award of damages is unlikely to be a practical remedy, given the difficulty of quantifying the loss sustained. An order for specific performance may be equally impracticable, since a party cannot be compelled to arbitrate if it does not wish to do so. As the saying goes, 'you can lead a horse to water, but you cannot make it drink'.[63]

1.56 In arbitration, this problem has been met both nationally and internationally by a policy of *indirect* enforcement. Rules of law are adopted that provide that if one of the parties to an arbitration agreement brings proceedings in a national court in breach of that agreement, those proceedings will be stopped at the request of any other party to the arbitration agreement (unless there is good reason why they should not be). This means that if a party wishes to pursue its claim, it must honour the agreement it has made and it must pursue its claim by arbitration, since this will be the only legal course of action open to it.[64]

1.57 It would be of little use to enforce an obligation to arbitrate in one country if that obligation could be evaded by commencing legal proceedings in another. Therefore, as far as possible, an agreement for international arbitration must be enforced internationally and not simply in the place where the agreement was made. This essential requirement is recognised in the international conventions, beginning with the 1923 Geneva Protocol, and it is endorsed in the New York Convention—although the title of the Convention fails to make this clear.[65]

---

[63] It should be noted, however, that in some jurisdictions, when the local court decides that a claim should be arbitrated, the court will order (a) that the court proceedings be discontinued, (b) that arbitration proceedings be commenced within a given period of time, and (c) that the court will retain jurisdiction to ensure that this is done. A distinction can be drawn in this regard between the effect of a 'dismissal' of court proceedings and a 'stay' of those proceedings: see, e.g., *Lloyd v Horensce LLC* 369 F.3d 263 (3rd Cir. 2004).

[64] Of course, the party concerned may decide to abandon its claim and is free to do so.

[65] The full title is the 'Convention on the Recognition and Enforcement of Foreign Arbitral Awards'. This fails to mention that the Convention *also* applies to the recognition and enforcement of agreements to arbitrate.

(v) Powers conferred by the arbitration agreement

1.58 An arbitration agreement does not merely serve to establish the obligation to arbitrate, but is also a basic source of the powers of the arbitral tribunal. In principle, and within the limits of public policy, an arbitral tribunal may exercise such powers as the parties are entitled to confer and do confer upon it, whether expressly or by implication, together with any additional or supplementary powers that may be conferred by the law governing the arbitration.[66] Parties to an arbitration are masters of the arbitral process to an extent impossible in proceedings in a court of law. Thus, for example (and with limits that will be considered later), the parties may determine the number of arbitrators on the arbitral tribunal, how this tribunal is to be appointed, in what country it should sit, what powers it should possess, and what procedure it should follow.

1.59 The 'agreement to arbitrate' also establishes the jurisdiction of the arbitral tribunal. In the ordinary legal process whereby disputes are resolved through the public courts, the jurisdiction of the relevant court may come from several sources. An agreement by the parties to submit to the jurisdiction will be only one of those sources. Indeed, a defendant will often find itself in court against its will. In the arbitral process, the jurisdiction of the arbitral tribunal is derived simply and solely from the express or implied consent of the parties.[67]

(j) Need for a dispute

1.60 At first glance, this may seem to be an unnecessary requirement. Surely, it might be asked, if there is no dispute, there is nothing to resolve? The problem arises when one party has what it regards as an 'open and shut' case to which there is no real defence. For example, someone who is faced with an unpaid cheque may take the view that there cannot be any *genuine* dispute about liability and that, if legal action has to be taken to collect the money that is due, he or she should be entitled to go to court and ask for summary judgment. However, if there is an arbitration clause in the underlying agreement with the debtor, the claimant may be directed to go to arbitration, rather than to the courts—even though, in the time it takes to establish an arbitral tribunal, a judge with summary powers may well have disposed of the case.

1.61 The expedient adopted in certain countries (including initially in England, when legislating for the enactment of the New York Convention) was to add words that were not in that Convention. This allowed the courts to deal with the case if the judge was satisfied 'that there is not in fact any dispute between the parties with

---

[66] See Chapter 3.
[67] It should be noted, however, that even when the parties think that they have agreed to a set of rules that will govern their dispute, a poorly drafted arbitration clause may mean the issue is taken before a national court: see, e.g., *Insigma Technology Co. Ltd v Alstom Technology Ltd* [2008] SGHC 134.

A. Introduction

regard to the matter agreed to be referred'.[68] In this way, it was possible to avoid a reference to arbitration and to obtain summary judgment. However, English law has now followed the strict wording of the New York Convention.[69] It can no longer be argued in England that, since there is no genuine dispute, the matter should not be referred to arbitration—although such an argument may remain sustainable in other countries.

(i) Existing and future disputes

1.62 A distinction is sometimes drawn between 'existing' and 'future' disputes. In the New York Convention, for instance, each contracting state recognises the validity of an agreement under which the parties undertake to submit to arbitration 'all or any differences which have arisen or *which may arise between them*'.[70] This distinction is principally of historical importance. Most of the states in the civil law tradition that did not originally enforce agreements for future disputes to be referred to arbitration now do so.[71]

1.63 In the common law systems, fewer difficulties were placed in the way of referring future disputes to arbitration.[72] Even so, states that follow common law traditions often find it convenient for other reasons to differentiate between 'existing' disputes and 'future' disputes. An arbitration clause is a blank cheque. It may be cashed for an unknown amount at an unknown future date. It is not surprising that states may adopt a more cautious attitude towards allowing future rights to be given away than they do towards the relinquishment of existing rights.

(ii) Arbitrability

1.64 Even if a dispute exists, this may not be sufficient; it must also be a dispute that, in the words of the New York Convention, is 'capable of settlement by arbitration'. The idea that a dispute may not be 'capable of settlement by arbitration' is

---

[68] Arbitration Act 1975, s. 1(i). This Act was repealed by the Arbitration Act 1996, although the New York Convention continues to be part of English law.
[69] Arbitration Act 1996, s. 9. Lord Saville stated:

> The action of the Courts in refusing to stay proceedings where the defendant has no defence is understandable. It is, however, an encroachment on the principle of party autonomy which I find difficult to justify. If the parties have agreed to arbitrate their disputes, why should a Court ignore that bargain, merely because with hindsight one party realises that he might be able to enforce his rights faster if he goes to Court?

See Lord Saville, 'The Denning Lecture 1995: Arbitration and the courts' (1995) 61(3) Arbitration 157, at 161.
[70] New York Convention, Art. II(1) (emphasis added).
[71] These states included France, which, as the country in which the ICC is based, is an important centre for arbitration. It was not until 1925, two years after acceding to the 1923 Geneva Protocol, that France altered its law to allow the arbitration of future disputes, in line with the Protocol.
[72] Although, in the United States, it was not until 1920 that the state of New York recognised arbitration clauses as valid and enforceable—and it was the first state to do so: see Coulson, 'Commercial arbitration in the United States' (1985) 51 Arbitration 367.

not meant as a criticism of arbitrators or of the arbitral process itself. Arbitrators are (or should be) just as 'capable' as judges of determining a dispute. But national laws may treat certain disputes as being more suitable for determination by their own public courts of law, rather than by a private arbitral tribunal. For instance, a dispute over matrimonial status may be regarded by the national law of a particular state as not being 'capable' of settlement by arbitration—although it would be more accurate to say that it is not 'permissible' to settle the dispute by arbitration.

1.65 It is important to know which disputes are 'arbitrable' and which are not. It is also important to note the correct definition of 'arbitrability', as used in international conventions, so as to avoid the confusion into which some courts and lawyers plunge.[73]

(k) Commencement of an arbitration

1.66 A formal notice must be given in order to start an arbitration. In ad hoc arbitrations, this notice will be sent or delivered to the opposing party.

1.67 The UNCITRAL Rules provide, for example, in Article 3(1) and (2), that:

1. The party or parties initiating recourse to arbitration (hereinafter called the 'claimant') shall communicate to the other party or parties (hereinafter called the 'respondent') a notice of arbitration.
2. Arbitration proceedings shall be deemed to commence on the date on which the notice of arbitration is received by the respondent.

1.68 The UNCITRAL Rules then state, in Article 3, what should be set out in the notice of arbitration. This includes a reference to the arbitration clause in the contract (or to any other form of arbitration agreement), a brief description of the claim, an indication of the amount involved, if any, and a statement of the relief or remedy sought. The notice of arbitration may also include proposals for the appointment of a sole arbitrator, or the appointment of the tribunal, as set out in Article 4 of the Rules.

1.69 In an institutional arbitration, it is usual for the notice to be given to the relevant institution by a 'request for arbitration' or similar document. The institution then

---

[73] Some writers (and indeed some judges, particularly in the United States) will describe a dispute as being not 'arbitrable' when what they mean is that it falls outside the jurisdiction of the tribunal, because of the limited scope of the arbitration clause or for some other reason. For example, the US Court of Appeals for the Tenth Circuit considered that a dispute was not 'arbitrable' because the reference to arbitration was made after the relevant time limit: see *Howsam v Dean Witter Reynolds Inc.* 537 US 79, 123 S.Ct 588 (2002). In fact, the dispute was perfectly arbitrable, but the reference to arbitration was not made in time. This unfortunate misuse of the term 'arbitrable' is so deeply entrenched that it cannot be eradicated; all that can be done is to watch out for the particular sense in which the word is being used. See further, e.g., Shore, 'Defining arbitrability: The United States vs the rest of the world', New York Law Journal, 15 June 2009. 'Arbitrability' is discussed more fully in Chapter 2.

A. Introduction

notifies the respondent or respondents. For instance, Article 4(1) of the ICC Rules provides as follows:

> A party wishing to have recourse to arbitration under the Rules shall submit its Request for Arbitration (the 'Request') to the Secretariat at any of the offices specified in the Internal Rules. The Secretariat shall notify the claimant and the respondent of the receipt of the Request and the date of such receipt.

Similar provisions are found in Article 1 of the LCIA Rules, Article 3 of the Rules of the Singapore International Arbitration Centre (SIAC), Article 2 of the Rules of the Stockholm Chamber of Commerce (SCC), and the rules of other arbitral institutions. **1.70**

(i) Choosing an arbitrator

It is evident that an arbitration cannot proceed without an arbitral tribunal.[74] Generally, parties are free to choose their own tribunal—although, sometimes, the parties may have surrendered this freedom by delegating the choice of a tribunal to a third party, such as an arbitral institution.[75] Where the freedom exists, the parties should make good use of it. A skilled, experienced, and impartial arbitrator is essential for a fair and effective arbitration. **1.71**

The choice of a suitable arbitrator involves many considerations.[76] What must be recognised is that an international arbitration demands different qualities in an arbitrator from those required for a national, or domestic, arbitration. In an international arbitration, different rules, and often different systems of law, will apply; the parties will almost certainly be of different nationalities; and the arbitration itself will usually take place in a country that is 'foreign' to the parties. Indeed, the place of arbitration will usually have been chosen precisely because it *is* foreign, so that no party has the advantage of 'playing at home', so to speak. **1.72**

If the arbitral tribunal consists of three arbitrators, each of the arbitrators may be of a different nationality, with each perhaps having grown up in a different cultural and legal environment.[77] Good international arbitrators will try hard to avoid misunderstandings that may arise because of this difference of background, or even of language. **1.73**

---

[74] The notice of arbitration may sometimes nominate an arbitrator on behalf of the claimant, but this denotes a three-member tribunal, with a second arbitrator to be chosen by the respondent and the presiding arbitrator to be chosen in a neutral fashion.

[75] In ICC arbitrations, e.g. in which the dispute is to be referred to a sole arbitrator, that person will be selected by the ICC itself unless (as is sensible) the parties agree on a suitable candidate: ICC Rules, Art. 12(3). Similarly, the ICC would select the presiding arbitrator if the parties were to fail to do so: Art. 12(5).

[76] See Chapter 4 for more discussion of these considerations.

[77] In the well-known *Aminoil* arbitration, in which the original authors took part as counsel, the members of the arbitral tribunal were respectively French, British, and Egyptian, and the registrar was Swiss; the parties, lawyers, and experts were Kuwaiti, American, Swiss, British, Egyptian, and Lebanese. The seat of the arbitration was France.

1.74 Making the right choice of arbitrator is important. Professor Lalive has said that '[t]he choice of the persons who compose the arbitral tribunal is vital and often the most decisive step in an arbitration. It has rightly been said that arbitration is only as good as the arbitrators'.[78]

1.75 More recently, Professor Park has observed that '[t]he profile of an ideal arbitrator might be described as someone knowledgeable in the substantive field, able to write awards in the relevant language, free of any nationality restrictions, and experienced in conducting complex proceedings'.[79]

1.76 A survey published in 2012 described the rise of what it called 'a third generation of arbitrators'.[80] According to this survey, the first generation were chosen as arbitrators for their general legal and social aura: they were 'the Grand Old Men' of arbitration. The second generation ('the Technocrats') were chosen for their legal or technical skills. The third, current, generation ('the Managers') are now being chosen for their expertise in arbitration and their skills in case management. The survey concluded, quoting a previous edition of this volume: 'Redfern and Hunter's dictum still seems to hold: "Probably the most important qualification for an international arbitrator is that he should be experienced in the law and practice of arbitration." '[81]

(l) Arbitral proceedings

1.77 There are no compulsory rules of procedure in international arbitration, no volumes containing 'the rules of court' to govern the conduct of the arbitration. Litigators who produce their own country's rulebook or code of civil procedure as a 'helpful guideline' will be told to put it aside.

1.78 The rules that govern an international arbitration are, first, the mandatory provisions of the *lex arbitri*—the law of the place of arbitration—which are usually cast in very broad terms,[82] and secondly, the rules that the parties themselves may have

---

[78] Lalive, 'Mélanges en l'honneur de Nicolas Valticos', in Dupuy (ed.) *Droit et Justice: Mélanges en l'honneur de Nicolas Valticos* (CEPANI, 1989), p. 289; see also, e.g., Derains and Levy (eds) *Is Arbitration Only as Good as the Arbitrator? Status, Powers and Role of the Arbitrator* (ICC Institute of World Business Law, 2011); Park, 'Arbitrators and accurancy' (2010) 1 J Intl Disp Settlement 25.

[79] Park, 'Arbitration in autumn' (2011) 2 J Intl Disp Settlement 287. Professor Park adds, at 311: 'To this laundry list, a claimant might add availability for hearings in the not too distant future. Yet someone who meets the bill with respect to experience and qualifications may have commitments that interfere with early hearings.'

[80] Schultz and Kovacs, 'The rise of a third generation of arbitrators? Fifteen years after Dezalay and Garth' (2012) 28 Arb Intl 161.

[81] Ibid., at 170. The reference is to *Redfern and Hunter on Law and Practice of International Commercial Arbitration* (3rd edn, Sweet & Maxwell, 1999), p. 205. The dictum was repeated in subsequent editions, but as many more women have become arbitrators, the statement should be corrected to read 'that he *or she* be experienced in the law and practice of arbitration'.

[82] For example, Model Law, Art. 18, simply states: 'The parties shall be treated with equality and each party shall be given a full opportunity of presenting his case.'

A. Introduction

chosen, such as the ICC or UNCITRAL Arbitration Rules. Under the rubric of 'General Provisions', Article 17(1)–(3) of the UNCITRAL Rules states:

1. Subject to these Rules, the arbitral tribunal may conduct the arbitration in such manner as it considers appropriate, provided that the parties are treated with equality and that at an appropriate stage of the proceedings each party is given a reasonable opportunity of presenting his case. The arbitral tribunal, in exercising its discretion, shall conduct the proceedings so as to avoid unnecessary delay and expense and to provide a fair and efficient process for resolving the parties' dispute.
2. As soon as practicable after its constitution and after inviting the parties to express their views, the tribunal shall establish the provisional timetable of the arbitration. The arbitral tribunal may, at any time, after inviting the parties to express their views, extend or abridge any period of time prescribed under these Rules or agreed by the parties.
3. If at an appropriate stage of the proceedings any party so requests, the arbitral tribunal shall hold hearings for the presentation of evidence by witnesses, including expert witnesses, or for oral argument. In the absence of such a request, the arbitral tribunal shall decide whether to hold such hearings or whether the proceedings shall be conducted on the basis of documents and other materials.

1.79 Some institutional rules of arbitration are more detailed than others, but within the broad outline of any applicable rules parties to an international arbitration are free to design a procedure suitable for the particular dispute with which they are concerned. This is another of the attractions of international arbitration. It is (or should be) a flexible method of dispute resolution: the procedure to be followed can be tailored by the parties and the arbitral tribunal to meet the law and facts of the dispute. It is not a Procrustean bed, enforcing conformity without regard to individual variation.

(m) Decision of the tribunal

1.80 It frequently happens that, in the course of arbitral proceedings, a settlement may be reached between the parties. Rules of arbitration usually make provision for this. Article 36(1) of the UNCITRAL Rules, for example, states:

If, before the award is made, the parties agree on a settlement of the dispute, the arbitral tribunal shall either issue an order for the termination of the arbitral proceedings or, if requested by both parties and accepted by the tribunal, record the settlement in the form of an arbitral award on agreed terms. The arbitral tribunal is not obliged to give reasons for such an award.

1.81 However, if the parties themselves cannot resolve their dispute, the task of the arbitral tribunal is to resolve it for them by making a decision, in the form of a written award. An arbitral tribunal does not have the powers or prerogatives of a court of law,[83] but in this respect it has a similar function to that of a court, being entrusted

---

[83] For a discussion of the differences between a judge and an arbitrator, see Lazareff, 'L'arbitre est-il un juge?', in Reymond (ed.) *Liber Amicorum* (Litec, 2004), p. 173; Rubino-Sammartano,

by the parties with both the power and the duty to reach a decision that will be binding upon the parties.

1.82 The power (and the duty) of an arbitral tribunal to make binding decisions distinguishes arbitration as a method of resolving disputes from other procedures, such as mediation and conciliation, which aim to arrive at a negotiated settlement. The *procedure* to be followed in order to arrive at a binding decision is flexible, adaptable to the circumstances of each particular case. Nevertheless, it is a *judicial* procedure and a failure by a tribunal to act judicially may be sanctioned by annulment or non-enforcement of that tribunal's award.[84] No similar enforceable requirement governs the procedures to be followed where parties are assisted in arriving at a negotiated settlement by mediation, conciliation, or some other process of this kind.[85]

1.83 How an arbitral tribunal reaches its decision is something that remains to be explored.[86] For a sole arbitrator, the task of decision making is a solitary one. Impressions as to the honesty and reliability of the witnesses; opinions on the merits, which have swayed from one side to another as the arbitral process unfolds; points that have seemed compelling under the eloquence of counsel: all will have to be reviewed and reconsidered, once the hearing is over and any post-hearing briefs are received. Money, reputations, and even friendships may depend on the arbitrator's verdict. The sole arbitrator's task, when the moment of decision arrives, is not an enviable one.

1.84 If the arbitral tribunal consists of three arbitrators, the task is both easier and more difficult. It is easier because the decision does not depend upon one person alone. The arguments of the parties can be reviewed, the opinions of each arbitrator can

---

'The decision-making mechanism of the arbitrator vis-à-vis the judge' (2008) 25 J Intl Arb 167; Ancel, 'L'arbitre juge' (2012) 4 Rev Arb 717.

[84] For example, s. 33(1)(a) of the English Arbitration Act 1996 states that the tribunal shall 'act fairly and impartially as between the parties, giving each party a reasonable opportunity of putting his case and dealing with that of his opponent'. This requirement mirrors Model Law, Art. 18, and is of general application.

[85] The arbitral process also produces a different *result* from that which might have been reached by the parties through negotiation, with or without the help of a mediator or conciliator, since a negotiated agreement will necessarily be in the form of a compromise acceptable to both parties.

[86] See, e.g., Lowenfeld, 'The party-appointed arbitrator: Further reflections', in Newman and Hill (eds) *The Leading Arbitrators' Guide to International Arbitration* (2nd edn, JurisNet, 2008), pp. 46–48; Fortier, 'The tribunal's deliberations', in Newman and Hill (eds) *The Leading Arbitrators' Guide to International Arbitration* (2nd edn, JurisNet, 2008), pp. 477–482; Puig, 'Deliberation and drafting awards in international arbitration', in Fernández-Ballesteros and Arias (eds) *Liber Amicorum Bernardo Cremades* (La Ley, 2010), pp. 131–158. On the importance of the tribunal's deliberations, see Bredin, 'Retour au délibéré arbitral', in Bernardini et al. (eds) *Liber Amicorum Claude Reymond* (Litec, 2004), p. 50; Derains, 'La pratique du délibéré arbitral', in Aksen (ed.) *Global Reflections in International Law, Commerce and Dispute Resolution: Liber Amicorum in Honour of Robert Briner* (ICC, 2005), pp. 221–224.

A. Introduction

be tested, the facts of the case and the relevant law can be discussed, and so forth. It is, at the same time, more difficult because three different opinions may well emerge during the course of the tribunal's deliberations. It will then be necessary for the presiding arbitrator to try to reconcile those differences, rather than face the unwelcome prospect of a dissenting opinion.

Experienced commentators remain divided on the question of whether or not dissenting opinions are of any benefit in international arbitration. Some see them as beneficial, allowing each arbitrator freedom of expression and demonstrating that the parties' arguments have been fully considered.[87] Others, whilst recognising that there are good dissenting awards, just as there are good dissenting judgments,[88] are concerned that a dissenting judgment may undermine the authority of the tribunal's award.[89] Indeed, a dissenting opinion 'may provide a platform for challenge to the award'.[90] 1.85

The debate about dissenting opinions has inevitably spilled over from commercial arbitration, in which awards are generally not publicly available, to investment arbitration, in which a dissenting opinion may have more impact because it is publicly available. One of the principal concerns is that dissenting opinions are almost always issued 'by the arbitrator appointed by the party that lost the case in whole or in part', which raises doubts as to the impartiality (or 'neutrality') of the arbitrator concerned.[91] It is to be expected that a party-nominated arbitrator will usually have some sympathy with the party that appointed him or her—but this should not prevent that arbitrator behaving impartially, as he or she is expected to do.[92] 1.86

---

[87] Rees and Rohn, 'Dissenting opinions: Can they fulfill a beneficial role?' (2009) 25 Arb Intl 329.

[88] In the famous English case of *Liversidge v Anderson* [1941] 3 All ER 336, Lord Atkins gave a dissenting speech in which he argued against the power of arbitrary arrest, even in times of war. Almost four years later, Lord Diplock said that the time had come to acknowledge that the majority were 'expediently and, at that time, perhaps excusably wrong and the dissenting speech of Lord Atkin was right': *Inland Revenue Commissioners v Rossminster* [1980] AC 952, at 1008.

[89] Redfern, 'Dissenting opinions in international commercial arbitration: The good, the bad and the ugly' (2004) 20 Arb Intl 223.

[90] Baker and Greenwood, 'Dissent—but only if you really feel you must: Why dissenting opinions in international commercial arbitration should only appear in exceptional circumstances' (2013) 7 Disp Res Intl 31.

[91] Van den Berg, 'Dissenting opinions by party-appointed arbitrators in investment arbitration', in Arsanjani, Katz Cogan, Sloane, and Wiessner (eds) *Looking to the Future: Essays in Honor of W Michael Reisman* (Koninklijke Brill, 2010), pp. 821–843.

[92] The debate continues. A response to the criticism of both party-appointed arbitrators and arbitrators dissenting in favour of their appointing party is offered in Brower and Rosenberg, 'The death of the two-headed nightingale: Why the Paulsson–van den Berg presumption that party-appointed arbitrators are untrustworthy is wrong' (2013) 29 Arb Intl 7 ; van den Berg, 'Charles Brower's problem with 10%: Dissenting opinions by party-appointed arbitrators in investment arbitration', in Caron et al. (eds) *Liber Amicorum for Charles Brower* (Oxford University Press, 2015).

(n) Enforcement of the award

1.87 Once an arbitral tribunal has made its final award, it has done what it was established to do. It has fulfilled its function.[93] The award itself, however, gives rise to important, lasting, and potentially public legal consequences. Although the award is the result of a private process of dispute resolution and is made by a private arbitral tribunal, it nevertheless constitutes a binding decision on the dispute between the parties. If the award is not carried out voluntarily, it may be enforced by legal proceedings—both locally (that is, by the courts at the place where it was made) and internationally, under such international conventions as the New York Convention.

1.88 An agreement to arbitrate is not only an agreement to take part in arbitral proceedings, but also an agreement to carry out any resulting arbitral award. It should not be necessary to state the obvious: that, in agreeing to arbitrate, the parties impliedly agree to carry out the award. However, such statements are made, as a precautionary measure, in many rules of arbitration. Article 34(6) of the ICC Rules, for example, states that:

> Every award shall be binding on the parties. By submitting the dispute to arbitration under the Rules, the parties undertake to carry out any award without delay and shall be deemed to have waived their right to any form of recourse insofar as such waiver can validly be made.

1.89 Most arbitral awards are carried out by the losing party or parties—reluctantly perhaps, but without any formal legal compulsion.[94] But while awards are binding, they are not always carried out voluntarily, and it may be necessary to seek enforcement by a court of law.

1.90 But which court of law? This is a something that the winning party will need to consider. The usual method for enforcing an award is to obtain judgment on it, and this will generally mean taking enforcement proceedings either (a) in the court of the country in which the losing party resides or has its place of business, or (b) in the court of the country in which the losing party has assets that may be seized.

1.91 It follows that, in order to have an effective system of international arbitration, it is necessary to have an interlinking system of national systems of law, so that the courts of country A will enforce an arbitration agreement or an arbitral award

---

[93] Save for incidental matters such as the interpretation of the award or correction of obvious errors for which the tribunal remains in being for a limited period of time, and save also for those rare cases in which the tribunal may be required by a court to reconsider its decision: see Chapter 9.

[94] See PricewaterhouseCoopers and Queen Mary University, *International Arbitration: Corporate Attitudes and Practices, 2008*, available online at http://www.arbitration.qmul.ac.uk/docs/123294.pdf.

made in country B. For this to happen, there must be international treaties or conventions providing for the recognition and enforcement of *both* arbitration agreements and arbitral awards by the courts of those countries that are party to that treaty or convention. The most important of these conventions have already been listed: amongst them, the New York Convention and the ICSID Convention are pre-eminent.[95]

(o) Summary

International arbitration is a hybrid. It begins as a private agreement between the parties. It continues by way of private proceedings, in which the wishes of the parties play a significant role. Yet it ends with an award that has binding legal force and effect, and which, under appropriate conditions, the courts of most countries of the world will recognise and enforce. In short, this essentially private process has a public effect, implemented with the support of the public authorities of each state and expressed through that state's national law. This interrelationship between national law and international treaties and conventions is of critical importance to the effective operation of international arbitration. **1.92**

The modern arbitral process has lost its early simplicity. It has become more complex, more legalistic, more institutionalised, and more expensive. Yet its essential features have not changed: the original element remains of two or more parties, faced with a dispute that they cannot resolve for themselves, agreeing that one or more private individuals will resolve it for them by arbitration, and that, if this arbitration runs its full course (that is, if the dispute is not settled in the course of the proceedings), it will not be resolved by a negotiated settlement or by mediation, or by some other form of compromise, but by a decision that is binding on the parties. That decision will be made by an arbitral tribunal, composed of one or more arbitrators, whose task is to consider the case put forward by each party and to decide the dispute. The tribunal's decision will be made in writing in the form of an award and will almost always set out the reasons on which it is based.[96] Such an award binds the parties (subject to any right of appeal or challenge that may exist[97]) and represents the final word on the dispute—and if the award is not carried out voluntarily, it may be enforced worldwide by national courts of law.[98] **1.93**

---

[95] These conventions are reviewed in more detail later in this chapter.
[96] Both institutional and international rules of arbitration usually require the arbitral tribunal to state the reasons upon which the tribunal bases its decision, although, under some rules, the parties may agree that this is not necessary: see, e.g., the UNCITRAL Rules, Art. 34(3).
[97] See Chapter 10.
[98] See Chapter 11.

B. Why Arbitrate?

(a) Introduction

1.94 There are many ways in which to settle a dispute. Disagreement about the correct spelling of a word can be resolved by reference to a dictionary. In a game of cricket, the toss of a coin will determine which side has the choice of whether to bat or to bowl. In a minor car accident, an apology and a handshake may be sufficient (although to suggest this perhaps represents a triumph of hope over experience).

1.95 Even where commercial interests are at stake, a dispute need not necessarily lead to all-out confrontation. Initially, the opposing parties will generally attempt to settle matters by meeting and negotiating, sometimes with the assistance of an expert mediator. There may come a point, however, at which attempts at negotiation have failed, it is clear that no agreement is possible, and what is needed is a decision by an outside party, which is both binding and enforceable. The choice then is generally between arbitration before a neutral tribunal and recourse to a court of law.

1.96 It might well be said that if the parties wish their dispute to be decided in a manner that is both binding and enforceable, they should have recourse to the established courts of law, rather than to a specially created arbitral tribunal. Why should parties to an international dispute choose to go to arbitration, rather than to a national court? Why has arbitration become accepted worldwide as the established way of resolving international disputes?

(b) Main reasons

1.97 There are two reasons of prime importance: the first is neutrality; the second is enforcement.

1.98 As to 'neutrality', international arbitration gives the parties an opportunity to choose a 'neutral' place for the resolution of their dispute and to choose a 'neutral' tribunal. As to 'enforcement', an international arbitration, if carried through to its end, leads to a decision that is enforceable against the losing party not only in the place where it is made, but also internationally.

(i) Neutrality

1.99 Parties to an international contract usually come from different countries and so the national court of one party will be a *foreign* court for the other party. Indeed, it will be 'foreign' in almost every sense of the word: it will have its own formalities, and its own rules and procedures developed to deal with domestic matters, *not* for international commercial or investment disputes. The court will also be 'foreign' in the sense that it will have its own language (which may or may not be the language of the contract), its own judges, and its own lawyers, accredited to the court. A party to an international contract that does *not* contain an agreement

B. Why Arbitrate?

to arbitrate may find that it is obliged, first, to commence proceedings in a foreign court, secondly, to employ lawyers other than those whom it usually employs, and thirdly, to embark upon the time-consuming and expensive task of translating the contract, the correspondence between the parties, and other relevant documents into the language of the foreign court. Such a party will also run the risk, if the case proceeds to a hearing, of sitting in court, but understanding very little of the evidence that is given or of how the case is progressing.

By contrast, a reference to arbitration means that the dispute will be determined in a neutral place of arbitration, rather than on the home ground of one party or the other. Each party will be given an opportunity to participate in the selection of the tribunal. If this tribunal is to consist of a single arbitrator, he or she will be chosen by agreement of the parties (or by such outside institution as the parties have agreed), and he or she will be required to be independent and impartial. If the tribunal is to consist of three arbitrators, two of them may be chosen by the parties' themselves, but each of them will be required to be independent and impartial (and may be dismissed if this proves not to be the case). In this sense, whether the tribunal consists of one arbitrator or three, it will be a strictly 'neutral' tribunal. 1.100

(ii) Enforcement

At the end of the arbitration (if no settlement has been reached), the arbitral tribunal will issue its decision in the form of an award. In this regard, three points should be emphasised. First, the end result of the arbitral process will be a binding decision and not (as in mediation or conciliation) a recommendation that the parties are free to accept or reject as they please. Secondly (and within limits that will be discussed later), the award will be final; it will not, as is the case with some court judgments, be the first step on a ladder of appeals, like an expensive game of 'snakes and ladders'. Thirdly, once the award has been made, it will be directly enforceable by court action, both nationally and internationally. 1.101

In this respect, an arbitral award differs from an agreement entered into as a result of mediation or some other form of alternative dispute resolution (ADR), which is binding only contractually. In its international enforceability, an award also differs from the judgment of a court of law, since the international treaties that govern the enforcement of an arbitral award have much greater acceptance internationally than do treaties for the reciprocal enforcement of judgments.[99] 1.102

---

[99] There is a multilateral treaty for the recognition and enforcement of court judgments made in the EU member states and Switzerland: Council Regulation (EC) No. 44/2001 of 22 December 2000 on jurisdiction and the recognition and enforcement of judgment in civil and commercial matters, OJ L 12/1, 16 January 2001 (formerly the Brussels and Lugano Conventions). The Common Market of the South (Mercado Común del Sur, or Mercosur), comprising Argentina, Brazil, Paraguay, and Uruguay, has also established the Las Leñas Protocol for the mutual recognition and enforcement of judgments from Mercosur states within the region. The Hague Conference on Private International Law has drawn up a Convention on Choice of Court Agreements, under which a judgment by the court of a contracting state designated in an exclusive 'choice of court

(c) Additional reasons

1.103 There are additional reasons that are often put forward as making arbitration an attractive alternative to litigation, at least four of which are worthy of comment.

(i) Flexibility

1.104 So long as the parties are treated fairly, an arbitration may be tailored to meet the specific requirements of the dispute, rather than conducted in accordance with fixed procedural rules. To this flexibility of the arbitral process must be added the opportunity to choose a tribunal that is sufficiently experienced that it can take advantage of its procedural freedom. Such a tribunal should be able to grasp quickly the salient issues of fact or law in dispute. This will save the parties time and money, as well as offer them the prospect of a sensible award.

(ii) Confidentiality

1.105 The privacy of arbitral proceedings and the confidentiality that surrounds the process are a powerful attraction to companies and institutions that may become involved (often against their will) in legal proceedings. There may be trade secrets or competitive practices to protect, or there may simply be a reluctance to have details of a commercial dispute (or some bad decision making) made the subject of adverse publicity. The once-general confidentiality of arbitral proceedings has been eroded in recent years, but it still remains a key attraction of arbitration.[100]

(iii) Additional powers of arbitrators

1.106 Sometimes, an arbitral tribunal may possess greater powers than those of a judge. For example, under some systems of law or some rules of arbitration, an arbitral tribunal may be empowered to award compound interest,[101] rather than simple interest, in cases in which the relevant court has no power to do so.[102]

---

agreement' would be recognised and enforced in other contracting states. At time of writing, the Convention has been signed by the European Union, the United States, Mexico, and Singapore, and is due to enter into force on 1 October 2015.

[100] Privacy and its counterpart—confidentiality—are discussed in detail in Chapter 2. Jennifer Kirby states that the new French Law 'takes an innovative position with respect to the presumption of confidentiality in international arbitration—it eliminates it. While the new law expressly provides that, unless the parties agree otherwise, French *domestic* arbitral proceedings shall be confidential, this new law consciously avoids any such provision with respect to international arbitration': Kirby, 'Introductory note to the 2011 French Law on Arbitration' (2011) 50 ILM 258, at 259. In this context, it is worth noting that the LCIA Rules contain, in Art. 30, detailed provisions for the confidentiality of the award, the materials created for the purpose of the arbitration, and the deliberations of the tribunal. By contrast, the ICC Rules contain no such provisions (although there are confidentiality provisions for the work of the ICC Court itself).

[101] One example is that of English law: under the Arbitration Act 1996, an arbitral tribunal is given the power to award compound interest if it thinks it appropriate to do so. Under the LCIA Rules, Art. 26(4), an arbitral tribunal may order the payment of simple *or* compound interest unless the parties have agreed otherwise.

[102] See, e.g., Secomb, 'A uniform, three-step approach to interest rates in international arbitration', in Kröll, Mistalis, Perales Viscasillas, and Rogers (eds) *International Arbitration and*

B. Why Arbitrate?

(iv) Continuity of role

Finally, there is a useful continuity in arbitration: an arbitral tribunal is appointed to deal with one particular case, and its task is to follow that case from beginning to end. This enables the tribunal to become acquainted with the parties, their advisers, and the case, as it develops through the documents, pleadings, and evidence. Such familiarity should help to move the case along—and it may indeed facilitate a settlement.

(d) Is arbitration perfect?

Is arbitration perfect? The answer is: 'Of course not.' Arbitration is based on principles of consent and party autonomy, and so procedures that are usual in litigation may not be available, or may not work very well, in international arbitration. Some examples of the problems to which this can give rise, and possible solutions to these problems, are given below.

(i) Multiparty arbitrations, joinder, and consolidation

Parties to an arbitration may wish to add (or join) a third party who is in some way involved in the dispute, for example as an insurer or in some other capacity. It would usually make sense to add (or join) this third party, so as to resolve all outstanding disputes in the same forum—but can this be done?

Alternatively, there may be two arbitrations between the same parties based on essentially the same facts, but with the claimant in the first arbitration being cited as the respondent in the second. It would make sense to consolidate the two arbitrations—that is, to bring them before the same arbitral tribunal—but, again, can this be done?

Problems such as these—multiparty arbitrations, the joinder of additional parties, the consolidation of arbitrations, and so forth—have troubled the users of arbitration for many years. In the celebrated *Dutco* case,[103] there were two respondents who each wanted to nominate an arbitrator. Under the former ICC Rules, they could not do this; they were instead required to nominate one arbitrator between them. They did so, under protest—but complaint was made to the French court, which said that the right of each party to nominate an arbitrator was part of French public policy and could not be waived. In consequence, the ICC had to devise new rules to deal with such a situation. These new Rules state that where there are multiple claimants or multiple respondents and the parties are unable to agree on a method for the constitution of the arbitral tribunal, the ICC Court itself may

---

International Commercial Law: Synergy, Convergence and Evolution (Kluwer Law International, 2011), pp. 431–450; Veeder, 'Whose arbitration is it anyway?', in Newman and Hill (eds) *The Leading Arbitrators' Guide to International Arbitration* (2nd edn, JurisNet, 2008), p. 356.

[103] *BKMI and Siemens v Dutco*, French Cass. Civ. 1ere, 7 January 1992, [1992] Bull Civ 1. This case is discussed more fully in Chapter 2.

appoint each member of the tribunal and designate one as president.[104] (The LCIA Rules adopt a similar position,[105] except that they state that the LCIA Court *shall* appoint the arbitral tribunal, rather than that it 'may' do so.[106])

1.112 As international trade, commerce, and investment becomes both more complex and more global, there are an increasing number of multiparty disputes.[107] For example, a car manufacturer based in Germany may have contracts with suppliers in other parts of Europe, or in Asia, for the manufacture and supply of components for its cars. Any defects in a given range of cars may mean that the German manufacturer will have claims against several suppliers, as it seeks to establish liability for the defects and compensation for its losses.

1.113 The leading arbitral institutions are well aware of the different problems that may arise and have taken (or are taking) action to address them,[108] so far as this is possible within the limits of 'party consent'. After consulting widely with business people and lawyers, the ICC introduced new Rules in 2012 in an attempt to deal with such problems. Under Article 7 of the ICC Rules, the joinder of third parties is now possible at any time up to confirmation or appointment of any arbitrator—or later, if all parties (including the third party) agree. Under Article 8, in an arbitration with multiple parties, claims may be made by one party against any other party, until signature or approval of the terms of reference[109]—or later, if authorised

---

[104] 2012 ICC Rules, Art. 12(6). This provision of the ICC Rules, first adopted in 1998, works well in practice, although it removes from the parties their right to nominate an arbitrator if they are unable to agree how this should be done. Interestingly, this is the very issue on which the French court took its stand, the right of a party to nominate its own arbitrator being stated to be fundamental! For a useful note on ICC practice, see Whitesell, 'Non-signatories in ICC arbitration', in Gaillard (ed.) *International Arbitration 2006: Back to Basics?* (Kluwer International, 2007), p. 366. Other institutional rules contain similar provisions.

[105] LCIA Rules, Art. 8(1). Article 8(2) goes on to provide that, in such circumstances, the arbitration agreement shall be treated as a written agreement for the nomination and appointment of the arbitral tribunal by the LCIA Court alone.

[106] 'May' is the formulation adopted in the ICC Rules.

[107] A total of 767 requests for arbitration were filed with the ICC Court in 2013; in 2014, there were 791, of which six were for emergency measures. The number of parties in 2013 was 2,120; in 2014, 2,222.

[108] For a detailed discussion of joinder, see Voser, 'Multi-party disputes and joinder of third parties', Presented at the International Council for Commercial Arbitration (ICCA) International Arbitration Conference, Dublin, 8–10 June 2008 . The ICC is not alone in allowing joinder. For example, Art. 4(2) of the Swiss Rules authorises the arbitral tribunal to decide whether a third person should be joined in the arbitration, after consulting all parties and taking into account all relevant circumstances. The LCIA Rules take a more restrictive approach: Art. 22(1)(viii) authorises the tribunal to allow one or more third persons to be joined in the arbitration as a party, provided that the applicant and any such third person consents in writing. Under Art. 9 of the ICC Rules, claims arising out of or in connection with more than one contract may be made in a single arbitration, on certain conditions. Finally, under Art. 10 of the ICC Rules, the ICC Court may order consolidation of two or more ICC arbitrations if the parties have agreed, or if all the claims are made under the same arbitration agreement, or where the claims in the arbitrations are made under more than one arbitration agreement, the arbitrations are between the same parties, the disputes arise in connection with the same legal relationship, and the Court finds the arbitration agreements compatible.

[109] See paragraph 1.167.

B. Why Arbitrate?

by the arbitral tribunal, which will consider the nature of the proposed claims, the stage that the arbitration has reached, and other relevant circumstances.[110]

(ii) Non-signatories

The problem of the so-called non-signatory occurs when a person or a legal entity that is *not* a party to the arbitration agreement wishes to join in the proceedings as a claimant. It occurs more usually, however, when one or more of the existing parties wishes to *add* another party. A common example is that of a claimant with a dispute under a contract between itself and the *subsidiary* of a major international corporation. The contract contains an arbitration clause, and so arbitration can be compelled against the subsidiary company—but the claimant would like to add the *parent* company to the arbitration, so as to improve its chances of being paid if it succeeds in its claim. Is it possible to do this if the parent company is not a party to the contract? **1.114**

While this problem is discussed in more detail later in the volume,[111] at this point it is sufficient to say (in very general terms) that the key issue is whether there is any 'deemed', or 'assumed', consent to arbitration. Various legal theories or doctrines have been developed to try to establish such assumed consent, including the 'group of companies' doctrine,[112] the 'reliance' theory, the concept of agency, and the US concept of 'piercing the corporate veil' (so that, for example, a parent company may be taken to be responsible for the actions of a subsidiary that is a mere shell and, accordingly, be treated as if it were a party to any contract made by that subsidiary). **1.115**

(iii) Conflicting awards

There is no system of binding precedents in international arbitration—that is, no rule that means that an award on a particular issue, or a particular set of facts, is binding on arbitrators confronted with similar issues or similar facts.[113] Each award stands on its own. An arbitral tribunal that is required, for example, to interpret a policy of reinsurance may arrive at a different conclusion from that of **1.116**

---

[110] See ICC Rules, Arts 8(1) and 23(4).
[111] See Chapter 2.
[112] The leading authority on this doctrine is *Chemical France and ors v Isover Saint Gobain* (1984) IX YBCA 131 (the *Dow Chemical* case), which is discussed in Chapter 2, at paragraphs 2.45–2.50. The doctrine is not recognised in all jurisdictions: see, e.g., *Peterson Farms Inc. v C&M Farming Ltd* [2004] EWHC 121 (Comm), at [62], in which an English court ruled that the 'group of companies' doctrine did not form part of the law of Arkansas (the substantive law governing the arbitration). On 'consent' generally, see Professor Hanatiou, who refers to the increasing complexity of modern business transactions, and argues for an approach that is pragmatic and no longer restricted to express consent, but tends to give more importance than before to the conduct of the parties: Hanatiou, 'Consent to arbitration: Do we all share a common vision?' (2011) 27 Arb Intl 539.
[113] See Kaufmann-Kohler, 'Arbitral precedent: Dream, necessity or excuse? The 2006 Freshfields Lecture' (2007) 23 Arb Intl 357.

An Overview of International Arbitration

another tribunal faced with the same problem. The award of the first tribunal, if it is known (and it may not be known, because of confidentiality) may be of persuasive effect, but no more.

1.117 The problem is a real one.[114] One solution that has been suggested is to create a new international court for resolving disputes over the enforcement of arbitral awards. But this has been described as 'the impossible dream',[115] and in cases in which different tribunals reach different conclusions on the same issues, the proposed international court would need to function, in effect, as a court of appeal rather than simply as an enforcement court. This would suit lawyers and arbitrators, who would welcome consistency of decisions, but it might not suit business people, who are looking for the solution to the particular dispute with which they are faced, rather than for the opportunity to contribute, at their own expense, to the development of the law.

(iv) Judicialisation

1.118 In recent years, there has been an almost endless discussion about the increasing 'judicialisation' of international arbitration—'meaning both that arbitrations tend to be conducted more frequently with the procedural intricacy and formality more native to litigation in national courts and that they are more often subjected to judicial intervention and control'.[116]

1.119 The problem appears to be at its most stark in the United States,[117] where there is a tradition of broad-ranging 'discovery', as well as the possibility of challenging

---

[114] For instance, in *Ronald Lauder v Czech Republic*, Final Award, UNCITRAL, 3 September 2001 and in *CME v Czech Republic*, Final Award, UNCITRAL, 14 March 2003, two claims brought in respect of a single dispute, involving virtually undisputed facts, produced conflicting awards from arbitral tribunals in London and Stockholm, as well as giving rise to litigation in the Czech Republic, the United States, and Sweden: see Brower, Brower II, and Sharpe, 'The coming crisis in the global adjudication system' (2003) 19 Arb Intl 424; Cremades and Madalena, 'Parallel proceedings in international arbitration' (2008) 24 Arb Intl 507. See also Professor Kaj Hobér's masterly review: Hobér, '*Res judicata* and *lis pendens* in international arbitration', in Hague Academy of International Law, *Collected Courses of the Hague Academy of International Law, Vol. 366* (Martinus Nijhoff, 2014), pp. 99–406.

[115] Howard M. Holtzmann, cited in Brower, Brower II, and Sharpe, 'The coming crisis in the global adjudication system' (2003) 19 Arb Intl 424, at 435.

[116] Brower, 'W(h)ither international commercial arbitration?' (2008) 24 Arb Intl 181, at 183.

[117] See, e.g., Seidenberg, 'International arbitration loses its grip: Are US lawyers to blame?', ABA Journal, April 2010, p. 51:

> Arbitration was supposed to be the solution for international companies seeking to resolve disputes without expensive and drawn-out court battles. But it is starting to look more like the problem...Arbitration of international commercial disputes has taken on many of the characteristics of litigation in US Courts. And this has upset many companies that rely on arbitration to resolve cross-border business disputes.

> See also the survey conducted by PricewaterhouseCoopers and Queen Mary University, *Corporate Choices in International Arbitration: Industry Perspectives, 2013*, available online at http://www.arbitration.qmul.ac.uk/research/2013/index.html, p. 22, which found that 'several interviewees linked concerns over increases in the costs of arbitration with...encroaching judicialisation'.

B. Why Arbitrate?

arbitral decisions. The US practice of 'discovery' (a term that is not used in international arbitration and for which there is no real equivalent outside the United States) describes a process of seeking out and collecting pre-trial evidence. Such evidence takes two forms: first, witness testimony; and secondly, the production of documents.

So far as witness testimony is concerned, witnesses may be required to give oral testimony, and to be cross-examined on oath, by the parties' counsel. Their testimony is recorded in a transcript, which is then made available for use in the arbitration proceedings as a 'pre-trial deposition'. So far as the production of documents is concerned, the parties to an arbitration will usually be ordered to disclose documents that are relevant and material to the issues in dispute, even if the party that has possession, custody, or control of the documents does not wish to produce them. In a major arbitration, the task of tracing and assembling these documents may take months and cost considerable sums of money, with phrases such as 'warehouse discovery' only palely reflecting the scope of the work to be done. Since 'documents' include emails and other electronically stored information (ESI), the time and costs involved in tracing and assembling the relevant material has increased dramatically.[118] One US lawyer summed up the position in an article, the title of which says it all: 'How the creep of United States litigation-style discovery and appellate rights affects the efficiency and cost-efficacy of arbitration in the United States.'[119]   **1.120**

This trend towards 'judicialisation' is not confined to the United States.[120] Arbitration has changed from the simple system of resolving disputes described earlier in this chapter to become big business. The arbitral process too has changed, from a system in which the arbitrator was expected to devise a satisfactory solution to the dispute[121] to one in which the arbitrator is required to make a decision in   **1.121**

---

[118] The problem posed by ESI has been addressed, amongst many others, by the British Chartered Institute of Arbitrators (CIArb), with its 2008 Protocol for E-Disclosure in Arbitration. The 2010 IBA Guidelines insist upon targeted disclosure of documents, rather than warehouse discovery.

[119] Rievman, Paper presented at a conference sponsored by the Centre for International Legal Studies, February 2005; see also Baker, 'At what price perfect justice?', Presented as part of a coursebook for the 2009 Annual Meeting of the International Institute for Conflict Prevention and Resolution, New York, 15–16 January 2009.

[120] See, e.g., Redfern, 'Stemming the tide of judicialisation in international arbitration' (2008) 2 World Arb & Med Rev 21, at 24: 'It would be comforting, at least for non US lawyers, if it could be assumed that the blight of increasing expense and delay in international arbitration is unique to the United States. It would be wrong, however, to make this assumption.'

[121] The late René David, a distinguished French arbitrator and author, wrote that, historically:

> The arbitrator was chosen *intuitu personae*, because the parties trusted him or were prepared to submit to his authority; he was a squire, a relative, a mutual friend or a man of wisdom, of whom it was expected that he would be able to devise a satisfactory solution for a dispute. The Italian Code of Procedure of 1865 significantly treated arbitration in a preliminary chapter 'On Conciliation and Arbitration'.

See David, *Arbitration in International Trade* (Economica, 1985), p. 29.

accordance with the law.[122] In reaching that decision, the arbitrator must proceed judicially—giving each party a proper opportunity to present its case and treating each party equally, on pain of having the arbitral award set aside for procedural irregularity.[123]

1.122 Various ways of dealing with the problem have been canvassed. Two of the most interesting proposals have been, first, a return to 'first principles', so that the arbitral tribunal would ask, in respect of each particular arbitration, what is the best way of dealing with this case, starting from zero,[124] and secondly, that, at the outset of the proceedings, the parties should be asked to make an informed choice—namely, do they want a full-blown trial of their dispute, whatever it costs, or, to save time and money, would they be prepared to accept some form of shortened procedure, recognising that this would limit their opportunity to develop their respective cases as meticulously as they might wish?

(v) Costs

1.123 International arbitration was once a relatively inexpensive method of dispute resolution. It is no longer so. There are several reasons for this. First, the fees and expenses of the arbitrators (unlike the salary of a judge) must be paid by the parties—and in international arbitrations of any significance, these charges are substantial.[125] Secondly, it may be necessary to pay the administrative fees and expenses of an arbitral institution—and these too may be substantial.[126] It may also be thought necessary to appoint a secretary or 'administrative assistant' to administer the proceedings. Once again, a fee must be paid. Finally, it will be necessary to hire rooms for meetings and hearings, rather than make use of the public facilities of the courts of law.

1.124 But the fees of the arbitrators and of the arbitral institutions, the charges for room hire, the costs of court reporters, and other such expenses are usually a drop in the ocean compared with the fees and expenses of the parties' legal advisers and expert witnesses. In a major arbitration, these will run into many millions, or even tens of millions, of dollars.[127] This means that international arbitration is not likely to be

---

[122] Under modern laws of arbitration and modern rules of arbitration, an arbitrator may decide *ex aequo et bono* only if the parties expressly authorise this: see paragraph 1.140.
[123] For instance, under New York Convention, Art. V, or Model Law, Art. 36.
[124] See, e.g., Rivkin, 'Towards a new paradigm in international arbitration: The town elder model revisited' (2008) 24 Arb Intl 3, at 378.
[125] See Chapter 4, paragraphs 4.192*ff*.
[126] See Chapter 4, paragraph 4.211.
[127] There are many reasons for this, including (a) the huge sums of money that are often at stake, (b) the increasing professionalism of lawyers, accountants, and others engaged in the arbitral process, with a determination to leave no stone unturned (which can—and does—lead to excessively lengthy and repetitive submissions), and (c) the increasing 'judicialisation' of international arbitration, which has been discussed earlier. For a helpful discussion of how such legal fees and expenses may be allocated between the parties by arbitral tribunals, see Williams and Walton, 'Seminar in print: Costs in international arbitration' (2014) 80 Arbitration 432.

B. Why Arbitrate?

cheaper than proceedings in a court of first instance unless there is a very conscious effort to make it so.[128]

However, one point that should not be forgotten in considering the cost of arbitration is that it is a form of 'one-stop shopping'. Although the initial cost is not likely to be less than that of proceedings in court, the award of the arbitrators is unlikely to be followed by a series of costly appeals to superior local courts.

1.125

(vi) Delay

Finally, a major complaint is that of delay, particularly at the beginning and at the end of the arbitral process. At the beginning, the complaint is of the time that it may take to constitute an arbitral tribunal, so that the arbitral process can start to move forward.[129] At the end of the arbitration, the complaint is of the time that some arbitral tribunals take to make their award, with months—and sometimes a year or more—passing between the submission of post-hearing briefs and the delivery of the long-awaited award.[130]

1.126

Once again, this is a problem of which the established arbitral institutions are aware. The ICC, for example, now requires arbitrators (before appointment) to confirm that they have reasonable availability,[131] to consider with the parties, at a procedural conference, how best the arbitration can be conducted, without unnecessary delay or expense,[132] and to deliver their award within six months of the signature of the terms of reference.[133]

1.127

(e) Summary

As the debate about costs and delay continues, it is important to remember that the aim of international arbitration is *not* simply to determine a dispute as quickly and cheaply as possible. That could be done with the spin of a coin. The aim of

1.128

---

[128] One of the objectives of this volume is to show how this can be achieved by means of skilled and effective case management.

[129] For example, under the ICDR Rules, forty-five days may elapse after receipt of the notice of arbitration before the administrator is requested to appoint the arbitrator(s) and designate the presiding arbitrator, and this process may take further time, with the need to find suitable candidates who have no conflict of interest: see ICDR Rules, Art. 6(3).

[130] One of the reasons for delay is the workload of the chosen arbitrators, particularly if they have other professional commitments, e.g. as counsel or as university professors.

[131] Article 11(2) of the 2012 ICC Rules states that:

'Before appointment or confirmation, a prospective arbitrator shall sign a statement of acceptance, availability, impartiality and independence'. Article 5(4) of the current LCIA Rules requires a potential arbitrator to make a written declaration that he or she 'is ready, willing and able to devote sufficient time, diligence and industry to ensure the expeditious and efficient conduct of the arbitration'.

(The arbitral institutions will need to check that such commitments are in fact honoured.)

[132] 2012 ICC Rules, Art. 22.

[133] 2012 ICC Rules, Art. 30(1). In practice, extensions of time are granted and awards are rarely made within the six-month time limit.

international arbitration is to arrive at a fair and reasoned decision on a dispute, based on a proper evaluation of the relevant contract, the facts, and the law. As Professor Park has written:

> Much of the criticism of arbitration's costs and delay thus tells only half the story, often with subtexts portending a cure worse than the disease. An arbitrator's main duty lies not in dictating a peace treaty, but in delivery of an accurate award that rests on a reasonable view of what happened and what the law says. Finding that reality in a fair manner does not always run quickly or smoothly. Although good case management values speed and economy, it does so with respect for the parties' interest in correct decisions. The parties have no less interest in correct decisions than in efficient proceedings. An arbitrator who makes the effort to listen before deciding will enhance both the prospect of accuracy and satisfaction of the litigant's taste for fairness. In the long run, little satisfaction will come from awards that are quick and cheap at the price of being systematically wrong.[134]

1.129 At one time, the comparative advantages and disadvantages of international arbitration versus litigation were much debated.[135] That debate is now over: opinion has moved strongly in favour of international arbitration for the resolution of international disputes.

1.130 In a domestic context, parties who are looking for a binding decision on a dispute will usually have an effective choice between a national court and national arbitration. In an international context, there is no such choice. There is no international court to deal with international business disputes.[136] The real choice is between recourse to a national court and recourse to international arbitration.

1.131 A party to an international contract that decides to take court proceedings will (in the absence of any agreed submission to the jurisdiction of a particular court) be obliged to have recourse to the courts of the defendant's home country, place of business, or residence.[137] To the claimant, this court (as already stated) will be 'foreign' in almost every sense of that word. If one of the parties to the contract is a state or state entity, the prospect becomes more daunting. The private party will usually have little or no knowledge of the law and practice of the national court of

---

[134] Park, 'Arbitration and accuracy' (2010) 1 J Intl Disp Settlement 27.

[135] For one of the most effective, and certainly the most entertaining, critiques of arbitration see Kerr, 'Arbitration v litigation: The *Macao Sardine* case', in Kerr, *As Far As I Remember* (Hart, 2002), Annex.

[136] Unless these disputes are between states, in which case the states concerned may, by agreement, submit their case to the International Court of Justice (ICJ) at The Hague. The Court of Justice of the European Union (CJEU) in Luxembourg may deal with disputes between private parties under EU law, but disputes of this kind are outside the scope of this book.

[137] A national court may allow service of its proceedings abroad, but this so-called extraterritorial jurisdiction is unlikely to be exercised if the foreign defendant has no connection with the country concerned. In any event, difficult problems of enforcement may arise, particularly if a judgment is obtained by default.

B. Why Arbitrate?

the state party—and it will be afraid of encountering judges predisposed to find in favour of the government to which they owe their appointment. For its part, the state (or state entity) concerned will not wish to submit to the national courts of the private party. Indeed, it will usually object to submitting to the jurisdiction of *any* foreign court.

1.132 In such situations, recourse to a neutral tribunal, in a convenient and neutral forum, is almost certainly preferable to recourse to national courts. It is plainly more attractive to establish a 'neutral' tribunal of experienced arbitrators, with knowledge of the language of the contract and an understanding of the commercial intentions of the parties, who will sit in a 'neutral' country and do their best to carry out the reasonable expectations of the parties, than it is to entrust the resolution of the dispute to the courts of one of the parties, which may lack experience of commercial matters or which may, quite simply, be biased in favour of the local party.

1.133 As one commentator has said:

> Although there are many reasons why parties might prefer international arbitration to national courts as a system of dispute resolution, the truth is that in many areas of international commercial activity, international arbitration is the only viable option, or as once famously put, 'the only game in town'. National courts may be considered unfamiliar, inexperienced, unreliable, inefficient, partial, amenable to pressure, or simply hostile. The larger and more significant the transaction in question, the less appropriate, or more risky, a national court may be. And so, where a third country's courts cannot be agreed upon, international arbitration becomes an essential mechanism actively to *avoid* a particular national court.[138]

1.134 An authoritative survey of the views of corporate counsel indicates that they agree with this analysis.[139]

---

[138] Landau, 'Arbitral lifelines: The protection of jurisdiction by arbitrators', in van den Berg (ed.) *International Arbitration 2006: Back to Basics?* (Kluwer Law International, 2007), pp. 282–287. Paulsson made a similar point, that *international* arbitration is 'the only game in town', in his talk at McGill University on 28 May 2008 entitled 'International arbitration is not arbitration'. He said that whilst national (or domestic) arbitration is an alternative to national courts of law, there is no alternative to international arbitration: '[I]n the transnational environment, international arbitration is the only game. It is a *de facto* monopoly.'

[139] 'Arbitration, because of its neutrality, gives a sense of fairness that litigation in foreign courts sometimes cannot provide': see PricewaterhouseCoopers and Queen Mary University, *Corporate Choices in International Arbitration: Industry Perspectives, 2013*, available online at http://www.arbitration.qmul.ac.uk/research/2013/index.html. Arbitration was the preferred method of resolving disputes for 52 per cent of the companies surveyed. It seems that even financial institutions, which have tended to prefer recourse to national courts in order to resolve disputes, are showing an increased interest in the use of arbitration. For instance, in 2013, the International Swaps and Derivatives Association, Inc. (ISDA) published its arbitration guide, which contains model arbitration clauses: see Freeman, 'The use of arbitration in the financial services industry' (2015) 16 Bus L Intl 77.

C. Alternative Dispute Resolution

1.135 It is becoming commonplace for parties to provide that if a dispute arises, they should attempt to resolve it by negotiation before going to arbitration. One particular formula, frequently found in long-term agreements, provides that, in the event of a dispute arising, the parties will first endeavour to reach a settlement by negotiations 'in good faith', before embarking upon arbitration. The problem is that an obligation to negotiate 'in good faith' is nebulous.[140] Who is to open negotiations? How long are they to last? How far does a party need to go in order to show 'good faith'?

1.136 Even where negotiations are conducted in good faith, they are unlikely to succeed unless those involved are capable of looking at the crucial issues objectively—and objectivity is difficult to maintain when vital interests (and perhaps even the future of the business itself) are at stake. It is here that an impartial third party may help to rescue discussions that are at risk of going nowhere. This is why international contracts sometimes provide that, before the parties embark upon litigation or arbitration, they will endeavour to settle any dispute by some form of ADR.[141]

(a) What is meant by alternative dispute resolution?

1.137 When something is described as an 'alternative', the obvious question is: 'alternative to what?' If 'alternative dispute resolution' is conceived as an 'alternative' to the formal procedures adopted by the courts of law, as part of a system of justice established and administered by the state, arbitration should be classified as a method of 'alternative' dispute resolution. It is indeed a very real alternative to the courts of law. However, the term is not always used in this wide sense. It is true that:

> Arbitration presents an alternative to the judicial process in offering privacy to the parties as well as procedural flexibility. However, it is nonetheless *fundamentally the same in that the role of the arbitrator is judgmental*. The function of the judge

---

[140] An agreement to try to settle disputes by mediation (which, in many legal systems, would be regarded as an unenforceable 'agreement to agree') may prove to be enforceable if there is sufficient certainty as to what procedure is to be followed, e.g. because there is provision for recourse to a recognised centre such as the Centre for Effective Dispute Resolution (CEDR): see Mackie, 'The future for ADR clauses after *Cable and Wireless*' (2003) 19 Arb Intl 345; Jarrosson, 'Observations on *Poiré v Tripier*' (2003) 19 Arb Intl 363. See also Kayali, 'Enforceability of multi-tiered dispute resolution clauses' (2010) 27 J Intl Arb 551.

[141] Construction disputes invariably need to be solved rapidly, if only on a temporary basis, and so those involved in the engineering and construction industry have, with the assistance of their lawyers, developed sophisticated techniques for resolving disputes. One frequently used technique, which might be termed the 'wedding cake approach', involves building up 'tiers' of dispute resolution, from mandatory discussions at senior management level, to mediation, dispute review boards, and finally arbitration. For a valuable discussion of these procedures, see Jenkins, *International Construction Arbitration Law* (2nd edn, Wolters Kluwer, 2014), esp. chs 3 and 6.

C. Alternative Dispute Resolution

and the arbitrator is not to decide how the problem resulting in the dispute can most readily be resolved so much as to apportion responsibility for that problem.[142]

1.138 There are many forms of ADR, too numerous to detail here.[143] It is sufficient to note the broad distinction between methods of ADR, such as mediation and conciliation,[144] in which an independent third party tries to bring the disputing parties to a compromise agreement and those methods in which a binding decision is imposed upon the parties without the formalities of litigation or arbitration.[145] Some forms of ADR combine binding and non-binding elements, for example what is known as 'med/arb' (unsurprisingly) involves a combination of mediation and arbitration.[146] The key point to emphasise for present purposes is that, unlike other methods of ADR, international arbitration leads to a binding award that is usually not open to challenge by national courts, and which can be enforced both nationally and internationally, under instruments such as the New York Convention.

(b) *Amiables compositeurs*, equity clauses, and decisions *ex aequo et bono*

1.139 Arbitration agreements sometimes specify that the arbitrators are to act as *amiables compositeurs* or, if the agreement has been drafted by public international lawyers or scholars,[147] that the arbitrators will decide *ex aequo et bono*. Such clauses may become more usual, since the Model Law specifically permits an arbitral tribunal to decide in accordance with equity if the parties authorise it to do so.[148] However,

---

[142] Dixon, 'Alternative dispute resolution developments in London' (1990) 4 Intl Construction L Rev 436, at 437 (emphasis added).

[143] For a general introduction, see Jenkins, *International Construction Arbitration Law* (2nd edn, Wolters Kluwer, 2014), ch. 6. For more specialist texts see, e.g., Brown and Marriott, *ADR Principles and Practice* (3rd edn, Sweet & Maxwell/Thomson Reuters, 2011); Boulle and Nesic, *Mediation: Principles, Process, Practice* (Butterworths, 2001); Newmark and Monaghan, *Butterworths Mediators on Mediation* (Tottel, 2005); Kendall, Freedman, and Farrell, *Expert Determination* (4th edn, Sweet & Maxwell, 2008).

[144] The terms 'mediation' and 'conciliation' are often used as if they were interchangeable. A mediator, as an independent third person, will move between the parties, listening first to one and then the other, and trying to persuade them to focus on their real interests rather than what they see as their legal rights. The role of the conciliator is to make proposals for settlement, or, in the words of the UNCITRAL Conciliation Rules, Art. 7(1), to 'assist the parties in an independent and impartial manner in their attempt to reach an amicable settlement of their dispute'.

[145] The best known of these methods being expert determination, as to which see, e.g., Kendall, Freedman, and Farrell, *Expert Determination* (4th edn, Sweet & Maxwell, 2008); McHugh, 'Expert determination' (2008) 74 Arbitration 148.

[146] There are broadly two versions of this procedure. In the first procedure, the mediator becomes the arbitrator if the mediation fails, whereas in the second, if the mediation fails, the role of the mediator is terminated and the dispute is submitted to a (separate) arbitral tribunal. The second method is plainly a more satisfactory way of proceeding. Moving the dispute from a mediator to an arbitrator makes clear the distinctive functions of a *mediator*, who attempts to facilitate negotiations for a settlement, and an *arbitrator*, who issues a decision on the dispute.

[147] The terms are not meant to be mutually exclusive.

[148] Model Law, Art. 28(3); see also, e.g., the English Arbitration Act 1996, s. 46, which allows the parties to agree what 'considerations' should govern the substance of the dispute.

an arbitration that is conducted under the provisions of such 'equity clauses' will still be an arbitration and not some species of ADR.[149]

D. What Kind of Arbitration?

(a) Introduction

1.140 Any arbitration, wherever it is conducted, is subject to the mandatory rules of the *lex arbitri*—that is, the law of the place of arbitration. Generally, these will be broad and non-specific. They will say, for instance, that the parties must be treated with equality,[150] but they will not set out the way in which this is to be achieved, with exchange of statements of case and defence, witness statements, disclosure of documents, and so forth. For this, more specific rules will be required. Here, the parties have a choice. Should the arbitration be conducted ad hoc—that is, without the involvement of an arbitral institution—or should it be conducted according to the rules of one of the established arbitral institutions?

(b) Ad hoc arbitration

1.141 Parties to an ad hoc arbitration may establish their own rules of procedure (so long as these rules treat the parties with equality and allow each party a reasonable opportunity of presenting its case).[151] Alternatively, and more usually, the parties may agree that the arbitration will be conducted without involving an arbitral institution, but according to an established set of rules, such as those of UNCITRAL, which provide a sensible framework within which the tribunal and the parties may add any detailed provisions as they wish—for example rules providing for the submission of pre-trial briefs or the agreement of expert reports.

1.142 If the issues at stake are sufficiently important (and in particular if a state or state entity is involved), it may be worth negotiating and agreeing detailed rules that take into account the status of the parties and the circumstances of the particular case. For example, any right to restitution may be expressly abandoned in favour of an award of damages.[152] Such specially drawn rules will generally be set out in a formal 'submission to arbitration', negotiated and agreed once the dispute has arisen. This submission agreement will confirm the appointment of the arbitral tribunal, set out the substantive law and the place (or 'seat') of the arbitration, and

---

[149] 'Choice of law' clauses are discussed in Chapter 3.
[150] See, e.g., Model Law, Art. 18.
[151] Many important arbitrations, e.g. reinsurance disputes under the so-called Bermuda form, are regularly conducted ad hoc.
[152] In the submission agreement, which was negotiated over a period of months and agreed by the Kuwait government and Aminoil as a basis for the *Aminoil* arbitration, the oil company gave up any claim for restitution of the oilfield that the Kuwait government had taken over.

D. What Kind of Arbitration?

detail any procedural rules upon which the parties have agreed for the exchange of documents, witness statements, and so forth.

(c) Ad hoc arbitration—advantages and disadvantages

(i) Advantages

One distinct advantage of an ad hoc arbitration is that it can be shaped to meet the wishes of the parties and the facts of the particular dispute. For this to be done efficiently and effectively, the cooperation of the parties and their advisers is necessary; if such cooperation is forthcoming, the difference between an ad hoc arbitration and an institutional arbitration is like the difference between a 'tailor-made' suit and one that is bought 'off the peg'. Many of the well-known arbitrations under oil concession agreements (including the *Sapphire*, *Texaco*, *BP*, *Liamco*, and *Aminoil* arbitrations) were conducted ad hoc.[153]

1.143

In practice, ad hoc arbitrations are now usually conducted on the basis of the UNCITRAL Arbitration Rules, which the parties agree to accept as a convenient and up-to-date set of rules.[154] States in particular are likely to regard the UNCITRAL Rules as a preferred option, since they do not derive their authority from an arbitral organisation based in a particular country, but from the United Nations itself.

1.144

(ii) Disadvantages

The principal disadvantage of ad hoc arbitration is that it depends for its full effectiveness on cooperation between the parties and their lawyers, supported by an adequate legal system in the place of arbitration. It is not difficult to delay arbitral proceedings, for example by refusing at the outset to appoint an arbitrator, so that there is no arbitral tribunal in existence and no agreed book of rules to say what

1.145

---

[153] These cases, which involved state parties, are considered in more detail in Chapter 3.

[154] It is not advisable to try to adopt or adapt institutional rules—such as those of the ICC—for use in an ad hoc arbitration, since such rules make repeated references to the institution concerned and are unlikely to work properly or effectively without it. It seems however (although it is not a practice that the authors would recommend) that it may be possible to involve two arbitral institutions in what would otherwise be an ad hoc arbitration (although quite why this should be done is another matter). The court in Singapore was faced with an arbitration clause stating that disputes should be resolved by arbitration before SIAC in accordance with the ICC Rules. The Singapore International Arbitration Centre was prepared to administer the arbitration under its rules, applying the ICC Rules to the 'essential features the parties would like to see' and the arbitration proceeded on this basis. The Singapore court upheld this arrangement: see *Insigma Technology Co. Ltd v Alstom Technology Ltd* [2008] SGHC 134, at [26]. More recently, in *HKL Group Co. Ltd v Rizq International Holdings Pte Ltd* [2013] SGHC 5, the Singapore High Court found that an arbitration clause in a contract that provided for disputes to be settled by arbitration in Singapore by a non-existent institution under the rules of the ICC was workable as long as the parties were able to secure the agreement of an arbitral institution in Singapore to conduct the arbitration. For its part, the ICC Court is unwilling to administer proceedings fundamentally different from its own basic concepts: see Craig, Park, and Paulsson, *International Chamber of Commerce Arbitration* (3rd edn, Oceana, 2000), para. 715.

is to be done.[155] It will then be necessary to rely on such provisions of law as may be available to offer the necessary support.[156] Only when an arbitral tribunal is in existence and a set of rules has been established will an ad hoc arbitration be able to proceed if one of the parties fails or refuses to play its part in the proceedings.

(d) Institutional arbitration

1.146 An 'institutional' arbitration is one that is administered[157] by a specialist arbitral institution under its own rules of arbitration. There are many such institutions, some better established than others. Amongst the most well known are the ICC, ICSID, the LCIA, and the International Centre for Dispute Resolution (ICDR).[158] There are also regional arbitral institutions (for instance in Beijing and Cairo) and there are chambers of commerce with a well-established reputation, including those of Stockholm, Switzerland, and Vienna.[159]

1.147 The rules of these arbitral institutions tend to follow a broadly similar pattern.[160] Some rulebooks reflect the influences of civil law (following the model of the ICC), whereas others derive greater inspiration from the common law (as exemplified by the LCIA). What is common to all sets of rules is that they are formulated specifically for arbitrations that are to be administered by the institution concerned, and they are usually incorporated into the main contract between the parties by means of an arbitration clause. The clause recommended by the ICC, for instance, states that: 'All disputes arising out of or in connection with the present contract shall be finally settled under the Rules of Arbitration of the International Chamber of Commerce by one or more arbitrators appointed in accordance with the said Rules.'

1.148 This clause is a convenient shorthand way of incorporating a detailed book of rules into the parties' contract, which rules will govern any arbitration that takes place under that contract. If, at some future date, one party proves reluctant to go ahead with arbitration proceedings, it will nevertheless be possible for the party or parties who wish to arbitrate to do so effectively, because there will be a set of rules to regulate both the way in which the arbitral tribunal is to be appointed, and the way in which the arbitration is to be conducted and carried through to its conclusion.

---

[155] Unless it has already been agreed that the UNCITRAL Rules are to govern the proceedings.
[156] See Chapter 3.
[157] As a further refinement, it should be mentioned that an arbitration may be wholly administered or semi-administered. An example of wholly administered arbitration is that of the ICSID, whereby the Centre provides a full service to the arbitral tribunal. An example of semi-administered arbitration is that of certain arbitrations conducted in England under the CIArb Rules: the Institute collects the initial advance on costs from the parties, appoints the arbitral tribunal, and then leaves it to the arbitral tribunal to communicate with the parties, arrange meetings and hearings, and so forth.
[158] As explained later, this is the international division of the AAA.
[159] As previously mentioned, six leading Swiss chambers of commerce, including those of Geneva and Zurich, now operate under the same rules of arbitration—namely, the Swiss Rules.
[160] But they may also diverge, e.g. by providing for 'fast-track' or expedited arbitration, as under the Swiss Rules, or for joinder of parties, as under the LCIA Rules.

D. What Kind of Arbitration?

(e) Institutional arbitration—advantages and disadvantages

(i) Advantages

1.149 Rules laid down by the established arbitral institutions will usually have been proven to work well in practice. They also will generally have undergone periodic revision in consultation with experienced practitioners, to take account of new developments in the law and practice of international arbitration. The rules themselves are generally set out in a small booklet, and parties who agree to submit any dispute to arbitration in accordance with the rules of a named institution effectively incorporate that institution's 'rulebook' into their arbitration agreement.

1.150 This automatic incorporation of an established 'rulebook' is one of the principal advantages of institutional arbitration. Suppose that there is a challenge to an arbitrator on the grounds of lack of independence or impartiality, or suppose that the arbitration is to take place before an arbitral tribunal of three arbitrators, and the defending party is unwilling to arbitrate and fails, or refuses, to appoint an arbitrator: the rulebook will provide for such a situation. It will also contain provisions under which the arbitration may proceed in the event of default by one of the parties. Article 26(2) of the ICC Rules, for instance, stipulates: 'If any of the parties, although duly summoned, fails to appear without valid excuse, the arbitral tribunal shall have the power to proceed with the hearing.' A rule such as this, which is also to be found in other institutional rules, as well as the UNCITRAL Arbitration Rules themselves, is extremely valuable to a tribunal (and to a party) faced with a defaulting party. It means that the arbitration may proceed, and an award may be made, even if a party fails or refuses to take part in the arbitration.

1.151 Another advantage of institutional arbitration is that most arbitral institutions provide specialist staff to administer the arbitration. They will ensure that the arbitral tribunal is appointed, that advance payments are made in respect of the fees and expenses of the arbitrators, that time limits are kept in mind, and generally that the arbitration is run as smoothly as possible.

1.152 A further feature of institutional arbitration is the situation in which the institution itself reviews the arbitral tribunal's award in draft form before sending it to the parties. A review of this kind, which is built into the ICC Rules, serves as a measure of 'quality control'. The ICC does not comment on the substance of the award and it does not interfere with the decision of the arbitral tribunal—but it does ensure that the tribunal has dealt with all of the issues before it, and that the award covers such matters as interest and costs (which are frequently forgotten, even by experienced arbitrators). The ICC's practice of 'scrutinising' awards in draft form is sometimes criticised as merely adding to the time taken to issue a tribunal's award. Its value, however, is well illustrated in a case described by Jennifer Kirby, a former deputy secretary general of the ICC Court, in which the ICC Secretariat pointed out to the arbitral tribunal that it had failed to take into account the fact that the contract contained an agreed limit on the amount of consequential damages that it could award.[161]

1.153 Finally, the assistance that an arbitral institution can give to the parties and their counsel in the course of the arbitral proceedings is appreciable. Even lawyers who are experienced in the conduct of arbitrations run into problems that they are grateful to discuss with the institution's secretariat.

(ii) Disadvantages

1.154 Under some institutional rules,[162] the parties pay a fixed fee in advance for the 'costs of the arbitration'—that is, the fees and expenses of the institution and of the arbitral tribunal. This fixed payment is assessed on an *ad valorem* basis. If the amounts at stake in the dispute are considerable and the parties are represented by advisers experienced in international arbitration, it may be less expensive to conduct the arbitration ad hoc.[163] On the other hand, the ability to pay a fixed amount for the arbitration, however long it takes, may work to the parties' advantage (and to the disadvantage of the arbitrators, in terms of their remuneration).[164]

1.155 The need to process certain steps in the arbitral proceedings through the machinery of an arbitral institution inevitably leads to some delay in the proceedings. Conversely, the time limits imposed by institutional rules are often unrealistically short. A claimant is unlikely to be troubled by this, since a claimant usually has plenty of time in which to prepare its case before submitting it to the respondent or to the relevant arbitral institution, so setting the clock running. However, a respondent is likely to be pressed for time, particularly in a case (such as a dispute under an international construction contract) that involves consideration of voluminous documents and in which the claim that is put forward may, in fact, prove to be a whole series of claims on a series of different grounds.

1.156 Although extensions of time will usually be granted either by the institution concerned or by the arbitral tribunal, the respondent is placed in the invidious position of having to seek extensions of time from the outset of the case. The respondent starts on the wrong foot, so to speak. The problem is worse if the respondent is a state or state entity. The time limits laid down in institutional rules usually fail to take account of the time that a state or state entity needs to obtain approval of important decisions, through its own official channels. In the ICC Rules, for

---

[161] See Kirby, 'What is an award, anyway?' (2014) 31 J Intl Arb 475.
[162] For example, those of the ICC and the Cairo regional centre.
[163] This may be done by agreement of the parties, even if the arbitration clause in the original agreement provided for institutional arbitration. To sound a cautionary note, however, such a course can lead to complete disaster, leaving the claimant without any effective remedy; see, e.g., ICC Case No. 3383 (1982) VII YBCA 119.
[164] The fixed amount itself takes no account of the time actually spent by the arbitrators, and so the fee paid to an arbitrator, if calculated at an hourly rate, may vary from as little as US$60 per hour to as much as US$1,000 or more.

D. What Kind of Arbitration?

example, the time limit for rendering a final award is six months, although this may be (and generally is) extended by the ICC.[165]

(f) Arbitral institutions

An increasing number of institutions administer, or claim to administer, arbitrations. Some serve a particular trade or industry;[166] others cater primarily for a particular country or geographic region. Each has its own set of rules, often based on the UNCITRAL Rules.[167] Each centre also generally has its own model form of arbitration clause. It is sensible (but not essential) to use one of these model forms if institutional arbitration is to be adopted.

1.157

Given the great number of arbitral institutions, or centres, in the world and the fact that new ones continue to come into existence, it is not practicable to list them all. What is proposed is, first, to set out the considerations that the parties (or their lawyers) should have in mind in choosing an arbitral institution, and secondly, to review briefly some of the better known institutions.

1.158

(i) What to look for in an arbitral institution

An arbitral institution will, of necessity, charge fees to cover the expenses of its premises, its staff, its publications, and so on. Payment starts only if it becomes necessary to make use of the institution's services, either for the appointment of an arbitrator or for the conduct of an arbitration. Since those fees will add to the cost of arbitration (in some cases substantially), parties and their lawyers should know what to look for in any given arbitral institution. It is suggested that the basic requirements should include the following.

1.159

Permanency Disputes between parties to an agreement frequently arise many years after the agreement was made, particularly with major projects (such as the construction of a dam or a motorway) or long-term contracts (such as for the supply of liquefied natural gas over a period of years). It is important that the institution named in the arbitration clause should be a genuine institution[168]

1.160

---

[165] One commentator has quoted, with approval, the authors' suggestion that institutional time limits 'are often unrealistically short' and has added that, although speed may be an undoubted good in standard commercial arbitrations, 'rules which cater to that desideratum may not be appropriate in cases involving difficult issues of public policy': Toope, *Mixed International Arbitration* (Grotius, 1990), p. 204.

[166] The London Maritime Arbitration Association (LMAA) receives literally thousands of requests for arbitration per year—although not all of these cases proceed to arbitration and others may be resolved on the basis of documents only: see term 12(b) of the LMAA Terms 2012.

[167] For example, the Swiss Rules state explicitly that they are based on the UNCITRAL Rules, with divergences where this was considered useful.

[168] Fake arbitral institutions are not unknown. In 2002, Citibank began receiving letters stating that it must arbitrate disputes under the rules of the 'National Arbitration Council' (NAC), a so-called arbitration service that was, in fact, provided by someone with a grudge against the bank. Citibank did not participate in any 'arbitrations', but customers who took advantage of the service received an 'award' for the amount of their credit card debt *plus* the fee of the NAC. Citibank

and that it should still be in existence when the dispute arises;[169] otherwise, the arbitration agreement may prove, in the words of the New York Convention, to be 'inoperative or incapable of being performed'. In that case, the only recourse (if any) will be to a national court (which is precisely what the arbitration agreement was designed to avoid).

1.161 It may well be said that this advice militates against the creation of new arbitral institutions and is unfairly biased in favour of established institutions. That is true—but the lawyer who advises a client to select a particular arbitration centre will need to be confident that the advice is good. It is easier to have such confidence if the institution or centre that is chosen has an established track record or, if it is a recent creation, has a reasonable guarantee of permanency.

1.162 **Modern rules of arbitration** The practice of international arbitration has changed rapidly in recent years, as new laws, rules, and procedures come into existence. The rules of arbitral institutions should not rest in some comfortable time warp. They should be brought up to date to reflect modern practice. It is difficult to conduct an effective modern arbitration under rules designed for a different era. Parties are entitled to expect that institutional rules will be reviewed and, if necessary, revised at regular intervals.[170]

1.163 **Specialised staff** Some arbitral institutions adopt a 'hands-on' approach to the conduct of arbitrations under their rules; others are content to leave matters to the arbitral tribunals appointed by them, whilst keeping an eye on the general progress of the arbitration. Whatever role the arbitral institution plays, it needs specialised—and often multilingual—staff. Their duties are likely to be many and varied, including not only explaining the rules, making sure that time limits are observed, collecting fees, arranging visas, and reserving accommodation, but also advising on appropriate procedures by reference to past experience.

1.164 **Reasonable charges** Some arbitral institutions assess their own administrative fees and expenses, and the fees payable to the arbitral tribunal, by reference to a

---

eventually obtained an injunction against the NAC to restrain this activity: see Rau, 'Arbitral jurisdiction and the dimensions of "consent"' (2008) 24 Arb Intl 204, at n. 19.

[169] In *Suzhou Canadian Solar Inc. v LDK Solar Co. Ltd*, May 2013, unreported, a Chinese court refused enforcement of an award issued by the former Shanghai subcommission of the China International Economic and Trade Arbitration Commission (CIETAC), following its break away from CIETAC to form a separate arbitral institution, on the basis that the parties had not consented to have their arbitration administered by a different arbitration commission from that specified in their contract.

[170] UNCITRAL published revised Rules in 2010; the ICC issued new rules effective from 1 January 2012, after a widespread consultation process. Other institutions have followed suit: the Swiss Rules were updated in 2012, as were the SIAC Rules, and those of the Hong Kong International Arbitration Centre in 2013. For a review of the revised rules of the ICC, UNCITRAL, CIETAC, and the Vienna International Arbitration Centre (VIAC), see the articles in (2012) 15(6) Intl Arb L Rev. The LCIA Rules, which dated from 1 January 1998, have also been revised, with new Rules becoming effective on 1 October 2014.

D. What Kind of Arbitration?

sliding scale, which is based on the amounts in dispute (including the amount of any counterclaim). This has the advantage of certainty, in that the parties can find out at an early stage what the total cost of the arbitration is likely to be. However, it operates as a disincentive to experienced arbitrators if the amounts in dispute are not substantial or if the arbitration takes a long time. Other institutions, such as the LCIA, assess their administrative costs and expenses, and the fees of the arbitrators, by reference to the time spent on the case (with an upper and lower limit, so far as the fees of the arbitrators are concerned).

(ii) Leading arbitral institutions

1.165 There are many arbitral institutions in the world, most, if not all, of which are equipped with their own rulebook and administrative staff, which may vary in number from one or two to fifty or more.

1.166 One of the world's leading international institutions is the ICC, which was established in Paris in 1923. Arbitrations under the ICC Rules are administered by a highly skilled, multilingual Secretariat, under the supervision of the ICC Court of Arbitration. However, as previously mentioned, the ICC Court is not a court of law; it is, in effect, the administrative body for ICC arbitrations, with members from all over the world.[171] Two special features of ICC arbitration are, first, the requirement for terms of reference to be drawn up at the outset of the proceedings, and secondly (as already touched upon), the Court's scrutiny of draft awards, to ensure that they are adequately reasoned and deal with all of the issues in the arbitration, including interest and costs.[172]

1.167 The AAA, which administers a considerable number of 'domestic' arbitrations within the United States (including, for example, labour disputes) also administers inter-state arbitrations.[173] In order to cope with the increasing number of such arbitrations, the AAA established the ICDR, which is based in the Irish Republic.

1.168 International arbitral institutions have also come into prominence in Asia. The China International Economic and Trade Arbitration Centre (CIETAC) was

---

[171] In *SNF SAS v Chambre de Commerce International*, Paris Cour d'Appel, 1ère Chambre, section C, 22 January 2009, it was held that the ICC, and not the court, possessed legal personality and was subject to French law, being based in Paris.

[172] There is an abundance of literature on the work of the ICC. The leading authorities are Craig, Park, and Paulsson, *International Chamber of Commerce Arbitration* (3rd edn, Oceana, 2000); Derains and Schwarz, *A Guide to the New ICC Rules of Arbitration* (2nd edn, Kluwer Law International, 2005); Schäffer, Verbist, and Imhoos, *ICC Arbitration in Practice* (Kluwer Law International, 2005). On the 2012 Rules, see Fry, Greenberg, and Mazza, *The Secretariat's Guide to ICC Arbitration* (ICC, 2012); Grierson and van Hooft, *Arbitrating under the 2012 ICC Rules* (Kluwer, 2012). In relation to the scrutiny of awards by the ICC Court, see paragraph 1.152.

[173] In addition to administering arbitrations under its own rules, the AAA also administers Inter-American Commercial Arbitration Commission (IACAC) arbitrations and makes its services available, if required, in arbitrations conducted under the UNCITRAL Rules, whether those arbitrations are held inside or outside the United States.

established in Beijing in April 1956 and has a regional arbitration centre in Hong Kong, which was established in 1985. The current CIETAC Arbitration Rules (the 'CIETAC Rules'), which came into force in May 2012, constitute a modern set of rules that is consistent with the internationalisation of Chinese arbitral practice and procedure.

1.169 A few years later, in 1991, SIAC was established in Singapore to provide a dispute resolution centre for Asia. Singapore's law on arbitration is based on the Model Law, and SIAC maintains a list of experienced arbitrators drawn from all parts of the world, from whom the parties may choose 'their' arbitrator, if they so wish. The revised SIAC Arbitration Rules, which came into effect on 1 April 2013, again constitute a complete modern set of rules.

1.170 Finally, mention must be made of the LCIA, which owes its origins to the London Chamber of Arbitration, founded on 23 November 1892.[174] At the time, it was said that:

> The chamber is to have all the virtues that the law lacks. It is to be expeditious where the law is slow, cheap where the law is costly, simple where the law is technical, a peace-maker instead of a stirrer up of strife.[175]

1.171 The LCIA has a relatively small administrative staff,[176] as compared to the ICC, for instance, but its rules are drawn in more detail than those of the ICC.[177] It has an important international caseload, including cases from Russia and countries within the former Russian confederation.

1.172 After a long and difficult gestation, the LCIA issued revised Rules to replace the previous 1998 Rules. These revised Rules, which came into effect in October 2014, will no doubt be the subject of detailed review, commentary, and criticism as they are applied in practice. Some of the language used would delight a Chancery lawyer practising at the time of Charles Dickens—the Preamble, for instance, refers to any agreement to arbitrate 'howsoever made', which provides 'in whatsoever manner' for arbitration under the LCIA Rules—but nevertheless the spirit of the 2014 Rules is refreshingly modern, making it evident that the drafting was carried out by lawyers who were well acquainted with the latest

---

[174] For the history of the LCIA, see Kerr, 'The London Court of International Arbitration 1892–1992' (1992) 8 Arb Intl 317; Delvolvé, 'Le centenaire de la LCIA (London Court of International Arbitration)' [1993] Rev Arb 599; Kerr, 'London Court of International Arbitration' (1996) 7 ICCA Congress Series 213.

[175] Manson (1893) IX LQR, cited in Veeder and Dye, 'Lord Bramwell's Arbitration Code' (1992) 8 Arb Intl 330.

[176] The LCIA is based in London, but has joined forces with the Dubai International Financial Centre to open an office in Dubai, for which purpose special rules of arbitration (and conciliation) have been formulated. An office has also been opened in Delhi, India, as a subsidiary of the LCIA.

[177] For a discussion of the decisions of the LCIA Court, see Nicholas and Partasides, 'LCIA Court decisions on challenges to arbitrators: A proposal to publish' (2007) 23 Arb Intl 1. For a commentary on the LCIA's 2014 Revised Rules, see Wade and Clauchy, *Commentary on the LCIA Arbitration Rules 2014* (Sweet & Maxwell, 2015).

D. What Kind of Arbitration?

developments in international arbitration and conscious of the justified concerns of business and other users.

There is explicit recognition of current methods of communication, making it clear (for instance) that a request for arbitration and all of its accompanying documents may be submitted in electronic form,[178] and that similar provisions apply to the response and indeed to communications generally.[179] There is recognition also of criticisms that are frequently expressed as to the time that arbitral proceedings often take and the costs involved. — 1.173

One way of speeding up the arbitral process is to provide for expedited arbitrations, as discussed earlier in this chapter. The LCIA Rules do not take this route. However, as in the previous Rules, they do provide for the expedited formation of the arbitral tribunal. They also impose, as has the ICC, a new requirement on a potential arbitrator to confirm that he or she is 'ready, willing and able to devote sufficient time, diligence and industry to ensure the expeditious and efficient conduct of the arbitration'.[180] In addition, parties and arbitrators are 'encouraged' to make contact with each other, within twenty-one days of notice of formation of the tribunal, so as to discuss and agree how the arbitration is to be conducted.[181] And when it comes to issuing a procedural order, the tribunal is under a newly articulated duty to provide for an 'expeditious means for the final resolution of the parties' dispute'.[182] — 1.174

The parties themselves are expected to do their best to make the proceedings run smoothly and efficiently. Failure to do so may result in one or other of them being sanctioned by a ruling on costs since, in assessing the amount to be awarded for 'legal costs' (that is, the legal and other expenses incurred by a party), the tribunal may take into account 'any non-co-operation resulting in undue delay and unnecessary expense'.[183] — 1.175

Sometimes, one of the parties to an arbitration agreement may need to seek interim relief *before* the arbitral tribunal is established. There may, for example, be good reason to believe that evidence is likely to be destroyed or assets liquidated before the arbitral proceedings can begin. The usual remedy in such cases is for the concerned party to apply to the appropriate court for a protective order, and it is generally recognised that such an application does not constitute a breach of the agreement to submit disputes to arbitration.[184] However, a new means of recourse has been established. — 1.176

---

[178] LCIA 2014 Revised Rules, Art. 1.
[179] LCIA 2014 Revised Rules, Arts 2 and 4.
[180] LCIA 2014 Revised Rules, Art. 5(4).
[181] LCIA 2014 Revised Rules, Art. 14(1) and (2).
[182] LCIA 2014 Revised Rules, Art. 14(4)(ii).
[183] LCIA 2014 Revised Rules, Art. 28(4).
[184] See, e.g., UNCITRAL Arbitration Rules, Art. 26(9), which provides that a request for interim measures addressed to a judicial authority 'shall not be deemed incompatible with the agreement to arbitrate, or as a waiver of that agreement'.

1.177 In the 2012 revision of its Rules, the ICC made detailed provision for the appointment of an 'emergency arbitrator' to whom applications for interim or conservatory relief may be made before the arbitral tribunal itself is established.[185] The intention is that, when justified, an 'emergency arbitrator' will be appointed within a matter of days, will immediately consider the parties' arguments, and will make his or her order within a matter of weeks. The LCIA has also brought in new Rules providing for the appointment of an 'emergency arbitrator' in circumstances in which this is justified.[186] The detailed provisions for 'emergency arbitrator' differ as between the two arbitral institutions, but both agree that the parties may 'opt out' of the emergency arbitrator rules,[187] and that any order of the emergency arbitrator may be confirmed, varied, or terminated by the arbitral tribunal, once it is constituted.[188]

1.178 More controversially, the LCIA Rules entitle the arbitral tribunal to exercise a measure of control over the 'legal representatives' of the parties. A new, longer, section of the Rules is devoted to 'Legal representatives',[189] replacing the former short section that referred to 'party representatives', who could be either 'legal practitioners or any other representatives'. This new section provides that, before the tribunal's formation, the registrar of the LCIA may request written confirmation of the names and addresses of each party's legal representatives in the arbitration. The point of this is to avoid any challenge to an arbitrator on the basis that he or she is not independent because of some perceived connection or association with a legal representative. Once the tribunal is formed, any intended change in a party's legal representation must be notified to all concerned and is subject to the approval of the tribunal. If the tribunal considers that the proposed change of legal representation might 'compromise the composition of the Arbitral Tribunal'[190]—or, in plain English, lead to challenge of an arbitrator—the tribunal may refuse to approve the proposed change.

1.179 A further measure of control by the tribunal over a party's legal representatives is provided by the Annex to the LCIA Rules. The Annex emulates the IBA Guidelines on Party Representation in International Arbitration, which, in their own words, seek to preserve 'the integrity and fairness of the arbitral proceedings'. The object of both sets of guidelines is indeed to achieve a fair hearing, and to 'level the playing field' as between lawyers from different legal backgrounds and traditions—but whereas the IBA Guidelines apply only if the parties to an arbitration choose to adopt them, the guidelines in the Annex to the LCIA Rules are mandatory. Under Article 18(5) of the LCIA Rules, each party to the arbitration *must* ensure that all

---

[185] ICC Rules, Art. 29 and Appendix V.
[186] LCIA 2014 Revised Rules, Art. 9B.
[187] ICC Rules, Art. 29(6)(b); LCIA Rules, Art. 9(14).
[188] ICC Rules, Art. 29(3); LCIA Rules, Art. 9(11).
[189] LCIA Rules, Art. 18.
[190] An example would be that of the arbitrator and the potential new legal representative coming from the same chambers or having some other kind of professional relationship.

D. What Kind of Arbitration?

of its legal representatives appearing by name before the tribunal have agreed to comply with the guidelines contained in the Annex.

1.180 The guidelines themselves warn, for instance, against repeated challenges to an arbitrator's appointment or to the jurisdiction of the arbitral tribunal; like the IBA guidelines, they also warn against knowingly making false statements, or putting forward false evidence, or concealing from the tribunal a document of which the tribunal has ordered production. Any failure of compliance by a legal representative may be sanctioned by (a) a written reprimand, (b) a written caution as to future conduct in the arbitration, and (c) 'any other measure necessary to fulfil within the arbitration the general duties required of the tribunal'—namely, to act fairly and impartially, and to adopt procedures that will avoid unnecessary delay and expense.

1.181 It will be interesting to see to what extent arbitrators (who, broadly speaking, depend for appointment upon the parties) will be prepared to impose cost or other sanctions on a party or its legal representative for conduct that may have added to the expense of the proceedings or delayed bringing them to a conclusion. There are obviously times when each party may be said to be at fault, for example by putting forward arguments that have little or no chance of success, but it is not always possible to point the finger of blame at one party alone. Professor Park, a former president of the LCIA, recognises that the availability of sanctions to promote compliance with professional guidelines 'will prove a challenge', and on the issue of guidelines generally, he concludes: 'In evaluating whether professional guidelines will make arbitration better or worse, the arbitration community must, for now at least, put the matter into a box labelled "Awaiting Further Light".'[191]

(g) Arbitrations involving a state

1.182 Disputes between states belong to the realm of public international law. However, where the state enters into a commercial agreement with a private party, either by itself or through a state entity, any disputes are likely to be referred either to the courts of the state concerned or to international arbitration. The private party to such a contract will almost certainly prefer to submit to arbitration as a 'neutral' process, rather than to the courts of the state with which it is in dispute.

1.183 Many factors have to be weighed in the balance when a state or state entity considers whether or not to submit to arbitration. There are political considerations, such as the effect that a refusal to go ahead with arbitration might have on relations with the state to which the foreign claimant belongs.[192] There are economic considerations, such as the loss of foreign investment that a refusal to arbitrate might bring

---

[191] Park, 'A fair fight: Professional guidelines in international arbitration' (2014) 30 Arb Intl 579.
[192] Investor–state arbitrations are dealt with in Chapter 8.

about. There are also, of course, considerations such as the effect of an award being granted *in absentia*, as happened in the Libyan oil nationalisation arbitrations.[193]

1.184 It is sometimes said that the right of a state to claim immunity from legal proceedings forms part of its sovereign 'dignity'. However, as a well-known English judge once said: 'It is more in keeping with the dignity of a foreign sovereign to submit himself to the rule of law than to claim to be above it.'[194]

1.185 Arbitrations in which one of the parties is a state or state entity often take place under the rules of institutions such as those already discussed.[195] There are, however, two institutions that are usually concerned only with disputes in which one of the parties is a state or state entity: ICSID in Washington DC and the Permanent Court of Arbitration (PCA) at The Hague.

(i) International Centre for the Settlement of Investment Disputes

1.186 The International Centre for the Settlement of Investment Disputes was established by the ICSID Convention and is based at the principal office of the World Bank in Washington. This convention, which is sometimes also known as the 'ICSID Convention', broke new ground. It gave both private individuals and corporations who were 'investors' in a foreign state the right to bring legal proceedings against that state, before an international arbitral tribunal. It was no longer necessary for such investors to ask their own governments to take up their case at an inter-state level, under the principle of 'diplomatic protection'. Instead, the ICSID Convention established a system under which individuals and corporations could demand redress directly against a foreign state by way of conciliation or arbitration.

1.187 It was only with the advent of BITs and such intergovernmental treaties as the North American Free Trade Agreement (NAFTA) that investors began to take advantage of their right of direct recourse against a foreign state, in their own names and on their own behalves. This was a major breakthrough. As one commentator pointed out:

> For the first time a system was instituted under which non State entities—corporations or individuals—could sue States directly; in which State immunity was much restricted; under which international law could be applied directly to the

---

[193] The three major international arbitrations arising out of the nationalisation by the Libyan government of oil concession agreements with foreign corporations, which still had many years to run, are discussed in Chapter 3. The Libyan government declined to take part in the arbitrations and so its case went if not unconsidered, at least unargued.

[194] *Rahimtoola v The Nizam of Hyderabad* [1958] AC 379, at 418 *per* Lord Denning.

[195] A number of arbitrations involving states or state entities take place under the ICC Rules. In 2012, the percentage of cases involving a state brought before the ICC was 9.9 per cent. However, PricewaterhouseCoopers and Queen Mary University, *International Arbitration: Corporate Attitudes and Practices, 2008*, available online at http://www.arbitration.qmul.ac.uk/docs/123294.pdf, states that 59 per cent of the participating arbitral institutions indicated that less than 25 per cent of their awards are rendered against states.

E. Sovereign States, Claims Commissions, and Tribunals

relationship between the investor and the host State; in which the operation of the local remedies rule was excluded; and in which the tribunal's award would be directly enforceable within the territories of the State's parties.[196]

1.188 An ICSID arbitration is truly 'delocalised' or 'denationalised' because it is governed by an international treaty, rather than by a national law. The Centre began life quietly, but what has been described as a 'tidal wave' of arbitrations between investors and states has led to a dramatic increase in its workload.[197]

(ii) Permanent Court of Arbitration

1.189 The PCA was established by the Convention for the Pacific Settlement of International Disputes, concluded at The Hague (hence known as the 'Hague Convention') in 1899 and revised in 1907. It was the product of the first Hague Peace Conference, which was convened on the initiative of Tsar Nicholas II of Russia 'with the object of seeking the most effective means of ensuring to all peoples the benefits of a real and durable peace'.[198] There was no 'real and durable peace', but some major inter-state disputes are, and have been, settled by arbitration.[199] In 1935, the PCA administered its first commercial arbitration between a private party and a state.[200] The PCA is not a court, as such, but an administrative body, with a list of potential arbitrators.

1.190 Over recent years, the Secretariat of the PCA has expanded its role to include not only the designation of appointing authorities for the appointment of arbitrators under the UNCITRAL Rules, but also the administration of arbitrations in disputes involving private parties, as well as states. Ad hoc and other tribunals may also take advantage of the established facilities of the Peace Palace at The Hague.[201]

E. Sovereign States, Claims Commissions, and Tribunals

1.191 The so-called Jay Treaty of 1794,[202] concluded between the United States and Britain following the American War of Independence, represented a 'new starting

---

[196] Lauterpacht, 'Foreword', in Schreuer, *The ICSID Convention: A Commentary* (Cambridge University Press, 2001), pp. xi–xii.
[197] As at 31 December 2013, ICSID had registered 459 cases under the ICSID Convention and Additional Facility Rules. The role of ICSID in such arbitrations is discussed in Chapter 8.
[198] Holls, *The Peace Conference at The Hague* (Macmillan, 1900), pp. 8–9.
[199] See Merrills, 'The contribution of the Permanent Court of Arbitration to international law and to the settlement of disputes by peaceful means', in Hamilton, Requena, van Scheltinga, and Shifman (eds) *The Permanent Court of Arbitration: International Arbitration and Dispute Resolution, Summaries of Awards, Settlement Agreements and Reports* (Kluwer, 1999), pp. 3–27.
[200] *Radio Corporation of America v China* (1941) 8 ILR 26.
[201] See the official PCA website online at http://www.pca-cpa.org.
[202] This was a general treaty of friendship, commerce, and navigation. It was called the 'Jay Treaty' after John Jay, the American Secretary of State.

point for the development of international arbitration'.[203] The Jay Treaty established various 'commissions' to resolve boundary and shipping disputes between the two countries. Each 'commission' consisted of one or two commissioners nominated by each party, with a 'neutral' president chosen by agreement or by drawing lots.

1.192 However, it was not until the *Alabama Claims* arbitration, almost a century later, that further progress was made towards the modern system of international arbitration, and again this was on an ad hoc basis, with the United States and Britain again as parties. The *Alabama Claims* arbitration, which took place in Geneva in 1871–72, arose because the British government did not prevent the *Alabama* and other vessels built in British yards from joining the US Civil War on the side of the southern states. The United States claimed that this was a breach of neutrality. A new type of tribunal was established to determine the dispute—one member from each side, with 'neutral' members being appointed by the king of Italy, the president of the Swiss Confederation, and the emperor of Brazil: '[A] collegiate international court, which was to set the pattern for many others, had emerged.'[204]

1.193 Arbitration, as already indicated, was an important part of the Hague Conventions of 1899 and 1907. The Hague Convention of 1899 stated that, in questions of a legal nature and particularly in the interpretation or application of treaties or conventions, '[a]rbitration is recognised by the Signatory Powers as the most effective, and at the same time the most equitable, means of settling disputes which diplomacy has failed to settle'.

1.194 This conclusion led first to the establishment at The Hague of the PCA and then a 'Permanent Court of Justice', which, as a standing judicial tribunal, adjudicated upon disputes that the states concerned were prepared to submit to it. In 1945, following the Second World War, the International Court of Justice (ICJ) was founded, as the successor to the Permanent Court of Justice and the principal judicial organ of the United Nations, also based at the Peace Palace in The Hague.

1.195 It is the Statute of the ICJ that serves as a guide both for the ICJ and for other tribunals (including arbitral tribunals) in ascertaining the applicable rules of public international law, to which reference is frequently made in investor–state arbitrations and, indeed, in other cases involving states or state entities. Article 38(1) of the Statute states:

> 1. The Court, whose function is to decide in accordance with international law[205] such disputes as are submitted to it, shall apply:
>   (a) international conventions, whether general or particular, establishing rules expressly recognised by the contesting States;

---

[203] For a full account of the Jay Treaty and of mixed commissions, see Simpson and Fox, *International Arbitration* (Stevens & Sons, 1959), p. 1.

[204] Ibid., at p. 8. The United Kingdom was required to pay US$15.5 million by way of compensation—a considerable sum at that time.

[205] The reference to 'international law' in Art. 38(1) is a reference to what is generally known as 'public international law', which generally regulates the relationship between sovereign states.

(b) international custom, as evidence of a general practice accepted as law;
(c) the general principles of law recognised by civilised nations;
(d) subject to the provisions of Article 59, judicial decisions and the teachings of the most highly qualified publicists of the various nations, as subsidiary means for the determination of rules of law.

2. This provision shall not prejudice the power of the Court to decide a case *ex aequo et bono*, if the parties agree thereto.

1.196 The practice of appointing 'mixed commissions' to resolve disputes in which sovereign states are involved continues. In recent years, various international 'claims commissions' or tribunals have been established to determine claims by individuals and corporations. Amongst the most significant of these are the Iran–United States Claims Tribunal,[206] the United Nations Compensation Commission (UNCC),[207] and the Claims Resolution Tribunal for Dormant Accounts in Switzerland (the 'Holocaust Tribunals').[208] The work of these tribunals and commissions has been discussed in detail in previous editions of this book. In particular, reference was made to the jurisprudence of the Iran–United States Claims Tribunal, which shows to advantage the UNCITRAL Rules in action and which, more importantly, demonstrates that arbitration has an important role to play as part of an overall political settlement between states.

F. Regulation of International Arbitration

(a) Introduction

1.197 A national or 'domestic' arbitration—that is, an arbitration between individuals, corporations, or entities resident in the same country—will usually involve only the domestic law of that country. International arbitration is different. As Sir Robert Jennings, former president of the ICJ, said in the preface to the first edition of this book:

> International commercial disputes do not fit into orthodox moulds of dispute procedures—they lie astraddle the frontiers of foreign and domestic law—and raise questions that do not fit into the categories of private international law either. Not least they raise peculiar problems of enforcement.

1.198 In practice this means, as already stated, that international arbitration depends for its effectiveness upon the support of different national systems of law, and in particular upon (a) the arbitration law of the country which is the place (or 'seat')

---

[206] This was established, following the release of American hostages in Iran, to deal with claims against Iran by US claimants.
[207] This was established to resolve the millions of claims resulting from the invasion of Kuwait by Iraq in 1990, which it did commendably despite its necessarily 'mass production' approach.
[208] This was established to deal with claims of the Holocaust victims and their successors.

of the arbitration, and (b) the law of the country or countries in which recognition and enforcement of the arbitral tribunal's award is sought.

(b) Role of national systems of law

1.199 An understanding of the interplay between the private arbitral process and the different national systems of law that may impinge upon that process is fundamental to a proper understanding of international arbitration. This interplay may take place at almost any phase of the arbitral process. It may be necessary at the outset of an arbitration for the claimant to ask the relevant national (or local) court to enforce an agreement to arbitrate, which the adverse party is seeking to circumvent by commencing legal proceedings, or it may be necessary to ask the relevant court to appoint the arbitral tribunal (if this cannot be done under the arbitration agreement or under the relevant rules of arbitration).

1.200 During the course of the arbitration, it may become necessary for a party to apply to the relevant court for assistance that it is empowered to give, for example the blocking of a bank account or the seizure of assets to prevent their disappearance.

1.201 When an award has been made, the losing party may seek to challenge it[209] on the basis that the arbitral tribunal exceeded its jurisdiction or on some other legally recognised ground. If the challenge succeeds, the award will either be amended or set aside completely.[210] By contrast, the winning party may need to apply to a national court for recognition and enforcement of the award[211] in a state (or states) in which the losing party has (or is believed to have) assets that can be sequestrated.

(c) State participation in the arbitral process

1.202 States that recognise international arbitration as a valid method of resolving international disputes are generally ready to give their assistance to the arbitral process. Indeed, in many cases, they are bound to do so by the international conventions to which they are parties. In return, it is to be expected that they will seek to exercise a measure of control over the arbitral process. Such control is usually exercised on a territorial basis: first, over arbitrations conducted in the territory of the state concerned; and secondly, over awards brought into the territory of the state concerned for the purpose of recognition and enforcement.

1.203 As to the first proposition, it would be unusual for a state to support arbitral tribunals operating within its jurisdiction *without* claiming some degree of control over

---

[209] Generally before courts of the place of arbitration.
[210] See Chapter 10.
[211] See Chapter 11.

the conduct of those arbitral tribunals—if only to ensure that certain minimum standards of justice are met, particularly in procedural matters.[212]

1.204 As to the second proposition, it is generally accepted that states that may be called upon to recognise and enforce an international arbitral award are entitled to ensure that certain minimum standards of due process have been observed in the making of that award, that the subject matter of the award is 'arbitrable' in terms of their own laws, and that the award itself does not offend public policy.[213]

1.205 The dependence of the international arbitral process upon national systems of law should be recognised, but not exaggerated. Across the world, there is a growing harmonisation of the national laws that govern both the conduct of international arbitrations, and the recognition and enforcement of international awards. This process of harmonisation was inspired by the New York Convention and has been given fresh impetus by the Model Law. Additionally, the importance of international arbitration, in terms both of its contribution to global trade and of the economic benefit that arbitrations can bring to the host country, is increasingly recognised, with new arbitration centres being established in different parts of the world. Some may have only a nominal existence, but taken as a whole they represent a potential source of revenue (and perhaps of prestige) to a country.[214]

(d) Role of international conventions and the Model Law

1.206 The most effective method of creating a 'universal' system of law governing international arbitration has been through international conventions (and, more recently, through the Model Law). International conventions have helped to link national systems of law into a network of laws that, while they may differ in their wording, have as their common objective the international enforcement of arbitration agreements and of arbitral awards.

---

[212] See Kerr, 'Arbitration and the courts: The UNCITRAL Model Law' (1984) 50 Arbitration 3, at 14:

> [T]here is virtually no body, tribunal, authority or individual in this country whose acts or decisions give rise to binding legal consequences for others, but who are altogether immune from judicial review in the event of improper conduct, breaches of the principles of natural justice, or decisions which clearly transcend any standard of objective reasonableness.

[213] For further discussion of 'arbitrability' and public policy, see Chapter 3.
[214] Mustill, 'The history of international commercial arbitration: A sketch', in Newman and Hill (eds) *The Leading Arbitrators' Guide to International Arbitration* (2nd edn, JurisNet, 2008), p. 17:

> National governments have also sought to gain economic advantage from the promotion of local arbitration by backing the establishment of arbitration or dispute resolution centres, the idea being that if there is in one's own country a focus of intellectual and practical activity in this field, with facilities for the conduct and study of arbitrations, contracting parties will choose to conclude agreements for arbitration there…

1.207 The first such convention, in modern times, was the Montevideo Convention.[215] This was established in 1889, and provided for the recognition and enforcement of arbitration agreements between certain Latin American states.[216] It was therefore essentially a regional convention. The first modern and genuinely *international* convention was the 1923 Geneva Protocol, which was drawn up on the initiative of the ICC and under the auspices of the League of Nations. It was quickly followed by the Geneva Convention of 1927.

(i) Geneva Protocol of 1923

1.208 The 1923 Geneva Protocol had two objectives. Its first and main objective was to ensure that *arbitration clauses* were enforceable *internationally*, so that parties to an arbitration agreement would be obliged to resolve their dispute by arbitration rather than through the courts. This was done, in effect, by requiring national courts to refuse to entertain legal proceedings brought in breach of an agreement to arbitrate. The second and subsidiary objective of the 1923 Geneva Protocol was to ensure that *arbitration awards* made pursuant to such arbitration agreements would be enforced in the territory of the states in which they were made.

1.209 The Geneva Protocol is now a spent force. It is still worthy of note, however, since its two objectives—the enforcement of both arbitration agreements and arbitral awards—remain the objectives of the New York Convention and of the Model Law.

(ii) Geneva Convention of 1927

1.210 The 1927 Geneva Convention[217] was intended to widen the scope of the Geneva Protocol by providing for the recognition and enforcement of Protocol awards made within the territory of *any* of the contracting states (and not merely within the territory of the state in which the award was made).[218] However, a party seeking enforcement of an award under the 1927 Geneva Convention had to *prove* the conditions necessary for enforcement. This led to what became known as the problem of 'double exequatur': to show that the award had become final in its country of origin, the successful party was often obliged to seek a declaration (an exequatur) in the courts of the country in which the arbitration took place to the effect that the award was enforceable in that country before it could go ahead and enforce the award (a second exequatur) in the courts of the place of enforcement.

---

[215] Treaty concerning the Union of South American States in respect of Procedural Law, signed at Montevideo on 11 January 1889. The Treaty is published, in an English translation, in United Nations, *Register of Texts of Conventions and Other Instruments Concerning International Trade Law*, Vol. II (UN, 1973), p. 5.
[216] Montevideo Convention, Arts 5–7.
[217] Convention for the Execution of Foreign Arbitral Awards, signed at Geneva on 26 September 1927.
[218] The states that have adhered to the Geneva Convention are substantially those that adhered to the Geneva Protocol (with some notable omissions, such as Brazil, Norway, and Poland).

(iii) New York Convention of 1958

1.211 The New York Convention is one of the cornerstones of international arbitration.[219] Indeed, it is principally because of the New York Convention that international arbitration has become the established method of resolving international disputes. The major trading nations of the world have become parties to the New York Convention. At the time of writing, the Convention has more than 145 parties, including Latin American states such as Argentina, Colombia, Mexico, and Venezuela, and Arab states such as Saudi Arabia, Egypt, Kuwait, and Dubai.

1.212 The New York Convention provides a simpler and more effective method of obtaining recognition and enforcement of foreign arbitral awards than was available under the 1927 Geneva Convention.[220] The title of the New York Convention suggests that it is concerned *only* with the recognition and enforcement of foreign arbitral *awards*. This is misleading. The Convention is also concerned with arbitration agreements, as is clear, for instance, in Article II—and indeed in other Articles, such as Articles IV(1)(b) and V(1)(a).

1.213 In order to enforce arbitration agreements, the New York Convention adopts the technique found in the 1923 Geneva Protocol. The courts of contracting states are required to refuse to allow a dispute that is subject to an arbitration agreement to be litigated before them if an objection to such litigation is raised by any party to the arbitration agreement.[221]

1.214 Courts of different countries have differed (and continue to differ) in their interpretation of the New York Convention.[222] This is often so for local, purely political, reasons, and thus the Convention itself, which was made for a simpler, less 'globalised', world, shows its age.[223]

(iv) Conventions after 1958

1.215 The New York Convention[224] represents a vital stage in the shaping of modern international arbitration. No convention since 1958 has had the same impact.

---

[219] In 1953, the ICC proposed a new treaty to govern international arbitration. The draft document produced by the ICC gave an early indication of the debate that has continued ever since, concerning the feasibility of a truly *international* award. The ICC's proposal for such an award, which would *not* be subject to control by the law of the place in which it was made, was unacceptable to the majority of states. It has also proved to be equally unacceptable in more modern times, when the Model Law was formulated.

[220] The New York Convention replaces the 1923 Geneva Protocol and the 1927 Geneva Convention as between states that are parties to both: see Art. VII(2).

[221] New York Convention, Art. 11(3).

[222] The ICCA's *Yearbook of Commercial Arbitration* (YBCA) reports, each year, court decisions made in different countries on the interpretation and application of the New York Convention, translated into English where necessary.

[223] Such as in the 'writing requirement'.

[224] The recognition and enforcement of awards under the New York Convention, and the grounds for refusal of such recognition and enforcement, are discussed in Chapters 10 and 11.

An Overview of International Arbitration

There are, however, other treaties and conventions, including original conventions, which may enable recognition and enforcement of arbitral awards in appropriate cases. These conventions are discussed in Chapter 11.

(v) Bilateral investment treaties

1.216 In the context of international treaties and conventions, a brief mention must be made of BITs. Historically, states doing business with each other often entered into 'treaties of friendship, commerce, and navigation'. In order to encourage trade and investment, the states concerned would grant each other favourable trading conditions and agree that any disputes would be resolved by arbitration. Such treaties have now given way to bilateral investment treaties, or BITs as they are more commonly known.[225]

1.217 The 'classic' agreement to arbitrate has already been described as one that is made between the parties themselves, either by means of an arbitration clause in their contract or by a subsequent submission to arbitration. The position is different in a BIT: the state party that is seeking foreign investment in effect makes a 'standing offer' to arbitrate any dispute that might arise in the future between itself and a qualifying foreign investor of the other state party to the treaty. Only when a dispute actually arises and the private investor accepts this 'standing offer' is an 'agreement to arbitrate' formed. The concept of a 'standing offer' to arbitrate with anyone who fits the required definition is different from the conventional model, in which the parties are known to each other when they make an agreement to arbitrate. The process has therefore been described as 'arbitration without privity'.[226] However, once the 'standing offer' has been accepted, an effective agreement to arbitrate, to which both the state or state entity and the investor are parties, comes into existence.

(vi) Model Law

1.218 The Model Law began with a proposal to reform the New York Convention. This led to a report from UNCITRAL[227] to the effect that harmonisation of the arbitration laws of the different countries of the world could be achieved more effectively by a model or uniform law. The final text of the Model Law was adopted by resolution of UNCITRAL, at its session in Vienna in June 1985, as a law to govern international commercial arbitration. A recommendation of the General Assembly

---

[225] According to the United Nations Conference on Trade and Development (UNCTAD), there are now more than 2,860 BITs and more than 340 'other' international investment agreements (such as free trade agreements, economic partnership agreements, or framework agreements with an investment element): see UNCTAD, 'International investment policymaking in transition: Challenges and opportunities of treaty renewal', IIA Issues Note No. 4 (June 2013), available online at http://unctad.org/en/PublicationsLibrary/webdiaepcb2013d9_en.pdf.
[226] Paulsson, 'Arbitration without privity' (1995) 10 ICSID Rev—Foreign Investment LJ 232.
[227] UNCITRAL, *Study on the Application and Interpretation of the Convention on the Recognition and Enforcement of Foreign Arbitral Awards*, UN Doc A/CN9/168 (UN, 1958).

F. Regulation of International Arbitration

of the United Nations commending the Model Law to Member States was adopted in December 1985.[228]

1.219 The Model Law has been a major success. The text goes through the arbitral process from beginning to end, in a simple and readily understandable form. It is a text that many states have adopted, either as it stands or with minor changes, as their own law of arbitration. So far, more than sixty states have adopted legislation based on the Model Law, with some, such as England, choosing to modernise their laws on arbitration without adopting the Model Law, whilst being careful to follow its format and to have close regard to its provisions.[229]

1.220 It may be said that if the New York Convention put international arbitration on the world stage, it was the Model Law that made it a star, with appearances in states across the world. Even so, the Model Law, which was enacted in 1985, has been overtaken by the fast-moving world of international arbitration in at least two respects: first, the requirement for an arbitration agreement to be in writing; and secondly, the provisions governing the power of an arbitral tribunal to order interim measures of relief.

1.221 To address these concerns, UNCITRAL established a working group in 2000 to consider revisions to the Model Law. This working group produced proposals that were adopted as revisions to the Model Law and approved by the United Nations in December 2006.[230]

1.222 As mentioned earlier in this chapter, the 'writing requirement' is now defined in very wide terms in the Revised Model Law, and there is also an 'option' allowing states to adopt this wide definition of 'in writing' or to dispense altogether with the requirement for writing.[231]

1.223 The UNCITRAL working group addressed a further controversial issue: whether an arbitral tribunal should have the power to issue interim measures on the application of one party, without the adverse party being aware of the application. Such *ex parte* applications are a common feature of litigation before the courts. If a party is told, for instance, that there is to be an application to prevent disposal of its assets, those assets may well have 'disappeared' before the application is heard. But are *ex parte* applications, made behind the back of a party, consistent with the underlying

---

[228] For a full account of the origins and aims of the Model Law, see the second edition of this book, pp. 508*ff*.
[229] The advisory committee established in the United Kingdom to report on the Bill that became the English Arbitration Act 1996 stated in Departmental Advisory Committee on Arbitration Law, *Report on the Arbitration Bill* (HMSO, 1996) (known as the 'DAC Report'), at para. 4: '[A]t every stage in preparing a new draft Bill, very close regard was paid to the Model Law, and it will be seen that both the structure and the content of the July draft bill, and the final bill, owe much to this model.'
[230] For example, New Zealand, Mauritius, Peru, Slovenia, Costa Rica, Ireland, and Belgium have adopted legislation based on the Model Law as revised.
[231] The 'writing requirement' and the 'option' provisions are discussed in Chapter 2.

basis of arbitration, with its emphasis on treating the parties with equality? The working group decided to allow such applications, but only on strictly limited conditions.[232]

(e) Practice of international arbitration

1.224 As this chapter has tried to make clear, there are no fixed, detailed rules of procedure governing an international arbitration: each case is different; each tribunal is different; and each dispute deserves to be treated differently. But there is a basic underlying structure, built upon three essential elements: first, the international conventions (and the Model Law) that have helped to form modern national laws of arbitration; secondly, established rules of international arbitration; and thirdly, the practice of experienced arbitrators and counsel.

(i) International conventions (and the Model Law)

1.225 The international conventions on arbitration do not prescribe (and they do not attempt to prescribe) the way in which an international arbitration should be conducted; instead, they lay down certain general principles. The New York Convention, for example, requires that a party should be given proper notice of the appointment of the arbitrator or of the arbitral proceedings, that the arbitral procedure should be in accordance with the agreement of the parties or the law of the country in which the arbitration takes place, and that each party should be given a proper opportunity to present its case. If this is not done, the national court or foreign courts in which enforcement is sought may refuse to recognise and enforce any arbitral award. These general principles of the New York Convention now form an integral part of the arbitration law (the *lex arbitri*) of countries throughout the world.

1.226 Other international conventions on arbitration, such as the ICSID Convention, which is concerned with investment disputes, go into more detail than the New York Convention but—like that convention—avoid setting down detailed rules of procedure.

1.227 The Model Law takes matters further. It contains detailed provisions for the appointment (and challenge) of arbitrators and for the appointment of substitute arbitrators, where necessary. It authorises an arbitral tribunal to rule on its own jurisdiction, treating an arbitration clause as an agreement that is independent of the contract of which it forms part. It authorises an arbitral tribunal to grant interim measures of relief, for instance to preserve assets or material evidence, and it deals in outline with the submission of statements of claim and defence, and other matters.

---

[232] See Chapter 7.

F. Regulation of International Arbitration

Countries that have adopted (or adapted) the Model Law thus have a national law governing arbitration that is 'arbitration friendly'. Those countries that have considered it necessary to go beyond the Model Law, in the sense of making more detailed provisions, have nevertheless taken full note of the Model Law in drafting their own 'arbitration friendly' legislation.[233] **1.228**

(ii) Established rules of international arbitration

Where, then, are the detailed rules to be found? It might be thought that they are to be found in the UNCITRAL Rules, or in the rules of arbitral institutions such as the ICC and the LCIA. **1.229**

It is true that these rules will usually contain provisions for selecting the place of arbitration (if this has not already been selected by the parties), the appointment of the arbitral tribunal, challenges to arbitrators or to their jurisdiction, the exchange of written submissions, the appointment of experts, the holding of a hearing, and so forth.[234] Such rules define the general 'shape' or outline of the arbitral proceedings, from the establishment of the arbitral tribunal to the publication of its eventual award. However, they do not prescribe *in detail* the way in which an arbitration should be conducted—and they do not attempt to do so. **1.230**

This means that, in each arbitration, there are important questions to be answered. Should there be written submissions? If so, how many and in what order—simultaneously or in sequence? Should evidence be called from witnesses? If so, in what manner and under what rules? If written witness statements are submitted, what status should they have? Are they to be taken into account only if the witness subsequently appears at the hearing, or should they be given some weight even if the person who made the statement fails to attend a subsequent hearing? Is the lawyer representing a party to the arbitration allowed to interview potential witnesses, or is this a breach of professional rules? Where a witness appears at a hearing, should he or she be cross-questioned, and if so, by whom: the representatives of the parties, the tribunal, or both? Should experts be appointed, and if so, by whom: the parties themselves or the tribunal? How should arguments of law be presented: in writing, orally, or both? **1.231**

These questions, and many others that arise in the course of an arbitration, are important practical questions. The answer to them is to be found in what has come to be known as the 'soft law' of international arbitration, and in the practice of experienced arbitrators and counsel. **1.232**

---

[233] See, e.g., the comment in the DAC Report, quoted in n. 229.
[234] Even if the arbitration is to be conducted ad hoc and without reference to any particular set of rules, an experienced tribunal will have well in mind the provisions of such rules, which are designed to ensure orderly and fair proceedings, leading to a reasoned award.

(iii) 'Hard law' and 'soft law'

1.233 The 'hard law' of international arbitration, as Professor Park has expressed it, 'looks at the process from the outside: the perspective of judges and legislators charged with providing a framework of statutes, treaties and cases setting the contours for judicial recognition and enforcement of arbitration agreements and awards'.[235]

1.234 This 'hard law' has already been discussed in outline, with reference to international treaties and national systems of law, and it will be discussed in much greater detail in the subsequent chapters of this book.

1.235 The 'soft law' of international arbitration looks at the process from the inside. Over the years, many sets of 'rules' and 'guidelines' have been drawn up by established professional bodies or arbitral institutions, and some have achieved recognition and endorsement within the arbitration community. For example, the Rules on the Taking of Evidence in International Arbitration, published by the International Bar Association (IBA) in 2010 in a revised edition, provide useful guidance on the testimony of witnesses and experts, and on the principles governing the disclosure of documents.[236] Again by way of example, certain 'case management techniques' have been advanced by the ICC as ways of controlling time and costs in arbitration.[237] In general, these rules and guidelines—this 'soft law' of international arbitration—is to be welcomed, but some voices warn against a proliferation of 'rules' and 'guidelines' that may deprive arbitration of its flexibility and adaptability.[238]

1.236 As already indicated, one particular area in which there is a tendency to create 'soft law' concerns the conduct of counsel in international arbitrations. Lawyers are subject to the rules and etiquette of their own particular bar or law society, but there is no 'international code of conduct' for counsel engaged in international arbitration. In consequence, conduct by counsel that may be regarded in some jurisdictions as perfectly acceptable, such as going through the evidence with a witness, will be regarded as 'unprofessional' in other jurisdictions. The IBA recognised

---

[235] Park, 'Arbitration in autumn' (2011) 2 J Intl Disp Settlement 1, at 3.
[236] The IBA has also issued Guidelines on Conflicts of Interest in International Arbitration to deal with problems (real or perceived) of conflict of interest on the part of arbitrators, as well as Guidelines on Party Representation in International Arbitration.
[237] These 'case management techniques' are now published as Appendix IV to the ICC's Rules of Arbitration. A better, and more complete, guide is to be found in ICC, *ICC Arbitration Commission Report on Techniques for Controlling Time and Costs in Arbitration* (2nd edn, ICC, 2014).
[238] The idea of a special code of procedure to deal with the arbitration of small claims was considered, but rejected by the Departmental Advisory Committee on Arbitration Law in the preparation of the English Arbitration Act 1996. It was considered that it would be wrong for the Act 'to lay down a rigid structure for any kind of case': see DAC Report and Supplementary Report, February 1996 and January 1997, at paras 167 and 168. Note also the comment of Professor Reymond that '[t]he reaction of certain people has been to propose the adoption of more and more detailed rules of procedure, which would deprive arbitration of one of its main advantages, subtlety and adaptability': Reymond, 'L'Arbitration Act 1996, convergence et originalité' (1997) 1 Rev Arb 45, at 54 (authors' translation).

F. Regulation of International Arbitration

this potential problem in the first edition of its Rules on the Taking of Evidence in International Arbitration, and the current edition states, at Article 4(3): 'It shall not be improper for a Party, its officers, employees, legal advisers or other representatives to interview its witnesses or potential witnesses and to discuss their prospective testimony with them.' This is helpful, but it plainly does not seek to set down a detailed practice rule indicating (for instance) to what extent counsel is entitled to 'rehearse' the evidence of his or her witnesses or otherwise to 'coach' them.

1.237 Efforts are being made by institutions such as the IBA and the ICC to formulate a 'code of conduct' for lawyers in international arbitration, but there are two principal problems: first, with identifying what standards of conduct will find universal acceptance; and secondly, with enforcing compliance with these standards.[239]

(iv) Practice of experienced arbitrators and counsel

1.238 What tends to happen, when experienced arbitrators and counsel are involved in an international arbitration, is that a mix of different national practices emerges, with the best of each selected and the worst rejected.[240] The idea that there is a 'common law approach' and a 'civil law' approach to the practice of international arbitration belongs to the rubbish bin of history. A common thread runs—or should run—through most international arbitrations along the following lines.

(1) An arbitral tribunal may decide for itself (subject to any later application to the courts) on any challenge to its jurisdiction.
(2) As the proceedings develop, an arbitral tribunal may be called upon to issue interim measures of relief, such as an order for security for costs or an order to prevent the flight of assets from the jurisdiction.
(3) At the stage of documentary disclosure, the usual procedure (using the IBA Rules on the Taking of Evidence in International Arbitration as guidelines) will be for each party to submit to the tribunal all of the documents on which it relies and to limit requests for disclosure of documents by the other side to such documents as are 'relevant and material to the outcome of the case'.[241]

---

[239] For instance, the IBA Guidelines on Party Representation in International Arbitration, as adopted by resolution of the IBA Council on 25 May 2013, prescribe certain standards of conduct for a 'party representative', but the sanctions for any 'misconduct' are admonishment, drawing appropriate inferences, or taking account of the misconduct in awarding costs. Such measures will generally fall short of the more draconian sanctions available to the professional body to which counsel (or the party representative) may belong, and 'the remedies for misconduct which appear at the end of the Guidelines are underwhelming': Cummins, 'The IBA Guidelines on Party Representation in International Arbitration: Levelling the playing field' (2014) 30 Arb Intl 429, at 455. The Guidelines draw on both civil law and common law traditions, but in their approach to evidentiary matters, the influence of the common law is significant: see Stephens-Chu and Spinelli, 'The gathering and taking of evidence under the IBA Guidelines on Party Representation in International Arbitration: Civil and common law perspectives' (2014) 8 Disp Res Intl 37.

[240] The conduct of an arbitration (including the different practices and procedures that may be adopted) is fully discussed in Chapter 6.

[241] IBA Rules, Art. 3.

If there are disputed requests for documents that are of any length, they will usually be dealt with by means of the so-called *Redfern* schedule (see Figure 1.1).[242]

Figure 1.1 Theoretical example of a claimant's *Redfern* schedule

Document requested	Relevance and materiality of the documents requested to the outcome of the dispute	Responses and objections to the claimant's request to produce documents	Decision of the arbitral tribunal
1. Any and all documents (including documents in electronic form) consisting of information on the general structure of management and the decision-making processes of the respondent, including minutes of board meetings, shareholders' meetings, and other documentation related to the decision-making process at the top level	The claimant asserts that the way in which the management processes were organised at respondent were inadequate and/or were the cause of the delays to production and the generally poor quality of the product. To prove these assertions, the claimant needs to know the respondent's management structure and needs documents normally produced for the purposes of a company's management at the level of top management (i.e. boards, shareholders' meetings, etc.).	This request is so wide that an order for their production would impose an unreasonable burden on the respondent: see the IBA Rules on the Taking of Evidence, Art. 9.	
2. A record of all previous complaints from customers since production began	Such documents will allow the claimant to establish the management methodology adopted by the respondent, and to demonstrate that this methodology was inadequate and unprofessional.	This request is too wide. However, the respondent is prepared to produce a list of complaints received over the last 18 months, whilst keeping the names of the customers confidential.	
3. All correspondence and other documents with the respondent's legal advisers concerning complaints by other customers	Such correspondence will demonstrate the steps to which the respondent went to deny liability for obvious deficiencies in the product.	To the extent that any such correspondence exists (which is denied), it would be covered by legal professional privilege.	

[242] In *Elektrim SA v Vivendi* [2007] EWHC 11 (Comm), [26], Aikens J referred to a procedural order by the arbitral tribunal, which dealt, inter alia, with the procedures to be adopted for the disclosure of documents. The judge said:

> The parties were to present their requests for production of documents in accordance with a procedure known in international arbitration as 'the Redfern Schedule'. The routine is that the party requesting the documents identifies the documents requested and the reasons for the request. The opposing party then sets out its reasons for its opposition to production (if any). The schedule then sets out the decision of the tribunal.

For the origins of the '*Redfern* schedule', see Redfern, 'Efficiency in arbitration: The *Redfern* schedule', ICCA Review, April 2013, pp. 9 and 12.

(4) The evidence of witnesses will usually be submitted in the form of written statements, with reply statements if considered necessary or appropriate, and the direct examination of witnesses will usually be limited, by agreement, to no more than 10 minutes or so.
(5) Old-fashioned advocacy, in terms of long speeches, theatrical flourishes, and 'jury-type' appeals to the emotions, is no longer the custom. It has been replaced by written briefs (although these are not always free of evocative words, or heartfelt appeals to 'honesty' and 'good faith').

G. Summary

1.239 The international conventions on arbitration, the Model Law, and the worldwide recognition of the importance of arbitration in resolving disputes in trade, commerce, and investment have brought about the modernisation and harmonisation across the globe of the laws that govern the process of international arbitration.

1.240 The international conventions operate through the national law of those states that have agreed to be bound by them. Although they may be adopted with reservations (such as to the 'commercial nature' of the dispute) and although states may apply their own criteria (such as to public policy grounds for refusing recognition of an arbitral award), these conventions nevertheless represent a compelling force for unification of national laws on arbitration. The same is true of the Model Law. Indeed, when looking at a particular local (or national) law, it is generally possible to look through the text of that law to a framework derived from a general treaty or convention—or indeed from the Model Law itself.[243]

1.241 Business people, lawyers, and arbitrators who are involved in international arbitration must abandon a parochial view of the law, as constituted by the particular national system with which they are familiar, in favour of a wider and more international outlook. In particular, they must be prepared to accept that there are other systems of law that may, in some respects, be better than their own and which must, in any event, be taken into account. As one commentator has said: 'International arbitration is a place where lawyers, counsel and arbitrators, trained in different legal systems, meet and work together. They have no choice but to find some common ground.'[244]

1.242 Similar considerations apply to the *practice* of international arbitration. There is no uniform practice or procedure. Arbitrators, parties, and counsel work together

---

[243] Consider, e.g., the German Arbitration Act 1998 and the Irish Arbitration Act 2010.
[244] Kaufmann-Kohler, 'Globalization of arbitral procedure' (2003) 36 Vanderbilt J Transnl L 1314, at 1323*ff*.

'to find some common ground' by devising a procedure that fits the dispute with which they are concerned.

1.243 International disputes take on many different forms. Any attempt to design a uniform arbitral procedure would be fraught with problems. It would also run the risk of defeating the purpose of international arbitration, which is to offer a *flexible* means of resolving disputes. Within the general framework of the 'hard law' of arbitration and taking advantage of the best features of the so-called soft law, it is possible both to adopt and to adapt procedures that are appropriate to the particular dispute with which the parties and the arbitrators are concerned. As this volume endeavours to show in the chapters that follow, this is part of the continuing challenge of the law and practice of international arbitration.

2

AGREEMENT TO ARBITRATE

A. Overview	2.01	E. Submission Agreements	2.119
B. Validity of an Arbitration Agreement	2.13	F. Arbitrability	2.124
		G. Confidentiality	2.161
C. Parties to an Arbitration Agreement	2.31	H. Defective Arbitration Clauses	2.197
		I. Waiver of the Right to Arbitrate	2.204
D. Analysis of an Arbitration Agreement	2.63	J. Multiparty Arbitrations	2.212

A. Overview

(a) Introduction

2.01 The agreement to arbitrate is the foundation stone of international arbitration.[1] It records the consent of the parties to submit to arbitration—a consent that is indispensable to any process of dispute resolution outside national courts.[2] Such processes depend for their very existence upon the agreement of the parties. Many attach great importance to the wishes of the parties—to *l'autonomie de la volonté*. Indeed, some go so far as to suggest that this consent, together with an appropriate set of rules, is sufficient to turn international arbitration into an autonomous, delocalised process that takes place independently of national law. For most, this goes too far.[3] It attaches too much importance to the wishes of the parties and not enough to the framework of national laws within which the arbitral process must take place. Nevertheless, the consent of the parties remains the essential basis of a voluntary system of international arbitration.[4]

---

[1] See Chapter 1, paragraph 1.40.

[2] As discussed later in this chapter, consent can be deemed by conduct or found in more than one document.

[3] Except for arbitrations conducted under the ICSID Convention. For further discussion of delocalised arbitration, see Chapter 3, paragraphs 3.76–3.77.

[4] Compulsory arbitration does exist. Nationally, it is used as a supposedly cheap and informal method of resolving disputes in particular areas. Internationally, the most striking example of compulsory arbitration was in the socialist countries of Central and Eastern Europe, where it

(b) Categories of arbitration agreement

2.02 There are two basic types of arbitration agreement: the arbitration clause and the submission agreement. An arbitration clause looks to the future, whereas a submission agreement looks to the past. The first, which is most common, is usually contained in the principal agreement between the parties and is an agreement to submit *future* disputes to arbitration. The second is an agreement to submit *existing* disputes to arbitration.

2.03 In this book, the terms 'arbitration clause' and 'submission agreement' are used according to these descriptions. Arbitration clauses are usually short, whilst submission agreements are often long. This is not because of any particular legal requirement; it is simply a reflection of the practicalities of the situation. An arbitration clause that deals with disputes that may arise in the future does not usually go into too much detail, since it is not known what kind of disputes will arise and how they should best be handled. Indeed, although the parties to a contract may agree to an arbitration clause, they hope that there will be no need to invoke it. Usually, they insert a short model clause, recommended by an arbitral institution, as a formality. By contrast, a submission agreement deals with a dispute that *has* in fact already arisen—and so it can be tailored to fit precisely the circumstances of the case. In addition to indicating the place of arbitration and the substantive law, it generally names the arbitrators, sets out the matters in dispute, and even (if thought appropriate) provides for the exchange of written submissions and other procedural matters.[5]

2.04 Most international commercial arbitrations take place pursuant to an arbitration clause in a commercial contract.[6] These clauses are often 'midnight clauses'—that is, the last clauses to be considered in contract negotiations, sometimes late at night or in the early hours of the morning. Insufficient thought is given to how disputes

---

was employed as the method of settling disputes under the provisions of the Convention on the Settlement of Arbitration of Civil Law Disputes Arising from Relations of Economic, Scientific and Technical Co-operation (Moscow Convention) of 1972. However, compulsory arbitration is outside the scope of this book, which is concerned with the mainstream of international arbitration—that is, with arbitration as a consensual process, taking place pursuant to an arbitration agreement.

[5] This is not a universal rule. A submission agreement may take the form of a brief agreement to submit an existing dispute to the procedures of an arbitral institution. Conversely, an arbitration clause providing for ad hoc arbitration could identify the procedure to be followed in detail, as well as the means of establishing the arbitral tribunal, filling vacancies, and so forth.

[6] It should be noted, however, that, in some Latin American states, e.g. Argentina and Uruguay, a clause to submit future disputes to arbitration is not operative until a submission agreement (or *compromiso*) has also been executed. (The same is also true of Brazil unless the arbitration clause incorporates a mechanism to constitute the arbitral tribunal, which it may do by reference to a set of institutional rules.) In these jurisdictions, the ICC Rules may be preferred because they provide for a functional equivalent of the *compromiso* (the terms of reference), which are not included in other institutional rules. See Blackaby, Lindsey, and Spinillo, *International Arbitration in Latin America* (Kluwer Law International, 2002), pp. 12, 31–32, and 73; Naón, 'Arbitration and Latin America: Progress and setbacks—2004 Freshfields Lecture' (2005) 21 Arb Intl 127; Blad (ed.), *International Comparative Legal Guide to International Arbitration* (5th edn, Global Legal Group, 2008), pp. 281 and 295.

A. Overview

are to be resolved (possibly because the parties are reluctant to contemplate falling into dispute), and an inappropriate and unwieldy compromise is often adopted,[7] for example a wrong choice (or no choice at all) of the substantive law or of the place of arbitration. If a dispute arises and arbitration proceedings begin, these matters must consequently be dealt with before any progress can be made with the real issues.

Later, this chapter deals separately with arbitration clauses and submission agreements, since different considerations apply to each. First, however, some general observations should be made. They apply equally to both types of arbitration agreement and derive from the international conventions governing arbitration. **2.05**

(c) International conventions

Although this topic is considered in Chapter 1, it is worth giving a brief summary here. The 1923 Geneva Protocol and the 1927 Geneva Convention dealt with the recognition and enforcement of international arbitration agreements and the execution of foreign arbitral awards. These were then followed by various regional conventions,[8] until eventually the most important convention in the field of international commercial arbitration, the New York Convention, was promulgated in 1958. **2.06**

The New York Convention continued where the Geneva treaties left off.[9] Its title as a 'Convention on the Recognition and Enforcement of Foreign Arbitral Awards' is a partial misnomer. The Convention's starting point is, in fact, the recognition and enforcement of arbitration agreements.[10] Having provided for recognition of the validity and enforceability of arbitration agreements, it also provides for the international enforcement of awards that comply with the specified criteria.[11] **2.07**

Closely modelled[12] on the New York Convention, the 1975 Panama Convention[13] was signed by the United States and a significant number of Latin American states, and marked another step forward in the recognition of arbitration as an established method of resolving disputes in a regional context. **2.08**

---

[7] For a step-by-step guide to drafting arbitration clauses, see Paulsson, Rawding, and Reed (eds) *The Freshfields Guide to Arbitration Clauses in International Contracts* (3rd edn, Kluwer Law International, 2010).
[8] See, e.g., the Bustamante Code of 1928 and the European Convention of 1961.
[9] The New York Convention replaces the Geneva treaties between states that have become bound by it: Art. VII(2).
[10] New York Convention, Arts II(1) and II(3).
[11] The Model Law follows a similar pattern.
[12] It too recognises the validity of an agreement that submits existing and future disputes to arbitration: Panama Convention, Art. 1.
[13] Its formal title is 'The Convention on the Settlement of Civil Law Disputes Resulting from Economic, Scientific and Technological Cooperation'. The text of the Convention appears in (1978) III YBCA 15.

(d) International standards

2.09 The effect of these and other conventions on arbitration,[14] whether international or regional, has been to establish the requirement for a valid international arbitration agreement and to indicate the parameters within which such an agreement will operate.

2.10 Unlike Venus, these Conventions did not arise fully formed from the sea.[15] Instead, they reflect the provisions to be found in developed arbitration laws and in the practice of arbitral institutions, such as the International Chamber of Commerce (ICC). In turn, they—together with the Model Law—have played an important part in modernising and harmonising state laws governing arbitration. An arbitration agreement that provides for international arbitration must take account of these international requirements. If it fails to do so, the arbitration agreement, and any award made under it, may not qualify for international recognition and enforcement.

2.11 In seeking to establish the 'international requirements', the starting point has to be the New York Convention. This has been described as 'the single most important pillar on which the edifice of international arbitration rests',[16] and one that 'perhaps could lay claim to be the most effective instance of international legislation in the entire history of commercial law'.[17] Under the Convention, each contracting state undertakes to recognise and give effect to an arbitration agreement when the following requirements are fulfilled:

- the agreement is in writing;
- it deals with existing or future disputes;
- these disputes arise in respect of a defined legal relationship, whether contractual or not; and
- they concern a subject matter capable of settlement by arbitration.

2.12 These are the four positive requirements of a valid arbitration agreement, laid down in Article II(1) of the New York Convention.[18] A further two requirements are, in

---

[14] Such as the European Convention of 1961 and the ICSID Convention.

[15] As in Botticelli's painting *The Birth of Venus* (c. 1486).

[16] Wetter, 'The present status of the International Court of Arbitration of the ICC: An appraisal' (1990) 1 Am Rev Intl Arb 91, at 93.

[17] Mustill, 'Arbitration: History and background' (1989) 6 J Intl Arb 43, at 49. See also Schwebel, 'A celebration of the United Nations' New York Convention' (1996) 12 Arb Intl 83.

[18] The first three are also contained in the Model Law, Art. 7(1) and (2), and the fourth in Arts 34(2)(b) and 36(2)(b)(i). More recently, however, the UN Commission on International Trade Law (UNCITRAL) formulated and adopted a recommendation regarding the interpretation of Arts II(2) and VII(1) of the New York Convention on 7 July 2006, by which it recognised that Art. II(2), which defines the way in which the 'writing' requirement must be fulfilled, must be applied 'recognizing that the circumstances described therein are not exhaustive'. See paragraphs 2.13*ff*.

effect, added by the provisions of Article V(1)(a),[19] which stipulates that recognition or enforcement of an award may be refused if the party requesting refusal is able to prove that the arbitration agreement was made by a person under incapacity or that the agreement was invalid under the applicable law. Expressed positively,[20] these represent additional requirements to the effect that:

- the parties to the arbitration agreement must have legal capacity under the law applicable to them;
- the arbitration agreement must be valid under the law to which the parties have subjected it or, failing any indication thereon, under the law of the country where the award was made. (In the words used earlier in the New York Convention, in Article II(3), the agreement must not be 'null and void, inoperative or incapable of being performed'.)

In Part B of this chapter, each of these requirements is considered in turn.

B. Validity of an Arbitration Agreement

(a) Formal validity—need for writing

All of the international conventions on arbitration that have already been mentioned, as well as Option 1 of the Model Law, require that an agreement to arbitrate shall be 'in writing'. The reason for imposing this requirement is self-evident. A valid agreement to arbitrate excludes the jurisdiction of the national courts[21] and means that any dispute between the parties must be resolved by a private method of dispute resolution—namely, arbitration. This is a serious step to take, albeit one that has become increasingly commonplace. Good reasons therefore exist for ensuring that the existence of such an agreement should be clearly established. This is best done by producing evidence in writing, although, as already noted in Chapter 1, the trend in modern national legislation has moved towards the relaxation of this formal requirement.[22]

2.13

Article II(2) of the New York Convention defines 'writing' as follows: 'The term "agreement in writing" shall include an arbitral clause in a contract or an arbitration agreement, signed by the parties or contained in an exchange of letters or telegrams.'

2.14

---

[19] They are also to be found in the Model Law, Arts 34(2)(a) and 36(1)(a)(i).
[20] Although it should be noted that the burden of proof is on the party opposing recognition or enforcement, who must prove lack of capacity or invalidity.
[21] See the discussion in Chapter 1, paragraph 1.39.
[22] In this regard, see Landau, 'The requirement of a written form for an arbitration agreement: When "written" means "oral" ', Sixteenth ICCA Congress, London, 12–15 May 2002.

2.15 The requirement for signature by the parties has given rise to problems in some states,[23] but the general view is that a signature is not necessary, provided that the arbitration agreement is in writing.[24]

2.16 There has, however, been a revolution in communications since the New York Convention was drawn up in 1958. Telegrams, which were a frequent method of communicating an urgent message in writing, were largely replaced first by telex, later by fax, and now by email. This change is reflected in the Model Law, which goes much further than the New York Convention in its definition of 'writing', and has itself been the subject of important recommended interpretations and revisions.[25]

2.17 As revised in December 2006, the version of the Model Law now contains both a long and a short form option for Article 7. Option 1 provides as follows:[26]

> [...]
> (3) An agreement is in writing if its content is recorded in any form, whether or not the arbitration agreement or contract has been concluded orally, by conduct, or by other means.
> (4) The requirement that an arbitration agreement be in writing is met by an electronic communication if the information contained therein is accessible so as to be useable for subsequent reference; 'electronic communication' means any communication that the parties make by means of data messages; 'data message' means information generated, sent, received or stored by electronic, magnetic, optical or similar means, including, but not limited to, electronic data interchange (EDI), electronic mail, telegram, telex or telecopy.
> (5) Furthermore, an arbitration agreement is in writing if it is contained in an exchange of statements of claim and defence in which the existence of an agreement is alleged by one party and not denied by the other.
> (6) The reference in a contract to any document containing an arbitration clause constitutes an arbitration agreement in writing, provided that the reference is such as to make that clause part of the contract.

---

[23] See, e.g., the cases cited in Cohen, 'Agreements in writing: Notes in the margin of the Sixth Goff Lecture' (1997) 13 Arb Intl 273. This article is a response to the earlier Kaplan, 'Is the need for writing as expressed in the New York Convention and Model Law out of step with commercial practice?' (1996) 12 Arb Intl 27. More recently, see also *Kanematsu USA Inc. v ATS—Advanced Telecommunications Systems do Brasil Ltda*, SEC 885, 18 April 2012, in which the Brazilian Supreme Court of Justice held that a signature is required where a party seeks to incorporate into a contract an arbitration clause contained in a set of standard terms and conditions.

[24] See Obergericht of Basle, 3 June 1971, (1979) IV YBCA 309; *Miserecchi v Agnesi*, Judgment No. 3620, Corte di Cassazione, 13 December 1971, (1976) I YBCA 190, with comment by Barone in [1972] Riv di Dir Internaz, Priv e Proc 563.

[25] On 7 July 2006, UNCITRAL issued a recommendation that Art. II(2) of the New York Convention be applied 'recognizing that the circumstances described therein are not exhaustive'. Subsequently, on 4 December 2006, the Model Law was amended pursuant to General Assembly Resolution 61/33 to include notable changes to Art. 7 on the writing requirement.

[26] Option 1 has been adopted by, e.g., Singapore in its 2012 revision to the Singapore International Arbitration Act, s. 2A.

B. Validity of an Arbitration Agreement

2.18 Option 1 has brought the Model Law into line with current practice, as reflected by national legislation and court decisions. For instance, an exchange of telexes between two firms of brokers in Paris containing the simple statement 'English law—arbitration, if any, London according ICC Rules' has been held to be a valid arbitration agreement, providing for arbitration in London under the ICC Rules, with English law as the substantive law of the contract.[27]

2.19 However, whilst the formal requirements may be relaxed, there *is* almost inevitably a requirement for at least a permanent record ('useable for subsequent reference' in the terms of the Model Law) from which a written transcription can be made. For example, the Netherlands Arbitration Act 1986 requires that the arbitration agreement shall be proven by an instrument in writing expressly or impliedly accepted by the parties.[28] For its part, as mentioned in Chapter 1, Swiss law requires an agreement to be made in writing or by means of communication that allows it to be evidenced by a text. Section 178(1) of the Swiss Private International Law Act 1987 (Swiss PIL) states simply: 'As regards its form, an arbitration agreement shall be valid if made in writing, by telegram, telex, telecopier or any other means of communication which permits it to be evidenced by a text.'[29]

2.20 Thus, for the purposes of the Model Law Option 1, the requirement for writing may now be satisfied where there is a record 'in any form' of the content of the arbitration agreement.

2.21 Moreover, where a party takes part in an arbitration without denying the existence of an arbitration agreement,[30] it will, in the normal course, be bound by implied consent. In some systems of law, an oral agreement to arbitrate will be regarded as being 'in writing' if it is made 'by reference to terms which are in writing', or if an oral agreement 'is recorded by one of the parties, or by a third party, with the authority of the parties to the agreement'.[31] In these modern arbitration laws,

---

[27] *Arab African Energy Corporation Ltd v Olieprodukten Nederland BV* [1983] 2 Lloyd's Rep 419; however, such a form is not recommended. See also *Jianxi Provincial Metal and Minerals Import and Export Corporation v Sulanser Co. Ltd* [1996] ADRLJ 249, in which an exchange of communications between a party to the contract and a third party, copied to the other party, could constitute an agreement in writing.

[28] Netherlands Arbitration Act 1986, s. 1021; see the commentary on this article in Sanders and van den Berg, *The Netherlands Arbitration Act 1986: Text and Notes, English* (Kluwer, 1987), p. 12, where it is said that the Act abolishes the possibility, which existed under the old Act, that an arbitration agreement could be concluded orally, but that an arbitration agreement is deemed to be concluded if the parties appear before the arbitral tribunal without invoking the lack of an agreement prior to raising any defence.

[29] Similar wording is contained in s. 7 of the Indian Arbitration and Conciliation Act 1996. See *Great Offshore Ltd v Iranian Offshore Engineering and Construction Co.* (2008) 14 SCC 240 for an analysis of the Indian law position.

[30] See Sanders, 'Arbitration', in Cappelletti (ed.) *Encyclopedia of International and Comparative Law, Vol. XVI* (Brill, 1987), ch. 12, para. 106.

[31] See, e.g., the English Arbitration Act 1996, s. 5(43)*ff*. The 'implied consent' provisions of the Model Law are also to be found in s. 5(5). In *Heifer International Inc. v Christiansen* [2007] EWHC 3015 (TCC), the court held that an arbitration agreement was validly concluded by reference to a written arbitration clause contained in another contract.

there has, in effect, been a triumph of substance over form: as long as there is some written evidence of an agreement to arbitrate, the form in which that agreement is recorded is immaterial.[32]

2.22 Option 2 goes a step further. It does not refer to a writing requirement at all, but rather provides that it is sufficient to show 'agreement by the parties to submit to arbitration all or certain disputes'.[33] This reflects the latest position under some systems of law that arbitration agreements are not subject to any requirements of form. For instance, article 1507 of French Decree 2011-48 provides that 'an arbitration agreement shall not be subject to any requirements as to its form'.[34]

2.23 However, a degree of caution is necessary. First, even courts in jurisdictions familiar with international arbitration still sometimes refuse to enforce arbitration agreements that are not in a written document signed by the parties or otherwise contained in an exchange of communications between the parties.[35] Secondly, an arbitration agreement that is regarded as valid by an arbitral tribunal or court in one country may not be so regarded by the courts of the country in which the award falls to be enforced.[36] By way of example, the Norwegian Court of Appeal refused recognition of an award rendered in London because an exchange of emails did not, in its view, satisfy the writing requirement of Article II(2) of the New York Convention. Although such an electronic exchange was valid and sufficient to evidence the existence of an arbitration agreement as a matter of the law of the place of arbitration— that is, English law—the Court held that the validity of the arbitration agreement was to be separately assessed by the local enforcement authority and that 'it should not be sufficient for enforcement that the arbitral award is valid according to the law of the country in question' (in this case, England, the place of arbitration).[37]

---

[32] See, e.g., Liebscher, 'Interpretation of the written form requirement Art. 7(2) UNCITRAL Model Law' (2005) 8 Int ALR 164 and the cases cited therein.

[33] In recent revisions to their respective arbitration laws, Belgium and Scotland have adopted the Option 2 wording. See art. 1681 of the Code Judiciaire and s. 4 of the Arbitration (Scotland) Act 2010, respectively.

[34] See also the New Zealand Arbitration Act 1996, s. 7(1), which provides that 'an arbitration agreement may be made orally or in writing'.

[35] See, e.g., the decision of the Second Circuit Court of Appeals in *Kahn Lucas Lancaster Inc. v Lark International Ltd* 186 F.3d 210 (2nd Cir. 1999). This decision has been applied by a number of other US courts, which have arrived at varying interpretations (some liberal; others less so) of an 'exchange of letters and telegrams'. See, e.g., the US District Court of the Southern District of California decision in *Chloe Z Fishing Co. Inc. v Odyssey Re (London) Ltd* 109 F.Supp.2d 1048 (SD Cal. 2000); the US District Court of the Western District of Washington decision in *Bothell Bothell v Hitachi Zosen Corporation* 97 F.Supp. 2d 1048 (WD Wash. 2000); the Third Circuit Court of Appeals decision in *Standard Bent Glass Corporation v Glassrobots Oy* 333 F.3d 440, 449 (3rd Cir. 2003). Most recently, the District Court of the Southern District of New York has affirmed the *Kahn Lucas* approach, but found that email exchanges between the parties 'comfortably satisf[ied] the standard set by the [New York] Convention': *Glencore Ltd v Degussa Engineered Carbons LP* 848 F.Supp.2d 410 (SDNY 2012).

[36] See the discussion in Chapter 3 on the law governing the arbitration agreement.

[37] Decision of the Halogaland Court of Appeal (Norway), 16 August 1999, (2002) XXVII YBCA 519.

B. Validity of an Arbitration Agreement

Finally, there remain states in which special requirements of form *are* imposed in respect of agreements to arbitrate.[38] Accordingly, the relevant national law must be examined if there is reason to believe that the formal validity of an arbitration agreement is likely to be questioned under that law.

2.24

(b) A defined legal relationship

Almost all international arbitrations arise out of contractual relationships between the parties. However, for the purposes of both the New York Convention and the Model Law, it is sufficient that there should be a 'defined legal relationship' between the parties, whether contractual or not. Plainly, there has to be some contractual relationship (real or implied) between the parties, since there must be an agreement to arbitrate to form the basis of the arbitral proceedings. Given the existence of such an agreement, the dispute submitted to arbitration may be governed by principles of delictual or tortious liability rather than (as is usually the case) by the law of contract.

2.25

Thus, in *Kaverit Steel Crane Ltd v Kone Corporation*,[39] Kaverit commenced court proceedings alleging that Kone had breached certain licence and distribution agreements. Kone sought a stay and a reference to arbitration pursuant to the arbitration clause in the agreements. The clause stated that all disputes 'arising out of or in connection with this contract' would be referred to arbitration. The Alberta Queen's Bench Division refused the stay on the grounds that some of the claims by Kaverit contained allegations that went beyond breach of contract, for example conspiracy and inducing breach of contract. The court held that these tort-based claims fell outside the scope of the arbitration clause.

2.26

However, the Alberta Court of Appeal held that the wording of the arbitration clause was wide enough to bring within its scope any claim that relied on the existence of a contractual relationship, even if the claim itself was a claim in tort.[40] To give an example: because the claim alleging 'conspiracy by unlawful means to harm [Kaverit]' relied upon a breach of contract as the source of the 'unlawfulness', that dispute should be referred to arbitration. However, it was held that those claims that were not based on the existence of a contract should proceed to trial, not arbitration.[41]

2.27

---

[38] Including, particularly, the requirement in some jurisdictions, e.g. Paraguay, that an arbitration clause is not operative until a submission agreement has also been executed: see n. 6.

[39] (1992) 87 DLR (4th) 129, (1994) XVII YBCA 346.

[40] The Court held that a dispute 'arises out of or in connection with a contract' if the 'existence of the contract is germane either to the claim or the defence': ibid., at 295–297.

[41] Courts around the world have adopted even wider interpretations of similar clauses, although the underlying principles are similar. The Chinese courts have held that 'all disputes arising out of or in connection with the contract' will capture tortious claims: see the view of the Supreme People's Court (SPC) in SPC, *The Second National Foreign-related Commercial and Maritime Trial Work Meeting Minutes* (26 December 2005), art. 7. See also Decision No. 506/2010 of the Greek Supreme Court of 10 February 2010, in which the Court held that tortious claims were within the scope of a standard ICC arbitration clause. See also *ABI Group Contractors Pty v Transfield Pty Ltd* (1999)

2.28 Thus, subject to any provisions of the relevant applicable law, the terms of an arbitrator's jurisdiction and powers in any particular case depend on a proper construction of the arbitration agreement. The arbitral tribunal must consider the dispute in question and then elicit from the arbitration agreement whether or not the parties intended a dispute of the kind in question to be resolved by arbitration.[42]

(c) A subject matter capable of settlement by arbitration

2.29 In determining whether a dispute is capable of settlement by arbitration, one is asking whether a dispute is 'arbitrable'. Arbitrability, in the sense in which it is used both in this book and generally, involves determining which types of dispute may be resolved by arbitration and which belong exclusively to the domain of the courts. Both the New York Convention and the Model Law are limited to disputes that are 'capable of settlement by arbitration'.[43]

2.30 This requirement is dealt with in more detail later in this chapter.[44] Suffice to say for now that, in principle, *any* dispute should be just as capable of being resolved by a private arbitral tribunal as by the judge of a national court. However, it is precisely because arbitration is a private proceeding with public consequences[45] that some types of dispute are reserved for national courts, the proceedings of which are generally in the public domain. It is in this sense that they are not 'capable of settlement by arbitration'. National laws establish the domain of arbitration as opposed to that of the local courts. Each state decides which matters may or may

---

14 Mealey's Intl Arb Rep G1, summarised in (1999) XXIV YBCA 591; *Multistar Leasing Ltd v Twinstar Leasing Ltd*, Civil Action Case No. 98-1330, US District Ct, Eastern District of Louisiana, 28 August 1998, summarised in (2000) XXV YBCA 871; *American Bureau of Shipping v Tencara SpA*, Judgment No. 8744, Italian Corte di Cassazione, Plenary Session, 26 June 2001, summarised in (2002) XXVII YBCA 509. See also the commentary by van den Berg, 'Scope of the arbitration agreement' (1996) XXI YBCA 415. Finally, see also the decision of the Federal Court of Australia in *Walter Rau Neusser Oel Und Fett Ag v Cross Pacific Trading Ltd* [2005] FCA 1102, discussed in Morrison, 'Defining the scope of arbitrable disputes in Australia: Towards a "liberal" approach?' (2005) 22 J Intl Arb 569.

[42] The decision of the English House of Lords in *Fiona Trust and Holding Corporation v Privalov* [2007] UKHL 40 offers further guidance. Lord Hoffmann considered the prior case law concerning the construction of arbitration clauses and the precise meaning of wording such as 'arising out of', and opined that 'the distinctions which they make reflect no credit upon English commercial law': at [12]. He continued, at [13]:

> [T]he construction of an arbitration clause should start from the assumption that the parties, as rational businessmen, are likely to have intended any dispute arising out of the relationship into which they have entered or purported to enter to be decided by the same tribunal. The clause should be construed in accordance with this presumption unless the language makes it clear that certain questions were intended to be excluded from the arbitrator's jurisdiction.

[43] New York Convention, Arts II(1) and V(2)(a); Model Law, Arts 34(2)(b)(i) and 36(1)(b)(i).
[44] See paragraphs 2.211*ff*.
[45] For example, in the recognition and enforcement of the award.

not be resolved by arbitration in accordance with its own political, social, and economic policy.

C. Parties to an Arbitration Agreement

(a) Capacity

2.31 Parties to a contract must have legal capacity to enter into that contract, otherwise it is invalid. The position is no different if the contract in question happens to be an arbitration agreement. The general rule is that any natural or legal person who has the capacity to enter into a valid contract has the capacity to enter into an arbitration agreement. Accordingly, the parties to such agreements include individuals, as well as partnerships, corporations, states, and state agencies.

2.32 If an arbitration agreement is entered into by a party who does not have the capacity to do so, the provisions of the New York Convention (or the Model Law, where applicable) may be brought into operation, either at the beginning or at the end of the arbitral process. At the beginning, the requesting party asks the competent court to stop the arbitration on the basis that the arbitration agreement is void, inoperative, or incapable of being performed.[46] At the end of the arbitral process, the requesting party asks the competent court to refuse recognition and enforcement of the award on the basis that one of the parties to the arbitration agreement is 'under some incapacity'[47] under the applicable law.

2.33 The rules governing capacity to contract can be found in the standard textbooks on the law of contract. They vary from state to state. In the context of an arbitration agreement, it is generally necessary to have regard to more than one system of law. In practice, the issue of capacity rarely arises in international arbitration. Nevertheless, it may be helpful to look briefly at the kind of questions that may arise, first in relation to individuals and corporate entities, and secondly—more importantly perhaps—in relation to states and state entities.

(i) Natural persons

2.34 The New York Convention and the Model Law, where applicable, require the parties to an arbitration agreement to have the capacity to enter into that agreement 'under the *law* applicable to them'.[48] More correctly, this should perhaps refer to the 'law or *laws*' applicable to them. The capacity of an individual to enter into a contract within the state of his or her place of domicile and residence will depend upon the law of that state—but, in the context of an international contract, it may

---

[46] New York Convention, Art. II(3); Model Law, Art. 8(1).
[47] New York Convention, Art. V(1)(a); Model Law, Art. 36(1)(a).
[48] Otherwise, the agreement will be regarded as invalid and accordingly unenforceable: see the provisions of the New York Convention and the Model Law cited above.

become necessary to have regard also to the law of the contract. For instance, a person aged 20 may well have the capacity to enter into an agreement under his or her own law, but not under the law governing the transaction in question. If that transaction were to turn out badly, a party who lacks capacity under one or other of the two systems of law might rely upon this as a reason for not carrying out the contract (or any agreement to arbitrate contained within it). However, there may be an applicable rule of law that defeats such ingenuity. For instance, Article 13 of the Rome I Regulation,[49] which applies among EU member states, provides:

> In a contract concluded between persons who are in the same country, a natural person who would have capacity under the law of that country may invoke his incapacity resulting from the law of another country, only if the other party to the contract was aware of that incapacity at the time of the conclusion of the contract or was not aware thereof as a result of negligence.

(ii) Corporations

2.35 The capacity of a corporation to enter into a contract is governed primarily by its constitution and the law of its place of incorporation. A corporation is required to act through its directors and officers in accordance with its constitution and its own governing law. If a corporation enters into a transaction that goes beyond its power (in other words, a transaction that is ultra vires) and the transaction turns out badly, it would be open to the corporation to contend that the agreement was not binding on it and that it was not obliged to arbitrate any dispute. To guard against this possibility, it is not unusual for states to have specific rules of law that restrict or abrogate the doctrine of ultra vires, so as to protect persons dealing in good faith with corporations.[50]

2.36 In addition to issues of corporate governance, the laws of some states may restrict a corporation from initiating arbitration in certain circumstances relating to the status of the corporate entity itself. For example, a number of states within the United States have statutes that restrict a corporation that is not 'in good standing' under the laws of that state from initiating any type of legal proceeding, including arbitration. Thus the failure of a corporation to maintain its good standing could be the basis of an application (or 'motion', to borrow from the US legal lexicon) to stay or dismiss an international arbitration filed by such corporation.

---

[49] Regulation (EC) No. 593/2008 of the European Parliament and of the Council of 17 June 2008 on the law applicable to contractual obligations (Rome I), OJ L 177/6, 4 July 2008. The uniform rules of this Regulation do not apply to questions involving the status or legal capacity of natural persons, except as stated.

[50] See, e.g., within the European Union, Directive 2009/101/EC of the European Parliament and of the Council of 16 September 2009 on coordination of safeguards which, for the protection of the interests of members and third parties, are required by Member States of companies within the meaning of the second paragraph of Article 48 of the Treaty, with a view to making such safeguards equivalent, OJ L 258/11, 1 October 2009.

C. Parties to an Arbitration Agreement

(iii) States and state agencies

It would be unusual to encounter a corporation that insisted, in its constitution, that any disputes should be referred to the courts, rather than to arbitration. It is less unusual, however, to find states or state agencies that are not permitted to refer disputes between themselves and a private party to arbitration. In France, for example, under article 2060 of the Civil Code, disputes concerning public collectives and public establishments, and all matters involving public policy, may not be referred to domestic arbitration.[51] However, certain industrial and commercial public entities may be authorised by decree to enter into arbitration agreements. Moreover, disputes arising out of industrial or commercial activities of public entities may be referred to *international* arbitration.[52] In Belgium, public law entities were at one time prohibited from concluding arbitration agreements. This prohibition has now been abolished, but some restrictions remain.[53] In Brazil, the higher courts have consistently ruled that a state body is not prohibited from agreeing to resolve disputes by arbitration and is bound by any such agreement.[54] In other countries, the state or state agency must obtain the approval of the relevant authorities before entering into an agreement for international commercial arbitration.[55]

2.37

---

[51] In 2007, the Labetoulle Report proposed to abolish the prohibition contained in art. 2060 and a draft law was prepared in order to 'broaden the possibility for recourse to arbitration for public bodies and to clarify the procedural regime of arbitrations involving public law': Groupe de travail sur l'arbitrage en matière administrative, *Rapport*, 13 March 2007, available online at http://www.justice.gouv.fr/art_pix/Rapport_final.pdf (in French). At the time of writing, no amendments have yet been made to art. 2060.

[52] See the decision of the Paris Cour d'Appel in *INSERM v Fondation F. Saugstad*, Paris Cour d'Appel, 13 November 2008. See also the decision of the Conseil d'État Libanais, *Etat Libanais v Societe FTML (Cellis) SAL*, 17 July 2001, in which the Lebanese State Council, with reference to French law, held that public entities could submit to international arbitration only those contracts that do not involve the exercise of the state's prerogatives of public power. This ruling was heavily criticised in Lebanon and resulted in a new Law No. 40 being enacted by the Lebanese Parliament establishing the validity of arbitration agreements in all contracts of the state and public entities, with the exception of administrative contracts being effective only after approval of the Council of Ministers. However, it is now generally accepted that, under French law, public entities cannot rely on provisions of French law to evade obligations contained in an international arbitration agreement that they have signed: Hanotiau and Olivier, 'Arbitrability, due process, and public policy under Article V of the New York Convention: Belgian and French perspectives' (2008) 25 J Intl Arb 721, at 724.

[53] The arbitration agreement must relate to the settlement of disputes regarding the formation or the performance of an agreement: see Code Judiciaire, art. 1676(3).

[54] See *Companhia Paranaense de Gas ('Compagás') v Carioca Passarelli Consortium ('Consortium')*, Appeal No. 247.646-0, Paraná Court of Appeals, 11 February 2004; *Copel v Energetica Rio Pedrinho S.A.*, Agravo de Instrumento No. 174.874-9, Paraná Court of Appeals, 11 May 2005; *Companhia Estadual de Energia Eléctrica ('CEEE') v AES*, Recurso Especial No. 612.439-RS, Paraná Superior Court of Justice, 14 September 2006.

[55] For example, in Venezuela, s. 4 of the Commercial Arbitration Act 1998 provides that when one of the parties to the arbitration agreement is a state entity (or an entity in which the state holds a stake of at least 50 per cent), the arbitration agreement must be specifically approved by the relevant minister. Similar restrictions are contained in art. 139 of the Iranian Constitution and s. 10 of the Saudi Arabian Law of Arbitration (Royal Decree No. M/34 of 16 April 2012).

2.38 This means that, before entering into an arbitration agreement with a foreign state or state entity, it is advisable to check that the persons entering into the contract on behalf of the state or state agency have the necessary authority to do so. It is also wise to check that any necessary procedures for obtaining consent to an arbitration agreement have been followed. Indeed, it is sensible to include a statement to this effect in the contract.[56]

2.39 It is plainly unsatisfactory for a state or state agency to be entitled to rely on its own law to defeat an agreement into which it has entered freely. A praiseworthy attempt to deal with this problem was made in the European Convention of 1961. This provided that persons considered by the law applicable to them to be 'legal persons of public law' should have the right to conclude valid arbitration agreements. It also provided that if a state were to wish to limit this facility in some way, it should say so on signing, ratifying, or acceding to the Convention.[57] Although the European Convention has met with only limited success, progressive states have dealt with the problem by adopting a similar approach. Swiss law, for example, provides that:

> If a party to the arbitration agreement is a state or enterprise or organisation controlled by it, it cannot rely on its own law in order to contest its capacity to be a party to an arbitration or the arbitrability of a dispute covered by the arbitration agreement.[58]

This is a provision that all states would do well to follow, and there is now, in any event, a growing international consensus to the effect that where a state entity has agreed to resolve disputes by international arbitration, it cannot rely on its own domestic laws in order to avoid submitting to the arbitral process.[59]

2.40 Some writers[60] have argued that restrictions imposed by a state on its capacity to enter into an arbitration agreement should not be qualified as issues of capacity, but rather as issues of arbitrability. It is argued that the restriction is self-imposed and could be waived at any time by the state concerned. It is not a true limitation on capacity, such as the protection of persons under mental disability. Accordingly,

---

[56] It would also be advisable to ensure that, under the relevant state law, the subject matter of the contract is 'arbitrable' in the sense discussed later.

[57] European Convention of 1961, Art. II(1) and (2).

[58] Swiss PIL, s. 177(2). Presumably, however, the state concerned might try to rely on its own law to defeat recognition or enforcement outside Switzerland of any arbitration award against it.

[59] See, e.g., *Benteler v State of Belgium*, Ad Hoc Award, 18 November 1983; Award in ICC Case No. 4381, 113 J du Droit Intl 1102 (1986); *Gatoil International Inc. v National Iranian Oil Co.*, High Court of Justice, Queen's Bench Division, 21 December 1988, (1988) XVII YBCA 587; *Buques Centroamericanos SA v Refinadora Costarricense de Petroleos SA* US Dist. LEXIS 5429 (SDNY 1989). See also the 1989 Resolution of the Institut de Droit International, which provides that '[a] State, a state enterprise, or a state entity cannot invoke incapacity to arbitrate in order to resist arbitration to which it has agreed.'

[60] See, e.g., Paulsson, 'May a state invoke its internal law to repudiate consent to international commercial arbitration?' (1986) 2 Arb Intl 90.

C. Parties to an Arbitration Agreement

it should be treated as a matter of 'subjective arbitrability', rather than as a matter of capacity.[61]

2.41 In practice, the important point is that there may be restrictions on the power of a state or state entity to enter into an arbitration agreement, whether these restrictions are qualified as matters of capacity or of subjective arbitrability. Legal advisers and others dealing with a state or state entity should be aware of this point.

(b) Third parties to the arbitration agreement

2.42 Party consent is a prerequisite for international arbitration. Such consent is embodied in an agreement to arbitrate, which, as discussed earlier,[62] will generally be concluded 'in writing' and signed by the parties. The requirement of a signed agreement in writing, however, does not altogether exclude the possibility that an arbitration agreement concluded in proper form between two or more parties might also bind other parties. Third parties to an arbitration agreement have been held to be bound by (or entitled to rely on) such an agreement in a variety of ways: first, by operation of the 'group of companies' doctrine, pursuant to which the benefits and duties arising from an arbitration agreement may, in certain circumstances, be extended to other members of the same group of companies; and secondly, by operation of general rules of private law—principally those governing assignment, agency, and succession. Thus, by way of example: the affiliate of a signatory to an arbitration clause may find itself a co-respondent in arbitration proceedings; an assignee of an insurance contract may be able to commence arbitration against the insurer of the original insured party; a principal may find itself bound by an arbitration agreement signed by its agent; or a merged entity may continue to prosecute arbitral proceedings commenced by one of its original constituent entities.

(i) The 'group of companies' doctrine

2.43 A number of arbitral tribunals and national courts have been called upon to consider whether an arbitration agreement concluded by a company may be binding on its group affiliates, by reason of the group being a 'single economic reality'.[63] Such attempts are often motivated by the stated aim of finding the 'true' party in interest—and, of greater practical importance, of targeting a more creditworthy member of the relevant group of companies.

---

[61] It is interesting to note in this context that the Swiss PIL, s. 177(2), refers both to 'capacity' and to 'arbitrability', so that—at the very least—the two concepts may merge.
[62] See paragraph 2.13.
[63] See generally Derains, 'L'extension de la clause d'arbitrage aux non-signatories: La doctrine des groupes de sociétés' (1994) 8 ASA Special Series 241; Jarosson, 'Conventions d'arbitrage et groupes de sociétés' (1994) 8 ASA Special Series 209; Derains and Schaf, 'Clauses d'arbitrage et groupes de sociétés' [1985] RDAI 231; Fadlallah, 'Clauses d'arbitrage et groupes de sociétés' [1984–85] Travaux du Comité Français de Droit International Privé 105; Gaillard and Savage (eds) *Fouchard Gaillard Goldman on International Commercial Arbitration* (Kluwer Law International, 1999), paras 500*ff*.

2.44 Although an objection of principle may readily be made—namely, that corporate personality is created precisely in order to contain liability within a particular corporate entity—in practice much will depend on the construction of the arbitration agreement in question, as well as the circumstances surrounding the entry into, and performance of, the underlying contract.[64]

2.45 The *Dow Chemical* case[65] has been invoked as the leading authority on the 'group of companies' doctrine. In that case, a claim was successfully brought before an ICC tribunal not only by the companies that had signed the relevant agreements, but also by their parent company, a US corporation, and a French subsidiary in the same group. However, a subsequent ICC tribunal ruled that 'there is no general rule in French international arbitration law that would provide that non-signatory parties members of the same group of companies would be bound by an arbitration clause.'[66] The Swiss and English courts have also refused to accept that a third party may be bound by an arbitration agreement merely because it has a legal or commercial connection to one of the parties.[67]

2.46 Some now argue that the *Dow Chemical* award and the judgment of the Paris Cour d'Appel confirming the award have been misinterpreted, and do not in fact lend support to an independent 'group of companies' doctrine. They note that, on a close reading of the decision, the tribunal's analysis was based on the parties' common intention, and its decision may be explained by reference to the traditional requirement for consent in international arbitration.[68]

2.47 In fact, the tribunal found that:

> [T]he arbitration clause expressly accepted by certain of the companies of the group should bind the other companies which, *by virtue of their role in the conclusion, performance, or termination of the contracts* containing said clauses, and *in accordance with the mutual intention of all parties* to the proceedings, appear to have

---

[64] Sandrock has argued that all of the cases usually discussed in connection with the 'group of companies' theory ought to be regarded (or to have been decided) on theories of agency, such as the theory of the undisclosed principal (or, in some legal systems, indirect representation), the reverse construction of mandat apparent, or principles of good faith and estoppel: Sandrock, 'Arbitration agreements and groups of companies', in Dominice, Patry, and Reymond (eds) *Études Pierre Lalive* (Helbing & Lichtenhahn, 1993), p. 625; Sandrock, 'The extension of arbitration agreements to non-signatories: An enigma still unresolved', in Baums, Hopt, and Hom (eds) *Corporations, Capital Markets and Business in the Law: Liber Amicorum Richard M Buxbaum* (Kluwer Law International, 2000), p. 461.

[65] ICC Case No. 4131/1982 (Interim Award) in *Dow Chemical France v ISOVER Saint Gobain (France)* (1983) 110 J du Droit Intl 899, noted by Derains in (1984) IX YBCA 131.

[66] ICC Case No. 11405/2001.

[67] See ICC Case No. 4504/1985–86 (1986) 113 J du Droit Intl 1118; *Peterson Farms Inc. v C&M Farming Ltd* [2004] EWHC 121; *City of London v Sancheti* [2008] EWCA Civ 1283.

[68] Hanotiau, 'Consent to arbitration: Do we share a common vision?', 2010 Annual Freshfields Lecture, London, 21 October 2010. See also Ferrario, 'The group of companies doctrine in international commercial arbitration: Is there any reason for this doctrine to exist?' (2009) 26 J Intl Arb 647.

C. Parties to an Arbitration Agreement

been veritable parties to these contracts or to have been principally concerned by them and the disputes to which they may give rise.[69]

The tribunal did refer to the relevant group of companies in that case as 'one and the same economic reality [*une réalité économique unique*]'.[70] However, it reached its decision on the basis of 'the intention common to all companies involved', and referred only 'subsidiarily' to the notion of a 'group of companies'.[71] 2.48

Recent case law confirms that where a court or tribunal is tasked with determining whether a third party is bound by an arbitration agreement, it will focus on the parties' common intention[72] and may consider a variety of factors in this regard, including: (a) whether the non-signatory actively participated in the conclusion of the contract containing the arbitration agreement;[73] (b) whether the non-signatory has a clear interest in the outcome of the dispute;[74] and (c) whether the non-signatory is party to a contract that is 'intrinsically inter-twined' with the contract under which the dispute has arisen.[75] 2.49

Accordingly, the *Dow Chemical* case may perhaps be best characterised as authority for the proposition that 'conduct can be an expression of consent and that among all the factual elements . . . the existence of a group of companies may be relevant'.[76] 2.50

---

[69] Derains, n. 65, at 135 (emphasis added).

[70] *Dow Chemical*, n. 65, at 904. The tribunal looked carefully at the parties' intentions in concluding the relevant arbitration clauses and said that the negotiating record showed that 'neither the "Sellers" nor the "Distributors" attached the slightest importance to the choice of the company within the Dow Group that would sign the contracts', and further (Derains, n. 65, at 132) that:

> [T]he arbitration clause expressly accepted by certain of the companies of the group should bind the other companies which, by virtue of their role in the conclusion, performance, or termination of the contracts containing said clauses, and in accordance with the mutual intention of all parties to the proceedings, appear to have been veritable parties to these contracts or to have been principally concerned by them and the disputes to which they may give rise.

[71] *Société Isover-Saint-Gobain v Société Dow Chemical France*, Paris Cour d'Appel, 22 October 1983, [1984] Rev Arb 98, at 100–101, n. Chapelle.

[72] See, e.g., *Chloro Controls (I) P Ltd v Severn Trent Water Purification Inc. and ors*, Supreme Court of India, 28 September 2012. The Court referred repeatedly to 'the real intention of the parties' to support its conclusion that an arbitration clause contained in a shareholders' agreement should be extended to a non-signatory company.

[73] See, e.g., *Sponsor AB v Lestrade*, Court of Appeal of Pau, 26 November 1986, [1988] Rev Arb 153 (the Court emphasised that Sponsor AB played an important role in the conclusion and execution of the contract, and in fact was 'the soul, inspirer and, in a word, the brains of the contracting party'); ICC Case No. 5103/1988 [1988] J du Droit Intl 1206; *Société Orthopaedic Hellas v Société Amplitude*, No. 11-25.891, Cass. Civ. 1ere, 7 November 2012.

[74] See, e.g., *Trelleborg do Brasil Ltda v Anel Empreendimentos Participações e Agropecuária Ltda*, Apelação Cível No. 267.450.4/6-00, 7th Private Chamber of São Paulo Court of Appeals, 24 May 2004.

[75] *Khatib Petroleum Services International Co. v Care Construction Co. and Care Service Co.*, Case No. 4729 of the Judicial Year 72, Egypt's Court of Cassation, June 2004; *Chaval v Liebherr*, Recurso Especial No. 653.733, Brazilian Superior Court of Justice, 3 August 2006.

[76] Hanotiau, 'Consent to arbitration: Do we share a common vision?' 2010 Annual Freshfields Lecture, London, 21 October 2010.

(ii) 'Piercing the corporate veil'

2.51 A court or tribunal may conclude that a third party is bound by an arbitration agreement where there is evidence that the party to the agreement is being used as 'a device or façade' in order to avoid or conceal liability.[77] In such circumstances, a party may also seek to rely on the 'alter ego' principle.[78]

(iii) Third-party beneficiaries of rights under a contract

2.52 Under some systems of law, a third party may also enforce rights conferred under the terms of a contract in certain circumstances. The English Contracts (Rights of Third Parties) Act 1999 provides that a third party ('A') may enforce a contractual term where the contract expressly provides that A may do so or purports to confer a benefit on A.[79] Where the contract contains an arbitration agreement, the third party is bound by the agreement and constrained to follow the arbitral process.[80]

2.53 A similar principle exists in France. The Cour de Cassation has held that where a contract conferring a benefit on a third party (*stipulation pour autrui*) contains an arbitration clause, the third party is obliged to refer any claim to arbitration. Moreover, that party is precluded from objecting to the tribunal's jurisdiction if it is joined to an action as a respondent.[81] The Italian courts have also confirmed that, in certain circumstances, once a third party decides to take the benefit of a contract, it can be bound to abide by all of the terms of the contract, including any arbitration agreement.[82] The US courts have invoked the principle of estoppel to similar effect.[83]

---

[77] See *Prest v Petrodel* [2013] UKSC 34, at [22] *per* Lord Sumption.

[78] See, e.g., *Wm Passalacqua Builders v Resnick Developers* 933 F.2d 131 (2nd Cir. 1991). The alter ego doctrine has also been successfully applied in respect of states and state entities: see *Bridas SAPIC, Bridas Energy International Ltd et al. v Government of Turkmenistan and Turkmennneft* 345 F.3d 347 (5th Cir. 2006), discussed in the news section of [2006] Int ALR N3334; cf. ICC Case No. 9151, *Joint Venture Yashlar and Bridas SAPIC v Government of Turkmenistan*, Interim Award of 8 June 1999.

[79] Contracts (Rights of Third Parties) Act 1999, s. 1.

[80] See Contracts (Rights of Third Parties) Act 1999, s. 8. See also *Nisshin Shipping Co. Ltd v Cleaves & Co. Ltd* [2003] EWHC 2602 (Comm), in which the English High Court held that brokers seeking to enforce the terms of charterparties that conferred benefits on them (the payment of commissions) were bound by the arbitration clause therein. However, see *Fortress Value Recovery Fund I LLC v Blue Skye Special Opportunities Fund LP* [2013] EWCA Civ 367, in which the English Court of Appeal held that a third party joined as *defendant* in a contract claim in the English courts could not invoke the arbitration clause in the contract to obtain a stay of proceedings under s. 9 of the English Arbitration Act 1996.

[81] *Banque populaire Loire et Iyonnais v Société Sangar*, Cour de Cassation (1ere Ch. Civ.), 11 July 2006.

[82] See, e.g., *Assicurazioni Generali SpA v Tassinari*, Judgment No. 2384, Corte di Cassazione, 18 March 1997; *L'Italia SpA v Milani*, Judgment No. 3207, Corte de Cassazione, 1 April 1994.

[83] See *Cargill International SA v M/T Pavel Dybenko* 991 F.2d 1012, 1019 (2nd Cir. 1993); *American Bureau of Shipping v Société Jet Flint SA* 170 F.3d 349, 353 (2nd Cir. 1999); *Avila Group Inc. v Norma J of California* 426 F.Supp. 537, 542 (DCNY 1977) ('To allow [a plaintiff] to claim the benefit of the contract and simultaneously avoid its burdens would both disregard equity and contravene the purpose underlying enactment of the Arbitration Act'); *Astra Oil Co. Inc. v Rover*

C. Parties to an Arbitration Agreement

(iv) Assignment, agency, and succession

Assignment The effect of an assignment of a contract on an arbitration clause contained therein will be determined principally by reference to the law governing the assignment in question, as well as the law governing the arbitration agreement. If the arbitration agreement is assignable under the relevant laws, there will be a further question as to the particular form, if any, which the assignment must take. This requirement must not be confused with the writing requirement that applies to the arbitration agreement itself. 2.54

Different laws take differing positions on whether an arbitration agreement should be presumed as having been assigned along with the main contract. Some laws, for example German, French, and English laws, make this presumption.[84] New York law also adopts this general presumption, albeit with certain limited exceptions.[85] The Swedish Supreme Court appears to have adopted a middle position—namely, that an arbitration clause will be presumed to be assignable if the parties have not expressly agreed otherwise, but that, once assigned, it will operate vis-à-vis the assignee only if that party has actual or constructive knowledge of the arbitration clause.[86] 2.55

Arbitration agreements concluded by agents The binding effect of an arbitration agreement concluded by an agent on behalf of a principal involves questions of authority (that is, the agent's ability to bind the principal to such agreements) and allied questions of necessary form.[87] Thus an ICC tribunal invited to determine 2.56

Navigation, Ltd 344 F.3d 276, 279, n. 2 (2nd Cir. 2003); *Birmingham Associates Ltd v Abbott Laboratories* 547 F.Supp.2d 295 (SDNY 2008), 2008 US Dist LEXIS 30321.

[84] See Bundesgerichtshof decision (1978) 71 BGHZ 162, 164–165, and (2000) 53 NJW 2346. Traditionally, French law required explicit consent to transfer the arbitration agreement on assignment of the main contract (arts 1166 and 1275 of the Code Civil make a distinction between perfect and imperfect novation, of which only the former discharges the original debtor of its obligations, but requires the original creditor's consent to that effect). However, recent case law has confirmed that transfer of the arbitration agreement is automatic on assignment of the main contract, whether domestic or international: *Sté Alcatel Business Systems et Alcatel Micro Electronics c/v and ors*, Cass. Civ. 1ere, 27 March 2007, (2007) 1 Bull Civ 129, (2007) 3 J du Droit Intl 18. For the English law position, see *West Tankers Inc. v RAS Riunione Adriatica di Sicurta SpA (The Front Comor)* [2005] 2 All ER (Comm) 240.

[85] There was a common law principle in New York law that arbitration was an 'obligation' not assumed by an assignee of a contract: see *United States v Panhandle Eastern Corporation et al.* 672 F.Supp. 149 (D. Del. 1987); *Gruntal & Co., Inc. v Ronald Steinberg et al.* 854 F.Supp. 324 (DNJ 1994); *Lachmar v Trunkline LNG Co.* 753 F.2d 8, 9–10 (2nd Cir. 1985); cf. *Banque de Paris v Amoco Oil* 573 F.Supp. 1465, 1472 (SDNY 1983). However, according to *GMAC Commer Credit LLC v Springs Indus* 171 F.Supp.2d 209 (SDNY 2001), 2001 US Dist LEXIS 5152, 44 UCC Rep. Serv. 2d 708 (6th Cir. 2001), this principle was superseded by New York's adoption of the Uniform Commercial Code (UCC) § 9-318 in 1964 (now § 9-404 after the UCC was revised in 2000). In *GMAC*, the Court held that 'the adoption of the Article 9 of the U.C.C. means that a finance assignee suing on an assigned contract is bound by that contract's arbitration clause unless it secured a waiver from the signatory seeking to arbitrate': *GMAC*, at 215.

[86] *Ms Emja Braack Shiffahrts KG v Wärtsilä Diesel AB*, Supreme Court of Sweden, 15 October 1997, [1998] Rev Arb 431, at 433, n. Hansson, Lecoanet, and Jarvin.

[87] See Reiner, 'The form of the agent's power to sign an arbitration agreement and Art. II(2) of the New York Convention' (1999) 9 ICCA Congress Series 82.

whether a principal was bound by an arbitration agreement concluded by its agent distinguished between the law governing the arbitration agreement (in that case, the law of the seat of the arbitration), the laws that governed the agent's capacity to conclude an arbitration agreement on behalf of the principal (the law of the principal's registered office), and the form in which such capacity should have been conferred on the agent (the law of the jurisdiction in which the agreement between the agent and the principal was concluded).[88]

2.57 National laws feature substantial differences on questions of necessary form (that is, whether the principal's written authorisation is required) and content (that is, whether the principal's authorisation need expressly envisage the conclusion of an arbitration agreement). For example, both Swiss and Austrian law require the principal expressly to authorise an agent to enter into an arbitration agreement on its behalf in order for that principal to be bound by such an agreement, but only Austrian law requires such express authorisation to be in writing.[89] Under Italian,[90] French,[91] and German[92] law, no particular form of authorisation is required.

2.58 Succession and novation Questions of succession in international arbitration arise most often in connection with companies, rather than natural persons.[93] The general rule is that arbitration agreements, like other contracts, enure to the benefit of universal successors of companies[94]—that is, the entities that succeed

---

[88] ICC Case No. 5832/1988 (1988) 115 J du Droit Intl 1198. Applying Austrian law, which requires authorisation to be given in writing by a principal to an agent in order for the latter validly to conclude an arbitration agreement ('to provide clear and simple evidence and to protect the parties against the waiver of procedural guarantees'), the tribunal refused to regard the principal as bound by the purported arbitration agreement. The conflict-of-laws rules on these different aspects of agency are notoriously complex. See further Dicey, Morris, and Collins, *The Conflict of Laws* (15th edn, Sweet & Maxwell, 2012), pp. 2109ff.

[89] On Austrian law, see s. 1008 of the Civil Code and n. 88; on Swiss law, see art. 396(3) of the Swiss Federal Code of Obligations.

[90] See *Rocco Giuseppe e Fli v Federal Commerce and Navigation Ltd*, Judgment No. 6915, Corte di Cassazione, 15 December 1982, (1985) 10 YBCA 464.

[91] See Code Civil, art. 1985; Code de Commerce, art. L1103 (formerly art. 109) (in respect of the contract of mandate or mandat); *Total v Achille Lauro*, Judgment No. 361, Corte di Cassazione, 25 January 1977, (1977) 17 Rassegna dell'Arbitrato 94, at 95. However, under art. 1989 of the Code Civil, the conclusion of an arbitration agreement requires specific authorisation.

[92] See Landesgericht Hamburg, Judgment of 19 December 1967, [1968] Arbitrale Rechtspraak 138, at 140 (in respect of a commercial broker or *Handelsmakler*, under s. 75h(2) of the German Commercial Code). In Sandrock, 'The extension of arbitration agreements to non-signatories: An enigma still unresolved', in Baums, Hopt, and Horn (eds) *Corporations, Capital Markets and Business in the Law: Liber Amicorum Richard M Buxbaum* (Kluwer Law International, 2000), p. 467, the author expresses a belief that an arbitration agreement concluded by an agent or representative without the principal's written authorisation would bind that principal only if, in the circumstances, third parties' legitimate expectations were to require protection.

[93] On natural persons, see s. 8(1) of the English Arbitration Act 1996: 'Unless otherwise agreed by the parties, an arbitration agreement is not discharged by the death of a party and may be enforced by or against the personal representatives of that party.'

[94] See, e.g., Interim Award in ICC Case No. 7337 (1999) 24 YBCA 149; *Fyrnetics Ltd v Quantum Group Inc.* 293 F.3d 1023 (7th Cir. 2002).

them as a result, for example, of a voluntary merger,[95] or by operation of law. Such questions involve the status of a company and are thus generally to be resolved by reference to the law of its incorporation (or, in respect of natural persons, by reference to the law of succession).[96]

(c) Joinder and intervention

2.59 Unlike litigation in state courts, in which third parties can often be joined to proceedings, the jurisdiction of an arbitral tribunal to allow for the joinder or intervention of third parties to an arbitration is limited. The tribunal's jurisdiction derives from the will of the parties to the arbitration agreement and therefore joinder or intervention is generally only possible with the consent of all parties concerned.[97] As between the original parties to the arbitration agreement, such consent may be either express, implied, or by reference to a particular set of arbitration rules agreed to by the parties that provide for joinder.[98]

2.60 Following recent revisions to many of the main institutional rules, most now contain a specific provision for joinder of third parties to an arbitration.[99] For example, Article 7(1) of the ICC Rules provides that:

> A party wishing to join an additional party to the arbitration shall submit its request for arbitration against the additional party (the 'Request for Joinder') to the Secretariat. The date on which the Request for Joinder is received by the Secretariat shall, for all purposes, be deemed to be the date of the commencement of arbitration against the additional party.... No additional party may be joined after the confirmation or appointment of any arbitrator, unless all parties, including the additional party, otherwise agree. The Secretariat may fix a time limit for the submission of a Request for Joinder.

---

[95] See Award in ICC Case No. 6223/1991 (1997) 8 ICC Bulletin 69. See also *AT&S Transportation LLC v Odyssey Logistics & Technology Corporation* 803 NYS 2d 118 (2005), in which the US courts held that the sale of substantially all of the assets of company A to company B constituted a de facto merger and bound company B to an arbitration agreement signed by company A.

[96] See the section on insolvency at paragraph 2.141.

[97] See, e.g., the Privy Council (Turks and Caicos Islands) decision in *The Bay Hotel and Resort Ltd v Cavalier Construction Co. Ltd* [2001] UKPC 34, discussed in Melnyk, 'The extent to which non-contracting parties can be encouraged or compelled to take part in arbitral proceedings: The English (Arbitration Act 1996) perspective' (2003) 6 Int ALR 59, at 63. On the issue of joinder generally, see Hanotiau, *Complex Arbitrations: Multiparty, Multicontract, Multi-issue and Class Actions* (Kluwer Law International, 2005), ch. IV; Voser, 'Multiparty disputes and joinder of third parties', Presented at the ICCA Congress, Dublin, 9 June 2008.

[98] See Platte, 'When should an arbitrator join cases?' (2002) 18 Arb Intl 67; Mohan and Teck, 'Some contractual approaches to the problem of inconsistent awards in multi-party, multi-contract arbitration proceedings' (2005) 1 Asian Intl Arb J 161, at 164.

[99] Besides the UNCITRAL Rules, see also: Hong Kong International Arbitration Centre (HKIAC) Rules, Art. 27; ICC Rules 2012, Art. 7; London Court of International Arbitration (LCIA) Rules, Art. 22(1)(viii); Singapore International Arbitration Centre (SIAC) Rules, Art. 24(1)(b); Swiss Rules, Art. 4(2).

2.61 Some rules now set out a detailed procedural framework for joinder applications,[100] but most are still silent on the issue. The Swiss Rules and the Rules of the Hong Kong International Arbitration Centre (HKIAC) also allow for intervention—that is, a third party may, of its own initiative, request to participate in the arbitration.[101]

2.62 Parties should be mindful that joining a third party to arbitration proceedings may be problematic if the tribunal has already been constituted. It is important to ensure that all parties are treated equally and, if relevant, that the procedure for participation in the appointment of the tribunal is respected.[102]

D. Analysis of an Arbitration Agreement

(a) Scope

2.63 An arbitration agreement confers a mandate upon an arbitral tribunal to decide any and all of the disputes that come within the ambit of that agreement. It is important that an arbitrator should not go beyond this mandate.[103] If he or she does so, there is a risk that his or her award will be refused recognition and enforcement under the provisions of the New York Convention. Article V(1)(c) provides that recognition and enforcement may be refused: 'If the award deals with a difference not contemplated by or not falling within the terms of the submission to arbitration, or if it contains decisions on matters beyond the scope of the submission to arbitration...' The Model Law contains an almost identical provision to the effect that an award may be set aside by the competent court, as well as refused recognition and enforcement, if it 'deals with a dispute not contemplated by or not falling within the terms of the submission to arbitration or contains decisions on matters beyond the scope of the submission to arbitration'.[104]

2.64 There are, in general, three categories of claim that are potentially within the scope of an arbitration agreement. These are:

- contractual claims (including claims incidental to the contract, such as *quantum meruit*);

---

[100] The ICC and the HKIAC Rules both contain detailed provisions on joinder procedure, including the required contents of the request for joinder and the written submissions of the other parties.
[101] Swiss Rules, Art. 4(2); HKIAC Rules, Art. 27(6).
[102] See Voser, 'Multiparty disputes and joinder of third parties', Presented at the ICCA Congress, Dublin, 9 June 2008, at 46–49.
[103] The poet's reflection that 'a man's reach should exceed his grasp, or what's a heaven for?' seems not to be apposite for an international arbitrator: Browning, 'Andrea del Sarto' (1855), line 97.
[104] Model Law, Arts 34(2)(iii) and 36(i)(a)(iii). The reference to a 'submission to arbitration' would include an arbitration clause and, e.g., the terms of reference in an ICC arbitration (as to which, see Chapter 1). There is a saving provision under both the Convention and the Model Law to the effect that if it is possible to separate the matters that *were* submitted to arbitration from those that were not, the award may be saved in respect of the matters that were submitted.

D. Analysis of an Arbitration Agreement

- claims in tort; and
- statutory claims.

The first two are self-explanatory. The third relates to those claims that arise out of legislation that might bind the parties, such as securities and antitrust legislation. In all three categories of claim, it is necessary to determine whether a particular claim or defence has a sufficient connection with the contract to be covered by the arbitration agreement on its terms.[105] Likewise, in relation to statutory claims, the arbitral tribunal or a judge may need to examine a claim or defence in relation to the wording of the arbitration agreement in order to decide whether there is a sufficiently close connection. In all such cases, the form of words used in the arbitration agreement will be important.

(i) Forms of wording

2.65 It is important to ensure that the wording adopted in an arbitration agreement is adequate to fulfil the intentions of the parties. Usually, when parties agree to resolve any disputes between them by arbitration, they intend such recourse to arbitration to be mandatory, rather than optional. Accordingly, the arbitration agreement should be drafted so as to make clear that resolving disputes by arbitration is not only the parties' right, but also their obligation.[106] Similarly, where parties include an arbitration agreement in their contract, they usually intend to resolve *all* disputes between them by this method (unless a specific exception is made). Accordingly, the arbitration agreement should be drafted in broad, inclusionary terms, rather than referring only certain categories of dispute to arbitration and leaving others to the jurisdiction of national courts.[107]

2.66 Fortunately, most national courts now regard arbitration as an appropriate way of resolving international commercial disputes and, accordingly, seek to give effect to arbitration agreements wherever possible,[108] rather than seek to narrow the scope

---

[105] For example, the Austrian Supreme Court held that 'disputes *resulting from* the agreement' does not cover non-contractual claims based on competition law that are connected to the underlying contract in no more than a 'functionally illustrative' way: Decision of the Supreme Court (*Oberster Gerichtshof*) No. 4 Ob. 80/08f, 26 August 2008, discussed in (2009) 12 Int ALR 40 (emphasis added).

[106] As a matter of Indian case law, arbitration clauses that state that 'parties *may* refer disputes to arbitration' have been held in the past to be optional rather than mandatory, thereby requiring the parties to agree afresh (by way of a submission agreement) to refer a particular dispute to arbitration: see the judgment of the Indian Supreme Court in *Wellington Associates Ltd v Mr Kirit Mehta* (2000) 4 SCC 272. See also the judgment of the Punjab and Haryana High Court in *Sudarshan Chopra and ors v Company Law Board and ors* (2004) 2 Arb LR 241.

[107] See the recommendations of the ICC, *Final Report of the Working Group on the ICC Standard Arbitration Clause*, ICC Doc. No. 420/318, 21 October 1991.

[108] A striking illustration of this policy can be seen in the decision of the US Federal District Court in *Warnes SA v Harvic International Ltd*, 3 December 1993, summarised in [1994] ADRLJ 65. The arbitration clause referred to the 'New York Commercial Arbitration Association', a non-existent association. The court held that it was clear that the parties intended to arbitrate and that an agreement on a non-existent forum was the equivalent of an agreement to arbitrate

of the agreement so as to preserve the court's jurisdiction. Thus the English Court of Appeal referred to a 'presumption of one-stop arbitration' in the interpretation of the arbitration agreement that is increasingly reflected in law and practice around the world.[109] Similarly, the Swiss Federal Tribunal tends to interpret arbitration clauses broadly: a general reference to 'disputes related to the agreement' may extend to claims arising out of ancillary or connected contracts, provided that those contracts do not contain different dispute resolution clauses.[110]

2.67 Where an issue *does* arise as to the scope of an arbitrator's jurisdiction, the issue may fall to be determined by the arbitrator (possibly at the outset of the arbitration) or by a competent court (for example where enforcement of the award is sought). There is a chance that the answer will differ according to the tribunal before which it is raised: in general, arbitrators are likely to take a less restrictive approach than the courts. This is understandable. An arbitrator is likely to consider that, because there *are* disputes between the parties, it would be sensible to try, as far as possible, to resolve them all in the same set of proceedings. A national court would no doubt be sympathetic to this approach—but it would nevertheless have it in mind that, unlike an arbitral award, its judgment might set a precedent for the future.[111] Whatever the tribunal, its decision will depend upon its interpretation of the words of the arbitration agreement and the intention of the parties, in the light of the law that governs that agreement.

2.68 General words such as 'claims', 'differences', and 'disputes' have been held by the English courts to encompass a wide jurisdiction in the context of the particular agreement in question.[112] In the United States, the words 'controversies or claims' have similarly been held to have a wide meaning, and if other words are used, it may be considered that the parties intended some limitation on the kind of disputes referred to arbitration.[113]

---

that does not specify a forum. Accordingly, the parties were directed to arbitrate in the American Arbitration Association (AAA) system.

[109] See *Fiona Trust & Holding Corporation v Yuri Privalov* [2007] EWCA Civ 20, at [19]. This pro-arbitration approach was endorsed by the House of Lords: *Premium Nafta Products Ltd (20th Defendant) and ors v Fili Shipping Co. Ltd and ors* [2007] UKHL 40.

[110] See, e.g., Decision No. 4A-103/2011, 20 September 2011, in which an arbitration clause contained in a licence agreement was held to be wide enough to cover a dispute arising out of a connected sale-and-purchase agreement. The English High Court's decision in *PT Thiess Contractors Indonesia v PT Kaltim Prima Coal and anor* [2011] EWHC 1842 (Comm) demonstrates the difficulties that may arise where separate, but related, contracts contain different dispute resolution clauses. The court was faced with a dispute that engaged two contracts: one containing an arbitration clause; the other submitting to the non-exclusive jurisdiction of the English courts. The court considered the scope of both dispute resolution provisions and the proper characterisation of the dispute, and ultimately decided that the English courts had jurisdiction.

[111] Or, even worse, might be overruled on appeal!

[112] See, e.g., *Woolf v Collis Removal Service* [1948] 1 KB 11, 18; *F & G Sykes (Wessex) Ltd v Fine Fare Ltd* [1967] 1 Lloyd's Rep 53; *The Angelic Grace* [1995] 1 Lloyd's Rep 87 (CA).

[113] In the case of *Prima Paint Corporation v Conklin Mfg Co.* 388 US 395, 87 S.Ct 1801, 18 L.Ed.2d 1270 (1967), the words 'any controversy or claim arising out of or relating to this agreement' were described as a broad arbitration clause; in *Scherk v Alberto-Culver* 417 US 506 (1974),

D. Analysis of an Arbitration Agreement

Linking words such as 'in connection with', 'in relation to', 'in respect of', 'with regard to', 'under',[114] and 'arising out of'[115] may also be important in any dispute as to the scope of an arbitration agreement. However, in *Fiona Trust*,[116] the English courts drew a line under this debate as a matter of English law. Arriving at a broad interpretation of the arbitration clause in question, the Court of Appeal held as follows: **2.69**

> For our part we consider that the time has now come for a line of some sort to be drawn and a fresh start made at any rate for cases arising in an international commercial context. Ordinary businessmen would be surprised at the nice distinctions drawn in the cases and the time taken up by argument in debating whether a particular case falls within one set of words or another very similar set of words…If any businessman did want to exclude disputes about the validity of a contract, it would be comparatively simple to say so.[117]

Finally, when considering the scope of the arbitration agreement and in addition to the form of words used, the parties, by their conduct in referring a matter to arbitration, may be taken as impliedly agreeing to confer on the arbitrator jurisdiction beyond that which would have existed pursuant to the arbitration clause. Accordingly, a claim in tort that may not be within the scope of the arbitration clause may nevertheless come within an arbitrator's jurisdiction where the parties address that claim in the arbitral proceedings, without reservation as to jurisdiction.[118] **2.70**

(b) Basic elements

There is no shortage of learned commentaries on the drafting of an arbitration agreement.[119] They are of little importance or relevance, except to those specialists **2.71**

'any controversy or claim' was held to include statutory claims under the Securities Exchange Act of 1934.

[114] For example, in *Onex Corporation v Ball Corporation*, 24 January 1994, summarised in [1996] ADRLJ 193 and (1995) XX YBCA 275, the Ontario Court of Justice held that a claim for rectification was a dispute arising 'under' the contract.

[115] See *The Angelic Grace* [1995] 1 Lloyd's Rep 87 (CA). In the United States, a decision of the Fifth Circuit Court of Appeals on 13 May 1998 evidenced an equally broad approach to the construction of a clause that referred to arbitration 'any dispute, controversy or claim arising out of or in relation to or in connection with "the agreement" ': *Pennzoil Exploration and Production Co. v Ramco Energy Ltd* 139 F.3d 1061, 1068 (5th Cir. 1998). The approach of the German courts appears to be much the same: see Oberlandesgericht, Frankfurt, 24 September 1985, summarised in (1990) XV YBCA 666, concerning the expression 'arising out of'. A similarly wide interpretation was given to the term 'concerning' in *Fletamentos Maritimos SA v Effjohn International BV* [1996] 2 Lloyd's Rep 304.

[116] *Fiona Trust & Holding Corporation v Yuri Privalov* [2007] EWCA Civ 20.

[117] Ibid., at [17]. This was expressly endorsed by the House of Lords in its rejection of the appeal: *Premium Nafta Products Ltd (20th Defendant) and ors v Fili Shipping Co. Ltd and ors* [2007] UKHL 40, at [13]. The English courts have followed this approach in subsequent cases: see, e.g., *Skype Technologies SA v Joltid Ltd* [2009] EWHC 2783 (Ch); *Starlight Shipping Co. v Allianz Marine & Aviation Versicherungs AG* [2011] EWHC 3381 (Comm).

[118] See, e.g., *The Almare Prima* [1989] 2 Lloyd's Rep 376.

[119] See, in particular, Gélinas, 'Arbitration clauses: Achieving effectiveness' (1998) 9 ICCA Congress Series 47. See also Paulsson, Rawding, and Reed (eds) *The Freshfields Guide to Arbitration*

in arbitration who may be called upon to draft a particularly complicated arbitration clause, or who may be asked to prepare a detailed submission agreement for use in a major arbitration.[120] International commercial arbitrations usually take place pursuant to a standard form arbitration clause, recommended either by the arbitral institution to which they refer, such as the ICC, International Centre for Dispute Resolution (ICDR), or the London Court of International Arbitration (LCIA), or by the United Nations Commission on International Trade Law (UNCITRAL). Any subsequent arbitration takes place according to the rules of either the institution concerned or of UNCITRAL, and these rules will generally be adequate to guide the process from beginning to end, including (if necessary) the constitution of the arbitral tribunal, the filling of any vacancies, the exchange of written submissions, and so on. Where the parties wish to provide for ad hoc arbitration, but not to make use of the UNCITRAL Rules, it will generally be sufficient to adopt a clause that makes it clear that all disputes are to be referred to arbitration. Also, the clause should specify that this is to take place in a state that has a modern law of arbitration, which, if necessary, will provide for the appointment of arbitrators, the filling of vacancies, and so on. In France, for example, a simple clause such as 'Resolution of disputes: arbitration, Paris', whilst not recommended, would be held as a valid submission to arbitration in an international commercial contract.[121] The French law on international arbitration would then give such support to the arbitral process as required, including appointment of the arbitral tribunal under article 1493 of the French New Code of Civil Procedure.

2.72 Arbitration clauses are usually drawn in wide terms, to ensure that all disputes that arise out of or in connection with a particular contract or contractual relationship are referred to arbitration. It is possible to limit arbitration to certain disputes, leaving others to the courts, but this is not generally desirable.[122] If a dispute does

---

(Kluwer Law International, 2010); Park, 'When and why arbitration matters', in Beresford Hartswell (ed.) *The Commercial Way to Justice* (Kluwer Law International, 1997), pp. 73–99, at p. 96; Derains, 'Rédaction de la clause d'arbitrage', in Desbois (ed.) *Le Droites Affaires Propriété Intellectuelle* (Libraries Techniques, 1987), p. 15. Also worth mentioning is Bernadini, 'The arbitration clause of an international contract' (1992) 9 J Intl Arb 45; Ball, 'Just do it: Drafting the arbitration clause in an international agreement' (1993) 10 J Intl Arb 29; Debevoise & Plimpton, *Annotated Model Arbitration Clauses for International Contracts* (Debevoise & Plimpton, 1996).

[120] In one arbitration between a state and a private corporation in which two of the authors took part as counsel, the negotiation and agreement of the detailed submission agreement took eighteen months, and involved consideration of several different systems of law and of transnational rules.

[121] Gaillard and Savage (eds) *Fouchard Gaillard Goldman on International Commercial Arbitration* (Kluwer Law International, 1999), para. 486; cf. the decision to similar effect in *Arab African Energy Corporation Ltd v Olieprodukten Nederland BV* [1983] 2 Lloyd's Rep 419.

[122] Gélinas, 'Arbitration clauses: Achieving effectiveness' (1998) 9 ICCA Congress Series 47, at 56, states: 'Unless the parties want to exclude from arbitration certain controversies…or to limit the arbitration procedure to precisely identified areas of conflict a broad clause is to be recommended over one that will attempt to list every possible type of dispute.' He points out that most modern judges are now prepared to give effect to broad wording such as that found in the standard ICC arbitration clause and adds that 'if no limitation is intended to the scope of the arbitration agreement, a broad clause must be preferred…'.

D. *Analysis of an Arbitration Agreement*

arise, there may well be a threshold issue as to whether or not it is a dispute that is covered by the arbitration clause—in other words, a dispute about what kind of dispute it is.

2.73 As already indicated, where parties agree to put an arbitration clause into their contract, they will usually select a standard form, or 'model', clause, either from one of the arbitral institutions or from an internationally recognised authority such as UNCITRAL. These model clauses are widely drawn. The UNCITRAL model refers to '[a]ny dispute, controversy or claim arising out of or relating to this contract, or the breach, termination or invalidity thereof'. Similar language is used in the ICC and LCIA model forms.

2.74 Where a model clause is used, it is sensible to supplement it by reference to the number of arbitrators, the place of arbitration, the law or laws governing the arbitration clause and the contract of which it forms part, the language of the arbitration, and so on. Otherwise any problems that arise in these respects and on which the parties cannot agree will have to be resolved by the relevant arbitral institution or by the arbitral tribunal itself.

2.75 There follows a note of the key elements of an arbitration clause, including those that may usefully supplement a model clause. Since these key elements have already been discussed, either in this or the preceding chapter, the note is brief.

(i) A valid arbitration agreement

2.76 First, there must be a valid arbitration agreement. In particular, it must be made clear, as it is in the model clauses, that the parties intend that any and all disputes between them shall be finally *resolved* by *arbitration*. Examples of defective clauses in which such an intention was not made clear are given later in this chapter.

(ii) Number of arbitrators

2.77 In an international arbitration, there should be an uneven number of arbitrators, and it is suggested that, in general, three at most will be sufficient.[123] The system of appointing only two arbitrators, with an 'umpire' or 'referee' to adjudicate between them if they cannot agree, may be appropriate for arbitrations within a defined trade or commodity association, but is impracticable for the generality of international arbitrations.

(iii) Establishment of the arbitral tribunal

2.78 This important subject is dealt with in Chapter 4.

---

[123] See Chapter 4, paragraph 4.29.

(iv) Ad hoc or institutional arbitration

2.79 Whether the tribunal will be ad hoc or institutional is one of the most important decisions that has to be taken—and, of course, it has to be taken at the wrong time. In an ideal world, it would be possible to wait until any disputes had arisen and then decide, according to their importance and complexity, how they should best be handled. Would a simple ad hoc agreement, backed by a modern system of arbitration law, be sufficient to dispose of the disputes without involving a national court[124] or an arbitral institution?[125] If not, would it be sensible to enlist the help and support (and the rules) of one of the arbitral institutions, and if so, which institution: the ICC, the LCIA, or the ICDR? Or would it be better, given the complexity of the dispute, the amount of money involved, the expertise likely to be required, and the importance of the issues to be resolved, to negotiate a detailed submission agreement?

2.80 These questions would be best answered when a dispute arises. But the reality is that, by this stage, the parties, like a divorcing couple, may not be talking to each other—or, at most, will be doing so only through their lawyers. Accordingly, good sense dictates that the agreement to arbitrate should be negotiated and concluded at the same time as the contract to which it relates. As one commentator has expressed it: 'The primary objective, in inserting an arbitration clause in a contract, is to ensure that when the time comes—that is, when a dispute parts the parties—neither one will be able to escape arbitration . . .'[126]

2.81 The choice between ad hoc and institutional arbitration has already been considered in Chapter 1,[127] and need not be repeated here. The criteria by which an arbitral institution should be judged are also considered in that chapter.[128]

(v) Filling vacancies in the tribunal

2.82 During the course of an arbitration, it may sometimes be necessary to replace an arbitrator, whether because his or her appointment has been successfully challenged, or because he or she has died, or for some other reason, such as incapacity. The rules of the established arbitral institutions contain comprehensive provisions to cover such contingencies,[129] as do modern laws of arbitration.[130] Where there is a submission agreement that is intended, as far as possible, to be self-contained,[131] provisions for filling any vacancies in the tribunal must be spelled out in some detail.

---

[124] For instance, to appoint the arbitrator or arbitrators.
[125] To provide a set of rules and to assist in the administration of the arbitration.
[126] Gélinas, 'Arbitration clauses: Achieving effectiveness' (1998) 9 ICCA Congress Series 47, at 51.
[127] See paragraphs 1.140*ff.*
[128] See paragraphs 1.159*ff.*
[129] See, e.g., the ICC Rules, Art. 15; LCIA Rules, Arts 10 and 11.
[130] See, e.g., the English Arbitration Act 1996, s. 27.
[131] In the sense that it will not need to be supplemented by the applicable law.

D. Analysis of an Arbitration Agreement

(vi) Place of arbitration

2.83 The place of arbitration is another decision of major importance. It constitutes the seat of the arbitration and the law of that place governs the arbitral proceedings. This is fully considered in Chapter 3. It is advisable for the parties themselves to choose a suitable place of arbitration, rather than to leave the choice to others. In doing so, as discussed in Chapter 3, they should locate their arbitration in a state the laws of which are adapted to the needs of modern international commercial arbitration and which is a party to the New York Convention. They should also take account of practical matters, such as distance, availability of adequate hearing rooms, backup services, and so on.

(vii) Governing law

2.84 The parties' contract should contain a choice of law clause and they should also consider making express provision for the governing law of the arbitration agreement. In *Sulamérica*,[132] the English Court of Appeal held that where parties have not expressly agreed on a governing law for their arbitration agreement, their choice of law for the main contract will be a 'strong indication' that they wished to adopt the same law for the arbitration agreement. Where the contract does not contain a 'choice of law' clause (or the arbitration agreement is not part of a contract), the court will turn to the parties' choice of seat in order to determine the law with which the arbitration agreement has its 'closest and most real connection'. Again, this topic is discussed in full in Chapter 3.[133]

(viii) Default clauses

2.85 It is important that the failure or refusal of one of the parties to take part should not frustrate an arbitration. The defaulting party is usually the respondent, who sees that it has nothing to win and may have much to lose by taking part in proceedings that are likely to lead to an award against it. Exceptionally, however, a claimant may lose heart in the face of a substantial counterclaim. It may then be the respondent who wishes to proceed. The rules of the arbitral institutions usually contain adequate default provisions; so too does Article 30 of the UNCITRAL Rules, which provides:

1. If, within the period of time fixed by these Rules or the arbitral tribunal, without showing sufficient cause:
   (a) The claimant has failed to communicate its statement of claim, the arbitral tribunal shall issue an order for the termination of the arbitral proceedings, unless there are remaining matters that may need to be decided and the arbitral tribunal considers it appropriate to do so;

---

[132] *Sulamérica CIA Nacional de Seguros SA v Enesa Engenharia SA* [2012] EWCA Civ 638. The Court of Appeal's decision in *Sulamérica* has recently been followed by the High Court in *Habas Sinai Ve Tibbi Gazlar Istihsal Endustrisi AS v VSC Steel Co. Ltd* [2013] EWHC 4071 (Comm).
[133] See paragraph 3.11.

(b) The respondent has failed to communicate its response to the notice of arbitration or its statement of defence, the arbitral tribunal shall order that the proceedings continue, without treating such failure in itself as an admission of the claimant's allegations; the provisions of this subparagraph also apply to a claimant's failure to submit a defence to a counterclaim or to a claim for the purpose of a set-off.

2. If a party, duly notified under these Rules, fails to appear at a hearing, without showing sufficient cause for such failure, the arbitral tribunal may proceed with the arbitration.

3. If a party, duly invited by the arbitral tribunal to produce documents, exhibits or other evidence, fails to do so within the established period of time, without showing sufficient cause for such failure, the arbitral tribunal may make the award on the evidence before it.

Where there is no default clause in the relevant rules of arbitration, it is sensible to include one in the arbitration clause.

(ix) Language

2.86 It is both customary and logical for the language of the arbitration to be the language of the contract. This will be the usual position in an institutional arbitration, although the arbitral tribunal usually has discretion to direct that other languages may be used or that documents may be admitted in their original language without the need for a translation. Thus, by way of notable example, Article 20 of the ICC Rules expressly provides that, 'in the absence of an agreement by the parties, the Arbitral Tribunal shall determine the language or languages of the arbitration, due regard being given to all relevant circumstances, including the language of the contract'.

2.87 Sometimes, a contract is made in two languages, each to be of equal authenticity. In such cases, simultaneous translations at the hearing of the arbitration may be unavoidable (although it slows down the proceedings and is not inexpensive).

(x) Multi-tier clauses

2.88 Parties to an arbitration agreement may decide that, prior to submitting any dispute to arbitration, they want to attempt an amicable settlement of the matter through direct negotiations or third-party assisted non-binding procedures such as mediation. Clauses that envisage an escalation of the dispute through at least two different forms of dispute resolution procedure are called 'multi-tier' dispute resolution clauses.[134]

---

[134] For a general discussion on multi-tier clauses in international arbitration, see Jolles, 'Consequences of multi-tier arbitration clauses: Issues of enforcement' (2006) 72 Arbitration 329; Jolles, 'Multi-tier dispute resolution: *Asghar and others v The Legal Services Commission and another*' (2005) 71 Arbitration 103. See also Chapter 1.

D. Analysis of an Arbitration Agreement

The advantage of such clauses is that they require the parties to explore fully the possibility of amicable settlement prior to the launch of often lengthy, expensive, and disruptive arbitral proceedings. The disadvantage is that if amicable settlement is possible, the parties are likely to explore the possibility in any event at the time that the dispute arises, and if it is not, the pre-arbitral tiers simply delay and obstruct the launch of determinative proceedings. Views therefore vary as to the merits of such clauses, although there tends to be general agreement on at least one aspect: if an arbitration clause is going to begin by requiring amicable negotiations between the parties, it should require that such discussions necessarily involve members of senior management who have not been personally implicated in the underlying dispute. **2.89**

Until recently, clauses providing for amicable discussions or negotiations have been dismissed by the English courts as 'a bare agreement to negotiate', which 'has no legal content' and is therefore unenforceable.[135] Following the decision in *Cable & Wireless*,[136] there has been a marked shift in the English courts' position. In that case, the High Court acknowledged that 'there is an obvious lack of certainty in a mere undertaking to negotiate ... because a court would have insufficient objective criteria to decide whether one or both parties were in compliance or breach of such a provision'.[137] However, it held that a multi-tier clause may be enforceable if it provides for 'a sufficiently certain and definable minimum duty of participation', and remarked that where the clause contains 'an unqualified reference to ADR [alternative dispute resolution]', that minimum duty 'should not be hard to find'.[138] **2.90**

Many multi-tier clauses have since failed the certainty threshold established in *Cable & Wireless*. In *Sulamérica*,[139] the English High Court held that the parties' agreement to ADR was unenforceable because there was no clear undertaking to enter into mediation, no clear provision for the appointment of a mediator, and no clearly defined mediation process. Most recently, in *Tang Chung Wah*,[140] the English High Court refused to enforce a multi-tier clause on the basis that it was 'too equivocal' and 'too nebulous', and contained no 'guidance as to the quality or nature of the attempts to be made to resolve a dispute'.[141] The Swiss courts adopted **2.91**

---

[135] *Walford v Miles* [1992] 2 WLR 174.
[136] *Cable & Wireless v IBM United Kingdom* [2002] EWHC 2059 (Comm), [2002] CLC 1319.
[137] Ibid., at 1326.
[138] Ibid., at 1327.
[139] *Sulamérica Cia Nacional de Seguros SA v Enesa Engenharia SA* [2012] EWHC 42 (Comm).
[140] *Tang Chung Wah v Grant Thornton International Ltd* [2013] All ER (Comm) 1226. In contrast, in the recent case of *Emirates Trading Agency LLC v Prime Mineral Exports Private Ltd* [2014] EWHC 2104, the English High Court upheld a multi-tier clause that required the parties to seek to resolve any dispute by 'friendly discussion' before referring such dispute to arbitration. The court's rationale was that the clause was sufficiently certain and complete to be enforceable in that the obligation in question was time-limited, and there was an implied and well-defined standard of good faith by which to judge compliance with it (i.e. fair, honest, and genuine discussions).
[141] *Tang Chung Wah*, at [72].

a similar approach in *X GmbH*,[142] in which the multi-tier clause did not provide any procedural framework for negotiations and did not prescribe a time limit for the initiation of conciliation proceedings.

2.92 Courts in other jurisdictions are more readily prepared to give effect to an agreement to engage in a non-binding ADR process. The Australian courts, for instance, consider that an agreement to negotiate in good faith entails an undertaking to behave in a particular manner and is therefore more than a mere 'agreement to agree'.[143] Similarly, the Singapore High Court has held that a bare agreement to mediate is valid and enforceable, referring to the traditional Asian value of promoting friendly negotiations and settlement whenever possible.[144]

2.93 Irrespective of the applicable law, care should always be taken when drafting multi-tier clauses to define the ADR procedure clearly (for example stipulating a specific time period, such as thirty days, for negotiations between senior management), along with the parties' respective obligations.[145]

(xi) Sole option clauses

2.94 Under 'sole option', or 'unilateral option', clauses, one party has a choice as to whether to bring a claim in a specified forum other than the dispute resolution forum that binds the other party.

2.95 The English courts have consistently ruled that sole option clauses are valid and enforceable under English law. In *Law Debenture Trust*,[146] the relevant legal instruments provided that disputes would be resolved by the English courts but the bondholders would have the right to refer a claim to arbitration if they so wished. The court stated:

> I give no weight to the use...of pejorative terms such as 'veto'. Nor is it correct so [*sic*] say that the provisions are somehow less than even handed in any relevant way. They give an additional advantage to one party, but so do many contractual provisions.[147]

---

[142] See the decision of the Swiss Federal Tribunal in *X GmbH v Y Sàrl*, Decision No. 4A_46/2011, 16 May 2011.

[143] See, e.g., *Hooper Bailie Associated v Natcon Group Pty* (1992) 28 NSWLR 206, in which the Supreme Court of New South Wales stated that what was enforced was not cooperation and consent, but participation in a process from which cooperation and consent might come. See also *United Group Rail Services v Rail Corporation New South Wales* [2002] CLC 1324.

[144] *International Research Corporation Plc v Lufthansa Systems Asia Pacific Pte Ltd* [2012] SGHC 226. See also Art. 13 of the UNCITRAL Model Law on International Commercial Conciliation, which states that courts and tribunals must give effect to agreements to attempt conciliation pre-arbitration.

[145] See, e.g., *Asghar v Legal Services Commission* [2004] EWHC 1803, [2004] Arb LR 43; Stockholm Institute, Interim Award of 17 July 1992, (1997) XXII YBCA 197, 201; Swiss Federal Tribunal decision of 6 June 2007, (2008) 1 ASA Bulletin 87, discussed in Boog, 'How to deal with multi-tiered dispute resolution clauses: Note on the Swiss Federal Supreme Court's Decision 4A_18/2007 of 6 June 2007' (2008) 26 ASA Bulletin 103.

[146] *Law Debenture Trust Corporation plc v Elektrim Finance BV* [2005] EWHC 1412 (Ch). See also *NB Three Shipping Ltd v Harebell Shipping Ltd* [2005] 1 Lloyd's Rep 205.

[147] *Law Debenture Trust*, at [44].

D. Analysis of an Arbitration Agreement

2.96 The courts of many other jurisdictions have also confirmed that sole option clauses are valid and enforceable under their domestic laws.[148]

2.97 In Russia, the position is more problematic. In *Russian Telephone Co.*,[149] the Presidium of the Supreme Arbitrazh Court held that an arbitration agreement that gave one party the sole option to refer disputes to the Russian courts instead of ICC arbitration in London violated the principle of procedural equality between litigating parties and was therefore unenforceable. However, it did not strike out the clause altogether; instead, it construed the clause so that *both* parties had the choice to either arbitrate or litigate.[150]

2.98 The position under French law is also uncertain following *X v Banque Privée Edmond de Rothschild Europe (Rothschild)*.[151] In that case, the dispute resolution clause restricted one party to litigate in a specific court, but provided that the other party (a bank) was free to select 'any other court of competent jurisdiction'. The Cour de Cassation held that the clause was 'potestative in nature' and 'for the sole benefit of the Bank', and was therefore contrary to the Brussels Regulation.[152] It remains to be seen whether the *Rothschild* case will prove authoritative where a sole option clause involves recourse to arbitration.[153]

(xii) Other procedural matters

2.99 Other procedural matters need to be covered only in a clause providing for ad hoc arbitration, or where the parties wish to deviate in certain respects from the rules that they have adopted in their arbitration clause. An example is where the parties adopt the UNCITRAL Rules, but wish the presiding arbitrator to make an award as if he or she were sole arbitrator in the event that a majority award is not possible.[154]

---

[148] In the United States, see, e.g., *DiMercurio v Sphere Drake Insurance plc* 202 F.3d 71 (1st Cir. 2000); in Italy, see *Astengo v Comune di Genova*, Judgment No. 2096, Corte di Cassazione, 22 October 1970; in Singapore, see *WSG Nimbus Pte Ltd v Board of Control For Cricket in Sri Lanka* [2002] SGHC 104; in Australia, see *PMT Partners Pty Ltd v Australian National Parks & Wildlife Service* (1995) 184 CLR 302.

[149] *Russian Telephone Co. v Sony Ericsson Mobile Communications Rus*, Case No. A40-49223/11-112-401, 19 June 2012.

[150] The Court did not address the validity of the arbitration agreement as such, but instead based its decision on the jurisprudence of the Russian Constitutional Court and the European Court of Human Rights concerning the right to a fair trial and the opportunity to present one's case.

[151] Cour de Cassation, 26 September 2012.

[152] Council Regulation (EC) No. 44/2001 of 22 December 2000 on jurisdiction and the recognition and enforcement of judgments in civil and commercial matters, OJ L 12/1, 16 January 2001. The English courts recently rejected an argument based on the *Rothschild* case and upheld a unilateral jurisdictional clause in *Mauritius Commercial Bank v Hestia Holdings Ltd* [2013] EWHC 1328 (Comm).

[153] If so, this would contradict earlier authority: see Cour d'Appel of Angers, 25 September 1972, [1973] Rev Arb 164.

[154] See the UNCITRAL Rules, Art. 33; only in relation to questions of procedure may the presiding arbitrator decide on his or her own in the absence of a majority.

2.100 The parties may also wish to confer special powers on the arbitral tribunal that do not normally exist under the law governing the arbitration or under the rules of the relevant arbitral institution, if any.[155] These additional powers may enable the arbitral tribunal to grant remedies that otherwise might not be available under the applicable law. For example, power may be given to order a party to provide security in relation to an amount in dispute, either by paying it into a special account established in the name of the arbitral tribunal or into some other blocked escrow account.[156]

(c) Separability

2.101 The concept of the separability of the arbitration clause[157] is both interesting in theory and useful in practice.[158] It means that the arbitration clause in a contract is considered to be separate from the main contract of which it forms part and, as such, survives the termination of that contract. Indeed, it would be entirely self-defeating if a breach of contract or a claim that the contract was voidable were sufficient to terminate the arbitration clause as well; this is one of the situations in which the arbitration clause is most needed.

2.102 Separability thus ensures that if, for example, one party claims that there has been a total breach of contract by the other, the contract is not destroyed for all purposes. Instead:

> It survives for the purpose of measuring the claims arising out of the breach, and the arbitration clause survives for determining the mode of their settlement. The purposes of the contract have failed, but the arbitration clause is not one of the purposes of the contract.[159]

2.103 Another method of analysing this position is that there are, in fact, two separate contracts: the primary, or main, contract concerns the commercial obligations of the parties; the secondary, or collateral, contract contains the obligation to resolve any disputes arising from the commercial relationship by arbitration. This secondary contract may never come into operation—but if it does, it will form the basis for the appointment of an arbitral tribunal and for the resolution of any dispute arising out of the main contract.

2.104 The doctrine of separability is endorsed by institutional and international rules of arbitration, such as those of UNCITRAL, which state in the context of pleas as to the jurisdiction of an arbitral tribunal that 'an arbitration clause that forms part of

---

[155] For the powers of an arbitral tribunal, see Chapter 5.
[156] Such an express power is contained, e.g., in the LCIA Rules, Art. 25.1(i).
[157] This concept is known in some systems of law as the autonomy of the arbitration clause (*l'autonomie de la clause compromissoire*).
[158] See Paulsson, 'Separability demystified', in *The Idea of Arbitration* (Oxford University Press, 2013), ch. 3, s. 1(c).
[159] *Heyman v Darwins Ltd* [1942] AC 356, at 374 *per* Lord MacMillan.

D. Analysis of an Arbitration Agreement

a contract shall be treated as an agreement independent of the other terms of the contract'.[160] Following the provisions of the UNCITRAL Rules, Article 16(1) of the Model Law provides that:

> The arbitral tribunal may rule on its own jurisdiction, including any objections with respect to the existence or validity of the arbitration agreement. For that purpose, an arbitration clause which forms part of a contract shall be treated as an agreement independent of the other terms of the contract. A decision by the arbitral tribunal that the contract is null and void shall not entail *ipso jure* the invalidity of the arbitration clause.

Similarly, Article 23(2) of the LCIA Rules stipulates that, for the purpose of a ruling on jurisdiction: **2.105**

> [A]n arbitration clause which forms or was intended to form part of another agreement shall be treated as an arbitration agreement independent of that other agreement. A decision by the Arbitral Tribunal that such other agreement is non-existent, invalid or ineffective shall not entail *(of itself)* the non-existence, invalidity or ineffectiveness of the arbitration clause.[161]

In the *Gosset* case,[162] the French Cour de Cassation recognised the doctrine of separability in very broad terms, as follows: **2.106**

> In international arbitration, the agreement to arbitrate, whether concluded separately or included in the contract to which it relates, is always save in exceptional circumstances... completely autonomous in law, which excludes the possibility of it being affected by the possible invalidity of the main contract.

Five years later, the US Supreme Court also recognised the separability of the arbitration clause in the *Prima Paint* case,[163] and modern laws on arbitration confirm the concept. Swiss law, for example, provides that '[t]he validity of an arbitration agreement cannot be contested on the ground that the main contract may not be valid'.[164] **2.107**

More recently, the Chinese courts have also accepted that: **2.108**

> Where the main contract is not concluded (null) or does not come into effect after conclusion (void), it will not influence the effect of the arbitration clause

---

[160] UNCITRAL Rules, Art. 23(1).
[161] See also ICC Rules, Art. 6(9) (emphasis added).
[162] Cass. Civ. 1ere, 7 May 1963 (Dalloz, 1963), 545.
[163] *Prima Paint Co. v Flood Conklin Manufacturing Corporation* 388 US 395, 402 (1967). In *Buckeye Check Cashing Inc. v John Cardegna et al.* 126 S.Ct 1204 (2006), the US Supreme Court confirmed that the *Prima Paint* separability rule applies equally in state and federal courts. For discussion of the doctrine in the United States, see McDougall and Ioannou, 'Separability saved: U.S. Supreme Court eliminates threat to international arbitration' (2006) 21 Mealey's Intl Arb Rep 15; Samuel, 'Separability and the U.S. Supreme Court decision in *Buckeye v Cardegna*' (2006) 22 Arb Intl 477. See also *Preston v Ferrer* 552 US 346 (2008). See also the Arbitration Fairness Act of 2015, introduced in the US Congress on 29 April 2015 after an earlier version failed to pass into law, which proposes to abolish the presumption of separability in the case of employment, consumer, antitrust, and civil rights disputes.
[164] Swiss PIL, s. 178(3).

agreed by the parties, as the arbitration clause is completely separable from the main contract.[165]

2.109 An increasing number of countries[166] have made their position clear by making the separability of the arbitration clause part of their laws on arbitration.[167] The number of states in which the concept has not yet been accepted is steadily diminishing.[168]

2.110 An independent (or autonomous) arbitration clause thus gives the arbitral tribunal a basis on which to decide on its own jurisdiction, even if it is alleged that the main contract has been terminated by performance or by some intervening event. Some laws and rules go further, to establish that the arbitration clause will survive even if the main contract that contains it proves to be null and void.[169] However, this must depend on the reason for which the contract is found to be null and void (that is, is it a reason that will also affect the 'separate' arbitration agreement?), and whether it is void *ab initio*.

2.111 While the doctrine of separability is now accepted in principle in all developed arbitral jurisdictions, application of the doctrine continues to vary—even within jurisdictions—in circumstances in which the main contract is argued never to have come into existence at all.

2.112 In England, section 7 of the Arbitration Act 1996 provides that an arbitration agreement contained in another agreement 'shall not be regarded as invalid, non-existent or ineffective because that other agreement...*did not come into existence*'.[170] The doctrine received approval and confirmation by the English

---

[165] *Interpretation on Certain Issues Relating to the Application of the PRC Arbitration Law*, Supreme People's Court, 23 August 2006; *Jiangsu Materials Group Light Industry and Weaving Co. v Hong Kong Top-Capital Holdings Ltd (Canada) & Prince Development Ltd* (the *Yuyi* case), Supreme People's Court, 1998. The courts of the Dominican Republic and the United Arab Emirates have also upheld the doctrine of separability: see *Bratex Dominicana, C por A v Vanity Fair Inc.*, Supreme Court of Justice of the Dominican Republic, 31 May 2005; Petition No. 353 of 2011, Abu Dhabi Court of Cassation, 24 August 2011.

[166] For instance, the Netherlands, in the Arbitration Act 1986, s. 1053; England, in the Arbitration Act 1996, s. 7; India, in the Arbitration and Conciliation Act 1996, s. 16; Brazil, in the Brazilian Arbitration Act of 1996, s. 8; and states that either adopt the Model Law or adapt their legislation to it.

[167] See Marrella, 'International business law and international commercial arbitration: The Italian approach' [1997] ADRLJ 25; Rogers and Launders, 'Separability: The indestructible arbitration clause' (1994) 10 Arb Intl 71; Svernlou, 'What isn't, ain't: The current status of the doctrine of separability' (1991) 8 J Intl Arb 37.

[168] See Sanders, 'Arbitration', in Cappelletti (ed.) *Encyclopedia of International and Comparative Law, Vol. XVI* (Brill, 1987), ch. 12, paras 106–112. It should be noted, however, that, as Sanders observes, a 'comparative study can only be made on the basis of the current situation' and 'situations change rapidly' (ibid., para. 102).

[169] Article 23(1) of the UNCITRAL Rules states that a decision by the arbitral tribunal that the contract is null and void 'shall not entail automatically the invalidity of the arbitration clause' and, as has been seen, the Model Law itself adopts this terminology, in Art. 16(1).

[170] Emphasis added. The doctrine was not recognised by the English courts until 1993, in *Harbour Assurance Co. Ltd v Kansa General International Insurance Co. Ltd* [1993] 1 Lloyd's Rep 455.

D. Analysis of an Arbitration Agreement

courts in *Fiona Trust*,[171] in which the House of Lords, confirming the decision of the Court of Appeal, held that the arbitrators, not the courts, should determine whether the underlying contract was void for illegality, unless the illegality was directed at the arbitration clause in particular.[172] By way of international comparison, in China, the courts are also now regularly applying the principle in accordance with international practice.[173]

2.113 It will be appreciated from what has been said that there is a direct connection between the autonomy of the arbitration clause and the power (or competence) of an arbitral tribunal to decide upon its own jurisdiction (or competence). This power (that of 'competence/competence', as it is sometimes known) is discussed in Chapter 5, which deals with jurisdiction and other issues.

(d) Summary

2.114 As already stated, most arbitrations take place pursuant to an arbitration clause in a 'contract'. Where the parties decide that any dispute between them will be submitted to arbitration under the rules of a particular arbitral institution, the model clause recommended by that institution should be incorporated into the contract. Where the parties decide that the services of an arbitral institution are unlikely to be required, but that they would nevertheless like to adopt an existing set of rules, they should incorporate the recommended UNCITRAL arbitration clause into the contract.

2.115 Where such arbitration clauses are adopted, most national courts will recognise and give effect to the parties' wishes to arbitrate any disputes between them. These model clauses bring with them a set of rules that are self-sufficient, and which should be enough to guide the arbitral tribunal and the parties from the beginning to the end of the arbitral process.

2.116 Nonetheless, it would be advisable to add to the model clause at least three of the basic elements of an arbitration agreement discussed—namely, the number of arbitrators, the place of arbitration, and the governing law of the contract. It may

---

[171] *Fiona Trust & Holding Corporation v Yuri Privalov* [2007] UKHL 40.
[172] See Altras, 'Bribery and separability: Who decides, the tribunal or the courts? *Fiona Trust & Holding Corp v Yuri Privalov*' (2007) 73 Arbitration 2; Merkin, 'Separability and illegality in arbitration' (2007) 17 Arb LM 1; Pengelley, 'Separability revisited: Arbitration clauses and bribery—*Fiona Trust & Holding Corp v Privalov*' (2007) 24 J Intl Arb 445; *Lesotho Highlands Development Authority v Impregilo SpA* [2005] UKHL 43, [2005] Arb LR 557, in particular the judgment of Lord Steyn. See also *Beijing Jianlong Heavy Industry Group v Golden Ocean Group Ltd* [2013] EWHC 1063 (Comm), in which the English High Court discussed the relevance of public policy considerations when examining the validity of an arbitration agreement.
[173] Arbitration Law of the People's Republic of China, s. 19; CIETAC Rules, Art. 5(4). See Wexia, 'China's search for complete separability of the arbitral agreement' (2007) 3 Asian Intl Arb J 163; Yeoh and Fu, 'The people's courts and arbitration: A snapshot of recent and judicial attitudes on arbitrability and enforcement' (2007) 24 J Intl Arb 635, at 638.

also be, or may become, necessary to identify the law governing the arbitration agreement.[174]

2.117 If the parties do not require the services of an arbitral institution and do not wish to adopt the UNCITRAL Rules, a simple submission to arbitration—adapted from one of the model clauses—would be sufficient in theory. In practice, however, it is sensible not only to provide for the number of arbitrators, the place of arbitration, and the governing law, but also to consider such provisions as those relating to the establishment of the arbitral tribunal, the filling of vacancies, and the failure or refusal of a party to take part in the arbitration.

2.118 The fact that the parties have agreed in their arbitration clause to an arbitration under institutional rules does not prevent them from agreeing, when a dispute has arisen, to a different method of resolving the dispute. Thus they may switch from, say, an ICC arbitration to an ad hoc arbitration or vice versa—but if they do so, a new arbitration agreement should be made, submitting the existing dispute (by way of submission agreement) to arbitration.

E. Submission Agreements

2.119 The position of the parties and their advisers in dealing with a submission agreement is radically different from the position that exists when an arbitration clause is being written into a contract. First, a dispute has actually arisen and usually this means that there will be a hostile element in the relationship. Secondly, the legal advisers know what kind of dispute they are facing, and they will wish to structure the arbitration to deal with it efficiently and appropriately. Thirdly, the interests of the parties may conflict, in that the claimant usually wants a speedy resolution, whereas the respondent may consider that it will be to its advantage to create delay.[175] For all of these reasons, the negotiation of a submission agreement may be a lengthy process. However, the importance of 'getting it right' cannot be overemphasised.

2.120 The submission agreement should contain many, if not all, of the basic elements of an arbitration agreement. In addition, it should contain a definition, or at least an outline, of the disputes that are to be arbitrated.

2.121 It is also possible to include in the submission agreement procedural arrangements, such as for production of documents, exchange of written submissions and

---

[174] See the discussion in Chapter 3, paragraphs 3.09*ff*.
[175] Although it should, of course, be borne in mind that the claimant may be compensated for the delay by an award of interest and that delay is usually achieved only by the expenditure of costs, e.g. the determination of a preliminary issue. Ultimately, the respondent may be directed to pay the costs of the arbitration, particularly if it is considered that its conduct has contributed to the delay. See Chapter 9.

witness statements, the timetable to be followed, and other matters. On balance, however, it is probably better to deal with such questions in a separate document, perhaps with the assistance of the arbitral tribunal once the arbitration has commenced.

The importance of ensuring that the submission agreement deals with all of these matters emerges clearly from the *Turriff* arbitration, which took place at the Peace Palace in The Hague.[176] During the course of the proceedings, two of the three arbitrators originally appointed resigned and the respondent withdrew, leaving the arbitration to proceed as a default arbitration.[177] The resignation of the presiding arbitrator on grounds of ill health was dealt with by agreement; the Canadian chairman was replaced by a Dutch judge. The withdrawal of the government from the arbitration could *not* be dealt with by agreement, since by then all cooperation between the parties had ceased. However, the arbitral tribunal had express power under the submission agreement to proceed in default (that is, in the absence of one of the parties). It decided to do so and a date was fixed for an adjourned hearing. A third crisis prevented this: the Sudanese arbitrator failed to attend the adjourned hearing. One of the arbitrators, who had been delegated by the arbitral tribunal to deal with procedural matters, fixed a new date for the hearing. He ordered that, in the absence of the Sudanese arbitrator, Turriff's oral argument and evidence should be presented before two members of the arbitral tribunal (that is, a truncated tribunal), and should be fully recorded, authenticated, and preserved.[178]

2.122

Under the submission agreement, it was for the government to appoint a new arbitrator[179] within sixty days. When it failed to do so, Turriff asked the president of the International Court of Justice (ICJ) to make the appointment, which he did, whereupon the remaining two arbitrators were deemed to have been reappointed. In this way, a new arbitral tribunal was constituted—and the hearing then continued *ex parte* as before, with the new arbitrator reading the transcript of the previous days' proceedings, in order to acquaint himself with the facts. In April 1970, the arbitral tribunal issued an award under which the government was ordered to pay

2.123

---

[176] A more recent example of a case involving the interpretation of a submission agreement is *Applied Industrial Materials Corporation v Ovalar Makne Ticaret Ve Sanayi AS*, No. OS Civ. 10540, 2006 WL 1816383 (SDNY 2006). In this case, the parties signed a submission agreement that required the arbitrators to disclose any circumstance that could impair their ability to render an unbiased award. In determining whether this was an ongoing obligation of disclosure, the court looked to the words of the submission agreement to interpret the parties' agreement in this regard.

[177] The case is briefly noted in Stuyt, *Survey of International Arbitrations 1794–1970* (Sijthoff/Oceana, 1976), App. I, Case No. A31 and more fully by Erades, 'The Sudan arbitration' [1970] NTIR 2, at 200–222. Erades became presiding arbitrator on the resignation of his predecessor. It is also commented upon in Schwebel, *International Arbitration: Three Salient Problems* (Grotius, 1987).

[178] Erades, 'The Sudan arbitration' [1970] NTIR 2, at 209.

[179] Although this was not known at the time, the government had in fact made an order revoking or purporting to revoke the Sudanese judge's appointment as an arbitrator.

compensatory damages, together with an additional sum to cover Turriff's legal costs and the costs, fees, and expenses of the arbitral tribunal.[180]

F. Arbitrability

(a) Introduction

2.124 Arbitrability, in the sense in which it is used both in this book and generally,[181] involves determining which types of dispute may be resolved by arbitration and which belong exclusively to the domain of the courts. Both the New York Convention and the Model Law are limited to disputes that are 'capable of settlement by arbitration'.[182]

2.125 In principle, *any* dispute should be just as capable of being resolved by a private arbitral tribunal as by the judge of a national court. Article 2059 of the French Civil Code, for example, provides that 'all persons may enter into arbitration agreements relating to the rights that they may freely dispose of'. Although article 2060 further provides that parties may not agree to arbitrate disputes in a series of particular fields (such as family law) and 'more generally in all matters that have a public interest [*plus généralement dans toutes les matières qui intéressent l'ordre public*]', this limitation has been construed in a very restrictive way by French courts. Similarly, section 1 of the Brazilian Arbitration Act of 1996 (Law No. 9307) states that parties may settle disputes through arbitration as long as the subject matter relates to freely transferable rights.[183]

2.126 However, it is precisely because arbitration is a private proceeding with public consequences[184] that some types of dispute are reserved for national courts, the proceedings of which are generally in the public domain. It is in this sense that they are not 'capable of settlement by arbitration'.

---

[180] Erades, 'The Sudan arbitration' [1970] NTIR 2, at 222. To complete the story, negotiations took place between the government and Turriff after the issue of the award, and the company accepted in settlement a substantial part of the sum awarded.

[181] In the United States and elsewhere, there is sometimes discussion by judges and others as to whether a particular dispute is 'arbitrable', in the sense that it falls within the scope of the arbitration agreement. The concern in such cases is with the court's jurisdiction over a particular dispute rather than a more general enquiry as to whether the dispute is of the type that comes within the domain of arbitration. See Zekos, 'Courts' intervention in commercial and maritime arbitration under US law' (1997) 14 J Intl Arb 99. For a general discussion of 'arbitrability' in the sense of 'legally capable of settlement by arbitration', see Sanders, 'The domain of arbitration', in Cappelletti (ed.) *Encyclopedia of International and Comparative Law, Vol. XVI* (Brill, 1987), ch. 12, pp. 113*ff*; see also Hanotiau, 'The law applicable to arbitrability' (1998) 9 ICCA Congress Series 146.

[182] New York Convention, Arts II(1) and V(2)(a); Model Law, Arts 34(2)(b)(i) and 36(1)(b)(i).

[183] See also art. 1030(1) and (2) of the German Code of Civil Procedure, which provides that any claim involving an economic interest (*Vermögensrechtlicher Anspruch*) may be the subject of arbitration, as may claims involving a non-economic interest of which the parties may freely dispose.

[184] For instance, in the recognition and enforcement of the award.

F. Arbitrability

National laws establish the domain of arbitration, as opposed to that of the local courts. Each state decides which matters may or may not be resolved by arbitration in accordance with its own political, social, and economic policy. In some Arab states, for example, contracts between a foreign corporation and its local agent are given special protection by law, and, to reinforce this protection, any disputes arising out of such contracts may be resolved only by the local courts.[185] In the United States, the arbitration of certain types of dispute that engage public policy appears to be under legislative attack. At the time of writing, a Bill (the 'Arbitration Fairness Act of 2015') in the United States, which has yet to be voted on, proposes to invalidate any pre-dispute arbitration clause in relation to employment, consumer, antitrust, and civil rights disputes on the grounds that the weaker of the parties in reality has little or no meaningful choice as to whether to select arbitration.[186] The legislators and courts in each country must balance the domestic importance of reserving certain matters of public interest to the courts against the more general public interest in allowing people the freedom to arrange their private affairs as they see fit.[187] In the international sphere, the interests of promoting international trade, as well as international comity, have proven important factors in persuading the courts to treat certain types of dispute as arbitrable.[188]

2.127

If the issue of arbitrability arises, it is necessary to have regard to the relevant laws of the different states that are, or may be, concerned. These are likely to include: the law governing the party involved, where the agreement is with a state or state entity; the law governing the arbitration agreement; the law of the seat of arbitration; and the law of the ultimate place of enforcement of the award.

2.128

---

[185] See also Mexico, where disputes concerning the administrative rescission of contracts entered into by a state entity are within the exclusive competence of the administrative courts. For a general discussion of restrictions on the arbitrability of disputes involving Mexican state companies, see Wöss, 'El orden público, derecho público, cosa juzgada e inarbitrabilidad en contratos públicos en México' (2012) 14 Spain Arb Rev 111.

[186] Other jurisdictions have grappled with consumer arbitration as well. Pursuant to s. 91(1) of the English Arbitration Act 1996, an arbitration agreement in a consumer contract is deemed unfair under the Unfair Terms in Consumer Contracts Regulations 1999 if it relates to a claim for a pecuniary remedy that does not exceed £5,000. An arbitration agreement with a consumer may also be unenforceable under English law pursuant to the Unfair Terms in Consumer Contracts Regulations 1999. See, e.g., *Mylcrist Builders Ltd v Buck* [2008] EWHC 2172 (TCC), in which the English High Court held that an arbitration clause in a building contract was unenforceable on the basis that it caused a significant imbalance between the parties by denying the consumer access to the courts.

[187] See Paulsson, *The Idea of Arbitration* (Oxford University Press, 2013), in particular ch. 1 on 'The impulse to arbitrate'.

[188] See *Mitsubishi Motors Corporation v Soler Chrysler Plymouth Inc.* 473 US 614, 105 S.Ct 3346 (1985), discussed at paragraph 2.136. However, the opposite is often argued in the context of less-developed countries. In that situation, it is suggested that the state should impose very strict limits on arbitrability, especially in respect of disputes involving state entities. The reason for such a policy is that this is the only way in which these states can retain control over foreign trade and investment where more economically powerful traders may have an unfair advantage. See Sornarajah, 'The UNCITRAL Model Law: A third world viewpoint' (1989) 6 J Intl Arb 7, at 16.

2.129 Whether or not a particular type of dispute is 'arbitrable' under a given law is, in essence, a matter of public policy for that law to determine. Public policy varies from one country to the next, and indeed changes over time.[189] The most that can be done here is to indicate the categories of dispute that may fall outside the domain of arbitration.

2.130 Reference has already been made in passing to contracts of agency, for which special provision may be made in some states as a matter of public policy. More generally, criminal matters and those that affect the status of an individual or a corporate entity (such as bankruptcy or insolvency) are usually considered to be non-arbitrable. In addition, disputes over the grant or validity of patents and trade marks may not be arbitrable under the applicable law. These various categories of dispute are now considered in greater detail.

(b) Categories of dispute for which questions of arbitrability arise

(i) Patents, trade marks, and copyright

2.131 Whether or not a patent or trade mark should be granted is plainly a matter for the public authorities of the state concerned, these being monopoly rights that only the state can grant. Any dispute as to their grant or validity is outside the domain of arbitration.[190] However, the owner of a patent or trade mark frequently issues licences to one or more corporations or individuals in order to exploit the patent or trade mark, and any disputes between the licensor and the licensee may be referred to arbitration. Indeed, disputes over such intellectual property rights are commonly referred to international arbitration—first, because this gives the parties an opportunity to select for themselves a tribunal of arbitrators experienced in such matters, and secondly (and perhaps more importantly), because of the confidentiality of arbitral proceedings, which helps to provide a safeguard for trade secrets.[191]

2.132 Unlike patents or trade marks, copyright is an intellectual property right that exists independently of any national or international registration and may be freely

---

[189] The concept of so-called international public policy, which may impose limits on the arbitrability of certain agreements such as an agreement to pay bribes (see paragraphs 2.122*ff*) is considered in Chapter 11, in the context of challenging the recognition and enforcement of arbitral awards.

[190] However, see, e.g., the Swiss Federal Office for Industrial Property Ruling of 15 December 1975, which stated that the Federal Office will execute awards dealing with intellectual property validity issues. The Paris Cour d'Appel has recently ruled that an arbitral tribunal may rule on the existence of an intellectual property right, provided that this issue is incidental to the dispute and the tribunal's determination will have effect only as between the parties: see *Liv Hidravlika v Diebolt*, No. 05-10577, Paris Cour d'Appel, 28 February 2008.

[191] See generally Lew, *Intellectual Property Disputes and Arbitration: Final Report of the Commission on International Arbitration* (ICC, 1997), esp. pp. 7–15. For a comparative overview of states' approaches to intellectual-property-related arbitration, see Hanotiau, 'L'arbitrabilité des litiges de propriété intellectuelle', in de Werra and Pauwelyn (eds) *La Resolution de Litiges de Propriété Intellectuelle* (Schulthess, 2010).

F. Arbitrability

disposed of by parties. There is therefore generally no doubt that disputes relating to such private rights may be referred to international arbitration.[192]

(ii) Antitrust and competition laws

Adam Smith, writing in the eighteenth century, said: 'People of the same trade seldom meet together, even for merriment and diversion, but the conversation ends in a conspiracy against the public, or in some contrivance to raise prices.'[193] This early distrust of monopolies and cartels finds its modern echo in increasingly wide-ranging antitrust (or competition) legislation across the world. Amongst national legislators, the United States has been prominent, beginning with the celebrated Shearman Act in 1890. Similarly, in 1958, the (then) European Community adopted rules of law that were to be directly applicable in all member states, and which prohibit agreements and arrangements having as their object or effect the prevention, restriction, or distortion of competition,[194] as well as any abuse of a dominant position,[195] within what is now the European Union. Articles 101 and 102 of the Treaty on the Functioning of the European Union (TFEU) have historically been enforced primarily by the European Commission, which has the power to investigate, to prohibit behaviours, to impose heavy fines, and also to grant exemptions pursuant to Article 101(3) TFEU where appropriate in light of the wider benefits of the activity or agreement that infringes Article 101.[196]

2.133

What can an arbitral tribunal do when confronted with an allegation that the contract under which the arbitration is brought is itself an illegal restraint of trade, or in some other way a breach of antitrust law? For example, in disputes between the licensor of a patent and the licensee, it has become almost standard practice for the licensor to allege (amongst a series of defences) that, in any event, the licence agreement is void for illegality. In general, an allegation of illegality should not prevent an arbitral tribunal from adjudicating on the dispute even if its finding is that

2.134

---

[192] In *Desputeaux v Éditions Chouette (1987) Inc.* [2003] 1 SCR 178, the Supreme Court of Canada confirmed that disputes over copyright ownership are arbitrable. The Court stated that although a creative work is a manifestation of the personality of the author, 'this issue is very far removed from questions relating to the status and capacity of persons and to family matters': ibid., at 181.
[193] Smith, *The Wealth of Nations* (Methuen, 1776), Bk 1, ch. 10, pt 2.
[194] Article 101 TFEU.
[195] Article 102 TFEU.
[196] Agreements that offend against Art. 101 are void under Art. 101(2), unless an exemption is granted under Art. 101(3). Until 1 May 2004, the power to grant exemptions fell to the European Commission alone. Since then, pursuant to Council Regulation (EC) No. 1/2003 of 16 December 2002 on the implementation of the rules on competition laid down in Articles 81 and 82 of the Treaty, OJ L 1/4, 4 January 2003, the power has been extended to national courts and competition authorities. Although the Regulation does not mention arbitral tribunals specifically, it changed the landscape of EU competition law and opened the door to arbitration as an arena for the private enforcement of EU competition rules. In this regard, see Dempegiotis, 'EC competition law and international arbitration in the light of EC Regulation 1/2003: Conceptual conflicts, common ground and corresponding legal issues' (2008) 25 J Intl Arb 365.

the agreement in question is indeed void for illegality. This is because, under the doctrine of separability,[197] the arbitration clause in a contract constitutes a separate agreement and survives the contract of which it forms part. More specifically, it is now widely accepted that antitrust issues are arbitrable. In France, the arbitrability of competition law issues is well established, having been acknowledged in the *Mors/Labinal* case in 1993[198] and reaffirmed by the Cour de Cassation in 1999.[199] Likewise, in Switzerland, the arbitrability of EU competition law was recognised by a decision of the Federal Tribunal in 1992,[200] in which the Tribunal found that '[n]either Article 85 of the [EU] Treaty nor Regulation 17 on its application forbids a national court or an arbitral tribunal to examine the validity of that contract'.

2.135 The US Supreme Court had already adopted this approach in the well-known *Mitsubishi* case.[201] At one time, it was held in the United States that claims under the antitrust laws were not capable of being resolved by arbitration, but had to be referred to the courts. In the *American Safety* case,[202] the reaction of the court was that:

> A claim under the antitrust laws is not merely a private matter... Antitrust violation can affect hundreds of thousands, perhaps millions, of people and inflict staggering economic damage. We do not believe Congress intended such claims to be resolved elsewhere than the Courts.[203]

2.136 However, in *Mitsubishi*, the US Supreme Court decided, by a majority of five to three, that antitrust issues arising out of international contracts were arbitrable under the Federal Arbitration Act. This was so despite the public importance of the antitrust laws, the significance of private parties seeking treble damages as a disincentive to violation of those laws, and the complexity of such cases. In its judgment, the Court stated:

> [W]e conclude that concerns of international comity, respect for the capacities of foreign and transnational tribunals and sensitivity to the need of the international commercial system for predictability in the resolution of disputes require

---

[197] Under this doctrine, the arbitration clause in a contract is regarded as separate from, and independent of, the contract of which it forms part: see paragraph 2.89.
[198] See the decision of the Paris Cour d'Appel of 19 May 1993, [1993] Rev Arb 645, n. Jarrosson.
[199] See the decision of the Cour de Cassation of 5 January 1999.
[200] Decision of the Tribunal Fédéral, 28 April 1992, [1992] ASA Bulletin 368. The same court reaffirmed this position in its decision of 13 November 1998, [1999] ASA Bulletin 529 and 455. The English courts have also held that 'there is no realistic doubt that such "competition" and "antitrust" claims are arbitrable': see *ET Plus SA v Jean Paul Welter & The Channel Tunnel Group* [2005] EWHC 2115 (Comm). However, merger control and state aid issues are within the exclusive competence of the European Commission and parties cannot agree to settle such issues by arbitration: see Blanke, 'The application of EU law to arbitration in England', in Lew, Bor, Fullelove, and Greenaway (eds) *Arbitration in England, with Chapters on Scotland and Ireland* (Kluwer Law International, 2013), p. 249.
[201] *Mitsubishi Motors Corporation v Soler Chrysler Plymouth Inc.* 473 US 614, 105 S.Ct 3346 (1985). And see generally Institute of International Business Law and Practice, *Competition and Arbitration* (ICC, 1993).
[202] *American Safety Equipment Corporation v JP Maguire Co.* 391 F.2d 821 (2nd Cir. 1968).
[203] Ibid., at 826.

that we enforce the parties' agreement, even assuming that a contrary result would be forthcoming in a domestic context.[204]

However, the Court went on to point out that the public interest in the enforcement of antitrust legislation could be asserted, if necessary, when it came to enforcement of any award made by the arbitral tribunal. It stated that:

> Having permitted the arbitration to go forward, the national courts of the United States will have the opportunity at the award enforcement stage to ensure that the legitimate interest in the enforcement of the antitrust laws has been addressed. The [New York Convention] reserves to each signatory country the right to refuse enforcement of an award where the 'recognition or enforcement of the award would be contrary to a public policy of that country'.[205]

In this way, rather than question whether antitrust issues are arbitrable, later decisions tend to focus—at least in the European Union and United States—on the extent of a state court's power to review arbitral awards in relation to disputes that raise competition issues. In its landmark decision in *Eco Swiss China Time Ltd v Benetton International NV*,[206] the European Court of Justice (ECJ) identified Article 81 of the EU Treaty (now Article 101 TFEU) as a matter of public policy that would justify the annulment or refusal of enforcement of an award that ignores it. In the context of a challenge to an award that gave effect to a licence agreement that was alleged, only after the award had been rendered, to violate Article 81 of the EU Treaty, the ECJ ruled that:

2.137

> ...a national court to which application is made for annulment of an arbitration award must grant that application if it considers that the award in question is in fact contrary to Article 85 of the Treaty [now Art. 81 TEU], where its domestic rules of procedure require it to grant an application for annulment founded on failure to observe national rules of public policy.[207]

Although, in *Eco Swiss*, the ECJ did not explicitly rule on whether arbitrators have a duty to apply Article 81 EC *ex officio* if the parties themselves made no reference to it, this decision is generally seen—at the very least—as implying that arbitrators should do so or risk the annulment of their award on grounds of a violation of public policy.[208] However, some uncertainty remains as to how serious the alleged

2.138

---

[204] *Mitsubishi Motors*, at 629.
[205] *Mitsubishi Motors*, at 628. However, see *Baxter International v Abbott Laboratories* 315 F.3d 163 (2nd Cir. 2004), in which the US Court's 'second look' was very limited in scope. In that case, the US Supreme Court limited its review to ensuring only that 'the tribunal took cognizance of antitrust claims and actually decided them'.
[206] Case C-126/97 [1999] ECR I-3079, (1999) XXIV YBCA 629.
[207] Ibid., at [41]. The decision arose from a preliminary reference made to the ECJ under Art. 234 TEU (ex Art. 177 EC) by the Supreme Court of the Netherlands.
[208] See Pinsolle, 'Note on Cass. Civ. 1ere, 6 July 2005' (2005) 4 Rev Arb 8; Dempegiotis, 'EC competition law and international arbitration in the light of EC Regulation 1/2003: Conceptual conflicts, common ground and corresponding legal issues' (2008) 25 J Intl Arb 365, at 380–386. The Organisation for Economic Co-operation and Development (OECD) has also adopted this view: see OECD, *Hearing Report on Arbitration and Competition* (13 December 2011), p. 12.

violation of competition law must be in order to justify the annulment of an award. The Paris Cour d'Appel has refused to annul an award that failed to address competition issues, on the basis that there was no 'flagrant, effective and concrete' violation of public policy.[209] Indeed, the prevailing view seems to be that a 'minimalist' standard of review is appropriate.[210]

(iii) Securities transactions

2.139 An earlier ruling by the Supreme Court in a dispute under the US Securities Act of 1933 foreshadowed the decision in *Mitsubishi*. In 1953, the Supreme Court had held that disputes under the Securities Act were not arbitrable.[211] In 1974, however, the Court held that such disputes *were* arbitrable in an international commercial arbitration. The case was *Scherk v Alberto-Culver*,[212] in which the Supreme Court said that a 'parochial refusal by the courts of one country to enforce an international arbitration agreement' would not only frustrate the purpose of the agreement, but also 'damage the fabric of international commerce and trade and imperil the willingness and ability of businessmen to enter into international commercial agreements'.[213] In subsequent cases, the Court went on to accept the arbitrability of securities disputes in US domestic arbitration.[214]

2.140 Other national securities laws, existing as they do to protect vulnerable consumers, restrict the resolution of disputes thereunder to the national courts. By way of example, German securities legislation expressly restricts the availability of

---

[209] *Thalès Air Défence v Euromissile*, Case No. 2002/60932, 18 November 2004.

[210] This so-called minimalist approach has been adopted by courts in Switzerland, in *Tensacciai SpA v Freyssinet Terra Armata Srl*, Case No. 4P_278/2005, Swiss Federal Tribunal, 8 March 2006; in New Zealand, in *Attorney-General v Mobil Oil NZ Ltd*, High Court, Wellington, 1 July 1987; in the United States, in *American Central Eastern Texas Gas Co. v Union Pacific Resources Group* 2004 US App LEXIS 1216; and in Sweden, in *Republic of Latvia v Latvijas Gaze*, Svea Court of Appeal, 4 May 2005. However, see also *SNF SAS v Cytec Industries BV (Holland)*, Cour de Cassation, Ch. Civ. 1ere, 4 June 2008, in which the French and Belgian courts initially applied differing standards of review to the same award. The Belgian Tribunal de Première Instance conducted a detailed review of the award for consistency with competition law and refused enforcement on this basis. However, its decision was overturned by the Belgian Court of Appeal, which adopted the 'minimalist approach' in line with the French courts' decisions in the same matter. For a general discussion of the different approaches taken by national courts, see Blanke, 'The minimalist and maximalist approach to reviewing competition law awards: A neverending saga' (2007) 2 SIAR 51.

[211] *Wilko v Swan* 346 US 427 (1953). See generally McCormack, 'Recent US legal decisions on arbitration law' (1994) 11 J Intl Arb 73.

[212] 417 US 506 (1974).

[213] Ibid., at 516–517.

[214] See, e.g., *Shearson v McMahon* 482 US 220, 107 S.Ct 2332 (1987); *Lipcon v Underwriters at Lloyd's* 148 F.3d 1285 (11th Cir. 1998) See also McCormack, 'Recent US legal decisions on arbitration law' (1994) 11 J Intl Arb 73; Ebenroth and Dillon, 'Arbitration clauses in international finance agreements' (1993) 10 J Intl Arb 5. In recent years, there has been a significant increase in the use of arbitration as a means of resolving disputes in this sector. In September 2013, the International Swaps and Derivatives Association, Inc. (ISDA) released its Arbitration Guide, which offers guidance on the use of arbitration clauses in the ISDA Master Agreement.

arbitration to commercial cases in which both parties are established businesses or companies.[215]

(iv) Insolvency

Issues of arbitrability arise in respect of insolvency law as a result of the conflict between the private nature of arbitration and the public-policy-driven collective procedures provided for under national insolvency laws.[216] Courts and tribunals in various countries have sought to identify where the boundary of arbitrability should lie and which insolvency issues are only suitable for resolution by a court. In this regard, a distinction can be made between 'core', or 'pure', insolvency issues, which are inherently non-arbitrable (for example matters relating to the adjudication of the insolvency itself or the verification of creditors' claims),[217] and the remaining circumstances of other cases involving the insolvency of one of the parties to a commercial arbitration agreement. The precise location of this dividing line varies between countries and will depend in part on national insolvency laws.

2.141

In the United States, the national bankruptcy courts were traditionally reluctant to defer their jurisdiction to arbitrators except in exceptional circumstances.[218] The approach now is for the courts to look at the type of dispute before them and to determine whether there are any core insolvency issues in play that deprive an arbitral tribunal of jurisdiction.[219]

2.142

In the European Union,[220] EC Council Regulation 1346/2000 establishes a common framework for insolvency proceedings. The Regulation provides, inter alia, that the law of the country in which insolvency proceedings are commenced shall determine the effect of those insolvency proceedings on other proceedings brought by individual creditors, including arbitration proceedings, with the exception of

2.143

---

[215] German Securities Trading Act (WpHG), s. 37h.
[216] See generally Lazic, *Insolvency Proceedings and Commercial Arbitration* (Wolters Kluwer, 1998), esp. pp. 154–177.
[217] See ibid., at pp. 154–157, and see also p. 155. See also Mantilla-Serrano, 'International arbitration and insolvency proceedings' (1995) 11 Arb Intl 69; Levy, 'Insolvency in arbitration (Swiss Law)' (2005) 23 Int ALR 28.
[218] See, e.g., *Zimmerman v Continental Airlines, Inc.* 712 F.2d 55 (3rd Cir. 1983). For a discussion of the development of the relationship between arbitration and insolvency in the United States, see Lazic, *Insolvency Proceedings and Commercial Arbitration* (Wolters Kluwer, 1998), pp. 165–175.
[219] In *Sonatrach (Algeria) v Distrigas Corp (US District Court) Massachusetts* (1995) XX YBCA 795 the Bankruptcy Court of Massachusetts held that the claim of damages before it did not implicate any major bankruptcy issue and therefore the dispute was arbitrable. However, in *United States Lines, Inc. et al. (US) v American Steamship Owners Mutual Protection and Indemnity Association, Inc. et al. (US)* (2000) XXV YBCA 1057, 1065 (2nd Cir., 1 November 1999), the Court of Appeal for the Second Circuit denied the arbitrability of the dispute, which it stated was 'integral to the bankruptcy court's ability to preserve and equitably distribute the Trust's assets'. See also *Larsen Oil and Gas Pte Ltd v Petroprod Ltd* [2010] 4 SLR 501, 501, in which the Singapore High Court stated, in relation to claims of unfair preference and transactions at an undervalue, the 'policy underlying the avoidance provisions…would be compromised if their enforcement is [*sic*] subject to private arrangements'.
[220] With the exception of Denmark, which opted out of the Regulation.

proceedings that are pending, which shall be determined by the law of the member state in which the lawsuit is pending.[221]

2.144 In Switzerland, the insolvency of one of the parties will not generally affect the arbitration agreement and arbitrators retain a wide jurisdiction to decide disputes relating to insolvency issues, including claims made on behalf of the estate itself.[222] German law also adopts a liberal approach to arbitrability in this context, with arbitrators having jurisdiction to determine all disputes relating to bankruptcy proceedings other than 'pure' insolvency issues, such as the appointment of an administrator, the collection and distribution of assets, and the reorganisation of a business.[223]

2.145 In Argentina, any arbitration agreement to which an insolvent company is party will automatically terminate upon the court entering a bankruptcy decree, unless the arbitral tribunal has already been constituted.[224] In Brazil, bankruptcy procedures are considered to be non-arbitrable.[225] However, a company's bankruptcy will not affect the validity of an arbitration agreement to which the company is party.[226]

2.146 Under English law, it is difficult to enforce an arbitration agreement against an insolvent party in circumstances under which the trustee in bankruptcy does not consent. The Arbitration Act 1996 introduced a specific procedure into the English Insolvency Act 1986, which allows a trustee in bankruptcy to adopt or reject an arbitration agreement. If it elects to reject the arbitration agreement, then arbitral proceedings can be brought only with the consent of the company's creditors and the court, which will look at all of the circumstances of the case to determine whether the dispute in question ought to be referred to arbitration.[227] This

---

[221] Article 4 of the Regulation. See also *Syska and anor v Vivendi and ors* [2009] EWCA Civ 677, in which the English courts confirmed that the 'proceedings pending' exception in Art. 15 of the Regulation applies to arbitration.

[222] See the Swiss Federal Tribunal Decision No. 4A_50/2012 of 16 October 2012, in which the Tribunal revisited its decision in *Vivendi v Elektrim*, Decision No. 4A_428_2008, 31 March 2009, and held that as long as the insolvent entity had legal personality according to the law of the place of incorporation, it was capable of being a party to foreign arbitral proceedings. See also generally Levy, 'Insolvency in arbitration (Swiss Law)' (2005) 8 Int ALR 23. For a more general discussion on insolvency in international arbitration from a Swiss law perspective, see Kohler and Levy, 'Insolvency and international arbitration', in Peter and Jeandin (eds) *The Challenges of Insolvency Law Reform in the 21st Century* (Schulthess, 2006), pp. 257–284.

[223] Lazic, *Insolvency Proceedings and Commercial Arbitration* (Wolters Kluwer, 1998), pp. 163–164.

[224] Article 134 of Argentina's Bankruptcy Law. See also *Bear Service SA v Cervecería Modelo SA de CV*, Argentine Federal Supreme Court, 5 April 2005.

[225] See *Jutaí 661 Equipamentos Eletrônicos Ltda v PSI Comércio e Prestação de Serviços em Telefones Celulares Ltda*, Superior Court of Justice, 12 March 2013.

[226] See *KwikasairCargasExpressas SA—Bankrupt Estate v AIG Venture Holdings Ltd*, Special Appeal No. 1.355.831, Superior Court of Justice, 19 March 2013.

[227] See Arbitration Act 1996, s. 107; Insolvency Act 1986, s. 349A. For a discussion of issues of insolvency and arbitration in English law, see Burn and Grubb, 'Insolvency and arbitration in English law' (2005) 8 Int ALR 124.

F. Arbitrability

apparently reflects the more general rule under English law that allows a trustee to refuse to acknowledge 'unprofitable' contracts. Should the trustee elect to confirm the arbitration agreement in a particular case, it becomes binding and enforceable both by and against the trustee.

(v) Bribery and corruption

2.147 Issues of bribery or corruption in the procurement or performance of a contract raise important questions of public policy. In its 2002 final report on public policy as a bar to the enforcement of international arbitral awards, the Committee on International Arbitration of the International Law Association (ILA) reviewed the development of the concept of public policy during the latter part of the twentieth century, and concluded that there was an international consensus that corruption and bribery are contrary to international public policy.[228]

2.148 So what is an arbitral tribunal to do if there is a dispute as to the performance of an international commercial agreement and it is said, as an excuse for non-performance, that the agreement had for its object the payment of bribes or some other fraudulent inducement? This issue was first raised in 1963 before a distinguished Swedish jurist, Judge Lagergren, who was acting as sole arbitrator in ICC Arbitration No. 1110.[229]

2.149 This landmark arbitration involved a dispute as to whether an agreement entered into in 1950 for the payment to Mr X of a 10 per cent commission on the value of industrial equipment then required for a particular public energy project in Argentina also covered the sale of equipment in 1958 for another similar project. Testifying before Judge Lagergren, Mr X stated that he ceded certain 'participations' to 'influential personalities' among a 'clique of people which had a controlling influence upon the Government's economic policy'. Witnesses for the respondent (a foreign supplier) testified that they understood that most of the money was for 'Peron and his boys' as the only way in which to 'get business of any scale in Argentina'.

2.150 Finding the contract to be 'condemned by public decency and morality' because it 'contemplated the bribing of Argentine officials for the purpose of obtaining the hoped-for business', Judge Lagergren found that such a dispute was not arbitrable, stating that the parties to such a contract had 'forfeited the right to ask for assistance of the machinery of justice'.[230]

---

[228] ILA Committee on International Commercial Arbitration, *Final Report on Public Policy as a Bar to Enforcement of International Arbitral Awards* (ILA, 2002). More generally on this topic, see Sayed, *Corruption in International Trade and Commercial Arbitration* (Kluwer Law International, 2004).

[229] Wetter, 'Issues of corruption before international tribunals: The authentic text and true meaning of Judge Gunnar Largegren's 1963 Award in ICC Case No. 1110' (1994) 10 Arb Intl 277.

[230] Ibid. Early commentators on this award criticised this approach as failing to give effect to the principle of the autonomy of the arbitration clause. However, as Wetter's publication of the award thirty years later revealed, there was no such contractual arbitration clause. The dispute had

2.151 The modern approach—based on the concept of separability,[231] which has now received widespread acceptance both nationally and internationally—is that an allegation of illegality does not in itself deprive the arbitral tribunal of jurisdiction.[232] On the contrary, it is generally held that the arbitral tribunal is entitled to hear the arguments and receive evidence, and to determine for itself the question of illegality.[233] Thus, in Switzerland, in a case involving a consultancy agreement, the Swiss Federal Tribunal decided that even if a consultancy agreement were, in effect, an agreement to pay a bribe (and this was not alleged, still less proven), the arbitration agreement would survive.[234]

2.152 Rather than raising questions of arbitrability, allegations of corruption made in an arbitration now raise the rather more substantive questions of proof and, if proven, the consequences of such impropriety under the relevant law.[235] Accepting without question the arbitrability of allegations of impropriety, an ad hoc arbitral tribunal acting under the UNCITRAL Rules addressed allegations of corruption put before it thus:

> The members of the Arbitral Tribunal do not live in an ivory tower. Nor do they view the arbitral process as one which operates in a vacuum divorced from reality. The arbitrators are well aware of the allegations that commitments by public

---

been the subject of a manifestly autonomous submission agreement. Judge Lagergren's decision was founded simply on the grounds of non-arbitrability. For further discussion on this decision, see Sayed, *Corruption in International Trade and Commercial Arbitration* (Kluwer Law International, 2004), pp. 59–65.

[231] See paragraphs 2.89*ff.*

[232] See Kreindler, 'Aspects of illegality in the formation and performance of contracts', Presented at the 16th ICCA Congress, London, May 2002. For a more recent review by the same author, see Kreindler, 'Public policy and corruption in international arbitration: A perspective for Russian related disputes' (2006) 72 Arbitration 236. See also Kosheri and Leboulanger, 'L'arbitrage face à la corruption et aux trafics d'influence' [1984] Rev Arb 3; Lalive, 'Ordre public transnational et arbitrage international' [1986] Rev Arb 329; Oppetit, 'Le paradoxe de la corruption à l'épreuve du droit de commerce international' (1987) 114 J du Droit Intl 5, at 5–21. See also Knoepfler, 'Corruption et arbitrage international', in Cherpilled (ed.) *Les Contrats de distribution: Contributions offertesau Professor Dessemontet* (CEDIDAC, 1998), p. 371; Derains, *Les Commissions Illicites* (ICC, 1992), pp. 65–68.

[233] For example, see *Fiona Trust & Holding Corporation v Yuri Privalov* [2007] EWCA Civ 20, in which the English courts confirmed that a claim that a disputed contract was induced by bribery should be decided by the arbitrator, not the courts, unless the allegation of illegality relates to the arbitration clause itself. See also Snodgrass, '*Fiona Trust v Privalov*: The Arbitration Act 1996 comes of age' [2007] Int ALR 27. For a contrary view, see *Hub Power Co. v Pakistan WAPDA*, Supreme Court of Pakistan, 14 June 2000, in which the Court held that allegations of corruption were not arbitrable, notwithstanding that the allegations did not impeach the arbitration agreement.

[234] Decision of the Tribunal Fédéral, *National Power Corporation (Philippines) v Westinghouse (USA)*, ATF 119 II 380, 2 September 1993.

[235] For an overview of how arbitral tribunals have dealt with allegations of corruption, see ICC, 'Tackling corruption in arbitration' (2013) 24 ICC International Court of Arbitration Bulletin, Supplement. The supplement contains extracts from awards rendered between 2001 and 2009 in ICC cases that involved corruption issues, along with a series of articles on the subject.

F. Arbitrability

sector entities have been made with respect to major projects in Indonesia without adequate heed to their economic contribution to public welfare, simply because they benefited a few influential people. The arbitrators believe that cronyism and other forms of abuse of public trust do indeed exist in many countries, causing great harm to untold millions of ordinary people in a myriad of insidious ways. They would rigorously oppose any attempt to use the arbitral process to give effect to contracts contaminated by corruption.

But such grave accusations must be proven... Rumours or innuendo will not do.[236]

If an allegation of corruption is made in plain language in the course of the arbitration proceedings, the arbitral tribunal is clearly under a duty to consider the allegation and to decide whether or not it is proven.[237] It remains less clear, however, whether an arbitral tribunal has a duty to assume an inquisitorial role and to address the question of corruption on its own initiative where none is alleged. Initiating its own investigation and rendering a decision on the outcome of such a self-initiated investigation might leave a tribunal open to charges of straying into territory that is *ultra petita*.[238] Conversely, a failure to address the existence of such illegality may threaten the enforceability of an award and thus may sit uncomfortably with an arbitral tribunal's duty under some modern rules of arbitration to use its best endeavours to ensure that its award is enforceable.[239] Striking the right balance between these competing considerations may not be easy. For now, the extent of an arbitral tribunal's duty—if any—to probe matters of illegality of its own motion remains unclear.[240]

2.153

(vi) Fraud

Where allegations of fraud in the procurement or performance of a contract are alleged, there appears to be no reason for the arbitral tribunal to decline

2.154

---

[236] *Himpurna California Energy Ltd v PT (Persero) Perusahaan Listruik Negara*, Final Award dated 4 May 1999, extracts of which are published in (2000) XXV YBCA 13. See also Partasides, 'Proving corruption in international arbitration: A balanced standard for the real world' (2010) 25 ICSID Rev 47.

[237] For a notable example of an award in which an international arbitral tribunal discusses the consequences of a finding of bribery, see *World Duty Free v Republic of Kenya*, Award, ICSID Case No. ARB/00/07, IIC 277 (2006), signed 25 September 2006, despatched 4 October 2006. In that case, the bribery was clearly established and the tribunal held that, as a matter of international public policy, the claims under a contract that had been procured by the payment of a cash bribe to the head of state, President Daniel arap Moi, should be dismissed immediately and in their entirety: see Anon, 'ICSID arbitrators: $2m payment to President Moi was a bribe' (2006) 21 Mealey's Intl Arb Rep 4.

[238] See Kreindler, 'Aspects of illegality in the formation and performance of contracts', Presented at the 16th ICCA Congress, London, May 2002, at n. 75.

[239] See, e.g., ICC Rules, Art. 41; LCIA Rules, Art. 32(2).

[240] See Kreindler, 'Public policy and corruption in international arbitration: A perspective for Russian related disputes' (2006) 72 Arbitration 236, esp. at 242–245. See also Sayed, *Corruption in International Trade and Commercial Arbitration* (Kluwer Law International, 2004), pp. 33–36, for discussion on an arbitrator's initiative in raising the non-arbitrability of public procurement-related matters in relation to suspected bribery.

jurisdiction.[241] Indeed, in the heat of battle, such allegations are frequently made, although much less frequently proven. Where a claim put forward in the course of an arbitration is found to be fraudulent, it will be for the arbitral tribunal to dismiss it. However, problems may arise, as they did in *Fougerolle*,[242] if the alleged fraud is not discovered until an award has been made. An ICC tribunal rejected a claim by Fougerolle, the subcontractor under a turnkey contract, to the effect that it had encountered unexpected ground conditions; in a partial award, the arbitrators ordered Fougerolle to repay monies to its main contractor. Some months later, it became known that the main contractor was relying on the same grounds as had been put forward by Fougerolle (which the main contractor had denied and which the tribunal arbitrators had rejected) in support of its own claims against the engineer. The arbitral tribunal refused to review its award, on the basis that it had been made and could not be reversed at that stage, the award having been approved by the ICC Court. The Paris Cour d'Appel stated that the award could be annulled if fraud was proved—but, in the event, it was decided that there had been no fraud.[243]

(vii) Natural resources

2.155   Although states enjoy sovereignty over natural resources found within their territories, in most jurisdictions of the world no questions of arbitrability arise in relation to commercial disputes relating to those natural resources. Arbitral tribunals have invariably distinguished between the sovereignty itself and the commercial decisions made by states in the exercise of that sovereignty.

2.156   Thus, in one 1982 case, the state party challenged the arbitrability of a dispute on the grounds that the arbitral tribunal could not 'pronounce upon the responsibility for the rupture of the Contract made between the parties' without simultaneously judging 'the decision made by the Utopian Government in the exercise of its national sovereignty to renounce the exploitation of natural resources'.[244] In order to avoid this problem, the tribunal made an important distinction between the governmental decision itself (to stop the exploitation of natural resources—that is, the exercise of sovereignty), which was unchallengable and the financial

---

[241] Note, however, the surprising decision of the Indian Supreme Court in *N Radakrishnan v Maestro Engineers* (2010) 1 SCC 72, in which it was held that the courts are better equipped to adjudicate allegations of fraud, and that of the Nigerian Court of Appeal in *BJ Export & Chemical Processing Co. v Kaduna Refining and Petrochemical Co.*, 31 October 2002, (2003) 24 WRN 74.

[242] *Fougerolle v Procoface*, Cass. Civ. 1ere, 25 May 1992.

[243] For a fuller account of this case, see de Boisésson, 'L'arbitrage et la fraude' [1993] Rev Arb 3. In the same article, de Boisséson also reviews the unpublished *Beltronic* case, which came before a French court of appeal. This was a somewhat unusual case, in that the arbitral process itself was fraudulent. A fake arbitration centre was set up, with the arbitrator and the fake centre sharing the damages awarded by the arbitrator against the unfortunate Canadian defendant!

[244] Award of 1982, *Company Z and ors (Republic of Xandu) v State Organisation ABC (Republic of Utopia)* (1983) VIII YBCA 93, at 111–115.

(viii) Corporate governance disputes

In most jurisdictions, parties are free to submit corporate governance disputes to arbitration. By way of example, the Dutch courts have held that a dispute concerning the validity of a shareholders' meeting or resolution is not arbitrable.[245]

2.157

But this is not the case everywhere: a series of decisions by the Russian courts, for example, has cast doubt on the arbitrability of corporate disputes under Russian law. In *Maximov v Novolipetsky Metallurgicheskiy Kombinat*,[246] both the lower courts and the Supreme Arbitrazh Court found that 'corporate' disputes are under the special jurisdiction of the arbitrazh courts pursuant to articles 33 and 225(1) of the Arbitrazh Procedural Code, and are therefore non-arbitrable.[247]

2.158

In England, the courts have recently reaffirmed that arbitral tribunals have wide powers to rule on corporate governance matters. In *Fulham Football Club*,[248] shareholder disputes were described as 'essentially internal disputes about alleged breaches of the terms or understandings upon which the parties were intended to co-exist as members of the company'.[249] The Court held that there was no reason why an 'unfair prejudice' claim should be 'inherently unsuitable' for determination by arbitration. The applicable test in each case is whether:

2.159

> ...the matters in dispute...engage third party rights or represent an attempt to delegate to the arbitrators what is a matter of public interest which cannot be determined within the limitations of a private contractual process.[250]

---

[245] *Groenselect Management NV v Van der Boogaard*, Dutch Supreme Court, NJ 2007, 561, 10 November 2006. However, see Case No. II ZR 255/08 of 6 April 2009, in which the German Federal Court of Justice held that disputes over the validity of shareholders' resolutions in German limited liability companies are arbitrable, provided that the arbitration agreement complies with the criteria set out in the judgment.

[246] Ruling of the Supreme Arbitrazh Court, VAS-15384/11, 30 January 2012.

[247] The Constitutional Court rejected Mr Maximov's challenge to art. 33 on the basis that it was unconstitutional later that year. The Court stated that the legislature had the right to establish specific procedures for hearing certain categories of disputes, although it did not address the *arbitrability* of corporate governance disputes as such: see Ruling of the Constitutional Court No. 1488-O, 17 July 2012. In January 2014, the Russian Ministry of Justice published a draft Bill aimed at reforming aspects of Russia's arbitration law. The Bill provided that corporate disputes are generally arbitrable, subject to certain specified exceptions. Public consultation on the draft Bill was completed in April 2014 and revised drafts were issued. However, at the time of writing, no legislation has been passed.

[248] *Fulham Football Club (1987) Ltd v Sir David Richards* [2011] EWCA Civ 855.

[249] Ibid., at [58].

[250] *Fulham Football Club*, at [107]. For further discussion of this case, see Lew and Marsden, 'Arbitrability', in Lew, Bor, Fullelove, and Greenaway (eds) *Arbitration in England, with Chapters on Scotland and Ireland* (Kluwer Law International, 2013), p. 410.

(c) Conclusion

2.160 The significance of 'arbitrability' should not be exaggerated. It is important to be aware that it may be an issue, but in broad terms most commercial disputes are now arbitrable under the laws of most countries.[251]

G. Confidentiality

2.161 The confidentiality of arbitral proceedings has traditionally been considered to be one of the important advantages of arbitration. Unlike proceedings in a court of law, where press and public are generally entitled to be present, an international arbitration is not a public proceeding. It is essentially a private process and therefore has the potential for remaining confidential. Increasingly, however, confidentiality cannot generally be relied upon as a clear duty of parties to arbitral proceedings. Parties concerned to ensure the confidentiality of their proceedings would therefore do well to include confidentiality provisions in their agreement to arbitrate, or in a separate confidentiality agreement concluded at the outset of the arbitration.

2.162 In this section, the authors explore:

- the distinction between privacy and confidentiality;
- the classical position and current trend as far as confidentiality is concerned;
- the confidentiality of the award;
- confidentiality in investor–state arbitrations; and
- institutional arbitral rules on confidentiality.

(a) Privacy and confidentiality

2.163 As far as the hearing is concerned, the major institutional rules are in agreement: the hearing is private. Article 26(3) of the ICC Rules states:

> The Arbitral Tribunal shall be in full charge of the hearings, at which all the parties shall be entitled to be present. Save with the approval of the Arbitral Tribunal and the parties, persons not involved in the proceedings shall not be admitted.

The rules of the ICDR, LCIA, International Centre for the Settlement of Investment Disputes (ICSID), and World Intellectual Property Organization (WIPO) contain similar provisions, as do the rules of such commercial arbitration organisations as the Austrian Federal Economic Chamber, the Swiss Chambers' Arbitration Institution, the China International Economic and Trade Arbitration

---

[251] See Kirry, 'Arbitrability: current trends in Europe' (1996) 12 Arb Intl 373; van den Berg, 'Arbitrability' (1996) XXI YBCA 450.

G. Confidentiality

Commission (CIETAC), and the Japanese Commercial Arbitration Association (JCAA).[252]

2.164 Article 28(3) of the UNCITRAL Rules spells out the position in similar terms:

> Hearings shall be held in camera unless the parties agree otherwise. The arbitral tribunal may require the retirement of any witness or witnesses, including expert witnesses, during the testimony of such other witnesses, except that a witness, including an expert witness, who is a party to the arbitration shall not, in principle, be asked to retire.

The 'privacy' of arbitration hearings is therefore uncontroversial. And if the hearing is to be held in private, it would seem to follow that the documents disclosed and the evidence given at that hearing should also be—and should remain—private. In principle, there would seem to be no point in excluding non-participants from an arbitration hearing if they can later read all about it in printed articles or on an authorised website. However, a broader duty of confidentiality in international arbitration is now far from clear.

(b) Confidentiality—classical position

2.165 A general principle of confidentiality in arbitrations under English law, which might be said to represent the classical view, was spelled out by the English Court of Appeal in *Dolling-Baker v Merrett*.[253] Subsequently, in *Hassneh Insurance Co of Israel v Mew*,[254] the English High Court recognised the existence of an implied duty of confidentiality as the natural extension of the undoubted privacy of the hearing in an international commercial arbitration:

> If it be correct that there is at least an implied term in every agreement to arbitrate that the hearing shall be held in private, the requirement of privacy must in principle extend to documents which are created for the purpose of that hearing. The most obvious example is a note or transcript of the evidence. The disclosure to a third party of such documents would be almost equivalent to opening the door of the arbitration room to that third party. Similarly witness statements, being so closely related to the hearing, must be within the obligation of confidentiality. So also must outline submissions tendered to the arbitrator. If outline submissions, then so must pleadings be included.[255]

2.166 In *Ali Shipping Corporation v 'Shipyard Trogir'*,[256] the English Court of Appeal reaffirmed this classical position. The Court stated that the confidentiality rule was founded on the privacy of arbitral proceedings and that an implied term as to the

---

[252] For research that points towards confidentiality as one of the reasons for choosing arbitration, see the references in Pryles, 'Confidentiality', in Hille and Newman (eds) *The Leading Arbitrators' Guide to International Arbitration* (Juris, 2004), p. 415.
[253] [1991] 2 All ER 890.
[254] [1993] 2 Lloyd's Rep 243.
[255] Ibid., at 247 *per* Colman J.
[256] [1998] 1 Lloyd's Rep 643.

confidentiality of arbitration was a term that 'arises as the nature of the contract itself implicitly requires', which the law would imply as a necessary incident of a definable category of contractual relationship.[257] The Court acknowledged, however, that 'the boundaries of the obligations of confidence which thereby arise have yet to be delineated'.[258]

2.167 The classical position was reaffirmed by the English Court of Appeal in the case of *John Forster Emmott v Michael Wilson & Partners Ltd*,[259] in which it was held that:

> [C]ase law over the last 20 years has established that there is an obligation, implied by law and arising out of the nature of arbitration, on both parties not to disclose or use for any other purpose any documents prepared for and used in the arbitration, or disclosed or produced in the course of the arbitration, or transcripts or notes of the evidence in the arbitration or the awards, and not to disclose in any other way what evidence has been given by any witness in the arbitration. The obligation is not limited to commercially confidential information in the traditional sense.[260]

2.168 In so reaffirming, the Court of Appeal nevertheless noted that the duty of confidentiality in arbitration proceedings was not absolute and went on to consider its limitations as follows:

> [T]he content of the obligation may depend on the context in which it arises and on the nature of the information or documents at issue. The limits of that obligation are still in the process of development on a case-by-case basis. On the authorities as they now stand, the principal cases in which disclosure will be permissible are these: the first is where there is consent, express or implied; second, where there is an order, or leave of the court (but that does not mean that the court has a general discretion to lift the obligation of confidentiality); third, where it is reasonably necessary for the protection of the legitimate interests of an arbitrating party; fourth, where the interests of justice require disclosure, and also (perhaps) where the public interest requires disclosure.[261]

2.169 This echoes what is a constant theme in English decisions on the implied duty of confidentiality—namely, that it exists, but is subject to limitations that remain to be determined on a case-by-case basis.[262] The Singapore courts have adopted a similar approach, accepting the existence of an implied duty of confidentiality, but stipulating that they will impose such a duty 'only to the extent that it is reasonable to do so'.[263]

---

[257] Ibid., at 651.
[258] Ibid.
[259] [2008] EWCA Civ 184.
[260] Ibid., at [105].
[261] Ibid., at [107].
[262] See, e.g., *Milsom v Ablyazov* [2011] EWHC 955 (Ch) and *Westwood Shipping Lines Inc. v Universal Schiffahrtsgesellschaft mbH* [2012] EWHC 3837 (Comm).
[263] *AAY and ors v AAZ (AAY)* [2011] 1 SLR 1093, 1120. The court found that the defendant had legitimate grounds to disclose certain materials to the relevant public authorities because 'there was reasonable cause to suspect criminal conduct' (at 1131). See also *Myanma Taung Chi Oo Co. Ltd v Win Win Nu* [2003] 2 SLR 945. In the same way, in New Zealand, every arbitration agreement entails a duty of confidentiality unless the parties expressly agree otherwise. An implied duty of confidentiality also applies by default in Scotland and Spain.

(c) Confidentiality—the current trend

2.170 Notwithstanding the foregoing, the current trend in international arbitration is to diminish—or at least to question—the confidentiality of arbitral proceedings as a whole. This trend seems to have been considerably influenced by arbitrations in which there was a genuine public interest—in the sense that the decision of the arbitral tribunal would in some way affect the general public. For example, in *Esso Australia Resources Ltd v The Honourable Sidney James Plowman and ors*,[264] the High Court of Australia concluded that whilst the privacy of the hearing should be respected, confidentiality was not an essential attribute of a private arbitration. Specifically, the court found that a requirement to conduct proceedings in camera did not translate into an obligation prohibiting disclosure of documents and information provided in, and for the purpose of, the arbitration. The court then concluded that although a certain degree of confidentiality might arise in certain situations, it was not absolute. In the particular case before the court, 'the public's legitimate interest in obtaining information about the affairs of public authorities' prevailed.[265]

2.171 In respect of this final point, one of the judges discussed the standards for disclosure in respect of information that is of legitimate interest to the public and held that:

> The courts have consistently viewed governmental secrets differently from personal and commercial secrets. As I stated in *The Commonwealth of Australia v John Fairfax and Sons Ltd*, the judiciary must view the disclosure of governmental information 'through different spectacles'. This involves a reversal of the onus of proof: the government must prove that the public interest demands non-disclosure.[266]

2.172 In another Australian case,[267] the appellate court decided that an arbitrator had no power to make a procedural direction imposing an obligation of confidentiality that would have had the effect of preventing the government from disclosing to a state agency, or to the public, information and documents generated in the course of the arbitration that ought to be made known to that authority or to the public. It was said that public health and environmental issues were involved:

> Whilst private arbitration will often have the advantage of securing for the parties a high level of confidentiality for their dealing, where one of those parties is a government, or an organ of government, neither the arbitral agreement nor the general procedural powers of the arbitrator will extend so far as to stamp on the governmental litigant a regime of confidentiality or secrecy which effectively destroys or limits the general governmental duty to pursue the public interest.[268]

---

[264] (1995) 193 CLR 10. The case is also set out in (1995) 11 Arb Intl, 3, 235.
[265] Ibid., at 249.
[266] Ibid., at 247 *per* Mason CJ.
[267] *Commonwealth of Australia v Cockatoo Dockyard Pty Ltd* [1995] 36 NSWLR 662.
[268] Ibid., at 682 *per* Kirby P. See also *Adesa Corporation v Bob Dickenson Auction Service Ltd* 73 OR (3d) 787, [56] (2004), in which the Canadian courts acknowledged that the 'confidentiality of arbitration proceedings should be fostered to maintain the integrity of the arbitration process', but stated that this should be balanced against any wider public interest in disclosure.

2.173 In the United States, neither the Federal Arbitration Act nor the Uniform Arbitration Act contain a provision requiring the parties or the arbitrators to keep secret arbitration proceedings in which they are involved. As a consequence, unless the parties' agreement or applicable arbitration rules provide otherwise, the parties are not required by US law to treat as confidential the arbitration proceedings and what transpires in them.[269]

2.174 In *United States v Panhandle Eastern Corporation*,[270] Panhandle brought a motion before a US federal district court for a protective order, preventing the disclosure of documents relating to arbitration proceedings between it and Sonatrach, the Algerian national oil and gas company. In support of its motion, Panhandle argued that disclosure to third parties of documents related to the arbitration would severely prejudice Panhandle's ongoing business relationship with both Sonatrach and the Algerian government.

2.175 The court denied the motion on the grounds that Panhandle had failed to satisfy the 'good cause' requirements of rule 26(c) of the Federal Rules of Civil Procedure and that the filing was untimely, but it proceeded to address the question of confidentiality and, having rejected the existence of an express confidentiality agreement between the parties, gave no credence to the existence of an implied obligation.[271] This decision has been followed in subsequent US cases in which the courts have refused to find a duty of confidentiality in the absence of an express contractual provision or the adoption of a set of arbitration rules containing such a provision.[272]

2.176 The Supreme Court of Sweden has also rejected the idea of a general implied duty of confidentiality in arbitration proceedings.[273] The same position prevails in Norway: absent an agreement to the contrary, arbitration proceedings and decisions by the tribunal are not subject to any duty of confidentiality.[274]

(d) Award

2.177 Some institutional rules of arbitration, including those of ICSID, provide that the award may be made public only with the consent of the parties.[275]

---

[269] See *Industrotech Constructors Inc. v Duke University* 67 NC App. 741, 314 S.E.2d 272 (1984); *Giacobassi Grandi Vini SpA v Renfield Corporation* US Dist. LEXIS 1783 (1987).

[270] 118 FRD 346 (D. Del. 1988).

[271] It would seem that the decision of the Court was *obiter*. Moreover, it has been suggested that too much should not be read into this decision. Panhandle was seeking a 'protective order' to shield the arbitration documents from disclosure and the onus of establishing 'good cause' is a heavy one: see Neill, 'Confidentiality in arbitration' (1996) 12 Arb Intl 303.

[272] See, e.g., *Contship Containerlines Ltd v PPG Industries Inc.*, 17 April 2003, 2003 US Dist. 6857.

[273] See *AI Trade Finance Inc. v Bulgarian Foreign Trade Bank Ltd*, Supreme Court of Sweden, 27 October 2000, (2000) 15 Mealey's Intl Arb Rep A1.

[274] Norwegian Arbitration Act 2004, s. 5.

[275] See ICSID Arbitration Rules, r. 48(4). See also, e.g., AAA Rules, Art. 27(4).

G. Confidentiality

It has always been recognised, however, that there are circumstances in which an award may need to be made public, for example for the purpose of enforcement by a national court. In *Hassneh Insurance Co of Israel v Mew*[276] —a case mentioned earlier—the judge concluded that an award and the reasons contained in that award were different in character from the other elements of the arbitration proceedings (such as notes and transcripts of evidence, witness statements, submissions, and pleadings, all of which were, in his view, covered by the principle of privacy stemming from the fact that arbitration hearings were held in private). He found that the award was potentially a public document for the purposes of supervision by the courts or enforcement in them, and therefore could be disclosed without the consent of the other party or the permission of the court if—but only if—the party seeking disclosure needed to do so in order to assert or protect its legal rights vis-à-vis a third party.[277] This position is now reflected in many of the institutional arbitration rules. **2.178**

In addition to the disclosure of awards where required by law, disclosure of a kind takes place when an arbitral institution—such as the ICC—publishes 'edited and redacted' copies of arbitral awards as a guide for the benefit of lawyers and arbitrators.[278] **2.179**

Article 27(4) of the ICDR Rules provides that an award may be made public 'only with the consent of all parties or as required by law'.[279] These Rules provide that, unless otherwise agreed by the parties, selected awards may be made publicly available, with the names of the parties and other identifying features removed. If the award has become publicly available through enforcement proceedings or otherwise, then the names need not be removed. **2.180**

In England, the Privy Council had to consider in *Aegis v European Re*[280] whether an arbitration award in one arbitration under a reinsurance agreement could be relied upon by the winning party in another arbitration under the same agreement, **2.181**

---

[276] [1993] 2 Lloyd's Rep 243.
[277] Article 30 of the LCIA Rules mirrors this position, as pointed out by Rawding and Seeger, 'Aegis v European Re and the confidentiality of arbitration awards' (2003) 19 Arb Intl 484. See also *City of Moscow v International Industrial Bank* [2004] 2 Lloyd's Rep 179, which concerned the publication of a court judgment dismissing a challenge to an arbitral award under s. 68 of the Arbitration Act 1996. The court stated that a public judgment was particularly desirable where it involved a point of law that may offer future guidance to practitioners, but emphasised that this must be balanced against the parties' expectations of privacy and confidentiality in arbitration. Ultimately, the court concluded that the judgment should remain private because the party 'had, objectively, no good reason for insisting on [its] publication'.
[278] The ICC has no specific rule as to the confidentiality of awards, although an ICC arbitral tribunal now has an express power under Art. 22(3) of the ICC Rules to make confidentiality orders in relation to arbitration proceedings or other matters in connection with the arbitration.
[279] Similarly, Art. 28(10) of the SIAC Rules states that SIAC may publish any award with the names of the parties and other identifying information redacted.
[280] *Associated Electric and Gas Insurance Services Ltd v European Reinsurance Co. of Zurich* [2003] UKPC 11.

despite an express confidentiality agreement in respect of the first arbitration. The case came to the Privy Council on appeal from the Court of Appeal of Bermuda and disclosure of the award was allowed. The Privy Council said that the legitimate use of an earlier award in a later, also private, arbitration between the same parties was not the kind of mischief against which the confidentiality agreement was directed. This decision has been rightly described as:

> ...eminently sensible in the circumstances of the case. The private and, in theory, confidential nature of arbitration should not mean that the parties can go on arbitrating the same point *ad infinitum* until they get the result they prefer.[281]

2.182 In France, the Paris Cour d'Appel ruled, in *Aita v Ojjeh*,[282] that the mere bringing of court proceedings to challenge an arbitration award violated the principle of confidentiality in that it caused 'a public debate of facts which should remain confidential'. The judgment also contains dicta to the effect that it is in 'the very nature of arbitral proceeding that they ensure the highest degree of discretion in the resolution of private disputes, as the two parties had agreed'.[283] More recently, however, and in line with the modern trend, the Paris Cour d'Appel in *Nafimco*[284] found that the claimant failed to 'show the existence and foundation of such a duty in French international arbitration law'.

(e) Confidentiality in investor–state arbitrations

2.183 In the *Cockatoo Dockyard* case,[285] the Australian court concluded that whilst there was a 'high level of confidentiality' in arbitral proceedings, this should not prevent disclosure where the public interest was concerned. It is this concern for the public interest—and for the public's 'right to know'—that has led to the erosion of the principle of confidentiality in arbitral proceedings. The need to balance the private interest in confidentiality against the possible public interest in disclosure may be seen in arbitrations that have taken place under the treaty that established the North American Free Trade Agreement (NAFTA).

---

[281] Rawding and Seeger, '*Aegis v European Re* and the confidentiality of arbitration awards' (2003) 19 Arb Intl 484, at 488–489.

[282] [1986] Rev Arb 583, 583.

[283] Ibid., at 584. Some commentators argue that the reasoning of the French court is unsatisfactory, and that the extreme position advanced must be seen in the context of the court's determination to punish what it evidently viewed as a hopeless and tactically motivated attempt to set aside an English award in the French courts: see Paulsson and Rawding, 'The trouble with confidentiality' (1994) 5 ICC International Court of Arbitration Bulletin 48.

[284] *Nafimco*, Paris Cour d'Appel, 22 January 2004. Under France's new Decree No. 2011-48, confidentiality obligations apply by default in domestic arbitration proceedings. However, the Decree does not provide for confidentiality in international arbitration proceedings. Accordingly, where parties agree to refer disputes to international arbitration, they should make express provision for confidentiality in the contract. See Code of Civil Procedure, arts 1464(4) and 1506.

[285] *Commonwealth of Australia v Cockatoo Dockyard Pty Ltd* [1995] 36 NSWLR 662.

G. Confidentiality

2.184 In the early 1980s, an international arbitral tribunal applying the ICSID Arbitration Rules in *Amco v Republic of Indonesia*[286] held that 'as to the "spirit of confidentiality" of the arbitral procedure, it is right to say that the Convention and the Rules do not prevent the parties from revealing their case'. Balanced against this finding, the *Amco* tribunal nonetheless referred to a general duty existing under international law not to exacerbate an ongoing international dispute, and relied on the existence of this duty to recommend to the parties that they should ensure that their public statements about cases in which they were involved were both short and accurate.

2.185 In the years since *Amco*, tribunals applying the ICSID Rules, including NAFTA tribunals, have striven to achieve the same balance. For example, in *Metalclad Corporation v United Mexican States*,[287] Mexico made an application for a confidentiality order, pursuant to Article 1134 of NAFTA ('Interim measures of protection') and Article 28 of the (then) ICSID Additional Facility Rules ('Procedural orders'). The tribunal dismissed the application, finding that:

> There remains nonetheless a question as to whether there exists any general principle of confidentiality that would operate to prohibit discussion of the arbitration proceedings by either party. Neither the NAFTA nor the ICSID (Additional Facility) Rules contain any express restriction on the freedom of the parties in this respect. Though it is frequently said that one of the reasons for recourse to arbitration is to avoid publicity, unless the agreement between the parties incorporates such a limitation, each of them is still free to speak publicly of the arbitration...Indeed, as has been pointed out by the Claimant in its comments, under US security laws, the Claimant, as a public company traded on a public stock exchange in the US, is under a positive duty to provide certain information about its activities to its shareholders, especially regarding its involvement in a process the outcome of which could perhaps significantly affect its share value.

> The above having been said, it still appears to the Arbitral Tribunal that it would be of advantage to the orderly unfolding of the arbitral process and conducive to the maintenance of working relationships between the Parties if during the proceedings they were both to limit public discussion of the case to a minimum, subject only to any externally imposed obligation by which either of them may be legally bound.[288]

2.186 In another NAFTA arbitration, *R Loewen and Loewen Corporation v United States of America*,[289] the US government requested that all filings, as well as the minutes of oral proceedings, be treated as open and available to the public. Loewen did not oppose public disclosure, but requested that the disclosure take place only after the conclusion of the arbitration. The tribunal rejected the US government's

---

[286] *Amco Corporation and ors v Republic of Indonesia*, Decision on Request for Provisional Measures, 9 December 1983, (1983) 1 ICSID Rep 410, at 412.
[287] Award, Ad hoc—ICSID Additional Facility Rules; ICSID Case No ARB (AF)/97/1; IIC 161 (2000).
[288] Ibid., at [13].
[289] Decision on Hearing of Respondent's Objection to Competence and Jurisdiction, ICSID Case No. ARB(AF)/98/3, IIC 253 (2001), 7 ICSID Rep 425, 128 ILR 339.

request, referring to Article 44(2) of the ICSID Additional Facility Rules, which provide that minutes of hearings should not be published without the consent of the parties.[290]

2.187 Although the tribunal rejected the US government's request, it did not recognise any general duty of confidentiality; rather, it rejected Loewen's submission that each party is under an obligation of confidentiality in relation to the proceedings. In its award on jurisdiction, the tribunal summarised its conclusions as follows:

> In its Decision the Tribunal rejected the Claimants' submission that each party is under a general obligation of confidentiality in relation to the proceedings. The Tribunal stated that in an arbitration under NAFTA, it is not to be supposed that, in the absence of express provision, the Convention or the Rules and Regulations impose a general obligation on the parties, the effect of which would be to preclude a Government (or the other party) from discussing the case in public, thereby depriving the public of knowledge and information concerning government and public affairs. The decision concluded by repeating the comment made by the *Metalclad* Tribunal, namely that it would be of advantage to the orderly unfolding of the arbitral process if during the proceedings, the parties were to limit public discussion to what is considered necessary.[291]

2.188 The trend towards greater transparency in investor–state arbitration has emerged more clearly in recent years. In *Biwater Gauff (Tanzania) Ltd v United Republic of Tanzania*,[292] the tribunal recognised that the 2006 ICSID Rules reflected this overall trend towards transparency. The tribunal considered the balance between transparency and what it referred to as the integrity of the arbitral process, and concluded that some confidentiality controls were warranted, but ought to be 'carefully and narrowly delimited'.[293] Ultimately, the tribunal did not prevent the parties from discussing the case in public, or from publishing awards and other decisions by the tribunal, but restricted the disclosure of records of hearings, submissions, and witness statements.

2.189 Reflecting this trend towards transparency, UNCITRAL has published the UNCITRAL Rules on Transparency in Treaty-based Investor–State Arbitration.[294] The rules provide for the publication of all documents, including the notice of

---

[290] Ibid., at [25]. (Although Art. 44 has since been excluded from the Additional Facility Rules, pursuant to the amendments that came into force on 1 January 2003, reg. 22 of the ICSID Administrative and Financial Regulations imposes the same prohibition.)
[291] Ibid., at [26].
[292] ICSID Case No ARB/05/22, Procedural Order No 3 (29 September 2006).
[293] Ibid.
[294] The Rules apply to UNCITRAL arbitrations under investment treaties concluded after 1 April 2014. They apply to disputes under existing treaties only if the parties so agree. They do not affect commercial or state-to-state arbitrations. Pro-transparency provisions are now also contained in the US and Canada model bilateral investment treaties (BITs), and the EU trade spokesperson has indicated that the Rules 'set a benchmark for all future EU investment treaties': see European Commission, 'EU backs new transparency standards for investor-state dispute settlement', Press release (11 February 2013), available online at http://trade.ec.europa.eu/doclib/press/index.cfm?id=868

G. Confidentiality

arbitration, written pleadings, and lists of exhibits (and expert reports and witness statements, if any person so requests). Public access to hearings is guaranteed and interested third parties are entitled to make submissions. However, tribunals have discretion to order that certain documents should remain confidential if they contain protected information or if their disclosure would undermine the integrity of the arbitral process.

(f) Revisions to rules of arbitration

2.190 The increasing number of arbitrations in which there is a legitimate public interest, such as the NAFTA arbitrations just discussed and the ICSID arbitrations to be discussed later, has led to an erosion of the concept of confidentiality, with pleadings and awards being publicly available on the Internet and elsewhere. Many arbitration institutions have therefore amended their rules to impose an express duty of confidentiality upon the parties, but this may be overridden if it is judged that the public interest so requires.

2.191 Article 30 of the LCIA Rules imposes an express duty of confidentiality on the parties to the arbitration as follows:

30.1 The parties undertake as a general principle to keep confidential all awards in the arbitration, together with all materials in the arbitration created for the purpose of the arbitration and all other documents produced by another party in the proceedings not otherwise in the public domain, save and to the extent that disclosure may be required of a party by legal duty, to protect or pursue a legal right, or to enforce or challenge an award in legal proceedings before a state court or other legal authority.

30.2 The deliberations of the Arbitral Tribunal shall remain confidential to its members, save as required by any applicable law and to the extent that disclosure of an arbitrator's refusal to participate in the arbitration is required of the other members of the Arbitral Tribunal under Articles 10, 12, 26 and 27.

30.3 The LCIA does not publish any award or any part of an award without the prior written consent of all parties and the Arbitral Tribunal.

2.192 Similar restrictions are imposed under other major institutional rules.[295] One notable exception is the ICC Rules, although its internal statutes stress the 'confidential nature' of the ICC Court's work, which must be respected by all participants in whatever capacity.[296] In general, many institutional rules recognise the importance of confidentiality in arbitral proceedings, which may well involve the disclosure of commercial or financial information, proprietary 'know-how', and other so-called trade secrets that the parties may not wish to be made publicly available.

---

[295] See, e.g., Swiss Rules, Art. 44; SCC Rules, Art. 46; HKIAC Rules, Art. 42. Article 35 of the SIAC Rules specifies that the duty of confidentiality extends to pleadings, evidence, and other materials in the arbitration proceedings, all documents produced by another party, the award, and the very existence of the proceedings.

[296] Article 6 of the Statutes of the International Court of Arbitration.

2.193 The WIPO Arbitration Rules carry the protection of 'trade secrets' much further, as might be expected from an organisation concerned with the protection of intellectual property rights. Article 52 of the WIPO Rules defines 'confidential information' as any information, regardless of the medium in which it is expressed:

(a) ...which is:
 (i) in the possession of a party;
 (ii) not accessible to the public;
 (iii) of commercial, financial or industrial significance; and
 (iv) treated as confidential by the person possessing it.
[...]

2.194 On application by the relevant party, the tribunal may classify such information as 'confidential',[297] effectively restricting its disclosure to the tribunal and the parties. In exceptional circumstances, the tribunal may delegate this duty to a 'confidentiality adviser' who will determine whether the information is to be so classified, and if so, to whom it may be disclosed, in whole or in part.[298] As an additional safeguard, the tribunal may appoint the 'confidentiality adviser' as an expert to report on specific issues on the basis of the confidential information, without disclosing that information either to the other party or to the tribunal itself.[299]

2.195 For completeness, it should be noted that the WIPO Rules extend the protection of confidentiality to the very existence of the arbitration,[300] to disclosures made during the arbitration,[301] and to the award.[302] The duty of confidentiality is also, of course, imposed upon the tribunal and the WIPO centre itself.[303]

(g) Conclusion

2.196 One of the advantages of arbitration is that it is a private proceeding, in which the parties may air their differences and grievances, and discuss their financial circumstances, their proprietary 'know-how', and so forth, without exposure to the gaze of the public and the reporting of the media. The fact that arbitral hearings are held in private still remains a constant feature of arbitration. However, to ensure the confidentiality of the entire proceedings, it is increasingly necessary to rely on an express provision of the relevant rules (for example those of the LCIA or of WIPO), or to enter into a specific confidentiality agreement as part of the agreement to arbitrate, or at the outset of proceedings[304] (and it seems that this may be

---

[297] WIPO Rules, Art. 52(c).
[298] WIPO Rules, Art. 52(d).
[299] WIPO Rules, Art. 52(e).
[300] WIPO Rules, Art. 73.
[301] WIPO Rules, Art. 74.
[302] WIPO Rules, Art. 75.
[303] WIPO Rules, Art. 76.
[304] See the concluding comments of Rawding and Seeger, '*Aegis v European Re* and the confidentiality of arbitration awards' (2003) 19 Arb Intl 484.

H. Defective Arbitration Clauses

overridden in some jurisdictions if the relevant court considers it to be in the public interest that it should be).

H. Defective Arbitration Clauses

The principal defects found in arbitration clauses are those of inconsistency, uncertainty, and inoperability. The argument as to whether an arbitration clause suffers from one or more of these defects is likely to be raised where, for example, a party takes action in a national court in relation to a dispute and the defendant seeks a stay of the proceedings on the basis of the existence of the arbitration clause. In such circumstances, the application for a stay may be opposed on the basis that the arbitration agreement was 'inoperative or incapable of being performed'.[305]

2.197

(a) Inconsistency

Where there is an apparent inconsistency in the clause, most national courts usually attempt to give a meaning to it, in order to give effect to the general intention of the parties, which was to submit disputes to arbitration. This is the case in England, where the courts uphold a clause and strike out an inconsistent provision if it is clear that the 'surviving clause' carries into effect the real intention of the parties and the 'discarded clause' would defeat the object of the agreement.[306]

2.198

> In the meantime, given the prevailing sense of confusion amongst practitioners as to the precise nature and scope of any implied duty of confidentiality in arbitration, and as to the exceptions to any such duty, parties would be well advised not to take anything for granted and to continue including express confidentiality provisions in their arbitration agreement or in procedural directions at the outset of the case.

The UNCITRAL Notes on Organizing Arbitral Proceedings, paras 31–32, make the very same recommendation. When drafting confidentiality clauses, parties may be aided by the Model Procedural Order on Confidentiality. See Hwang and Thio, 'A proposed model procedural order on confidentiality in international arbitration: A comprehensive and self-governing code' (2012) 29 J Intl Arb 137.

[305] These terms are used in the New York Convention, Art. II(3), and in the Model Law, Art. 8(1). For a discussion of defective arbitration clauses, see Schmitthoff, 'Defective arbitration clauses' [1975] JBL 9. For a further discussion of the approach of national courts to the interpretation of defective arbitration clauses generally, see Auchie, 'The liberal interpretation of defective arbitration clauses in international commercial contracts: A sensible approach?' [2007] Int ALR 206. See also Mistelis and Lew, *Pervasive Problems in International Arbitration* (Kluwer Law International, 2006), pp. 163–165.

[306] See *Central Meat Products Ltd v JV McDaniel Ltd* [1952] 1 Lloyd's Rep 562; note also *EJR Lovelock Ltd v Exportles* [1968] 1 Lloyd's Rep 163, in which inconsistencies and uncertainties were exposed in the clause itself. See too *Mangistaumunaigoz Oil v United World Trade Inc.* [1995] 1 Lloyd's Rep 617, in which the arbitration clause provided for 'arbitration, if any, by ICC Rules in London'. The words 'if any' could be rejected as surplus usage. See also *Braes of Doune Wind Farm v Alfred McAlpine* [2008] EWHC 426 (TCC) and the decision of the Swiss Federal Tribunal in Case No. 4A_376/2008 of 5 December 2008, discussed by Scherer, 'Introduction to the case law section' (2009) 4 ASA Bulletin 735.

(b) Uncertainty

2.199 Similarly, as regards uncertainty, the courts of most countries generally try to uphold an arbitration provision[307] unless the uncertainty is such that it is difficult to make sense of it. The same is true of institutions. By way of example, the German courts have shown themselves time and again ready to give effect to clauses that are a long way from certain. In 2006, the Stuttgart court found that a clause referring disputes 'without resource [*sic*] to the ordinary court to Stockholm, Sweden' to be a reference to arbitration under the Stockholm Chamber of Commerce.[308] In the same year, the Oldenburg court held that a reference to 'the International Court of Arbitration (*Internationales Schiedsgericht*) in Austria' was a reference to the international arbitration centre of the Austrian Federal Economic Chamber.[309] The Singapore courts have recently upheld an agreement to refer disputes to 'the Arbitration Committee at Singapore under the rules of the International Chamber of Commerce'.[310] For its part, the ICC has in the past accepted the following vague and imprecise formulations as references to the ICC Court: 'the official Chamber of Commerce in Paris, France'; 'the Arbitration Commission of the Chamber of Commerce and Industry of Paris'; and 'a Commission of Arbitration of French Chamber of Commerce, Paris'.[311]

2.200 From time to time, however, courts and institutions are confronted with clauses that simply fail for lack of certainty.[312] Examples are:

(1) 'In the event of any unresolved dispute, the matter will be referred to the International Chamber of Commerce';
(2) 'All disputes arising in connection with the present agreement shall be submitted in the first instance to arbitration. The arbitrator shall be a well-known Chamber of Commerce (like the ICC) designated by mutual agreement between both parties';
(3) 'Any and all disputes arising under the arrangements contemplated hereunder...will be referred to mutually agreed mechanisms or procedures

---

[307] See *Star Shipping AS v China National Foreign Trade Transportation Corporation* [1993] 2 Lloyd's Rep 445 (CA); *Nokia Maillefer SA v Mosser*, Tribunal Cantonal (Court of Appeal), 30 March 1993, (1996) XXI YBCA 681, (1995) 1 ASA Bulletin 64.
[308] [2006] OLG Report Stuttgart 685.
[309] [2006] Schieds VZ 223 (OLG Oldenburg).
[310] The Singapore High Court concluded that it was open to the parties to approach any arbitral institution in Singapore to administer the arbitration, applying the ICC Rules: *HKL Group Co. Ltd v Rizq International Holdings Pte Ltd* [2013] SGHC 5.
[311] Derains and Schwartz, *A Guide to the ICC Rules of Arbitration* (2nd edn, Kluwer Law International, 2005), p. 86.
[312] For a recent example, see the Swiss Federal Tribunal's Decision No. 4A_279/2010 of 25 October 2010, in which it refused to uphold an arbitration clause that referred disputes to 'The American Arbitration Association or to any other US court'. The tribunal held that it was impossible to ascertain whether the parties had agreed to arbitrate to the exclusion of the state courts' primary jurisdiction.

of international arbitration, such as the rules of the London Arbitration Association'; and

(4) 'For both parties is a decision of Lloyd or Vienna stock exchange binding and both will subjugate to the International Chamber of Commerce'.

The problem with the first example is that even if the broad reference to the ICC is taken to be a reference to the ICC Court in Paris, the clause by itself does not stipulate whether the unresolved dispute is to be settled by arbitration or by conciliation or by some other procedure. The second example provides for arbitration 'in the first instance', but fails to provide intelligibly for the appointment of an arbitral tribunal. Even if the parties were to agree upon 'a well-known Chamber of Commerce' as arbitrator, this would be of no avail, since arbitrators must be individuals. The third example requires the future agreement of the parties on 'mutually agreed mechanisms or procedures'. The fourth is simply meaningless.

Further examples of what have been referred to as 'pathological arbitration clauses' are to be found in Craig, Park, and Paulsson's commentary on ICC arbitration.[313] Two of the more flagrant examples include: **2.201**

(1) 'In case of dispute (*contestation*), the parties undertake to submit to arbitration but in case of litigation the Tribunal de la Seine shall have exclusive jurisdiction';[314] and

(2) 'Disputes hereunder shall be referred to arbitration, to be carried out by arbitrators named by the International Chamber of Commerce in Geneva in accordance with the arbitration procedure set forth in the Civil Code of Venezuela and in the Civil Code of France, with due regard for the law of the place of arbitration'.[315]

The latter clause is given as an example of a 'disastrous compromise', which might lead to extensive litigation (unrelated to the merits of the dispute) to sort out any contradictions in the various laws stated to be applicable.[316]

(c) Inoperability

Article II(3) of the New York Convention states that: **2.202**

> The court of a Contracting State, when seized of an action in a matter in respect of which the parties have made an agreement within the meaning of this article, shall, at the request of one of the parties, refer the parties to arbitration, unless it

---

[313] Craig, Park, and Paulsson, *International Chamber of Commerce Arbitration* (3rd edn, Oceana, 2000), pp. 127–135.
[314] Ibid., at p. 128.
[315] Ibid., at pp. 132–133.
[316] Ibid. For further discussion on pathological arbitration clauses, see also Eisemann, 'La clause d'arbitrage pathologique', in Minoli (ed.) *Commercial Arbitration Essays in Memoriam Eugenio Minoli* (UTET, 1974); Davis, 'Pathological clauses: Eisemann's still vital criteria' (1991) 7 Arb Intl 365.

finds that the said agreement is null and void, inoperative or incapable of being performed.[317]

The reference to the agreement being 'null and void' refers to the arbitration agreement itself, since, as seen in the discussion of the principle of separability, in most countries the nullity of the main contract does not necessarily affect the validity of the arbitration agreement. An arbitration agreement is 'null and void' if it is 'devoid of legal effect', for example owing to mistake, duress, or fraud.[318] At first sight, it is difficult to see a distinction between the terms 'inoperative' and 'incapable of being performed'. However, an arbitration clause is inoperative where it has 'ceased to have legal effect'[319] as a result, for example, of a failure by the parties to comply with a time limit, or where the parties have repudiated,[320] or by their conduct impliedly revoked, the arbitration agreement.[321] By contrast, the expression 'incapable of being performed' appears to refer to more practical aspects of the prospective arbitration proceedings. It applies, for example, if it is for some reason impossible to establish the arbitral tribunal.[322] Courts tend to construe these provisions narrowly, to avoid offering a 'back door' for a party wishing to escape the arbitration agreement.[323]

2.203 An inability to pay advances on the costs of the arbitration,[324] or to make payment of an award,[325] should not mean that an arbitration clause is inoperative or incapable of being performed. However, in India, it has been held in the past that a stay of court proceedings should be refused on the grounds that exchange control regulations would prevent payments in foreign currency to the arbitrators and other overseas expenses of those participating in a foreign arbitration.[326]

---

[317] Similar words are contained in the Model Law, Art. 8(1).

[318] See, e.g., *Rhone Mediterranee v Achille Lauro* 712 F.2d 50 (3rd Cir.1983); *Albon v Naza Motor Trading Sdn Bhd* [2007] EWHC 665 (Ch). See also ICCA, 'Request for the enforcement of an arbitration agreement', in ICCA (ed.) *ICCA's Guide to the Interpretation of the 1958 New York Convention: A Handbook for Judges* (ICCA, 2011), pp. 51–52.

[319] *Albon v Naza Motor Trading Sdn Bhd* [2007] EWHC 665 (Ch).

[320] *Downing v Al Tameer Establishment* [2002] EWCA Civ 721.

[321] *Corcoran v Ardra Insurance Co. Ltd* 842 F.2d 31 (2nd Cir. 1988), also reported in (1989) XIV YBCA 773. For the continuation of the saga, see (1991) XVI YBCA 663 and (1992) XVII YBCA 666. See also Pryles, 'Inoperative and operative arbitration agreements: Developments in Australian law' (2006) 23 J Intl Arb 227.

[322] In *Aminoil v Government of Kuwait* (1982) XXI ILM 976, the original arbitration clause provided that the third arbitrator was to be appointed by the 'British Political Resident in the Gulf', an official whose post had ceased to exist at the time that the dispute arose; this defect was, in the event, cured by the conclusion of a new submission agreement.

[323] See, e.g., the decision of the Supreme Court of Canada in *Seidel v Telus Communications Inc.* [2011] 1 SCR 531.

[324] See *El Nasharty v J Sainsbury plc* [2007] EWHC 2618 (Comm), at [4].

[325] See *The Rena K* [1979] QB 377. See also Amparo Directo 465/2005, Tercer Tribunal Colegiado en Materia Civil del Primer Circuito, Servicios Administrativos de Emergencia, 2 September 2005, in which the Mexican courts held that an arbitration agreement cannot be 'inoperative' as a result of external factors that do not pertain to the agreement itself, such as the financial situation of the parties.

[326] See van den Berg, *The New York Arbitration Convention of 1958* (Kluwer Law International, 1981), p. 160.

I. Waiver of the Right to Arbitrate

2.204 In certain circumstances, a party may waive its right under an arbitration agreement to have a dispute finally settled by arbitration. Under most laws, such a waiver will typically require a statement, or conduct, that amounts to a clear and unequivocal renunciation of the right to arbitrate. Such a renunciation can be found in a party's participation in national court proceedings in which the parties, subject matter, and the relief sought[327] are identical to actual or prospective arbitration proceedings.

2.205 Article 8(1) of the Model Law provides:

> A court before which an action is brought in a matter which is the subject of an arbitration agreement shall, *if a party so requests not later than when submitting his first statement on the* substance *of the dispute*, refer the parties to arbitration unless it finds that the agreement is null and void, inoperative or incapable of being performed.[328]

2.206 Under section 9(3) and (4) of the English Arbitration Act 1996, a party wishing to stay court proceedings brought in breach of an arbitration agreement must make its application before taking any step in those proceedings in answer to the other party's substantive claim. In *Eagle Star Insurance*,[329] the English House of Lords (now the Supreme Court) summarised the position as follows:

> [I]n order to deprive a defendant of his recourse to arbitration a 'step in the proceedings' must be one which impliedly affirms the correctness of the proceedings and the willingness of the defendant to go along with a determination by the Courts of law instead of arbitration.[330]

Applying this test, the Law Lords concluded that an application to strike out a defective statement of claim did not constitute a 'step in the proceedings'.[331]

---

[327] It is not unusual for parties to bring administrative and court proceedings in parallel to arbitration proceedings in relation to the same underlying subject matter when the relief sought in the administrative and court proceedings is not available from an arbitral tribunal. Such parallel administrative and/or court proceedings would not amount to a waiver of the right to arbitrate. This can happen, e.g., where parties bring administrative and court proceedings to reverse a tax assessment, in parallel to bringing a contractual claim in international arbitration in relation to the consequences of a tax assessment. Whilst an arbitral tribunal can award contractual relief, it cannot take the administrative act of reversing a tax assessment. As a consequence, an administrative or judicial proceeding to reverse the tax assessment could not amount to a waiver of the right to arbitrate a contractual claim.

[328] Emphasis added.

[329] *Eagle Star Insurance Co. v Yuval Insurance Co.* [1978] 1 Lloyd's Rep 357 (a case decided under the Arbitration Act 1950).

[330] Ibid., at 361. The courts have adopted the same approach under the Arbitration Act 1996: see *Patel v Patel* [2000] QB 551; *Bilta (UK) Ltd (in liquidation) v Nazir* [2010] EWHC 1086 (Ch).

[331] See also *Capital Trust Investments Ltd v Radio Design TJ AB* [2002] EWCA Civ 135, in which a party was held not to have waived its right to arbitrate notwithstanding its application for summary judgment in the court proceedings. The summary judgment application was expressed to be in the alternative to the stay application.

2.207 A similar approach prevails in Australia. The courts require proof that a party has 'unequivocally abandoned' its right to arbitrate by taking steps that are wholly inconsistent with an intention to have the dispute finally settled by arbitration.[332] In *La Donna v Wolford*,[333] the Supreme Court of Victoria found that a party had waived its right to arbitrate by applying for security for costs in court proceedings. The Court reasoned as follows:

> [The party] sought an advantage, or at least sought to impose upon La Donna a burden, which was based upon the proposition that the litigation would proceed in this Court, that the defendant would take steps, and that the defendant would incur costs in taking those steps, in that litigation in this Court. This step was an unequivocal abandonment of the alternative course, being an application for a stay and a consequent arbitration.[334]

2.208 In certain circumstances, a party may maintain its right to arbitrate while taking substantive steps in court proceedings, for example by expressly reserving its rights under the arbitration agreement. In *Eisenwerk Hensel Bayreuth GmbH v Australian Granites Ltd*,[335] a party filed a defence in court proceedings and the Australian courts held that there had been no waiver, noting that the party was faced with the immediate threat of a default judgment and had filed a cover letter with its defence, confirming that it had no intention of discontinuing the arbitration proceedings that it had already instituted.

2.209 Under Canadian law, a party may waive its right to arbitrate if it files a defence or counterclaim in court proceedings.[336] In China, the first court hearing is the final opportunity for any party to raise any objection to the court's jurisdiction on the ground that the dispute is covered by an arbitration agreement.[337]

2.210 The US courts have traditionally been reluctant to find that a party has waived its right to arbitrate unless: (a) the party had knowledge of its right to arbitrate; (b) the party acted inconsistently with that right, and (c) the inconsistency caused prejudice.[338] In *Louisiana Stadium v Merrill Lynch*,[339] this test was satisfied in

---

[332] See, e.g., *ACD Tridon Inc. v Tridon Australia Pty Ltd* [2002] NSWSC 896, in which the Supreme Court of New South Wales held that a party had not waived its right to arbitrate although it had consented to directions, obtained an order for document production, and even agreed to be joined as a party to the New South Wales proceedings. The Court considered that the parties were simply 'exploring various ways of resolving of the whole or parts of the disputes' (at [75]).

[333] *La Donna Pty Ltd v Wolford AG* [2005] VSC 359.

[334] Ibid., at [26].

[335] [2001] 1 QDR 461.

[336] See, e.g., *Granville Shipping Co. v Pegasus Lines Ltd (TD)* [1996] 2 FC 853, Federal Court of Canada.

[337] Article 26 of the Arbitration Law of the People's Republic of China.

[338] See, e.g., *Airbus SAS v Aviation Partners Inc.*, No. C12-1228JLR, United States District Court, Western District of Washington, 25 October 2012; *Citibank NA v Stok & Associates PA*, No. 09-13556, 11th Circuit, 20 July 2010.

[339] *Louisiana Stadium & Exposition District, State of Louisiana v Merrill Lynch*, No. 10-889-CV, 2nd Circuit, 22 November 2010. See also *Great Western Mortgage Corporation v Peacock* 110 F.3d 222 (3rd Cir. 1997).

circumstances under which a party filed and pursued an action in the courts, then waited eleven months to invoke the arbitration agreement.

A party may also lose its right to arbitrate if there is a lengthy delay in the prosecution of its claim(s). Under the English Arbitration Act 1996, an arbitral tribunal has the power to dismiss a claim on broadly the same grounds as a national court may strike out claims in litigation.[340] The 1996 Act provides that, unless otherwise agreed by the parties, the tribunal may dismiss the claim if it is satisfied that there has been inordinate and inexcusable delay on the part of the claimant in pursuing its claim, and that the delay either gives rise (or is likely to give rise) to a 'substantial risk' that a fair resolution of the dispute is not possible, or that it has caused (or is likely to cause) serious prejudice to the respondent.[341] **2.211**

J. Multiparty Arbitrations

(a) Introduction

When several parties are involved in a dispute, it is usually considered desirable that the issues should be dealt with in the same proceedings, rather than in a series of separate proceedings. In general terms, this saves time and money. More importantly, it avoids the possibility of conflicting decisions on the same issues of law and fact, since all issues are determined by the same tribunal at the same time. In national courts, it is generally possible to join additional parties, or to consolidate separate sets of proceedings. In arbitration, however, it is difficult, and sometimes impossible, to achieve this, because the arbitral process is based upon the agreement of the parties. As a working group of the ICC's Commission on International Arbitration noted in its *Final Report on Multi-party Arbitrations*: **2.212**

> The difficulties of multi-party arbitrations all result from a single cause. Arbitration has a contractual basis; only the common will of the contracting parties can entitle a person to bring a proceeding before an arbitral tribunal against another person and oblige that other person to appear before it. The greater the number of such persons, the greater the degree of care which should be taken to ensure that none of them is joined in the proceeding against its will.[342]

---

[340] This provision was incorporated into the Arbitration Act 1950 by the Courts and Legal Services Act 1990. It was later incorporated into the English Arbitration Act 1996, s. 41(3).

[341] The position is similar in Hong Kong. If a claimant unreasonably delays the prosecution of a claim, it may be dismissed: Arbitration Ordinance, s. 59.

[342] Commission on International Arbitration, *Final Report on Multiparty Arbitrations*, Paris, June 1994, published in (1995) 6 ICC Bulletin 26 (the 'Delvolvé Report'), para. 5. See also generally Hanotiau, *Complex Arbitrations: Multiparty, Multicontract, Multi-issue and Class Actions* (Kluwer Law International, 2005). For an illustration of judicial reluctance to order consolidation unless the agreement of all parties is express, see the US courts, e.g. in *Stolt-Nielsen SA v Animal Feeds Intern Corporation* 2008 WL 4779582 (2nd Cir. 4 November 2008); *Glencore Ltd v Schnitzer Steel Products* 189 F.3d 264, 265–266 (2nd Cir. 1999); *Champ v Siegel Trading Co.* 55 F.3d.269 (7th Cir. 1995).

2.213 Where there is a multiparty arbitration, it may be because there are several parties to one contract, or it may be because there are several contracts with different parties that have a bearing on the matters in dispute. It is helpful to distinguish between the two.

(i) Several parties to one contract

2.214 It is increasingly common—particularly in international trade and commerce—for individuals, corporations, or state agencies to join together in a joint venture, or consortium, or in some other legal relationship of this kind, in order to enter into a contract with another party or parties. Where such a contract contains an arbitration clause and a dispute arises, the members of the consortium or joint venture may decide that they would each like to appoint an arbitrator. This is what happened in *Dutco*.[343] Dutco had entered into a contract with a consortium of two German companies and, when disputes arose, brought arbitral proceedings under the ICC Rules against those two companies. Each of the companies claimed to be entitled to appoint an arbitrator. This created problems, because the ICC Rules do not contemplate an arbitral tribunal of more than three arbitrators.[344] The ICC requested the two German companies to make a joint nomination of an arbitrator. They did so, but reserved their right to challenge the ICC's decision, which they regarded as depriving each of them of the right to nominate an arbitrator. The French Cour de Cassation agreed with the German companies: the court regarded the principle of equality in the appointment of arbitrators as a matter of public policy.

2.215 Many arbitration rules now make express provision for arbitration proceedings arising under multiparty contracts, so as to avoid the *Dutco* dilemma. For example, Article 12 of the ICC Rules states:

> [...]
>
> 6 Where there are multiple claimants or multiple respondents, and where the dispute is to be referred to three arbitrators, the multiple claimants, jointly, and the multiple respondents, jointly, shall nominate an arbitrator for confirmation...
>
> [...]
>
> 8 In the absence of a joint nomination... and where all parties are unable to agree to a method for the constitution of the arbitral tribunal, the Court may appoint each member of the arbitral tribunal and shall designate one of them to act as president....

---

[343] *BKMI and Siemens v Dutco*, French Cass. Civ. 1ere, 7 January 1992, (1992) 1 Bull Civ, (1992) 119 J du Droit Intl 707, 2nd document; commentary by Bellet [1992] Rev Arb 470, at 473–482; excerpts in (1993) XVII YBCA 140.
[344] ICC Rules, Art. 12 (ex Art. 8(4)).

J. Multiparty Arbitrations

Article 8 of the LCIA Rules adopts a similar procedure: **2.216**

8.1 Where the Arbitration Agreement entitles each party howsoever to nominate an arbitrator, the parties to the dispute number more than two and such parties have not all agreed in writing that the disputant parties represent collectively two separate 'sides' for the formation of the Arbitral Tribunal (as Claimants on one side and Respondents on the other side, each side nominating a single arbitrator), the LCIA Court shall appoint the Arbitral Tribunal without regard to any party's entitlement or nomination.

8.2 In such circumstances, the Arbitration Agreement shall be treated for all purposes as a written agreement by the parties for the nomination and appointment of the Arbitral Tribunal by the LCIA Court alone.

These and other arbitration rules[345] recognise the right of the parties to nominate a member of the arbitral tribunal if they are able to agree, but takes this right away from all parties equally and vests it in the institution if they cannot do so. This is a sensible solution to the problem of constituting an arbitral tribunal where there are three or more parties who are unable to agree amongst themselves. However, there may be difficulties when it comes to obtaining recognition and enforcement of an award made by a tribunal that has been established *for* the parties, rather than *by* the parties. The New York Convention, in Article V(1)(d), states that recognition and enforcement of an award may be refused on proof that '[t]he composition of the arbitral authority or the arbitral procedure was not in accordance with the agreement of the parties, or, failing such agreement, was not in accordance with the law of the country where the arbitration took place'. The Model Law contains a similar provision.[346]

If a losing party in an arbitration were to ask the competent court to refuse recognition or enforcement of an award on these grounds, the party seeking enforcement would presumably argue that the composition of the arbitral tribunal *was* in accordance with the agreement of the parties, since, by adopting the institutional rules, they had agreed, inter alia, to this particular provision. The only question that might then arise would be whether such an agreement, made before the arbitration proceedings began, was permitted by the *lex arbitri*—that is, the law of the state in which the arbitration took place. **2.217**

(ii) Several contracts with different parties

A different problem arises where there are several contracts with different parties, each of which has a bearing on the issues in dispute. Again, this is a situation that is not uncommon in modern international trade and commerce. A major international construction project is likely to involve not only the employer and the main contractor (which itself may be a consortium of companies), but also a host of specialised suppliers and subcontractors. Each of these parties will be operating under **2.218**

---

[345] See the UNCITRAL Rules, Art. 10; SIAC Rules, Art. 9; Swiss Rules, Art. 8; HKIAC Rules, Art. 8(2); SCC Rules, Art. 13(4) and (6).
[346] In Model Law, Art. 36(1)(a)(iv).

Agreement to Arbitrate

a different contract, often with different choice-of-law and arbitration clauses—and yet any dispute between, say, the employer and the main contractor is likely to involve one or more of the suppliers or subcontractors.[347]

2.219 What happens when a dispute between the employer and the main contractor is referred to arbitration, and the main contractor wishes to join the subcontractor in the proceedings, on the basis that if there is any liability, it is a liability that the main contractor is entitled to pass on to the subcontractor? This was the issue raised in the *Adgas* case.[348] Adgas[349] was the owner of a plant that produced liquefied natural gas in the Arabian Gulf. The company started an arbitration in England against the main contractors under an international construction contract, alleging that one of the huge tanks that had been constructed to store the gas was defective. The main contractor denied liability, but added that if the tank were defective, it would be the fault of the Japanese subcontractor. Adgas brought ad hoc arbitration proceedings against the main contractor before a sole arbitrator in London. The main contractor then brought separate arbitration proceedings, also in London, against the Japanese subcontractor.

2.220 There is little doubt that if the matter had been litigated in an English court, the Japanese company would have been joined as a party to the action. However, Adgas did not agree that the Japanese subcontractor should be brought into its arbitration with the main contractor, since this would have lengthened and complicated the proceedings,[350] nor did the Japanese subcontractor agree to be joined. It preferred to await the outcome of the main arbitration, to see whether or not there was a case to answer.

2.221 Lord Denning, giving judgment in the English Court of Appeal, plainly wished that an order could be made consolidating the two sets of arbitral proceedings, so as to save time and money and to avoid the risk of inconsistent awards:

> As we have often pointed out, there is a danger in having two separate arbitrations in a case like this. You might get inconsistent findings if there were two separate arbitrators. This has been said in many cases...it is most undesirable that there should be inconsistent findings by two separate arbitrators on virtually the selfsame question, such as causation. It is very desirable that everything should be done to avoid such a circumstance.[351]

---

[347] Another common situation arises in connection with bank guarantees concluded in connection with the main agreement: see Hanotiau, *Complex Arbitrations: Multiparty, Multicontract, Multi-issue and Class Actions* (Kluwer Law International, 2005), pp. 129–132 ; Wessel and Gsell, 'ITSA v SATCOM & BBVA: Spanish court extends an arbitration agreement to guarantor not a party to the contract' [2006] Int ALR N16.

[348] *Abu Dhabi Gas Liquefaction Co. Ltd v Eastern Bechtel Corporation* [1982] 2 Lloyd's Rep 425 (CA), (1982) XXI ILM 1057, [1983] Rev Arb 119 (with comment by Paulsson), (1984) IX YBCA 448.

[349] That is, the Abu Dhabi Gas Liquefaction Co. Ltd, which itself was owned by a consortium consisting of the Abu Dhabi National Oil Corporation and several international corporations.

[350] There was also a different choice-of-law clause in the two contracts.

[351] *Abu Dhabi Gas*, at 427.

J. Multiparty Arbitrations

The Court recognised that it was powerless to order consolidation without the consent of all parties:

> There is no power in this court or any other court to do more upon an application such as this than to appoint an arbitrator or arbitrators, as the case may be; we have no powers to attach conditions to that appointment, and certainly no power to inform or direct an arbitrator as to how he should thereafter conduct the arbitration or arbitrations.[352]

However, the Court was able to go some way towards meeting the problem of conflicting decisions. The case had come before the Court on an application for the appointment of an arbitrator, and the Court decided that it could appoint the *same* arbitrator in each case, if that arbitrator was ready to accept the appointment (as indeed he was). Lord Denning said: 'It seems to me that there is ample power in the court to appoint in each arbitration the same arbitrator. It seems to me highly desirable that this should be done so as to avoid inconsistent findings.'[353] This was one practical solution to the problem of conflicting decisions—but it still meant that there would be two separate arbitrations arising out of the same dispute.

2.222 Other solutions have been adopted, as will be seen, but none is entirely satisfactory. As a former secretary-general at the ICC Court pointed out: 'No generally acceptable solution to the manifold issues arising from multi-party arbitrations has yet been found by either the ICC or any of the dozens of other scholars, lawyers and arbitral institutes working on this issue.'[354]

2.223 Partial solutions have, however, now emerged in national arbitration laws and recent revisions of many of the major arbitral rules, and these are described later in the discussion of consolidation.[355]

(b) Class arbitrations

2.224 A 'class', or 'representative', action is a legal proceeding that enables the claims of a number of persons with the same interest (the 'class members') to be brought by one or a number of claimants (the 'representative claimant(s)') against the same respondent. In a class action, only the representative claimant(s) is a party to the action, and although the class members do not take an active part in the proceedings, they are bound by the outcome.

---

[352] *Abu Dhabi Gas*, at 427 *per* Watkins LJ. See also *Hartford Accident and Indemnity Co. v Swiss Reinsurance America Corporation* 87 F.Supp.2d 300 (SDNY 2000), in which the US courts acknowledged the risk of inconsistent decisions, but stated that this did not give courts 'the authority to reform...private contracts'.

[353] *Abu Dhabi Gas*, at 427.

[354] Bond, 'Recent developments in International Chamber of Commerce arbitration', in Practising Law Institute (ed.) *International Commercial Arbitration: Recent Developments* (PLI, 1988), pp. 55–101, at 89.

[355] See paragraphs 2.238*ff.*

2.225 Although, for many years, class actions have been peculiar to the US litigation landscape, variations on the theme have begun to make an appearance in other legal systems.[356] Perhaps more surprisingly, class actions have begun to make an appearance in international arbitration. 'Surprisingly' because one might take the view that a representative action is anathema to the principles of privity and party autonomy that tend to lead to the classic constellation of claimants facing respondents in the same proceedings who are party to the same contract. But US courts, no doubt more comfortable with the concept of class actions than other courts around the world, have started to see no reason why class action cannot be exported to international arbitration.

2.226 Thus, in the US Supreme Court's 2003 landmark decision in *Green Tree Financial Corporation v Bazzle*,[357] the plurality of a divided Supreme Court opened the door to class-wide arbitrations. The case involved a lender who had entered into standard-form contracts for home improvement loans with a number of borrowers. As is typical in contracts of this type, the contracts contained an arbitration clause, referring all disputes to 'binding arbitration by one arbitrator selected by us [the lender] with the consent of you'. The matter was commenced by two sets of consumers, who first brought two separate lawsuits before state courts challenging the lender's practices. Both lawsuits were referred to arbitration at the lender's demand, and in both cases the sole arbitrator (who was, in fact, the same individual in both cases) administered the cases as class-wide arbitrations and issued class awards in favour of the borrowers.[358]

2.227 The lender challenged the award, submitting that, in 'selecting an' arbitrator that was 'consented to by' one of its customers as required by the express terms of the arbitration agreement, it was not selecting an arbitrator to determine its dispute with its other customers. On this basis, it argued that the terms of the arbitration agreement did not accommodate, but rather forbade, class-wide arbitration.

2.228 The South Carolina Supreme Court upheld the class awards, reasoning that there was nothing in either the contracts or the Federal Arbitration Act to preclude class-wide arbitration. Unable to arrive at a majority opinion, the US Supreme Court nevertheless affirmed the judgment and found in the process that an arbitrator, rather than a court, must determine whether the contracts forbid class arbitration.

2.229 The response to *Green Tree* in the United States was immediate. Many companies—particularly in consumer businesses—modified their standard arbitration

---

[356] In England, procedural rules of court now exist for collective and representative actions (see Pt 19 of the Civil Procedure Rules). Similar procedural rules have, since 2003, been introduced for the courts in Sweden, Norway, Finland, Germany, and Italy.
[357] 539 US 444 (2003).
[358] In one of the two cases, the court had certified it as a class action before it was removed to arbitration. In the second case, the arbitrator certified it as a class-wide arbitration himself.

clauses to add an express prohibition on class-wide proceedings. This led to another wave of litigation, challenging the enforceability of such class-action waivers. The Californian courts, for instance, have consistently refused to give effect to waivers contained in consumer contracts on the basis that they are unconscionable.[359]

2.230 In 2003, US arbitral institutions promulgated new rules that deal with class-action scenarios. The American Arbitration Association (AAA) promulgated Supplementary Rules for Class Actions, which:

- require the arbitrator first to decide whether a class action is permissible under the contract in question and applicable state law;
- provide guidance for the arbitrator thereafter in determining whether to 'certify' the existence of a class;[360] and
- in particular, require the arbitrator to set forth his or her ruling on the class-action issues in a 'class construction award' that may itself be enforced or set aside in court.[361]

2.231 As for the courts, until recently there appeared to be a discernible trend toward allowing class treatment of issues that were arbitrable under most standard arbitration clauses, at least where the clause did not explicitly prohibit or restrict class treatment.[362] However, the tide changed following the Supreme Court's decision in *Stolt-Nielsen SA v Animalfeeds International Corporation*.[363] The Court overturned an arbitral award that determined issues on a class basis on the ground that the tribunal had exceeded its powers, stating that:

> An implicit agreement to authorize class-action arbitration ... is not a term that the arbitrator may infer solely from the fact of the parties' agreement to arbitrate. This is so because class-action arbitration changes the nature of arbitration to such a degree that it cannot be presumed the parties consented to it by simply agreeing to submit their disputes to an arbitrator.[364]

2.232 The Court noted that a shift from an ordinary bilateral or multilateral arbitration to a class-action arbitration involved 'fundamental changes', including a larger number of parties, lack of privacy and confidentiality, the adjudication of rights of absent parties, and the potential for high-value awards that were subject to only minimal judicial review on the merits. It stated that tribunals should therefore not

---

[359] See, in particular, *Discover Bank v Superior Court* 36 Cal. 4th 148 (2005); *Thibodeau v Comcast Corporation* 2006 Pa. Super. 306 (2006).
[360] In this regard, the Rules, for the most part, mirror the standards set forth in r. 23 of the Federal Rules of Civil Procedure.
[361] Of particular interest for international practitioners, as part of its rules for class arbitrations, the AAA explicitly waived the normal policy of confidentiality.
[362] See the decision of the Southern District of New York in *JSC Surtneftegat v President & Fellows of Harvard College*, SDNY 04 Civ 6069, 11 October 2007.
[363] 130 S.Ct 1758 (2010).
[364] Ibid., at 1775.

presume that the parties' mere silence on the issue of class arbitration constitutes consent.[365]

2.233 The recent case of *Oxford Health Plans LLC v Sutter*[366] indicates that a tribunal may still have some room for manoeuvre in circumstances in which parties have made no express provision for class arbitration. The US Supreme Court refused to overturn an arbitral award in which the tribunal found party consent to class arbitration in the absence of express wording, stating that it was for the tribunal to decide such matters on a case-by-case basis on a proper construction of the relevant contracts.[367]

2.234 After much debate, the related question of the validity of class arbitration waivers has also reached the US Supreme Court. In *AT&T Mobility LLC v Concepcion*,[368] it was held that such provisions are enforceable. The Court noted the 'liberal federal policy favouring arbitration', and held that arbitration agreements should be placed on an equal footing with other contracts and enforced according to their terms. Most recently, in *American Express Co. v Italian Colors Restaurant*,[369] the Supreme Court refused to carve out an exception to this principle where the cost of pursuing separate arbitrations is prohibitively high.

2.235 The concept of class arbitration has found little support outside the United States.[370] The European Commission launched a public consultation on 'collective redress' mechanisms in EU member states, as a result of which non-binding policy was published on 11 June 2013.[371] Whether class arbitration can be extended beyond the United States, and the resulting awards enforced internationally, remains an open question.[372]

(c) **Concurrent hearings**

2.236 Another possible solution to the problem is to appoint the same arbitrator to both arbitrations. As mentioned earlier, this may be possible where, for instance, a

---

[365] Ibid.
[366] 133 S.Ct 2064 (2013).
[367] The Court distinguished *Stolt-Nielsen SA v Animal Feeds Intern Corporation* 2008 WL 4779582 (2nd Cir., 4 November 2008), in which the parties 'had entered into an unusual stipulation that they had never reached an agreement on class arbitration'.
[368] *AT&T Mobility LLC v Concepcion*, Supreme Court of the United States, 131 S. Ct. 1740 (2011).
[369] No. 12-133, Supreme Court of the United States, 20 June 2013.
[370] However, see *Luis Alberto Duran Valencia v Bancolombia*, 24 April 2003, in which a Colombian tribunal allowed a class arbitration to proceed in a post-acquisition dispute involving multiple shareholders.
[371] European Commission, *Public Consultation: Towards a Coherent European Approach to Collective Redress* (4 February 2011); Commission Recommendation of 11 June 2013 on common principles for injunctive and compensatory collective redress mechanisms in the Member States concerning violations of rights granted under Union Law, OJ L 201/60, 26 July 2013.
[372] Strong, 'Enforcing class arbitration in the international sphere: Due process and public policy concerns' (2008) 30 U Penn JIL 89.

J. Multiparty Arbitrations

national court appoints the arbitrator.[373] If it is done, the procedures to be followed need to be considered carefully. The arbitrator may direct that (subject to any necessary provisions as to confidentiality) documents disclosed in one arbitration should be made available to the parties in the other,[374] and that a transcript of the witness evidence should be made, so that evidence given in one arbitration may be used in the other (with the parties being given the opportunity to question or comment upon it).

There is no reason in principle why this practice should not be adopted by the parties themselves, without any need for the court to intervene. It would depend upon the agreement of *all* of the parties concerned and, once again, appropriate procedural rules would have to be worked out. This could no doubt be done more easily in an ad hoc arbitration than in one that is subject to institutional rules.[375] 2.237

(d) Court-ordered consolidation

A solution that has been adopted in different parts of the world has been to enact legislation that enables the relevant national court to order consolidation of arbitrations.[376] In the Netherlands, for example, under the 1986 Arbitration Act, the president of the District Court in Amsterdam may order the whole or partial consolidation of two or more connected arbitrations in the Netherlands, unless the parties agree otherwise.[377] Some provinces of Canada also allow for court-ordered consolidation of connected proceedings.[378] 2.238

There is no provision in the Model Law for the consolidation of arbitrations, but nevertheless several states that have adopted it have added a provision providing for court-ordered consolidation. In any given case, it is necessary to consider the relevant legislation of the state concerned to see exactly what provision is made, but two examples illustrate what might be expected. Under the Hong Kong Arbitration 2.239

---

[373] It was the solution adopted by the English Court of Appeal in *Abu Dhabi Gas Liquefaction Co. Ltd v Eastern Bechtel Corporation* [1982] 2 Lloyd's Rep 425: see paragraph 2.219.

[374] In this regard, see *Aegis v European Re* [2003] 1 WLR 1041; Rawding and Seeger, 'Aegis v European Re and the confidentiality of arbitration awards' (2003) 19 Arb Intl 483.

[375] However, the Rules of the London Maritime Arbitrators Association (LMAA) contain provisions enabling arbitrators to order concurrent hearings of arbitrations, even where the tribunals are not identical: LMAA Rules, Art. 14(b).

[376] See generally Hanotiau, *Complex Arbitrations: Multiparty, Multicontract, Multi-issue and Class Actions* (Kluwer Law International, 2005), pp. 179–190.

[377] Code of Civil Procedure 1986, art. 1046. Proposals submitted to the Dutch Parliament to amend this provision were approved on 27 May 2014. The amended art. 1046 contains three material differences. First, the parties may now nominate a third party (e.g. an arbitral institution) to decide on a party's request to consolidate arbitration proceedings. This was a power previously held only by the president of the District Court of Amsterdam. Secondly, such third party's power to consolidate is broader than that of the president (who may order consolidation only where both sets of proceedings are in the Netherlands), in that the third party may also decide on a request to consolidate a Netherlands-seated arbitration with an arbitration seated *outside* of the Netherlands. Thirdly, the requirement that the subject matter of the arbitrations be connected has been removed.

[378] See *Western Oil Sands Inc. v Allianz Insurance Co. of Canada* [2004] ABQB 79.

Ordinance, the court may consolidate proceedings or order them to be heard concurrently or consecutively if: (a) a common question of law or fact arises in both proceedings; (b) the disputes arise out of the same transaction or series of transactions; or (c) the court considers it desirable to do so for any other reason.[379] In California, the court may order consolidation on such terms as it considers just and necessary. If the parties cannot agree upon the arbitrators, the court will appoint them. The court will also determine any other matters on which the parties cannot agree and which are necessary for the conduct of the arbitration.[380]

2.240 At first sight, court-ordered consolidation seems to be the ideal solution to the problem of ensuring consistent decisions, when the same or similar issues of law and fact would otherwise come before different arbitral tribunals. There are, however, likely to be practical and legal problems. The different arbitration agreements may differ in their provisions as to number and method of appointment of arbitrators, as to the relevant rules of arbitration, as to the power to issue interim awards, and so on. They may also differ as to the law governing the merits of the dispute.[381] Finally, there may be a problem in obtaining recognition and enforcement for such awards. Reference has already been made to the requirement of Article V(1)(d) of the New York Convention to the effect that the composition of the arbitral authority, and the arbitral procedure, must be in accordance with the agreement of the parties. Where an arbitral tribunal that has been imposed upon the parties makes an award, it may be argued that the award should be refused recognition and enforcement under this provision of the Convention.[382] There is strong support, however, for the view that where a court *has* ordered a consolidated arbitration, the award *will* be enforceable under the New York Convention provided that the parties have at least agreed to arbitration and to the same arbitral jurisdiction.[383]

2.241 In England, when the Arbitration Act 1996 was being drafted, it was proposed that there should be a provision in the Act that would empower either the arbitral tribunal or the court (or both) to order consolidation or concurrent hearings. The

---

[379] See the Hong Kong Arbitration Ordinance 2011, Sch. 2, s. 2. However, parties must 'opt in' to this provision: see also *Chun Wo Building Construction v China Merchants Tower Co.* [2000] 2 HKC 255.

[380] California Code of Civil Procedure, § 1297.272. For a note of other states that adopted the Model Law, but added a provision for consolidation of arbitrations, see Sanders, 'Arbitration', in Cappelletti (ed.) *Encyclopedia of International and Comparative Law, Vol. XVI* (Brill, 1987), ch. 12, para. 45. See also Leboulanger, 'Multi-contract arbitrations' (1996) 13 J Intl Arb 43.

[381] As in *Abu Dhabi Gas Liquefaction Co. Ltd v Eastern Bechtel Corporation* [1982] 2 Lloyd's Rep 425 (CA): see paragraph 2.219.

[382] See Hascher, 'Consolidation of arbitration by American courts: Fostering or hampering international commercial arbitration?' (1984) 1 J Intl Arb 127.

[383] See van den Berg, 'Consolidated arbitrations and the 1958 New York Arbitration Convention' (1986) 2 Arb Intl 367; see also Jarvin, 'Consolidated arbitrations, the New York Arbitration Convention and the Dutch Arbitration Act 1986: A critique of Dr van den Berg' (1987) 3 Arb Intl 254; van den Berg, 'A replique to Mr Jarvin' (1987) 3 Arb Intl 259. See also *Karaha Bodas Co. v Perusahaan Pertambangan Minyak* 364 F.3d 274 (5th Cir. 2004); *Riverstone Ins Ltd v Liquidators of ICD*, Case No. 08/12816, Paris Cour d'Appel, 5 November 2009.

J. Multiparty Arbitrations

Departmental Advisory Committee (DAC) on Arbitration Law considered these proposals carefully, but rejected them. The DAC wrote:

> In our view it would amount to a negation of the principle of party autonomy to give the tribunal or the Court power to order consolidation or concurrent hearings. Indeed it would to our minds go far towards frustrating the agreement of the parties to have their own tribunal for their own disputes. Further difficulties could well arise, such as the disclosure of documents from one arbitration to another. Accordingly we would be opposed to giving the tribunal or the Court this power. However, if the parties agree to invest the tribunal with such a power, then we would have no objection.[384]

The DAC went on to state that it appreciated the common sense behind the proposal for compulsory consolidation, but nevertheless was of the opinion that the problem would best be solved by agreement of the parties. It was suggested that arbitration agreements could be drafted so as to permit consolidation or concurrent hearings; by way of example, reference was made to the Rules of the London Maritime Arbitrators Association (LMAA).[385] In order to make it plain that such procedures are permissible under English law, section 35 of the 1996 Act provides that: **2.242**

> (1) The parties are free to agree—
>   (a) that the arbitral proceedings shall be consolidated with other arbitral proceedings, or
>   (b) that concurrent hearings shall be held,
>   on such terms as may be agreed.
> (2) Unless the parties agree to confer such power on the tribunal, the tribunal has no power to order consolidation of proceedings or concurrent hearings.

Provisions such as this emphasise the consensual nature of arbitration. They make it clear that, in principle, it is right to allow the parties themselves to decide whether there should be a consolidated arbitration or concurrent hearings in any given dispute.

(e) Consolidation by consent

(i) *Under an arbitration agreement*

The ICC Commission on International Arbitration's *Final Report on Multi-party Arbitrations* summarised its work as follows: **2.243**

> Reaching the end of its investigations, the Working Group has come to the conclusion that it is improper to deal with multi-party arbitration as if it were susceptible of simple and uniform treatment. International trade gives rise to situations which have become extremely complex.[386]

---

[384] Departmental Advisory Committee on Arbitration Law, *Report on the Arbitration Bill*, February 1996, para. 180.
[385] See paragraph 2.208.
[386] Delvolvé Report, n. 344, para. 114.

The Working Group suggested that the problem posed called for 'a wide range of solutions'. One was for the parties to agree in advance that any dispute between them would be referred to a multiparty arbitration.[387] The report stated that, '[i]n a multilateral relationship, whether involving a single contract or separate related contracts, it may be appropriate or necessary to have a multi-party arbitration clause'.[388]

2.244 Drafting such a clause is not easy. It requires a close understanding of the nature of the relationship between the different parties and of the type of disputes that may conceivably arise, and it calls for careful and detailed drafting. It is miles away from the standard, or model, form of arbitration clause under which most arbitrations are conducted. The report includes as an annexe examples of multiparty arbitration agreements that have been drawn from various sources.[389]

(ii) Under institutional rules

2.245 Neither the Model Law nor the UNCITRAL Rules contain any provision for the consolidation of different arbitrations. However, the problem is a real one—and it is a problem to which arbitral institutions such as the ICC and the LCIA have given long and careful consideration. Under Article 10 of the ICC Rules, the ICC Court may, at the request of a party, consolidate two or more pending arbitrations where: (a) the parties agree; (b) all claims are made under the same arbitration agreement; or (c) in the case of claims under multiple contracts, the arbitrations are between the same parties, the disputes arise in connection with the same legal relationship, and the Court considers that the terms of the arbitration agreements are compatible.

2.246 Article 4(1) of the Swiss Rules allows for consolidation in the following circumstances:

> Where a notice of arbitration is submitted between parties already involved in other arbitral proceedings pending under these Rules, the Court may decide, after consulting with the parties and any confirmed arbitrator in all proceedings, that the new case shall be consolidated with the pending arbitral proceedings. The Court may proceed in the same way where a Notice of Arbitration is submitted between parties that are not identical to the parties in the pending arbitral proceedings. When rendering its decision, the Court shall take into account all relevant circumstances, including the links between the cases and the progress already made in the pending arbitral proceedings.[390]

---

[387] Delvolvé Report, para. 114
[388] Delvolvé Report, para. 113.
[389] They are not, however, to be regarded as approved by the Working Group. For further guidance, see Paulsson, Rawding, and Reed (eds) *The Freshfields Guide to Arbitration Clauses in International Contracts* (3rd edn, Kluwer Law International, 2010).
[390] See also the Rules of the Belgian Centre for Arbitration and Mediation (CEPANI), Art. 13, which adopts a similar approach.

J. Multiparty Arbitrations

In an appropriate case, provisions such as these should prove useful in bringing everyone concerned before the same arbitral tribunal. However, the procedure to be followed in the conduct of such a consolidated arbitration would have to be carefully worked out, so as to ensure that each party is given a proper opportunity to present its case. Otherwise, any award may be refused recognition or enforcement.[391]

2.247

---

[391] Under the provisions of the New York Convention, Art. V1(b), or the Model Law, Art. 36(1)(a)(ii).

3

APPLICABLE LAWS

A.	Overview	3.01	D. Law Applicable to the Substance	3.91
B.	Law Governing the Agreement to Arbitrate	3.09	E. Conflict Rules and the Search for the Applicable Law	3.198
C.	Law Governing the Arbitration	3.37	F. Other Applicable Rules and Guidelines	3.221

A. Overview

(a) Introduction

Many disputes that are referred to arbitration are determined by arbitral tribunals with no more than a passing reference to the law. They turn on matters of fact: what was said and what was not said; what was promised and what was not promised; what was done and what was not done. A plant for the manufacture of glass pharmaceutical bottles is erected and put into operation on a turnkey basis, but fails to produce bottles of the right quality and quantity, and the plant operates at a loss: was this because of some defect in the plant, for which the supplier is responsible, or was it the result of mismanagement by the owner in the operation of the plant? A major bank is involved in a financial scandal and the bank's institutional shareholders agree to compensate depositors for their loss: are these payments recoverable under a policy of insurance, or reinsurance, or are they not covered? **3.01**

In such cases, the arbitral tribunal first needs to resolve the issues of fact, as best it can, before moving on to interpret the contract and, if need be, to refer to any underlying system of law. Just as an arbitral tribunal frequently reaches its decision on the merits of a dispute without detailed reference to the law applicable to those merits, so an arbitral tribunal may well pay little, or no, attention to the law that governs its own existence and proceedings as an arbitral tribunal. Indeed, it may even give no more than fleeting recognition to the fact that such a law exists—any more than the average purchaser of a motor car gives, at best, fleeting recognition to the law of contract that underpins the transaction. **3.02**

(b) No legal vacuum

3.03 It would be wrong to deduce from this, however, that international arbitration exists in a legal vacuum. That would be like suggesting that there is no need for a law of contract, since parties to a contract make their own law. Millions of contracts—most of them made orally, rather than in writing—are made every day throughout the world. They may be as simple as the purchase of a bus ticket or the hire of a taxi, or they may be as complex as the purchase of a car on credit terms. Most are made, performed—and forgotten. Disputes are rare; the involvement of lawyers, rarer still. Yet law governs each of these situations. The apparent simplicity of the purchase of a bus ticket or the hire of a taxi is deceptive. They are transactions that involve a contractual relationship and such relationships are underpinned by complex rules of law. These may not be referred to expressly, but they exist nonetheless:

> It is often said that the parties to a contract make their own law, and it is, of course, true that, subject to the rules of public policy and *ordre public*, the parties are free to agree upon such terms as they may choose. Nevertheless, agreements that are intended to have a legal operation (as opposed to a merely social operation) create legal rights and duties, and legal rights and duties cannot exist in a vacuum but must have a place within a legal system which is available for dealing with such questions as the validity, application and interpretation of contracts, and, generally, for supplementing their express provisions.[1]

3.04 Like a contract, an arbitration does not exist in a legal vacuum. It is regulated, first, by the rules of procedure that have been agreed or adopted by the parties and the arbitral tribunal; secondly, it is regulated by the law of the place of arbitration. It is important to recognise at the outset—as even distinguished judges and commentators sometimes fail to do—that this dualism exists.

3.05 For the most part, modern laws of arbitration are content to leave parties and arbitrators free to decide upon their own particular, detailed rules of procedure, so long as the parties are treated equally. Under these modern laws, it is accepted that the courts of law should be slow to intervene in an arbitration, if they intervene at all.[2] Nevertheless, rules need the sanction of law if they are to be effective and,

---

[1] Lord McNair, 'The general principles of law recognised by civilised nations' (1957) 33 BYIL 1, at 7.

[2] The lead is given by the Model Law, which states categorically (in Art. 5) that, '[i]n matters governed by this Law, no court shall intervene except where so provided in this Law'. Even states that have not adopted the Model Law per se have thought it appropriate to make a similar statement: for instance, Swiss law states that its courts will 'decline jurisdiction' where there is an agreement to arbitrate, except in limited circumstances (Swiss Private International Law Act 1987, or Swiss PIL, s. 7). The Swedish Arbitration Act 1999 contains a similar provision, at s. 4, although ss 5 and 6 contain exceptions to this rule; the French Code of Civil Procedure provides for the same at art. 1448; and the Spanish Arbitration Act 2003, which is based on the Model Law with

in this context, the relevant law is the law of the place or seat of the arbitration. This is referred to as the *lex arbitri*.

3.06 This is an important—and frequently misunderstood—topic, to which it will be necessary to return later in this chapter.

(c) A complex interaction of laws

3.07 International arbitration, unlike its domestic counterpart, usually involves more than one system of law or of legal rules. Indeed, it is possible, without undue sophistication, to identify at least five different systems of law that, in practice, may have a bearing on an international arbitration:

(1) the law governing the arbitration agreement and the performance of that agreement;
(2) the law governing the existence and proceedings of the arbitral tribunal (the *lex arbitri*);
(3) the law, or the relevant legal rules, governing the substantive issues in dispute (generally described as the 'applicable law', the 'governing law', 'the proper law of the contract', or 'the substantive law');
(4) other applicable rules and non-binding guidelines and recommendations;[3] and
(5) the law governing recognition and enforcement of the award (which may, in practice, prove to be not one law, but two or more, if recognition and enforcement is sought in more than one country in which the losing party has, or is thought to have, assets).[4]

3.08 This chapter deals with: the law governing the agreement to arbitrate; the law governing the arbitration itself (the *lex arbitri*); the law governing the substantive matters in dispute (the substantive law); the law or rules governing conflicts of law; and certain non-national guidelines and rules that are increasingly relied upon in international arbitration. The law governing the parties' capacity to enter into an arbitration agreement has been dealt with in Chapter 2, and issues relating to the laws governing the arbitral award (including challenge, recognition, and enforcement) are dealt with in Chapters 10 and 11.

---

significant changes, states unequivocally at s. 7 that, '[i]n matters governed by this Act, no court shall intervene except where so provided in this Act'.

[3] What some have referred to as the procedural 'soft law' of international arbitration: see Park, 'The procedural soft law of international arbitration: Non-governmental instruments', in Mistelis and Lew (eds) *Pervasive Problems in International Arbitration* (Kluwer Law International, 2006), pp. 141–154.
[4] See Chapter 11.

B. Law Governing the Agreement to Arbitrate

3.09 An agreement to arbitrate, as discussed in Chapter 2, may be set out in a purpose-made submission agreement or—as is the case much more frequently—in an arbitration clause. Both submission agreements and arbitration clauses have been considered in detail in the previous chapter. It is appropriate, however, to consider the law governing arbitration agreements here.

3.10 It might be assumed that this is the same law as that which the parties chose to govern the substantive issues in dispute—but this is not necessarily a safe assumption. An 'applicable law clause' will usually refer only to the 'substantive issues in dispute'. It will not usually refer in terms to disputes that might arise in relation to the arbitration agreement itself. It would therefore be sensible, in drafting an arbitration agreement, also to make clear what law is to apply to that agreement.

3.11 If no such express designation has been made and it becomes necessary to determine the law applicable to the agreement to arbitrate, what are the choices?[5] There are other possibilities, but the principal choice—in the absence of any express or implied choice by the parties—lies between the law of the seat of the arbitration and the law that governs the contract as a whole.

(a) Law of the contract

3.12 Since the arbitration clause is only one of many clauses in a contract, it might seem reasonable to assume that the law chosen by the parties to govern the contract will also govern the arbitration clause.[6] If the parties expressly choose a particular law to govern their agreement, why should some other law—which the parties have not chosen—be applied to only one of the clauses in the agreement, simply because it happens to be the arbitration clause? It seems reasonable to say, as has Professor Lew, that:

> There is a very strong presumption in favour of the law governing the substantive agreement which contains the arbitration clause also governing the arbitration agreement. This principle has been followed in many cases. This could even be *implied* as an agreement of the parties as to the law applicable to the arbitration clause.[7]

---

[5] For an in-depth discussion of this issue, see Lew, 'The law applicable to the form and substance of the arbitration clause' (1999) 9 ICCA Congress Series 114.

[6] See *Sulamérica Cia Nacional de Seguros SA and ors v Enesa Engenharia SA and ors* [2012] EWCA Civ 638, at [11], in which the English Court of Appeal observed:

> It has long been recognised that in principle the proper law of an arbitration agreement which itself forms part of a substantive contract may differ from that of the contract as a whole, but it is probably fair to start from the assumption that, in the absence of any indication to the contrary, the parties intended the whole of their relationship to be governed by the same system of law.

[7] Lew, n. 5, at 143 (emphasis added). It could also be seen as an *express* choice, if the arbitration clause is considered to be simply one of the rights and obligations assumed by the parties in their contract, to be governed by the law which governs that contract.

B. Law Governing the Agreement to Arbitrate

A French commentator has offered a similar view: **3.13**

> The autonomy of the arbitration clause and of the principal contract does not mean that they are totally independent one from the other, as evidenced by the fact that acceptance of the contract entails acceptance of the clause, without any other formality.[8]

This supports the view that the arbitration clause is generally governed by the same law as the rest of the contract. However, the reference here to the 'autonomy' of the arbitration clause points towards the problem that may arise. An arbitration clause is taken to be autonomous and to be separable from other clauses in the agreement.[9] If necessary, it may stand alone. In this respect, it is comparable to a submission agreement. It is this separability of an arbitration clause that opens the way for the possibility that it may be governed by a different law from that which governs the main agreement.

The New York Convention points towards this conclusion.[10] In the provisions relating to enforcement, the Convention stipulates that the agreement under which the award is made must be valid 'under the law to which the parties have subjected it', or, failing any indication thereon, 'under the law of the country where the award was made' (which will be the law of the seat of the arbitration). **3.14**

(b) Law of the seat of the arbitration

Taking as their point of departure the separability of the arbitration clause, there are cases in different jurisdictions in which a court or arbitral tribunal has taken the law of the seat of the arbitration to be the appropriate law to govern the parties' arbitration agreement. This approach has been adopted in the London Court of International Arbitration (LCIA) Rules, which provide at Article 16(4) that: **3.15**

> The law applicable to the Arbitration Agreement and the arbitration shall be the law applicable at the seat of the arbitration, unless and to the extent that the parties have agreed in writing on the application of other laws or rules of law and such agreement is not prohibited by the law applicable at the arbitral seat.

The following examples illustrate this approach.

In *Sulamérica Cia Nacional de Seguros SA and ors v Enesa Engenharia SA and ors*,[11] the English Court of Appeal held that English law was the governing law of an arbitration agreement, even though it appeared in a contract that was governed by **3.16**

---

[8] Derains, 'The ICC arbitral process, Part VIII: Choice of law applicable to the contract and international arbitration' (2006) 6 ICC International Court of Arbitration Bulletin 10, at 16–17.

[9] Separability is discussed in Chapter 2. See *Fiona Trust & Holding Corporation and ors v Privalov and ors* [2007] EWCA Civ 20; *Fili Shipping Co. Ltd v Premium Nafta Products Ltd* [2007] UKHL 40 (on appeal from *Fiona Trust*). See also *Sulamérica*, at [9].

[10] New York Convention, Art. V(1)(a). There is a similar provision in Model Law, Art. 34(2)(a).

[11] [2012] EWCA Civ 638.

Brazilian law and which also reserved exclusive jurisdiction in relation to any disputes under the contract to the Brazilian courts. In addition to the Brazilian governing law and jurisdiction clause, the contract separately provided for arbitration seated in London under the Aida Reinsurance and Insurance Arbitration Society (ARIAS) Arbitration Rules.

3.17 The case concerned two insurance policies covering various risks arising in connection with the construction of a hydroelectric generating plant in Brazil. A dispute had arisen between the parties over Sulamérica's liability for certain claims made by Enesa under the policies and Sulamérica gave notice of arbitration to Enesa. In response, Enesa commenced proceedings in the Brazilian courts, where it obtained an anti-suit injunction restraining Sulamérica from pursuing the arbitration. Sulamérica, in turn, obtained an anti-suit injunction in the English Commercial Court, restraining Enesa from pursuing the action in the Brazilian courts. Enesa appealed to the English Court of Appeal, arguing (among other things) that it was not bound to arbitrate because the arbitration agreement was governed by the law of Brazil, under which the arbitration agreement could be invoked only with Enesa's consent.

3.18 The English Court of Appeal upheld Sulamérica's anti-suit injunction, finding (among other things) that the proper law of the arbitration agreement was English law. The central question concerned the relative importance to be attached to the parties' express choice of proper law and their choice of London as the seat of arbitration.

3.19 The English Court of Appeal held that the law of the arbitration agreement was to be determined by application of the three-stage enquiry established at common law.

(1) If the parties made an express choice of law to govern the arbitration agreement, that choice would be effective, regardless of the law applicable to the contract as a whole.
(2) Where the parties failed expressly to specify the law of the arbitration agreement, it was necessary to consider whether the parties had made an implied choice of law.
(3) Where it was not possible to establish the law of the arbitration agreement by implication, it was necessary to consider what would be the law with the 'closest and most real connection' with the arbitration agreement.

3.20 Where the parties had not made an express choice of law, the English Court of Appeal accepted that it was fair to start from the assumption that, in the absence of any contrary indication, the parties intended the whole of their relationship to be governed by the same system of law. Starting from that assumption, the 'natural inference' was that the parties intended that law chosen to govern the substantive contract also to govern the agreement to arbitrate. Such

B. Law Governing the Agreement to Arbitrate

an approach accorded with previous authority recognising that the proper law of the arbitration agreement would typically be the same as the substantive law of the contract, whereas the *lex arbitri* would usually be the law of the seat of the arbitration.[12]

3.21 However, the English Court of Appeal held that, in the present case, two specific factors indicated that the parties did not intend that Brazilian law should govern the arbitration agreement.

3.22 First, it was argued that, under Brazilian law, the arbitration agreement was enforceable only with Enesa's consent. The English Court of Appeal recognised that there was no indication that the parties intended the arbitration agreement to be enforceable by only one party and, accordingly, there was a serious risk that a choice of Brazilian law would entirely undermine the arbitration agreement. Such a risk militated against an implied choice of Brazilian law as the proper law of the arbitration agreement.

3.23 Secondly, the choice of London as the seat of arbitration entailed acceptance by the parties that English law would apply to the conduct and supervision of the arbitration, which suggested that the parties intended English law to govern all aspects of the arbitration agreement. The English Court of Appeal was fortified on this point by two prior decisions, *C v D*[13] and *XL Insurance Ltd v Owens Corning*.[14] Both cases concerned insurance contracts containing a New York applicable law clause, along with a clause providing for arbitration in London under the English Arbitration Act 1996. In both cases, the relevant court recognised that the choice of London as the seat of the arbitration implied a choice of English law as the law governing the arbitration agreement.

3.24 Accordingly, turning to the third stage of the enquiry, the English Court of Appeal held that, in the circumstances of the case, the arbitration agreement had its closest and most real connection with the law of the place where the arbitration was to be held, which would exercise the supporting and supervisory jurisdiction necessary to ensure the effectiveness of the arbitral procedure. In arriving at its decision, however, the Court conceded that prior authority on establishing the proper law of the arbitration agreement was 'not...entirely consistent'.[15]

---

[12] *Channel Tunnel Group Ltd v Balfour Beatty Construction Ltd* [1993] AC 334; *Black Clawson International Ltd v Papierwerke Waldhof-Aschaffenburg AG* [1982] 2 Lloyd's Rep 446; *Sonatrach Petroleum Corporation v Ferrell International Ltd* [2002] 1 All ER (Comm) 627; *Sumitomo Heavy Industries Ltd v Oil & Natural Gas Commission* [1994] 1 Lloyd's Rep 45; *Leibinger v Stryker Trauma GmbH* [2005] EWHC 690 (Comm). See also Dicey, Morris, and Collins, *The Conflict of Laws* (14th edn, Sweet & Maxwell, 2000), paras 16-016*ff*; Mustill and Boyd, *Commercial Arbitration* (2nd edn, LexisNexis Butterworths, 1989).
[13] [2007] EWCA Civ 1282, [2008] 1 All ER (Comm) 1001.
[14] [2001] All ER (Comm) 530.
[15] [2012] EWCA Civ 638, at [52] *per* Lord Neuberger of Abbotsbury MR.

> [handwritten margin note: contract containing the clause — not the clause itself.]

Applicable Laws

3.25 In the *Bulbank* case, the Bulgarian Foreign Trade Bank (Bulbank) concluded a contract with an Austrian bank.[16] The contract containing the arbitration clause expressed a choice of Austrian law. A dispute arose between the two parties and arbitral proceedings were initiated in Stockholm. Bulbank challenged the award in the Swedish courts on the basis that the arbitration agreement was void for breach of an allegedly implied term of confidentiality. The Supreme Court of Sweden held that the arbitration agreement was valid under the law of the seat of arbitration, Swedish law, stating that:

> ... no particular provision concerning the applicable law for the arbitration agreement itself was indicated [by the parties]. In such circumstances the issue of the validity of the arbitration clause should be determined in accordance with the law of the state in which the arbitration proceedings have taken place, that is to say, Swedish law.[17]

The Supreme Court thus ignored the parties' choice of Austrian law to govern the underlying contract, considering that the arbitration clause ought to be treated as a separate agreement subject to a separate law.

3.26 In a Belgian case, *Matermaco v PPM Cranes*,[18] the law of the place of arbitration, Belgium, was applied to questions of arbitrability despite the fact that the laws of the State of Wisconsin had been chosen by the parties to apply to the underlying contract. The Brussels Tribunal de Commerce considered Articles II(1) and V(2)(a) of the New York Convention, stating that their similarity:

> ... and a consistent interpretation of the Convention require that the arbitrable nature of the dispute be determined, under the said Articles II and V, under the same law, that is, the *lex fori*. Hence it is according to Belgian law that the arbitrable nature of the present dispute must be determined.[19]

3.27 In all of these cases, it is plain that the effect of the decision (and perhaps one of the driving forces behind it) was to validate the arbitration agreement. The parties had agreed to arbitrate disputes, but when the time came to do so, one party sought to renege on that agreement.

3.28 The importance of the law of the seat of arbitration is particularly marked in the United States. The Federal Arbitration Act of 1925 (FAA) controls arbitrations involving interstate or foreign commerce and maritime transactions, and it also

---

[16] *Bulgarian Foreign Trade Bank Ltd v Al Trade Finance Inc.*, Case No. T1881–99, Swedish Supreme Court, 27 October 2000, (2001) XXVI YBCA 291. It should be noted that the Swedish Arbitration Act 1999 provides, in s. 48, that where an arbitration agreement has an international connection and the parties have not agreed upon a choice of law, the arbitration agreement is governed by the law of the seat of the arbitration.

[17] *Bulgarian Foreign Trade Bank Ltd*, at 293.

[18] *Matermaco SA v PPM Cranes Inc.*, Brussels Tribunal de Commerce, 20 September 1999, (2000) XXV YBCA 673.

[19] Ibid., at 675.

B. Law Governing the Agreement to Arbitrate

implements the New York Convention. One commentator has written: 'The FAA creates a body of federal substantive law of arbitrability and pre-empts contrary state law policies. Hence, once the dispute is covered by the FAA, federal law applies to all questions of interpretation, construction, validity, revocability and enforceability.'[20]

3.29 The scope of the FAA is therefore such that it appears, of itself, to constitute the law governing the arbitration agreement. This analysis is confirmed by recent US cases focusing on the relationship between the FAA and state (or even foreign) law, which emphasise the former's pre-eminence as the law governing the arbitration where there is an express choice of state (or foreign law) in relation to the arbitration clause or agreement itself that is inconsistent with the FAA's policies.

3.30 In *Pedcor Mgt Co. Inc. Welfare Benefit Plan v North American Indemnity*,[21] which concerned a class arbitration and in which the arbitration agreement expressed a choice of Texan law, the court stated: '[I]t is well established that the FAA pre-empts state laws that contradict the purpose of the FAA by "requiring a judicial forum for the resolution of claims which the contracting parties agreed to resolve by arbitration." '[22]

3.31 In *AT&T Mobility LLC v Concepcion*,[23] the US Supreme Court held that a rule under California law, which deemed class arbitration waivers in consumer contracts of adhesion unconscionable, was 'an obstacle to the accomplishment and execution of the full purposes and objectives of Congress' and was therefore preempted by the FAA. In particular, the Court determined that '[a]lthough § 2's saving clause preserves generally applicable contract defenses, nothing in it suggests an intent to preserve state law rules that stand as an obstacle to the accomplishment of the FAA's objectives'.[24]

3.32 Similarly, in *County of Nassau v Chase*,[25] it was held that, in the absence of inconsistency, federal law did not pre-empt New York state law and that the relevant standard for determining whether an arbitrator has so far exceeded the scope of authority that the award should be overturned was that specified by state law.[26]

---

[20] Zekos, 'Problems of applicable law in commercial and maritime arbitration' (1999) 16 J Intl Arb 173, at 180–181.
[21] 343 F 3d 355 (5th Cir 2003).
[22] Ibid., at 363.
[23] 131 S.Ct 1740, 1753 (2011); see also *Ferguson v Corinthian Colleges, Inc.* 733 F.3d 928, 936 (9th Cir. 2013).
[24] *AT&T Mobility LLC v Concepcion*, at 1748.
[25] 402 Fed. Appx 540 (2nd Cir. 2010).
[26] See also *American Express Co. v Italian Colors Restaurant* 133 S.Ct 2304, 2310 (2013), in which the US Supreme Court observed that the text of the FAA 'reflects the overarching principle that arbitration is a matter of contract' and 'courts must "rigorously enforce" arbitration agreements according to their terms'.

(c) Parties' common intention—a French 'third way'

3.33 The solutions considered so far have focused on establishing the law governing the arbitration agreement by reference to a national law, be it the law of the contract or the law of the seat of arbitration. The French courts, however, have adopted a different method whereby the existence and scope of the arbitration agreement is determined exclusively by reference to the parties' discernible common intentions. In this way, the arbitration agreement remains independent of the various national laws that might, in other jurisdictions, be deemed to apply to it. This approach avoids the difficulties of categorising the arbitration agreement for conflict-of-laws purposes, as well as the particularities of private international law regimes.

3.34 This French 'third way' came about as a result of a number of decisions by the Paris Cour d'Appel from the early 1970s through to the early 1990s, which culminated in the Cour de Cassation's decision in *Dalico* in 1993:[27]

> [B]y virtue of a substantive rule of international arbitration, the arbitration agreement is legally independent of the main contract containing or referring to it, and the existence and effectiveness of the arbitration agreement are to be assessed, subject to the mandatory rules of French law and international public policy, on the basis of the parties' common intention, there being no need to refer to any national law.[28]

References in this context to the independence of the arbitration agreement are to its autonomy from the national laws that otherwise might apply to it, as opposed to autonomy from the main contract in terms of its existence.[29] The French Supreme Court thus stopped short of a complete delocalisation of the arbitration agreement, by subjecting it to the mandatory provisions of French law.[30] Moreover, it does remain open to the parties, if such is their common intention, to expressly designate a national legal system or set of conflict laws, as the French Supreme Court clarified in the *Uni-Kod* decision.[31]

---

[27] *Municipalité de Khoms El Mergeb c/Sté Dalico*, Cass. Civ. 1ere, 20 December 1993, [1994] Rev Arb 116. The case was brought by a Libyan municipal authority against a Danish contractor after the latter had initiated arbitration proceedings. The Libyan party argued that the arbitration agreement was governed by Libyan law and that it was invalid under Libyan law. The Paris Cour d'Appel rejected these arguments without deciding what law applied.

[28] Ibid., at 117, as translated by Professor Gaillard in Savage and Gaillard (eds) *Fouchard, Gaillard, Goldman on International Commercial Arbitration* (Kluwer Law International, 1999), para. 437.

[29] Professor Gaillard refers to the 'dual meaning' of 'autonomy' in Savage and Gaillard (eds) *Fouchard, Gaillard, Goldman on International Commercial Arbitration* (Kluwer Law International, 1999), para. 388. See also ibid., paras 420–421 and 435–451, and in particular 441 for an endorsement of the French third way. Regarding the separability of the arbitration agreement from the main contract under French law, see *Sté Omenex c/Hugon*, Cass. Civ. 1ère, [2006] Rev Arb 103, in which the court held that an arbitration agreement survives the invalidity of the underlying agreement.

[30] Lew, Mistelis, and Kröll, *Comparative International Commercial Arbitration* (Kluwer Law International, 2003), para. 6-66.

[31] *Uni-Kod c/Sté Ouralkali*, Cass. Civ. 1ere, 30 March 2004, [2005] Rev Arb 959.

B. Law Governing the Agreement to Arbitrate

The French approach was examined by the UK Supreme Court in its decision of 3 November 2010 in *Dallah Real Estate and Tourism Holding Co. v Ministry of Religious Affairs, Government of Pakistan*.[32] The decision related to an agreement between Dallah Real Estate and a Pakistani government trust dated 10 September 1996, relating to commercial services for pilgrimages to Saudi Arabia, including an International Chamber of Commerce (ICC) arbitration clause, seated in Paris. Dallah initiated arbitration proceedings against the Pakistani government and against the trust, despite the latter being only a contractual counterparty. An arbitral tribunal seated in Paris accepted jurisdiction over the Pakistani government and rendered an award in favour of Dallah. The award was challenged in Paris, the seat of the arbitration, and its enforcement was challenged in the United Kingdom on the basis (among other things) that the tribunal had no jurisdiction over the non-signatory Pakistani government. The Supreme Court of England and Wales, applying French law, accepted that, as a starting point, French law (the law of the seat) refers to supranational law:

3.35

> [Under French law,] arbitration agreements derive their existence, validity and effect from supra-national law, without it being necessary to refer to any national law. If so, that would not avoid the need to have regard to French law 'as the law of the country where the award was made' under Article V(1)(a) of the Convention and s. 103(2)(b) of the 1996 Act. The Cour de Cassation is, however, a national court, giving a French legal view of international arbitration; and Dallah and the Government agree that the true analysis is that French law recognises transnational principles as potentially applicable to determine the existence, validity and effectiveness of an international arbitration agreement, such principles being part of French law.[33]

(d) Combining several approaches—a Swiss model

The final approach in determining the law or rules applicable to an arbitration agreement is to combine several approaches, as is the case in Switzerland. Section 178(2) of the Swiss Federal Statute of Private International Law (Swiss PIL) provides:

3.36

> As regards its substance, the arbitration agreement shall be valid if it conforms either to the law chosen by the parties, or to the law governing the subject-matter of the dispute, in particular the law governing the main contract, or if it conforms to Swiss law.

This formulation allows Swiss courts maximum opportunity to uphold the validity of the arbitration agreement.

---

[32] [2010] UKSC 4.
[33] Ibid., at [15]. A few months later, the Paris Cour d'Appel, in *Gouvernement du Pakistan—Ministère des Affaires Religieuses v Dallah Real Estate and Tourism Holding Co.*, Case No. 09/28533, 17 February 2011, reached a different conclusion as to whether the Pakistani government was bound by the arbitration clause as a non-signatory to the contract.

C. Law Governing the Arbitration

(a) Introduction

3.37 An international arbitration usually takes place in a country that is 'neutral', in the sense that none of the parties to the arbitration has a place of business or residence there.[34] This means that, in practice, the law of the country in which territory the arbitration takes place—that is, the *lex arbitri*—will generally be different from the law that governs the substantive matters in dispute. An arbitral tribunal with a seat in the Netherlands, for example, may be required to decide the substantive issues in dispute between the parties in accordance with the law of Switzerland or the law of the State of New York or some other law, as the case may be. Nevertheless, the arbitration itself, and the way in which it is conducted, will be governed (if only in outline) by the relevant Dutch law on international arbitration.

3.38 This difference between the *lex arbitri* (the law of the place, or 'seat', of the arbitration) and the law governing the substance of the dispute was part of the juridical tradition of continental Europe, but is now firmly established in international arbitration.[35]

3.39 It is right that there should be a distinction between the *lex arbitri* and the substantive law of the contract. Where parties to an international arbitration agreement choose for themselves a seat of arbitration, they usually choose a place that has no connection with either themselves or their commercial relationship. They choose a 'neutral' place.[36] By doing so, they do not necessarily intend to choose the law of that place to govern their relationship.[37] Indeed, as well as choosing a place of arbitration, they may well choose a substantive law that has no connection with that place.

---

[34] A study into corporate attitudes on international arbitration has shown that factors such as 'formal legal infrastructure' (including neutrality, impartiality, and the record of the courts in enforcing agreements to arbitrate and arbitral awards), the law governing the contract, and convenience are key to parties' choice of the place of arbitration: see White & Case and Queen Mary School of International Arbitration, University of London, *2010 International Arbitration Survey: Choices in International Arbitration*, available online at http://www.arbitrationonline.org/docs/2010_InternationalArbitrationSurveyReport.pdf. See also dicta by Lord Hoffman in delivering the leading judgment for the House of Lords in *West Tankers v RAS (the Front Comor)* [2007] 1 Lloyd's Rep 391, at [12]: in the case of arbitration, 'the situs and governing law are generally chosen by the parties on grounds of neutrality, availability of legal services and the unobtrusive effectiveness of the supervisory jurisdiction'.

[35] Savage and Gaillard (eds) *Fouchard, Gaillard, Goldman on International Commercial Arbitration* (Kluwer Law International, 1999), para. 1428. Early recognition of this principle in English law may be seen in *Compagnie Tunisienne de Navigation SA v Compagnie d'Armament Maritime SA* [1971] AC 572, at 604.

[36] For choice of place, see paragraph 3.37 and n. 34.

[37] For choice of law, see paragraph 3.12.

If the parties do not make an express choice of the place of arbitration, the choice will **3.40** have to be made for them, either by the arbitral tribunal itself or by a designated arbitral institution. Article 18(1) of the United Nations Commission on International Trade Law (UNCITRAL) Arbitration Rules, for instance, states: 'If the parties have not previously agreed on the place of arbitration, the place of arbitration shall be determined by the arbitral tribunal having regard to the circumstances of the case.' Article 18(1) of the ICC Rules leaves the choice to the ICC Court: 'The place of arbitration shall be fixed by the Court, unless agreed upon by the parties.'

In cases of this kind, which are not uncommon in both institutional and ad hoc **3.41** arbitration, the choice of the place of arbitration has little or nothing to do with the parties or with the contract under which the dispute arises. It is, so to speak, an unconnected choice. In these circumstances, it would be illogical to hold that the *lex arbitri*, the law of the place of arbitration, was necessarily the law applicable to the issues in dispute. (Occasionally, it may be otherwise if the parties have chosen a place of arbitration, but have not chosen a law to govern their contractual relationship.[38])

(b) What is the *lex arbitri*?

It is appropriate, at this stage, to consider what is meant by the *lex arbitri*. The question was posed rhetorically by a distinguished English judge: **3.42**

> What then is the law governing the arbitration? It is, as the present authors trenchantly explain,[39] a body of rules which sets a standard external to the arbitration agreement, and the wishes of the parties, for the conduct of the arbitration. The law governing the arbitration comprises the rules governing interim measures (eg Court orders for the preservation or storage of goods), the rules empowering the exercise by the Court of supportive measures to assist an arbitration which has run into difficulties (eg filling a vacancy in the composition of the arbitral tribunal if there is no other mechanism) and the rules providing for the exercise by the Court of its supervisory jurisdiction over arbitrations (eg removing an arbitrator for misconduct).[40]

(c) The content of the *lex arbitri*

Each state will decide for itself what laws it wishes to lay down to govern the conduct **3.43** of arbitrations within its own territory. Some states will wish to build an element of consumer protection into their law, so as to protect private individuals. For example, section 6 of the Swedish Arbitration Act 1999[41] provides that an arbitration

---

[38] Under s. 48 of the Swedish Arbitration Act 1999, e.g. where parties have not chosen a substantive law to govern their contract, it will be governed by the law of the seat of the arbitration. This situation is discussed later in this chapter.
[39] The reference was to the second edition of this book.
[40] *Smith Ltd v H International* [1991] 2 Lloyd's Rep 127, at 130.
[41] For an English translation of the Act, see online at http://www.sccinstitute.com/?id=23746. See also (2001) 17(4) Arb Intl 426; for commentaries on the Act throughout.

agreement with a consumer involving goods or services for private use is invalid if made before a dispute arises. Again, for example, the Swedish Act provides that the arbitral tribunal may order the parties to pay the arbitrators' fees and, if it does so, must set out in its final award its decision as to the fees payable to each of the arbitrators.[42] The arbitral tribunal must also provide clear instruction to the parties of the steps that must be taken to appeal to the district court against this decision.[43]

3.44 In recognition of the distinction between domestic arbitration and international arbitration—in which the sums at issue are likely to be larger and the parties better able to look after themselves—some states have (sensibly, it may be thought) introduced a code of law specifically designed for international arbitrations. Such a code of law is usually fairly short: the French Code, for example, comprises only twenty-four articles,[44] some of which consist of a single sentence, and the Swiss PIL, comprising only sixteen articles, is even more concise.

3.45 Reference has already been made to the Model Law, which the authors have described as the baseline for any state wishing to modernise its law of arbitration.[45] Although the Model Law contains more provisions than those to be found in the comparable French or Swiss laws, these provisions are drawn in relatively broad terms. They do not purport to lay down any detailed procedural rules as to the actual conduct of an arbitration—such as rules on the submission and exchange of witness statements, the order in which witnesses are to be called, the time to be allotted for the questioning and cross-questioning of witnesses, and so forth. Indeed, Article 19 of the Model Law expressly provides that:

(1) Subject to the provisions of this Law, the parties are free to agree on the procedure to be followed by the arbitral tribunal in conducting the proceedings.
(2) Failing such agreement, the arbitral tribunal may, subject to the provisions of this Law, conduct the arbitration in such manner as it considers appropriate. The power conferred upon the arbitral tribunal includes the power to determine the admissibility, relevance, materiality and weight of any evidence.

3.46 It may be helpful at this point to give examples of the matters with which the *lex arbitri* might be expected to deal, although the exact position under the relevant *lex arbitri* should be checked, particularly where these legal provisions are mandatory. With this qualification, the *lex arbitri* is likely to extend to:

- the definition and form of an agreement to arbitrate;
- whether a dispute is capable of being referred to arbitration (that is, whether it is 'arbitrable' under the *lex arbitri*);

---

[42] Swedish Arbitration Act 1999, s. 37.
[43] Swedish Arbitration Act 1999, s. 41. It is an unattractive proposition for arbitrators whose work has been accomplished and whose role is over to face a possible challenge before the local courts in relation to their fees.
[44] French Code of Civil Procedure, Bk IV, Title V ('International arbitration').
[45] See Chapter 1.

- the constitution of the arbitral tribunal and any grounds for challenge of that tribunal;
- the entitlement of the arbitral tribunal to rule on its own jurisdiction;
- equal treatment of the parties;
- freedom to agree upon detailed rules of procedure;
- interim measures of protection;
- statements of claim and defence;
- hearings;
- default proceedings;
- court assistance, if required;
- the powers of the arbitrators, including any powers to decide as *amiables compositeurs*;
- the form and validity of the arbitration award; and
- the finality of the award, including any right to challenge it in the courts of the place of arbitration.

These are all important aspects of international arbitration. They may well arise in practice and are all addressed later in this commentary. Three essential points should, however, be made now.

(1) The effective conduct of an international arbitration may depend upon the provisions of the law of the place of arbitration. One way of illustrating this dependence is by reference to any provisions of the local law for judicial assistance in the conduct of the arbitration. Even if the arbitrators have the power to order interim measures of protection, such as orders for the preservation and inspection of property, they are unlikely to have the power to enforce such orders—particularly if the property in question is in the possession of a third party. For this, it is necessary to turn to national courts for assistance.[46]

(2) The choice of a particular place of arbitration may have important and unintended consequences. This is because the law of that place may confer powers on the courts or on the arbitrators that the parties did not expect. An example of this is the power to consolidate arbitrations. Whether or not a court or arbitral tribunal has the power to consolidate two or more

---

[46] See, e.g., Swiss PIL, Ch. 12, s. 183, which provides that the arbitral tribunal may request the assistance of the court where a party does not voluntarily comply with a protective measure; the Netherlands Arbitration Act 1986, s. 1022(2), which provides for a party to request a court to grant interim measures of protection; the English Arbitration Act 1996, s. 44(1) and (2), which gives the court the same powers to order the inspection, photocopying, preservation, custody, or detention of property in relation to an arbitration as it has in relation to litigation; and the Model Law, Art. 9, which allows a party to seek interim measures of protection from a court. It should be noted that while the courts of the seat play the lead role in supporting the arbitral process, inter alia, in terms of granting interim relief, it may also be necessary to seek relief from other courts beyond the seat, where, e.g., assets might be located. Various national laws (e.g. Dutch and German law) foresee this possibility, and courts in various other jurisdictions including Hong Kong have intervened in support of arbitrations being conducted overseas: see *The Lady Muriel* [1995] 2 HKC 320 (CA).

arbitrations that involve the same basic issues of fact or law is a controversial question. In the present context, it is necessary to note only that such a power may exist under the *lex arbitri* and that this may come as a disagreeable surprise to a party who does not wish to have other parties joined in its arbitration.[47]

(3) There is an obvious prospect of conflict between the *lex arbitri* and a different system of law that may be equally relevant. Consider, for example, the question of arbitrability—that is, whether or not the subject matter of the dispute is 'capable' of being resolved by arbitration. The concept of arbitrability is basic to the arbitral process. Both the New York Convention and the Model Law refer explicitly to disputes that are 'capable of being resolved by arbitration'.

3.47 It may be said that if a dispute is capable of being resolved by litigation in the courts, which will lead to a decision that (subject to any appeal) puts an end to that dispute, surely the same dispute is equally capable of being resolved by arbitration? Theoretically, this may well be correct. In practice, however,[48] every state reserves for itself, as a matter of public policy, what might perhaps be called a 'state monopoly' over certain types of dispute. Accordingly, whether or not a particular dispute—for example over the disposal of assets belonging to a bankrupt company—is legally 'capable of being resolved by arbitration' is a matter that each state will decide for itself. It is a matter on which states may well differ, with some taking a more restrictive attitude than others. This obviously results in an element of forum shopping and is 'good for business' for those jurisdictions adopting a liberal approach to arbitrability: for example, because of their liberal approach to arbitrating intellectual property disputes, Geneva or London might be preferred over Paris as the seat chosen for an arbitration of a trade mark dispute. However, a claim may be arbitrable under the law governing the arbitration agreement and under the *lex arbitri*, but not under the law of the place of enforcement. An award in such a case, although validly made under the *lex arbitri*, might prove to be unenforceable under the New York Convention.

(d) Procedural rules and the *lex arbitri*

3.48 The preceding discussion about the content of the *lex arbitri* indicates that most, if not all, national laws governing arbitration deal with general propositions, such

---

[47] The Netherlands Arbitration Act 1986 provides, in s. 1046, that related arbitral proceedings before another arbitral tribunal in the Netherlands may be consolidated by order of the court notwithstanding the objection of one of the parties, unless the parties have agreed otherwise. Amendments to s. 1046, approved by the Dutch Parliament on 27 May 2014, now allow third parties (e.g. arbitral institutions) to make similar orders to consolidate proceedings: see Chapter 2. British Columbia has adapted the Model Law, in s. 27(2) of the International Commercial Arbitration Act of 1996, to allow court-ordered consolidation where the parties to two or more arbitration agreements have agreed to consolidate the arbitrations arising out of those agreements.

[48] As discussed in more detail in Chapter 2, paragraph 2.59.

C. Law Governing the Arbitration

as the need to treat each party equally, rather than with detailed rules of procedure, such as the time for exchange of witness statements or the submission of pre-hearing briefs.

Nevertheless, at some stage in the conduct of an arbitration—and, indeed, at a fairly early stage—the parties will need to know where they stand in terms of the detailed procedure to be followed. There are many points to be clarified: will the claimant's statement of claim simply outline the facts supporting the claim, or will it be accompanied by the documents that are relied upon and perhaps by legal submissions? When the respondent has submitted its defence, will the claimant have the right to submit a reply, or is that the end of the written submissions? What about the evidence of witnesses? Are there to be written statements of witnesses, and if so, in what order, within what time limits, and with what (if any) right of reply? **3.49**

It is plainly necessary for the parties and the arbitral tribunal to know what procedural rules they are required to follow, particularly in an international arbitration in which the parties will usually come from different backgrounds, with a different approach to such questions as the interviewing of witnesses, the production of documents, and so forth. **3.50**

All that needs to be understood at this point is that there is a great difference between the general provisions of the law governing the arbitration (the *lex arbitri*) and the detailed procedural rules that will need to be adopted, or adapted, for the fair and efficient conduct of the proceedings. The rules of the arbitral institutions, such as the ICC and the LCIA, provide an overall framework within which to operate, as do the UNCITRAL Rules. However, it is important to note that even these rules will need to be supplemented by more detailed provisions by the parties or the arbitral tribunal, as discussed in Chapter 6. **3.51**

It is therefore often advisable, particularly where parties and their counsel are from different legal backgrounds, to agree such rules at the outset of an arbitration. This may be done by agreement of the parties, or by order of the arbitral tribunal at the first procedural meeting. As part of this process, the parties may agree, or the arbitral tribunal may order, that they adopt or have regard to a pre-existing set of detailed rules, for example the International Bar Association (IBA) Rules on the Taking of Evidence in International Arbitration. By ensuring that the rules are clearly established early on, the administration of the case will (or at least should) be simplified, and the scope for delay and dilatory tactics reduced. **3.52**

(e) Seat theory

The concept that an arbitration is governed by the law of the place in which it is held, which is the 'seat' (or 'forum', or *locus arbitri*) of the arbitration, is well established **3.53** in both the theory and practice of international arbitration.[49] It has influenced the wording of international conventions from the 1923 Geneva Protocol to the New York Convention. Article 2 of the 1923 Geneva Protocol states: 'The arbitral procedure, including the constitution of the arbitral tribunal, shall be governed *by the will of the parties and by the law of the country* in whose territory the arbitration takes place.'[50]

3.54 The New York Convention[51] maintains the reference to 'the law of the country where the arbitration took place'[52] and, synonymously, to 'the law of the country where the award is made'.[53] This continues the clear territorial link between the place of arbitration and the law governing that arbitration: the *lex arbitri*. This territorial link is again maintained in Article 1(2) of the Model Law: 'The provisions of this Law, except articles 8, 9, 35 and 36, apply only if the place of arbitration is in the territory of this State.'[54]

3.55 Amongst modern laws on arbitration, those of Switzerland and of England are perhaps particularly clear on the link between the seat of the arbitration and the *lex arbitri*. Swiss law states:

> The provisions of this chapter shall apply to any arbitration *if the seat of the arbitral tribunal is in Switzerland* and if, at the time when the arbitration agreement was concluded, at least one of the parties had neither its domicile nor its habitual residence in Switzerland.[55]

In English law, certain provisions of the Arbitration Act 1996 apply only where the seat of the arbitration is in England, Wales, or Northern Ireland, whereas other provisions (for example for the stay of court proceedings commenced in breach of an arbitration agreement) apply even if the seat of the arbitration is not in those countries or if no seat has been designated.[56] The 'seat of the arbitration' is defined as 'the juridical seat of the arbitration' designated by the parties, or by an arbitral institution or the arbitrators themselves, as the case may be.[57] Unless the parties

---

[49] See, e.g., Park, 'The *lex loci arbitri* and international commercial arbitration' (1983) 32 ICLQ 21; Jarvin, 'Le lieu de l'arbitrage' (1993) 4 ICC Bulletin 7; Born, *International Commercial Arbitration* (2nd edn, Kluwer Law International, 2014), pp 1530–1531. See also Kaufmann-Kohler, 'Identifying and applying the law governing the arbitral procedure: The role of the law of the place of arbitration' (1999) 9 ICCA Congress Series 336.
[50] Emphasis added.
[51] Which, by means of Art. VII(2), replaces the 1923 Geneva Protocol to the extent that contracting states become bound by the New York Convention.
[52] New York Convention, Art. V(1)(d).
[53] New York Convention, Art. V(1)(a) and (e).
[54] Articles 8 and 9 are concerned with enforcing the arbitration agreement and interim measures of protection respectively; Arts 35 and 36 are concerned with recognition and enforcement of the award.
[55] Swiss PIL, Ch. 12, s. 176(1) (emphasis added).
[56] English Arbitration Act 1996, s. 2.
[57] English Arbitration Act 1996, s. 3.

C. Law Governing the Arbitration

agree otherwise, the seat of the arbitration must be stated in the award of the arbitrators.[58]

3.56 As this introduction tries to make clear, the place, or 'seat', of the arbitration is not merely a matter of geography. It is the territorial link between the arbitration itself and the law of the place in which that arbitration is legally situated:

> When one says that London, Paris or Geneva is the place of arbitration, one does not refer solely to a geographical location. One means that the arbitration is conducted within the framework of the law of arbitration of England, France or Switzerland or, to use an English expression, under the curial law of the relevant country. The geographical place of arbitration is the factual connecting factor between that arbitration law and the arbitration proper, considered as a nexus of contractual and procedural rights and obligations between the parties and the arbitrators.[59]

The seat of an arbitration is thus often intended to be its legal centre of gravity. This does not mean that all of the proceedings of the arbitration have to take place there, although preferably some should do so:

> Although the choice of a 'seat' also indicates the geographical place for the arbitration, this does not mean that the parties have limited themselves to that place. As is pointed out[60]...in a passage approved by the Court of Appeal in *Naviera Amazonia Peruana SA v Compania Internacional de Seguros del Peru* [1988] 1 Lloyd's Rep 116 at 121, it may often be convenient to hold meetings or even hearings in other countries. This does not mean that the 'seat' of the arbitration changes with each change of country. The legal place of the arbitration remains the same even if the physical place changes from time to time, unless of course the parties agree to change it.[61]

3.57 Arbitrators and the parties to an international arbitration often come from different countries. It may not always be convenient for everyone concerned to travel to the country that is the seat of the arbitration for the purpose of a meeting or a hearing. Alternatively, it may simply be easier and less expensive to meet elsewhere. In recognition of this reality, the ICC Rules allow hearings and meetings to be held elsewhere than at the place (or seat) of the arbitration. The relevant rule, Article 18, reads as follows:

1) The place of the arbitration shall be fixed by the Court, unless agreed upon by the parties.

---

[58] English Arbitration Act 1996, s. 52(5).
[59] Reymond, 'Where is an arbitral award made?' (1992) 108 LQR 1, at 3. As indicated at paragraph 3.57, there is no such 'curial' law in ICSID arbitration proceedings. In accordance with Art. 62 of the ICSID Convention, the place of the proceedings is the seat of the centre unless otherwise agreed, but this does not impose the curial law of Washington, DC.
[60] In the second edition of this book.
[61] *Union of India v McDonnell Douglas Corporation* [1993] 2 Lloyd's Rep 48. (The Peruvian case referred to in this citation is generally known as 'the *Peruvian Insurance* case'.)

2) The arbitral tribunal may, after consultation with the parties, conduct hearings and meetings at any location it considers appropriate, unless otherwise agreed by the parties.

3) The arbitral tribunal may deliberate at any location it considers appropriate.

3.58 The LCIA has a similar rule. Article 16(3) of the LCIA Rules provides that:

> The Arbitral Tribunal may hold any hearing at any convenient geographical place in consultation with the parties and hold its deliberations at any geographical place of its own choice; and if such place(s) should be elsewhere than the seat of the arbitration, the arbitration shall nonetheless be treated for all purposes as an arbitration conducted at the arbitral seat and any order or award as having been made at that seat.

Article 20(2) of the Model Law also allows the arbitral tribunal to meet at any place it considers appropriate for its deliberations or to hear witnesses, unless the parties object.[62]

3.59 These are sensible provisions. They recognise the realities of international arbitration, with parties, lawyers, and arbitrators likely to be based in different parts of the world. They give flexibility to the tribunal and to the parties in selecting a convenient location for procedural meetings, hearings, and deliberations. It may be, for example, that although the seat of the arbitration is Jakarta, the arbitral tribunal finds it convenient to meet to hold hearings in Singapore.[63] In international construction disputes, it is often necessary for an arbitral tribunal sitting in one country to visit the site of the project in another country to carry out an inspection. Equally, it may be more convenient for an arbitral tribunal sitting in one country to conduct a hearing in another country or continent, for example for the purpose of taking evidence.

3.60 An arbitral tribunal that visits another country must, of course, respect the law of that country. For example, if the purpose of the visit is to take evidence from witnesses, the arbitral tribunal should respect any provisions of the local law that govern the taking of evidence.[64] However, each move of the arbitral tribunal does not of itself mean that the seat of the arbitration changes. The

---

[62] The Netherlands Arbitration Act 1986, s. 1037(3), is to like effect; cf. the law in the United States that requires that hearings be conducted in the place of the arbitration unless the parties agree otherwise: see, e.g., *Spring Hope Rockwool v Industrial Clean Air Inc.* 504 F.Supp. 1385 (EDNC 1981); *Snyder v Smith* 736 F.2d 409 (7th Cir. 1984), cert. denied, 469 US 1037 (1984); *Jain v de Méré* 51 F.3d 686, 692 (7th Cir. 1995); *National Iranian Oil Co. v Ashland Oil, Inc.* 817 F.2d 326, 334 (5th Cir. 1987). Under the FAA, where the parties have not agreed on the location of the arbitration, a court may order the parties to conduct the arbitration in its own district: *Clarendon National Insurance Co. v Lan* 152 F.Supp.2d 506, 524 (SDNY 2001).

[63] This was the case in *PT Garuda Indonesia v Birgen Air* [2002] 1 SLR 393 (CA), in which it was held that there was no legal nexus between the arbitration and Singapore simply because hearings were held there.

[64] For example, the local law may not permit arbitrators to take evidence from witnesses on oath.

seat of the arbitration remains the place initially agreed by, or on behalf of, the parties.[65]

What is the legal position if, as sometimes happens, the arbitral tribunal—having consulted the parties and perhaps against the objection of one of them—holds all meetings, hearings, and deliberations in a place that is not the seat of the arbitration? To proceed in this manner reduces the seat of the arbitration to a legal fiction: a place of arbitration in which nothing takes place. In the light of the provisions set out above, and subject to any particular restrictions contained in the *lex arbitri* and the views of the parties,[66] this would seem to be permissible. It conforms with the letter, if not the spirit, of the law or the applicable rules. **3.61**

(f) Is the *lex arbitri* a procedural law?

In some countries, the law governing arbitration, including international arbitration, is part of a code of civil procedure. This is so, for example, in France and in Germany—and it is sometimes said that the *lex arbitri* is a law of procedure, as if that is all that it is. It is true, of course, that the *lex arbitri* may deal with procedural matters—such as the constitution of an arbitral tribunal where there is no relevant contractual provision—but the authors suggest that the *lex arbitri* is much more than a purely procedural law. It may stipulate that a given type of dispute—over patent rights, for instance, or (as in Belgium and some Arab states) over a local agency agreement—is not capable of settlement by arbitration under the local law: this is surely not simply a matter of procedure?[67] Or again, by way of example, an award may be set aside on the basis that it is contrary to the public policy of the *lex arbitri*: once more, this would not seem to be merely a matter of procedure. **3.62**

---

[65] The preceding two paragraphs were cited with approval by the court in *Naviera Amazonia Peruana SA v Compania Internacional de Seguros del Peru* [1988] 1 Lloyd's Rep 116.

[66] In ICC Case No. 10623 (2003) 21 ASA Bulletin 60 (including summary by Professor Crivellaro), the tribunal held all meetings, etc., in Paris, although the seat of the arbitration was in Ethiopia. The Ethiopian government, a party to the arbitration, contested the tribunal's jurisdiction both by challenging it unsuccessfully before the ICC Court and by applying to its local courts, the interference of which the tribunal ignored. Interference by local courts is further discussed at paragraph 3.98. See also the decision of the Svea Court of Appeal in *Titan Corporation v Alcatel CIT SA* (Svea Court of Appeal), RH 2005:1 (T 1038-05) YCA XXX (2005), 139, in which the Court denied jurisdiction to consider an *ex parte* application to set aside an award that stated that the seat of arbitration was Stockholm. The Court based its decision in part on the fact that all of the hearings (in which one of the authors was counsel for the claimant) had taken place in Paris and in London, and not in Stockholm; hence, in its view, the arbitration could not be considered to have any connection to Sweden as required for the Swedish Arbitration Act 1999 to apply. This decision was subsequently reversed (in relevant part) by the Swedish Supreme Court.

[67] Another good reason for not labelling the *lex arbitri* 'procedural' is that different countries have different notions of what is a matter of procedure and what is a matter of substance: cf. the treatment of time limits in English law, discussed in Chapter 4, paragraph 4.04.

3.63 It is also sometimes said that parties have selected the procedural law that will govern their arbitration by providing for arbitration in a particular country.[68] This is too elliptical and, as an English court itself held in *Braes of Doune Wind Farm*,[69] it does not always hold true. What the parties have done is to choose a place of arbitration in a particular country. That choice brings with it submission to the laws of that country, including any mandatory provisions of its law on arbitration. To say that the parties have 'chosen' that particular law to govern the arbitration is rather like saying that an English woman who takes her car to France has 'chosen' French traffic law, which will oblige her to drive on the right-hand side of the road, to give priority to vehicles approaching from the right, and generally to obey traffic laws to which she may not be accustomed. But it would be an odd use of language to say that this notional motorist had opted for 'French traffic law'; rather, she has chosen to go to France—and the applicability of French law then follows automatically. It is not a matter of choice.

3.64 Parties may well choose a particular place of arbitration precisely because its *lex arbitri* is one that they find attractive.[70] Nevertheless, once a place of arbitration has been chosen, it brings with it its own law. If that law contains provisions that are mandatory as far as arbitrations are concerned, those provisions must be obeyed.[71] It is not a matter of choice, any more than the notional motorist is free to choose which local traffic laws to obey and which to disregard.

(g) Choice of another procedural law

3.65 The concept of subjecting an arbitration in one state to the procedural law of another has been the subject of much theoretical discussion. Thus, for example, an arbitration could be held in Switzerland, but, by agreement between the parties, made subject to the procedural law of Germany. In this regard, Swiss law provides that the parties to an arbitration may 'subject the arbitral procedure to the procedural law of their choice'.[72]

---

[68] See, e.g., the reference of Lord Diplock to the 'selection' of a particular *lex arbitri* by the choice of a place of arbitration, in *Compagnie Tunisienne de Navigation SA v Compagnie d'Armament Maritime SA* [1971] AC 572, at 604.

[69] The English Technology and Construction Court, in *Braes of Doune Wind Farm (Scotland) v Alfred McAlpine Business Services* [2008] EWHC 426 (TCC), stated that the parties' designation of 'Glasgow, Scotland' as the place of arbitration referred only to the place where it was intended to hold hearings. England was deemed to be the juridical seat owing to the fact that the parties had referred to the application of the English Arbitration Act 1996. This case demonstrates that the parties' choice of procedural law may be determinative of the seat of the arbitration. According to the court at [17], 'one needs to consider what, in substance, the parties agreed was the law of the country which would juridically control the arbitration'.

[70] See Chapter 6.

[71] See, e.g., consolidation under Dutch law and the mandatory provisions of other national laws governing arbitration, such as the mandatory provisions of the English Arbitration Act 1996.

[72] Swiss PIL, Ch. 12, s. 182; there are provisions in Dutch and Italian law to the same effect, and in the French Code of Civil Procedure, at art. 1509. However, non-compliance with public policy rules would be a ground for setting an award aside even if another procedural law were chosen.

C. Law Governing the Arbitration

It is not easy to understand why parties might wish to complicate the conduct of an arbitration in this way (unless, as is possible, they do not understand what they are doing). It means that the parties and the arbitral tribunal would need to have regard to two procedural laws: that of Germany, as the chosen procedural law; and that of Switzerland, to the extent that the provisions of Swiss law (such as the requirement of equality of treatment of the parties) are mandatory.[73] Nor is this all: if it becomes necessary during the course of the arbitration to have recourse to the courts—for example on a challenge of one of the arbitrators—to which court would the complainant go? The Swiss court would presumably be reluctant to give a ruling on German procedural law; the German court might well prove unwilling to give a ruling on a procedural matter that it could not directly enforce, since the arbitration was not conducted within its territorial jurisdiction.

3.66

It is tempting to suggest that if the procedural law of a particular country is either so attractive or so familiar to the parties that they wish to adopt it, they would do better to locate their arbitration in that country. One need look only at the difficulties that a party would face in obtaining a subpoena against a reluctant witness, however, to recognise the problems inherent in a choice of foreign procedural law.[74]

3.67

In a Peruvian insurance case,[75] the English Court of Appeal considered a contract that had been held by the court of first instance to provide for an arbitration to be located in Peru, but subject to English procedural law. The Court of Appeal construed the contract as providing for arbitration in London under English law, but noted that a situation (such as that contemplated by the Florida International Commercial Arbitration Act of 2011) involving a choice of foreign procedural law was theoretically possible. However, practical difficulties were foreseen:

3.68

> There is equally no reason in theory which precludes parties to agree that an arbitration shall be held at a place or in country X but subject to the procedural laws of Y. The limits and implications of any such agreement have been much discussed in the literature, but apart from the decision in the instant case there appears to be no reported case where this has happened. This is not surprising when one considers the complexities and inconveniences which such an agreement would involve. Thus, at any rate under the principles of English law, which rest upon the territorially limited jurisdiction of our courts, an agreement to arbitrate in X subject to English procedural law would not empower our courts to exercise jurisdiction over the arbitration in X.[76]

---

[73] Swiss PIL, Ch. 12, s. 182(3).
[74] In many countries, an arbitrator has no power to issue a subpoena and the parties must rely upon the relevant court for such process: see, e.g., Model Law, Art. 27. The United States does allow for an arbitrator to summon a witness to attend and to bring any material documents or evidence, but the local federal district court must be called in to assist in compelling a reluctant witness to attend or to punish a witness who fails to attend: FAA, s. 7. See Chapter 7.
[75] *Naviera Amazonia Peruana SA v Compania Internacional de Seguros de Peru* [1988] 1 Lloyd's Rep 116.
[76] Ibid., at 120.

Applicable Laws

(h) Where an award is made

3.69 From time to time, it may become necessary to determine where an award is made. The point is an important one. For example, recognition and enforcement of an award may be refused on the basis that the arbitration agreement was not valid 'under the law of the country where the award was made, or on the basis that the award itself had been 'set aside or suspended' by a court of the country in which it was made.[77]

3.70 Some arbitration rules and some national laws deal expressly with the place at which an award is 'made'. For example, the ICC Rules provide that an award is deemed to be made at the place (or seat) of the arbitration and on the date stated therein.[78] This is a sensible provision when arbitrators who live in different countries may well have agreed on the final terms of the award by email or other forms of communication. The Model Law contains a similar provision,[79] as do the Netherlands 1986 Act[80] and the English Arbitration Act 1996.[81]

3.71 But what happens when there is no provision in the rules of arbitration or in the *lex arbitri* as to where the award is made? Is this then a question of fact, or is there some relevant legal presumption? In an international arbitration, with a tribunal of three arbitrators, the award in its final form may well be signed in three different countries, each member of the tribunal adding his or her signature in turn. There is a strong argument that, in such circumstances, the award should be deemed to have been made at the seat of the arbitration:

> The award, it is submitted, is no more than a part, the final and vital part of a procedure which must have a territorial, central point or seat. It would be very odd if, possibly without the knowledge of the parties or even unwittingly, the arbitrators had the power to sever that part from the preceding procedure and thus give a totally different character to the whole.[82]

This analysis is persuasive, but it does assume, of course, that the 'central point or seat' was real, in the sense that the arbitral proceedings (or most of them) actually took place there.

3.72 An alternative view is that an award is 'made' at the place where it is signed. This was the view taken by the English court,[83] but the ruling was reversed by the

---

[77] New York Convention, Art. V(1)(e); Model Law, Art. 36(1)(a)(v). Note that these provisions are discretionary: recognition and enforcement may be refused. See Chapter 10.
[78] ICC Rules, Art. 31.3.
[79] Model Law, Art. 31(3).
[80] Netherlands Arbitration Act 1986, Art. 1037(1).
[81] English Arbitration Act 1996, ss 52(5) and 53.
[82] Mann, 'Where is an award "made"?' (1985) 1 Arb Intl 107, at 108. However, the view of Dr Mann that an award is 'made' at the arbitral seat and not necessarily at the place where it is signed was not accepted in *Hiscox v Outhwaite* [1992] AC 562.
[83] In *Hiscox v Outhwaite*, at 594, where the arbitration was conducted in London, but the award was signed in Paris.

C. Law Governing the Arbitration

Arbitration Act 1996.[84] Nevertheless, it is a view that may still prevail elsewhere in the world. The question is important and is discussed in more detail in Chapter 9.

(i) Delocalisation

As far as international arbitration is concerned, it would save considerable time, trouble, and expense if the laws governing arbitrations were the same throughout the world, so that there were—so to speak—a universal *lex arbitri*. There would then be a 'level playing field' for the conduct of international arbitrations wherever they took place. An arbitral tribunal would not have to enquire whether there were any special provisions governing arbitration that were peculiar to the law of the country that was the seat of the arbitration. On this aspect of the arbitral process, all laws would be the same.

3.73

In practice, however, the idea of a universal *lex arbitri* is as illusory as that of universal peace. Each state has its own national characteristics, its own interests to protect, and its own concepts of how arbitrations should be conducted in its territory. Although the Model Law offers states a simple, yet well-recognised approach to reaching a common standard for the practice of international arbitration, certain states that have adopted the Model Law have been unable to resist adding their own particular provisions to it.[85] Also, states with a long history of arbitration, and a highly developed law and practice, are particularly unlikely to adopt simplified models that may, in themselves, create fresh problems.[86] Nevertheless, it is inconvenient (to put it no higher) that the regulation of international arbitration should differ from one country to another—and this has led to the search for an escape route.

3.74

In this connection, two separate developments are seen. The first is for the state to relax the control that it seeks to exercise over international arbitrations conducted on its territory. This is the route taken by modern laws of arbitration. These laws take careful note of the theme of the Model Law, which is that their courts should not intervene in arbitrations unless authorised to do so. The role of the courts should be supportive, not interventionist.[87]

3.75

---

[84] English Arbitration Act 1996, s. 3.
[85] For example, Egypt has adopted the Model Law, but has added a provision that provides for annulment if the award fails to apply the law agreed by the parties—thus opening the way for the Egyptian courts to review awards on issues of law, which is not permitted under the Model Law. For an authoritative commentary on the Egyptian Code, see Atallah, 'The 1994 Egyptian Arbitration Law ten years on' (2003) 14 ICC Bulletin 16. In Latin America, while several states have now adopted the Model Law with limited modifications (Bolivia, Chile, Guatemala, Nicaragua, Paraguay, Peru, and Venezuela), Brazil and Costa Rica chose to tinker with the Model Law's formulation and have added their own customised elements.
[86] This was the view of the Mustill Committee, which recommended that the Model Law should not be adopted, but that the English law of arbitration should nevertheless take careful account of it—as has been done, in the Arbitration Act 1996.
[87] See, e.g., Mustill and Boyd, 'A survey of the 1996 Act', in *Commercial Arbitration* (2nd edn with 2001 Companion Volume, LexisNexis Butterworths, 2001), pp. 28–30, commenting on the

3.76 The second development is to detach an international arbitration from control by the law of the place in which it is held. This is the so-called delocalisation theory, the idea being that instead of a dual system of control, first by the *lex arbitri* and then by the courts of the place of enforcement of the award, there should be only one point of control: that of the place of enforcement. In this way, the whole world (or most of it) would be available for international arbitrations, and international arbitration itself would be 'supranational', 'a-national', 'transnational', 'delocalised', or even 'expatriate'. More poetically, such an arbitration would be a 'floating arbitration', resulting in a 'floating award'.[88]

3.77 A recent judicial manifestation of the delocalisation theory is provided by the French Cour de Cassation, which, in enforcing an arbitral award set aside by the English High Court, held that:

> [A]n international arbitral award, *which does not* belong *to any state legal system*, is an international decision of justice and its validity must be examined according to the applicable rules of the country where its recognition and enforcement are sought.[89]

As noted earlier, this French approach was considered by the UK Supreme Court in *Dallah Real Estate*, in which, without endorsing such an approach under English law, the Court noted that, under French law, 'arbitration agreements derive their existence, validity and effect from supra-national law, without it being necessary to refer to any national law'.[90]

English Arbitration Act 1996. See also Mustill and Boyd, *Commercial Arbitration* (2nd edn with 2001 Companion Volume, LexisNexis Butterworths, 2001), Preface, where it is said that:

> The Act has however given English arbitration law an entirely new face, a new policy, and new foundations. The English judicial authorities...have been replaced by the statute as the principal source of law. The influence of foreign and international methods and concepts is apparent in the text and structure of the Act, and has been openly acknowledged as such. Finally, the Act embodies a new balancing of the relationships between parties, advocates, arbitrators and courts which is not only designed to achieve a policy proclaimed within Parliament and outside, but may also have changed their juristic nature.

[88] See in particular Lew, 'Achieving the dream: Autonomous arbitration' (2006) 22 Arb Intl 178, at 202; Fouchard, *L'Arbitrage Commercial International* (Litec, 1965), pp. 22–27; Paulsson, 'Arbitration unbound: Award detached from the law of its country of origin' (1981) 30 ICLQ 358; Paulsson, 'Delocalisation of international commercial arbitration: When and why it matters' (1983) 32 ICLQ 53. For a continuation of the debate, see Nakamura, 'The place of arbitration: Its fictitious nature and *lex arbitri*' (2000) 15 Mealey's Intl Arb Rep 23; Rubins, 'The arbitral seat is no fiction: A brief reply to Tatsuya Nakamura's Commentary, "The place of arbitration: Its fictitious nature and *lex arbitri*" ' (2001) 16 Mealey's Intl Arb Rep 23; Pinsolle, 'Parties to an international arbitration with the seat in France are at full liberty to organise the procedure as they see fit: A reply to the article by Noah Rubins' (2001) 16 Mealey's Intl Arb Rep 30; Nakamura, 'The fictitious nature of the place of arbitration may not be denied' (2001) 16 Mealey's Intl Arb Rep 22.

[89] *Société PT Putrabali Adyamulia v Société Rena Holding et Société Mnugotia Est Epices* [2007] Rev Arb 507, at 514 (emphasis added).

[90] *Dallah Real Estate and Tourism Holding Co. v Ministry of Religious Affairs, Government of Pakistan* [2010] UKSC 4, at 15.

C. Law Governing the Arbitration

3.78 The delocalisation theory takes as its starting point the autonomy of the parties—the fact that it is their agreement to arbitrate that brings the proceedings into being—and rests upon two basic (yet frequently confused) arguments.[91] The first assumes that international arbitration is sufficiently regulated by its own rules, which are either adopted by the parties (as an expression of their autonomy) or drawn up by the arbitral tribunal itself. The second assumes that control should come only from the law of the place of enforcement of the award.

(i) Arguments considered

3.79 The first argument is, in effect, that an international arbitration is self-regulating and that this is, or should be, sufficient. It is true that the parties to an international arbitration will generally (but not always) have a set of procedural rules to follow, whether they are those of an arbitral institution or are formulated ad hoc. It is also true that the arbitral tribunal will generally (but again, not always) have the power to fill any gaps in these rules by giving procedural directions—and this set of rules, whether agreed by the parties or laid down by the arbitral tribunal, may perhaps be said to constitute 'the law of the arbitration', in the same way as a contract may be said to constitute 'the law of the parties'. Finally, when the arbitration is being administered by an arbitral institution (such as the ICC or LCIA), that institution may be said to have taken over the state's regulatory functions, by itself laying down rules for the confirmation or removal of arbitrators, terms of reference, time limits, scrutiny of awards, and so on.[92]

3.80 Most arbitrations are conducted without any reference to the law that governs them. Nonetheless, to repeat a point that has already been made, this law—the *lex arbitri*—exists.[93] Its support may be needed not only to fill any gaps in the arbitral process (such as the appointment of arbitrators), but also to give the force of law to orders of the arbitral tribunal that reach beyond the parties themselves, for example for the 'freezing' of a bank account or for the detention of goods. More crucially, this law will confer its nationality on the award of the arbitral tribunal, so that it is recognised, for example, as a Swiss award or a Dutch award and may benefit from any international treaties (such as the New York Convention) to which its country of origin is a party.

---

[91] In this discussion, 'delocalisation' is used (as it was originally) to signify the detachment of international arbitration from control by the law of the place of arbitration. Somewhat confusingly, the term is now sometimes used to indicate not only detachment from the *lex arbitri*, but also the replacement of a national law governing the substance of the dispute by general principles or some other non-national concept: see, e.g., Toope, *Mixed International Arbitration* (Grotius, 1990), p. 19, who states: 'Some [specialists] would preclude the delocalisation of procedure, but allow delocalisation of the substantive law, through the application of "general principles", "a *lex mercatoria*" or international law *per se*.'

[92] See Fouchard, *L'Arbitrage Commercial International* (Litec, 1965), pp. 22–27.

[93] The point is no doubt so obvious as to need no comment, but the statement of Professor Weil seems particularly apt in this context: 'The principle of *pacta sunt servanda* and that of party autonomy do not float in space; a system of law is necessary to give them legal force and effect.'

3.81 The second argument in support of the delocalisation theory is that any control of the process of international arbitration should come only at the place of enforcement of the award. If this were the position, it would mean that the place of arbitration would be, in legal terms, irrelevant. This may or may not be a desirable solution—but it is significant that one state, Belgium, which had compulsorily 'delocalised' international arbitrations has (as will be described shortly[94]) since changed its mind. For the rest, the prevailing emphasis, both nationally and internationally, is on a necessary connection between the place of arbitration and the law of that place. This may be seen, as has already been demonstrated, in the New York Convention[95] and in the Model Law.[96]

(ii) Position in reality

3.82 The delocalisation theory has attracted powerful and eloquent advocates. Professor Gaillard describes this 'representation' of international arbitration as one that:

> ...accepts the idea that the juridicity of arbitration is rooted in a distinct, transnational legal order, that could be labelled as the arbitral legal order, and not in a national system, be it that of the country of the seat or that of the place or places of enforcement. This representation corresponds to the international arbitrators' strong perception that they do not administer justice on behalf of any given State, but that they nonetheless play a judicial role for the benefit of the international community.[97]

Seductive as such theories might be, the reality is that the delocalisation of arbitrations—other than those, like those of the International Centre for the Settlement of Investment Disputes (ICSID), which are governed directly by international law—is possible only if the local law (the *lex arbitri*) permits it. Assessing the theory of 'delocalisation', Professor Paulsson concludes in his treatise *The Idea of Arbitration* as follows:

> [T]he development of international arbitration owes a disproportionately large debt to French law and to the conceptual advances of French judges and scholars. Nowhere else have the twin lodestars of freedom and internationalization combined in the conception of a voluntary process that accommodates the reality of a transnational society, shone so bright. Yet the zeal of those who make extravagant claims may do more harm than the resistance of non-believers and scoffers. The proposition that an effective legal order may be built upon diaphanous abstractions like *positive perspectives* or *transnational dynamics* are more likely to impede than to facilitate respect for the arbitral process.[98]

See Weil, 'Problèmes relatifs aux contrats passés entre un état et un particulier' (1969) 128 Hague Recueil 95, at 181 (authors' translation).

[94] See paragraph 3.82 and n. 103.
[95] Article V(1)(a) and (e).
[96] Article 36(1)(a)(i) and (v).
[97] Gaillard, *Legal Theory of International Arbitration* (Martinus Nijhoff, 2010), p. 35.
[98] Paulsson, *The Idea of Arbitration* (Oxford University Press, 2013), p. 44.

C. Law Governing the Arbitration

One country that opted in favour of a substantial degree of delocalisation was Belgium. By its law of 27 March 1985, a provision was added to article 1717 of the Belgian Code Judiciaire to the effect that a losing party was not permitted to challenge in the Belgian courts an award made in an international arbitration held in Belgium, unless at least one of the parties had a place of business or other connection with Belgium. In the event, however, it appears that this legal provision discouraged parties from choosing Belgium as the seat of the arbitration and the law has since been changed.[99]

(j) Seat theory and the *lex arbitri*

The strength of the seat theory is that it gives an established legal framework to an international arbitration, so that instead of 'floating in the transnational firmament, unconnected with any municipal system of law',[100] the arbitration is firmly anchored in a given legal system. Just as the law of contracts helps to ensure that contracts are performed as they should be and are not mere social engagements, so the *lex arbitri* helps to ensure that the arbitral process works as it should. The necessity for such support for (and control of) the arbitral process is, of course, reflected in the Model Law, which allows for certain functions (such as the appointment of arbitrators, where there is a vacancy) and for certain sanctions (such as the setting aside of an award) to be exercised by the courts of the place of arbitration.[101]

3.84

For this reason, the English courts have held that although, under English law and subject to certain mandatory provisions, parties are free to agree the law and procedure that will govern how proceedings are conducted, the law chosen must indeed satisfy this function. In *Halpern v Halpern*,[102] Jewish law as a religious law was deemed not to be a 'realistic candidate as the law of the arbitration', and in addition was said to lack any supervisory or appellate jurisdiction over arbitrations.

3.85

The fact that different states have different laws governing international arbitration and that some of these laws may not be well suited to this task has two practical consequences. First, it means that, wherever an international arbitration is held, the provisions of the local law should be checked to see whether there are any

3.86

---

[99] The original authors commented, in the second edition of this book, that while claimants would no doubt welcome the 'hands-off' attitude of the Belgian legislature, respondents were likely to be less enthusiastic and their lawyers might be expected to advise against Belgium as a suitable place for arbitration. This has proved to be the case. Belgian law now allows parties to an international arbitration to opt out of local control if they so wish, but no longer provides for compulsory delocalisations: Law of 19 May 1998, art. 1717.
[100] *Bank Mellat v Helliniki Techniki SA* [1984] QB 291, 301, [1983] 3 All ER 428 (CA).
[101] See Model Law, Arts 6 (which allocates various functions to the local courts) and 34 (which allows the local court to set aside awards made in its territory, on certain limited grounds).
[102] [2006] EWHC 603 (Comm); aff'd on this point in [2007] EWCA Civ 291.

particular mandatory rules that must be observed in order to obtain a valid award. Secondly, it means that not every country is a suitable *situs* for international arbitration and that a certain amount of 'forum shopping' is advisable.

3.87 The first point is almost self-evident. For example, if the local law requires an award to be made within a defined period of time or to be lodged with a local court for it to be valid, then the necessary action must be taken to conform to this requirement. The second point is less evident, but equally important. Since the law and practice of international arbitration differs from one state to the next (and may even differ from place to place within the same state), care should be taken to choose a place of arbitration in a state that is favourable, rather than in one that is unfavourable. This is a matter of considerable practical importance and should be considered at the time the parties are drafting their arbitration agreement.[103]

3.88 One final comment is necessary before leaving the discussion of delocalisation and the *lex arbitri*. It seems, for now, that the movement in favour of total delocalisation, in the sense of freeing an international arbitration from control by the *lex arbitri*, remains aspirational. As the Belgian experiment showed, delocalisation is possible only to the extent that it is permitted by the *lex arbitri*, and parties to an arbitration may well prefer an arbitral tribunal that is subject to some rational legal control. However, there is still discontent amongst practitioners regarding the impact of local laws that are seen to operate unfairly and, at times, almost arbitrarily, and so there have been cases of what may perhaps be described as 'delocalisation by a side door'.

3.89 In *Chromalloy*,[104] for example, the Egyptian court annulled an arbitral tribunal's award made in Cairo in favour of a US corporation. Despite this annulment by the courts of the place of arbitration, the award was granted recognition and enforcement by the US District Court in Washington, DC—'to the advantage of the home team', in the words of certain distinguished US commentators.[105] And *Chromalloy* is but one example of national courts enforcing awards that have been annulled by the courts of the place of arbitration.[106]

3.90 Then there are the problems caused by local courts that issue injunctions at the seat of the arbitration to prevent arbitral tribunals from carrying out their task. Some tribunals continue with the arbitral proceedings despite the injunction (even when

---

[103] See Chapter 2.
[104] *Chromalloy Aeroservices Inc. v Arab Republic of Egypt*, 939 F.Supp. 907 (DDC 1996), (2003) 19 Arab Intl 424, (2003) 12 Intl Arab Rep 8.
[105] Brower, Brower, II and Sharpe, 'The coming crisis in the global adjudication system' (2003) 19 Arb Intl 415, at 424.
[106] See, e.g., *Corporacion Mexicana de Mantenimiento Integral, S. de R.L. de C.V. v PEMEX-Exploracion y Produccion*, No 10 Civ 206 (AKH) 2013 WL 4517225 (SDNY, August 27, 2013), in which the district court in the Southern District of New York confirmed a US$400 million arbitral award that had been set aside in the seat in Mexico City. Such examples are considered in greater detail in Chapter 11.

they are within the territorial jurisdiction of the court concerned) on the basis that the injunction is not justified.[107] In effect, these arbitrators 'delocalise' their arbitration by refusing to accept the rulings of the local court under the *lex arbitri*.[108]

D. Law Applicable to the Substance

(a) Introduction

When questions of procedure have been settled, the principal task of the arbitral tribunal is to establish the material facts of the dispute. It does this by examining the agreement between the parties, by considering other relevant documents (including correspondence, minutes of meetings, and so on), and by hearing witnesses, if necessary. The arbitral tribunal then builds its award on this foundation of facts, making its decision either on the basis of the relevant law or exceptionally, and then only if expressly authorised by the parties, on the basis of what seems to be fair and reasonable in all of the circumstances. 3.91

Once the relevant facts have been established, the arbitral tribunal may not need to go outside the confines of the agreement originally made between the parties in order to determine the dispute. This agreement, particularly in international commercial transactions, will generally be quite detailed. For example, international construction contracts run to many hundreds of closely printed pages, accompanied by detailed drawings and specifications. Properly understood, such an agreement will generally make clear what the parties intended, what duties and responsibilities they each assumed, and therefore which of them must be held liable for any failure of performance that has occurred. 3.92

But, as already stated, an agreement intended to create legal relations does not exist in a legal vacuum. It is supported by a system of law that is generally known as 'the substantive law', 'the applicable law', or 'the governing law' of the contract.[109] These terms all denote the particular system of law that governs the interpretation and validity of the contract, the rights and obligations of the parties, the mode of performance, and the consequences of breaches of the contract.[110] 3.93

---

[107] See, e.g., *Himpurna California Energy Ltd v Republic of Indonesia* (2000) XXV YBCA 11, at 176, in which the tribunal, in its interim award dated 26 September 1999, ruled that an injunction (ordered by the Central District Court of Jakarta that arbitral proceedings be suspended) was 'the consequence of the refusal of the Republic of Indonesia to submit to an arbitration to which it [had] previously consented [and] therefore [it did] not, under Art. 28 of the UNCITRAL Rules [on the submission of evidence], excuse the Republic of Indonesia's default'. See also ICC Case No. 10623 (2003) 21 ASA Bulletin 60.

[108] Again, this is discussed in more detail in Chapter 7, especially at paragraphs 7.51–7.61.

[109] In English private international law, it is also known as the 'proper law' of the contract.

[110] *Compagnie Tunisienne de Navigation SA v Compagnie d'Armament Maritime SA* [1971] AC 572, at 603 *per* Lord Diplock.

3.94 Changes in the law applicable to the contract may bring about changes in the contract itself. For instance, a country may enact currency regulations; these regulations will then apply to contracts that are governed by the law of that country. This happened in a case in which the delivery of bearer bonds to their lawful owner was refused because, under the law of then Czechoslovakia, it had become illegal for the bonds to be delivered without the consent of the Central Bank. The Central Bank refused that consent. The owner of the bonds sued for their delivery, but was unsuccessful:

> If the proper law of the contract is the law of Czechoslovakia, that law not merely sustains but, because it sustains, may also modify or dissolve the contractual bond. The currency law is not part of the contract, but the rights and obligations under the contract are part of the legal system to which the currency law belongs.[111]

Accordingly, it is not enough to know what agreement the parties have made. It is also essential to know what law is applicable to that agreement. In a purely domestic contract, the applicable law will usually be that of the country concerned. If a French woman purchases a dress in a Paris boutique, French law will be the applicable or substantive law of that contract. However, where the contract is in respect of an international transaction, the position is more complicated: there may then be two, or more, different national systems of law capable of qualifying as the substantive law of the contract, and—although it is important not to exaggerate the possibilities—these different national systems may contain contradictory rules of law on the particular point or points in issue.

(i) Crossing national frontiers

3.95 An individual who crosses a national frontier on foot or by car, passport in hand, realises that he or she is moving from one country to another. After a moment's thought, the traveller will realise that he or she is transferring from one legal system to another—and indeed that what is lawful in one country is not necessarily so in another.

3.96 This transition from one legal system to another is less apparent, or at least more easily forgotten, when national frontiers are crossed by electronic signals from telephones, telexes, faxes, or email. For example, an oil trader in New York may enter into an agreement by fax to buy crude oil on the spot market in Rotterdam, for shipment to a refinery in Germany. A bullion dealer in London may buy gold over the telephone from Zurich for delivery to a bank in Italy, on the basis that payment is to be made by an irrevocable letter of credit drawn on a bank in Chicago. These transactions cross national frontiers as unmistakably as travellers by road or train. Although there are no frontier posts to go through, complex questions of law may

---

[111] *Kahler v Midland Bank Ltd* [1950] AC 24, at 56. Similar problems have arisen in relation to Argentine investments under which obligations payable in foreign currency were forcibly redenominated in Argentine pesos at a rate of one dollar to one peso. This applied only to contracts governed by Argentinian law.

D. Law Applicable to the Substance

still arise because of the crossing of national boundaries. Transactions such as these take place constantly and rules of law govern each transaction. Yet problems still arise, first, in identifying what law applies, and secondly, in dealing with any conflict between the applicable laws.

(b) Autonomy of the parties

3.97 It is generally recognised that parties to an international commercial agreement are free to choose for themselves the law (or the legal rules) applicable to that agreement.[112] The doctrine of party autonomy, which was first developed by academic writers and then adopted by national courts, has gained extensive acceptance in national systems of law:[113]

> [D]espite their differences, common law, civil law and socialist countries have all equally been affected by the movement towards the rule allowing the parties to choose the law to govern their contractual relations. This development has come about independently in every country and without any concerted effort by the nations of the world; it is the result of separate, contemporaneous and pragmatic evolutions within the various national systems of conflict of laws.[114]

3.98 The doctrine has also found expression in international conventions, such as the Rome I Regulation.[115] Rome I, which is applicable to contractual obligations within the European Union, accepts as a basic principle the right of parties to a contract to choose, expressly or by implication, the law that is to govern their contractual relationship.[116]

3.99 If national courts are prepared (as most of them are) to recognise the principle of party autonomy in the choice of the law applicable to a contract, then, *a fortiori*, arbitral tribunals should also be prepared to do so. An international arbitral tribunal owes its existence to the agreement of the parties and, in applying the law chosen by the parties, an arbitral tribunal is simply carrying out their agreement.

---

[112] The point as to 'legal rules', by which is meant something other than a national system of law, is developed at paragraphs 3.131–3.197. The Model Law (and the UNCITRAL Rules) allows the parties to choose the 'rules of law' applicable to their contract (which may include, e.g., the *lex mercatoria*), but stipulates that if the parties fail to make such a choice, the arbitral tribunal shall apply 'the law' applicable to the dispute (which would not include the *lex mercatoria*).

[113] See, e.g., Brazilian Arbitration Act 1996, s. 2; China New Interpretation, s. 16; English Arbitration Act 1996, s. 46(1); French Code of Civil Procedure, Art. 1511; German ZPO 1998, Art. 1051(10); Indian Arbitration and Conciliation Act 1996, s. 28(10)(b); Russian International Arbitration Law 1993, s. 28; Swiss PIL, s. 187(1).

[114] Lew, *Applicable Law in International Commercial Arbitration* (Oceana/Sigthoff & Noorthoff, 1978), p. 75.

[115] Regulation (EC) No. 593/2008 of the European Parliament and of the Council of 17 June 2008 on the law applicable to contractual obligations, OJ L 177/6, 4 July 2008.

[116] Rome I, Art. 3(1). The Regulation does not apply to arbitration agreements, but the subject under discussion here is not that of arbitration agreements, but of the contract between the parties under which a dispute has arisen.

(i) Recognition by international conventions

3.100 Both international conventions and the model rules on international arbitration confirm that the parties are free to choose for themselves the law applicable to their contract. For example, Article 42 of the ICSID Convention provides: 'The Tribunal shall decide a dispute in accordance with such rules of law as may be agreed by the parties.' Article 35(1) of the UNCITRAL Rules provides: 'The arbitral tribunal shall apply the rules of law designated by the parties as applicable to the substance of the dispute.' And, amongst the rules of arbitral institutions,[117] Article 21(1) of the ICC Rules provides: 'The parties shall be free to agree upon the rules of law to be applied by the arbitral tribunal to the merits of the dispute...' As one commentator has stated:

> There are few principles more universally admitted in private international law than that referred to by the standard terms of the 'proper law of the contract'—according to which the law governing the contract is that which has been chosen by the parties, whether expressly or (with certain differences or variations according to the various systems) tacitly.[118]

(ii) Time of choice

3.101 At its origin, the rule of party autonomy related to the freedom of the parties to choose the applicable law at the time of making their contract. It now extends (under the international conventions and rules cited) to the right of the parties to choose the law as it is to be applied at the time of the dispute.

3.102 It is logical to allow the parties to choose the law that is to govern their contract at the time when they make it. In their contract, the parties set out the rights and duties that they undertake to uphold towards each other. It is appropriate that they should, at the same time, refer to the system of law by which that contract is to be governed, because that law forms an essential element of the bargain between them.

3.103 There is less logic in allowing the parties to choose the applicable law once a dispute has arisen and yet, in practice, it seems that parties may do so, even if their choice of law differs from that which they had chosen previously. Indeed, the Rome I Regulation makes express provision for this.[119] If any justification for this delayed choice (or even change) of law is sought in legal philosophy, it must lie more generally in the concept of the autonomy of the parties. Parties are generally free to vary

---

[117] Other examples include the Rules of the American Arbitration Association's (AAA) International Centre for Dispute Resolution (ICDR), Art. 28(1); LCIA Rules, Art. 22(3); the Rules of the Russian Federation's Chamber of Commerce and Industry (RF CCI), Art. 26(1); the Rules of the Arbitration Institute of the Stockholm Chamber of Commerce (SCC), Art. 22(1); the Arbitration Rules of the World Intellectual Property Organization (WIPO), Art. 59(a).

[118] Lalive, cited in Lew, *Applicable Law in International Commercial Arbitration* (Oceana/Sigthoff & Noorthoff, 1978), p. 87.

[119] Rome I Regulation, Art. 3, provides that a choice of law, or a variation of a choice, can be made at any time after the conclusion of the contract by agreement between the parties.

D. Law Applicable to the Substance

the terms of their contract by agreement; in the same way, they should be free to vary by agreement the law applicable to a dispute arising out of that contract.

(iii) Restrictions on party autonomy

For lawyers who practise in the resolution of international trade disputes and who are accustomed to wending their way through a maze of national laws, the existence of a general transnational rule of law supporting the autonomy of the parties is almost too good to be true. The natural inclination is to ask whether there are any restrictions on the rule, and if so, what?[120]   **3.104**

The answer is that there may be limited restrictions on the rule, designed to ensure that the choice of law is bona fide and is not contrary to public policy. Thus the Rome I Regulation, for example, does not allow the choice of a foreign law to override the mandatory rules of law of a country towards which all of the factual elements of the contract point—so that, for example, the choice of a foreign law for the purposes of tax evasion or avoiding competition regulation would not be permissible.[121] Thus, in *Soleimany v Soleimany*,[122] the English Court of Appeal refused to enforce an award where the transaction was not illegal under the applicable law, but was illegal under English law.   **3.105**

The case concerned a contract between a father and son, which involved the smuggling of carpets out of Iran in breach of Iranian revenue laws and export controls. The father and son had agreed to submit their dispute to arbitration by the Beth Din, the Court of the Chief Rabbi in London, which applied Jewish law. Under the applicable Jewish law, the illegal purpose of the contract had no effect on the rights of the parties and the Beth Din proceeded to make an award enforcing the contract. In declining to enforce the award, the English Court of Appeal stated: **3.106**

> The Court is in our view concerned to preserve the integrity of its process, and to see that it is not abused. The parties cannot override that concern by private agreement. They cannot by procuring an arbitration conceal that they, or rather one of them, is seeking to enforce an illegal contract. Public policy will not allow it.[123]

(iv) Choices

Subject only to the qualifications of good faith, legality, and no public policy objection, the conventions and rules on arbitration that have been mentioned make it   **3.107**

---

[120] See Moss, 'Can an arbitral tribunal disregard the choice of law made by the parties?' (2005) 1 Stockholm Intl Arb Rev 6.

[121] By way of illustration of the point, the European Court of Justice (ECJ), in *Eco Swiss China Ltd v Benetton International NV* [1999] ECR I–3055, ruled that a breach of EU competition law constitutes a violation of the *ordre public*. In *Marketing Displays International Inc. v VR Van Raalte Reclame BV*, Case Nos 04/694 and 04/695, 24 March 2005, the Dutch Court of Appeal upheld a lower court's refusal to grant exequatur to three US arbitral awards, because the awards were considered incompatible with Art. 81 EC and thus violated public policy.

[122] [1999] QB 785.

[123] Ibid, at 800.

plain that the parties may choose for themselves the law applicable to the dispute. Parties to an international commercial agreement should make full and proper use of this freedom, inserting a 'choice of law' clause into their contract.

3.108 If they fail to do so, it will almost certainly be a matter for regret should a dispute arise, since (as will be seen) the search for the proper law can be a long and expensive process. A choice-of-law clause may be drawn in very simple terms. It is usually sufficient to say: 'This agreement shall in all respects be governed by the law of England' (or of Singapore, or of the State of New York, or of any other state that has in place a modern law of contract).

3.109 The question that then arises is: given a free choice, what system of law should the parties choose as the law applicable to the dispute? Is their choice limited to the choice of a national system of law, or may it extend beyond this, perhaps to rules of law such as those of the law merchant (*lex mercatoria*)? Indeed, are the parties limited to a choice of law or of legal rules? May they not, for instance, agree that the dispute should be decided according to considerations of equity and good conscience?

3.110 It is to these questions that attention must now be turned. The choices that may be available to the parties include:

- national law;
- public international law (including the general principles of law);
- concurrent laws (and combined laws—the *tronc commun* doctrine);
- transnational law (including international development law, the *lex mercatoria*, codified terms and practices, and trade usages); and
- equity and good conscience.

(c) National law

3.111 In most international commercial contracts, including those in which a state or state entity is one of the parties, it is usual for a given system of law to be chosen as the law applicable to the contract itself. There is much sense in such a choice. Parties who choose a law to govern their contract, or any subsequent dispute between them, will generally choose an autonomous system of law. Such a system is not merely a set of general principles or of isolated legal rules;[124] rather, it is an interconnecting, interdependent collection of laws, regulations, and ordinances, enacted by or on behalf of the state, and interpreted and applied by the courts. It is a complete legal system, designed to provide an answer to any legal question that might be posed. Furthermore, a national system of law will, in principle, be a known and existing system, capable of reasonably accurate interpretation by experienced practitioners.

---

[124] Which, in this context, will be referred to as a 'national' system of law, the term being intended to cover not merely a 'national law' properly so-called, such as that of France, but also the law of a 'state' within a federal system, such as New York or California.

D. Law Applicable to the Substance

In law, as in life, there is no certainty. However, a national system of law provides a known (or at least determinable) legal standard against which the rights and responsibilities of the parties can be measured. In the event of a dispute, the parties can be advised with reasonable confidence as to their legal position—or, at the very least, they can be given a broad indication of their chances of success or failure. If, for example, parties to a dispute that is to be heard in Switzerland agree that the arbitral tribunal shall apply the law of France, then all concerned (arbitrators, parties, and advisers alike) know where they stand. The arbitrators will know to what system of law they have to refer, if such reference becomes necessary. The parties and their advisers will be able to evaluate their prospects of success against the known content of French law. They will know, too, what sort of legal arguments they will have to present and what sort of legal arguments (as to fault, compensation, and so on) they may be required to address. 3.112

(i) Choice of a system of national law

The standard arbitration clauses recommended by arbitral institutions, such as the ICC, are usually followed by a note pointing out that, in addition to incorporating the arbitration clause in their agreement, the parties should also add a 'choice of law' clause. In-house lawyers and others who are concerned with the drafting of contracts will invariably do this, so that, in most commercial contracts, it is usual to find an arbitration clause, followed by a 'choice of law' clause. 3.113

Almost invariably, the law chosen is a national law. This may be because of that law's connection with the parties to the contract, or it may simply be because the parties regard it as a system of law that is well suited to governing their commercial relations. Indeed, many contracts incorporate the choice of a particular country's law, although they have no connection with that country. For example, commodity contracts, shipping and freight contracts, and contracts of insurance often contain a choice of English law, because the commercial law of England is considered to reflect, and to be responsive to, the needs of modern international commerce. For similar reasons, many major reinsurance contracts contain a choice of the law of the State of New York. 3.114

In an ideal world, almost any national system of law should be suitable, as long as that law has been drawn up, or has developed, in a manner that suits the requirements of modern commerce. In the real world, some national systems of law will be found to contain outdated laws and regulations that make them unsuitable for use in international contracts. 3.115

Indeed, even well-developed and modern codes of law are not necessarily best suited to the needs of international (as opposed to purely domestic) commerce. The law of a country reflects the social, economic, and (above all) political environment of that particular country. If a country habitually controls the import and export trade (perhaps permitting such activities only through state corporations), and prohibits the free flow of currency across the exchanges, these restrictions will 3.116

permeate the national law. This may or may not benefit the country concerned, but it is not an environment in which international trade and commerce is likely to flourish. A national law that does not permit the free flow of goods and services across national frontiers is probably not the most suitable law to govern international commercial contracts and the disputes that may arise from them.

3.117 Parties to an international commercial contract will need to bear these kinds of considerations in mind in choosing a given system of law to govern their contractual relationships. Even in countries that favour international trade and development, problems may arise, particularly where the contract is made with the state itself or with a state agency. The problem, shortly stated, is that the state (as legislator) may change the law and so change the terms of the contract lawfully, but without the agreement of the other party to the contract. The state may, for instance, impose labour or import restrictions, which render performance of the contract more expensive. Unless the contract has been drafted with such possible contingencies in mind—and such contingencies may be difficult to foresee—it is the private party who will suffer from this change in the equilibrium of the contract.

3.118 The problem of protecting a party from changes in the local law was considered in the *Sapphire* arbitration:[125]

> Under the present agreement, the foreign company was bringing financial and technical assistance to Iran, which involved it in investments, responsibilities and considerable risks. It therefore seems normal that they should be protected against any legislative changes which might alter the character of the contract and that they should be assured of some legal security. This would not be guaranteed to them by the outright application of Iranian law, which it is within the power of the Iranian State to change.[126]

(ii) Precluding unfair treatment

3.119 Various devices have been borrowed from private law contracts in an attempt to maintain the balance of the contract. These include revision clauses, hardship clauses, and *force majeure* clauses, all of which have a part to play in helping to maintain the balance of the contractual relationship. In some long-term economic development agreements, the national law has been 'frozen' by means of the parties agreeing that the law of the state party will be applied as it stood on a given date. Strictly speaking, the state law does not then operate as the applicable law, but as an immutable code of law incorporated into the contract. It will not change no matter what amendments are made to the state law itself. The problem, however (apart from the lack of flexibility that this device introduces into the contract), is that thes party may still introduce a law avoiding such clauses in its own territory. In other words, the problem of entrenching such clauses has to be faced, and whilst

---

[125] *Sapphire International Petroleum Ltd v The National Iranian Oil Co.* (1964) 13 ICLQ 1011.
[126] Ibid., at 1012.

D. Law Applicable to the Substance

initially attractive, the 'freezing' solution may fly in the face of political, social, and economic realities.

(iii) Stabilisation clauses

3.120 One method of introducing a 'freezing' solution, particularly in long-term agreements, has been the inclusion of stabilisation clauses. These are undertakings on the part of the contracting state that it will not annul or change the terms of the contract by legislative or administrative action without the consent of the other party to the contract. In one of the arbitrations that arose out of the Libyan oil nationalisations, the arbitrator held that the Libyan government's act of nationalisation was in breach of certain stabilisation clauses and was, accordingly, an illegal act under international law, entitling the companies to restitution of their concessions.[127] This decision is generally criticised as going too far, not only in its rejection of Libyan law as a basic ingredient of the governing law clause and in its so-called internationalisation of the oil concession agreement, but also in its decision in favour of *restitutio in integrum*.[128] In any event, restitution was obviously impracticable. The only purpose that it could serve was to indicate the basis on which damages should be paid for the allegedly illegal expropriation.[129]

3.121 In another of the Libyan oil nationalisation arbitrations, in which the facts were almost identical, the sole arbitrator did *not* regard the stabilisation clauses as preventing the government's act of nationalisation; rather, he held that this nationalisation was a legitimate exercise of sovereign power, as long as it was accompanied by 'equitable compensation'.[130] In the *Aminoil* arbitration, the arbitral tribunal held by a majority (with a separate opinion attached to the award) that, properly interpreted, the stabilisation clause in the concession agreement (which was to run for a period of sixty years) did not prevent the Kuwaiti government's act of nationalisation.[131]

3.122 Stabilisation clauses attempt to maintain a particular legal regime in existence, often for a considerable period of time, irrespective of any changes that may occur in the political, social, and economic environments of the country concerned.[132]

---

[127] *Texaco Overseas Petroleum Co. v Government of Libyan Arab Republic* (1978) 17 ILM 3.

[128] See, in particular, Rigaux, 'Des dieux et des héros: Réflexions sur une sentence arbitrale' [1978] Revue Critique de Droit International Privé 435; Stern, 'Trois arbitrages, un même problème, trois solutions' [1980] Rev Arb 3.

[129] See Chapter 8, paragraphs 8.146*ff.*

[130] *Libyan American Oil Co. (Liamco) v Government of the Libyan Arab Republic* (1981) 20 ILM 1, (1981) VI YBCA 89, at 104 and 113. For further discussion of the three Libyan oil nationalisation arbitrations, see Greenwood, 'State contracts in international law: The Libyan oil arbitrations' (1982) 53 BYIL 27.

[131] *American Independent Oil Co. Inc. (Aminoil) v Government of the State of Kuwait* [1982] 21 ILM 976, at 1027 (separate opinion of Sir Gerald Fitzmaurice QC).

[132] For further discussion of stabilisation clauses, see, e.g., Wetter, *The International Arbitral Process: Public and Private, Vol. 1* (Oceana, 1979), p. 407; Toope, *Mixed International Arbitration* (Grotius, 1990), pp. 52*ff*; Nassar, *The Sanctity of Contracts Revisited* (Martinus Nijhoff, 1994);

Traditionally, lenders have viewed stabilisation clauses as an essential component of investment projects, especially in developing states and those states in which political risk is deemed to be high. States keen to attract foreign investment have, in the past, seen stabilisation clauses as a valuable way of reassuring investors that the state can offer a stable investment environment.[133]

3.123 However, stabilisation clauses have come under increasing scrutiny and pressure from civil society groups, who argue that private investors should not be in a position to limit a host state's ability to modernise its laws. Indeed, some have criticised stabilisation clauses as being responsible for so-called regulatory chill.

3.124 Perhaps as a result of such increasing scrutiny, some commentators now distinguish stabilisation clauses into broadly two distinct groups—namely, traditional stabilisation clauses and economic equilibrium clauses.[134] This should not obscure the fact, however, that the variety of drafting variations of stabilisation clauses has resulted in a wide spectrum that stretches from 'freezing' clauses, on the one hand, to a proximity with *force majeure* and hardship clauses, on the other.

3.125 Traditional stabilisation clauses are often called 'freezing' clauses because, in their most basic form, these clauses state that the law in force at the time that the contract is made will be the law that governs the contract for its entire duration. Some freezing clauses seek to achieve this by stating that any new law will not apply to the parties to the contract by virtue of the freezing clause. Others are drafted to state that, in the event of a conflict between the law applicable at the time of making the contract and a newly enacted law, the former will prevail. Some are more limited and seek to cover only particular matters, for example changes to tax and customs regulations. It should be noted that freezing clauses may face enforceability issues on public policy grounds.[135]

Bernardini, 'Stabilization and adaptation in oil and gas investments' (2008) 1 J World Energy L & Bus 98; Maniruzzaman, 'The pursuit of stability in international energy investment contracts: A critical appraisal of the emerging trends' (2008) 1 J World Energy L & Bus 121; Cotula, 'Reconciling regulatory stability and evolution of environmental standards in investment contracts: Towards a rethink of stabilization clauses' (2008) 1 J World Energy L & Bus 158. For an example of a stabilisation clause in a liquefied natural gas (LNG) contract that worked against the party that it was intended to protect, see Gaillard, 'The role of the arbitrator in determining the applicable law', in Newman and Hill (eds) *The Leading Arbitrators' Guide to International Arbitration* (Juris, 2004), p. 186.

[133] On how stabilisation clauses may have helped to create a secure and favourable legal regime, and thereby encouraged investment, see, e.g., the Nigerian LNG venture, discussed by Rawding, 'Protecting Investments under state contracts: Some legal and ethical issues' (1995) 99 Arb Intl 341.

[134] See Al Faruque, 'Typologies, efficacy, and political economy of stabilisation clauses: A critical appraisal' (2007) 4 OGEL; Maniruzzaman, 'Damages for breach of stabilisation clauses in international investment law: Where do we stand today?' [2007] IELTR 11; Bernardini, 'Stabilization and adaptation in oil and gas investments' (2008) 1 J World Energy L & Bus 98; Cotula, 'Reconciling regulatory stability and evolution of environmental standards in investment contracts: Towards a rethink of stabilization clauses' (2008) 1 J World Energy L & Bus 158.

[135] See Wälde and Ndi, 'Stabilizing international investment commitments: International law versus contract interpretation' (1996) 31 Tex Intl LJ 215.

D. Law Applicable to the Substance

As their name implies, 'economic equilibrium', or 'renegotiation', clauses attempt to maintain the original economic equilibrium of the parties at the time of contracting, where subsequent measures might otherwise alter the expected economic benefits to which the parties have subscribed.[136] These clauses do not aim to freeze the law; thus newly enacted laws will apply to the investment. However, they will provide the investor with a contractual entitlement to be compensated for the cost of complying with new laws or, alternatively, may require the parties to negotiate in good faith to restore the original economic equilibrium of the contract. Avoiding any purported restriction on the development of local law, such clauses thereby steer clear of the principal ground of criticism of 'freezing' clauses.[137]

3.126

Both categories of stabilisation clause therefore present different ways of allocating 'change of law' risk between investors and host states. Moreover, such clauses could support claims by investors pursuant to the 'expropriation', 'fair and equitable treatment', or 'umbrella' provisions in investment treaties.

3.127

(d) Mandatory law

Although it is generally recognised that parties to an international commercial agreement are free to choose for themselves the law (or legal rules) applicable to that agreement, there are limits to this freedom. Mandatory rules have been defined as those that 'cannot be derogated from by way of Contract',[138] and may feature in the determination of a contractual dispute in addition to the governing law selected by the parties.

3.128

Thus, by way of example, Russian law may feature in the determination of corporate governance issues relating to a Russian company even if the arbitration arises from a shareholders agreement governed by Swedish law. In the same way, again by way of example, US-quoted companies cannot exclude the application of the Foreign Corrupt Practices Act of 1977 from the operations simply by concluding an investment agreement in Kazakhstan that is subject to Kazakh law. Moreover, in yet another example that the authors have seen in practice in an ICC case in Paris, the commercial export of defence technology from the United States to the Gulf region will be subject to the US International Trade in Arms Regulations even if the supply contract in question is governed by the law of the United Arab Emirates. However, perhaps the most frequently encountered instance of the application of

3.129

---

[136] Maniruzzaman, in turn, divides economic equilibrium clauses into three categories: stipulated economic balancing provisions, non-specified economic balancing provisions, and negotiated economic balancing provisions. See Maniruzzaman, 'Damages for breach of stabilisation clauses in international investment law: Where do we stand today?' [2007] IELTR 11, at 127*ff*.

[137] For further discussion of economic equilibrium clauses, see Berger, 'Renegotiation and adaptation of international investment contracts: The role of contract drafters and arbitrators' (2003) 36 Vanderbilt J Transl L 1348; Al Qurashi, 'Renegotiation of international petroleum agreements' (2005) 22 J Intl Arb 261.

[138] Rome I Regulation, Art. 3(3).

mandatory law is competition, or antitrust, law, and the authors now proceed to use that as an illustration.

3.130 As already discussed in Chapter 2,[139] at one time it was widely considered that the private forum of arbitration was not appropriate for the determination of claims under competition law. Landmark judgments such as that of the US Supreme Court in *Mitsubishi Motor Corporation v Soler Chrysler-Plymouth*,[140] however, have long since confirmed the arbitrability of competition law issues. A decision of the European Court of Justice (ECJ) goes further,[141] and suggests that, in Europe at least, arbitral tribunals may be duty-bound—or may at least have a discretion—to address issues of European competition law *ex officio* even where they have not been raised by the parties themselves, because such issues constitute a matter of public policy.[142] Indeed, as a matter of public policy, European competition law would need to be taken into account even if the substantive law chosen by the parties were not a European national law.[143]

(e) Public international law and general principles of law

3.131 Public international law is concerned primarily with states, but not exclusively so.[144] As Dame Rosalyn Higgins, a former president of the International Court of Justice (ICJ) in The Hague, has contended, international law is a dynamic (not static) decision-making process, in which there are a variety of participants:

> Now, in this model, there are no 'subjects' and 'objects', but only *participants*. Individuals *are* participants, along with states, international organizations (such as the United Nations, or the International Monetary Fund (IMF) or the [International Labour Organization] ILO) [*sic*], multinational corporations, and indeed private non-governmental groups.[145]

---

[139] See Chapter 2, paragraphs 2.133*ff*.
[140] (1986) XI YBCA 555.
[141] *Eco Swiss China Ltd v Benetton Investment NV* [1999] ECR I–3055.
[142] For a discussion of this subject, see Partasides and Burger, 'The Swiss Federal Tribunal's Decision of 8 March 2006: A deepening of the arbitrator's public policy dilemma?' (2006) 3 Concurrences 26. See also Berman, 'Navigating EU law and the law of international arbitration' (2012) 28 Arb Intl 397.
[143] Thus, in *Eco Swiss China Ltd v Benetton Investment NV* [1999] ECR I–3055, an arbitral tribunal seated in the Netherlands found Benetton liable for wrongfully terminating an exclusive licensing agreement by which Eco Swiss was given the exclusive right to sell watches and clocks bearing the words 'Benetton by Bulova' throughout Europe. Benetton challenged the award before the Dutch courts, claiming annulment on the grounds, inter alia, that the exclusive licensing agreement was anti-competitive under Art. 81 TEU and that therefore an award that enforced such an agreement was contrary to public policy. This issue had been raised neither by the parties nor by the arbitrators during the arbitration. The Dutch courts sent several questions of European law to the ECJ for determination and the ECJ found that a violation of European community law made an award liable to be set aside by a national court, because European competition law qualified as a matter of public policy.
[144] Higgins, *Problems Process: International Law and How We Use It* (Clarendon, 1994), p. 39.
[145] Ibid., at p. 50.

D. Law Applicable to the Substance

Amongst the 'participants' to whom President Higgins referred are those individuals and corporations who brought claims before the Iran–United States Claims Tribunal and those 'investors' who seek to protect their investment through the machinery of ICSID.[146] This has brought public international law into sharper focus as far as private individuals and corporations—and their lawyers—are concerned. Increasingly, 'international law' may be specified as the substantive law of a contract, particularly where that contract is with a state or state agency. The reference may be to 'international law' on its own, or it may be used in conjunction with a national system of law.

3.132

Reference has already been made to the freedom that parties (generally) have in selecting the law or the legal rules applicable to their contract. There is no reason, in principle, why they should not select public international law as the law that is to govern their contractual relationship.[147] To quote President Higgins again:

3.133

> The increasing importance of international arbitration is an area that we should perhaps be watching. It is now commonplace for a foreign private corporation and a state who have entered into contractual relations to agree to international arbitration in the event of a dispute. (And, in principle, the private party could be an *individual*, though as such he will probably have less leverage than a foreign corporation and may well have to accept the local legal system rather than reference to international arbitration). The applicable law clause may designate a national legal system, but more usually it will refer to 'general principles of law' or 'the law of country X and the relevant principles of general international law', or some such similar formula. At one bound, therefore, the private party has escaped the need to have his claim brought by his national government, and can invoke international law. Thus, if State X and Mr Y have a contract, State X's ability to vary the terms of that contract will be interpreted by reference to the relevant principles of international law; and compensation due to Mr Y will likewise be appraised by reference to international law…Arbitral clauses which refer to international law as the applicable law effectively remove the alleged inability of individuals to be the bearer of rights under international law. This is being done by mutual consent, of course—but the point is that there is *no inherent reason* why the individual should not be able directly to invoke international law and to be the beneficiary of international law.[148]

There are many sources of public international law, including international conventions and international custom, but probably the most relevant, as far as non-state parties are concerned, are 'the general principles of law recognised by

3.134

---

[146] See Chapter 8 in relation to the applicable law in disputes under investment treaties.

[147] Compare the observation of the court in *Orion Compania Espanola de Seguros v Belfort Maatschappij Voor Algemene Verzekgringeen* [1962] 2 Lloyd's Rep 257, at 264, a case brought many years ago:

> Thus, it may be, though perhaps it would be unusual, that the parties could validly agree that a part, or the whole, of their legal relations should be decided by the arbitral tribunal on the basis of a foreign system of law, or perhaps on the basis of principles of international law; eg, in a contract to which a Sovereign State was a party.

[148] Higgins, *Problems Process: International Law and How We Use It* (Clarendon Press, 1994), p. 54.

civilised nations'.[149] These have been defined as 'the general principles of municipal jurisprudence, in particular of private law, in so far as they are applicable to relations of States'.[150]

3.135 However, the problem of adopting public international law as the system of law that is to govern a commercial relationship is not a problem of principle, but of practice. Public international law, being concerned primarily with the relationships between states, is not particularly well equipped to deal with detailed contractual issues—such as mistake, misrepresentation, time of performance, the effect of bankruptcy or liquidation, *force majeure*, or the measure of damages, and so forth. The same criticism may be directed at the choice of 'general principles of law' as the governing law of a commercial contract. The problem with the general principles is they are just that: they deal with such topics as the principle of good faith in treaty relations, abuse of rights, and the concept of state and individual responsibility. They are excellent as generalisations, but may lack sufficient detail for contractual relations.[151] That is why the authors suggest that if they are to be used in a contract, they should be used as a concurrent law, rather than on their own.

(f) Concurrent laws, combined laws, and the *tronc commun* doctrine

3.136 As already indicated in the discussion of contracts to which a state or state entity is a party,[152] one of the main anxieties among commercial organisations engaged in trading or other business relationships with a sovereign state is that, after the bargain has been struck and the contract has been signed, the state may change its own law to the disadvantage of the private party.

3.137 One established safeguard against unfair or arbitrary action by the state party to the contract is to stipulate that the state's own law will apply only in so far as it accords with either public international law, the general principles of law, or some other system with accepted minimum standards.

3.138 The ICSID Convention, which established ICSID,[153] makes use of this system of concurrent laws. The Convention provides for the resolution of disputes between

---

[149] Article 38 of the Statute of the ICJ (which was established in 1945 and is generally known as the 'World Court') states that, in applying international law to the disputes before it, the Court is to apply, inter alia, those general principles of law.
[150] Jennings and Watts (eds) *Oppenheim's International Law, Vol. I* (9th edn, Oxford University Press, 1992), p. 29, cited with approval in Brownlie, *Principles of Public International Law* (Oxford University Press, 2012), p. 34. Professor Brownlie goes on to add that, in practice, tribunals exercise considerable discretion in how they choose, edit, and adapt elements of municipal jurisprudence: ibid., at p. 35.
[151] For an excellent (and, it must be admitted, detailed) work on this topic, see Cheng, *General Principles of Law as Applied by International Courts and Tribunals* (Cambridge University Press, 1987).
[152] See paragraphs 3.117*ff*.
[153] See the discussion of this Convention in Chapter 1.

D. Law Applicable to the Substance

a state (or a state entity) and a private party;[154] it stipulates that if a dispute arises and there has been no express choice of law by the parties, the arbitral tribunal will apply the law of the contracting state party to the arbitration *and* 'such rules of international law as may be applicable'. Thus honour is satisfied. The state's own law is given proper recognition. Yet some fetter is imposed upon possibly unfair or arbitrary action by means of the reference to public international law.[155]

This is a system of concurrent laws. For example, if a state were to terminate a long-term investment contract by an act of nationalisation, it would presumably do so in a way that would be valid under its own law. However, such an act of nationalisation would not be valid under international law unless it were shown to be non-discriminatory and to serve a public purpose, with proper compensation being offered. In this way, international law would be brought into play to set a minimum standard, which the arbitral tribunal would be empowered to uphold in its award.[156]   **3.139**

(i) Libyan oil nationalisation arbitrations

The coupling of national law with international law is seen in the three arbitrations that arose out of the Libyan oil nationalisations, the *Texaco*, *BP*, and *Liamco* arbitrations, although it worked effectively in only one of them.[157]   **3.140**

The choice-of-law clause was identical in the different concession agreements that came before three different arbitrators. It read as follows: **3.141**

> This concession shall be governed by and interpreted in accordance with the principles of law of Libya common to the principles of international law and, in the absence of such common principles, then by and in accordance with the general

---

[154] Provided that the state has adopted the ICSID Convention.

[155] Rawding, 'Protecting Investments under state contracts: Some legal and ethical issues' (1995) 99 Arb Intl 341 describes this option as subjecting national law to 'international quality control'. The issue of applicable law in cases brought under investment treaties is addressed in Chapter 8. For examples of ICSID cases resolved on the basis of international law (to the extent that there were gaps in the applicable host state law, or where its application would have produced a result inconsistent with international law), see *Klöckner Industrie-Anlagen v Republic of Cameroon*, ICSID Case No. ARB/81/2, 3 May 1995; *Amco Asia Corporation v Republic of Indonesia*, ICSID Case No. ARB/81/1, 16 May 1986; *Wena Hotels Ltd v Arab Republic of Egypt*, Decision on Annulment Application, ICSID Case No. ARB/98/4, IIC 274 (2002), (2002) 41 ILM 933, (2004) 6 ICSID Rep 129, (2003) 130 Clunet J du Droit Intl 167, signed 28 January 2002; *Sempra Energy International v Republic of Argentina*, Award, ICSID Case No. ARB/02/16, IIC 304 (2007), signed 18 September 2007, despatched 28 September 2007.

[156] For a discussion of compensation, see Chapter 8, paragraphs 8.79–8.97.

[157] *Texaco Overseas Petroleum Co. v Government of Libyan Arab Republic* (1978) 17 ILM 3; *BP Exploration Co. (Libya) Ltd v Government of the Libyan Arab Republic* (1979) 53 ILR 297; *Libyan American Oil Co. (Liamco) v Government of the Libyan Arab Republic* (1981) 20 ILM 1, (1981) VI YBCA 89. See also Greenwood, 'State contracts in international law: The Libyan oil arbitrations' (1982) 17 ILM 14; Rigaux, 'Des dieux et des héros: Réflexions sur une sentence arbitrale' [1978] Revue Critique de Droit International Privé 435; Stern, 'Trois arbitrages, un même problème, trois solutions' [1980] Rev Arb 3.

principles of law, including such of those principles as may have been applied by international tribunals.[158]

In the event, this clause was interpreted in three different ways by the three different arbitrators:

- in the *Texaco* arbitration, the sole arbitrator held that the clause was primarily a choice of public international law;
- in the *BP* arbitration, the sole arbitrator appears to have regarded it as a choice of the general principles of law;[159] and
- in the *Liamco* arbitration, the sole arbitrator held that the governing law of the contract was the law of Libya, but that the clause excluded any part of that law that was in conflict with the principles of international law.[160]

3.142 The arbitral tribunal in the *Aminoil* arbitration arrived at a similar conclusion in respect of a concession agreement that had been brought to an end by an act of nationalisation, coupled with an offer of 'fair compensation'.[161] Aminoil and the Government of Kuwait agreed in the submission agreement that their dispute should be settled by arbitration 'on the basis of law', but left the choice of law to the tribunal, with the stipulation that the tribunal should have regard to 'the quality of the parties, the transnational character of their relations and the principles of law and practice prevailing in the modern world'.[162] On this basis, Aminoil argued that the concession agreement was governed by transnational law, which it equated with the general principles of law, including the principles of *pacta sunt servanda*, reparation for injury, respect for acquired rights, the prohibition of unjust enrichment, and the requirement of good faith (including the prohibition against abuse of rights and estoppel or preclusion). The government, for its part, argued for the application of the law of Kuwait, of which public international law formed part.

3.143 It is useful to look at the tribunal's decision on the applicable law for two reasons: first, the state actually took part in the *Aminoil* arbitration, unlike Libya in the Libyan arbitrations; and secondly, the dramatic increase in the length of ICSID arbitrations has focused attention on concurrent law clauses.

---

[158] For this text, see the *Texaco* arbitration, n. 157.
[159] 'The governing system of law is what that clause expressly provides—namely, in the absence of principles common to the law of Libya and international law, the general principles of law, including such of those principles as may have been applied by international tribunals': *BP*, n. 157, *per* Judge Lagergren.
[160] *Liamco v Libya* (1982) 62 ILR 140, at 143. The fact that three different arbitrators could arrive at three different conclusions on the meaning of the same choice-of-law clause highlights one of the weaknesses of the arbitral system, which is the possibility of conflicting awards on the same basic problem: see Stern, 'Trois arbitrages, un même problème, trois solutions' [1980] Rev Arb 3.
[161] *American Independent Oil Co. Inc. (Aminoil) v Government of the State of Kuwait* [1982] 21 ILM 976.
[162] *Aminoil*, at 980.

D. Law Applicable to the Substance

The tribunal in *Aminoil* stated that the question of the law applicable to the substantive issues in dispute before it was a simple one. The law of Kuwait applied to many matters with which it was directly concerned, but, as the government had argued, established public international law was part of the law of Kuwait and the general principles of law were part of public international law.[163] The tribunal concluded:

3.144

> The different sources of the law thus to be applied are not—at least in the present case—in contradiction with one another. Indeed, if, as recalled above, international law constitutes an integral part of the law of Kuwait, the general principles of law correspondingly recognize the rights of the State in its capacity of supreme protector of the general interest. If the different legal elements involved do not always and everywhere blend as successfully as in the present case, it is nevertheless on taking advantage of their resources, and encouraging their trend towards unification, that the future of a truly international economic order in the investment field will depend.[164]

The use of a system of concurrent laws, such as that envisaged by the ICSID Convention in the absence of an express choice of law by the parties to the dispute, seems to be the way forward for international contracts to which a state or state entity is a party. The reference to the law of the state concerned gives proper importance to the sovereign position of the state party, yet the reference to international law, or possibly to the general principles of law, provides a measure of protection to the private party to the contract. There is a balance to be struck between state law and international law. It is important that arbitral tribunals should be prepared to give due weight to both.

3.145

While this discussion has shown where the search for a 'neutral' law may lead, particularly in relation to state contracts,[165] the search for such a law is not confined to state contracts. One solution, which has been canvassed in theory and occasionally adopted in practice, is to choose the national laws of both parties and so obtain the best (or possibly the worst) of both worlds. This *tronc commun* doctrine is based on the proposition that, if free to do so, each party to an international commercial transaction would choose its own national law to govern that transaction. If this proves unacceptable, why not go some way towards achieving this objective by identifying the common core of the two different systems of law and applying this to the matters in dispute?[166]

3.146

The *Sapphire* arbitration has already been mentioned as an illustration of the problem of affording protection to the private party to a state contract against

3.147

---

[163] *Aminoil*, at 1000.
[164] *Aminoil*, at 1001.
[165] See paragraph 3.141*ff.*
[166] The *tronc commun* doctrine was first elaborated by Rubino-Sammartano in 1987: see Rubino-Sammartano, 'Le tronc commun des lois nationales en presence: Réflexions sur le droit applicable par l'arbitre international' [1987] Rev Arb 133; Rubino-Sammartano, *International Arbitration Law and Practice* (Kluwer Law International, 1990), p. 274.

Applicable Laws

changes in the national law enacted by the state party.[167] There was no express choice of law in the contract. There were, however, choice-of-law clauses in similar concession agreements previously made by the respondent, the National Iranian Oil Company, which were in the following terms:

> In view of the diverse nationalities of the parties to this Agreement, it shall be governed by and interpreted and applied in accordance with the principles of law common to Iran and the several nations in which the other parties to this Agreement are incorporated, and in the absence of such common principles then by and in accordance with principles of law recognised by civilised nations in general, including such of those principles as may have been applied by international tribunals.[168]

3.148 This choice-of-law clause appears to be an adoption of the *tronc commun* solution to the choice-of-law problem. It would require the arbitrator to find out what principles existed in the law of Iran, which were also to be found in the national laws of the other parties to the agreement, and to apply those common principles to the matters in dispute before him or her. However, the arbitrator in the case adopted a different approach: he read the clause as entitling him to disregard the law of Iran (although this was specifically mentioned in the choice-of-law clause) and to apply the general principles of law. The arbitrator asserted that:

> It is quite clear from the above that the parties intended to exclude the application of Iranian law. But they have not chosen another positive legal system and this omission is on all the evidence deliberate. All the connecting factors cited above point to the fact that the parties therefore intended to submit the interpretation and performance of their contract to principles of law generally recognised by civilised nations, to which article 37 of the agreement refers, being the only clause which contains an express reference to an applicable law.[169]

3.149 Many years after the *Sapphire* arbitration, another important example of combined laws (or again, more correctly, of combined legal principles) came to be generally reported (and sometimes misreported). In the Channel Tunnel project, the concessionnaire Eurotunnel entered into a construction contract with a group of Anglo–French companies, known as Trans-Manche Link. Surprisingly, this agreement between two private entities referred not to the national law of either party, nor indeed to any national system of law, but instead to the common principles of both systems of law.[170] The relevant clause provided that the contract would:

> ... in all respects be governed by and interpreted in accordance with the principles common to both English law and French law, and in the absence of such common

---

[167] *Sapphire International Petroleum Ltd v The National Iranian Oil Co.* (1964) 13 ICLQ 1011.
[168] Quoted ibid., at 1014.
[169] Ibid., at 1015.
[170] It is surprising in that the *tronc commun* is generally chosen as the 'politically correct' choice of law in cases involving a foreign state, rather than cases involving only private parties.

D. Law Applicable to the Substance

principles by such general principles of international trade law as have been applied by national and international tribunals.[171]

3.150 A dispute under the construction contract went to the English High Court, and this choice of law clause was considered both by the Court of Appeal and by the highest court in England, the House of Lords (now the Supreme Court).[172] In the Court of Appeal, one of the judges said:

> Since both Eurotunnel and the contractors were partly French and partly English, I wonder why they did not choose either English law or French law exclusively—and for that matter why they chose Brussels as the seat of any arbitration. The hybrid system of law which they did choose has a superficial attraction, but I suspect that it will lead to lengthy and expensive dispute.[173]

3.151 This comment proved prescient.[174] The search for common principles of English and French law meant that, for each dispute that arose under the construction contract—and there were many—teams of French and English lawyers on each side had to determine what the answer was likely to be under the applicable principles of their own law and then work out to what extent, if at all, these principles were common to both systems of law. As one of the construction group's external counsel has commented:

> The main reason for the difficulty in applying a clause providing for the application of common principles between English and French law is that although both systems tend to produce the same or very similar results, they fall short of providing the set of common principles which is necessary to cover all contractual disputes.[175]

3.152 Although the Court of Appeal was, in passing, critical of this choice-of-law clause—as a hybrid system of law—it did not suggest that it was anything other than a binding and enforceable agreement. This emerges even more strongly in the decision of the House of Lords:

> The parties chose an indeterminate 'law' to govern their substantive rights; an elaborate process for ascertaining those rights; and a location for that purpose

---

[171] *Channel Tunnel Group Ltd and France Manche SA v Balfour Beatty Construction Ltd and ors* [1993] AC 334, 347.
[172] When Eurotunnel sought an injunction to prevent Trans-Manche from carrying out a threat to cease work on part of the project.
[173] *Channel Tunnel Group Ltd v Balfour Beatty Construction Ltd* [1992] 1 QB 656, at 675.
[174] Rubino-Sammartano, 'The Channel Tunnel and the tronc commun doctrine' (1993) 10 J Intl Arb 59, at 61, asserts that: 'The Channel Tunnel contract is an example of an express choice by the parties and as such it does not seem to leave the door open to possible argument. The view expressed by Staughton LJ, "I suspect it will lead to lengthy and expensive dispute" cannot consequently be shared.' In fact, as stated above, it was entirely accurate, in that two teams of lawyers, French and English, had to be engaged by each of the parties in order to advise on the many disputes that arose. It is true that the choice-of-law clause was clear; this is not the issue. What was not clear was what were the 'common principles' of French and English law that were applicable to the various different disputes that arose—including, e.g., disputes as to whether a particular claim was or was not barred (or extinguished) by lapse of time.
[175] Duval, 'English and French law: The search for common principles' (1997) 25 Intl Business Lawyer 181, at 182.

outside the territories of the participants. This conspicuously neutral, 'a-national' and extra-judicial structure may well have been the first choice for the special needs of the Channel Tunnel venture. But whether it was right or wrong, it is the choice which the parties have made.[176]

3.153 The Channel Tunnel project was one of the major international construction contracts of the twentieth century.[177] Of course, even if only one system of law had been chosen as the applicable law, both French and English lawyers would have been needed to deal with the financing of the project, as well as 'domestic' issues such as staff accommodation on either side of the Channel, labour relations, and so on—but the dispute resolution process itself would have been simpler, less expensive, and, it is suggested, more predictable.

3.154 There are many large international projects in which lawyers from different countries are likely to be needed. In such major projects, the expense involved in searching for the common principles of two national systems of law, or for 'the common core' of these two national laws, may perhaps be justified (particularly if the two systems are known to have much in common).[178] However, in ordinary trading contracts of the kind that constitute the day-to-day substance of international commerce, it must be doubtful whether the additional trouble and expense can be justified.

3.155 In summary, it is suggested that, in ordinary international commercial contracts, including construction contracts, the parties would do well to try to agree upon a given national law as the law of the contract. It may take time to reach agreement, but it will be time well spent. Where one of the parties to the contract is a state or a state agency, it may be necessary to adopt a system of concurrent laws (which may not be easy to operate, but which will probably be better than a system of combined laws).

(g) Transnational law (including the *lex mercatoria*, the UNIDROIT Principles, trade usages, and Shari'ah)

(i) Introduction

3.156 The reference to 'such rules of international law as may be agreed by the parties' (such as in Article 42 of the ICSID Convention), or to 'the relevant principles of international law' (as in the Channel Tunnel Treaty) serve to remind us that

---

[176] *Channel Tunnel Group Ltd v Balfour Beatty Construction Ltd* [1993] AC 334, at 368. In the same judgment, Lord Mustill said, at 353, 'having promised to take their complaints to the experts and if necessary to the arbitrators, that is where the appellants should go'.

[177] For further comment on the House of Lords' decision, see Reymond, 'The Channel Tunnel case and the law of international arbitration' (1993) 109 LQR 337; Veeder, 'L'Arret Channel Tunnel de la Chambre des Lords' (1993) 4 Rev Arb 705.

[178] Rubino-Sammartano, 'The Channel Tunnel and the tronc commun doctrine' (1993) 10 J Intl Arb 59, at 61: '[T]he common part of these two national laws must be treated as that chosen by the parties.'

D. Law Applicable to the Substance

it is not the whole corpus of law, but only certain specific rules of law that are likely to be relevant in any given dispute. For example, an international contract for the sale of goods governed by the law of Austria will usually bring into consideration only those provisions of Austrian law that deal with the sale of goods. An international construction project that is governed by the law of England will principally involve consideration of those particular areas of law that are concerned with construction contracts. This breaking down of the whole body of the law into specific, discrete sections is reflected by increased specialisation within the legal profession itself. Thus, for example, within an association of lawyers such as the IBA, there are specialist groups whose primary expertise is in energy law, or intellectual property, or construction law—and so forth.[179]

3.157 In these circumstances, it seems appropriate to ask whether or not a particular group of bankers, or merchants, or traders may develop their own special rules of conduct that gradually acquire the force of law, either by themselves or by incorporation into national law or international treaty. Experience suggests that the answer to this question is a cautious 'yes'.[180] Indeed, in the past, this is how much of our law developed. Colombus, for example, tells of the early maritime codes such as the Rhodian Sea Law, which dated from the second or third century BC and which was 'of great authority in the Mediterranean, for its principles were accepted by both Greeks and Romans and its memory lasted for a thousand years'.[181] This was an early form of transnational law, as indeed was the celebrated Consolato des Mare which, again according to Colombus, 'throughout the Middle Ages, reigned supreme in the Mediterranean until the advent of sovereign states, national legislation superseding the customary laws of the sea, so often incorporating many of its rules'.[182]

3.158 It is significant that, within time, the 'customary laws of the sea' were superseded by legislation. As states evolve, this is almost inevitable. In the present-day world of sovereign states and complex legislation, it may be questioned whether there is still room for the crystallisation of customary practices into rules of law. Even if there is, it is likely to be confined to particular usages and to particular trades—and to grow, so to speak, in the interstices of existing laws, rather than to form one vast corpus of law.

---

[179] The same division into specialist groups may be seen within law firms from which, increasingly, clients are seeking specialist business sector advice or expertise.
[180] This can be seen in White & Case and Queen Mary School of International Arbitration, University of London, *2010 International Arbitration Survey: Choices in International Arbitration*, available online at http://www.arbitrationonline.org/docs/2010_InternationalArbitrationSurveyReport.pdf, which indicated that 50 per cent of respondents have 'sometimes' used transnational laws and rules to govern contracts.
[181] Colombus, *International Law of the Sea* (1967).
[182] Ibid.

3.159 There are many different communities carrying on activities that may be as diverse (and have as little in common) as the transport of goods or the establishment of an international telecommunications network. The rules of law that are relevant to these different commercial activities are in themselves likely to be very different. They may share certain basic legal concepts—such as the sanctity of contracts (*pacta sunt servanda*)—but even here different considerations are likely to apply. For example, an international contract for the sale of goods will be performed within a comparatively short timescale—but compare this to a major infrastructure project that will take many years to perform and during the course of which the basis upon which the original bargain was struck may change dramatically.

3.160 Given these words of caution, the approach adopted in this book is pragmatic, rather than theoretical. This is probably the most useful approach, since in practice lawyers and arbitrators are concerned with a particular dispute or series of disputes rather than with some 'general theory' of law. In a report on transnational rules, the author referred to the approach adopted by the International Law Association (ILA) formulated as follows:

> The Committee's approach in its continuing study of transnational law has been to step back from the highly contentious issues that arise from any theoretical consideration of transnational law, or *lex mercatoria*, as a discrete body of principles and to examine, in a pragmatic way, the application of individual identifiable principles at least as a phenomenon of international commercial arbitration, which it undoubtedly is.[183]

(ii) Lex mercatoria

3.161 One of the most important developments in the field of transnational law was that of the *lex mercatoria*. This draws on the sources of law that have already been mentioned, including public international law generally and the general principles of law specifically. It also draws on the UNIDROIT Principles of International Commercial Law (the UNIDROIT Principles, recently updated in 2010) and the 1998 Principles of European Contract Law,[184] which are discussed later in this chapter.

3.162 This modern version of a 'law merchant' is taken to consist of rules and practices that have evolved within the international business communities. The late Professor Goldman, who named this new 'law' and who contributed greatly to its development,[185] refers to it as having had 'an illustrious precursor in the Roman

---

[183] Bowden, *Transnational Rules in International Commercial Arbitration*, ICC Publication No. 480/4 (ICC, 1993), p. 127.
[184] Prepared by the Lando Commission and sometimes called the 'Lando Principles'. See paragraphs 3.177–3.181.
[185] See Goldman, '*Lex mercatoria*' (1983) 3 Forum Internationale 21. The late Professor Goldman, having referred to the codification of international commercial practices, such as the ICC's UCP and Incoterms, as evidence of the emergence of an *international* business practice (on which, see paragraph 3.189), stated, ibid., at 5:

D. Law Applicable to the Substance

jus gentium',[186] which he describes as 'an autonomous source of law proper to the economic relations (*commercium*) between citizens and foreigners (*peregrine*)'.[187]

The advantage of such a code of law is obvious: it would be adapted to the needs of modern international commerce and it would be of uniform application. The problem is whether such a system of law, which might have existed in Roman times or in the Middle Ages, can arise spontaneously—as it were—amongst states that already possess in full measure their own laws, orders, and regulations. Amongst some commentators, the new *lex mercatoria* has been greeted with approval.[188] Others have been politely sceptical,[189] or (in the context of state contracts) have dismissed it as an idea of which the time has passed, since more sophisticated laws and rules now exist.[190] Others still have been openly hostile.[191] What, then, is this new 'law' that has aroused so much controversy, and which, from time to time, has made its appearance in arbitral awards and in court proceedings?   3.163

For Professor Goldman, the distinguishing features of the *lex mercatoria* were its 'customary' and 'spontaneous' nature.[192] It was his view that international commercial relationships: 3.164

> ...may perfectly well be governed by a body of specific rules, including transnational custom, general principles of law and arbitral case law. It makes no difference

---

Commentators in the early 1960s began to take note of this evolution. Clive Schmithoff was the first in England to salute the new Law Merchant; in France, Philippe Kahn, with respect to international sales, Philippe Fouchard, with respect to international arbitration and Jean Stoufflet, with respect to documentary credits, undertook to study this law. As for myself, I concluded that a place could be acknowledged for the *lex mercatoria*—a name which stuck—within the boundaries of the law.

[186] Ibid, at 3.
[187] Ibid.
[188] Goldman, 'La *lex mercatoria* dans les contrats d'arbitrage internationaux: Réalité et perspectives' (1979) 106 Clunet J du Droit Intl 475; Lalive, 'Transnational (or truly international) public policy and international arbitration' (1986) 3 ICC Congress Series 257; Gaillard, *Transnational Rules in International Arbitration 1993*, ICC Publication No. 480/4 (ICC, 1993) (a very helpful review of aspects of transnational law by distinguished contributors).
[189] See, e.g., Mustill LJ, 'The new *lex mercatoria*: The first twenty-five years' (1987) 4 Arb Intl 86, at 86, in which he notes that '[t]he Lex Mercatoria has sufficient intellectual credentials to merit serious study, and yet is not so generally accepted as to escape the sceptical eye'.
[190] See, e.g., Delaume, 'The proper law of state contracts and the *lex mercatoria*: A reappraisal' (1988) 3 ICSID Rev—Foreign Investments LJ 79, at 106, where this experienced international practitioner suggests that the risk of changes in state law to the detriment of the private party to a state contract may be insured under the Convention Establishing the Multilateral Investment Guarantee Agency (1985) 24 ILM 1589, and that this is far more adapted to the commercial realities 'than the Lex Mercatoria which remains, both in scope and in practical significance, an elusive system and a mythical view of a transnational law of State Contracts whose sources are elsewhere'.
[191] See, e.g., Mann, 'The proper law in the conflict of laws' (1987) 36 ICLQ 437, at 448; Toope, *Mixed International Arbitration* (Grotius, 1990), esp. p. 96, where the author concludes: 'It would appear that the so-called *lex mercatoria* is largely an effort to legitimise as "law" the economic interests of Western corporations.'
[192] Goldman, 'La *lex mercatoria* dans les contrats d'arbitrage internationaux: Réalité et perspectives' (1979) 106 Clunet J du Droit Intl 475, at 481.

if this body of rules is not part of a legal order[193] comporting its own legislative and judicial organs. Within this body of rules, the general principles of law are not only those referred to in Article 38(a) of the Statute of the International Court of Justice; there may be added to it principles progressively established by the general and constant usage of international trade.[194]

3.165 It is not difficult to envisage rules developing in a particular area of international trade—such as documentary credits—and eventually being codified, either in national legislation or by international treaty, so as to attain the force of law.[195] But the custom in question is usually that of a particular trade or industry. The point has already been made that international traders do not constitute a homogeneous community; instead, they constitute myriad communities, each with their own different customary rules. How are these very different and specific rules to evolve into universal rules of international trade law?

3.166 Rather than pose these theoretical questions, it is perhaps more useful to ask: what is this new law? What principles does it embody? What specific rules does it lay down? In short, what is its content?

3.167 There appear to be two alternative approaches towards assessing the content of the new *lex mercatoria*: the 'list' method and the 'functional' approach.

3.168 **List method** As far as the 'list' method is concerned, various lists of rules or principles have been prepared over the past decade,[196] drawing, amongst other things, upon the UNIDROIT Principles and the 1998 Principles of European Contract Law. The list process has been criticised as lacking flexibility. To counter this criticism, Professor Berger has proposed 'creeping codification':

> Creeping codification is to be distinguished from more formalized techniques for defining the *lex mercatoria* (UNIDROIT and Lando Principles): it is intended to avoid the 'static element' characteristic of other approaches and to provide the openness and flexibility required in order to take account of the rapid development of international trade and commerce.[197]

Creeping codification is intended to ensure that a list of transnational commercial principles is capable of being rapidly, and continually, revised and updated. Professor Berger established the Central Transnational Law Database[198] as the

---

[193] Although Professor Goldman himself contended that it was part of a legal order.
[194] Ibid., at 496.
[195] Both the ICC Rules (Art. 21(2)) and the UNCITRAL Rules (Art. 35(3)) require arbitrators to take account of relevant trade usages.
[196] See, e.g., Berger, *The Creeping Codification of* Lex Mercatoria (Kluwer Law International, 1999), p. 212. See also Mustill LJ, 'The new *lex mercatoria*: The first twenty-five years' (1987) 4 Arb Intl 86—although he thought the results 'a modest haul for twenty-five years of international arbitration'. See too Paulsson, 'La *lex mercatoria* dans l'arbitrage de la CCI' [1990] Rev Arb 55; Dalhuisen, 'Legal orders and their manifestation: The operation of the international commercial and financial legal order and its *lex mercatoria*' (2006) 24 BJIL 129, at 179*ff*.
[197] Berger, *The Creeping Codification of* Lex Mercatoria (Kluwer Law International, 1999), p. 192.
[198] See Berger, '*Lex mercatoria* online: The Central Transnational Law Database at http://www.tldb.de' (2002) 18 Arb Intl 83.

D. Law Applicable to the Substance

institutional framework within which to develop and update the list on an ongoing basis.[199]

Functional approach The alternative approach involves identifying particular rules of the *lex mercatoria* as and when specific questions arise. This 'functional' approach regards the *lex mercatoria* as a method for determining the appropriate rule or principle. Professor Gaillard is a leading exponent of this approach,[200] who emphasises that the controversy, which initially focused on the existence of transnational rules, has shifted. He says that it is now: **3.169**

> ...concentrating more recently on the establishment in further detail of the *content* of those rules or the more systematic assessment of the means to do so. As a result, very significant differences of opinion on how such goals may be achieved have emerged.[201]

According to Gaillard, the functional approach presents the advantage that any claim made by a party in a given case would necessarily find an answer, which may not be the position under the list method.[202] **3.170**

As a practical matter, when arbitrators seek to identify the content of the *lex mercatoria*, they draw increasingly on the UNIDROIT Principles: **3.171**

> If the Unidroit Principles embody concepts already in the *lex mercatoria*,...these Principles would seem to provide a point of explicit reference for arbitral tribunals. And this is exactly what appears to be happening: the Unidroit Principles have already been referred to in about thirty ICC cases, it is recently reported, in order to identify general legal principles.[203]

The usefulness of the UNIDROIT Principles and of the 1998 Principles of European Contract Law (which set out rules common to the main legal systems surveyed) has also been recognised by Fortier: 'The result—a concrete, usable list of principles and rules—addresses head-on the traditional concern of practitioners that the *lex* is too abstract and impractical to be of any use in the real world.'[204] **3.172**

The fact that the UNIDROIT Principles embody concepts within the *lex mercatoria*, but are not a source of it, has similarly been stressed by Professor Mayer in a useful survey of ICC awards on the issue: **3.173**

> Each arbitral award stands on its own. There is no doctrine of precedence or of *stare decisis* as between different awards; and in general there is no appellate court to sort

---

[199] Fortier, 'The new, new *lex mercatoria*, or back to the future' (2001) 17 Arb Intl 121, at 126.
[200] Gaillard, 'Transnational law: A legal system or a method of decision-making?' (2001) 17 Arb Intl 62.
[201] Ibid., at 60; see also Fortier, n. 199.
[202] Gaillard, n. 200, at 64.
[203] Molineaux, 'Applicable law in arbitration: The coming convergence of civil and Anglo-Saxon law via Unidroit and *lex mercatoria*' (2000) 1 JWIT 127, at 130.
[204] Fortier, 'The new, new *lex mercatoria*, or back to the future' (2001) 17 Arb Intl 121, at 124–125.

the wheat from the chaff. There is, in this sense, no formal control of the arbitral process.[205] Arbitrators are free to decide as they choose. Conscientious arbitrators will obviously do their utmost to ensure that their decision is made in accordance with the law governing the contract. Their professional conscience will demand no less; and they will not decide *ex aequo et bono* without the express authorisation of the parties. But if the law governing the contract consists of those rules or principles which the arbitrators consider most appropriate, and which may conveniently be labelled as part of the *lex mercatoria*, those arbitrators are in effect free to decide in accordance with what they consider to be just and equitable, whilst purporting to decide in accordance with legal rules.[206]

This is a pertinent observation. Under the guise of applying the *lex mercatoria*, an arbitral tribunal may in effect pick such rules as seem to the tribunal to be just and reasonable—which may or may not be what the parties intended when they made their contract.

3.174 The *lex mercatoria* has had an impact upon the law of international arbitration,[207] and has been described as a body of 'substantive and procedural practices which parties and tribunals expect to apply and are applied in international arbitration'.[208] It has also served to remind both the parties to international arbitration and the arbitral tribunals called upon to resolve their disputes that they are operating at an international level, and that different considerations may come into play from those to be found in purely national, or domestic, arbitrations.

3.175 Where the *lex mercatoria* is said to govern the parties' contract, either by agreement of the parties themselves or by a decision of the tribunal, will a court enforce that choice of law, if called upon to do so? And will such a court enforce an award made in conformity with the *lex mercatoria*, if called upon to do so?

3.176 In principle, the answer to both questions appears to be 'yes'. If the parties have agreed upon a particular method of dispute resolution, the court should be prepared to enforce that agreement following normal contractual principles.[209] Again, if the arbitral tribunal has carried out the mission entrusted to it and has decided the case in accordance with the rules of law chosen by the parties, there would seem to be no reason why a court should refuse to enforce the award. The tribunal has simply done what the parties empowered it to do. As regards enforcement of

---

[205] Except on procedural matters, which are not under consideration here.
[206] Mayer, 'The UNIDROIT Principles in contemporary contract practice' (2002) ICC Bulletin (Special Supplement) 111.
[207] For instance, in authorising arbitrators to choose the governing law of the contract, where the parties have not done so, without necessarily following the conflict rules of the place of arbitration.
[208] Lew, 'Is there a "global free-standing body of substantive arbitration law?" ', in van den Berg (ed) *International Arbitration: The Coming of a New Age?* (Kluwer Law International, 2013), pp. 53–61.
[209] Compare the statement of Lord Mustill in *Channel Tunnel Group Ltd v Balfour Beatty Construction Ltd* [1993] AC 334, at 353: '[H]aving promised to take their complaints to the experts and if necessary to the arbitrators, that is where the appellants should go.'

D. Law Applicable to the Substance

the award, the Resolution adopted by the ILA expresses the position that should sensibly be taken:[210]

> The fact that an international arbitrator has based an award on transnational rules (general principles of law, principles common to several jurisdictions, international law, usages of trade, etc) rather than on the law of a particular State should not itself affect the validity or enforceability of the award:
> (i) where the parties have agreed that the arbitrator may apply transnational rules; or
> (ii) where the parties have remained silent concerning the applicable law.[211]

This position has been adopted by various national courts, including the French Cour de Cassation, the Austrian Supreme Court, and the English Court of Appeal.[212]

(iii) UNIDROIT Principles

The influence of codified terms and practices in the concept and development of a new *lex mercatoria* has already been noted. For example, the ICC's Uniform Customs and Practice for Documentary Credits (UCP), formulated as long ago as 1933,[213] have helped significantly in moving towards a single, uniform international standard for the interpretation of documentary credits—those valuable pieces of paper upon which much of international trade depends. Similarly, the ICC's International Rules for the Interpretation of Trade Terms (known as 'Incoterms') are intended to give a consistent, uniform meaning to terms that are in frequent use in international trade—so that expressions such as 'exw' (meaning 'ex works'), 'cif' (meaning cost, insurance, and freight), and 'fob' (meaning 'free on board') should mean the same to businessmen and traders in São Paulo as they do to those based in London or New York.[214]   **3.177**

Reference has already been made to the UNIDROIT Principles of International Commercial Contracts.[215] They are, in nature, a restatement of the general principles of contract law. The principles are comprehensive,[216] covering not only the   **3.178**

---

[210] At its conference in Cairo, April 1992.
[211] Quoted in ICC, *Transnational Rules in International Commercial Arbitration*, ICC Publication No. 480/4 (ICC, 1993), p. 247. Note, however, that if no choice of law has been made by the parties, the arbitral tribunal may not be free to choose anything other than national law. This is because the relevant rules of arbitration, or the relevant state law, may not allow any other option.
[212] *Banque du Proche-Orient v Société Fougerolle*, Cass. Civ. 2eme, 9 December 1981 (second decision) and Cass. Civ. 1ere, 22 October 1991; Judgment of the Austrian Supreme Court, 18 November 1982, reproduced in (1984) IX YBCA 161; *Deutsche Schachtbau und Tiefbohrgesellschaft GmbH (F/Germ) v R'as Al Khaimah National Oil Co. (R'as Al Khaimah, UAE) Shell International Petroleum Co. Ltd (UK)* [1987] 3 WLR 1023, rev'd on other grounds [1990] 1 AC 295. See also Rivkin, 'Enforceability of awards based on *lex mercatoria*' (1993) 19 Arb Intl 47.
[213] The latest version of which is the UCP 600, published in 2007: ICC Publication No. 600.
[214] The latest version of which is the 2010 edition: ICC Publication No. 715. Both Incoterms and documentary credits are discussed with trade usages at paragraph 3.189.
[215] See paragraphs 3.174, 3.177, and 3.179.
[216] The UNIDROIT Principles were revised in May 2011 and are available online at http://www.unidroit.org/english/principles/contracts/principles2010/integralversionprinciples2010-e.pdf.

interpretation and performance of contractual obligations, but also the conduct of negotiations leading to the formation of a contract. In 2010, they were developed to include new rules relating to failed contracts, illegality, and conditions, as well as the plurality of obligors and obligees. The emphasis is, not surprisingly, on good faith and fair dealing.[217] The aim of the UNIDROIT Principles is to establish a neutral set of rules that may be used throughout the world without any particular bias to one system of law over another. As one experienced commentator has said: 'They were not drafted in the interest of a specific party or lobbying group. They will strike a fair balance between the rights and obligations of all parties to the contract.'[218]

3.179 The UNIDROIT Principles 'represent a system of rules of contract law'.[219] They apply only when the parties choose to apply them to their contract, or have agreed that their contract will be governed by 'general principles of law', the *lex mercatoria*, or the like.[220] However, in practice, arbitral tribunals may themselves decide to refer to the UNIDROIT Principles as an aid to the interpretation of contract terms and conditions—or even as a standard to be observed, for example in the negotiation of a contract.[221]

3.180 Indeed, in a Swedish arbitration, the European claimant argued in favour of Swedish law, basing itself on the choice of Sweden as a place of arbitration. The Chinese party argued in favour of Chinese law, because China had the closest connection with the contract. The tribunal relied on Article 24(1)[222] of the Rules of the Arbitration Institute of the Stockholm Chamber of Commerce (SCC), which permitted it to apply 'the law or rules of law which the tribunal considers to be most appropriate'. Having decided that no common intention as to a particular national system of law could be found, the tribunal decided as follows:

> In the Tribunal's view, it is reasonable to assume that the contracting parties expected that the eventual law chosen to be applicable would protect their interest in a way that any normal business man would consider adequate and reasonable, given the nature of the contract and any breach thereof, and without any surprises

---

[217] Article 1(7) states: 'Each party must act in accordance with good faith and fair dealing in international trade. The parties may not exclude or limit this duty.'

[218] See van Houtte, 'The UNIDROIT Principles of International Commercial Contracts' (1995) 11 Arb Intl 373, at 374.

[219] UNIDROIT has published a commentary on the revised principles entitled *UNIDROIT Principles of International Commercial Contracts, 2010*.

[220] More precisely, the opening words to the Preamble to the UNIDROIT Principles state:

> These Principles set forth general rules for international commercial contracts. They shall be applied when the parties have agreed that their contract be governed by them. They may be applied when the parties have agreed that their contract be governed by 'general principles of law', the '*lex mercatoria*' or the like.

[221] For a review of the application of the UNIDROIT Principles in arbitration practice, see Piers and Erauw, 'Application of the UNIDROIT Principles of International Commercial Contracts in Arbitration' (2012) 8 J Priv Intl L 441.

[222] Now Art. 22(1) of the Rules of the Arbitration Institute of the SCC.

D. Law Applicable to the Substance

that could result from the application of domestic laws of which they had no deeper knowledge. This leads the Tribunal to conclude that the issues in dispute between the parties should primarily be based, not on the law of any particular jurisdiction, but on such rules of law that have found their way into international codifications or such like that enjoy a widespread recognition among countries involved in international trade... the only codification that can be considered to have this status is the UNIDROIT Principles of International Commercial Contracts... The Tribunal determines that the rules contained therein shall be the first source employed in reaching a decision on the issues in dispute in the present arbitration.[223]

One example will indicate how the UNIDROIT Principles are intended to work. In many forms of contract, the party that bears the major responsibility for performance will seek either to limit its liability or even to exclude liability altogether. Thus a clause in a construction contract may, for example, stipulate that the contractor has no liability for loss of profit arising out of any breach of the contract, whether caused by negligence or any other breach of duty. The question then arises as to the scope of this clause and, in particular, whether, in specific circumstances, it may be set aside altogether.[224] In relation to such a claim, Article 7(1)(6) of the UNIDROIT Principles states: **3.181**

> A clause which limits or excludes one party's liability for non-performance or which permits one party to render performance substantially different from what the other party reasonably expected may not be invoked if it would be grossly unfair to do so, having regard to the purpose of the contract.

The effect of such a clause, in a dispute to which the UNIDROIT Principles are applicable, is to permit an arbitral tribunal to disregard the exemption clause in appropriate circumstances. In each case, it will be for the tribunal to decide what was the purpose of the contract and whether, in all of the circumstances, it would be 'grossly unfair' to apply the exemption clause.

(iv) Trade usages

As already mentioned, institutional rules (such as those of the ICC) and international arbitration rules (such as those of UNCITRAL) require an arbitral tribunal to take account of relevant trade usage.[225] A similar requirement is to be found in the Model Law[226] and in some national legislation, such as the Netherlands Arbitration Act 1986.[227]   **3.182**

The relevant trade usages will have to be established by evidence in any given case (unless the arbitrators are familiar with them and make this clear to the parties).   **3.183**

---

[223] See Arbitration Institute of the SCC, *Stockholm Arbitration Report* (SCC, 2002), p. 59, with commentary by Fernandez-Armesto.
[224] In the same manner as an exemption clause might be disregarded under domestic legislation to protect consumers.
[225] ICC Rules, Art. 21(2); UNCITRAL Rules, Art. 35(3).
[226] Article 28(4).
[227] Article 1054(4).

However, organisations such as the ICC have been prominent in attempting to establish a commonly understood meaning for expressions that are in frequent use in international trade contracts. Terms such as 'exw', 'cif', 'fob', and so forth are expressions that are in common use and which are intended to set out, in an abbreviated form, the rights and obligations of the parties. It is obviously important that they should have the same meaning worldwide. To this end, the precise extent of these rights and obligations is spelt out in the Incoterms. In much the same way, the UCP have proved valuable in moving towards a single international standard for the interpretation of these important instruments of world trade.

3.184 Standard-form contracts are commonplace in many fields, including the shipping trade, the commodity markets, and the oil industry. The step from the establishment of international terms and conditions to the establishment of uniform rules for the interpretation of these terms and conditions is a small, but important, one. Such uniform rules may apply only within the ambit of a national system of law. But if the same rules are uniformly applied by different national courts, or by arbitral tribunals, the basis is laid for the establishment of a customary law, which will have been created by merchants and traders themselves (rather than by lawyers) and which may achieve international recognition.

(v) Shari'ah law

3.185 Islamic law, which applies to some degree across a broad swathe of Muslim countries,[228] embodies not only the Qur'an, but also other sources of Islamic law.[229] Modern codes of law in Islamic countries take account of Shari'ah, often as a principal source of law.[230] Shari'ah itself contains general principles that are basic to any civilised system of law, such as good faith in the performance of obligations and the observance of due process in the settlement of disputes.[231] Although there are differences from country to country (partly as a result of the different schools of Islamic law and partly because some states are more open to Western influences than others), Islamic law, traditions, and language give these states a common heritage and, to some extent, a common approach to arbitration.[232]

---

[228] These range from Arab countries such as Saudi Arabia, the United Arab Emirates, Kuwait, Oman, Bahrain, Syria, Yemen, Iraq, and Iran, to African states such as Egypt, Tunisia, Sudan, Morocco, and Algeria, and to Asian states such as Pakistan, Bangladesh, Malaysia, and Indonesia.

[229] Namely, for Sunni schools of law, the Sunnah (the sayings and practices of the Prophet Muhammad), Ijma (consensus among recognised religious authorities), and Qiyas (inference by precedent). For a general introduction to the structure and evolution of Islamic law, see Coulson, *A History of Islamic Law* (Edinburgh University Press, 1964).

[230] For example, the constitutions of Yemen, Qatar, and Egypt state that Shari'ah is a primary source of law.

[231] See Majeed, 'Good faith and due process: Lessons from the Shari'ah' (2004) 20 Arb Intl 97.

[232] See Darwazeh, 'Arbitration in the Arab world: An interview with Professor Ahmed Sadek El-Kosheri' (2008) 25 J Intl Arb 203.

D. Law Applicable to the Substance

In a case that came before the English High Court, a financial transaction had been structured in a manner (an 'Estisna form') that ensured that the transaction conformed with orthodox Islamic banking practice.[233] There was provision for any disputes to be settled by arbitration in London under the ICC Rules and there was a choice-of-law clause that provided for any dispute to be 'governed by the Law of England except to the extent it may conflict with Islamic Shari'ah, which shall prevail'. A dispute arose and the ICC appointed as sole arbitrator Mr Samir Saleh, an experienced lawyer and expert on Shari'ah law. The losing party challenged the arbitrator's award, but the English court rejected this challenge, holding that the award was a clear and full evaluation of the issues, and had all the appearances of being right.[234]

3.186

According to Professor Fadlallah, however, 'the landscape was clouded'[235] by three well-known awards, which, in his view, are not confined to history[236] and continue to have 'harmful effects' on the development of Euro–Arab arbitration.[237] In *Sheikh Abu Dhabi v Petroleum Development Ltd*,[238] *Ruler of Qatar v International Marine Oil Co. Ltd*,[239] and *Aramco v Government of Saudi Arabia*,[240] the tribunals refused to apply Shari'ah on the grounds that it did not contain a 'body of legal principles applicable to the construction of modern commercial instruments'.[241] Ironically, according to Professor Fadlallah, the outcome in each case would have been the same even if Shari'ah had been applied.[242]

3.187

(vi) Authority to apply non-national law

The authority of an arbitral tribunal to apply a non-national system of law (such as the general principles of law, or the *lex mercatoria*) will depend upon (a) the agreement of the parties, and (b) the provisions of the applicable law.

3.188

---

[233] *Sanghi Polyesters Ltd (India) v The International Investor KCFC (Kuwait)* [2000] 1 Lloyd's Rep 480.

[234] See also *Musawi v R E International (UK) Ltd and ors* [2007] EWHC 2981, discussed at paragraph 3.189.

[235] Fadlallah, 'Arbitration facing conflicts of culture: The 2008 Freshfields Lecture' (2009) 25 Arb Intl 303.

[236] See, for example, *Beximco Pharmaceuticals Ltd and ors v Shamil Bank of Bahrain EC* [2004] EWCA Civ 19, discussed by Fadlallah, ibid. Also of interest is a recent question posed in the English Parliament on 15 December 2008 regarding which 'Islamic tribunals' have authority to act under the English Arbitration Act 1996. The Minister for Business, Enterprise and Regulatory Reform responded that there is 'no specific provision in the Arbitration Act 1996 for "Islamic Tribunals"', but that '[t]he Act allows all parties to have their disputes decided by a set of principles of their choice rather than by national law': HC Deb, 15 December 2008, cols 465–466W. He also referred to the Muslim Arbitration Tribunals (MAT), established in 2007 to provide an alternative route to resolve civil issues in accordance with Shari'ah principles. The MAT operates according to the principles of the Arbitration Act 1996.

[237] Fadlallah, n. 235.

[238] [1952] ICLQ 247.

[239] (1956) 20 Int L Rep 534.

[240] (1963) 27 Int L Rep 117.

[241] *Sheikh Abu Dhabi v Petroleum Development Ltd* [1952] ICLQ 247.

[242] Fadlallah, 'Arbitration facing conflicts of culture: The 2008 Freshfields Lecture' (2009) 25 Arb Intl 303.

3.189 The ICSID Convention, for example, is clear on this point. Article 42 states: 'The Tribunal shall decide a dispute in accordance with such *rules of law* as may be agreed by the parties.'[243] The reference to 'rules of law', rather than to 'law' or 'a system of law', is a coded reference to the applicability of appropriate legal rules even though these may fall short of being an established and autonomous system of law.

3.190 Within different states, different positions are adopted. France and Switzerland, for example, allow arbitrators to decide according to rules of law.[244] By contrast, the Model Law, whilst leaving it to the parties to make an express choice of such '*rules of law*' as they wish, requires an arbitral tribunal, if the choice is left to the tribunal, to apply 'the law determined by the conflict of laws rules which it considers applicable'.[245] English law follows this approach: the arbitral tribunal has to decide the dispute (a) in accordance with the law chosen by the parties, or (b) if the parties agree, in accordance with 'such other considerations as are agreed by them or determined by the tribunal'; if there is no choice or agreement by the parties, the tribunal must apply 'the law' determined by the appropriate conflict rules.[246] English courts have considered the meaning of 'such other considerations' under section 46(1)(b) of the Arbitration Act 1996 in the following cases:

- in *Musawi v R E International (UK) Ltd and ors*,[247] the court held that section 46(1)(b) of the 1996 Act entitled the parties to the arbitration to require the *ayatollah* arbitrator to apply Shari'ah law as the applicable law; and
- in *Halpern v Halpern*,[248] which concerned the application of Jewish law, the Court of Appeal ruled that if the seat of arbitration were England, then section 46(1)(b) of the 1996 Act would permit the tribunal to apply the parties' choice of some form of rules or non-national law to govern the merits of their dispute.[249]

Nevertheless, the meaning of 'such other considerations' is not yet entirely settled and it is difficult to transpose interpretations from other jurisdictions in which similar concepts may have different meanings. In Switzerland, for instance, *ex aequo et bono* is understood to mean the application of principles other than legal rules, while the concept of *amiable compositeur* requires the application of legal

---

[243] Emphasis added.
[244] Article 1511 of the Code of Civil Procedure, Decree No. 81–500 of 12 May 1981; Swiss PIL, Ch. 12, s. 187. The ICC Rules also now refer to 'the rules of law' (in Art. 21) rather than to 'the law' to be applied.
[245] Model Law, Art. 28(2) (emphasis added). Despite the early approach of the common law to require tribunals to apply a fixed and recognisable system of law, the adoption of the Model Law in various common law countries, including Australia, Canada, Hong Kong, and New Zealand, means that there is now growing express recognition of the concept.
[246] English Arbitration Act 1996, s. 46.
[247] [2007] EWHC 2981.
[248] [2007] EWCA Civ 291.
[249] As noted earlier, however, an arbitration agreement must be governed by the law of a country (in this case, Swiss or English law—the decision was never made) and cannot be governed by Jewish law.

D. Law Applicable to the Substance

rules, but allows arbitrators to moderate the effect of such rules. In France, meanwhile, the two concepts are given a similar meaning.

3.191 The ICC Rules, on the other hand, clearly go further than the Model Law (and the English Arbitration Act 1996): they not only allow the parties to choose the application of 'rules of law' to govern the dispute, but also allow the arbitral tribunal, in the absence of an agreement by the parties, to apply 'the rules of law which it determines to be appropriate'.[250] Thus, by confirming their ability to choose rules of law other than those of a single state, the rules confer greater flexibility on both the arbitrators and the parties.[251]

(h) Equity and good conscience

3.192 Arbitrators may, from time to time, be required to settle a dispute by determining it on the basis of what is 'fair and reasonable', rather than on the basis of law. Such power is conferred upon them by so-called equity clauses, which state, for example, that the arbitrators shall 'decide according to an equitable rather than a strictly legal interpretation', or, more simply, that they shall decide as *amiables compositeurs*.

3.193 This power to decide 'in equity', as it is sometimes expressed, is open to several different interpretations. It may mean, for instance, that the arbitral tribunal:

- should apply relevant rules of law to the dispute, but may ignore any rules that are purely formalistic (for example a requirement that the contract should have been made in some particular form); or
- should apply relevant rules of law to the dispute, but may ignore any rules that appear to operate harshly or unfairly in the particular case before it; or
- should decide according to general principles of law; or
- may ignore completely any rules of law and decide the case on its merits, as these strike the arbitral tribunal.

Commentators generally reject this fourth alternative. To the extent that they do agree, commentators seem to suggest that even an arbitral tribunal that decides 'in equity' must act in accordance with some generally accepted legal principles. In many (or perhaps most) cases, this means, as indicated at the outset of this chapter, that the arbitral tribunal will reach its decision based largely on a consideration of the facts and on the provisions of the contract, whilst trying to ensure that these provisions do not operate unfairly to the detriment of one or the other of the parties.

3.194 French law, for example, allows the arbitrators to act as *amiables compositeurs*, but requires them to satisfy certain standards.[252] The Paris Cour d'Appel has held that

---

[250] ICC Rules, Art. 21(1).
[251] For example, they may choose general principles of law, or the *lex mercatoria*, or the UNIDROIT Principles.
[252] See Loquin, *L'Amiable Compositeur en Droit Comparé et International: Contribution à l'Étude du Non-Droit dans l'Arbitrage International* (Librairie Techniques, 1980).

'arbitrators acting as *amiables compositeurs* have an obligation to ensure that their decision is equitable or else they would betray their duty and give rise to a cause for annulment'.[253]

3.195 For an 'equity clause' to be effective, there are, in principle, two basic requirements: first, that the parties have *expressly* agreed to it; and secondly, that it should be permitted by the applicable law. Both requirements are seen in such provisions as Article 35(2) of the UNCITRAL Rules, which provides: 'The arbitral tribunal shall decide as *amiable compositeur* or *ex aequo et bono* only if the parties have expressly authorised the arbitral tribunal to do so and if the law applicable to the arbitral procedure permits such arbitration.'

3.196 It is noteworthy that the UNCITRAL Rules refer to *amiable compositeur* and *ex aequo et bono* as distinct concepts. Although a historical distinction has been drawn between them,[254] the increasing practice of international arbitral tribunals appears to be to view both concepts as granting a discretion to arbitral tribunals to put aside strict legal rules and to decide a dispute by reference to general principles of fairness.[255]

3.197 The arbitration laws of some states go even further: they assume that the arbitrators will decide in equity unless it is expressly stated that they must decide in law. This recalls a time when arbitration was considered a 'friendly' method of dispute resolution, rather than the law-based process that it has become. If the arbitration is to take place in such a state, parties should take care to specify if they do not want the arbitrators to decide in accordance with principles of equity.[256]

E. Conflict Rules and the Search for the Applicable Law

(a) Introduction

3.198 As the foregoing discussion has endeavoured to make clear, parties to a contract are entitled to choose the law that is to govern their contractual relationship, and parties should exercise this entitlement with proper care and consideration in any

---

[253] Paris Cour d'Appel, 11 January 1996, 351.

[254] See Rubino-Sammartano, '*Amiable compositor* (joint mandate to settle) and *ex bono et aequo* (discretional authority to mitigate strict law): Apparent synonyms revisited' (1992) 9 J Intl Arb 5.

[255] See Grierson and van Hooft, *Arbitrating under the 2012 ICC Rules* (Kluwer Law International, 2012), pp. 319–335 (glossary entries for *amiable compositeur* and *ex aequo et bono*); *Halsbury's Laws of England*, Vol. 2 (5th edn, LexisNexis, 2008), footnote to para. 1208; Born, *International Commercial Arbitration* (2nd edn, Kluwer Law International, 2014), pp 2770–2776.

[256] See, e.g., Ecuador's Law of Arbitration No. 145/1997, which states at s. 3: 'The parties will decide whether the arbitrator shall decide in law or in equity. Unless otherwise agreed, the award shall be in equity.' Other countries reverse this presumption: see Chile's Judicial Code, Art. 235 ('If the parties have not indicated the type of arbitrator, the law presumes that he will be an arbitrator at law').

E. Conflict Rules and the Search for the Applicable Law

international commercial contract into which they may enter. In the event of a dispute, such care and consideration may prove to be very valuable indeed.

The choices generally open to parties have been set out throughout this chapter. If disputes arise and no choice of law has been agreed, it is difficult to make a proper assessment of the rights and obligations of the parties, because there is no known legal framework within which to make this assessment. **3.199**

If arbitration proceedings are commenced, one of the first tasks of the arbitral tribunal will be to do what the parties have failed to do—that is, to establish what law is applicable to the contract. In some cases, it might be appropriate for the arbitral tribunal to identify some non-national rule or custom to decide the issue in question, as opposed to a national law.[257] This search for the applicable substantive law may be a time-consuming and unpredictable process. The next section indicates how arbitrators are likely to approach the task if obliged to do so. By way of general introduction, the ILA's Committee for International Commercial Arbitration has recognised the need for guidance and development of best practices for parties, counsel, and arbitrators in ascertaining the contents of the applicable law to an international commercial arbitration. The recommendations made in the report, *Ascertaining of the Content of the Applicable Law in International Commercial Arbitration*, are commended to arbitral tribunals, with a view to facilitating uniformity and consistency in identifying the potentially applicable laws or rules.[258] **3.200**

(b) Implied or tacit choice

In the absence of an express choice of law, the arbitral tribunal will usually look first for the law that the parties are presumed to have intended to choose. This is often referred to as a 'tacit' choice of law. It may also be known as an implied, inferred, or implicit choice. There is a certain artificiality involved in selecting a substantive law for the parties and attributing it to their tacit choice, where (as often happens in **3.201**

---

[257] See Mayer, 'Reflections on the international arbitrator's duty to apply the law: The 2000 Freshfields Lecture' (2001) 17 Arb Intl 235, at 237–240, for a discussion of how arbitrators may not be bound to apply the law.

[258] The report issued after the ILA's Seventy-third Conference, held in Rio in August 2008, is available online at http://www.ila-hq.org/en/committees/index.cfm/cid/19. The Annex Resolution No. 6/2008 contains guidance split into the following sections: general considerations; acquiring information relevant to the ascertainment of the applicable law; interaction with the parties; making use of information about the law's content; and guidance in special circumstances, e.g. where public policy is implicated. Recommendations of particular note are: Recommendation 4, that the rules governing the ascertainment of the contents of law by national courts are not necessarily suitable for arbitration and that arbitrators should not rely on unexpressed presumptions as to the contents of the applicable law, including any presumption that it is the same as the law best known to the tribunal or to any of its members, or even that is the same as the law of the seat of arbitration; Recommendation 5, that arbitrators should primarily receive information about the contents of the applicable law from the parties; and Recommendation 6, that arbitrators should not introduce legal issues (propositions of law that may bear on the outcome of the dispute) that the parties have not raised.

practice) it is apparent that the parties themselves have given little, or no, thought to the question of the substantive law that is applicable to their contract.

3.202 Article 3(1) of the Rome I Regulation recognises this artificiality when it provides that a choice of law must be 'expressed or *demonstrated with reasonable certainty* by the terms of the contract or the circumstances of the case'.[259] The report by Professors Guiliano and Lagarde that was published alongside the Convention has a special status in its interpretation.[260] The report states that the parties may have made a real choice of law, although not expressly stated in their contract, but the court may not be permitted to infer a choice of law that the parties might have made *where they had no clear intention of making a choice*.[261]

3.203 In such an event, the court—or the arbitral tribunal—will generally decide that the contract is to be governed by the law of the country with which it is most closely connected. It will be presumed that this is the country that is the place of business or residence of the party that is to effect the performance characteristic of the contract. However, this presumption does not apply if the place of characteristic performance cannot be determined. Indeed, it will be disregarded altogether if it appears that the contract is more closely connected with another country.[262]

3.204 In practice, as already indicated, parties to an international commercial contract would do well to make a specific choice of law, rather than to leave the matter to be determined by a court or arbitral tribunal.

(c) Choice of forum as choice of law

3.205 One criterion for attributing a choice of law to the parties, in the absence of any express choice, is that of a choice of forum by the parties. If the parties make no express choice of law, but agree that any disputes between them shall be litigated in a particular country, it is generally assumed that they intend the law of that country to apply to the substance of their disputes. This assumption is expressed in the maxim *qui indicem forum elegit jus* ('a choice of forum is a choice of law').

3.206 The assumption makes sense when the reference is to a court of law. For instance, if the parties fail to put a choice-of-law clause into their contract, but provide for the resolution of any disputes by the courts of New York, it would seem to be a reasonable assumption that they intended those courts to apply their own law—that is, the law of the State of New York. The assumption is less compelling, however, when the dispute resolution clause provides for arbitration in a particular country,

---

[259] Emphasis added.
[260] Giuliano and Lagarde, *Council Report on the Convention on the Law Applicable to Contractual Obligations*, OJ C 282/1, 31 October 1980.
[261] Ibid., p. 17 (emphasis added). See also Dicey, Morris, and Collins, *The Conflict of Laws* (15th edn, Sweet & Maxwell, 2012), pp. 1809*ff.*
[262] Rome I Regulation, Art. 4; see also Dicey, Morris, and Collins, n. 261, pp. 1818*ff*, for a commentary on this provision of the Convention, which is based on Swiss and, subsequently, Dutch law.

E. Conflict Rules and the Search for the Applicable Law

rather than litigation in the courts of that country. A place of arbitration may be chosen for many reasons unconnected with the law of that place. It may be chosen because of its geographical convenience to the parties, or because it is a suitably neutral venue, or because of the high reputation of the arbitration services to be found there, or for some other, equally valid, reason. In one case before the SCC's Arbitration Institute, the tribunal highlighted the fallacy of the principle that a choice of forum is a choice of law in the context of arbitration in the following terms:

> [I]t is highly debatable whether a preferred choice of the *situs* of the arbitration is sufficient to indicate a choice of governing law. There has for several years been a distinct tendency in international arbitration to disregard this element, chiefly on the ground that the choice of the place of arbitration may be influenced by a number of practical considerations that have no bearing on the issue of applicable law.[263]

3.207 Nevertheless, where the parties have not made an express choice of the substantive law of their contract, but have included a reference to arbitration and have chosen the place of arbitration, that choice may—absent other indications—influence the decision as to what the substantive law of the contract should be. Thus, in a case in which the choice of the substantive law of the contract was unenforceable because it was too uncertain, but the arbitration clause was clear in its provision for arbitration in London, it was held that the arbitration agreement was a valid agreement and was governed by English law.[264]

(d) Conflict rules

3.208 In the absence of an express or implied choice by the parties, an arbitral tribunal is faced with the problem of choosing a system of law or a set of legal rules to govern the contract. It must first decide whether it has a free choice, or whether it must follow the conflict-of-law rules of the seat of the arbitration—that is, the conflict rules of the *lex fori*. Every developed national system of law contains its own rules for the conflict of laws (sometimes called private international law, in the narrower sense of that phrase). These conflict rules usually serve to indicate what law is to be chosen as the law applicable to a contract.

3.209 To carry out this role, the relevant conflict rules generally select particular criteria that serve to link or connect the contract in question with a given system of law. These criteria are often referred to as 'connecting factors'. However, they differ from country to country; accordingly, the answer to the question 'what is the applicable law?' will also differ from country to country. Some of the rules that are applied to connect a particular contract with a particular national law or set of legal

---

[263] See Arbitration Institute of the SCC, *Stockholm Arbitration Report* (SCC, 2002), p. 59, with commentary by Fernandez-Armesto.
[264] *Sonatrach Petroleum Corp v Ferrell International Ltd* [2002] 1 All ER (Comm) 627.

rules now look decidedly out of date. For example, under the conflict rules of some states, the applicable law (in the absence of an express or tacit choice) is likely to be the law of the place where the contract was concluded (the *lex locus contractus*). The place of conclusion of a contract may, at one time, have been a factor of some significance, since it would usually be the place of business or residence of one of the parties and might well also have been the place in which the contract was to be performed. However, with contracts now being concluded by email or by fax, or by meetings at an airport or some other location, the place in which the contract is finally concluded is often a matter of little, or no, significance.

3.210 A modern set of conflict rules is that adopted in the Rome I Regulation,[265] which provides at Article 4(1) that, in the absence of an express choice by the parties, 'the contract shall be governed by the law of the country with which it is most closely connected'.[266] In this regard, there is a rebuttable presumption that the contract is most closely connected with the country in which the party which is to effect the 'performance characteristic of the contract' has its central administration, principal place of business, or other place of business through which the performance is to be effected.[267]

(e) Does an international arbitral tribunal have a *lex fori*?

3.211 As already stated, conflict-of-law rules differ from one country to another. A judge or arbitral tribunal in one country may select the applicable law by reference to the place where the contract was made, whereas in another country it may be selected by reference to the law with which the contract has the closest connection. In short, the same question may produce different answers, depending upon where the judge or arbitral tribunal happens to be sitting.

3.212 In the context of international arbitration, this is plainly unsatisfactory. The seat of the arbitration is invariably chosen for reasons that have nothing to do with the conflict rules of the law of the place of arbitration. This has led to the formulation of a doctrine that has found support in both the rules of arbitral institutions and the practice of international arbitration—namely, that, unlike the judge of a national court, an international arbitral tribunal is not bound to follow the conflict-of-law rules of the country in which it has its seat.

3.213 A leading commentator has spoken of 'the almost total abandonment of the application of the rules of conflict of the so-called arbitral forum',[268] and the

---

[265] It is worth noting that arbitral agreements are expressly excluded from the scope of the Convention by Art. 1(2)(d), but the discussion in the present section is about contracts as a whole and not about a separate (or separable) agreement to arbitrate.
[266] Rome I Regulation, Art. 4(1).
[267] Rome I Regulation, Art. 4(2).
[268] Goldman, 'La *lex mercatoria* dans les contrats et l'arbitrage internationaux: Réalité et perspectives' [1979] J du Droit Intl 475, at 491.

E. Conflict Rules and the Search for the Applicable Law

point was emphasised in the *Sapphire* arbitration,[269] in which the tribunal commented that, unlike the judge of a national court, an international arbitral tribunal has no *lex fori*:

> Contrary to a State judge, who is bound to conform to the conflict law rules of the State in whose name he metes out justice, the arbitrator is not bound by such rules. He must look for the common intention of the parties, and use the connecting factors generally used in doctrine and in case law and must disregard national peculiarities.[270]

This was an early enunciation of what has come to be known as the 'direct choice' (*voie directe*) method of choosing the substantive law, which in reality gives arbitrators the freedom to choose as they please.

(f) International conventions, rules of arbitration, and national laws

3.214 Article 42(1) of the ICSID Convention states that, in the absence of any choice of the applicable or governing law of the contract by the parties, the arbitral tribunal must apply the law of the contracting state that is a party to the dispute, together with such rules of international law as may be applicable. The ICSID Convention, however, is necessarily concerned with states or state entities. Accordingly, it follows the traditional practice of giving considerable weight to the law of the *state* party to a contract, in the absence of any choice of law.

3.215 Other conventions are content to leave the choice to the arbitral tribunal. Article VII of the European Convention of 1961, for instance, provides that '[f]ailing any indication by the parties as to the applicable law, the arbitrators shall apply the proper law under the rules of conflict that the arbitrators deem applicable'. Although the European Convention of 1961 refers to 'rules of conflict', these are *not* necessarily the rules of conflict of the country in which the arbitration has its seat; on the contrary, the reference is to the conflict rules that the arbitrators deem applicable.

3.216 A similar approach is adopted in the Model Law.[271] The intention is to make it clear that the arbitral tribunal is entitled to choose the governing law of the contract in the absence of any express or implied choice of law by the parties themselves. In doing this, the arbitrators proceed objectively—but should they still be obliged to proceed by way of particular conflict rules? The point may be academic, since in practice an arbitral tribunal will seek to apply the law (or, if permitted, the rules of law) that it considers to be appropriate. Whether this choice is reached through conflict rules or more directly may not matter.

---

[269] *Sapphire International Petroleum Ltd v The National Iranian Oil Co.* (1964) 13 ICLQ 1011.
[270] Ibid.
[271] Model Law, Art. 28(2).

3.217 It should be noted, however, that French law omits any reference to conflict rules. This is both logical and sensible. French law states that: 'The arbitral tribunal shall decide the dispute in accordance with the rules of law chosen by the parties or, where no such choice has been made, in accordance with the rules of law it considers appropriate.'[272] This provision contains two propositions: first, an international arbitral tribunal is not obliged to proceed to its choice of law by the adoption of any national conflict of laws rules; and secondly, it is not obliged to choose a *system* of law as the substantive law of the contract, but may instead choose such *rules* of law as it considers appropriate for the resolution of the dispute.[273] The trail blazed by French law has since been followed by other countries, including Canada, India, Kenya, and the Netherlands.[274]

(g) Conclusion

3.218 In reaching its decision on the law to be applied in the absence of any choice by the parties, an arbitral tribunal is entitled (unless otherwise directed by the applicable rules or the *lex arbitri*) to select any of the systems or rules of law upon which the parties themselves might have agreed, had they chosen to do so.

3.219 When it comes to determining how an arbitral tribunal should proceed to its decision, then once again (as so often in international arbitration) no universal rule can be identified. Some systems of law insist that, in making its choice, an arbitral tribunal should follow the rules of conflict of the seat of the arbitration—an attitude that looks increasingly anachronistic. The modern tendency is for international conventions and rules of arbitration to give considerable latitude to arbitral tribunals in making their choice of law, whilst still requiring them to do so by way of appropriate or applicable conflict rules. Some national laws (including the French, the Swiss, and the Dutch) carry the matter to its logical conclusion: by abandoning the reference to conflict rules altogether, they allow an arbitral tribunal to decide for itself what law (or rules of law) the tribunal considers appropriate to settle the dispute.

3.220 This is an approach to be commended. If an arbitral tribunal can be trusted to decide a dispute, so too can it be trusted to determine the set of legal rules by which it will be guided in reaching its decision. If the parties do not wish the arbitral tribunal to have such freedom of action, the remedy is in their own hands: they should agree upon the applicable law or set of legal rules, preferably in their

---

[272] Article 1511 of the French Code of Civil Procedure. The same formulation is now used at Art. 35 of the UNCITRAL Rules 2010.
[273] ICC Rules, Art. 21(1); LCIA Rules, Art. 22(3). The SCC Rules, Art. 22(1), and WIPO Rules, Art. 59(1), also endorse the direct approach.
[274] In Canada, by the Ontario International Commercial Arbitration Act 1990, s. 6; In India, the Arbitration and Conciliation Act 1996, s. 28(1)(b)(iii); in Kenya, the Arbitration Act 1995, s. 29(3); in the Netherlands, the Arbitration Act 1986, s. 1054(3). Swiss law also comes close to the same position, in s. 187 of the Swiss PIL.

contract, but if not, then at any time after the dispute has arisen. If they do not do so, it will fall to the arbitral tribunal to make a decision that is likely to impact on the outcome of the arbitration. In order to reach this decision (which may be given as a ruling on a preliminary issue by way of an interim or partial award), the arbitral tribunal will usually have to consider detailed arguments of law and fact. This is an expense that could readily have been avoided if the parties had taken the time and the trouble to agree on one of the many choices open to them.

F. Other Applicable Rules and Guidelines

(a) Ethical rules

Much has been said and written about the duties to which arbitrators are subject[275]—but what of arbitration practitioners who appear as counsel in international arbitrations, often outside their home jurisdictions? A lawyer appearing in a court action before his or her own local courts will clearly be subject to the rules of professional ethics of his or her local bar. But what if that lawyer practises outside his or her home jurisdiction? And what if he or she is appearing in an arbitration? And what if that arbitration is taking place in yet another different jurisdiction? Will the lawyer remain subject to his or her local bar rules? Will he or she also be subject to the ethical rules applying to lawyers practising in the jurisdiction in which he or she is now based? Will the lawyer also be subject to the ethical rules applying to lawyers conducting legal proceedings in the place of arbitration, if different?   **3.221**

The answers to these myriad questions can have a significant impact on the conduct of the arbitration. Let us consider, for example, the question of how much contact a lawyer should have with a witness prior to a hearing. In some jurisdictions, such as England, it is impermissible for a lawyer to 'coach' a witness on the evidence to be given at a hearing.[276] In others, constraints on lawyers appear to be far more limited.   **3.222**

In her comparison of standards of professional conduct, one commentator put it thus: 'An Australian lawyer felt that from his perspective it would be unethical to prepare a witness; a Canadian lawyer said it would be illegal; and an American lawyer's view was that not to prepare a witness would be malpractice.'[277] Therein lies the problem: counsel in the same procedure, playing to very different rules, with a possible concrete impact on the substantive outcome of the arbitration.

---

[275] Indeed, this is the subject of Chapter 5.
[276] Bar Council of England and Wales Code of Conduct, Pt VII, s. 705(a). See, e.g., *R v Momdou and anor* [2005] EWCA Crim 177, [45]: 'There is no place for witness training in this country, we do not do it. It is unlawful.'
[277] Miller, 'Zip to nil? A comparison of American and English lawyers' standards of professional conduct', CA 32 ALI-ABA 199, 204 (1995).

Applicable Laws

3.223 Until recently, there had been little alternative for counsel other than to ascertain individually the answers to the following questions.

(1) 'Am I subject to my professional bar rules when I am acting in an arbitration, and even when I am acting in an arbitration abroad?'[278]
(2) 'If I am practising abroad, am I also subject to the professional ethical rules of the jurisdiction in which I am practising?'[279]
(3) 'If the seat of the arbitration is in a third jurisdiction, am I also subject to the ethical rules of a third bar?'

3.224 It is a matter of concern that the answers to these questions may not be the same for all counsel participating in the same arbitration proceedings. However, some commentators have for some time posited the possibility of a harmonisation of professional bar rules to the extent that they apply to practitioners in international arbitration.[280] The idea is attractive, particularly for those concerned to ensure that the playing field for the participants in international arbitration is level. However, the changes necessary to achieve this should not be underestimated, requiring national bar rules around the world to make express exceptions to their general codes as far as practitioners in arbitral proceedings are concerned.[281] If such changes are to happen at all, they are unlikely to happen quickly.

3.225 An alternative means of harmonisation lies in non-binding guidelines. As with so much else, the IBA has taken a lead in this, publishing its Guidelines on Party Representation in International Arbitration on 25 May 2013. Intended to provide practical assistance in dealing with ethical issues that arise in international arbitration, the Guidelines provide situational guidance in relation to the most frequent issues encountered by practitioners.

3.226 The Guidelines address five substantive ethical issues that arise in practice, relating to:

- conflicts of interest (Guidelines 5 and 6);
- *ex parte* communications with arbitrators (Guidelines 7 and 8);

---

[278] van Houtte, 'Counsel–witness relations and professional misconduct in civil law systems' (2003) 19 Arb Intl 457. Professor van Houtte argues that Art. 4 ('Applicable Rules of Conduct in Court') of the Code of Conduct for European Lawyers has the effect that whenever the seat of the arbitration is within the European Union, the ethical standards of the seat apply. For standards that should apply to participants in the arbitral process, see Veeder, 'The 2001 Goff Lecture: The lawyer's duty to arbitrate in good faith' (2002) 18 Arb Intl 431.

[279] In many jurisdictions, it is a requirement for foreign lawyers practising in the jurisdiction to register with the local bar.

[280] Paulsson, 'Standards of conduct for counsel in international arbitration' (1992) 3 Am Rev Intl Arb 214. In a similar vein, the Code of Conduct for European Lawyers was originally drawn up and adopted in 1998 by the Conseil des Barreaux de la Communauté Européene (CCBE).

[281] The Brussels Bar Rules contain such express exceptions. For a further discussion of the issue, see van Houtte, 'Counsel–witness relations and professional misconduct in civil law systems' (2003) 19 Arb Intl 457.

F. Other Applicable Rules and Guidelines

- misleading submissions to the arbitral tribunal (Guidelines 9–11);
- improper information exchange and disclosure (Guidelines 12–17); and
- assistance to witnesses and experts (Guidelines 19–24).

In relation to each, the Guidelines set out best practices and recommended approaches. They also propose certain remedies and sanctions, including admonishing the representative, drawing adverse inferences, and altering the apportionment of costs, as well as a broader reference to any 'other measures' that might ensure the fairness and integrity of proceedings.

3.227 The leading international arbitral institutions have also taken their first cautious steps towards regulating the conduct of counsel (and parties) in international arbitration. The ICC, for instance, envisages that an arbitral tribunal may sanction unreasonable conduct in making its award of costs. Article 37(5) of the ICC Rules provides that, in making a decision on costs, the tribunal shall take account of 'such circumstance as it considers relevant, including the extent to which each party has conducted the arbitration in an expeditious and cost-effective manner'.

3.228 More boldly, the LCIA provides, in Article 18 of its Rules, certain provisions governing a party's legal representatives. These include, at Article 18(5), a provision that each party 'shall ensure that all its legal representatives appearing by name before the Arbitral Tribunal have agreed to comply with the general guidelines contained in the Annex to the LCIA Rules, as a condition of such representation'. The general guidelines in the Annex are designed to promote 'the good and equal conduct of the parties' legal representatives appearing by name within the arbitration', and they provide, by way of example, that a legal representative should not knowingly make any false statement to the arbitral tribunal, should not conceal or assist in the concealment of any document of which production is ordered, and should not initiate any undisclosed contact with an arbitrator. Notably, Article 18(6) of the LCIA Rules also now endows an arbitral tribunal with the power to order sanctions for the violation of the guidelines, including (broadly) the taking of any measure 'necessary to fulfill within the arbitration the general duties required of the Arbitral Tribunal', as defined elsewhere in the Rules.

(b) Guidelines

3.229 One of the recognised advantages of international arbitration is the flexibility that results from the paucity of rules (and the corresponding preponderance of discretion) that enables arbitrators to tailor proceedings precisely to the characters, cultures, and claims that feature in any particular arbitration. Thus every international arbitration—at least in theory—is a microcosm of potential procedural reform. That potentiality is undoubtedly a quality of the arbitral process—but that quality has a price: procedural unpredictability. And it is a price that many in the expanding constituency of arbitration users are increasingly unwilling to pay.

3.230 To address this unpredictability, in recent years the world of international arbitration has seen the steady growth of procedural guidelines and recommendations, which now occupy a prominent place in the practice of international arbitration. In this regard, another commentator has referred to the growth during the last decade of the procedural 'soft law' of international arbitration[282]—growth that has indeed been quite remarkable. By way of notable example:

- in 1996, UNCITRAL published its detailed Notes on Organising Arbitral Proceedings;
- in 1999, and again in 2010, the IBA's Arbitration and Alternative Dispute Resolution (ADR) Committee D revised its now ubiquitous Rules on the Taking of Evidence in International Arbitration;
- in 2004, and again in 2014, the same IBA Committee published its Guidelines on Conflicts of Interest in International Arbitration;
- in 2013, as we have seen, the same IBA Committee published its Guidelines on Party Representation;
- in 2006, the American College of Commercial Arbitrators (CCA) developed a compendium of Best Practices for Business Arbitration, which was also revised in 2010; and
- in 2008, the ILA published its *Report on Ascertaining the Contents of the Applicable Law in International Commercial Arbitration*.

3.231 To be clear, the many guidelines that have been formulated, not to mention those yet to come, do not (and indeed cannot) alter any national rules and regulations in relation to the conduct of party representatives, nor do they imbue arbitral tribunals with any of the powers held by national bodies to enforce national rules and regulations. Instead, these guidelines are intended as a tool that can be adopted by the parties to an arbitration agreement. Nevertheless, many will now feature prominently—side-by-side with the applicable laws—in the conduct of international arbitrations and are referred to, where appropriate, throughout the subsequent chapters of this book.

---

[282] See n. 3.

4

ESTABLISHMENT AND ORGANISATION OF AN ARBITRAL TRIBUNAL

A.	Background	4.01	E.	Challenge and Replacement of Arbitrators	4.89
B.	Appointment of Arbitrators	4.33	F.	Organisation of the Arbitral Tribunal	4.169
C.	Qualities Required in International Arbitrators	4.49	G.	Fees and Expenses of the Arbitral Tribunal	4.202
D.	Independence and Impartiality of Arbitrators	4.75			

A. Background

(a) Introduction

4.01 Once the decision to start an arbitration has been taken and the appropriate form of notice or request for arbitration has been delivered, the next step is to establish the arbitral tribunal. Whilst a national court of law is a standing body to which an application may be made at almost any time, an arbitral tribunal must be brought into existence before it can exercise any jurisdiction over the parties and the dispute. The contrast between the two is seen most clearly when a dispute has arisen, attempts at settlement have failed, and one of the parties has decided that the time has come to pursue its legal rights. If the dispute is to be taken to court, the claimant need only initiate whatever form of originating process is appropriate to set the machinery of justice into operation before the court. The parties will have no role to play in the composition of that court. It is different if the dispute is to be referred to arbitration: there is no permanent standing body of arbitrators and, absent some specific mechanism in the applicable rules for a separate 'pre-arbitral' phase for urgent decisions,[1] no decisions can be taken or relief sought until the tribunal has been established.

---

[1] Such pre-arbitral mechanisms are becoming more common: see paragraphs 4.03 and 4.18*ff*.

4.02 The establishment of the tribunal may be a relatively lengthy process, especially where one party (almost always the respondent) fails to nominate an arbitrator. Even where the relevant rules provide for the institution to make the remaining appointments, including the president of the tribunal, such process can be time-consuming as the institution consults regarding suitable candidates.[2] Other than in cases that are expedited, the establishment of the tribunal takes at least two months from the submission of the notice or request for arbitration.

4.03 The question then arises: what can be done pending constitution of the arbitral tribunal if urgent measures are required? The traditional response is to rely on the relevant national courts for critical relief. Most modern arbitral systems permit an application for interim measures to be sought from national courts pending the formation of the tribunal, without such application constituting a waiver of the arbitration agreement.[3] However, the need to rely on the national court system to decide upon what may be a critical issue in the arbitration right at the start of that process goes against one of the very purposes of arbitration: to grant to an expert authority outside the formal court system the power to make decisions related to a dispute. To address the need of the parties to obtain a quick decision, most institutions have therefore adopted a specific mechanism in their rules.[4]

---

[2] The International Chamber of Commerce (ICC) may consult with the relevant national committees with regard to suitable candidates and may appoint the presiding arbitrator or make default appointments based on the proposal of that committee. If the Court does not accept the proposal, it may repeat its request or seek a proposal from another national committee, or appoint directly any person it deems suitable (ICC Rules, Art. 13(3)). The Court also has the power to make direct appointments without consulting national committees in certain prescribed circumstances, including where one or more parties is a state or state entity (ICC Rules, Art. 13(4)). The London Court of International Arbitration (LCIA) makes all final appointments, taking into account any written agreement or joint nomination by the parties (LCIA Rules, Art. 5(7)) and any particular method or criteria for selection agreed in writing by the parties (LCIA Rules, Art. 5(9)). See also the comment of Turner and Mohtashami, *A Guide to the LCIA Arbitration Rules* (Oxford University Press, 2009), p. 61, on Art. 5(5) of the previous Rules. Article 37(2) of the ICSID Convention and Rule 2 of the International Centre for Settlement of Investment Disputes (ICSID) Rules of Procedure for Arbitration Proceedings provide for a rather cumbersome process whereby the claimant has to propose an appointment mechanism, which, if not accepted by the other party within sixty days, defaults to an institutional system.

[3] See, e.g., ICC Rules, Art. 28(2):

> Before the file is transmitted to the Arbitral Tribunal, and in appropriate circumstances even thereafter, the parties may apply to any competent judicial authority for interim or conservatory measures. The application of a party to a judicial authority for such measures or for the implementation of any such measures ordered by an Arbitral Tribunal shall not be deemed to be an infringement or a waiver of the arbitration agreement...

For more detail on the legitimate support that can be obtained in favour of an arbitration from national courts, see Chapter 7.

[4] LCIA Rules, Art. 9; International Centre for Dispute Resolution (ICDR) Rules, Art. 37, Netherlands Arbitration Institute (NAI) Arbitration Rules, Art. 42. The 2012 ICC Rules have introduced an emergency arbitrator procedure in Art. 29 and Appendix V. Previously, parties could rely only on the separate ICC Rules for Pre-Arbitral Referee Procedure, which required parties expressly to opt in. These were rarely used in practice.

The different approaches among arbitral institutions include summary arbitral proceedings,[5] expedited formation of the tribunal,[6] and (increasingly) the expeditious appointment of an 'emergency arbitrator'.[7]

(b) Commencement of an arbitration

4.04 The commencement of an arbitration is a significant step, not merely as evidence of a real conflict between the parties, but also in terms of compliance with any limitation period for the presentation of claims.

4.05 Time limits for bringing legal proceedings by way of arbitration or litigation are imposed by the law of most, if not all, countries. It is said that the interest of the state is that litigation should be started within a reasonable time of the events that gave rise to it. Time limits in litigation or arbitration must always be considered with care. Failure to observe them may be fatal in terms of both commencing a claim and complying with any time agreed for rendering the award. Time usually starts to run from the date on which the cause of action arises. It may well be necessary to take some positive step to commence an arbitration (such as the notification of a request for arbitration, or the service of a notice requiring the appointment of an arbitrator) in order to prevent a claim failing through time bar. Prescriptive time limits may also be imposed by contract (as in many standard forms of contract—whether for the charter of a ship or for the carrying out of a major civil engineering project).

4.06 Whereas contractual time limits are often short—generally, a matter of months—those imposed by law are longer—generally, a number of years. This in itself creates no special problem. In principle, it is right that a claimant should have adequate time in which to prepare and bring a claim.

4.07 Most problems arise in the area of conflict of laws. In particular, there may be a difference in both the length and the nature of the time limits laid down by different national systems of law. One system of law, for example, may provide that claims under a contract are to be brought within three years, whilst another system of law may allow six years. More importantly, one system of law may classify time limits as matters of procedure, to be governed by the law of the place of arbitration, while another system may classify time limits as matters of substance, governed by the same law as that which governs all of the other substantive matters in issue.

---

[5] NAI Rules, Art. 42k.
[6] LCIA Rules, Art. 9A.
[7] See, e.g., ICDR Rules, Art. 37.3; ICC Rules, Art. 29 and Appendix V. See paragraphs 4.18*ff* for a more detailed discussion on emergency arbitrators and how these solutions have been working in practice.

(c) Commencement of an arbitration under institutional rules

4.08 In order to stop time running, arbitration proceedings must be commenced in accordance with the contract or relevant applicable law, or both (see Chapter 1). If there is any difference between this law and any institutional rules of arbitration adopted by the parties, the non-waivable provisions of the applicable law will prevail. In most cases, however, national laws permit parties to modify rules for commencement of arbitration by agreement, in which case the claimant need only be concerned with complying with the relevant institutional rules (or rules set out in the arbitration clause itself). By way of example, the Rules of the International Chamber of Commerce (ICC) require a party wishing to have recourse to arbitration to submit a 'request for arbitration', which must contain, inter alia, a description of the nature and circumstances of the dispute, details of the relief sought, and particulars concerning the number and choice of arbitrators. Article 4(2) of the ICC Rules state that: 'The date on which the Request is received by the Secretariat shall, for all purposes, be deemed to be the date of commencement of the arbitral proceedings.'

4.09 The date designated under the ICC Rules as being 'for all purposes' the date of commencement of the arbitral proceedings may well be the same date under a particular national system of law. This is the case in English and French law, under which time will stop running if and when a request for arbitration is made in conformity with the relevant arbitration clause. In other cases, the institutional requirements for the commencement of an arbitration may differ from what is required by national systems of law. For example, an arbitration under the International Centre for the Settlement of Investment Disputes (ICSID) is deemed to have commenced on the date of ICSID's registration of the request for arbitration.[8]

4.10 These issues can be summarised as follows.

- Institutional rules providing for the date on which an arbitration shall be deemed to commence are valid for the purposes of the institution concerned.
- Institutional rules may also mark the 'commencement of an arbitration' for the purpose of any time limit contained in the contract, where the contract refers disputes to arbitration in accordance with the rules of that particular institution.
- Institutional rules may mark the 'commencement of an arbitration' for the purpose of statutory time limits, *but only if* the provisions of the relevant legislation permit the parties to override the statutory limits or coincide with the rules of the institution.
- If there is any conflict between the institutional rules and the relevant legislation, the latter determines the 'date of commencement of the arbitration' for the purpose of any statutory time limits that must be observed.

---

[8] ICSID Arbitration Rules, r. 6(2): 'A proceeding under the Convention shall be deemed to have been instituted on the date of the registration of the request.'

A. Background

(d) Commencement of an ad hoc arbitration under the applicable law

4.11 If the dispute resolution clause refers only to arbitration, without referring to an arbitral institution, the relevant legislation usually prescribes the steps required to achieve the 'commencement of arbitration proceedings'. These steps differ from one arbitration clause to another and from country to country. The relevant country in this regard will be that of the seat of the arbitration, the law of which will govern the mechanism for commencing an arbitration in the absence of the application of institutional or other pre-agreed rules. It may be necessary:

- to send a notice of arbitration to the opposing party, briefly describing the dispute, nominating an arbitrator, and requiring the opposing party to nominate its own arbitrator within a given time period; or[9]
- to commence the procedure for designation of the arbitral tribunal, as provided in the arbitration agreement; or
- to require the opposing party to appoint or to concur in the appointment of an arbitrator.

4.12 By way of example, the Swiss Private International Law Act 1987 (Swiss PIL) provides that, in the absence of contrary agreement, proceedings are commenced 'when one of the parties initiates the procedure for the constitution of the arbitral tribunal'.[10] In contrast, the Brazilian Arbitration Act 1996 provides that 'an arbitral procedure is commenced when the appointment is accepted by the sole arbitrator or by the arbitrators if several'.[11]

(e) Selecting an arbitral tribunal

4.13 Once a decision to refer a dispute to arbitration has been made, choosing the right arbitral tribunal is critical to the success of the arbitral process. It is an important choice not only for the parties to the particular dispute, but also for the reputation and standing of the process itself. It is, above all, the quality of the arbitral tribunal that makes or breaks the arbitration, and it is one of the unique distinguishing factors of arbitration as opposed to national judicial proceedings.[12]

---

[9] In this respect, Art. 21 of the Model Law provides that: 'Unless otherwise agreed by the parties, the arbitral proceedings in respect of a particular dispute commence on the date on which a request for that dispute to be referred to arbitration is received by the respondent.'

[10] Swiss PIL, Ch. 12, s. 181. In England, the parties may agree upon when the proceedings are to be regarded as commenced for limitation purposes. Failing agreement, it is when one party gives a written notice to the other party or the appointing authority seeking the establishment of the tribunal: English Arbitration Act 1996, s. 14.

[11] Brazil–Law No. 9.307 of 23 September 1996, s. 19.

[12] For a comprehensive review of the complex criteria involved in the selection of arbitrators, see Lalive, 'Requirements of international arbitration: The selection of Arbitrators', in Reymond and Bucher (eds) *Swiss Essays on International Arbitration* (Schulthess, 1984), p. 23; Lalive, 'On the neutrality of arbitrators and the place of arbitration', in Reymond and Bucher (eds) *Swiss Essays on International Arbitration* (Schulthess, 1984), p. 33. See also Timmer, 'The quality,

4.14 In addition to choosing an arbitrator with appropriate knowledge of the relevant substantive area of law, it is particularly important for parties to recognise the importance of experience in arbitration, particularly for a sole arbitrator or the presiding arbitrator, who must take control of the proceedings. The rights of the parties—and, in particular, the right to a fair hearing—must be scrupulously observed. The sole or presiding arbitrator may have to perform this function against a background of a conflict of culture and legal backgrounds of the parties' representatives. At the same time, the proceedings must maintain their momentum. They must not be allowed to sink in a quagmire of procedural problems. There may be language problems, both in relation to communications between members of the arbitral tribunal and in the reception of evidence. A timetable must be set for the various steps to be taken in the arbitration (production of documents, exchange of witness statements, and so on), as well as dealing with travel and hotel arrangements, and other administrative matters. These are all tasks that call for skill and, above all, experience in the practice of international arbitration.

4.15 It is difficult to choose the qualifications of an arbitrator before the dispute has arisen. Will a claim be large or small? Is it essentially a legal problem, or does it turn mostly on the facts? Is particular expertise required to evaluate the facts quickly and correctly? These are the kinds of question that need to be answered before the most suitable arbitrator(s) can be chosen; 'horses for courses' is a rule that applies beyond the race track and is one best applied once the parties know the nature of the dispute.

4.16 In principle, the parties should be free to choose their own arbitrators, so that the dispute may be resolved by 'judges of their own choice'.[13] Sometimes, however, parties to an arbitration will find that this choice is limited by the restrictions placed on that choice by the clause, the institution, or the applicable statutory rules. For example, the qualifications of the arbitrator may have been designated in advance of any conflict, requiring a lawyer of 'not less than five years' standing', or 'a native English speaker with experience in Brazilian law and the oil and gas industry'. While such qualifications may seem like a good idea at the time that an arbitration clause is drafted, they are usually more trouble than they are worth: not only may they cause delay in ascertaining whether or not a particular arbitrator comes

---

independence and impartiality of the arbitrator in international commercial arbitration' (2012) 78 Arbitration 348.

[13] This phrase comes from the Hague Conventions on the Pacific Settlement of International Disputes of 1899 (Art. 15) and 1907 (Art. 37). However, in recent years, a debate has arisen as to the pros and cons of accommodating unilateral party appointments within the arbitral process. See Paulsson, 'Moral hazard in international dispute resolution', Inaugural lecture as holder of Michael R. Klein Distinguished Scholar Chair, University of Miami School of Law, Miami, FL, 29 April 2010; Brower and Rosenberg, 'The death of the two-headed nightingale: Why the Paulsson–van den Berg presumption that party-appointed arbitrators are untrustworthy is wrongheaded' (2013) 29 Arb Intl 43. The authors take no position on this debate, save to note that, at the time of writing, no sea change had taken place in the ubiquity of party appointment.

A. Background

within the qualification (or, indeed, whether any such person exists who would be ready and available to act), but they may also create unnecessary additional grounds for an obstreperous losing party to challenge an unfavourable award.

(f) Emergency arbitrators

Emergency arbitrator procedures are increasingly common in the main institutional arbitration rules as an alternative to the parties seeking interim relief from national courts prior to the arbitral tribunal being constituted. At the time of writing, the following institutional rules provide for the appointment of emergency arbitrators: the ICC Rules;[14] the London Court of International Arbitration (LCIA) Rules;[15] the International Centre for Dispute Resolution (ICDR) Rules;[16] the Swiss Rules of International Arbitration (Swiss Rules);[17] the Rules of the Stockholm Chamber of Commerce (SCC);[18] the Hong Kong International Arbitration Centre (HKIAC) Rules;[19] and the Singapore International Arbitration Centre (SIAC) Rules.[20]

4.17

It is hoped that these new rules will be more effective and useful to parties than their precursors, which required parties expressly to opt in. The new emergency arbitrator procedures apply automatically to arbitrations under the given arbitration rules, unless the parties expressly opt out of their application.[21]

4.18

In general, these rules allow parties to appoint an 'emergency arbitrator' to determine applications for interim relief as soon as a request for arbitration has been filed, or, in some cases, even earlier.[22] Indeed, some institutional rules now give the emergency arbitrator the power to order *ex parte* relief,[23] subject to the other party being heard immediately after the preliminary order is granted.

4.19

---

[14] ICC Rules, Art. 29 and Appendix V.
[15] In addition to providing for the expedited formation of the arbitral tribunal (Art. 9A), the LCIA Rules provide, at Art. 9B, for the appointment of an emergency arbitrator at any time prior to the formation or expedited formation of the arbitral tribunal. Any such application must set out the specific grounds for requiring the appointment of an emergency arbitrator and the specific claim for emergency relief. Importantly, the Rules provide that any such application will not prejudice a party's right to apply to a national court for interim or conservatory measures before the formation of the arbitral tribunal.
[16] ICDR Rules, Art. 37.
[17] See the 2012 Swiss Rules, Art. 43.
[18] SCC Rules, Appendix II.
[19] HKIAC Rules, Sch. 4.
[20] SIAC Rules, Sch. 1.
[21] Nine emergency arbitrator applications had been made under the SCC Rules by the beginning of 2014, in which the tribunals took the consistent approach that an interim measure can be granted only if the applicant shows that the harm that is to be prevented by the measure is irreparable, and of an urgent or imminent nature. See Lundstedt, *SCC Practice: Emergency Arbitrator Decisions, 1 January 2010–31 December 2013* (SCC, 2014), p. 25.
[22] The LCIA, ICC, SCC, and Swiss Rules permit the appointment of an emergency arbitrator before the notice of arbitration is filed. Others, including the SIAC, ICDR, and Australian Centre for International Commercial Arbitration (ACICA) Rules, require that it be filed with or after the notice of arbitration.
[23] For example, Swiss Rules, Art. 26(3).

4.20 A notable example of an 'emergency arbitrator' procedure is that found in the latest version of the ICC Rules. Pursuant to Article 29 and Appendix V to those Rules, a party may make an application for such measures by sending an application to the Secretariat, together with the relevant supporting documentation required under the Rules and payment of the prescribed fee.[24] Although an application can be made before the applicant files its request for arbitration, a request for arbitration must be sent to the Secretariat within ten days of the application to avoid the termination of the emergency proceedings.[25] The emergency arbitrator will be appointed within two days of the Secretariat receiving the application and may make an order within fifteen days of receiving the file (although this can be extended by the president of the International Court of Arbitration of the ICC if deemed necessary).[26] The procedure will not be available, however, if: (a) the arbitration agreement under the Rules was concluded *before* the date on which the latest Rules came into force; (b) the parties have agreed to opt out of these provisions; or (c) the parties have agreed to another pre-arbitral procedure that provides for the granting of conservatory, interim, or similar measures.[27]

4.21 Under most rules, including the ICC Rules, the emergency arbitrator's decision is interim in nature and will not bind the arbitral tribunal with respect to any question, issue, or dispute determined in the order.[28] Although Article 29(2) of the ICC Rules requires the parties to undertake to comply with any order made by the emergency arbitrator, the consequences of non-compliance are uncertain. Parties will still need to rely on the support of the national courts to enforce interim measures granted by an emergency arbitrator against non-compliant parties. It is not yet clear how local courts will react to such requests, given that an interim 'order' is unlikely to qualify as an award under the New York Convention. In some jurisdictions, specific legislative changes have been introduced to ensure that orders of emergency arbitrators are treated in the same way as those of an arbitral tribunal.[29]

(g) Sole arbitrators and multi-arbitrator tribunals

4.22 The establishment of an arbitral tribunal involves many considerations. First is the question of numbers: should there be more than one arbitrator, and if so, how

---

[24] ICC Rules, Art. 29(1) and Appendix V, Art. 1(3). The costs of an emergency arbitrator proceeding is set out in Art. 7(1) and Appendix V. Between 2012, when the 'emergency arbitrator' procedure was adopted, and 31 May 2014, the emergency arbitrator provisions were applied in ten cases: see Carlevaris and Feris, 'Running in the ICC Emergency Arbitration Rules: The first ten cases' (2014) 25 ICC International Court of Arbitration Bulletin 25. The authors suggest that these cases confirm the need amongst users of arbitration for such provisions.
[25] ICC Rules, Art. 29(1) and Appendix V, Art. 1(6).
[26] ICC Rules, Art. 2(1) and Appendix V, Art. 6(4).
[27] ICC Rules, Art. 29(6).
[28] ICC Rules, Art. 29(2).
[29] For example, the Singapore International Arbitration Act 2012 was amended so that the definition of 'arbitral tribunal' included emergency arbitrators: see Brock and Feldman, 'Recent trends in the conduct of arbitrations' (2013) 30 J Intl Arb 177, at 198.

A. Background

many? Is there any general rule as to the number of arbitrators that should be appointed, or does this depend upon the circumstances of the particular dispute? The laws of some countries sensibly provide that the number of arbitrators must be uneven and this should be borne in mind by the drafters of arbitration clauses. Clauses providing for two arbitrators and an 'umpire', used principally (but not exclusively) in shipping and commodities disputes, are unsuitable for modern international arbitration. Tribunals of five (or more) arbitrators are best reserved for arbitrations between states.[30] Thus an important consideration in the drafting of an arbitration clause or a submission agreement is the number of arbitrators to be appointed. In commercial cases, the choice, in practice, is between one and three.

(i) Sole arbitrators

Article 12(2) of the ICC Rules provides that, where the parties have not agreed upon the number of arbitrators, a sole arbitrator will be appointed unless 'the dispute is such as to warrant the appointment of three arbitrators'. Following the same policy, Article 5(8) of the LCIA Rules states: 'A sole arbitrator shall be appointed unless the parties have agreed in writing otherwise, or if the LCIA Court determines that in the circumstances a three-member tribunal is appropriate (or, exceptionally, more than three).' **4.23**

The ICDR Rules follow the same approach, with a sole arbitrator the default solution, but adding the criteria of size and complexity to the administrator's discretion as to whether to constitute a three-member tribunal. Article 5 provides: **4.24**

> If the parties have not agreed on the number of arbitrators, one arbitrator shall be appointed unless the administrator determines in its discretion that three arbitrators are appropriate because of the large size, complexity or other circumstances of the case.

There is much to be said for such a provision on grounds of speed and economy. The advantages of referring a dispute to a sole arbitrator are self-evident. Appointments for meetings or hearings can be more easily arranged with a sole arbitrator than with a tribunal of three arbitrators. The interests of economy are also served, since the parties will have to bear the fees and expenses of only one arbitrator rather than three. Moreover, the arbitral proceedings should be completed more quickly, since a sole arbitrator does not need to 'deliberate' with **4.25**

---

[30] For example, in the North American Free Trade Agreement (NAFTA) state-to-state arbitrations under NAFTA, Ch. 20, under which five arbitrators are appointed: see, e.g., *Mexico v USA (Cross-Border Trucking)* USA-98-2008-01, 6 February 2001, in which one of the authors was the chairman of the tribunal, available online at http://www.nafta-sec-alena.org/. Other examples may be found online at http://www.pca-cpa.org/, e.g. *Ireland v United Kingdom (Mox Plant)*, an arbitration pursuant to Annexe VII of the 1982 United Nations Convention on the Law of the Sea (UNCLOS), and *Channel Tunnel Group Ltd and France-Manche SA v United Kingdom and France*, Partial Award, UNCITRAL, PCA, 30 January 2007, IIC 58 (2007), an arbitration brought under a concession agreement between the parties in accordance with Art. 19 of the Treaty of Canterbury between the United Kingdom and France, dated 12 February 1986.

colleagues in an attempt to arrive at an agreed, or majority, determination of the matters in dispute. If the parties to an international arbitration are able to agree upon the appointment of a sole arbitrator in whom they both have confidence, it makes sense for them to do so.

4.26 However, if the parties cannot agree on the identity of a sole arbitrator, an arbitrator will be 'imposed' upon them—that is, an arbitrator will be chosen by a national court or by a designated appointing authority, such as the president of a professional body or one of the specialised arbitral institutions.[31] The arbitrator so chosen may or may not be suitable for the task. What is certain is that he or she will not have been chosen by the parties, but by someone else on their behalf, thus depriving the parties of one of the fundamental benefits of arbitration: choosing the judge. There is also a greater risk of error resulting from the failings of a sole arbitrator who does not benefit from the balancing factor of two further arbitrators analysing the issues in dispute.

4.27 As a consequence, there is typically a preference for the appointment of three arbitrators in all but the smallest cases. The Arbitration Rules of the United Nations Commission on International Trade Law (UNCITRAL) reflect this preference by providing that if the parties have not previously agreed otherwise, three arbitrators will be appointed.[32] A similar provision is contained in the Model Law.[33]

(ii) Two arbitrators

4.28 In certain trades and specialised markets, the practice is to submit disputes to an arbitral tribunal of two arbitrators, with a subsequent reference to an umpire if the two party-nominated arbitrators cannot agree between themselves. This practice derives from the concept of arbitration as a 'friendly' method of settling disputes and it is a system that may work reasonably well within the context of a defined trade or market. However, it is not a practice to be recommended more generally in international arbitrations. It is important, particularly in a highly contentious dispute, that there should be someone who can take the lead within the arbitral tribunal. If there is only one arbitrator, there is no problem: a sole arbitrator is unmistakably in charge of the proceedings. The position is the same with a tribunal of three arbitrators, in which case the presiding arbitrator is plainly in charge. However, if there are two arbitrators, which of them is to lead? How much time are they required to spend in discussion before deciding (if such is the case) that they cannot agree? If they cannot agree, whose responsibility is it to inform the parties and to ensure that steps are taken to appoint an umpire? Within the confines of a trade association, these kinds of problems rarely arise; if they do arise, they may be dealt with relatively easily by trade practice. In mainstream international

---

[31] The procedure for the appointment of arbitrators is discussed paragraphs 4.33*ff.*
[32] UNCITRAL Rules, Art. 7(1).
[33] Model Law, Art. 10(2).

A. Background

arbitration, it is preferable to avoid such problems by avoiding altogether the 'two arbitrator' system.

(iii) Three arbitrators

4.29 Modern preference is for international disputes to be referred to an arbitral tribunal comprising three arbitrators, unless the amount in dispute is small. This preference has much to commend it. Each of the parties will usually have the right to nominate at least one arbitrator, leaving the third arbitrator to be chosen by agreement or by a third-party institution.

4.30 The advantage to a party of being able to nominate an arbitrator is that it gives the party concerned a sense of investment in the arbitral tribunal. Each party will have at least one 'judge of its choice' to listen to its case. This is particularly important in an international arbitration, in which, in addition to the matters formally in issue, there may well be differences of language, tradition, and culture between the parties, and, indeed, between the members of the arbitral tribunal themselves. An arbitrator nominated by a party will be able to make sure that the arbitral tribunal properly understands the case of the appointing party. In particular, such an arbitrator should be able to ensure that any misunderstandings that may arise during the deliberations of the arbitral tribunal (for example because of differences of legal practice, culture, or language) are resolved before they lead to injustice. In this way, a party-nominated arbitrator can fulfil a useful role in ensuring due process for the party that nominated him or her, without stepping outside the bounds of independence and impartiality.[34]

4.31 A three-member tribunal is more expensive than an arbitration conducted by a sole arbitrator and will usually take longer to render an award. However, the 'quality of justice' is likely to be less subject to the foibles and failings of an individual member. Indeed, in a process in which there is no effective appeal on the merits, the risk of an error of law or fact by a three-member tribunal is far lower than that of a sole arbitrator with no colleagues to correct or with whom to debate an inadvertent mistake or misunderstanding.

(iv) Four or more arbitrators

4.32 It is difficult to envisage circumstances in which it would make sense to appoint four arbitrators—or, indeed (leaving aside trade tribunals), any even number. As far as the mainstream of international arbitration is concerned, it is sensible to follow the lead of those countries that make it compulsory for an uneven number of arbitrators to be appointed. Nor is there usually any good reason for appointing an arbitral tribunal of more than three members. Even in a case of major importance, three carefully chosen and appropriately qualified arbitrators should be sufficient to dispose satisfactorily of the issues in dispute. The practice of states in appointing

---

[34] See paragraphs 4.75*ff.*

arbitral tribunals of five, seven, or more is usually dictated by political, rather than by practical, considerations.

B. Appointment of Arbitrators

(a) Introduction

4.33 There are several different methods of appointing an arbitral tribunal. The most usual are:

- by agreement of the parties;
- by an arbitral institution;
- by means of a list system;
- by means of the co-arbitrators appointing a presiding arbitrator;
- by a professional institution or a trade association; or
- by a national court.

Each method is now considered in turn.

(i) Agreement of the parties

4.34 A major attraction of arbitration is that it allows parties to submit a dispute to judges of their own choice rather than requiring that choice to be exercised by a third party on their behalf.[35] Where an arbitral tribunal is to consist of more than one arbitrator, it is usual for each party to nominate one arbitrator, leaving the third arbitrator to be appointed by one of the other methods mentioned above.

4.35 Sometimes, a party seeking to undermine an arbitration will refuse to appoint an arbitrator, or a party-appointed arbitrator will refuse to agree on a third arbitrator. This situation can best be avoided by a provision in the arbitration agreement, or in the applicable arbitration rules, that allows an experienced institution to intervene and make the appointment in the event of default.[36] In an ad hoc arbitration, it is often necessary to fall back on the *lex arbitri*, which normally provides for the appointment to be made by the court of the seat of the arbitration. Although most national courts will make an appointment in such a situation, relying on national courts inevitably leads to greater delay and relative uncertainty. Furthermore, national courts may not have a sufficiently international perspective to make a suitable appointment in an international case. It is therefore wise to ensure that there is a fallback position in the clause, by choosing either an institutional arbitration or, in the case of an ad hoc arbitration, an

---

[35] See n. 13 in respect of the debate that has arisen as to the pros and cons of what Paulsson has referred to as 'unilateral party appointments'.
[36] See, e.g., ICC Rules, Art. 12(2); LCIA Rules, Art. 7(2).

B. Appointment of Arbitrators

appointing authority that will take responsibility for the appointment of the remaining arbitrators.

(ii) Appointment by arbitral institutions

Arbitral institutions invariably have their own rules for appointing arbitrators. The ICC Rules, for example, provide that, where there is to be a sole arbitrator and the parties fail to reach an agreed nomination within thirty days from the communication of the request for arbitration to the other party, the arbitrator will be appointed by the ICC Court. The Rules also provide that, where there is to be an arbitral tribunal of three arbitrators, the third arbitrator will be appointed by the ICC Court, unless the parties have agreed upon another procedure, in which case the agreed appointment must be made within a limited time.[37] The rules of each of the ICDR, LCIA, and the World Intellectual Property Organization (WIPO) contain similar provisions.[38] In contrast, the China International Economic and Trade Arbitration Commission (CIETAC) Rules require parties to nominate their respective arbitrators from CIETAC's designated panel of arbitrators; alternatively, if they agree to nominate from outside the panel of arbitrators, then that nomination is subject to confirmation by the chairman of CIETAC.[39]

4.36

In an ad hoc arbitration, there is no automatic intervention by an arbitral institution if agreement is not reached between the parties. The default procedure of most national arbitration systems is appointment of the remaining arbitrators by the relevant national court. As a preferred alternative, the parties may choose an arbitral institution as appointing authority in their arbitration clause. Many arbitral institutions offer their services as appointing authority for a fee, including the ICC, the ICDR, the LCIA, and the Permanent Court of Arbitration (PCA) in The Hague.[40] The secretary-general of ICSID is also prepared to act as 'designating', or appointing, authority for ad hoc arbitration agreements that do not fall within the scope of the ICSID Convention. What the arbitral institutions and international bodies have to offer, compared to professional societies and trade associations, are their day-to-day involvement in international arbitration and their access to a pool of highly qualified arbitrators. They know the qualities required in the persons whom they appoint and they usually know the potential candidates.

4.37

(iii) List system

When a 'list system' is used, each party compiles a list of three or four persons considered to be acceptable arbitrators, perhaps with a brief note of the relevant

4.38

---

[37] ICC Rules, Art. 12(4) and (5).
[38] ICDR Rules, Art. 6; LCIA Rules, Art. 5; WIPO Rules, Art. 19.
[39] CIETAC Rules, Art. 23.
[40] Fees for this service are typically £1,250 for the LCIA, €1,500 for the secretary-general of the PCA, and US$3,000 for the ICC. These figures are available on each institution's website.

experience and qualifications of each. The lists are then exchanged in an attempt to reach agreement. The procedure has several advantages. Sometimes, the same person may be named on each list. Even if this is not the case, the process focuses the thinking of the parties and their advisers on the type of arbitrator required, and may help to pave the way towards agreement.[41]

4.39 A variation on this system, sometimes used by arbitral institutions—particularly the ICDR, the SCC, and the Netherlands Arbitration Institute (NAI)—is the dispatch by the institution of the *same* list of names to each party. Each party returns the list, deleting any name to which it objects and grading the remainder in order of preference. The appointing authority then chooses an arbitrator from the list, in accordance with the order of preference indicated by the parties. The system is slower than that of direct appointment by an arbitral institution, but has the advantage of offering the parties an element of choice (even though this choice is necessarily restricted to persons initially named by the institution on its list).[42] The same procedure may also be used to choose the presiding arbitrator for an arbitral tribunal of three arbitrators.[43]

(iv) Appointment by co-arbitrators of the presiding arbitrator

4.40 Where a tribunal of three arbitrators is to be constituted, the arbitration clause or submission agreement often provides that each party is to nominate one arbitrator and that the two arbitrators so nominated will choose the third, who acts as the presiding arbitrator. This is perhaps the most satisfactory way of nominating a third arbitrator, since the party-nominated arbitrators will presumably have confidence in their chosen candidate. It is usual for each of the arbitrators to consult with the party who nominated them as to the identity of the presiding arbitrator and, by this means, to ensure that the appointee is acceptable to all concerned.[44] In this context, the party-nominated arbitrators should inform each other that this procedure is being followed.

---

[41] One problem that has arisen in practice when the list system has failed and the appointment has been left to a third-party institution, or court, relates to the appointing authority appointing a person who has appeared on one of the party's lists. It is not uncommon for the other party to object to such an appointment on the basis that the candidate has already been discussed by the parties, thereby 'burning' all of those names. To avoid this risk, it is useful to agree in advance of using a list system that the inclusion of a name on the list will not operate as a bar to the eventual appointment of such a person by the arbitral institution or appointing authority. Another, more tactical, approach is for a party not to nominate the person whom it wants on the first list, but to keep the name in reserve, so that it might emerge in subsequent negotiations. However, such gamesmanship may prove to be self-defeating if the other party agrees to a person named on the first list!

[42] UNCITRAL Rules, Art. 8(2).

[43] UNCITRAL Rules, Art. 9(3).

[44] The IBA Guidelines on Party Representation in International Arbitration, published in May 2013, provide that communications between a party representative and a prospective or party-nominated arbitrator relating to the selection of the presiding arbitrator fall outside the general rule that party representatives should not engage in *ex parte* communications with an arbitrator concerning the arbitration (see Guideline 8(b)).

B. Appointment of Arbitrators

(v) Professional institution

The president or a senior officer of a professional institution may be named as the appointing authority in arbitration clauses. The persons so-named are usually ready to discharge this duty. Indeed, professional institutions often maintain lists of members ready to serve as arbitrators. However, a professional institution should be used as an appointing authority only where the dispute is almost certainly likely to be of a highly technical nature in which that institution specialises. **4.41**

(vi) National courts

If the parties are unable to reach agreement upon the appointment of an arbitrator and where no one is expressly empowered to make the appointment for them, it is necessary to consider whether there is any national court that has the jurisdiction and the power to make the necessary appointment. The parties should look first to the seat of the arbitration (if this has been determined), since it is usually the courts of the seat that have the power to nominate any remaining members of the tribunal, irrespective of the nationality of the parties or the law governing the substance of the dispute. The relevant rules are usually set out in the arbitration law of the seat (which may be a separate statute or part of a wider code of civil procedure). It is usually sufficient for the claimant (who is invariably the party most interested in proceeding speedily) to apply to the relevant court for the appropriate appointment. For example, under the English Arbitration Act 1996, the courts have default powers: **4.42**

- to give directions as to the making of any necessary appointments;
- to direct that the tribunal shall be constituted by such appointments (or any one or more of them) as have been made;
- to revoke any appointments already made; or
- to make any necessary appointments itself.[45]

In making any appointments, a court will often ask the parties' lawyers, or the party-nominated arbitrators, to suggest possible candidates.

In principle, a national court will have *jurisdiction* where the arbitration is to be conducted on its territory.[46] Accordingly, there should be no problem where the seat of arbitration is specified in the arbitration clause or submission agreement: the party wishing to proceed with the arbitration simply applies to the appropriate national court for the appointment to be made. However, a problem arises if the seat of arbitration has not been specified in the arbitration clause or submission agreement. It may be possible to persuade a court to assume jurisdiction, for example on the basis that the law governing the substantive issues in dispute is the law **4.43**

---

[45] English Arbitration Act 1996, s. 18(3).
[46] See the discussion concerning the *lex arbitri* in Chapter 2, paragraphs 2.08*ff*.

of the country of that court, or that the respondent is within the jurisdiction of the court (and so capable of being compelled to carry out its orders).[47]

4.44 This situation offers a clear example of the dangers inherent in a defective, or 'pathological', arbitration clause. A clause that fails to provide either for an effective method of constituting the arbitral tribunal or for the place of arbitration may turn out to be inoperable. It is likely to lead to the claimant being unable to enforce the arbitration agreement. If a claimant takes its case to a national court, it may be met by an application for a stay of the proceedings on the grounds of the existence of an arbitration clause. At best, there is considerable potential for delay. At worst, there is the possibility that the claimant may find that there is no effective remedy at all, since the courts will refuse to entertain an action and the arbitration clause is defective.

4.45 The powers of a national court to appoint an arbitrator are less likely to give rise to problems. Countries with developed systems of arbitration law recognise the role that needs to be played by their law and by their courts in assisting the arbitral process. Accordingly, national courts are usually empowered to appoint arbitrators in circumstances in which it becomes necessary for one of the parties to a dispute to request them to do so. Wide powers to appoint arbitrators and umpires are contained in most modern national codes of law governing arbitration.[48] However, it should not be assumed that the relevant court will necessarily have the requisite power, nor should it be assumed that any powers that it does possess will necessarily apply to the particular situation that has arisen. The position under the relevant local law should be checked carefully at the time of selecting the place of arbitration, particularly if no specific method of establishing the arbitral tribunal has been agreed.

(vii) Appointing authority

4.46 Parties should recognise that, in the case of an ad hoc arbitration, it is in their common interest to choose an appointing authority by agreement—or, at least, to

---

[47] For example, the English court may appoint an arbitrator where the seat of arbitration has not been designated, provided that the proceedings have sufficient connection with England: English Arbitration Act 1996, ss 2(4) and 18. Under the new French Arbitration Act, the president of the Paris Tribunal de Grande Instance may act in support of an international arbitration located abroad if (a) the parties have agreed that French procedural law shall apply to the arbitration, or (b) the parties have expressly granted jurisdiction to French courts over disputes relating to the arbitral procedure, or (c) one of the parties is exposed to a risk of a denial of justice (understood as the impossibility to constitute the arbitral tribunal by any other means): French Code of Civil Procedure, art. 1505(2), (3), and (4). See also Seraglini and Ortscheidt, *Droit de l'Arbitrage Interne et International* (Prix du Cercle Montesquieu, 2013), paras 765–772.

[48] See, e.g., Swiss PIL, Ch. 12, s. 179; French Code of Civil Procedure, Decree Law No. 2011–48 of 13 January 2011, art. 1452. Article 11 of the Model Law confers upon the appropriate national courts the power to appoint arbitrators where necessary. In England, the Arbitration Act 1996, s. 18, gives the court the power to make an appointment where the arbitration agreement provides for an appointing authority to perform the task and the authority refuses or fails to do so.

B. Appointment of Arbitrators

choose a method of designating an appointing authority. One way of doing this is to adopt the UNCITRAL Rules, or simply the Articles of those Rules that relate to the designation of the appointing authority and its functions. Under these Rules, if the parties have not agreed upon an appointing authority, then, after fulfilling certain preliminary requirements, a party may request the secretary-general of the PCA to designate one.[49]

(viii) Designation by the secretary-general of the Permanent Court of Arbitration

The UNCITRAL Rules do not specify the information that must be supplied to the secretary-general for the purposes of designating an appointing authority, but, in practice, the PCA asks for the same documents that are to be provided to an appointing authority under Article 8(1) of the Rules for the purposes of appointing an arbitrator. These include the notice of arbitration, the contract out of which the dispute has arisen, and (if it is not contained in that contract) the arbitration agreement. The secretary-general will usually also request copies of correspondence indicating that the designation of an appointing authority is necessary because a party has failed to appoint an arbitrator, or that it has been impossible to reach agreement on a sole or presiding arbitrator, or that there is a contested challenge of an arbitrator.

4.47

If the respondent does not participate in making a request, the secretary-general writes to the respondent to invite comments and specifies a reasonable time for reply. Before designating an appointing authority, the secretary-general may also ask for the names of potential arbitrators and appointing authorities that have been discussed between the parties and rejected.[50] After reviewing the documents submitted and considering any comments from the parties, the secretary-general selects the organisation or individual that he or she considers best placed to perform the function of appointing authority.[51] The secretary-general then enquires whether that organisation or individual is willing to accept the designation. If the

4.48

---

[49] UNCITRAL Rules, Art. 6(2).

[50] Hence the need to be clear, before discussing candidates between the parties, whether candidates discussed and rejected may subsequently be appointed by an appointing authority, or if they are excluded as a result.

[51] The views of the parties, as well as concerns of speed and cost, may influence the secretary-general's choice of an individual, rather than an organisation. the secretary-general's designations of organisations include ACICA, the American Arbitration Association (AAA), the Arbitral Centre of the Austrian Federal Economic Chamber, the Bombay Incorporated Law Society, the Cairo Regional Centre for International Commercial Arbitration (CRCICA), the Chartered Institute of Arbitrators (CIArb), the German Arbitration Institute (DIS), the HKIAC, the ICC, ICSID, the Kuala Lumpur Regional Centre for Arbitration (KLRCA), the LCIA, SIAC, and the Swiss Arbitration Association. Examples of designations of individuals include: a former chief justice of New South Wales, Australia, in a dispute between a Korean company and an Asian state entity; an international arbitration practitioner based in the United Kingdom, in a dispute between a French company and the government of a Central European Republic; and an international arbitration practitioner based in the United States, in a dispute between a Dutch company and an African state entity.

answer is in the affirmative, the parties are informed of that decision and requested to approach the appointing authority direct for the next step to be taken in the arbitration. The secretary-general does not give reasons for the decision.[52]

C. Qualities Required in International Arbitrators

(a) Introduction

4.49 In most arbitration systems, any natural person may be chosen to act as an arbitrator, the only general requirement being that the person chosen must have legal capacity. However, the choice of an arbitrator is critical and information as to the potential candidates' experience in the subject matter of the arbitration, as well as his or her specific procedural and substantive tendencies, should be sought.[53] Much of this information may be obtained from informal discussion within the arbitration community—either by asking other members of the community, or hearing the candidates speak at conferences. Within law firms with specialist arbitration teams, such consultation is effective and quick, given the combined experience of the group. Once armed with this information, a decision can be taken as to the person to whom the dispute will be entrusted.

(b) Restrictions imposed by the contract

4.50 Some standard forms of international contracts—particularly those used in the shipping and commodity trades, and the insurance and reinsurance industries—identify the kind of arbitrator to be chosen in the event of a dispute. Some institutional rules require that the arbitrator be nominated from a list held by that institution; others require that the chairman or sole arbitrator be a qualified lawyer.[54] In general terms, it is not advisable to fix a list of arbitrator qualifications, since there may not be someone who fulfils those criteria and is available to act as arbitrator at the time that a dispute arises, with the corresponding risk that the arbitral clause will be inoperable. Much will depend on the nature of the restriction. It may be acceptable to include limitations requiring that all arbitrators be fluent in the language of the contract (or the likely language of the dispute) and, occasionally, there are limitations on the residence or nationality of the arbitrators (with the aim of avoiding arbitrators with the same nationality as one of the parties).[55] However, the establishment of strict qualifications prior

---

[52] By 2014, the secretary-general had dealt with more than 550 requests to designate an appointing authority or to act directly as the appointing authority, forty-one of which were in 2014 alone. See PCA, *Annual Report of the Permanent Court of Arbitration* (PCA, 2014), p. 25.
[53] See the discussion in Chapter 1.
[54] See DIS Rules, Art. 2(2).
[55] In this regard, see the discussion of the English courts' decisions in *Jivraj v Hashwani* on the validity of nationality limitations on arbitrator appointments at para 4.62.

C. Qualities Required in International Arbitrators

to the dispute arising may give rise to problems, since the same contract may generate disputes of a very differing nature. As a matter of experience, it is best not to stipulate criteria before a particular dispute has arisen. This then gives the parties the greatest flexibility to nominate the most appropriate arbitrators for the circumstances of the particular dispute.

Where such contractual criteria do nevertheless exist, it is good practice for the selected arbitrator to obtain a clear written confirmation from the parties at the beginning of the arbitral process that the criteria are considered fulfilled, or a clear waiver that a particular requirement is no longer considered necessary. In this way, the arbitrator will avoid the risk of the issue being later deployed by a party as a defence to enforcement in the event that it has lost the arbitration.[56] **4.51**

(c) Restrictions imposed by the applicable law

The number of countries that impose restrictions on the choice of an arbitrator has decreased since the early editions of this work. In its latest arbitration legislation, Spain, for example, repealed its former rule that the arbitrator must be a qualified lawyer where the dispute involves issues of law.[57] In 2012, Saudi Arabia removed the requirement that all arbitrators be male and have knowledge of Shari'ah law (although the presiding arbitrator in a panel of three is still required to hold a degree in Shari'ah).[58] **4.52**

(d) Professional qualifications

International disputes are too varied and too numerous for it to be sensible to identify any general rule as to the kind of person who should be chosen to act as an arbitrator. Parties must make up their own minds as to the qualifications that they require in an arbitrator. The most that can be done is to indicate some of the more important considerations. **4.53**

(i) Sole arbitrator

In international arbitrations (as distinct from domestic arbitrations) before a sole arbitrator, it is usual to appoint a lawyer. Even where the dispute is relatively simple, difficult problems of procedure and of conflict of laws can regularly arise. These are problems that a lawyer with suitable procedural and legal experience is generally **4.54**

---

[56] For example, on the basis that the arbitral tribunal was not constituted in accordance with the agreement of the parties: see New York Convention, Art. V(1)(d).
[57] Spanish Arbitration Act 2003, s. 13, repealing the 1988 Act, s. 12(2).
[58] Saudi Arabia's new arbitration law came into force in July 2012. The new Arbitration Regulation (Royal Decree No. M/34) is based on the principles of the UNCITRAL Model Law and has significantly modernised the pre-existing law in many respects, including in the requirements of arbitrators: see Harb and Leventhal, 'The new Saudi Arbitration Law: Modernization to the tune of Shari'a' (2013) 30 J Intl Arb 113.

better equipped to handle than a person whose expertise lies in another area. In ICC arbitrations, for example, most arbitrators are lawyers or professors of law.[59]

(ii) Three arbitrators

4.55 Where the arbitral tribunal is to consist of three arbitrators, at least one member of the arbitral tribunal (preferably the presiding arbitrator) should be a lawyer, or at least a person who has considerable experience of acting as arbitrator in international disputes, since someone will need to understand how to drive the process forward.[60]

4.56 There is no reason why the other two members of the arbitral tribunal should also always be lawyers, unless the dispute is one in which the issues involved are principally complex issues of law. Part of the attraction of arbitration is the way in which the expertise necessary for the understanding and resolution of the dispute may be found amongst the arbitrators themselves. For example, if a dispute arises out of an international construction contract involving matters of a technical nature, it may be appropriate that one (or more) of the members of the arbitral tribunal should be a civil engineer, or someone skilled in the particular technical matters that are in issue.

4.57 However, if the presiding arbitrator is likely to be a lawyer, a party should consider carefully before nominating a technical arbitrator in cases in which the other party has nominated a lawyer. This combination may result in the arbitral tribunal having two lawyers 'against' a technical expert arbitrator. It may therefore be better 'tactically' for the parties to seek to agree that, given the technical nature of a particular dispute, each will appoint, say, an engineer or an economist, with a lawyer as the presiding arbitrator.

(e) Language

4.58 An arbitrator must have an adequate working knowledge of the language in which the arbitration is to take place, so that he or she will understand the evidence and be able to draft an award in that language. Quite separately, the arbitrator should also understand the language in which most of the written evidence is drafted, or in which most of the oral evidence will be given. Whilst English has generally been adopted as the working language of international commerce for contracts between parties that speak different languages, it is far from clear that the underlying documents and evidence will be in that language. If an arbitrator is appointed who does not have a sufficient knowledge of the language of the evidence, it becomes

---

[59] For a view on the varied profiles of arbitrators in investment treaty arbitration, which now regularly includes retired diplomats, migrating commercial arbitrators, and former judges, see van den Berg, 'Qualified investment arbitrators?', in Wautelet, Kruger, and Coppens (eds) *The Practice of Arbitration: Essays in Honour of Hans van Houtte* (Hart, 2012), p. 54.

[60] Ibid.

C. Qualities Required in International Arbitrators

necessary to engage translators and interpreters to translate the evidence of the witnesses and the documents into a language that the arbitrator concerned *can* understand.

(f) Experience and outlook

4.59 Careful thought should be given to the particular experience or outlook of a particular arbitrator. Since most arbitrations are private, it is often difficult for newcomers to the field to assess whether or not a particular candidate may be an appropriate appointment. Will the person be organised and efficient? What is his or her ability to handle complex arbitration issues? Does he or she have sufficient knowledge of the applicable substantive law? Is he or she likely to be a consensus builder? What kind of approach does he or she have to contractual interpretation? Many of these questions can be answered only by experienced arbitration practitioners familiar with the community of international arbitrators and the manner in which they conduct proceedings. In this context, it is worthwhile considering consulting with experienced practitioners in respect of this vital decision, lest one of the key benefits of arbitration—that of choosing a judge—become something of a lottery.

(g) Availability

4.60 The criterion of experience may conflict with the criterion of availability. Some of the most experienced international arbitrators are also the busiest. Their consequent lack of availability, resulting in significant delays in convening hearings and rendering awards, has become a major frustration for users of a process that was originally intended to be quicker than the courts of law. For this reason, there are increasingly compelling reasons to look beyond the 'usual suspects' in appointing arbitrators.[61] Indeed, ascertaining a prospective arbitrator's availability (by asking concrete, rather than general, questions about competing commitments) before making an appointment may be as important in ensuring an efficient and effective process as establishing his or her experience. The ICC now requires all prospective arbitrators to disclose in how many cases they are sitting as co-arbitrator and chairman, and to confirm that they have adequate availability to discharge their mandate, at the time that they complete their 'statement of acceptance, availability, impartiality and independence'.[62] This allows either party to make objections

---

[61] As far as gender diversity is concerned, the number of female arbitrators, whilst growing, remains disappointingly low. As at August 2014, only 5.61 per cent of the appointed arbitrators in concluded ICSID cases were female. In 2013, 13 per cent of LCIA arbitrators were female: see Greenwood and Barber, 'Is the balance getting better? An update on the issue of gender diversity in international arbitration' (2015) Arb Intl, online at http://arbitration.oxfordjournals.org/content/early/2015/05/02/arbint.aiv034. See also Rothman, 'Gender diversity in arbitrator selection', Dispute Resolution Magazine, Spring 2012, p. 22.

[62] The latest version of the statement was introduced in January 2012 and is sent by the ICC to arbitrators when they are appointed to complete. The statement requires arbitrators to confirm their acceptance of the relevant appointment, their ability to 'devote the time necessary to conduct

based on perceived lack of availability, and the ICC may refuse to confirm appointments on this basis. In Article 5(4) of its 2014 Rules, the LCIA requires candidates for appointment as arbitrators to confirm that they are 'ready, willing and able to devote sufficient time, diligence and industry to ensure the expeditious and efficient conduct of the arbitration'.

(h) Nationality

4.61 In an ideal world, the country in which the arbitrator was born or the passport that he or she carries should be irrelevant. The qualifications, experience, and integrity of the arbitrator should be the essential criteria. It ought to be possible to proceed in the spirit of the Model Law, which, addressing this question, provides simply: 'No person shall be precluded by reason of his nationality from acting as an arbitrator, unless otherwise agreed by the parties.'[63] Nevertheless, in the interests of the perception of neutrality, the usual practice in international arbitration is to appoint a sole arbitrator (or a presiding arbitrator) of a different nationality from that of the parties to the dispute.

4.62 The validity of nationality limitations on arbitrator appointments, which are found in most institutional rules, was recently cast into doubt following a ruling of the English Court of Appeal in *Jivraj v Hashwani*.[64] In a decision that caused surprise around the world, the Court found that arbitrators are 'employed' by the parties and therefore subject to employment equality laws that made 'nationality' restrictions illegal. In a welcome reversal, however, the Supreme Court of England and Wales subsequently confirmed that arbitrators are not 'employees' of the parties and therefore not subject to such employment equality laws.[65] This decision confirms the long-standing (and entirely understandable) practice of requiring the nationalities of sole or presiding arbitrators, unless the parties agree otherwise, to differ from those of the parties.[66]

4.63 Indeed, the current practice under most sets of institutional rules is that the sole or presiding arbitrator will almost certainly be someone of a different nationality from that of the parties to the dispute. Article 6(7) of the UNCITRAL Rules, for example, provides that, in making the appointment:

> The appointing authority shall have regard to such considerations as are likely to secure the appointment of an independent and impartial arbitrator and shall take

---

[the] arbitration diligently, efficiently and in accordance with the time limits in the Rules', and the number of pending cases in which they are involved.

[63] Model Law, Art. 11(1).
[64] [2011] 1 WLR 1872.
[65] *Jivraj v Hashwani* [2011] UKSC 40.
[66] More generally, this decision upholds the principle of party autonomy in the selection of arbitrators, since the Court refused to use public policy to fetter the parties' freedom to agree what qualities and attributes their arbitrators should have. The judgment is discussed in depth in Style and Cleobury, '*Jivraj v Hashwani*: Public interest and party autonomy' (2012) 27 Arb Intl 563.

C. Qualities Required in International Arbitrators

into account as well the *advisability* of appointing an arbitrator of a nationality other than the nationalities of the parties.[67]

4.64 Article 13(5) of the ICC Rules goes further and provides that '[t]he sole arbitrator or the chairman of an arbitral tribunal *shall* be of a nationality other than those of the parties'.[68] Another provision allows an exception to this rule 'in suitable circumstances and provided that neither of the parties objects', but nevertheless the general rule is clear: it is a rule of neutral nationality. The LCIA and HKIAC Rules take a similar line. Article 6(1) of the LCIA Rules provides:

> Where the parties are of different nationalities, a sole arbitrator or the presiding arbitrator shall not have the same nationality as any party unless the parties who are not of the same nationality as the arbitral candidate all agree in writing otherwise.[69]

4.65 Article 6(4) of the ICDR Rules takes a slightly different approach, whilst broadly embracing the same principle:

> In making such appointments, the administrator, after inviting consultation with the parties, shall endeavour to select suitable arbitrators. At the request of any party or on its own initiative, the administrator may appoint nationals of a country other than that of any of the parties.

4.66 The CIETAC Rules are less prescriptive, Article 28 simply listing 'the nationalities of the parties' as one of several considerations for the chairman to take into account when appointing arbitrators pursuant to the rules.

4.67 In light of a swathe of recent cases from other parts of the world—in particular, Latin America and Asia—there is now a growing community of arbitrators from those regions who bring a fresh perspective to arbitration. Relevant statistics are not easy to find, but there are signs that more arbitrators from developing countries are being appointed. The ICC's statistics, for example, show that tribunals in a growing number of cases include arbitrators from outside Western Europe and North America, from countries such as Brazil, Mexico, and Poland.[70] Evidence from ICSID also bears witness to a broad geographic spread of arbitral appointments, ranging from the Philippines to Argentina.[71]

---

[67] Emphasis added.
[68] Emphasis added.
[69] See similar provision in HKIAC Rules, Art. 11(2), which is described as a general rule that, subject to Art. 11(3), allows an exception in 'appropriate circumstances' and provided that none of the parties objects within a time limit set by HKIAC.
[70] ICC, 'ICC arbitration: A ten-year statistical overview' (2008) 19 ICC International Court of Arbitration Bulletin 1, at 10. In 2012, arbitrators of seventy-six nationalities were appointed or confirmed under the ICC Rules. By contrast, there were seventy-three in 2009, sixty-six in 2007, sixty-one in 2004, and fifty-seven in 1999: http://www.iccwbo.org/.
[71] For an indication of the geographic diversity, see the list of ICSID arbitrators on the ICSID website.

(i) Education and training

4.68 The most important qualification for an international arbitrator is experience in the law and practice of arbitration. There is no sense in appointing an experienced lawyer as sole or presiding arbitrator responsible for advancing the process if that experience does not include practical experience of arbitration. The reputation and acceptability of international arbitration depends upon the quality of the arbitrators themselves. The task of presiding over the conduct of an international commercial arbitration is no less skilled than that of a surgeon conducting an operation, or a pilot flying an aircraft. It should not be entrusted to someone with no practical experience of it.

4.69 It follows that there should be some recognised and effective process by which potential international arbitration practitioners, who may eventually become arbitrators, can acquire the necessary skills. There must always be a new generation in prospect. This has been recognised by some arbitral institutions and some now run training programmes for prospective arbitrators. Such programmes are to be encouraged, although institutions should be careful to avoid any perception that they offer these products purely for the purposes of generating profits.[72]

4.70 In order to ensure that there is continuity between generations, the ICC, the PCA, and UNCITRAL operate internship schemes under which young lawyers and postgraduate students work inside those institutions for a period of several months. The different arbitral institutions have also established 'young practitioner' groups that enable the younger members of the arbitration practitioner community to meet each other and debate arbitration topics, thus creating a network of future potential arbitrators.[73]

4.71 Another practical proposal that has gained popularity is that young practitioners and students from different parts of the world are invited—with the consent of the parties—to attend hearings as observers. They are also offered internships by leading international arbitrators, who—again with the consent of the parties—arrange for them to serve as arbitral secretaries. Furthermore, because many firms now have dedicated arbitration practices, young associates have an opportunity to observe the conduct of an arbitration from the perspective of counsel and secretary.

---

[72] The Chartered Institute of Arbitrators (CIArb), headquartered in London, offers courses that include a two-part examination structure and a system of 'pupillage' under which, with the consent of the parties, trainee arbitrators may attend hearings. The Institute also provides special programmes for potential international arbitrators, which are held all over the world. The ICDR also conducts training programmes for arbitrators on its various panels and offers courses in a number of different countries.

[73] The LCIA established the 'Young International Arbitration Group' in 1997. This has since been followed by the ICC 'Under 40' Group, ICDR's 'Young & International', the Swiss Arbitration Association's 'Below 40' Group, and 'Young ICCA'.

C. Qualities Required in International Arbitrators

(j) Interviewing prospective arbitrators

4.72 It is common for counsel to draw up a list of prospective party-nominated arbitrators who are invited to interviews by representatives of a party. In the past, a number of eminent European arbitrators declined to participate in such interviews on the grounds that they were, at best, demeaning and, at worst, improper. However, this practice should not be objectionable in principle, provided that it is engaged in openly and that the scope of the discussion is appropriately restricted. A prospective arbitrator may be questioned, for example, as to potential conflicts of interest. In this regard, the candidate should be supplied with the names of the parties and counsel. He or she may also be questioned on his or her experience in the relevant field, qualifications for the case in hand, and availability. It is also reasonable for a party's representatives to have an opportunity to assess the candidate's physical and mental health. However, there should be no attempt to ascertain (directly or indirectly) the prospective arbitrator's views on the substantive or procedural issues that are expected to arise in the case.[74]

4.73 One distinguished US arbitrator has identified his own guidelines, having informed the interviewers of them in advance. First, other than in exceptional circumstances, the interviewers must travel to see him in his office (that is, he will not respond to a 'summons' to the premises of the party concerned or their representatives). Secondly, the interviewing delegation must be led by an *external* lawyer retained by the party in question (that is, he will not see the party's employees on their own). Thirdly, the meeting should not be conducted over lunch or other event involving hospitality—regardless of who will pay the bill. Fourthly, he will take a note of the discussion that he will regard as disclosable to interested parties if appropriate. And fifthly, if appointed, he will inform the arbitrator nominated by the other party of both the fact and the content of the discussion with the party that appointed him. These are sensible guidelines that should avoid any real risk of impropriety—and prospective arbitrators would be wise to adopt a similar system, or to adapt them in a way that seems appropriate to the circumstances of individual cases.[75]

4.74 More difficult is the question of interviewing prospective sole or presiding arbitrators in cases in which the arbitration agreement calls for the appointment to be made by agreement between the parties. Again, there can be no objection in principle, provided that both parties' representatives are present and the discussion is carefully controlled.

---

[74] Parties can agree in advance to adhere to specific guidelines during interviews, e.g. CIArb's 2011 Guidelines on the Interviewing of Prospective Arbitrators.

[75] See Chartered Institute Guidelines and IBA Guidelines on Party Representation in International Arbitration (2013). See also Bishop and Reed, 'Practical guidelines for interviewing, selecting and challenging party-appointed arbitrators in international commercial arbitration' (1998) 4 Arb Intl 395.

D. Independence and Impartiality of Arbitrators

(a) Introduction

4.75 It is a fundamental principle in international arbitration that every arbitrator must be, and must remain, independent and impartial of the parties and the dispute.[76] Although some confusion arose from the former practice in US domestic arbitrations whereby party-nominated arbitrators were to be considered 'non-neutral',[77] the 2004 Revision of the American Arbitration Association (AAA)/American Bar Association (ABA) Code of Ethics for Arbitrators in Commercial Disputes reversed this domestic arbitration presumption. There is now a presumption of neutrality for all arbitrators, including party-appointed arbitrators, to be applied unless the parties' agreement, the arbitration rules agreed to by the parties, or applicable laws provide otherwise.[78] This was already the case in international commercial arbitration conducted in the United States,[79] and so this has 'brought the American system of arbitrator ethics substantially into line with international norms'.[80]

4.76 Experienced practitioners recognise that the deliberate appointment of a partisan arbitrator is, in any event, often counterproductive: the remaining arbitrators will very soon perceive what is happening and the influence of the partisan arbitrator during the tribunal's deliberations will be—at the very least—diminished. It is a far better practice to appoint a person who may, by reason of culture or background, be broadly in sympathy with the case theory to be put forward, but who will be strictly impartial when it comes to assessing the facts and evaluating the arguments on fact and law.

---

[76] See the discussion in Chapter 1. See LCIA Rules, Art. 10(1) and (3); ICC Rules 2012, Art. 14(1); UNCITRAL Rules 2010, Art. 12; ICDR Rules, Art. 8(1); SIAC Rules 2010, Art. 11(1); HKIAC Rules, Art. 11(4); CIETAC Rules 2012, Art. 29(2).

[77] The 1977 AAA/ABA Code of Ethics for Arbitrators in Commercial Disputes (Canon VII, Introductory Note) provided for this presumption. According to one commentator, this resulted from a conception that arbitration was to be considered to be a form of alternative dispute resolution (ADR) rather than neutral adjudication: see Finizio, 'The partial arbitrator: US developments relating to arbitrator bias' (2004) 7 Intl Arb L Rev 88. This approach was fully supported by the courts, which states that 'a party-appointed arbitrator is permitted, and should be expected, to be predisposed towards the nominating party's case': *Del Monte Corporation v Sunkist Growers* 10 F.3d 753, 760 (11th Cir. 1993).

[78] AAA/ABA Code of Ethics for Arbitrators in Commercial Disputes (2004). The approach set out in the Code has been approved by subsequent court judgments: see, e.g., *Borst v Allstate Insurance Co.* 717 NW.2d 42, 48 (Wis. 2006); *Applied Industrial Materials Corporation v Ovalar Makine Ticaret Ve Sanayi, AS* 492 F.3d 132, 139 (2nd Cir. 2007). The Code was referred to as non-binding authority in *New Regency Productions, Inc. v Nippon Herald Films, Inc.* USCA 05-55224, Ninth Circuit, 4 September 2007.

[79] The AAA's International Arbitration Rules provide, in Art. 7, that all arbitrators appointed under those Rules shall be impartial and independent. The ICDR is the international division of the AAA, with offices in New York and Dublin.

[80] Sheppard, Jr, 'The new era of arbitrator ethics for the United States: The 2004 Revision to the AAA/ABA Code of Ethics for Arbitrators in Commercial Disputes' (2005) 21 Arb Intl 91, at 92.

D. Independence and Impartiality of Arbitrators

'Independence' is generally considered to be concerned with questions arising out of the relationship between an arbitrator and one of the parties, whether financial or otherwise. This is thought to be susceptible to an *objective* test, because it has nothing to do with an arbitrator's (or prospective arbitrator's) state of mind.

4.77

By contrast, the concept of 'impartiality' is considered to be connected with actual or apparent bias of an arbitrator—either in favour of one of the parties, or in relation to the issues in dispute. Impartiality is thus a *subjective* and more abstract concept than independence, in that it involves primarily a state of mind.[81]

4.78

(b) Disclosure

(i) Test to be applied

In order to avoid any risk of being declared in violation of the obligation of impartiality and independence, a prospective arbitrator should disclose all of the facts that could reasonably be considered to be grounds for disqualification. If he or she does so (and no objection is made), any subsequent challenge during or after the proceedings should be unsuccessful. The right to an independent and impartial arbitrator is deemed to have been waived in respect of objections founded upon facts contained in the disclosure statement.

4.79

The duty of impartiality—to maintain an open mind and to decide the case on the evidence presented, free from any preconceptions or connection with the parties or witnesses—nevertheless remains. If new circumstances arise that might give cause for any doubt as to an arbitrator's independence and/or impartiality, the arbitrator concerned should disclose them immediately to the parties and to the other arbitrators. A question has arisen as to whether the ongoing standard of disclosure should depend on the stage that the arbitration has reached.[82] Certain commentators consider that disclosure at the end of an arbitration should be judged on a weaker standard to ensure that the arbitration reaches its conclusion.[83]

4.80

In practice, a person approached to act as a party-nominated arbitrator usually discloses any relevant facts informally to the prospective appointing party in the first instance. If the circumstances disclosed do not give any cause for concern either to the prospective arbitrator or to the nominating party, then the prospective arbitrator accepts the nomination and writes formally to both parties, setting

4.81

---

[81] A comprehensive analysis of challenge and disqualification on grounds of both independence and impartiality under each of the different arbitration rules can be found in Daele, *Challenge and Disqualification of Arbitrators in International Arbitration* (Kluwer Law International, 2012), chs 7–8.

[82] 2004 IBA Guidelines on Conflicts of Interest in International Arbitration, Explanatory Note to General Standard 3(d).

[83] See Veeder, 'L'indépendance et l'impartialité de l'arbitre dans l'arbitrage international', in Cadiet (ed.) *Clay, Jeuland, Médiation et Arbitrage* (Litec, 2005), p. 219; Lord Steyn, 'England: The independence and/or impartiality of arbitrators in international commercial arbitration' (2007) Supplement ICC International Court of Arbitration Bulletin 91, at 96.

out the relevant facts if they are of a nature that should be disclosed on the basis that they might be considered 'in the eyes of' the other party to give rise to doubts as to the prospective arbitrator's independence or impartiality.

4.82 There is thus a subtle difference, in this context, between the *objective* test as to whether the relevant facts would cause doubt in the mind of a reasonable third party and the *subjective* test as to whether they might cause doubt in the minds of the parties involved in the specific case in question. The Explanatory Notes to the IBA's 2004 Guidelines on Conflicts of Interest provide as follows:

> [B]ecause of varying considerations with respect to disclosure the proper standard for disclosure may be different. A purely objective test for disclosure exists in the majority of the jurisdictions analysed and in the UNCITRAL Model Law. Nevertheless, the Working Group recognizes that the parties have an interest in being fully informed about any circumstances that may be relevant in their view. Because of the strongly held views of many arbitration institutions (as reflected in their rules and as stated to the Working Group) that the disclosure test should reflect the perspectives of the parties, the Working Group in principle accepted, after much debate, a subjective approach for disclosure. The Working Group has adapted the language of Article 7.2 of the ICC Rules for this standard.[84]

4.83 In the case of a third arbitrator, who is normally approached jointly by the parties or by the two party-nominated arbitrators, the two-stage process that generally operates in relation to a party-nominated arbitrator is not necessary; any circumstances that should be disclosed should be made known to both parties simultaneously. It is highly desirable that any matters disclosed should be confirmed to the parties in writing. Some arbitral institutions have a specific declaration form that every arbitrator is required to sign before an appointment is confirmed.[85]

(ii) International Bar Association Guidelines on Conflicts of Interest

4.84 An arbitrator's assessment of whether or not particular circumstances might give rise to doubts as to his or her impartiality or independence are likely to differ from one person to the next. Many of the remote 'relationships' disclosed by an arbitrator trained in the United States would not be considered disclosable by a lawyer trained in the civil law systems.[86] The obvious risk is that disclosure statements are not being made on the same basis. The IBA decided to tackle this issue 'head-on' in its 2004 Guidelines on Conflicts of Interest in International Commercial Arbitration,[87] which proved

---

[84] 2004 IBA Guidelines on Conflicts of Interest in International Arbitration, Explanation to General Standard 3. The text was approved by the IBA Council on 22 May 2004.

[85] See ICC Rules, Art. 11(2); ICSID Arbitration Rules, r. 6(2); LCIA Rules, Art. 5(4).

[86] One author recalls an arbitration in which an American co-arbitrator made three pages of disclosures, including references to congresses in which he had been present with counsel for one of the parties, whereas the other European arbitrator did not consider it relevant to disclose that he spent most summer vacations with counsel to the party that appointed him!

[87] The IBA 2004 Guidelines are not the only source in this regard. The LCIA Court's publication of abstracts of its reasoned decisions on challenges to arbitrators has provided an important additional source of information about how the duties of independence and impartiality are

D. Independence and Impartiality of Arbitrators

relatively successful. The IBA subsequently updated the Guidelines in light of experience in practice and, on October 2014, issued its revised Guidelines on Conflicts of Interest in International Arbitration.[88]

The IBA Guidelines aim to establish a common set of principles addressing concrete situations and thus to avoid the risk of arbitrators from different cultures applying radically different standards of disclosure. They drew on the combined experience of a working group comprising nineteen experienced practitioners from different jurisdictions.[89] **4.85**

How do the Guidelines work? They start with a general introduction, continue by setting out 'General Standards Regarding Impartiality, Independence and Disclosure', and conclude with a section on the 'Practical Application of the General Standards'. This last section divides a non-exhaustive list of 'circumstances' into four separate colour groups. **4.86**

- The 'Non-Waivable Red List' contains examples of situations in which an arbitrator should not act even with the consent of all parties and illustrate the principle that no person should be a judge in his or her own cause.
- The 'Waivable Red List' contains examples of situations that, while potentially leading to disqualification, may be accepted by express agreement of the parties to the dispute as not requiring disqualification in the circumstances of the particular case.
- The 'Orange List' is a non-exhaustive enumeration of specific situations, which (depending on the facts of a given case) in the eyes of the parties may give rise to justifiable doubts as to the arbitrator's impartiality or independence. This category is intended to deal with circumstances that a prospective arbitrator has a duty to disclose. It is contemplated that, once properly disclosed, the parties will be deemed to have waived their rights if they fail to make a timely challenge in relation to the disclosed circumstances.
- The 'Green List' contains examples of situations in which no appearance of (or actual) conflict of interest arises from an objective viewpoint. Thus there is no duty on a prospective arbitrator to disclose such circumstances.

---

applied *in concreto*. Although the LCIA Court has, on occasion, referred to the IBA Guidelines as guidance on the parameters of independence and impartiality, this has been only as one factor in a broader analysis of prevailing standards: Walsh and Teitelbaum, 'The LCIA Court decisions on challenges to arbitrators: An introduction' (2011) 27 Arb Intl 283.

[88] It will be noted that the term 'commercial' was dropped from the title of the 2014 Guidelines.
[89] The IBA Conflicts of Interest Subcommittee, established to monitor the use of the 2004 Guidelines, published a report summarising the use of the Guidelines in their first five years between 2004 and 2009. The Subcommittee found that, whilst the Guidelines are generally not applied directly by those making decisions on independence and impartiality, they are nevertheless increasingly referred to in the reaching of those decisions. For a review of the first five years of the 2004 Guidelines, see Scherer, 'The IBA Guidelines on Conflicts of Interest in International Arbitration: The first five years 2004-2009' (2010) 4 Disp Res Intl 15.

4.87 It is the Orange List that has raised the most debate, since the Guidelines do not provide any substantive guidance on what, if any, conflicts of interest falling within the scope of the Orange List (commercial or relationship conflicts) ought to result in disqualification.[90] Moreover, any attempt to provide lists of precise circumstances result in accusations of incompleteness. That is the difficulty inherent in their application. Yet the reference to precise factual circumstances is also their inherent virtue.

4.88 After ten years, the Guidelines have gained general acceptance as a non-binding set of principles with which most international arbitrators seek to comply. In the experience of the authors, the Guidelines are relied upon heavily by parties challenging arbitrators and those defending such challenges. And whilst the Guidelines may not always be directly cited, they are nonetheless also present in the minds of the authorities when reaching decisions on concepts of independence and impartiality. According to research conducted by the ICC, of 187 challenges and contested confirmations handled by the ICC Court between July 2004 and 1 August 2009, 106 referred to at least one example contained in one of the non-exhaustive lists in the Guidelines.[91]

E. Challenge and Replacement of Arbitrators

(a) Introduction

4.89 Challenges of arbitrators were, at one time, a rare event. If a vacancy occurred, it was usually because of the death or resignation of an arbitrator. However, modern commercial and investment arbitrations often involve vast sums of money and the parties have become more inclined to engage specialist lawyers, who are expert in manoeuvres designed to obtain a tactical advantage, or at least to minimise a potential disadvantage.[92] Statistics on arbitrator challenges are available from

---

[90] El-Kosheri and Youssef, 'The independence of international arbitrators: An arbitrator's perspective' (2007) Supplement ICC International Court of Arbitration Bulletin 43, at 43; Whitesell, 'Independence in ICC arbitration: ICC Court practice concerning the appointment, confirmation, challenge and replacement of arbitrators' (2007) Supplement ICC International Court of Arbitration Bulletin 7, at 36.

[91] See Feris and Greenberg, 'References to the IBA Guidelines on Conflicts of Interest in International Arbitration when deciding on arbitrator independence in ICC cases', in Fry and Greenberg, 'The arbitral tribunal: Applications of Articles 7–12 of the ICC Rules in recent cases' (2009) 20 ICC International Court of Arbitration Bulletin 12, Appendix.

[92] Between 1 January 2000 and 31 December 2009, 3.43 per cent of the arbitrators appointed in ICC arbitrations were challenged; between 1 January 2006 and 31 December 2010, 3 per cent of LCIA arbitrations involved a challenge to at least one arbitrator; between 1 January 1999 and 31 December 2010, challenges were made in 3.5 per cent of SCC arbitrations: Daele, *Challenge and Disqualification of Arbitrators in International Arbitration* (Kluwer Law International, 2012), pp. 66–68. The use of challenges to delay and disrupt an arbitration, and the measures that can be used to respond to and minimise the effectiveness of such tactics, was discussed at the 1990 ICCA Congress in Stockholm: see van den Berg, 'Preventing delay or disruption of arbitration' (1991) 5 ICCA Congress Series 131.

E. Challenge and Replacement of Arbitrators

most of the main institutions, and some commentators have concluded that the practice has increased to the extent that it is at risk of affecting the efficiency and legitimacy of the process.[93] This is particularly noteworthy in the investment arbitration scenario.[94]

In recent years, parties have generally been prepared to accept the arbitrator that they had for better or for worse, even if, as sometimes happened, an arbitrator was clearly not independent—being, for example, a senior official of a state party to the arbitration! There is now very much more readiness to challenge arbitrators on the grounds of perceived lack of independence or impartiality. Some challenges are undoubtedly meritorious, for example an arbitrator may have failed (inadvertently or not) to disclose a relationship that, once revealed, gives rise to justifiable doubts as to his or her independence or impartiality. In other cases, however, challenges are made to obtain a tactical advantage, for example at the start of an arbitration, to hinder the formation of the arbitral tribunal, or in the course of an arbitration, because the party making the challenge suspects that the tribunal (or an influential member of it) is not persuaded of the merits of the challenging parties' case. Such challenges pose problems for the institutions that are obliged to adjudicate upon them. They also cause delay and add to the expense of the arbitral proceedings, since the parties, the challenged arbitrator, and the other members of the tribunal will be asked to comment upon the challenges and often go to great lengths to do so.[95]

4.90

---

[93] See Nicholas and Partasides, 'LCIA Court decisions on challenges to arbitrators: A proposal to publish' (2007) 23 Arb Intl 1, at 1. For a more recent analysis of the available data on challenges in both international commercial arbitrations and investment treaty arbitrations, see Baker and Greenwood, 'Are challenges overused in international arbitration?' (2013) 30 J Intl Arb 101.

[94] By way of example, in the case of treaty claims against Argentina, Argentina mounted arbitrator challenges against the entire tribunal in the ICSID cases *Sempra Energy International v Argentine Republic*, Award, Case No. ARB/02/16, and *Camuzzi International SA v Argentine Republic*, Award, Case No. ARB/03/2, both heard 28 September 2007, available online at http://www.italaw.com/documents/SempraAward.pdf; against a party-nominated arbitrator in the case of *BG Group PLC v Argentine Republic*, Award, UNCITRAL, 24 December 2007, available online at http://www.italaw.com/sites/default/files/case-documents/ita0081.pdf; against the president and a party-nominated arbitrator in each of *National Grid Group plc v Argentine Republic*, Decision on Jurisdiction, UNCITRAL, 20 June 2006, available online at http://www.italaw.com/sites/default/files/case-documents/ita0553.pdf, and Decision on the Challenge to Mr Judd L. Kessler, 3 December 2007, available online at http://www.italaw.com/sites/default/files/case-documents/italaw1171.pdf, and *Abaclat and ors v Argentine Republic* (formerly *Giovanna a Beccara and ors v. Argentine Republic*), Request for the Disqualification of President Pierre Tercier and Arbitrator Albert Jan van den Berg, ICSID Case No. ARB/07/5, 15 September 2011, available online at http://www.italaw.com/sites/default/files/case-documents/ita0238.pdf; and twice against the same party-appointed arbitrator in *Suez, Sociedad General de Aguas de Barcelona S.A., and InterAguas Servicios Integrales del Agua S.A v Argentine Republic*, Decision on Liability, ICSID Case No. ARB/03/17, 30 July 2010, available online at http://www.italaw.com/sites/default/files/case-documents/ita0813.pdf, at [22]–[27]. In all cases, the challenges were dismissed.

[95] However, the best advice for an arbitrator who is challenged is to say nothing. There have been cases in which an arbitrator who is challenged reacted so intemperately that the institution that considered the challenge thought that it would be unwise to allow him to continue as an arbitrator.

4.91 The increasing use of challenges in the arbitral process has caused institutions to review the traditional practice of maintaining the confidentiality of the challenge decision. The LCIA has begun to publish such decisions in redacted form in the interests of transparency.[96] This has the added benefits of clarifying for arbitrators the standards applied and of assisting uniformity in disclosure practice.

(b) Grounds for challenge

4.92 Before a challenge can be considered, the applicable rules need to be established. In the event of an arbitration taking place in accordance with an established set of arbitration rules, the test will be set out in those rules, with a challenge being made to the relevant institution, or (in the case of UNCITRAL) to the appointing authority designated by the PCA. In the event of a pure ad hoc arbitration (that is, one with no chosen set of rules), the test will be set out in the local arbitration law and, in the absence of an appointing authority, any challenge will usually be decided by the judicial courts of the seat of the arbitration.

(i) Arbitral rules

4.93 In general, the parties to an arbitration may challenge an arbitrator only where they have reasonable doubts as to his or her impartiality or independence. However, the main arbitral rules contain a variety of tests and it would be wrong to assume that the test is effectively the same in each case.

4.94 Article 12 of the UNCITRAL Rules provides:

1. Any arbitrator may be challenged if circumstances exist that give rise to justifiable doubts as to the arbitrator's impartiality or independence.
2. A party may challenge the arbitrator appointed by him only for reasons of which he becomes aware after the appointment has been made.

[…]

Commentators on the UNCITRAL Rules note that the inclusion of the word 'justifiable' in Article 12(1) to define the kind of doubt required to sustain a challenge reflects UNCITRAL's clear intention of establishing an objective standard for impartiality and independence: 'While a party's subjective concerns about an arbitrator's bias may prompt a challenge, it is the objective reasonableness of these concerns that is ultimately determinative.'[97]

---

[96] The first abstracts of the LCIA's challenge decisions were published in (2011) 27(3) Arb Intl. To date, the LCIA is the only commercial arbitration institution to provide reasoned decisions, although ICSID and the Iran–United States Claims Tribunal also provide reasoned decisions to the parties: see Baker and Greenwood, 'Are challenges overused in international arbitration?' (2013) 30 J Intl Arb 101.

[97] Caron and Caplan, *The UNCITRAL Arbitration Rules: A Commentary* (2nd edn, Oxford University Press, 2013), p. 208.

E. Challenge and Replacement of Arbitrators

4.95 The relevant case law supports this position. The appointing authority in a well-known UNCITRAL challenge decision of January 1995 noted that:

> If the doubt had merely to arise in the mind of a party contesting the impartiality of an arbitrator, 'justifiable' would have been almost redundant. The word must import some other standard—a doubt that is justifiable in an objective sense. In other words, the claimant here has to furnish adequate and solid grounds for doubts. Those grounds must respond to reasonable criteria. In sum, would a reasonably well informed person believe that the perceived apprehension—the doubt—is justifiable? Is it ascertainable by that person and so serious as to warrant the removal of the arbitrators?[98]

4.96 The ICC Rules are succinct on the issue. Article 14(1) simply notes that:

> A challenge of an arbitrator, whether for an alleged lack of impartiality, or independence *or otherwise*, shall be made by submission to the Secretariat of a written statement specifying the facts and circumstances on which the challenge is based.

The breadth of this provision is striking and would appear to grant the ICC Court considerable discretion to remove an arbitrator. Since the ICC Court procedure for deciding challenges is an administrative one with no reasons provided, the application in practice of this rule is visible only in the results. It has been noted by commentators that challenges more frequently succeed based on a failure to disclose a relationship with one or more of the parties than on alleged misconduct during the arbitral proceeding.[99]

4.97 The LCIA Rules are more explicit. Article 10(3) states: 'An arbitrator may also be challenged by any party if circumstances exist that give rise to justifiable doubts as to his impartiality or independence.' The ICDR, SCC, SIAC, and HKIAC Arbitration Rules also adopt a 'justifiable doubts' test for determining impartiality and independence.[100]

4.98 The ICSID Convention, which governs arbitrations between investors and states under the auspices of ICSID, states that:

> A party may propose to a Commission or Tribunal the disqualification of any of its members on account of any fact indicating a manifest lack of the qualities required by paragraph (1) of Article 14. A party to arbitration proceedings may, in addition, propose the disqualification of an arbitrator on the ground that he was ineligible for appointment to the Tribunal under Section 2 of Chapter IV.[101]

---

[98] Challenge Decision of 11 January 1995, reprinted in (1997) XXII YBCA 227, at 234 (i.e. at [23]). The objective test has been repeatedly confirmed in more recent UNCITRAL challenge decisions, including, e.g., in *ICS Inspection and Control Services Ltd v Argentine Republic*, Challenge Decision of 17 December 2009, available online at http://italaw.com/sites/default/files/case-documents/ita0415.pdf, at [2]: '[The] conflict in question is sufficiently serious to give rise to objectively justifiable doubts as to...impartiality and independence.'

[99] See Derains and Schwartz, *A Guide to the New ICC Rules of Arbitration* (2nd edn, Kluwer Law International, 2005), p. 187.

[100] See SCC Rules, Art. 15(1); ICDR Rules, Art. 8(1); SIAC Rules, Art. 11(1); HKIAC Rules, Art. 11(6).

[101] ICSID Convention, Art. 57.

4.99 The qualities required by Article 14(1) include the ability to 'exercise independent judgment'; the grounds on which an arbitrator is 'ineligible for appointment' refer to the nationality provisions, which are designed to ensure that (unless the parties agree otherwise) the majority of arbitrators are not of the nationality of the state party or of the private party to the dispute.[102] The Authoritative Notes to the ICSID Arbitration Rules explain the effect of this provision as follows:

> [A]n arbitrator is to [resign] if, for instance, he may have an interest in the result of the dispute. In fact, in view of the qualities he is required to possess, a candidate is unlikely to accept an appointment as arbitrator where his personal interest is involved and, if he realises such involvement after the appointment, he may be trusted to resign. The experience of other international arbitration bodies has, in this respect, apparently been reassuring; it therefore seems unnecessary to particularise grounds for resignation.[103]

4.100 In one challenge decision under the ICSID Rules, the respondent state challenged the claimant's party-nominated arbitrator on the basis that she had recently decided against the same respondent state in an unrelated case and that the award revealed a prima facie lack of impartiality 'made evident through the most prominent inconsistencies of the award that result in the total lack of reliability towards [the arbitrator]'.[104] The remaining members of the tribunal called upon to decide the challenge noted that there had been no allegation of any link of any nature between the arbitrator and the parties, and that they had witnessed no evidence of any lack of independence or impartiality in the course of the tribunal's deliberations over the four years of the case's history. The participation in an award that had found against the respondent state (where such an award had been made unanimously) did not of itself show any 'manifest lack of independence'. The remaining members concluded that Article 14 of the Convention established an objective standard:

> Implicit in Article 57 and its requirement for a challenger to allege a fact indicating a manifest lack of the qualities required of an arbitrator by Article 14, is the requirement that such lack be proven by objective evidence and that the mere belief by the challenge of the contest arbitrator's lack of independence or impartiality is not sufficient to disqualify the contested arbitrator.[105]

---

[102] ICSID Convention, Arts 38 and 39.
[103] ICSID Arbitration Rules, r. 8, n. C.
[104] *Suez and ors v Republic of Argentina*, Disqualification Decision, ICSID Case No. ARB/03/17. IIC 312 (2007), at [8], available online at http://icsid.worldbank.org.
[105] Ibid., at [40]. This objective standard has been applied consistently by ICSID tribunals, e.g. in *ConocoPhillips Co. et al. v Bolivarian Republic of Venezuela*, Decision on the Proposal to Disqualify L. Yves Fortier, QC, Arbitrator, ICSID Case No. ARB/07/30, 27 February 2012, at [54]–[56]; *Abaclat and ors v Argentine Republic*, Recommendation on Proposal for Disqualification of Prof. Pierre Tercier and Prof. Albert Jan van den Berg, ICSID Case No. ARB/07/05, 19 December 2011, at [54]–[65]; *Universal Compression International Holdings, SLU v Bolivian Republic of Venezuela*, Decision on the Proposal to Disqualify Professor Brigitte Stern and Professor Guido Santiago Tawil, Arbitrators, ICSID Case No. ARB/10/9, 20 May 2011, at [65], [70]–[71].

E. Challenge and Replacement of Arbitrators

4.101 This was consistent with the decision on the challenge to the president of the annulment committee in *Compañía de Aguas del Aconquija SA and Vivendi Universal v Argentine Republic*,[106] in which it was concluded that the challenging party must rely on established facts and 'not on any mere speculation or inference'.[107]

(ii) National laws

4.102 National arbitration laws also contain tests that operate in the case of a pure ad hoc arbitration with a seat in the country. For example, section 1033 of the Netherlands Arbitration Act 1986 provides that an arbitrator may be challenged if circumstances exist that give rise to justifiable doubts as to his or her impartiality or independence. By contrast, the Swiss PIL retains the justifiable doubts standard, but refers only to doubts as to independence, not impartiality. This has been said potentially to allow for bias by an arbitrator in favour of the nominating party,[108] but the better view is that strict impartiality remains a requirement of Swiss law.[109]

4.103 Section 24(1) of the English Arbitration Act 1996 is more comprehensive:

(1) A party to arbitral proceedings may (upon notice to the other parties, to the arbitrator concerned and to any other arbitrator) apply to the court to remove an arbitrator on any of the following grounds:
   (a) that circumstances exist that give rise to justifiable doubts as to his impartiality;
   (b) that he does not possess the qualifications required by the arbitration agreement;
   (c) that he is physically or mentally incapable of conducting the proceedings or there are justifiable doubts as to his capacity to do so;
   (d) that he has refused or failed—
      (i) properly to conduct the proceedings, or
      (ii) to use all reasonable despatch in conducting the proceedings or making an award,
   and that substantial injustice has been or will be caused to the applicant.[110]

---

[106] ICSID Case No. ARB/97/3, IIC 69 (2001), (2002) 17 ICSID Rev—Foreign Investment LJ 168, (2004) 6 ICSID Rep 330, (2004) 125 ILR 46.

[107] The interpretation of 'manifest' itself has been equivocal. To some tribunals, it has referred 'not to the seriousness of the allegation but to the ease with which [the allegation] may be perceived': *EDF International SA v Argentina*, Challenge Decision of 25 June 2008, at [65]–[69]. Others have taken the view that 'manifest' must relate to the substance of the conflict itself, such that, from the perspective of an informed reasonable person, established facts 'make it obvious and highly probable, not just possible, that the challenged arbitrator is a person who may not be relied upon to exercise independent and impartial judgment': *Suez, Sociedad General de Aguas de Barcelona SA v Argentine Republic*, ICSID Cases Nos ARB/03/17 and ARB/03/19, Decision on Second Proposal for Disqualification, at [29].

[108] Blessing, 'The new international arbitration law in Switzerland' (1988) 5 J Intl Arb 9, at 39.

[109] Smith, 'Impartiality of the party-appointed arbitrator' (1990) 6 Arb Intl 320, at 328.

[110] This has been held to import a 'fair-minded and reasonable observer' test and to require a demonstration of a real possibility of apparent bias, rather than a real possibility of unconscious bias: see *A v B and X* [2011] EWHC 2345 (Comm).

4.104 In the United States, the duty of avoiding evident partiality is established by section 10(a) of the Federal Arbitration Act of 1925 (FAA):

> (a) In any of the following cases the United States court in and for the district wherein the award was made may make an order vacating the award upon the application of any party to the arbitration—
> [...]
> (1) where there was evident partiality or corruption in the arbitrators, or either of them;
> [...]

This section has been interpreted as including a strict duty of disclosure. The US Supreme Court set a high standard in *Commonwealth Coatings*[111] by requiring disclosure of any dealings that might create an impression of bias. In that case, an arbitral award was set aside for failure to disclose business connections with one of the parties, even though the award was unanimous and the Court found that there was no *actual* bias.[112]

4.105 French law was amended in January 2011 to codify an arbitrator's duty of disclosure. Article 1456(2) of the Code of Civil Procedure now explicitly requires 'an arbitrator to disclose any circumstance that may affect his or her independence or impartiality'.[113]

(c) Procedure for challenge

4.106 The procedure for challenge of an arbitrator appears in the rules of arbitration that have been adopted by the parties or, in the event of an ad hoc arbitration, in the rules of the applicable arbitration law at the place of arbitration (usually the local courts). Where a challenge falls to be dealt with by the courts, the procedure to be followed is specified in the applicable law. Where the rules of an arbitral institution apply, the procedure is normally that a complaint should be made in the first instance *either* to the arbitral institution *or* to the arbitral tribunal itself, with a right of review by the courts.

4.107 Most national laws provide for a challenge to an arbitrator to be made during the course of the arbitration, as well as on an application to set aside the award.[114]

---

[111] *Commonwealth Coatings Corporation v Continental Casualty Co.* 393 US 145 (1968).

[112] However, more recently, Justice White noted that an arbitrator, who must not be held to the same standard as a judge, has no duty to disclose 'remote commercial connections...He cannot be expected to provide the parties with his complete and unexpurgated business biography': *Commonwealth Coatings Corporation v Continental Casualty Co.* 393 US 145, 151 (1968). Lower courts have tended to followed this approach: see, e.g., *Positive Software Solutions, Inc. v New Century Finance Corporation* 476 F.3d 278, 281–282 (5th Cir. 2007).

[113] Decree No. 2011-48 of 13 January 2011. See Cohen, 'Indépendence des arbitres et conflits d'intérêts' [2011] Rev Arb 614.

[114] English Arbitration Act 1996, s. 24; Model Law, Art. 13; Swiss PIL, Ch. 12, s. 180; Netherlands Arbitration Act 1986, ss 1034 and 1035.

E. Challenge and Replacement of Arbitrators

Delays are often minimised by provisions that restrict challenges to objections founded on information that has recently come to the attention of the challenging party, prohibit any appeal from the initial ruling on the challenge, and permit the arbitration to proceed while the challenge is pending. Such provisions are to be found in the Model Law and, for example, in the English Arbitration Act 1996.[115]

A curious gap in the US FAA leaves the parties no avenue of judicial review of an appointment until after an award has been rendered, unless the rules of procedure adopted by the parties provide for earlier review.[116] This means that a party with a valid objection to the composition of the tribunal would have to make the objection 'on the record' and then wait until the end of the case before challenging the award (with the attendant waste of time and money if the challenge is successful). 4.108

(i) ICC challenge procedure

The ICC Rules provide that a party seeking to challenge an arbitrator must do so within thirty days of the date of notification of the appointment or the date on which that party became aware of the circumstances giving rise to the challenge. The challenge must be made in writing, specifying the facts and circumstances on which it is based. The ICC Court will then decide on the challenge after the Secretariat has afforded an opportunity to the arbitrator concerned, the other party, and any other members of the arbitral tribunal to comment in writing within a suitable period of time.[117] 4.109

Those comments are to be communicated to the parties and to the arbitrators. No reasons are provided on the challenge decision and the decision is not published. These aspects have been criticised as lacking transparency with regards to the affected party and to the public interest in understanding the basis of a challenge decision. Indeed, in one case in which a respondent state had accepted the ICC as appointing authority, having received an adverse challenge decision the state decided to sue the ICC in its own courts on the basis that it had not received reasons.[118] In a subsequent challenge made by the same respondent state in another 4.110

---

[115] Model Law, Art. 13; English Arbitration Act 1996, s. 24(3).
[116] *Morelite Construction Corporation v New York City District Carpenters Benefit Funds* 748 F.2d 79 (2nd Cir. 1984). This was confirmed more recently in *Gulf Guaranteed Life Insurance Co. v Connecticut General Life Insurance Co.* 304 F.3d 476, 490 (5th Cir. 2002), in which the court held that 'there is no authorisation under the FAA's express terms for a court to *remove* an arbitrator from service. Rather, even where arbitrator bias is at issue, the FAA does not provide for removal of an arbitrator from service prior to an award, but only for potential vacatur of any award' (emphasis original).
[117] ICC Rules, Art. 14(2) and (3).
[118] Recurso filed by the Republic of Argentina against the ICC on 8 February 2006, requesting that the ICC's decision be overturned for failure to provide reasons. Two preliminary injunctions were granted by the National Contentious-Administrative Court of Appeals in *Estado Nacional—Procuración del Tesoro de la Nación c/Cámara de Comercio Internacional*, dated 3 July 2007 and 17 July 2008 (unpublished).

arbitration, the parties agreed to refer the challenge decision to the LCIA, which renders reasoned challenge decisions.[119]

4.111 The publication of the reasons for ICC decisions on challenge (or any other matter) is currently prohibited under Article 11(4) of its Rules,[120] and this prohibition was not lifted with the recent revision of the ICC Rules. There would seem to be two principal reasons for this: first, if reasons are given and published, this might encourage more challenges; and secondly, when a decision is made by a large assembly of Court members, as in the monthly plenary sessions, there may well be a variety of reasons for that decision.[121] In the interests of greater transparency, however, the ICC has published three reports containing general summaries of, and themes arising from, its challenge decisions.[122]

(ii) LCIA challenge procedure

4.112 Under the LCIA Rules, a party who intends to challenge an arbitrator must send a written statement of the reasons for challenge to the LCIA within fourteen days of the establishment of the arbitral tribunal, or within fourteen days of becoming aware of the circumstances justifying the challenge if this is later. The LCIA Court will give the other parties and the challenged arbitrator a chance to comment on the written statement. Unless the challenged arbitrator withdraws (or the other party agrees to the challenge) within fourteen days of receipt of the written statement of reasons, the LCIA Court decides whether or not the challenge should be upheld.[123] The LCIA Rules now expressly require that the decision of the LCIA Court—which, in practice, will comprise a three-person division—shall be made in writing, with reasons.[124] Indeed, if the parties so request, the division may even hold an oral hearing in this regard.

---

[119] *Decision on the Challenge in the Arbitration National Grid Plc v Republic of Argentina*, LCIA Case No. UN7949, 3 December 2007.

[120] Article 11(4) reads: 'The decisions of the Court as to the appointment, confirmation, challenge or replacement of an arbitrator shall be final and the reasons for such decisions shall not be communicated.'

[121] Since 2010, most decisions on challenges are taken in a *comité restraint*, which consists of three Court members. The composition of that comité varies from week to week, although the presiding member is either the president of the Court or a vice-president. The comité decides whether a challenge should be rejected or transferred to the plenary session, if it seems likely to succeed: Daele, *Challenge and Disqualification of Arbitrators in International Arbitration* (Kluwer Law International, 2012), paras 4.026–4.027.

[122] The first report was authored by Stephen Bond in 1991: Bond, 'The experience of the ICC in the confirmation/appointment stage of an arbitration', in Hunter (ed.) *The Arbitral Process and the Independence of Arbitrators*, ICC Pub No. 472 (ICC, 1991), pp. 9–14. The second was authored by Dominique Hascher in 1995: Hascher, 'ICC practice in relation to appointment, confirmation, challenge and replacement of arbitrators' (1995) 6 ICC International Court of Arbitration Bulletin 16. The third was authored by Anne Marie Whitesell in 2008: Whitesell, 'Independence in ICC arbitration: ICC Court practice concerning the appointment, confirmation, challenge and replacement of arbitrators' (2007) Supplement ICC International Court of Arbitration Bulletin 36.

[123] LCIA Rules, Art. 10(3)–(6).

[124] LCIA Rules, Art. 10(6).

E. *Challenge and Replacement of Arbitrators*

In 2006, in order to assist the transparency of the process, the LCIA resolved to **4.113** publish decisions on challenge in a suitably redacted form. This has given rise to a discussion in other institutions about adopting similar measures. The first publication of such decisions appeared in *Arbitration International* in 2011.[125]

(iii) UNCITRAL challenge procedure

Under the UNCITRAL Rules, any challenge must be notified to the other party **4.114** and to the members of the arbitral tribunal, including the challenged arbitrator. A fifteen-day time limit for submitting a challenge is adopted and the time limit is applied strictly.[126] The merits of challenges are decided upon by the appointing authority,[127] and whether or not reasons will accompany the challenge decision will depend upon who the appointing authority is.

(iv) Challenges under the ICSID Rules

Any challenge of an arbitrator made under the provisions of the ICSID Convention **4.115** must be made 'promptly, and in any event before the proceeding is declared closed'.[128] This is not an open-ended time delay. In *Suez and ors v Argentina*,[129] the remaining members of the tribunal considered that a challenge brought fifty-two days after the party had become aware of the facts giving rise to the challenge (and incidentally just before the final hearing in the case) had not been brought promptly.

The party making the challenge (or 'proposing the disqualification of an arbitra- **4.116** tor', as it is phrased in the ICSID Arbitration Rules) must state the reasons in a document to be filed with the secretary-general of ICSID. This proposal for disqualification is then transmitted to all of the members of the arbitral tribunal and to the opposing party. If the challenge is directed at a sole arbitrator, or to a majority of the arbitrators, it is also transmitted to the chairman of the Administrative Council of ICSID (de facto, the president of the World Bank). The arbitrator whose position is challenged may then, 'without delay', furnish any appropriate explanations to the arbitral tribunal or the chairman, as the case may be.[130]

If the challenge is directed against one arbitrator in an arbitral tribunal of three, **4.117** the decision is taken by the other two arbitrators, who may accept or reject it. If

---

[125] See (2011) 27(3) Arb Intl 281–536.
[126] For an attempt by a party to challenge facts after expiry of the fifteen-day time limit, see *AWG Group v Argentine Republic*, Challenge Decision of 22 October 2007, at [21], reported as part of the challenge decision in the parallel ICSID case of *Suez and ors v Argentine Republic*, available online at http://www.worldbank/icsid.org.
[127] UNCITRAL Rules, Art. 13.
[128] ICSID Arbitration Rules, r. 9(1). If the grounds for challenge become known only when the proceedings are closed, then the remedy is a request for an annulment of the award under Rule 50.
[129] *Suez and ors v Republic of Argentina*, Disqualification Decision, ICSID Case No. ARB/03/17, IIC 312 (2007), at [22]–[26].
[130] ICSID Arbitration Rules, r. 9(3).

they cannot agree, the decision will be made by the chairman. The decision will also be made by the chairman if the challenge is directed against a sole arbitrator, or against the majority of the arbitral tribunal.[131] The decision must be reasoned.[132] For as long as the constitution of the arbitral tribunal is in doubt because of a challenge to one or more of the arbitrators, the arbitral proceedings are suspended.[133] If the challenge is upheld, a vacancy is created in the arbitral tribunal, which must be filled before the proceedings resume. If the challenge is rejected, the arbitration proceeds.[134]

(d) Principal bases for challenge

4.118 Any discussion of standards and tests is likely to remain esoteric without a practical understanding of the way in which challenge decisions are actually taken. In the following illustrations of the real operation of these standards, we will consider some of the responses given by the competent decision-making bodies in contexts such as:

- where there is an alleged connection between the arbitrator and one of the parties;
- where there is an alleged connection between the arbitrator and counsel for one of the parties (which can include, by way of example, where an arbitrator and counsel for one of the parties belong to the same barristers' chambers);
- where the arbitrator acts as counsel for a third party in a dispute involving similar issues, in which he or she is advancing a case contrary to that of one of the parties to the dispute before him or her as arbitrator (the so-called double-hat dilemma); and
- where the arbitrator makes a statement that is alleged to involve a pre-judgment of an issue in the dispute.

(i) Connection with one of the parties

4.119 A connection with one of the parties can arise in a number of different scenarios. The IBA Guidelines[135] provide detailed advice on a range of specific disqualifying

---

[131] ICSID Arbitration Rules, r. 9(4)–(5).

[132] ICSID challenge decisions are usually publicly available. For recent examples, see *Saint-Gobain Performance Plastics Europe v Bolivarian Republic of Venezuela*, Decision on Claimant Proposal to Disqualify Mr Gabriel Bottini from the Tribunal under Article 57 of the ICSID Convention, ICSID Case No. ARB/12/13, 27 February 2013; *ConocoPhillips Co. et al. v Bolivarian Republic of Venezuela*, Decision on the Proposal to Disqualify L. Yves Fortier, QC, Arbitrator, ICSID Case No. ARB/07/30, 27 February 2012. Both decisions are available online at http://icsid.worldbank.org.

[133] ICSID Arbitration Rules, r. 9(6).

[134] Unlike Art. 48 ('The Award') of the ICSID Convention, Art. 58 ('Replacement and Disqualification of Conciliators and Arbitrators') does not state that a challenge decision must give reasons. However, the ad hoc committee in *Azurix v Argentina II*, Annulment Decision of 1 September 2009, at [290], held that 'a duty to state reasons for a decision under Article 58 might be considered implicity [sic]'.

[135] See paragraphs 4.89*ff* above.

E. Challenge and Replacement of Arbitrators

connections. Most obviously, the arbitrator (or a close family member[136]) could have a significant financial interest in one of the parties, or in the subject matter in dispute in the arbitration, which would clearly be disqualifying.[137]

4.120 In an ICSID case (with a parallel UNCITRAL case heard by the same tribunal), disqualification was sought by the respondent based on the fact that the arbitrator in question was a non-executive director (NED) of an investment bank that held a small participation in two of the claimants, principally as a portfolio investor on behalf of others.[138] The challenged arbitrator confirmed that she had no knowledge of such investments, and that investment banks invest in a wide variety of stocks and shares. In the role of NED, the arbitrator had no influence or participation in such investment decisions and had to be independent of the management of the bank. The remaining members took a pragmatic view of the realities of modern life, noting that the mere fact of a remote connection could not be sufficient in and of itself, and holding that:

> [T]he fact of an alleged connection between a party and an arbitrator in and of itself is not sufficient to establish a fact that would establish a manifest lack of that arbitrator's impartiality and independence. Arbitrators are not disembodied spirits dwelling on Mars, who descend to earth to arbitrate a case and then immediately return to their Martian retreat to await inertly the call to arbitrate another. Like other professionals living and working in the world, arbitrators have a variety of complex connections with all sorts of persons and institutions.[139]

4.121 A further step is required: the alleged connection must be evaluated *qualitatively* in order to decide whether it constitutes a fact indicating a manifest lack of the quality of independence of judgment and impartiality required of an ICSID arbitrator. This was addressed by means of a four-point test.

- *Proximity* How closely connected is the challenged arbitrator to one of the parties by reason of the alleged connection? The closer the connection between an arbitrator and a party, the more likely it is that the relationship may influence an arbitrator's independence of judgment and impartiality.
- *Intensity* How intense and frequent are the interactions between the challenged arbitrator and one of the parties as a result of the alleged connection? The more frequent and intense the interaction by virtue of the relationship between an arbitrator and a party, the more probable it is that such a relationship will affect the arbitrator's independence of judgment and impartiality.

---

[136] The Guidelines define 'close family member' as a spouse, sibling, child, parent, or life partner, in addition to any other family member with whom a close relationship exists.
[137] See paragraph 1.3 of the Non-Waivable Red List (for the arbitrator) and paragraph 2.2.2 of the Waivable Red List (for close family members).
[138] *Suez, Sociedad General de Aguas de Barcelona SA, and InterAguas Servicios Integrales del Agua SA v Argentine Republic*, ICSID Case No. ARB/03/17; *Suez, Sociedad General de Aguas de Barcelona SA, and Vivendi Universal SA v Argentine Republic*, Decision on a Second Proposal for the Disqualification of a Member of the Arbitral Tribunal, ICSID Case No. ARB/03/19, 12 May 2008.
[139] Ibid., at [32].

- *Dependence* To what extent is the challenged arbitrator dependent on one of the parties for benefits as a result of the connection? The more dependent an arbitrator is on a relationship for benefits or advantages, the more likely it is that the relationship may influence the arbitrator's independence of judgment and impartiality.
- *Materiality* To what extent are any benefits accruing to the challenged arbitrator as a result of the alleged connection significant and therefore likely to influence the arbitrator's judgment in some way? Obviously significant benefits derived from a relationship will be more likely to influence an arbitrator's judgment and impartiality than negligible or insignificant benefits.

4.122 On the basis of this test, the connection between the arbitrator and the parties was considered not to give rise to a manifest lack of independent judgment: as a passive investor, the bank obtained dividends only through its participation, which represented a tiny fraction of its operations. Those dividends would not have a material effect on the bank's profitability and thus its own success. Further, the very purpose of a non-executive independent director under the applicable banking rules was to act as an independent supervisor and not be involved in business decisions.[140]

4.123 A connection can also exist on the basis of advice provided to one of the parties.[141] In another ICSID case, the respondent state challenged the president of an ad hoc annulment committee based on the fact that another partner in his law firm had given limited advice to one of the parties in an unrelated area, which advice was continuing, but nearing completion.[142] The fact had been disclosed by the president, who had no personal involvement in the advice in question. The remaining panel members dismissed the challenge and noted the following relevant facts:

> ...(a) that the relationship in question was immediately and fully disclosed and that further information about it was forthcoming on request, thus maintaining

---

[140] Less seriously, infrequent social contact between arbitrators and counsel has sometimes been relied on to found a challenge. In *Zhinvali Development Ltd v Republic of Georgia*, Decision on Respondent's Proposal to Disqualify Arbitrator, ICSID Case No. ARB/00/1, 19 January 2001, an arbitrator was challenged unsuccessfully for attending a dinner party with a senior executive of one of the three shareholders of Zhinvali. Similarly, the Advisory Committee on Judicial Ethics of the New York State Unified Court System recently opined that 'the mere status of being a "Facebook friend," *without more*, is an insufficient basis to require recusal': *Recent New York State Judicial Ethics Opinions related to Social Networks and Relationships* (May 2013), Opinion 13-29, available online at http://www.transnational-dispute-management.com/legal-and-regulatory-detail.asp?key=9493

[141] The fact that an arbitrator regularly advises the appointing party or an affiliate of the appointing party and he or she (or his or her firm) derives significant financial income from such advice is on the Non-Waivable Red List (paragraph 1.4). Also on the Red List, although capable of being waived by express agreement of the parties, are instances in which an arbitrator has previously given legal advice or provided an expert opinion to one of the parties or an affiliate of one of the parties (paragraph 2.1.1), or he or she is currently representing or advising one of the parties or an affiliate of one of the parties (paragraph 2.3.1).

[142] *Compañía de Aguas del Aconquija SA and Vivendi Universal v Argentina*, Decision on the Challenge to the President of the Committee, ICSID Case No. ARB/97/3, IIC 69 (2001), (2002) 17 ICSID Rev—Foreign Investment LJ 168, (2004) 6 ICSID Rep 330, (2004) 125 ILR 46.

E. Challenge and Replacement of Arbitrators

full transparency; (b) that [the arbitrator] personally has and has had no lawyer-client relationship with the Claimants or its affiliates; (c) that the work done by his colleague has nothing to do with the present case; (d) that the work concerned does not consist in giving general legal or strategic advice to the Claimants but concerns a specific transaction, in which [law firm] are not the lead firm; (e) that the legal relationship will soon come to an end with the closure of the transaction concerned.[143]

(ii) Connection with one of the counsel

4.124 A connection with counsel can also arise in a variety of ways. An arbitrator cannot sit in a case in which he or she has a financial relationship with one of the counsel. Most obviously, this will arise if they are colleagues in the same law firm.[144] Similarly, an arbitrator who receives a significant number of repeat appointments from the same law firm could be said to have developed a financial relationship with that firm.[145]

4.125 A recent decision by the French Cour de Cassation in *Tecso*[146] involved a challenge to an award based on an arbitrator's failure to disclose a shared history with the law firm in which counsel for one of the parties, Neoelectra Group, practised. The arbitrator had left the law firm in question before the lawyer began working for the firm, although he had since provided the firm with two or three legal opinions. Neoelectra's counsel was also representing Neoelectra in her capacity as a self-employed lawyer and not on behalf of the firm. The Paris Cour d'Appel set aside the award for the failure of the arbitrator to disclose this connection, but its decision was later reversed by the Cour de Cassation. It held that, without explaining how the connection was susceptible to trigger reasonable doubts in the parties' minds as to the arbitrator's independence and impartiality, the Cour d'Appel had not enabled the Cour de Cassation to exercise its control to annul the award.[147]

---

[143] Ibid., at [26].
[144] The situation of an arbitrator and counsel for one of the parties being at the same law firm is on the Waivable Red List, at paragraph 2.3.3.
[145] In this regard, paragraph 3.3.8 of the Orange List encourages arbitrators to make a disclosure if they have 'within the past three years received more than three appointments by the same counsel or the same law firm'.
[146] *Tecso*, Case No. 11-20.299, Cass. Civ. 1, 10 October 2012.
[147] Thomas Clay has argued that the language used by the Cour de Cassation simply states that the burden lies with that party which doubts the arbitrator's independence to substantiate such doubts: see Clay, 'Arbitrage et modes alternatifs de règlement des litiges' [2012] Recueil Dalloz 2991. He contests the contentions made by other scholars, such as Christophe Seraglini and Laura Weiller, according to whom this decision marked a return to a more stringent control on the alleged lack of independence: see Henry, 'Devoir de révélation de l'arbitre: Consécration du critère de l'incidence raisonnable sur l'indépendance et l'impartialité de l'arbitre' (2012) 46 La Semaine Juridique 1675; Weiller, 'Rejet de la prétendue faute de l'arbitre' (2012) 10 Procédures, comm. 284. See also *Tecnimont SPA v J&P Avax*, Case No. 11-26.529, Cass. Civ. 1ere, 25 June 2014.

4.126 A similar issue arose in relation to an arbitrator challenge in an ICSID arbitration. In *Universal Compression International Holdings v Venezuela*,[148] Venezuela challenged the appointment of the claimant-appointed arbitrator on the basis of two separate connections with counsel for the claimant. First, it was alleged that the claimant 'enjoyed a privileged position' because the arbitrator had served as joint counsel with the claimant's counsel in three arbitrations, one of which occurred two years prior to the challenge. This first ground was dismissed, because the facts and parties of those matters were different, and the respondent had not demonstrated the extent to which similar legal issues would arise in the present dispute.[149] Secondly, it was alleged that the independence and impartiality of the arbitrator were impugned because a member of the claimant's counsel team had formerly worked as a junior lawyer in the same firm and team as that arbitrator. This second ground was also rejected. In this regard, it appears that the deciding arbitrators were influenced by the fact that the junior lawyer had been one of several team members in the arbitrator's former team and had resigned to join the claimant's law firm five years earlier.[150]

4.127 England's divided legal profession, comprising solicitors and barristers, poses a particular question when it comes to considering an arbitrator's connection with counsel. Unlike partners and associates at law firms, barristers within chambers work as sole practitioners, sharing operating expenses, but neither income nor case information. For this reason, in English court proceedings, there has never been any constraint preventing barristers from appearing against each other in the same case nor, indeed, before a former member of chambers who is now a judge. The situation is less straightforward in international arbitration proceedings, which will typically involve lawyers and parties who are far less familiar with the role and workings of barristers' chambers.

4.128 In *Hrvatska Elektroprivreda, dd v Republic of Slovenia*,[151] the respondent state identified the addition of a barrister to its legal team at a very late stage of the proceedings. The barrister in question was a member of the same chambers as the chairman of the arbitral tribunal, which led to an objection by the claimant and its non-English legal counsel. Exercising an inherent jurisdiction, the tribunal decided that the best way in which to safeguard the proceedings was to order the counsel in question to withdraw from the proceedings. In so ordering, the tribunal began its discussion by observing that '[b]arristers are sole practitioners' and 'chambers are not law firms'—but it observed that '[i]t is, however, equally true that

---

[148] *Universal Compression International Holdings, SLU v Bolivian Republic of Venezuela*, Decision on the Proposal to Disqualify Professor Brigitte Stern and Professor Guido Santiago Tawil, Arbitrators, ICSID Case No. ARB/10/9, 20 May 2011, at [52].
[149] Ibid., at [97]–[102].
[150] Ibid., at [105]–[107].
[151] Tribunal's Ruling on the Participation of Counsel, ICSID Case No. ARB/05/24, 6 May 2008.

E. Challenge and Replacement of Arbitrators

this practice is not universally understood let alone universally agreed, and that Chambers themselves have evolved in the modern market place for professional services with the consequence that they often present themselves with a collective connotation'.[152] Although the tribunal did 'not believe there is a hard-and-fast rule to the effect that barristers from the same Chambers are always precluded from being involved as, respectively, counsel and arbitrator in the same case', neither was the converse true, and a determination of partiality 'depends on all relevant circumstances'.[153] Taking into account that the claimant was entirely unfamiliar with the barristers' chambers system of England and Wales, that the respondent consciously decided not to disclose the identity of the barrister until a very late stage in the proceedings, and that the respondent refused to reveal the extent of his participation, the tribunal found it necessary for counsel to step down in order to 'dispel' the 'atmosphere of apprehension and mistrust'.[154]

4.129 Similarly, in *Brescla Calcio SpA v West Ham United FC Plc*,[155] the Board of the International Council of Arbitration for Sport (ICAS) upheld a challenge against the respondent's party-appointed arbitrator because counsel for the respondent was from the same chambers. In the submission of the Italian claimant, this circumstance 'cast some doubts, at least in appearance, as to the arbitrator's independence'.[156] The ICAS Board applied an objective test to the assessment of independence and referred explicitly to the IBA Guidelines in coming to this decision, noting that it was convinced that the arbitrator in question was perfectly independent and impartial. In 2010, the ICC also upheld a challenge to the claimant-appointed arbitrator on the basis that she was a member of the same barristers' chambers as two members of the claimant's additional counsel.[157]

4.130 It remains to be seen whether, in the words of the *Hrvatska Elektroprivreda* tribunal, a 'hard-and-fast' rule will develop against barristers appearing before other barristers from the same chambers. It also remains to be seen what steps the English bar may seek to take to address the concerns that are clearly growing internationally.[158]

---

[152] Ibid., at [17]–[18].
[153] Ibid., at [31].
[154] Ibid.
[155] (2012) 3 ISLR 40.
[156] Ibid., at 52.
[157] ICC Case No. 16553/GZ. See Gorvath and Berzero, 'Arbitrator and counsel: The double-hat dilemma' (2013) 10 TDM, available online at http://www.transnational-dispute-management.com/article.asp?key=1985
[158] The Bar Council of England and Wales has recently issued an information note regarding barristers in international arbitration and, in so doing, avoided a blanket ban on members of the same chambers appearing in the same case as counsel and arbitrator. According to the Bar Council:

> As a matter of English and Welsh law, there is no prohibition against an advocate appearing before an arbitration tribunal which includes a member of his or her chambers...Nevertheless, good practice would dictate that in circumstances where a barrister comes to understand that he or she has been instructed in an arbitration where one or more of the members of the Tribunal are barristers in the same set of chambers, prompt disclosure ought to be made by those instructing the barrister advocate to the

For now, and as the IBA Guidelines make clear, it is undoubtedly necessary for disclosure to take place if the arbitrator and another arbitrator, or the counsel for one of the parties, are members of the same barristers' chambers.[159]

4.131 Moreover, an increasing number of arbitration rules are requiring the parties to identify their representatives and authorising the tribunal to dismiss counsel from the case if the tribunal considers this necessary to maintain the integrity of the proceedings.[160] The IBA Guidelines require a party to disclose the identity of its counsel 'on its own initiative' and 'at the earliest opportunity'.[161] In the same way, the IBA Rules on Party Representation in International Arbitration provide that, after the constitution of the tribunal, no person should accept representation of a party where there is a conflict of interest with one of the arbitrators and permit the tribunal to take measures necessary to safeguard the integrity of the proceedings, including by excluding the new party representative.[162] It is also becoming usual for arbitral tribunals to adopt similar provisions on their own initiative.

(iii) Issue conflict

4.132 An 'issue conflict' may arise where a lawyer is sitting in one case as an arbitrator in which a point of law is being argued, whilst acting in another case as counsel to a party arguing that same point of law. There is no suggestion of any links with the parties, but rather an allegation that the arbitrator will not be able to be impartial with regard to a decision on a point of law that may be determinative in the case in which he or she is defending the interests of a client as counsel. This scenario—sometimes referred to as the 'double-hat dilemma'—is particularly prevalent in investment arbitration cases, given the discrete number of recurring legal concepts at issue,[163] the publicity of the investment arbitration awards, and the repeat participation by well-known international lawyers as counsel and arbitrator.[164]

---

legal representatives of the other side. This will ensure as far as possible that the guidance set out in the IBA Guidelines on Conflicts of Interest in International Arbitration is followed (see further below). A failure to make prompt disclosure, could ultimately, lead to a challenge to the independence of the member(s) of the Tribunal in question.

See Bar Council of England and Wales, *Information Note Regarding Barristers In International Arbitration*, 6 July 2015, available online at http://www.barcouncil.org.uk/media/376302/bc_information_note_-_perceived_conflicts_in_international_arbitration_-_060715.pdf, p. 4.

[159] IBA Guidelines on Conflicts of Interest in International Arbitration, paragraph 3.3.2.
[160] LCIA Rules, Art. 18.
[161] IBA Guidelines on Conflicts of Interest in International Arbitration, Guideline 7(b).
[162] IBA Guidelines on Party Representation in International Arbitration, Guidelines 5 and 6.
[163] International investment law applied as the substantive law in these arbitrations is largely focused on specific concepts of expropriation, fair and equitable treatment, and unreasonable or discriminatory measures. See Chapter 8 for more details.
[164] See *Vito G. Gallo v Canada*, Decision on the Challenge to an Arbitrator, 14 October 2009, IIC 404 (2009). See also Daele, *Challenge and Disqualification of Arbitrators in International Arbitration* (Kluwer Law International, 2012), paras 7.010–7.012.

E. Challenge and Replacement of Arbitrators

This arose in the *Telekom Malaysia* arbitration,[165] in which Telekom Malaysia claimed against the Republic of Ghana pursuant to the Malaysia–Ghana bilateral investment treaty (BIT) in relation to an alleged expropriation of its investment in Ghana Telecommunications Co. Ltd. The arbitration was held in accordance with the UNCITRAL Rules and administered by the PCA. Following a successful challenge by each party as to the other's selected arbitrator, Telekom Malaysia appointed an eminent French practitioner and academic as replacement arbitrator. By reason of the arbitrator's role as counsel to an investor in a similar investment arbitration, Ghana challenged his appointment. Ghana argued that, given that the arbitrator was simultaneously acting for an investor in relation to similar points of law, he would be likely to adopt a position favourable to Telekom Malaysia. As a result, he lacked independence and impartiality as an arbitrator.[166]   4.133

While the other members of the tribunal and the Secretariat of the PCA both rejected challenges brought by Ghana, Ghana brought the matter for review to the Dutch courts, The Hague being the agreed seat of the arbitration. In its decision of 18 October 2004, the District Court of The Hague emphasised the 'incompatibility' of the arbitrator's role as attorney and arbitrator, placing much weight on the appearance, rather than the actual existence of bias.[167] It has been reported that the Court held that: 4.134

> Even if this arbitrator were able to sufficiently distance himself in chambers from his role as attorney in the reversal proceedings…account should be taken of the appearance of his not being able to observe the said distance. Since he has to play these two parts, it is in any case impossible for him to avoid the appearance of not being able to keep these two parts strictly separated.[168]

To avoid giving rise to 'justifiable doubts' as to the arbitrator's impartiality and independence as arbitrator, the Court permitted him to continue serving on the tribunal, on the condition that he resign as counsel in the other arbitration within ten days. This decision raises questions of the compatibility of acting as arbitrator and counsel, particularly in investment arbitrations.   4.135

In a more recent case, *ICS v Argentina*,[169] Argentina sought the removal of the investor-appointed arbitrator, who was also acting as counsel for another investor   4.136

---

[165] *Telekom Malaysia Berhad v Republic of Ghana*, Decision No. HA/RK2004.667, District Court of The Hague, 18 October 2004, available online at http://www.italaw.com/sites/default/files/case-documents/ita0857_0.pdf.

[166] Levine, 'Dealing with arbitrator "issue conflicts" in international arbitration' (2006) 3 Disp Res J 60, at 62; Peterson, 'Dutch Court finds arbitrator in conflict due to role of counsel to another investor', Investment Law and Policy Weekly News Bulletin, 17 December 2004.

[167] District Court of The Hague, Civil Law Section, Provisional Measures Judge, Challenge No. 13/2004, Petition No. HA/RK2004/667, Decision of 18 October 2004, cited in Levine, n. 164 and Peterson, n. 164.

[168] Ibid., at 63.

[169] Challenge Decision, UNCITRAL, PCA Case No. 2010-9, 17 December 2009. See also, Daele, *Challenge and Disqualification of Arbitrators in International Arbitration* (Kluwer Law International, 2012), paras 7.013–7.015; IBA Conflicts of Interest Subcommittee, 'The IBA

in ICSID annulment proceedings involving Argentina. In response, ICS argued that the annulment proceedings would soon be completed and that the arbitrator would therefore not be arguing for his investor client at the same time as he was sitting in judgment in the instant arbitration. Perhaps unsurprisingly, the appointing authority was unconvinced by such temporal distinctions and, referring to the IBA Guidelines, held that the conflict was 'sufficiently serious to give rise to objectively justifiable doubts as to [the arbitrator's] impartiality and independence'.[170]

4.137 Along the same lines, in September 2009, ICAS amended its rules to prohibit arbitrators from serving as counsel before the Court of Arbitration for Sport (CAS) at the same time.[171] It is questionable, however, if such issue conflicts will exist more broadly in purely commercial cases in which the applicable legal systems, facts, and legal issues are extremely varied and the ultimate awards rarely published.

(iv) Pre-judgment

4.138 In one UNCITRAL case, the respondent state challenged one of the arbitrators on the basis of comments made during the hearing on the merits based on Article 12 of the UNCITRAL Rules, which states: 'Any arbitrator may be challenged if circumstances exist that give rise to justifiable doubts as to the arbitrator's impartiality and independence.' The respondent state submitted that the particular statement pre-judged one of the issues in the arbitration.[172] The claimant noted that the statement had been made in the course of posing a hypothetical question to the claimant's expert. No allegation was made of any connections between the arbitrator and one of the parties, and the analysis was consequently limited to a review of whether there was a lack of impartiality. The challenge was heard by a division of the LCIA Court by agreement of the parties.

4.139 The division applied an objective test of impartiality. It concluded that any statement had to be analysed as a whole and in its context, and that if this exercise was done by a reasonable third party in the case in question, there was no reasonable apprehension of bias. The context of hypothetical questions to an expert and the immediate correction by the arbitrator of the concern raised orally by the

---

Guidelines on Conflicts of Interest in International Arbitration: The first five years 2004–2009' (2010) 4 Disp Res Intl 51.

[170] *ICS v Argentina*, at [3]. See also the recent decision of the chairman of the ICSID Administrative Council in *Blue Bank International & Trust (Barbados) Ltd v Bolivarian Republic of Venezuela*, Decision on the Parties' Proposal to Disqualify a Majority of the Tribunal, ICSID Case No. ARB/12/20, 12 November 2013. See also the IBA Guidelines on Conflicts of Interest, Pt II, para. 6.

[171] Statutes of the Bodies Working for the Settlement of Sports-Related Disputes, s. 18 ('CAS arbitrators and mediators may not act as counsel for a party before the CAS'). See also Perry, 'Stockholm: Arbitrator and counsel—The double-hat syndrome' (2012) 7 Global Arb Rev 4.

[172] *National Grid PLC v Republic of Argentina*, Decision on the Challenge dated 3 December 2007, LCIA Case No. UN7949, at [38].

E. Challenge and Replacement of Arbitrators

respondent state following the statement was such that 'any appearance of bias which may have been created by the challenged sentence was eliminated'.[173]

Even when comments made do show how an arbitrator is thinking, the US courts have made it clear that this is a natural result of evaluating evidence on an ongoing basis as a case progresses. For example, in *Fairchild & Co. Inc. v Richmond*,[174] it was held that:

4.140

> [An a]rbitrator's legitimate efforts to move the proceedings along expeditiously may be viewed as abrasive or disruptive to a disappointed party... such displeasure does not constitute grounds for vacating an arbitration award... [E]vident partiality is not demonstrated where an arbitrator consistently relies upon the evidence and reaches the conclusions favourable to one party... The mere fact that arbitrators are persuaded by one party's arguments and choose to agree with them is not of itself sufficient to raise a question as to the evident partiality of the arbitrators.

Allegations of pre-judgment are not always limited to an arbitrator's conduct in the instant case. Challenges have been mounted on the basis of prior publication by an arbitrator of opinions that pertain to an issue in dispute. In an ICSID case, it was held that if an arbitrator has previously published a general opinion about a particular legal issue that also arises in the present arbitration, then this will not normally give rise to any conflict issues.[175] Rejecting the challenge, the tribunal found that the taking of a general position on an issue raised in the arbitration was not sufficient to establish bias, or even the appearance of bias, since a reasonable person would consider that the arbitrator would still give proper consideration to the facts, circumstances, and arguments presented by the parties in the particular case.

4.141

The situation may be different where the arbitrator concerned is deemed to have publicly commented on the arbitration itself, and not merely on a particular legal issue arising in the case. In *Perenco Ecuador Ltd v Republic of Ecuador & Empresa Estatal Petroleos del Ecuador*,[176] the challenge arose out of a published interview with the arbitrator, in which he made various comments about Ecuador's disobedient behaviour in the proceedings, including Ecuador's refusal to comply with orders for provisional measures. The comments were made in the context of a broader discussion about the issue of recalcitrant states in international arbitration. The secretary-general of the PCA found that, although the arbitrator did not specifically refer to the arbitration, his combination of chosen words and the context in which he used them had the overall effect of painting an unfavourable view

4.142

---

[173] Ibid., at [96].
[174] *Fairchild & Co. Inc. v Richmond F & PR Co.* 516 F.Supp 1305, 1313 (DDC 1981).
[175] *Urbaser SA and ors v Argentine Republic*, Decision on Claimants' Proposal to Disqualify Professor Campbell McLachlan, Arbitrator, ICSID Case No. ARB/07/26, 12 August 2010, available online at http://italaw.com/sites/default/files/case-documents/ita0887.pdf.
[176] Decision on Challenge to Arbitrator, ICSID Case No. ARB/08/6, PCA Case No. IR-2009/1, 8 December 2009, available online at http://italaw.com/sites/default/files/case-documents/ita0625.pdf.

of Ecuador (which had brought the challenge) in such a way as to give a reasonable and informed third party justifiable doubts as to his impartiality.[177]

(e) Waiver

4.143 A question arises concerning the obligation of a party to raise promptly any objection concerning the independence or impartiality of an arbitrator (or any other ground of challenge) when the facts upon which the challenge is based come to the attention of the objecting party.

4.144 In the ICSID Arbitration Rules, Rule 27 ('Waiver') states clearly that a party who fails to object promptly to an alleged violation of a relevant rule is deemed to have waived its right to object:

> A party which knows or should have known that a provision of the Administrative and Financial Regulations, of these Rules, of any other rules or agreement applicable to the proceeding, or of an order of the Tribunal has not been complied with and which fails to state *promptly* its objections thereto, shall be deemed—subject to Article 45 of the Convention—to have waived its right to object.

4.145 Under Article 13(2) of the Model Law, challenges related to impartiality or independence must be filed with the arbitral tribunal within fifteen days of the party becoming aware of the circumstances giving rise to justifiable doubts as to those issues. Is the objection to be deemed to be waived if the time limit is not met, or may the objection be raised in a challenge to the award or on enforcement proceedings? This question has not been resolved definitively. The better view is that, on policy grounds, a failure to comply with the time limits should bar any attack of the award on this basis.

4.146 In common law jurisdictions, the concept of waiver is well established: a party may not 'lie in ambush' with an objection to await the decision of the tribunal. The Supreme Court of Canada has stated that '[t]here is no doubt that, generally speaking, an award will not be set aside if the circumstances alleged to disqualify an arbitrator were known to both parties before the arbitration commenced and they proceeded without objection'.[178]

4.147 The concept of waiver is also known in civil law countries. A challenge to an arbitrator under the Swiss PIL must be brought 'without delay'.[179] An unreasonable delay in bringing a challenge amounts to a 'forfeiture', which is a reflection of the bona fides principle in Swiss law.[180] Under French law, parties have one month from discovery of the fact at issue to file a challenge application.[181]

---

[177] Ibid., at [48].
[178] *Ghirardosi v Minister of Highways (BC)* 56 DLR (2d) 469, 473 (1996).
[179] Swiss PIL, Ch. 12, s. 180(2).
[180] See Blessing, 'The new international arbitration law in Switzerland' (1988) 5 J Intl Arb 9, at 40.
[181] French Code of Civil Procedure, art. 1456(3).

E. Challenge and Replacement of Arbitrators

4.148 The prominent place of 'waiver' in the challenge landscape is reflected in the IBA Guidelines. With the exception of circumstances that fall within the Waivable and Non-Waivable Red Lists, the Guidelines require, in General Standard 4(a), that a party make an explicit objection within thirty days of any disclosure by the arbitrator, or of a party, learning of facts or circumstances that could constitute a potential conflict of interest for an arbitrator, otherwise the party is deemed to have waived the potential conflict. With regards to circumstances falling within the Waivable Red List, General Standard 4(c)(ii) requires an express waiver by all parties in order for the arbitrator to accept appointment or continue to act as an arbitrator.

4.149 A discussion of waiver is incomplete without a consideration of the emerging phenomenon of 'advance' waivers. With the growth in the number of arbitrators who work at large law firms, a practice is developing in international arbitration whereby such arbitrators send advance waivers to the parties prior to accepting an appointment. Such waivers vary in form, but typically amount to a request for advance clearance from the parties to the effect that the acceptance of the arbitral appointment will not inhibit other lawyers from the same law firm from acting for or against any party involved in the arbitration, as long as such separate mandate is unrelated to the arbitration. Waivers by the parties in advance raise questions of party autonomy and informed consent. At the time of writing, the approach of the leading institutions to such waivers appears to be neither fixed nor consistent. For its part, the 2014 version of the IBA Guidelines acknowledges the increasing use of such advanced waivers, but does not take a position on their validity and effect, save to confirm that they do not discharge an arbitrator's ongoing duty of disclosure.[182]

(f) Conclusion on challenges

4.150 So where does this leave us? A prospective arbitrator should not accept an appointment if there is reason to believe that either party will genuinely feel that he or she is not independent, or is not capable of approaching the issues impartially. The position is more difficult where a party objects *after* the arbitrator has been appointed. If both parties agree that the arbitrator should resign, then this is determinative. The arbitrator should also resign if it seems, on reflection, that the objection is, or appears to be, well founded, whether or not the parties agree.

4.151 However, if the objection appears to be without merit, the arbitrator should not resign, but should permit the matter to be dealt with by the relevant challenge procedure. Even though this course may create delay, it helps to discourage unmeritorious

---

[182] IBA Guidelines, General Standard 3(b). The explanation of General Standard 3(b) provides that the Guidelines 'do not otherwise take a position as to the validity and effect of advance declarations or waivers, because the validity and effect of any advance declaration or waiver must be assessed in view of the specific text of the advance declaration or waiver, the particular circumstances at hand and the applicable law'.

disruptive tactics. If a party nominates a perfectly acceptable arbitrator—the 'judge of its choice'—and wishes that arbitrator to remain even though an objection has been made, that arbitrator should, in principle, remain unless the appropriate authority, whether it is a national court or another body, issues a ruling to the contrary. The same general principle applies in the case of a presiding arbitrator, although a presiding arbitrator is probably under a greater duty to examine the grounds for objection carefully before deciding whether or not to proceed with the case.

(g) **Filling a vacancy**

4.152 A replacement arbitrator must be appointed where a member of a three-person tribunal resigns or is successfully challenged and the other two members do not proceed as a truncated tribunal.[183] If the arbitration is being conducted under international or institutional rules, or under a properly drawn submission agreement, the procedure for replacing an arbitrator will be specified. In general, the new appointment is made in the same way as the original appointment.[184]

4.153 Problems are likely to arise in replacing an arbitrator only in pure ad hoc arbitrations. The parties themselves may be able to reach an agreement as to the method by which the arbitrator should be replaced and this approach should certainly be attempted first. However, if the parties cannot agree, either on the choice of a replacement arbitrator or on the way of making that choice, then an approach to the relevant national court must be considered. Since, by definition, an arbitral tribunal is already in existence and the place of arbitration will almost certainly have been decided, the request for the appointment of a replacement arbitrator is made to the courts at the seat of arbitration. It is necessary to ensure that the court has the power to make the necessary appointment, but, as with the appointment of arbitrators *ab initio*, most developed national systems of law confer such powers upon their courts.[185] Nevertheless, it is best not to rely upon recourse to national courts if it can be avoided. The following guidelines are therefore suggested.

- Where provision is to be made for an arbitration to be conducted according to the rules of one of the arbitral institutions, those rules should be checked to make sure that they contain adequate provision for the filling of a vacancy.

---

[183] Exceptionally, in the case of a three-member arbitral tribunal, the arbitration may proceed with the two remaining members. See the discussion of truncated tribunals at paras 4.154*ff*.

[184] A notable exception arises under the ICSID Arbitration Rules, r. 11(2), where, in order to prevent abuse, a party-nominated arbitrator who resigns will be replaced by a person nominated by the chairman of the Administrative Council of ICSID rather than by the relevant party, unless the remaining members of the arbitral tribunal have consented to his resignation, under r. 8(2).

[185] For example, in English law, the court has wide powers to give directions as to the making of any appointments and, indeed, to make any necessary appointments itself: English Arbitration Act 1996, s. 18. See also Goldman, 'The complementary roles of judges and arbitrators in ensuring that international commercial arbitration is effective', in ICC (ed.) *60 Years of ICC Arbitration: A Look at the Future*, ICC Publication No 412 (ICC, 1984), p. 275.

E. Challenge and Replacement of Arbitrators

- Where an arbitration is to be conducted ad hoc under the terms of a submission agreement, adequate provisions for the filling of any vacancy in the arbitral tribunal should be written into the submission agreement.
- Where an arbitration is to be conducted ad hoc without any formal submission agreement, it should be held only in a country in which the local law contains adequate provision for filling any vacancy that may arise.

(h) Truncated tribunals

4.154 Most party-appointed arbitrators act properly and in good faith. It occasionally happens, however, that a party-appointed arbitrator refuses to participate in the arbitration, or submits a resignation without sufficient reason. If this takes place early in the proceedings, or if the case is one in which the interests of justice do not require a quick decision, a replacement may be appointed.[186]

4.155 Appointing a new arbitrator may, however, be impractical when the resignation, or refusal to participate, occurs late in the arbitral proceedings. Finding and appointing a replacement, and allowing the new arbitrator to become familiar with the case, inevitably causes delay. The situation is particularly aggravated if the arbitrator chooses to resign, or refuses to participate, when the stage of the tribunal's deliberations is reached. In such cases, and in cases in which a quick conclusion to the arbitration is essential, the only sensible course may be for the two remaining arbitrators to continue with the proceedings and to render an award without the participation of the third arbitrator.

4.156 A number of celebrated cases provide examples of situations in which arbitral tribunals have continued proceedings and rendered awards as truncated tribunals.[187] Most of these have been ad hoc arbitrations, but there have been cases under the UNCITRAL Rules[188] and the ICC Rules[189] in which proceedings have been continued and awards rendered by truncated tribunals. The AAA International Arbitration Rules (1991 edition) appear to have been the first set of rules to provide expressly for the two remaining arbitrators to continue where their colleague third

---

[186] In which case, the procedures for filling vacancies would apply as described above.

[187] These cases were discussed at the 1990 ICCA Congress: see Schwebel and Böckstiegel, 'Preventing delay or disruption of arbitration' (1991) 5 ICCA Congress Series 241, at 270–274. See also the French-Mexican Claims Commission cases, discussed in Feller, *The Mexican Claims Commissions* (Macmillan, 1935), pp. 70–77. See also Schwebel, *International Arbitration: Three Salient Problems* (Grotius, 1987), pp. 144–296.

[188] See, e.g., Order of 17 May 1985, in *Sedco Inc. v National Iranian Oil Co.*, Case No. 129, reprinted in (1985) 8 Iran–US CTR 34, with concurring opinion of Judge Bower at 40; *Uiterwiyk Corporation v Islamic Republic of Iran*, Award No. 375–381–1, 6 July 1988, (1988) 19 Iran–US CTR 107, at 116; also dissenting letter and supplemental opinion in (1988) 19 Iran–US CTR 107, at 161 and 169.

[189] See Böckstiegel, 'Preventing delay or disruption of arbitration' (1991) 5 ICCA Congress Series 271.

arbitrator fails to participate.[190] If the parties have agreed that the arbitration may proceed with two arbitrators, national courts may be expected to enforce an otherwise valid award.[191]

4.157 One US commentator has written:

> I find it very hard to imagine that, even in the absence of an express rule or agreement, a modern court in a state that otherwise has a public policy of supporting international commercial arbitration would invalidate an award issued by a majority of arbitrators because a party-appointed arbitrator, in an effort to frustrate the arbitration, chooses to absent himself at a late stage of the proceedings, or refuses to sign an award. National laws that refer to participation by three arbitrators should be interpreted to have been satisfied, as Professor Gaillard suggests, when all three have had a fair and equal *opportunity* to participate.[192]

4.158 Nevertheless, most of the world's leading international arbitral institutions followed the example of the AAA (as the ICDR was then known). The LCIA and WIPO followed the philosophy of leaving the question of whether or not to proceed on a truncated basis entirely to the discretion of the remaining arbitrators. However, the ICC adopted a more restrictive approach:

> 5 Subsequent to the closing of the proceedings, instead of replacing an arbitrator who has died or been removed by the Court pursuant to Articles 15(1) and 15(2), the Court may decide, when it considers it appropriate, that the remaining arbitrators shall continue the arbitration. In making such determination, the Court shall take into account the views of the remaining arbitrators and of the parties and such other matters that it considers appropriate in the circumstances.[193]

Thus not only does the ICC limit the possibility of a truncated tribunal to the deliberations phase, but also it is the ICC Court that takes the decision, rather than the remaining members of the tribunal.

4.159 Several cases in which arbitral tribunals have decided to proceed in truncated form have come into the public domain. The most sensational involved the government of a country in south-east Asia, which exerted considerable pressure on the arbitrator whom it had appointed to withdraw. The final award contains a passage stating comprehensively the relevant facts and analysing the legal consequences. The conclusion of the two remaining arbitrators, relying on the published works of a

---

[190] AAA International Arbitration Rules, effective 1 March 1991, Art. 11. The provision remained unaltered in the ICDR's 2003 edition and now exists as Art. 11 of the current Rules, effective from 1 June 2009.
[191] See Gaillard and Veeder, 'Failure by a party-appointed arbitrator to participate in the arbitral proceedings' (1999) 5 ICCA Congress Series, Topic 7. Moreover, Veeder notes in his report that the Model Law may be construed to authorise truncated tribunals.
[192] See Holtzmann, 'How to prevent delay and disruption of arbitration: Lessons of the 1990 ICCA Stockholm Congress' (1991) 5 ICCA Congress Series 28 (emphasis original).
[193] ICC Rules, Art. 15(5).

E. Challenge and Replacement of Arbitrators

well-known international jurist, was that it could—and indeed should—proceed in truncated form to render a final award.[194]

So far as the UNCITRAL Rules are concerned, there is therefore respectable authority supporting the legitimacy of a truncated tribunal's decision to proceed and render an award where appropriate. In institutional arbitration, the most modern sets of rules have created their own individual regimes—mostly leaving it to the governing bodies of the institutions concerned to decide, rather than to the remaining arbitrators. In ad hoc arbitrations in which the parties have not chosen to arbitrate under the UNCITRAL Rules, it is wise for the remaining arbitrators to proceed with caution; at the very least, they should review any relevant provisions of the *lex arbitri* and (if they are aware of it) the law of the place of likely enforcement of the award.

4.160

It seems clear that the option of proceeding as a truncated tribunal, rather than as a reconstituted full tribunal, will remain as an exceptional measure to be adopted only when the arbitration is nearing its end and where there is clear evidence that the arbitrator concerned, voluntarily or involuntarily, has been associated with an abuse of the process.[195]

4.161

(i) Procedure following the filling of a vacancy

A question of considerable practical importance arises when a vacancy does occur in the arbitral tribunal and is filled: to what extent must the arbitral tribunal retrace its steps? If the oral hearings have not begun when the vacancy arises, it should not be necessary for either the newly constituted arbitral tribunal or the parties themselves to go back over old ground. It is sufficient for the replacement arbitrator to be given time to read the pleadings and other documents exchanged between the parties, to consider any procedural directions given by the former arbitral tribunal, and to signify his or her assent to them. This assent should be recorded in writing as a matter of practice, although no particular form is required. However, if the vacancy arises *after* the oral proceedings have begun, it will necessarily bring them to a close for a period of time, unless the proceedings continue before a truncated tribunal. When the arbitral tribunal has been reconstituted, the question arises as to whether or not evidence that has already been heard and legal arguments that have already been advanced orally should be repeated for the

4.162

---

[194] *Himpurna California Energy Ltd v Republic of Indonesia* (2000) XXV YBCA 186, citing Schwebel's Cambridge Lauterpacht lectures, in which he referred to *Republic of Colombia v Cauca Co.*, the *French-Mexican Claims Commission* cases, the *Lena Goldfields* arbitration, the *Sabotage* cases, and the Advisory Opinion of the International Court of Justice (ICJ) in Interpretation of Peace Treaties with Bulgaria, Hungary and Romania.

[195] For consideration of the treatment of truncated tribunals by various institutions' rules, see Maniruzzaman, 'The authority of a truncated arbitral tribunal: Straight path or puzzle?' (2012) 90 Amicus Curiae 22.

benefit of the replacement arbitrator. Such repetition is both time-consuming and expensive. It is in the interests of both parties to the arbitration to try to avoid it, if at all possible.

4.163 Where a transcript is available, it should be sufficient for the replacement arbitrator to read the transcript and so bring himself or herself up to date with the proceedings. If, as a result of such reading, the replacement arbitrator wishes to have a particular witness recalled, or a particular argument explained in more detail, it may be in the interests of both parties to agree that this should be done, rather than run the risk of having to start the oral proceedings again from the beginning. Where there is no transcript of the oral hearing, the extent to which oral evidence and argument already presented needs to be repeated is a question that can be resolved only by discussion between the members of the arbitral tribunal (including the replacement member), the parties, and their legal advisers.

4.164 The parties may generally be relied upon to cooperate in such matters. Once an arbitration has progressed so far, it is usually in the interests of all parties that the proceedings continue without the need for repetition, because the costs are invariably substantial. Thus it is for the replacement arbitrator, in consultation with the remaining members of the tribunal, to decide the extent to which the previous steps in the proceedings should be retraced.

4.165 It is difficult to lay down any specific rule as to the attitude that the replacement arbitrator should adopt. The UNCITRAL Rules provide that, where an arbitrator is replaced, 'the proceedings shall resume at the stage where the arbitrator who was replaced ceased to perform his or her functions, unless the arbitral tribunal decides otherwise'.[196] The ICC Rules provide that the reconstituted tribunal will determine, after having invited parties to comment, whether and to what extent any prior proceedings shall be repeated. However, if the parties agree on the matter, the tribunal will usually follow such agreement.[197]

By contrast, Article 34 of the WIPO Rules provides that '[w]henever a substitute arbitrator is appointed, the Tribunal shall, having regard to any observations of the parties, determine in its sole discretion whether all or part of any prior hearings are to be repeated'.

4.166 The 2010 version of the ICDR Rules contains broadly similar provisions,[198] but the 2014 version of the LCIA Rules does not cover the position expressly.

---

[196] UNCITRAL Rules, Art. 15.
[197] UNCITRAL Rules, Art. 15(4). See also Daele, *Challenge and Disqualification of Arbitrators in International Arbitration* (Kluwer Law International, 2012), para. 4.103.
[198] ICDR Rules, Art. 11(2).

(j) Insuring against a vacancy

4.167 At one time, it was not unusual, in large and expensive international commercial arbitrations, for insurance to be taken out on the lives of the members of the arbitral tribunal. This was usually done when the oral hearings were about to begin and, in itself, was a recognition of the fact that the oral hearings might have to be repeated if one of the members of the arbitral tribunal (and in particular the presiding arbitrator) were to die. The advantage of taking out insurance is that if an arbitrator were to die or become incapacitated, the proceeds of the insurance policy would be available to cover at least part of the considerable expenses involved in adjourning the hearing, reconstituting the arbitral tribunal, reconvening the hearing, and, perhaps, going over again the ground already covered.

4.168 One problem, apart from that of the cost of such insurance, is that the members of the arbitral tribunal must be told that insurance on their lives is being taken out—if only because the insurance company will need medical information, and perhaps a medical examination, which only the arbitrators themselves can provide. It is a delicate, and sometimes invidious, task to suggest, or to appear to suggest, to members of the arbitral tribunal that they may not survive the proceedings! They may not like the message, or the messenger. If it is to be done, it is best done by both parties acting jointly, rather than by one party acting on its own.[199]

F. Organisation of the Arbitral Tribunal

(a) Introduction

4.169 There is much work to be done 'behind the scenes' to ensure that an international arbitration runs smoothly. The arbitrators are generally of different nationalities, as are the parties, their advisers, and experts. This mixture of nationalities is one of the most intriguing challenges involved in the practice of international commercial arbitration. It needs more careful planning and organisation to bring together such a mixed group of people in what will be a foreign city for most of them than it does to arrange a domestic arbitration. Indeed, arranging a hearing in a large international commercial arbitration has much in common with arranging a series of performances for a company of opera singers or actors embarking upon an international tour: there is a venue to be arranged, times and dates to be fixed, hotel rooms to be booked, technicians (in the form of interpreters, transcription services, and so forth) to be engaged, and the whole performance has to be so organised that, when the time comes, the assembled cast of parties, lawyers, experts, and witnesses are ready to present their offerings to their small, but important, audience—the

---

[199] As far as the authors are aware, the practice of the parties insuring the lives or health of the arbitrators appears to have virtually disappeared.

arbitral tribunal. The work involved in making the administrative arrangements has led to it becoming the established practice in larger and more complex international arbitrations for the arbitral tribunal to appoint an arbitral secretary or registrar, whose function includes taking care of the practical arrangements.[200]

(b) Meetings and hearings

4.170 In arbitrations in which the arbitral tribunal consists of more than a sole arbitrator, it is usually necessary for the members of the arbitral tribunal to meet from time to time for consultation amongst themselves. There is no reason why such meetings should be held at the seat of the arbitration. If it is more convenient for the members of the arbitral tribunal to meet elsewhere, they may do so, subject to any provisions to the contrary in the submission agreement or in the applicable rules of arbitration.[201] The arbitrators may be required, however, to meet at the seat of the arbitration for the purpose of drawing up or signing their award.[202]

(i) Meetings and hearings at which the parties are present

4.171 In all but the simplest cases, it is likely that in-person or teleconference/video conference meetings will take place from time to time between the arbitral tribunal, the parties, and their representatives, so that procedural orders or directions may be considered. Unless the applicable law or rules forbid it, the arbitral tribunal may decide to hold meetings with the parties elsewhere if this is more convenient and, in particular, if savings of costs may be achieved. However, the arbitral tribunal should consult the parties before doing so. If the parties agree to hold all meetings and/or hearings at the place of arbitration, this should guide the arbitral tribunal. It is nevertheless noteworthy that, in recent years, with the advances of video-conferencing technology, many steps may be taken without the need for a physical meeting. This is particularly to be encouraged where the amounts in dispute are limited and the costs of organising the meeting considerable.

4.172 Unless the case is to be decided on the basis of documents only, there is also a final hearing, or a series of hearings, at which the parties and their representatives attend in order to put forward the evidence of their witnesses and their legal arguments.[203] Witness hearings are generally, but not always, held at the seat of the arbitration; provision is sometimes made for the arbitral tribunal to meet elsewhere,[204] when,

---

[200] For a discussion of the role and functions of an arbitral secretary or registrar, see paragraphs 4.192*ff.*

[201] The UNCITRAL Rules give the arbitral tribunal complete freedom in this respect: see Art. 18(2). So also do the LCIA Rules: see Art. 16(3). The ICSID Arbitration Rules, however, appear to contemplate that even meetings for consultation between the members of the arbitral tribunal should take place 'at the seat of the Centre or at such other place that may have been agreed by the parties': see r. 13(3). See Chapter 3, paragraph 3.57.

[202] See Chapter 3.

[203] For a more detailed account of the issues to consider for a final oral hearing, see Chapter 6.

[204] See, e.g., the UNCITRAL Rules, Art. 18(2); LCIA Rules, Art. 16(3).

for instance, the evidence of an important witness is required, and it is more convenient for the arbitral tribunal and the parties to go to the witness than it is for the witness to go to the arbitral tribunal.[205]

(ii) Fixing dates for hearings

Where the arbitral tribunal consists of more than a sole arbitrator, the date of the hearing will generally be fixed by the presiding arbitrator, in consultation with the co-arbitrators, the parties, and their advisers. It is good practice to fix final hearing dates as early as possible, so that the many actors involved will book the dates in their diaries. It is inevitably difficult to coordinate the agendas of arbitrators, parties, and witnesses for a period that may be between one to three weeks. A good idea is to fix the dates in the procedural calendar at the first procedural meeting (or terms of reference meeting, in ICC cases), usually annexed to a procedural order. Once fixed, the final hearing dates will act as a backstop beyond which the arbitration cannot be delayed. This helps to concentrate the minds of counsel and the arbitral tribunal in the face of any subsequent attempts to extend the procedural schedule. **4.173**

If a reasonable agreement on a date cannot be reached between the parties and the arbitral tribunal, the arbitral tribunal must fix a date without such agreement. There can be little objection to this, as long as the parties are given reasonable notice.[206] **4.174**

In fixing a date for the hearing, the sole or presiding arbitrator should take account of holiday periods in the countries of the arbitrators and the parties. The arbitrator is unlikely to wish to work during religious or family holidays in his or her own country, and should not unreasonably insist that others must work during such periods in their countries. This is not a legal obligation; rather, it is a matter of courtesy and of consideration for the other participants. It may also be difficult—or even impossible, in some countries—to provide the necessary infrastructure for a hearing on a public holiday. **4.175**

(iii) Length of hearings

In fixing a date for the start of the hearings, the sole or presiding arbitrator must keep in mind the length of time that the hearing is likely to take. Indeed, this is a question that will be asked repeatedly when making travel and hotel arrangements, when booking rooms in which the hearing is to take place, when making arrangements for the attendance of the parties and their witnesses, and so on. It is extremely difficult to estimate accurately how long a case is likely to last. As **4.176**

---

[205] This may be the case if witnesses are unable to travel for health reasons, or if the witnesses are high-ranking government officials or ministers. However, once again, it is now common for witnesses who, for good reason, cannot be physically present to be heard by video conference.
[206] ICSID Arbitration Rules, r. 13(4).

a general rule, it is safer to overbook time at the beginning of a case and then release time later if it appears that the hearing will not take up all of the allotted days than it is to try to reconvene the entire proceeding at a later date if insufficient time has been set aside. Similarly, finding availability of all participants for a longer hearing will be more difficult and thus will itself cause delays. As in many aspects of procedure in international arbitration, it is for the tribunal to strike a balance between affording the parties a reasonable opportunity to present their case and not succumbing to some parties' (or counsel's) tendencies towards procedural excess.

(c) Administrative aspects

4.177 The place of the arbitration is chosen before any hearing is held—but it is necessary to fix a specific venue in appropriate premises offered by an arbitral institution, conference centre, or other suitable building. In deciding on a venue, the primary consideration must be to find accommodation that is fit for the purpose. Two particular requirements stand out. First, the venue chosen must provide adequate space not only for the arbitral tribunal, but also for the parties and their lawyers, for screens, charts, drawings, and other documents, all of which may be voluminous, and for anyone else who is to assist in the conduct of the arbitration, including experts, stenographers, and interpreters. In modern times, electronic aids of one kind or another are routinely deployed and should be available at the proposed venue.[207] Secondly, as far as possible, the facilities chosen must be available for the purposes of the arbitration throughout the whole period of the hearing. It is both irritating and inconvenient when the hearing room (at a hotel, for example) must be completely cleared at the end of the day's proceedings, to make way for a dinner or other function.

4.178 For a meeting between the arbitral tribunal and the parties, it is usually sufficient if one room is available, provided that the room is big enough. For a witness hearing—particularly a hearing that is likely to last for more than two or three days—it is usual (and, in some cases, essential) for other rooms to be available as 'breakout' rooms in which each party can store documents, check transcripts, prepare for the next day's hearings, and generally engage in the often frantic activity that goes on behind the scenes in any international commercial arbitration. The arbitral tribunal should also have a room available for its own deliberations, because it is often inconvenient or impracticable to ask the parties to withdraw completely from the hearing room. Security can also present problems: the parties (and the arbitral tribunal) usually wish to be able to leave documents at the venue without fear of their being seen by others. Suitable accommodation, particularly for a lengthy hearing, is not easy to find. Specialist international arbitration groups

---

[207] Such as PowerPoint displays on a screen.

F. Organisation of the Arbitral Tribunal

within law firms often keep comprehensive lists of the facilities available in their localities, categorising them in terms of relative expense and convenience. Some of the commonly used alternatives are as follows.

(i) Arbitration centres

Most major arbitration institutions and centres are able to provide, or at least to recommend, accommodation that is suitable for almost every type of hearing. Where one of the parties is a government or other state enterprises, it is worth considering whether the arbitration can be brought within the facilities of either the PCA at the Peace Palace in The Hague, or of ICSID (that is, the facilities of the World Bank in Washington or Paris). Even where an arbitration does not fall within the PCA Rules, the secretary-general of the PCA is generally willing to accommodate arbitrations between private parties, as well as those under the PCA's Rules, provided that space is available. Likewise, ICSID has agreed to hold hearings under the UNCITRAL Rules where there is a connection with other cases that are being heard under the ICSID umbrella.

4.179

Some of the established international arbitral institutions, such as the ICC, ICDR, and LCIA, can also provide accommodation for use both as hearing rooms and conference rooms. The LCIA has arrangements with the International Dispute Resolution Centre (IDRC) in Fleet Street, London, which includes a suite of over fifty rooms (including fourteen hearing/meeting rooms and more than thirty-five breakout rooms).[208] The ICC also has its own set of arbitration facilities in Paris, the ICC Hearing Centre, which is separate from the ICC premises themselves.[209] The ICDR headquarters in New York can host eight hearings at the same time, which capacity is supplemented by ICDR's international offices in Mexico, Dublin, and Bahrain.[210] Maxwell Chamber in Singapore can accommodate up to four arbitration cases simultaneously, whilst Arbitration Place in Toronto offers sixteen different hearing rooms of varying sizes.

4.180

(ii) Hotels

If the seat of the arbitration is not within one of the leading arbitration venues at which specialist accommodation is available, then it is common to rely on the leading hotels of the town or city in which the arbitration is to take place. Such hotels are mostly accustomed to looking after business visitors and will be able to offer, in addition to conference or other function rooms, photocopying, fax, and other services. Again, the critical concern is to ensure that the same room is available for the duration of the hearing to avoid expensive and time-consuming room changes mid-hearing.

4.181

---

[208] See http://www.idrc.co.uk/facilities.
[209] See http://www.iccwbo.org/products-and-services/hearing-centre/facilities/services/.
[210] See http://www.adr.org.

(iii) Interpreters

4.182 Some witnesses may be unable to express themselves easily, if at all, in the language of the arbitration. It should be regarded as a fundamental right of a party or a witness to speak at a hearing in his or her mother tongue.[211] In such circumstances, it is necessary to arrange for professional interpreters to be available, so that the witnesses may give testimony in their own language. Arrangements for the engagement of interpreters are usually undertaken by the party who requires their services. If a witness is to give evidence through an interpreter, it is usual to notify both the arbitral tribunal and the other party of this fact well in advance of the hearing.

4.183 The use of an interpreter may slow down the proceedings. This is something that the arbitral tribunal must take into account in assessing the duration of the hearing. Some techniques are available to minimise the inevitable delays involved in the use of interpreters. One is for the parties to agree a neutral interpreter in advance of the hearing, holding interviews to that effect. This reduces the risk of disputes over the possible partiality of an interpreter. If the witness has some command of the language of the arbitration, then the witness may use the interpreter simply to help him or her to understand the questions and formulate the answers. With modern technology, simultaneous interpretation can work relatively well, particularly where the facilities (such as those of ICSID) are especially designed for its use. In some ICSID cases, there has even been agreement to hold bilingual arbitrations, whereby there is interpretation into two languages.

(iv) Transcripts

4.184 A verbatim transcript, particularly of the evidence, can be of great importance in international arbitrations in which (as almost invariably occurs) the members of the arbitral tribunal have different levels of comprehension of the language of the proceedings. Indeed, the experience of the authors is that international arbitrators (and parties' counsel) rely heavily on transcripts of the proceedings when these are available for the purposes of preparing post-hearing submissions[212] and for drafting the award. They also constitute a permanent record of the proceedings, which may be beneficial later if, for example, a vacancy on the arbitral tribunal has to be filled, or if there are subsequent court proceedings for recourse against, or for enforcement of, the award.

4.185 Transcripts are prepared by means of professional transcript writers. One of the best systems is 'Livenote', whereby the testimony of the witness is shown

---

[211] It is not unreasonable, however, for an arbitral tribunal to require a party who wishes to engage lawyers to present his or her case to retain representatives who are able to perform their functions in the working language of the arbitration.

[212] It is usual to give such references by citing the day, page, and paragraph number of the transcript; so, e.g., the arbitral tribunal might be referred to the evidence of a particular witness at 'Day 10, page 70, paragraph B'.

F. Organisation of the Arbitral Tribunal

instantaneously on laptop computer screens available to the participants in the arbitration room. Whilst expensive, this can very useful (particularly for counsel in the course of a cross-examination). For most arbitrators, however, the value of the transcript lies in its availability during the deliberations and for drafting the award. A method cheaper than Livenote is to organise 'daily transcripts' that arrive on the same evening of each hearing day.

(v) Hearing hours

4.186 In most countries, judges sit in their courts for only a relatively short period each day: perhaps no more than five hours. This is sensible in that it allows judges time to read through their notes of the evidence and argument, and to reflect on what they have heard and what they would like to hear. Judges also have other duties to perform, and they do not usually accept judicial appointments on the basis that they will spend their weekends writing judgments or doing other paperwork. Relatively short working hours also allow the parties and their advisers essential time in which to produce any evidence, information, or data that the court may request, and it also gives them time to prepare for the next session.

4.187 This practice is not generally followed by arbitral tribunals engaged in international arbitrations. People who are present at the hearing may have travelled a long way to be there. They will usually be staying in hotels, and the cost of the proceedings will be substantial and will increase on a daily basis. The resulting tendency is to propose longer hearing hours, but this may be unfair to the parties and to their counsel, because it does not allow sufficient time (including time for reflection) in which they can present their respective cases. Moreover, shorter hours do not necessarily make for longer hearings. Lawyers can more readily condense their speeches if they have additional time for preparation during the course of the hearing. The arbitral tribunal may then put pressure on the parties to tailor their presentations to fit within an agreed timetable—subject to each party being allowed a reasonable period of time in which to present its case.

4.188 Above all, the arbitral tribunal should take charge of the hearings by imposing a timing discipline on the parties.[213] The allocation of time can be effectively applied by use of a 'chess clock' system, whereby, once the hearing days are fixed, each party is given a particular quota of hours. Within that quota, they must engage in direct examination of their own witnesses, cross-examination of the other party's witnesses, and oral submission. The use of the allotted time as between witnesses, or between submission and examination, is left to the discretion of the parties. At the hearing itself, the time is usually accounted for by a secretary to the tribunal or the president. It is nevertheless wise for each party to keep its own record and confirm that record with the tribunal at the end of each day, to avoid unpleasant surprises on the last day! If this system is adopted, the

---

[213] See ICC Rules, Art. 26(3): 'The arbitrator shall be in full charge of the hearings…'

tribunal should allow plenty of time for breaks and tribunal interventions. Thus, in a hearing day from 9.30 a.m. to 5.30 p.m., probably no more than six hours should be taken as party time, given the need for lunch and breaks and interventions from the tribunal.

(vi) Relations between the parties and the arbitral tribunal

4.189 It is important to remember that an arbitration, with its relatively informal atmosphere, is regarded as being a more friendly method of resolving disputes than proceedings before judges in national courts. There are more opportunities in an arbitration for informal meetings between the parties, their lawyers, and experts, on the one hand, and the members of the arbitral tribunal, on the other. This is something to be encouraged, provided that contacts take place openly. It is perfectly normal and reasonable for the parties and their counsel to converse with the members of the arbitral tribunal in coffee breaks, provided that such conversations are public and do not raise any issue concerning the case. (Sport, weather, and the quality of the coffee are always safe topics!)

(vii) Functions of the presiding arbitrator

4.190 The presiding arbitrator acts as chairman of the arbitral tribunal and will often be referred to as 'the president', or 'the chairman', not only in established rules of arbitration, but also by the parties and their lawyers during the course of the proceedings. The task of the presiding arbitrator is to take charge of the deliberations of the arbitral tribunal, and of the conduct of any meetings and hearings. It is the presiding arbitrator's responsibility to make sure that the proceedings move forward as smoothly and effectively as possible.

4.191 Depending on the rules under which the arbitration is being conducted, the presiding arbitrator may have no more than a voice equal to that of the co-arbitrators when it comes to making decisions, but the presiding arbitrator is nevertheless first amongst equals. A presiding arbitrator sometimes receives greater remuneration than the other members of the arbitral tribunal (usually described as the 'co-arbitrators') because of the greater investment in time as a result of additional responsibilities involved.[214] This is frequently the case when fees are fixed on a lump-sum basis. If the arbitrators' fees are based on an hourly rate, the presiding arbitrator is likely to be paid more than the others because of the additional hours that he or she will spend on the case compared with the co-arbitrators.

---

[214] For a comprehensive review of the functions of the presiding arbitrator, see Kaplan and Mills, 'The role of the chair in international commercial arbitration', in Prylles (ed.) *The Asian Leading Arbitrators' Guide to International Arbitration* (JurisNet, 2007), ch. 6. See also Reymond, 'Le président du tribunal arbitral', in *Etudes Offertes a Pierre Bellet* (Litec, 1991), pp. 467–482, subsequently translated into English and published as Reymond, 'The president of the arbitral tribunal' (1994) 1 ICSID Rev—Foreign Investment LJ 1.

F. Organisation of the Arbitral Tribunal

(d) Role of an arbitral secretary

4.192 The conduct of an international commercial arbitration may involve the sole or presiding arbitrator in a considerable amount of administrative work. As mentioned already, arrangements must be made for meetings between the parties and the arbitral tribunal. In a three-member arbitral tribunal, there is necessarily a certain amount of interchange between the arbitrators themselves, as well as between the arbitrators and the parties or their representatives.

4.193 When it comes to hearings, it may be necessary for the arbitral tribunal to arrange for the presence of interpreters and for a transcript of the proceedings to be made. It is essential for the smooth running of the arbitration that these arrangements should be made and in good time. Since the arrangements fall to be made by, or on behalf of, the arbitral tribunal itself, rather than by the parties, it is an established practice in large and complex international commercial arbitrations for the arbitral tribunal to appoint an arbitral secretary to take charge of all of the administrative arrangements that would otherwise fall to be made by the arbitral tribunal, to act as a link between the parties and the arbitral tribunal[215]

4.194 In performing his or her function, the arbitral secretary normally attends all meetings of the arbitral tribunal and also usually attends the hearings, so as to ensure that the various administrative procedures are running smoothly. For example, the secretary may organise the attendance of witnesses and verify that the transcript accurately records the evidence given. However, the arbitral secretary should not take an active part in the private deliberations of the arbitral tribunal that lead to the award.

4.195 The legitimate limits of the role and function of an arbitral secretary have been the subject of much debate within the arbitral community over many years. There are some who are of the view that the role of the arbitral secretary should be limited to the purely administrative; others consider there to be nothing illegitimate in an arbitrator delegating more substantive tasks to a secretary, in the same way as national judges have, for many years, made use of judicial clerks.[216] Notwithstanding such differences, however, there is broad consensus

---

[215] The increased acceptance and use of arbitral secretaries is evidenced in part by recent revisions to leading arbitral rules. By way of notable example, the *travaux preparatoires* of the UNCITRAL Rules 2010 reveal that some of the revisions were aimed at explicitly accommodating the use of secretaries: see the express references to assistance being provided to the tribunal at Arts 5, 16, and 40. Moreover, a recent survey indicates that, overall, arbitral secretaries are used in 35 per cent of arbitrations. They are more common in civil law proceedings (46 per cent) than in common law proceedings (24 per cent), and more so in Latin American (62 per cent) than in Asian (26 per cent) arbitrations: see White & Case and Queen Mary University of London, *Current and Preferred Practices in the Arbitral Process* (2012), available online at http://www.arbitration.qmul.ac.uk/research/2012/index.html, pp. 10–15.

[216] Ibid. In preparation for ICCA Singapore 2012, one of the authors was involved in conducting a survey among more than 200 members of the arbitration community, looking at various issues relating to the legitimate role of arbitral secretaries. While 95 per cent of participants agreed

that an arbitral secretary should be appointed only with the knowledge and consent of the parties, and that it remains the responsibility of the arbitral tribunal to ensure that its decision-making function is not delegated in any way. The task is to assist the arbitral tribunal, not to usurp its function.[217]

(i) Institutional arbitrations

4.196 Even in an administered arbitration, many detailed arrangements still fall to be made by the arbitral tribunal itself and the assistance of a secretary is extremely valuable in this regard. According to the ICC's Note on the Appointment, Duties and Remuneration of Administrative Secretaries of August 2012, the tasks of the arbitral secretary can include:

- organising meetings and hearings with the parties;
- taking a note of who is present at the hearing;
- checking and filing new exhibits;
- identifying relevant extracts in the record;
- preparing drafts of the procedural history;
- preparing a chronology of key events;
- performing legal or similar research;
- looking after witnesses who are in the course of giving evidence during the breaks;
- helping witnesses to find documents and passages to which they have been referred; and
- reminding parties of deadlines and communicating with the arbitral institution.[218]

4.197 All of these tasks free up the arbitral tribunal to focus on its core role: listening carefully to the evidence and weighing up the arguments, in order to reach a decision on the merits. When an appointment is made, a special arrangement may need to be made to meet the related fees and expenses, since these do not traditionally form part of the institution's administrative expenses or the arbitrator's fees.

---

with the use of arbitral secretaries, there was less consensus on the extent to which the arbitral secretary's role should go beyond the purely administrative. Following the session on arbitral secretaries at ICCA Singapore 2012, at which the results of the survey were discussed, Young ICCA developed guidelines for practitioners and tribunals in the appointment, role, and cost of arbitral secretaries: ICCA, *Young ICCA Guide on Arbitral Secretaries*, The ICCA Reports No. 1 (Kluwer Law International, 2014).

[217] See generally Partasides, 'The fourth arbitrator: The role of secretaries to tribunals in international arbitration' (2002) 18 Arb Intl 147; Partasides, 'Secretaries to arbitral tribunals', in Hanotiau and Mourre (eds) *Players' Interaction in International Arbitration* (Kluwer Law International, 2012), p. 87.

[218] See the duties listed in ICC, 'Note on the appointment, duties and remuneration of administrative secretaries' (2012) 23 ICC International Court of Arbitration Bulletin. See also *Young ICCA Guide on Arbitral Secretaries*, n. 216, Art. 2.

(ii) Whom to appoint

The obvious person to appoint as an arbitral secretary or registrar is a young lawyer with some experience of international commercial arbitration and of the administrative problems to which it can give rise. The usual procedure is for the arbitral tribunal to choose its own secretary or registrar, who is generally (although not invariably) a junior practising lawyer based in the same city as the presiding arbitrator (and, where the presiding arbitrator works for a firm, often a junior associate from that firm). A moderate hourly fee is paid, appropriate to the nature of the duties.   **4.198**

It is important to obtain the agreement of the parties before any appointment is made, with a clear explanation to the parties of the nature of the secretary's role and the benefits that such an appointment will give to the process, in terms of efficiency and cost savings. Some arbitral institutions offer clear guidelines on how to appoint arbitral secretaries and the proper scope of their role.[219]   **4.199**

(iii) Costs of an arbitral secretary

One of the key reasons for using an arbitral secretary is to save costs for the parties. It is surely uncontroversial, therefore, for the *Young ICCA Guide on Arbitral Secretaries* to record as 'a general principle' that 'the use of an arbitral secretary should reduce rather than increase the overall costs of the arbitration'.[220]   **4.200**

What this means in practice is likely to depend on the applicable rules of arbitration. Where the arbitral tribunal is remunerated on the basis of the amount in dispute, the costs and expenses associated with the arbitral secretary are more appropriately borne by the arbitral tribunal rather than the parties. Where the arbitral tribunal is remunerated on an hourly basis, the costs and expenses associated with the arbitral secretary may be more appropriately borne by the parties, owing to the efficiency of having many routine tasks performed at a lower rate by an arbitral secretary.   **4.201**

G. Fees and Expenses of the Arbitral Tribunal

(a) Introduction

The cost of bringing or defending a claim before an international arbitral tribunal is likely to be considerably higher than that of bringing or defending the same claim before a national court. This is because, in addition to the usual expenses of litigation, it is necessary for the parties to pay the fees and expenses of the arbitral tribunal (including international travel) and the cost of hiring suitable   **4.202**

---

[219] See ICC, 'Note', n. 218.
[220] *Young ICCA Guide on Arbitral Secretaries*, n. 216, Art. 4(I).

accommodation for hearings. In addition, where the arbitration is administered by an arbitral institution, the fees and expenses of that institution must be paid. This contrasts sharply with proceedings before a national court, in which the court rooms, the attendants, and the judges themselves are provided and paid for by the state. The parties often make no more than a nominal contribution to the state by way of a registration fee or other levy.[221] The fact that arbitration before a private arbitral tribunal attracts these additional charges makes it more desirable that arbitrations should not be conducted with all of the time-consuming formalities of proceedings in a national court. The aim should be to make use of the informality and flexibility of the arbitral process, so as to reduce both the time spent on the case and the cost of conducting it. In this way, the financial burden on the parties will be alleviated, to some extent.

(b) Who fixes fees?

4.203 Where an arbitration is conducted under the auspices of an arbitral institution, it is not necessary for the parties to engage in any direct negotiations with the tribunal concerning the basis of its fees. These are generally fixed by the institution, sometimes acting independently, sometimes after consultation with the sole or presiding arbitrator. The parties have no say in the matter. In an ad hoc arbitration, however, it is necessary for the parties to make their own arrangements with the arbitrators as to their fees. The arbitrators should do this at an early stage in the proceedings, in order to avoid misunderstandings later. To avoid any suggestion of impropriety, any discussions with arbitrators concerning the amount to be paid to them should take place only in the presence of all of the parties to the dispute, or their representatives.

(c) Methods of assessing fees

4.204 No universally established method exists for assessing the fees payable to an arbitrator for taking part in an international commercial arbitration. At least three methods are in current use:

- the *ad valorem* method, whereby the fee is calculated as a proportion of the amounts in dispute;
- the 'time spent' method, which establishes an hourly or daily rate for work done by an arbitrator on the case; and
- the 'fixed fee' method, whereby the sum payable to the arbitrator by way of remuneration is fixed at the outset, without direct reference either to the amounts in dispute or to the time that the arbitrator spends on the case.

---

[221] Although, in some countries, the court fees are calculated on an *ad valorem* basis and may become substantial when large sums of money are in dispute.

(i) Ad valorem method

4.205 The *ad valorem* method entails assessing the arbitrators' fees as a percentage of the total amount in dispute (including any counterclaim). It has the merit of being easy to use and capable of uniform application. It is necessary to know only (a) the total amount in dispute, and (b) the percentage figure to be applied. With this information, the parties can work out for themselves what fees they are likely to have to pay, if they take their dispute to arbitration. The ICC is the most prominent among the institutions that adopt this method. The ICC Rules contain a 'scale of administrative costs and fees', which shows how the administrative charges of the ICC Secretariat are calculated by applying a different percentage to each successive slice of the sum in dispute. The fees payable to the arbitrator or arbitrators may be calculated on a similar basis, except that the percentages are different and, for each successive slice of the sum in dispute, minimum and maximum percentages are given, to establish a 'range'.[222] In practice, the ICC Court fixes the fees of the arbitrators within the overall range, taking into account the diligence of the arbitrators, the time spent, the rapidity of the proceedings, and the complexity of the dispute.[223]

4.206 It was once common for fees in many professions to be assessed on an *ad valorem* basis. In effect, it means that the large cases subsidise the small ones. However, the modern tendency is for the amount involved in a particular case (whilst being of some significance as showing the degree of responsibility carried) to be regarded as only *one* of the factors to be taken into account in assessing professional fees; the time spent on a particular case, reflecting as it does a more accurate measure of the cost of doing the work, is regarded as the dominant factor.

(ii) 'Time spent' method

4.207 The usual method of assessing fees is to establish a rate at which the arbitrators will be paid for the time spent working on the case. This rate covers not only work done at the hearing of the arbitration, but also any work done outside the hearing. It is usual to establish an hourly or daily rate, or sometimes a combination of both. A lower daily or hourly rate is sometimes fixed for travelling time, when the arbitrator is not available to undertake other work.

4.208 The successful operation of a method of payment based on a time spent rate depends on the arbitrators keeping an accurate record of the time that they actually spend on the case. It also depends on the parties being prepared to trust this record, since (apart from time spent at meetings with the parties and at the hearing) it is not something that can easily be checked. It may be that the presiding arbitrator should consider it to be one of his or her functions to monitor the fee invoices submitted

---

[222] Where the case is submitted to more than one arbitrator, the ICC Court has discretion to increase the fee up to a maximum of three times the fee payable to a single arbitrator.
[223] ICC Rules, Appendix III, Art. 2(2), available online at http://www.iccarbitration.org (search 'arbitration costs calculator').

by the co-arbitrators. In an UNCITRAL arbitration, this is more or less inevitable, since Article 40 of the UNCITRAL Rules provides that the arbitrators' fees shall be 'reasonable in amount' and shall be stated separately as to each arbitrator in the award. The hourly and/or daily rate is likely to vary according to the status of the arbitrator and the size, importance, and complexity of the arbitration. It is in this context that the amount in dispute will be taken into account when the time spent method is used.[224] Most international arbitrators with recognised reputations are prepared to accept that smaller cases should be undertaken at a rate lower than their 'normal' rate.

(iii) 'Fixed fee' method

4.209 There are cases in which arbitrators ask to be paid on a fixed fee basis. These cases are usually cases of major importance, involving arbitrators of high international standing. Where remuneration is to be paid to the arbitrators on a fixed fee basis, the sum agreed is intended to cover all of the work done by the arbitrators on the case, including time spent at the hearing, however long it may last. The problem is that it is difficult to know at the outset of a case what figure to agree as a fixed fee. It is difficult to know how the case will develop, whether or not it will settle before it reaches a hearing, and if it does not settle, how long the hearing itself is likely to take. The best that can be done, in such circumstances, is to make an intelligent assessment of the total number of days likely to be spent by the arbitrators on the case, assuming that it runs its full course, and then to multiply this total by an appropriate daily rate, so as to arrive at a figure for the fixed fee. The arbitrators may have done a similar calculation; alternatively, they may have applied a percentage to the total amount in dispute, so as to calculate the fee to which they consider themselves entitled! It may then be necessary for a certain amount of bargaining to take place between the arbitrators, on the one hand, and the parties, on the other, in order to arrive at an agreed figure. In general terms, fixed fees are increasingly rare and most prestigious arbitrators are prepared to work on one of the other two, more reasonable, bases.

(d) Negotiating arbitrators' fees

4.210 Parties and their legal advisers may find themselves obliged to negotiate with arbitrators over the question of their fees if they think that the arbitrators are asking

---

[224] In 2009, typical daily fees fell in the range US$3,000–6,000 and hourly rates ranged from approximately $450 to $800 for ad hoc arbitrations. At the time of writing (July 2015), the LCIA's range remained up to £450 per hour (US$699 at rates of exchange prevalent at time of writing), covering both hearings and preparatory work. The ICSID fee scale provides for US$3,000 per day or per eight-hour period of work. The ICDR simply asks individual arbitrators to propose rates in the biographical notes kept by the institution, on the basis that market forces will provide adequate checks and balances. The ICC operates a scale fee system, in which time spent is only one of several factors taken into account when fees are fixed by its Court. Most of the other major arbitral institutions operate a scale based on the amount in dispute.

G. Fees and Expenses of the Arbitral Tribunal

for too much. There is no reason why this should not be the case. The problem is that each party is reluctant to upset the arbitrators by appearing to criticise their fees, because each party has it clearly in mind that the same arbitrators will be sitting in judgment on its case. It may seem foolish to bargain over a few hundred dollars a day if, by doing so, a claim worth many millions of dollars may be put in jeopardy.

4.211 However, it is wrong to think in this way. Arbitrators of the right calibre should not take offence if it is suggested to them that they are proposing to charge rather more than the 'going rate' for the job, as long as the suggestion is made with proper courtesy. However, it is essential that, if such a suggestion is made to the arbitrators, it should be made by *all* of the lawyers representing parties to the dispute. On this issue at least, the lawyers involved in the case should present a united front to the arbitrators.

(e) Commitment or cancellation fees

4.212 A complex arbitration may involve protracted proceedings in several separate stages. Arbitrators are invariably asked to reserve weeks, or even months, for hearings in complicated cases. Substantial blocks of time are carved out of the arbitrators' diaries and they must refuse other remunerative work during the reserved period. Three factors may lead to this time being lost to the arbitrator: first, the parties may settle their dispute; secondly, the parties may terminate the mandate of an arbitrator for some other reason; and thirdly—and most commonly—a procedural schedule may have been fixed that turns out to have been too ambitious, with the result that witness hearings have to be postponed.

4.213 Courts in England have held that the right to a commitment fee is not an implied term of the contract created when an appointment is accepted, and that it would be misconduct if an arbitrator were to require a commitment fee as a condition of continuing to perform his or her services if the appointment had been accepted without such a reservation.[225] Where the arbitrators were asked to hold available a sixty-day period some two years in the future, it was not improper for the arbitrators to *request* a commitment fee, although 'it did not accord happily with their status to become involved in negotiations about fees' after their appointment.[226] Further, it would be inappropriate if an arbitrator were to conclude an agreement for a commitment fee with one of the parties when the other party had refused to participate in the negotiations. In any event, once the appointment is accepted, the parties are under no obligation to agree to any commitment or cancellation fees.

---

[225] *K/S Norjarl A/S v Hyundai Heavy Industries Co. Ltd* [1991] 1 Lloyd's Rep 260; appeal dismissed, [1992] QB 863, [1991] 1 Lloyd's Rep 524.
[226] Ibid., at [268].

4.214 It is therefore important for the arbitrators, if they wish to have a commitment or cancellation fee in place, to agree such arrangements with the parties at the time of accepting the appointment. Furthermore, it is important for international arbitrators to understand that commitment and/or cancellation fees are acceptable in some cultural environments, but so unusual as to be unacceptable in others. It is common for such fees not to represent the full time cost of the days not used, on the assumption that the arbitrator will be able to undertake some remunerative work during that period; accordingly, commitment fees ranging between 50 and 75 per cent are usual.

(f) Expenses of the arbitral tribunal

4.215 The question of the expenses incurred by the arbitrators will also have to be settled, unless the arbitration is being conducted under the auspices of an arbitral institution (such institutions collecting money from the parties and reimbursing the arbitrators as part of their routine administrative functions). This falls naturally to be dealt with at the same time as the question of the arbitrators' fees. The costs of air or train travel are invariably simply reimbursed on an 'as incurred' basis. Two points must be clarified between the arbitral tribunal and the parties: the first concerns the class of travel,[227] which, in order to avoid embarrassment later, should be established at the beginning; the second is whether the arbitrators may claim immediate reimbursement of their expenses, rather than wait for the end of the case, or for the next-stage payment date for fees. There is no justification for asking the arbitrators to fund the cash flow for the arbitral process. This is all relatively straightforward. Less easy is the question of subsistence expenses. Broadly speaking, there are two methods of dealing with arbitrators' subsistence expenses: the first may be described as the 'reimbursement method'; the second, as the *per diem* method'.

(i) Reimbursement method

4.216 If the reimbursement method is adopted, the arbitrators must keep a detailed note of their expenditure in connection with their work on the case, including air fares, hotel expenses, and so on. Then, from time to time, they will arrange to have these expenses reimbursed, by submitting details to the relevant arbitral institution, to a designated member or member of the arbitral tribunal (if there is one), to the administrative secretary or registrar, or to the parties direct, as the case may be. Sometimes, a limit may be imposed on the amount for which an arbitrator is reimbursed (for example in respect of hotel expenses), and any expenditure over this limit is then for the account of the arbitrator personally.

---

[227] The ICC's instructions to arbitrators enables them to be reimbursed for business class travel for flights of less than six hours' duration and first class for longer flights. Thus flights between the United States and Europe are generally mandated for first-class travel—although, in fact, most ICC arbitrators make transatlantic flights in business class other than in exceptional circumstances.

G. Fees and Expenses of the Arbitral Tribunal

(ii) Per diem method

The alternative method is for the parties to pay an amount fixed at a daily rate to cover hotel and other subsistence expenses. This daily, or *per diem*, rate is fixed at a level sufficient to cover the costs of living away from home at a hotel of good standard at the place of arbitration. It will also cover incidental expenses such as meals, taxis, telephone calls, and so on. It is paid to the arbitrator as a fixed amount of money, calculated on a *per diem* basis by reference to the number of days spent on the case, away from home. It is then for the arbitrator to meet the actual expenses out of this fixed allowance and to pay any excess personally. The ICC operates a *per diem* rate for reimbursement of subsistence expenses.[228] There can be little doubt that, of the two methods discussed, this method is better. It avoids the detailed clerical work of checking payments against receipts or other vouchers; it also avoids prying into an arbitrator's style of living, so as to decide whether a particular expense was or was not necessary in the interests of the proper conduct of the arbitration. The *per diem* method should generally be adopted in any international commercial arbitration in which payment of the arbitrators' expenses is the direct responsibility of the parties themselves, or of the administrative secretary or registrar appointed by the arbitral tribunal.

4.217

(iii) ICSID system

Although these methods are the methods most commonly encountered in practice for the payment of arbitrators' expenses, variations on these basic themes may be found. For instance, ICSID offers arbitrators some choice in the method of claiming their expenses. An arbitrator in an ICSID arbitration is entitled to the following allowances for attending meetings or hearings in connection with the case:

4.218

- the actual cost of air travel at 'one class above coach', by air or other means of transport ('coach' being economy class);
- an 'in–out' allowance of a fixed sum, to cover the costs of porterage, taxis, tips, and other expenses of travelling;
- the actual cost of transport within the city in which the arbitration is taking place; and
- a *per diem* allowance, either at the full rate or at the so-called mixed rate.[229]

The last item on this list merits particular comment. Under the ICSID system, the full *per diem* rate varies from place to place, with different rates being established for different cities, according to whether or not they are 'high-cost cities'. As an

4.219

---

[228] The standard ICC *per diem* allowance at time of writing (July 2015) remain US$1,200 for an overnight stay and $400 for a day's expenses, if no overnight stay in hotel accommodation is involved.

[229] The standard ICSID *per diem* allowance for subsistence expenses (i.e. meals, taxis, etc.) fixed on 6 July 2005 and still in effect in 2015 was US$115; however, special *per diem* allowances of $135, $170, or $185 applied for certain high-cost cities (e.g. $170 for Washington, DC, which is in the second highest cost category).

alternative to claiming the full *per diem* rate, arbitrators may claim reimbursement under the 'mixed rate'. On this basis, reimbursement may be claimed for the actual cost of a hotel room (plus tax and service charge), together with an allowance of one half of the applicable full *per diem* rate to cover meals, tips, and other expenses. In practice, arbitrators taking part in an ICSID arbitration tend to choose reimbursement on the mixed rate basis unless otherwise agreed, since this comes nearest to covering the expenses likely to be incurred in staying, for instance, at a hotel in Washington, DC, where arbitrations under the ICSID Rules usually take place.

(g) Securing payment of the fees and expenses of the arbitral tribunal

4.220 The question of establishing effective arrangements with regard to fees and expenses is as important for the arbitrators as it is for the parties. The fact that arbitrators may become *functus officio* instantly at the joint will of the parties emphasises the importance for the arbitrators of obtaining adequate security for payment of their fees and expenses. The acceptance by the arbitrators of the functions bestowed upon them creates a legal relationship between the parties and the members of the arbitral tribunal. This relationship carries with it an implied undertaking by the parties to compensate the members of the arbitral tribunal fairly in respect of their work and expenses, whether or not an award is issued. However, even under those national systems of law in which this is clear,[230] arbitrators do not usually wish to go to the trouble and cost of suing the parties for their fees and expenses.

4.221 Where the arbitration is being administered by an established arbitral institution, the arbitral tribunal need not concern itself with the collection of payments on account of its fees and expenses. This part of the administration of the case is handled by the arbitral institution concerned. In any other case, however, the arbitral tribunal should arrange for the parties to make sufficient deposits in respect of its fees and expenses.[231] There are two reasons for this: first, it helps the parties to keep a check on expenses as the case proceeds; and secondly, it is easier to collect payments from the parties whilst the arbitration is in progress than when the proceedings are over.

4.222 A bank account should be opened for receipt of the deposits made by the parties. This account may then also be used for paying fees and expenses to the members of the arbitral tribunal as and when payments fall due. Any interest earned on the account should be credited to the account (and, accordingly, be accrued for the benefit of the parties). The account is usually opened in the name of the arbitral tribunal, with the sole arbitrator or the presiding arbitrator as signatory on the account. If an administrative secretary or registrar has been appointed, the maintenance and operation of the account may be one of that person's responsibilities.

---

[230] See, e.g., English Arbitration Act 1996, s. 28.
[231] The UNCITRAL Rules make provision for this in Art. 43.

G. Fees and Expenses of the Arbitral Tribunal

As noted, however, some institutions offer this fundholding service irrespective of whether the arbitration is taking place under their rules.[232] This is to be recommended in large cases, since the arbitral institutions are far better equipped to undertake this kind of service than arbitrators and usually do so based on an hourly cost basis far lower than that of the arbitrator.[233]

---

[232] The LCIA provides a fundholding service for arbitrations conducted under the UNCITRAL Rules and also for ad hoc arbitrations. Where acting as fundholder, the LCIA sets up a dedicated bank account in either dollars, sterling, or euro, into which advances on costs and other administrative costs should be lodged by the parties. The LCIA will then monitor the account to ensure that it has enough funds to cover the arbitration costs and will make disbursement as determined by the tribunal: http://www.lcia.org/.

[233] In 2013, the costs of the LCIA fundholding service were £150 per hour.

5

POWERS, DUTIES, AND JURISDICTION OF AN ARBITRAL TRIBUNAL

| A. Background | 5.01 | C. Duties of Arbitrators | 5.43 |
| B. Powers of Arbitrators | 5.06 | D. Jurisdiction | 5.91 |

A. Background

(a) Introduction

An arbitral tribunal established to determine an international dispute operates in an entirely different context from that of a judge sitting in a national court. Judges sit in a legal environment that clearly defines the extent of their powers and duties. They are generally given full immunity in respect of any potential liability arising out of the conduct of their judicial function. Their jurisdiction, and the extent to which decisions in relation to jurisdiction may be reviewed by an appellate court, are clearly established in the law governing the proceedings. **5.01**

The position differs in arbitration—particularly in international arbitration, in which the powers, duties, and jurisdiction of an arbitral tribunal arise from a complex mixture of the will of the parties, the law governing the arbitration agreement, the law of the place of arbitration,[1] and the law of the place in which recognition or enforcement of the award may be sought. **5.02**

(b) Practical considerations

A balance must be struck between the sanctions that may be imposed on arbitrators who carry out their functions in a careless or improper manner and the equally necessary requirement that an arbitral tribunal be free to perform its task without **5.03**

---

[1] Or, exceptionally, the law to which the parties have agreed to subject the arbitration. See Chapter 3.

constantly 'looking over its shoulder' in the fear of being challenged by means of legal process. On one view, it may be argued that arbitrators should be given virtually unlimited powers, in order to adapt the process to the dispute in question, and to encourage speed and effectiveness in the arbitral process. However, the requirements of public policy, whether national or international,[2] make some control necessary, so as to ensure that the parties are not without recourse if the arbitral tribunal acts beyond its jurisdiction,[3] treats the parties unequally, or fails to conduct a fair hearing.

5.04 The system for the protection of parties against excesses on the part of arbitral tribunals is usually contained in the framework for recourse against the award itself, or at the moment of recognition and enforcement.[4] However, arbitrators may be removed for certain types of wrongful conduct during the arbitral process pursuant to the rules of an applicable arbitral institution,[5] or under the law governing the arbitration,[6] by an application to the courts of the country in which the arbitration has its seat.

5.05 The powers and duties of an arbitral tribunal are also closely linked to the question of its jurisdiction (particularly in defining the extent of that jurisdiction) and the difficult question of determining the validity of the arbitration agreement. Before turning to the question of the jurisdiction of the arbitral tribunal to decide the particular dispute before it, the powers and duties of the arbitral tribunal will be considered.

B. Powers of Arbitrators

(a) Introduction

5.06 The powers of an arbitral tribunal are those conferred upon it by the parties within the limits allowed by the applicable law,[7] together with any additional powers that may be conferred automatically by operation of law. These powers are established to enable the arbitral tribunal to carry out its task properly and effectively.

---

[2] See Chapter 10, paragraphs 10.81*ff.*
[3] See Chapter 10.
[4] For further discussion of this subject, see Chapter 11.
[5] For instance, under Art. 15(2) of the Arbitration Rules of the International Chamber of Commerce (ICC Rules), the ICC's International Court of Arbitration may remove an arbitrator for not fulfilling his or her functions in accordance with the Rules or within the prescribed time limit.
[6] For instance, under s. 24(1) of the English Arbitration Act 1996, the English court may remove an arbitrator for 'justifiable doubts' as to that arbitrator's impartiality.
[7] As far as the tribunal's *powers* are concerned, the applicable law is usually the proper law of the arbitration agreement and the law of the place of arbitration. For discussion of applicable law generally, see Chapter 3.

B. Powers of Arbitrators

5.07 In a well-conducted international arbitration, control of the proceedings moves smoothly from the parties to the arbitral tribunal. At first, the parties are fully in charge. They alone know the issues in dispute, how they intend to set about proving the facts upon which they rely, and the arguments of law that they propose to advance. The case that is to be put to the arbitral tribunal is 'their' case. Indeed, the arbitral tribunal owes its very existence to the parties: it is 'their' tribunal. As the proceedings develop, however, the arbitral tribunal becomes increasingly familiar with the matters in dispute. It begins to decide for itself which facts it regards as relevant and which questions of law it regards as important. It is in a position to start making known its views as to how the case should be presented within the framework of the particular rules that govern the proceedings. The balance of power, in effect, shifts from the parties to the arbitral tribunal. It is right that this should be so: the arbitrators, not the parties, are the final judges of the matters in dispute. However, this shift in the balance of power happens only if the arbitrators know when and how to take charge of the proceedings, and understand the tools at their disposal.

(b) Sources of arbitrators' powers

(i) Powers conferred by the parties

5.08 The parties may confer powers upon the arbitral tribunal directly or indirectly, but only within the limits of the applicable law. Any excess of power (that is, any power granted over and above that allowed by the applicable law) is invalid, even if it is contained in international or institutional rules of arbitration.

5.09 A 'direct' conferment of powers takes place when the parties agree expressly upon the powers that they wish the arbitrators to exercise, possibly by setting them out in the terms of appointment or a submission agreement. Such powers are likely to include the powers to order production of documents, to appoint experts, to hold hearings, to require the presence of witnesses, to receive evidence, and to inspect the subject matter of the dispute. The ways in which these powers may be expressly conferred upon the arbitral tribunal in submission agreements have been described in more detail elsewhere in this volume.[8]

5.10 An 'indirect' conferment of powers takes place when the parties have agreed that the arbitration is to be conducted according to pre-established rules of arbitration that set out the powers of the tribunal. In the case of the International Chamber of Commerce (ICC), some of these powers are conferred on the ICC's International Court of Arbitration itself. For example, the place of arbitration is determined by the ICC Court, unless it has been chosen by agreement of the parties.[9]

---

[8] See Chapter 2, paragraphs 2.119*ff.*
[9] ICC Rules, Art. 18.1.

(ii) Powers conferred by operation of law

5.11 The powers conferred upon an arbitral tribunal by the parties, whether directly or indirectly, fall short of the powers that may be exercised by a national court. Such courts derive their authority from the state, which grants to them formidable coercive powers to ensure obedience to their orders. An arbitral tribunal does not usually possess such powers.[10] The parties cannot confer upon a private tribunal the coercive powers over property and persons that are conferred by the state on a national court. In recognition of this fact, many systems of law supplement the powers of arbitral tribunals by:

- giving powers directly to arbitral tribunals;
- authorising national courts to exercise powers on behalf of arbitral tribunals or the parties themselves; or
- a combination of these two methods.

5.12 A good example of procedural powers being conferred on an international arbitral tribunal by law is provided by the English Arbitration Act 1996. The tribunal is given various powers, including the powers to order a claimant to provide security for costs,[11] to administer oaths to witnesses,[12] and generally to determine procedural matters.[13]

5.13 It is consequently not enough simply to refer to the arbitration agreement (including any institutional or international rules that may be incorporated within that agreement) in order to determine the powers of the arbitral tribunal; any relevant mandatory provisions of the law governing the arbitration agreement, and of the law governing the arbitration, must also be taken into account. These provisions usually extend the powers conferred by the parties. In some circumstances, however, they may restrict the powers that the parties have sought to confer upon the arbitral tribunal. As already indicated, any such 'excess' power is invalid, as are any orders or decisions made in reliance upon it.

5.14 In practice, the best approach when considering the powers of an arbitral tribunal is to look first at the arbitration agreement (including any applicable rules), then at the law governing the arbitration agreement, and finally at the law governing the arbitration (if different). The arbitration agreement should be considered to establish

---

[10] Some Latin American states, such as Colombia and Ecuador, do not follow this rule and grant to arbitrators a degree of *imperium*, such that they can call upon public officers to enforce their orders directly as if they were a court of law. See, e.g., s. 9 of Ecuador's 2006 Arbitration and Mediation Law: '[Arbitrators] shall request the aid of public, judicial, police and administrative officers as shall be necessary without having to resort to any ordinary judge at the place where . . . it is necessary to adopt those measures.' See, for a fuller description, Marchan, 'Ecuador', in Newman and Ong (eds) *Interim Measures in International Arbitration* (Juris, 2014), pp. 21*ff*.

[11] English Arbitration Act 1996, s. 38(3). The arbitral tribunal can enforce this order by dismissing the claim if it is not complied with: s. 41(6).

[12] English Arbitration Act 1996, s. 38(5).

[13] English Arbitration Act 1996, s. 34. This power is also granted by Model Law, Art. 19(1).

what powers the parties themselves have agreed to confer on the arbitral tribunal. In general, those powers are set out in the rules to which the arbitration has been subjected. The law governing the arbitration agreement should then be considered to identify how those powers may have been supplemented or restricted. The law of the arbitration agreement, which governs its validity, effect, and interpretation, may confer specific powers (or impose certain limitations) upon the arbitral tribunal.[14] Finally, if different, the law governing the arbitration itself, the *lex arbitri*, should be similarly considered. An example of such a restriction is an arbitration agreement governed by English law, but which provides for the arbitration to take place in Zurich. The arbitration agreement might include an express provision that the arbitrator is entitled to administer oaths to any witnesses in the arbitration; if it did not do so, English law (if it were the *lex arbitri*) would imply such a provision.[15] The law of Switzerland, however, does not permit a private individual, such as an arbitrator, to administer oaths. This is a mandatory provision of Swiss law, which, as the law governing the arbitration, would override the express or implied provisions of the arbitration agreement.

(c) Common powers of arbitral tribunals

(i) *Establishing the arbitral procedure*

In general terms, the arbitral tribunal enjoys a very broad power to determine the appropriate procedure. Indeed, this is one of the defining features of arbitration as opposed to courts, in which a fixed procedure exists. It is, however, subject to an overarching respect of due process or natural justice—that is, equality of treatment and an opportunity to be heard. For example, Article 17(1) of the UNCITRAL Rules contain a general power for the arbitral tribunal to 'conduct the arbitration in such manner as it considers appropriate, provided that the parties are treated with equality and that at an appropriate stage of the proceedings, each party is given a reasonable opportunity of presenting its case'.[16]   **5.15**

(ii) *Determining the applicable law and seat*

Occasionally, parties omit to decide important matters in the arbitration agreement, such as the seat of the arbitration or the applicable law. In order to prevent the clause from failing, with a consequent remission to state courts, the arbitral tribunal is usually provided with the power to determine the seat[17] and the applicable rules of law.[18] Such important decisions will normally be made only once both   **5.16**

---

[14] See, e.g., New Zealand Arbitration Act 1996, s. 12; Swiss Private International Law Act 1987 (Swiss PIL), s. 183; Brazilian Arbitration Law 1996, s. 22.
[15] English Arbitration Act 1996, s. 12.
[16] Similar rules apply under institutional rules: see the Rules of the China International Economic and Trade Arbitration Commission (CIETAC), Art. 33(1).
[17] UNCITRAL Rules, Art. 18(1).
[18] UNCITRAL Rules, Art. 35(1).

parties have had an opportunity to be heard on the issue.[19] The determination of the seat or place of arbitration by an institution or by the arbitral tribunal is important, since the choice will determine the *lex arbitri* and consequently establish a state jurisdiction to supervise the arbitration. It is common practice for arbitral tribunals in these circumstances to establish a seat in a jurisdiction that is a signatory to the New York Convention (for recognition and enforcement purposes) and which has an established reputation as a seat in international disputes.

(iii) Determining the language of the arbitration

5.17 Where the language of the arbitration is not established by the arbitration agreement and the institutional rules do not provide for determination of this question, the arbitral tribunal must determine the language(s) to be used in the proceedings.[20] Usually, tribunals fix the language of the arbitration as that of the underlying contract, since this is most likely to be the 'common' language of the parties.[21] However, where the parties have used two working languages in negotiations (or have authentic versions of the contract in two languages), the tribunal may agree to a bilingual arbitration in which two languages may be used interchangeably by the parties, with or without the need for translation or interpretation.

(iv) Requiring the production of documents

5.18 Where a party has requested disclosure of specific, or a narrow category of, documents by the other party and that party has raised objections, the arbitral tribunal will usually receive a request for an order requiring such production. If the arbitral tribunal concludes that the document or category of documents is indeed relevant to the resolution of the dispute, it has the power to order production.[22] In the event that the requested party does not produce the ordered documents, the tribunal has no power (*imperium*) to force production, but may nevertheless 'draw adverse inferences' from such failure or (in French law) impose a financial penalty.[23] A further limitation is that this power may not be exercised against non-parties to the arbitration.[24]

5.19 The law of the place of arbitration may provide supplementary state powers to assist the tribunal. For example, in a tribunal with a seat in the United States, the

---

[19] The determination of the applicable law is addressed in detail in Chapter 3.
[20] UNCITRAL Rules, Art. 19(1).
[21] See Chapter 2, paragraph 2.86.
[22] The question of the production of documentary evidence is discussed in detail in Chapter 6, paragraphs 6.92*ff.*
[23] New French Code of Civil Procedure (as amended in 2011), art. 1467: '*Si une partie détient un élément de preuve, le tribunal arbitral peut lui enjoindre de le produire selon les modalités qu'il détermine et au besoin à peine d'astreinte.* [If a party is in possession of evidence, the arbitral tribunal may order it to be produced in a manner that the tribunal decides and if necessary under penalty for failure to do so.]'
[24] For more detail, see Chapter 6, paragraph 6.111.

tribunal may issue a subpoena requiring a person present within the jurisdiction to produce documents. However, the arbitral subpoena can be enforced by a court of the state in which the arbitration is taking place only against a person resident or present within the jurisdiction of that court.[25]

(v) Requiring the presence of witnesses/subpoenas

5.20 The arbitral tribunal has the power to require the presence of witnesses under the control of the parties. However, absent any powers to call upon the forces of public order, if such a witness fails to appear, the arbitral tribunal is usually limited to drawing adverse inferences from the party's failure to secure the presence of the witness. Once again, the tribunal's powers may be supplemented by the law governing the proceedings (*lex arbitri*) by providing judicial support to the enforceability of orders. For example, in England and Wales, a party may seek a peremptory order from the tribunal requiring the attendance of a witness in the power of a party, which, if disobeyed, may be followed by a court order in support. If the court order is disobeyed, it is a contempt of court, which may lead to a criminal prosecution.[26] In the United States, using the same subpoena procedure outlined above for documents, an arbitral subpoena can be issued in respect of a third-party witness present in the jurisdiction of the state in which the arbitration is to take place. In Switzerland, a tribunal may also obtain court assistance for the taking of evidence, such as compelling a witness to appear.[27]

(vi) Administrating oaths

5.21 In practice, witnesses in an international arbitration are not usually required to swear an oath. It is generally sufficient for arbitrators simply to seek confirmation that the witness will tell the truth and to alert the witness to the fact that failure to do so may constitute a breach of applicable laws. Indeed, French law prohibits arbitrators from administering oaths: 'The arbitral tribunal may call upon any person to provide testimony. Witnesses shall not be sworn in.'[28] By contrast, in some jurisdictions such as the United Arab Emirates (UAE), witnesses are *required* to take an oath in a prescribed manner,[29] and if they fail to do so, the award is at risk

---

[25] United States Federal Arbitration Act of 1925 (FAA), § 7, which states that arbitrators 'may summon in writing any person to attend before them...as a witness and in a proper case to bring with him or them any book, record, document, or paper which may be deemed material as evidence in the case'. For an example of the use of the power and confirmation of its application to non-parties see *Stolt-Nielson SA v Celanese AG* 430 F.3d 567 (2nd Cir. 2005).

[26] See paragraph 5.35.

[27] Swiss PIL, s. 184(2).

[28] French Code of Civil Procedure, art. 1467: '*Le tribunal arbitral peut entendre toute personne. Cette audition a lieu sans prestation de serment.*' This provision was unaltered by the 2011 French Arbitration Law.

[29] UAE Civil Procedure Code, art. 211(1): 'The arbitrators shall cause the witnesses to take oath. Whoever makes a false statement before the arbitrators shall be deemed to have committed the crime of perjury.'

of being set aside.[30] Some states and rules adopt a middle ground, and grant to the tribunal the power to administer oaths.[31]

(vii) Examining the subject matter of the dispute

5.22 Where the dispute concerns the status of the subject matter of the contract, such as the condition of a cargo or faults in a particular structure in a construction project, it may be useful for the tribunal to see for itself the cargo or the structure in question. The tribunal usually has this power under relevant institutional rules[32] or national laws. The possibility of a 'site visit' is also addressed in the International Bar Association (IBA) Rules on the Taking of Evidence in International Arbitration.[33] Such visits need to be carefully planned in advance, with appropriate protocols in place. The tribunal will usually make the site visit in the presence of the parties and any relevant party or tribunal-appointed experts.

(viii) Appointing experts

5.23 Many rules of arbitration permit the tribunal to appoint its own expert.[34] The IBA Rules make specific provision for this possibility and establish useful ground rules for such appointment.[35] Where questions of technical expertise are required in an international arbitration, whether arising out of liability or quantum issues, it is usual for the parties to present expert reports from independent experts retained for the purpose.[36] It is then for the arbitral tribunal to weigh and compare the value of that expert testimony, in order to reach a conclusion. Sometimes, the evidence of the experts is of such technical complexity that the tribunal has difficulty in reaching a decision. The tribunal may then decide to seek assistance from a neutral expert, either at the outset of a technically complex case or at a later stage, to assist in evaluating the technical evidence.

5.24 If the tribunal decides to exercise this power, it is better done sooner rather than later; in any event, it should be done before the final hearing, so that the expert can be present during the oral testimony of the party-appointed experts. Generally, the tribunal will wish to make its own choice of expert, after consultation with the parties. However, a possible variation from this general practice would be for the

---

[30] In the US case *In re Arbitration between International Bechtel Co. Ltd v Department of Civil Aviation of the Government of Dubai* 300 F.Supp.2d 112 (DDC 2005), the US District Court for Columbia refused to enforce an award set aside in Dubai on the basis of the failure properly to administer the oath in accordance with the UAE Civil Code.

[31] See, e.g., English Arbitration Act 1996, s. 38(5); Arbitration Rules of the International Centre for the Settlement of Investment Disputes (ICSID), r. 38(5).

[32] For example, London Court of International Arbitration (LCIA) Rules, Art. 22(1)(iv); 2012 Arbitration Rules of the Permanent Court of Arbitration (PCA), Art. 27(3): the 'arbitral tribunal may, after consultation with the parties, perform a site visit'.

[33] See IBA Rules, Art. 7 ('Inspection').

[34] For example, UNCITRAL Rules, Art. 29(1); CIETAC Rules, Art. 42(1).

[35] See IBA Rules, Art. 6 ('Tribunal-appointed experts').

[36] See Chapter 6, paragraphs 6.133*ff*.

B. Powers of Arbitrators

tribunal to appoint two experts, one chosen from each of two lists provided by the parties. This 'expert team' would then provide the tribunal with a single report on the relevant technical issues, based on a single set of questions established in consultation between the arbitrators and the parties.[37]

When an arbitral tribunal exercises its power to appoint an expert, terms of reference should be established setting out the scope of the exercise, with a list of specific questions and issues to consider (on which the parties should be allowed to comment prior to its delivery to the expert). These questions should be limited to those that require technical expertise and must not, in any circumstance, delegate any legal question. The tribunal expert should be asked to prepare a draft report in response to the issues, which should include the methodology and evidence used to arrive at the conclusion. This should then be circulated to the parties for comment. Once comments are received, the expert should either prepare a final report and/or be made available for oral examination.[38] — 5.25

It is important to note that the final report of the tribunal's expert(s) is simply another evidentiary element for the arbitral tribunal to consider in its deliberations. It should not be considered as binding the tribunal in any way. The tribunal should not delegate its obligation to reach its own decision on all of the issues (including technical or quantum issues) in dispute.[39] — 5.26

(ix) Interim measures

During the course of an arbitration, it may become necessary for the arbitral tribunal or a national court to issue orders intended to preserve evidence, to protect assets, to respect procedural rights, and otherwise to maintain the status quo pending the outcome of the arbitration proceedings.[40] Such orders take different forms and are known by different names. In the Model Law and in the UNCITRAL Rules, they are known as 'interim measures';[41] in the English version of the ICC Rules, they are known as 'conservatory and interim measures'.[42] Whatever their designation, they are intended to operate as holding orders to protect the status quo and the integrity of the proceedings, pending the outcome of the arbitral process. — 5.27

---

[37] The details of this proposal are set out in Sachs, 'Protocol on expert teaming: A new approach to expert evidence', in ICCA (ed.) *Arbitration Advocacy in Changing Times* (Kluwer, 2011), pp. 135*ff*.

[38] One comprehensive procedure, which may be incorporated or used as a checklist, is established at IBA Rules, Art. 6.

[39] Similar 'ground rules' are established in IBA Rules, Art. 6.

[40] As the tribunal noted in *Burlington Resources v Republic of Ecuador*, Procedural Order No. 1 on Burlington Oriente's Request for Provisional Measures, ICSID Case No. ARB/08/5, 29 June 2009, at [60]: 'In the Tribunal's view, the rights to be preserved by provisional measures are not limited to those which form the subject-matter of the dispute or substantive rights as referred to by the Respondents, but may extend to procedural rights, including the general right to the status quo and to the non-aggravation of the dispute...'

[41] UNCITRAL Rules, Art. 26.

[42] ICC Arbitration Rules, Art. 28.

Most of the major institutional rules now empower arbitral institutions to appoint 'emergency arbitrators' for the purpose of providing rapid interim relief before the constitution of a tribunal.[43] An emergency arbitrator usually enjoys the same power as the definitive tribunal to order interim relief—but once constituted, the arbitral tribunal may review that relief.[44]

5.28 Where interim measures of protection are required, the arbitral tribunal itself generally has the power to issue them. For example, Article 28(1) of the ICC Rules provides that 'the Arbitral Tribunal may, at the request of a party, order any interim or conservatory measure it deems appropriate'. There are similar provisions in many arbitration laws.[45] For example, Article 17 of the Model Law (as amended in 2006) states, '[u]nless otherwise agreed by the parties, the arbitral tribunal may, at the request of a party, grant interim measures'.

5.29 The International Centre for the Settlement of Investment Disputes (ICSID) is different, in that it appears to limit the power of the arbitral tribunal to that of 'recommending' interim measures:

> At any time during the proceeding a party may request that provisional measures for the preservation of its rights be recommended by the Tribunal. The request shall specify the rights to be preserved, the measures the recommendation of which is requested, and the circumstances that require such measures.[46]

5.30 The use of the word 'recommended' in this context stems from the concern of the drafters of the ICSID Convention to be seen as respectful of national sovereignty by not granting powers to private tribunals to order a state to do, or not do, something on a purely provisional basis. Arbitral jurisprudence, however, indicates that these measures may nevertheless be taken to constitute binding obligations.[47] As most recently confirmed by the *Perenco v Ecuador*[48] tribunal, it is now 'generally

---

[43] LCIA Rules, Art. 9B; Stockholm Chamber of Commerce Arbitration Rules (SCC Rules), Art. 32(4) and Appendix II, Art. 3; ICC Rules, Art. 29(1) and Appendix V, Art. 1(2); International Centre for Dispute Resolution (ICDR) Arbitration Rules, Art. 6; Singapore International Arbitration Centre (SIAC) Rules, Art. 26(2), with proceedings governed by Sch. 1.

[44] See Chapter 4, paragraphs 4.17*ff* for a review of the role of emergency arbitrators.

[45] For example, UNCITRAL Rules, Art. 26; LCIA Rules, Art. 25; ICDR Rules, Art. 21; ICSID Rules, r. 39.

[46] ICSID Convention, Art. 47; ICSID Rules, r. 39.

[47] In this regard, in *Emilio Agustín Maffezini v Kingdom of Spain*, Decision on Request for Provisional Measures, ICSID Case No. ARB/97/7, IIC 85 (2000), (2001) 16 ICSID Rev—Foreign Investment LJ 212, at [9], the ICSID tribunal came to the following conclusion: 'The Tribunal's authority to rule on provisional measures is not less binding than that of a final award. Accordingly, for the purposes of this order, the tribunal deems the word "recommend" to be of equivalent value as the word "order".' See also *City Oriente v Republic of Ecuador and Petroecuador*, Decision on Interim Measures, ICSID Case No. ARB/06/21, IIC 309 (2007), at [52]. The case law is addressed in Kaufmann-Kohler and Antonietti, 'Interim relief in international investment agreements', in Yannaka-Small (ed.) *Arbitration under International Investment Agreements* (Oxford University Press, 2010), pp. 507–550.

[48] *Perenco Ecuador Ltd v Republic of Ecuador and Empresa Estatal Petróleos del Ecuador (Petroecuador)*, Decision on Provisional Measures, ICSID Case No. ARB/08/6, IIC 375 (2009), at [74].

accepted' that provisional measures before ICSID are tantamount to orders and are binding on the party to which they are directed.

Whilst most arbitration rules and laws of arbitration permit interim measures to be granted at the tribunal's discretion, they provide little guidance as to how that discretion should be exercised. Traditionally, arbitrators have looked to concepts common to most legal systems in the granting of such measures—such as the need to establish a prima facie case on the merits and the risk of serious and irreparable harm if the measure is not granted. The publication of decisions on interim measures in ICSID cases has allowed some conclusions to be drawn in respect of the tribunal's decision-making process. In particular, recent ICSID jurisprudence suggests that provisional measures are 'extraordinary measures', which are recommended in only limited circumstances, such as when such measures are (a) necessary to avoid imminent and irreparable harm, and (b) urgent. In *Occidental v Ecuador*,[49] for example, the tribunal noted: **5.31**

> It is also well-established that provisional measures should only be granted in situations of necessity and urgency in order to protect rights that could, absent such measures, be definitively lost...In other words the circumstances in which the provisional measures are required under Article 47 of the ICSID Convention are those in which the measures are necessary to preserve a party's rights and where the need is *urgent* in order *to avoid irreparable harm*.

As already stated, the applicable test for interim measures is rarely enunciated in applicable laws of arbitration. This lack of guidance was addressed in the revised UNCITRAL Model Law of 2006, in which Article 17A ('Conditions for granting interim measures') sets out the applicable test as follows: **5.32**

> (1) The party requesting an interim measure under article 17(2)*(a), (b)* and *(c)* shall satisfy the arbitral tribunal that:
> (a) Harm not adequately reparable by an award of damages is likely to result if the measure is not ordered, and such harm substantially outweighs the harm that is likely to result to the party against whom the measure is directed if the measure is granted; and
> (b) There is a reasonable possibility that the requesting party will succeed on the merits of the claim. The determination on this possibility shall not affect the discretion of the arbitral tribunal in making any subsequent determination.
>
> [...]

This test follows earlier arbitral practice. It confirms that the key elements to take into account are: (a) the risk of irreparable harm, if the order is not granted; (b) that the harm to the requesting party, if the order is not granted, will be greater than the harm to the other party if it *is* granted (the 'balance of convenience' test); and

---

[49] *Occidental Petroleum Corporation and Occidental Exploration and Production Co. v Republic of Ecuador*, Decision on Provisional Measures, ICSID Case No. ARB/06/11, IIC 305 (2007), at [59] (emphasis original).

(c) that the requesting party has a reasonable chance of success on the merits (that is, a prima facie case).

5.33 In most jurisdictions, an arbitral tribunal has the power to issue interim measures provided that both parties are heard (thereby preserving the essential right to be heard as one of the cornerstones of due process). The problem arises when one party seeks to obtain interim measures *ex parte*—that is, in the absence of the opposing party or parties. Institutional rules sometimes authorise the tribunal to grant *ex parte* interim measures under 'exceptional circumstances', subject to the opposing party's right to be heard later.[50] However, some commentators have suggested that such a power is incompatible with the consensual nature of arbitration and with proper respect for due process.[51]

5.34 Article 17B of the revised UNCITRAL Model Law sets out a compromise, which provides for emergency relief in the form of a 'preliminary order'. This can be requested on an *ex parte* basis simultaneously with the request for interim relief. An order for preliminary relief is subject to a twenty-day time-limit, pursuant to Article 17C(4), and the same conditions apply as for interim measures. Within that twenty-day period, an application may be made to the arbitral tribunal, on notice to the other party, to adopt or vary the preliminary order. In addition, a preliminary order may be granted on an *ex parte* basis if the arbitrator decides that disclosure of the request for interim relief would frustrate the purpose of the measure (for example because the opposing party might seek to hide or remove relevant assets). Article 17C(5) provides that a preliminary order of emergency relief, whilst binding on the parties, is not enforceable by a court.[52]

(x) Security for costs

5.35 Security for costs is a special form of interim relief, to which the criteria outlined so far do not apply. Instead, the tribunal must weigh the costs to a respondent of defending a claim in which there is a possibility of not recovering those costs even if successful against the risk of stifling a genuine claim by a claimant who is short of funds, possibly because of the very conduct of the respondent that has given rise to the arbitration.

---

[50] Swiss Rules, Art. 26(3) (emphasis added):

> In *exceptional circumstances*, the arbitral tribunal may rule on a request for interim measures by way of a preliminary order before the request has been communicated to any other party, provided that such communication is made at the latest together with the preliminary order and that the other parties are immediately *granted an opportunity to be heard*.

[51] See van Houtte, 'Ten reasons against a proposal for *ex parte* interim measures of protection in arbitration' (2004) 20 Arb Intl 85, at 89.

[52] Indeed, it is questionable whether any provisional or interim relief ordered by an arbitral tribunal is enforceable by state courts under the New York Convention absent specific authority, since, by definition, such decisions will not be final: see Chapter 7, paragraphs 7.19*ff*.

B. Powers of Arbitrators

The point has already been made that the costs of presenting or defending a claim in an international arbitration may run into millions of dollars.[53] Where a claimant considers launching arbitral proceedings, this is—or should be—one of the factors to be taken into account. But what about the respondent, who has no such luxury of choice? If there is a valid arbitration agreement to which the respondent is a party, that respondent is obliged to take part in the arbitration, like it or not—or risk a default award. In such circumstances, the respondent may well ask if there is any way in which it can be assured that if it wins and is awarded costs, there will at least be a fund out of which the costs award will be paid.

5.36

The answer is that, in certain circumstances, it may be possible to ask the arbitral tribunal to make an order to the effect that a claimant (or counter-claimant) should provide security for costs. Article 25(2) of the Rules of the London Court of International Arbitration (LCIA), for example, confers upon an arbitral tribunal the power to order a claimant or counter-claimant 'to provide or procure security for Legal Costs and Arbitration Costs by way of deposit or bank guarantee or in any other manner and upon such terms as the Arbitral Tribunal considers appropriate in the circumstances'. The English Arbitration Act 1996 contains a similar provision. Under other rules of arbitration, such as those of UNCITRAL, the ICC, and ICSID, security for costs may be ordered under the general provision that authorises an arbitral tribunal to issue interim measures of protection.[54]

5.37

Whether or not to order security for costs has come under scrutiny in the context of investment arbitration. Where a claimant's principal producing asset has been seized by a state without compensation, it is not surprising that the claimant may suffer acute financial constraints; in such circumstances, some states have attempted to obtain security for costs in respect of the claim. Tribunals have been cautious about granting security in such a situation: in *Commerce Group v El Salvador*, for example, the annulment committee noted that 'the power to order security for costs should be exercised only in extreme circumstances, for example, where abuse or serious misconduct has been evidenced'.[55]

5.38

A more difficult issue arises where a claimant has obtained third-party funding— that is, where its legal costs are paid in whole or part by a professional funder, who will usually be repaid only in the event of success. Respondent states have argued that the mere existence of third-party funding should require the posting of security, since, in the event of a failed claim, there will be no ability to recuperate costs

5.39

---

[53] See Chapter 1, paragraph 1.124.
[54] See, for ICSID, *Libananco Holdings v Republic of Turkey*, Decision on Preliminary Issues, ICSID Case No. ARB 06/8, 23 June 2008, at [59]. For UNCITRAL, see *Guaracachi America, Inc. and Rurelec plc v Plurinational State of Bolivia*, Procedural Order No. 14, PCA Case No. 2011-17, 11 March 2013 (*Guaracachi* PO14), available online at http://www.pca-cpa.org/.
[55] *Commerce Group Corporation & San Sebastian Gold Mines, Inc. v Republic of El Salvador*, Annulment Proceeding, Decision on El Salvador's Application for Security for Costs, ICSID Case No. ARB/09/17, 20 September 2012, at [45].

from the funder, which is not a party to the arbitration. In *Guaracachi and Rurelec v Bolivia*,[56] the tribunal was circumspect about this argument, noting:

> ...As a factual matter, the Respondent has not shown a sufficient causal link such that the Tribunal can infer from the mere existence of third party funding that the Claimants will not be able to pay an eventual award of costs rendered against them, regardless of whether the funder is liable for costs or not....

In *RSM Production Corporation v Saint Lucia*,[57] the claimant's history of consistently failing to pay advances or costs orders in other ICSID cases caused the tribunal to reach a decision in favour of granting security.[58]

(xi) Power to sanction counsel

5.40 Following concerns about increased abuse by counsel of certain procedural tools at their disposal with which to delay arbitrations, to cause hearings to be annulled, or otherwise to frustrate an efficient process, one arbitral institution (the LCIA) has introduced a new power to sanction counsel.[59] The tribunal may thus exercise its discretion to issue a written reprimand or caution as to future conduct in the arbitration, or take any other measure necessary to fulfil its general duties if counsel were to:

- engage in activities intended unfairly to obstruct the arbitration or to jeopardise the finality of any award, including repeated challenges to an arbitrator's appointment or to the jurisdiction or authority of the tribunal known to be unfounded by counsel;
- knowingly make any false statement to the tribunal or the LCIA Court;
- knowingly procure or assist in the preparation of, or rely upon, any false evidence presented to the tribunal or the LCIA Court; or
- knowingly conceal or assist in the concealment of any document ordered to be produced by the tribunal.

(d) **Supporting powers of the courts**

5.41 National courts with an 'arbitration-friendly' law can usually lend support to arbitral tribunals, where needed. The United States, for example, provides a formidable array of tools to enable courts to assist international arbitral tribunals, including, in some cases, arbitral tribunals with seats outside of the United States, where relevant evidence is in the United States. These include the power to order depositions, the power to subpoena witnesses present in the jurisdiction to give evidence or to

---

[56] See *Guaracachi* PO14 supra, at [7].
[57] *RSM Production, Inc. v Saint Lucia*, Decision on Saint Lucia's Request for Security for Costs, ICSID Case No. ARB 12/10, 12 August 2014.
[58] In a heavily debated assenting opinion, Dr Gavan Griffith went further and suggested that security for costs be ordered wherever third-party funding is involved.
[59] See LCIA Rules, Art. 18(5) and (6), and Annex.

produce documents, and the power to order production of documents sought by a party to an arbitration with a foreign seat.[60]

5.42 Another example is provided by the English system, in which the court can act as a 'backup' to the arbitration by ordering a party to comply with any peremptory order made by the tribunal.[61] This effectively converts the breach of the tribunal's order into a contempt of court. A court can also assist a tribunal by making its own orders in relation to the proceedings.[62] These include orders freezing a party's assets,[63] orders permitting the seizure of relevant evidence,[64] and orders securing the attendance of witnesses.[65] This range of powers, whether exercised directly by the arbitral tribunal itself or indirectly by application to the courts, provides the support from *national* legal systems that *international* arbitration requires to achieve its purpose.[66]

C. Duties of Arbitrators

(a) Introduction

5.43 The duties of an arbitrator may be divided into three categories: duties imposed by the parties; duties imposed by law; and ethical duties. It is a useful discipline for an arbitral tribunal to draw up for itself a checklist of its specific duties, whatever their origin. Such a list will differ from case to case, since it must allow for the impact of different rules of arbitration and for the differing laws applicable to each case.

(b) Duties imposed by the parties

5.44 Specific duties may be imposed upon an arbitral tribunal by the parties. This may be done before the arbitrators are appointed, or during the course of the arbitration, or both. If it is done before the appointment of arbitrators (for example in an ad hoc submission agreement), each arbitrator should check the agreement before accepting the appointment, in case it imposes unreasonable duties or duties that are incapable of fulfilment. For example, there might be a provision that the award should be made within a limited time after the appointment of the arbitral tribunal. If the agreed timescale is unacceptable to the arbitrator and cannot be changed, the appointment should be declined.

---

[60] See Chapter 7 for more details on these powers.
[61] English Arbitration Act 1996, s. 42. A court can make such orders only if it is satisfied that the person to whom the tribunal's order was directed has had sufficient time to comply.
[62] English Arbitration Act 1996, ss 43 and 44.
[63] Ibid., s. 44(3).
[64] Ibid., s. 44(2)(c).
[65] Ibid., s. 43(2).
[66] This will be examined in more detail in Chapter 7.

5.45 Duties may also be imposed on the arbitral tribunal during the course of the proceedings by the parties, but usually only after consultation with the arbitral tribunal. For example, in a dispute arising out of a construction project in a warzone, the parties may decide in the course of the arbitration that they wish the arbitral tribunal to inspect the construction site. The proposal for such a site inspection would usually be discussed with, and agreed by, the arbitral tribunal—but if a particular arbitrator were unwilling to accept the proposal and the parties were to insist upon it, that arbitrator would have to resign.

5.46 Where the arbitration is conducted under specific rules, those rules usually impose particular duties on the arbitral tribunal in addition to any imposed by the parties. A review of the rules of two arbitral institutions indicates what sort of duties these might be. Under the ICSID Arbitration Rules, arbitrators must, before or at the first session, sign a declaration of independence and readiness to judge fairly as between the parties, in default of which they are deemed to have resigned.[67] Under the same Rules, the arbitral tribunal must meet for its first session within sixty days of its constitution, or such other period as the parties to the arbitration may agree;[68] it must keep its deliberations secret;[69] it must take decisions by a majority vote;[70] and it must give reasons for its award.[71] The ICC Rules also impose their own obligations upon arbitral tribunals—such as to confirm their availability,[72] to draw up terms of reference,[73] to make an award within a defined period of time,[74] and to submit the award in draft form to the ICC's Court for scrutiny.[75]

(c) Duties imposed by law

5.47 Other duties are imposed by law. For instance, the law may require an arbitral tribunal to decide all procedural and evidential matters,[76] to treat the parties fairly and impartially,[77] or to make the award in a particular form.[78]

(i) Duty to act with due care

5.48 It is generally recognised that members of a profession, such as lawyers, doctors, accountants, architects, and engineers, are under a duty to carry out their

---

[67] ICSID Rules, r. 6(2).
[68] Ibid., r. 13(1).
[69] Ibid., r. 15(1).
[70] Ibid., r. 16(1).
[71] Ibid., r. 47(1)(i).
[72] ICC Rules, Art. 11(2).
[73] Ibid., Art. 23(1).
[74] Ibid., Art. 30(1). Unless extended by the ICC's Court under Art. 30(2), this time limit is six months.
[75] Ibid., Art. 33.
[76] English Arbitration Act 1996, s. 34.
[77] Ibid., s. 33(1)(a).
[78] Such as in writing or with reasons: see, e.g., art. 1448 of the Mexican Commercial Code and art. 1054(1) and (2) of the German Code of Civil Procedure (ZPO).

C. Duties of Arbitrators

professional work with proper skill and care—and that they may be held liable in damages at the suit of an injured party if they fail to do so. In the course of their professional work, such professionals may well be required to formulate a decision that is binding upon two or more parties. For example, an architect may be required, under a standard form of building contract, to certify the value of work as it is performed, by issuing interim certificates. If due care is not taken so that (for instance) the amount certified is too large and the employer loses money as a consequence, the architect may be compelled by legal action to make good the loss caused by his or her negligence.[79] Equally, an accountant may be asked to determine the value of shares in a private company in a way that will be binding upon the parties to an agreement. In this case also, if the accountant acts without due care and a party suffers loss, the accountant may be sued in respect of negligence.[80]

5.49 The distinction between a professional adviser, who formulates a decision binding upon two or more parties in the course of a professional activity, and an arbitrator, who formulates a decision binding upon two or more parties in the course of an arbitration, is not easy to identify. It seems appropriate to expect the same standard of professional care from a lawyer (or an accountant, or an architect, or an engineer) who is serving as an arbitrator as would be expected in the course of his or her other professional work. The parties to an arbitration entrust an arbitral tribunal with an important task, for which they are prepared to pay—often quite generously. They therefore expect the arbitrator to perform the task with due care and there exists an obvious moral duty for him or her to do so. The question is whether there is also a legal duty.

5.50 This question goes to the heart of the relationship between the arbitrator and the parties. As the practice of international arbitration becomes increasingly sophisticated and as the sums at stake grow in size, a party that has suffered loss as a result of an arbitrator's manifest lack of care may wish to seek to recover that loss from the arbitrator personally. How can a breach by the arbitrator of the obligation to act with due care be sanctioned? This will depend on the nature of the relationship with the parties. There are two schools of thought:[81] the first considers that the relationship between the arbitrator and the parties is established by contract; the second may be identified as the 'status school', which considers that the judicial nature of an arbitrator's function should result in treatment comparable to that of a judge.[82] In some jurisdictions, such like treatment may give rise to immunity from

---

[79] As in the English case *Sutcliffe v Thackrah* [1974] AC 727; [1974] 1 Lloyd's Rep 312 (HL).
[80] *Arenson v Arenson* [1977] AC 405; [1976] 1 Lloyd's Rep 179 (HL).
[81] The two schools are analysed in Mullerat, 'The liability of arbitrators: A survey of current practice', Paper presented at the IBA Commission on Arbitration, Chicago, IL, 21 September 2006.
[82] The position in English law appeared to favour a hybrid approach. In *K/s Norjari A/s v Hyundai Heavy Industries Co. Ltd* [1992] QB 863, [1991] 3 All ER 211, [1991] 3 WLR 1025, at [7], Sir Nicholas Browne-Wilkinson VC noted in the Court of Appeal that:

> For myself, I find it impossible to divorce the contractual and status considerations: in truth the arbitrator's rights and duties flow from the conjunction of those two elements. The arbitration agreement is a bilateral contract between the parties to the main contract.

legal proceedings; in others, it simply results in the application of rules on judicial liability.[83]

5.51 The 'contractual school' considers that an arbitrator is appointed by or on behalf of the parties to an arbitration to perform a service (that of resolving a dispute between them) for a fee. In these circumstances, a contractual relationship arises between the parties and the arbitrator. The terms of this contract may be set out in the submission to arbitration, the relevant rules of arbitration, the terms of reference, and/or the terms of appointment. Other terms may be imposed by operation of law, and include the duties to act with due diligence and to act judicially.

5.52 The contractual approach finds favour in most continental European jurisdictions.[84] Austrian law, for instance, takes the position that there is a contract between the arbitrator and the parties. This contract (*Schiedsrichtervertrag*), although it resembles a contract for services, is considered to be *sui generis* by some authors.[85] Certain duties, as well as rights, are imposed upon an arbitrator under the contract. One of the rights is a right to remuneration. The duties include conducting the proceedings in an appropriate way and making an award. The Austrian Code of Civil Procedure provides that an arbitrator who does not fulfil the duties assumed by accepting an appointment, or who does not fulfil them in due time, may be liable to the parties for loss caused by wrongful behaviour.[86] Nevertheless, liability in

> On appointment, the arbitrator becomes a third party to that arbitration agreement, which becomes a trilateral contract. Under that trilateral contract, the arbitrator undertakes his quasi-judicial functions in consideration of the parties agreeing to pay him remuneration. By accepting appointment, the arbitrator assumes the status of a quasi-judicial adjudicator, together with all the duties and disabilities inherent in that status.

However, the English Supreme Court now seems to have firmly embraced the contractual approach in the case of *Jivraj v Hashwani* [2011] UKSC 40, at [23]: 'It is common ground, at any rate in this class of case, that there is a contract between the parties and the arbitrator or arbitrators appointed under a contract and that his or their services are rendered pursuant to that contract...'

[83] For a detailed study on the sources of arbitral liability and the implications in connection with immunity, see Franck, 'The liability of international arbitrators: A comparative analysis and proposal for qualified immunity' (2000) 20 NYL Sch J Intl Comp L 1. For a discussion of the status of the arbitrator, see Fouchard, 'Relationships between the arbitrator and the parties and the arbitral institution' (1995) 12 ICC International Court of Arbitration Bulletin 22.

[84] Whilst there is a degree of unity in European civil law jurisdictions on this issue, several civil law jurisdictions in Latin America (such as Colombia and Ecuador) have taken a firm view in favour of the status approach by considering the arbitrator a 'temporary judge', with the same powers and duties as a state-appointed judge during the pendency of his or her appointment.

[85] See Melis, 'Austria', in Lew (ed.) *The Immunity of Arbitrators* (Lloyd's of London Press, 1990), p. 18. Swiss law adopts a similar position: see Voser and Fischer, 'The arbitral tribunal', in Geisinger and Voser (eds) *International Arbitration in Switzerland: A Handbook for Practitioners* (Kluwer Law International, 2013), pp. 52–54.

[86] Article 594(4) of the Austrian Code of Civil Procedure states: 'An arbitrator who does not fulfil his obligations resulting from the acceptance of his appointment or do so in a timely fashion, shall be liable to the parties for all damages caused by his culpable refusal or delay.' However, a recent decision of the Austrian Supreme Court (OG 6 June 2006, 9 Ob. 207/06v) limited the scope of this provision by ruling that an arbitrator's liability is limited to violations that constitute grounds for setting aside an arbitral award under art. 595 of the Austrian Code of Civil Procedure and can be triggered only in situations in which the award has successfully been set aside.

C. Duties of Arbitrators

respect of procedural mistakes and wrong decisions is limited to wilful harm or gross negligence.[87]

5.53 A similar position is adopted by Dutch law. An arbitrator is held to be in a contractual relationship with the parties and may be liable for damages in the event of committing 'gross negligence'.[88] Other jurisdictions, such as Argentina, consider that the arbitral contract renders arbitrators liable for losses caused by any failure to perform duties: '[A]cceptance by arbitrators of their appointment shall entitle the parties to compel them to carry out their duties and to hold them liable for costs and damages derived from the non-performance of arbitral duties.'[89] Chinese law provides for liability for certain arbitral conduct, in addition to sanctions such as removal from the relevant list of arbitrators.[90]

5.54 The 'status school' is based on the performance by arbitrators of a judicial or quasi-judicial function, which grants an element of 'status' entitling them to treatment similar to that of a judge. Certain rights and duties are conferred on the arbitrator by the very fact of having assumed that office. The arbitrator exercises a compulsory jurisdictional function and enjoys statutory powers. In most common law jurisdictions, this leads to certain immunities,[91] although the immunity may be qualified where the arbitrator has acted in bad faith.[92]

5.55 Specifically, arbitrators and arbitral institutions in the United States enjoy a broad degree of immunity from suit for actions taken within their mandate.[93] Arbitrators acting in England cannot be held liable for the performance of their arbitral functions, unless bad faith can be proved.[94] Similarly, arbitrators in New Zealand,

---

[87] See Melis, 'Austria', in Paulsson (ed.) *International Handbook on Commercial Arbitration* (Wolters Kluwer Law & Business, 2007), p. 16.
[88] van den Berg, 'The Netherlands', in Lew (ed.) *The Immunity of Arbitrators* (Lloyd's of London Press, 1990), p. 59.
[89] Argentine National Code of Civil and Commercial Procedure, art. 745.
[90] Arbitration Law of the People's Republic of China, s. 38.
[91] See, e.g., *Corey v New York Stock Exchange* 691 F.2d 1205, 1209 (6th Cir. 1982); *Sutcliffe v Thackrah* [1974] AC 727, at 735D; *Pickens v Templeton* [1994] 2 NZLR 718, at 727–728 (although a valuer was technically classified as an arbitrator by the Arbitration Act 1908, his actions were not sufficiently judicial to justify immunity, because they were based on his expertise and he did not make a final determination of the dispute). See also *Sport Maska Inc. v Zittrerm* [1988] 1 SCR 564.
[92] The laws of Australia, Canada, England, and New Zealand all provide that arbitrators may be liable for fraud, bad faith, or intentional actions. In the United States, however, arbitrator immunity is subject only to rare exceptions: see, e.g., *Lundgren v Freeman* 307 F.2d 104, 118 (9th Cir. 1962).
[93] Wallace, 'United States', in Lew (ed.) *The Immunity of Arbitrators* (Lloyd's of London Press, 1990), p. 85. See also *Corey v New York Stock Exchange* 691 F.2d 1205 (6th Cir. 1982). Immunity of arbitrators in the United States derives from the view that they are functioning as judges, and is to be contrasted with qualified immunity in Austria, Germany, and Norway, and no immunity in France, Spain, and Sweden: see Lew, 'Introduction', in Lew (ed.) *The Immunity of Arbitrators* (Lloyd's of London Press, 1990).
[94] English Arbitration Act 1996, s. 29. See also s. 74, which grants the same immunity to arbitral institutions, appointing authorities, and their respective employees.

Australia, Kenya, and Ireland cannot be held liable for negligence.[95] This common law approach has now been followed by institutions such as the ICC and the LCIA, which have adopted rules seeking to exclude liability for arbitrators.[96] Nevertheless, some commentators from common law systems have questioned the appropriateness of almost absolute immunity for arbitrators, and several have argued that arbitrators have professional duties of care, skill, and diligence, and that they should be liable for breach of such duties.[97]

5.56 A rigid categorisation of the source of an arbitrator's obligation to act with due care risks obscuring the real debate: whether it is appropriate, as a matter of policy, to accord immunity, or partial immunity, to arbitrators. Public policy in this context is mainly concerned with the independence and integrity of the decision-making process, which could be jeopardised if, as a result of liability, arbitrators were to be subject to reprisals by disappointed parties.[98]

5.57 Other arguments in favour of immunity are that:

- it helps to ensure the finality of arbitral awards, by preventing an unsuccessful party from suing the arbitrator;[99]
- fewer skilled persons would be prepared to act as arbitrators if they were to run the risk of incurring substantial liability;[100]
- arbitrators have no interest in the outcome of the dispute and should not be compelled to become parties to it; and
- it ensures the protection of the public, in those cases in which truly judicial functions are exercised (presumably by unburdening the courts of many disputes).

Some commentators go so far as to base arbitral immunity entirely on public policy grounds, arguing that immunity can be explained satisfactorily only as a concession from the state, which weighs the potential wrongs caused by such immunity against the benefits of arbitration.[101]

---

[95] New Zealand's Arbitration Act 1996, s. 13; Australian International Arbitration Act 1974, s. 28 (which Act was amended in 1992 to incorporate the UNCITRAL Model Law); ICC Rules, Art. 34; Kenyan Arbitration (Amendment) Act No. 11 of 2009, s. 16B(1); Irish Arbitration Act 2010, s. 22(1) ('An arbitrator shall not be liable in any proceedings for anything done or omitted in the discharge or purported discharge of his or her functions').

[96] See LCIA Rules, Art. 31(1), excluding 'conscious and deliberate wrongdoing'; ICC Rules, Art. 40, which excludes only conduct prohibited by applicable law.

[97] See, e.g., Brown, 'Expansion of arbitral immunity: Is absolute immunity a foregone conclusion' [2009] J Disp Res 225, which contends that qualified immunity is the appropriate type of immunity that would 'protect arbitral decision making while not shielding non-decisional acts'.

[98] See, e.g., *Cort v AAA* 795 F.Supp.970, 972 (N.D.Ca. 1992), determining that, in order to encourage independent judgments, the arbitration process is granted immunity.

[99] See Yat-Sen Li, 'Arbitral immunity: A profession comes of age' (1998) 64 Arbitration 51, at 53.

[100] See, e.g., *Cort*, at 973. However, some comment that arbitration is now a fully developed profession, the members of which should accept personal responsibility, including full legal liability for loss caused by any failure: see Yat-Sen Li, n. 99, at 55.

[101] See Lin Yu and Sauzier, 'From arbitrator's immunity to the fifth theory of international commercial arbitration' (2000) 3 Intl Arb L Rev 114.

5.58 But the arguments are not all one-way. There are a number of policy arguments against immunity: immunity may encourage carelessness; the finality of the decision is given priority over individual justice; disciplinary remedies are generally unavailable against arbitrators; and alternative remedies, such as *vacatur* of the award and withholding of fees, may be inadequate.

5.59 One substantial concern is the lack of uniformity in approach. The source of the arbitrator's duties and the public policy of the state in which the arbitrator is acting need to be examined on a case-by-case basis. It would be helpful if some overriding principles could be established at an international level to provide comfort to arbitrators in the exercise of their functions, irrespective of the seat of arbitration.

5.60 The IBA states its position in its 1987 Rules of Ethics for International Arbitrators[102]—that is, that 'international arbitrators should in principle be granted immunity from suit under national laws, except in extreme cases of wilful or reckless disregard of their legal obligations'. This appears to be a suitable middle ground, but it remains a wish, rather than a reality, in many jurisdictions. Pending the establishment of uniform or harmonised rules in this regard, potential arbitrators should ascertain the potential scope of their liability, principally in accordance with the law of the seat.

5.61 Meanwhile, perhaps the practical answer is that where arbitrators are exposed to a risk of personal liability, by reason of the law under which the arbitration is to take place, they might refuse to accept appointment unless given an indemnity by the parties. In this way, they would obtain immunity from liability by contract, even if they were not entitled to it by operation of law. Whether such an indemnity would be enforceable as a matter of public policy is uncertain. Professional liability insurance should also be available to cover the risks, but the cost would presumably have to be passed on to the parties.

5.62 A separate issue that is increasingly the subject of discussion is the potential liability of the arbitral institution: aggrieved parties who have lost an arbitration may look indiscriminately for defendants, and arbitral institutions have not escaped this trend.[103]

---

[102] The IBA Rules of Ethics were superseded by the Guidelines on Conflicts of Interest in International Arbitration, published in 2004 (and amended in 2014), for the matters addressed therein. However, the question of arbitrator immunity was not addressed in the Guidelines, for which the Rules of Ethics continue to apply.

[103] For example, in 2013, RSM, a US oil company, filed a lawsuit in the United States against ICSID and its secretary-general over the alleged mishandling of an annulment proceeding: see *Global Arbitration Review*, 3 June 2013. For a more detailed analysis of arbitral institution liability, see van Houtte and McAsey, 'The liability of arbitrators and arbitral institutions', in Habegger, Hochstrasser, Nater-Bass, and Weber-Stecher (eds) *Arbitral Institutions under Scrutiny* (Juris, 2013), p. 133; Rasmussen, 'Overextending immunity: Arbitral institutional liability in the United States, England, and France' (2002) 26 Fordham Intl LJ 1824.

5.63 Like the relationship between the arbitrators and the parties, the relationship between parties to the arbitration and the arbitral institution administering the arbitration is generally considered to be contractual. Whereas, in common law jurisdictions, arbitral institutions have more or less absolute immunity from liability,[104] in civil law jurisdictions, they may be held liable for wrongful acts, and such liability will usually be based on general principles of contractual liability. For example, in January 2009, in a case against the ICC, the Paris Cour d'Appel held that the waiver of liability contained in the ICC Arbitration Rules ran contrary to the duty of the ICC as an arbitral institution and should be treated as if it were not written.[105]

5.64 The basis for immunity of arbitral institutions in common law jurisdictions is different from that relating to arbitrators. It is based on the fact that they operate as quasi-judicial organisations[106] in order to protect those functions that are closely related to the arbitral process and sufficiently related to the adjudicative phase of the arbitration, thereby ensuring that the policies behind immunity are fulfilled. Without this immunity, it is argued (mainly in the United States) that the immunity of arbitrators themselves would be meaningless, because liability would merely shift from the arbitrator to the arbitral organisation.[107]

5.65 In the United States, breaches by an institution of its own rules and failure to abide by the arbitration agreement usually attract immunity. In France, however, arbitration institutions are required to adhere to their own rules and are potentially liable for their failure to adhere to the arbitration agreement.[108]

5.66 Institutional rules usually provide for the institution's immunity in relation to any act or omission in connection with the arbitration, subject to applicable law,[109] but for the LCIA, there is an exclusion for conscious or deliberate wrongdoing.[110] The

---

[104] In the United States, institutions, like arbitrators, have absolute immunity. In *Austern v Chicago Board Options Exchange* 716 F.Supp.121 (SDNY 1989), the plaintiffs sued an arbitral institution for damages for mental anguish, but were barred by the doctrine of immunity. In England, the Arbitration Act 1996, s. 74, provides for immunity in relation to the discharge by the institution of its duties, unless it acts in bad faith.

[105] See *SNF v Chambre de Commerce Internationale*, Paris Cour d'Appel, Ch. 1ere, section C, 22 January 2009.

[106] See *Rubenstein v Otterbourg* 357 NYS.2d 62, 64 (NY Misc. 1973); *Boraks v AAA* 517 NW.2d 771, 772 (Mich. App. 1994).

[107] See *Corey v New York Stock Exchange* 691 F.2d 1205, 1211 (6th Cir. 1982).

[108] In *Société Cubic Défense Système v Chambre de Commerce Internationale* [1997] Rev Arb 417, a French court stated that an arbitral institution could be liable for a failure to adhere to the parties' agreement. See also see *SNF v Chambre de Commerce Internationale*, Paris Cour d'Appel, Ch. 1ere, section C, 22 January 2009. However, French courts make a distinction between the institution's jurisdictional role (decisions intimately linked with the process, such as arbitrator challenges) and non-jurisdictional conduct, such as when the institution fails to run the arbitration properly: see Dupeyré, 'Les arbitres et centres d'arbitrage face à leurs responsabilités: Le droit français à son point d'équilibre' (2014) 32 ASA Bulletin 265.

[109] See ICC Rules, Art. 40; ICSID Convention, Art. 20; Netherlands Arbitration Institute (NAI) Rules, Art. 66; SIAC Rules, Art. 34(1); ICDR Rules, Art. 38.

[110] LCIA Rules, Art. 31.

C. Duties of Arbitrators

rules of the arbitral institution are usually incorporated in the contract between the parties and the institution, and as such may operate as an exclusion of liability. However, any mandatory rules of the forum providing for liability would be likely to trump such exclusion.[111]

(ii) Duty to act promptly

An arbitral tribunal has an obvious moral obligation to carry out its task with due diligence. Justice delayed is justice denied. Some systems of law endeavour to ensure that an arbitration is carried out with reasonable speed by setting a time limit within which the arbitral tribunal must make its award.[112] The time limit fixed is sometimes as short as six months (as indeed it is in the ICC Rules[113]), although generally it may be extended by consent of the parties, or at the initiative of the institution[114] or the tribunal.[115] If an award is not made within the time allowed, the authority of the arbitral tribunal terminates, and the award will be null and void.[116] Some systems of law provide that an arbitrator who fails to proceed with reasonable speed in conducting the arbitration and making his or her award may be removed by a competent court,[117] and deprived of any entitlement to remuneration. The Model Law provides that the mandate of an arbitrator terminates if he or she 'fails to act without undue delay'.[118]

5.67

Whilst these sanctions may act as a spur to the indolent arbitrator, they do nothing to compensate a party who has suffered financial loss as a result of delay in the conduct of the arbitration. Delay in the conduct of an arbitration may have serious financial consequences; awards of interest rarely compensate the successful party for the financial loss suffered in the interim. The question accordingly arises as to whether or not an arbitrator may be made liable in damages for undue delay. No liability is imposed under the established international or institutional rules, and it would be most unusual to find a term imposing liability for delay in an ad hoc submission agreement. Liability might, however, be established on the basis of the

5.68

---

[111] As occurred in *Société Cubic Défense Système v Chambre de Commerce Internationale* [1997] Rev Arb 417.
[112] For example, the Italian Code of Civil Procedure, as amended in 2006, arts 813 and 820 (240 days from date of acceptance of appointment by the tribunal); the 2006 Ecuadorean Law of Arbitration and Mediation, s. 25 (150 days from the final hearing).
[113] ICC Rules, Art. 30(1).
[114] Ibid., Art. 30(2). See also art. 1463(2) of the French Code of Civil Procedure (2011 amendments): 'The statutory or contractual time limit may be extended by agreement between the parties or, where there is no such agreement, by the judge acting in support of the arbitration.'
[115] Section 25 of the 2006 Ecuadorean Law of Arbitration and Mediation permits the tribunal 'where strictly necessary' to grant itself *ex officio* an extension of the 150-day time limit by a further 150 days.
[116] See arts 760 and 771 of the National Code of Civil Procedure of Argentina.
[117] As in England: Arbitration Act 1996, s. 33(1)(b). An arbitrator has a duty to act fairly and without unnecessary delay. Breach of this duty may result in the removal of the arbitrator by the court (s. 24(2)) and/or a challenge to the award (s. 68).
[118] Model Law, Art. 14.

contractual duty of care,[119] in those jurisdictions in which the arbitrator does not benefit from immunity.

5.69 Faced with increasing delays in the conduct of arbitrations, the major institutions have revised their rules to improve the speed and efficiency of arbitrations. For example, the ICC Rules now require the tribunal and the parties to 'make every effort' to 'conduct the arbitration in an expeditious and cost-effective manner'. This includes a compulsory case management conference,[120] in which the use of specific case management techniques is encouraged.[121] The tribunal is also required to set an expected date for issue of the award, following the close of the proceedings.[122] Appendix IV sets out case management techniques, and is supplemented by the ICC Commission's updated report on controlling time and costs in arbitration.[123]

(iii) Duty to act judicially

5.70 It is important that an arbitral tribunal should act, and should be seen to act, judicially (that is, respecting the rules of due process). This is more than a mere moral obligation; it is also one that, to some extent at least, may be enforced under international or institutional rules, or under the applicable law. The duty to act judicially is a duty that extends to all aspects of the proceedings.

5.71 What does this mean in practice? Neither the arbitral tribunal as a whole nor any of its individual members should, for instance, discuss the case with one party in the absence of the other, unless in connection with the nomination of the president of the arbitral tribunal (where this has been agreed), or if the absent party has failed to attend a meeting or a hearing, having been given proper notice to do so. At the hearing, the duty to act judicially means that each party must be accorded equality of treatment and given a fair opportunity to present its case. It would be wrong, for instance, to allow one party to call witnesses and to deny the other party a similar opportunity. Similarly, it would be improper to allow one party to address the arbitral tribunal orally and to deny the same to the other party. International and institutional rules, which are usually silent as to the duties of the arbitral tribunal, also find common ground on this point. Article 17 of the UNCITRAL Rules provides that the arbitral tribunal may conduct the arbitration in such a manner as it considers appropriate 'provided that the parties are treated with equality and that at an appropriate stage of the proceedings each party is given a reasonable opportunity of presenting its case'.[124] The ICSID Rules do not contain such a general statement, but detailed provisions ensure equality of treatment, and if any party fails to appear or

---

[119] See paragraphs 5.48*ff*.
[120] ICC Rules, Art. 22(2).
[121] Ibid., Appendix VI.
[122] Ibid., Art. 27.
[123] ICC Commission on Arbitration and ADR, *ICC Commission Report: Controlling Time and Costs in Arbitration* (2nd edn, ICC, 2014).
[124] The ICC Arbitration Rules contain provisions to a similar effect: see Art. 22(4).

C. Duties of Arbitrators

present its case, a special default procedure must be followed.[125] Article 14(4)(i) of the LCIA Rules require arbitrators at all times 'to act fairly and impartially as between all parties, giving each a reasonable opportunity of putting its case and dealing with that of its opponent'.

5.72 The law applicable to the arbitration proceedings often states explicitly that due process must be observed by the arbitral tribunal. For example, section 21(2) of the Brazilian Arbitration Law of 1996 states that 'the principles of the presence of both parties to the dispute, equal treatment of the parties, impartiality of the arbitrator and freedom of decision, shall always be respected'.[126] English law has gone even further. Section 33(1) of the Arbitration Act 1996 provides that an arbitral tribunal shall:

[...]
(a) act fairly and impartially as between the parties giving each party a reasonable opportunity of putting his case and dealing with that of his opponent, and
(b) adopt procedures suitable to the circumstances of the particular case, avoiding unnecessary delay or expense, so as to provide a fair means for the resolution of the matters falling to be determined.

This is a mandatory provision, from which neither the parties nor the tribunal may derogate.[127] An arbitrator acting in breach of this duty can be removed.[128] Perhaps more significantly, awards made in breach of it are open to challenge[129] and would face difficulties of enforcement.[130]

5.73 The duty to act judicially is not simply a matter of ensuring equality between the parties and giving each the right to respond to the other party's position; it also arises where the arbitral tribunal decides to base its decision on an issue not specifically raised by the parties. It is an accepted principle that the tribunal is free to apply any element of applicable law (even where not commented or argued by the parties) under the maxim *juris novit curia* ('the court knows the law'). But what is the consequence under the applicable law of relying on a legal argument not addressed by the parties?

5.74 English law is clear in this respect: a tribunal must give the parties an opportunity to be heard. If it fails to do so, then the duty to act judicially will have been infringed. In one case, the English courts noted that an arbitral tribunal must have provided each party with a fair opportunity to address all of the essential building blocks in its conclusion.[131] On the facts of the case, the claimant had been deprived

---

[125] ICSID Rules, r. 42.
[126] See also art. 1434 of the Mexican Commercial Code: 'The parties shall be treated with equality and each party shall be given a full opportunity to present its case.'
[127] English Arbitration Act 1996, s. 4(1) and Sch. 1.
[128] Ibid., s. 24.
[129] Ibid., s. 68(2)(a).
[130] New York Convention, Art. V(1)(d) and possibly also Art. V(2)(b).
[131] *OAO Northern Shipping Co. v Remolcadores De Marin SL (Remmar)* [2007] EWHC 1821. See also 'Serious irregularity sends award back to arbitrators' (2007) 22 Mealey's Intl Arb Rep 20.

of the opportunity to advance submissions on an issue that had formed part of the tribunal's reasoning in the award, but had not been debated by the parties. The court held that such action amounted to a serious irregularity capable of causing substantial injustice, thus meeting the criteria for the setting aside of an award under section 68 of the 1996 Act. The court set aside the award and remitted the issue to the arbitral tribunal for further consideration.

5.75 The position is less clear in continental Europe, where Switzerland and other civil law jurisdictions allow arbitrators to reach their conclusions on legal theories not advanced by the parties, without inviting them to comment.[132] This distinction is not helpful in tribunals composed of arbitrators from different legal cultures and there has been a call for harmonisation.[133]

5.76 Where a tribunal fails in its duty to act judicially, the immediate sanction is for it to be removed. In some circumstances, this can be done without waiting for the award, either under the rules of the relevant arbitral institution[134] or by a national court, where the applicable law permits the courts at the place of arbitration to intervene.[135] However, in some jurisdictions, such as the United States, there is no opportunity for concurrent court control and the aggrieved party must wait until the end of the proceedings before challenging the award.[136]

5.77 The duty to act judicially is to be clearly distinguished from the duty to be independent and impartial. By way of illustration, in a decision of the LCIA Court, a sole arbitrator was challenged for conducting a meeting with representatives of the respondent during two consecutive days in the absence of the claimant or any

---

In *Vee Networks Ltd v Econet Wireless International Ltd* [2005] 1 Lloyd's Rep 192, at 79–91, the Court of Appeal remanded a partial award to the arbitrator for not giving the parties the opportunity to comment on a new legal theory. However, the test is not easily met and if the award would have reached the same conclusion absent the issue not placed before the parties, the challenge is unlikely to succeed: see *ABB AG v Hochtief Airport GmbH* [2006] EWHC 388 (Comm), [2006] Arb LR 33.

[132] *X. v 1. Union Cycliste Internationale (UCI), 2. Fédération Z.*, Decision 4A_110/2012, Federal Supreme Court of Switzerland, 1st Civil Law Chamber, 9 October 2012, at [3.1.1]:

> In Switzerland, the right to be heard is in connection with the appreciation of the facts. The right of the parties to be consulted on legal questions is only recognised in a very limited manner. As a general rules under the principle of jua novit curia, state or arbitral tribunals may freely consider the legal consequences of the facts and may rule on the basis of legal rules not invoked by the parties.

[133] Giovannini, 'International arbitration and *jura novit curia*: Towards harmonization', in Fernández-Ballesteros and Arias (eds) *Liber Amicorum Bernardo Cremades* (La Ley, 2010). See also Arroyo, 'Which is the better approach to *jura novit arbiter*: The Swiss or the English?', in Müller and Rigozzi (eds) *New Developments in Commercial Arbitration* (Schulthess, 2010).

[134] For example, ICC Rules, Art. 15(2).

[135] For example, English Arbitration Act 1996, s. 24.

[136] In *PK Time Group, LLC v Robert*, No. 12 Civ 8200 (PAC), 2013 WL 3833084 (SDNY 13 July 2013), a federal district court denied a petition to remove a panel of arbitrators before a final award on damages had been issued, based on alleged misconduct and bias. The court dismissed the application and confirmed its view that the FAA prohibits pre-award challenges to arbitrators.

C. Duties of Arbitrators

of its representatives. A verbatim transcript of the meeting was produced for the parties, in which the arbitrator had made clear that the meeting was not a formal hearing. The claimant challenged the arbitrator. The LCIA Court, considering the manner in which the arbitration had been conducted, stated that it had no reason to doubt the arbitrator's independence or impartiality, but, in considering whether the arbitrator had acted fairly between the parties, found that '[f]or the Arbitrator to meet with the representatives of one party in the absence of the other, and to permit any discussion of the merits of the dispute at such a meeting is, to put it no higher, an error of judgment', which in the Court's view, constituted a failure to act fairly between the parties.[137]

Normally, the sanctions for a failure to act judicially do not include financial compensation to the aggrieved party. Nevertheless, a party who has suffered financial loss as a result of such a failure may wish to claim personally against the arbitrator. The term 'failure to act judicially' may cover a variety of conduct. Where the behaviour is wilful misconduct or bad faith (for example the acceptance of a bribe), the party who has suffered loss would be entitled to claim against the offending arbitrator, even in countries that traditionally confer immunity, such as Australia, England, and New Zealand.[138] **5.78**

(d) Ethical duties

In addition to specific duties imposed on arbitrators, either by the parties or by law, it is generally considered that an arbitrator has certain moral or ethical obligations. One obvious example, discussed earlier, is the obligation to decline to accept an appointment if sufficient time and attention cannot be given to the case.[139] There has been much discussion as to how these ethical standards—sometimes described as the 'deontology' of arbitrators—might be defined or established in some form of internationally accepted 'code of conduct'. This was achieved in the context of domestic arbitration in the United States, where the American Bar Association (ABA)/American Arbitration Association (AAA) Code of Ethics for Arbitrators was introduced in 1977 (with substantial modifications in 2004). **5.79**

In the international arena, the IBA established its Rules of Ethics for International Arbitrators in 1987. This is a set of principles designed to guide international arbitrators as to how the required arbitrator qualities of impartiality, competence, diligence, and discretion might be applied in practice in order to ensure a degree of harmonisation. The IBA subsequently adopted Guidelines on Conflicts of Interest **5.80**

---

[137] See Nicholas and Partasides, 'LCIA Court decisions on challenges to arbitrators: A proposal to publish' (2007) 23 Arb Intl 16, referring to Decision No. 10 of the LCIA Court, dated 13 February 2002.
[138] See Arbitration Act 1996, s. 29, for England; Arbitration Act 1996, s. 13, for New Zealand; International Arbitration Act 1974, s. 28(1), for Australia.
[139] See paragraph 5.44.

in International Arbitration in 2004, which replaced the Rules of Ethics only to the extent that they covered the same ground, and the IBA issued a revised version of the Guidelines in 2014.[140]

5.81 The IBA recognised the problems posed by conflicts of interest in international arbitration and the ever-increasing recourse to arbitrator challenges as a means of delaying arbitrations or depriving a party of the arbitrator of its choice. This trend was fuelled by the lack of clear guidance on the standards to apply in making disclosures and by different cultural perspectives of what was appropriate. The Guidelines have sought to inject a greater degree of objectivity and clarity into conflict and disclosure obligations, but have failed to stem the tide of arbitrator challenges.[141]

(i) Use of arbitration to further criminal purposes

5.82 Other ethical duties may arise where an arbitrator suspects that the arbitral process is being hijacked for a criminal purpose.[142] One important concern is the laundering of the proceeds of crime through a fraudulent dispute, which is rapidly settled. The parties ask the tribunal to embody a settlement of their 'dispute' in a consent award, through which an unlawful payment is successfully hidden. The award may then be enforced internationally and the money is 'laundered'. A tribunal should therefore be particularly cautious in agreeing to an early consent award that simply involves the payment of money. A consent award is of real utility only where there is an element of future performance that may need to be enforced. An obligation to pay money is usually sufficiently protected by mutual releases in a settlement agreement conditional upon the receipt of funds. Other parties who wish to abuse the arbitral process may be more sophisticated and simply put up a weak defence. There are often 'tell-tale' signs: the entities involved are often recently incorporated; their activities are usually of a nature that does not require any real investment; and the contract in question is rarely detailed or well drafted.

5.83 What is an arbitrator to do when confronted with possible criminal activity linked to an arbitration? There is a balance to be struck. It is not the job of the arbitrator to seek to uncover criminal activity, but rather to resolve the dispute within the scope of the arbitration agreement. Nevertheless, an EU Directive now requires 'auditors, external accountants and tax advisors', as well as 'notaries and other independent legal professionals', to report on their own initiative 'any fact which might indicate money laundering' and to provide the authorities with any information requested.[143] Particular reference is made to the legal profession in respect

---

[140] As discussed earlier in this volume. See Chapter 4 paragraph 4.84.
[141] See Chapter 4, paragraphs 4.84ff, for further discussion of the IBA Guidelines on Conflicts of Interest and Disclosure in International Arbitration.
[142] For a thorough analysis of the interplay between arbitration and criminal law, see Mourre, 'Arbitration and criminal law: Reflections on the duties of the arbitrator' (2006) 22 Arb Intl 95.
[143] Directive 2001/97/EC of the European Parliament and of the Council of 4 December 2001 amending Council Directive 91/308/EEC on prevention of the use of the financial system for the

C. Duties of Arbitrators

of assisting clients in the implementation of transactions. A further Directive was passed in 2005 aimed at preventing use of the financial system for the purpose of money laundering and terrorist financing.[144]

5.84 It is questionable whether the definition of 'independent legal professionals' would include arbitrators, or whether resolving a dispute could be said to be assisting a 'client' in the implementation of a transaction. Indeed, the 2005 Directive envisages reporting obligations for legal professionals when assisting in financial or corporate transactions, but excludes such obligations when information is obtained before, during, or after legal proceedings.[145] The position of mediators is clearly closer to this definition. Nevertheless, it would seem inappropriate for an arbitrator to ignore the question where there are clear signs of criminal activity. In any event, an arbitrator who is suspicious of criminal activity and is sitting in the European Union would do well to see how the terms of the directives have been implemented by local legislation.

5.85 If an arbitrator has grounds for suspecting a criminal offence, each party should be given an opportunity to provide an explanation. Once the tribunal believes it has sufficient justification, it can then evaluate the facts. In cases of fraud or corruption, this is likely to have an impact on the outcome of the dispute. In cases of money laundering or other manipulation of the process by the parties, the tribunal should terminate the proceedings on the basis that there is no genuine dispute. In cases of a consent award, the tribunal may issue a ruling refusing to approve the settlement.

5.86 Opinions nevertheless appear to be split as to whether the arbitrators should inform the appropriate authorities (whoever they might be). An ICC Task Force concluded that 'it appeared contrary to the nature of arbitration, contrary in particular to the trust that the parties place in the arbitrator, for an arbitral tribunal to report to the authorities the offences found'.[146] But if the parties' trust is simply that the arbitral tribunal act as a mute observer of a criminal offence, then it should not be respected. It seems wrong that the confidential nature of arbitral proceedings and the ultimate enforceability of an award should be open to abuse by international crime. The arbitration community must therefore be vigilant to ensure that it does not unwittingly assist in such ends.

---

purpose of money laundering, OJ L 344/76, 28 December 2001. The United Kingdom implemented the Directive by means of the Money Laundering Regulations 2003, SI 2003/3075, and the Proceeds of Crime Act 2002.

[144] Following the passage of the Third Directive—Directive 2005/60/EC of the European Parliament and of the Council of 26 October 2005 on the prevention of the use of the financial system for the purpose of money laundering and terrorist financing, OJ L 309/15, 25 November 2005—the UK Regulations were updated: see now the Money Laundering Regulations 2007, SI 2007/2157.

[145] Directive 2005/60/EC, Recitals 19 and 20.

[146] ICC French National Committee of the Commission on Arbitration, *Report of Task Force on Criminal Law and Arbitration*, Doc. 420/492 (ICC), p. 13.

5.87 One issue of increasing concern in international commerce is bribery and corruption.[147] These issues may arise in at least three distinct circumstances: first, there is the question of the corruption of the arbitrator; secondly, there is the dispute that arises out of a contract the very purpose of which is the bribery of state officials (usually denominated 'consultancy agreements'); and thirdly, there is the case in which the contract in question was procured by a bribe.

5.88 It goes without saying that one of the ethical duties of an arbitrator is to decide fairly in the absence of any corruption or bribe. Unfortunately, arbitration has not escaped the tentacles of corruption that taint many legal systems and there have been various initiatives to combat corruption in international arbitration over recent years. One such initiative is the Additional Protocol to the Criminal Law Convention on Corruption,[148] which entered into force on 1 February 2005, following ratification by five member states of the Council of Europe. As of October 2014, the Protocol had been ratified by thirty-six member states. The Protocol was developed by the Council of Europe to supplement the Criminal Law Convention on Corruption, which entered into force on 1 July 2002, by widening its scope to cover arbitrators. The Protocol requires state parties to create a criminal offence of bribery of a domestic or foreign arbitrator, whether bribery is instigated by an individual ('active bribery') or an arbitrator ('passive bribery').

5.89 The question of the contract the object of which is the exercise of influence over state officials was addressed in a famous decision of Judge Gunnar Lagergren, acting as arbitrator.[149] Although neither party had alleged the nullity of the contract based on its purpose, the arbitrator raised the issue of his own motion and concluded, on the basis of the evidence before him, that the object of the contract was the trafficking of influence. He consequently dismissed the claim on the basis that the contract was illegal.

5.90 The issue of the contract obtained through a bribe was considered by the arbitral tribunal in the ICSID case *World Duty Free v Kenya*.[150] In this case, the arbitral tribunal was shown evidence that the contract upon which the arbitration was based was procured by the payment of a bribe. The tribunal had no hesitation in

---

[147] For a deep analysis of this complex topic, see Sayed, *Corruption in International Trade and Commercial Arbitration* (Kluwer Law International, 2004). See also (2013) 24 ICC Bulletin, Supplement entitled 'Tackling Corruption in Arbitration', and Lamm, Moloo, and Pham, 'Fraud and corruption in international arbitration' (2013) 3 TDM.

[148] CETS No. 191, available online at http://conventions.coe.int.

[149] Award by Gunnar Lagergren, ICC Case No. 1110, (1996) XXI YBCA 47, (1994) 10 Arb Intl 286.

[150] *World Duty Free Co. Ltd v Republic of Kenya*, Award, ICSID Case No. ARB/00/7, IIC 277 (2006), 4 October 2006. Similarly, in the case of *Inceysa Vallisoletana SL v Republic of El Salvador*, Award, ICSID Case No. ARB/03/26, 2 August 2006, a systematic fraud in securing a contract with the Republic of El Salvador, for the operation of vehicle inspection stations, caused the tribunal to deny jurisdiction on a number of grounds, including that the investment was not made in accordance with the laws of El Salvador.

dismissing the claim, which it considered in clear breach of international public policy. The arbitral tribunal concluded that:

> In light of domestic laws and international conventions relating to corruption, and in light of the decisions taken in this matter by courts and arbitral tribunals, this Tribunal is convinced that bribery is contrary to international public policy of most, if not all, States, or, to use another formula, to transnational public policy. Thus, claims based on contracts of corruption or on contracts obtained by corruption cannot be upheld by this Arbitral Tribunal.[151]

These decisions have sent an important message that international arbitration may not be used as a tool to further unlawful contracts. Any party that resorts to bribery to obtain a contract is likely to find that the mechanism of international arbitral justice is no longer open to it.

D. Jurisdiction

(a) Introduction

5.91 An arbitral tribunal may validly resolve only those disputes that the parties have agreed that it should resolve. This rule is an inevitable and proper consequence of the voluntary nature of arbitration. It is the parties who give to a private tribunal the authority to decide disputes between them, and the arbitral tribunal must take care to stay within the terms of its mandate. The rule to this effect is expressed in several different ways. Sometimes, it is said that an arbitral tribunal must conform to the mission entrusted to it,[152] or that it must not exceed its mandate, or that it must stay within its terms of reference,[153] competence, or authority. Another way of expressing the rule (which is followed in this volume) is to state that an arbitral tribunal must not exceed its jurisdiction (this term being used in the sense of mandate, competence, or authority).

(b) Challenges to jurisdiction

5.92 A challenge to the jurisdiction of an arbitral tribunal may be partial or total. A *partial* challenge raises the question of whether certain (but not all) of the claims or counterclaims that have been submitted to the arbitral tribunal are within its jurisdiction. A challenge of this kind does not amount to a fundamental attack on the jurisdiction of the arbitral tribunal. A *total* challenge, by contrast, questions the whole basis upon which the arbitral tribunal is acting or purporting to act.

---

[151] *World Duty Free*, at [157].
[152] See, e.g., French Code of Civil Procedure (2011 amendment), art. 1457: 'Arbitrators shall carry out their mission until it is completed.'
[153] Under the ICC Rules, Art. 23, an arbitral tribunal must draw up its own 'terms of reference' for signature by the parties and the tribunal and for approval by the ICC Court, before proceeding with the arbitration.

A partial challenge is usually dependent on whether the particular matters referred to arbitration fall within the scope of the arbitration agreement. A total challenge usually questions whether there is a valid arbitration agreement at all.

(i) Partial challenge

5.93 A partial challenge exists where it is asserted that *some* of the claims (or counterclaims) that have been brought before the arbitral tribunal do not properly come within its jurisdiction. For instance, a construction contract may require all claims for varied or additional work first to be decided by an engineer before being referred to arbitration. If a claimant brings certain claims without asking or waiting for the engineer's decision, the respondent may argue that this failure means that the claims concerned were not properly submitted to arbitration and so were not within the jurisdiction of the arbitral tribunal. Similar issues have been tested in ICSID arbitrations, in which there is usually a requirement to notify disputes for the purpose of seeking an amicable settlement for a period before commencing an arbitration. Respondent states have often argued that certain claims fall outside of the originally notified dispute.[154]

5.94 Any lack of jurisdiction in this sense may be cured by agreement of the parties. Even if certain claims or counterclaims are outside the scope of the initial reference to arbitration, the parties may agree that new matters should, for convenience, be brought within the arbitration. By signing a submission agreement to this effect, they may effectively bring new claims within the jurisdiction of the arbitral tribunal. This is not always as straightforward as might appear: under some arbitration rules, where the arbitral process has already begun, new claims may be added only with the permission of the arbitral tribunal.[155]

5.95 Nevertheless, there are many cases in which the other party objects to new claims being brought into the arbitration and has good legal grounds for its objection. In these cases (and indeed in any case in which it seems that it may be exceeding its jurisdiction), the arbitral tribunal should proceed with caution. This issue is of particular concern where there are two or more contracts. In one case, a claim was brought before an arbitral tribunal constituted under the ICC Rules pursuant to a loan agreement. The loan agreement did not specify the seat of the arbitration and Paris was agreed by the parties. In its counterclaim, the respondent raised claims under a second loan agreement, which provided for an ICC arbitration

---

[154] See, e.g., *CMS Gas Transmission Co. v Republic of Argentina*, Decision on Objections to Jurisdiction, ICSID Case No. ARB/01/8, IIC 64 (2003), (2003) 42 ILM 788, signed 17 July 2003, in which the later claims were considered to have been an evolution of a dispute already notified. In contrast, in the case of *Burlington Resources, Inc. v Ecuador*, Jurisdictional Decision, ICSID Case No. ARB 08/5, 2 June 2010, the tribunal rejected jurisdiction over an unrelated claim that had not been the subject of prior notification.

[155] See, e.g., ICC Rules, Art. 23(4), which allows claims made after the drafting of the terms of reference only in the discretion of the arbitral tribunal.

with a seat in Madrid. The claimant objected to the inclusion of the counterclaim brought under the second loan agreement and noted that the counterclaim was incompatible with the arbitration in light of the different seat. The arbitral tribunal nevertheless proceeded to review the claim under the second loan within the original arbitration, on the basis that the two loans were commercially connected. The claimant successfully set aside the award before the Paris Cour d'Appel on the basis of a lack of jurisdiction over the second loan agreement in light of the lack of consent of the claimant.[156] It can therefore be seen that if a tribunal does exceed its jurisdiction, its award will be imperilled, and may be set aside or refused recognition and enforcement in whole or in part by a competent court.[157]

5.96 National laws and the international conventions on arbitration emphasise how important it is that an arbitral tribunal should not exceed its jurisdiction. In French law, for example, an award may be challenged where 'the arbitral tribunal wrongly upheld or declined jurisdiction'.[158] Internationally, the New York Convention provides that recognition and enforcement of an award may be refused on proof that '[t]he award deals with a difference not contemplated by or not falling within the terms of the submission to arbitration, or it contains decisions on matters beyond the scope of the submission to arbitration'.[159]

5.97 Partial challenges to the jurisdiction of an arbitral tribunal have become relatively common in modern times, and they do not in themselves raise any fundamental problems. It is different, however, when there is a total challenge to the jurisdiction of the arbitral tribunal that raises the more fundamental question of whether there is a valid arbitration agreement at all.

(ii) Total challenge

5.98 An arbitral tribunal that derives its authority from a submission agreement is unlikely to face a total challenge to its jurisdiction. The purpose of a submission agreement is to give the arbitral tribunal jurisdiction to determine specific disputes between specific parties. Total challenges to jurisdiction are therefore likely to arise in practice only where the authority (or purported authority) of the arbitral tribunal is derived from an arbitration clause.

---

[156] *Societe Empresa de Telecomunicaciones de Cuba SA (ETECSA) v Telefonica Antillana SA and SNC Banco Nacional de Comercio Exterior*, Paris Cour d'Appel, Ch. 1ere, section C, Decision of 16 November 2006.
[157] In *ETECSA*, although the issue of complaint was the exercise of jurisdiction in relation to the second loan agreement, the Paris Cour d'Appel was unable to sever the part related to the original loan agreement and the entire award was consequently set aside.
[158] French Code of Civil Procedure (2011 amendments), art. 1520.
[159] New York Convention, Art. V(1)(c). It should be pointed out, however, that the possibility of the 'good' parts of an award being separated from the 'bad' is explicitly recognised, since this paragraph of the New York Convention goes on to state that if the decision on matters submitted to arbitration can be separated from those that were not submitted, 'that part of the award which contains decisions on matters submitted to arbitration may be recognised and enforced'.

5.99 The grounds for a challenge to jurisdiction are often related to the basic elements of arbitration clauses, as discussed in Chapter 2. One of the alleged parties to an arbitration agreement may argue that it is not bound by the agreement, because the arbitration clause was contained in a document to which it had not consented, or it may claim that the legal entity signing the agreement was a different and distinct legal person. Alternatively, it may be argued that the arbitration agreement is not an agreement in writing,[160] or that the whole dispute in issue is outside the scope of the arbitration agreement, or not arbitrable under the applicable law. The respondent may say that the claim is time-barred, or that, for some other reason, the arbitration clause is inoperative or incapable of being performed. Challenges to the jurisdiction of the arbitral tribunal of this type raise questions as to who should decide the challenge—the arbitral tribunal or a national court—and whether a ruling on jurisdiction by the arbitral tribunal may be reviewed by a national court and at what stage.

(c) Autonomy (or separability) of the arbitration clause

5.100 Closely linked to the question of *who* decides a total jurisdiction challenge is another issue—namely, whether the arbitration clause can be regarded (a) as having an independent existence, or (b) as existing only as a part of the contract within which it is contained. The issue is important because, without an independent existence, any party could seek to avoid arbitration by simply alleging the invalidity of the contract in which the arbitration agreement is contained. If the contract (and hence the arbitration clause) is not valid or is non-existent, then the basis for the tribunal to convene to decide whether or not the arbitration clause is valid is not immediately apparent.

5.101 This concern has been addressed by most jurisdictions by means of the adoption of what is known as the 'doctrine of separability'. In other words, an arbitration clause is considered to be a separate and autonomous agreement from the contract in which it is contained. Consequently, its validity does not depend on the validity of the contract as a whole.[161] By surviving termination of the main contract, the clause also constitutes the necessary agreement of the parties that any disputes between them (even concerning the validity or termination of the contract in which it is contained) should be referred to arbitration. In this way, it provides a legal basis for the appointment of an arbitral tribunal.

---

[160] See Chapter 2, paragraph 2.13*ff*.
[161] See, e.g., the UNCITRAL Rules, Art. 23; ICC Rules, Art. 6(9); LCIA Rules, Art. 23; ICDR Rules, Art. 19; Model Law, Art. 16(1); English Arbitration Act 1996, s. 7. This is the reason why most authors refer to the 'law governing the arbitration agreement', rather than to the 'law governing the contract.' An arbitration clause may be valid even if the contract of which it forms a part is found, under the same law, to be invalid.

D. Jurisdiction

5.102 In short, if the tribunal is to decide on its own jurisdiction, it must first assume that jurisdiction. This is what the doctrine of separability allows it to do. It is apparent that the doctrine is, in many ways, a convenient and pragmatic fiction. If the arbitral tribunal decides that the clause is not a valid agreement to arbitrate, then the basis for its authority disappears. In reality, if the clause is not an enforceable agreement to arbitrate, that authority was never there. Nevertheless, because of its obvious practical advantages, this doctrine is widely accepted both by arbitration rules and in national laws.[162] The question of separability was reviewed by the English courts in *Fiona Trust & Holding Corporation and ors v Privalov and ors*. The case concerned charterparties made between, inter alia, the claimants and the defendant charterers. The claimants alleged that the charterparties had been procured by bribery, and that both the charterparties and the arbitration agreements contained within them were rescinded as a result of that bribery. The Court of Appeal, confirming the doctrine of separability of the arbitration agreement from the underlying contract, held that the arbitration agreement would continue to apply unless it was directly impeached for some specific reason.[163] On the facts of the case, there was no special reason indicating that the bribery impeached the arbitration clause in particular. The House of Lords (now the English Supreme Court) upheld the decision of the Court of Appeal, concluding that the principle of separability means that the invalidity or rescission of the main contract does not necessarily entail the invalidity or rescission of the arbitration agreement: the arbitration agreement must be treated as a distinct agreement and can be void or voidable only on grounds that relate directly to the arbitration agreement.[164] The validity, existence, or effectiveness of the arbitration agreement is not dependent upon the effectiveness, existence, or validity of the underlying substantive contract unless the parties have agreed to this.[165] The doctrine of separability requires direct impeachment of the arbitration agreement before it can be set aside. This is an exacting test.[166]

5.103 But a decision that the arbitration clause is legally separate from the main contract does not answer the procedural question: if a challenge to the jurisdiction of the arbitral tribunal is made, by whom is the challenge to be determined? Is it to be determined by the arbitral tribunal itself, by an arbitral institution, by an appointing authority, or by a court of competent jurisdiction?

(i) Who judges?

5.104 It is generally accepted that an arbitral tribunal has power to investigate its own jurisdiction. This is a power inherent in the appointment of an arbitral tribunal.

---

[162] See Chapter 2, paragraphs 2.101*ff*.
[163] [2007] EWCA Civ 20.
[164] [2007] UKHL 40, at [17].
[165] Ibid., at [32].
[166] Ibid., at [35].

Indeed, it is an essential power if the arbitral tribunal is to carry out its task properly. An arbitral tribunal must be able to look at the arbitration agreement, the terms of its appointment, and any relevant evidence in order to decide whether or not a particular claim, or series of claims, comes within its jurisdiction. The arbitral tribunal's decision on the issue may be reviewed subsequently by a competent national court—but it is commonly accepted that this does not prevent the tribunal from making the decision in the first place.

(ii) Competence-competence

5.105 The usual practice under modern international and institutional rules of arbitration is to spell out in express terms the power of an arbitral tribunal to decide upon its own jurisdiction, or (as it is often put) its competence to decide upon its own competence.[167] For example, Article 23(1) of the UNCITRAL Rules provides:

> The arbitral tribunal shall have the power to rule on its own jurisdiction, including any objections with respect to the existence or validity of the arbitration agreement. For that purpose, an arbitration clause that forms part of a contract shall be treated as an agreement independent of the other terms of the contract. A decision by the arbitral tribunal that the contract is null shall not entail automatically the invalidity of the arbitration clause.

5.106 Similarly, under Article 6(9) of the ICC Rules:

> Unless otherwise agreed, the arbitral tribunal shall not cease to have jurisdiction by reason of any claim that the contract is non-existent or null and void, provided that the arbitral tribunal upholds the validity of the arbitration agreement. The arbitral tribunal shall continue to have jurisdiction to determine the parties' respective rights and to decide their claims and pleas even though the contract itself may be non-existent or null and void.

5.107 The ICC process nevertheless provides for the possibility of a provisional check on the prima facie existence of the arbitration agreement by the ICC Court, at the discretion of the secretary-general, who may refer the case to the Court for decision.[168] If the Court is satisfied that such an agreement may exist, 'the arbitration shall proceed' and 'any decision as to the jurisdiction of the arbitral tribunal… shall then be taken by the arbitral tribunal itself'. If the Court is not so satisfied, then the arbitration cannot proceed under the ICC Rules in respect of the parties or claims in question.

---

[167] This is sometimes described in a form of shorthand as 'competence-competence'. It is expressed in German as *Kompetenz/Kompetenz* and in French as *compétence de la compétence*.
[168] ICC Rules, Art. 6(3). The 2012 ICC Rules have made a significant change to the 2008 ICC Rules, which required a two-stage process whereby a decision of the prima facie existence of an arbitration agreement would have to be made by the ICC Court in each case. No guidance is given as to how the secretary-general is expected to exercise the discretion.

D. Jurisdiction

Most modern national laws governing international arbitration also spell out the power of an arbitral tribunal to rule on its own jurisdiction. For example, Article 16 of the Model Law provides that: **5.108**

> The arbitral tribunal may rule on its own jurisdiction, including any objections with respect to the existence or validity of the arbitration agreement. For that purpose, an arbitration clause which forms part of a contract shall be treated as an agreement independent of the other terms of the contract. A decision by the arbitral tribunal that the contract is null and void shall not entail *ipso jure* the invalidity of the arbitration clause.[169]

Support of the principle has not, however, been universal. In India, a series of cases appeared to reject the concept, but a recent decision of the Bombay High Court suggests that the approach is changing.[170]

As identified earlier, there are essentially two elements to the separability rule: first, that an arbitral tribunal can rule upon its own jurisdiction; and secondly, that, for this purpose, the arbitration clause is separate and independent from the terms of the contract containing the transaction between the parties. Most countries, including those that have adopted the Model Law, embrace both propositions.[171] However, the two are interrelated, not identical. To understand the real scope of an arbitrator's power in any given country, it is always important to check whether both propositions appear in its national law. In the English Arbitration Act 1996, for example, the competence of an arbitral tribunal to rule on its own jurisdiction is established in section 30; the separability of the arbitration clause is established in section 7. The relationship between the two provisions was addressed in *Vee Networks Ltd v Econet Wireless International Ltd*.[172] The case held that separability, as provided in section 7, insulates the arbitration agreement from the underlying contract, and that 'competence-competence', as provided in section 30, reflects the doctrine of separability, but leaves intact the requirement that the arbitration agreement should be valid and binding.[173] **5.109**

---

[169] For a discussion of the competence-competence principle in the United States, see, e.g., Graves and Davydan, 'Competence-competence and separability—American style', in Kröll, Mistelis, Perales Viscasillas, and Rogers (eds) *International Arbitration and International Commercial Law: Synergy, Convergence and Evolution* (Kluwer Law International, 2011), pp. 157–178.

[170] Concern about the application of the concept in India was voiced by Ray and Sabharwal, 'Competence-competence: An Indian trilogy' (2007) 22 Mealey's Intl Arb Rep 15, but this position appears to have softened: see, e.g., *Kvaerner Cementation India Ltd v Bajranglal Aggaral* (2012) 5 SCC 214, in which the Bombay High Court found that once an arbitration is initiated, it has no power to rule on the existence or validity of the arbitration clause, and referred the parties to the arbitrator under s. 16 of the Arbitration and Conciliation Act 1996.

[171] See, e.g., the Swiss PIL, Ch. 12, s. 178(3); Brazilian Arbitration Law, s. 8; English Arbitration Act 1996, ss 7 and 30.

[172] [2004] EWHC 2909 (QB), [2004] Arb LR 729.

[173] Ibid., at [20]. For commentary on this decision, see Dundas, 'Separability and jurisdiction: Court assistance to arbitration and a costs horror story—Three recent cases in the English courts' (2005) 71 Arbitration 3.

(iii) Limitations on jurisdiction

5.110 In addition to checking the applicable rules of procedure that set out the power of an arbitral tribunal to decide on its own jurisdiction, parties should examine carefully the law of the arbitral seat to establish to what extent those powers may be limited by the public policy of the seat. Further, whilst the conventions and rules referred to may define 'the jurisdiction of the arbitrators', that jurisdiction itself is derived not from any international source, but from the arbitration agreement—and the arbitration agreement can confer only powers that are permissible under the law applicable to the arbitration agreement and under the *lex arbitri*.

(iv) Award made without jurisdiction

5.111 The nullity of an award in the absence of a valid arbitration agreement is recognised both in national laws and in the international conventions governing arbitration. In the Model Law, for example, one of the limited cases in which it is possible to challenge an award is that in which 'the [arbitration] agreement is not valid under the law to which the parties have subjected to it'.[174] Likewise, under the New York Convention, recognition and enforcement of an award may be refused if the arbitration agreement 'is not valid under the law to which the parties have subjected it or, failing any indication thereon, under the law of the country where the award was made'.[175] This apparent consistency between the applicable tests at the setting aside and enforcement stages has not avoided conflict. For example, in *Dallah v Pakistan*,[176] the Supreme Court of England and Wales and the Paris Cour d'Appel reached opposite conclusions regarding the validity of an ICC award that had been rendered in Paris. The Supreme Court refused to enforce the award, finding that the tribunal incorrectly assumed jurisdiction over the Government of Pakistan because it had not signed the relevant arbitration agreement. But, shortly thereafter, the Paris Cour d'Appel upheld the tribunal's decision that it had jurisdiction, which was based on its determination that the government *was* a party to the arbitration agreement. In so finding, the Paris Cour d'Appel rejected the government's application to annul the award.[177]

(d) Court control

5.112 A decision given by an arbitral tribunal as to its jurisdiction is subject to control by the courts of law, which in this respect have the final word. The relevant procedure, degree of deference, and burden of proof vary from country to country, and sometimes even within countries. In practice, recourse to the courts on issues of jurisdiction is likely to take place at one of three stages: at the beginning of the arbitral

---

[174] Model Law, Art. 34(2)(a)(i).
[175] New York Convention, Art. V(1)(a).
[176] [2010] UKSC 46, [2011] 1 All ER 485.
[177] For commentary on this decision, see, e.g., Grierson and Taok, '*Dallah*: Conflicting judgments from the UK Supreme Court and the Paris Cour d'Appel' (2011) 28 J Intl Arb 407.

D. Jurisdiction

process; during the course of the process; or following the making of the award. These different stages, and the options open both to the arbitral tribunal and to the challenging party, are considered later in this chapter. First, however, it is necessary to review the question of concurrent court control.

(i) Concurrent control

Any challenge to jurisdiction during the course of the arbitral proceedings is usually made to the arbitral tribunal itself. The arbitral tribunal will decide whether (a) to 'bifurcate' the proceedings, asking for separate pleadings and holding a jurisdictional hearing before issuing an interim award on jurisdiction, or (b) join the jurisdictional objection to the merits, which will then be addressed as part of the final award. In many jurisdictions, an interim award on jurisdiction may be challenged immediately in the local courts,[178] which permits a challenge to the arbitral tribunal's jurisdiction *before* any award on the merits has been issued.[179] By this means, a final decision on the issue of jurisdiction may be obtained at an early stage in the arbitral proceedings. One notable exception is the ICSID regime, under which no application to local courts to review a jurisdictional decision is possible and the internal annulment process applies only in respect of final awards, which must 'deal with every question submitted to the tribunal'.[180] The annulment process is consequently open only in respect of negative jurisdictional decisions that finally dispose of the dispute.[181]

5.113

The system under which a national court may review the issue of jurisdiction before the arbitral tribunal has issued a final award on the merits is known as 'concurrent control'. The advantage of this system is that it will save the cost and time of preparing a case on the merits if the court denies arbitral jurisdiction. There are broadly two arguments against concurrent control. First, it is argued that recourse to the courts during the course of arbitral proceedings should not be encouraged, since arbitral proceedings should, as far as possible, be conducted without outside 'interference'. Secondly, and more pragmatically, it is argued that to allow recourse to the courts during the course of an arbitration is likely to encourage delaying tactics on the part of a reluctant respondent. This question was much debated during the preparation of the Model Law—but the solution of concurrent control *was* adopted.[182]

5.114

---

[178] For example, in England, under the Arbitration Act 1996, ss 32 and 67.
[179] For example, English Arbitration Act 1996, s. 32. This particular option for challenging jurisdiction is narrowly drawn, and may be pursued only with the permission of the other party (or parties) and the tribunal. It was intended for cases in which it is clear that a challenge to the courts on jurisdiction would almost inevitably follow an arbitral award on this matter.
[180] ICSID Convention, Art. 48(3).
[181] In two cases in which one of the authors has been involved, the ICSID Secretariat refused attempts to register applications for annulment of positive jurisdictional decisions. Indeed, where the jurisdictional decision is positive, they are called 'decisions on jurisdiction', and where they are negative and the case is effectively dismissed, they are called 'awards on jurisdiction'. Only awards are subject to a possible annulment process.
[182] Model Law, Art. 16. The jurisdictional award must be challenged within thirty days of its notification to the competent courts of the seat.

(ii) Choices open to the arbitral tribunal

5.115 As the practice of international arbitration becomes more sophisticated, challenges to the jurisdiction of arbitral tribunals become more frequent. An arbitral tribunal faced with a challenge to its jurisdiction will need to decide whether to examine the jurisdictional issue separately or to join it to the merits.

5.116 Usually, the arbitral tribunal will require the claimant to plead its full case (including presentation of witness statements and expert reports) and then allow the respondent time in which to indicate whether it wishes to seek to bifurcate the proceedings. If the respondent seeks bifurcation, the claimant will be given a brief opportunity to respond and the tribunal will then rule. If bifurcation is decided, any hearing on the merits is usually suspended and the jurisdictional issue is made subject to a pleading schedule, a hearing, and an interim award. Otherwise, the jurisdictional issue will be joined to the merits and the respondent will raise the objection in its defence. The tribunal's decision will usually depend on whether the objection is a self-contained legal question that can be properly addressed without detailed knowledge of the underlying facts (in which case, bifurcation may well be ordered), or a question that is linked to the merits and facts of the case (in which case, the tribunal is likely to consider it more efficient to address jurisdiction and merits together in a single hearing and award).

5.117 Any award on jurisdiction made by an arbitral tribunal, whether as an interim or final award, is binding on the parties to the arbitration. However, it may be set aside by a competent court, and it may be refused recognition or enforcement. This is the principle adopted in the Model Law with regard to both setting aside and refusal of recognition or enforcement.[183] It is also the principle adopted in the New York Convention with regard to the recognition and enforcement of awards.[184]

(e) Procedural aspects of resolving issues of jurisdiction

5.118 Objections to the jurisdiction of the arbitral tribunal are usually raised by a respondent in the early stages of the arbitration (or by a claimant in relation to any counterclaims).[185] Indeed, most institutional rules require that an objection be raised no later than the statement of defence, or (for counterclaims) in the reply to the counterclaim.[186] This is a sensible and practical provision. It is undesirable that a party who feels that the case is beginning to go against it should be able to raise objections to jurisdiction at a late stage of the proceedings. National laws often

---

[183] Model Law, Art. 16(3). See Chapter 9.
[184] See Chapter 11.
[185] Certain laws require pleas as to the lack of jurisdiction of the tribunal to be raised before the submission of the defence on the merit: see, e.g., Model Law, Art. 16(2). See also the English Arbitration Act 1996, s. 31(1), which requires this plea to be made not later than 'the time [when the objecting party] takes the first step in the proceedings to contest the merits of any matter in relation to which he challenges the tribunal's jurisdiction'.
[186] For example, UNCITRAL Rules, Art. 23(2); LCIA Rules, Art. 23(3).

D. Jurisdiction

support this position. Under section 31(1) of the English Arbitration Act 1996, an objection to jurisdiction cannot be raised later than 'the time [the party raising the objection] takes the first step in the proceedings to contest the merits'.[187] In Venezuela, any objection to jurisdiction has to be raised within five business days of the procedural hearing.[188]

(f) Options open to the respondent

A respondent has four methods of challenging the jurisdiction of an arbitral tribunal established contrary to its assertion that the tribunal has no jurisdiction. It may: **5.119**

- boycott the arbitration;
- raise its objections with the tribunal;
- apply to the national court to resolve the issue; or
- challenge the award, once it has been made.

(i) Boycott the arbitration

The first, and most extreme course of action, is to boycott the arbitration altogether. In this event, the arbitration will proceed on an *ex parte* basis and the respondent will seek to set aside the award, or to resist enforcement on the grounds of lack of jurisdiction, after the final award has been issued. The Libyan government took this course in the oil nationalisation cases[189] after writing to the arbitrator in each case to contend that the arbitral proceedings were invalid. Liberia behaved in the same way in *Letco v Liberia* before an ICSID tribunal.[190] It is ill-advised, since, provided that the party has been properly notified of the constitution of the tribunal and of relevant procedural deadlines and hearings, an award will be enforceable against it notwithstanding its non-participation. Further, a costs award against the recalcitrant party is likely.[191] This situation is increasingly rare, because most parties (both states and private parties) are advised about the adverse consequences of such conduct.   **5.120**

(ii) Raise objections with the arbitral tribunal

The second course of action (which is the most conventional) is to raise objections with the arbitral tribunal itself and to request bifurcation of the jurisdictional question. As noted earlier,[192] the tribunal will order the bifurcation and schedule an   **5.121**

---

[187] For the purposes of this section, the 'first step' does not include any participation in the appointment of an arbitrator. See also the Swiss PIL, s. 186(2).
[188] Venezuelan Law on Commercial Arbitration 1998, s. 25.
[189] See Chapter 1, paragraph 1.183.
[190] See Award dated 31 March 1986, (1986) 2 ICSID Rep 356, at 378.
[191] In *Letco v Liberia*, the tribunal awarded full costs against Liberia on the basis of 'Liberia's procedural bad faith': ibid., at 378.
[192] See paragraph 5.116.

exchange of written briefs on the jurisdictional issue, usually followed by an oral hearing and an interim award. Alternatively, if the issue has a close connection to the merits, or appears to be a dilatory tactic, the tribunal may join the objection to the merits and address it in the final award.

(iii) Apply to a national court

5.122 The third course of action is for the respondent to ignore the arbitral tribunal and to go to court to resolve the issue of jurisdiction. There are various ways in which this may be done. The respondent may, for example, seek an injunction or similar remedy to restrain the arbitral tribunal from proceeding (an 'anti-arbitration injunction'), or the respondent may seek a declaration to the effect that the arbitral tribunal does not have jurisdiction in respect of the particular claim(s) put forward by the claimant, for example on the basis that there was no valid arbitration agreement. Alternatively, the respondent may take the offensive and commence court litigation in respect of the matters in dispute. The claimant in the arbitration would presumably defend such a challenge to the jurisdiction of the arbitral tribunal by seeking to have the arbitration agreement enforced, relying on Article II of the New York Convention, or the relevant provision of domestic law implementing the New York Convention.[193]

5.123 Such challenges to the jurisdiction of an arbitral tribunal are usually addressed to the courts at the seat of arbitration, if these courts have power to intervene concurrently in an international arbitration during the course of the proceedings.[194] The main disadvantage for a respondent who adopts this course is the risk of an adverse court decision upholding arbitral jurisdiction. This will enhance the standing of the arbitration and make it more difficult to challenge the award subsequently, or to resist enforcement of any subsequent award against the respondent on the grounds of lack of jurisdiction.

(iv) Attack the award

5.124 The fourth course of action is for the respondent to participate in the arbitration and to remain passive until after the final award has been issued by the arbitral tribunal. It may then either challenge the award in the courts of the country in which the arbitration took place, or refuse to implement the award and wait for the successful claimant to attempt to enforce it. When an action for enforcement is taken, the losing party might then argue the objections to jurisdiction as a ground for refusal of enforcement. The disadvantage of this tactic is that most systems of

---

[193] Article II requires courts of signatory states to decline jurisdiction and refer the parties to arbitration where an arbitration agreement exists. The relevant national court must simply decide whether the arbitration agreement is null and void, inoperative, or incapable of being performed. If it is not, the parties will be referred to arbitration.

[194] For example, it would be possible in such countries as England and Switzerland, where the policy is that issues of jurisdiction should be finally resolved at the earliest possible stage by means of concurrent court control. Such control is not possible in the United States.

D. Jurisdiction

law will consider a failure to raise an objection to jurisdiction promptly as a waiver of the objection, particularly where the applicable institutional rules require that it be made at a particular phase of the arbitration.[195]

(v) A combined approach

What, then, is the reluctant party to do when requested to take part in an arbitration under an agreement that it considers to be non-existent or invalid? It should take part in the proceedings and raise the matter with the arbitral tribunal itself at the earliest possible stage; it should insist that all objections be fully argued before the arbitral tribunal and contend that the determination of these objections should be the subject of an interim award. If the arbitral tribunal upholds its own jurisdiction, as it frequently does, the respondent should continue to participate in the arbitration, having expressly reserved its position in relation to the issue of jurisdiction, so that this issue may be considered again after the final award is issued, either by way of a challenge to the award in the courts of the place of arbitration, or by resisting attempts to obtain recognition or enforcement of the award.

5.125

(iv) Form of court intervention

Although a national court's role in reviewing a tribunal's award on jurisdiction is well established, the type of intervention that the court is meant to undertake is not so clear. Is the court to have a *de novo* hearing, considering the jurisdictional question afresh, or is it merely to review the tribunal's decision, applying a presumption that this decision is correct? In other words, what degree of deference should it show to the original decision? The United States has adopted a distinction depending on the nature of the jurisdictional decision. If jurisdiction is denied by the arbitral tribunal based upon a failure to comply with a procedural precondition (what the US courts call 'procedural arbitrability' and other jurisdictions would call 'admissibility'), the US Supreme Court has held that the arbitrators must be given deference. They can answer the question 'when' there is a duty to arbitrate. If, on the other hand, jurisdiction has been denied based on an alleged absence of an arbitration agreement, failure of the dispute to fall within the scope of the arbitration agreement, or lack of arbitrability of the dispute given its nature (what the US courts call 'substantive arbitrability'), then the court may exercise a *de novo* review.[196] The court therefore will have the ultimate right to answer the question of 'whether' there is a duty to arbitrate.

5.126

---

[195] This would be the position under Model Law, Art. 4. If a party has appeared and participated in the arbitration without raising any objections to the jurisdiction of the tribunal, it may be deemed to have impliedly submitted to the arbitration and any challenge to jurisdiction thereafter might be viewed as a mere device. It is significant, though, that Art. 4 refers to provisions from which the parties 'may derogate', and thus a party is not capable of waiving a mandatory provision of the applicable law.
[196] *Howsam v Dean Witter Reynolds, Inc.* 537 US 79, 84 (2002).

5.127 This issue was reviewed in *BG v Argentina*,[197] in which an arbitration under the United Kingdom–Argentina bilateral investment treaty (BIT) had taken place under the UNCITRAL Rules with Washington, DC, as the seat of the arbitration. Following BG's victory in the arbitration, Argentina challenged the award before the District Court, alleging that the arbitrators had no jurisdiction because the claimant had not complied with the BIT's requirement of first submitting the dispute to the courts of Argentina for eighteen months (a requirement that did not require any decision from the courts and under which, even if a decision were issued, the right to arbitrate remained).[198] The arbitral tribunal had analysed and rejected this argument, based on the futility of the requirement in light of restrictions on accessing the Argentine courts and certain provisions of the 1969 Vienna Convention on the Law of Treaties. The District Court rejected the challenge to the award. However, the District of Columbia Court of Appeals upheld it, by reviewing the treaty directly and deciding that the Court need not show deference to the arbitrators' views, but could review the question *de novo*. BG successfully appealed to the US Supreme Court, which confirmed that the eighteen-month requirement was simply a procedural precondition or threshold provision, since the dispute could be definitively resolved only by arbitration. As a consequence, it was no different from any other procedural precondition, since it did not affect 'whether' the dispute could be arbitrated, but only 'when' it could be arbitrated. In accordance with existing case law on procedural preconditions, arbitrators should be given deference and a *de novo* analysis of the question was not permissible.

(g) International agreements on the jurisdiction of national courts

5.128 Whilst any challenge to an arbitral award should be brought before the courts of the seat of the arbitration, the proper judicial forum for other applications may be less clear, particularly where jurisdictional treaties apply. Within the European Union, for example, a measure of uniformity as to which state courts may accept jurisdiction is established by the 2001 Brussels Regulation.[199] Article 1(2)(d) of the Regulation specifically excludes arbitrations from the application of the Regulation. Article 2 establishes a basic rule (subject to limited exceptions) that persons shall be sued in the courts of the state in which they are domiciled. A potential conflict consequently arises when a legal action is brought in one of the member states, but there is a claim that the dispute is covered by an arbitration clause providing for arbitration in a different member state. The party seeking to avoid arbitration may claim that there was no binding arbitration agreement, and that therefore the

---

[197] *BG Group PLC v Republic of Argentina*, No. 12-138, 572 US (5 March 2014).
[198] The obligation did not require any decision to be made, nor did it prevent any party from subsequently submitting the dispute to arbitration after eighteen months or a decision with which it was not satisfied.
[199] Council Regulation (EC) No. 44/2001 of 22 December 2000 on jurisdiction and the recognition and enforcement of judgments in civil and commercial matters, OJ L 12/1, 16 January 2001.

D. Jurisdiction

court of the defendant's domicile has jurisdiction and not the courts at the seat of the arbitration. The other party may reply that a question as to the validity of an arbitration agreement is itself excluded from the application of the Regulation, under Article 1(2), as being connected with an arbitration.

5.129 This precise situation occurred in the *Marc Rich* case,[200] in which an English court was asked to rule on the validity of an arbitration agreement as part of the process of considering an application for support of the arbitral process (in the appointment of an arbitrator), while simultaneously an Italian court (which would have had jurisdiction under the Regulation were it not for the arbitration agreement) was asked to act as if no valid arbitration agreement existed. The European Court of Justice (ECJ) held that the arbitration exclusion of the (then) Brussels Convention (now Article 1(2)(d) of the Brussels Regulation) extended to litigation before a national court in respect of the arbitrator. As a consequence, it was admissible for the English courts to intervene in the appointment of an arbitrator, notwithstanding the domicile of the defendant in Italy. This appears to be sound. The exclusion exception of Article 1(2)(d) would be deprived of any real meaning if the Regulation were to apply to applications in support of arbitration.

5.130 Another area of tension between the EU jurisdiction regime and the arbitration exception was exposed in *Van Uden Maritime v Deco-Line*.[201] The claimant was a Dutch corporation, which had started an arbitration against a German respondent in the Netherlands for monies due under a charterparty. The claimant also sought an interim payment from the national courts in the Netherlands pursuant to the Netherlands Arbitration Act 1986. The Hoge Raad of the Netherlands referred the question to the ECJ as to whether it had jurisdiction to make a provisional order pending determination of a dispute by an arbitral tribunal on the basis of Article 24 of the Brussels Convention (now Article 31 of the Brussels Regulation), which states:

> Application may be made to the courts of a Contracting State for such provisional, including protective, measures as may be available under the law of that State, even if, under this Convention, the courts of another Contracting State have jurisdiction as to the substance of the matter.

5.131 The respondent argued that there was no such jurisdiction, since the arbitration exception applied. The ECJ disagreed, holding that:

> [P]rovisional measures are not in principle ancillary to arbitration proceedings but are ordered in parallel to such proceedings and are intended as measures of support. They concern not arbitration as such *but the protection of a wide variety of rights*.[202]

---

[200] *Marc Rich Co. AG v Societa Italiana Impianti PA (The Atlantic Emperor)* [1989] 1 Lloyd's Rep 548 (CA); appealed to the ECJ and heard on 17 October 1990, [1992] 1 Lloyd's Rep 342 (ECJ). See also the discussion in Hascher, 'Arbitration under the Brussels Convention' (1997) 13 Arb Intl 33.
[201] Case C-391/95 *Van Uden Maritime BV v Kommanditgesellschaft in Firma Deco Line and anor* [1999] 2 WLR 1181.
[202] Ibid., at [33] (emphasis added).

The net result is that such applications benefit from the protection of the Brussels Regulation such that there can be no concurrent proceedings (Articles 21–23). Further, an application for interim measures from an EU national court in support of an arbitration can be enforced under the Regulation in any other court in the European Union. This is a strong incentive to seek such measures therein, since interim measures from a national court may not be enforced automatically elsewhere pursuant to the New York Convention.

5.132 The same area of conflict was addressed in the case of *Allianz SpA and anr v West Tankers Inc*. West Tankers Inc. had chartered a vessel to Erg SpA pursuant to a charterparty that provided for disputes to be resolved by arbitration in England. The vessel had collided with a jetty in an Italian port. Erg claimed compensation from its insurer up to the limit of its insurance cover and commenced arbitration proceedings in London against West Tankers for the excess. West Tankers denied liability for the damage caused by the collision. Having paid Erg compensation under the insurance policies for the loss that it had suffered, the insurer brought proceedings against West Tankers before the Italian courts in order to recover the sums that it had paid to Erg, based on its statutory right of subrogation. West Tankers raised an objection of lack of jurisdiction on the basis of the existence of the arbitration agreement.

5.133 In parallel, West Tankers brought proceedings before the English courts, seeking a declaration that the dispute with the insurer was to be settled by arbitration pursuant to the arbitration agreement and an 'anti-suit' injunction restraining the insurer from pursuing the proceedings commenced before the Italian courts. The English High Court upheld West Tankers' claims and granted the anti-suit injunction sought against the insurer.[203] The latter appealed against that judgment to the House of Lords, arguing that the grant of such an injunction was contrary to the Brussels Regulation, since it had a right to bring a claim in the Italian courts, and if the Italian courts took jurisdiction, that should be the end of the matter.

5.134 The House of Lords (now the UK Supreme Court) first referred to judgments in which it was held that an anti-suit injunction restraining a party from commencing or continuing proceedings in a court of another member state cannot be compatible with the system established by the Brussels Regulation, even where it is granted by the court having jurisdiction under that regulation.[204] That is because the Regulation provides a complete set of uniform rules on the allocation of jurisdiction between the courts of the member states, which must trust each other to apply those rules correctly. However, that principle could not, in the view of the House of Lords, be extended to arbitration, which was excluded from the scope of the Regulation by virtue of Article 1(2)(d). Since there was no set of uniform rules

---

[203] *West Tankers Inc. v Allianz SpA and anor* [2005] EWHC 454 (Comm).
[204] *West Tankers Inc. v Allianz SpA and anor* [2007] UKHL 4.

D. Jurisdiction

in relation to arbitration, it was clear from the *Marc Rich* case that the exclusion in Article 1(2)(d) applies both to arbitration proceedings and legal proceedings in relation to arbitration. As a consequence, the House of Lords concluded that an anti-suit injunction addressed to the Italian court would not infringe the regulation. However, it stayed its proceedings, pending a preliminary ruling to address the question: 'Is it consistent with Regulation No. 44/2001 for a court of a Member State to make an order to restrain a person from commencing or continuing proceedings in another Member State on the ground that such proceedings are in breach of an arbitration agreement?'

The ECJ concluded that, although the subject matter of the proceedings was arbitration (and thus outside of the scope of the Regulation), an anti-suit injunction against a court of another member state that considered it had validly taken jurisdiction under the Regulation would have consequences that could undermine its effectiveness.[205] This was particularly so where proceedings were seeking to prevent the exercise by the courts of a member state of their jurisdictional privileges under the Regulation. In these circumstances, it was exclusively a matter for the courts first seised of the dispute (in this case, the Italian courts) to determine the validity of an arbitration agreement relied upon by a respondent in order to contest its jurisdiction. Otherwise, it would amount to stripping that court of the power to determine its own jurisdiction under the Brussels Regulation. Such anti-suit injunctions were consequently held to be incompatible with the Regulation. The ECJ noted too that this solution was consistent with Article II(3) of the New York Convention, which vests the courts of a state seised of a matter in respect of which an arbitration agreement exists with the power to refer the matter to arbitration. **5.135**

The European Court's decision in the *West Tankers* case has been widely criticised by commentators for not taking into account the fundamental principles of arbitration law and the reality of arbitral practice—namely, that parties select specific jurisdictions as seats for their arbitrations because of their arbitration-friendly judicial systems.[206] It is argued that parties expect the national courts at the seat of the arbitration to enforce agreements to arbitrate and to protect their supervisory jurisdiction. Nevertheless, some commentators have suggested that courts at the seat of the arbitration may continue to enforce arbitration agreements by alternative means, such as declaring the validity of the arbitration agreement, ordering its specific performance, or awarding damages for the breach of agreements to arbitrate.[207] **5.136**

---

[205] Case C-185/07 *Allianz SpA and anor v West Tankers Inc.* [2009] ECR I-663.
[206] See, e.g., Merkin, 'Anti-suit injunctions: The future of anti-suit injunctions in Europe' (2009) 9 Arb LM 1; Clifford and Browne, 'Lost at sea or a storm in a teacup? Anti-suit injunctions after *Allianz SPA (formerly Riunione Adriatica di Sucurta SPA) v West Tankers Inc*' (2009) 12 Intl Arb L Rev 19; Noussia, 'Antisuit injunctions and arbitration proceedings: What does the future hold?' (2009) 26 J Intl Arb 311.
[207] See Byford and Sarwar, 'Arbitration clauses after *West Tankers*: The unanswerable conundrum? Practical solutions for enforcing arbitration clauses' (2009) 12 Intl Arb L Rev 29; Merkin,

5.137 Recently, the scope of the Brussels Regulation was clarified by the superseding Regulation 1215/2012 (the Recast Regulation),[208] which came into force on 10 January 2015.[209] Article 1(2)(d) of the Recast Regulation continues to exclude arbitrations from its application, but provides guidance to courts seised of arbitration matters. Recital 12 states that when a member state court is seised of an action that is subject to an arbitration agreement, the Recast Regulation does not prevent the court from (a) referring those parties to arbitration, (b) staying or dismissing the proceedings, or (c) examining the validity of the arbitration agreement. Recital 12 also excludes rulings from member state courts on the validity of arbitration agreements from the recognition and enforcement regime of the Recast Regulation, regardless of whether the court decided the matter as a principal or incidental issue. However, if a member state court has determined that an arbitration agreement is invalid, then that court's judgment on the substance of the dispute may be recognised or enforced under the Regulation. Recital 12 states that this is without prejudice to member state courts' competence to recognise and enforce arbitral awards in accordance with the New York Convention, 'which takes precedence over' the Recast Regulation.[210] Finally, Recital 12 provides that the Regulation is not applicable to any action or ancillary proceedings relating to the establishment of an arbitral tribunal, the powers of the arbitrators, or the conduct or any other aspect of arbitral procedure, nor to any action or judgment regarding the annulment, review, appeal, recognition, or enforcement of an arbitral award.

'Anti-suit injunctions: The future of anti-suit injunctions in Europe' (2009) 9 Arb LM 1; Michaelson and Blanke, 'Anti-suit injunctions and the recoverability of legal costs as damages for breach of an arbitration agreement' (2008) 74 Arbitration 12; Veeder, 'The Brussels Regulation, the Lugano Convention, the Arbitration Exception and the New Schlosser Report', Paper presented at the ICC UK Annual Arbitration Conference, London, 6 November 2008.

[208] Regulation (EU) No. 1215/2012 of the European Parliament and of the Council of 12 December 2012 on jurisdiction and the recognition and enforcement of judgments in civil and commercial matters (recast), OJ L 351/1, 20 December 2012.

[209] Articles 75 and 76 of Regulation 1215/2012 came into force on 10 January 2014.

[210] Article 73(2) of Regulation 1215/2012 also provides that '[t]his Regulation shall not affect the application of the 1958 New York Convention'.

6

CONDUCT OF THE PROCEEDINGS

A. Overview	6.01	E. Collecting Evidence	6.75
B. Expedited Procedures	6.26	F. Hearings	6.155
C. Preliminary Steps	6.41	G. Proceedings after the Hearing	6.200
D. Written Submissions	6.65		

A. Overview

(a) Introduction

6.01 An international arbitration may be conducted in many different ways; there are few fixed rules. Institutional and ad hoc rules of arbitration often provide an outline of the various steps to be taken, but detailed regulation of the procedure to be followed is established either by agreement of the parties, or by directions from the arbitral tribunal, or a combination of the two. The flexibility that this confers on the arbitral process is one of the reasons why parties choose international arbitration over other forms of dispute resolution in international trade. The only certainty is that the parties' counsel should not bring with them the rulebooks from their home courts: the rules of civil procedure that govern proceedings in national courts have no place in arbitrations unless the parties expressly agree to adopt them.

6.02 In general, an arbitral tribunal must conduct the arbitration in accordance with the procedure agreed by the parties. If it fails to do so, the award may be set aside, or refused recognition and enforcement.[1] However, the freedom of the parties to dictate the procedure to be followed in an international arbitration is not unrestricted. The procedure that they establish must comply with any mandatory rules[2]

---

[1] An award may be set aside under the Model Law if 'the arbitral procedure was not in accordance with the agreement of the parties', and this is also a ground for refusal of recognition or enforcement: Arts 34(2)(a)(iv) and 36(1)(a)(iv). See also New York Convention, Art. V(1)(d).
[2] See the above provisions of the Model Law and the New York Convention, and see Chapter 2.

and public policy requirements of the law of the juridical seat of the arbitration.[3] It must also take into account the provisions of the international conventions on arbitration, which aim to ensure that arbitral proceedings are conducted fairly.[4] Accordingly, a balance must be struck between the parties' wishes concerning the procedure to be followed and any overriding requirements of the legal regime that governs the arbitration.

6.03 In some respects, an international arbitration is like a ship. An arbitration may be said to be 'owned' by the parties, just as a ship is owned by shipowners. But the ship is under the day-to-day command of the captain, to whom the owners hand control. The owners may dismiss the captain if they wish and hire a replacement, but there will always be someone on board who is in command[5]—and, behind the captain, there will always be someone with ultimate control.

6.04 At the beginning of an international arbitration, the parties are firmly in control of the process. In ad hoc arbitration, in which there is no institution involved, they may—and sometimes do—write a complete set of procedural rules to govern the way in which the proceedings are to be handled. When they subsequently appoint an arbitral tribunal, by whatever method they have agreed, that tribunal is constrained by that agreed procedural framework. In institutional arbitration, the procedural framework is provided by the institution's rules, to which the parties agreed when they signed the arbitration agreement and which they put into effect when they referred the resolution of disputes between them to the rules of the institution concerned.

6.05 When the arbitral tribunal is established, day-to-day control of the proceedings begins to pass to the tribunal. However, the transfer of control is not total and is not immediate. The tribunal usually engages in a dialogue with the parties on procedural matters, and often a first 'procedural order' is issued to design the essential elements of the process and the time limits within which each stage is to take place.

6.06 Many tribunals make considerable efforts, often adopting compromises in the process, to enable 'Procedural Order No. 1' to carry the subheading 'By Consent'. However, whether or not the procedural order is made by consent, once it is made the procedure will acquire a desirable degree of predictability and authenticity. The tribunal will be more firmly in control, to ensure that the procedural steps are completed on time, and will have a firm basis for determining the almost inevitable procedural issues that will arise between the parties as the arbitration moves forward.[6] By the time of the witness hearings, the tribunal is fully in command

---

[3] For a discussion of the seat of the arbitration, see Chapter 3, paragraph 3.53*ff*.

[4] See Chapter 1 for an introduction to the arbitral process.

[5] See Veeder, 'Whose arbitration is it anyway: The parties' or the arbitration tribunal's? An interesting question', in Hill and Newman (eds) *The Leading Arbitrators' Guide to International Arbitration* (2nd edn, Juris, 2008), p. 337, at pp. 340–341.

[6] Rowley and Wisner, 'Party autonomy and its discontents: The limits imposed by arbitrators and mandatory laws' (2011) 5 World Arb & Med Rev 321, at 321, conceive of this as an expression

A. Overview

(in the sense of being 'captain of the ship'); in any event, by that stage the parties usually find it easier to ask the tribunal for directions on disputed procedural issues than to attempt to reach agreement between themselves.

(b) Party autonomy

Party autonomy is the guiding principle in determining the procedure to be followed in an international arbitration. It is a principle that is endorsed not only in national laws, but also by international arbitral institutions worldwide, as well as by international instruments such as the New York Convention and the Model Law. The legislative history of the Model Law shows that the principle was adopted without opposition,[7] and Article 19(1) of the Model Law itself provides that: 'Subject to the provisions of this Law, the parties are free to agree on the procedure to be followed by the arbitral tribunal in conducting the proceedings.' This principle follows Article 2 of the 1923 Geneva Protocol, which provides that '[t]he arbitral procedure, including the constitution of the arbitral tribunal, shall be governed by the will of the parties...', and Article V(1)(d) of the New York Convention, under which recognition and enforcement of a foreign arbitral award may be refused if 'the arbitral procedure was not in accordance with the agreement of the parties'.

6.07

Article 19 of the Arbitration Rules of the International Chamber of Commerce (ICC)—historically, a champion of the principle of autonomy of the parties—provides:

6.08

> The proceedings before the arbitral tribunal shall be governed by the Rules and, where the Rules are silent, by any rules which the parties or, failing them, the arbitral tribunal may settle on, whether or not reference is thereby made to the rules of procedure of a national law to be applied to the arbitration.

Adopting a similar approach, Article 14(2) of the Rules of the London Court of International Arbitration (LCIA) states that: 'The parties may agree on joint proposals for the conduct of their arbitration for consideration by the Arbitral Tribunal. They are encouraged to do so in consultation with the Arbitral Tribunal...' In the field of investor–state arbitrations, the International Centre for the Settlement of Investment Disputes (ICSID) adopts a similar approach, its Arbitration Rule 20(1) requiring that, '[a]s early as possible after the constitution of a Tribunal, its

---

of party autonomy in which the arbitrator 'giv[es] effect to the parties' choices in running the arbitration'. Pryles, 'Limits to party autonomy in arbitral procedure' (2007) 24 J Intl Arb 327 explains the procedural autonomy of the tribunal as a product of a tripartite contract between parties and tribunal, mandatory law, and institutional rules.

[7] See, e.g., United Nations Commission on International Trade Law (UNCITRAL), *Report of the Secretary-General: Possible Features of a Model Law on International Commercial Arbitration*, UN Doc. A/CN.9/207 (UN, 1981), para. 17: 'Probably the most important principle on which the Model Law should be based is the freedom of the parties in order to facilitate the proper functioning of international commercial arbitration according to their expectations.'

President shall endeavor to ascertain the views of the parties regarding questions of procedure'.

(c) Limitations on party autonomy

6.09 In the exercise of their autonomous authority, the parties may confer upon the arbitral tribunal such powers and duties as they consider appropriate to the specific case. They may choose formal or informal methods of conducting the arbitration, adversarial or inquisitorial procedures, documentary or oral methods of presenting evidence, and so forth. The exercise of this autonomy is, however, limited by certain requirements that may be categorised under the following headings.

(i) Equal treatment

6.10 If party autonomy is the first principle to be applied in relation to procedure in international arbitration, equality of treatment is the second—and it is of equal importance. This principle is given express recognition both in the New York Convention[8] and in the Model Law, Article 18 of which states: 'The parties shall be treated with equality and each party shall be given a full opportunity of presenting his case.'

6.11 The concept of treating the parties with equality is fundamental in all civilised systems of civil justice. The provision in the Arbitration Rules of the United Nations Commission on International Trade Law (UNCITRAL) to the effect that the arbitral tribunal may conduct the arbitration in such manner as it considers appropriate[9] is qualified by the proviso that it must treat the parties with equality. The same concept underlies other sets of arbitration rules.[10]

6.12 The requirement that the parties must be treated with equality thus operates as a limitation on party autonomy. For instance, a provision in a submission agreement that only one party should be heard by the arbitral tribunal might well be treated as invalid (for example by an enforcement court) even if both parties originally agreed to it. The UNCITRAL Secretariat recognised the dilemma in the report that led to the Model Law:

> [I]t will be one of the more delicate and complex problems of the preparation of a model law to strike a balance between the interest of the parties to freely determine

---

[8] New York Convention, Art. V(1)(b): 'Recognition and enforcement of the award may be refused...if...[t]he party against whom the award is invoked was...unable to present his case...'
[9] UNCITRAL Rules, Art. 17(1).
[10] See, e.g., World Intellectual Property Organization (WIPO) Arbitration Rules, Art. 38(b); International Centre for Dispute Resolution (ICDR) Rules, Art. 16(1); American Arbitration Association (AAA) Commercial Arbitration Rules, Art. 32(a). See also the Swiss Rules, Art. 15(1), and the Rules of the Hong Kong International Arbitration Centre (HKIAC), Art. 13(1), which both refer to 'equal treatment'. The corresponding provisions of the ICC Rules, Art. 22(4), the LCIA Rules, Art. 14(4)(i), and the Dubai International Arbitration Centre (DIAC) Rules, Art. 17(2) do not expressly mention 'equality', but the phrase 'fairly and impartially' must encompass it.

A. Overview

the procedure to be followed and the interests of the legal system expected to give recognition and effect thereto.[11]

(ii) Public policy

The parties must not purport to confer powers upon an arbitral tribunal that would cause the arbitration to be conducted in a manner contrary to the mandatory rules or public policy of the state in which the arbitration is held. One important mandatory rule that has already been considered requires that each party should be given a fair hearing or, as the Model Law expresses it, 'a full opportunity of presenting his case'. **6.13**

At first sight, the word 'full' can be misleading: it conjures visions of a party having an entitlement to present as much argument and evidence as it sees fit. But, in this context, the word 'full' must be given a sensible meaning, and in practice it seems unlikely that a national court would set aside an award where the tribunal took a clearly reasonable and proportionate approach to limiting the scope of the evidence that a party wished to present. Confirming this, most sets of modern arbitration rules now expressly provide that a party need be given only a *'reasonable* opportunity to present its case', which should encourage arbitral tribunals to balance opportunity with efficiency in determining appropriate arbitral procedures.[12] **6.14**

Any agreement between the parties purporting to confer power on the arbitral tribunal to perform an act that would be contrary to a mandatory rule (or to the public policy) of the country in which the arbitration is taking place would be unenforceable in that country, at least to the extent of the offending provision. So would any provision that purports to give the arbitral tribunal power to perform an act that is not capable of being performed by arbitrators under the law applicable to the arbitration agreement, or under the law of the seat of arbitration.[13] **6.15**

(iii) Arbitration rules

Limitations may also be introduced by the operation of the arbitration rules chosen by the parties. Such rules usually contain few mandatory provisions in relation to the conduct of the proceedings. For example, the UNCITRAL Rules specify only the following: **6.16**

- under Article 17(1), the parties must be treated with equality and, at an appropriate stage of the proceedings, each party must be given a reasonable opportunity of presenting its case;

---

[11] UNCITRAL, n. 7, para. 21.
[12] See, e.g., UNCITRAL Rules, Art. 17(1); ICC Rules, Art. 22(4); LCIA Rules, Art. 14(4)(i); Rules of the Stockholm Chamber of Commerce (SCC), Art. 19(2); China International Economic and Trade Arbitration Commission (CIETAC) Rules, Art. 33(1); HKIAC Rules, Art. 13(1). Compare DIAC Rules, Art. 17(2); Vienna International Arbitration Centre (VIAC) Rules, Art. 28(1); Swiss Rules, Art. 15(1).
[13] For example, the administration of oaths by arbitrators in a country in which the law allows oaths to be administered only by judicial officers.

- under Article 17(3), the tribunal must hold a hearing if either party requests one at an appropriate stage of the proceedings;
- under Articles 20 and 21, there must be one consecutive exchange of written submissions (a 'statement of claim' and a 'statement of defence'); and
- under Article 29(5), if the tribunal appoints an expert, it may give the parties the opportunity to question that expert at a hearing and the parties must be given an opportunity to present their own expert witnesses on the points at issue.

(iv) Third parties

6.17 The parties may not validly agree to confer powers on an arbitral tribunal that directly affect persons who are not parties to the arbitration agreement, unless a special provision of the applicable law enables them to do so. This is rare.[14] This principle applies to matters of substance, as well as procedure. For example, an arbitral tribunal cannot direct a person who is not a party to the arbitration agreement to pay a sum of money or to perform a particular act.

6.18 Concerning procedural matters, an arbitral tribunal may direct the parties to produce documents, to attend hearings, or to submit to examination—but it usually has no power to compel third parties to do so, even if the parties to the arbitration have purported to confer such a power on the tribunal. The participation of third parties in arbitration proceedings, whether by giving evidence or producing documents, may usually be compelled only by invoking the assistance of a national court of competent jurisdiction.[15]

(d) International practice

6.19 There is no universally recognised comprehensive set of detailed procedural rules governing international arbitrations. As described in Chapter 1, each arbitral tribunal is different, each dispute is different, and each case deserves to be treated differently. But there are basic underlying structures, built on three elements: first, the international conventions (and the Model Law), to which reference has been made; secondly, the various established sets of international arbitration rules; and thirdly, the practice of experienced arbitrators and counsel.

6.20 The international conventions and the Model Law do not prescribe the way in which an international arbitration should be conducted, but merely establish

---

[14] For example, in the United States, the Federal Arbitration Act of 1925 (FAA), § 7, allows an arbitrator to issue a summons to order the attendance of a third party as a witness at the arbitral proceedings; but court assistance is necessary to enforce the summons if the third party refuses to obey it.

[15] This is considered in more detail in Chapter 7, paragraphs 7.13*ff*.

A. Overview

general principles intended to ensure a fair procedure and an award that is enforceable both nationally and internationally.

Even the established sets of international rules—such as those of the ICC, the International Centre for Dispute Resolution (ICDR), and the LCIA and, for ad hoc arbitrations, those of UNCITRAL—do not describe in any detail the way in which an international arbitration should be conducted. This means that, in practice, it is for the arbitral tribunal and the parties to work together to establish procedures suitable to the circumstances of the particular case. Indeed, as many sets of arbitration rules now expressly provide, the tribunal and the parties have a positive duty to design the procedure so that it provides a fair, expeditious, and cost-effective means for the resolution of the matters in dispute.[16] In doing so, the arbitral tribunal and the parties should consider, and find answers to, a series of practical questions, such as the following.

6.21

- Is a confidentiality agreement required?
- Is this a case in which it would be helpful for the tribunal to determine preliminary issues, and if so, what type of issue(s)?
- If, as is usual, there are to be written submissions, should they be exchanged sequentially or simultaneously?
- How is the production of documentary evidence to be handled?
- How is the evidence of witnesses to be presented? Are there to be written witness statements and reply statements, and if so, are there are any special considerations to take into account, other than the timing of such statements?
- Is an oral hearing necessary, and if so, how long does it need to be in light of the parties' written submissions and evidence?
- Should there be a pre-hearing conference (if one is not prescribed by the rules adopted by the parties), and if so, at what stage of the proceedings?
- How much time should be reserved for the witness hearing, and when is it likely to be possible to fix dates and make the necessary bookings of hearing rooms, breakout rooms, court reporters, and so forth?

These are all important practical questions that are discussed in this chapter. First, however, it is useful to consider the way in which the procedural 'shape' of an international arbitration differs from that of civil dispute resolution in national courts.

(e) Procedural structure of a typical international arbitration

Two elements in particular distinguish the procedural shape of an international arbitration from civil dispute resolution procedures in national courts. The first is that, unlike judges, it would be unusual for all of the arbitrators to be resident at

6.22

---

[16] See, e.g., ICC Rules, Art. 22; UNCITRAL Rules, Art. 17(1); LCIA Rules, Art. 14(4) and (5); Swiss Rules, Art. 15(1) and (7); SCC Rules, Art. 19(2); ICDR Rules, Art. 16(1) and (2); SIAC Rules, Art. 16(1); HKIAC Rules, Art. 13(1).

Conduct of the Proceedings

```
┌─────────────────────────────────────────────────────────┐
│                Initial written submissions              │
│  (Request for arbitration/notice of arbitration, answer/│
│                    response and reply)                  │
└─────────────────────────────────────────────────────────┘
                            ↓
┌─────────────────────────────────────────────────────────┐
│                 Constituting the tribunal               │
└─────────────────────────────────────────────────────────┘
                            ↓
┌─────────────────────────────────────────────────────────┐
│          Preliminary meeting/case management conference │
│      (If prescribed by the relevant rules or otherwise  │
│       agreed or requested by the arbitral tribunal)     │
└─────────────────────────────────────────────────────────┘
                            ↓
┌─────────────────────────────────────────────────────────┐
│                   First procedural order                │
└─────────────────────────────────────────────────────────┘
                            ↓
┌─────────────────────────────────────────────────────────┐
│              Exchange of written submissions            │
│  (Sequential or simultaneous? One round or two rounds?  │
│  Accompanied by documents, written statements, and      │
│  expert reports, or do those follow in subsequent       │
│  rounds?)                                               │
└─────────────────────────────────────────────────────────┘
                            ↓
┌─────────────────────────────────────────────────────────┐
│                  Case review conference                 │
└─────────────────────────────────────────────────────────┘
                            ↓
┌─────────────────────────────────────────────────────────┐
│        Request for production of additional documents   │
│  (Typically, after the first round of written           │
│   submissions and before a second round)                │
└─────────────────────────────────────────────────────────┘
                            ↓
┌─────────────────────────────────────────────────────────┐
│                  Pre-hearing conference                 │
└─────────────────────────────────────────────────────────┘
                            ↓
┌─────────────────────────────────────────────────────────┐
│                     Witness hearing                     │
└─────────────────────────────────────────────────────────┘
                            ↓
┌─────────────────────────────────────────────────────────┐
│                   Post-hearing briefs                   │
│     (Sequential or simultaneous? One round or two?)     │
└─────────────────────────────────────────────────────────┘
                            ↓
┌─────────────────────────────────────────────────────────┐
│       Closure of the proceedings by the arbitral tribunal│
└─────────────────────────────────────────────────────────┘
                            ↓
┌─────────────────────────────────────────────────────────┐
│                          Award                          │
└─────────────────────────────────────────────────────────┘
                            ↓
┌─────────────────────────────────────────────────────────┐
│                Proceedings after the award              │
│     (Correction, interpretation, or additional awards)  │
└─────────────────────────────────────────────────────────┘
```

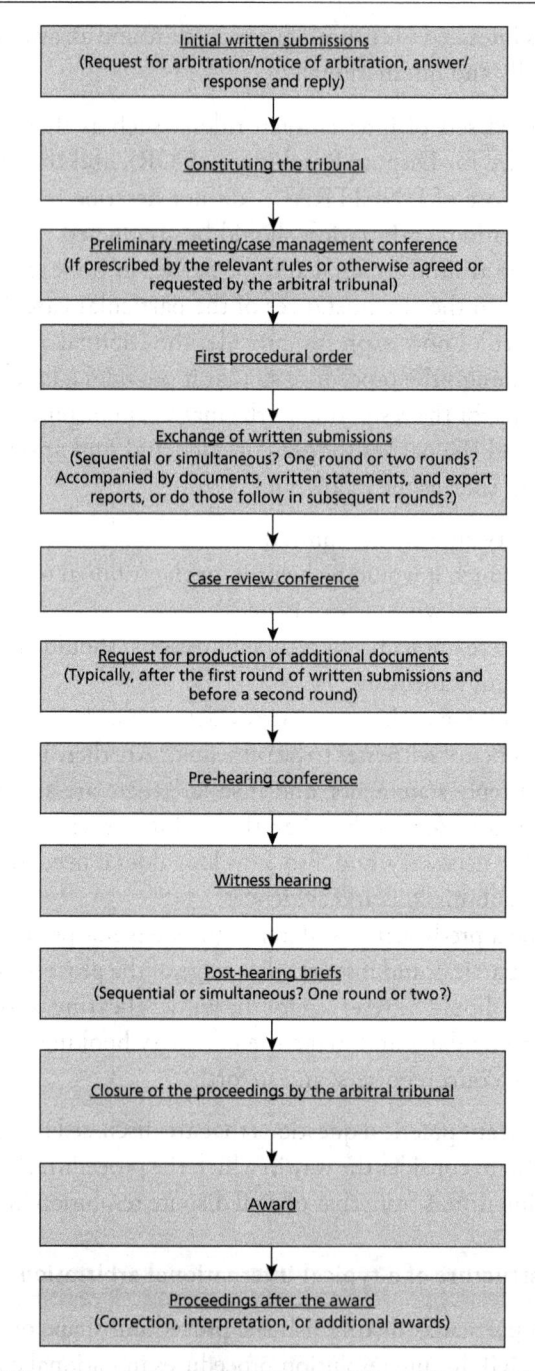

Figure 6.1 Initial written submissions (request for arbitration/notice of arbitration,[a] answer/response, and reply)

[a] 'A request' (in the United States, sometimes described as a 'demand for arbitration') is delivered to the institution in an institutional arbitration; a 'notice' is delivered to the opposing party in ad hoc arbitrations, e.g. under the UNCITRAL Rules.

B. Expedited Procedures

the seat of the arbitration. This means that it is difficult to convene a hearing, or procedural meeting, at short notice and at relatively low cost.

6.23 The second element is that time spent at hearings is 'premium time' in terms of cost to the parties. Not only is each day for which the tribunal is in session extraordinarily costly, but the longer the arbitrators and the parties' counsel are expected to spend together, the more difficult it will be to find a date (or dates) on which all concerned can be assembled.

6.24 The result is that, in formulating a first procedural order,[17] arbitral tribunals routinely try to ensure that the procedure is able to keep to a minimum in-person meetings prior to the witness hearing. While there are many different variations—and emphasising that a 'standard form' procedure should never replace the design process that is the essence of arbitration procedure—a typical modern international arbitration will usually proceed along a path such as that illustrated in Figure 6.1.

6.25 This chapter is concerned with the stages that take place after the arbitral tribunal has been established until the proceedings are closed by the arbitral tribunal following delivery of the parties' last submissions. Starting the arbitration and establishing the arbitral tribunal have been covered earlier in this volume;[18] the award, and proceedings after the award, are covered later.[19]

B. Expedited Procedures

(a) Introduction

6.26 Before turning to the various procedural steps that are normally followed in an international arbitration, brief consideration is given to the procedural options available for expedited determinations. Expedited dispute resolution processes are not a recent development. Brief procedures were, for instance, known in Venice between the twelfth and sixteenth centuries, in which decisions were rendered within very short time frames.[20]

6.27 Nevertheless, in recent years, there has been a growing sense of frustration among businessmen involved in international commerce, because of the lengthy delays involved in obtaining the hoped-for promised land of the arbitral tribunal's award. A few solutions have emerged that deserve mention.[21]

---

[17] See Chapter 4.
[18] See Chapter 4.
[19] See Chapter 9.
[20] Marrella and Mozzato, *Alle origini dell'arbitrato commerciale internazionale: L'arbitrato a Venezia tra Medioevo ed età moderna* (CEDAM, 2001).
[21] The debate that followed also gave birth to the notion of 'fast-track' arbitration. The aim of such processes is to accelerate all of the steps, thereby achieving a binding result as quickly as possible, reducing overall costs, and encouraging settlements.

Conduct of the Proceedings

(b) Expedited formation

(i) Emergency arbitrator procedures

6.28 As described in more detail in Chapter 4, 'emergency arbitrator' procedures have become a common feature of the main institutional arbitration rules.[22] These procedures provide parties with a means of obtaining interim relief from an emergency arbitrator appointed on an expedited basis (usually within one or two business days) prior to the constitution of the arbitral tribunal, providing an alternative to seeking relief before the national courts. Under some rules, an emergency arbitrator can be appointed before the notice of arbitration is filed[23] and can hear applications *ex parte*.[24]

(ii) Expedited formation of the arbitral tribunal

6.29 The LCIA Rules provide that, in cases of exceptional urgency, a party may apply to the LCIA Court for the expedited formation of an arbitral tribunal.[25] The application must be made in writing to the LCIA Court, with copies sent to all other parties to the arbitration, and must set out the specific grounds for the exceptional urgency in the formation of the arbitral tribunal. For obvious reasons, it is usually the claimant who requests expedited formation.[26]

6.30 The LCIA Court has discretion to shorten the time limits for the formation of the arbitral tribunal. There have been a few cases in which the time limit has been 'significantly abridged' and one case in which a sole arbitrator was appointed within 48 hours of receipt of the request for arbitration.[27]

---

[22] ICC Rules, Art. 29 and Appendix V; ICDR Rules, Art. 37; Swiss Rules, Art. 43; SCC Rules, Appendix II; HKIAC Rules, Sch. 4; SIAC Rules, Sch. 1; LCIA Rules, Art. 9B. Since 1990, the ICC has offered the option to parties to expressly adopt the Pre-Arbitral Referee Rules, which provide for the immediate appointment of a pre-arbitral referee empowered to make certain interim orders prior to the constitution of the arbitral tribunal. However, the Rules have rarely been used, primarily because they require parties to opt in, and are now rendered practically obsolete by the introduction of the emergency arbitrator provisions in Art. 29 and Appendix V of the 2012 ICC Rules, which apply unless the parties expressly opt out.

[23] See, e.g., the ICC, SCC, and Swiss Rules.

[24] Swiss Rules, Art. 26(3).

[25] LCIA Rules, Art. 9A ('Expedited Formation of Arbitral Tribunal') provides:

9.1 In exceptional urgency, any party may apply for the emergency formation of the Arbitral Tribunal by the LCIA Court under Article 5.

9.2 Such an application shall be made in writing to the Registrar (preferably by electronic means), together with the Request (if made by a Claimant) or a copy of the Response (if made by a Respondent), delivered or notified to all other parties to the arbitration. The application shall set out the specific grounds for exceptional urgency in the formation of the Arbitral Tribunal.

9.3 For the purpose of forming the Arbitral Tribunal, the LCIA Court may abridge any period of time under the Arbitration Agreement or other agreement of the parties (pursuant to Article 22.5).

[26] Turner and Mohtashami, *Guide to the LCIA Arbitration Rules* (Oxford University Press, 2009), paras 4.86*ff*.

[27] Information provided by the LCIA's Registrar.

B. Expedited Procedures

Amongst more recent entrants into the arbitration field, the Dubai International Arbitration Centre (DIAC) has adopted a similar approach to expedited formation of the arbitral tribunal.[28] Nevertheless, examples of such expedited formation remain few and far between, with the criterion of 'exceptional urgency' interpreted and applied strictly.

6.31

(c) Fast-track procedures

Following the constitution of the arbitral tribunal, expedition can be achieved by the adoption of 'fast-track' procedures, either by means of simplified procedures available under certain arbitral rules, or by the tribunal exercising its discretion to abridge time limits.

6.32

Arbitrations can be put on a 'fast track' by adopting simplified procedures and avoiding some of the procedural excesses of modern arbitral practice. Several arbitral institutions have developed rules for the faster resolution of disputes by means of a simplified procedure.[29] As might be expected, the rules differ from one institution to another, but the Swiss Rules serve as a good example of how the procedure can work significantly to reduce the duration of an average arbitration. Under these Rules:

6.33

- a sole arbitrator is appointed, unless the arbitration agreement otherwise provides and the parties are unable to agree to the appointment of a sole arbitrator;
- written pleadings are limited to a statement of case, a defence, and (if applicable) a counterclaim and reply;
- unless the parties agree to a documents-only arbitration, a single hearing is held for the examination of witnesses and experts, and for oral argument; and
- the award is made within six months of the date of the transmittal of the file to the arbitral tribunal, which states the arbitrator's reasons in summary form (or does not give reasons at all if the parties so agree).

---

[28] DIAC Rules, Art. 12 ('Expedited Formation') provides:
  12.1 On or after the commencement of the arbitration, any party may apply to the Centre for the expedited formation of the Tribunal, including the appointment of any replacement arbitrator where appropriate.
  12.2 Any such application shall be made to the Centre in writing, copied to all other parties to the arbitration and shall set out the specific grounds for exceptional urgency in establishing the Tribunal.
  12.3 The Centre may, in its complete discretion, adjust any time-limit under these Rules for formation of the Tribunal, including service of the Answer and of any matters or documents adjudged to be missing from the Request.

[29] These include the AAA, SIAC, CIETAC, HKIAC, WIPO, SCC, and the Swiss Chambers' Arbitration Institution. See, e.g., AAA Commercial Arbitration Rules, Expedited Procedures, Sections E-1–E-10; see also the ICDR Arbitration Model Clause for Expedited Cases; SIAC Rules, Art. 5; CIETAC Rules, Ch. IV (titled 'Summary Procedure'); HKIAC Rules, Art. 41; WIPO Expedited Arbitration Rules; SCC Rules for Expedited Arbitrations; Swiss Rules, Art. 42.

Conduct of the Proceedings

It is noteworthy that, while this procedure is mandatory for cases in which the total amount in dispute does not exceed CHF1 million,[30] it is available for disputes of a greater amount if the parties so agree. Such processes offer hope for parties who wish to avoid the delay and cost involved in a traditional international arbitration process.[31]

6.34 A notable example of a fast-track arbitration under standard arbitral rules involved the fast world of Formula One (F1) motor racing.[32] At the time that the dispute arose, the first grand prix of the season was traditionally held in Melbourne in March. In preparation for the race, teams shipped their cars from Europe in mid-February. At the end of one season, in the mid-1990s, one team fell into dispute with the Federation Internationale de l'Automobile (FIA), headquartered in Paris, which regulates the F1 championship in accordance with a comprehensive set of rules. The team in question, which was sponsored by a tobacco company, wished to paint one of its cars in the colours of one of its brands of cigarettes and the other, in the livery of another of its brands. The FIA objected, on the grounds that the championship is a team event, and insisted that all cars from the same team must be painted in identical livery. The constitution of the FIA, to which every team must sign up when entering the championship, contained an ICC arbitration clause.

6.35 By Christmas Eve in the year in question, it became apparent that a resolution of the dispute would not be achieved by negotiation. The team and the FIA agreed that they would submit to a 'fast-track' ICC arbitration with a view to obtaining a final decision by the end of January, so that the cars could be painted and shipped in time to reach Australia by the end of February.

6.36 The F1 team filed a request for arbitration with the ICC between Christmas Day and New Year's Eve. A three-member arbitral tribunal was appointed on New Year's Day. This tribunal circulated draft terms of reference on the same day, which all concerned signed within two more days. A sequential exchange of 'memoranda', to which the parties attached the documents on which they relied, then took place at seven-day intervals, followed by a simultaneous exchange of written witness statements within a few more days. A handful of disputed document requests were resolved by prompt procedural orders from the tribunal and an eight-hour witness hearing took place on

---

[30] Swiss Rules, Art. 6(4).
[31] The Swiss Federal Supreme Court ruled on a challenge to an award rendered in accordance with the Swiss Chamber's expedited procedure and held, in the circumstances, that the respondent had not been denied its right to be heard nor had it been treated unequally: Decision No. 4A_294/2008, Swiss Federal Supreme Court, 28 October 2008.
[32] ICC Case No. 10211. None of the material published in this book is confidential, because the proceedings and the procedure were fully reported in various motor racing journals. See also Kaufmann-Kohler and Peter, 'Formula 1 racing and arbitration: The FIA tailor-made system for fast track dispute resolution' (2001) 17 Arb Intl 173.

B. Expedited Procedures

the last Saturday of January. The tribunal deliberated on the Sunday, and sent its final award to the ICC Court for scrutiny by fax and courier at lunchtime the next day (Monday), together with separate signed, but undated, signature pages.

The award was approved at an emergency session of the ICC Court the same afternoon, and the decision was notified to the parties by fax and overnight courier on the same day. The parties received the fully reasoned award on the last day of January, one month precisely from the day on which the tribunal was appointed, and the cars were painted and shipped to Australia in good time for the first grand prix race of the season.[33] This case demonstrates what speed can be achieved (even before a grand prix begins) when the parties have a joint will to obtain early resolution, and the arbitral tribunal is disposed and available to act on that will.[34]

6.37

(d) Early, or summary, determinations

An alternative to 'fast-track' procedures is early, or summary, determination. This involves the early determination of one or more claims or defences, upon application by a party or on the tribunal's own initiative, on the basis that the claim or defence in question has no prospect of success.[35]

6.38

Such procedures remain uncommon in international arbitration and very few arbitration rules provide for them expressly. Rule 41(5) of the ICSID Arbitration Rules is one such exception, and permits a party to raise a preliminary objection that a claim is 'manifestly without legal merit'.[36]

6.39

---

[33] As a postscript, one of the present authors, who was a member of the tribunal (which unanimously upheld the FIA's position), recalls one of the other arbitrators during the deliberation making the observation: 'Of course, you know what they [the F1 team] will do...they'll paint each car the same, one side of the car in the livery of one brand and the other side in the livery of the other brand.' His instinct served him well: this is precisely what the team did.

[34] See also Rawding, Fullelove, and Martin, 'International arbitration in England: A procedural overview', in Greenaway, Fullelove, Lew, and Bor (eds) *Arbitration in England, with Chapters on Scotland and Ireland* (Kluwer Law International, 2013), p. 361, at paras 18-34–18-38.

[35] Gill, 'Applications for the early disposition of claims in arbitration proceedings' (2009) 14 ICCA Congress Series 513. National court procedures often permit a court to make a summary judgment where a plaintiff or a defendant has no reasonable prospects of succeeding on its claim or defence. However, as Gill points out, 'it is uncontroversial to suggest that tribunals generally do not possess the powers of summary disposition conferred on national courts': ibid., at 515. See also the Centre for Public Resources (CPR) International Committee on Arbitration, Guidelines on Early Disposition of Issues in Arbitration, available online at http://www.cpradr.org/RulesCaseServices/CPRRules/GuidelinesonEarlyDispositionofIssuesinArbitration.aspx.

[36] ICSID Rules, r. 41(6), provides that: 'If the Tribunal decides that the dispute is not within the jurisdiction of the Centre or not within its own competence, or that all claims are manifestly without legal merit, it shall render an award to that effect.' See also AAA Rules, Art. 33. More generally, IBA Rules, Art. 2.3, encourages the arbitral tribunal 'to identify to the Parties, as soon as it considers it to be appropriate, any issues:...(b) for which a preliminary determination may be appropriate'. See also 1999 IBA Working Party and 2010 IBA Rules of Evidence Review Subcommittee, 'Commentary on the Revised Text of the 2010 IBA Rules on the Taking of Evidence

6.40 In the absence of specific provisions contemplating early disposition or the agreement of the parties, the use of summary procedures are believed by some to introduce 'due process' risk at the enforcement stage of proceedings.[37] How consistent are such procedures, so the question goes, with the requirement to provide a party with a 'reasonable' opportunity to be heard? While such a question is perhaps understandable (particularly when considering the approach to enforcement taken by some national courts), a summary procedure need not prejudice the 'reasonable' opportunity to be heard. Moreover, approached with prudence, such procedures can, in the right circumstances, be entirely consistent with an arbitral tribunal's duty to adopt procedures that avoid unnecessary delay or expense.

C. Preliminary Steps

(a) Introduction

(i) Preliminary meetings

6.41 Preliminary meetings at a very early stage of a dispute process are not customary in some countries. Nevertheless, especially where the parties and their representatives come from different legal systems or different cultural backgrounds, it is sensible for the tribunal to convene a meeting with the parties as early as possible in the proceedings. This ensures that the arbitral tribunal and the parties have a common understanding of how the arbitration is to be conducted, and enables a carefully designed framework for the conduct of the arbitration to be established.[38] In modern times, it is common practice for preliminary meetings to be conducted by teleconference or video conference. This saves the costs inevitably incurred when one (or more) of the arbitrators or counsel has to travel across national boundaries, even across oceans, in order to be present in person. However, there is no real substitute for all of the players coming together in one room as soon as possible after the arbitration has started.

6.42 Some institutional rules now provide expressly for the convening of a 'preliminary meeting',[39] or 'case management conference',[40] whilst others provide for such a meeting to be convened at the discretion of the tribunal.[41]

---

in International Arbitration' (2011) 5(1) DRI 45, at 51: 'While the Working Party did not want to encourage litigation-style motion practice, the Working Party recognised that in some cases certain issues may resolve all or part of a case.'

[37] Born and Beale, 'Party autonomy and default rules: Reframing the debate over summary disposition in international arbitration' (2010) 21 ICC International Court of Arbitration Bulletin 19.

[38] It is necessary to distinguish between a preliminary meeting (or preliminary hearing) and a pre-hearing conference. A preliminary meeting takes place as early as possible in the proceedings, and certainly before the written stage. A pre-hearing conference takes place after the written stage, and has as its primary objective the organisation and order of proceedings at the evidentiary hearing.

[39] SIAC Rules, Art. 16(3); DIAC Rules, Art. 22.

[40] ICC Rules, Art. 24. See also ICC Rules, Appendix IV ('Case Management Techniques').

[41] AAA Rules, Art. 21 (and Sections P-1 and P-2); ICDR Rules, Art. 16(2). Most rules require the tribunal to consult with the parties before it prepares the procedural timetable for the arbitration: see,

C. Preliminary Steps

In practice, a preliminary meeting proceeds through various stages. The members of the arbitral tribunal usually arrange to meet privately, before meeting the parties. This is partly to effect introductions and partly to discuss provisional views as to the organisation of the arbitration. **6.43**

Similarly, substantial benefits may be gained if the representatives of the parties have an opportunity to interact before attending the preliminary meeting with the arbitral tribunal. This is particularly important in ad hoc arbitrations, since matters such as the fees and expenses of the arbitrators are normally dealt with at this stage. To avoid embarrassment, in ad hoc arbitrations, it is important that the representatives of the parties should be able to present an agreed position to the arbitral tribunal on the question of the arbitrators' fees and expenses. **6.44**

(ii) Representation at preliminary meetings

In order to obtain the maximum benefit from a preliminary meeting with the arbitral tribunal, each party should be represented by persons with sufficient authority and knowledge of the case to take 'on the spot' decisions, both in discussion with the other party's representatives and during the course of the meeting with the arbitral tribunal itself. This means that it is usually necessary for the leader of each party's team of lawyers, as well as a person with appropriate executive authority from the client itself, to attend. It is common practice, particularly where a government is involved, for an 'agent' to be nominated.[42] The agent is the person to whom both the arbitral tribunal and the other party are entitled to address communications, and from whom they may seek an authoritative statement on behalf of the government concerned. **6.45**

(iii) Items to be covered at preliminary meetings

The agenda items to be addressed at a preliminary meeting depend partly on the law governing the arbitration (for example, in some jurisdictions, it may be necessary to establish a submission agreement)[43] and partly on whether the parties have already subjected the arbitration to a set of international or institutional rules, either for administered or for non-administered arbitration. If the arbitration is subject to the rules of one of the major international arbitration institutions, it will not be necessary, for example, for the parties to deal directly with the arbitrators in connection with the tribunal's fees, which will be handled by the institution concerned. **6.46**

---

e.g., ICSID Rules, r. 20; HKIAC Rules, Art. 13(2); SCC Rules, Art. 23; Swiss Rules, Art. 15(3). See also UNCITRAL Rules, Art. 17(2).

[42] As in the *Aminoil* arbitration: *Government of the State of Kuwait v The American Independent Oil Co. (Aminoil)* (1982) 21 ILM 976, at 983.

[43] By the twenty-first century, this had become rare: see Chapter 2, n. 6.

6.47 Whether an arbitration is ad hoc or institutional, the procedure and schedule for the following items will usually be addressed during a preliminary meeting:[44]

- preliminary issues—such as jurisdictional objections, interim relief applications, and/or bifurcation;
- written submissions—including number of rounds, their timing, structure, and length, and whether they are to be accompanied by documentary and witness evidence;
- document production;
- witnesses—including their number, the timing of submission of witness statements or expert reports, and any use of tribunal-appointed experts;
- the pre-hearing conference—including the venue and timing;
- the evidentiary hearing—including its venue and timing; and
- other procedural and administrative matters—such as the role of the IBA Rules on the Taking of Evidence in International Arbitration, the chairman's power to make procedural orders alone, the appointment of an arbitral secretary, and the means of communication with the tribunal.

(iv) 'Time out'

6.48 As mentioned in the last section, private meetings of the arbitral tribunal and between the parties themselves may take place before the main case management meeting of the arbitral tribunal and the parties. Indeed, it is not uncommon for the main meeting to be adjourned, or even for there to be several short adjournments, while the arbitrators confer in private (or 'caucus', as lawyers sometimes describe it). This also gives the parties' representatives an opportunity for further private discussions. In this way, and with the guidance of the arbitral tribunal, the parties may be able to agree on the basic framework and organisation of the proceedings.

6.49 Arbitral tribunals usually prefer to avoid making rulings on disputed procedural matters in the early stages of the arbitration. Where there is disagreement between the parties, arbitrators often suggest compromise solutions. This appears to derive from the complexities of tribunal psychology,[45] as a result of which individual members of the arbitral tribunal (and particularly the presiding arbitrator) are reluctant to make rulings at the start of the arbitration that one of the parties may regard (however unjustifiably) as amounting to unfair treatment.

6.50 Nevertheless, if, at the end of a case management meeting, there are still matters outstanding upon which the parties are unable to agree, the arbitral tribunal must make a decision. Sometimes, this is done immediately; sometimes, it is reserved and notified to the parties later. It is unusual for a preliminary meeting to extend beyond one day, as a maximum, and it may well be disposed of within half a day or less. This means that, with careful planning, it is sometimes possible to hold a

---

[44] See also Böckstiegel, 'Party autonomy and case management: Experiences and suggestions of an arbitrator' [2013] SchiedsVZ 1.
[45] See Chapter 9.

C. Preliminary Steps

preliminary meeting without the need for any of the participants to make an overnight stay in a hotel unless intercontinental travel is involved.

(v) UNCITRAL Notes on Organizing Arbitral Proceedings

6.51 It may be useful, at the beginning of an arbitration, for the parties to consult the UNCITRAL Notes on Organizing Arbitral Proceedings.[46] These Notes provide a list of matters that the parties and the tribunal may wish to consider in establishing the procedural rules for their arbitration. Some of these matters—such as establishing the language of the arbitration—may be thought to be fairly obvious; others are more helpful, including arrangements to protect the confidentiality of proprietary information, arrangements for the exchange of memorials and other written submissions, means of communication between the parties (including the extent to which email, fax, or other electronic forms of communication should be used), and so forth.

(vi) 'Procedural Order No. 1'

6.52 Many experienced international arbitrators have their own model forms of procedural orders. These are sent to the parties' counsel as a first step towards discussing and agreeing the terms of the first procedural order, which will establish an overall procedural scheme for the arbitration in question. Such a procedural order will usually include dates (or time limits) for the delivery of memorials, and for the production of documents, witness statements, and expert reports. It may also contain provisional dates for a witness hearing. A procedural order of this type serves as a useful guideline to the parties and to the tribunal in discussing what is required for the actual arbitration with which they are concerned. However, there is a risk that the use of such 'model forms', which often go into a considerable degree of detail, may result in the indiscriminate adoption of rigid procedures that are not appropriately tailored to the particular dispute in question. Indeed, an automatic (one might almost say 'lazy') reliance on procedures devised for other arbitrations may lead to a failure to acquire a proper understanding of the case and a consequent failure to deliver on the key procedural 'promise' of arbitration—namely, tailor-made efficiency.

(b) Preliminary issues

6.53 One of the elements that may emerge from the answers to such a questionnaire is whether or not there are some issues that should be decided as 'preliminary issues' or 'separate issues'. Apart from jurisdictional issues,[47] other questions may arise that either should be determined as preliminary issues before the arbitral tribunal considers the substance of the claims or, alternatively, may be dealt with more

---

[46] These are set out at in Appendix I. The UNCITRAL Working Group II (Arbitration and Conciliation) produced a draft revised version of the Notes in its Sixty-second Session in New York, 2–6 February 2015, but at the time of writing this draft had yet to be approved.
[47] See Chapter 5.

conveniently at an early stage as separate issues, in order to facilitate the efficient and economical conduct of the proceedings.

(i) 'Bifurcation' of liability and quantum

6.54 A question that often arises is whether or not issues of liability and quantum should be dealt with separately. In many modern disputes arising out of international trade, particularly in relation to construction projects or intellectual property disputes, the quantification of claims is a major exercise. It may involve both the parties and the arbitral tribunal in considering large numbers of documents, as well as complex technical matters involving experts appointed by the parties, or by the arbitral tribunal, or both. In such cases, it may involve savings in costs and overall efficiency if the arbitral tribunal determines questions of liability first. In this way, the parties avoid the expense and time involved in submitting evidence and argument on detailed aspects of quantification that may turn out to be irrelevant following the arbitral tribunal's decision on liability.[48]

6.55 There are sometimes clear arguments in favour of separating issues of liability from issues of quantum in a large and complex case. For example, a claimant may have suffered a substantial loss (including loss of profit) as a result of the breakdown or failure of an important piece of plant or equipment. The claimant may seek to recover this loss by way of arbitration proceedings against a respondent responsible for the manufacture and/or installation of the equipment. In its defence, the respondent may allege, first, that it is instead a supplier who is liable for any breakdown or failure in the plant or equipment supplied, secondly, that liability is limited under the terms of the contract to a sum much smaller than the amount claimed, and, thirdly, that, in any event, some of the losses claimed (such as loss of profit) are irrecoverable (because of the conditions of contract) and others are not fully recoverable, because they have been quantified on the wrong basis.

6.56 This is a common situation in international disputes, with the respondent putting forward a succession of defences, any one of which, if successful, may limit—or even defeat—the claim. How should an arbitral tribunal deal with such a situation?

6.57 There are various possibilities. First, the tribunal might decide to hear legal argument as to the effect of the clause limiting liability—on the basis that if the clause is found to be effective, the respondent may pay the limited amount stated in the clause and the case will then be concluded.

6.58 At first sight, this seems to be an attractive option for both parties. There is no point in spending time and money on a complicated factual investigation if the dispute

---

[48] See also the discussion of partial and interim awards in relation to the separation of liability and quantum in Chapter 9. See also ICC Rules, Appendix IV, para. (a); ICDR Rules, Art. 16(3); AAA Rules, Art. 32(b); SIAC Rules, Art. 16(4).

C. Preliminary Steps

may be resolved by the determination of a legal point as a preliminary issue. It may emerge, however, that the correct legal interpretation to be put upon the clause that limits, or purports to limit, liability depends on the facts—and that, in order to ascertain and understand the factual situation, it is necessary to enquire fully into all of the circumstances of the case, with the assistance of both fact and expert witnesses on each side. Thus the findings of the arbitral tribunal on the legal issue might be so dependent on its finding on the fact issues as to make it difficult (and indeed undesirable) to disentangle them. In this event, it would be appropriate for the arbitral tribunal to investigate the relevant facts rather than to attempt to deal with the legal issue in isolation.

Although, in practice, issues of liability and quantum may, from time to time, prove to be inextricably interwoven, it is sometimes possible to see a broad division between them. It is also sometimes possible to determine the principles on which damages should be awarded, while leaving the pure arithmetical calculations to a second stage. **6.59**

(ii) Separation of other issues

It is rarer for an arbitral tribunal to separate issues where there is no clear dividing line—to say, in effect, 'there are only a limited number of issues on which we wish to hear evidence and argument from the parties, and these are as follows'. This course should not be attempted lightly. Before an arbitral tribunal can safely isolate some of the issues for its attention, it must be satisfied that it has been adequately informed of all of the issues that are relevant or likely to be relevant to its decision. This stage is not likely to be reached until the written phase of the proceedings is under way. Where, however, an arbitral tribunal is satisfied that it has been adequately briefed on all of the issues and that the time has come for it to take the initiative in this way, the effect can be dramatic in terms of saving both time and money. **6.60**

The *Aminoil* arbitration provides a classic example.[49] Many hundreds of millions of dollars were at stake, depending upon whether the Kuwait government's act of nationalisation was unlawful (as claimed by Aminoil), thereby giving rise to the possibility of an award of damages on a full indemnity basis, which would have a punitive effect, or lawful (as the government claimed), and thus susceptible to resolution by the payment of fair compensation. **6.61**

At the close of the written stage of the proceedings, the arbitral tribunal convened a meeting with the parties and their counsel to consider various procedural matters relating to the forthcoming oral hearings. Following this meeting, the arbitral tribunal made an order fixing the hearing date in Paris and specifying, amongst other **6.62**

---

[49] See Redfern, 'The arbitration between the Government of Kuwait and Aminoil' (1984) 55 BYIL 65.

things, seven specific issues that the parties should address, the order in which they would be taken, and which side should speak first on each issue. This is how the hearing was conducted—and there is no doubt that this intervention by the arbitral tribunal led to a significant saving in time and money for both parties, and, in the end, to an outcome that both parties regarded as fair.[50]

6.63 At that time, in the early 1980s, it was relatively rare for an arbitral tribunal to take control of the proceedings in this way.[51] However, since then, international arbitrations have become more complex and costly. As both arbitral tribunals and practitioners search for quicker and more cost-effective ways of handling disputes, it seems essential that arbitrators should seek to direct the conduct of arbitrations from an early stage—and, in particular, that they should seek to cut through the foliage in order to reach the root issues as quickly as possible. Although, like the shipowner mentioned earlier,[52] the parties can agree to dismiss the arbitrators if they jointly lose confidence in them, it is no longer appropriate for arbitrators to sit passively behind their tables and say to themselves, 'this is clearly the wrong way of conducting this case, but the parties have agreed to do it like this so we'll go along with it'.[53]

6.64 To this end, one experienced arbitrator has advocated the introduction of an early hearing for opening arguments and initial exchanges with the tribunal on the merits prior to the evidentiary hearing.[54] This is to be welcomed: such early substantive 'case review conferences' would permit an arbitral tribunal to be actively involved in the streamlining of procedures to focus on those issues and evidence that will be material to the outcome of the case. The timing of such a case review conference would be key. It cannot happen too early, for example at the first case management conference, because at that stage arbitrators and even counsel are often not endowed with sufficient information about the case to reach informed decisions about the most efficient procedure to be followed. In the same way, such a 'case review conference' should not happen too late in the process, because that will defeat the purpose. Timed well, such early substantive engagement by the tribunal can be very effective in fulfilling arbitration's promise as a tailored and efficient process.

---

[50] See Hunter and Sinclair, '*Aminoil* revisited: Reflections on a story of changing circumstances', in Weiler (ed.) *International Investment Law and Arbitration: Leading Cases from the ICSID, NAFTA, Bilateral Treaties and Customary International Law* (Cameron May, 2005), pp. 347–381.

[51] Note that a number of sets of institutional rules permit the tribunal to 'direct the parties to focus their presentations on issues the decision of which could dispose of all or part of the case': ICDR Rules, Art. 16(3); AAA Rules, Art. 32(b); SIAC Rules, Art. 16(4). See also ICC Rules, Appendix IV, para. (a); LCIA Rules, Art. 19(2).

[52] See paragraph 6.03.

[53] In this vein, one arbitrator has remarked, 'I am sometimes shocked when I write the award that although we heard 25 witnesses, I am only referring to two, and I think, "why did we spend time hearing them, why did the parties bear the costs of preparing them…" ': 'Due process must trump efficiency, says Derains', Global Arbitration Review, 23 September 2014.

[54] Kaplan, 'If it ain't broke, don't change it' (2014) 80 Arbitration 172. See also Partasides and Vesel, pp. 167–168.

D. Written Submissions

(a) Introduction

6.65 In ad hoc international arbitrations, when the procedure to be followed has been established, the first step taken in almost all cases is an exchange between the parties of some form of written submission.

6.66 The immediate purposes of the parties' initial statements are to facilitate the appointment of the arbitral tribunal, to guide the institution or the arbitral tribunal in establishing the amount of the deposit to be paid by the parties to secure the costs of the arbitration, to enable the arbitral tribunal to identify the issues that arise for determination, and to make appropriate procedural orders for the next steps. In nearly all cases of any substance, however, the arbitral tribunal orders the exchange of further, fuller written pleadings, as well as an appropriate level of evidence gathering, before the oral stage of proceedings is reached.

6.67 The LCIA Rules provide that, after the parties have delivered the request for arbitration and response, written pleadings consisting of a 'statement of case', 'statement of defence', and 'statement of reply' (and further equivalent written pleadings in the event of a counterclaim, referred to as a 'cross-claim') follow each other within certain time limits. It is clear from these Rules that (subject to any contrary agreement of the parties or directions from the arbitral tribunal) the written statements are intended, in principle, to be the only pre-hearing written submissions in the arbitration.[55]

6.68 The ICDR Rules provide for the exchange of initial statements of claim and defence,[56] and state that the arbitral tribunal may 'decide whether the parties shall present any written statements in addition'.[57] The Swiss Rules adopt a similar approach, and also require a party's statement to be accompanied by 'all documents and other evidence on which it relies'.[58]

6.69 The ICSID Arbitration Rules entitle the documents that are to be filed by the parties as a 'memorial' and a 'counter-memorial', followed, if necessary, by a reply and a rejoinder. These Rules also allow for simultaneous exchange of written submissions, if the request for arbitration was made jointly.[59] The Rules provide that a memorial should contain a statement of the relevant facts, a statement of law, and submissions, and that the counter-memorial, reply, or rejoinder should respond to these statements and submissions, and add any additional facts, statements of law,

---

[55] LCIA Rules, Art. 15(1).
[56] ICDR Rules, Arts 2 and 3.
[57] ICDR Rules, Art. 17(1).
[58] Swiss Rules, Arts 18(3) and 19(2).
[59] ICSID Rules, r. 31(1) and (2).

or submissions of its own.[60] The Explanatory Note states that the scope of these pleadings represents:

> ...an adaptation of common law practice to the procedure of the civil law. These provisions, tested by international arbitration practice, are designed to prevent procedural arguments concerning the scope of pleadings, even if the parties have differing legal backgrounds. Where, however, the parties share a common experience with an identical or similar system of procedure, they may agree on different contents and functions for the pleadings.[61]

6.70 Written pleadings are usually exchanged sequentially, so that the claimant fires the first shot, the statement of claim, and the respondent answers with the statement of defence (and counterclaim, if any). Exceptionally, however, the arbitral tribunal may direct that the parties should submit their written pleadings simultaneously, so that each party delivers a written submission of its claims against the other on a set date, and then, on a subsequent date, the parties exchange their written answers and so forth. Whilst simultaneous exchanges can reduce the overall duration of the written phase, they are more likely to lead to the arbitral equivalent of 'ships passing in the night'. For this reason, simultaneous exchange remains less common than sequential exchange for pre-hearing submissions.[62]

(b) **Terminology**

6.71 Many different expressions are used to describe written submissions. Examples are 'statement of claim', 'statement of case', 'memorial', and 'points of claim'. These lead to corresponding expressions such as 'statement of defence', 'statement of reply', 'counter-memorial', and so forth, with 'reply', 'rejoinder', 'replique', 'duplique', and similar phrases being used for additional rounds of written submissions.

6.72 The different expressions used to describe written submissions are not wholly interchangeable and none are capable of precise definition. In general, it may be said that the term 'points of claim' indicates a relatively short document, the primary purpose of which is to define the issues and state the facts upon which the claimant's claims are founded. By contrast, the expressions 'statement of claim' and 'memorial' imply a more comprehensive documentary submission, intended to include argument relating to the legal issues, as well as incorporating (in annexes

---

[60] ICSID Rules, r. 31(3).
[61] The Note was included in the Rules of Procedure for Arbitration Proceedings (Arbitration Rules) of January 1968, referring to r. 30(3), which is r. 31(3) in the current 2006 edition of the Rules: see Rayfuse, *ISCID Reports, Vol. 1: Reports of Cases Decided under the Convention on the Settlement of Investment Disputes between States and Nationals of Other States, 1965* (Grotius, 1993), p. 93.
[62] White & Case and Queen Mary University of London, *Current and Preferred Practices in the Arbitral Process* (2012), available online at http://www.arbitration.qmul.ac.uk/research/2012/index.html, found that 82 per cent of respondents said that sequential exchange was the most common approach, with 79 per cent expressing a preference for it.

E. Collecting Evidence

or appendices) the documentary evidence relied upon and the written testimony of witnesses, together with any experts' reports on matters of opinion.

(c) Time and length limits

6.73 The practice of arbitral tribunals varies greatly. Sometimes, a tribunal will fix time limits for the submission of written pleadings that are tacitly accepted from the beginning as being unrealistic and which serve merely as targets to make sure that the parties start their preparatory work without delay. Such arbitral tribunals expect applications for extensions of time to be made and will grant them readily. Other arbitral tribunals regard this approach as both artificial and inappropriate, and prefer to assess realistic time limits at an early stage, in the expectation that they will be observed. The second approach is more common and is to be preferred.[63]

6.74 There is no such thing as a standard time limit in international arbitration, although periods of up to three months between submissions are not uncommon. Arbitrators should recognise, however, that the longer the time limits, the lengthier the written submissions are likely to be. Whilst this might be considered a matter for the parties (who pay their lawyers' resulting fees), a trend appears to be developing in international arbitration for the submission of exhaustive written submissions, which are heavy with hyperbole and repetition. Not only does this add considerably to the time and cost of proceedings, but it can hinder a tribunal's understanding of a case. Increasingly, therefore, arbitral tribunals are now considering the imposition of page limits on (at least some of) the parties' written submissions.[64]

E. Collecting Evidence

(a) Introduction

6.75 It is impossible to collect comprehensive and reliable statistics in relation to private international arbitrations, but it is reasonable to assume that the eventual outcomes in the majority of international arbitrations (perhaps 60–70 per cent) usually turn on the facts rather than on the application of the relevant principles of law. A good

---

[63] The practice developed under the UNCITRAL Rules by the Iran–United States Claims Tribunal is summarised, with case citations, in Holtzmann, 'Fact-finding by the Iran–United States Claims Tribunal', in Lillich (ed.) *Fact-Finding before International Tribunals: Eleventh Sokol Colloquium* (Transnational, 1991), pp. 101–133. In deciding upon the admissibility of late-filed submissions, the tribunal considered, in light of the circumstances of each case, the needs for equality and fairness, the possibility of prejudice to the other party, and the requirements for orderly conduct of the proceedings.

[64] The Iran–United States Claims Tribunal considered 'the reasons for the delay, the prejudice to the other party, and the effect of admitting the late-filed counterclaim on the orderly progress of the case': Holtzmann, 'Some lessons of the Iran–United States Claims Tribunal', in Landwehr (ed.) *Private Investors Abroad: Problems and Solutions in International Business* (Bender, 1988), p. 5. See also UNCITRAL Rules, Art. 22.

proportion of the remainder turn on a combination of facts and law, and only in a minority of cases is the outcome dependent solely on issues of law, with the underlying facts being undisputed or irrelevant.

6.76 It follows that fact-finding is one of the most significant functions of an arbitral tribunal and it is a function that all tribunals take seriously. The relevant facts are determined by international arbitral tribunals either following the presentation by the parties (usually via experienced counsel) of documentary and/or oral evidence, or by arbitral tribunals making their own efforts, with the assistance of the parties, to ascertain the evidence that they consider necessary to establish the relevant facts.

(i) Civil law and common law procedures

6.77 In court procedures in most common law countries, the initiative for the collection and presentation of evidence is almost wholly in the hands of the parties. The judge acts as a kind of referee, to administer the applicable rules of evidence and to give a decision at the end on who has 'won' the argument in a combative sense. The judge listens to the evidence and may question the witnesses; in general, however, common law judges leave it to the parties to present their respective cases and then form a judgment on the basis of what the parties elect to present to the court. By contrast, in the courts of most civil law countries, the judge takes a far more active role in the conduct of the proceedings and in the collection of evidence, including the examination of witnesses.[65]

6.78 The impression given by these brief summaries of the two systems is that the differences are fundamental. Yet there is a considerable risk of overgeneralisation in drawing distinctions between the so-called common law and civil law systems. Each system has many variations. The rules of procedure in the United States are different from those in England, just as the German and French rules of procedure are different.

6.79 Emphasising this point, a Swiss international arbitration specialist stated:

> ...My first remark is that there is no such thing as '*Civil Law procedure*' in civil and commercial litigation. In Common Law countries, there are undoubtedly certain common basic principles of procedure, which go back to the procedure practised in the English courts. In continental Europe, there is no such common origin. In each country, one finds a different blend of civil procedure, largely influenced by local custom, the legal education received by judges and by counsel, and, to a varied extent, by the influence of the procedure practised in the old ecclesiastical courts, although such courts were abolished, in Protestant countries, at the time of the Reformation....

---

[65] See the discussion of comparative arbitration practices in (1987) 3 ICCA Congress Series 98. The extent to which the Iran–United States Claims Tribunal took an active role in obtaining evidence is described by Holtzmann, 'Fact-finding by the Iran–United States Claims Tribunal', in Lillich (ed.) *Fact-Finding before International Tribunals: Eleventh Sokol Colloquium* (Transnational, 1991), pp. 106–110.

E. Collecting Evidence

The result of this is that there is possibly as much difference between the outlook and practice of a French avocat and of a German Rechtsanwalt as between those of an English and of an Italian lawyer. The same applies within my own country, Switzerland, where civil and criminal procedure remain in the realm of the 26 sovereign States of the Confederation, thus leading to the existence of 26 different codes of civil or criminal procedure, plus a Civil Procedure Act for the Federal Supreme Court. There is as much difference between the type of civil procedure practised in Geneva and that practised in Zurich as between those featured in Madrid and Stockholm.

These differences are experienced daily in international arbitration, where they are sometimes the source of great difficulties. Certainly these difficulties are due, to a large extent, to the different patterns of civil procedure law, but, in my experience, to a far greater extent to the undisclosed assumptions and prejudices of municipal lawyers faced for the first time in their lives with a system of which they are not aware. Just to take a simple example, a common lawyer expects the claimant as a matter of course to have the last word at the end of the day, whereas a continental lawyer considers it a requirement of natural justice that the defendant should be the last to address the Court.[66]

6.80 Nevertheless, there is just enough uniformity in the general approach to questions concerning the presentation of evidence to justify using the expression 'civil law countries' by way of contrast to the 'common law countries' when discussing the presentation of evidence to international tribunals. Where there are differences between the two systems, they are most noticeable in the area of the procedures that lead to fact-finding. The most important elements include the following.

(ii) Admissibility

6.81 In practice, tribunals composed of three experienced international arbitrators from different legal systems approach the question of the reception of evidence in a pragmatic way. Whether they are from common law or civil law countries, they tend to focus on establishing the facts necessary for the determination of the issues between the parties and are reluctant to be limited by technical rules of evidence that might prevent them from achieving this goal. This is especially so where the rules in question were originally designed for use in jury trials, centuries ago, at a time when many jurors were not able to read or write, so that it was necessary for documents to be read aloud at hearings.

6.82 It is essential for practitioners who have been raised in the common law tradition to appreciate this and to learn not to rely overly on technical rules concerning the admissibility of evidence during the course of the proceedings, particularly at witness hearings. Conversely, where all three arbitrators come from a common law background, practitioners from civil law countries should take care that their cases do not depend on proving facts that can be established only by means of the

---

[66] Reymond, 'Part 2: Common law and civil law procedures—Which is the more inquisitorial?' (1989) 55 Arbitration 155, at 159.

presentation of evidence that may be technically inadmissible under the system with which all members of the arbitral tribunals concerned are familiar.

6.83 Most international arbitral tribunals are 'hybrid', in the sense that they will comprise members with backgrounds in different systems of law. Where a 'non-hybrid' arbitral tribunal is established, the team of lawyers retained to represent each party should preferably include a member who is familiar with the approach to the presentation and reception of evidence that the arbitral tribunal is likely to apply. This precaution should not be necessary where the arbitral tribunal is 'hybrid', because such tribunals nearly always adopt a flexible approach to admissibility of evidence; it is unlikely that a party will be prevented from submitting evidence that may genuinely assist the arbitral tribunal in establishing the facts, should they be disputed.[67]

(iii) Burden of proof

6.84 One question that often arises in an international arbitration is that of knowing which party has the responsibility for proving a particular allegation or set of allegations. The generally accepted answer is that the 'burden of proof' of any particular factual allegation is upon that party which makes the allegation. This is recognised explicitly in Article 27(1) of the UNCITRAL Rules: 'Each party will have the burden of proving the facts relied on to support its claim or defence.' The UNCITRAL Rules then go on to make it clear that this burden of proof may be discharged by the evidence of witnesses, including expert witnesses, or by the production of documents, exhibits, or other evidence, or (of course) by a combination of the two. Further, there are some propositions that are so obvious that proof is not required.[68]

(iv) Standard of proof

6.85 The degree of proof that must be achieved in practice before an international arbitral tribunal is not capable of precise definition, but it may be safely assumed that it is close to the test of the 'balance of probability' (that is, 'more likely than not'). This standard is to be distinguished from the concept of 'beyond all reasonable doubt' required, for example, in countries such as the United States and England to prove guilt in a criminal trial before a jury.[69]

---

[67] Holtzmann, 'Fact-finding by the Iran–United States Claims Tribunal', in Lillich (ed.) *Fact-Finding before International Tribunals: Eleventh Sokol Colloquium* (Transnational, 1991), pp. 118–119. See also Holtzmann, 'Streamlining arbitral proceedings: Some techniques of the Iran–United States Claims Tribunal' (1995) 11 Arb Intl 39; Straus, 'The practice of the Iran–US Claims Tribunal in receiving evidence from parties and from experts' (1986) 3 J Intl Arb 57. See also IBA Rules, Art. 9(1).

[68] One such proposition might be that the earth is a sphere, although members of the flat earth society would not agree.

[69] In *Parker* (1926) 4 Rep Intl Arb Awards 25, at 39, the Mexican–US General Claims Commission held that, '...when the claimant has established a *prima facie* case and the respondent has offered no evidence in rebuttal the latter may not insist that the former pile up evidence to establish its allegations beyond a reasonable doubt without pointing out some reason for doubting'. See

E. Collecting Evidence

The practice of arbitral tribunals in international arbitrations is to assess the weight to be given to the evidence presented in favour of any particular proposition by reference to the nature of the proposition to be proved. For example, if the weather at a particular airport on a particular day is an important element in the factual matrix, it is probably sufficient to produce a copy of a contemporary report from a reputable newspaper, rather than to engage a meteorological expert to advise the tribunal. **6.86**

In general, the more startling the proposition that a party seeks to prove, the more rigorous the arbitral tribunal will be in requiring that proposition to be fully established. A classic example of this general rule involves allegations of fraud or illegality. Whilst the standard will remain the 'balance of probabilities', an arbitral tribunal is likely to look even more closely at the evidence to determine whether such a standard has been adequately met. In the words of an English case heard in the (then) House of Lords: **6.87**

> The civil standard of proof always means more likely than not. The only higher degree of probability required by the law is the criminal standard. But, as Lord Nicholls of Birkenhead explained in *In re H (Sexual Abuse, Standard of Proof) (Minors)* [1996] AC 563 at 586, some things are inherently more likely than others. It would need more cogent evidence to satisfy one that the creature seen walking in Regent's Park was more likely than not to have been a lioness than to be satisfied to the same standard of probability that it was an Alsatian. In this basis, cogent evidence is generally required to satisfy a civil tribunal that a person has been fraudulent or behaved in some other reprehensible manner. But the question is always whether the tribunal thinks it more probable than not.[70]

In deciding what evidence to produce and the means by which it should be presented, the practitioner should therefore make an evaluation of the degree of proof that the tribunal is likely to require before being sufficiently satisfied to make the finding of fact that his or her client is seeking. **6.88**

(b) Categories of evidence

The evidence presented to arbitral tribunals on disputed issues of fact may be divided into four categories: **6.89**

(1) production of contemporaneous documents;
(2) testimony of witnesses of fact (written and/or oral);
(3) opinions of expert witnesses (written and/or oral); and
(4) inspection of the subject matter of the dispute.

---

also Eveleigh, Hanotiau, Menzies, Philip, Redfern, Reiner, and Reymond, 'The standards and burden of proof in international arbitration' (1994) 10 Arb Intl 317, at 320–321; Pietrowski, 'Evidence in international arbitration' (2006) 22 Arb Intl 373.

[70] *Secretary of State for the Home Department v Rehman* [2001] UKHL 47, at [140]–[141] *per* Lord Hoffmann. See also Partasides, 'Proving corruption in international arbitration: A balanced standard for the real world' (2010) 25 ICSID Rev—Foreign Investment LJ 472.

These methods may be used, or combined, in many different ways for the purpose of discharging the burden of proof to the standard required by an arbitral tribunal. It is important to recognise that each different arbitral tribunal may adopt a different approach not only to the manner in which it wishes the evidence to be presented, but also to the weight that it is willing to give to any particular type of evidence.

6.90 Modern international arbitral tribunals accord greater weight to the contents of contemporary documents than to oral testimony given, possibly years after the event, by witnesses who have obviously been 'prepared'[71] by lawyers representing the parties. In international arbitrations, the best evidence that can be presented in relation to any issue of fact is almost invariably contained in the documents that came into existence at the time of the events giving rise to the dispute.[72]

6.91 Unsurprisingly, the evidence-gathering activity in international arbitrations usually takes place in the period after the facts in dispute have been identified, through the written submissions delivered by the parties, and before the witness hearings begin.

(c) Documentary evidence

6.92 The parties produce the documents on which they intend to rely at an early stage in an international arbitration. This will usually be with their written submissions, which has the merit of placing the principal documents 'on the table' at the earliest practicable moment.

6.93 The story becomes more complicated in the context of documents that the parties have not chosen to produce voluntarily. The phrase 'culture clash' is overused in the lexicon of modern arbitration, but it often seems appropriate in the context of document production.

6.94 It is thus not unusual for US lawyers to come to hearings in European (and other) prominent arbitration venues carrying with them a belief in the entitlement to 'discovery'[73] of a certain document, or groups of documents. By contrast, in some

---

[71] Sometimes actually rehearsed with the aid of video cameras.
[72] In two cases before the Iran–United States Claims Tribunal, fact-finding on jurisdictional issues was based entirely on documentary evidence consisting of official documents, corporate documents prepared in the ordinary course of business, publications of which the Tribunal took judicial notice, certificates by independent certified public accountants, and affidavits of corporate officers: see Holtzmann, 'Fact-finding by the Iran–United States Claims Tribunal', in Lillich (ed.) *Fact-Finding before International Tribunals: Eleventh Sokol Colloquium* (Transnational, 1991), pp. 110–114.
[73] The word 'discovery' is a term of art used in the United States and some other common law countries (no longer in England, where the term was abolished under the Civil Procedure Rules 1996) to describe a process whereby the parties (and their lawyers) are legally obliged to produce documents that are 'relevant to the pleaded issues', even if they are prejudicial to that party's case. Subject to any mandatory rules of the *lex arbitri*, or agreement of the parties, the process known as 'discovery' has no place in international arbitration.

E. Collecting Evidence

civil law countries, it may be professional malpractice for a lawyer to disclose such documents to the arbitral tribunal or to the opposing party.[74] The result can be that a huge amount of time and expense is incurred in dealing with disputes concerning document production.

(i) IBA Rules on the Taking of Evidence in International Arbitration

In the late 1990s, building on experience gained from the (not particularly successful) Supplementary Rules Governing the Presentation and Reception of Evidence in International Commercial Arbitration that it had adopted in 1983, the International Bar Association (IBA) embarked on a project to produce a new more 'internationalised' version. This project led to the 1999 edition, entitled the IBA Rules on the Taking of Evidence in International Commercial Arbitration, which became almost universally recognised as the international standard for an effective, pragmatic, and relatively economical document production regime. Following a two-year review process that included a public consultation, a substantially revised version of the Rules (now titled the IBA Rules on the Taking of Evidence in International Arbitration[75]) was adopted by the IBA Council on 29 May 2010. The 2010 edition retains the general principles of the 1999 edition and also reflects new developments in arbitral practice in the intervening decade. The remainder of this section of the current chapter is therefore presented by reference to the principles and provisions contained in the 2010 edition.[76] 6.95

Article 3 of the IBA Rules deals with document production. Its main provisions are as follows: 6.96

1. Within the time ordered by the Arbitral Tribunal, each Party shall submit to the Arbitral Tribunal and to the other Parties all Documents available to it on which it relies, including public Documents and those in the public domain, except for any Documents that have already been submitted by another Party.
2. Within the time ordered by the Arbitral Tribunal, any Party may submit to the Arbitral Tribunal and to the other Parties a Request to Produce.

---

[74] Other than where the applicable arbitration rules expressly permit such an order.
[75] The deletion of the word 'Commercial' from their title was intended to reflect the fact that the Rules may be, and indeed already are, applied in both commercial and investment treaty arbitration.
[76] The Preamble to the Rules provides that:

They are designed to supplement the legal provisions and the institutional, *ad hoc* or other rules that apply to the conduct of the arbitration... Parties and Arbitral Tribunals may adopt the IBA Rules of Evidence, in whole or in part, to govern arbitration proceedings, or they may vary them or use them as guidelines in developing their own procedures. The Rules are not intended to limit the flexibility that is inherent in, and an advantage of, international arbitration, and Parties and Arbitral Tribunals are free to adapt them to the particular circumstances of each arbitration.

Article 1 of the Rules further includes various provisions aimed at resolving conflicts between the Rules, mandatory provisions of law, and the institutional, ad hoc, or other rules that apply to the conduct of the arbitration.

3. A Request to Produce shall contain:
   (a) (i) a description of each requested Document sufficient to identify it, or
       (ii) a description in sufficient detail (including subject matter) of a narrow and specific requested category of Documents that are reasonably believed to exist; in the case of Documents maintained in electronic form, the requesting Party may, or the Arbitral Tribunal may order that it shall be required to, identify specific files, search terms, individuals or other means of searching for such Documents in an efficient and economical manner;
   (b) a statement as to how the Documents requested are relevant to the case and material to its outcome; and
   (c) (i) a statement that the Documents requested are not in the possession, custody or control of the requesting Party or a statement of the reasons why it would be unreasonably burdensome for the requesting Party to produce such Documents, and
       (ii) a statement of the reasons why the requesting Party assumes the Documents requested are in the possession, custody or control of another Party.
4. Within the time ordered by the Arbitral Tribunal, the Party to whom the Request to Produce is addressed shall produce to the other Parties and, if the Arbitral Tribunal so orders, to it, all the Documents requested in its possession, custody or control as to which it makes no objection.

[...]

6.97 These provisions are admirably clear and self-explanatory. They establish the principle, referred to earlier, that the parties should produce the evidentiary documents on which they rely as the first stage. They make provision for requests by each party to the other(s) for further documents, with appropriate limitations. The most significant limitation is in the expression 'relevant to the case and material to its outcome' in Article 3(3)(b), which is considered further later in this chapter.[77]

6.98 Most legal practitioners are accustomed to the obligation to satisfy a court, or arbitral tribunal, as to the question of relevance of documents or other information that they are seeking from the opposing party. But the requirement of showing 'materiality' to the outcome of the case is an increased burden. It also enables arbitral tribunals to deny document requests where, although the requested documents would generally be relevant, they consider that their production will not affect the outcome of the proceedings.

6.99 Dealing with disputed document production requests can be a laborious and time-consuming process for all concerned, and different arbitral tribunals adopt

---

[77] See paragraph 6.102. This formulation was intended to be a clarification, rather than a modification, of the criteria under the 1999 Rules, which required a document to be 'relevant and material to the outcome of the case'. The change of wording is not mentioned in the IBA Commentary on the 2010 Rules: Ashford, *The IBA Rules on the Taking of Evidence in International Arbitration: A Guide* (Cambridge University Press, 2013), paras P-5–P-38. See also Kläsener, 'The duty of good faith in the 2010 IBA Rules on the Taking of Evidence in International Arbitration' (2010) 13 Intl Arb LR 160.

E. Collecting Evidence

various techniques to cut through the detail involved in resolving such disputed requests. Article 3 of the IBA Rules (to continue the extract set out above), contains the following relevant provisions:

> [...]
> 5. If the Party to whom the Request to Produce is addressed has an objection to some or all of the Documents requested, it shall state the objection in writing to the Arbitral Tribunal and the other Parties within the time ordered by the Arbitral Tribunal. The reasons for such objection shall be any of those set forth in Article 9.2[78] or a failure to satisfy any of the requirements of Article 3.3.
> 6. Upon receipt of any such objection, the Arbitral Tribunal may invite the relevant Parties to consult with each other with a view to resolving the objection.
> 7. Either Party may, within the time ordered by the Arbitral Tribunal, request the Arbitral Tribunal to rule on the objection. The Arbitral Tribunal shall then, in consultation with the Parties and in timely fashion, consider the Request to Produce and the objection. The Arbitral Tribunal may order the Party to whom such Request is addressed to produce any requested Document in its possession, custody or control as to which the Arbitral Tribunal determines that *(i)* the issues that the requesting Party wishes to prove are relevant to the case and material to its outcome; *(ii)* none of the reasons for objection set forth in Article 9.2 applies; and *(iii)* the requirements of Article 3.3 have been satisfied. Any such Document shall be produced to the other Parties and, if the Arbitral Tribunal so orders, to it.
> [...]

6.100 An increasingly common formatting tool for organising and presenting this process of document request, objection and decision is to use a so-called *Redfern* schedule, devised by one of the authors.[79] When one party issues a 'request to produce' to the other, an exchange of views takes place between the parties' lawyers, usually

---

[78] Article 9(2) states:
> 2. The Arbitral Tribunal shall, at the request of a Party or on its own motion, exclude from evidence or production any Document, statement, oral testimony or inspection for any of the following reasons:
> (a) lack of sufficient relevance to the case or materiality to its outcome;
> (b) legal impediment or privilege under the legal or ethical rules determined by the Arbitral Tribunal to be applicable;
> (c) unreasonable burden to produce the requested evidence;
> (d) loss or destruction of the Document that has been shown with reasonable likelihood to have occurred;
> (e) grounds of commercial or technical confidentiality that the Arbitral Tribunal determines to be compelling;
> (f) grounds of special political or institutional sensitivity (including evidence that has been classified as secret by a government or a public international institution) that the Arbitral Tribunal determines to be compelling; or
> (g) considerations of procedural economy, proportionality, fairness or equality of the Parties that the Arbitral Tribunal determines to be compelling.

[79] See Chapter 1, paragraph 1.238 and Figure 1.1.

by correspondence, but sometimes at a meeting. During this exchange, the parties' positions become clearer: for example, the 'requested party' may say 'we are prepared to produce documents covering this period of time, but not longer, because that would be oppressive', or 'we don't have the management committee minutes, but we are prepared to disclose the relevant board minutes'. In this way, the nature of the requests and the objections may change as the discussion proceeds.

6.101 The purpose of the *Redfern* schedule is to crystallise the precise issues in dispute, so that the arbitral tribunal knows the position that the parties have reached following the exchanges between them.[80] This makes it possible for the arbitral tribunal to make an informed decision as to whether or not a particular document, or class of documents, should be produced, without having to be involved in the details of the exchanges between the parties' lawyers and, usually, without the need for a meeting.

6.102 To achieve this purpose, a schedule with at least four columns is drawn up. Each column of the schedule is intended to be completed as briefly as possible by the parties' lawyers.

- In the first column, the 'requesting party' sets out (a) a brief description of the requested document in sufficient detail to identify it, or (b) a description in sufficient detail to identify a narrow and specific category of documents that are reasonably believed to exist.
- In the second column, the requesting party states why the requested document(s) are both relevant to the case and material to its outcome, as well as the statements required by Article 3(3)(c)(i) and (ii) of the IBA Rules.
- In the third column, the requested party states the extent to which, if at all, it is prepared to accede to the request, and if it objects, the grounds on which it does so.[81]
- The fourth column is left blank for the arbitral tribunal's decision.

If the tribunal considers that the schedule as it stands does not contain sufficient information for it to make a properly informed decision, the arbitral tribunal will

---

[80] The requirement to present document requests in the form of a *Redfern* schedule is often set out in the first procedural order, or a subsequent procedural order dealing with document production issues. Successive iterations of the parties' *Redfern* schedules are then filed with the arbitral tribunal. Typically, the *Redfern* schedules are the primary, or may even be the sole, channel of consultation between the parties on their objections to the other party's document production requests.

[81] As a further efficiency on the use of *Redfern* schedules, VV Veeder QC has proposed a set of 'Veeder codes', in the form of abbreviations of the reasons for objection set out in IBA Rules, Art. 3(5), for use in the drafting of objections to documents requests made in *Redfern* schedules. For example, where the requested party objects on the grounds that the requested document is not material to the outcome of the case (pursuant to Arts 3(3)(b) and 9(2)(a)), it would enter the code 'M' in the third column of the *Redfern* schedule; where the requested party objects on the basis that the request is excessively broad (pursuant to Art. 3(3)(a)(ii)), it would enter the code 'B'.

either (a) call for additional information, or (b) exceptionally, arrange a meeting with the parties to consider the disputed requests in more detail.

To reach a determination, where practicable, the arbitral tribunal may convene a case review conference with the parties' counsel with the objective of working out a way forward on most of the categories of documents requested.[82] Indeed, not only can such a physical hearing prove to be an efficient way in which to resolve document production disputes, but it can also prove to be a valuable early opportunity for the tribunal to engage the parties directly on the substance of the dispute.

6.103

(ii) Production of electronic documents

It has been said that at least 90 per cent of documents, correspondence, and other information generated is now stored in electronic form.[83] It is therefore not surprising that there has been much discussion concerning the ways in which such materials (known generically as electronically stored information, or ESI) may, or should, be used in commercial litigation.

6.104

In national court procedures in civil law countries, there is generally no obligation on the parties to produce documents other than those on which they rely unless, exceptionally, the judge orders a party to produce documents as part of his or her investigation of the facts. It follows that, in many civil law systems, the existence of many hundreds of thousands of pages of ESI relating to a transaction does not give rise to practical problems.

6.105

However, in many common law countries,[84] the rules of procedure in civil litigation place an obligation on the parties to disclose all documents 'relevant' to the issues in dispute. The sheer scale of complying with this obligation may place an intolerable burden in terms of cost and effort not only on the producing party, but also on the opposing party, and on the judges who have to make the findings of fact on which their judgments are based.

6.106

In the litigation context, a partial solution was developed in the form of the so-called Sedona Principles,[85] which are aimed primarily at containing to a reasonable level

6.107

---

[82] Such an approach is now expressly encouraged by IBA Rules, Art. 3(6), and may be agreed in advance by the parties during the consultation on evidentiary issues that is now provided for by Art. 2(1). See also IBA Rules, Art. 2(2)(c); ICC Rules, Appendix IV, para. (d)(v).

[83] In 2003, a project of the School of Information Management and Systems at the University of California at Berkeley, entitled How Much Information?, estimated that 92 per cent of the new information produced in 2002 was stored in magnetic form—usually on a hard drive—and 70 per cent of this information is never printed: see online at http://groups.ischool.berkeley.edu/archive/how-much-info-2003/

[84] See paragraph 6.77.

[85] *Best Practices, Recommendations and Principles for Addressing Electronic Document Production* (2nd edn, 2007), named after The Sedona Conference (held at the Sedona Hilton in the United States). The first edition of the Principles published in 2004 clearly inspired the conclusions reached by the Cresswell Committee in England, whose report in turn led to a Practice Direction under the English Civil Procedure Rules, Pt 31, and, later, to an amendment of the US Federal Rules of Civil Procedure. See also Hedges, 'Litigation lessons? US Federal Rules of Civil Procedure, The Sedona

the extent of the human resources that parties may be obliged to expend in identifying documents that might be required to be disclosed in litigation.

6.108 As stated earlier in this chapter,[86] rules of court do not apply in international arbitrations unless either the parties agree to adopt them or, exceptionally, the arbitral tribunal imposes them by a procedural direction.[87] It follows that, absent agreement of the parties, the basis for production of documents is in the discretion of the arbitral tribunal.

6.109 It is therefore appropriate to assess the question of production of ESI against the background of the current version of the IBA Rules, by which many tribunals will today be guided in the exercise of their discretion. First, the IBA Rules define the term 'document' as 'a writing, communication, picture, drawing, program or data of any kind, whether recorded or maintained on paper or by electronic, audio, visual or any other means'.[88]

6.110 In the context of production of documents pursuant to Article 3 of the IBA Rules, it seems clear that there is no difference in principle between 'hard copy' documents and 'soft copy' documents. It follows that the same general criteria should apply to the approach by arbitral tribunals to resolving disputes between the parties as to whether or not they should order the production of requested documents. The most important of these are 'unreasonable burden', 'proportionality', and 'considerations of procedural economy, fairness or equality'. To a certain extent, these elements are intertwined. It is for the arbitral tribunal to weigh the 'materiality to the outcome' against 'proportionality' (including the cost and burden involved in complying with the contemplated procedural order).[89]

Principles, and Part 31 of the English Civil Procedure Rules', in Howell (ed.) *Electronic Disclosure in International Arbitration* (JurisNet, 2008), pp. 107–117.

[86] See paragraph 6.01.

[87] Which would generally be inappropriate unless both parties come from the seat of the arbitration, in which case the arbitration would not, in fact, be an *international* arbitration.

[88] IBA Rules, Definitions. The Introduction to the Sedona Principles defines ESI as including:

> ...email, web pages, word processing files, audio and video files, images, computer databases...including but not limited to servers, desktops, laptops, cell phones, hard drives, flash drives, PDAs and MP3 players. Technically, information is 'electronic' if it exists in a medium that can only be read through the use of computers. Such media include cache memory, magnetic disks (such as computer hard drives or floppy disks), optical disks (such as DVDs or CDs), and magnetic tapes.

As the definition of 'Documents' contained in the 1999 edition of the IBA Rules was sufficiently broad to encompass most forms of ESI, it was decided that minor changes would be made in the 2010 edition to ensure that all known forms of ESI evidence would be subject to the IBA Rules: 1999 IBA Working Party and 2010 IBA Rules of Evidence Review Subcommittee, 'Commentary on the Revised Text of the 2010 IBA Rules on the Taking of Evidence in International Arbitration' (2011) 5(1) DRI 45, at 49.

[89] In respect of the production of electronic documents, the power of the tribunal under IBA Rules, Art. 3(3)(a)(ii), to require a requesting party to 'identify specific files, search terms, individuals or other means of searching for such Documents in an efficient and economical manner' provides a way in which to reduce the burden imposed on a requested party. See also Art. 3(12)(b) (a party need produce electronic documents only 'in the form most convenient or economical to it that

E. Collecting Evidence

(iii) Documents in the possession of third parties

An arbitral tribunal lacks power to order production of documents in the possession of a third party even where such documents may be relevant to the matters in issue. However, in some countries, a third party may be compelled by subpoena to attend at the hearings to give evidence and the courts can assist the arbitral tribunal in enforcing the attendance of such witnesses. In England, a party may apply to a court to compel the attendance of a witness who is within the jurisdiction of the court and to bring with him or her any material documents in his or her possession.[90] Similarly in the United States, the Federal Arbitration Act of 1925 (FAA) provides that the arbitrators may summon a person to attend before them and to produce any material documents.[91]

6.111

It sometimes happens in arbitration proceedings that a third party appears voluntarily at the request of one of the parties to provide testimony helpful to that party. On questioning by the other party's counsel, the witness may then object to the production of requested documents. While the arbitral tribunal may not have the power to order such a third party to produce documents, it may draw an adverse inference in respect of the evidence of the witness in question if it appears to the tribunal that the witness is withholding documents without good reason.

6.112

(iv) Adverse inferences

A technique followed by arbitral tribunals coming from different systems and cultures is to draw an 'adverse inference' from the silence of a party, or failure to comply with an order of the arbitral tribunal for the production of documentary or witness evidence.[92] This is covered in Article 9(5) and (6) of the IBA Rules, which state:

6.113

> 5. If a Party fails without satisfactory explanation to produce any Document requested in a Request to Produce to which it has not objected in due time or fails to produce any Document ordered to be produced by the Arbitral Tribunal, the Arbitral Tribunal may infer that such document would be adverse to the interests of that Party.
> 6. If a Party fails without satisfactory explanation to make available any other relevant evidence, including testimony, sought by one Party to which the Party to whom the request was addressed has not objected in due time or fails to make

---

is reasonably usable by the recipients') and (c) (a party is not required to produce 'multiple copies of Documents which are essentially identical'). See also Smit, 'E-disclosure under the Revised IBA Rules on the Taking of Evidence in International Arbitration' (2010) 13 Int ALR 201.

[90] English Arbitration Act 1996, s. 43.
[91] US FAA, § 7.
[92] The Iran–United States Claims Tribunal drew adverse inferences from the silence of a party in the face of alleged breach or non-performance of the contract when some complaint would have been expected, and from failure of a party to mention a point in a contract or in contemporaneous correspondence consistent with that party's position in the arbitration: Holtzmann, 'Fact-finding by the Iran–United States Claims Tribunal', in Lillich (ed.) *Fact-Finding before International Tribunals: Eleventh Sokol Colloquium* (Transnational, 1991), pp. 126–127.

available any evidence, including testimony, ordered by the Arbitral Tribunal to be produced, the Arbitral Tribunal may infer that such evidence would be adverse to the interests of that Party.

6.114 In this way, two important limitations apply where the IBA Rules are applicable. The first is that there must have been an order of the arbitral tribunal for production of the documents or other testimony concerned; the second is that the requested party must have failed to provide a 'satisfactory explanation' for not having produced the material in question. Whether or not an explanation to the effect that the material 'does not exist' or 'no longer exists' is satisfactory is a matter for the arbitral tribunal to decide after taking all of the relevant circumstances into consideration.

6.115 For example, if a document had been destroyed before the dispute arose, pursuant to a well-established (and reasonable) corporate document retention policy, many arbitral tribunals would consider such an explanation to be reasonable. However, if a document had been destroyed soon after a new document retention policy had been implemented, particularly if the policy was devised after the dispute arose, it would not be surprising if the tribunal were to take a sceptical view of the explanation.

(v) Presentation of documents

6.116 It is of considerable assistance to the arbitral tribunal if the parties are able to present the documentary evidence in the form of a volume (or volumes) of documents, in chronological order, with each page numbered like those of a book, for use at the hearing. In this way, each member of the arbitral tribunal, and each party, has a complete set of documents with identical numbering. If there is a huge number of documents, it may be a good idea to identify the most important documents and include them in a separate volume, or volumes (sometimes known as a 'core bundle'). This has the additional benefit of avoiding tiresome and unnecessary duplication of documents.

6.117 The use of the word 'agreed' in the context of volumes of documents occasionally gives rise to misunderstanding. The word is not intended to indicate that the parties are agreed on the meaning of the contents of the document, or its evidentiary weight, or even its admissibility. It simply indicates that the authenticity of the document is 'agreed' in the sense that each party agrees that it is an accurate copy of an existing document.

6.118 When the authenticity of documents is disputed, the arbitral tribunal usually orders that the originals (or certified copies, when appropriate) must be produced for inspection.[93] This may be carried out by forensic experts, if necessary. If the

---

[93] IBA Rules, Art. 3(12)(a).

E. Collecting Evidence

originals are not produced, the arbitral tribunal may disregard the documents in question as unreliable.

(vi) Translations

It is usually necessary to provide translations of any documents that are not already in the language of the arbitration. Such translations should, if possible, be submitted to the arbitral tribunal jointly by the parties as 'agreed translations'. The most convenient practice is to include the document in its original language first, immediately following it in the volume with the translation into the language of the arbitration.[94] If the correctness of the translation is disputed, each party's version may be inserted following the original and the tribunal may involve an expert translator of its own to resolve such a dispute.

6.119

(d) Fact witness evidence

The role of fact witnesses is to explain or supplement the evidentiary documents, so as to help the arbitral tribunal to perform its fact-finding function. In commercial transactions, as compared with accident cases, for example, most of the witnesses are likely to have had some connection with the transaction on one side or the other. They therefore tend to have a direct or indirect interest in the outcome of the case. It is not surprising that most arbitral tribunals regard the testimony of fact witnesses as sometimes less reliable than the documents that were brought into existence at the time of the events that gave rise to the dispute.

6.120

Article 4 of the IBA Rules deals with the presentation of fact witness evidence. It provides, in part, as follows:

6.121

1. Within the time ordered by the Arbitral Tribunal, each Party shall identify the witnesses on whose testimony it intends to rely and the subject matter of that testimony.
2. Any person may present evidence as a witness, including a Party or a Party's officer, employee or other representative.
3. It shall not be improper for a Party, its officers, employees, legal advisors or other representatives to interview its witnesses or potential witnesses and to discuss their prospective testimony with them.
4. The Arbitral Tribunal may order each Party to submit within a specified time to the Arbitral Tribunal and to the other Parties Witness Statements by each witness on whose testimony it intends to rely, except for those witnesses whose testimony is sought pursuant to Articles 4.9 or 4.10. If Evidentiary Hearings are organised into separate issues or phases (such as jursidiction, preliminary determinations, liability or damages), the Arbitral Tribunal or the Parties by agreement may schedule the submission of Witness Statements separately for each issue or phase.

---

[94] IBA Rules, Art. 3(12)(d).

5. Each Witness Statement shall contain:
   (a) the full name and address of the witness, a statement regarding his or her present and past relationship (if any) with any of the Parties, and a description of his or her background, qualifications, training and experience, if such a description may be relevant to the dispute or to the contents of the statement;
   (b) a full and detailed description of the facts, and the source of the witness's information as to those facts, sufficient to serve as that witness's evidence in the matter in dispute. Documents on which the witness relies that have not already been submitted shall be provided;
   (c) a statement as to the language in which the Witness Statement was originally prepared and the language in which the witness anticipates giving testimony at the Evidentiary Hearing;
   (d) an affirmation of the truth of the Witness Statement; and
   (e) the signature of the witness and its date and place.

[…]

7. If a witness whose appearance has been requested pursuant to Article 8.1 fails without a valid reason to appear for testimony at an Evidentiary Hearing, the Arbitral Tribunal shall disregard any Witness Statement related to that Evidentiary Hearing by that witness unless, in exceptional circumstances, the Arbitral Tribunal decides otherwise.
8. If the appearance of a witness has not been requested pursuant to Article 8.1, none of the other Parties shall be deemed to have agreed to the correctness of the content of the Witness Statement.[95]

[…]

In effect, this scheme codifies the procedures that have been developed by international arbitrators and arbitral institutions over the years,[96] during which it has gradually become common practice to present the direct testimony of fact witnesses in writing in advance of the witness hearing.

(i) Presentation of witness evidence

6.122 It is increasingly rare for the written witness statements to be submitted on oath in the form of affidavits. More frequently, the statements are simply signed by the witnesses. The IBA Rules requires each party to indicate to the arbitral tribunal which of the other party's witnesses should be required to attend the hearing for oral examination; the arbitral tribunal itself indicates to the parties which, if any, of the other witnesses it wishes to hear in person.[97] It is relatively rare for the arbitral

---

[95] This provision and Art. 8(1) are intended to save on time and expense by requiring witnesses to attend only where they are requested to do so, and by providing that a witness statement is not deemed to be accepted by the other parties in the absence of any such request (whether by agreement or otherwise): 1999 IBA Working Party and 2010 IBA Rules of Evidence Review Subcommittee, 'Commentary on the Revised Text of the 2010 IBA Rules on the Taking of Evidence in International Arbitration' (2011) 5(1) DRI 45, at 64–66; Ashford, *The IBA Rules on the Taking of Evidence in International Arbitration: A Guide* (Cambridge University Press, 2013), paras 4-13–4-14.

[96] See, e.g., LCIA Rules, Art. 20; SIAC Rules, Art. 22.

[97] This was a revision introduced in 2010 that was intended to align the IBA Rules with current best practice: 1999 IBA Working Party, n. 95, at 65. Article 8(2) provides that the right to call witnesses is subject to the tribunal's power to exclude any appearance that it considers to be 'irrelevant,

E. Collecting Evidence

tribunal to require a witness to be present if neither party requires that witness to attend.[98]

(ii) Preparation of witnesses

An important aspect of the presentation of witness evidence is the question of whether, **6.123** and if so, to what extent, it is permissible for a party, its employees, or counsel to interview and prepare those witnesses whose testimony they intend to present to the arbitral tribunal. This is largely a cultural matter, although the rules of some national courts (and/or bar associations) forbid, or make it unethical for, parties or their counsel to contact witnesses before they give their testimony in person.[99]

In international arbitration, it is well recognised that witnesses may be interviewed **6.124** and prepared prior to giving their oral testimony.[100] This is confirmed by at least three of the sets of institutional rules in common use. The LCIA Rules expressly permit it, subject to any mandatory provisions of any law governing the arbitration, other rules of law, or an order of the tribunal to the contrary,[101] and the Swiss Rules and the Rules of the Singapore International Arbitration Centre (SIAC) also permit such contact.[102] Article 4(3) of the IBA Rules also provides: 'It shall not be improper for a Party, its officers, employees, legal advisors or other representatives to interview its witnesses or potential witnesses and to discuss their prospective testimony with them.'[103] However, it is generally accepted that there are certain limits. It would be professional misconduct if a lawyer were to try to persuade a fact witness to tell a story that both the lawyer and the witness know to be untrue, and to prepare the witness to make such a story sound as credible as possible.[104]

---

immaterial, unreasonably burdensome, duplicative or otherwise covered by a reason for objection set forth in Article 9.2'.

[98] See also IBA Rules, Arts 3(10) and 8(5).

[99] See the paper presented by Doak Bishop at the 2012 ICCA Congress held in Singapore in the context of a panel discussion on the merits of uniform ethical regulation of international arbitration. See also Bishop and Stevens, 'The compelling need for a code of ethics in international arbitration: Transparency, integrity and legitimacy' (2011) 15 ICCA Congress Series 391, at 394.

[100] Blackaby, 'Witness preparation: A key to effective advocacy in international arbitration' (2010) 15 ICCA Congress Series 118.

[101] LCIA Rules, Art. 20(5).

[102] Swiss Rules, Art. 25(2); SIAC Rules, Art. 22(5).

[103] The final phrase, 'and to discuss their prospective testimony with them', was introduced in the 2010 edition to clarify 'that such an interview need not remain general, but may indeed relate to the subject-matter of the prospective testimony': 1999 IBA Working Party and 2010 IBA Rules of Evidence Review Subcommittee, 'Commentary on the Revised Text of the 2010 IBA Rules on the Taking of Evidence in International Arbitration' (2011) 5(1) DRI 45, at 63–64; Ashford, *The IBA Rules on the Taking of Evidence in International Arbitration: A Guide* (Cambridge University Press, 2013), paras 4-7–4-8. See also the IBA Guidelines on Party Representation in International Arbitration, Guideline 24, which similarly provides that: 'A Party Representative...may meet or interact with Witnesses and Experts in order to discuss and prepare their prospective testimony.' See also the UNCITRAL Notes on Organizing Arbitral Proceedings, paras 61 and 67. However, in exercise of its discretion under IBA Rules, Art. 9(1), a tribunal may take into account extensive interviewing and preparation in determining the weight that it will accord to a witness's evidence.

[104] See the IBA Guidelines on Party Representation in International Arbitration, Guidelines 26 and 27. See also LCIA Rules, Annex.

It would also almost always be counterproductive. Experienced arbitral tribunals tend to have good 'noses' for sniffing out inaccuracies in stories told by witnesses, and invariably cross-check oral testimony against the available corroborative documentary and other evidence.

(iii) Parties as witnesses

6.125 Another cultural division arises between lawyers from jurisdictions in which a party cannot be a 'witness' as such. This stems from the rules of court in some civil law countries under which a person (or officer, or employee, in the case of corporate entities) cannot be treated as a witness in his or her own cause.[105] However, even in the courts of these countries, a party can be heard; the rule merely forbids him or her from being categorised as a witness.

6.126 As in the case of other rules of national court procedure, this rule does not apply in international arbitrations,[106] unless the parties have expressly agreed that such rules should be applied. It may be that an arbitral tribunal will tend to give greater weight to the testimony of a witness who has no financial or other interest in the outcome of the arbitration, but that is a different question.[107]

(iv) Admissibility and weight of witness evidence

6.127 The rules concerning admissibility of witness testimony are, in principle, the same for written testimony as those that are applied to witnesses when they are giving oral testimony at a hearing before the arbitral tribunal.[108] In practice, it is rare for an arbitral tribunal to order written witness testimony to be withdrawn as inadmissible; rather, an arbitral tribunal is far more likely to address such issues as a matter of the evidentiary weight to be accorded the contents of the witness evidence concerned.

6.128 An arbitral tribunal has discretion to determine the evidentiary weight to be given to witness evidence.[109] This arises from the general principles applicable to arbitration proceedings and is expressly affirmed, for example, in Article 27(4) of the UNCITRAL Rules.[110]

---

[105] Germany is a significant example, followed by countries in which the code of civil procedure broadly follows the German tradition, such as Austria and the Czech Republic. See also 1999 IBA Working Party, n. 103, at 63.

[106] IBA Rules, Art. 4(2).

[107] 1999 IBA Working Party, n. 103, at 63.

[108] See above.

[109] IBA Rules, Art. 9(1). The practice of the Iran–United States Claims Tribunal concerning the weight to be given to affidavits is discussed by Holtzmann, 'Fact-finding by the Iran–United States Claims Tribunal', in Lillich (ed.) *Fact-Finding before International Tribunals: Eleventh Sokol Colloquium* (Transnational, 1991), pp. 113–114.

[110] See also, e.g., LCIA Rules, Art. 22(1)(vi); Swiss Rules, Art. 24(2); SCC Rules, Art. 26(1); HKIAC Rules, Art. 22(1).

E. Collecting Evidence

In general, arbitral tribunals tend to give less weight to uncorroborated witness testimony than to evidence contained in contemporaneous documents. Arbitral tribunals also give greater weight to the evidence of a witness that has been tested by cross-examination, or by an examination by the arbitral tribunal itself. Arbitral tribunals usually reject any submission that they should not hear the evidence of any particular witness, even if it is secondary or 'hearsay' evidence. However, an arbitral tribunal will give less weight to secondary evidence if, in its opinion, the party calling that evidence could have produced a witness who would have been able to give direct first-hand evidence on the factual issue in question.

6.129

(v) Taking evidence outside the seat

Problems arise when an arbitral tribunal wishes to obtain evidence from outside of the jurisdiction in which the arbitration takes place. In most countries, arbitrators do not have subpoena powers and thus have to request the assistance of courts if they want to compel the attendance of third-party witnesses, or to compel the production of documents in the possession of third parties, whether they are located within the seat of the arbitration or beyond.

6.130

The 1970 Hague Convention on the Taking of Evidence Abroad in Civil or Commercial Matters streamlines procedures for obtaining evidence in response to a request for assistance from 'judicial authorities'—but an arbitral tribunal is not a judicial authority. Accordingly, a request made from an arbitral tribunal does not fall within the scope of the 1970 Hague Convention. Nonetheless, many of the signatory states to the Hague Convention lend their judicial assistance to an arbitral tribunal with its juridical seat in another contracting state, or have otherwise enacted legislation that permits courts to provide assistance to foreign tribunals.[111] In the United States, courts have the power to order non-parties within their jurisdiction to give testimony or to produce documents for use in proceedings 'in a foreign or international tribunal' at the request of the tribunal or 'any interested person'.[112] Although this power is designed principally to provide judicial assistance with foreign judicial proceedings, parties are increasingly seeking to rely on it to secure court-ordered documentary evidence in aid of foreign arbitrations.[113] However, there remains controversy both as to whether the courts' power applies to foreign arbitral proceedings and the circumstances

6.131

---

[111] For example, s. 44 of the English Arbitration Act 1996 permits English courts to provide assistance to foreign arbitral tribunals, but s. 2(3) provides that the courts can refuse to do so if 'the fact that the seat of the arbitration is outside England and Wales or Northern Ireland, or that when designated or determined the seat is likely to be outside England and Wales or Northern Ireland, makes it inappropriate to do so'.

[112] 28 USC § 1782.

[113] This is particularly so after the US Supreme Court's decision in *Intel Corporation v Advanced Micro Devices, Inc.* 542 US 241 (2004), in which it adopted an expansive view of the scope of § 1782, holding that the Court's power extends to 'administrative and quasi judicial proceedings abroad'.

in which an order can be made at the unilateral request of a party without the tribunal's approval.[114]

6.132 The Model Law also deals with court assistance in the production of evidence.[115] However, it was determined that questions of international cooperation in the taking of evidence should not be governed by a model law, but through bilateral or multilateral conventions. Thus it is restricted to obtaining evidence where both the state in which the arbitration takes place and the state in which the evidence is located are signatories of the Model Law. In the light of inherent limitations, the most common way of compelling the production of evidence in arbitration is indirectly, by means of the ability of arbitrators to draw adverse inferences from unexcused failure to produce the requested evidence.[116]

(e) Experts

(i) Role of experts in international arbitration

6.133 We have already discussed the presentation of evidence to a tribunal, first by means of the production of contemporaneous documents, and secondly, by means of the testimony of witnesses of fact. The third method of presenting evidence to an arbitral tribunal is by means of the use of expert witnesses. Some issues can be determined only by the arbitral tribunal deciding on differences that are essentially matters of opinion. Thus, in a construction dispute, the contemporary documents, comprising correspondence, progress reports, and other memoranda, and the evidence of witnesses who were present on the site may enable the arbitral tribunal to determine what actually happened. There may then be a further question to be determined—namely, whether or not what actually happened was the result of, for example, a design error or defective construction practices. The determination of such an issue can be made by the arbitral tribunal only with the assistance of experts, unless it possesses the relevant expertise itself. Equally, in shipping arbitrations, the performance of a vessel or its equipment may need to be evaluated by experts, so that the arbitral tribunal may make the relevant findings of fact.

6.134 There are two basic methods of proceeding in a situation in which the arbitral tribunal itself does not have the relevant expertise. The first is for the arbitral tribunal

---

[114] See the discussion in Chapter 7, at paragraphs 7.39–7.44. See also Beale, Lugar, and Schwartz, 'Solving the § 1782 puzzle: Bringing certainty to the debate over 28 USC § 1782's application to international arbitration' (2011) 47 SJIL 51. However, it has been noted that '[f]ederal courts uniformly agree that Section 1782 applies to investment arbitration and they routinely order liberal, American-style discovery in aid of such international proceedings': Alford, 'Ancillary discovery to prove denial of justice' (2013) 53 VJIL 127, at 128 and 136–137. See, e.g., *In re Application of Chevron Corporation (Berlinger)* 709 F.Supp.2d 283 (SDNY 2010); aff'd *Chevron Corporation v Berlinger* 629 F.3d 297 (2nd Cir. 2011). See also IBA Rules, Art. 3(9).
[115] Model Law, Art. 27.
[116] IBA Rules, Art. 9(4) and (5).

E. Collecting Evidence

to appoint its own expert or experts; the second is for the parties to present expert evidence to the tribunal and, since this evidence will presumably be in conflict, for the arbitral tribunal to evaluate it. This evaluation is usually carried out after it has been tested by cross-examination, or by some other method, which may include the appointment by the arbitral tribunal of its own expert.

(ii) Experts appointed by the arbitral tribunal

In international arbitration, the arbitral tribunal is usually composed of lawyers.[117] Where matters of a specialist or technical nature arise, such an arbitral tribunal often needs expert assistance in reaching its conclusions, in order 'to obtain any technical information that might guide it in the search for the truth'.[118]

6.135

International arbitral tribunals have the power to appoint experts under most arbitration rules.[119] Although it is a well-established principle of most national systems of law that someone to whom a duty has been delegated must not delegate that duty to someone else, it is difficult to see any objection in principle to the appointment of an expert by an arbitral tribunal.[120] If an arbitral tribunal needs expert technical assistance in order to understand complex technical matters and it decides that it is in need of expert assistance to understand these matters in order to arrive at a proper decision, there is no good reason to prevent it from obtaining such assistance.

6.136

As a corollary to this power, the arbitral tribunal should give the parties an opportunity to comment on any expertise upon which the arbitrators have relied. The measures adopted by the Iran–United States Claims Tribunal in certain of its cases to involve the parties in the appointment and work of a tribunal appointed expert are instructive. In naming an expert, the Tribunal has first given the parties the opportunity to agree on an expert, then presented the parties with a list of individuals and institutions from which to choose, stating that if the parties are still unable to agree, the Tribunal will choose the expert itself. Similarly, the Tribunal

6.137

---

[117] See Chapter 4, paragraphs 4.55*ff*.

[118] See *Starrett Housing Corporation v Government of the Islamic Republic of Iran* (1987) 16 Iran–US CTR 112, Award No. 314-21-1, 14 August 1987, at [264], quoting the International Court of Justice (ICJ) in *United Kingdom of Great Britain and Northern Ireland v Albania (Corfu Channel)* [1949] ICJ Rep 4, at 20.

[119] See, e.g., UNCITRAL Rules, Art. 29; ICC Rules, Art. 25(4); Swiss Rules, Art. 27; SCC Rules, Art. 29; ICDR Rules, Art. 22; SIAC Rules, Art. 23; HKIAC Rules, Art. 25; LCIA Rules, Art. 21.

[120] This principle was expressed by the Iran–United States Claims Tribunal in *Starrett Housing*, at [266]: 'No matter how well qualified an expert may be, however, it is fundamental that an arbitral tribunal cannot delegate to him the duty of deciding the case.' In applying this principle, the Tribunal cited earlier international tribunals and stated, at [273]: '[T]he Tribunal adopts as its own the conclusions of the Expert on matters within his area of expertise when it is satisfied that sufficient reasons have not been shown that the Expert's view is contrary to the evidence, the governing law, or common sense.' See also the comment and cases cited at [271]–[272]. See also IBA Rules, Art. 6(7).

Conduct of the Proceedings

has also sought input from the parties concerning the expert's terms of reference. Once the expert has prepared a preliminary report, the parties are given an opportunity to comment and the expert is expected to take these comments into account when finalising his or her report.[121] In this way, the parties can assist the expert in making the report complete, while being reassured that important aspects of the case are not being decided without their involvement.[122]

(iii) Expert witnesses presented by the parties

6.138 One of the least satisfactory features of modern international arbitrations is the prevailing practice of presenting conflicting expert evidence of opinion on matters of great technical complexity. However well the advocates for the parties are able to test evidence of expert opinion presented by the other side through cross-examination, 'how can the jury judge between two statements each founded upon an experience confessedly foreign in kind to their own?'[123]

6.139 Although professional triers of fact should fare better than a jury, it is sometimes difficult for an arbitral tribunal to make a reasoned judgment as between two conflicting professional opinions on complex technical matters. Nevertheless, this remains by far the most common method of presenting expert evidence, regardless of where the arbitration takes place.[124]

6.140 The parties' expert evidence is normally delivered initially in the form of written expert reports, usually at the same time as any written statements of witnesses of fact, or shortly thereafter, but in any event well in advance of the hearing.[125]

6.141 Article 5(2) of the IBA Rules provides a useful summary of the expected contents of a party-appointed expert report:[126]

> 2. The Expert Report shall contain:
>   (a) the full name and address of the Party-Appointed Expert, a statement regarding his or her present and past relationship (if any) with any of the

---

[121] See *Starrett Housing*, at [6].

[122] In the same way, the IBA Rules provide for the involvement of the parties in the appointment of the expert, and also recommend that the parties (or their experts) have an opportunity to comment on and question the expert's report: see IBA Rules, Art. 6(1), (2), (5), and (6).

[123] Learned Hand, 'Historical and practical considerations regarding expert testimony' (1901) 15 Harv L Rev 40, at 54–55.

[124] A number of international arbitration rules provide for the use of party-appointed experts: see, e.g., UNCITRAL Rules, Art. 27(2); LCIA Rules, Art. 20; Swiss Rules, Art. 25(2) and (4); SCC Rules, Art. 28; SIAC Rules, Art. 22; HKIAC Rules, Art. 22(5).

[125] IBA Rules, Art. 5(1). See also Ashford, *The IBA Rules on the Taking of Evidence in International Arbitration: A Guide* (Cambridge University Press, 2013), para. 2-10.

[126] The key amendments introduced in the 2010 edition of the Rules were the requirements to (a) include a description of expert's instructions, (b) provide a statement of independence, and (c) append copies of the documents on which the experts relies, unless they are already on the record of the arbitration. The report must also now include statements regarding translation and be signed with an affirmation of genuine belief in the opinions expressed (rather than an affirmation of the truth of the report, as was required under the 1999 edition of the Rules). See also

E. Collecting Evidence

Parties, their legal advisors and the Arbitral Tribunal, and a description of his or her background, qualifications, training and experience;
(b) a description of the instructions pursuant to which he or she is providing his or her opinions and conclusions;
(c) a statement of his or her independence from the Parties, their legal advisors and the Arbitral Tribunal;
(d) a statement of the facts on which he or she is basing his or her expert opinions and conclusions;
(e) his or her expert opinions and conclusions, including a description of the methods, evidence and information used in arriving at the conclusions. Documents on which the Party-Appointed Expert relies that have not already been submitted shall be provided;
(f) if the Expert Report has been translated, a statement as to the language in which it was originally prepared, and the language in which the Party-Appointed Expert anticipates giving testimony at the Evidentiary Hearing;
(g) an affirmation of his or her genuine belief in the opinions expressed in the Expert Report;
(h) the signature of the Party-Appointed Expert and its date and place; and
(i) if the Expert Report has been signed by more than one person, an attribution of the entirety or specific parts of the Expert Report to each author.

(iv) Admissibility of expert evidence

6.142 Where expert evidence is introduced by the parties, the rules regarding the admissibility of expert evidence applied by arbitral tribunals will be, in general, the same as those applied to other forms of evidence in the same arbitration. If the evidence of technical opinion is conflicting (which is usually the case), the expert witnesses must be prepared to appear in person before the arbitral tribunal for examination. Consistent with the approach to fact witnesses, the IBA Rules provide that party-appointed experts need not appear for testimony at an evidentiary hearing unless they are requested to do so and that, in the absence of any such request, the other parties shall not be deemed to have accepted the correctness of the expert's report.[127]

(v) Categories of expert evidence

6.143 The evidence of experts is presented in relation to all kinds of matters of opinion. Engineers and scientists are frequently called upon to present reports, and to give evidence, in relation to disputes in which the quality of building work or the performance of plant and equipment is in issue. Accountants are called upon to give evidence as to the quantum of claims; lawyers may sometimes be required to give evidence where provisions of a 'foreign' system of law have to be explained to the arbitral tribunal. In addition, it is not unknown for handwriting experts, or other persons expert in the forensic examination of documents, to be called upon where the authenticity of a document is in question.

---

ibid., at paras 5-4–5-27, and the Chartered Institute of Arbitrators (CIArb) Protocol for the Use of Party-Appointed Expert Witnesses in International Arbitration.

[127] IBA Rules, Arts 8(1), and 5(5) and (6).

(vi) Experts on 'foreign' law

6.144 In the common law system, judges sitting in their national courts expect the substantive law of a foreign country to be 'proved as fact' by expert evidence. This convenient fiction has worked satisfactorily for hundreds of years in the court system. However, it takes only a brief moment of reflection to appreciate that the convenient fiction that 'foreign law is fact' does not work in the context of an international arbitration. Imagine three French lawyer arbitrators, sitting in England, with French avocats presenting arguments on the applicable French substantive law: any suggestion that English procedural law would require the relevant 'foreign' French substantive law to be proved as 'fact' would surely be greeted with some hilarity.

6.145 In practice, the international arbitration community has solved this dilemma in a pragmatic and efficient way. Nowadays, in almost all international arbitrations, 'law' is treated as 'law'. Such law is proven either as a matter of submission by counsel (or its local co-counsel), or by way of expert testimony in the form of an expert opinion by a legal expert of the substantive law in issue. Whilst different tribunals will have different preferences, there is a natural scepticism amongst many arbitrators as to the value of receiving such evidence as testimony involving lawyers being cross-examined by lawyers before other lawyers.

(f) Inspection of the subject matter of the dispute

6.146 The fourth method of presenting evidence to an arbitral tribunal is for the arbitral tribunal itself to inspect the subject matter of the dispute. This is usually a site inspection, and mainly arises in connection with construction contracts and disputes arising out of the performance of process plant and so forth. However, it may also apply in other types of case, for example it is common in commodity arbitrations for the arbitrator to inspect the cargo or consignment if the dispute concerns the quality of the goods supplied.[128]

6.147 Article 7 of the IBA Rules provides that:

> Subject to the provisions of Article 9.2, the Arbitral Tribunal may, at the request of a Party or on its own motion, inspect or require the inspection by a Tribunal-Appointed Expert or a Party-Appointed Expert of any site, property, machinery or any other goods, samples, systems, processes or Documents, as it deems appropriate. The Arbitral Tribunal shall, in consultation with the Parties, determine the timing and arrangement for the inspection. The Parties and their representatives shall have the right to attend any such inspection.[129]

---

[128] Ashford, *The IBA Rules on the Taking of Evidence in International Arbitration: A Guide* (Cambridge University Press, 2013), para. 7-02.
[129] See IBA Rules, Art. 6(3) and (5), subject to Art. 9(2). See also the ICDR Guidelines for Arbitrators Concerning Exchanges of Information, para. 5.

E. Collecting Evidence

Although this power exists, arbitral tribunals do not often use this opportunity to supplement the information and evidence available to them, probably because the additional expense involved is likely to be substantial in relation to the benefit gained. It is more common, in modern practice, for models, photographs, drawings, or even films to be used to fulfil the purpose that would have been served by a site inspection. For example, in an ICC arbitration, it was proposed to charter a helicopter to make a video showing the terrain in which a road was constructed over a length of some 60 km.[130] And in public international law cases between states, for example involving a boundary dispute, film and photographic evidence is often presented at hearings.[131]

(i) Procedure for inspection

An arbitral tribunal has broad discretion as to the manner in which it undertakes an inspection of the subject matter of the dispute. Unless the parties specifically agree otherwise, the arbitral tribunal will normally be careful to ensure that the principle of equality of treatment is strictly observed. In particular, the arbitral tribunal will not normally make a site inspection except in the presence of representatives of both parties, and the arbitrators will not normally put questions directly concerning the case to persons working on the site unless counsel for each of the parties also has the right to ask additional questions of those persons.

Occasionally, parties may agree that the arbitral tribunal should inspect a site, or the subject matter of the dispute, without being accompanied at all. However, it would be inappropriate, and potentially dangerous when the award comes to be enforced, if the arbitral tribunal were to make an inspection in the presence of one party alone.[132]

If a site inspection is to be made, it is good practice for the arbitral tribunal to issue a procedural direction in advance. Who is to be present? Who will make the arrangements? Will questions and answers or any discussion be transcribed and form part of the record? In general, it is suggested that best practice is to direct that there will be no transcript and that what is said should not form part of the record.[133] Otherwise, much of the usefulness of the inspection may be lost as a result of the inevitable delay and formality that accompanies the presence of a reporter.

6.148

6.149

6.150

6.151

(ii) Inspection under ad hoc and institutional rules of arbitration

The UNCITRAL Rules and the ICC Rules are silent on the question of inspection of the subject matter of the dispute, although the UNCITRAL Rules refer to the

6.152

---

[130] In fact, the dispute was settled before this was done.
[131] Regarding inspections, see Art. 66 of the 1978 ICJ Rules of Court (adopted on 14 April 1978 and entered into force on 1 July 1978).
[132] UNICTRAL Notes on Organizing Arbitral Proceedings, para. 57.
[133] Ibid., para. 58.

Conduct of the Proceedings

obligation of the parties to make available to any experts appointed by the arbitral tribunal any relevant information for inspection.[134] The LCIA Rules,[135] the SIAC Rules,[136] the Rules of the China International Economic and Trade Arbitration Commission (CIETAC),[137] the DIAC Rules,[138] the American Arbitration Association (AAA) Rules,[139] and the World Intellectual Property Organization (WIPO) Rules[140] make specific provision for any inspection or investigation that the arbitral tribunal may require.

6.153 The ICSID Arbitration Rules contemplate that a site inspection may be necessary. They contain power for the arbitral tribunal to 'visit any place connected with the dispute or conduct inquiries there' if the arbitral tribunal deems it necessary,[141] and they call upon the parties to cooperate in this, with the expenses forming part of the expenses of the parties.[142]

6.154 The WIPO Rules also provide for experiments to be conducted,[143] and for the provision by the parties of 'primers' and 'models'.[144]

F. Hearings

(a) Introduction

6.155 It has been said that the only thing wrong with 'documents only' arbitrations is that there are not enough of them. Such arbitrations are commonplace in certain categories of domestic arbitrations—notably, in relation to small claims cases. In the international context, the main examples of 'documents only' arbitrations are those conducted under the Rules of the London Maritime Arbitrators Association (LMAA) in connection with disputes arising out of charterparties and related documents.

6.156 However, in mainstream international arbitration, it is unusual for the arbitral proceedings to be concluded without at least a brief hearing at which the representatives of the parties have an opportunity to make oral submissions to the arbitral tribunal, and at which the arbitral tribunal itself is able to ask for clarification

---

[134] UNCITRAL Rules, Art. 29(3). See also the LCIA Rules, Art. 21(3); Swiss Rules, Art. 27(2); ICDR Rules, Art. 22(2); SIAC Rules, Art. 23(1)(b); HKIAC Rules, Art. 25(2); CIETAC Rules, Art. 42(2).
[135] LCIA Rules, Art. 22(1)(iv).
[136] SIAC Rules, Art. 24(e).
[137] CIETAC Rules, Art. 41.
[138] DIAC Rules, Art. 27(4).
[139] AAA Rules, Art. 36.
[140] WIPO Rules, Art. 50.
[141] ICSID Rules, r. 24(2)(b).
[142] ICSID Rules, r. 34(3) and (4).
[143] WIPO Rules, Art. 49 (on motion of a party).
[144] WIPO Rules, Art. 51 (with the agreement of the parties).

F. Hearings

of matters contained in the written submissions and in the written evidence of witnesses.

All of the rules of the major international arbitration institutions provide for a hearing to take place at the request of either party, or at the instigation of the arbitral tribunal itself. Whilst an arbitral tribunal must proceed to make its award without a hearing if the parties have expressly so agreed,[145] such an agreement is rare in modern international arbitration.

6.157

(b) Organisation of hearings

Hearings are normally held on a date fixed by the arbitral tribunal, either at the request of one or both of the parties, or on its own initiative. The administrative arrangements may be made by one of the parties, often the claimant, with the agreement of the other. Alternatively, they may be made by the sole or presiding arbitrator, or by the arbitral secretary (if there is one).

6.158

In fully administered arbitrations, the institution itself (for example the AAA or the LCIA) sometimes makes the arrangements; in others, these matters are left to the arbitral tribunal and the parties.[146]

6.159

The task of organising hearings in a major international commercial arbitration should not be underestimated nor should the cost. A suitable hearing room must be provided, with ancillary breakout rooms and facilities for the parties and the arbitral tribunal. Access to printing facilities, and a Wi-Fi connection, is invariably essential. A live transcript and verbatim record of the proceedings is often considered essential. Accommodation is also required for witnesses, experts, and the parties' legal teams.[147]

6.160

In short, oral hearings are the most cost-intensive periods of any arbitration and their scheduling often leads to the greatest delays, because availability of all essential participants must be coordinated. Efforts should therefore be made by arbitrators and counsel to limit their duration. To this end, the following matters should be considered.

6.161

- Should there be one hearing or several?
- Should there be time limits for the presentation of oral arguments?
- Should there be a limit on the time allowed for the examination and re-examination of witnesses?
- Should there be post-hearing briefs, rather than oral closing submissions?[148]

---

[145] See, e.g., LCIA Rules, Art. 19(1).
[146] See UNCITRAL Notes on Organizing Arbitral Proceedings, paras 24–25. The ICC Secretariat is usually willing to make the necessary arrangements if requested to do so by the arbitral tribunal.
[147] For further discussion of administrative arrangements of an arbitral tribunal, see Chapter 4, paragraphs 4.169*ff.*
[148] See UNCITRAL Notes on Organizing Arbitral Proceedings, paras 76–79.

(i) Location

6.162 In most cases, hearings may be held at any location that is convenient for all concerned. Subject to any mandatory provisions of law in the seat of the arbitration, there is generally no requirement that all hearings be physically conducted in the territory of the seat of the arbitration.[149] As a result, most modern arbitration rules allow for the conduct of oral hearings at any location that the tribunal considers appropriate.[150] While it remains common to hold the main evidential hearing in the place of arbitration, the option not to do so can, on occasion, bring real benefits and savings in convenience and cost (for example when many of the participants in a hearing are all based in another city), and should be exploited in appropriate cases.

(ii) Pre-hearing conference

6.163 In large and complex cases, a properly planned pre-hearing meeting or conference can pay substantial dividends in terms of saving time and money at the hearing itself. Such conferences should be organised efficiently, both as to timing and content. The timing is extremely important. If a pre-hearing conference takes place too near to the hearing itself, it will be too late for the 'shape' of the hearing to be influenced. However, if it takes place too early, the arbitral tribunal is not sufficiently well informed about the issues or the evidence needed to supplement the material submitted in writing to enable useful decisions to be taken with regard to the structure of the hearing.

6.164 Agenda items to be covered at a pre-hearing conference can include tribunal sitting times, the division of time between the parties, the running order, length, and format of opening statements, the sequestration of witnesses, the scope and length of direct cross- and redirect examination, oral closing statements and/or post-hearing briefs, transcription, and the preparation of hearing bundles. These matters may be agreed by the parties, and if they cannot agree, decided by the tribunal, and memorialised in a procedural order.[151]

---

[149] In a decision that was widely criticised, the Swedish Svea Court of Appeal held, in *Titan Corporation v Alcatel CIT SA*, Case No. RH 2005:1 (T 1038-05) YCA XXX (2005), 139, that Titan Corporation could not request the Swedish courts to set aside an ICC award in an arbitration in which the seat was Stockholm because the parties had not conducted any of the hearings in Stockholm (consistent with the discretion to hold hearings other than in the place of arbitration that exists under the ICC Rules). In 2010, the Supreme Court reversed the decision. See 'Decision by the Svea Court of Appeal in Sweden rendered in 2005 Case No. T 1038–05' (2005) 2 Stockholm Intl Arb Rev 259; Ewerlöf, 'Chapter 10 application of the New York Convention by Swedish courts', in Wallin, Regnwaldh, Magnusson, and Franke (eds) *International Arbitration in Sweden: A Practitioner's Guide* (Kluwer Law International, 2013), p. 267, at pp. 270–271.

[150] See, e.g., SCC Rules, Art. 20(2); ICC Rules, Art. 18(2); UNCITRAL Rules, Art. 18(2); LCIA Rules, Art. 16(3). See also Model Law, Art. 20(2).

[151] Michael Moser has proposed a useful 'pre-hearing checklist' to be distributed to the parties well in advance of the hearing: Moser, 'The "pre-hearing checklist": A technique for enhancing efficiency in international arbitral proceedings' (2013) 30 J Intl Arb 155.

F. Hearings

Pre-hearing conferences have been used to considerable effect by arbitral tribunals since the early days of the Iran–United States Claims Tribunal. The potential value of pre-hearing conferences has also been accepted by ICSID, which formulated a Rule to provide for them: **6.165**

> (1) At the request of the Secretary-General or at the discretion of the President of the Tribunal, a pre-hearing conference between the Tribunal and the parties may be held to arrange for an exchange of information and the stipulation of uncontested facts in order to expedite the proceeding.
>
> (2) At the request of the parties, a pre-hearing conference between the Tribunal and the parties, duly represented by their authorized representatives, may be held to consider the issues in dispute with a view to reaching an amicable settlement.[152]

The first part of this Rule envisages a conventional role for the pre-hearing conference—namely, that of helping to ensure that time is saved at the hearing itself. The second part of the Rule is less conventional. It seeks to take advantage of the fact that the claims and counterclaims of the opposing parties tend to change shape under the hammer of contested proceedings, as each side begins to understand its opponent's case better, and it envisages that, at the request of the parties, a conference may be held, with a view to arriving at an amicable settlement of the dispute prior to the main hearing. **6.166**

Whether rules provide for oral pre-hearing conferences explicitly or not,[153] they have become common practice in the exercise of an arbitral tribunal's general procedural discretion. Indeed, the most proactive tribunals will use them to go beyond a purely organisational agenda and indicate to the parties issues on which it would like the parties to focus at the hearing.[154] **6.167**

(c) Procedure at hearings

Individual arbitral tribunals approach the determination of the procedure to be followed at the hearing in different ways. Most have the common aim of keeping the duration of the hearing to a minimum so far as practicable, in order to assist the busy schedules of the arbitrators and parties and to reduce expense. **6.168**

Ideas as to what is a reasonable length of time for a hearing differ. Formerly,[155] in English court practice, hearings could last for many weeks, causing great inconvenience, expense, and exhaustion to all concerned.[156] By contrast, **6.169**

---

[152] ICSID Rules, r. 21.
[153] Only a few do: see WIPO Rules, Art. 47; CIETAC Rules, Art. 33(5).
[154] In this regard, see ICC Rules, Appendix IV, para. (g) ('Case Management Techniques').
[155] Under the English Civil Procedure Rules 1998, however, the length of the hearing is restricted according to the value or complexity of the case.
[156] The oral tradition in England owes its origin to the 'man who is no longer there'—that is, the juror. Jury trials led to two inescapable procedural features. First, once started, the oral proceedings had to be completed, because, once assembled, there was no real practical possibility of reconvening

arbitrators from the civil law countries tend to regard any hearing that takes more than three days as a long one. Although one hears of exceptions, the general tendency in international arbitration is towards shorter hearings, with greater reliance upon documentary evidence. This is a necessary step in the interests of economy of time and costs in cases that often involve arbitrators, lawyers, experts, company executives, and other participants operating away from their home bases.

6.170 The procedure at a hearing is not fixed in stone. As the UNCITRAL Notes on Organizing Arbitral Proceedings describe:

> Arbitration rules typically give broad latitude to the arbitral tribunal to determine the order of presentations at the hearings. Within that latitude, practices differ, for example, as to whether opening or closing statements are heard and their level of detail; the sequence in which the claimant and the respondent present their opening statements, arguments, witnesses and other evidence; and whether the respondent or the claimant has the last word. In view of such differences, or when no arbitration rules apply, it may foster efficiency of the proceedings if the arbitral tribunal clarifies to the parties, in advance of the hearings, the manner in which it will conduct the hearings, at least in broad lines.[157]

6.171 Against the backdrop of procedural freedom, a usual practice (or practices) has emerged in international arbitration that is described next.

(i) Opening statements

6.172 The usual practice in international arbitration, given the necessary time limits, is to allocate to each side only a limited opening statement, in which the advocates assume that the arbitrators have a full knowledge of the written submissions and evidence that is already on the record. This is followed by the main event: the oral testimony of the witnesses for each party. An English international arbitrator put it thus:

> Finally, since the arbitrators are likely to be busy professional people and often from different countries, the oral hearings will usually be remarkably short by English standards. Their main purpose is to hear the cross-examination of the witnesses, bracketed by short opening and closing remarks from both sides, which are often supplemented by written post-hearing submissions.[158]

(ii) Examination of witnesses

6.173 Although the examination of witnesses owes much to the common law tradition, it has become a standard feature of evidential hearings in international arbitration.

---

the same jury many weeks, or even months, later. Secondly, although jurors had to be property owners, there was no guarantee that they were literate; hence the need for all of the documents to be read aloud at the hearing.

[157] UNCITRAL Notes on Organising Arbitral Proceedings, para. 80.
[158] Kerr, 'Concord and conflict in international arbitration' (1997) 13 Arb Intl 121, at 126–127.

F. Hearings

For this reason, witness preparation has become a significant part of hearing preparation for parties involved in international arbitration and cross-examination has become a key arbitration counsel skill in the conduct of a hearing.

Of course, there are important limits in the preparation of witnesses. The role of counsel should be to assist witnesses 'in developing the confidence and clarity of thought required to testify truthfully and effectively based upon their own knowledge or recollection of the facts'.[159] Counsel should not be instructing witnesses to change their evidence. In this regard, the IBA Guidelines on Party Representation contain advice as to the appropriate limits of such preparation, providing that contact between counsel and witnesses should not 'alter the genuiness of the Witness or Expert evidence, which should always reflect the Witness's own account of relevant facts, events or circumstances'.[160] It should be borne in mind that being examined in the 'witness box' is, for most witnesses, an unfamiliar and intimidating experience.[161] Once the hearing begins, styles of witness examination vary and tribunals will typically allow counsel some leeway to test the evidence in the way that they prefer. As a general matter, however, tribunals tend not to appreciate overly aggressive or discourteous attacks by counsel. Since being examined in the 'witness box' is, for most witnesses, an intimidating experience, an aggressive comportment by counsel can easily backfire. Experienced arbitrators often discount severe or bullying cross-examinations on the basis that they evidence the self-importance of the cross-examiner rather than the lack of credibility of the witness.[162]

6.174

Article 8 of the IBA Rules confirms the current international standard previously adopted by many international arbitral tribunals:

6.175

[…]
2. The Arbitral Tribunal shall at all times have complete control over the Evidentiary Hearing. The Arbitral Tribunal may limit or exclude any question to, answer by or appearance of a witness, if it considers such question, answer or appearance to be irrelevant, immaterial, unreasonably burdensome, duplicative or otherwise covered by a reason for objection set forth in Article 9.2. Questions to a witness during direct and re-direct testimony may not be unreasonably leading.
3. With respect to oral testimony at an Evidentiary Hearing:

    (a) the Claimant shall ordinarily first present the testimony of its witnesses, followed by the Respondent presenting testimony of its witnesses;
    (b) following direct testimony, any other Party may question such witness, in an order to be determined by the Arbitral Tribunal. The Party who initially

---

[159] Roney, 'Effective witness preparation for international commercial arbitration: A practical guide for counsel' (2003) 20 J Intl Arb 429, at 430. This article provides a useful practical six-step guide for the preparation of witnesses.
[160] See IBA Guidelines on Party Representation, Guidelines 20–24, and the accompanying commentary.
[161] Ibid.
[162] Veeder, 'The 2001 Goff Lecture: The lawyer's duty to arbitrate in good faith' (2002) 18 Arb Intl 431, at 445.

presented the witness shall subsequently have the opportunity to ask additional questions on the matters raised in the other Parties' questioning;
(c) thereafter, the Claimant shall ordinarily first present the testimony of its Party-Appointed Experts, followed by the Respondent presenting the testimony of its Party-Appointed Experts. The Party who initially presented the Party-Appointed Expert shall subsequently have the opportunity to ask additional questions on the matters raised in the other Parties' questioning;
(d) the Arbitral Tribunal may question a Tribunal-Appointed Expert, and he or she may be questioned by the Parties or by any Party-Appointed Expert, on issues raised in the Tribunal-Appointed Expert Report, in the Parties' submissions or in the Expert Reports made by the Party-Appointed Experts;
(e) if the arbitration is organised into separate issues or phases (such as jurisdiction, preliminary determinations, liability and damages), the Parties may agree or the Arbitral Tribunal may order the scheduling of testimony separately on each issue or phase;
(f) the Arbitral Tribunal, upon request of a Party or on its own motion, may vary this order of proceeding, including the arrangement of testimony by particular issues or in such a manner that witnesses be questioned at the same time and in confrontation with each other (witness conferencing);
(g) the Arbitral Tribunal may ask questions to a witness at any time.
4. A witness of fact providing testimony shall first affirm, in a manner determined appropriate by the Arbitral Tribunal, that he or she commits to tell the truth or, in the case of an expert witness, his or her genuine belief in the opinions to be expressed at the Evidentiary Hearing. If the witness has submitted a Witness Statement or an Expert Report, the witness shall confirm it. The Parties may agree or the Arbitral Tribunal may order that the Witness Statement or Expert Report shall serve as that witness's direct testimony.
5. Subject to the provisions of Article 9.2, the Arbitral Tribunal may request any person to give oral or written evidence on any issue that the Arbitral Tribunal considers to be relevant to the case and material to its outcome. Any witness called and questioned by the Arbitral Tribunal may also be questioned by the Parties.

6.176 In the courts of common law countries, elaborate rules of evidence are still deployed even though they were designed for use in jury trials, which (other than in the United States) are largely used only in criminal cases. Such rules of evidence are not necessary in the courts of civil law countries because, in general, fact-finding is the responsibility of the judge based on his or her own enquiries and collection of the evidence. In any event, the civil procedure rules applicable in national courts do not apply to international arbitrations unless the parties agree otherwise, or the local law at the seat of arbitration provides that they do apply to international arbitrations held in that country as the juridical seat.

6.177 Fact witnesses are usually first 'examined' by counsel for the party presenting that witness, then 'cross-examined' by counsel for the other party, then 're-examined' by the first counsel, if necessary. Additional cross-examination may be introduced,

F. Hearings

with permission of the arbitral tribunal, where the witness has given new 'direct' testimony during the re-examination.[163]

6.178 Arbitral tribunals may sustain objections to direct or redirect examination questions based on characterising them as 'leading', or 'closed' (that is, questions that prompt the answer that the examining counsel wishes to obtain).[164] This is not because there is a binding evidential rule against putting such questions in international arbitration, but because the value of a witness's testimony is reduced if it is given pursuant to a question that has suggested the answer. This constraint does not apply to cross-examining counsel, who may ask any type of question as long as it is fair and relevant to the issues in dispute.

6.179 Witnesses are sometimes excluded, or 'sequestered', until they have given their testimony, although this practice is often dispensed with, particularly if a witness also happens to be a party representative. Much depends on whether or not a party is likely to gain an unfair advantage by having a particular witness present while the corresponding witness presented by the opposing party gives evidence. Fact witnesses are not allowed to discuss the case with any member of the 'team', whether lawyers or other witnesses presented by the same party, during overnight or refreshment breaks whilst they are under examination. This is an obvious way of ensuring that the witness is not 'coached' on how to answer questions during an examination or re-examination ('redirect'). Sometimes, they are permitted to eat meals together, or drink coffee, on the understanding that the case will not be discussed in his presence.

(iii) 'Witness conferencing'

6.180 An alternative to traditional cross-examination is to put two or more witnesses together to answer questions from the tribunal. This technique, which was described in the 1999 edition of the IBA Rules as 'witness confrontation', is now better known as 'witness conferencing'. Where fact witnesses are concerned, it is a somewhat adventurous path for an arbitral tribunal to take. But, used together with traditional cross-examination, it may provide an effective way of identifying areas of agreement and disagreement between witnesses. It also offers an opportunity for an immediate and direct comparison between the witness's earlier testimony, both in writing and at the hearing.

6.181 In the context of expert witnesses, the practice of 'witness conferencing' is much better established. It can be a very effective way of highlighting the points of agreement and disagreement between the experts, and it often leads if not to agreement, then at least to a narrowing of the points of difference—that is, the conflicting expert testimony between which the arbitral tribunal may have difficulty deciding.[165]

---

[163] Although witnesses 'shall' appear in person, the tribunal may permit a witness to provide testimony by 'videoconference or similar technology': IBA Rules, Art. 8(1).
[164] See IBA Rules, Art. 8(2).
[165] See Peter above.

6.182 Where a bridge has collapsed into a river, for example, a fact witness will testify as to what he or she saw and in what way the bridge fell, while the expert witness will testify as to what, in his or her opinion, caused the bridge to collapse. Was it defective design, or defective workmanship or materials? Where the parties' respective experts disagree, after submitting lengthy and persuasive expert reports, how is the arbitral tribunal to decide which explanation is more persuasive?

6.183 The role of experts in this context is to assist, educate, and advise the arbitral tribunal, in a fair and impartial manner, in specialist fields (such as technical, forensic accountancy, or legal) relevant to specific issues in dispute between the parties in which (some of) the arbitrators do not themselves have relevant expertise. The result is that arbitral tribunals find themselves faced with deciding between the opinions of opposing experts who have provided diametrically opposite opinions to questions such as, 'why did the bridge fall down?',[166] with little or no unbiased expert advice to guide them.

6.184 In an effort to find a practical solution, a number of experienced international arbitrators[167] developed 'expert conferencing' techniques instead of, or (more typically) in addition to, traditional cross-examination. In this kind of procedure, either before or (more commonly) after the experts have drafted their written expert reports, the experts are required to meet and draw up lists of (a) matters on which they agree, and (b) matters on which they do not agree, and the reasons for their disagreement.[168]

6.185 Based on list (b), the arbitral tribunal prepares an agenda designed to encompass the matters on which the experts are not agreed, and presents it to the parties and their advocates in advance of the hearing. Then, after all of the fact witnesses from both sides have been heard and often after the experts have been subject to individual cross-examination, the independent experts retained by the opposing parties come before the arbitral tribunal, seated alongside each other at the witness table.[169]

6.186 The chairman of the arbitral tribunal then takes the experts through the agenda, item by item. The experts are requested to explain in their own words the basis for reaching the opinions set out in their written reports and to answer each other's main points. They may also be encouraged to debate these points directly with each other if the arbitral tribunal considers that this would be useful.

---

[166] One side's expert says, with great conviction, 'faulty design of the bridge'; equally convincingly, the other side's expert says, 'defective materials used in construction of the bridge'. Cross-examination of experts by counsel is considered by many international arbitrators to be an inadequate tool to help them to make a determination between the opposing views of such experts.

[167] Notably Peter, 'Witness conferencing' (2002) 18 Arb Intl 47.

[168] IBA Rules, Art. 5(4). See also the CIArb Protocol for the Use of Party-Appointed Expert Witnesses in International Arbitration, Arts 6 and 7(2).

[169] IBA Rules, Art. 8(3)(f).

F. Hearings

(iv) Closing submissions

6.187 As with opening statements, it is relatively rare in modern international arbitration for lengthy oral submissions to be made after the witness testimony has been heard. There are two reasons for this. The first relates to time and cost. It has been noted already that the most expensive phase of an international arbitration is the time during which all of the players must be gathered in a city that will be foreign to most of them. The accommodation costs are high, but these are dwarfed by the 'time costs' of the parties: the tribunal, the parties' representatives, their counsel, and the witnesses. The second reason is that it can be challenging, alongside intensive witness examination, for counsel to review quickly and evaluate the transcripts obtained throughout the hearing, and to craft a closing statement that will deal adequately with the tribunal's concerns.

6.188 It is more usual, in modern international arbitrations, for the closing submissions to be in writing, in the form of post-hearing briefs, delivered after the parties have had the opportunity to review (and, where necessary, correct) the transcripts, within a time for delivery to be agreed between the parties or fixed by the arbitral tribunal. These documents will contain footnote references to the transcripts of the evidence and are designed to facilitate the drafting of the award.

6.189 However, this does not exclude the possibility of counsel being permitted to present some form of oral closing statement after the witness testimony has been heard, if they prefer, or to answer questions from the arbitral tribunal.

(v) Who has the last word?

6.190 In common law practice, it is the claimant (or 'plaintiff', in some jurisdictions) in a national court that is given the 'last word', on the basis that the claimant bears the burden of proof. In international arbitrations, however, this practice is rarely followed, since arbitrators tend to feel, instinctively, that due process is generally served only if the respondent has the privilege of having the last word to balance the claimant's privilege of going first. Furthermore, the 'burden of proof' point is not wholly valid, because, in most international arbitrations, the burden falls on each party to prove the facts on which it relies.

(d) Default hearings

6.191 An arbitral tribunal may, and indeed should, proceed *ex parte* if one of the parties (almost invariably the respondent) refuses or fails to appear. In such cases, the arbitral tribunal should proceed with the hearing and issue its award, making sure that the precise circumstances in which the proceedings have taken place are specified in the award itself.[170]

---

[170] For a discussion of practice under various arbitration rules and national laws, see van den Berg, 'Preventing delay and disruption of arbitration' (1990) 5 ICCA Congress Series 17. See also

6.192 This is necessary because it is likely that a party who boycotts an international arbitration intends to resist enforcement of any award ultimately rendered. Since it is a legitimate ground for refusal of recognition or enforcement of an award, whether under the New York Convention or otherwise, that a party has not had a reasonable opportunity to present its case, it is desirable that the award should itself show, on its face, the circumstances in which the respondent did not participate. Two main problems commonly arise in relation to such *ex parte* hearings: the first is what constitutes a 'refusal' to participate; the second is how the arbitral tribunal should proceed in such circumstances.

(i) Refusal to participate

6.193 In some circumstances, the situation is clear. This was so in the three Libyan oil nationalisation cases[171] in which the Libyan government stated at the outset that it refused to take any part in the proceedings, on the grounds that the arbitral tribunals, in each case, had no jurisdiction. It will also be clear if a respondent expressly refuses to reply to correspondence from the arbitral tribunal, or to comply with any procedural directions as to the submission of written pleadings, and so forth.

6.194 There are two other circumstances in which an arbitral tribunal should proceed *ex parte*, but these are more difficult to identify. The first is where a party does not notify its unwillingness to participate, but creates a delay so unreasonable that the arbitral tribunal (on the application of the other party) would be justified if it were to treat the party in default as having abandoned its right to present its case. It is impossible to specify precisely when this point arises in any given proceedings and an arbitral tribunal must use its best judgment, balancing the various factors involved. However, the arbitral tribunal should bear in mind that it may not be doing the claimant any favours if it accedes too early to an application to proceed *ex parte*, because the award may become the subject of a successful challenge when the claimant seeks to enforce it.[172]

6.195 The second situation is where a party so disrupts the hearing that it becomes impossible to conduct it in an orderly manner. Experience of such a situation is hard to find, but theoretically it could happen; the arbitral tribunal would then need to treat the defaulting party's conduct as being equivalent to a refusal to participate.

ICSID Rules, r. 42; UNICTRAL Rules, Art. 30; Swiss Rules, Art. 28; SCC Rules, Art. 30; ICDR Rules, Art. 23; AAA Rules, Art. 31; HKIAC Rules, Art. 26.

[171] The *Texaco*, *BP*, and *Liamco* arbitrations; see Chapter 3, paragraphs 3.140*ff*.

[172] It is rare, but not unknown, for the respondent to want the proceedings to go ahead, when the claimant has failed to take them forward, in order to obtain an award that will put an end to the claim. In such a case, similar considerations will apply: the respondent will require a solid award, capable of being *recognised* by the courts, if this becomes necessary.

G. Proceedings after the Hearing

(ii) Procedure in default hearings

Unlike a court, an arbitral tribunal has no authority to issue an award akin to a default judgment. Its task is to make a determination of the disputes submitted to it. Accordingly, even if a party fails to present its case, the arbitral tribunal must consider the merits and make a determination of the substance of the dispute. Where it is clear from the beginning that a party (usually the respondent) does not propose to take part, the arbitral tribunal usually ensures that all notifications of hearings and correspondence continue to be sent to the defaulting party, and that all of the participating party's submissions and evidence are placed before the defaulting party in written form. The tribunal will then be justified in holding only a brief hearing, on an *ex parte* basis, to review the claims and raise any questions. **6.196**

A reliable guideline as to how such a proceeding should take place is that the party who is taking part must prove its case to the satisfaction of the arbitral tribunal. The arbitral tribunal has no duty to act as advocate for a party who has elected not to appear, but it must examine the merits of the arguments of law and fact put to it by the participating party, so as to satisfy itself that these are well founded. It must then make a reasoned determination of the issues. **6.197**

The practice of arbitral tribunals varies as regards hearings in such situations. Much will depend on the form in which the written stages of the arbitration have taken place. If the written stages have been comprehensive, the arbitral tribunal may feel justified in holding a brief and purely formal hearing prior to issuing its award. If, on the other hand, the written pleadings have been skeletal, formal documents in which only the issues have been defined and no documentary or witness evidence has been submitted in writing, the arbitral tribunal would probably consider it necessary to hear oral evidence before being satisfied that the participating party has discharged the burden of proof in relation to its claims (or defences). **6.198**

The Model Law contains a provision empowering the arbitral tribunal to continue the proceedings and to make an award where a party fails to comply with the requirements of the procedure agreed by the parties or established by the arbitral tribunal.[173] Similar provisions are to be found in modern laws of arbitration, even if they are not directly based on the Model Law. **6.199**

G. Proceedings after the Hearing

(a) Introduction

In theory, the hearing should conclude the participation of the parties in the arbitration. Indeed, it is good practice for the arbitral tribunal to declare the evidentiary **6.200**

---

[173] Model Law, Art. 25.

record closed.[174] This will not prevent the parties, if so agreed by the tribunal, from submitting post-hearing briefs, but it will prevent them from submitting new unsolicited material after the hearing, which will require further procedural orders to enable the other party to reply.

(b) Post-hearing briefs

6.201 It is increasingly common for the parties to submit post-hearing briefs, often of limited length, summarising the main points that have emerged in evidence and argument. The emergence of such a practice may be seen as a direct corollary of the practice of limiting the length of the hearing—and, indeed, of imposing time constraints on the parties at the hearing.[175]

6.202 Thus the most frequently adopted form of proceedings after the closure of the hearings is an exchange of post-hearing briefs. Such a final written opportunity to make submissions is particularly useful where the arbitral tribunal has raised questions during the closing arguments and the parties' counsel wish to have time to undertake research before giving their answers. One of the authors experienced such a situation at a hearing, when the question of whether or not the United Nations Convention on Contracts for the International Sale of Goods 1980 (Vienna Sales Convention) applied to the transaction in question was raised during the closing arguments. This was not a matter upon which the parties' counsel could reasonably be expected to respond 'off the cuff' and, accordingly, the parties were directed to submit post-hearing memoranda on the question.[176]

(c) Introduction of new evidence

6.203 The post-hearing briefs may not always be the end of the proceedings. First, fresh evidence may come to light after the hearing, but before the arbitral tribunal has issued its award. In these circumstances, the arbitral tribunal has discretion to reopen the proceedings at the request of the party wishing to present the new evidence.[177] Clearly, it should refuse to do so where the fresh evidence is not needed for the deliberations, or if the new material appears to be a spurious attempt to delay the proceedings. But, in general, arbitral tribunals prefer to determine a dispute with the benefit of all of the relevant evidence in their possession. If the fresh evidence turns out to be valueless, or without merit, the opposing party may be compensated by the arbitral tribunal in relation to the additional costs incurred, and by an award of interest where this is appropriate.

---

[174] Some sets of institutional rules require it: e.g., ICC Rules, Art. 27; DIAC Rules, Art. 34; SIAC Rules, Art. 28(1).
[175] See section on 'Hearings' above.
[176] AAA Case No. 13T1810031097.
[177] See, e.g., UNCITRAL Rules, Art. 31(2); Swiss Rules, Art. 34; VIAC Rules, Art. 32; SIAC Rules, Art. 28(1).

G. *Proceedings after the Hearing*

6.204 The course that should be adopted by the arbitral tribunal depends on the circumstances of each case and the nature of the material to which a response must be made. However, arbitral tribunals normally (and rightly) try to ensure that additional hearings do not take place unless they are really necessary; they generally permit one party to put in further written evidence and submissions only if the other has presented fresh material at, or subsequent to, the hearing.

7

ROLE OF NATIONAL COURTS DURING THE PROCEEDINGS

A. Introduction	7.01	C. During the Arbitral Proceedings	7.13
B. At the Beginning of the Arbitration	7.09	D. At the End of the Arbitration	7.62
		E. Conclusion	7.63

A. Introduction

The relationship between national courts and arbitral tribunals swings between forced cohabitation and true partnership. Arbitration is dependent on the underlying support of the courts, which alone have the power to rescue the system when one party seeks to sabotage it. As a former senior English judge has stated: **7.01**

> [T]here is plainly a tension here. On the one hand the concept of arbitration as a consensual process reinforced by the ideas of transnationalism leans against the involvement of the mechanisms of state through the medium of a municipal court. On the other side there is the plain fact, palatable or not, that it is only a Court possessing coercive powers which could rescue the arbitration if it is in danger of foundering.[1]

A party who agrees to refer disputes to arbitration chooses a private system of justice and this in itself raises issues of public policy. There are limits upon this freedom of choice. Most states restrict the possibility of arbitration to disputes that the state itself regards as being legally capable of being settled by arbitration—that is, to disputes that are, because of their subject matter, 'arbitrable' in the sense discussed elsewhere in this volume.[2] However, as has been seen, the concept of what is and what is not 'arbitrable' differs from one country to another, and even across time.[3] The state prescribes the boundaries of arbitration and enforces these **7.02**

---

[1] *Coppée Levalin NV v Ken-Ren Fertilisers and Chemicals* [1994] 2 Lloyd's Rep 109 (HL), at 116 *per* Lord Mustill.
[2] See Chapter 2, paragraphs 2.29*ff*.
[3] See, e.g., the changed attitude of the US courts towards the arbitration of antitrust, securities, or patent issues.

boundaries through its courts. The state also determines other limitations upon the arbitral process: whether, for instance, arbitrators have the power to compel the attendance of witnesses or the disclosure of documents, and, more importantly, whether or not any appeal to the national court is possible, and if so, how, when, and upon what terms.[4]

7.03 To the extent that the relationship between national courts and arbitral tribunals is said to be one of 'partnership',[5] it is not a partnership of equals. Arbitration may depend upon the agreement of the parties, but it is also a system built on law, which relies upon that law to make it effective both nationally and internationally. National courts could exist without arbitration, but arbitration could not exist without the courts. The real issue is to define the point at which this reliance of arbitration on the national courts begins and that at which it ends.

(a) Increasing independence of arbitration

7.04 As noted in Chapter 1, arbitration is now the principal method of resolving international disputes involving states, individuals, and corporations. This reality has led the arbitral process to distance itself, where possible, from the risk of domestic judicial parochialism. Modern international arbitration has consequently achieved a considerable degree of independence from national courts. For example, the arbitration clause in an international contract is generally recognised as being an independent agreement, which survives any termination of the contract in which it is contained.[6] The parties themselves are generally free to determine how their disputes are to be resolved, subject only to such safeguards as may be considered necessary as a matter of public policy; arbitrators are free to decide on their own jurisdiction, subject only to differing degrees of review by the national court of the seat of the arbitration, or place of recognition or enforcement. The parties are free to choose which system of law will govern the dispute between them—and, indeed, may even elect general principles, such as the UNIDROIT Principles of International Commercial Contracts.[7] Finally, judicial control of errors of law in international arbitration has been virtually abandoned, leaving courts the limited role of policing procedural due process, such as the obligation of the tribunal to give each party a fair hearing.

---

[4] See Chapter 10.
[5] See, e.g., Goldman, *The Complementary Role of Judges and Arbitrators*, ICC Publication No. 412 (ICC, 1984), p. 259.
[6] See the discussion of separability in Chapter 2, paragraphs 2.101*ff*.
[7] One of the largest arbitrated disputes in history was decided under the UNIDROIT Principles of International Commercial Contracts: see Bonell, 'A "global" arbitration decided on the basis of the UNIDROIT Principles' (2001) 17 Arb Intl 249. See also Bonell, *An International Restatement of Contract Law: The UNIDROIT Principles of International Commercial Contracts* (Brill, 2005), pp. 273–274. For a detailed analysis, see Vogenauer and Kleinheisterkamp (eds) *Commentary on the UNIDROIT Principles of International Commercial Contracts (PICC)* (Oxford University Press, 2009).

A. Introduction

Nonetheless, the arbitral process remains subject to the arbitration law of the country in which it has its juridical seat and that of the country, or countries, in which a winning party may seek to recognise or enforce the eventual award. In other words, the involvement of national courts in the international arbitration process remains essential to its effectiveness. Indeed, experiments that some countries have made in unbounded 'party autonomy' ultimately resulted in a backlash in favour of a controlling role for the courts. For example, Belgium set out to attract international arbitrations by denying any right of review for the local courts only to discover that such 'anational' arbitration dissuaded potential users and reintroduced supervisory control unless both parties agreed expressly to exclude it.[8] Equally, the ever-increasing trend to seek interim measures has placed a renewed focus on the respective roles of the arbitral tribunal and the courts.

7.05

(b) Limitations on independence

UNCITRAL Model Law seeks to exclude the involvement of the courts as far as possible. Article 5 states: 'In matters governed by this Law, no court shall intervene except where so provided in this Law.' At first sight, this is a striking declaration of independence. Yet the Model Law does not seek to exclude the participation of what it calls the 'competent court'[9] in carrying out 'certain functions of arbitration assistance and supervision'. On closer examination of the Model Law itself, it becomes apparent that, of its thirty-six Articles, no fewer than ten recognise a possible role for the 'competent court'. For example, Article 11 acknowledges that the help of the competent court may be necessary to constitute the arbitral tribunal;[10] Article 13 acknowledges that the competent court may have to decide upon a challenge to an arbitrator if there are justifiable doubts as to that arbitrator's impartiality or independence;[11] Article 16 acknowledges that a party to an international arbitration may apply to the competent court to review the decision of the arbitral tribunal on jurisdiction—in which case, it is the decision of that court (and not the decision of the arbitral tribunal) that is

7.06

---

[8] See Chapter 10, paragraph 10.69.
[9] The competent court is defined in Model Law, Art. 6, as the court or other authority specified by each state as being competent to perform the functions entrusted to it by the Model Law.
[10] See *Montpelier Reinsurance Ltd v Manufacturers Property & Casualty Ltd* [2008] SC (Bda) 27 Com (24 April 2008), at [7]:

> ...Article 11(4) of the Model Law requires the Court to help constitute an arbitration panel wherever it is clear that the agreed appointment procedures have broken down. The Court's primary statutory duty is to ensure that the parties can resolve their dispute before an independent and impartial arbitral tribunal without delay. This overriding policy consideration trumps deference to the particular contractual procedure which appears to have broken down....

[11] See *Progressive Career Academy Pvt. Ltd v FIIT JEE Ltd* (2011) 5 RAJ 7 Delhi, at [20]: 'The UNCITRAL Model Law, in Article 13(3), explicitly enables the party challenging the decision of the Arbitral Tribunal to approach the Court on the subject of bias or impartiality of the Arbitral Tribunal.'

final and binding.[12] The Model Law also acknowledges that the assistance of the competent court may be necessary in the taking of evidence,[13] and that, in any challenge to the arbitral award, or to its recognition and enforcement, the judgment of the competent court will be decisive.[14]

(c) 'A relay race'

7.07 If there is a partnership between arbitrators and the national courts, it is one in which each has a different role to play at different times. The relationship between courts and arbitrators has been compared by a former senior English judge, Lord Mustill, to a relay race:

> Ideally, the handling of arbitral disputes should resemble a relay race. In the initial stages, before the arbitrators are seized of the dispute, the baton is in the grasp of the court; for at that stage there is no other organisation which could take steps to prevent the arbitration agreement from being ineffectual. When the arbitrators take charge they take over the baton and retain it until they have made an award. At this point, having no longer a function to fulfil, the arbitrators hand back the baton so that the court can in case of need lend its coercive powers to the enforcement of the award.[15]

In principle, there should be no disputes as to where the frontier between the public world of the courts and the private world of arbitration lies. At the beginning of an arbitration, national courts (not the arbitrators) have the task of enforcing the agreement to arbitrate if one of the parties should seek to avoid it. At the end of the arbitral process, national courts (not the arbitrators) must also enforce the arbitral award if the losing party is not prepared to comply with it voluntarily. During the arbitral process, the arbitrators (not the courts) must take charge of

---

[12] *PT Tugu Pratama Indonesia v Magma Nusantara Ltd* [2003] SGHC 204, at [12]:

> The Model Law, when it comes to questions relating to the jurisdiction of the arbitral tribunal, gives a party who is questioning such jurisdiction two opportunities to challenge the jurisdiction. The first is before the appointed arbitral tribunal itself. The second opportunity, which can only be taken after the first challenge before the tribunal has failed in that the tribunal has given a ruling that it has jurisdiction, is an application to the High Court to decide on the matter. This is the right given to parties to an arbitration by Art 16(3) of the Model Law and this is the right that PT Tugu invoked by filing this application.

[13] Model Law, Art. 27. For an application of this rule, see, e.g., *Jardine Lloyd Thompson Canada Inc. v SJO Catlin* [2006] ABCA 18, at [25]:

> The parties to the arbitration can craft an arbitration agreement to suit their own purposes but they cannot, without more, exercise powers over third persons. The Legislature has seen fit, however, to empower tribunals to request the court's assistance in taking evidence. It is common ground, and properly so, that Article 27 can be used to obtain the evidence of third persons at the arbitration hearing....

[14] See Model Law, Arts 34–36.

[15] Lord Mustill, 'Comments and conclusions', in International Chamber of Commerce (ICC) (ed.) *Conservatory Provisional Measures in International Arbitration: 9th Joint Colloquium* (ICC, 1993), p. 118.

B. At the Beginning of the Arbitration

the proceedings, set time limits, organise meetings and hearings, issue procedural directions, consider the arguments of fact and law put forward by, or on behalf of, the parties, and make their award.

Unfortunately, the respective domains of arbitral tribunals and national courts may not be so clearly distinguished. As Lord Mustill went on to observe: **7.08**

> In real life the position is not so clear-cut. Very few commentators would now assert that the legitimate functions of the Court entirely cease when the arbitrators receive the file, and conversely very few would doubt that there is a point at which the Court takes on a purely subordinate role. But when does this happen? And what is the position at the further end of the process? Does the Court retake the baton only if and when invited to enforce the award, or does it have functions to be exercised at an earlier stage, if something has gone wrong with the arbitration, by setting aside the award or intervening in some other way?[16]

B. At the Beginning of the Arbitration

It is possible to identify at least three situations in which the intervention of the court may be necessary at the beginning of the arbitral process: **7.09**

- the enforcement of the arbitration agreement;
- the establishment of the tribunal; and
- challenges to jurisdiction.

(a) Enforcing the arbitration agreement

A party to an arbitration agreement might decide to issue proceedings in a court of law, rather than to take the dispute to arbitration. In the unlikely situation of the respondent's acquiescence without reservation, the arbitration agreement will have been deemed waived and the court action will proceed. However, having entered into an arbitration agreement, the respondent usually wishes to insist on its right to have the dispute decided by arbitrators rather than by a national court. For their part, most courts are obliged to enforce the agreement to arbitrate pursuant to Article II of the New York Convention,[17] by refusing to accept such proceedings in court and by referring the parties instead to arbitration. This is also reflected in the Model Law, Article 8 of which provides: **7.10**

> (1) A court before which an action is brought in a matter which is the subject of an arbitration agreement shall, if a party so requests not later than when

---

[16] Ibid.
[17] New York Convention, Art. II(3), states:

> The court of a Contracting State, when seized of an action in a matter in respect of which the parties have made an agreement within the meaning of this article, shall, at the request of one of the parties, refer the parties to arbitration, unless it finds that the said agreement is null and void, inoperative or incapable of being performed.

submitting his first statement on the substance of the dispute, refer the parties to arbitration unless it finds that the agreement is null and void, inoperative or incapable of being performed.

(2) Where an action referred to in paragraph (1) of this article has been brought, arbitral proceedings may nevertheless be commenced or continued, and an award may be made, while the issue is pending before the court.

(b) Establishing the arbitral tribunal

7.11 If the parties have failed to make adequate provision for the constitution of an arbitral tribunal and if there are no applicable institutional or other rules (such as the UNCITRAL Rules), the intervention of a national court may be required to appoint the chairperson or the respondent's arbitrator.[18] In the absence of any such rules, the national court must also intervene to decide any challenge to the independence or impartiality of an arbitrator.[19]

(c) Challenges to jurisdiction

7.12 If any issue is raised as to the jurisdiction of the arbitral tribunal, it will generally (although not always) be made at the beginning of the arbitration. If the objection is successful, the arbitration will be terminated. The issue of challenge to jurisdiction is one of growing importance and is dealt with in Chapter 5. The only point that should be made here, in the context of the relationship between national courts and arbitral tribunals, is that it is recognised in the Model Law (and in many national systems of law) that whilst any challenge to the jurisdiction of an arbitral tribunal may be dealt with *initially* by the tribunal itself, the final decision on jurisdiction rests with the relevant national court.[20] This is either the court at the seat of the arbitration, or the court of the state(s) in which recognition and enforcement of the arbitral award is sought.

C. During the Arbitral Proceedings

7.13 What happens in the most important phase of an arbitration, when the arbitrators begin their task? The baton has been passed to them. Is there any need for national courts to be involved in the arbitral process? The answer in almost every case is 'no'. Once an arbitral tribunal has been constituted, most arbitrations are conducted without any need to refer to a national court, even if one of the parties fails or refuses to take part in the proceedings. There may be times, however, at which the involvement of a national court is necessary in order to ensure the proper conduct of the arbitration. It may become necessary, for instance, to ask the competent

---

[18] Model Law, Art. 11.
[19] Ibid., Art. 13(3).
[20] Ibid., Art. 16(3).

C. During the Arbitral Proceedings

court to assist in taking evidence, or to make an order for the preservation of property that is the subject of the dispute, or to take some other interim measure of protection. The question that then arises is whether a national court may (or indeed should) become involved in a dispute that is subject to arbitration, and if so, how far this involvement should extend.

(a) Interim measures—powers of the arbitral tribunal

7.14 During the course of an arbitration, it may be necessary for the arbitral tribunal or a national court to issue orders intended to preserve evidence, to protect assets, or in some other way to maintain the status quo pending the outcome of the arbitration. Such orders take different forms and go under different names. In the Model Law[21] and in the UNCITRAL Rules,[22] they are known as 'interim measures'. In the English version of the Arbitration Rules of the International Chamber of Commerce (ICC), they are known as 'interim or conservatory measures', and in the French version, as *'mesures conservatoires ou provisoires'*.[23] In the Swiss law governing international arbitration, they are referred to as 'provisional or conservatory measures'.[24] Whatever their designation, however, they are intended in principle to operate as holding orders and apply only pending the issue of a final arbitral award.

7.15 In many cases in which interim measures of protection are required, the arbitral tribunal itself has the power to issue them, as considered in Chapter 5. In these circumstances, it may be asked why, if the arbitral tribunal itself has the power to issue interim measures, the help or intervention of a national court might be necessary? There are, however, five situations in which the tribunal's powers may be insufficient and which thus lead a party favouring recourse to a national court.

(i) No powers

7.16 First, the arbitral tribunal *may not have* the necessary powers. This is usually a result of antique domestic legislation harking back to a time when the power to grant such measures was considered to be a prerogative of the national courts for public policy reasons. Article 753 of the Argentine Code of Civil Procedure, for example, states: 'Arbitrators shall not issue compulsory or enforcement measures, these shall be requested to the judge who shall give the aid of his jurisdiction for the faster and more effective operation of the arbitral process.' Such limitations are nevertheless very rare in practice.

---

[21] Ibid., Art. 17.
[22] UNCITRAL Rules, Art. 26.
[23] ICC Arbitration Rules, Art. 28. Similarly, London Court of International Arbitration (LCIA) Rules, Art. 25, refers to 'interim and conservatory measures'.
[24] Swiss Private International Law Act 1987 (Swiss PIL), Ch. 12, s. 183.

(ii) Inability to act prior to the formation of the tribunal

7.17 Secondly, the arbitral tribunal cannot issue interim measures until the tribunal itself has been established.[25] The point may seem obvious, yet it is frequently overlooked until a crisis arises. It takes time to establish an arbitral tribunal and, during that time, vital evidence or assets may disappear. National courts may be expected to deal with such urgent matters. Most international institutional rules have sought to address this lacuna in their most recent revisions through the appointment of so-called emergency arbitrators. For example, the Rules of the Netherlands Arbitration Institute (NAI) provide for the NAI's prompt appointment of a single arbitrator to resolve interim measure issues prior to the constitution of the formal tribunal (summary arbitral proceedings).[26] Once the measures have been issued, that arbitrator may take no further role in the proceedings. Other arbitration institutions such as the ICC, Stockholm Chamber of Commerce (SCC), Singapore International Arbitration Centre (SIAC), International Centre for Dispute Resolution (ICDR), and London Court of International Arbitration (LCIA) have adopted similar provisions in their most recent arbitration rules making it possible for parties to obtain interim relief before the tribunal has been constituted, by allowing the appointment of 'emergency arbitrators'.[27] Following these developments in arbitration rules, legislation has also been implemented in certain jurisdictions to facilitate the enforcement of emergency relief orders. Notably, the Hong Kong Arbitration Ordinance of 2013 allows Hong Kong courts to enforce relief granted by emergency arbitrators whether the order is issued in Hong Kong or abroad.[28] However, where there is no specific provision for the enforcement of the orders of an emergency arbitrator, a party may still prefer to rely on the competent national court to ensure state-backed enforcement of an interim order.

(iii) An order can affect only the parties to the arbitration

7.18 The third factor in understanding why the assistance of a national court may be necessary is that the powers of an arbitral tribunal are generally limited to the parties to the arbitration. The Model Law makes it plain that an arbitral tribunal may order interim measures only against 'a party'.[29] A third-party order, for example, addressed to a bank holding deposits of a party would not be enforceable against the bank, and multiparty or multi-contract disputes may also pose similar problems, requiring national court assistance.

---

[25] Indeed, in the case of ICC arbitrations, interim measures cannot be issued by the tribunal until the file has been transmitted to it: see ICC Rules, Art. 28.
[26] NAI Rules, Art. 42(f).
[27] SCC Rules, Art. 32(4) and Appendix II, Art. 3; ICC Rules, Art. 29(1) and Appendix V, Art. 1(2); SIAC Rules, Art. 26.2, with proceedings governed by Sch. 1; HKIAC Rules, Art. 23(1) and Sch. 4, Art. 1; ICDR Rules, Art. 6; LCIA Rules, Art. 9B.
[28] Hong Kong Arbitration Ordinance of 2013, ss 22A and 22B.
[29] Model Law, Art. 17(2).

C. During the Arbitral Proceedings

(iv) Enforcement difficulties

Fourthly, interim measures ordered by an arbitral tribunal do not, by definition, finally resolve any point in dispute. An order or award of interim measures is therefore unlikely to satisfy the requirement of finality under the New York Convention, which may render it unenforceable internationally.[30] As a consequence, where there may be a need for international enforcement of the interim measure, parties should consider applying for such measures before the courts of the place of execution.

7.19

Notwithstanding this limitation, some states have sought to label certain interim measures ordered by tribunals as 'awards', at least as far as their own legislation is concerned. This is the case in Israel and Malaysia, which define 'award' to include an interim award,[31] or New Zealand,[32] which makes the provisions on enforcement of awards applicable to an interim measures order (unless the tribunal provides otherwise). Arbitral practice varies on this question, although the recent tendency appears to be in favour of tribunals making orders, rather than awards. In the context of an ICC arbitration, that may add considerably to the speed of the process, because an order, unlike an award, will not need to be scrutinised by the ICC Court before issue.[33]

7.20

(v) No ex parte application

Fifthly, a party may need to make an application *ex parte* (that is, without notice to the party against whom the measure is directed), for example to freeze a bank account of the other party to prevent the transfer of funds abroad. As discussed in Chapter 5, the revised UNCITRAL Model Law offers the possibility of limited *ex parte* applications to the arbitral tribunal.[34] However, it will take a considerable time before those changes are made to the actual arbitration laws in force in the most popular arbitration seats, and the rules of the leading institutions do not currently expressly envisage such a power for arbitrators.[35] As a consequence, in most cases in which *ex parte* relief is important, such as where there is a risk of dissipation of assets or of important evidence being destroyed, the courts are the only option.

7.21

---

[30] See, e.g., *Société Sardisud v Société Technip*, Paris Cour d'Appel, 1ere Ch. Civ., 25 March 1994, [1994] Rev Arb 391. The Supreme Court of Queensland refused to enforce an interlocutory injunction issued by an Indiana state court on the basis that it was not an 'arbitral award' within the meaning of the New York Convention: *Resort Condominiums Inc. v Bolwell* (1995) XX YBCA 628. See also *Hall Steel Co. v Metalloyd Ltd*. 492 F.Supp.2d 215, 217 (ED Mich. 2007): 'Whether enforcement of an arbitration award is sought under the FAA or the New York Convention, the courts are agreed that the award in question must be "final" in order to be eligible for judicial confirmation.'

[31] Israel Arbitration Law of 1968, s. 1; Malaysia Arbitration Act 2005, s. 2.

[32] New Zealand Arbitration Act 1996, Sch. 1, art. 17L.

[33] ICC Rules, Art. 33.

[34] Model Law, Art. 17B(1): 'Unless otherwise agreed by the parties, a party may, without notice to any other party, make a request for an interim measure together with an application for a preliminary order directing a party not to frustrate the purpose of the interim measure requested.'

[35] Jurisdictions that have adopted legislation based on the revised UNCITRAL Model Law allowing for *ex parte* preliminary orders include Australia, Colombia, Costa Rica, Hong Kong, Ireland, Lithuania, Panama, Peru, and Rwanda.

(b) Interim measures—powers of the competent court

7.22 For all of these reasons, it is important that the competent court should have the power to issue interim measures in support of the arbitral process. In situations of extreme urgency, in which third parties need to be involved or in which there is a strong possibility that a party will not voluntarily execute the tribunal's order, there may be little option but to identify the appropriate state court and make the application there. The measures requested may include the granting of injunctions to preserve the status quo or to prevent the disappearance of assets, the taking of evidence from witnesses, or the preservation of property or evidence.

7.23 Applying for interim measures before a court may give rise to at least two issues. First, if a party to an arbitration agreement makes an application for interim measures to the court rather than to the arbitral tribunal, will this be regarded as a breach of the agreement to arbitrate? Secondly, if the choice between seeking interim measures from the courts or from the arbitral tribunal is truly an open choice, should the application be made to the courts or to the arbitral tribunal?

(i) Incompatibility with the arbitration agreement?

7.24 The risk that resort to interim measures before a court might operate as a waiver of the arbitration agreement, or that any order so obtained might be dissolved in the face of a valid arbitration clause, appears to be consigned to history. Most arbitration rules are explicit in confirming that an application for interim relief from a court is not incompatible with an arbitration agreement. For example, Article 28(2) of the ICC Rules states clearly that:

> The application of a party to a judicial authority for such [interim or conservatory] measures or for the implementation of any such measures ordered by an arbitral tribunal shall not be deemed to be an infringement or a waiver of the arbitration agreement…

A similar provision is to be found in the UNCITRAL Rules, Article 26(9) of which provides that '[a] request for interim measures addressed by any party to a judicial authority shall not be deemed incompatible with the agreement to arbitrate, or as a waiver of that agreement'.[36] Article 9 of the Model Law also states categorically that: 'It is not incompatible with an arbitration agreement for a party to request, before or during arbitral proceedings, from a court an interim measure of protection and for a court to grant such measure.'

7.25 Nevertheless, where an application is made to a national court for interim measures, a judge may be reluctant to make a decision that risks prejudicing the outcome of the arbitration. As was stated in the English (then) House of Lords:

> There is always a tension when the court is asked to order, by way of interim relief in support of an arbitration, a remedy of the same kind as will ultimately be sought

---

[36] See also ICDR Rules, Art. 24(3); SCC Rules, Art. 32(5); ICC Rules, Art. 29(7); SIAC Rules, Art. 26(3); HKIAC Rules, Art. 23(9); LCIA Rules, Art. 9B, para. 9.12.

C. During the Arbitral Proceedings

from the arbitrators: between, on the one hand, the need for the court to make a tentative assessment of the merits in order to decide whether the plaintiff's claim is strong enough to merit protection, and on the other the duty of the court to respect the choice of tribunal which both parties have made, and not to take out of the hands of the arbitrators (or other decision makers) a power of decision which the parties have entrusted to them alone. In the present instance I consider that the latter consideration must prevail...If the court now itself orders an interlocutory mandatory injunction, there will be very little left for the arbitrators to decide.[37]

(ii) Should application be made to a national court or to the arbitrators?

7.26 As to the question of whether to seek interim relief from the relevant court or the arbitral tribunal, much depends on the relevant law and the nature of the relief sought. The relevant law may make it clear, for instance, that any application should be made first to the arbitral tribunal, and only then to the court of the seat of arbitration. This is the position taken by Swiss law, which empowers the arbitral tribunal to take 'provisional', or conservatory, measures (unless the parties otherwise agree), then states that if the party against whom the order is made fails to comply, the arbitral tribunal may request assistance from the competent court.[38]

7.27 English law is equally careful to spell out the position. It does so in three provisos to the court's 'powers exercisable in support of arbitral proceedings', including the preservation of evidence, the inspection of property, the granting of an interim injunction, and the appointment of a receiver. These three provisos are set out at section 44(3)–(5) of the Arbitration Act 1996:

(3) If the case is one of urgency, the court may, on the application of a party or proposed party to the arbitral proceedings, make such order as it thinks necessary for the purpose of preserving evidence or assets.
(4) If the case is not one of urgency, the court shall act only on the application of a party to the arbitral proceedings...made with the permission of the tribunal or with the agreement in writing of the other parties.
(5) In any case the court shall act only if or to the extent that the arbitral tribunal ...has no power or is unable for the time being to act effectively.

7.28 Where the position is not spelled out as clearly as this, the answer to the question of whether to seek interim relief from the court or from the arbitral tribunal is likely to depend upon the particular circumstances of each case. If, for example, a tribunal has not been constituted, the matter is one of urgency, and there is a concern

---

[37] *Channel Tunnel Group Ltd v Balfour Beatty Construction Ltd* [1993] AC 334, at 367–368. See also *Patel v Patel* [1999] All ER (D) 327 (CA).
[38] Swiss PIL, Ch. 12, s. 183(1) and (2). In France, in a 2012 decision, the Reims Cour d'Appel held that, after the tribunal has been constituted, applications for provisional or conservatory measures or measures relating to the taking of evidence can no longer be made to domestic courts: see *SA Clinique de Champagne v Enrico Ambrosini*, Reims Cour d'Appel, 1ere Ch. Civ., 3 July 2012, [2012] Rev Arb 681.

that an emergency arbitrator order may not be voluntarily executed,[39] the only possibility is to apply to the relevant national court for interim measures. At the same time, the party seeking such an order should take steps to advance the arbitration, so as to show that there is every intention of respecting the agreement to arbitrate. Where the arbitral tribunal *is* in existence, or appointing an emergency arbitrator is possible and likely to be effective, it is appropriate to apply first to that tribunal or emergency arbitrator for interim measures, unless international enforcement may be required.[40]

7.29 This is not simply a question of division of labour. Although an arbitral tribunal or an emergency arbitrator lacks the coercive powers of a court of law, and in spite of questions concerning the international enforceability of an order for interim measures, parties should not forget that any order is binding as between them. Furthermore, it is a brave (or foolish) party who deliberately chooses to ignore interim measures ordered by the tribunal charged with deciding the merits of its dispute. As one experienced commentator has asserted:

> Ultimately, of course, the arbitrators' greatest source of coercive power lies in their position as arbiters of the merits of the dispute between the parties. Parties seeking to appear before arbitrators as good citizens who have been wronged by their adversary would generally not wish to defy instructions given to them by those whom they wished to convince of the justice of their claims.[41]

7.30 There are other logistical problems inherent in applying to a court for interim measures. Often, the merits of the dispute will be under a foreign law, which the local court will be ill-prepared to consider at an interim stage; likewise, the language of the dispute and the contract may be different. Finally, the chosen court is likely to be at the place of execution of the order to avoid concerns as to enforceability. This may give rise to problems of bias if the measures sought are against a state entity or a local entity in favour of a foreign corporation.[42]

7.31 The nature of the relief sought is also likely to have an important bearing on the question of whether to go to a national court or to the arbitral tribunal. Interim measures of relief take many forms and differ from state to state. Moreover, new

---

[39] See paragraph 7.17.
[40] This appears to be the thinking behind the ICC Arbitration Rules, Art. 28(2) of which provides that the parties may apply to any competent judicial authority either '[b]efore the file is transmitted to the arbitral tribunal' (that is, before the arbitral tribunal is in a position to make an order), or 'in appropriate circumstances even thereafter'.
[41] Schwartz, 'The practices and experience of the ICC Court', in ICC (ed.) *Conservatory and Provisional Measures in International Arbitration*, ICC Publication No. 519 (ICC, 1993), p. 59.
[42] In an ICC arbitration in which one of the authors was involved (ICC Case No. 11681), the parties had to consider whether to apply to the tribunal or to the local courts of the respondent for an interim measure. Given that the applicable law and language were foreign to the local court, and that the measure sought to stop an important commercial transaction of an entity local to the court, a decision was taken to apply to the arbitral tribunal. The measure was awarded and the respondent complied voluntarily.

C. During the Arbitral Proceedings

and important forms of relief may be crafted by the courts or set out in legislation, so that it would be unwise to regard the categories of interim measures as being in any sense closed. The following classification may, however, be helpful.

- measures relating to the attendance of witnesses;
- measures related to preservation of evidence;
- measures related to documentary disclosure;
- measures aimed at preserving the status quo; and
- measures aimed at relief in respect of parallel proceedings.

(c) Measures relating to the attendance of witnesses

7.32 The first category of interim measures, directed towards the taking and preservation of evidence, is one of obvious concern. Since an arbitral tribunal does not generally possess the power to compel the attendance of relevant witnesses, it may be necessary to resort to the courts, particularly if the witness whose presence is required is not in any employment or other dependent relationship to the parties to the arbitration and so cannot be persuaded to attend voluntarily. This need for the assistance of the court is recognised by Article 27 of the Model Law:

> The arbitral tribunal or a party with the approval of the arbitral tribunal may request from a competent court of this State assistance in taking evidence. The court may execute the request within its competence and according to its rules on taking evidence.

7.33 Some national arbitration laws, including those of countries such as Switzerland, which have not adopted the Model Law per se, follow this form of wording very closely.[43] In other arbitration laws, the position may be set out more fully. For example, section 43 of the English Arbitration Act 1996 provides that:

> (1) A party to arbitral proceedings may use the same court procedures as are available in relation to legal proceedings to secure the attendance before the tribunal of a witness in order to give oral testimony or to produce documents or other material evidence.
> (2) This may only be done with the permission of the tribunal or the agreement of the other parties.
> (3) The court procedures may only be used if—
>   (a) the witness is in the United Kingdom, and
>   (b) the arbitral proceedings are being conducted in England and Wales or, as the case may be, Northern Ireland.
> (4) A person shall not be compelled by virtue of this section to produce any document or other material evidence which he could not be compelled to produce in legal proceedings.[44]

---

[43] Swiss PIL, s. 184(2).
[44] Under Arbitration Act 1996, s. 2(3), this section of the Act (and that concerning court powers exercisable in support of arbitral proceedings) applies even if (a) the seat of the arbitration is outside England, Wales, or Northern Ireland, or (b) no seat has been designated or determined.

Role of National Courts during the Proceedings

In addition, English courts have the same power in relation to arbitration proceedings as they have for their own purposes in relation, inter alia, to the taking of the evidence of witnesses and the preservation of evidence.[45]

7.34 In an arbitration with a seat in the United States, section 7 of the Federal Arbitration Act of 1925 (FAA) grants arbitrators the power to subpoena witnesses within the jurisdiction either to appear to give oral evidence or to disclose relevant documentary evidence in their possession.[46]

7.35 Practically, a subpoena can be issued by tribunals only in respect of witnesses present in the jurisdiction, and there appear to be few instances of the power having been exercised in the context of international arbitrations.[47] In one unreported ICC case, a tribunal refused to exercise its power to issue a subpoena to produce documents against a foreign national present in New York only for the arbitration hearing. The tribunal considered that the parties would not have contemplated the exercise of such power when selecting New York as a seat for a dispute that otherwise had no connection with the United States.

7.36 Another emerging limitation arising out of the consensual nature of arbitration is that section 7 subpoenas can be issued only against entities who are parties to

---

[45] Arbitration Act 1996, s. 44(1).

[46] The section reads:

> The arbitrators selected either as prescribed in this title or otherwise, or a majority of them, may summon in writing any person to attend before them or any of them as a witness and in a proper case to bring with him or them any book, record, document, or paper which may be deemed material as evidence in the case.... Said summons shall issue in the name of the arbitrator or arbitrators, or a majority of them, and shall be signed by the arbitrators, or a majority of them, and shall be directed to the said person and shall be served in the same manner as subpoenas to appear and testify before the court; if any person or persons so summoned to testify shall refuse or neglect to obey said summons, upon petition the United States district court for the district in which such arbitrators, or a majority of them are sitting may compel the attendance of such person or persons before said arbitrator or arbitrators, or punish said person or persons for contempt in the same manner provided by law for securing the attendance of witnesses or their punishment for neglect or refusal to attend in the courts of the United States.

[47] In the United States, it is not entirely clear whether the Federal Rules of Civil Procedure (FRCP), applicable to US courts, impose a territorial limit on an arbitral tribunal's power to subpoena witnesses. The relevant provision is r. 45(b)(2), under which a subpoena 'may be served at any place within the district of the court by which it is issued, or at any place without the district that is within 100 miles of the place of the deposition, hearing, trial, production, or inspection specified in the subpoena'. The view taken by the Eighth Circuit is that such territorial limit is not applicable to arbitral tribunals: *In re Security Life Insurance Co. of America* 228 F.3d 865, 872 (8th Cir. 2000). However, the Second Circuit and a district court in Illinois have concluded that r. 45(b)(2) does impose such a limit, because a US court cannot enforce a subpoena served outside its jurisdiction: *Dynegy Midstream Services v Trammochem* 451 F.3d 89, 96 (2nd Cir. 2006); *Alliance Healthcare Services, Inc. v Argonaut Private Equity, LLC* 804 F.Supp.2d 808, 811 (ND Ill. 2011).

the arbitration agreement.[48] Once a witness is called to testify before the tribunal, section 7 allows the tribunal to subpoena documents in the witness's possession.[49] However, this limitation varies among US courts, and several courts have held that section 7 applies to pre-hearing discovery of documents in the possession of third parties,[50] or to pre-hearing discovery of non-parties where a party demonstrates a special need or unusual circumstances.[51]

(d) Measures related to the preservation of evidence

7.37 As far as the preservation of evidence is concerned, it is obviously important that evidence should *not* be destroyed before a proper record can be made of it. If, for example, the dispute is over the quality of a consignment of coffee or cocoa beans, then some measurement of that quality must be made before the consignment is either sold or perishes. If, for example, the dispute is over the number or quality of reinforcing bars used in the concrete foundations of a road, bridge, or a dam, some record must be preserved, preferably by independent experts, before those foundations are covered over. Given that the preservation of evidence is a matter of particular concern right at the beginning of the case, before the formation of the arbitral tribunal, this is an area in which parties are likely to rely heavily on the emergency arbitrator procedure.

7.38 Arbitration laws may grant specific powers to national courts to support arbitration by means of the granting of interim injunctions to preserve evidence. For example, section 44 of the English Arbitration Act 1996 grants to the courts in cases of urgency the same powers in arbitration to order the preservation of evidence, or the inspection, photographing, or preservation of property, as in court proceedings.[52] In one case, pending initiation of an arbitration, the Court of Appeal granted a freezing order preventing a respondent from disposing or otherwise dealing with shares in order to protect a disputed right to purchase under a share purchase agreement.[53] The Court considered that property could include contractual rights and that there was no bar to the issuing of a mandatory injunction. The key question was the need to protect the rights that would be the subject of the arbitration.

---

[48] See *Life Receivables Trust v Syndicate 102 at Lloyd's of London* 549 F.3d 210, 216–217 (2nd Cir. 2008); *Hay Group, Inc. v EBS Acquisition Corporation*, 360 F.3d 404, 410 (3rd Cir. 2004). In both, it was held that FAA, § 7, does not authorise arbitrators to compel pre-hearing document discovery from entities not party to the arbitration proceedings.
[49] See *Life Receivables Trust*, at 218.
[50] See *Stanton v Paine Webber Jackson Curtis Inc.* 685 F.Supp. 1241 (SD Fla. 1988); *Meadows Indemnity Co. Ltd v Nutmeg Insurance Co.* 157 FRD 42 (MD Tenn. 1994). In both, it was held in favour of the arbitrators' power to order subpoenas of third-party documents.
[51] See *COMSAT Corporation v NSF* 190 F.3d 269, 276 (4th Cir. 1999), holding that, at a minimum, a party must demonstrate that the information it seeks is otherwise unavailable.
[52] English Arbitration Act 1996, s. 44(3).
[53] *Cetelem SA v Roust Holdings Ltd* [2005] EWCA Civ 618.

(e) Measures related to documentary disclosure

7.39 As observed in Chapter 6, the arbitral tribunal's power to order disclosure of documents is generally limited to the parties to the arbitration. Yet, in certain circumstances, relevant documents may be in the hands of a third party. Whilst the courts of the seat of the arbitration may offer some assistance, it has usually been chosen for its neutrality, and so the relevant third party is unlikely to be within its jurisdiction. The usual result is that third-party documents remain outside the scope of the arbitral process. However, this limitation does not apply in all jurisdictions in the United States, where an application to obtain disclosure of documents in support of a foreign arbitration is possible.

7.40 This power arises from section 1782 of Title 28 of the US Code, which permits a district court to order a person who 'resides or is found' in the district to give testimony or produce documents 'for use in a foreign or international tribunal… upon the application of any interested person'. Until 2006, case law had limited the meaning of the word 'tribunal' to a judicial court, with the result that this power did not extend to arbitration proceedings.[54] The US Supreme Court rejected this position in *Intel Corporation v Advanced Micro Devices, Inc.*,[55] which extended the narrow interpretation of 'tribunal' to encompass requests made by the Directorate-General of Competition for the Commission of the European Union. Notably, the Supreme Court concluded that Congress's deletion of the words 'in any judicial proceeding pending in any court in a foreign country' and replacement of them with the words 'in a proceeding in a foreign or international tribunal' was intended to provide the possibility of US judicial assistance to administrative bodies with adjudicative powers such as the Commission.[56] It was only a matter of time before this reasoning was applied to the case of a private arbitral tribunal. This happened in *In re Roz Trading Ltd*,[57] a case from the Northern District of Georgia.

7.41 Roz Trading had entered into a joint venture with a subsidiary of Coca-Cola and the Government of Uzbekistan. Roz alleged that Uzbekistan violently seized its interests in the joint venture and that Coca-Cola had assisted Uzbekistan in eliminating Roz from the joint venture. It initiated arbitral proceedings against Coca-Cola, Uzbekistan, and others before the International Arbitral Centre of the Austrian Federal Economic Chamber in Vienna under the joint venture agreement. Roz then applied to the district court in Georgia for an order, pursuant to section 1782, to compel Coca-Cola to produce documents for use before the arbitral tribunal in Austria. Coca-Cola argued that an arbitral panel convened before the Vienna Centre was not a 'tribunal' within the meaning of section 1782.

---

[54] *National Broadcasting Co., Inc. v Bear Stearns & Co., Inc.* 165 F.3d 184 (2nd Cir. 1999); *Republic of Kazakhstan v Biedermann International* 168 F.3d 880 (5th Cir. 1999).
[55] 542 US 241, 124 S.Ct 2466, 159 L.Ed.2d 355 (2004).
[56] Ibid., at 248–249.
[57] 469 F.Supp.2d 1221 (ND Ga. 2006).

C. During the Arbitral Proceedings

Applying the Supreme Court's reasoning from *Intel*, the district court ruled that an **7.42** arbitral panel of the Centre is a 'tribunal' within the meaning of section 1782, such that the court's assistance was available. The court then proceeded to exercise its discretion to grant discovery on the basis that '[d]iscovery is particularly appropriate where, as here, the practical availability of documents requested through other means of discovery is uncertain'.[58]

This decision has been followed by the Eleventh Circuit and a slim majority **7.43** of district courts,[59] and in respect of arbitrations conducted pursuant to the dispute resolution provisions in investment treaties in the case of *Oxus Gold*.[60] However, other circuits (including the Fifth and the Second) have adopted a contrary view.[61]

The possibility of seeking such evidence has also been the subject of academic **7.44** criticism. One author has argued that it runs contrary to the consensual nature of arbitration.[62] Another commentator has noted the disparity of access to evidence that could result from use of this section, because the foreign interested party would have access to section 1782 to obtain disclosure from the US entity, whereas the US entity would probably have no such access to obtain disclosure from the foreign entity.[63] Other commentators argue that the discretionary nature of the grant of the section 1782 order permits the court to 'weed out' abusive applications from those that are genuinely needed in order to have a fair arbitration.[64] It has been argued that courts will generally not grant an order where the target of the order is a party, where there is evidence to suggest that the foreign tribunal will not be receptive to the evidence, where it appears that the application is being made in an attempt to circumvent restrictions placed by the foreign tribunal, and where

---

[58] Ibid., at 1230.
[59] See, e.g., *In re Consorcio Ecuatoriano de Telecomuniciaciones SA v JAS Forwarding, Inc.* 685 F.3d 987 (11th Cir. 2012); *OJSC Ukrnafta v Carpatsky Petroleum Corporation*, Case No. 3.09 MC 265 (JBA), 2009 WL 2877156 (D. Conn., 27 Aug. 2009); *In Re Application of Chevron Corporation* 709 F.Supp.2d 283 (SDNY 2010); *In re Application of Mesa Power Group LLC*, Case No. 2:11-mc-270-ES, 2013 WL 1890222 (DNJ, 19 April 2013); *Ecuador, et al. v Stratus Consulting, Inc.*, Case No. 13-cv-01112-REB-KLM, 2013 WL 2352425 (D. Colo., 29 May 2013); *Republic of Ecuador v Bjorkman* 801 F.Supp.2d 1121 (D. Col., 2011); *In re Application of the Republic of Ecuador* 2011 WL 4434816 (ND Cal., 2011).
[60] *In re Oxus Gold plc*, Case No Misc 06-82-GEB, 2007 US Dist. LEXIS 24061 (DNJ, 2 April 2007).
[61] *El Paso Corporation v La Comision Ejecutiva Hidroelectrica Del Rio Lempa* 341 Fed.Appx 31 (5th Cir. 2009); *Norfolk Southern Corporation v General Securities Insurance Co.* 626 F.Supp.2d 882 (ND Ill. 2009); *In re Operadora DB Mex., SA* 2009 US Dist. LEXIS 68091, at [18]–[20] (MD Fla., 1 August 2009); *In re Application by Rhodianyl SAS* 2011 U.S. Dist. LEXIS 72918, at [26], [43] (D. Kan., 25 March 2011); *In re Dubey* 2013 US Dist. LEXIS 83972, at [7.15] (CD Cal., 7 June 2013).
[62] Rutledge, 'Discovery, judicial assistance and arbitration: A new tool for cases involving US entities?' (2008) 25 J Intl Arb 171.
[63] Fellas, 'Using US courts in aid of arbitration proceedings in other countries' (2008) 11 Intl ALR 3.
[64] Wessal, 'A tribunal by any other name: US discovery in aid of non-US arbitration' (2005) 8 Intl ALR 139.

the scope of disclosure is intrusive or burdensome.[65] It seems therefore that the use of section 1782 will ultimately be restricted only to those cases in which there is no other true avenue available to obtain necessary documents and evidence, rather than as a 'back door' to US-style discovery in the arbitral process.[66]

(f) Measures aimed at preserving the status quo

7.45 There are many cases in which an award of damages, however substantial, does not fully compensate the injured party for the loss that it has suffered. This may include damage to reputation, loss of business opportunities, and similar heads of claim, which are real enough, but difficult to prove and to quantify, even if they are considered to be legally admissible. For example, a manufacturer may refuse to continue supplies under a distribution agreement, alleging breach of contract. If the distributor does not receive the supplies for which it has contracted, it may not be able to fulfil the contracts that it, in turn, has made. This may damage the distributor's reputation. In such a case, the distributor would no doubt wish to argue that the status quo should be maintained and that the manufacturer should continue to supply, pending resolution of the dispute by arbitration. Similarly, a pharmaceutical company may produce a particular drug under licence, then decide to manufacture and market a competing product under its own name, claiming that there is nothing in the licence agreement to prevent it doing so. In such a case, the licensor probably wishes to argue that, until the dispute is resolved by arbitration, the licensee should be restrained from manufacturing and marketing the competing product.

7.46 Such protection could be granted by the tribunal once constituted under the relevant rules permitting interim measures.[67] However, if the application for interim measures is made to a national court, rather than to the arbitral tribunal itself, the court will have to consider whether it has the power to act, and if so, whether, in the particular circumstances, it *should* act. This problem confronted the English courts in the *Channel Tunnel* case. This was a case that went on appeal from the court of

---

[65] In fact, the court in *Roz Trading* did restrict the scope of the discovery granted to the applicant: *In re Roz Trading Ltd.* 469 F.Supp.2d 1221, 1230 (ND Ga. 2006).

[66] Recent decisions have sought to impose certain contours on applications under § 1782. See *In re Application of Caratube International Oil Co., LLP* 730 F.Supp.2d 101 (DDC 2010), holding that discovery should be denied where it appears that the party is attempting to circumvent agreed upon procedures; *In re Application of Thai-Lao Lignite (Thailand) Co., Ltd.* 821 F.Supp.2d 289 (DDC 2011), holding that, for discovery to be allowed in enforcement proceedings, there must be sufficient contacts in order to establish jurisdiction; *Thai-Lao Lignite (Thailand) Co., Ltd., et al. v Laos* 2012 WL 966042 (SDNY 2012), holding that foreign governments are not 'persons' under § 1782 and therefore cannot be compelled to produce witnesses, documents, or any other discovery materials; *In re the Republic of Ecuador* 2010 U.S. Dist. LEXIS 132045 (ND Cal., 1 December 2010), holding that foreign governments can invoke § 1782; *CE International Residential Holdings, LLC v SA Minerals Ltd. Partnership, et al.*, Case No. 12-CV-08087 (CM)(SN), 2013 WL 2661037 (SDNY, 12 June 2013), noting that comity concerns can prevent discovery requested in domestic courts.

[67] See Chapter 5.

C. During the Arbitral Proceedings

first instance to the Court of Appeal and then to the (then) highest English court, the House of Lords. Each court gave a different answer to the two questions posed.

The contract for the construction of the Channel Tunnel was an international contract that contained a 'two-stage' provision for the resolution of any disputes that might arise between Eurotunnel (the owner and intended operator of the tunnel) and Trans-Manche Link (TML), a consortium of five French and five British construction companies that had agreed to construct the land terminals, bore and equip the tunnels,[68] and provide the necessary rolling stock. At the first stage, any dispute between Eurotunnel and TML was to go to a panel of experts, who had to give a decision within ninety days. If either party disagreed with the panel's decision, the dispute was to be referred to arbitration in Brussels under the ICC Rules. 7.47

One serious dispute that arose between the parties was about payment for the Tunnel's cooling system. This was not part of the original specification, but was added by a variation order. TML claimed that the monthly payments it received for the cooling system were insufficient. By the end of September 1991, the gap between what Eurotunnel had paid and what TML claimed had grown to approximately £17 million. In October 1991, TML wrote to Eurotunnel, threatening to suspend work on the cooling system unless its claim was met in full and pointing out the 'very serious' consequences that this would have for completion of the project, with subcontractors and other workers having to be laid off, equipment orders being delayed or cancelled, and so forth. In reply, Eurotunnel applied to the English court for an interim injunction to restrain TML from carrying out its threat. TML argued that the English courts had no power to intervene by granting the injunction that was sought; instead, it said, the court should stay the litigation and refer the parties to arbitration, in accordance with the then governing statute.[69] 7.48

The judge who heard the case at first instance decided that he *did* have the power to grant an injunction and would have done so, but for an undertaking by TML to continue working pending further court proceedings.[70] The Court of Appeal considered that it was an appropriate case for an injunction, but that it had no power to grant one, because of the arbitration agreement.[71] The House of Lords considered that it *did* have power to grant an injunction, but thought it inappropriate to do so.[72] In giving the House of Lords' judgment, Lord Mustill highlighted the problem to which this kind of application for interim relief may give rise: 7.49

> It is true that mandatory interlocutory relief may be granted even where it substantially overlaps the final relief claimed in the action; and I also accept that it is possible for the court at the pre-trial stage of the dispute arising under a construction

---

[68] In fact, there were three tunnels: two running tunnels (for the trains) and a service tunnel.
[69] The English Arbitration Act 1975.
[70] *Channel Tunnel Group v Balfour Beatty Ltd*, Commercial Court, 27 November 1991.
[71] *Channel Tunnel Group v Balfour Beatty Ltd*, Court of Appeal, 22 January 2002.
[72] *Channel Tunnel Group v Balfour Beatty Ltd* [1993] AC 334.

contract to order the defendant to continue with a performance of the works. But the court should approach the making of such an order with the utmost caution and should be prepared to act only when the balance of advantage plainly favours the grant of relief. In the combination of circumstances which we find in the present case, I would have hesitated long before proposing that such an order should be made, even if the action had been destined to remain in the High Court.[73]

7.50 The fact that, in the *Channel Tunnel* case, three different courts gave different answers to the questions of whether or not there was power to issue an injunction, and if so, whether it would be appropriate to do so, underlines the difficulties posed by such questions.[74] It is no comfort to the practitioner to say so, but there is no clear rule as to whether or not an injunction will be issued in particular circumstances.[75] Each case has to be assessed individually.

(g) Interim relief in respect of parallel proceedings

7.51 Whilst an uneasy truce may have been signed between the courts and arbitral tribunals in the developed arbitral jurisdictions,[76] a 'turf war' continues to rage in other parts of the world, where there is an uncomfortable trend towards the issue of 'anti-arbitration' injunctions, either by the courts of the seat or by the courts of the place of eventual enforcement. The fact pattern is often similar: a dispute arises between a foreign party and a state, or state-owned entity, which has signed an arbitration agreement. The state entity wishes to sabotage the arbitral proceedings

---

[73] Ibid., at 367.

[74] The former English arbitration legislation was amended to take account, inter alia, of some of the difficulties that the courts faced in the *Channel Tunnel* case. The Court of Appeal, which would have been prepared to grant an injunction, considered that it had no power to do so, because the arbitration agreement provided for arbitration in Brussels. The English Arbitration Act 1996, s. 44 (2)(e), provides that the powers of the court that are 'exercisable in support of arbitral proceedings' include the granting of an interim injunction, and this section of the Act applies even if the seat of the arbitration is outside England (s. 2(3)). There may be resort to the courts if, or to the extent that, the arbitral tribunal or any other person empowered by the parties to decide the case 'has no power or is unable for the time being to act effectively' (s. 44(5)).

[75] For different approaches to the granting of court injunctions pending arbitration, see *NCC International AB v Alliance Concrete Singapore Pte Ltd*, Case No. CA 47/2007, Singapore Court of Appeal, 26 February 2008; *Mobil Cerro Negro Ltd v Petroleos De Venezuela SA*, High Court of Justice, Queen's Bench Division (Commercial Court), 18 March 2008, [2008] Folio 61; *Fisichella Motor Sport International SpA v Héctor*, Audencia Provincial, Barcelona, 4 March 2010; *Toyo Tire Holdings of Americas, Inc. v Continental Tire North America, Inc. and ors*, Case No. 10-55145, United States Court of Appeals for the Ninth Circuit, 17 June 2010; *ENRC Marketing AG and ors v OJSC 'Magnitogorsk Metallurgical Kombinat'*, Case No. NSD 2110 of 2011, Federal Court of Australia, 25 November 2011; *Petrobras v Tractebel Energia & MSGAS*, Case No. AgRg MC 19.226-MS (2012/0080171-0), Superior Court of Justice of Brazil, 29 June 2012; *Discovery Geo Corporation v STP Energy Pte Ltd*, High Court of New Zealand, 19 December 2013.

[76] For example, in a 2010 decision, a Paris court held that French courts cannot interfere with arbitral proceedings: *SA Elf Aquitaine and Total v Mattei, Lai. Kamara and Reiner*, Paris Court of First Instance, 6 January 2010. While in less categorical terms, US and English courts have expressed great reluctance to issue anti-arbitration injunctions: see Reisman and Iravani, 'The changing relation of national courts and international commercial arbitration' (2010) 21 Am Rev Intl Arb 33.

C. During the Arbitral Proceedings

and have the case remitted for judicial determination in its own courts. It therefore seeks an injunction before those courts, seeking to challenge the jurisdiction of the tribunal, and an order requiring the arbitrators and adverse party to suspend or abandon the arbitral proceedings on pain of daily fines (or worse). This problem has raised serious challenges to the modern arbitrator: should such orders be obeyed, even where patently the product of improper government intervention, or should the arbitrator seek to ensure justice in the individual case, often at risk of monetary penalties (or worse)?

7.52 In one such case, a subsidiary of a US corporation, Himpurna, had entered into a contract with the Indonesian state electricity corporation, PLN, to explore and develop geothermal resources in Indonesia and subsequently to sell the power to PLN. In the wake of the Asian economic crisis, PLN failed to purchase the electricity supplied. Himpurna relied on the arbitration clause in the contract to commence an arbitration under the UNCITRAL Rules against PLN. A final award was made in favour of Himpurna, which PLN refused to pay. Himpurna subsequently commenced a second arbitration proceeding against Indonesia, based on Indonesia's pledge to secure PLN's performance. Shortly after serving the statement of claim, proceedings were commenced by both PLN and Indonesia in the Indonesian courts, which resulted in interim injunctions ordering the suspension of the arbitral proceedings pending a court decision on the merits, with an attached fine of US$1 million per day for breach of the order.

7.53 The tribunal considered that the injunction was a transparent attempt to avoid the consequences of a freely signed arbitration agreement and refused to abandon the arbitration. To avoid the risk of breaching the Indonesian court order, the tribunal moved the place of the hearing to The Hague and convened witnesses. Indonesia tried to stop such hearings from proceeding by seeking an injunction from the Dutch courts. This attempt failed, and the hearings were held (albeit in truncated form without the presence of the Indonesian arbitrator) and a final award issued.

7.54 The colourful facts of this case raise important questions as to how an arbitral tribunal can seek to avoid injunctions of national courts in extreme circumstances. First, the place of hearings in an UNCITRAL case can be held 'at any place [the tribunal] deems appropriate', and so the physical transfer of the hearings to The Hague was permitted by the Rules. In connection with the injunction itself, Article 28 of the UNCITRAL Rules allows a tribunal to proceed with the arbitration notwithstanding one party's default whenever the defaulting party has failed to show 'sufficient cause' for its default. In this regard, the arbitral tribunal found that the Indonesian injunction did not constitute 'sufficient cause', because (a) it was sought and obtained by a state agency that was under the *de jure* control of the Government of Indonesia, and (b) the Government of Indonesia had *de facto* made no attempt to rein in those actions that were inconsistent with its obligations under the parties' arbitration agreement.

7.55 As a second ground, the arbitral tribunal held that the very existence of an arbitration agreement, and the involvement of a state party, entitled the tribunal to apply international law. As a matter of international law, the actions of the Indonesian courts were attributable to the Republic of Indonesia. In *Benteler v Belgium*,[77] an international tribunal had held that 'a state which has signed an arbitration clause or agreement would be acting contrary to international public policy if it subsequently relied on the incompatibility of such an obligation with its internal legal system'.[78] The arbitral tribunal held that it would constitute 'a denial of justice for the courts of a State to prevent a foreign party from pursuing its remedies before a forum to the authority of which the State consented'.[79] Thirdly, the tribunal held that an international arbitral tribunal is not 'unconditionally subject' to the jurisdiction of the courts at the seat of the arbitration. Specifically, the 'adjudicatory authority' of an international tribunal 'does not emanate from a discrete sovereign but rather from an international order'.[80]

7.56 Similar issues were addressed in another matter concerning an arbitration between a European construction company and an Ethiopian municipal authority. It related to an infrastructure project to be undertaken in Addis Ababa under an International Federation of Consulting Engineers (FIDIC) standard form contract comprising a number of the FIDIC 'general conditions', which were supplemented by 'special conditions' specifically negotiated by the parties. Confusingly, one of the FIDIC general conditions that was adopted was a standard ICC arbitration clause providing for ICC arbitration in Addis Ababa, while one of the parties' special conditions was a separate arbitration clause that provided for arbitration in Addis Ababa pursuant to the Civil Code of Ethiopia. When a dispute arose between the parties and the European contractor commenced ICC proceedings, the Ethiopian municipal authority raised jurisdictional objections. It argued that, in specifically negotiating an arbitration agreement that did not make reference to the ICC in the 'special conditions', the parties had evinced a clear intention not to refer disputes to ICC arbitration. A hearing on the merits was scheduled in Paris to include the appearance of a number of witnesses resident in Ethiopia, even though the seat of the arbitration was Addis Ababa. In holding the hearing on the merits in a place other than the seat of the arbitration, the tribunal relied on Article 14(2) of the ICC Rules, which allowed it to conduct hearings at any location it considered 'appropriate' (a provision that had been restated in the parties' terms of reference).

7.57 The Ethiopian party was outraged and applied to the ICC's Court to remove the arbitrators, claiming that, in having regard to its own convenience and that of the claimant alone, the tribunal's decision to hold hearings outside of Ethiopia gave

---

[77] (1985) 8 European Commercial Cases 101.
[78] Quoted in *Himpurna California Energy Ltd (Bermuda) v Republic of Indonesia* (2000) XXV YBCA 11, [169].
[79] Ibid., at [184].
[80] Ibid., at [181].

C. During the Arbitral Proceedings

the respondent reason to doubt the tribunal's impartiality. This application was rejected by the ICC's Court. Following this, and pursuant to the Ethiopian Civil Code, the Ethiopian party applied to the Ethiopian courts to remove the arbitrators. Pending its decision on the challenge, the Ethiopian Supreme Court issued an injunction enjoining the proceedings.

In an interim award in which it found that it did have jurisdiction over the parties' dispute, the ICC tribunal also held that it had the discretion—indeed the duty—not to comply with the Ethiopian Supreme Court's injunction. How was the tribunal able to reach this decision? As a practical matter, the arbitrators were personally insulated from the effects of the injunction. As a result of the tribunal's procedural ruling, the hearing took place outside Ethiopia and none of the three arbitrators were Ethiopian nationals. How did the tribunal justify ignoring the orders of the courts that had supervisory jurisdiction over the arbitration? At least four grounds were given. First, the tribunal noted that, as a tribunal, it was not an organ of state, but a creature of contract. As a result, it held that its primary duty was to the parties to ensure that their agreement to arbitrate was not frustrated.[81] Secondly, the tribunal found that an agreement to submit disputes to international arbitration 'is not anchored exclusively in the legal order of the seat... [but is] validated by a range of international sources and norms extending beyond the domestic seat'.[82] As to what these international sources were, the tribunal referred in particular to the New York Convention, which it suggested 'embodied principles of general [recognition]'.[83] Thirdly, the tribunal held that although Article 35 of the ICC Rules imposes a duty on tribunals to 'ensure' that their awards are 'enforceable at law' and, in this case, the likely place of enforcement was Ethiopia, this did not mean that an arbitral tribunal: **7.58**

> ...should simply abdicate to the courts of the seat the tribunal's own judgment about what is fair and right...In the event that the arbitral tribunal considers that to follow a decision of a court would conflict fundamentally with the tribunal's understanding of its duty to the parties, derived from the parties' arbitration agreement, the tribunal *must follow its own judgment*, even if that requires non-compliance with a court order.[84]

Finally, the tribunal concluded that to comply with the injunction would lead to a denial of justice.[85] Specifically, it held that in the same way as a state cannot rely on changes in its own laws to justify breach of contract, so a state entity cannot resort to the state's courts to frustrate an arbitration agreement.[86] **7.59**

---

[81] *Salini Construttori Spa v Federal Democratic Republic of Ethiopia, Addis Ababa Water and Sewerage Authority*, ICC Case No. 10623, 7 December 2001, available online at http://italaw.com/documents/Salini_v._Ethiopia_Award.pdf, at [128].
[82] Ibid., at [129].
[83] Ibid., at [130].
[84] Ibid., at [142] (emphasis added).
[85] Ibid., at [143].
[86] Ibid., at [174].

7.60 There are also examples of national courts with no supervisory jurisdiction that have sought to stay foreign arbitral proceedings. In *National Grid v Argentina*,[87] the claimant had instituted proceedings under the UNCITRAL Arbitration Rules against Argentina, pursuant to the United Kingdom–Argentina bilateral investment treaty (BIT). The parties agreed to a juridical seat of Washington, DC, and the ICC was designated as appointing authority. In the course of proceedings, Argentina unsuccessfully challenged the president of the tribunal before the ICC and then brought a claim against the ICC before its own courts in Buenos Aires. Less than a week before the final hearing, Argentina obtained an interim injunction in its domestic proceedings against the ICC to stay the arbitration in Washington, DC. The tribunal refused to suspend the proceedings, noting that the procedure for the challenge of arbitrators was a self-contained procedure under the UNCITRAL Rules, agreed by the parties, and further that the supervisory courts were those of the agreed seat, being Washington, DC, and not Argentina. Similarly, in *SGS v Pakistan*,[88] the Pakistan Supreme Court issued an order against SGS restraining it from taking any action to pursue arbitration proceedings that it had commenced under the Arbitration Rules of the International Centre for the Settlement of Investment Disputes (ICSID) on the basis of a BIT. SGS nevertheless pursued its case, considering that the Pakistani courts had no supervisory jurisdiction over an ICSID claim.

7.61 Such cases nevertheless remain rare. The vast majority of arbitrations are pursued without interference from domestic courts. Nevertheless, the evolution of an international law to which tribunals must respond, even if in conflict with the dictates of the courts of the seat, may cause such courts to curtail their partisan zeal and conform to accepted international norms.

D. At the End of the Arbitration

(a) Judicial control of the proceedings and the award

7.62 One final aspect of the relationship between national courts and arbitral tribunals remains to be considered: the extent to which, if at all, national courts should exercise judicial control over the conduct of international arbitrations and the resulting award. There are two extreme positions. As one English judge recognised:

> It can be said on the one side that if parties agree to resolve their disputes through the use of a private rather than a public tribunal, then the court system should play

---

[87] Decision of the Fourth Chamber of the Camara Contencioso-Administrativo Federal, 2 July 2007.
[88] *Société Générate de Surveillance SA (SGS) v Islamic Republic of Pakistan*, Pakistan Supreme Court, 3 July 2002. For a detailed analysis of the case, see Lau, 'Note on *Société Générale de Surveillance v Pakistan*' (2003) 19 Arb Intl 179.

no part at all, save perhaps to enforce awards in the same way as they enforce any other rights and obligations to which the parties have agreed. To do otherwise is unwarrantably to interfere with the parties' right to conduct their affairs as they choose.

The other extreme position reaches a very different conclusion. Arbitration has this in common with the court system; both are a form of dispute resolution which depends on the decision of a third party. Justice dictates that certain rules should apply to dispute resolution of this kind. Since the state is in overall charge of justice, and since justice is an integral part of any civilised democratic society, the courts should not hesitate to intervene as and when necessary, so as to ensure that justice is done in private as well as public tribunals.[89]

The extent to which there should be judicial control at the seat of the arbitration over both the conduct of the arbitration and the resulting award is a matter on which different commentators and, more importantly, different states have taken different views. It is an important matter, and is considered in more detail in Chapters 9 and 10.

E. Conclusion

7.63 Powers that have been conferred on national courts by legislation, or which have been developed by the courts themselves, such as the powers to attach bank accounts, to appoint liquidators, or to issue injunctions, are there to serve the interests of justice. They are there to ensure that the ultimate purpose of legal proceedings is not frustrated by evidence or assets disappearing, or by parties taking the law into their own hands. As international commercial transactions and foreign direct investment increase, recourse to the courts, even where there is an arbitration agreement, may be essential if the aims of justice are to be properly served. As one experienced Swiss arbitrator expressed it:

> [T]he development of law and international arbitration has been marked by an obvious tendency to limit the possibilities of court intervention in the course of an arbitration.
>
> ...It may be that the tide is now turning: it is increasingly realised in international arbitration circles that the intervention of the courts is not *necessarily* disruptive of the arbitration. It may equally be definitely *supportive*...[90]

7.64 As in all relationships, the appropriate balance must be found between the rights of the courts to supervise arbitrations and the rights of parties to solicit the courts' assistance in times of need.

---

[89] Lord Saville, 'The Denning Lecture 1995: Arbitration and the courts' (1995) 61 Arbitration 157, at 157.
[90] Reymond, 'The *Channel Tunnel* case and the law of international arbitration' (1993) 109 LQR 337, at 341 (emphasis added).

8

ARBITRATION UNDER INVESTMENT TREATIES

A.	Introduction	8.01	D.	Merits of the Dispute	8.78
B.	Jurisdictional Issues	8.14	E.	Measures of Compensation under Bilateral Investment Treaties	8.141
C.	Law Applicable to the Substance of the Dispute	8.62			

A. Introduction

8.01 Historically, an individual or a corporation who wished to assert a claim against a foreign state for breach of customary international law could not do so directly. Instead, the individual or corporation had to petition its government to take up, or 'espouse', the claim on its behalf. In the course of the nineteenth century, influential individuals or corporations would convince their government to send a small contingent of warships to moor off the coast of the offending state until reparation was forthcoming. This form of 'gunboat diplomacy' was exercised frequently by European powers on behalf of their subjects in the not-so-distant past. For example, when faced with Venezuela's default on its sovereign debt in 1902, the governments of Great Britain, Germany, and Italy sent warships to the Venezuelan coast to demand reparation for the losses incurred by their nationals.

8.02 Argentine jurist and diplomat Carlos Calvo fought for the right of newly independent states to be free of such intervention by foreign powers, promoting the so-called Calvo doctrine, whereby foreign investors should be in no better position than local investors, with their rights and obligations to be determined through the exclusive jurisdiction of the courts of that state.[1] His position was adopted by the First International Conference of American States in 1889, the

---

[1] This thesis was first published in 1868 in the seminal Calvo, *Derecho internacional teórico y práctico de Europa y América* (Paris, 1868).

ad hoc Commission on International Law of which (without the support of the United States) concluded:

> Foreigners are entitled to enjoy all the civil rights enjoyed by natives and they shall be accorded all the benefits of said rights in all that is essential as well as in the form or procedure, and the legal remedies incident thereto, absolutely in like manner as said natives. A nation has not, nor recognizes in favour to foreigners, any other obligations or responsibilities than those which in favour of the natives are established in like cases by the constitution and the laws.[2]

8.03 The doctrine was incorporated into the forerunner of the modern investment treaty, the 'treaty of friendship, commerce and navigation' (FCN treaty). For example, Article 21 of the FCN treaty between Italy and Colombia of 1894 stated as follows:

> The Contracting Parties express their desire to avoid all types of dispute which might affect their cordial relations and agree that, in connection with disputes which involve individuals arising out of criminal, civil or administrative matters, their diplomatic agents will abstain from intervening except in cases of denial of justice or extraordinary or unlawful delay in the administration of justice.[3]

8.04 Gunboat diplomacy as a means of asserting rights of nationals was finally laid to rest at the Second International Peace Conference of The Hague in 1907, when the Convention on the Peaceful Resolution of International Disputes was signed. The Convention provided the framework for the conclusion of bilateral arbitration treaties. In accordance with these treaties, in the event of a dispute between two states arising out of the particular interests of a national of the other state, an independent arbitral tribunal would be formed. In effect, a state could espouse the claim of its national (the so-called right of diplomatic protection) by means of a horizontal inter-state procedure. There was no direct cause of action by the foreign national whose interests had been harmed.

8.05 The legal basis of the right of 'diplomatic protection', in the words of the Permanent Court of International Justice (PCIJ) in the *Panevezys-Saldutiskis Railway* case, was that:

> [I]n taking up the case of one of its nationals, by resorting to diplomatic action or international judicial proceedings on his behalf, a state is in reality asserting its own right, the right to ensure in the person of its nationals respect for the rules of international law. This right is necessarily limited to the intervention on behalf of its own nationals because, in the absence of a special agreement, it is the bond of nationality between the state and the individual which alone confers upon the state the right of diplomatic protection, and it is as a part of the function of diplomatic protection that the right to take up a claim and to ensure respect for the rules of international law must be envisaged.[4]

---

[2] Scott, *The International Conferences of American States (1889–1928)* (Oxford University Press, 1931), p. 45.
[3] Free translation from the Italian.
[4] *Panevezys-Saldutiskis Railway (Estonia v Lithuania)* [1939] PCIJ Series A/B 76, ICGJ 328 (1939), at [16].

A. Introduction

As one learned commentator stated, the procedure was unsatisfactory from the individual claimant's point of view: 8.06

> He has no remedy of his own, and the state to which he belongs may be unwilling to take up his case for reasons which have nothing to do with its merits; and even if it is willing to do so, there may be interminable delays before, if ever, the defendant state can be induced to let the matter go to arbitration.... It has been suggested that a solution might be found by allowing individuals access in their own right to some form of international tribunal for the purpose, and if proper safeguards against merely frivolous or vexatious claims could be devised, that is a possible reform which deserves to be considered. For the time being, however, the prospect of states accepting such a change is not very great.[5]

Since that text was written in 1963, the situation has changed dramatically and what Professor Brierley thought unlikely has become a commonplace reality. The validity of his concerns, and the inevitable 'politicisation' of disputes 'leaving investors, particularly small and medium-sized enterprises, with little recourse save what their government cares to give them after weighing the diplomatic pros and cons of bringing any particular claim',[6] led to a radical reform in the dispute-settlement provisions of many BITs. 8.07

This reform was made possible by the conclusion of the Convention on the Settlement of Investment Disputes between States and Nationals of Other States of 1965 (the ICSID Convention).[7] The Convention was aimed primarily at creating a new arbitral forum for the resolution of disputes between investors and states by means of the inclusion of arbitration clauses in state contracts. Nevertheless, the *travaux préparatoires* of the Convention also made clear that the consent of the state to arbitration could be established through the provisions of an investment law.[8] Following the 1959 Abs-Shawcross Draft Convention on Investments 8.08

---

[5] Brierley, *The Law of Nations* (6th edn, Oxford University Press, 1963), p. 277.
[6] Testimony of Dan Price, one of the negotiators of the North American Free Trade Agreement (NAFTA), addressing investment protection issues before a US Senate Ways and Means Committee Hearing on the Free Trade Area of the Americas.
[7] The International Centre for the Settlement of Investment Disputes (ICSID) was established by the 1965 Convention on the Settlement of Investment Disputes between States and Nationals of Other States, known as the 'ICSID Convention', or sometimes the 'Washington Convention'. The Convention has been ratified by 151 states. The history of the Convention is detailed in Parra, *The History of ICSID* (Oxford University Press, 2012). For a detailed analysis of the provisions of the ICSID Convention, see Schreuer, Malintoppi, Reinisch, and Sinclair, *The ICSID Convention: A Commentary* (2nd edn, Cambridge University Press, 2009). A simple guide to the ICSID arbitration process is contained in Reed, Paulsson, and Blackaby, *Guide to ICSID Arbitration* (2nd edn, Kluwer Law International, 2011).
[8] See ICSID, 'Report of the Executive Directors of the International Bank for Reconstruction and Development on the [ICSID Convention]', in *ICSID Convention, Regulations and Rules* (ICSID, 2006), p. 43, para. 24:

> ...Nor does the Convention require that the consent of both parties be expressed in a single instrument. Thus, a Host State might in its investment protection legislation offer to submit disputes arising out of certain classes of investments to the jurisdiction of the Centre, and the investor might give his consent by accepting the offer in writing.

Abroad and the 1967 Organisation for Economic Co-operation and Development (OECD) Draft Convention on the Protection of Foreign Property,[9] many states had begun a programme of bilateral treaties for the promotion and protection of investments (the so-called BITs) that set out explicit protections in favour of foreign investment.[10] They were a natural successor to the FCN treaties of the early part of the twentieth century, but still suffered from the limitations imposed by diplomatic protection. Once the ICSID Convention was in place, treaty drafters from signatory states quickly seized upon the possibility of using this specialist forum for the resolution of treaty disputes between states and investors, and did so by incorporating a clause establishing the consent of the state to arbitrate with covered investors. Professor Brierley's vision of a diagonal clause, permitting investors to claim directly under a treaty against the state in which the investment was made (the 'host state'), thus became a reality. Switzerland, for example, inserted a diagonal clause for the first time in its 1981 BIT with Sri Lanka,[11] and has done so systematically ever since.[12]

8.09 This right of direct recourse ensures that the investor's claim is not subject to the political considerations inherent in diplomatic protection. Even if there is no agreement between the investor and the host state, the investor may usually commence arbitration directly against the host state.[13] Foreign investors were nevertheless slow to take up their newfound rights: the first case brought by an investor under the investment protections of a BIT was not decided until 1990.[14]

8.10 In light of the dramatic increase in the number of BITs[15] and the emergence of clearer legal principles through case law, the number of investor–state arbitrations has mushroomed. In 2014, ICSID registered thirty-eight new arbitration cases—nearly seven times the number of cases registered during the whole of

---

[9] See 1967 OECD Draft Convention on the Protection of Foreign Property (1968) 7 ILM 117; see also earlier draft at (1963) 2 ILM 241.

[10] The history of BITs is described in greater detail in Vandevelde, *Bilateral Investment Treaties: History, Policy, and Interpretation* (Oxford University Press, 2010).

[11] Agreement between the Government of the Swiss Confederation and the Government of the Democratic Socialist Republic of Sri Lanka for the Reciprocal Promotion and Protection of Investments, signed on 23 September 1981, entered into force on 12 February 1982.

[12] See Liebeskind, 'State–investor dispute settlement clauses in Swiss bilateral investment treaties' (2002) 20 ASA Bulletin 1, at 27.

[13] Obviously, the investor could have access to litigation before the courts of the host state. However, this would clearly be a last resort, since it raises serious questions of neutrality of forum and ultimate enforceability of the judgment elsewhere. On the advantages of international arbitration to resolve investment disputes, see Parra, 'Provisions on the settlement of investment disputes in modern investment laws, bilateral investment treaties and multilateral instruments on investment' (1997) 12 ICSID Rev—Foreign Investment LJ 287, at 288–289.

[14] *Asian Agricultural Products Ltd (AAPL) v Republic of Sri Lanka*, Final Award, ICSID Case No. ARB/87/3, IIC 18 (1990).

[15] According to United Nations Conference on Trade and Development (UNCTAD), the number of BITs increased from 385 at the end of the 1980s to a total of 2,926 by the end of 2014: see UNCTAD, *World Investment Report* (UN, 2015), available online at http://unctad.org/en/PublicationsLibrary/wir2015_en.pdf.

A. Introduction

ICSID's first ten years of existence.[16] By the end of 2014, the number of known treaty-based investor–state cases had reached 608—approximately ten times the figure as it stood at 2000.[17]

The dramatic growth of BITs since the mid-1980s has led to the adoption of similar provisions in the 'investment chapters', or collateral agreements, to multilateral economic cooperation treaties. These include the Association of Southeast Asian Nations (ASEAN) Comprehensive Investment Agreement,[18] the North American Free Trade Agreement (NAFTA),[19] the Energy Charter Treaty (ECT),[20] and the Dominican Republic and Central America–United States Free Trade Agreement (DR-CAFTA).[21] Similar provisions have found their way into bilateral free trade agreements (FTAs) such as the United States–Chile FTA[22] and the 2010 Canada–Panama FTA.[23] **8.11**

As the number of investment treaty arbitrations has grown, concerns over the investment treaty system have arisen. These concerns include a perceived deficit of legitimacy given that states are being judged on their conduct by private non-elected individuals. Concerns have also arisen in respect of inconsistent arbitral awards, the independence and impartiality of arbitrators, and the delays and costs of arbitral procedures.[24] These complaints have resonated in some scholarly publications[25] and popular media outlets.[26] At the same time, between 2007 and 2012, a small group of Latin American countries defending multiple claims—Bolivia, **8.12**

---

[16] See ICSID, *The ICSID Caseload—Statistics (Issue 2015-1)* (ICSID, 2015), available online at https://icsid.worldbank.org.

[17] See UNCTAD, *Recent Trends in IIAs and ISDS*, International Investment Agreements (IIA) Issues Notes 1 (UN, 2015), available online at http://unctad.org/.

[18] Signed on 26 February 2009, entered into force on 29 March 2012. This agreement covers investments from investors of Brunei, Cambodia, Indonesia, Laos, Malaysia, Myanmar, Philippines, Singapore, Thailand, and Vietnam in the territory of these states.

[19] NAFTA, Ch. 11 ('Investment'), signed on 17 December 1992, entered into force on 1 January 1994. This agreement covers investments from investors of Canada, Mexico, and the United States in the territory of these states.

[20] Signed on 17 December 1994, entered into force on 16 April 1998. The ECT covers investments in the energy sector for investors of its state parties (which number more than fifty) within the territory of those states.

[21] DR-CAFTA, Ch. 10 ('Investment'), signed on 5 August 2004, entered into force between 2006 and 2009 in seven signatory countries. This agreement covers investments from investors from the United States, Costa Rica, El Salvador, Guatemala, Honduras, Nicaragua, and the Dominican Republic in the territory of these states.

[22] Signed on 6 June 2003, entered into force on 1 January 2004.

[23] Canada–Panama Free Trade Agreement, signed on 14 May 2010, entered into force on 1 April 2013.

[24] See UNCTAD, *World Investment Report 2015* (UN, 2015), available online at http://unctad.org.

[25] See, e.g., Waibel, Kaushal, Chung, and Balchin, *The Backlash against Investment Arbitration* (Kluwer Law International, 2010).

[26] See, e.g., Weisbrot, 'The Trans-Pacific Partnership Treaty is the complete opposite of "free trade" ', The Guardian, 19 November 2013; Weisman, 'Trans-Pacific Partnership seen as Door for Foreign Suits against U.S.', New York Times, 25 March 2015.

Ecuador, and Venezuela—denounced the ICSID Convention and certain BITs.[27] These concerns and isolated denunciations are not symptomatic of an exodus from the investment treaty system. According to the United Nations Conference on Trade and Development (UNCTAD), 330 new investment treaties were concluded between 2010 and 2014,[28] including more than two dozen in Latin America alone. During that same period, ICSID gained seven new member states.[29] Systemic reforms are being considered[30] and implemented, including the introduction of new transparency provisions.[31]

8.13 As a result of the growth in investment treaties, many foreign investments are protected by investment treaties. The question is whether an investor can rely on one or more of these investment treaties to vindicate its legal rights in a particular case. This raises fundamental issues relating to the scope and application of those treaties, which issues are addressed next.

B. Jurisdictional Issues

(a) Existence of an applicable treaty

8.14 To determine whether an investor enjoys investment treaty protection, an applicable treaty between the state in which the investment was made and the home state of the investor must be identified.[32] It is easy to identify multilateral investment

---

[27] See UNCTAD, *Denunciation of the ICSID Convention and BITs: Impact on Investor–State Claims*, IIA Issue Notes No. 2 (UN, 2010), available online at http://unctad.org/en/Docs/webdiaeia20106_en.pdf; State Department and the Trade Representative, Office of the United States, *Notice of Termination of United States–Bolivia Bilateral Investment Treaty*, Federal Register, 23 May 2012; Blackaby, 'ICSID withdrawal: A storm in a teacup' (2010) 1 Les Cahiers de l'Arbitrage 45; ICSID, 'Venezuela submits a notice under Article 71 of the ICSID Convention', ICSID News Release, 26 January 2012, available online at https://icsid.worldbank.org.

[28] See UNCTAD, *World Investment Reports* (UN, 2011–15), available online at http://unctad.org.

[29] See the list of ICSID contracting states online at https://icsid.worldbank.org/.

[30] See UNCTAD, *Reform of Investor–State Dispute Settlement: In Search of a Roadmap*, IIA Issues Notes No. 2 (UN, 2013), available online at http://unctad.org/.

[31] See ICSID Arbitration Rules, r. 37; ICSID Arbitration (Additional Facility) Rules, r. 41; UNCITRAL Rules on Transparency in Treaty-based Investor–State Arbitration, Resolution 68/109 adopted by the United Nations General Assembly on 16 December 2013, effective as of 1 April 2014; UNCITRAL Draft Convention on Transparency in Treaty-Based Investor-State Arbitration, Doc. No. A/CN.9/WG.II/WP.181, February 2014.

[32] An investor may derive protections for the same investment from more than one treaty or from other non-treaty sources, such as foreign investment laws or contracts. It may be possible for claims based on different instruments to be dealt with in the same arbitral proceedings: see *Pac Rim Cayman LLC v The Republic of El Salvador*, Decision on the Respondent's Jurisdictional Objections, ICSID Case No. ARB/09/12, IIC 543 (2012), at [4.45]: '[T]he Tribunal finds no juridical difficulty in having an ICSID arbitration based on different claims arising from separate

B. Jurisdictional Issues

treaties, because they are sufficiently notorious. It is, however, more difficult to detect applicable BITs, considering their number and the absence of a comprehensive list.[33] Although the UNCTAD list is helpful, the only accurate means of verifying the existence of a BIT, and whether it is in force,[34] is by contacting the treaty section of the relevant government or embassy.

Most BITs contain provisions with respect to their effective date and duration. An issue may arise as to whether investments made prior to the date on which the BIT came into effect are eligible for protection under it. Tribunals have generally taken the position that prior investments are afforded protection and some treaties are explicit in this regard. The Argentina–United States BIT, for example, provides that it shall apply to investments existing at the time of entry into force, as well as to investments made or acquired thereafter.[35] A distinction should be drawn between application of a BIT to investments made prior to its entry in force and its application to alleged breaches that occurred prior to that date. In *Técnicas Medioambientales Tecmed SA v The United Mexican States*,[36] the tribunal held that while the concerned investment was eligible for protection under the BIT, the BIT could not have retrospective application to actions by the host state prior to its entry into force. **8.15**

Bilateral investment treaties also commonly include provisions regarding the legal status of investments after the termination or expiry of the particular BIT. Generally, such provisions indicate that investments that were otherwise covered by the treaty whilst in force will continue to benefit from the same protection for a specified 'sunset' period, usually of between ten and fifteen years after termination or expiry.[37] **8.16**

---

investment protections and separate but identical arbitration provisions, here CAFTA and the Investment Law.'

[33] The UNCTAD website provides a database of international investment agreements at http://investmentpolicyhub.unctad.org/IIA.

[34] Treaties that have been signed may not necessarily be in force. A treaty enters into force in accordance with the procedure provided for within the treaty itself. This usually involves the exchange of instruments of ratification between the contracting states.

[35] Treaty between the United States and the Argentine Republic Concerning the Reciprocal Encouragement and Protection of Investment, signed on 14 November 1991, entered into force on 20 October 1994, Art. XIV(1).

[36] Award, ICSID Case No. ARB(AF)/00/02, IIC 247 (2003). The tribunal noted, however, that the pre-BIT acts of the host state would be relevant to consider a continuing or aggravating breach of the BIT. See also *Empresas Lucchetti, SA and Lucchetti Peru, SA v Republic of Peru*, Award, ICSID Case No. ARB/03/4, IIC 88 (2005), at [53]; *Phoenix Action Ltd v The Czech Republic*, Award, ICSID Case No. ARB/06/5, IIC 367 (2009), at [68].

[37] For instance, in May 2008, the Bolivarian Republic of Venezuela denounced its BIT with the Netherlands. In accordance with its terms, the termination of the BIT took effect on 1 November 2008. However, in view of its fifteen-year survival clause, investments made prior to 1 November 2008 remain protected by the BIT until 2023: see Agreement on Encouragement and Reciprocal Protection of Investments between the Kingdom of the Netherlands and the Republic of Venezuela, signed on 22 October 1991, entered into force 1 November 1993, Art. 14.

(b) Protected investors

8.17 Once a potentially applicable treaty has been identified, the relevant treaty provisions defining the eligible 'investors', or 'nationals', should be reviewed. Although treaties may vary substantially in this respect, the following provision of the Switzerland–Pakistan BIT is representative:

> For the purposes of this Agreement:
>
> (1) The term 'investor' refers with regard to either Contracting Party to:
> (a) natural persons who, according to the law of that Contracting Party, are considered to be its nationals;
> (b) legal entities, including companies, corporations, business associations and other organisations, which are constituted or otherwise duly organised under the law of that Contracting Party and have their seat, together with real economic activities, in the territory of that same Contracting Party;
> (c) legal entities established under the law of any country which are, directly or indirectly, controlled by nationals of that Contracting Party or by legal entities having their seat, together with real economic activities, in the territory of that same Contracting Party.[38]

Investors covered by protection of investment treaties can thus be divided into natural persons and legal entities.

(i) Natural persons

8.18 Most BIT provisions establish the nationality of a natural person by reference to the domestic laws of the respective contracting states. This is consistent with the concept of state sovereignty in deciding the criteria for identifying its nationals. Certain BITs may contain an additional requirement of residence,[39] or domicile.[40]

8.19 Difficulties may arise where the purported investor is a national of both state parties to the BIT. The ICSID Convention precludes individuals from suing any state of which they are nationals.[41] Tribunals have favoured formal nationality, rather than the test of effective (or dominant) nationality, in determining whether an individual qualifies as a 'national of another [ICSID] Contracting State' under the Convention.[42] This preclusion of an investor who also holds the nationality

---

[38] Agreement between the Swiss Confederation and the Islamic Republic of Pakistan concerning the Reciprocal Promotion and Protection of Investments, signed on 11 July 1995, entered into force on 6 May 1996, Art. 1. Free translation from the French original.

[39] See, e.g., Treaty between the Federal Republic of Germany and the State of Israel concerning the Encouragement and the Reciprocal Protection of Investments, signed on 24 June 1976, entered into force on 14 April 1980, Art. 1(3)(b).

[40] See, e.g., Agreement between the Government of Denmark and the Government of the Republic of Indonesia Concerning the Encouragement and the Reciprocal Protection of Investments, signed on 30 January 1968, entered into force on 10 March 1970, Art. 1.

[41] ICSID Convention, Art. 25(2)(a).

[42] See *Ioan Micula and ors v Romania*, Decision on Jurisdiction and Admissibility, ICSID Case No. ARB/05/20, IIC 339 (2008), at [101]; *Waguih Elie George Siag and Clorinda Vecchi v The Arab Republic of Egypt*, Decision on Jurisdiction, ICSID Case No. ARB/05/15, IIC 288 (2007).

B. Jurisdictional Issues

of the host state does not apply where other arbitration mechanisms, such as the UNCITRAL arbitration rules, are used, provided that there is no separate express prohibition on dual nationals in the BIT itself.[43]

(ii) Legal entities

All investment treaties extend the benefit of their protection to legal entities such as companies. Many BITs simply require that the entity be incorporated or constituted under the laws of one of the contracting parties. Some treaties add other requirements, such as the need actually to carry out business in the home state.[44] **8.20**

Where no such additional requirements have been stipulated, tribunals generally conduct a review limited to determining whether the legal entity satisfies the formal definition of investor under the treaty and refuse to incorporate additional requirements that the treaty drafters did not include. For instance, in *Yukos Universal Ltd (Isle of Man) v Russian Federation*,[45] Russia argued that the claimant should not qualify as an investor under the ECT (which defines 'investors' based on the law under which an entity is organised), because it was a shell company that was owned and controlled by Russian nationals. In rejecting this argument, the tribunal held that it knew of 'no general principles of international law that would require investigating how a company or another organization operates when the applicable treaty simply requires it to be organized in accordance with the laws of a Contracting Party' and refused to 'write new, additional requirements—which the drafters did not include—into a treaty, no matter how auspicious or appropriate they may appear'.[46] **8.21**

---

[43] Most BITs contain no such exclusions. An exception to this general practice is the Canada–Venezuela BIT, which excludes persons holding citizenship of both the contracting states from the definition of 'investors' for the purposes of the agreement: see Agreement between the Government of Canada and the Government of the Republic of Venezuela for the Promotion and Protection of Investments, signed on 1 July 1996, entered into force on 28 January 1998, Art. I(g).

[44] See, e.g., Agreement on Encouragement and Reciprocal Protection of Investments between the Kingdom of the Netherlands and the Argentine Republic, signed on 20 October 1992, entered into force on 1 October 1994, Art. 1(b):

> [T]he term 'investor' shall comprise with regard to either Contracting Party:...
> (ii)...legal persons constituted under the law of that Contracting Party and actually doing business under the laws in force in any part of the territory of that Contracting Party in which a place of effective management is situated; and (iii) legal persons, wherever located, controlled, directly or indirectly, by nationals of that Contracting Party.

[45] Interim Award on Jurisdiction and Admissibility, UNCITRAL, PCA Case No. AA 228, IIC 416 (2009).

[46] Ibid., at [415]. Similarly, in *Mobil Corporation, Venezuela Holdings BV and ors v Bolivarian Republic of Venezuela*, Decision on Jurisdiction, ICSID Case No. ARB/07/27, IIC 435 (2010), the host state, Venezuela, argued, among other things, that the exercise of genuine control by a Dutch national over a non-Dutch investor entity was required for the nationality requirement under the Netherlands–Venezuela BIT to be met, even though this was not provided for in the BIT. The tribunal held that formal control was sufficient and that the exercise of genuine control was not relevant.

8.22 Similarly, in *Tokios Tokelės v Ukraine*,[47] a majority of the arbitrators held that an investor incorporated in Lithuania qualified as an investor under the Lithuania–Ukraine BIT,[48] even though 99 per cent of its shares were owned by Ukrainian nationals. By contrast, in *TSA Spectrum de Argentina SA v Argentine Republic*,[49] a majority denied jurisdiction under the Netherlands–Argentina BIT[50] over a claim against Argentina brought by an Argentine company claiming to be 'controlled' by its Dutch parent (which owned 100 per cent of its shares). The tribunal looked beyond the claimant's immediate (Dutch) parent company and found that its 'ultimate owner' was an Argentine national. The tribunal then held that Article 25(2)(b) of the ICSID Convention's 'foreign control' requirement for juridical entities having the nationality of the state party to the arbitration had not been met.

8.23 The natural consequence of the formalistic language of most treaties is that adopting a particular corporate structure for the purposes of attracting the protection of an investment treaty is wholly legitimate (as it is in the case of tax structuring). In *Aguas del Tunari SA v Republic of Bolivia*,[51] the tribunal rejected Bolivia's objection that the 'availability of the BIT was the result of strategic changes in the corporate structure', noting that:

> [I]t is not uncommon in practice, and – absent a particular limitation – not illegal to locate one's operations in a jurisdiction perceived to provide a beneficial regulatory and legal environment in terms, for examples, of taxation or the substantive law of the jurisdiction, including the availability of a BIT.[52]

8.24 Some tribunals have nevertheless drawn the line where the restructuring of an investment has been undertaken solely to gain BIT protections in relation to an earlier dispute, holding that this would amount to a lack of good faith and an 'abusive manipulation of the system'.[53] Thus, in *Mobil Corporation Venezuela Holdings*

---

[47] Decision on Jurisdiction, ICSID Case No. ARB/02/18, IIC 258 (2004). The tribunal refused to pierce the corporate veil because there was no evidence that the claimant had used its status as a Lithuanian entity for an improper purpose, noting, at [56], that 'the Claimant manifestly did not create Tokios Tokelės for the purpose of gaining access to ICSID arbitration under the BIT against Ukraine, as the enterprise was founded six years before the BIT between Ukraine and Lithuania entered into force'. See also *The Rompetrol Group NV v Romania*, Decision on Preliminary Objections, ICSID Case No. ARB/06/3, IIC 322 (2008).

[48] Agreement between the Government of Lithuania and the Government of Ukraine Concerning the Protection and Promotion of Investment, signed on 8 February 1994, entered into force on 6 March 1995.

[49] Award, ICSID Case No. ARB/05/5, IIC 358 (2008), at [160]–[162].

[50] Agreement on Encouragement and Reciprocal Protection of Investments between the Kingdom of the Netherlands and the Argentine Republic, signed on 20 October 1992, entered into force on 1 October 1994.

[51] Decision on Respondent's Objections to Jurisdiction, ICSID Case No ARB/02/3, IIC 8 (2005).

[52] Ibid., at [330].

[53] *Mobil Corporation Venezuela Holdings BV and ors v Bolivarian Republic of Venezuela*, Decision on Jurisdiction, n. 46, at [405], citing *Phoenix Action Ltd v The Czech Republic*, Award, n. 36, at [93] and [144]. See also *Tidewater Inc. and ors v The Bolivarian Republic of Venezuela*, Decision on Jurisdiction, ICSID Case No. ARB/10/5, IIC 573 (2013), at [146].

B. Jurisdictional Issues

BV v Bolivarian Republic of Venezuela,[54] the tribunal held that it had jurisdiction over claims relating to nationalisation measures taken by Venezuela after the corporate restructuring in question had taken place, but not claims relating to disputes over royalty and tax rates that had arisen prior to the restructuring.

Some treaties seek to limit the scope of protection to protected investors by means of treaty clauses allowing the state parties to deny treaty benefits to investors that do not have substantial business activities in their home state and which are controlled by entities or persons of a third state (known as 'denial of benefits' clauses).[55] While it remains a matter of debate whether these clauses can be applied retroactively (that is, after an investment is made),[56] tribunals have held that respondent states bear the burden of proving that the requisite elements have been satisfied.[57] **8.25**

Legal entities established in the host state (and therefore having the nationality of the respondent state) may receive treaty protection if (a) they are controlled by entities incorporated in the other contracting state, and (b) both states have agreed in the applicable treaty to extend the protection of the treaty to such controlled entities. This extension is expressly permitted by Article 25(2)(b) of the ICSID Convention.[58] For example, Article 1(2)(c) of the Argentina–France BIT extends protection to: **8.26**

> ...legal persons effectively controlled directly or indirectly by nationals of one of the Contracting Parties or by legal persons having their registered office in the

---

[54] See n. 46.
[55] See, e.g., Treaty between the Government of the United States of America and the Government of the Republic of Bolivia Concerning the Encouragement and Reciprocal Protection of Investment, Art. XII:

> Each Party reserves the right to deny to a company of the other Party the benefits of this Treaty if nationals of a third country own or control the company and: (a) the denying Party does not maintain normal economic relations with the third country; or (b) the company has no substantial business activities in the territory of the Party under whose laws it is constituted or organized.

[56] See *Plama Consortium Ltd v Republic of Bulgaria*, Decision on Jurisdiction, ICSID Case No. ARB/03/24, IIC 189 (2005), at [162]–[165] (holding that denial-of-benefits clause cannot be invoked retroactively, after an investment has been made); *Guaracachi America Inc. and Rurelec Plc v The Plurinational State of Bolivia*, Award, PCA Case No. 2011-17, IIC 628 (2014), at [376]–[378] (holding the denial-of-benefits clause under the United States–Bolivia BIT could be validly invoked after the dispute arose).
[57] See, e.g., *Ulysseas Inc. v The Republic of Ecuador*, Interim Award, UNCITRAL, 28 September 2010, at [166].
[58] Article 25(2)(b) states:

> National of another Contracting state means:...any juridical person which had the nationality of the Contracting state party to the dispute...and which, because of foreign control, the parties have agreed should be treated as a national of another Contracting state for the purposes of this Convention.

This 'agreement' is usually explicit (e.g. in the definition of 'investor' in a BIT). It may also be implicit: see *Millicom International Operations BV & Sentel GSM SA v The Republic of Senegal*, Decision on Jurisdiction, ICSID Case No. ARB/08/20, IIC 450 (2010), at [109]–[115] (holding that consent can be implied where the host state entered into an agreement with a local entity containing an ICSID arbitration clause).

territory of one of the Contracting Parties and constituted in accordance with legislation of the latter.[59]

8.27 Thus a locally incorporated entity may claim against its state of incorporation if controlled by a national or company of the other contracting state. This is significant because it is often expedient, or even necessary, to incorporate a local entity to hold an investment, and this extension of protection allows the local entity to bring a claim for its direct losses. It also enables minority shareholders in the local entity (many of whom may be local investors) to obtain indirect relief through treaty arbitration.

(c) Protected investments

8.28 In order to rely on an investment treaty, a qualifying 'investor' must establish that it has made a protected 'investment'. Most investment treaties contain a definition of what constitutes an 'investment'.[60] They tend to provide a definition that commences with a broad statement, often referring to 'every kind of asset',[61] or 'every kind of investment in the territory',[62] and then add a non-exhaustive list of examples. The United Kingdom–Chile treaty[63] is typical in this respect and provides, at Article 1(a), that:

> ... 'investment' means every kind of asset and in particular, though not exclusively, includes:
> (i) movable and immovable property and any other property rights such as mortgages, liens and pledges;
> (ii) shares in, and stock and debentures of a company, and any other form of participation in a company;
> (iii) claims to money or to any performance under contract having a financial value;
> (iv) intellectual property rights, goodwill, technical processes and know-how;
> (v) business concessions conferred by law or under contract, including concessions to search for, cultivate or extract or exploitation of natural resources.

---

[59] Agreement between the Government of the French Republic and the Government of the Republic of Argentina on the Encouragement and the Reciprocal Protection of Investments, signed on 3 July 1991, entered into force on 3 March 1993, Art. 1(2)(c). Free translation from the French original.

[60] See UNCTAD, *Scope and Definitions (A Sequel)*, Series on Issues in International Investment Agreements II (UN, 2011), available online at http://unctad.org/.

[61] See Agreement between the Government of the Union of Soviet Socialist Republics and the Government of the United Kingdom of Great Britain and Northern Ireland for the Promotion and Reciprocal Protection of Investments, signed on 6 April 1989, entered into force on 3 July 1991, Art. 1(a); ECT, Art. 1(6).

[62] See Treaty between the United States of America and the Argentine Republic Concerning the Reciprocal Encouragement and Protection of Investments, n. 35, Art. I(1)(a).

[63] Agreement between the Government of the United Kingdom of Great Britain and Northern Ireland and the Government of Chile for the Promotion and Protection of Investments, signed on 8 January 1996, entered into force on 21 April 1997.

B. Jurisdictional Issues

The open-ended definition acknowledges that the concept of 'investment' is **8.29** dynamic and may evolve over time. A tribunal entertaining an investment treaty claim must therefore analyse whether the claimant's investment satisfies the definition in the treaty that has been invoked.

Most treaties provide that a shareholding in a company established in the host **8.30** country constitutes an investment. In *AMT v Zaire*,[64] the ICSID tribunal rejected Zaire's argument that AMT, an American company, had not made any direct investment in Zaire, because it had merely participated in the share capital of a Zairian company. The arbitral tribunal held that investments via the share capital of a local entity were eligible for protection under the United States–Zaire BIT.[65] And, in *CMS v Argentina*,[66] the tribunal held that the American claimant's minority shareholding in an Argentine company qualified as a protected investment. Such decisions are important because host states often impose an obligation that the ultimate investment vehicle be a locally incorporated entity.

The definition of 'investment' has been interpreted to cover direct and indirect **8.31** investments, and modern contractual and other transactions having economic value.[67]

An indirect shareholding in a local company via one or several intermediary com- **8.32** panies has been held to constitute a protected investment, even where the treaty's definition of 'investment' does not expressly include 'indirect' investments. In *Tza Yap Shum v Peru*,[68] the tribunal held that a Chinese national's indirect shareholding in a local Peruvian company, which was held via an intermediary company established in the British Virgin Islands, could be considered a protected investment for the purposes of the Peru–China BIT.

---

[64] *American Manufacturing and Trading Inc. v Republic of Zaire*, Award, ICSID Case No. ARB/93/1, IIC 14 (1997), at [5.08]–[5.15].
[65] Treaty between the United States of America and the Republic of Zaire concerning the Reciprocal Encouragement and Protection of Investment, signed on 3 August 1994, entered into force on 28 July 1989, defining 'investments' as including 'a company or shares of stock or other interests in a company or interests in the assets thereof'.
[66] *CMS Gas Transmission Co. v The Republic of Argentina*, Decision on Jurisdiction, ICSID Case No. ARB/01/8, IIC 64 (2003), at [36]–[65]. See also *Suez, Sociedad General de Aguas de Barcelona SA and InterAguas Servicios Integrales del Agua SA v The Argentine Republic*, Decision on Jurisdiction, ICSID Case No. ARB/03/17, IIC 236 (2006), at [51].
[67] See, e.g., Parra, 'The scope of new investment laws and international instruments', in Pritchard (ed.) *Economic Development, Foreign Investment and the Law* (Kluwer Law International, 1996), p. 35. See also UNCTAD, *Scope and Definitions (A Sequel)*, Agreements II (UN, 2011), n. 60.
[68] *Sr Tza Yap Shum v Republic of Peru*, Decision on Jurisdiction and Competence, ICSID Case No. ARB/07/6, IIC 382 (2009); Agreement between the Government of the Republic of Peru and the Government of the People's Republic of China Concerning the Encouragement and Reciprocal Protection of Investments, signed on 9 June 1994, entered into force on 1 February 1995.

8.33 Indirect investments in assets, rather than shareholdings, have also been held to be protected. In *Mobil Corporation v Bolivarian Republic of Venezuela*[69] the tribunal held that a Dutch company had a qualifying investment in a Venezuelan joint venture, even though the party to that agreement was its Bahamian subsidiary, and the Netherlands–Argentina BIT[70] did not expressly specify that both direct and indirect investments were covered.[71]

8.34 Tribunals have also recognised that financial investments qualify for protection under BITs, even though they do not correspond to the conventional notion of 'foreign investment' in that they do not necessarily involve an inflow of funds into the host state or the active management of an investment.[72] For example, in *Fedax NV v Republic of Venezuela*,[73] the arbitral tribunal held that promissory notes issued by Venezuela, acquired by the claimant from the original holder in the secondary market by way of endorsement, constituted an investment under the Netherlands–Venezuela BIT. The relevant BIT included 'titles to money' as a category of investment, and the tribunal rejected the contention of the Republic of Venezuela that this item was restricted to classic forms of direct foreign investment—that is, 'the laying out of money or property in business ventures, so that it may produce a revenue or income'.[74] The tribunal also held that 'it is a standard feature of many international finance transactions that the funds involved are not physically transferred to the territory of the host country but are put at its disposal elsewhere'.[75]

8.35 Subsequent tribunals have opined that loans,[76] government bonds, and related security entitlements[77] can constitute protected 'investments' under the broad

---

[69] See n. 46.
[70] See n. 37.
[71] But see *Standard Chartered Bank v United Republic of Tanzania*, Award, ICSID Case No. ARB/10/12, IIC 581 (2012). In this case, the tribunal held that a loan made in Tanzania was not a protected investment. The passive indirect ownership of the loan by the claimant, a British company, did not suffice for the purposes of the United Kingdom–Tanzania BIT, which it interpreted as requiring an investor to contribute actively to an investment.
[72] See also *Tokios Tokelės v Ukraine*, Decision on Jurisdiction, n. 47, at [77]–[80], in which the tribunal noted that the requirement that there be a transfer of capital was absent from the text, and contrary to the object and purpose of the BIT.
[73] Decision on Objections to Jurisdiction, ICSID Case No ARB/96/3, IIC 101 (1997). The definition contained in the applicable BIT was substantially the same as that one quoted at paragraph 8.28.
[74] Ibid., at [41].
[75] Ibid.
[76] *Ceskoslovenska Obchodni Banka AS v The Slovak Republic*, Decision on Objections to Jurisdiction, ICSID Case No. ARB/97/4, IIC 49 (1999). In this case, no funds were actually transferred to the Slovak Republic pursuant to the loan. However, owing to the close connection of the loan facility to the development of banking facilities in the Slovak Republic, the same was held to be an investment.
[77] *Abaclat and ors v The Argentine Republic*, Decision on Jurisdiction and Admissibility, ICSID Case No. ARB/07/5, IIC 504 (2011); see also *Ambiente Ufficio SPA and ors v The*

B. Jurisdictional Issues

headings of the relevant BIT's definition of investment, such as 'assets', 'claims to money', or 'obligations'. Some tribunals have held that whilst certain financial transactions taken in isolation might not qualify as investments, they may nevertheless be so considered if the overall operation of which they are part, or to which they are connected, constitutes an investment.[78]

8.36 In order to determine whether a purported 'investment' qualifies for protection under the treaty, it may be necessary to consider the conditions under which the investment was admitted into the host state.[79] Investments procured by fraud or corruption, or made in violation of the host state's public policy laws or international principles of good faith, will generally not be protected. For instance, the tribunal in *Inceysa Vallisoletana SL v Republic of El Salvador*[80] declined jurisdiction on the basis that the investment, a concession contract, was obtained through fraud. And in *Phoenix Action Ltd v Czech Republic*,[81] the tribunal declined jurisdiction on the basis that the claimant's acquisition of an interest in two Czech companies for the sole purpose of bringing a claim against the Czech Republic was not an 'investment' under the BIT, because it was not made in good faith.

8.37 Moreover, some treaties contain conditions requiring that the investment be specifically approved, or 'classified', by the host state. In *Philippe Gruslin v Malaysia*,[82] the tribunal declined jurisdiction on the ground that the concerned investment was not made in a project *approved* by Malaysia, which was a precondition to accessing the protection of the agreement. However, some tribunals have prevented states from relying on formal requirements where the investment has otherwise been clearly approved by the state. In *Desert Line Projects LLC v The Republic of Yemen*,[83] the tribunal upheld its jurisdiction despite the claimant's failure to produce an 'investment certificate'—a requirement under the BIT. The tribunal did not consider that the granting of a specific certificate was an indispensable formality for jurisdictional purposes and it emphasised that the investment had been endorsed at the highest level of the state.

Argentine Republic, Decision on Jurisdiction and Admissibility, ICSID Case No. ARB/08/9, IIC 576 (2013).

[78] *Ceskoslovenska Obchodni Banka*, n. 76.

[79] See, e.g., Agreement between the Government of Canada and the Government of the Republic of Argentina for the Protection and Promotion of Investments, signed on 5 November 1991, entered into force on 29 April 1993, Art. 1(a), requiring that the investment be 'made in accordance with the laws' of the host state.

[80] Decision on Jurisdiction, ICSID Case No. ARB/03/26, IIC 134 (2006). See also *Gustav F W Hamester GmbH & Co. KG v Republic of Ghana*, Award, ICSID Case No. ARB/07/24, IIC 456 (2010), at [122]–[124].

[81] See n. 36. See also *Cementownia 'Nowa Huta' SA v Republic of Turkey*, Award, ICSID Case No. ARB(AF)/06/2, IIC 390 (2009), at [146]–[149].

[82] Award, ICSID Case No. ARB/99/3, IIC 129 (2000), (2000) 5 ICSID Rep 492.

[83] Award, ICSID Case No. ARB/05/17, IIC 319 (2008), at [116]–[118].

8.38 In addition to satisfying the definition of 'investment' in the BIT, several tribunals have required that an investment also possess certain objective characteristics in order to qualify for protection. This case law was developed in the context of Article 25 of the ICSID Convention, which requires that legal disputes arise directly out of an 'investment'.[84] The Convention, however, does not define the term 'investment',[85] leaving it to contracting states to do so, such as by means of BIT clauses. However, certain tribunals and commentators have opined that the term 'investment' in the ICSID Convention must be understood as setting 'outer limits' to, or mandatory requirements for, ICSID's jurisdiction that cannot be left to the discretion of the parties.[86] In this regard, it is often noted that a simple contract for the sale of goods, without more, could not qualify as an investment under Article 25 of the Convention, even if this were the subject of an agreement by the parties.[87]

8.39 The tribunals that adhere to this view typically apply some version of the so-called *Salini* test, which was laid out in *Salini v Morocco*—although it originally derives from *Fedax v Venezuela*.[88] The tribunal in that latter case opined that '[t]he basic features of an investment have been described as involving a certain duration, a certain regularity of profit and return, assumption of risk, a substantial commitment and a significance for the host State's development'.[89]

8.40 Among the tribunals that have applied the *Salini* test, there is disagreement as to how it should be applied and which factors should be considered. Perhaps the most controversial aspect is whether (and to what extent) investments must contribute to the economic development of a state (a factor drawn from the Preamble of the ICSID Convention[90]). The tribunal in *LESI SpA and ASTALDI SpA v People's*

---

[84] See 8.42.
[85] ICSID, 'Report of the Executive Directors of the International Bank for Reconstruction and Development on the ICSID Convention', n. 8, p. 44, para. 27 explains that:

> [N]o attempt was made to define the term 'investment' given the essential requirement of consent by the parties, and the mechanism through which Contracting States can make known in advance, if they so desire, the classes of disputes which they would or would not consider submitting to the Centre (Article 25(4)).

[86] Schreuer, Malintoppi, Reinisch, and Sinclair, *The ICSID Convention: A Commentary*, n. 7, p. 83.
[87] See, e.g., *SGS Société Générale de Surveillance SA v Republic of Paraguay*, Decision on Jurisdiction, ICSID Case No. ARB/07/29, IIC 525 (2010), at [93].
[88] *Salini Costruttori SpA and Italstrade SpA v Morocco*, Decision on Jurisdiction, ICSID Case No. ARB/00/4, IIC 207 (2004); *Fedax NV v Republic of Venezuela*, Decision on Objections to Jurisdiction, n. 73.
[89] *Fedax NV v Republic of Venezuela*, ibid., at [43].
[90] The first paragraph of the Preamble to the ICSID Convention reads: 'Considering the need for international cooperation for economic development, and the role of private international investment therein...'

B. Jurisdictional Issues

Democratic Republic of Algeria[91] considered this requirement to be irrelevant. By contrast, the ad hoc committee in *Patrick Mitchell v Democratic Republic of the Congo*[92] held that 'the existence of a contribution to the economic development of the host State as an essential – although not sufficient – characteristic or unquestionable criterion of the investment, does not mean that this contribution must always be sizable or successful'.[93]

Other tribunals, however, reject the *Salini* test as inappropriately narrowing the definition of 'investment' in the investment treaty. The annulment committee in *Malaysian Historical Salvors, SDN, BHD v Malaysia*[94] decided, by majority, to annul the original sole arbitrator's decision that a salvage contract was not an 'investment' under Article 25 of the ICSID Convention because it did not sufficiently contribute to Malaysia's economic development. The decision rejected the elevation of the *Salini* criteria to jurisdictional conditions and criticised the arbitrator's failure to apply the broad definition of investment in the applicable BIT. 8.41

This doctrine of the objective notion of investment has recently been applied outside the ICSID context, in an UNCITRAL case: *Romak SA (Switzerland) v Republic of Uzbekistan*.[95] In that case, the tribunal was asked to determine whether a transfer of title to wheat amounted to an investment. Referring to the 'inherent meaning' of the term 'investments' under the BIT—which the tribunal held included a contribution over a certain period of time involving some risk—the tribunal concluded that this one-off transaction did not constitute an investment. This approach in a non-ICSID context was criticised in *Guaracachi America Inc. and Rurelec Plc v Plurinational State of Bolivia*,[96] in which it was held that: 8.42

> [I]t is not appropriate to import 'objective' definitions of investment... when in the context of a non-ICSID arbitration such as the present case. On the contrary, the definition of protected investment, at least in non-ICSID arbitrations, is to be obtained only from the (very broad) definition contained in the BIT...

Whilst the notion of investment has been expanding, it has its limitations. As noted already, ordinary commercial transactions are generally not protected 8.43

---

[91] Award, ICSID Case No. ARB/05/3, IIC 354 (2008). See also *Mr Saba Fakes v Republic of Turkey*, Award, ICSID Case No. ARB/07/20, IIC 439 (2010), at [110].
[92] Decision on the Application for Annulment of the Award, ICSID Case No ARB/99/7, IIC 172 (2006).
[93] Ibid., at [33].
[94] Decision on Jurisdiction, ICSID Case No. ARB/05/10, IIC 289 (2007).
[95] Award, PCA Case No. AA280, IIC 400 (2009).
[96] See n. 56, at [364].

by investment treaties or the ICSID Convention.[97] In other cases, tribunals have found that bank guarantees contingent on a sales contract[98] and expenses incurred in bidding for a public contract were not investments under the applicable BIT.[99]

8.44 Moreover, in some recent BITs, states have narrowed the scope of protection by expressly excluding portfolio investments[100] and commercial contracts,[101] or by requiring that investments have certain inherent characteristics by reference to criteria associated with the *Salini* test.[102] Other states have limited the scope of their BITs by excluding certain classes of dispute arising out of investments in certain sectors, which they are permitted to do under Article 25(4) of the ICSID Convention, although such exclusions are unlikely to affect treaties already in place.[103]

(d) Consent and conditions to access investment treaty arbitration

8.45 In order to access arbitration under a treaty, both parties must consent. Host states set out their consent in the text of the investment treaties. Typically, the consent will include procedural preconditions to be fulfilled, such as the written notification of a dispute and the expiry of a specified period within which the investor seeks to engage the host state in amicable consultations (also known as a 'cooling-off period'). Other treaties require the investor to pursue remedies before the courts of the host state for a minimum period prior to commencing arbitration. The question arises: what happens if an investor fails to comply with such conditions?

---

[97] See paragraph 8.38. However, in *GEA Group Aktiengesellschaft v Ukraine*, Award, ICSID Case No. ARB/05/18, IIC 487 (2011), the tribunal found that a conversion contract involving the delivery of diesel, catalysts, and other materials, as well as know-how on logistics and market and other services, was a 'complex relationship going far beyond the simple sale of raw materials', and therefore constituted a protected investment.

[98] *Joy Mining Machinery Ltd v Arab Republic of Egypt*, Award on Jurisdiction, ICSID Case No. ARB/03/11, IIC 147 (2004), at [44]–[47]. The tribunal reached this conclusion notwithstanding the fact that the BIT defined 'investment' as every kind of asset, including mortgage, lien or pledge, and claims to money or to any other performance under contract having a financial value: see ibid., at [38].

[99] *Mihaly International Corporation v Democratic Socialist Republic of Sri Lanka*, Award, ICSID Case No. ARB/00/2, IIC 170 (2002).

[100] See, e.g., European Free Trade Association (EFTA)–Mexico FTA, signed 27 November 2000, entered into force on 1 July 2001, Art. 45.

[101] See, e.g., Canada Model BIT (2004), Art. 1.

[102] See, e.g., United States Model BIT (2012), Art. 1, which defines 'investment' as 'every asset that an investor owns or controls, directly or indirectly, that has the characteristics of an investment, including such characteristics as the commitment of capital or other resources, the expectation of gain or profit, or the assumption of risk'.

[103] For instance, in 1974, Jamaica excluded legal disputes arising directly out of an investment relating to minerals or other natural resources. In 2007, Ecuador provided a similar notice under Art. 25(4) of the ICSID Convention in respect of disputes arising out of investments in the natural resources sector. (Ecuador then notified its denunciation of the Convention on 6 July 2009.)

B. Jurisdictional Issues

The level of detail required for notifications of dispute sent under investment **8.46** treaties depends upon the requirements set out in the text of the treaty and their interpretation. Several tribunals have held it to be unnecessary for the investor to 'spell out its legal case in detail',[104] or even to allege a breach of the BIT itself,[105] during the initial negotiation process and that it is sufficient for it to inform the state of the allegations that may later be invoked to engage the host state's international responsibility before an international tribunal.[106] Other tribunals, including the tribunal in *Burlington Resources Inc. v Republic of Ecuador*,[107] have held that a notification must refer to specific breaches of the BIT and have declined jurisdiction over one of several claims on the basis that it had not been specifically notified.

An important question arises as to whether consultation periods are procedural or **8.47** jurisdictional in nature. If procedural, then failure to comply where the purpose of the clause is frustrated (for example when the host state has failed to engage in discussions) does not impact on the consent to arbitrate.[108] For example, in *Ronald S Lauder v The Czech Republic*,[109] the tribunal waived the waiting period in the following terms:

> However, the Arbitral Tribunal considers that this requirement of a six-month waiting period of Art VI(3)(a) of the Treaty is not a jurisdictional provision, ie a limit set to the authority of the Arbitral Tribunal to decide on the merits of the dispute, but a procedural rule that must be satisfied by the Claimant (*Ethyl Corp v Canada*, UNCITRAL June 24, 1998, 38 ILM 708 (1999), paras 74–88). As stated above, the purpose of this rule is to allow the parties to engage in good-faith negotiations before initiating arbitration.[110]

Similarly, the tribunal in *Biwater Gauff (Tanzania) Ltd v United Republic of* **8.48** *Tanzania*[111] held that the six-month amicable settlement period under the BIT was 'procedural and directory in nature', the purpose of which was 'to facilitate

---

[104] *Tulip Real Estate Investment and Development Netherlands BV v Republic of Turkey*, Decision on Bifurcated Jurisdictional Issue, ICSID Case No. ARB/11/28, IIC 583 (2013), at [83].
[105] *Compañía de Aguas del Aconquija SA and Vivendi Universal SA v Argentine Republic*, Decision on Annulment, ICSID Case No. ARB/97/3, IIC 307 (2007).
[106] *Tulip Real Estate*, n. 104, at [83].
[107] Decision on Jurisdiction, ICSID Case No. ARB/08/5, IIC 436 (2010), at [334]–[337]. See also *Murphy Exploration and Production Co. International v Republic of Ecuador*, Award on Jurisdiction, ICSID Case No. ARB/08/4, 15 December 2010, at [102]–[105].
[108] See, e.g., *Abaclat and ors v The Argentine Republic*, Decision on Jurisdiction and Admissibility, n. 77; *Alps Finance and Trade AG v Slovak Republic*, Award, UNCITRAL, 5 March 2011, IIC 489 (2011), at [200]–[212]; *Teinver SA, Transportes de Cercanias SA, Audobuses Urbanos del Sur SA v Argentine Republic*, Decision on Jurisdiction, ICSID Case No. ARB/09/1, IIC 570 (2012), at [107]*ff*.
[109] Final Award UNCITRAL 3 September 2001 1 IIC 205 (2001).
[110] Ibid., at [187]. Moreover, in the tribunal's view (at [190]), '[t]o insist that the arbitration proceedings cannot be commenced until six months after the 19 August 1999 Notice of Arbitration would, in the circumstances of this case, amount to an unnecessary, overly formalistic approach which would not serve to protect any legitimate interests of the Parties'.
[111] Award, ICSID Case No. ARB/05/22, IIC 330 (2008), at [343].

opportunities for amicable settlement...not to impede or obstruct arbitration proceedings'.

8.49 Similar approaches have been adopted with other preconditions to arbitration, such as the obligation to pursue local court remedies for a set period of time before accessing arbitration irrespective of whether or not the local court had issued a decision. In the case of *BG Group v Republic of Argentina*,[112] a treaty requirement to submit the dispute to the Argentine courts for eighteen months (without any obligation to be bound by the result, or even to reach a decision) before accessing arbitration was not held to be 'an absolute impediment to arbitration' in the particular circumstances. The circumstances were that the host state had severely restricted access to those local courts.[113]

8.50 Other tribunals, however, have held that conditions to access arbitration under a BIT, such as consultation periods, are jurisdictional prerequisites. For instance, in *Guaracachi America Inc. and Rurelec PLC v Plurinational State of Bolivia*,[114] the tribunal concluded that it lacked jurisdiction over certain claims because the claimants failed to observe a six-month 'cooling-off period', even though it considered that to have done so would have been likely to prove futile.

8.51 A separate issue is whether preconditions to arbitration can be avoided (or replaced) by relying on the 'most favoured nation' (MFN) clause of the applicable treaty in order to access more favourable preconditions in other treaties concluded by the host state of the investment. There is much debate as to whether MFN clauses can be applied to dispute settlement clauses in investment treaties.

8.52 This possibility was upheld by an ICSID tribunal in the *Maffezini* case.[115] Mr Maffezini was an Argentine investor, who had a dispute with the Government of

---

[112] Final Award, UNCITRAL, IIC 321 (2007).

[113] Ibid., at [147]. The conclusion of the tribunal on this point led Argentina to challenge the award before the courts of the seat, which was Washington, DC. Under the terms of the *lex arbitri*, the US Federal Arbitration Act of 1925 (FAA), the district court confirmed the award. However, the award was subsequently vacated by the district appellate court. An application for certiorari to the US Supreme Court was made and granted. This was the first time that an investment arbitration had been reviewed by the Supreme Court. The justices overruled the appellate court and held that the obligation to go to local courts for a set period without any obligation to await a final decision (or to agree to the final decision) was effectively a procedural precondition, which, in light of Supreme Court precedent, meant that deference should be given to the arbitral tribunal's decision.

[114] See n. 56 at [386] and [388]. See also *Enron Corporation and Ponderosa Assets LP v Argentine Republic*, Decision on Jurisdiction, ICSID Case No. ARB/01/3, IIC 92 (2004); *Burlington Resources Inc. v Republic of Ecuador*, Decision on Jurisdiction, n. 107; *Tulip Real Estate Investment and Development Netherlands BV v Republic of Turkey*, Decision on Bifurcated Jurisdictional Issue, n. 104.

[115] *Emilio Agustín Maffezini v The Kingdom of Spain*, Award on Jurisdiction, ICSID Case No. ARB/97/7, IIC 85 (2000).

B. Jurisdictional Issues

Spain arising out of an investment that he had made in Spain. He submitted his dispute to ICSID arbitration under the Spain–Argentina BIT,[116] despite the fact that the treaty had a dispute settlement clause requiring prior recourse to local courts for a period of eighteen months. Mr Maffezini pointed out that the MFN clause of the Spanish treaty obliged Spain to treat investors of Argentina no less favourably than third-party investors. Consequently, rather than taking his dispute to local courts, he invoked the MFN clause of the Spanish treaty in order to rely on the more favourable dispute settlement clause of another BIT concluded between Spain and Chile.[117] This treaty provided for access to international arbitration after only a six-month negotiation period.

The ICSID tribunal held that the text of the MFN clause of the Spanish treaty embraced the dispute settlement provisions of that treaty. Therefore, relying on the more favourable arrangements contained in the Chile–Spain BIT and, inter alia, the legal policy adopted by Spain with regard to the treatment of its own investors abroad (whereby it generally tried to secure for them the right to access international remedies without prior recourse to local remedies), Mr Maffezini had the right to submit the dispute to international arbitration without first accessing the Spanish courts. This position was upheld by a number of later tribunals,[118] but has not been unanimously adopted. In *Wintershall Aktiengesellschaft v Argentine Republic*,[119] the tribunal declined jurisdiction on the basis that the MFN clause did not embrace the dispute resolution provision. **8.53**

(e) Bilateral investment treaties and contractual dispute resolution clauses

Another issue is whether a state's consent to arbitration in a BIT is overridden by an exclusive choice-of-forum clause in a related investment contract. Tribunals have generally held that, as long as the arbitration claims allege a cause of action under the BIT, they are not subject to the contractually elected jurisdiction. In **8.54**

---

[116] Agreement between the Government of the Argentine Republic and the Kingdom of Spain for the Promotion and Reciprocal Protection of Investments, signed on 3 October 1991, entered into force on 28 September 1992.

[117] Agreement between the Republic of Chile and the Kingdom of Spain concerning the Reciprocal Encouragement and Protection of Investments, signed on 2 October 1991, entered into force on 29 March 1994.

[118] Since *Maffezini*, several tribunals have applied MFN clauses in order to bypass conditions for access to arbitration: see e.g. *Gas Natural SDG, SA v Argentine Republic*, Decision on Jurisdiction, ICSID Case No. ARB/03/10, IIC 115 (2005), at [30]–[31]; *Suez, Sociedad General de Aguas de Barcelona SA and InterAguas Servicios Integrales del Agua SA v The Argentine Republic*, Decision on Jurisdiction, n. 66.

[119] Award, ICSID Case No. ARB/04/14, IIC 357 (2008). Similarly, in *Daimler Financial Services v Argentine Republic*, Award, ICSID Case No. ARB/05/1, IIC 669 (2012), the tribunal held, by majority, that the clause requiring the pursuit of remedies before local courts for eighteen months was a condition precedent to arbitration that could not be altered through the application of the MFN clause.

Lanco v Argentina,[120] for example, the contract contained an exclusive jurisdiction clause in favour of the Argentine courts. Argentina argued that this clause applied and that the dispute was not within the jurisdiction of the ICSID tribunal. The tribunal rejected this argument, holding that the exclusive jurisdiction clause in the contract could not exclude the jurisdiction of the ICSID tribunal in relation to the BIT claim. Each claim had a separate source (one was based in contract and the other on the BIT) and each source had a separate dispute resolution provision.

8.55 In the *Vivendi* case,[121] the relevant investment was a concession contract concluded by the claimant with Tucumán, a province of Argentina. The claims concerned acts by Tucumán authorities interfering with the claimant's rights under the concession contract. Argentina argued that the dispute resolution clause of the contract, establishing the jurisdiction of the local courts for the purpose of interpretation and application of the contract, precluded jurisdiction under the French treaty. Rejecting this argument, an ICSID annulment committee held that:

> [W]here 'the fundamental basis of a claim' is a treaty laying down an *independent standard* by which the conduct of the parties is to be judged, the existence of an exclusive jurisdiction clause in the contract between the Claimant and the respondent state or one of its subdivisions cannot operate as a bar to the application of the treaty standard.[122]

The committee went on to state that BIT claims often involve taking into account the terms of a contract in determining whether there has been a breach of the BIT. This does not prevent the claims being BIT claims for which treaty arbitration is available.

8.56 The case law also suggests, however, that there may be cases in which the claims are, in reality, linked to the underlying contract only, so that the contract is the 'fundamental basis' of the claims, rather than the BIT. In this case, the contract clause may apply even if the claims are formally 'dressed up' as BIT claims.[123] This issue is further complicated by the issue of 'observance of undertakings', or 'umbrella', clauses in which the treaty apparently elevates contractual rights to the level of treaty rights. In such cases, purely contractual claims may also be categorised as treaty claims and jurisdiction should be granted. In such cases, there may be issues of admissibility where the relevant contract also includes an exclusive jurisdiction clause.[124]

---

[120] *Lanco International Inc. v Argentine Republic*, Award, ICSID Case No. ARB/97/6, 5 ICSID Rep 367, IIC 148 (1998).
[121] *Compañía de Aguas del Aconquija SA and Vivendi Universal SA v Argentine Republic*, Decision on Annulment, n. 105.
[122] Ibid., at [101] (emphasis added).
[123] See, e.g., *Camuzzi International SA v Argentine Republic*, Decision on Objections to Jurisdiction, ICSID Case No. ARB/03/2, IIC 41 (2005), at [89].
[124] See paragraphs 8.134–8.140 for a more detailed discussion of the scope of the 'umbrella clause' provisions.

B. Jurisdictional Issues

(f) Parallel claims before local courts

8.57 Another question that arises is whether consent to arbitration is affected by the pursuit of remedies before a local court through the operation of a so-called fork in the road provision. Many dispute settlement clauses of BITs provide that investors may choose to submit a dispute *either* to the local courts of the host state *or* to arbitration, and once made, the choice is final.[125] Thus if the investor has already submitted the investment dispute to the local courts, it may no longer resort to arbitration. Hence the 'fork in the road'.

8.58 Most tribunals have generally held that 'fork in the road' clauses bar arbitration claims under a treaty only where there is a 'triple identity', with the same object, parties, and cause of action being pursued simultaneously before local courts and in arbitration. As the tribunal in *Toto Construzioni Generali Spa v Lebanon* held:

> In order for a fork-in-the-road clause to preclude claims from being considered by the Tribunal, the Tribunal has to consider whether the same claim is 'on a different road,' ie that a claim with the same object, parties and cause of action, is already brought before a different judicial forum.[126]

8.59 Since disputes submitted to local courts tend to relate to contractual or regulatory issues that are distinct from the BIT breach issues submitted to arbitration, they do not usually trigger the fork-in-the-road provision.[127] As stated by the *CMS* tribunal in its decision on jurisdiction: 'As contractual claims are different from treaty claims, even if there had been or there currently was a recourse to local courts for breach of contract, this would not have prevented submission of the treaty claims to arbitration.'[128]

8.60 The case law, however, is not unanimous on this subject. In the *Pantechniki* award,[129] the tribunal dismissed a claim by the same claimant based on a fork-in-the-road clause because the 'fundamental basis of the claim' in the arbitration matched that of the local court proceeding. In this regard, the tribunal noted that

---

[125] See, e.g., Agreement between the Republic of Korea and the Republic of Chile on the Reciprocal Promotion and Protection of Investments, signed on 6 September 1996, entered into force on 16 September 1999, Art. 8(4): 'Once the investor has submitted the dispute to the competent tribunal of [the Host State], that selection shall be final.'

[126] *Toto Costruzioni Generali SpA v Republic of Lebanon*, Decision on Jurisdiction, ICSID Case No. ARB/07/12, IIC 391 (2009), at [211].

[127] Ibid., at [211]–[212]; *Total SA v The Argentine Republic*, Decision on Liability, ICSID Case No. ARB/04/01, IIC 484 (2010), at [443].

[128] *CMS Gas Transmission Co. v Argentine Republic*, Decision on Jurisdiction, n. 66. See Schreuer, 'Travelling the BIT route: Of waiting periods, umbrella clauses and forks in the road' (2004) 5 JWIT 231, at 247.

[129] *Pantechniki SA Contractors & Engineers (Greece) v The Republic of Albania*, Award, ICSID Case No. ARB/07/21, IIC 383 (2009), at [61] and [67].

the prayer for relief in the local court proceedings—namely, of payment amounts due under a contract—matched the relief sought before the tribunal:

> To the extent that this prayer was accepted it would grant the Claimant exactly what it is seeking before ICSID – and on the same 'fundamental basis'. The Claimant's grievance thus arises out of the same purported entitlement that it invoked in the contractual debate it began with the General Roads Directorate. The Claimant chose to take this matter to the Albanian courts. It cannot now adopt the same fundamental basis as the foundation of a Treaty claim. Having made the election to seize the national jurisdiction the Claimant is no longer permitted to raise the same contention before ICSID.[130]

8.61 Moreover, much may depend on the language of the treaty. Where a claimant is simultaneously pursuing a local remedy in respect of the same measures,[131] a tribunal constituted under an investment treaty should look carefully at whether the fork-in-the-road provision is limited to claims under the treaty, or merely to the resolution of a dispute arising out of the investment.

C. Law Applicable to the Substance of the Dispute

8.62 Bilateral investment treaties do not always contain specific provisions on the law to be applied by arbitral tribunals appointed to resolve disputes under the treaties. Those BITs that do contain applicable law provisions often list both international law and domestic law, without indicating which is pre-eminent or how they are to be combined. By way of example, Article 8 of the United Kingdom–Argentina BIT[132] provides that:

> The arbitral tribunal shall decide the dispute in accordance with the provisions of this Agreement, the laws of the Contracting Party involved in the dispute, including its rules on conflicts of laws, the terms of any specific agreement concluded in relation to such an investment and the applicable principles of international law.

8.63 Where the investment treaty is silent as to the applicable law, other instruments may provide guidance. Article 35(1) of the 2010 UNCITRAL Arbitration Rules provides that, failing a designation of the applicable law by the parties, 'the arbitral tribunal shall apply the law which it determines to be appropriate'.[133] Article 42 of

---

[130] Ibid., at [67].

[131] Defensive local actions that challenge measures impairing investments have been found not to trigger fork-in-the-road clauses: see, e.g., *Genin and ors v Republic of Estonia*, Award, ICSID Case No. ARB/99/2, IIC 10 (2001).

[132] Agreement between the Government of the United Kingdom of Great Britain and Northern Ireland and the Government of the Republic of Argentina for the Promotion and Protection of Investments, signed on 11 December 1990, entered into force on 19 February 1993.

[133] This stands in contrast to the less flexible approach set out in the 1976 UNCITRAL Rules, Art. 33(1) which provided that 'failing such designation by the parties, the arbitral tribunal shall apply the law determined by the conflict of laws rules which it considers applicable'. See Caron and Caplan, *The UNCITRAL Arbitration Rules* (2nd edn, Oxford University Press, 2012), pp. 112*ff*.

C. Law Applicable to the Substance of the Dispute

the ICSID Convention provides that, in the absence of an agreement on the applicable law, 'the Tribunal shall apply the law of the Contracting State party to the dispute (including its rules on the conflict of laws) and such rules of international law as may be applicable'.

Ultimately, however, whether or not a BIT specifies the applicable law, the tribunal will apply and accord a controlling role to international law.[134] Because BITs are international law instruments, international law is applicable by virtue of the 1969 Vienna Convention on the Law of Treaties, which provides that treaties are 'governed by international law' and must be interpreted in the light of 'any relevant rules of international law applicable'.[135]

8.64

In this regard, in the *AAPL v Sri Lanka* case,[136] which was brought under the Sri Lanka–United Kingdom BIT,[137] the tribunal held the BIT to be the 'primary source of the applicable legal rules', and added that the BIT was not a 'closed legal system', but had to be seen in the 'wider juridical context' of international law. This led the tribunal to apply general international law to complement the provisions of the BIT. Similarly, the annulment committee in the *Vivendi* case held that:

8.65

> [I]n respect of a claim based upon a substantive provision of that BIT...the inquiry which the ICSID tribunal is required to undertake is one governed by the ICSID Convention, by the BIT and by applicable international law. Such an inquiry is neither in principle determined, nor precluded, by any issue of municipal law...[138]

International law provides the standard by reference to which the legality of the conduct of the host state is to be assessed.[139] This is made clear in Article 3 of the International Law Commission's Draft Articles on State Responsibility,[140] which

8.66

---

[134] *Middle East Cement Shipping and Handling Co. SA v Arab Republic of Egypt*, Award, ICSID Case No. ARB/99/6, IIC 169 (2002), at [86]. See also Kjos, *Applicable Law in Investor–State Arbitration: The Interplay Between National and International Law* (Oxford University Press, 2013).

[135] Vienna Convention on the Law of Treaties, opened for signature 23 May 1969, Arts 2(1)(a) and 31(3)(c), 1155 United Nations Treaty Series 331, reprinted in 8 ILM 679 (1969). See also *Asian Agricultural Products Ltd (AAPL) v Republic of Sri Lanka*, n. 14, at [20]–[21].

[136] Ibid.

[137] Agreement between the Government of the United Kingdom of Great Britain and Northern Ireland and the Government of Sri Lanka for the Promotion and Protection of Investments, signed on 13 February 1980, entered into force on 18 December 1980.

[138] *Compañía de Aguas del Aconquija SA and Vivendi Universal SA v Argentine Republic*, Decision on Annulment, n. 105, at [102].

[139] See Parra, 'Applicable law in investor–state arbitration', in Rovine (ed.) *Contemporary Issues in International Arbitration and Mediation: The Fordham Papers* (Brill, 2008). See also *Azurix Corporation v The Argentine Republic*, Award, ICSID Case No. ARB/01/12, IIC 24 (2006), at [67].

[140] See the ICSID Annulment Committee's reliance on this provision in *Compañía de Aguas del Aconquija*, n. 105, at [95]–[96].

provides that the 'characterisation of an act of a State as internationally wrongful is governed by international law'.

8.67 In this sense, it may be necessary to refer to international law in order to interpret the terms of an investment treaty. For instance, while investment treaties generally include provisions regarding the expropriation of investments, they typically do not define the term 'expropriation'. Tribunals can therefore refer to the concept of expropriation under customary international law in order to interpret the scope and content of the investment treaty.[141] The application of international law, however, does not allow claimants to assert claims under customary international law as an independent cause of action.[142]

8.68 The applicable law provisions in investment contracts or other agreements forming part of the background of the dispute do not preclude the application of international law. In *Wena Hotels Ltd v Egypt*,[143] the annulment committee rejected the argument that the applicable law clauses of the lease agreements between Wena Hotels and an Egyptian state authority, which selected Egyptian law, applied to the BIT dispute:

> The leases deal with questions that are by definition of a commercial nature. The [BIT] deals with questions that are essentially of a governmental nature, namely the standards of treatment accorded by the State to foreign investors. It is therefore apparent that Wena and EHC agreed to a particular contract, the applicable law and the dispute settlement arrangement in respect of one kind of subject, that relating to commercial problems under the leases. It is also apparent that Wena as a national of a contracting state could invoke the [BIT] for the purpose of a different kind of dispute, that concerning the treatment of foreign investors by Egypt. This other mechanism has a different and separate dispute settlement arrangement and might include a different choice of law provision or make no choice at all.
>
> [...]
>
> This Committee accordingly concludes that the subject matter of the lease agreements submitted to Egyptian law was different from the subject matter brought before ICSID arbitration under the [BIT].[144]

8.69 This approach does not ignore domestic law or the text of Article 42(1) of the ICSID Convention set out earlier.[145] However, it should be remembered that the Convention was itself drafted principally with investor–state contracts in

---

[141] *Accession Mezzanine Capital LP v Hungary*, Decision on Respondent's Objection under Arbitration Rule 41(5), ICSID Case No. ARB/12/3, IIC 577 (2013), at [68.70]. See also 2012 United States Model BIT, Annex B, which states the 'shared understanding' of the parties that expropriation (Art. 6(1)) 'is intended to reflect customary international law concerning the obligation of States with respect to expropriation'.

[142] *Generation Ukraine Inc. v Ukraine*, Award, ICSID Case No. ARB/00/9, IIC 116 (2003), at [11.3].

[143] *Wena Hotels Ltd v Arab Republic of Egypt*, Decision on Annulment Application, ICSID Case No. ARB/98/4, IIC 274 (2002).

[144] Ibid., at [31]–[36].

[145] See paragraph 8.63.

C. Law Applicable to the Substance of the Dispute

mind, in which domestic law would play the critical, if not exclusive, role.[146] Treaty interpretation, however, calls for a different approach. If a domestic legal system were to provide rules of decision, then a state could simply legislate itself out of a breach of treaty, contrary to Article 27 of the Vienna Convention ('[a state] may not invoke the provisions of its internal law as justification for its failure to perform a treaty'). As the tribunal held in the *Santa Elena* case:

> To the extent that there may be any inconsistency between the two bodies of law, the rules of public international law must prevail. Were this not so in relation to takings of property, the protection of international law would be denied to the foreign investor and the purpose of the ICSID Convention would, in this respect, be frustrated.[147]

This does not mean that the domestic law of the host state does not have a role to play. The domestic law of the host state will be taken into consideration in order to establish the facts to be analysed in determining whether the state is liable under the investment treaty. For instance, a tribunal will consider domestic law in determining whether particular assets or rights constituting an alleged investment exist and in whom they vest; the question of whether these assets or rights constitute an investment under the treaty will, however, be a question governed by the treaty and international law. **8.70**

Similarly, the domestic law of the host state will typically constitute evidence of the measures taken by the state that are alleged to be in breach of the treaty, since the misconduct of the state will usually manifest itself through internal legal acts. The analysis of whether these acts or measures engage the host state's liability under the treaty will, however, be governed by the terms of the treaty and international law. **8.71**

The practice of BIT tribunals has been summarised by one commentator as follows: **8.72**

> The principle that treaties are on the plane of international law is too well established to warrant much argument. Therefore, alleged breaches of a BIT by a state are prima facie governed by international law. Be that as it may, the complex questions that arise in foreign investment disputes cannot simply be answered by a prior assumption of the sole applicability of international law. As is always the case, foreign investments are intrinsically connected to the national law of the host state. Suffice to say that questions as to whether an investment is properly made or whether a measure or regulation taken by a state meets the threshold of treaty violation may not be disposed of without a thorough examination of that state's

---

[146] See *Autopista Concessionada de Venezuela CA v Bolivarian Republic of Venezuela*, Award, ICSID Case No. ARB/00/5, IIC 20 (2003), at [336]: '[T]his Tribunal believes that there is no reason in this case, especially considering that it is a contract and not a treaty arbitration, to go beyond the corrective and supplemental functions of international law.'

[147] *Compañía del Desarrollo de Santa Elena SA v The Republic of Costa Rica*, Final Award, ICSID Case No. ARB/96/1, IIC 73 (2000), at [64]. See also *Enron Corporation and Ponderosa Assets LP v Argentine Republic*, Decision on Jurisdiction, n. 114, at [206]–[209]; *LG&E Energy Corporation and ors v Argentine Republic*, Decision on Liability, ICSID Case No. ARB/02/1, IIC 152 (2006), at [98].

national law. Even if the relevant treaty does not provide for a choice of substantive law, arbitrators still have the obligation to consider the relevant national laws of the host state, with the caveat that such law may not be applicable if it is contrary to the obligations assumed by the state under the treaty – the principle that a state cannot rely on its internal laws to derogate from or modify its treaty obligations. To that extent, it is conceded that the arbitrators may have a certain margin and power of interpretation.[148]

8.73 Potential conflicts between international and domestic law often fall away when tribunals take note that international legal principles and treaties are frequently incorporated into domestic law, as did the tribunal in *BG Group PLC v Republic of Argentina*:

> [T]he challenge of discerning the role that international law ought to play in the settlement of this dispute, vis-à-vis domestic law, disappears if one were to take into account that the BIT and underlying principles of international law, as 'the supreme law of the land', are incorporated into Argentine domestic law, superseding conflicting domestic statutes.[149]

8.74 As for conflicts between two international law instruments, these also often fall away, because it is possible to interpret both instruments harmoniously. Such issues have arisen in the context of BITs entered into by a non-EU member state with an EU member state when the former accedes to the European Union. The newly acceded states have argued that their BIT obligations were terminated, or modified, as a result of their accession. For instance, in *Achmea BV v Slovak Republic*,[150] the Slovak Republic argued that the Netherlands–Slovakia BIT was terminated, and its dispute settlement clause inapplicable, as a consequence of Slovakia's accession to the European Union, because the BIT was incompatible with Slovakia's obligations under EU law. The tribunal disagreed, holding that the BIT established rights that were neither duplicated by nor incompatible with EU law. The tribunal also held that the fact that it was bound to apply EU law to the extent that it formed part of the applicable laws did not deprive it of jurisdiction.[151]

8.75 In *Electrabel SA v Republic of Hungary*,[152] the claimant brought a claim under the ECT (of which the European Union is a member) in relation to the termination of an agreement by Hungary, carried out in compliance with a European Commission

---

[148] Igbokwe, 'Determination, interpretation and application of substantive law in foreign investment treaty arbitrations' (2006) 23 J Intl Arb 267, at 297–298. See also *MTD Equity Sdn Bhd & MTD Chile SA v Republic of Chile*, Decision on Annulment, ICSID Case No. ARB/01/17, IIC 77 (2007), at [72].

[149] *BG Group PLC v Republic of Argentina*, Final Award, n. 112, at [97]. See also *Siemens AG v Argentine Republic*, Award, ICSID Case No. ARB/02/8, IIC 227 (2007), at [78]–[79].

[150] *Achmea BV (formerly known as Eureko BV) v Slovak Republic*, Award on Jurisdiction, Arbitrability and Suspension, UNCITRAL, PCA Case No. 2008-13 (2010), IIC 46 (2010), at [244]–[246].

[151] Ibid., at [281]–[283].

[152] Decision on Jurisdiction, Applicable Law and Liability, ICSID Case No. ARB/07/19, IIC 567 (2012), at [4.195].

C. Law Applicable to the Substance of the Dispute

directive. The tribunal held that (a) European law formed part of international law, and was therefore applicable to the dispute under the ECT, and (b) European law, as part of Hungary's national law, should also be taken into account as a fact relevant to the dispute.[153] The tribunal held that there was no inconsistency between the ECT and European law, which should, in any event, be interpreted harmoniously. However, the tribunal held that, had it found an inconsistency between the two, EU law would prevail over the ECT.[154]

8.76 Finally, it should be noted that although there is 'a progressive emergence of rules through lines of consistent cases on certain issues',[155] there is no doctrine of precedent in investment treaty arbitration.[156] Therefore while investment treaty case law may be a subsidiary means for the determination of rules of international law,[157] tribunals are not bound by the decisions of other tribunals. Commenting on this issue, the tribunal in the *SGS Société Générale de Surveillance SA v Republic of the Philippines* case noted:

> Moreover there is no doctrine of precedent in international law, if by precedent is meant a rule of the binding effect of a single decision. There is no hierarchy of international tribunals, and even if there were, there is no good reason for allowing the first tribunal in time to resolve issues for all later tribunals. It must be initially for the control mechanisms provided for under the BIT and the ICSID Convention, and in the longer term for the development of a common legal opinion or *jurisprudence constante*, to resolve the difficult legal questions…[158]

8.77 The consequences of failing to identify and apply the applicable law may be grave. It can expose the tribunal's award to a challenge, or even annulment. Indeed, in

---

[153] By contrast, in *AES Summit Generation Ltd and AES-Tisza Erömü Kft v Republic of Hungary*, Decision of the Ad Hoc Committee on the Application for Annulment, ICSID Case No. ARB/07/22, IIC 592 (2012), at [161], and [168]–[174], the tribunal held that the applicable law of the arbitration was the ECT and that EU law was a fact only potentially relevant to whether Hungary had violated its ECT obligations.

[154] Ibid., at [191].

[155] Kaufmann-Kohler, 'Arbitral precedent: Dream, necessity or excuse? The 2006 Freshfields Lecture' (2007) 23 Arb Intl 357. See also *Daimler Financial Services v Argentine Republic*, n. 119, at [52].

[156] Indeed, tribunals have reached different conclusions based on the same facts and law. See, e.g., the decisions in *CME Czech Republic BV (The Netherlands) v Czech Republic*, Partial Award, UNCITRAL, 13 September 2001, IIC 61 (2001); *Ronald S Lauder v Czech Republic*, Final Award, n. 109, in which claims were brought under two different treaties based on identical facts. In *Lauder*, the case was dismissed. In *CME*, the Czech state was ordered to pay over US$300 million. On legal issues, there has been a clear split on the scope of the so-called umbrella clause in the cases of *Bureau Veritas, Inspection, Valuation, Assessment and Control, BIVAC BV v Republic of Paraguay*, Decision on Jurisdiction, ICSID Case No. ARB/07/9, IIC 428 (2009), and *SGS Société Générale de Surveillance SA v Republic of Paraguay*, Decision on Jurisdiction, n. 87. Both cases were based on nearly identical facts.

[157] ICJ Statute, Art. 38(d).

[158] *SGS Société Générale de Surveillance SA v Republic of the Philippines*, Decision on Jurisdiction, ICSID Case No. ARB/02/6, IIC 224 (2004), at [97]. See also *Suez, Sociedad General de Aguas de Barcelona SA and InterAguas Servicios Integrales del Agua SA v Argentine Republic*, Decision on Jurisdiction, n. 66, at [189].

the ICSID context, ad hoc committees annulled the awards rendered in *Enron v Argentina* and *Sempra v Argentina* on the basis that the arbitral tribunals exceeded their powers by failing to apply the applicable law.[159]

D. Merits of the Dispute

8.78 If jurisdictional hurdles are overcome, the question arises whether the host state has breached its substantive treaty obligations. There is a surprising degree of uniformity between substantive protections in the treaties, aided by model treaties established as negotiating models by the main capital-exporting nations. The essential protections are:

- the protection against expropriation or measures equivalent to expropriation without compensation;
- the right to be treated fairly and equitably;
- the right to full protection and security;
- the protection against arbitrary or discriminatory treatment;
- the right to national and MFN treatment;
- the right to the free transfer of funds and assets; and
- the protection against a state's breaches of its investment obligations and undertakings.[160]

(a) No expropriation without prompt, adequate, and effective compensation

8.79 The obligation to compensate for expropriation is among the most crucial protections provided by investment treaties. This provision is frequently relied upon by foreign investors in treaty arbitration. The expropriation provisions in investment treaties are quite similar. A typical provision is, for example, Article 3(1) of the United States–Argentina BIT,[161] which states:

> Investments shall not be expropriated or nationalized either directly or indirectly through measures tantamount to expropriation or nationalization ('expropriation') except for a public purpose; in a non-discriminatory manner; upon

---

[159] *Enron Creditors Recovery Corporation (formerly Enron Corporation) and Ponderosa Assets LP v Argentine Republic*, Decision on Application for Annulment, ICSID Case No. ARB/01/3, IIC 441 (2010); *Sempra Energy International v Argentine Republic*, Decision on Annulment, ICSID Case No. ARB/02/16, IIC 438 (2010).

[160] For a detailed analysis of these substantive treaty obligations, see Reinisch (ed.) *Standards of Investment Protection* (Oxford University Press, 2008); Newcombe and Paradell, *Law and Practice of Investment Treaties: Standards of Treatment* (Kluwer Law International, 2009); Vandevelde, *Bilateral Investment Treaties* (Oxford University Press, 2010); Salacuse, *The Law of Investment Treaties* (2nd edn, Oxford University Press, 2015); Schreuer and Dolzer, *Principles of International Investment Law* (Oxford University Press, 2012).

[161] See n. 35.

D. Merits of the Dispute

payment of prompt, adequate and effective compensation; and in accordance with due process of law and the general principles of treatment provided for in Article II(2). Compensation shall be equivalent to the fair market value of the expropriated investment immediately before the expropriatory action was taken or became known, whichever is earlier; be paid without delay; include interest at a commercially reasonable rate from the date of expropriation; be fully realizable; and be freely transferable at the prevailing market rate of exchange on the date of expropriation.

8.80 Thus, in order to be lawful, BITs generally require that the expropriation be (a) for a public purpose, (b) non-discriminatory, (c) in accordance with due process, and (d) upon payment of prompt, adequate, and effective compensation.

(i) Direct expropriation

8.81 A direct expropriation involves the outright physical seizure of a foreign investor's property, or the title to such property, by the host state. In such cases, 'there is an open, deliberate and unequivocal intent, as reflected in a formal law or decree or physical act, to deprive the owner of his or her property through the transfer of title or outright seizure'.[162] For instance, in *Funnekotter v Zimbabwe*,[163] the tribunal held that Zimbabwe had expropriated the claimants' investments in commercial farms by means of a government land acquisition programme, as well as by means of actual physical invasions.

(ii) Indirect expropriation

8.82 It is now a well-accepted principle of international law that expropriation may occur indirectly, by measures resulting in a substantial deprivation of the use and value of the investment, even though the actual title of the asset remains with the investor.[164] As explained in *Ronald S Lauder v The Czech Republic*: 'The concept of indirect (or "de facto", or "creeping") expropriation is not clearly defined. Indirect expropriation or nationalization is a measure that does not involve an overt taking, but that effectively neutralized the enjoyment of the property.'[165]

8.83 International arbitral tribunals have recognised this principle and upheld claims for indirect expropriation when the state has not seized the investment, but has taken measures that have destroyed its value.

---

[162] UNCTAD, *Expropriation: A Sequel*, Series on Issues in International Investment Agreements II (UN, 2012), available online at http://unctad.org/en/Docs/unctaddiaeia2011d7_en.pdf, p. 7.

[163] *Bernardus Henricus Funnekotter and ors v Republic of Zimbabwe*, Award, ICSID Case No. ARB/05/6, IIC 370 (2009).

[164] OECD, ' "Indirect expropriation" and the "right to regulate" in international investment law', Working Paper on International Investment No. 2004/4 (September 2004), available online at http://www.oecd.org/daf/inv/investment-policy/WP-2004_4.pdf.

[165] *Ronald S Lauder v Czech Republic*, Final Award, n. 109, at [200].

8.84 For example, in *Total v Argentina*, the tribunal explained:

> [U]nder international law a measure which does not have all the features of a formal expropriation could be equivalent to an expropriation if an effective deprivation of the investment is thereby caused. An effective deprivation requires, however, a total loss of value of the property such as when the property affected is rendered worthless by the measure, as in case of direct expropriation, even if formal title continues to be held.[166]

8.85 Indirect expropriation can also arise from a deprivation of control or interference in management by the state, thus preventing the investor from controlling the day-to-day operation of the investment. Such measures would include:

> ...depriving the investor of control over the investment, managing the day-to-day operations of the company, arresting and detaining company officials or employees, supervising the work of officials, interfering in administration, impeding the distribution of dividends, interfering in the appointment of officials or managers, or depriving the company of its property or control in whole or in part.[167]

In evaluating the degree to which the host state's measures have interfered with the investor's rights, tribunals typically consider the economic impact of the measures on the investment, their interference with the investor's reasonable expectations, and their duration.[168]

8.86 Under exceptional or 'extreme' circumstances, the imposition of taxes, which are considered part of a state's regulatory powers, can be expropriatory. In the *Burlington* case,[169] the tribunal explained that 'a tax measure may be tantamount to expropriation if (i) it produces the effects required for any indirect expropriation and (ii) in addition, it is discriminatory, arbitrary, involves a denial of due process or an abuse of rights'.

---

[166] *Total SA v Argentine Republic*, Decision on Liability, n. 127, at [195]–[196].

[167] *Sempra Energy International v Argentine Republic*, Award, ICSID Case No. ARB/02/16, IIC 304 (2007), at [284], endorsing the criteria set out in *Pope & Talbot Inc. v Government of Canada*, Award on Damages, UNCITRAL, 31 May 2002, IIC 195 (2002). See also *PSEG Global, Inc., The North American Coal Corporation, and Konya Ingin Electrik Üretim ve Ticaret Ltd Şirketi v Republic of Turkey*, Award, ICSID Case No. ARB/02/5, IIC 198 (2007), at [278]:

> The Tribunal has no doubt that indirect expropriation can take many forms. Yet, as the tribunal in *Pope & Talbot* found, there must be some form of deprivation of the investor in the control of the investment, the management of day-to-day operations of the company, interfering in the administration, impeding the distribution of dividends, interfering in the appoint of officials and managers, or depriving the company of its property or control in total or in part.

[168] *LG&E Energy Corporation and ors v Argentine Republic*, Decision on Liability, n. 147, at [190].

[169] *Burlington Resources Inc. v Republic of Ecuador*, Decision on Liability, ICSID Case No. ARB/08/5, IIC 568 (2012), at [375].

D. Merits of the Dispute

(iii) Acts contrary to undertakings and assurances granted to investors may constitute indirect expropriation

States may also expropriate foreign investments by means of measures that interfere with assurances that they offered to investors to induce them to invest. The assurances that states offer to create a favourable investment environment may amount to essential conditions for those investments and, as such, may form part of the legal framework underlying, and protecting, those investments. A failure by the state to honour those undertakings may give investors who reasonably relied on them a right to compensation. **8.87**

International arbitral tribunals have held that government assurances and undertakings create 'acquired rights' for investors.[170] The rationale is simple. Investors looking to invest in developing countries cannot predict with confidence that conditions of stability and security will exist throughout the period of their investment; thus the state provides certain core promises to foreign investors (in contracts or licenses), which motivate the decision to invest. If those promises are unilaterally withdrawn by the state within the agreed lifespan of the investment (for example a thirty-year concession) in a manner that destroys the value of the investment, then an indirect expropriation may have occurred.[171] **8.88**

The tribunal in *CME v Czech Republic*[172] reached such a conclusion when it was asked to consider the expropriation claim of an investor in a joint venture in the Czech Republic. The investor alleged that the joint venture collapsed after the Czech broadcasting authority forced the investor to give up its exclusive licensing rights and changed other key terms of the joint venture agreement. The tribunal held that the acts of the Czech regulatory authority interfered with the 'economic and legal basis of CME's investment' and 'destroy[ed] the legal basis ("the safety net") of the Claimant's investment', which ruined the 'commercial value of the investment' and thus amounted to expropriation. **8.89**

However, in the absence of such government assurances or undertakings, the effects alone (as grave as they may be) may be insufficient to constitute expropriation. In the *Methanex* case,[173] the tribunal held that a non-discriminatory, bona fide **8.90**

---

[170] Acquired rights have been defined as follows:

> Acquired rights are any rights, corporeal or incorporeal, properly vested under municipal law in a natural or juristic person and of an assessable monetary value. Within the scope of such rights fall interests which have their basis in contract as well as in property, provided they concern an undertaking or investment of a more or less permanent character.

See O'Connell, *International Law, Vol. II* (2nd edn, Stevens & Sons, 1970), pp. 763–764.
[171] Fatouros, *Government Guarantees to Foreign Investors* (Columbia University Press, 1962).
[172] *CME Czech Republic BV (The Netherlands) v Czech Republic*, n. 156, at [551], [554]–[555], and [591].
[173] *Methanex Corporation v United States of America*, Final Award on Jurisdiction and Merits, UNCITRAL, 19 August 2005, IIC 167 (2005), at [7].

regulation within the police powers of the state, which banned a harmful gasoline additive containing methanol, had not expropriated Methanex, a Canadian producer of methanol, in the absence of a breach of specific commitments by the state.

8.91 Similarly, a simple breach of contract by a state does not amount to an expropriation in the absence of an act of the state in its sovereign (as opposed to contractual) capacity.[174] The *Waste Management*[175] tribunal explained: '[I]t is one thing to expropriate a right under a contract and another to fail to comply with the contract. Non-compliance by a government with contractual obligations is not the same thing as, or equivalent or tantamount to, an expropriation.' Tribunals have nevertheless found that contractual rights were expropriated where a state acted in a sovereign manner by terminating a contract by decree,[176] and following a series of 'sovereign acts designed illegitimately to end the concession or to force its renegotiation'.[177]

8.92 In sum, the paramount concern of tribunals in indirect expropriation cases is whether a state's interference with prior assurances that it gave to an investor, be it direct or indirect, express or covert, creeping or not, deprives the investor, in whole or in significant part, of the use or reasonably expected benefit of its investment.[178]

(iv) Purpose of the host state's measures does not affect their characterisation

8.93 The form of measures or their motive is irrelevant if the effect is to deprive the owner of the economic benefit of the asset. This is an enquiry based on effect, rather than intention.[179] Arbitral tribunals have held that it is immaterial that the

---

[174] See *Parkerings-Compagniet AS v Republic of Lithuania*, Award, ICSID Case No. ARB/05/8, IIC 302 (2007), at [443]–[445]; *Azurix Corporation v Argentine Republic*, Award, n. 139, at [315]; *Suez, Sociedad General de Aguas de Barcelona SA and InterAguas Servicios Integrales del Agua SA v Argentine Republic*, Decision on Liability, ICSID Case No. ARB/03/17, IIC 442 (2010), at [140]–[145].

[175] *Waste Management Inc. v United Mexican States*, Award, ICSID Case No. ARB(AF)/00/3, IIC 270 (2004), at [175]. See also *Biwater Gauff (Tanzania) Ltd v United Republic of Tanzania*, Award, n. 111, at [458].

[176] *Siemens AG v Argentine Republic*, Award, n. 149, at [271].

[177] *Compañía de Aguas del Aconquija SA and Vivendi Universal SA v Argentine Republic*, Award, ICSID Case No. ARB/97/3, IIC 307 (2007), at [7.5.22].

[178] *Eureko BV v Republic of Poland*, Partial Award of the Ad Hoc Committee, UNCITRAL, 19 August 2005, IIC 98 (2005), at [242]; *Fireman's Fund Insurance Co. v The United Mexican States*, Award, ICSID Case No. ARB(AF)/02/01, IIC 291 (2006), at [176]; *ADC Affiliate Ltd and ADC & ADMC Management Ltd v Republic of Hungary*, Award, ICSID Case No. ARB/03/16, IIC 1 (2006), at [424]; *LG&E Energy Corporation and ors v Argentine Republic*, Decision on Liability, n. 147, at [190].

[179] *Compañia de Aguas del Aconquija*, at [7.5.20]:

> There is extensive authority for the proposition that the state's intent, or its subjective motives are at most a secondary consideration. While intent will weigh in favour of showing a measure to be expropriatory, it is not a requirement, because the effect of the measure on the investor, not the state's intent, is the critical factor.

D. Merits of the Dispute

property was expropriated for laudable environmental reasons,[180] or as part of the political reorientation of the country.[181]

Although the purpose of an expropriatory measure may affect its legality, it does not affect the host state's obligation to provide the expropriated investor with prompt and adequate compensation. This point was affirmed by the ICSID tribunal in *Compañía del Desarrollo de Santa Elena SA v Republic of Costa Rica*: **8.94**

> Expropriatory environmental measures – no matter how laudable and beneficial to society as a whole – are, in this respect, similar to any other expropriatory measures that a state may take in order to implement its policies: where property is expropriated, even for environmental purposes, whether domestic or international, the state's obligation to pay compensation remains.[182]

Whilst considering whether there has been expropriation in a particular case, a tribunal need not examine each state measure in isolation. If the cumulative effect of multiple state measures is substantially to deprive the investor of the use, value, and enjoyment of its investment, expropriation may still be construed.[183] This is known as 'creeping expropriation'. As the tribunal noted in *Siemens AG v The Argentine Republic*: **8.95**

> By definition, creeping expropriation refers to a process, to steps that eventually have the effect of an expropriation. Obviously, each step must have an adverse effect but by itself may not be significant or considered an illegal act. The last step in a creeping expropriation that tilts the balance is similar to the straw that breaks the camel's back. The preceding straws may not have a perceptible effect but are part of the process that led to the break.[184]

(b) 'Fair and equitable treatment' and the international minimum standard

Almost all investment treaties require host states to accord 'fair and equitable treatment' to investors of the other contracting state.[185] It is the treaty standard most **8.96**

---

[180] *Compañía del Desarrollo de Santa Elena SA v Republic of Costa Rica*, Final Award, n. 147, at [71]–[72].
[181] *Phillips Petroleum Co. Iran v Islamic Republic of Iran* (1989) 21 Iran–US CTR 79, at 115–116.
[182] *Compañía del Desarrollo de Santa Elena*, n. 147, at [71]–[72].
[183] *Biwater Gauff (Tanzania) Ltd v United Republic of Tanzania*, Award, ICSID Case No. ARB/05/22, IIC 330 (2008), at [455]; *Walter Bau AG v The Kingdom of Thailand*, Award, UNCITRAL, 1 July 2009, IIC 429 (2009), at [10.10]. See also Weston, 'Constructive takings under international law: A modest foray into the problem of creeping expropriation' (1976) 16 VJIL 103; UNCTAD, *Taking of Property*, Series on Issues in International Investment Agreements (UN, 2000), available online at http://unctad.org/en/docs/psiteiitd15.en.pdf, p. 11; Restatement (Third) of Foreign Relations Law of the United States, § 712.
[184] *Siemens AG v Argentine Republic*, Award, n. 149, at [263].
[185] UNCTAD, *Fair and Equitable Treatment: A Sequel*, Series on Issues in International Investment Agreements II (UN, 2012), available online at http://unctad.org/en/Docs/unctaddiaeia2011d5_en.pdf, pp. 17–35 (identifying the five 'most important and widespread approaches to the FET standard in treaty practice').

frequently invoked before investment tribunals and the one most frequently found to be breached. To highlight the significance of this standard of protection, it is frequently addressed at the beginning of the general treatment clauses. For example, Article II(2)(a) of the United States–Argentina BIT[186] provides: 'Investment shall at all times be accorded fair and equitable treatment, shall enjoy full protection and security and shall in no case be accorded treatment less than that required by international law.'

8.97 It is difficult to reduce the words 'fair and equitable treatment' to a precise statement of a legal obligation. They grant considerable discretion to tribunals to review the 'fairness' and 'equity' of government actions in light of all of the facts and circumstances of the case.[187]

8.98 International arbitral tribunals called upon to decide cases on the basis of the 'fair and equitable treatment' standard have developed the elements of the obligation that it imposes upon states.[188] In accordance with the 'plain meaning' approach required by the Vienna Convention, tribunals have concluded, based on the object and purpose of the treaties, that the standard is intended to accord to foreign investors broad objective protections. These include a stable and predictable investment environment, in order to maximise investments.[189] As the tribunal noted in *LG&E Energy Corporation and ors v Argentine Republic*:

> [T]he stability of the legal and business framework in the State party is an essential element in the standard of what is fair and equitable treatment. As such, the Tribunal considers this interpretation to be an emerging standard of fair and equitable treatment in international law.[190]

---

[186] See n. 35.

[187] See, e.g., Schreuer, 'Fair and equitable treatment in arbitral practice' (2005) 6 JWIT 357; Kalicki and Medeiros, 'Fair, equitable and ambiguous: What is fair and equitable treatment in international investment law?' (2007) 22 ICSID Rev—Foreign Investment LJ 24; Kinnear, 'The continuing development of the fair and equitable treatment standard', in Bjorklund, Laird, and Ripinsky (eds) *Investment Treaty Law: Current Issues III* (British Institute of International and Comparative Law, 2009), p. 214; Yannaca-Small, 'Fair and equitable treatment standard', in Yannaca-Small (ed.) *Arbitration under International Investment Agreements* (Oxford University Press, 2010), pp. 385–410; UNCTAD, *Fair and Equitable Treatment: A Sequel*, Series on Issues in International Investment Agreements II (UN, 2012), available online at http://unctad.org/en/Docs/unctaddiaeia2011d5_en.pdf.

[188] *Enron Corporation and Ponderosa Assets LP v Argentine Republic*, Award, ICSID Case No. ARB/01/3, IIC 292 (2007), at [256]–[257].

[189] See decisions in which tribunals have referred to the object and purpose of the BIT to interpret the fair and equitable treatment standard: *Azurix Corporation v Argentine Republic*, Award, n. 139, at [360]; *MTD Equity Sdn Bhd & MTD Chile SA v Republic of Chile*, Award, ICSID Case No. ARB/01/17, IIC 174 (2004), at [109]–[113]; *Saluka Investments BV v Czech Republic*, Partial Award, UNCITRAL, 17 March 2006, ICGJ 368 (PCA 2006), at [300].

[190] Decision on Liability, n. 147, at [12].

D. Merits of the Dispute

8.99 International arbitral tribunals have identified the protection of investors' legitimate expectations as the 'dominant element'[191] of the fair and equitable treatment standard. In order to determine if a state's measures violate the standard, tribunals frequently examine 'the impact of the measure on the reasonable investment-backed expectations of the investor; and whether the state is attempting to avoid investment-backed expectations that the state created or reinforced through its own acts'.[192] It is on this basis that the UNCITRAL ad hoc tribunal in *CME v Czech Republic*[193] found that the Czech Republic's legislative and regulatory changes had unlawfully harmed CME's investment by altering the country's investment framework, and held that the government had 'breached its obligation of fair and equitable treatment by evisceration of the arrangements in reliance upon [which] the foreign investor was induced to invest'.

8.100 In *Técnicas Medioambientales Tecmed SA v The United Mexican States*,[194] the basic expectation of the claimant was that the laws applicable to its investment in a landfill for hazardous waste would be used by the government for the purpose of assuring compliance with the environmental and health goals underlying such laws. In particular, upon making its investment, the claimant 'reasonably trusted, on the basis of existing agreements and of the good faith principle' that the permit it acquired in order to make its investment would continue in full force and effect.[195] As held by the tribunal, however, the relevant Mexican federal agency later refused to renew the claimant's permit for political reasons arising from local community opposition unrelated to the underlying environmental and health goals.[196] This conduct constituted a breach of the fair and equitable treatment standard.

8.101 In order to qualify for protection, the investor's expectations must be reasonable, based on the conduct of the state and reasonable reliance by the investor in making the investment, as explained by the tribunal in *LG&E*:

> [T]he investor's fair expectations have the following characteristics: they are based on the conditions offered by the host State at the time of the investment; they may not be established unilaterally by one of the parties; they must exist and be enforceable by law; in the event of infringement by the host State, a duty to compensate the investor for damages arises except for those caused in the event of state of necessity; however, the investor's fair expectations cannot fail to consider parameters such as business risk or industry's regular patterns.[197]

---

[191] *Saluka*, n. 189, at [302].
[192] Paulsson, 'Investment protection provisions in treaties', in ICC (ed.) *Investment Protection* (ICC, 2000), p. 22, para. 19.
[193] *CME Czech Republic BV (The Netherlands) v Czech Republic*, n. 156, at [611].
[194] Award, ICSID Case No ARB(AF)/00/02, IIC 247 (2003), at [157].
[195] Ibid., at [160].
[196] Ibid., at [164].
[197] *LG&E Energy Corporation and ors v Argentine Republic*, Decision on Liability, n. 147, at [130]; *Saluka Investments BV v Czech Republic*, n. 189, at [304]. Tribunals have enquired on the level of investors' due diligence in considering the extent to which the investor actually relied on

8.102 It has been held that failure to ensure due process, consistency, and transparency in the functioning of public authorities,[198] and the lack of a predictable and stable framework for investment contrary to the legitimate expectations of the investor and commitments made by the host state,[199] are breaches of fair and equitable treatment standards.[200] The legal stability requirement does not require that a state's legal system remain frozen in time. However, legislative changes that are unfair and inequitable in the face of specific commitments to the contrary may constitute a compensable treaty breach:

> Save for the existence of an agreement, in the form of a stabilisation clause or otherwise, there is nothing objectionable about the amendment brought to the regulatory framework existing at the time an investor made its investment... What is prohibited however is for a State to act unfairly, unreasonably or inequitably in the exercise of its legislative power.[201]

8.103 The fair and equitable standard has also been held to be breached by the effective discrimination of host states in favour of domestic entities. In *Eastern Sugar BV v The Czech Republic*,[202] the claimant invested in sugar factories in the Czech Republic. Those subsidiaries were then targeted by a decree passed by the Czech authorities in a very different manner from its application to domestic entities.[203] As explained by the tribunal, 'the Czech Republic penalized a foreign company that had done nothing illegal in the previous years, while Czech newcomers who had exceeded their quota within the previous years were now rewarded for having done so'.[204] As a result, the tribunal held that the effect of one of the decrees was

---

the state's representations when investing: see *Parkerings-Compagniet AS v Republic of Lithuania*, Award, n. 174, at [335]–[336]; *MTD Equity Sdn Bhd & MTD Chile SA v Republic of Chile*, n. 189, at [176]–[178].

[198] *Emilio Agustín Maffezini v Kingdom of Spain*, Award, ICSID Case No. ARB/97/7, IIC 86 (2000), at [83]; *Encana Corporation v Republic of Ecuador*, Award, LCIA Case No. UN3481, IIC 91 (2006), at [158].

[199] *CME Czech Republic BV (The Netherlands) v Czech Republic*, Partial Award, n. 156, at [611]; *PSEG Global, Inc., The North American Coal Corporation, and Konya Ingin Electrik Üretim ve Ticaret Ltd Şirketi v Republic of Turkey*, Award, n. 167, at [253]–[254]; *Saluka Investments BV v Czech Republic*, Partial Award, n. 189, at [279] and [309].

[200] *CMS Gas Transmission Co. v Republic of Argentina*, Award, ICSID Case No. ARB/01/8, IIC 65 (2005), at [276] ('fair and equitable treatment is inseparable from stability and predictability'); see also *Occidental Petroleum Corporation and ors v Republic of Ecuador*, Final Award, LCIA Case No. UN 3467, IIC 202 (2004), at [183].

[201] *Parkerings-Compagniet AS v Republic of Lithuania*, Award, n. 174, at [332]; *CMS Gas Transmission Co. v Republic of Argentina*, n. 200, at [277] ('It is not a question of whether the legal framework might need to be frozen as it can always evolve and be adapted to changing circumstances, but neither is it a question of whether the framework can be dispensed with altogether when specific commitments to the contrary have been made').

[202] Partial Award, SCC Case No. 088/2004, IIC 310 (2007).

[203] Ibid., at [335].

[204] Ibid., at [337].

D. Merits of the Dispute

discriminatory, and therefore in violation of the Netherlands–Czech and Slovak Federal Republic BIT.[205]

8.104 The standard also requires host states to offer basic protections in their internal judicial systems. Failure to provide such protection is categorised as 'denial of justice'.[206] Such a finding can be made 'whenever an uncorrected national judgment is vitiated by fundamental unfairness'.[207] Specifically, the tribunal in *Azinian v Mexico*[208] explained how such a claim could be advanced in the following terms:

> [A] denial of justice could be pleaded if the relevant courts refuse to entertain a suit, if they subject it to undue delay, of if they administer justice in a seriously inadequate way... There is a fourth type of denial if justice, namely the clear and malicious misapplication of the law.[209]

8.105 In summary, it is therefore now possible to identify certain kinds of conduct and treatment that would be likely to constitute a violation of the fair and equitable treatment standard. As explained by the tribunal in *Joseph Charles Lemire v Ukraine*,[210] the standard requires 'an action or omission by the State which violates a certain threshold of propriety, causing harm to the investor, and with a causal link between action or omission and harm'. In assessing that threshold of propriety, that tribunal will consider whether:

- the state has failed to offer a stable and predictable legal framework;
- the state made specific representations to the investor;
- due process has been denied to the investor;
- there is an absence of transparency in the legal procedure or in the actions of the state;
- there has been harassment, coercion, abuse of power, or other bad faith conduct by the host state; and
- any of the actions of the state can be labelled as arbitrary, discriminatory, or inconsistent.[211]

---

[205] Ibid., at [338].
[206] NAFTA tribunals have held that a denial of justice would constitute a breach of the standard: see *The Loewen Group Inc. and Raymond L Loewen v United States of America*, Award, ICSID Case No. ARB(AF)/98/3, IIC 254 (2003), at [132]; *Waste Management Inc. v United Mexican States*, Award, n. 175, at [98]; *International Thunderbird Gaming Corporation v The United Mexican States*, Award, UNCITRAL, 26 January 2006, IIC 136 (2006), at [194], rejecting the investors' denial of justice claims. For a comprehensive analysis, see Paulsson, *Denial of Justice in International Law* (Cambridge University Press, 2005).
[207] Ibid., p. 5.
[208] *Azinian and ors v Mexico*, Award on Jurisdiction and Merits, ICSID Case No. ARB(AF)/97/2, IIC 22 (1999).
[209] Ibid., at [102]–[103].
[210] Decision on Jurisdiction and Liability, ICSID Case No ARB/06/18, IIC 424 (2010), at [284].
[211] Ibid.

(i) International minimum standard and fair and equitable treatment

8.106 There is disagreement over whether the concept of 'fair and equitable treatment' is synonymous with the minimum standard of protection required by customary international law, or whether it represents an independent concept requiring greater protection.[212] Under customary international law, the minimum standard has traditionally been understood to be based on a standard of review that was set out in the 1926 *Neer* decision of the United States–Mexico General Claims Commission:

> [T]he treatment of an alien, in order to constitute an international delinquency, should amount to an outrage, to bad faith, to wilful neglect of duty, or to an insufficiency of governmental action so far short of international standards that every reasonable and impartial man would readily recognize its insufficiency.[213]

8.107 The *Neer* standard, however, has been subject to considerable criticism on the grounds that 'it did not lay down a general rule' and is of only 'limited import' in the interpretation of investment treaties.[214]

8.108 In an oft-cited article on British investment treaty practice, one commentator concluded that:

> [T]he terms 'fair and equitable treatment' envisage conduct which goes far beyond the minimum standard and afford protection to a greater extent and according to a much more objective standard than any previously employed form of words... The terms are likely to be understood and applied independently and autonomously.[215]

8.109 Unless there is a clear and express link with the minimum international standard, tribunals have overwhelmingly interpreted fair and equitable treatment provisions in BITs as an independent and self-contained treaty standard with an autonomous meaning, which provides protections beyond the customary international law standard.[216]

8.110 A difficulty occurs when treaties link the fair and equitable standard to 'international law'. Typical language is 'fair and equitable treatment in accordance with international law'. The argument has frequently been made that this type

---

[212] See Dolzer and Stevens, *Bilateral Investment Treaties* (Martinus Nijhoff, 1995), p. 59; *BG Group PLC v Republic of Argentina*, Final Award, UNCITRAL, 24 December 2007, IIC 321 (2007), at [275]–[310].

[213] *Neer v Mexico*, Opinion, United States–Mexico General Claims Commission, (1926) 4 RIAA 60, at 61–62.

[214] Paulsson and Petrochilos, 'Neer-ly misled?' (2007) 22 ICSID Rev—Foreign Investment LJ 242, at 257.

[215] Mann, 'British treaties for the promotion and protection of investments' (1981) 52 BYIL 241, at 244.

[216] See, e.g., *Enron Corporation and Ponderosa Assets LP v Argentine Republic*, n. 188, at [258]; *Compañia de Aguas del Aconquija SA and Vivendi Universal SA v Argentine Republic*, Award, n. 177, at [7.4.5]. See generally Schreuer and Dolzer, *Principles of International Investment Law*, n. 160, pp. 137–138.

D. Merits of the Dispute

of reference restricts the protection to the customary international law minimum standard of treatment.[217] However, several tribunals have concluded that this cannot be the case, since 'international law', as a general reference, must also take into account treaty practice. As the tribunal in the *Vivendi* case held:

> The Tribunal sees no basis for equating principles of international law with the minimum standard of treatment. First, the reference to principles of international law supports a broader reading that invites consideration of a wider range of international law principles than the minimum standard alone.... [T]he language of the provision suggests that one should also look to contemporary principles of international law, not only to principles from almost a century ago.[218]

But what happens where there is a clear reference to the customary international law standard, and is it different from a stand-alone fair and equitable treatment standard? Some tribunals have concluded that the evolution of the customary standard makes the analysis a distinction without a difference.[219] For example, the NAFTA tribunal in *Mondev v United States*,[220] applying the customary international law standard, made a clear distinction with the Neer standard and held that: 'To the modern eye, what is unfair or inequitable need not equate with the outrageous or the egregious. In particular, a State may treat foreign investment unfairly and inequitably without necessarily acting in bad faith.'[221]

8.111

It is clear that there is significant overlap between the customary and the treaty standards, and that the distinctions between the two 'may well be more apparent than real'.[222] In recent years, BIT tribunals have 'seemed to be less interested in the theoretical discussion on the relationship between the FET and the MST [minimum standard of treatment] and turned their attention primarily to the content

8.112

---

[217] The content of the international minimum standard is itself open to debate: see UNCTAD, *Fair and Equitable Treatment*, Series on Issues in International Investment Agreements (UN, 1999), available online at http://unctad.org/en/Docs/psiteiitd11v3.en.pdf, pp. 39–40. See also Paulsson and Petrochilos, 'Neer-ly misled?' (2007) 22 ICSID Rev—Foreign Investment LJ 242.

[218] *Compañia de Aguas del Aconquija SA and Vivendi Universal SA v Argentine Republic*, Decision on Annulment, n. 77, at [7.4.7].

[219] *Pope & Talbot Inc. v Government of Canada*, Award on Damages, UNCITRAL, 31 May 2002, IIC 195 (2002), at [52] and [55]; *International Thunderbird Gaming Corporation v The United Mexican States*, Award, n. 206, at [194].

[220] *Mondev International Ltd v United States of America*, Final Award, ICSID Case No. ARB(AF)/99/2, IIC 173 (2002).

[221] Ibid., at [116].

[222] *Saluka Investments BV v Czech Republic*, Partial Award, n. 189, at [292]–[295]. See also *CMS Gas Transmission Co. v Republic of Argentina*, n. 200, at [284]:

> While the choice between requiring a higher treaty standard and that of equating it with the international minimum standard might have relevance in the context of some disputes, the Tribunal is not persuaded that it is relevant in this case. In fact, the Treaty standard of fair and equitable treatment and its connection with the required stability and predictability of the business environment, founded on solemn legal and contractual commitments, is not different from the international law minimum standard and its evolution under customary law.

of the FET [fair and equitable treatment] obligation, whether or not it is qualified by the MST'.[223]

(c) Full protection and security

8.113 As in the case of 'fair and equitable treatment', it is difficult to give a precise meaning to the notion of 'full protection and security'. However, its scope may be illustrated by reference to its practical application. In contrast with most of the other investor protections, which impose restrictions or prohibitions on certain types of host state activity, the 'full protection and security' clause seeks to impose certain positive obligations on the host state to protect investments.

8.114 Arbitral tribunals have traditionally found breaches of the 'full protection and security' obligation in situations in which the host state failed to prevent physical damage to qualifying investments by not taking measures that fell within the normal exercise of governmental functions of policing and maintenance of law and order.[224] In *AAPL v Sri Lanka*,[225] the tribunal held that Sri Lanka violated its obligation of full protection and security by not taking all possible measures to prevent the destruction of an investor's shrimp farm and the killing of more than twenty of its employees during a counterinsurgency operation.

8.115 The standard applied is one of 'due diligence', or an *obligation de moyens*, requiring the host state to exercise reasonable care, within its means,[226] to protect investments, rather than a 'strict liability' standard. However, there is no need for the claimant to establish negligence or bad faith.

8.116 The obligation of the host state to provide full protection and security to investors is independent, and not relative to the level of protection provided by the state to its own nationals or to nationals of other states. Therefore the fact that the state did not protect the property of its own nationals is no defence to a claim by an investor of breach of this obligation.[227] However, the resources available to a

---

[223] UNCTAD, *Fair and Equitable Treatment: A Sequel*, Series on Issues in International Investment Agreements II (UN, 2012), available online at http://unctad.org/en/Docs/unctaddiaeia2011d5_en.pdf, p. 59.
[224] *Asian Agricultural Products Ltd (AAPL) v Republic of Sri Lanka*, Final Award, n. 14; *American Manufacturing and Trading Inc. v Republic of Zaire*, Award, n. 64; *Rumeli Telekom AS and Telsim Mobil Telekomunikasyon Hizmetleri AS v Republic of Kazakhstan*, Award, ICSID Case No. ARB/05/16, IIC 344 (2008). See generally Schreuer, 'Full protection and security' (2010) 1 J Intl Disp Settlement 353.
[225] *Asian Agricultural Products Ltd (AAPL) v Republic of Sri Lanka*, Final Award, n. 14.
[226] *Pantechniki SA Contractors & Engineers v Republic of Albania*, Award, n. 129, at [81]–[84].
[227] *American Manufacturing and Trading Inc. v Republic of Zaire*, Award, n. 64.

D. Merits of the Dispute

state and the reasonable deployment of those resources will be elements that are taken into account. For example, if, in the context of civil disturbances, a factory belonging to a foreign investor were burned down because all of the police were protecting a neighbouring domestically owned installation, liability might well be established. If, however, the police were fully engaged in protecting the population, and many local businesses, whether locally or foreign-owned, were damaged, it may be difficult to establish liability.

Whilst this standard has normally been applied in situations of physical protection of real and tangible property, its scope has been extended to other circumstances.[228] For instance, it has been held that withdrawal of an authorisation vital to the operation of the investment amounts to a breach of 'full protection and security'.[229] Similarly, a change in the legal framework, making it impossible to preserve and continue contractual arrangements underpinning the investment, has also been found incompatible with a BIT's 'full protection and security' provision.[230] 8.117

(d) No arbitrary or discriminatory measures impairing the investment

Most investment treaties impose an obligation upon the host state not to impair the management or operation of the investment by arbitrary or discriminatory measures.[231] For instance, Article II(3)(b) of the United States–Ecuador BIT[232] provides: 'Neither Party shall in any way impair by arbitrary or discriminatory measures the management, operation, maintenance, use, enjoyment, acquisition, expansion, or disposal of investments…' 8.118

---

[228] *Waguih Elie George Siag and Clorinda Vecchi v Arab Republic of Egypt*, Award, ICSID Case No. ARB/05/15, IIC 374 (2009), at [445]–[448]; *AES Summit Generation Ltd and AES-Tisza Erömü Kft v Republic of Hungary*, Award, ICSID Case No. ARB/07/22, IIC 455 (2010), at [13.3.2]; *Marion Unglaube and Reinhard Unglaube v Republic of Costa Rica*, Award, ICSID Case Nos ARB/08/1 and ARB/09/20, IIC 554 (2012), at [281]. Other tribunals, however, have rejected this extension of the standard: see, e.g., *Rumeli Telekom AS and Telsim Mobil Telekomunikasyon Hizmetleri AS v Republic of Kazakhstan*, Award, n. 224, at [668]–[669]; *AWG Group Ltd v Argentine Republic*, Decision on Liability, UNCITRAL, 30 July 2010, IIC 443 (2010), at [174]–[177].

[229] *Antoine Goetz and ors v République du Burundi*, Award, ICSID Case No. ARB/95/3, IIC 16 (1999), at [125]–[131].

[230] *CME Czech Republic BV (The Netherlands) v Czech Republic*, Partial Award, n. 156, at [613]; *National Grid Plc v Argentine Republic*, Award, UNCITRAL, 3 November 2008, IIC 361 (2008), at [189]; *Azurix Corporation v Argentine Republic*, Award, n. 189, at [408].

[231] Not all investment treaties use the term 'arbitrary'; some instead refer to 'unreasonable or discriminatory' measures. As explained by the tribunal in *National Grid*, n. 230, at 197, the terms are synonymous: 'It is the view of the Tribunal that the plain meaning of the terms "unreasonable" and "arbitrary" is substantially the same in the sense of something done capriciously, without reason.'

[232] Treaty between the United States of America and the Republic of Ecuador Concerning the Encouragement and Reciprocal Protection of Investment, signed on 27 August 1993, entered into force on 11 May 1997.

8.119 The concepts of 'arbitrary', or 'discriminatory', measures are not defined in the treaties. The International Court of Justice (ICJ) formulated the test of 'arbitrariness' in the context of investment protection in the *ELSI* case.[233] The court observed:

> Arbitrariness is not so much something opposed to a rule of law, as something opposed to the rule of law...It is a wilful disregard of due process of law, an act which shocks, or at least surprises, a sense of juridical propriety.[234]

8.120 In the words of the tribunal in *Joseph Charles Lemire v Ukraine*,[235] arbitrariness is defined as:

> [...]
> a. a measure that inflicts damage on the investor without serving any apparent legitimate purpose;
> b. a measure that is not based on legal standards but on discretion, prejudice or personal preference;
> c. a measure taken for reasons that are different from those put forward by the decision maker;
> d. a measure taken in wilful disregard of due process and proper procedure.[236]

8.121 For instance, in the *Azurix* case,[237] involving an investment in a water concession, government measures that included inciting consumers not to pay their bills, requiring the concessionaire not to apply the new tariffs resulting from a review, and denying the concessionaire access to documentation on the basis of which it had been sanctioned, were considered to be arbitrary.

8.122 To take another example, in the *El Paso* case,[238] the tribunal concluded that measures taken by Argentina to address the economic crisis at the end of 2001 were reasonable, consistent with the aim pursued, had the desired result, and therefore were not tainted by arbitrariness. The tribunal observed that there were several methods that Argentina could have employed to address the crisis, that evidence presented by the experts demonstrated a difference of opinion as to which would

---

[233] *Case Concerning Elettronica Sicula SpA (ELSI) (United States of America v Italy)*, Judgment, 15 ICJ 76 (1999), ICGJ 95 (1989). See also *LG&E Energy Corporation and ors v Argentine Republic*, Decision on Liability, n. 147, at [158]. For a definition based on the plain meaning of the term 'arbitrary', *see Azurix Corporation v Argentine Republic*, Award, n. 189, at [392] ('In its ordinary meaning, "arbitrary" means "derived from mere opinion", "capricious", "unrestrained", "despotic" ').
[234] *ELSI*, at [128].
[235] Decision on Jurisdiction and Liability ICSID Case No. ARB/06/18, IIC 424 (2010).
[236] Ibid., at [262].
[237] *Azurix Corporation v Argentine Republic*, Award, n. 181, at [393].
[238] *El Paso Energy International Co. v Argentine Republic*, Award, ICSID Case No. ARB/03/15, IIC 519 (2011), at [319]–[325].

D. Merits of the Dispute

have been the preferred solution, and that, ultimately, the measures resulted in the positive evolution of Argentina's economy.

8.123 In relation to 'discriminatory' treatment, a measure is considered discriminatory if (a) 'the intent of the measure is to discriminate', or (b) 'if the measure has a discriminatory effect'.[239] As a result, although evidence of discriminatory intent may be relevant, it is 'the fact of unequal treatment which is key'.[240] Thus it is not essential to establish any bad faith on the part of the host state.[241] It has been held that, in general, a measure is discriminatory in effect if it results in a treatment of an investor that is different from that accorded to other investors in a similar or comparable situation, where there appears to be no reasonable basis for such differentiation.[242] The issue of whether investors are in such a comparable situation is a question of fact. Typically, tribunals have been reluctant to find that investors are in sufficiently comparable positions to take advantage of this protection.

(e) National and 'most favoured nation' treatment

8.124 Investment treaties also provide comparative protection standards—that is, standards that do not set an autonomous standard of treatment, but rather require treatment no less favourable than that of nationals and companies of the host state (national treatment), or of any other state (MFN treatment). Article 3(1) of the United Kingdom–Egypt BIT[243] is a representative provision:

> Neither Contracting Party shall in its territory subject investments or returns of investors of the other Contracting Party to treatment less favourable than that which it accords to investment or returns of its own nationals or companies or to investments or returns of nationals or companies of any third State.

8.125 Being relative standards of protection, their scope cannot be defined in the abstract, but will vary according to the circumstances of each case. This requires an analysis of facts, including the protections and assurances granted by the host state to other investors.

---

[239] *LG&E Energy Corporation and ors v Argentine Republic*, n. 147, at [262].
[240] *Marion Unglaube and Reinhard Unglaube v Republic of Costa Rica*, Award, n. 228, at [263].
[241] *The Loewen Group Inc. and Raymond L Loewen v United States of America*, Award, n. 206, at [127]. The tribunal was considering the judgment of a US trial court. The tribunal observed that bad faith or malicious intention is not an essential element of unfair and inequitable treatment, and it is sufficient if there is a lack of due process that offends a sense of judicial propriety. Although the tribunal found the trial court proceedings to be improper and discreditable, it held against the claimant, as a result of its failure to exhaust all remedies under the US legal system.
[242] *Antoine Goetz and ors v République du Burundi*, Award, n. 229, at [121]; *Nykomb Synergetics Technology Holding AB v Republic of Latvia*, Award, Stockholm Rules, IIC 182 (2003), at [64]; *Saluka Investments BV v Czech Republic*, Partial Award, n. 189, at [313] ('State conduct is discriminatory, if (i) similar cases are (ii) treated differently (iii) and without reasonable justification').
[243] Treaty between the United States of America and the Arab Republic of Egypt Concerning the Reciprocal Encouragement and Protection of Investments, signed on 29 September 1982, entered into force on 27 June 1992.

8.126 In order to succeed in a claim based on the national treatment or MFN provisions of a BIT, a claimant must establish that *more* favourable treatment has been granted to another foreign investor or national in similar circumstances.[244] The requirement for a similar basis of comparison is explicit in NAFTA, which provides that national treatment applies only where the foreign and domestic investor are 'in like circumstances'.[245] Tribunals do not require proof of discriminatory or protectionist intent in order to find a treaty breach. However, the pursuit of legitimate policy objectives may justify differential treatment.[246]

8.127 Traditionally, the MFN clause is relied on in the context of substantive rights. For example, the host state of an investment may provide tax concessions to French investors in the oil industry, but not to British investors in that industry. In those circumstances, the British investor could rely on the MFN clause to claim the same treatment or compensation for the loss suffered as a result of the discrimination. However, as seen earlier, tribunals in *Maffezini* and other cases[247] have extended the application of this provision from substantive to procedural matters, such as the dispute resolution mechanism between the host state and investors.[248] This trend has led to a new generation of investment treaties that include more deliberate language to exclude procedural rights from the reach of the MFN clause.[249]

8.128 The presence of MFN clauses in investment treaties creates a diffusive effect of investor protection, as additional gains obtained by one state flow to other states. This can lead to the creation of a single 'highest' standard for all contracting parties to BITs with a particular state.

(f) **Free transfer of funds related to investments**

8.129 Many investment treaties provide guarantees relating to the free movement of funds. Article IV of the United States–Ecuador BIT[250] provides:

> Each Party shall permit all transfers related to an investment to be made freely and without delay into and out of its territory. Such transfers include: (a) returns;

---

[244] *Parkerings-Compagniet AS v Republic of Lithuania*, Award, n. 174, at [368]; *United Parcel Service of America Inc. v Government of Canada*, Award, UNCITRAL, 24 May 2007, IIC 306 (2007), at [173]–[184].

[245] NAFTA, Art. 1102(1).

[246] *Gami Investments Inc. v The Government of the United Mexican States*, Award, UNCITRAL, 15 November 2004, IIC 109 (2004), at [114]; *Parkerings-Compagniet AS v Republic of Lithuania*, Award, n. 174, at [371].

[247] See *EDF International and ors v Argentine Republic*, Award, ICSID Case No. ARB/03/23, IIC 556 (2012), at [929].

[248] See paragraphs 8.51–8.53.

[249] See, e.g., UNCTAD, *Most-Favored-Nation Treatment: A Sequel*, Series on Issues in International Investment Agreements II (UN, 2010), available online at http://unctad.org/en/Docs/diaeia20101_en.pdf, pp. 85–86 (referring to the Chile–Colombia FTA of 2006, Annex 9.3, the Canada–Peru FTA of 2008, Annex 804.1, and the Japan–Switzerland EPA of 2009, Art. 88).

[250] Treaty between the United States of America and the Republic of Ecuador Concerning the Encouragement and Reciprocal Protection of Investment, signed on 27 August 1993, entered into force on 11 May 1997.

D. Merits of the Dispute

(b) compensation 'pursuant to provisions of the treaty'; (c) payments arising out of an investment dispute; (d) payments made under a contract, including amortization of principal and accrued interest payments made pursuant to a loan agreement; (e) proceeds from the sale or liquidation of all or any part of an investment; and (f) additional contributions to capital for the maintenance or development of an investment.

Transfers shall be made in a freely usable currency at the prevailing market rate of exchange on the data of transfer with respect to spot transactions in the currency to be transferred.

This obligation entitles foreign investors to compensation if suddenly affected by currency control regulations, or other host state acts, which effectively confine the investor's money in the host state. As is evident from the provision in the United States–Ecuador BIT, the free transfer provisions are broad in scope, being not limited to the invested funds, but covering any amounts derived from or associated with the investment, including profit, dividend, interest, capital gain, royalty payment, management, technical assistance or other fee, or returns in kind.   8.130

However, treaties often provide for exceptions to the free movement of funds by allowing host states to restrict transfers during unusual periods of low foreign exchange or balance-of-payments problems.[251] Further, it may be permissible for the host state to maintain laws and regulations requiring reports of currency transfer, or to take measures for protection of creditor interests. Such regulations must nevertheless comply with the other investor treaty provisions requiring equitable and non-discriminatory treatment.   8.131

Despite their fundamental importance,[252] few awards have considered free transfer of funds provisions in BITs. Following Argentina's imposition of a 'ring fence' restricting transfers of currency abroad, several investors claimed a breach of 'free transfer of funds' BIT provisions. The tribunal in *Metalpar v Argentina*[253] held that the claimants had not complied with the established procedure for transferring funds abroad (that is, seeking the authorisation of the central bank) and could not therefore complain that Argentina had breached the free transfer of funds provision in the Chile–Argentina BIT. The tribunal in *Continental Casualty Co. v Argentine Republic*[254] noted that not every cross-border movement of funds will be 'related to the investment' and protected by the BIT. It held that the frustrated   8.132

---

[251] See, e.g., the Protocol attached to the Treaty between the United States of America and the Arab Republic of Egypt Concerning the Reciprocal Encouragement and Protection of Investments, 29 September 1982, para. 10.
[252] One tribunal noted that the guarantees provided by free transfer of funds provisions are 'fundamental to the freedom to make a foreign investment and an essential element of the promotional role of BITs': see *Continental Casualty Co. v Argentine Republic*, Award, ICSID Case No. ARB/03/9, IIC 336 (2008), at [245].
[253] *Metalpar SA and Buen Aire SA v Argentine Republic*, Award, ICSID Case No. ARB/03/5, IIC 326 (2008), at [179].
[254] *Continental Casualty*, n. 252, at [242].

transfer at issue—a short-term placement to a bank account outside Argentina for the purpose of protecting the funds from the impeding devaluation—was not a transfer protected by the BIT.

8.133 In *White Industries v India*,[255] the claimant alleged that the retention of bank guarantees by Coal India (a state-owned company) was a violation of India's obligation to 'permit all funds of an investor related to an investment to be transferred freely without unreasonable delay' under the BIT. The tribunal, however, dismissed the claim, finding, inter alia, that the provision was meant to apply to the movement of capital and exchange of currency, not assertions of contractual rights.

(g) Observance of specific investment undertakings

8.134 Treaties often contain a so-called umbrella clause—that is, the obligation of the host state to respect specific undertakings towards investors. The final sentence of Article 2(2) of the United States–Argentina Treaty[256] sets out such an 'umbrella clause', whereby the host state is required to observe specific obligations entered into with the investor: 'Each Party shall observe any obligation it may have entered into with regard to investments.'

8.135 Unlike other treaty terms, umbrella clauses come in many varieties, and it is particularly important to consider the language of the specific clause in question. These linguistic differences have given rise to different interpretations as to the scope and meaning of these clauses.

8.136 There is disagreement as to the whether the legal effect of umbrella clauses is to elevate any breach of contractual obligations in direct agreements between states and investors to the level of treaty breach.[257] The award in *SGS v Pakistan*[258] was the first to consider the issue of the scope of umbrella clauses. The tribunal concluded, on the terms of the particular clause in question, that it did 'not believe that transmutation of SGS's contract claims into BIT claims has occurred' through the operation of such a clause.

---

[255] *White Industries Australia Ltd v Republic of India*, Final Award, UNCITRAL, 30 November 2011, IIC 529 (2011), at [13.2.1]–[13.2.4].

[256] See n. 35.

[257] See OECD, 'Interpretation of the umbrella clause in investment agreements', Working Paper on International Investment No. 2006/3 (October 2006), available online at http://www.oecd.org/daf/inv/investment-policy/WP-2006_3.pdf; Crawford, 'Treaty and contract in investment arbitration' (2008) 24 Arb Intl 351; Kunoy, 'Singing in the rain: Developments in the interpretation of umbrella clauses' (2006) 7 JWIT 275.

[258] *SGS Société Générale de Surveillance SA v Islamic Republic of Pakistan*, Decision on Jurisdiction, ICSID Case No. ARB/01/13, IIC 223 (2003), at [156].

D. Merits of the Dispute

8.137 The arbitral tribunal concluded that the legal consequences of such an interpretation of the BIT were 'so far-reaching in scope, and so automatic and unqualified and sweeping in their apparent operation, so burdensome in their potential impact upon the contracting party',[259] that clear and convincing evidence had to be adduced by the claimant to demonstrate that such was the shared intent of the contracting parties to the BIT. In the absence of such evidence, the arbitral tribunal rejected the claimant's interpretation, which would, according to the tribunal, amount to 'incorporating by reference an unlimited number of state contracts as well as other municipal law instruments setting out state commitments including unilateral commitments to an investor of the other contracting party'.[260]

8.138 This limitative interpretation of umbrella clauses was rejected in another case[261] brought by the same investor against the Philippines under the Switzerland–Philippines BIT.[262] That case concerned Article X(2): 'Each Contracting Party shall observe any obligation it has assumed with regard to specific investments in its territory by investors of the other Contracting Party.' The tribunal concluded that this clause did make it a breach of the BIT for the host state to fail to observe binding contractual commitments, but that the scope of the obligations contained in the investment agreement remained governed by the applicable law of the contract and were not elevated to international law. The practical impact of the decision was further limited by the conclusion that compliance with undertakings was a 'two-way street' and that the investor first had to comply with its obligation to submit its claim to local jurisdiction in accordance with the dispute resolution clause.[263]

8.139 The diverging approaches adopted by the *SGS v Pakistan* and *SGS v Philippines* tribunals have led to the development of conflicting lines of jurisprudence, which one leading commentator has grouped into four 'camps':

> The first camp adopts an extremely narrow interpretation of umbrella clauses, holding that they are operative only where it is possible to discern a shared intent of the parties that any breach of contract is a breach of the BIT (*SGS v Pakistan*; *Joy Mining v Egypt*).
>
> The second camp seeks to limit umbrella clauses to breaches of contract committed by the host State in the exercise of sovereign authority (*Pan American Energy v Argentina*; *El Paso Energy v Argentina*).

---

[259] Ibid., at [167].
[260] Ibid., at [168].
[261] *SGS Société Générale de Surveillance SA v Republic of the Philippines*, Decision on Jurisdiction, n. 158.
[262] Agreement between the Swiss Confederation and the Republic of the Philippines on the Promotion and Reciprocal Protection of Investments, signed on 23 August 1991, entered into force on 23 April 1999.
[263] *SGS Société Générale de Surveillance SA v Republic of the Philippines*, Decision on Jurisdiction, n. 158, at [155].

A third view goes to the other extreme: the effect of Umbrella clauses is to internationalise investment contracts, thereby transforming contractual claims into treaty claims directly subject to treaty rules (*Fedax v Venezuela*; *Eureko v Republic of Poland*; *Noble Ventures v Romania*).

Finally there is the view that an umbrella clause is operative and may form the basis for a substantive treaty claim, but that it does not convert a contractual claim into a treaty claim. On the one hand it provides, or at least may provide, a basis for a treaty claim even if the BIT in question contains no generic claims clause (*SGS v Philippines*; *CMS v Argentina (Annulment)*); on the other hand, the umbrella clause does not change the proper law of the contract or its legal incidents, including its provisions for dispute settlement.[264]

8.140 Recent cases involving umbrella clauses have continued to divide into these camps.[265] For instance, in interpreting nearly identical umbrella clauses, the tribunals in *BIVAC v Paraguay* and *SGS v Paraguay* came to opposite conclusions. Both tribunals determined that the umbrella clause imports contractual obligations into the investment treaty. However, the *BIVAC* tribunal determined that the claim was inadmissible because the parties had agreed to the exclusive jurisdiction of national courts,[266] whereas the *SGS* tribunal determined that the forum selection clause was not a bar to its jurisdiction.[267] In the words of one commentator, 'the situation seems to remain as uncertain today as it was 10 years ago when the first two *SGS* Tribunals were called to interpret and apply the clause for the first time in a legal vacuum'.[268]

E. Measures of Compensation under Bilateral Investment Treaties

8.141 In the context of investment treaty arbitration, the term 'compensation' is commonly used to describe (a) a prerequisite for a lawful expropriation of private property, (b) one form of reparation for injury caused by a state's unlawful act under international law, and/or (c) the obligation to pay damages as a consequence for a breach of contract.[269] In customary international law, compensation is considered

---

[264] Crawford, 'Treaty and contract in investment arbitration' (2008) 24 Arb Intl 351, at 366–367.
[265] See, e.g., *Gustav F W Hamester GmbH & Co. KG v Republic of Ghana*, Award, n. 80; *EDF International SA and ors v Argentine Republic*, Award, n. 247; *Bosh International, Inc. and B&P Ltd Foreign Investments Enterprise v Ukraine*, Award, ICSID Case No. ARB/08/11, IIC 565 (2012).
[266] *Bureau Veritas, Inspection, Valuation, Assessment and Control, BIVAC BV v Republic of Paraguay*, Decision on Jurisdiction, n. 156, at [141]–[142], and [159].
[267] *SGS Société Générale de Surveillance SA v Republic of Paraguay*, Decision on Jurisdiction, n. 156, at [162]–[171].
[268] Yannaca-Small, '*BIVAC BV v Paraguay* versus *SGS v Paraguay*: The umbrella clause still in search of one identity' (2013) 28 ICSID Rev—Foreign Investment LJ 307, at 313.
[269] Marboe, 'Compensation in investment law and arbitration', in Bjorklund, Laird, and Ripinsky (eds) *Investment Treaty Law: Current Issues III* (British Institute of International and Comparative Law, 2009), pp. 29–32.

E. Measures of Compensation under Bilateral Investment Treaties

an alternative to restitution in the sense that 'restitution is a primary remedy for international wrongs, while compensation has a supplementary function in achieving the ultimate objective of reparation, viz wiping out all the consequences of the illegal act'.[270]

The quantification of compensation is left to the arbitral tribunal's discretion: **8.142**

> This is not a matter to be resolved simply on the basis of the burden of proof. To be sure, the tribunal must be satisfied that the claimant has suffered some damage under the relevant head as a result of the respondent's breach. But once it is satisfied of this, *the determination of the precise amount of this damage is a matter for the tribunal's informed estimation* in the light of all the evidence available to it.[271]

A tribunal will award compensation, however, only if the party seeking it has established causation. As articulated by the majority in *Biwater Gauff (Tanzania) Ltd v United Republic of Tanzania*: **8.143**

> Compensation for any violation of the BIT, whether in the context of unlawful expropriation or the breach of any other treaty standard, will only be due if there is a sufficient causal link between the actual breach of the BIT and the loss sustained by [the claimant].[272]

The elements of causation include, inter alia, '(a) a sufficient link between the wrongful act and the damage in question, and (b) a threshold beyond which damage, albeit linked to the wrongful act, is considered too indirect or remote'.[273] In other words, proof of causation requires cause, effect, and a logical link between the two.[274] **8.144**

---

[270] Ripinsky and Williams, *Damages in International Investment Law* (British Institute of International and Comparative Law, 2008), p. 55, citing the ruling in *Chorzów Factory* that the state was under 'the obligation to restore the undertaking [i.e. restitution] and, if this be not possible, to pay its value at the time of the indemnification [i.e. compensation], which value is designed to take the place of restitution which has become impossible': see *Case Concerning the Factory at Chorzów (Claim for Indemnity) (Germany v Poland)* [1928] PCIJ Series A No. 17, at 48.

[271] *Rumeli Telekom AS and Telsim Mobil Telekomunikasyon Hizmetleri AS v Republic of Kazakhstan*, Award, n. 224, at [147] (emphasis added); see also Kantor, *Valuation for Arbitration* (Kluwer Law International, 2008), pp. 1–2.

[272] *Biwater Gauff (Tanzania) Ltd v United Republic of Tanzania*, Award, n. 111, at [779].

[273] Ibid., at [785], citing Crawford, *The International Law Commission's Articles on State Responsibility: Introduction, Text and Commentaries* (Cambridge University Press, 2002), pp. 204–205. The majority determined that although Tanzania had violated the BIT, none of the violations caused the loss and damage in question: *Biwater Gauff*, n. 111, at [797]–[798]. The concurring and dissenting opinion, at [16]–[19], considered the majority's analysis to confuse issues of causation, on the one hand, and quantum of damages, on the other. Tanzania seized the claimant's business, which clearly caused injury to it. However, the claimant had failed to demonstrate damages, so the majority's analytical confusion was not decisive in the outcome.

[274] *Joseph Charles Lemire v Ukraine*, Decision on Jurisdiction and Liability, n. 210, at [157]. That a claimant could potentially recover against a respondent state on the basis of a contract does not preclude the claimant for recovering damages for the state's breach of the relevant BIT: see, e.g.,

8.145 The issue of compensation can be usefully considered first in terms of remedies for expropriation and remedies for other international law breaches, before turning to certain ancillary issues (moral damages, interest, costs, and attorneys' fees).

(a) Expropriation remedies

8.146 The almost universal standard of compensation in expropriation established by BITs for lawful expropriations is the 'fair market value' of the investment immediately prior to the expropriatory measure. This standard dates from 1938 and is known as the 'Hull formula' after US Secretary of State Cordell Hull, who declared, in a dispute between the United States and Mexico concerning the expropriation of US oil fields, that international law required Mexico to pay 'prompt, adequate and effective' compensation.[275] The standard requires the payment of full market value of the expropriated asset speedily in a convertible currency. The World Bank Guidelines on the Treatment of Foreign Direct Investment state:

> 1. Compensation for a specific investment taken by the State will, according to the details provided below, be deemed 'appropriate' if it is adequate, effective and prompt.
> 2. Compensation will be deemed 'adequate' if it is based on the fair market value of the taken asset as such value is determined immediately before the time at which the taking occurred or the decision to take the asset became publicly known.[276]

8.147 Fair market value is generally accepted to mean the price at which a willing buyer and willing seller would conclude an arm's-length transaction.[277] As the tribunal in *Starrett Housing Corporation v Iran*[278] summarised it:

> ...the price [at which] a willing buyer would buy...and the price at which a willing seller would sell...on condition that none of the two parties [is] under any kind of duress and that both parties have good information about all relevant circumstances involved in the purchase.[279]

8.148 There are various accepted methods of calculating the fair market value of an asset. The fair market value of an income-producing asset, or 'going concern', is often

---

Deutsche Bank AG v Democratic Socialist Republic of Sri Lanka, Award, ICSID Case No. ARB/09/2, IIC 578 (2012), at [556]–[565].

[275] Hackworth, *Digest of International Law*, vol. 3, 659 (1942).

[276] Reprinted in Shihata, *Legal Treatment of Foreign Investment: The World Bank Guidelines* (Martinus Nijhoff, 1993), p. 193.

[277] Ripinsky and Williams, *Damages in International Investment Law* (British Institute of International and Comparative Law, 2008), pp. 183–186, citing *Black's Law Dictionary*.

[278] *Starrett Housing Corporation, et al. v Iran*, Iran–United States Claims Tribunal Award No. 314-24-1, 14 August 1987.

[279] Ibid., at [18], [27], and [274].

E. Measures of Compensation under Bilateral Investment Treaties

calculated by measuring its future prospects by using the discounted cash flow (DCF) analysis. The World Bank Guidelines define DCF as:

> ...the cash receipts realistically expected from the enterprise in each future year of its economic life as reasonably projected minus that year's expected cash expenditure, after discounting this net cash flow for each year by a factor which reflects the time value of money, expected inflation, and the risk associated with such cash flow under realistic circumstances.[280]

This is exactly what a willing buyer and seller would do in the real world when fixing a price for a business. In order to calculate future cash flows, future revenues, operating expenditure, capital expenditure, and applicable taxes will all need to be estimated.[281] The discount rate will, in turn, be established using a formula that takes into account the particular risk of the industry in question by means of what is known as the 'beta'[282] and the relevant country risk. This exercise is usually undertaken by expert economist witnesses. **8.149**

Once a figure is obtained from the DCF analysis, it is often supported by reference to comparative transactions, which show what comparable assets in comparable countries have been sold for at similar moments in time. **8.150**

Another common valuation methodology where the affected asset is part of a publicly traded company is to look to the stock market valuation. This is of greater value where the affected asset represents the whole (or the bulk of) the traded corporation and the market in question is liquid. **8.151**

Where the affected asset is not publicly traded, is not a going concern and has no clear prospect of future earning power (for example a factory as yet unopened, which was to make a product in respect of which the local market is uncertain), tribunals have looked to book value (using the numbers appearing in the asset's accounting books or balance sheets) or 'sunk costs' (the repayment of investments undertaken that cannot be recovered), with interest appropriate to the country in which the asset is located.[283] **8.152**

In this context, it is important to consider whether the asset in question has a history of producing income. In *AAPL v Sri Lanka*,[284] the tribunal refused to award lost profits, since the future profitability of a shrimp farm could not be reasonably established with a sufficient degree of certainty. This approach had been adopted earlier by the Iran–United States Claims Tribunal, where an American investor **8.153**

---

[280] *World Bank Guidelines on the Treatment of Foreign Direct Investment*, s. IV(6).
[281] See *Phillips Petroleum Co. Iran v Islamic Republic of Iran*, n 181, at [111].
[282] The 'beta' measures the volatility of the particular industry vis-à-vis the stock market as a whole.
[283] See Marboe, *Calculation of Compensation and Damages in International Investment Law* (Oxford University Press, 2009), pp. 269–270, 279–280.
[284] *Asian Agricultural Products Ltd (AAPL) v Republic of Sri Lanka*, Final Award, n. 14.

was unable to obtain lost profits from a factory that had been expropriated before it had started operations.[285]

8.154 The question remains as to the circumstances in which an asset with no history of revenue production may properly give rise to a DCF-type calculation. In the *Karaha Bodas* and *Himpurna* arbitrations, which involved a geothermal power project that was terminated, damages were awarded for lost profits notwithstanding the absence of any revenue-generating activity based on expected future demand.[286]

8.155 Similarly, assets linked to natural resources with proven or probable reserves (such as oil fields or mines) are one class of investments the market value of which is intrinsically linked to those reserves, rather than simply the result of a historic analysis of revenue generation. In such circumstances, whether the assets are in production or not will not affect market value materially, because the market values the resources proven in the ground, which will be eventually extracted by a 'willing buyer'.[287]

8.156 Recent awards have distinguished between the standard of compensation for lawful expropriations[288] and unlawful expropriations.[289] In *ADC v Hungary*,[290] the tribunal stated that:

> [T]he BIT only stipulates the standard of compensation that is payable in the case of a lawful expropriation, and these cannot be used to determine the issue of damages payable in the case of an unlawful expropriation since this would be to conflate compensation for a lawful expropriation with damages for an unlawful expropriation.

8.157 In other words, if any of the cumulative conditions set out in the treaty expropriation article are not met, then (by definition) the expropriation has not complied with the treaty obligations and the treaty standard need no longer apply. As a consequence, tribunals have held that unlawful expropriations are to be compensated under the customary international law standard, rather than under the express terms of the BIT.[291] The customary standard of compensation is set out in the famous *Chorzów Factory* case as one of full reparation, which 'must, as far

---

[285] *Phelps Dodge Corporation v Iran* (1986) 10 Iran–US CTR 121.
[286] *Karaha Bodas Co. LLC v Perusahaan Pertambangan Minyak Dan Gasi Bumi Nehara*, Award, UNCITRAL, 18 December 2000; *Himpurna California Energy Ltd v PT PLN*, Award, UNCITRAL, 4 May 1999, both available at (2000) XXV YBCA 13.
[287] *Occidental Petroleum Corporation and ors v Republic of Ecuador*, Award, ICSID Case No. ARB/06/11, IIC 561 (2012), at [707]–[708], [722], [733], and [737]–[738] (awarding US$1.77 billion—US$2.3 billion with interest applied).
[288] Namely, the treaty standard described at paragraph s 8.79–8.95.
[289] Sheppard, 'The distinction between lawful and unlawful expropriation', in Ribeiro (ed.) *Investment Arbitration and the Energy Charter Treaty* (Juris, 2007).
[290] *ADC Affiliate Ltd and ADC & ADMC Management Ltd v Republic of Hungary*, Award, n. 178, at [481]. See also *Saipem SpA v People's Republic of Bangladesh*, Award, ICSID Case No. ARB/05/07, IIC 378 (2009), at [201].
[291] *ADC v Hungary*, n. 178.

E. Measures of Compensation under Bilateral Investment Treaties

as possible, wipe out all the consequences of the illegal act and re-establish the situation which would, in all probability, have existed if that act had not been committed'.[292]

The application of this standard may lead to higher compensation than for lawful expropriation.[293] For example, in *ADC v Hungary*,[294] the asset expropriated—an airport concession—increased in value after its expropriation by the state. The tribunal held that, in order to restore the investor to the position in which it would have been 'but for' the expropriation, the investor should be awarded the higher value of the asset at the time of the award, rather than the value of the asset at the time of expropriation (the valuation date set out in the BIT).[295] This approach was recently adopted by the majority in the *ConocoPhillips v Venezuela* arbitration.[296] Other tribunals, however, have found that, in certain circumstances, 'the distinction between compensation for a lawful expropriation and compensation for an unlawful expropriation may not make a significant practical difference'.[297]

8.158

(b) Compensation for other treaty breaches

As in the expropriation context, a claimant who has prevailed in establishing other types of treaty breach—that is, breaches of the 'fair and equitable', and other, treatment protections provided in the treaties—must also establish its entitlement to compensation for those breaches. For instance, the tribunal in *Rompetrol Group NV v Romania*[298] found that the claimant had established Romania's breach of the BIT's fair and equitable treatment provision, but had not proven that it suffered economic loss or damage as a result of that breach. Consequently, the tribunal awarded no compensation. To take another example, in *Joseph Charles Lemire v Ukraine*,[299] the claimant demonstrated a causal link between the host state's wrongful denial of public tenders and the loss in value of his broadcasting

8.159

---

[292] *Case Concerning the Factory at Chorzów (Claim for Indemnity) (Germany v Poland)* [1928] PCIJ Series A No. 17, at 47. See Abdala and Spiller, '*Chorzow*'s standard rejuvenated: Assessing damages in investment treaty arbitrations' (2008) 25 J Intl Arb 103.
[293] *Compañía de Aguas del Aconquija SA and Vivendi Universal SA v Argentine Republic*, Award, n. 177, at [8.2.5].
[294] *ADC Affiliate Ltd and ADC & ADMC Management Ltd v Republic of Hungary*, Award, n. 178.
[295] Ibid., at [496].
[296] *ConocoPhillips Petrozuata BV and ors v Bolivarian Republic of Venezuela*, Decision on Jurisdiction and the Merits, ICSID Case No. ARB/07/30, IIC 605 (2013), at [343].
[297] *Waguih Elie George Siag and Clorinda Vecchi v Arab Republic of Egypt*, Award, n. 228, at [539]–[542]; *Bernardus Henricus Funnekotter and ors v Republic of Zimbabwe*, Award, n. 163, at [124]; *Marion Unglaube and Reinhard Unglaube v Republic of Costa Rica*, Award, n. 228, at [305] and [307].
[298] Award, ICSID Case No. ARB/06/3, IIC 591 (2013), at [283], [286], and [288]. See also *Nordzucker AG v Republic of Poland*, Third Partial and Final Award, UNCITRAL, 28 January 2009.
[299] See n. 210, at [163]*ff.* Ukraine objected that any such analysis would be inherently speculative.

company, showing that it was 'probable—and not simply possible' that his company would have been awarded the tender but for the wrongful acts.

8.160 Bilateral investment treaties usually do not specify the damages to which the claimant would be entitled as compensation for the host state's other treaty breaches. However, international tribunals have awarded damages for breach of the fair and equitable treatment standard according to the *Chorzów Factory* case—that is, the 'wiping out' of all consequences of the illegal act.

8.161 International tribunals have applied the *Chorzów Factory* principle, confirming that, under international law, treaty breaches give rise to the obligation to compensate the economic harm that they cause in an amount equivalent to the losses that the claimant can prove were caused by the measures in question.[300] It should be noted that, in case of successful claims for expropriation and other treaty breaches, compensation will not be cumulative.

8.162 In applying the *Chorzów Factory* principle, several tribunals have used the standard of fair market value in determining damages for violations of fair and equitable treatment.[301] Although 'fair market value' is a standard employed in compensating for an expropriation, in *CMS v Argentina*,[302] the tribunal resorted to the fair market value standard in assessing damages arising out of Argentina's breach of the treaty, noting that the standard 'might be appropriate for breaches different from expropriation if their effect results in important long-term losses'. The tribunal established the quantum of damages using the DCF method to calculate the net present value (NPV) of expected cash flows. It adopted a (hypothetical) scenario *without* the adverse measures, from which it subtracted the NPV of expected cash flows in the (actual) scenario *with* the adverse measures.[303]

8.163 Restitution also remains available as a remedy for fair and equitable treatment breaches. In *Mr Franck Charles Arif v Republic of Moldova*,[304] the respondent

---

[300] *MTD Equity Sdn Bhd & MTD Chile SA v Republic of Chile*, n. 189; *Petrobart Ltd v Kyrgyz Republic*, Award, SCC Arbitration No. 126/2003, IIC 184 (2005); *Azurix Corporation v Argentine Republic*, Award, n. 189; *S D Myers Inc. v Government of Canada*, Final Award on the Merits, UNCITRAL, 30 December 2000, IIC 249 (2000); *Metalclad Corporation v United Mexican States*, Award, ICSID Case No. ARB(AF)/97/1, IIC 161 (2000).

[301] Reed and Bray, *Fair and Equitable Treatment: Fairly and Equitably Applied In Lieu of Unlawful Indirect Expropriation?* (Brill, 2007); *CMS Gas Transmission Co. v Republic of Argentina*, n. 200; *Enron Corporation and Ponderosa Assets LP v Argentine Republic*, n. 188; *Azurix Corporation v Argentine Republic*, Award, n. 189; *Saluka Investments BV v Czech Republic*, Partial Award, n. 189.

[302] *CMS Gas Transmission*, n. 200, at [410].

[303] One possible measure of the value of a claimant's investment in a company 'but for' the respondent state's measures is the actual price paid for the claimant's shares: see *EDF International and ors v Argentine Republic*, Award, n. 247, at [1232].

[304] *Mr Franck Charles Arif v Republic of Moldova*, Award, ICSID Case No. ARB/11/23, IIC 585 (2013).

E. Measures of Compensation under Bilateral Investment Treaties

requested the option to offer restitution instead of damages were it found to have breached its treaty obligations. The tribunal obliged, noting that 'restitution is more consistent with the objective of bilateral investment treaties, as it preserves both the investment and the relationship between the investor and Host State'.[305] The tribunal gave Moldova sixty days in which to make proposals for restitution and allowed the claimant to accept or reject those proposals.[306]

(c) Moral damages

In recent years, an increasing number of arbitral tribunals have been presented with claims for 'moral damages', a compensatory remedy for a category of intangible harm.[307] The first example of an award of such damages was the 2008 decision in *Desert Line v Yemen*.[308] The *Desert Line* tribunal found that it had jurisdiction to award moral damages, which may be requested in 'exceptional circumstances' and by corporate claimants only in 'specific circumstances'. It then awarded US$1 million in damages for physical duress suffered by executives of the claimant company at the hands of government security forces, as well as for the company's loss to its 'credit and reputation'.[309]

8.164

In the wake of *Desert Line*, a significant number of claimants have, unsuccessfully, sought moral damages. In denying a claim for moral damages, the *Lemire* majority articulated a test that has been adopted in several subsequent cases, holding that moral damages can be awarded only in exceptional cases in which:

8.165

– the State's actions imply physical threat, illegal detention or other analogous situations in which the ill-treatment contravenes the norms according to which civilised nations are expected to act;
– the State's actions cause a deterioration of health, stress, anxiety, other mental suffering such as humiliation, shame and degradation, or loss of reputation, credit and social position; and
– both cause and effect are grave or substantial.[310]

---

[305] Ibid., at [570].
[306] Ibid., at [633].
[307] Jagusch and Sebastian, 'Moral damages in investment arbitration: Punitive damages in compensatory clothing?' (2013) 29 Arb Intl 45, at 45–46.
[308] *Desert Line Projects LLC v Republic of Yemen*, Award, n. 83. The previous case was *SARL Benvenuti & Bonfant v People's Republic of the Congo*, Award, ICSID Case No. ARB/77/2, 8 August 1980, (1982) 21 ILM 740, which was decided *ex aequo et bono* rather than under a BIT.
[309] *Desert Line*, n. 83, at [289]–[290].
[310] *Joseph Charles Lemire v Ukraine*, n. 210, at [333]. The majority was sympathetic to the claimant's claim that recurring rejections of his applications had a negative impact on his entrepreneurial image, which would be likely to satisfy the second requirement for moral damages. Nevertheless, the 'gravity' required under the moral damages standard was not present, for Lemire's situations could not be compared to the armed threats or witnessing of deaths for which other tribunals have awarded moral damages: ibid., at [339]. The *Lemire* test has been adopted in other cases: see, e.g.,

(d) Interest

8.166 Investment arbitration tribunals routinely award interest, which forms part of the overall compensation for loss owed to a prevailing party. For example, in the case of an expropriation, the obligation to pay arises prior to the expropriatory act. Failure to make such payment causes the affected investor to lose the use of those funds in the period between the taking and payment of the compensation, and is part of the loss. As noted by one leading commentator: 'The most commonly cited reason for awarding interest is to compensate the claimant for the loss of the ability to benefit from the use of the principal sum.'[311]

8.167 Many BITs provide for payment of interest in their expropriation clauses, and the International Law Commission's Draft Articles of State Responsibility codify the customary international law view that interest is part of full reparation for other types of breach.[312] In deciding whether to award interest, investment arbitration tribunals consider the applicable interest rate, the starting date for the calculation (for example date of expropriation), whether compounding of interest is appropriate, and whether to grant post-award interest.[313] In the terms of the rate of interest, tribunals have adopted a number of different approaches, including the rate in the host country,[314] the cost of capital of the investor,[315] or the borrowing rate that an investor would have been charged,[316] among others.[317] As to the award of simple versus compound interest, the 'overwhelming trend' is to award compound interest,[318] such that there is now a 'jurisprudence *constante* where the presumption has shifted from a decade or so ago with the result that it would now be more appropriate to order compound interest'.[319]

Sr Tza Yap Shum v Republic of Peru, n. 68, IIC 382 (2009); *Mr Franck Charles Arif v Republic of Moldova*, Award, n. 304, at [584]–[592], and [615].

[311] Crawford, *State Responsibility: The General Part* (Oxford University Press, 2013), pp. 532–533.

[312] Ibid., citing the International Law Commission's Draft Articles of State Responsibility, Art. 38.

[313] See Ripinsky and Williams, *Damages in International Investment Law*, n. 270, p. 362; Marboe, *Calculation of Compensation and Damages in International Investment Law*, n. 283, pp. 371–392; Sabahi, *Compensation and Restitution in Investor–State Arbitration: Principles and Practice* (Oxford University Press, 2011), pp. 148–153. For a detailed discussion of interest in international commercial arbitrations, see Chapter 9.

[314] *CME Czech Republic BV (The Netherlands) v Czech Republic*, Final Award, n. 156, at [636]–[641].

[315] *Compañía de Aguas del Aconquija SA and Vivendi Universal SA v Argentine Republic*, Award, n. 177, at [9.2.8].

[316] *Alpha Projektholding GmbH v Ukraine*, Award, ICSID Case No. ARB/07/16, IIC 464 (2010), at [514].

[317] See generally Marboe, n. 283, ch. 6; Ripinsky and Williams, n. 270, ch. 9.

[318] *Ioan Micula and ors v Romania*, Decision on Jurisdiction and Admissibility, ICSID Case No. ARB/05/20, IIC 339 (2008), at [1266].

[319] *Gemplus SA and ors v The United Mexican States*, Award, ICSID Case No. ARB(AF)/04/3, IIC 488 (2010); *Talsud SA v The United Mexican States*, Award, ICSID Case No. ARB(AF)04/4, IIC 488 (2010), at Pt XVI, [26].

E. Measures of Compensation under Bilateral Investment Treaties

(e) Costs and attorneys' fees

8.168 The traditional position in investment treaty arbitration, in comparison to commercial arbitration, has been for each party to bear its own costs of legal representation and related expenses, and to divide tribunal costs equally.[320] More recently, however, there has been a trend toward requiring the losing party to pay the costs and legal fees of the prevailing party in certain circumstances, based on the parties' degree of success and/or conduct.[321] As summarised by one commentator, those circumstances may include where the unsuccessful party (a) advances patently unmeritorious or legally untenable claims, (b) abuses the investment arbitration process, (c) presents poor and inefficient pleadings, or (d) engages in egregious underlying conduct.[322]

8.169 This practice is consistent with the ICSID Arbitration Rules and the UNCITRAL Arbitration Rules, both of which give tribunals considerable discretion in awarding costs. Indeed, Article 42 of the UNCITRAL Rules was revised in 2010, and now includes a default principle that costs *and* legal fees shall be borne by the unsuccessful party.[323] ICSID Arbitration Rule 28(1), however, does not contain any default principle concerning the allocation of costs and legal fees.[324]

---

[320] See, e.g., *ICS Inspection and Control Services Ltd (United Kingdom) v Republic of Argentina*, Award on Jurisdiction, PCA Case No. 2010-9, UNCITRAL, IIC 528 (2012), at [340]; *Chevron Corporation and Texaco Petroleum Co. v Republic of Ecuador*, Final Award, UNCITRAL, 31 August 2011, IIC 505 (2011), at [375]. For a detailed discussion of costs and fees in international commercial arbitrations, see Chapter 9.

[321] See, e.g., *Libananco Holdings Co. Ltd v Republic of Turkey*, Award, ICSID Case No. ARB/06/8, IIC 506 (2011), at [565]–[569] (ordering the claimant to pay the Republic of Turkey US$15 million and to reimburse the Republic for its arbitration costs); *TECO Guatemala Holdings LLC v Republic of Guatemala*, Award, ICSID Case No. ARB/10/17, IIC 623 (2013), at [769]–[779] (ordering the Republic of Guatemala to reimburse 75 per cent of the claimant's costs, amounting to US$7.5 million). See also a detailed survey of costs allocation in more than 200 investment arbitration awards in Hodgson, 'Counting the costs of investment treaty arbitration', Global Arbitration Review, 24 March 2014.

[322] Reed, 'Allocation of costs in international arbitration' (2011) 26 ICSID Rev—Foreign Investment LJ 76.

[323] See Caron and Caplan, *The UNCITRAL Arbitration Rules* (Oxford University Press, 2013), p. 867 (noting that Art. 40(1) of the 1976 UNCITRAL Arbitration Rules addressed the costs of legal representation and assistance, but did not apply any default principle to those costs).

[324] See Gotanda, 'Consistently inconsistent: The need for predictability in awarding costs and fees in investment treaty arbitrations' (2013) 28 ICSID Rev—Foreign Investment LJ 420, at 433 (arguing that '[t]he system for awarding costs and fees in investment treaty arbitrations can be greatly improved by ICSID's adoption of a clearer allocation rule').

9

AWARD

A. Introduction	9.01	E. Form and Content of Awards	9.139
B. Categories of Award	9.18	F. Effect of Awards	9.173
C. Remedies	9.40	G. Proceedings after the Award	9.186
D. Deliberations and Decisions of the Tribunal	9.100		

A. Introduction

(a) Destination of an international arbitration—the award

Parties to transborder transactions who go to the trouble and expense of taking their disputes to international arbitration do so in the expectation that, unless a settlement is reached along the way, the process will lead to an award. They also expect that, subject to any right of appeal or recourse, the award will be final and binding upon them. Both international and institutional rules of arbitration reflect this expectation. Article 34(2) of the Arbitration Rules of the United Nations Commission on International Trade Law (UNCITRAL) states simply: 'All awards shall be made in writing and shall be final and binding on the parties. The parties shall carry out all awards without delay.' The Rules of the International Chamber of Commerce (ICC), recognising the possibility of some form of challenge to an award at the place of arbitration under the *lex arbitri*, are more circumspect: **9.01**

> Every award shall be binding on the parties. By submitting the dispute to arbitration under the Rules, the parties undertake to carry out any award without delay and shall be deemed to have waived their right to any form of recourse insofar as such waiver can validly be made.[1]

As the UNCITRAL Rules suggest, there may be more than one award in any given dispute. An arbitral tribunal may be called upon to decide procedural issues, or to make partial awards that decide certain issues between the parties on a partial **9.02**

---

[1] ICC Rules, Art. 34(6).

or final basis.[2] For example, the tribunal may make a preliminary decision on its jurisdiction, rather than take the risk of proceeding to the merits of the case and then, perhaps, deciding later that it lacks jurisdiction. Alternatively, it may make a partial award of a sum of money that it considers to be indisputably due and payable by one party to the other.[3]

9.03 All 'awards' are 'final' in the sense that they dispose 'finally' of the issues decided in them (subject to any challenge or procedure for correction or interpretation), and they are 'binding' on the parties.[4] The award that disposes 'finally' of all outstanding issues is known as the 'final award'. A final award, in this sense, is usually the outcome of arbitral proceedings that have been contested throughout. However, it may embody an agreed settlement between the parties, in which case it is generally known as a 'consent award', or an 'award on agreed terms'. Another category is an award in proceedings in which a party has failed or refused to participate, in which case it is usually described as a 'default award'.

9.04 Each of these different types of award are considered in this chapter. Since all awards are dispositive of the issues that they determine, it is important that the arbitral tribunal does its best to ensure not only that the award is correct, but also that it is enforceable across international frontiers.[5]

(b) Definition of an award

9.05 There is no internationally accepted definition of the term 'award'. Indeed, no definition is to be found in the main international conventions dealing with arbitration, including the Geneva treaties, the New York Convention, and the Model Law. Although the New York Convention is directed to the recognition

---

[2] The authors recommend use of the term 'partial awards', rather than 'interim', or 'provisional', awards. The latter terms, particularly in the civil law context, can be interpreted to mean that such awards are not final, when they are indeed final; there is nothing 'provisional' about an award rendered before the conclusion of the arbitration.

[3] Some modern arbitration statutes make a specific distinction between interim, partial, and final awards. The Netherlands Arbitration Act 1986, s. 1049, provides that: 'The arbitral tribunal may render a final award, a partial award, or an interim award.' The commentary on this article by Sanders and van den Berg, *The Netherlands Arbitration Act 1986* (Kluwer International Law, 1987) suggests that: partial awards are given in respect of substantive issues that are separated, such as liability and quantum; interim awards are given on jurisdictional issues; and simple orders are made in respect of procedural issues. The Swiss Private International Law Act 1987 (Swiss PIL), Ch. 12, provides for 'preliminary awards' in relation to jurisdictional issues in s. 186(3), while 'partial awards' that finally determine the issue are provided for in s. 188: see Geisinger, *International Arbitration in Switzerland: A Handbook for Practitioners* (2nd edn, Wolters Kluwer, 2013), pp. 226–227.

[4] The English Arbitration Act 1996, s. 39, is an exception to this general rule in granting a power to make 'provisional awards' if the parties agree that the arbitral tribunal shall have such power. Interestingly, s. 39 mentions the word 'award' only in the marginal note and the body of the section refers to 'orders'. Whether such orders are enforceable under the New York Convention is questionable and would be a matter for the courts of the country in which enforcement is sought: see Hunter and Landau, *The English Arbitration Act 1996: Text and Notes* (Wolters Kluwer, 1998), p. 35.

[5] See, e.g., ICC Rules, Art. 41.

A. Introduction

and enforcement of arbitral awards,[6] the nearest that it comes to a definition is in Article I(2): 'The term "arbitral awards" shall include not only awards made by arbitrators appointed for each case but also those made by permanent arbitral bodies to which the parties have submitted.'

At one stage, it was proposed that there should be a definition of the term 'award' in the Model Law, but ultimately none was adopted. One suggested solution illustrates the difficulty of finding a definition that encompasses not only final awards, but also partial awards, which dispose of only some issues. The proposed definition was as follows: **9.06**

> 'Award' means a final award which disposes of all issues submitted to the arbitral tribunal and any other decision of the arbitral tribunal which finally determines any question of substance or the question of its competence or any other question of procedure but, in the latter case, only if the arbitral tribunal terms its decision an award.[7]

As this proposed definition shows, the need to distinguish between awards that are final and other decisions of a tribunal that are not is a complicating factor. The possible solution of defining each separately was not adopted. The Model Law also plainly contemplates that there may be more than one award during the course of an arbitration. For example, a plea that the arbitral tribunal does not have jurisdiction may be dealt with either in the final award or as a 'preliminary question'; thus, in a 'Model Law country', if the tribunal takes the second course, its partial award may be challenged in the competent court within thirty days of its notification to the parties.[8]

The time limit for challenge of an award begins to run from the date on which the award was issued. Once the final award has been made, it may be impossible for a party to challenge any element in it that flows from a previously unchallenged partial award. Moreover, only an 'award' will qualify for recognition and enforcement under the relevant international conventions, including the New York Convention. Thus important consequences flow from a ruling or decision of the arbitral tribunal that has the status of an award. **9.07**

The term 'award' should generally be reserved for decisions that finally determine the substantive issues with which they deal.[9] This involves distinguishing between awards, which are concerned with substantive issues, and procedural orders and directions, which are concerned with the conduct of the arbitration. Procedural **9.08**

---

[6] And of arbitration agreements: see Chapter 2.
[7] Broches, 'Recourse against the award; Enforcement of the award: UNCITRAL's Project for a Model Law on International Commercial Arbitration' (1984) 2 ICCA Congress Series 201, at 208.
[8] Model Law, Art. 16(3).
[9] Some commentators have suggested that a 'preliminary award' may be treated as 'provisional'. However, this concept seems to be fraught with peril; the authors suggest that any decision that is *not* finally determinative of the issues with which it deals should not be described as an 'award'.

orders and directions help to move the arbitration forward; they deal with such matters as the exchange of written evidence, the production of documents, and the arrangements for the conduct of the hearing. They do not have the status of awards and they may perhaps be called into question after the final award has been made (for example as evidence of 'bias', or 'lack of due process').[10]

(c) Which rulings/orders have the status of an award?

9.09 Distinguishing between an 'award' and an 'order' may not be as easy as simply reading the title that an arbitral tribunal chooses to give to its ruling. Both the Paris Cour d'Appel and a US Federal Court of Appeals have classified certain arbitral decisions entitled 'orders' by tribunals as 'awards'. This makes them susceptible to annulment and/or recognition and enforcement proceedings in national courts.

9.10 The Paris Cour d'Appel decision in *Brasoil*[11] arose from an ICC arbitration under a contract whereby Brasoil agreed to drill a number of wells in the Libyan desert for the Management and Implementation Authority of the 'Great Man-Made River Project'. Brasoil started an ICC arbitration following termination of the contract by the Authority in 1990. In 1995, the arbitral tribunal issued a partial award in which it held Brasoil liable for the malfunctioning of the wells that it had constructed. In 1997, during the damages phase of the proceedings, the Authority submitted certain documents that Brasoil alleged had been fraudulently withheld during the liability phase. Brasoil requested that the tribunal review its partial award on liability. In May 1998, the tribunal denied Brasoil's request in what it described as an 'order'. Brasoil sought to have the 'order' set aside and the Paris Cour d'Appel granted its request on the grounds that, although described as an 'order', the tribunal's decision was, in fact, an 'award', because it purported to make a final determination of a substantive issue between the parties.[12] In so finding, the Cour d'Appel reasoned as follows:

> The qualification of [a decision as an] award does not depend on the terms used by the arbitrators or by the parties...after a five-month deliberation, the arbitral tribunal rendered the 'order' of 14 May 1998, by which, after a lengthy examination of the parties' positions, it declared that the request could not be granted because Brasoil had not proven that there had been fraud as alleged. This reasoned decision—by which the arbitrators considered the contradictory theories

---

[10] If a party is aggrieved by a procedural order or direction, it is sensible for that party to make a formal protest. In this way, it will reserve the position in case it emerges, at a later stage, that the ruling in question has, e.g., denied that party a proper opportunity to present its case or to respond to the case submitted by the opposing party.

[11] *Braspetro Oil Services Co. v The Management and Implementation Authority of the Great Man-Made River Project*, Paris Cour d'Appel, 1 July 1999, (1999) 14 Mealey's Intl Arb Rep 8, at [G-1]–[G-7].

[12] For a commentary on this decision, see Gill, 'The definition of award under the New York Convention' (2008) 2 Disp Res Intl 114, at 119, in which the author writes that 'the court found that the "procedural order" was effectively an award because it settled a substantive issue between the parties. The tribunal was exercising its jurisdictional power and its decision was therefore an award'.

A. Introduction

of the parties and examined in detail whether they were founded, and solved, in a final manner, the dispute between the parties concerning the admissibility of Brasoil's request for a review, by denying it and thereby ending the dispute submitted to them—appears to be an exercise of its jurisdictional power by the arbitral tribunal... Notwithstanding its qualification as an 'order', the decision of 14 May 1998... is thus indeed an award.[13]

Some years later, the French Supreme Court provided a definition of an arbitral award that supported this interpretation. Addressing a challenge to an award on the basis of an alleged professional relationship between the chairman of the arbitral tribunal and the parent company of the guarantor of debts owed by the respondent, the Cour de Cassation held that 'only proper arbitral awards may be challenged through an action to set aside' and went on to define awards as: **9.11**

> ...decisions made by the arbitrators which resolve in a definitive manner all or part of the dispute that is submitted to them on the merits, jurisdiction or a procedural matter which leads them to put an end to the proceedings.[14]

The decision of the Seventh Circuit Federal Court of Appeal in *True North*[15] addressed similar issues. True North, a US advertising company, and Publicis Communications, an affiliate of the Publicis global communications group, entered into a joint venture in 1989, which eventually led the parties to arbitration in London. As one of its requests for relief in the arbitration, True North requested that Publicis disclose tax records filed with the US Internal Revenue Service and the Securities and Exchange Commission (SEC). In October 1998, the chairman of the arbitral tribunal, 'for and on behalf of the arbitrators', signed an unreasoned 'order' directing Publicis to disclose the requested tax records to True North. Publicis failed to comply and True North applied to the court to confirm the arbitral decision. Publicis argued that the tribunal's decision constituted no more than a procedural order and that only finally determinative 'awards' are subject to confirmation or enforcement. The issue ultimately came before the Seventh Circuit Federal Court of Appeals, which disagreed, reasoning that the finality of a decision was the key to its recognition or enforcement under the New York Convention. In so doing, it described Publicis's approach as 'extreme and untenable formalism', and observed: **9.12**

> Although Publicis suggests that our ruling will cause the international arbitration earth to quake and mountains to crumble, resolving this case actually requires determining only whether or not this particular order by this particular arbitration tribunal regarding these particular tax records was final. If the arbitration tribunal's 30 October 1998 decision was final, then [the district court judge] had the

---

[13] *Braspetro Oil Services Co. v The Management and Implementation Authority of the Great Man-Made River Project*, Paris Cour d'Appel, 1 July 1999, (1999) XXIVa YBCA 297, at [1]–[4].
[14] *Groupe Antoine Tabet v République du Congo*, Case No. 09-72.439, Cass. Civ. 1ere, 12 October 2011, n.p.
[15] *Publicis Communications and Publicis SA v True North Communications Inc.* (2000) XXV YBCA 1152.

authority to confirm it. If the arbitrators' decision was not final, then the district court jumped the gun.[16]

9.13 Referring to an earlier edition of this volume, the Federal Court of Appeals noted that the arbitral tribunal's decision on the tax records was intended to be final and stated that the fact that the 'order' was issued prior to the conclusion of the arbitration was no bar to its enforceability or finality:

> The tribunal's order resolved the dispute, or was supposed to, at any rate. Producing the documents wasn't just some procedural matter—it was the very issue True North wanted arbitrated... The tribunal explicitly carved out the tax records issue for immediate action from the bulk of the matter still pending, stating that 'the delivery of the documents should not await final confirmation in the Final Award'. Requiring the unrelated issues to be arbitrated to finality before allowing True North to enforce a decision the tribunal called urgent would defeat the purpose of the tribunal's order. A ruling on a discreet, time-sensitive issue may be final and ripe for confirmation even though other claims remain to be addressed by arbitrators.[17]

(d) Rendering an internationally enforceable award

9.14 No arbitral tribunal can be expected to *guarantee* that its award will be enforceable in whatever country the winner chooses to enforce it. However, every arbitral tribunal must do its best. As Article 41 of the ICC Rules provides: 'In all matters not expressly provided for in the Rules, the Court and the arbitral tribunal shall act in the spirit of these Rules and shall make every effort to make sure that the award is enforceable at law.'[18] Phrases such as 'make every effort' imply an 'obligation to perform', rather than an 'obligation to achieve a defined result'. Nonetheless, the message is clear: in principle, the eventual outcome of every arbitration is intended to be a final, enforceable, award—as opposed to the outcome of a mediation, which is intended to be an agreement between the parties.

9.15 For an arbitral tribunal to achieve the standard of performance required to make an internationally enforceable award, it must first ensure that it has jurisdiction to decide all of the issues before it. The arbitral tribunal must also comply with any procedural rules governing the arbitration. Such rules commonly include, for

---

[16] Ibid., at [4].

[17] Ibid., at [9]. For a commentary on this decision, see Murphy, 'Enforceability of foreign arbitral decisions' (2001) 67 Arbitration 369, at 371, in which the author concludes that:

> [T]his decision has clearly announced that all orders or awards made in the arbitral process are capable of recognition and enforcement abroad by means of the New York Convention, so long as the finality test is satisfied... when rendering any decision, it may be prudent to determine whether or not the issue is being dealt with finally, to recite that in the decision and, despite the approach of the Seventh Circuit, to label the decision or order as an award to ensure that no argument of form over substance can take place.

[18] See also LCIA Rules, Art. 32.2.

example, allocation of the costs of the arbitration,[19] identifying the seat of the arbitration, and having the award formally approved by an arbitral institution (as with an ICC award).[20] The arbitral tribunal must also sign and date the award, and arrange for it to be delivered to the parties in the manner laid down in the relevant law or by the rules that apply to the arbitration. If the arbitral tribunal has carried out its work adequately, it should not be called upon to 'correct', or 'interpret, its award, although this does sometimes happen.[21]

Moreover, Article V(2)(b) of the New York Convention provides that, even when these conditions have been met, an award need not be enforced if it violates the public policy of the place of enforcement: 9.16

> Recognition and enforcement of an arbitral award may also be refused if the competent authority in the country where recognition and enforcement is sought finds that...the recognition or enforcement of the award would be contrary to the public policy of that country.

This provision gives discretion to the judicial authority at the recognition and enforcement stage, highlighting the impossibility of ensuring international enforceability at the time of issuing the award.

Given the complexity of the task facing an arbitral tribunal, the arbitrators should be adequately trained and experienced.[22] An award may comply meticulously with the agreed rules of procedure and with the law governing the arbitration, but may fail to comply with some special requirement of the law of the place of enforcement, so that the award may be unenforceable in that jurisdiction. 9.17

B. Categories of Award

All awards are final and binding, subject to any available challenges.[23] However, the term 'final award' is customarily reserved for an award that completes the mission of the arbitral tribunal. Subject to certain exceptions, the delivery of a final award renders the arbitral tribunal *functus officio*: it ceases to have any further jurisdiction in respect of the dispute, and the special relationship that exists between the arbitral tribunal and the parties during the currency of the arbitration ends. This has significant consequences. An arbitral tribunal should not issue a final award until it is satisfied that its mission has actually been completed. If there are outstanding matters to be determined, such as questions relating to costs 9.18

---

[19] For example, ICC Rules, Art. 37(3); UNCITRAL Rules, Art. 40.
[20] ICC Rules, Art. 33.
[21] For further discussion of interpretation, correction, and revision of awards, see paragraphs 9.200*ff*.
[22] See Chapter 10, paragraphs 10.02, 10.08 and 10.64.
[23] See, e.g., UNCITRAL Rules, Art. 34(2).

(including the arbitral tribunal's own costs), the arbitral tribunal should issue an award expressly designated as a partial award.

(a) Partial awards

9.19 The power to issue a partial award is a useful weapon in the armoury of an arbitral tribunal. A partial award is an effective way of determining matters that are susceptible to determination during the course of the proceedings, and which, once determined, may save considerable time and money for all involved.[24] One obvious example that has already been given is where an issue of jurisdiction is involved: a partial award on such an issue may shorten, or at least simplify, the proceedings considerably. An arbitral tribunal that spent months hearing a dispute, only to rule in its final award that it had no jurisdiction, would (to put it mildly) appear inefficient (unless the issue of jurisdiction were inseparably bound up with the merits of the case).

9.20 The power of an arbitral tribunal to issue partial awards may derive from the arbitration agreement or from the applicable law. Where the arbitration agreement incorporates international or institutional rules of arbitration, these rules generally contain provisions for the making of such awards.[25]

9.21 The ICC Rules, for instance, define the term 'award' to include 'an interim, partial, or final award'.[26] In practice, partial awards are frequently made in ICC arbitrations, particularly where jurisdiction is challenged or the proper law has to be determined by the arbitral tribunal.[27] The Rules of the London Court of International

---

[24] See the discussion of enforceability of partial awards in the United States in von Mehren, 'The enforcement of arbitral awards under conventions and United States law' (1985) 9 Yale Journal of World Public Order 343, at 362. The approach of the case that von Mehren cites, *Sperry International Trade, Inc. v Government of Israel* 532 F.Supp. 901 (SDNY 1982), continues to be followed for its proposition that partial awards disposing of issues separable from those that continue to be disputed are final for the purposes of judicial review and enforcement:

> The New York Convention, the United Nations arbitration rules, and the commentators' consistent use of the label 'award' when discussing final arbitral decisions does not bestow transcendental significance on the term. Their treatment of 'award' as interchangeable with final does not necessarily mean that synonyms such as decision, opinion, order, or ruling could not also be final. The content of a decision—not its nomenclature—determines finality.

See also, e.g., *Santos v GE Co*. No. 10 Civ. 6948, 2011 US Dist. LEXIS 131925 (SDNY 2011), at [14]–[15]; *Yonir Techs, Inc. v Duration System (1992) Ltd* 244 F.Supp.2d 195, 204 (SDNY 2002). '[T]hese authorities suggest that, regardless of whether the form of the arbitral measure (*e.g.*, an award or order) resembles a final award, if the substance of the measure serves a discrete function and effects a final disposition of a particular issue, the interim measure is confirmable and enforceable': Sherwin and Rennie, 'Interim relief under international arbitration rules and guidelines: A comparative analysis' (2009) 20 Am Rev Int'l Arb 318, at 326.

[25] See, e.g., UNCITRAL Rules, Art. 26 ('Interim measures').

[26] ICC Rules, Art. 2(v).

[27] For further discussion of partial awards in ICC arbitrations, see ICC, *Final Report on Interim and Partial Awards of a Working Party of the ICC's Commission on International Arbitration* (1990) 2 ICC International Court of Arbitration Bulletin 26, at 30, in particular

B. Categories of Award

Arbitration (LCIA) follow the same approach: 'The Arbitral Tribunal may make separate awards on different issues at different times. Such awards shall have the same status and effect as any other award made by the Arbitral Tribunal.'[28]

In an ad hoc arbitration, it is usual to make express provision in the submission agreement for the arbitral tribunal to issue partial awards, if it sees fit to do so. Where the power is not conferred expressly upon the arbitral tribunal by the agreement of the parties, it may nevertheless be conferred by operation of law. For example, section 47 of the English Arbitration Act 1996 provides: **9.22**

> (1) Unless otherwise agreed by the parties, the tribunal may make more than one award at different times on different aspects of the matters to be determined.
> (2) The tribunal may, in particular, make an award relating to:
> (a) an issue affecting the whole claim, or
> (b) a part only of the claims or cross-claims submitted to it for decision.
> (3) If the tribunal does so, it shall specify in its award the issue, or the claim or part of a claim, that is the subject-matter of the award.

Other modern arbitration laws contain similar provisions. Although the Model Law itself does not otherwise expressly refer to partial awards, it is clear from the context in which the expression 'final award' is used, and from the *travaux préparatoires*, that the draftsmen intended that the arbitral tribunal should have such a power.[29] However, if there is no express or implied provision for an arbitral tribunal to make a partial award—either in the arbitration agreement, the applicable arbitration rules, or the applicable law—it is doubtful that the tribunal has power to do so.[30] It is usually apparent from its content that a partial award is not the 'last' award; nevertheless, the award should state clearly that it is a partial award. As mentioned earlier,[31] the issuance of a final award renders the arbitral tribunal *functus officio*, except for the purpose of correcting minor or clerical errors. It is important not to allow either party an opportunity to claim that the arbitral tribunal has no further jurisdiction on the grounds that it has issued a final award, when it intended to issue only a partial award. **9.23**

The main disadvantage of a partial award is that a further avenue for judicial review (and consequent delay) is created. Judicial intervention during the course of the arbitration may occur on an application by one of the parties to annul (or set aside) **9.24**

---

the discussion about terminology. The term 'interlocutory award' should never be used, because it leads to confusion with procedural directions, which are not given in the form of an award.

[28] LCIA Rules, Art. 26(7).
[29] Model Law, Art. 32(1). See Holtzmann and Neuhaus, *A Guide to the UNCITRAL Model Law on International Commercial Arbitration* (Kluwer Law, 1989), p. 868. The Model Law, Ch. IVA, does, however, expressly refer to interim measures and preliminary orders.
[30] It was perhaps to avoid uncertainty in this respect that some jurisdictions amended the Model Law to provide specifically so that the arbitral tribunal may make a partial award on any matter on which it may make a final award: see, e.g., the British Columbia International Commercial Arbitration Act, s. 31(6).
[31] See paragraph 9.18.

the partial award, or on an application to confirm it.[32] The Model Law limits the potential for delay by specifying that an application to review a partial award on jurisdiction must be lodged within thirty days of receipt of notice of the ruling, with no appeal beyond the first level of court in which the decision is made.[33] As noted above, the relevant decision need not have the title 'award' to be subject to judicial review or confirmation.[34]

(i) Issues concerning the applicable law

9.25 An example of a situation in which a partial award is likely to prove useful is where there is a dispute between the parties as to the law(s) applicable to the merits of the case. If this is not resolved at an early stage, the parties must argue their respective cases by reference to different systems of law. They may even need to introduce evidence from lawyers experienced in each of these different systems. In such circumstances, it may be sensible for the arbitral tribunal to issue a preliminary decision on the question of the applicable law.

(ii) Separation of issues (jurisdiction, liability, quantum)

9.26 A further example of the type of case in which it may be convenient to issue a partial award is where issues of liability may be separated from those of quantum, which is often worth doing if it is possible to disentangle these issues. Most obviously, the determination of a particular issue of liability in favour of the respondent may make it unnecessary for the arbitral tribunal to investigate questions of *quantum*.[35] Even if it is not determinative, a decision by an arbitral tribunal on certain issues of principle in a dispute may well encourage the parties to reach a settlement on quantum. They are usually well aware of the costs likely to be involved if the arbitral tribunal itself has to go into the detailed quantification of a claim—a process that often involves taking evidence from accountants, technical experts, and others.

9.27 However, there are real dangers in attempting to isolate determinative issues at an early stage of the proceedings. The nature of the dispute and the way in which the

---

[32] In the United States, a partial award for the payment of freight was 'confirmed' by a court while there were still outstanding matters in dispute in the arbitration: *Metallgesellschaft AG v M/V Capitan Constante and Yacimientos Petroliferos Fiscales* 790 F.2d 280 (2nd Cir. 1986). The majority judgment lists cases endorsing the 'proposition that an award which finally and definitely disposes of a separate independent claim may be confirmed although it does not dispose of all the claims that were submitted to arbitration': ibid., at [3]. However, the dissent of Feinberg CJ noted the dangers of piecemeal review of arbitral awards. Since then, case law has followed the separability rule of the majority; see, e.g., *In re Chevron USA, Inc.* Case No. 08-08-00082-CV, 2010 Tex. App. LEXIS 459 (8th Cir. 2010), at [19]–[20]; *Zeiler v Deitsch* 500 F.3d 157, 168 (2nd Cir. 2007); *Hart Surgical, Inc. v Ultracision Inc.* 244 F.3d 231 (1st Cir. 2001); *Publicis Communication v True North Communications Inc.* 206 F.3d 725, 727 (7th Cir. 2000).
[33] Model Law, Art. 16(3).
[34] See paragraphs 9.11–9.15.
[35] See Chapter 6, paragraphs 6.54*ff*.

B. Categories of Award

parties present their cases may change during the course of the proceedings, and it is not unknown for parties to amend their cases radically in order to take advantage of a preliminary award on liability. Where this happens, savings of time and cost will not be achieved, and the result will be the opposite of that intended. Moreover, the process of rendering a preliminary award can itself be a time-consuming and expensive one. It is suggested that an arbitral tribunal should not normally decide to issue a partial award on its own initiative,[36] but should do so only following a request by one of the parties. Where both parties agree that a partial award should be made, the arbitral tribunal must follow the agreement of the parties. Where only one party requests a partial award, a tribunal with the power to make such an award should reach its decision as to whether or not to comply with the request only after receiving the submissions of both parties and giving each party a reasonable opportunity to explain its position.

(iii) Limitation clauses in a contract

Major commercial contracts—for example for the supply of a process plant or for a construction project—often contain a clause that limits, or purports to limit, the type or amount of damages payable in the event of breach. A typical example is a clause providing that in no event will loss of profits be payable. There may be occasions on which a partial award on the meaning and effect of such clauses will help to define the amount of the claim, and may make the prospect of settlement more likely.

9.28

(b) Foreign and domestic awards

The distinction between foreign and domestic awards is especially significant in the context of challenging and enforcement of awards in national courts, which is addressed in Chapter 10. In India, the Foreign Awards (Recognition & Enforcement) Act 1961 defines a foreign award as an award made in another country on differences between persons arising out of legal relationships, whether contractual or not, considered to be commercial under the law in force in India.[37] The Indian Supreme Court considered the expression 'foreign awards', and held that a lawsuit could be stayed only upon the Court being satisfied that the relationship of the parties to the arbitration agreement is one that should be considered 'commercial' and that this term should be given a broad meaning.[38] Conversely, the

9.29

---

[36] Except in relation to issues of jurisdiction, where the respondent has not raised them, or has elected not to participate, as in *Liberian Eastern Timber Corporation v Government of the Republic of Liberia* (1987) 26 ILM 647, in which the government nominated one of the authors as an arbitrator, but then refused to take part in the proceedings, and the arbitral tribunal examined its jurisdiction—as required by the ICSID Arbitration Rules, r. 42(4)—and issued a partial award.

[37] Indian Foreign Awards (Recognition & Enforcement) Act 1961, s. 2.

[38] *RM Investment & Trading Company v Boeing Company*, 1994 (4) SCC 541, (1997) XXII Ybk Comm Arb 711.

Indian Supreme Court has held that the term 'domestic award' means an award made in India whether or not this is in a purely domestic context; thus the definition will include a 'domestically rendered' award in a domestic arbitration or in an international arbitration.

(c) Default awards

9.30 Occasionally, international arbitrations are commenced in which one party (usually the respondent) fails or refuses to take part. This failure or refusal may be complete—that is, it occurs from the outset of the proceedings—or it may happen during the proceedings as a result of a change of mind or strategy. The arbitral tribunal is compelled to take a more positive role in these circumstances, making its task more difficult. The task of an arbitral tribunal is not to 'rubber stamp' claims that are presented to it; rather, it must make a *determination* of these claims, so the tribunal must take upon itself the burden of testing the assertions made by the active party, and it must call for such evidence and legal argument as it may require for this purpose.[39]

9.31 If the arbitral tribunal makes an award in favour of the active party in the proceedings, it will wish to ensure that the award is effective. To this end, it should ensure, in particular, that the award recites in considerable detail the procedure followed by the arbitral tribunal and the efforts made by the arbitral tribunal to communicate the active party's case to the defaulting party, so as to give that party every opportunity to present its own arguments and evidence. Further, the motivation, or reasons, given in the award should (without necessarily being lengthy) reflect the fact that the arbitral tribunal has genuinely addressed the merits of the case, in order to show that a reasoned determination has been made.

9.32 The award should also deal with any questions of jurisdiction that appear to the arbitral tribunal to be relevant, whether or not such issues have been raised by one or other of the parties. In this context, the Arbitration Rules of the International Centre for the Settlement of Investment Disputes (ICSID), which contain detailed provisions for default proceedings, expressly stipulate, at Rule 42(4), that '[t]he Tribunal shall examine the jurisdiction of the Centre and its own competence in the dispute and, if it is satisfied, decide whether the submissions made are well-founded in fact and in law'. If the arbitral tribunal follows these guidelines, there is less risk of the money spent by the active party in obtaining the award being wasted as a result of a subsequent decision by national courts that the award is unenforceable.

---

[39] For a discussion of the procedure to be followed where one party fails or refuses to participate in an arbitration, see Chapter 6.

(d) Additional awards

When the tribunal renders an award that does not address all of the issues presented, the parties may, within a limited time frame, request an additional award to remedy this gap. Many arbitration rules expressly provide for additional awards,[40] and even where they are not expressly provided for, there is generally a procedural tool by which they can, in essence, be accomplished.[41] The ICC Rules are an exception. They provide for the correction of clerical or typographical errors, as well as the interpretation of awards,[42] but they do not provide for the rendering of an award based on a party's objection that the tribunal failed to consider an issue presented. This is no doubt the result of the scrutiny process of the ICC Court.

9.33

(e) Consent awards and termination of proceedings without an award

As in litigation in national courts, parties to an international arbitration often arrive at a settlement during the proceedings. Where this occurs, the parties may simply implement the settlement agreement and thus revoke the mandate of the arbitral tribunal. This means that the jurisdiction and powers conferred on the arbitral tribunal by the parties are terminated.[43]

9.34

In many cases, however, the parties find it desirable for the terms of settlement to be embodied in an award. There are many reasons for this. The most important is that it is usually easier for a party to enforce performance by the other party of a future obligation if that obligation is contained in an award (in respect of which the assistance of the New York Convention may be available), rather than to take further steps to enforce a settlement agreement. Other reasons for obtaining a consent award include the desirability (particularly where a state or state agency is involved) of having a definite and identifiable 'result' of the arbitral proceedings, in the form of an award, which may be passed to the appropriate paying authority for implementation. In this context, the signatures of the arbitrators on the consent award indicate a measure of approval by the arbitral tribunal to the agreement reached by the parties. This may help to meet politically motivated criticism of those responsible for taking the decision to reach a compromise settlement.

9.35

There should be little or no problem as far as capacity to compromise is concerned. Many countries adopt as their definition of matters that are capable of resolution by arbitration (that is, matters that are 'arbitrable') the concept that parties may refer to arbitration any disputes in respect of which they are entitled

9.36

---

[40] See UNCITRAL Rules, Art. 39; LCIA Rules, Art. 27; International Dispute Resolution Procedures (International Arbitration), Art. 30; Stockholm Chamber of Commerce (SCC) Rules, Art. 42; English Arbitration Act 1996, s. 57(3)(b); Model Law, Art. 33(1)(b).
[41] See, e.g., ICSID Rules, r. 49(2).
[42] ICC Rules, Art. 35.
[43] This follows from the consensual nature of arbitration: see Chapter 5, paragraph 5.33.

to reach a compromise. The reverse holds good: if parties are entitled to refer a dispute to arbitration, they are entitled to reach a compromise in respect of that dispute.

9.37 No restrictions are imposed by national law, or international or institutional rules of arbitration, to the effect that, once arbitral proceedings have been commenced, the parties cannot terminate them by agreement. On the contrary, a settlement is invariably welcomed, and it may be possible to have it recorded in an agreed award. Article 30 of the Model Law provides for such an agreed award; Article 36(1) of the UNCITRAL Rules provides for a settlement to be recorded by an order or by an award:

> If, before the award is made, the parties agree on a settlement of the dispute, the arbitral tribunal shall either issue an order for the termination of the arbitral proceedings or, if requested by the parties and accepted by the tribunal, record the settlement in the form of an arbitral award on agreed terms. The arbitral tribunal is not obliged to give reasons for such an award.

The ICC Rules contain a similar provision, at Article 32: if the parties reach a settlement, after the file has been transmitted to the arbitral tribunal in accordance with Article 13, then 'the settlement *shall* be recorded in the form of an award made by consent of the parties, if so requested by the parties and if the arbitral tribunal agrees to do so'.[44] The word 'shall' is mandatory and suggests an obligation to record any settlement in a consent award. However, it is qualified by the requirements that the parties must request such an award and the tribunal must agree to it. This indicates that, under the UNCITRAL and ICC Rules, there is no obligation for either the parties or the tribunal to make a consent award.

9.38 Under whatever rules the parties are proceeding, however, it would be a normal act of courtesy to inform the arbitral tribunal (and the appropriate arbitral institution, if one is involved) of any settlement agreement reached between the parties, particularly if meetings or hearings have already been held. There may also be sound financial reasons for doing what normal courtesy demands. First, notifying the arbitral tribunal of a settlement will ensure that it does not incur further fees and expenses (other than any cancellation fees that may have been agreed). Secondly, such notification might lead to a refund of advance payments made to cover fees and expenses, since the actual costs incurred may well be less than expected if the case has been settled without a hearing. Thirdly, as already indicated, it is desirable to put the terms of settlement into an enforceable form when there is an element of future performance. Although most settlements involve immediate implementation of the agreed terms, it is nevertheless not unusual for there to be provision for payment by instalments, or for some future transaction between the parties to be carried out.

---

[44] Emphasis added.

C. Remedies

A question occasionally arises as to the role of an arbitral tribunal that is requested 9.39
by the parties to make a consent award ordering the performance of an unlawful
act. Examples might be the manufacture of an internationally banned drug, or
the smuggling of contraband or—perhaps more realistically—an agreement that
manifestly contravenes relevant competition or antitrust laws. At one time, various
sets of rules (including the ICC Rules prior to 1998) seemed to leave the tribunal
with no discretion, but modern rules and legislation permit the arbitral tribunal to
refuse to make a consent award.[45]

C. Remedies

The arbitral tribunal's power to grant appropriate relief is based on the arbitra- 9.40
tion agreement and the applicable arbitration law. The basis on which an arbitral
tribunal orders a remedial measure flows from the arbitration agreement and subsequent submission of the dispute to arbitration. While an arbitration agreement
could specify the remedial measures to be conferred upon the tribunal, the common practice is that the tribunal will be silent on that point. In such circumstances,
the tribunal must look into the relevant arbitration rules or applicable national law
on arbitration to determine the types of relief available to it. Arbitration awards
may cover a range of remedies, including:

- monetary compensation;
- punitive damages and other penalties;
- specific performance and restitution;
- injunctions;
- declaratory relief;
- rectification;
- filling gaps and adaptation of contracts;
- interest; and
- costs.

(a) Monetary compensation

The type of award most often made by an international arbitral tribunal is one that 9.41
directs the payment of a sum of money by one party to the other. This payment may
represent money due under a contract (debt), or compensation (damages) for loss
suffered, or both. The sum of money awarded is usually expressed in the currency
of the contract or the currency of the loss. In large transnational projects, however,
it is not unusual for reference to be made to several different currencies—so that,
for example, plant and equipment manufactured or purchased overseas may be
paid for in US dollars, whilst labour, plant, and equipment made or purchased

---

[45] See, e.g., ICC Rules, Art. 32.

Award

locally may be paid for in the local currency. In such cases, unless the parties agree, the arbitral tribunal must receive written or oral submissions as to the currency or currencies in which the award is to be made.

9.42 Under many national arbitration laws, arbitral tribunals have discretion to make awards in any currency deemed appropriate. The *Lesotho Highlands* case is illustrative of both the exercise of such discretion and the potential consequences of doing so. The case concerned the construction of a dam in Lesotho by a consortium of foreign companies. The consortium claimed amounts that, had they been paid when due, would have been payable in Lesotho loti, as owed under the relevant contract. However, by the time the award was made, the value of the loti had diminished against international currency values. The consortium therefore claimed payment of the award in four European currencies contractually designated as currencies for non-loti payments. In rendering the award in the currencies requested, the arbitral tribunal invoked section 48 of the English Arbitration Act 1996, which allows a tribunal to order payment of an award in any currency (unless agreed otherwise by the parties).

9.43 Once the right of appeal on a point of law was excluded under section 69 of the English Arbitration Act 1996, the employer challenged the award in the English courts, under section 68(2)(b), for excess of power.[46] The employer claimed that the provisions in the contract on currencies effectively excluded the tribunal's power to select the currency of the award. On appeal to the House of Lords, the employer's challenge was dismissed by a majority of four to one.[47]

(b) Punitive damages and other penalties

9.44 Punitive damages are not awarded to compensate the wronged party, but instead to punish and deter the wrongdoer. In general, punitive damages are an exceptional and extreme measure permitted only, for example, in cases of fraud and substantial malice.[48] In the context of awarding punitive damages, it is tempting to think that an arbitral tribunal has precisely parallel jurisdiction to that of a national court to award damages in accordance with the law applicable to the substantive merits of the dispute. However, the powers of an arbitral tribunal are not necessarily the same as those of a court.

9.45 An arbitral tribunal may, in certain respects, have *wider* powers than those of a judge, because the tribunal's powers flow from, inter alia, the arbitration agreement. Thus, in England, a court applying US law has no power to order the payment of triple damages—a power provided under US antitrust legislation.[49]

---

[46] *Lesotho Highlands Development Authority v Impregilo SpA and ors* [2003] EWCA Civ 1159.
[47] *Lesotho Highlands Development Authority v Impregilo SpA and ors* [2005] UKHL 43.
[48] Lew, Mistelis, and Kröll, *Comparative International Commercial Arbitration* (Kluwer Law International, 2003), p. 651.
[49] *British Airways Board v Laker Airways Ltd* [1985] AC 58 (HL).

C. Remedies

But an arbitral tribunal sitting in England *does* have the power to award triple damages provided that the parties' arbitration agreement was sufficiently wide to encompass the determination of US antitrust law claims—although, for public policy reasons, there may be problems of enforcement, as will be discussed later.[50] It is necessary to look at the law applicable to the substance of the dispute, as well as the law of the seat of the arbitration. In civil law countries, the concept of punitive damages is almost unknown, whether in breach-of-contract cases or otherwise, with a limited exception in some countries where there has been a wilful intention to harm the claimant amounting, in effect, to fraud.[51] Under French and German law, punitive damages are not recoverable. Under English law, punitive damages may be awarded only in actions in tort—and even then only in three categories of case.[52] Punitive damages may not be awarded in an action for breach of contract.[53] However, such claims are permissible in the United States, where statutes may provide expressly for the payment of multiple damages by one party to the other.[54]

Thus there may be occasional circumstances in which claims for damages in civil lawsuits go beyond the concept of compensating the winning party for its losses. But two other matters arise in the context of claims for punitive damages in arbitrations: the first concerns the threshold question of the power of an arbitral tribunal to impose penal sanctions; the second relates to enforceability. 9.46

The question of whether an arbitral tribunal has the power to impose penal sanctions depends on the law of the place of arbitration (the *lex arbitri*) and the provisions of the arbitration agreement. The *lex arbitri* may be unsympathetic. In one case in the United States, the court stated that 'the prohibition against an arbitrator 9.47

---

[50] See paragraphs 9.49ff. It would lead to an absurd result if an arbitral tribunal applying US antitrust law could determine the issue of liability under that law, but not award the mandatory remedy provided for in that law. The point was considered by a US court in *PPG Inc v Pilkington Plc* (1995) XX YBCA 885.

[51] In ICC Case No. 5946 (1991) XVI YBCA 97, at 113, an ICC arbitration held in Geneva, a claim was made for exemplary damages, but this claim was refused on the basis that:

> ...damages that go beyond compensatory damages to constitute a punishment of the wrongdoer... [punitive or exemplary damages], are considered contrary to Swiss public policy, which must be respected by an arbitral tribunal sitting in Switzerland even if the arbitral tribunal must decide a dispute according to a law that may allow punitive or exemplary damages as such: see Art 135(2) Switzerland's Federal Code on Private International Law of December 1987, which refuses to allow enforcement of a judgment awarding damages that cannot be awarded in Switzerland...

[52] See *Rookes v Barnard* [1964] AC 1129. The three categories are: (a) abuse of power by servants of the government; (b) conduct that was motivated by the pursuit of profits; and (c) where punitive, or 'exemplary', damages expressly authorised by statute.

[53] For contract cases, see *Addis v Gramophone Co. Ltd* [1909] AC 488, with exceptions to the general rule at 495. For actions in tort, see *Rookes v Barnard* [1964] AC 1129, [1967] 1 Lloyd's Rep 28 (HL).

[54] Examples of statutes that provide for multiple damages in the United States are the Racketeer Influenced and Corrupt Organizations Act of 1970 (RICO) and antitrust laws that provide for triple damages.

awarding punitive damages is based on strong public policy indeed'.[55] However, there are also US cases in which the arbitration clause was held to be wide enough to confer an express or implied power to award punitive damages, for example where the context of the underlying transaction manifestly implied that any dispute would be likely to incorporate a claim for multiple damages.[56]

9.48 The same principles apply in the context of an ad hoc submission agreement. Little has been disclosed publicly about the *Greenpeace* arbitration.[57] This case arose from the sinking of the ship *Rainbow Warrior* by agents apparently working for the French government. It is widely assumed that the damages awarded to Greenpeace were not restricted to the cost of refloating and repairing the vessel, and other direct damages, and that the submission agreement was drawn widely enough to justify an award of punitive damages. But this case, even if published, would be of limited general interest in the present context, since it was not a case arising out of a breach of contract.

9.49 With regard to enforcement, the key question is whether an award of punitive damages would be enforceable under the New York Convention in a country that does not itself recognise such a remedy. The ground for refusal of enforcement would be Article V(2) of the Convention, which allows refusal of recognition or enforcement of an award if recognition or enforcement would be contrary to public policy. For example, in a leading judgment rendered in Germany in 1992, the Federal Supreme Court (*Bundesgerichtshof*) refused to enforce part of a US court decision that provided for the recovery of punitive damages, on the grounds that such recovery was contrary to German public policy.[58] The authors are not aware of any German court decisions relating to attempts to enforce a foreign arbitral award providing for the recovery of punitive damages, but the same result is likely.[59]

9.50 In summary, it is suggested that arbitral tribunals should treat claims for punitive damages and other penalties with considerable caution. They should examine the question of whether or not such damages may be awarded under the law applicable to the substance of the dispute. They should also address themselves to the threshold question as to whether or not they have power to make such an award, even if a

---

[55] *Garrity v Lyle Stuart Inc.* 40 NY 2d 354, 353 NE 2d 793 (1976).
[56] *Willoughby Roofing Supply Co. v Kajima International Inc.* 776 F.2d 269 (11th Cir. 1985), in which an arbitral award of punitive damages for wilful fraud in the inducement of a contract was upheld; *Mitsubishi v Soler Chrysler-Plymouth Inc.* 473 US 614 (1985), in which arbitral awards of statutory treble damages were approved for antitrust violations.
[57] Reymond, 'The *Rainbow Warrior* arbitration between Greenpeace and France' (1992) 9 J Intl Arb 92, at 93.
[58] *Bundesgerichtshof* (Neue Juristische Wochenschrift, 1992), at 3096*ff.* The Court has affirmed it in two more recent decisions: BVerfG, Beschluß vom 24.01.2007—2 BvR 1133/04; BVerfG, Beschluß vom 14.06.2007—2 BvR 2247/06.
[59] Similarly, Dutch courts have held that a judgment to pay punitive damages cannot be recognised and enforced in the Netherlands without further enquiry: see the decision of the District Court of Rotterdam, 17 February 1995, [1996] NIPR 205, at 207.

C. Remedies

claim for punitive damages is admissible under the law applicable to the substance of the dispute, by examining both the *lex arbitri* and the scope of the arbitration agreement.[60]

Problems concerning enforceability should be left for the courts at the place of enforcement. However, it is preferable for arbitral tribunals to treat any award in respect of punitive damages or any other penalties as an entirely separate claim, in order to ensure that the punitive portion of the award is severable in the event of a successful challenge in the courts at the place of enforcement.   9.51

(c) Specific performance

An arbitral tribunal may be authorised by the parties or by the applicable law (either the substantive law or the *lex arbitri*, depending on the conflict-of-laws rule applicable) to order specific performance of a contract. An international arbitral tribunal sitting in the United States will have the power to award specific performance,[61] and English law empowers an arbitral tribunal sitting in England 'to order specific performance of a contract (other than a contract relating to land)' unless a contrary intention is expressed in the arbitration agreement.[62] In civil law jurisdictions, specific performance is a recognised remedy for breach of contract, but less so in common law systems. In international arbitration, various tribunals have ordered specific performance, and their decisions have been upheld by state courts.[63] The question of whether an arbitral tribunal is empowered to order specific performance is thus rarely an issue in international arbitration. However, the question of whether it is an appropriate remedy, and whether it can be effectively granted in the circumstances of any particular case, was not definitively established at the time of writing.   9.52

(d) Restitution

Restitution seeks to put the aggrieved party in the same position as that in which it would have been had the wrongful act not taken place. In common law terminology, it is a form of specific performance. In the field of commercial arbitration, it   9.53

---

[60] For a comprehensive review of the powers of arbitrators to award punitive damages, see Gotanda, *Supplemental Damages in Private International Law* (Kluwer Law International, 1998), pp. 226–229.

[61] While neither the US Federal Arbitration Act of 1925 (FAA) nor the Uniform Arbitration Act of 1955, as amended (UAA), expressly specifies the remedies available in international arbitrations taking place in the United States (e.g. the UAA, § 21, empowers arbitrators to 'order such remedies as the arbitrator considers just and appropriate under the circumstances of the arbitration proceeding'), courts have confirmed that arbitrators have the power to award specific performance even if the arbitration agreement does not specify this remedy: see, e.g., *Brandon v MedPartners Inc.* 203 FRD 677, 686 (SD Fla. 2001).

[62] English Arbitration Act 1996, s. 48(5)(b).

[63] Lew, Mistelis, and Kroll, *Comparative International Commercial Arbitration* (Kluwer Law International, 2003), p. 650.

is a remedy that is hardly ever used in practice—perhaps because international tribunals rightly tend to avoid making awards that are difficult to enforce. There have also been doubts as to whether an arbitral tribunal has power to award restitution. In England, at least, the question was resolved by the Arbitration Act 1996: unless the parties otherwise agree, an arbitral tribunal has the same powers as an English court 'to order a party to do or refrain from doing anything'.[64]

9.54 An example of the use of this remedy in public international law is provided by the *Temple of Preah-Vihear* case,[65] in which the International Court of Justice (ICJ) ordered the Government of Thailand to restore to Cambodia certain sculptures and other objects that it had removed from the temple on the border between the two countries. Even in the field of public international law, however, the remedy is little used. It seems rather to set a standard for the assessment of monetary compensation:

> The essential principle contained in the actual notion of an illegal act—a principle which seems to be established by international practice and in particular by the decisions of arbitral tribunals—is that reparation must, as far as possible, wipe out all the consequences of the illegal act and re-establish the situation which would, in all probability, have existed if that act had not been committed. Restitution in kind, or, if this is not possible, *payment of a sum corresponding to the value which a restitution in kind would bear*; the award, if need be, of damages for loss sustained which would not be covered by restitution in kind or payment in place of it—such are the principles which should serve to determine the amount of compensation due for an act contrary to international law.[66]

9.55 In practice, restitution is rarely ordered, since it is usually impracticable to undo the effects of the relevant breach(es) and to place the claimant in the position in which it would have been but for such breach(es). An award of monetary compensation is generally the appropriate remedy, particularly in commercial disputes. An apparent exception is the award of the sole arbitrator in the *Texaco* arbitration.[67] On examination, however, it is difficult to accept this award as a precedent for the effective granting of restitution in international arbitration. The sole arbitrator found that the Libyan government had acted in breach of its obligations by nationalising the company's property and other assets in Libya. He held that *restitutio in integrum* was, 'both under the principles of Libyan law and under the principles of international law, the normal sanction for non-performance of contractual obligations'.[68] Although this award reads well at a scholarly level, it has been severely criticised and, on the same facts, a different conclusion was reached in the *BP*

---

[64] English Arbitration Act 1996, s. 48(5)(a).
[65] *Cambodia v Thailand* [1962] ICJ Rep 6.
[66] *Case Concerning the Factory at Chorzów (Claim for Indemnity) (Germany v Poland)* (the *Chorzów Factory* case) [1928] PCIJ Series A No. 17, at 47 (emphasis added).
[67] *Texas Overseas Petroleum Co. and California Asiatic Oil Co. (Texaco) v Government of the Libyan Arab Republic* (1978) 17 ILM 3.
[68] Ibid., at 36.

C. Remedies

arbitration.[69] The arbitrator's decision in the *Texaco* arbitration in favour of restitution is, indeed, hard to accept. First, whilst it may be practicable for a state to hand back objects taken from a temple, it seems wholly impracticable for a state to hand back to a foreign company oil fields and installations that have been taken over by the state and which are in that state's own territory.[70] Secondly, it must be doubted whether the award was intended to be enforceable. At a preliminary meeting with the sole arbitrator at which only the agents and counsel of the company appeared,[71] and in a subsequent memorial, the claimants stated (according to the arbitrator) that 'they intended that the present arbitration should be an arbitration on matters of principle, a fact which the Sole Arbitrator did not fail to note on the occasion of the oral hearings'.[72]

It seems that the claimants themselves were seeking an authoritative legal opinion on the merits of the case, rather than an enforceable award. There is no objection in principle to the use of the arbitral process in this way; indeed, this was done, by agreement of the parties, in the *Aramco* arbitration.[73] However, such cases cannot serve as a reliable precedent for most commercial arbitrations, in which what is sought is not a legal opinion, but an award that is capable of enforcement. **9.56**

The relief sought and granted in the growing number of investor–state arbitrations confirms that, in practice, monetary compensation, rather than restitution, is the principal remedy sought and granted in international arbitration. By way of example, Article 1135 of Chapter 11 of the North American Free Trade Agreement (NAFTA) provides that although a tribunal may award 'restitution of property', such awards 'shall provide that the disputing party may pay monetary damages and any applicable interest in lieu of restitution'. Thus the host state of an investment that is condemned under a Chapter 11 arbitral award will always have the right to pay damages in place of restitution. And so it has proved more generally in practice: a review of the ICSID Reports over the last two decades confirms that restitution has been sought in only a handful of ICSID arbitrations and has (at the time of writing) never been awarded. **9.57**

In *Occidental Petroleum Corporation and Occidental Exploration and Production Co. v Ecuador*,[74] the claimants sought an order from the tribunal that Ecuador fully reinstate the claimants' rights under the relevant contracts. In an interim award **9.58**

---

[69] *British Petroleum Co. (Libya) Ltd v Government of the Libyan Arab Republic* (1979) 53 ILR 297.
[70] This impracticability was recognised by the parties in the *Aminoil* arbitration: *Government of the State of Kuwait v American Independent Oil Co. (Aminoil)* (1982) 21 ILM 976. To avoid any doubt, it was specifically agreed in that case that restitution was not sought.
[71] The Libyan government boycotted the proceedings throughout, after claiming that the dispute was not arbitrable because the acts of nationalisation were acts of sovereignty.
[72] *Texas Overseas Petroleum Co. and California Asiatic Oil Co. (Texaco) v Government of the Libyan Arab Republic* (1978) 17 ILM 3, at 8.
[73] *Saudi Arabia v Arabian American Oil Co. (Aramco)* (1963) 27 ILR 117.
[74] Decision on Provisional Measures, ICSID Case No. ARB/06/11, 17 August 2007, IIC 305 (2007).

dated 17 August 2007,[75] the tribunal refused to grant interim protection of the claimants' rights under the relevant contracts partly on the basis that the claimants could not establish a right to an award of specific performance of the contracts. The tribunal held that an order reinstating the claimants' contract could be made only if (a) it was not legally impossible to revive the contract, (b) such a remedy would not involve a disproportionate interference with state sovereignty, as compared to an award of damages, and (c) damages could not otherwise make the claimants whole for their losses. Indeed, of growing relevance in investor–state arbitration is the opposite question of whether a victorious investor must relinquish title to property that it has claimed—successfully—has been expropriated.[76]

(e) Injunctions

9.59 There is no objection in principle to an arbitral tribunal granting relief by way of injunction, if requested to do so, either on an interim basis or as final relief. Injunctive relief is addressed in detail in Chapter 7. For present purposes, it is sufficient to state that an arbitral tribunal is not usually empowered to make effective orders against third parties, and if injunctive relief against third parties is required, it is generally quicker and more effective to seek it directly from a national court. Most sets of international and institutional rules make it clear that an arbitration clause is not to be taken as excluding the jurisdiction of the relevant national court to make orders for interim measures of protection.[77] However, Article 26(3) of the UNCITRAL Rules, for example, contains the qualification requiring that an applicant must satisfy the tribunal that:

> [...]
>
> (i) harm not adequately reparable by an award of damages is likely to result if the measure is not ordered, and such harm substantially outweighs the harm that is likely to result to the party against whom the measure is directed if the measure is granted; and
>
> (ii) there is a reasonable possibility that the requesting party will succeed on the merits of the claim.

Some national courts have also chosen to limit their ability to grant interim relief to cases involving arbitration proceedings with a domestic seat. In India, for example, the Supreme Court in *Bhatia International*[78] apprently intended to make interim relief available to parties in foreign arbitration proceedings; however, the application of the decision in subsequent cases has resulted in a distortion of Indian arbitration law. The Court in *Bhatia* concluded that Part I of the Indian Arbitration

---

[75] IIC 305 (2007).
[76] In this regard, see Rubins, 'Must the victorious investor-claimant relinquish title to expropriated property?' (2003) 4 JWIT 3, at 481; *CMS Gas Transmission Co. v Argentine Republic*, Award, ICSID Case No. ARB/01/08, 12 May 2005, IIC 65 (2005).
[77] See, e.g., ICC Rules, Art. 28; UNCITRAL Rules, Art. 26. See paragraphs 7.22*ff.*
[78] *Bhatia International v Bulk Trading S.A.* (2002) 4 SCC 105.

C. Remedies

and Conciliation Act 1996 was applicable to all arbitrations, including foreign arbitrations, unless expressly or impliedly excluded by agreement of the parties. Subsequently, in *Venture Global Engineering v Satyan Computer Services Ltd*,[79] the Supreme Court held that Indian courts could set aside awards made outside India, by applying section 34 (under Part I) of the 1996 Act. However, in 2012, the Supreme Court in *Balco*[80] categorically overruled *Bhatia* and *Venture Global*, holding that Part I of the Arbitration and Conciliation Act 1996 are not applicable to an international arbitration in which the seat of the arbitration is not India. As a result, where an international arbitration is seated in a country other than India, no application under section 9 of the 1996 Act for interim relief is available.

(f) Declaratory relief

9.60 An arbitral tribunal may be asked to make an award that is simply declaratory of the rights of the parties. Modern arbitration legislation[81] often makes express provision for the granting of declaratory relief. Even when there is no such provision, however, there is no reason in principle why an arbitral tribunal should not grant such relief. Indeed, declaratory relief has become a common remedy in international arbitration, with requests for contractual damages usually coupled with a request for a declaration that there has been a breach of contract.

9.61 The *Aramco* arbitration provides an example of an arbitration in which the parties only claimed declaratory relief.[82] Aramco claimed that its exclusive right to transport oil from its concession area in Saudi Arabia had been infringed by the agreement made between the Saudi Arabian government and the late Aristotle Onassis, the Greek shipping magnate, and his company, Aramco. The dispute was significant—but neither party wished it to jeopardise their trading relationship, which was a continuing relationship dating back many years.[83] Accordingly, it was agreed that the dispute should be referred to an ad hoc tribunal of three arbitrators based in Geneva. It was further agreed that the award should be of declaratory effect only, with neither of the parties claiming damages for any alleged injury. The arbitral tribunal said:

> There is no objection whatsoever to Parties limiting the scope of the arbitration agreement to the question of what exactly is their legal position. When the competence of the arbitrators is limited to such a statement of the law and does not allow them to impose the execution of an obligation on either of the Parties, the Arbitration Tribunal can only give a declaratory award.[84]

---

[79] [2008] INSC 40.
[80] *Bharat Aluminium Co. v Kaiser Aluminium Technical Services Inc.* (2012) 9 SCC 552.
[81] See, e.g., the English Arbitration Act 1996, s. 48(3); LCIA Rules, Art. 22(1)(g) (granting tribunals the express power to rectify).
[82] For further discussion of this arbitration, see Chapter 3.
[83] The original concession was granted by King Saud of Saudi Arabia in 1933, for a period of sixty years.
[84] *Saudi Arabia v Arabian American Oil Co. (Aramco)* (1963) 27 ILR 117, at 145.

9.62 A declaratory award establishes the legal position definitively and has a binding effect as between the parties. It is a useful device, particularly where the parties have a continuing relationship and want to resolve a dispute without the risk of damaging that relationship by a demand for monetary compensation. It is capable of recognition, but it is not itself capable of enforcement; for the purposes of enforcement, an award must also involve an obligation to pay compensation or to take, or refrain from taking, a particular course of action.

(g) Rectification

9.63 Rectification essentially is a common law equitable remedy. Rectification of a contract is a remedy virtually unknown in civil law countries, where it tends to be treated in the same sense as adaptation of contracts and 'filling gaps'. In common law countries, these concepts are considered separately. However, in general, an arbitral tribunal may make an order for rectification of a contract if empowered to do so by the parties.

9.64 If no express power is conferred by the arbitration agreement, the question of the arbitral tribunal's jurisdiction to order rectification requires closer examination. For example, a standard-form arbitration clause that refers to 'disputes arising under the contract' is probably not wide enough to include a claim for rectification, since what is sought by rectification is a rewriting of the contract to reflect what one party claims to have been the agreement actually made. The phrase 'in connection with' in the arbitration clause may, however, be considered to give the arbitral tribunal a wider power. In England, any doubt about the position was resolved by the Arbitration Act 1996: an arbitral tribunal has the power 'to order the rectification, setting aside or cancellation of a deed or other document', unless the parties agree otherwise.[85] This express power to rectify is also reflected in the LCIA Rules, Article 22(1)(g) of which gives arbitral tribunals the 'additional' power:

> ...to order the correction of any contract between the parties or the arbitration agreement, but only to the extent required to rectify any mistake which the Arbitral Tribunal determines to be common to the parties and then only if and to the extent to which the law(s) or rules of law applicable to the contract or arbitration agreement permit such correction.

(h) Filling gaps and adaptation of contracts

9.65 An arbitral tribunal does not, in general, have power to create, or write, a contract between the parties. Its role in a contractual dispute is usually to interpret the contract as signed by the parties. However, almost anything is possible by clear consent of the parties.[86] In particular, it is generally accepted in modern times that

---

[85] English Arbitration Act 1996, s. 48(5)(c). See also the discussion of the scope of the arbitration clause and adaptation and filling gaps in Chapter 2, paragraphs 2.63*ff*.
[86] Provided that it is not unlawful or contrary to public policy.

C. Remedies

an arbitral tribunal has implied consent to 'fill gaps' by making a determination as to the presumed intention of the parties in order to make a contract operable. In England, a relatively mature authority for this proposition may be found in the famous 'chickens' case,[87] to which reference is still made from time to time by the English courts.

9.66 The principle was clarified and expanded in the later *Mamidoil* line of cases. In *Mamidoil*,[88] the English Court of Appeal stated:

> [...]
> (vi) Particularly in the case of contracts for future performance over a period, where the parties may desire or need to leave matters to be adjusted in the working out of their contract, the courts will assist the parties to do so, so as to preserve rather than destroy bargains, on the basis that what can be made certain is itself certain. *Certum est quod certum reddi potest.*
> [...]
> (viii) For these purposes, an express stipulation for a reasonable fair measure or price will be a sufficient criterion for the courts to act on. But even in the absence of express language, the courts are prepared to imply an obligation in terms of what is reasonable.
> [...]
> (x) The presence of an arbitration clause may assist the courts to hold a contract to be sufficiently certain or to be capable of being rendered so, as indicating a commercial and contractual mechanism which can be operated with the assistance of experts in the field, by which the parties, in the absence of agreement, may resolve their dispute.

9.67 A similar position exists in civil law countries, where the courts appear to go directly to what they call the 'intention of the parties', rather than use the 'implied term' device that is a feature of English contractual interpretation. In a note on 'L'Interprétation Arbitrale',[89] a distinguished Swiss commentator suggested that, in French law, the arbitrator takes account of the commercial context in which an agreement is made—but if the parties have omitted an important provision from their contract on a particular point, it is perhaps because they prefer to leave it open, rather than not to agree upon a contract at all.

9.68 A more difficult question is whether or not an arbitral tribunal has power to change the unambiguous terms of a contract. This is certainly possible where the relevant contract contains a provision authorising the arbitral tribunal to do so. Such provisions are commonly found in long-term supply contracts concerned with hydrocarbons such as oil and gas, and minerals such as copper and bauxite, as well as

---

[87] *F & G Sykes (Wessex) Ltd v Fine Fare Ltd* [1967] 1 Lloyd's Rep 53. See also Veeder, 'England', in Paulsson and Bosman (eds) *ICCA International Handbook on Commercial Arbitration* (Kluwer Law International, 1984).
[88] *Mamidoil-Jetoil Greek Petroleum Co. SA v Okta Crude Oil Refinery AD* [2001] 2 All ER (Comm) 193, at 215.
[89] Levy, 'L'interprétation arbitrale' (2013–14) 4 Rev Arb 861.

pharmaceutical products. Many such contracts contain clauses that provide for price adjustments or other adaptations by means of direct negotiation between the parties and/or by 'third-party-assisted negotiation' (mediation). However, in modern times, the increasingly competitive scenarios in which international business transactions are concluded, and subsequently implemented, sometimes make it difficult for corporate entities with powerful investors standing behind them to agree to the adaptation of clear contractual terms. This is especially so when one party stands to make a substantial financial gain by holding the other party to an unambiguous contractual commitment. The concept of fairness sometimes appears to take second place behind the prospect of profit. Direct or third-party-assisted negotiation may hold out little prospect of leading to a solution in this kind of scenario. Nevertheless, the concept of an award made by an international arbitration tribunal imposing upon the parties material changes to an unambiguous and freely negotiated contract remains controversial.

9.69 A device used for the adaptation of contracts during the latter part of the twentieth century was the so-called hardship clause. Attempts to create a workable solution may be seen in the 1978 ICC Rules for the Adaptation of Contracts and the Model Exploration and Production Sharing Agreement of Qatar of 1994. In the twenty-first century, Principles 6.2.2 and 6.2.3 of the 2004 UNIDROIT Principles of International Commercial Contracts[90] served as a 'blueprint' for many such provisions. However, none of these has gained widespread acceptance. In any event, most of these solutions require an express provision in the relevant contract to bring them into operation. In practice, such standard form clauses are rarely seen in modern contracts, and commercial parties (and their lawyers) tend to insert tailor-made 'balancing' provisions in long-term supply contracts to enable mediators and/or arbitral tribunals to help the parties to adapt their contracts when circumstances change in a manner that was unforeseen at the time that the contract was signed.

9.70 Professional mediators are well placed to operate in this way, even if there is no express provision in the relevant contract for adjustments in changed circumstances, because their function is designed specifically to assist the parties to look for possible solutions that may be acceptable to all of them. This is different from the function of an arbitral tribunal, which is to impose an 'award' that is designed to be binding on the disputing parties even if they (or one of them) may find it unacceptable. Some sets of international arbitration rules make it clear that the arbitral tribunal must decide 'according to law'. This is generally interpreted to mean that while they may (and indeed should) *interpret* the underlying contract, they must not alter its express and unambiguous terms without express authorisation from the disputing parties. Article 35 of the UNCITRAL Arbitration Rules

---

[90] Available online at http://www.unidroit.org/english/principles/contracts/principles2004/blackletter2004.pdf.

C. Remedies

provides a classic example of this approach, while most of the major sets of institutional arbitration rules remain silent on the issue.

Occasionally, arbitral tribunals issue awards that have the effect of changing the express terms of a contract in which there is no clear provision authorising them to do so. Where the applicable substantive law is that of a civil law jurisdiction, the justification usually given is the application of the doctrine of *rebus sic stantibus*. In the common law world, the parties' legal representatives and arbitrators tend to place reliance on 'implied terms'. However, parties to long-term contracts rarely take this kind of dispute to arbitration; they usually adopt modern direct negotiation techniques,[91] or third-party-assisted negotiation (mediation) processes.

9.71

(i) Interest

The payment of interest on a loan, or in respect of money that is paid later than it should have been, is a common feature of modern business relationships, and the award of interest in international arbitration has likewise become routine.[92] Indeed, it has become rare for interest not to be awarded where an award provides for the payment of monies due. As one international arbitrator has said:

9.72

> In all international commercial arbitrations where a claim for the payment of money is advanced, whether debt or damages, it is highly probable that the claimant has also suffered a financial loss resulting from late payment of the principal amount. That loss can amount to a significant proportion of the total claim; and in certain cases, it can exceed the principal amount. In a modern arbitration régime, it is unthinkable that a claimant should not have the right to recover that loss in the form of interest.[93]

However, the situation is different in Muslim countries—such as Saudi Arabia—in which the law against usury (*riba*) prevents the levying of interest:

> The proposition of interest, strictly applied in Hanbali law (Saudi Arabia, Qatar) nd Zayydi law (North Yemen) is linked in the minds of Muslim lawyers and economists with the rejection of the idea of the *homo economicus* as devised by the West, and with the integration of religious principles into the commercial life of the Muslim businessman, while the businessman should be solvent he should also conform to Qur'anic teaching, for although the Prophet did not condemn

---

[91] Such as those taught by the Program on Negotiation at Harvard Law School.
[92] The exceptions to this are arbitrations in which Islamic law may be applicable and in respect of which the law against usury (*riba*) may prevent the levying of interest: see Saleh, 'The recognition and enforcement of foreign arbitral awards in the states of the Arab Middle East', in Lew (ed.) *Contemporary Problems in International Arbitration* (CCLS/Kluwer, 1986), pp. 348–349. See, however, the decision of the English courts in *Sanghi Polyesters Ltd (India) v The International Investor KCFC (Kuwait)* [2000] 1 Lloyd's Rep 480, which suggests that, in some Islamic jurisdictions, interest may be awarded under another name.
[93] Veeder, 'Whose arbitration is it anyway: The parties' or the arbitration tribunal's? An interesting question?', in Newman and Hill (eds) *The Leading Arbitrators' Guide to International Arbitration* (2nd edn, Juris, 2008), p. 344. See also Brower and Sharpe, 'Awards of compound interest in international arbitration: The *Aminoil* non-precedent' (2006) 3 TDM 5.

profit arising from sale or from a partnership he did prohibit the charging of interest on a loan...[94]

(i) Basis upon which interest can be awarded

9.73 The basis upon which interest is awarded in international arbitration does, however, vary. Most institutional rules of arbitration do not contain express provisions for the payment of interest, largely because their drafters assumed that an arbitral tribunal has the power to make an award in respect of interest in just the same way as it has the power to make an award in respect of any other claims submitted to it.[95] The right to interest will therefore flow from the parties' underlying contract (that is, from a contractual provision for the levying of late payment interest), or by virtue of the applicable law.[96] The laws that govern the power of a tribunal to award interest also vary. In some jurisdictions, for example Bermuda, Hong Kong, England, and Scotland, the power to award interest is governed by the law of the place of arbitration.[97] In others, for example under German conflict-of-laws rules, the liability to pay interest is a question of substantive law and thus governed by the law of the contract.[98]

(ii) How much interest to award

9.74 More problematic in practice than the question of whether an arbitral tribunal can award interest in principle are the more practical questions of the rate of interest to be awarded, from which start date, and in which currency. Most applicable laws leave these questions to the tribunal's discretion. Thus the English Arbitration Act 1996 empowers a tribunal seated in England to award interest 'from such dates, at such rates and with such rests as it considers meets the justice of the case'.[99] Similarly, the law of Australia permits a tribunal to award interest 'at such reasonable rate as the tribunal determines for the whole or any part of the money, for the whole or any part of the period between the date on which the cause of action arose and the date on which the award is made', and thereafter 'from the day of the making of the award or such later day as the tribunal specifies, on so much of the money

---

[94] Saleh, 'The recognition and enforcement of foreign arbitral awards in the states of the Arab Middle East', in Lew (ed.) *Contemporary Problems in International Arbitration* (CCLS/Kluwer, 1986), pp. 348–349.

[95] Exceptionally, the LCIA Rules, Art. 26(6), provides that the arbitral tribunal may award compound interest not limited to the period up to the date of the award. For a discussion of compound interest, see paragraphs 9.76*ff*.

[96] See Gotanda, 'Awarding interest in international arbitration' (1996) 90 Am J Intl L 40, at 50*ff*; Gotanda, 'A study of interest', Villanova University School of Law Working Paper Series No. 83 (August 2007), available online at http://digitalcommons.law.villanova.edu/wps/art83/, pp. 3*ff*.

[97] See, e.g., the English Arbitration Act 1996, s. 49.

[98] Accordingly, under German conflict-of-laws rules, if an arbitral tribunal sitting in Germany were to conclude that the substantive law of the contract was English, it would apply not only those rules of English law governing interest that English law classifies as substantive, but also those rules that English law classifies as procedural, because a court of arbitral tribunal sitting in Germany would classify such *procedural* rules as being of a *substantive* nature for this purpose.

[99] English Arbitration Act 1996, s. 49(3). Almost identical provisions are found in the Irish Arbitration (International) Commercial Act 1998, s. 10(2).

as is from time to time unpaid'.[100] Other jurisdictions, such as Hong Kong, India, and Singapore, have also enacted laws that give arbitrators similar discretion in the award of interest.[101]

In exercising this discretion, the tribunal will typically invite submissions and evidence from the parties on these issues in the same way as it would in respect of any other request for relief. Thus parties will usually have an opportunity to set out their respective positions on the rate of interest to be applied, the period for which it should be applied, and whether a different rate (such as a statutory legal interest rate) should be applied for the period following the rendering of an award up until payment. In making such submissions, parties would do well to make an award of interest as easy for a tribunal as possible by providing the calculations upon which such an award would be based.[102]

9.75

(iii) Compound interest

Most systems of national law expressly permit arbitral tribunals to award some form of interest on an amount awarded in respect of a claim or counterclaim, whether the principal amount awarded is due under a contract or as compensation or as restitution. However, the award of compound—as opposed to simple—interest remains less clear.[103] Although the Model Law does not contain any express provisions concerning interest, recent arbitration legislation in common law jurisdictions such as England, Ireland, Hong Kong, and Bermuda give arbitral tribunals express power to award compound interest. Thus section 49 of the English Arbitration Act 1996 provides that, unless otherwise agreed by the parties, the tribunal may award simple or compound interest. This is, however, by no means a feature of all common law jurisdictions: in Canada and the United States, the power to award compound interest varies from state to state and province to province; in Australia and New Zealand, the power to award compound interest is strictly limited.

9.76

In civil law jurisdictions, arbitral tribunals typically have the power to award a statutory (or legal) rate of interest, which is simple interest at a rate defined by statute. Like the common law, however, there are once again exceptions to the rule: the Dutch and Japanese civil codes provide, for example, that statutory interest is automatically capitalised at the end of each year. Moreover, an ICC arbitral

9.77

---

[100] Australian International Arbitration Acts 1974–1989, ss 25(1) and 26; equivalent provisions are also found in the Maltese Arbitration Act 1996, ss 63(1) and 64.
[101] Hong Kong Arbitration Ordinance 1997, Ch. 341, ss 2GH and 2GI; Indian Arbitration and Conciliation Act 1996, s. 31(7)(a) and (b); Singapore International Arbitration Act (Ch. 143A) 2002, ss 12(5)(b) and 20.
[102] As Professor Park observed in his 2002 Freshfields Lecture, there are, in theory, three kinds of arbitrator—namely, those who can count and those who cannot: see Park, 'Arbitration's Protean nature: The value of rules and the risks of discretion' (2003) 19 Arb Intl 279.
[103] For the avoidance of doubt, compounding interest involves capitalising interest and accruing further interest on such capitalised interest. The difference between simple and compound interest can be significant where the amount in dispute is large and the time periods involved are lengthy.

tribunal in Geneva awarded compound interest in a dispute between a state and a French entity on the application of trade usage under Article 13 of the ICC Rules.[104] Sources of international law are no clearer. Article 38 of the International Law Commission's Draft Articles on Responsibility of States for Internationally Wrongful Acts[105] provides simply that 'interest shall be payable on any principal sum when necessary in order to ensure full reparation'.

9.78 Although the law on this issue varies from jurisdiction to jurisdiction, awards of compound interest are becoming more common. In the *Santa Elena* arbitration,[106] an international tribunal found that although simple interest seemed, at that time, to be awarded more frequently than compound interest, 'no uniform rule of law has emerged from the practice in international arbitration as regards the determination of whether compound or simple interest is appropriate in any given case'. In *Wena Hotels*,[107] an ICSID tribunal went further and found that an award of compound interest is generally appropriate in modern arbitration. In recent years, the approach in the *Santa Elena* and *Wena Hotels* arbitrations has been followed by a large number of arbitral tribunals, such that the award of compound interest is no longer an exception.[108]

9.79 The reason for this shift has been that, where the applicable law allows, international arbitral tribunals appear to be reaching the same view as that reached over thirty years ago by Judge Howard Holtzmann in his dissenting opinion in *Starrett Housing Corporation v Iran*[109]—namely, that simple interest may not always, in the language of Article 38 of the Draft Articles on Responsibility of States, 'ensure *full* reparation of loss suffered'. As a leading academic in this field has observed:

> [A]lmost all financing and investment vehicles involve compound interest… if the claimant could have received compound interest merely by placing its money in a

---

[104] Arnaldez, Derains, and Hascher, *Collection of ICC Arbitral Awards 1991–1995* (Kluwer Law International, 1997), p. 459.

[105] Official Records of the General Assembly, F50, 6th Session, Supplement No. 10 (AR/56/10), Ch. IV, E.1.

[106] *Compañía del Desarollo de Santa Elena SA v Republic of Costa Rica* (2000) 39 ILM 1317, at [103].

[107] *Wena Hotels Ltd v Egypt*, Award, ICSID Case No. ARB/98/4; IIC 273 (2000), (2002) 41 ILM 896.

[108] With respect to NAFTA claims, see *Pope Talbot v Government of Canada*, Award on Damages, Ad hoc UNCITRAL, IIC 195 (2002); *SD Myers Inc. v Government of Canada*, Second Partial Award, Ad hoc UNCITRAL, IIC 250 (2002). Other awards include *Middle East Cement Shipping and Handling G SA v Arab Republic of Egypt*, Award, ICSID Case No. ARB/99/6, IIC 169 (2002); *CME Czech Republic BV v Czech Republic*, Final Award and Separate Opinion, Ad hoc UNCITRAL, IIC 62 (2003); *Azurix Corporation v Argentine Republic*, Award, ICSID Case No. ARB/01/12, IIC 24 (2006); *ADC Affiliate Ltd, ADC & ADMC Management Ltd v Republic of Hungary*, Award, ICSID Case No. ARB/03/16, IIC 1 (2006); *Siemens AG v Argentine Republic*, Award, ICSID Case No. ARB/02/8, IIC 227 (2007); *LG&E Energy Corporation, LG&E Capital Corporation, and LG&E International Inc. v Argentine Republic*, Award, ICSID Case No. ARB/02/1, IIC 295 (2007). All of these decisions are in the public domain and can be found online at http://icsid.worldbank.org.

[109] Iran–US CTR 122, 269 (1983).

C. Remedies

readily available and commonly used investment vehicle, it is neither logical nor equitable to award the claimant only simple interest.[110]

(iv) Enforcing awards that carry interest

It has already been seen that an award of interest (whether simple or compound) may be prohibited by a relevant national law. If this is the law of the arbitration agreement, or of the contract under which the dispute arises, it seems that an arbitral tribunal has no option but to apply it. Where parties to a contract have chosen (or are deemed to have chosen) as the substantive law of their agreement a law that prohibits the payment of interest, they can scarcely complain if interest is not payable.

9.80

If the law of the place of arbitration (the *lex arbitri*) forbids the payment of interest, it may theoretically be possible for the arbitral tribunal to disregard this local law and apply the substantive law of the contract. But if the provisions of the local law are mandatory, there is a risk that the award could be attacked and rendered invalid under the law of the place where it was made. It follows that an arbitral tribunal sitting in Saudi Arabia, but applying French law as the substantive law of the contract, should be cautious when considering an award in respect of interest, even though this is permitted by the substantive law of the contract; certainly, any award of interest should be clearly separated from the other parts of the award.

9.81

What of the law of the place of enforcement? If an award cannot be enforced, it is worth no more than a bargaining chip. However, at the time of the arbitration, it is hardly possible for an arbitral tribunal to do more than make an informed guess as to the likely place of enforcement of its eventual award—and even this will be difficult until the arbitral tribunal has formed a view as to which party is likely to win the arbitration. It is suggested that, in deciding whether or not to award interest, an arbitral tribunal cannot be expected to take into account the likely consequences of such an award in a potential place of enforcement unless the point is expressly brought to its attention by one or both of the parties, in which case the point would no doubt have to be considered.

9.82

(v) Post-award interest

In general, it is also open to arbitrators to set a rate of post-award interest in any amount that they deem appropriate.[111] This is often the rate that would apply to a judgment in the country in which the award is made. But, in modern practice, arbitral tribunals often decline to distinguish between pre- and post-award interest; instead, arbitral tribunals often award a single rate of interest to run for the whole period from a certain date (which may include the date of the breach, or

9.83

---

[110] Gotanda, 'Awarding interest in international arbitration' (1996) 90 Am J Intl L 40, at 61.
[111] See paragraphs 9.81–9.82.

Award

the date on which the loss was suffered, or the date of the request for arbitration, depending on the applicable law and on the way in which the arbitral tribunal decides to exercise any discretion available to it) up to the date of payment of the award.[112]

9.84 In some instances, once an arbitral award is enforced in a particular country as a judgment of a court, the post-award interest rate may be replaced by the rate applicable to civil judgments. In England, however, section 49(3) of the English Arbitration Act 1996 permits the arbitral tribunal to exercise its discretion to award interest up to the date of payment.

(j) Costs

9.85 A claim in respect of the costs incurred by a party in connection with an international arbitration is, in principle, no different from any other claim, except that it usually cannot be quantified until the end of the arbitral proceedings. However, while no significant changes have been made to most national laws since the previous edition of this volume, there have been considerable changes to the rules and practices of some of the major international arbitration institutions during that period, as well as to the practices adopted by tribunals.

9.86 These changes appear to have been driven by a number of factors, including pressure on corporate executives, and the in-house counsel who advise and report to them, to reduce the levels of expenditure incurred on pursuing international arbitrations. Governments have also been subjected to the same kind of budgetary pressures. This, in turn, seems to have led some of the world's major institutions to amend the terminology traditionally used in connection with costs. The institutions presumably wish to draw a clear distinction between their own administration charges, and the tribunal's fees and expenses, and the expenses over which they have no real control, such as the hiring of hearing rooms, and transcription and translation services, among other things.

9.87 In previous editions, costs claims were considered under *two* headings—namely, 'costs of the arbitration' and 'costs of the parties'. These are broad summaries of the terminology used in the UNCITRAL Rules,[113] the ICC Rules,[114] the ICDR Rules,[115] the Rules of the Stockholm Chamber of Commerce (SCC),[116] the Rules of the Singapore International Arbitration Centre (SIAC),[117] and the LCIA Rules.[118]

---

[112] For a comprehensive review of the power of arbitrators to award post-award interest, see Gotanda, *Supplemental Damages in Private International Law* (Kluwer Law International, 1998), pp. 85–93.
[113] UNCITRAL Rules, Art. 40(1) and (2).
[114] ICC Rules, Art. 37(1).
[115] ICDR Rules, r. 34.
[116] SCC Rules, Arts 43 and 44.
[117] SIAC Rules, Art. 31(1) and (2).
[118] LCIA Rules, Art. 28(1).

C. Remedies

However, in light of the changes in approach since the previous edition, it is proposed in this edition to adopt three separate categories for the purpose of discussing claims in respect of costs:

- 'costs of the tribunal' (including the charges for administration of the arbitration by any arbitral institution);
- 'costs of the arbitration' (including hiring the hearing rooms, interpreters, transcript preparation, among other things); and
- 'costs of the parties' (including the costs of legal representation, expert witnesses, witness and other travel-related expenditure, among other things).

Each of these categories is now considered in turn.

(i) Costs of the tribunal

9.88 The costs of the tribunal usually include not only the fees, and travel-related and other expenses, payable to the individual members of the arbitral tribunal itself, but also any directly related expenses, such as the fees and expenses of any experts appointed by the arbitral tribunal. Also included in the tribunal costs are the fees and expenses of any administrative secretary or registrar, and any other incidental expenses incurred by the arbitral tribunal for the account of the case. In institutional arbitration, the tribunal costs are usually fixed or approved by the institution.

(ii) Costs of the arbitration

9.89 The costs of (the) arbitration include hiring rooms for hearings, and other meetings, between the parties and the tribunal, as well as the fees and expenses of the reporters who prepare the transcripts. These are usually organised and paid directly by the parties, and are disbursed by the parties in equal shares pending the tribunal's final award. Occasionally, where the arrangements are made by the chairman of the tribunal, or by an administering institution, such costs are paid from the deposits held by the arbitral tribunal or the institution. In general, however, the parties usually prefer to control these costs themselves rather than give the tribunal what may amount to a 'blank cheque' to buy in such services. The UNCITRAL Rules avoid this issue by requiring the tribunal to inform the parties of the methodology that it proposes to use in determining its costs and expenses. This methodology is then subject to challenge by the parties. Thereafter, in any award rendered, the tribunal must fix its costs and expenses consistently with this methodology, and any party may request the appointing authority or the secretary-general of the Permanent Court of Arbitration (PCA) to review the calculations.[119]

(iii) Costs of the parties

9.90 The costs of the parties include not only the fees and expenses of the legal representatives engaged to represent the parties at the arbitration hearing, but also the

---

[119] UNCITRAL Rules, Art. 41(3) and (4).

Award

costs incurred in the preparation of the case. There will also be other professional fees and expenses, such as those of accountants or expert witnesses, as well as the hotel and travelling expenses of the lawyers, witnesses, and others concerned, and copying and printing charges, as well as telephone, fax, and email expenses. All of these costs are likely to be substantial in a major case.

9.91 Nevertheless, these costs rarely include any allowance for the time spent on the case by senior officials, directors, or employees of the parties themselves, or the indirect costs of disruption to their ordinary business. The hidden cost of such 'executive', or 'management', time may be high. It may occasionally even exceed the direct costs. In general, the larger the case, the more executive time is spent on it. If it is possible to recover the legal costs and expenses of bringing or defending a claim in arbitration, should it be unusual to recover the cost of executive time, particularly if this includes—as it often does—the cost of in-house counsel?

9.92 Traditionally, such costs have been regarded as part of the normal cost of running a business enterprise or a government department, rather than the recoverable costs of the winning party.[120] The UNCITRAL Rules, for example, do not include such costs in the definition of what constitutes the 'costs of the arbitration', although, for instance, the 'travel and other expenses of witnesses' and 'the costs for legal representation and assistance' *are* included.[121]

9.93 The ICC Rules not only refer to 'the reasonable legal and other costs incurred by the parties', but also indicate that the tribunal may consider such circumstances as it considers relevant (including the extent to which each party has conducted the arbitration in an expeditious and cost-effective manner) before making a decision on the amount of costs to be awarded.[122] A similar provision has been introduced in the 2014 version of the LCIA Rules.[123] The UNCITRAL Rules adopt a more conservative approach: while recognising that the arbitral tribunal may take into account the circumstances of the case when allocating costs between the parties, they do not explicitly mention cooperative or disruptive behaviour of the parties as a factor.

9.94 However, there is no necessary correlation between the time spent on a particular line of research or argument and the value of that time, in terms of the end result. Even if it is assumed that every minute spent on the case was of value—a somewhat brave assumption—the relevant hourly charging rate may vary from one country to another, and even from place to place within the same country.[124]

---

[120] See Gotanda, *Supplemental Damages in Private International Law* (Kluwer Law International, 1998), p. 191.
[121] UNCITRAL Rules, Art. 40.
[122] ICC Rules, Art. 37(1).
[123] LCIA Rules, Art. 28(4).
[124] In one UNCITRAL case in the late 1990s, the hourly rate claimed for a senior partner in a New York law firm was more than double the hourly rate of a senior partner of a New Orleans firm.

C. Remedies

Another problem is that of deciding when the assessment of costs should be made. **9.95**
Arbitration rules, such as those of UNCITRAL[125] and the SCC,[126] provide for the costs of the arbitration to be fixed in the award. The ICC Rules[127] provide differently, permitting the tribunal to fix costs at any time during the arbitration. The arbitral tribunal then has a choice: it can either ask each of the parties for details of their costs and expenses before making its award, so as to deal with them in that award; or it can deal with costs in a separate final award, which will then reduce what was intended to be a 'final' award on the merits of the case to the status of a partial award.

Practical problems of this kind have led many international arbitral tribunals to **9.96**
refrain from ordering the unsuccessful party to pay the legal costs of the winning party, or simply to order the losing party to pay an arbitrarily chosen fixed sum towards the winner's legal costs. This practice may well change, as more attention is directed by lawyers and their clients to the costs of the arbitration, including the cost of executive time. Indeed, a costs order is one of the few means at a tribunal's disposal to discourage—and, in appropriate circumstances, to punish—a party's wasteful procedural tactics during an arbitration. At the time of writing, however, most international arbitral tribunals that decide to make an award of costs in favour of the winning party tend to adopt a broad approach in assessing the amount to be paid. In doing so, they tend to adopt the approach of an arbitrator in a case in the Iran–United States Claims Tribunal, who, in a separate opinion, proposed criteria along the following lines.

- Were costs claimed in the arbitration?
- Was it necessary to employ lawyers in the case in question?
- Is the amount of the costs reasonable?
- Are the circumstances of the particular case such as to make it reasonable to apportion such costs?

After asserting that the first two tests are normally satisfied in complex arbitra- **9.97**
tions, he commented on the reasonableness criterion as follows:

> The classic test of reasonableness is not, however, an invitation to mere subjectivity. Objective tests of reasonableness of lawyers' fees are well known. Such tests typically assign weight primarily to the time spent and complexity of the case. In modern practice, the amount of time required to be spent is often a gauge of the extent of the complexities involved. Where the Tribunal is presented with copies of bills for services, or other appropriate evidence, indicating the time spent, the hourly billing rate, and a general description of the professional services rendered, its task need be neither onerous nor mysterious. The range of typical hourly billing rates is generally known and, as evidence before the Tribunal in various cases including this one indicates, it does not greatly differ between the US and

---

[125] UNCITRAL Rules, Art. 40.
[126] SCC Rules, Art. 43(4).
[127] ICC Rules, Art. 37(3).

countries of Western Europe, where both claimants and respondents before the Tribunal typically hire their outside counsel. Just how much time any lawyer reasonably needs to accomplish a task can be measured by the number of issues involved in a case and the amount of evidence requiring analysis and presentation. While legal fees are not to be calculated on the basis of the pounds of paper involved, the Tribunal by the end of a case is able to have a fair idea, on the basis of the submissions made by both sides, of the approximate extent of the effort that was reasonably required. Nor should the Tribunal neglect to consider the reality that legal bills are usually first submitted to businessmen. The pragmatic fact that a businessman has agreed to pay a bill, not knowing whether or not the Tribunal would reimburse the expenses, is a strong indication that the amount billed was considered reasonable by a reasonable man spending his own money, or the money of the corporation he serves.[128]

9.98 A number of subsequent Iran–United States Claims Tribunal awards have referred to, and adopted, this test as a guide.[129] Furthermore, in the more recent, much publicised, very substantial *Yukos* cases,[130] a highly distinguished tribunal, also applying the UNCITRAL Rules, adopted a similar approach. These cases may provide a practical, common-sense, guide to the practice that international tribunals may adopt when they are required to exercise their discretion in relation to an award in respect of costs.

(k) Requirements imposed by national law

9.99 Most national legislation is silent concerning awards of costs in international arbitrations. The Model Law also does not address this question. Some states that have adopted the Model Law have added provisions regarding awards of the costs of arbitration, but not many.[131] As with interest, and indeed all other matters concerning the powers of the tribunal, any specific provisions of the *lex arbitri* concerning costs must be respected. However, the practices of national courts in following their own rules in relation to awarding costs do not appear to be an appropriate guide for the way in which an international tribunal should exercise the discretion granted to it under either the relevant set of rules or the *lex arbitri*.[132] It is suggested that international tribunals, wherever the seat of arbitration, should be guided by the *lex arbitri* and by the applicable substantive law as to the scope of its discretion, and by the applicable arbitration rules (if any) as to the exercise of that discretion.

---

[128] Separate opinion of Judge Holtzmann, reported in [1985] Iranian Assets Litigation Reporter 10860, at 10863; (1985) 8 Iran–US CTR 329, at 332–333.

[129] For a detailed review of the practices of the Iran–United States Claims Tribunal, see van Hof, *Commentary on the UNCITRAL Arbitration Rules* (Kluwer Law International, 1991), pp. 293–311.

[130] For example, see *Yukos Universal Ltd (Isle of Man) v. The Russian Federation*, PCA Case No. AA 227, UNCITRAL, 18 July 2014, at [1887].

[131] Born, *International Commercial Arbitration* (2nd edn, Kluwer Law International, 2014), p. 3087.

[132] For a comprehensive review of the practices of international tribunals concerning the award of costs, see Gotanda, *Supplemental Damages in Private International Law* (Kluwer Law International, 1998), pp. 173–192.

D. Deliberations and Decisions of the Tribunal

(a) Introduction

9.100 So the purpose of an arbitration is to arrive at a binding and enforceable decision. For the parties and their lawyers, it is the dispositive section of an award that is most important. Yet there is more to an award, including how a tribunal of arbitrators goes about reaching its decision, which is largely neglected in the literature concerning international arbitration.

9.101 The task that faces arbitral tribunals is not easy. A leading English judge described judicial decision making as follows:

> The judge's role in determining what happened at some time in the past is not of course peculiar to him. Historians, auditors, accident investigators of all kinds, loss adjusters and doctors are among those who, to a greater or lesser extent, may be called upon to perform a similar function. But there are three features of the judge's role which will not apply to all these other investigations. First, he is always presented with conflicting versions of the events in question: if there is no effective dispute, there is nothing for him to decide. Secondly, his determination necessarily takes place subject to formality and restraints (evidential or otherwise) attendant upon proceedings in court. Thirdly, his determination has a direct practical effect upon people's lives in terms of their pockets, activities or reputations.[133]

9.102 The same task faces an arbitral tribunal, but with a difference: in a tribunal of judges—a court of appeal, for instance—the judges are likely to have a shared legal background and, for the most part, to be of the same nationality; this is not usually so in major international commercial disputes, which usually involve a tribunal of three arbitrators, rather than a sole arbitrator.

9.103 First, such an arbitral tribunal is not a permanent court or tribunal except in special cases such as the Iran–US Claims Tribunal. Secondly, the tribunal may be composed of arbitrators of different professions: accountants, engineers, or whatever the case may require. Thirdly, even if all of the members of the tribunal are lawyers, they will often be of different nationalities, with different languages and different legal backgrounds—common law, civil law, Shari'ah, and so forth. They may know each other personally or professionally, or they may (as is often the case) meet for the first time when they come together as a tribunal chosen to resolve a dispute.

9.104 How will this disparate, ad hoc group of people set about trying to reach their decision? They will read the parties' submissions, the witness statements, and the lever arch files full of photocopied documents; they will listen to evidence and argument. After this, although (as the saying goes) they may not be any wiser, they should certainly be better informed. As a case proceeds, each arbitrator will

---

[133] Lord Bingham, *The Business of Judging* (Oxford University Press, 2000), p. 4.

no doubt begin to form his or her own view as to how the various issues that have arisen ought to be determined, but the tribunal should arrive at a decision together. If the tribunal consists of three arbitrators, there must be some exchange of views, some dialogue between them, if they are to do so.

9.105 There are no set rules as to how a decision should be made. Each arbitration is different and each arbitral tribunal is different. What works well with one tribunal may not work at all with another. However, the advice written by a former president of the LCIA may serve as a useful guideline:

> While it is important for the chairman not to rush his fellow arbitrators into reaching a definitive decision on all outstanding issues—indeed, it is incumbent on the chairman to remind the members of the tribunal that their work is only just beginning and that any opinions expressed will be considered to be provisional—it is, however, crucial to ascertain whether or not a consensus seems likely to emerge on one or more of the issues to be decided. If there is disagreement between the two party-appointed arbitrators, the chairman will begin to earn his extra stipend. In the event a consensus on certain issues is clear, the chairman will generally offer to prepare a first draft of an eventual award, for discussion at a later date.
>
> No member of the tribunal must exert any pressure on his colleagues during this first session. This initial session should provide an opportunity for all arbitrators to engage in a relaxed dialogue with one another.
>
> Each arbitrator must feel that he is allowed to 'think out loud' in this informal setting. Personally, whether I serve as chairman or party-designated arbitrator, I tend to listen at least as much as to speak during such a first encounter. I wish my colleagues to know what my initial views are, but I also want to know how my colleagues believe they can inform the decision-making process which has begun.[134]

9.106 This passage raises an interesting question as to whether there is any difference between, on the one hand, informal discussions among members of the tribunal (for example over a meal or during a coffee break) and, on the other, formal deliberations (in the French sense). Among the reasons why deliberations are infrequently addressed is undoubtedly the fact that some systems encourage secrecy in the deliberative process. For example, in French law, as in some other civil law countries, the deliberations of the arbitrators are 'secret'.[135] In French law, the interchange of views between arbitrators is formalised as a '*deliberation*'. The Civil Code that governs French internal (or domestic) arbitrations requires the arbitrators to fix the date at which their deliberations will start (*le délibéré sera pronouncé*),[136] after which no further submissions by the parties are allowed. One distinguished French academician and author considers the rule that there must be a '*deliberation*' before

---

[134] Fortier, 'The tribunal's deliberations', in Newman and Hill (eds) *The Leading Arbitrators' Guide to International Arbitration* (2nd edn, Juris, 2008), pp. 479–480.
[135] French Civil Code, art. 1479, states: 'Les délibérations du tribunal arbitral sont secretes.'
[136] French Civil Code, art. 1468, states: 'Le tribunal arbitral fixe la date à laquelle le délibéré sera prononcé. Au cours du délibéré, aucune demande ne peut être formée, aucun moyen soulevé et aucune pièce produite, si ce n'est à la demande du tribunal arbitral.'

there is any award by the tribunal to be a rule of international public order.[137] Although it does not necessarily follow that the deliberations should be secret, for another French commentator the rule that such a '*deliberation*' should be, and should remain, so is a 'fundamental principle, which constitutes one of the main-springs of arbitration, as it does of all judicial decisions'.[138] However, this is not solely a French position. Rule 15 of the ICSID Arbitration Rules states:

(1) The deliberations of the Tribunal shall take place in private and remain secret.
(2) Only members of the Tribunal shall take part in its deliberations. No other person shall be admitted unless the Tribunal decides otherwise.

9.107 In a well-known case,[139] the Swedish Court of Appeal discussed what is necessary for a proper deliberation when considering a request by the Czech Republic to set aside an arbitral award. One of the grounds put forward was that the arbitrator nominated by the Czech Republic had, as he alleged in his dissenting opinion, been deliberately excluded by his fellow arbitrators from the deliberations of the tribunal. The Court referred to a seemingly conflicting balance of considerations: the equality of the arbitrators, balanced against the need for the tribunal to reach a conclusion without undue delay. The Court said, in summary, that the arbitrators should be treated equally, but that the procedures adopted should also be cost-effective and flexible. There were no formal rules, and so the deliberations might be oral or written, or both; deadlines could be set, but could also be changed as required, and so forth. The Swedish Court of Appeal added that whilst due process must be guaranteed:

[W]hen two arbitrators have agreed upon the outcome of the dispute, the third arbitrator cannot prolong the deliberations by demanding continued discussions in an attempt to persuade the others as to the correctness of his opinion. The dissenting arbitrator is thus not afforded any opportunity to delay the writing of the award.[140]

9.108 The rule as to the secrecy, or confidentiality, of the tribunal's discussions has significant consequences.[141] It was considered by a former president of the ICJ, in

---

[137] Bredin, 'Le secret du délibéré arbitral', in *Études Offertes à Pierre Bellet* (Litec, 1991).
[138] De Boisséson, *Le Droit Français de l'Arbitrage National et International* (Joly, 1990), p. 296. See also the comment in Robert, *L'Arbitrage: Droit Interne, Droit International Privé* (5th edn, Dalloz, 1983), para. 360 (authors' translation): 'Although it is practised according to a certain number of foreign laws, notably Anglo-Saxon, the dissenting opinion is prohibited in French domestic law since it violates the secrecy of the tribunal's deliberation...' Under German law, unless provided otherwise by the arbitration agreement, deliberations are secret: see *Münchener Kommentar zur Zivilprozessordnung: ZPO*, § 1052 Rn 1-5.
[139] *Czech Republic v CME Czech Republic BV*, Case No. T 8735–01, Svea Court of Appeal, IIC 63 (2003). An English translation of the judgment can be found online at http://italaw.com/sites/default/files/case-documents/ita0182.pdf; a case summary is available at [2003] Stockholm Arb Rep 167.
[140] *Czech Republic*, in the English translation, at 87; in the case summary, at 180.
[141] See Gaillard and Savage (eds) *Fouchard, Gaillard, and Goldman on International Commercial Arbitration* (Kluwer Law International, 1999), para. 1374.

considering a challenge to one of the members of the Iran–United States Claims Tribunal, whose impartiality had been questioned on the basis of a dissenting opinion that he had issued. In the course of the decision on the challenge, it was held that:

> A rule of the confidentiality of the deliberations must, if it is to be effective, apply generally to the deliberation stage of a tribunal's proceedings and cannot realistically be confined to what is said in a formal meeting of all the members in the deliberation room. The form or forms the deliberation takes varies greatly from one tribunal to another. Anybody who has had experience of courts and tribunals knows perfectly well that much of the deliberation work, even in courts like the ICJ which have formal rules governing the deliberation, is done less formally. In particular the task of drafting is better done in small groups rather than by the whole court attempting to draft round the table. Revelations of such informal discussion and of suggestions made could be very damaging and seriously threaten the whole deliberation process.[142]

9.109 As noted, there must obviously be some interchange of views between the members of the tribunal as they try to arrive at a decision that can be expressed in their award. This interchange of views may be characterised, as it is in the ICSID Arbitration Rules and in the French Civil Code, as a '*deliberation*', but this does not mean that the members of the tribunal have to sit together in solemn conclave, like cardinals electing a pope, until a decision is reached.

9.110 What is likely to happen in practice is that the arbitrators exchange views informally, as the case progresses—particularly in the course of the hearing—and then decide how to proceed with the formulation of their award. The chairman of the tribunal often prepares a list of the issues that he or she considers critical, then asks the co-arbitrators to amend, or add to, this list and perhaps express a preliminary view on the issues raised—either orally or, more commonly, in writing—with each arbitrator being given the opportunity to comment upon what the others have written.

9.111 Where the arbitral tribunal consists of a sole arbitrator, the need to consult with other members of the tribunal and to try to reconcile possibly differing opinions does not arise. However, the sole arbitrator will still need to consider the evidence and arguments of the parties, work through a list of the significant issues, and generally come to a conclusion on the matters in dispute as part of the process of drafting an award.

9.112 For a sole arbitrator, it is only his or her decision that counts. But what happens when there is a tribunal of three arbitrators and, despite their best efforts, they find themselves unable to agree? Ideally, decisions are made unanimously; but there must be a 'fall-back' position, and, on this, the international and institutional rules

---

[142] Sir Robert Jennings, Decision of 7 May 2001, at 7. A summary of the decision was published at (2001) 16 Mealey's Int Arb Rep 2. The full text is available for purchase from Mealey's online.

D. Deliberations and Decisions of the Tribunal

of arbitration differ. Some favour majority voting; others give the presiding arbitrator a decisive role.

(b) Tribunal psychology

9.113 Most international arbitrations are determined by an arbitral tribunal composed of three arbitrators. The aim of their deliberations must be to achieve a unanimous award, since this will be seen as both authoritative and conclusive. If unanimity cannot be achieved, however, the next best thing is to have a majority award, rather than an award by the chairman alone—or no award at all. In one of the Iran–United States arbitrations, a US-appointed arbitrator concurred in a majority award, although he thought that the damages awarded were half what they should have been. 'Why then do I concur in this inadequate award?' he asked rhetorically; 'Because', he answered, 'there are circumstances in which "something is better than nothing".'[143]

9.114 There may be concern over the way in which arbitrators will conduct themselves in deliberations when they have been directly appointed by one of the parties to a dispute. However, parties rarely abuse the arbitral process to the extent of nominating an arbitrator whose specific function is to vote for the party who nominated him or her, although they do appoint arbitrators whom they believe are likely to be sympathetic to the case that they wish to advance during the proceedings. As has been said:

> It should not be surprising if party appointed arbitrators tend to view the facts and law in a light similar to their appointing parties. After all, the parties are careful to select arbitrators with views similar to theirs. But this does not mean that arbitrators will violate their duty of impartiality and independence.[144]

9.115 In an international arbitration, each arbitrator, however appointed, is under a duty to act impartially and to reach a determination of the issues in a fair and unbiased manner.[145] It follows that it would be improper if a party-nominated arbitrator were to hold private discussions with the party who nominated that arbitrator about the substance of the dispute. However, it is not improper for a party-nominated arbitrator to ensure that the arbitral tribunal properly understands the case being advanced by that party,[146] and a party-nominated arbitrator who is convinced of

---

[143] *Economy Forms Corporation v Islamic Republic of Iran*, Award, Case No. 55-165-1, 13 June 1983, quoted in Schwebel, 'The majority vote of an arbitral tribunal' (1991) 2 Am Rev Intl Arb 402, at 409.
[144] Mosk and Ginsburg, *Dissenting Opinions in International Arbitration* (Liber Amicorum Bengt Broms, 1999), p. 275.
[145] See Chapter 5, paragraphs 5.79ff.
[146] Indeed, this is a material part of the duties of party-nominated arbitrators. A party-nominated arbitrator should do his or her best to ensure that he or she understands the case being put forward by the party that nominated him or her and should seek to make sure that the arbitral tribunal as a whole is in the same position. It is, of course, necessary for party-nominated arbitrators to consider carefully the merits of the arguments on both sides and not to be seen as favouring appointing

the merits of the case being put forward by the appointing party can have a significant impact on the private deliberations of the arbitral tribunal when the award is discussed. Interestingly, the UNCITRAL Rules extend the duty of the arbitrator in relation to disclosing circumstances giving rise to a potential conflict of interest so that it is owed not only to the parties, but also to the other members of the tribunal.[147]

9.116 The behaviour of the party-appointed arbitrators affects the dynamics of deliberations for the presiding arbitrator, although the presiding arbitrator will form his or her own view of the case. If it is difficult to achieve a majority award, inevitably the presiding arbitrator leans towards a compromise with a party-nominated arbitrator who follows the proceedings intelligently, asks good questions of each party, and puts forward well-reasoned arguments, rather than with someone who shows little interest in the proceedings and gives the impression of being there simply as the advocate nominee of the appointing party.

(c) Bargaining process

9.117 An award of monetary compensation arrived at by a majority vote is sometimes the result of a bargaining process in the deliberations that might be more common in a marketplace than in a judicial, or quasi-judicial, proceeding. To describe it as a process of eliminating alternatives by 'a proper sequence of votes' is an attractive euphemism. However, particularly when carried out in a structured manner and in relation to predefined issues, 'bargaining' may be a sensible way in which to proceed. Such a procedure is envisaged in the 1966 European Convention providing a Uniform Law on Arbitration (known as the 'Strasbourg Uniform Law'), which provides that:

> Except where otherwise stipulated, if the arbitrators are to award a sum of money, and a majority cannot be obtained for any particular sum, the votes for the highest sum shall be counted as votes for the next highest sum until a majority is obtained.[148]

9.118 Where there are a number of different issues, it is theoretically possible for the members of the arbitral tribunal to be split on some issues and unanimous on others. In such cases, the question arises as to whether all of the issues should be decided by the presiding arbitrator alone (if this is permitted under the relevant rules of arbitration) or whether the award may be divided into various parts. If there is lack of unanimity in relation to one of many issues, the award as a whole will usually be issued by a majority. If there is no majority in relation to a number of issues, the award as a whole should be that of the presiding arbitrator if the

---

parties. For further discussion of this subject, see Smith, 'Impartiality of the party-appointed arbitrator' (1990) 6 Arb Intl 320.

[147] UNCITRAL Rules, Art. 11.
[148] Strasbourg Uniform Law, Annex I, Art. 22(3).

D. Deliberations and Decisions of the Tribunal

relevant rules permit; otherwise, the arbitrators will have to continue, in one way or another, to try to reach a majority decision. It is unusual for an arbitral tribunal to split its award into a number of different parts in which the operative directions in the award have been reached by different processes.

(d) Majority voting

As an example of majority voting, Article 33(1) of the UNCITRAL Rules provides: 'When there is more than one arbitrator, any award or other decision of the arbitral tribunal shall be made by a majority of the arbitrators.' However, Article 33(2) makes an exception to this rule in relation to questions of procedure and allows the presiding arbitrator to decide such questions on his or her own, subject to revision by the tribunal. This provision gives rise to two potential problems. **9.119**

The first is how to identify procedural issues: for example, is a determination of the place of arbitration under Article 18 of the Rules a question of procedure? If it is, then, in the absence of a majority, the presiding arbitrator may decide. However, Professor Pieter Sanders, as special consultant to the UNCITRAL Secretariat, played a major role in drafting the UNCITRAL Rules. He expressed the view that the determination of the place of arbitration should *not* be considered a procedural question; and should therefore not be a function of the presiding arbitrator alone.[149] **9.120**

The second problem is that, in order to achieve an award, a majority must be reached, because there is no fall-back position. Professor Sanders stated that 'the arbitrators are...forced to continue their deliberations until a majority, and probably a compromise solution, has been reached'.[150] **9.121**

This is a potentially serious defect in the UNCITRAL Rules, since there may be cases in which it is genuinely impossible to achieve a majority. In construction industry arbitrations, for example, there are often many different issues in relation to separate claims and it is possible for each individual arbitrator to have a different view on these different issues. Furthermore, the arbitrators may have widely differing views on questions of quantum in such cases, with no real possibility of a compromise solution being achieved in order to obtain a majority award.[151] The Model Law, Article 29 of which adopts the same position as the UNCITRAL Rules, is open to the same criticism. **9.122**

---

[149] (1977) II YBCA 172, at 194.
[150] Ibid., at 208.
[151] An arbitral tribunal has no mandate to return a verdict of *non liquet*. See, e.g., ICSID Convention, Art. 42(2). Therefore, if it is not possible to form a majority, the proper course is for the arbitrators to resign and for a replacement tribunal to be appointed. For an example in which this occurred, see *Tokios Tokeles v Ukraine*, Decision on Jurisdiction, ICSID Case No. ARB/02/18, 29 April 2004.

9.123 The approach in the ICC Rules is different. These rules provide that where the arbitral tribunal is composed of more than one arbitrator, the award, if not unanimous, may be made by a majority of the tribunal; if there is no majority, the chairman of the arbitral tribunal makes the decision alone.[152] The same approach is adopted in the Swiss Private International Law Act 1987 (Swiss PIL), the Swiss Rules of International Arbitration, the English Arbitration Act 1996, and the LCIA Rules.[153]

9.124 In contrast to the UNCITRAL Rules, under the ICC Rules, the Swiss Rules, and the LCIA Rules, the pressure is on the other arbitrators to join the presiding arbitrator in forming a majority. This is because of the presiding arbitrator's power to make an award alone. However, if this happens, the party-chosen arbitrators will not participate in the award;[154] instead, the award will have been made by a person who has often been chosen for the parties by an arbitral institution or by some other appointing authority.

9.125 In ICSID arbitrations, majority rule also prevails. The ICSID Convention provides that '[t]he Tribunal shall decide questions by a majority of the votes of all its members',[155] and this provision is carried into effect by the ICSID Arbitration Rules, Rule 16(1) of which states: 'Decisions of the Commission shall be taken by a majority of the votes of all its members. Abstention shall count as a negative vote.' In this context, 'majority rule' means that at least two of the three members of the arbitral tribunal must be prepared to agree with each other, whatever element of bargaining or compromise this might involve. An arbitral tribunal is bound to render a decision. It is not permitted to say that it is undecided and unable to make an award. It may not bring in a finding of *non liquet* (on the ground of silence, or obscurity of the law, or otherwise).[156]

9.126 It may well be difficult for individual members of an arbitral tribunal to alter their respective positions so as to achieve the necessary majority. The notes to the ICSID Arbitration Rules record that, when the Rules were originally formulated, consideration was given to providing for the possibility of the arbitral tribunal being unable to reach a majority decision. It was concluded, however, that no problem would arise with questions that admitted only a positive or a negative answer. If a positive proposition, such as a submission, were to fail to achieve a majority, it

---

[152] ICC Rules, Art. 31(1). In such a case, the presiding arbitrator's role is very similar, but not identical, to that of an umpire. The difference is that an umpire is not required to make a decision unless and until the arbitrators appointed by the parties disagree. If they disagree, they take no further part in the proceedings and the umpire proceeds as if he or she were sole arbitrator.
[153] LCIA Rules, Art. 26(3); Swiss PIL, Ch. 12, s. 189; English Arbitration Act 1996, s. 20(3)–(4); Swiss Rules, Art. 31(1).
[154] LCIA Rules, Art. 26(3).
[155] ICSID Convention, Art. 48(1).
[156] ICSID Convention, Art. 42(2).

D. Deliberations and Decisions of the Tribunal

would automatically fail since, under the ICSID Rules, an abstention is counted as a negative vote. Where the question could not be answered by a simple 'yes' or 'no', as in the determination of the amount of compensation to be awarded, it was concluded that 'a decision can normally be reached by a proper sequence of votes by which alternatives are successively eliminated'.[157]

9.127 Thus there are various ways in which the awards of three-member arbitral tribunals may be made. They may be made unanimously, or by a majority, or by the presiding arbitrator alone if he or she is empowered to decide alone under the rules governing the proceedings.

(e) Concurring and dissenting opinions

(i) Concurring opinions

9.128 A 'separate', or 'concurring', opinion is one that is given by an arbitrator who agrees with the result of the arbitration, but who either does not agree with the reasoning or does not agree with the way in which the award is formulated. These opinions are rarely given in commercial arbitrations. They are more frequently found in public law arbitrations, in which the practice of the ICJ tends to be followed.[158]

(ii) Dissenting opinions

9.129 Dissenting opinions pose greater problems and are less frequently delivered. There is a broad division of philosophy and practice as to whether the giving of dissenting opinions should be permitted. In arbitrations between states, the right to submit a dissenting opinion was asserted as long ago as the middle of the nineteenth century, in the *Alabama Claims* arbitration[159] between the United Kingdom and the United States. The Statute of the ICJ expressly entitles judges in the minority to deliver dissenting opinions,[160] and this right has been exercised frequently not only in judgments, but also in connection with procedural orders, advisory opinions, and interim proceedings.

9.130 When arbitrators dissent in international arbitrations, they often simply refuse to sign the award. Where this is done, the dissenting opinion may be annexed to the award if the other arbitrators agree, or it may be delivered to the parties separately.

---

[157] Note D to Arbitration Rule 47 of 1968, (1968) 1 ICSID Reports 108.
[158] Article 57 of the ICJ Statute is generally interpreted as permitting the practice of giving separate opinions: see Born, *International Commercial Arbitration* (2nd edn, Kluwer Law International, 2014), pp. 3052–3053.
[159] Alabama Claims of the United States of America against Great Britain, Award rendered on 14 September 1872 by the Tribunal of Arbitration established by Article I of the Treaty of Washington of 8 May 1871. For a discussion of the proceedings, see Cushing, *The Treaty of Washington: Its Negotiation, Execution, and the Discussions Relating Thereto* (Harper & Bros, 1873).
[160] ICJ Statute, Art. 57.

In either case, the dissenting opinion does not form part of the award itself: it is not an 'award', but an *opinion*.[161]

(iii) Position in national laws

9.131 Modern arbitration legislation tends not to refer expressly to dissenting opinions. For example, there is no mention of dissenting opinions in the Swiss PIL, although a commentator states that an arbitrator has the right to give reasons for his dissent.[162] The Netherlands Arbitration Act 1986[163] similarly contains no express provision, but the authoritative commentary notes state that whilst dissenting opinions are not customary in the Netherlands, they are not excluded.[164] In France, it is sometimes said that the principle of the secrecy of the deliberations is such that even to disclose that the decision was unanimous is a breach thereof.[165] This is not an approach that is favourable to the concept of a dissenting opinion, yet such opinions are given in international arbitrations—even in France. No prohibition against dissenting opinions is known in the common law countries. Indeed, it is not unusual for common law arbitrators to consider themselves under a duty to inform the parties of their reasons for any dissent.

(iv) Position under institutional rules

9.132 Of the world's arbitral institutions, ICSID is alone in expressly recognising in its Rules the right of an arbitrator to issue an individual opinion and, in particular, a dissenting opinion: 'Any member of the Tribunal may attach his individual opinion to the award, whether he dissents from the majority or not, or a statement of his dissent.'[166] The LCIA Rules do not mention dissenting opinions, although the right of an arbitrator to issue a dissenting opinion is recognised in England[167]

---

[161] See, e.g., Redfern, 'Dissenting opinions in international commercial arbitration: The good, the bad and the ugly' (2004) 20 Arb Intl 223, at 236, arguing that dissenting opinions are unwelcome in international commercial arbitration, because:

> It is the *decision* which matters; and it matters *not* as a guide to the opinions of a particular arbitrator, or as an indication of the future development of the law, but because it resolves the particular dispute that divides the parties; and it resolves that dispute as part of a private, not public, dispute resolution process that the parties themselves have chosen.

[162] Blessing, 'The new International Arbitration Law in Switzerland' (1988) 5 J Intl Arb 9, at 66.
[163] At the time of writing, the Netherlands was updating its 1986 Act.
[164] Sanders and van den Berg, *The Netherlands Arbitration Act 1986* (Kluwer Law and Taxation, 1987), p. 33.
[165] Cass. Soc. 9 November 1945, Gaz. Pal. 1946 1.22. Note, however, Professor Bredin's comment that legal opinion on this point seems to be divided: Bredin, 'Le secret du délibéré arbitral', in *Études Offertes à Pierre Bellet* (Litec, 1991), p. 71.
[166] ICSID Arbitration Rules, r. 47(3); ICSID Convention, Art. 48(4).
[167] See, e.g., *Bank Mellat v GAA Development Construction Co.* [1988] 2 Lloyd's Rep 44, *per* Steyn J, (1990) XV YBCA 521.

D. *Deliberations and Decisions of the Tribunal*

and it may be assumed that the draftsmen considered that no express provision was necessary. Nor do the ICDR or ICC Rules contain any provision relating to dissenting opinions.

The way in which dissenting opinions are be handled in ICC arbitrations is unique because of the provisions of the ICC Rules relating to scrutiny of awards.[168] Should the ICC Court 'scrutinise' the dissenting opinion—or, indeed, take any notice of it at all? At one time, the ICC discouraged the submission of dissenting opinions, but in 1985 a working party was set up to consider dissenting opinions, the final report of which was adopted in 1988.[169] The report did not attempt to rule out dissenting opinions; rather, it suggested that the only circumstances in which a dissenting opinion should not be sent to the parties with the award was where it is prohibited by law, or where the validity of the award might be imperiled, either in the place of arbitration or (to the extent that this could be foreseen) in the country of enforcement. The ICC has issued guidelines to its staff that reflect the conclusions of the working group and, in practice, dissenting opinions are sent out by the ICC with the majority award. **9.133**

(v) *Practice at the Iran–United States Claims Tribunal*

Separate and dissenting opinions were submitted by both the Iranian and US arbitrators in many reported cases. In one of these, the dissenting arbitrator went too far, when the dissenting judge indicated that the other two arbitrators had agreed with one of his views in deliberations.[170] In another case, problems were also caused when the dissenting opinion was issued after the majority decision was published and contained allegations of procedural misconduct on the part of the majority arbitrators.[171] The majority arbitrators felt compelled to file an additional opinion, whereupon the dissenting arbitrator continued the process by issuing yet another opinion. This was, in turn, followed by a second additional opinion by the chairman, who, whilst stating that he would make no further response, indicated that he considered this exceptional procedure to be necessary to vindicate the integrity of the tribunal and its staff, and to answer allegations that were factually incorrect. Acrimonious trading of allegations and insults could go on indefinitely, and it is clearly desirable that the arbitrators should disclose their concerns to each other in an exchange of draft opinions *before* the formal issue of the majority award and the dissenting opinion. **9.134**

---

[168] Discussed further in paragraph 9.202. Article 33 of the ICC Rules provides that no award shall be rendered by the arbitral tribunal until it has been approved by the ICC Court.
[169] ICC, *Final Report of the Working Party on Dissenting Opinions* (1991) 2 ICC International Court of Arbitration Bulletin 32.
[170] Decision of 7 May 2001, at 7.
[171] *Grainger Associates v Islamic Republic of Iran* (1987) 16 Iran–US CTR 317.

(vi) When and how should dissenting opinions be given in international arbitrations?

9.135 As already indicated, there is no tradition of dissenting opinions in civil law systems.[172] Dissenting opinions have come to international arbitration from the common law tradition and it is a disputed question whether they have added value to the arbitral process.[173] The traditional justification for dissenting opinions in common law judicial systems is that they may contribute to the development of the law. Although rare, there are examples of higher courts adopting dissenting opinions rather than the judgment of the majority. It might well be said—particularly by common lawyers—that if dissenting opinions can contribute in this way to a national judicial system of justice, why might they not also contribute to the system of international arbitration? To this, there are at least three responses.

9.136 First, in most cases, there is no appeal from the award of an arbitral tribunal and, moreover, there exists no system of *stare decisis* in international arbitration. A dissenting opinion cannot therefore inform an appellate arbitral jurisdiction nor will it guide future arbitral tribunals searching for the wisdom of precedent. Dissenting opinions therefore have far less to contribute to the arbitral process than to a common law judicial system. An exception to this may be in the context of ICSID arbitrations, in which the award is expressly defined to include any individual or dissenting opinions.[174]

9.137 Secondly, rather than contribute to the arbitral process, dissenting opinions may endanger the efficacy of the process by threatening the validity and enforceability of the award. One might imagine an argument in response to this concern along the following lines: if an award is flawed, then a dissenting arbitrator has a right—indeed perhaps even a duty—to provide ammunition that may assist the losing party in challenging the award. However, such an argument ignores the very purpose of an arbitration: to arrive at a determinative decision. Depending on the rules of arbitration agreed by the parties, that decision can be a majority decision or the decision of the presiding arbitrator alone. It is the *decision* that matters, and it matters not as a guide to the opinions of a particular arbitrator or as an indication of the future development of the law, but because it resolves the particular dispute that divides the parties, in the manner chosen by the parties, even if one of the arbitrators believes that decision to be wrong.

9.138 The third and final reason is more sensitive, and follows from the different way in which arbitrators—as opposed to judges—are appointed. Judges are appointed by the state. They do not depend in any way on the parties who appear before

---

[172] Lévy, 'Dissenting opinions in international arbitration in Switzerland' (1989) 5 Arb Intl 35, at 35.
[173] This question was asked and answered in Alan Redfern's 2003 Queen Mary College/Freshfields Lecture: Redfern, 'Dissenting opinions in international commercial arbitration: The good, the bad and the ugly' (2004) 20 Arb Intl 223.
[174] ICSID Arbitration Rules, r. 46.

them. In an international arbitration, by contrast, two of the three members of the tribunal will usually have been appointed (or nominated) by the parties. When a dissenting arbitrator disagrees with the majority, and does so in terms that favour the party that appointed him or her, it may cause some concern: does the dissent arise from an honest difference of opinion, or is it influenced by a desire to keep favour with the party that appointed the dissenting arbitrator? As one commentator has said:

> Certain arbitrators, so as not to lose the confidence of the company or the state which appointed them, will be tempted, if they have not put their point of view successfully in the course of the tribunal's deliberation, systematically to draw up a dissenting opinion and to insist that it be communicated to the parties.[175]

Other authors concur:

> Although party-appointed arbitrators are supposed to be impartial and independent in international arbitrations, some believe that with the availability of dissent, arbitrators may feel pressure to support the party that appointed them and to disclose that support.[176]

E. Form and Content of Awards

(a) Generally

9.139 The best awards are short, reasoned, and simply written in clear, unambiguous language. An arbitral tribunal should aim at rendering a correct, valid, and enforceable award. It may have to do so as a matter of legal duty to the parties, under some systems of law,[177] or it may be under an obligation to do so under rules of arbitration, such as those of the ICC, which state at Article 35 that an arbitral tribunal 'shall make every effort to make sure that the Award is enforceable at law'. Whether or not there is a legal obligation, the arbitral tribunal will want to do its best, as a matter of professional pride, to ensure that the award is enforceable: having been entrusted with the duty of determining a dispute for the parties, it will naturally wish to ensure that its duty is properly and effectively discharged.

9.140 A distinguished arbitrator has suggested that:

> A valid yardstick for assessing the diligence shown by the arbitrators in drawing up an arbitral award that is enforceable and likely to be recognised, is to apply the criteria established under the New York Convention, since compliance therewith will enable recognition and enforcement of the arbitral award in all the signatory countries. Consequently, no arbitral tribunal could be held responsible in a case

---

[175] De Boisséson, *Le Droit Français de l'Arbitrage National et International* (Joly, 1990), p. 802 (author's translation).
[176] Mosk and Ginsburg, *Dissenting Opinions in International Arbitration* (Liber Amicorum Bengt Broms, 1999), p. 275. See also De Boisséson, *Le Droit Français de l'Arbitrage National et International* (Joly, 1990), p. 802.
[177] See Chapter 5.

Award

where its decision was not recognised in a given country for failing to fulfil some mandatory requirement imposed by that country's domestic law, unless the parties had expressly advised the tribunal of this circumstance, which should rightly have been taken into account when the arbitral award was drawn up.[178]

9.141 The award of an international arbitral tribunal may be challenged in the courts of the juridical seat of arbitration.[179] In other circumstances, recognition and enforcement of the award may be refused by a competent court in the place(s) in which such recognition or enforcement is sought. This subject is discussed in detail later.[180] The point to be made here is that an arbitral tribunal should bear the possibilities of challenge and recourse in mind when drawing up its award. In the English procedure, the term 'reasoned award' is used to describe a form in which the arbitrator's reason are set out in the award and form part of it.[181] Against this background, the validity of an award must be considered under two headings: form and content.

(b) Form of the award

9.142 In general, the requirements of form are dictated by the arbitration agreement (including the rules of any arbitral institution chosen by the parties) and the law governing the arbitration (the *lex arbitri*).

(i) Arbitration agreement

9.143 It is necessary to check whether the arbitration agreement specifies any particular formalities for the award. In practice, this means examining any set of rules that the parties have adopted. The UNCITRAL Rules, for example, lay down the following requirements:

- the award shall be made in writing;
- the reasons upon which the award is based shall be stated;
- the award shall be signed by the arbitrators, and shall contain the date on which and the place where it was made; and
- where there are three arbitrators and one of them fails to sign, the award shall state the reason for the absence of the signature.[182]

9.144 The only arbitral institution that sets out the detailed obligations for an arbitrator when writing an award is ICSID. Rule 47 of the ICSID Rules states:

(1) The award shall be in writing and shall contain:
 (a) a precise designation of each party;
 (b) a statement that the Tribunal was established under the Convention, and a description of the method of its constitution;

---

[178] Cremades, 'The arbitral award', in Newman and Hill (eds) *The Leading Arbitrators' Guide to International Arbitration* (2nd edn, Juris, 2008), p. 500.
[179] Or, exceptionally, if the parties have agreed to subject the arbitration to the law of a 'foreign' country, in the courts of that country.
[180] See Chapter 11, paragraphs 11.55*ff*.
[181] Beresford-Hartwell, 'The reasoned award' (1988) 54 Arbitration 36, at 44.
[182] UNCITRAL Rules, Art. 34. See also Swiss Rules, Art. 32.

E. Form and Content of Awards

    (c) the name of each member of the Tribunal, and an identification of the appointing authority of each;
    (d) the names of the agents, counsel and advocates of the parties;
    (e) the dates and place of the sittings of the Tribunal;
    (f) a summary of the proceeding;
    (g) a statement of the facts as found by the Tribunal;
    (h) the submissions of the parties;
    (i) the decision of the Tribunal on every question submitted to it, together with the reasons upon which the decision is based; and
    (j) any decision of the Tribunal regarding the cost of the proceeding.
(2) The award shall be signed by the members of the Tribunal who voted for it; the date of each signature shall be indicated.
(3) Any member of the Tribunal may attach his individual opinion to the award, whether he dissents from the majority or not, or a statement of his dissent.

9.145 These two examples, drawn from institutional rules of arbitration, indicate the importance for the arbitral tribunal of checking the form (and contents) of its award against the relevant rules.

(ii) Law governing the arbitration

9.146 The requirements of form imposed by national systems of law vary from the comprehensive to the virtually non-existent. The Swiss Code of Civil Procedure, under Part III, which govern domestic arbitrations in Switzerland, lays down detailed requirements,[183] but for international cases, these are narrowed to just four—namely, that the award be in writing, reasoned, dated, and signed.[184] Section 52 of the English Arbitration Act 1996 follows the same lines:

(1) The parties are free to agree on the form of an award.
(2) If or to the extent that there is no such agreement, the following provisions apply.
(3) The award shall be in writing signed by all the arbitrators or all those assenting to the award.
(4) The award shall contain the reasons for the award unless it is an agreed award or the parties have agreed to dispense with reasons.
(5) The award shall state the seat of the arbitration and the date when the award is made.

(iii) Introductory section of an award

9.147 Awards will often begin by setting out the names and addresses of the parties, and the names and contact details of their representatives. The award will then usually contain a brief narrative setting out a number of facts relating to the arbitration. These may include an identification of the arbitration agreement or document containing the arbitration clause, a brief description of the disputes that have arisen between the parties, the relief claimed, and the way in which the arbitral tribunal

---

[183] Swiss Code of Civil Procedure, Pt III, art. 384.
[184] Swiss PIL, Ch 12, s. 189.

(iv) Signatures

9.148 Some national systems of law require that all arbitrators should sign the award in order for it to be valid.[186] This is highly unsatisfactory, since, in such cases, a dissenting arbitrator may frustrate an arbitration simply by refusing to sign the award. Any country the law of which contains such a mandatory rule without any means of 'rescue' is unsuitable for international arbitration.[187] Formalities with regards to signature have survived in the United Arab Emirates (UAE), for example, and are important to follow. A 2009 decision by the Dubai Court of Cassation[188] distinguished between awards in which the grounds were included in the same document as the award itself and awards in which the grounds and the award were in separate documents. It was held that arbitrators can sign the final page on which the award appears if it is attached to the grounds; if they are in separate documents, then the Court held that the award must be signed as well as *each* page of the award by all of the arbitrators. In practice, arbitrators sitting in arbitration proceedings in the UAE normally sign every page of the award.

9.149 The rules of arbitration of the major international arbitral institutions all deal expressly or impliedly with signature of the award. The ICC Rules make it clear that the award must be signed, but that the award of a majority of the arbitrators or, if there is no majority, the award of the presiding arbitrator alone is effective.[189] A similar provision is found in the LCIA Rules.[190]

(v) Language of the award

9.150 The award will normally be rendered in the language of the arbitration, although occasionally it may be made either in the language that is the *de facto* working language of the arbitral tribunal or in the language that is most convenient for the parties.[191] Any mandatory rule of law of the place of arbitration concerning the language of the award must be respected. It is a condition of recognition and enforcement under the New York Convention that a foreign arbitral award must

---

[185] Ibid.
[186] See Paulsson and Bosman (eds) *ICCA International Handbook on Commercial Arbitration* (Kluwer Law International, 1984).
[187] This situation does not apply to countries such as Switzerland, which require an award to be signed, but allow for the signature of the majority or the presiding arbitrator, as the case may be: Swiss PIL, Ch. 12, s. 189(2); Swiss Rules, Art. 32(4).
[188] Dubai Court of Cassation, Petition No. 156/2009.
[189] ICC Rules, Art. 31(1).
[190] LCIA Rules, Art. 26(4).
[191] See, e.g., United Nations Economic Commission for Europe (UNECE) Arbitration Rules for Certain Categories of Perishable Agricultural Products, Art. 29.

E. Form and Content of Awards

be accompanied by an officially certified translation into the language of the place in which recognition or enforcement of the award is sought, when this is not the language of the award.[192]

(c) Contents of the award

The contents of an award, like its form, are dictated primarily by the arbitration agreement and the law governing the arbitration (the *lex arbitri*). **9.151**

(i) Arbitration agreement

Arbitration agreements usually provide that the award is to be final and binding upon the parties. It follows that the award should deal with all matters referred to arbitration, in so far as they have not been dealt with by any interim or partial awards. However, arbitration agreements rarely go on to describe the content of the award; the nearest they get is to incorporate a set of arbitration rules. Such rules invariably also provide that the award should deal with such matters as the costs of the arbitration[193] and the payment of interest. The rules may also provide that the award shall state the reasons upon which it is based.[194] Even if not specifically required, the giving of reasons is a practice that should be followed unless there is some very good reason why it should not be.[195] **9.152**

(ii) Unambiguous

Most national systems of law require an award to be unambiguous and dispositive. Ambiguity is often capable of being cured, either by the arbitral tribunal interpreting the award at the request of the parties (or occasionally at the request of only one of them),[196] or by an application to the relevant national court for an order that the award should be remitted to the arbitral tribunal for clarification. The position is similar where the award contains provisions that are inconsistent. **9.153**

(iii) Determination of the issues

An award must also be *dispositive*, in that it must constitute an effective determination of the issues in dispute. It is not sufficient for the arbitral tribunal to issue a vague expression of opinion. The award must be formulated in an imperative tone: 'we award', 'we direct', 'we order', or the equivalent.[197] **9.154**

---

[192] New York Convention, Art. IV(2).
[193] See, e.g., UNCITRAL Rules, Art. 40; ICC Rules, Art. 37; LCIA Rules, Art. 28(2).
[194] See, e.g., UNCITRAL Rules, Art. 34(3); ICSID Arbitration Rules, r. 47(1)(i).
[195] For further discussion on this topic, see paragraphs 9.157*ff*.
[196] See paragraph 9.186.
[197] This is less important with a declaratory award, which, by its nature, is not enforceable per se. Nevertheless, a declaratory award should be clear as to its findings if it is to be of real assistance to the parties.

9.155 Equally, if there is more than one respondent and a monetary award is made in favour of the claimant, it is essential for the arbitral tribunal to make it clear whether one of the respondents, and if so, which one, has the obligation to make the payment, or whether the obligation is joint and several.

9.156 An award should not direct the parties to perform an illegal act or require the parties to do anything that may be considered contrary to public policy,[198] nor may the award contain any directions that are outside the scope of authority of the arbitral tribunal.

(iv) Reasons

9.157 The way in which reasons are given in arbitral awards varies considerably. Sometimes, the reasoning, or 'motivation', is set out with extreme brevity. However, a mere statement that the arbitral tribunal accepted the evidence of one party and rejected the evidence of the other, which was common practice for some arbitrators, had rightly fallen into disrepute by the end of the twentieth century. Certainly, such a practice would be regarded as being defective as a matter of form by the ICC Court. In other cases, awards may run into hundreds of pages, including a detailed review of the evidence and arguments put forward by the parties, followed by a closely reasoned conclusion.

9.158 Even in modern times, there are arbitrations in which providing reasons is likely to seem superfluous. An arbitrator in a quality arbitration, for example, who is asked to decide whether goods supplied do or do not correspond to sample, can hardly do more than answer 'yes' or 'no'.

9.159 The ICSID Convention calls for a reasoned award, without any exceptions,[199] and in practice the ICC Court deems awards that are insufficiently reasoned to be defective as to form. They are therefore remitted to the arbitral tribunal for amendment before they can be approved in accordance with Article 33 of the ICC Rules. The UNCITRAL Rules take the same approach as the Model Law: reasons should be given, unless the parties agree otherwise.[200]

9.160 The general consensus in favour of a reasoned, or 'motivated', award is reflected in the European Convention on International Commercial Arbitration of 1961, Article VIII of which states:

> The parties shall be presumed to have agreed that reasons shall be given for the award unless they
> (a) either expressly declare that reasons shall not be given; or

---

[198] However, since public policy considerations vary from country to country, it may be difficult to avoid this in all cases, e.g. an award of interest may be acceptable in the country in which the award is made, but not in the country of enforcement.
[199] ICSID Convention, Art. 48(3).
[200] UNCITRAL Rules, Art. 34(3).

(b) have assented to an arbitral procedure under which it is not customary to give reasons for awards, provided that in this case neither party requests before the end of the hearing, or if there has not been a hearing then before the making of the award, that reasons be given.

(v) Different ways of giving reasons

The general practice of arbitral tribunals in international cases is to devote more time and space in the award to giving the reasons for its determination of the legal arguments than to a review of the factual issues. This is not surprising, since most arbitral tribunals in international cases are composed of lawyers.[201] However, it should be borne in mind by such tribunals that what is needed is an intelligible decision, rather than a legal dissertation. The object should be to keep the reasons for a decision as concise as possible, according to the nature of the dispute. The parties want to read the essential *reasoning* underlying the decision, not a lesson in the law.[202]

9.161

(d) Time limits

A limit may be imposed as to the time within which the arbitral tribunal must make its award. When this limit is reached, the authority or mandate of the arbitral tribunal is at an end and it no longer has jurisdiction to make a valid award. This means that, where a time limit exists, care must be taken to see that either the time limit is observed, or the time limit is extended before it expires. The purpose of time limits is to ensure that the case is dealt with speedily. Such limits may be imposed on the arbitral tribunal by the rules of an arbitral institution, by the relevant law, or by agreement of the parties.

9.162

The laws of a number of countries provide for time limits within which an award must be made, sometimes starting from the date upon which the arbitration itself commenced. In India, the Arbitration and Conciliation Act 1996 has dispensed with the time limit that was imposed by the previous law. In the United States, the position varies from state to state. In some states, the limit is thirty days from the date on which the hearings are closed. However, time limits in the United States may also be extended by mutual agreement of the parties or by court order.

9.163

It is important that a fixed time limit for rendering the award should not enable one of the parties to frustrate the arbitration. This might happen if a fixed limit were to run from the date of the appointment of the arbitral tribunal, rather than, for example, that of the end of the hearings. If a court has no power to intervene on the

9.164

---

[201] Even where the party-nominated arbitrators are technical specialists, expert in the subject matter of the project or transaction, it is usual for the presiding arbitrator to be a lawyer.
[202] See Lord Bingham, *The Business of Judging* (Oxford University Press, 2000). For the risks that the alleged absence of reasons may lead to an arbitral award being overturned, see Redfern, 'ICSID: Losing its appeal?' (1987) 3 Arb Intl 98.

application of one party alone and the time limit can be extended only by agreement of the parties, a party might frustrate the proceedings simply by refusing to agree to any extension of time. However, the courts of many countries would be reluctant to invalidate a late award in such a case. For example, in New York, it was held that an untimely award was not a nullity, even though the issue of timeliness was properly raised: the court stated that, without a finding of prejudice, there was no justification for denying confirmation of the award.[203]

(i) Disadvantages of mandatory time limits

9.165 It is rare to find time limits for delivery of the award in non-institutional rules. Where such limits are imposed, it is usually by an express agreement between the parties, contained in the arbitration clause or the submission agreement. Undoubtedly, such a provision is inserted with the intention of putting pressure on the arbitral tribunal to complete its work with due despatch and in order to minimise the opportunities for delaying the resolution of disputes by the parties themselves. However, it is a strategy that may well prove to be counterproductive. In most substantial international cases before an arbitral tribunal consisting of three arbitrators, it is usually impracticable to complete the arbitration within such a short period of time as three or six months. The result is that the arbitral tribunal may be forced into a situation in which, in order to comply with the time limit, it must issue its award without giving the respondent a proper opportunity to present its case. Such an award is vulnerable to an action for nullity or to a successful defence to enforcement proceedings. Thus the successful party finds that, far from the time limit having assisted in a speedy resolution of the dispute, it contributes to overall delay and ineffectiveness in the arbitral process.[204] In addition, certain arbitral institutions have introduced simplified or expedited procedures for the conduct of an international arbitration, and a standard feature of these procedures is a provision for the award to be made within a relatively short time.[205]

9.166 In general, it is preferable that no time limit should be prescribed for the making of the award in an arbitration clause or submission agreement. However, if the parties consider it desirable to set a limit, or if it is necessary to do so under the applicable law, the time limit should, if possible, be related to the closure of the hearings and not to the appointment of the arbitral tribunal, or to some other stage in the arbitration at which the respondent will have opportunities to create

---

[203] *State of New York Department of Taxation and Finance v Valenti* 57 AD 2d 174, 393 NYS 2d 797 (1977).
[204] For a potential horror story, see *Staatsrechtliche v ICC Schiedsgerichtsentschied*, Bundesgericht, I. Zivilabteilung (Federal Court, First Civil Division), 24 March 1997, (1997) 2 ASA Bulletin 316. For commentary, see Kreindler and Kautz, 'Agreed deadlines and the setting aside of arbitral awards' (1997) 4 ASA Bulletin 576.
[205] See Chapters 1 and 6.

E. Form and Content of Awards

delay. A provision that the award must be issued within a certain time after the closure of the hearings helps to ensure that the arbitral tribunal proceeds diligently with its task. It is frustrating for the parties if the arbitral tribunal takes many months to deliberate and to issue its award. However, any time limit should be realistic and not merely one that incites the arbitral tribunal to make the award in too great a hurry, thus potentially exposing the award to a successful challenge.

(ii) Non-mandatory provisions

9.167 Perhaps the best way in which the parties can put time pressure on an arbitral tribunal, without placing the effectiveness of the proceedings at risk, is to insert some form of non-mandatory provision. In one ICC case,[206] the arbitration clause contained a provision to the effect that 'the parties wish that the award shall be issued within five months of the date of the appointment of the third arbitrator'.

9.168 The arbitral tribunal considered it necessary to clarify the position and, at its request, the parties confirmed that this provision:

- superseded the provision of Article 18(1) of the then applicable 1998 ICC Rules, which provided that the award was to be made within six months of the signing of the terms of reference; and
- did not affect the power of the ICC Court to extend the time limit provided for by the parties, in accordance with Article 18(2) of the then applicable 1998 ICC Rules.

In effect, therefore, the parties set a *target* for the arbitral tribunal in their arbitration agreement, without imposing any mandatory provision that might have placed at risk the effectiveness of that agreement.

(e) Notification of awards

9.169 International and institutional rules of arbitration generally make provision for the notification of the award to the parties. The UNCITRAL Rules provide, at Article 34(6), that '[c]opies of the award signed by the arbitrators shall be communicated to the parties by the arbitral tribunal'. However, no time limit is imposed within which this must be done. The position is similar under the ICSID Arbitration Rules, Rule 48(1) of which merely states that a certified copy of the award (including individual opinions and statements of dissent) will be sent to the parties 'promptly' when the last arbitrator has signed it. Article 34(1) of the ICC Rules provides that the Secretariat will notify the parties once an award has been made, provided that the costs have been fully paid.

---

[206] ICC Case No. 5051.

9.170 That party which expects to have won the case will invariably make it its business to obtain a copy of the award as soon as practicable, either directly from the arbitral tribunal or from the relevant arbitral institution. If that party has won, it will immediately communicate the award to the unsuccessful party. The time limit within which a party may apply to the appropriate court for recourse against the award often runs from the date of communication of the award and not from the making of the award itself.[207] If this were not so, the possibility of injustice would arise: the arbitral tribunal might make its award and then fail to communicate it to the unsuccessful party until after the time limit for recourse had expired. However, the position should be checked under the law of the place in which recourse may be sought, which is normally the place of arbitration.

(f) Registration or deposit of awards

9.171 In some countries, it may be necessary to register or deposit the award with the national court, generally on payment of an appropriate fee.[208] In other countries, registration for the purposes of recognition by the courts is optional. In some, it may be a necessary prelude to enforcement of a foreign award. In such cases, there may be an element of 'double *exequatur*', which has been strongly criticised by the ICC and by the draftsmen of the New York Convention, amongst others.[209] The principle on which the New York Convention is based is that the award needs only to be binding on the parties in order for it to be enforceable. Nonetheless, registration is a matter that may affect the validity of the award if the mandatory provisions of the place in which the arbitration is held require it.[210] Where the requirement is mandatory, it *must* be deposited in order to protect the validity of the award.

9.172 Even when it is not mandatory, registration or deposit of an award may be desirable in order to put pressure on the unsuccessful party. In some cases, registration of the award is relevant for the purposes of the time limit within which any application for nullification of the award must be made. Although registration will not necessarily assist the successful party in relation to enforcement actions in other countries, it may protect the award from any further challenge in the country in which the arbitration took place.

---

[207] For example, in England, communication of the award to the parties is an essential ingredient, since the time limits for challenging an award run from its delivery to the parties: see Arbitration Act 1996, ss 55(2) and 70(3).

[208] For example, Germany, India, and Indonesia: see Paulsson and Bosman (eds) *ICCA International Handbook on Commercial Arbitration* (Kluwer Law International, 1984).

[209] See Chapter 11.

[210] This must be considered separately from any requirement for the deposit of the award with an arbitral institution.

F. Effect of Awards

(a) *Res judicata*

9.173 The basic principle of *res judicata* is that a legal right or obligation, or any facts, specifically put in issue and determined by a court or tribunal of competent jurisdiction cannot later be put back into question as between the same parties.[211]

9.174 Despite general recognition, the application of the principle of *res judicata* varies as between jurisdictions. In common law jurisdictions, the estoppel of *res judicata* broadly falls into two categories: cause-of-action estoppel, which prevents either party from relitigating the same action against the other; and issue estoppel, which prevents a party from questioning or denying an issue already decided in previous proceedings between the parties. Many civil law jurisdictions apply *res judicata* only as a cause-of-action estoppel, and the estoppel is said to attach only to the dispositive part of the judgment/award, not to the reasons. This is strictly applied in Switzerland, Germany, and Sweden, but less so in France, Belgium, the Netherlands, and Italy.[212]

9.175 Given the difficulties that can arise as a result of the varying interpretations of the principle of *res judicata*, the International Commercial Arbitration Committee of the International Law Association (ILA) set about creating a transnational body of rules that could be referred to as guidance, or adopted by the parties if they so choose, in international arbitrations. Since 2004, the Committee has published interim and final reports on *res judicata* and *lis pendens*, and, at the same time as its final report, the Committee adopted its Recommendations on *Lis Pendens* and *Res Judicata* and Arbitration.[213] In setting forth a transnational approach, the Committee commented in its final report that:

> *Res judicata* regarding international arbitral awards should not necessarily be equated to *res judicata* effects of judgments of state courts and, thus, may be treated differently than *res judicata* under domestic law. International arbitral awards in accordance with the Recommendations are to be treated differently than judgments. This is due to the differences between international arbitration and domestic court dispute settlement, as well as to the international character of arbitration, which should not be reduced to domestic notions regarding *res*

---

[211] See the award in *Amco Asia Corporation v Indonesia (Resubmission: Jurisdiction)*, ICSID Case No. ARB/81/1, (1992) 89 ILR 552, at 560.

[212] In France, Belgium, and the Netherlands, recourse can be had to the reasons in order to explain the meaning and scope of the *dispositif*. In Italy, certain cases suggest that *res judicata* may include the entire reasoning. See, in this regard, ILA, *Interim Report on* Res Judicata *and Arbitration* (2009) 25 Intl Arb 1, at 51, 52, and 65.

[213] The ILA interim report, the final report, and the ILA Recommendations can all be found at (2009) 25 Arb Intl or online at http://www.ila-hq.org.

judicata that are valid in a domestic setting but are hardly appropriate in an international context.[214]

9.176 The doctrine of *res judicata* can be applicable in international arbitration in a variety of ways. Broadly, there are three different aspects of *res judicata*: first, the effect of an award on existing disputes between the parties; secondly, its effect on subsequent disputes between the parties; and thirdly, its effect on third parties.

(b) Existing disputes

9.177 As far as the parties themselves are concerned, it is clear that (subject to challenge before a competent court) the award disposes of those disputes between the parties that were submitted to arbitration.[215] This even extends to cases in which the arbitrators acted as *amiables compositeurs*.[216] If one party were to bring a court or arbitral action against the other in relation to the subject matter of the arbitration, based on the same cause of action between the same parties, the court or tribunal would dismiss the action on the ground that the issues had been disposed of and were *res judicata*.[217] In the United States, courts have often applied *res judicata* (also referred to as 'claim preclusion') to bar claims that could have been, but were not, asserted in a prior arbitral proceeding. However, if the award is deemed invalid and is set aside by a court of competent jurisdiction, the nullified award does not operate as *res judicata* in any subsequent proceedings. An example of this is the *Pyramids* arbitration, in which the claimant started an ICSID arbitration after the award in the ICC arbitration was nullified in the French courts.[218]

9.178 The ILA's Committee has endorsed this basic application of *res judicata*, which depends on the 'triple identity test' (the same parties, the same subject matter, and same claim for relief). In particular, Recommendation 3 of Part II of the ILA Recommendations provides as follows:

> 3. An arbitral award has conclusive and preclusive effects in further arbitral proceedings if:
> - it has become final and binding in the country of origin and there is no impediment to recognition in the country of the place of subsequent arbitration;

---

[214] ILA, *Final Report on Res Judicata and Arbitration* (2009) 25 Intl Arb 72, para. 25.
[215] See the commentary on the award in ICC Case No. 3383, Jarvin and Derains, *Collection of ICC Arbitral Awards 1974–1985* (Kluwer Law International, 1994), pp. 394 and 397.
[216] Söderlund, '*Lis pendens, res judicata* and the issue of parallel judicial proceedings' (2005) 22 J Intl Arb 4.
[217] In France, arts 1476 and 1500 of the *Nouveau Code de Procédure Civile* provide that an arbitral award has a *res judicata* effect with respect to the dispute that it determines. Similar provisions also exist in Belgium, Spain, Germany, Austria, and Switzerland. See Hanotiau, 'The *res judicata* effect of arbitral awards' (2003) *Supplement* ICC International Court of Arbitration Bulletin 43.
[218] For further discussion of the *Pyramids* arbitration, see Chapter 11.

F. Effect of Awards

- it has decided on or disposed of a claim for relief which is sought or is being reargued in the further arbitration proceedings;
- it is based upon a cause of action which is invoked in the further arbitration proceedings or which forms the basis for the subsequent arbitration proceedings; and
- it has been rendered between the same parties.

(c) Subsequent disputes

9.179 Where there are subsequent disputes between the same parties, more difficult questions arise. Because there is no doctrine of *stare decisis* in arbitration, the previous decision of an arbitral tribunal will not be binding on any subsequent disputes that arise between the same parties over different subject matter or a different cause of action (even if related). But it does not follow that a previous decision will necessarily be irrelevant to the resolution of a subsequent dispute between the same parties. It is necessary to consider the principle of issue estoppel. This precludes a party in subsequent proceedings from contradicting an issue of fact or the legal consequences of a fact that has already been raised and decided in earlier proceedings between the same parties, even if the causes of action in both proceedings are not identical.[219]

9.180 By way of example, the English Privy Council decided that, notwithstanding a confidentiality agreement concluded by the parties to an arbitration not to disclose material generated therein to third parties, an award rendered in that arbitration could be relied upon by one of the parties in a subsequent arbitration to found a plea of issue estoppel. The second arbitration took place between the same parties and concerned the same clause under the same reinsurance agreement as the first arbitration. In so finding, the Privy Council reasoned that relying on an issue estoppel in a subsequent arbitration was 'a species of the enforcement of the rights given by the [previous] award' and that this legitimate use of the earlier award was not a breach of the confidentiality agreement.[220] In the same way, US courts have also invoked principles of collateral estoppel, or 'issue preclusion', to exclude issues raised in litigation that were previously adjudicated fully and fairly during an arbitration, and vice versa.[221]

---

[219] Cremades and Madalena, 'Parallel proceedings in international arbitration' (2008) 24 Arb Intl 4, at 507; Sheppard, 'Res judicata and estoppel', in ICC (ed.) *Parallel State and Arbitral Procedures in International Arbitration*, ICC Publications No. 692 (ICC, 2005), p. 225; Barnett, *Res Judicata, Estoppel, and Foreign Judgments: The Preclusive Effects of Foreign Judgments in Private International Law* (Oxford University Press, 2001), p. 135.

[220] *Associated Electric and Gas Insurance Services Ltd v European Reinsurance Co. of Zurich* [2003] 1 WLR 1041.

[221] *In the matter of petition of Gemstar TV Guide International Inc. v Henry C Yuen*, Index No. 602094/07, NY Sup., New York Co., NY Misc LEXIS 7845 (2007).

9.181 The ILA Committee has endorsed the application of 'issue estoppel' in international arbitration,[222] including as Recommendations 4 and 5 of Part II of the ILA Recommendations as follows:

> 4. An arbitral award has conclusive and preclusive effects in the further arbitral proceedings as to:
> - Determinations and relief contained in its dispositive part as well as in all reasoning necessary thereto;
> - Issues of fact or law which have actually been arbitrated and determined by it, provided any such determination was essential or fundamental to the dispositive part of the arbitral award.
> 5. An arbitral award has preclusive effects in the further arbitral proceedings as to a claim, cause of action or issue of fact or law, which could have been raised, but was not, in the proceedings resulting in that award, provided that the raising of any such new claim, cause of action or new issue of fact or law amounts to procedural unfairness or abuse.

(d) Effect of award on third parties

9.182 An arbitral tribunal has no power to make orders or to give directions against someone who is not a party to the arbitration agreement, unless that party has in some way acquiesced in a manner that, without actually making him or her a party to the arbitration agreement, indicates an intention on his or her part to be bound by the award.

9.183 It follows that an award can neither directly confer rights nor impose obligations upon a person who is not a party to the arbitration agreement. For example, the award of an arbitral tribunal in the main arbitration between an employer and a contractor under a building contract does not have the effect of *res judicata* in respect of a claim for an indemnity by the contractor against its subcontractor in a subsequent arbitration. Although the facts in both arbitrations may be substantially the same, the second arbitral tribunal may come to a different conclusion from the first—and there is very little that the subcontractor can do apart from agreeing (with the consent of both parties to the main arbitration) to be joined as an additional party in the main arbitration. This gives the subcontractor the right to present evidence and argument in relation to any claims that affected it.[223]

9.184 Nonetheless, an award may often have a significant *indirect* effect on persons who were not parties to the arbitration. For example, a third party may be affected by an award where one person is jointly liable with another who is a party to the arbitration. The award would not be *res judicata* in any subsequent claim against that third party, but it should be of persuasive significance in that a tribunal is likely to

---

[222] ILA, *Final Report on Res Judicata and Arbitration* (2009) 25 Intl Arb 72, at 77; ILA Recommendations on *Lis Pendens* and *Res Judicata* and Arbitration, Pt II, paras 4 and 5, (2009) 25 Intl Arb 1, at 85.

[223] For further discussion of consolidation of arbitrations, see Chapter 2, paragraph 2.238.

G. Proceedings after the Award

consider the findings of the earlier award to inform its own findings. Conversely, it is possible that an award (even if unsatisfied) against one of the persons who was jointly liable would have the effect of discharging the third party's liability. Finally, where an award orders performance (for example in relation to the delivery of property by one of the parties), it is doubtful whether it is effective if the property concerned is temporarily in the hands of a third party under a licence.

In the United States, issue estoppel can, in certain circumstances, be relied upon in subsequent litigation involving a different party.[224] Further, in both the United States and England, certain parties that are closely linked to the original parties might be bound by an earlier award where the connection is close enough to establish privity between such parties. In an English case, the court held that a director of the claimant company was a privy of the company and therefore had an interest in the arbitration.[225] It has been argued in the international sphere that 'sister companies' constituting a single 'economic entity' should all be bound by the *res judicata* effect of an award involving one of those companies.[226] The ILA Committee noted, in its interim report, that ICSID tribunals have followed this 'single economic entity' analysis in relation to questions of jurisdiction, and asked whether it might also usefully be relied upon in relation to *res judicata* in order to prevent companies from a corporate group 'endlessly re-litigat[ing] the same dispute under the disguise of formally separate legal identities'.[227] However, for the time being, this approach has not been adopted and the ILA has made no recommendation in this regard.

9.185

G. Proceedings after the Award

Exceptions to the general rule that an arbitral tribunal becomes *functus officio* on the issue of a final award arise from specific provisions of the national system of law governing the arbitration, from the parties' arbitration agreement, or from any rules of arbitration adopted by them.[228]

9.186

The 'interpretation', or 'clarification', of a final award is a different matter. The Model Law provides for interpretation of a specific point or a part of the award *only* when the parties agree that such a request should be made to the tribunal.[229] The problem with 'interpretation', as opposed to 'correction', of an award is that it risks giving the aggrieved party an opportunity to reopen the case.

9.187

---

[224] See, e.g., *Parklane Hoisery Co. v Shore* 439 US 322 (1979); ILA, *Interim Report on* Res Judicata *and Arbitration* (2009) 25 Intl Arb 1, at 48.
[225] *Dadourian Group International Inc. v Simms and ors* [2004] EWHC 450 (Ch), [2004] Arb LR 17, with commentary in 'The effect of an arbitration award' (2005) 5 Arb LM 4.
[226] ILA, *Interim Report on* Res Judicata *and Arbitration* (2009) 25 Intl Arb 1, at 21.
[227] Ibid., at 58 and 59.
[228] See Chapter 10.
[229] Model Law, Art. 33(1)(b). See also the English Arbitration Act 1996, s. 57(3).

(a) Under national law

9.188 Many systems of national law with developed arbitral rules permit the correction of minor clerical or typographical errors in awards, either at the request of one or both of the parties, or by the arbitral tribunal on its own initiative. For example, in England, this power is conferred expressly by statute. Section 57 of the Arbitration Act 1996 provides:

> (1) The parties are free to agree on the powers of the tribunal to correct an award or make an additional award.
> (2) If or to the extent there is no such agreement, the following provisions apply.
> (3) The tribunal may on its own initiative or on the application of a party:
>> (a) correct an award so as to remove any clerical mistake or error arising from an accidental slip or omission or clarify or remove any ambiguity in the award, or
>> (b) make an additional award in respect of any claim (including a claim for interest or costs) which was presented to the tribunal but was not dealt with in the award.
>
> These powers shall not be exercised without first affording the other parties a reasonable opportunity to make representations to the tribunal.[230]
>
> [...]

9.189 The US Federal Arbitration Act of 1925 (FAA) provides that the relevant district court may make an order modifying or correcting errors.[231] The grounds for modifying or correcting an award include 'evident material miscalculation', 'evident material mistake', and 'imperfect[ions] in a manner of form not affecting the merits'.[232] Similar provisions are contained in the arbitration statutes of many individual states in the United States, some of which also permit corrections and modifications on the initiative of the arbitral tribunal. Additionally, in some countries, the arbitral tribunal may complete the award where a determination of a claim, or ruling as to costs, has been omitted.[233]

(b) Under rules of arbitration

9.190 Exceptions to the general rule of *functus officio* vary considerably under different sets of arbitration rules. The LCIA Rules contain an express power for the arbitral tribunal to correct accidental mistakes or omissions, but not to make interpretations of awards.[234] Prior to 1998, the ICC Rules did not mention either correction or interpretation. This was presumably on the basis that the process of scrutiny under

---

[230] For an example of how and when awards can be considered under s. 57, see *Gold Coast Ltd v Naval Gijon SA* [2006] EWHC 1044 (Comm), [2006] Arb LR 381.
[231] FAA, § 11.
[232] FAA, § 11(c). See *Hall Street Associates LLC v Mattel Inc.* 552 US 576 (2008).
[233] For the powers of an arbitral tribunal to correct or complete an award in various national states, see the national reports in Paulsson and Bosman (eds) *ICCA International Handbook on Commercial Arbitration* (Kluwer Law International, 1984).
[234] LCIA Rules, Art. 27.

G. Proceedings after the Award

Article 21 of the previous version of the Rules should be sufficient to ensure that all mistakes would be identified. However, the 2012 Rules contain the following provision:

> On its own initiative, the arbitral tribunal may correct a clerical, computational or typographical error, or any errors of similar nature contained in an award, provided such correction is submitted for approval to the Court within 30 days of the date of such award.[235]

Similarly, the SCC Rules contain an explicit provision granting the arbitral tribunal power to give a written interpretation of its award at the request of a party, in addition to the power to correct clerical errors: **9.191**

> Within 30 days of receiving an award, a party may, upon notice to the other party, request that the Arbitral Tribunal correct any clerical, typographical or computational errors in the award, or provide an interpretation of a specific point or part of the award. If the Arbitral Tribunal considers the request justified, it shall make the correction or provide the interpretation within 30 days of receiving the request.[236]

The UNCITRAL Rules contain powers for the arbitral tribunal to correct its award, issue additional awards, and interpret its award (if so requested) within narrow time limits. The *correction* of an award (normally in relation to clerical or typographical errors) may take place either at the request of the party or on the initiative of the arbitral tribunal itself.[237] Yet the arbitral tribunal may issue an interpretation only at the request of a party, not on its own initiative.[238] Similarly, the arbitral tribunal may issue an additional award only at the request of a party.[239] The purpose of the provision relating to additional awards is to ensure that the arbitrators may complete their mission if they have omitted from their award decisions in relation to any of the claims presented in the proceedings. Time limits for complying with each of these provisions are set out in the relevant Articles. In each case, the provisions of Article 34, relating to the formalities required in making an award, must be observed. **9.192**

Where the arbitral tribunal is asked to issue an interpretation of its award,[240] whether under the UNCITRAL Rules or otherwise,[241] this may pose difficulties **9.193**

---

[235] ICC Rules, Art. 35(1). For a comprehensive survey of applications for correction and/or interpretation of awards under the ICC Rules that have been made since the introduction of Art. 29, see Brooks Daly, 'Correction and interpretation of arbitral awards under the ICC Rules of Arbitration' (2002) 13 ICC International Court of Arbitration Bulletin 1.
[236] SCC Rules, Art. 41(1).
[237] UNCITRAL Rules, Art. 38(2).
[238] UNCITRAL Rules, Art. 37(1). Curiously, Art. 37(2) does not contain the express safeguard for the arbitral tribunal that appears in Art. 39(2), '[i]f the arbitral tribunal considers the request for an award or additional award to be justified'. But common sense dictates that the literal language meaning of Art. 37(2) could not be used to force the arbitral tribunal to give an interpretation, at least when it considers the request to be spurious.
[239] UNCITRAL Rules, Art. 39(1).
[240] In a case in which one of the authors was an arbitrator, the losing respondent requested an interpretation, but the arbitral tribunal determined that this was a manifest attempt by that party to cause the arbitral tribunal to review its decision on the merits of the case.
[241] The ICDR Rules, Art. 30, contain similar provisions to those of the UNCITRAL Rules.

for the tribunal. Its members will have to recapitulate their thinking as best they can and clarify what is unclear—unless they take the view that the request is without substance and may be dealt with in a summary manner.

9.194 The ICSID Arbitration Rules go further than those of other arbitral institutions. They permit applications for the award to be interpreted and revised not only by the original arbitral tribunal,[242] but also, if that arbitral tribunal cannot be reconstituted, by a new one specially appointed for the purpose.[243] This is a cumbersome procedure, but it appears to be part of the price to be paid for the self-contained and autonomous nature of ICSID arbitrations, which means that even obvious errors may be corrected only within the system and not by an outside authority such as a national court.[244]

(c) Review procedures other than by national courts

9.195 Challenging awards in national courts is considered in Chapter 10. However, in a limited number of cases, there may be a prior review of awards by some other authority. The main instances in which this arises are as follows. First, in certain specialised types of arbitration, particularly in the commodity trades, there is usually provision for either party to appeal to a specially constituted arbitral appeals tribunal.[245] Secondly, in a small number of countries, parties may raise an objection to an award before a body other than a national court. One example is Saudi Arabia, where a party can submit an objection to the Committee for the Settlement of Commercial Disputes. Thirdly, in the ICC system, the award must not be signed by the arbitral tribunal until it has been scrutinised by the ICC Court. This provision, which has provoked some controversy, states:

> Before signing any award, the arbitral tribunal shall submit it in draft form to the Court. The Court may lay down modifications as to the form of the award and, without affecting the arbitral tribunal's liberty of decision, may also draw its attention to points of substance. No award shall be rendered by the arbitral tribunal until it has been approved by the Court as to its form.[246]

It calls for two different standards of review: the first is as to *form*, with respect to which the ICC Court may 'lay down' modifications; the second is as to points of *substance*, which the ICC Court may only 'draw to the attention' of the arbitrator.

9.196 The review of awards by the ICC Court causes concern to some arbitrators, who consider it unnecessary and time-consuming. It also arouses suspicion on the part of some parties, who fear that the case will be reviewed by a 'court' before which

---

[242] ICSID Arbitration Rules, rr 50–52.
[243] ICSID Arbitration Rules, r. 51(3).
[244] For an example of the relevant ICSID Rules in practice, see *Marvin Feldman v Mexico*, Correction and Interpretation of the Award, ICSID Case No. ARB(AF)/99/1, IIC 158 (2003).
[245] See Chapter 10, paragraph 10.75.
[246] ICC Rules, Art. 33.

they have had no opportunity of presenting their cases. However, the Swiss Federal Court has ruled that this particular provision of the ICC Rules does not contravene Swiss law. By adopting the Rules, the parties have agreed that the ICC Court should act as the auxiliary of the arbitral tribunal in relation to the form of the award and as adviser to the tribunal in relation to the substance of the award.[247]

The advantages and disadvantages of the ICC's scrutiny process were subject to extensive consultation and debate in the period preceding the formulation of the 2012 version of the ICC Rules. Overall, it was found that a substantial majority of arbitrators and other arbitral practitioners considered the scrutiny process to be valuable, and that the advantages outweighed the disadvantages. The ICC prides itself on the overall quality of ICC awards and the scrutiny process acts as a measure of quality control,[248] ensuring, amongst other things, that the arbitrators deal with all of the claims. These include interest and costs, with which the arbitrators are called upon to deal.

9.197

(d) Review of the award by way of settlement

After the award has been made, parties can also settle a dispute by voluntarily agreeing to vary the terms of the award themselves. In a study of the record of compliance with, and variation of, awards once rendered, it was found that more than 18 per cent had been renegotiated post-award to establish final settlement claims.[249] Citing even higher figures, another study found that 40 per cent of corporations negotiated a settlement after the arbitral award was rendered.[250] Accordingly, it seems that parties commonly conclude the matter by entering into a negotiation either to establish terms of payment or to establish a new settlement, using the award as a bargaining tool.

9.198

(e) Publication of awards

A conflict emerged during the 1990s between the 'inherent confidentiality' of the arbitral process and the desire for publication of awards in the interests of establishing a body of precedent that might guide—if not bind—other arbitrators. The prevailing trend appears to favour publication. Awards of the Iran–United States Claims Tribunal have been comprehensively reported and have been used for guidance in other arbitrations. The ICDR Rules provide that, unless otherwise agreed

9.199

---

[247] *Syrian Petroleum Co. v GTM-Entrepose SA*, Proc. No. 58/1990, Swiss Federal Court Decision of 16 July 1990 (unpublished).
[248] For a description of the procedures followed by the ICC Court in scrutinising awards, see Craig, Park, and Paulsson, *International Chamber of Commerce Arbitration* (3rd edn, Oceana, 2000), ch. 20.
[249] Of 118 cases, 22 had been renegotiated: Naimark and Keer, 'Post-award experience in international commercial arbitration' (2005) 60 Disp Res J 94.
[250] Mistelis and Baltag, 'Recognition and enforcement of arbitral awards and settlement in international arbitration: Corporate attitudes and practices' (2008) 19 Am Rev Intl Arb 319, at 324.

by the parties, selected awards may be made publicly available, with the names of the parties and other identifying features removed. There are other circumstances in which, even without the consent of the parties, an award may find its way into the public domain. This may occur, for example, during court proceedings to challenge or enforce an award,[251] or when a publicly quoted corporation is obliged to disclose in its published accounts material information relating to its liabilities.[252]

9.200 In a less official context, in a form of post-Soviet legal *samizdat*,[253] it is becoming increasingly common for awards rendered in investment treaty arbitrations to be circulated via email and the Internet between practitioners and academics active in the field. During the second decade of the twenty-first century, online communities sprung up to exchange information and views on matters related to arbitration and international law. One of the most prominent among these is the Oil Gas Energy Mining Infrastructure Dispute Management (OGEMID) email list.[254]

9.201 Together with other similar forums,[255] OGEMID informally introduced an era of greater (although haphazard) transparency within the world of international arbitration. The advantages and disadvantages of transparency versus confidentiality continue to be debated within the international arbitration community, with many drawing a distinction between investment treaty arbitration and commercial arbitration arising between parties to private contracts.

9.202 Further, after several years of debate, UNCITRAL completed its deliberations on *transparency* in 'treaty-based investor-state arbitrations' in July 2014. This should herald a new—and significantly changed—era concerning not only the awards in such arbitrations, but also the written memorials and evidence submitted to international arbitral tribunals. At the time of writing, it is too early to predict the extent to which this will result in a new level of transparency in treaty-based investor–state arbitrations; and whether, in the medium or long term, the trend towards greater transparency will be extended to international arbitrations between private commercial parties.

---

[251] See, e.g. *Emmott v Michael Wilson & Partners Ltd* [2008] EWCA Civ 184.
[252] See Chapter 2. See also Paulsson and Rawding, 'The trouble with confidentiality' (1995) 11 Arb Intl 303.
[253] *Samizdat*, meaning literally 'self-publishing', was the clandestine copying and onward distribution of government-suppressed literature in Soviet states. Individuals who received a copy of a censored text would be expected to make copies, often by hand, and then to hand those out for further consumption, copying, and distribution.
[254] The list, set up by the late Professor Thomas Wälde, has been described as a 'vehicle where the blue-eyed theorists meet the rock of reality ... [where] theoreticians [can no longer] graze on the prairies of theory in groups of like-minded people rather than slog it out at the coalface of legal practice': 'OGEMID: An exchange practice–theory vehicle', posted online at OGEMID, 23 May 2008.
[255] See, e.g., Laird and Weiler's http://www.investmentclaims.com, or Professor Newcombe's Investment Treaty Arbitration website, online at http://ita.law.uvic.ca/.

10

CHALLENGE OF ARBITRAL AWARDS

A. Introduction	10.01	D. Effects of Challenge	10.89
B. Methods of Challenge	10.11	E. State Responsibility for	
C. Grounds for Challenge	10.34	Wrongful Setting Aside	10.93

A. Introduction

No one likes losing. So it is not surprising that, when a client is disappointed with an arbitral award, the first question the lawyer is asked is: 'How can I appeal?' As is so often the case when a lawyer is asked a question, the answer is: 'It depends.' **10.01**

First, it depends on whether the relevant rules of arbitration establish any internal appeal procedure, as is the case in certain maritime and commodity arbitration systems. It is noteworthy that most arbitration rules do not provide such an appeal. Indeed, most institutional rules provide unequivocally that an arbitral award is final and binding.[1] These are not intended to be empty words. One of the advantages of arbitration is that it is intended to result in the final determination of the dispute between the parties. If the parties want a compromise solution to be proposed, they should opt for mediation. If they are prepared to fight the case to the highest court in the land, they should opt for litigation. By choosing arbitration, the parties choose, in principle, finality. An arbitral award is not intended to be a mere proposal as to how the dispute might be resolved, nor is it intended to be the first step on a ladder of appeals through national courts. **10.02**

To the losing party, this 'advantage' of arbitration may seem, in retrospect, to be the very opposite. However, the laws of many countries, reflecting the policy of the New York Convention and the Model Law, have what has been described by the **10.03**

---

[1] See, e.g, LCIA Rules, Art. 26(8); ICC Arbitration Rules, Art. 34(6); ICDR Arbitration Rules, Art. 30(1).

US federal courts as 'a pro-enforcement bias'.[2] This means that whilst it may be possible to challenge an arbitral award, the available options are likely to be limited—and intentionally so.

10.04 It is usually the law of the seat of the arbitration[3] that contains these limited provisions for challenging an arbitral award.[4] They are principally focused on ensuring that the arbitration has been conducted in accordance with basic rules of due process, respecting the parties' equal right to be heard before an independent and impartial arbitral tribunal within the boundaries of their arbitration agreement. Grounds of challenge are rarely concerned with a review of the merits of the tribunal's decision, thus distinguishing challenge from an appeal.

10.05 It is worth clarifying at the outset the distinction between actions to challenge, or set aside, an award[5] and those opposing the enforcement of an award. A challenge to an award (usually) takes place in the courts of the seat of the arbitration and it is an attempt by the losing party to invalidate the award on the basis of the statutory grounds available under the law of the seat. In contrast, actions opposing enforcement, which are discussed in Chapter 11, may take place in any jurisdiction in which the winning party seeks to enforce an award. At that point, as long as the state of enforcement is a signatory to the New York Convention, the party against whom enforcement is sought has the opportunity to rely on the limited exceptions contained in Article V to block such enforcement. The statutory grounds for challenging an award under domestic law often closely resemble the exceptions to enforcement in the New York Convention. As a consequence, a party who is dissatisfied with the outcome of an arbitration will have at least two available methods to prevent an award from being given effect: it can affirmatively challenge the validity of the award in the courts of the seat; and/or it can attempt to thwart a party seeking to enforce the award under the New York Convention. As will be shown in this chapter and the next, success in the former almost always ensures success in the latter.

(a) Purpose of challenge

10.06 The purpose of challenging an award before a national court at the seat of arbitration is to have that court declare all, or part, of the award null and void. If an award is set aside or annulled by the relevant court, it will usually be treated as invalid, and accordingly unenforceable, not only by the courts of the seat of arbitration, but also by national courts elsewhere.[6] This is because, under both

---

[2] *Parsons Whittemore Overseas Co. Inc. v Société Générale de l'Industrie du Papier* 508 F.2d 969, 973 (2nd Cir. 1974).
[3] Or, if the parties have chosen a different procedural law to govern the arbitration, under that law: New York Convention, Art. V.1(e); Model Law, Art. 36(1)(a)(v).
[4] Including a partial, or interim, award that is final as to the issue(s) with which it deals.
[5] Also referred to as 'actions seeking annulment of the award'.
[6] New York Convention, Art. V, provides only that a competent national authority *may* refuse to enforce an award that has been annulled at the seat. It is not obliged to do so; accordingly, an award that has been set aside by the court of the seat of arbitration may be granted recognition

A. Introduction

the New York Convention and the Model Law, a competent court may refuse to grant recognition and enforcement of an award that has been set aside by a court of the seat of arbitration.[7] It is important to note that, following complete annulment, the claimant can recommence proceedings because the award simply does not exist—that is, the *status quo ante* is restored. The reviewing court cannot alter the terms of an award nor can it decide the dispute based on its own vision of the merits. Unless the reviewing court has a power to remit the fault to the original tribunal,[8] any new submission of the dispute to arbitration after annulment has to be undertaken by commencement of a new arbitration with a new arbitral tribunal.

(b) Preconditions to challenge

10.07 Before challenging an award before the relevant court, it will usually be necessary to consider other available remedies, which may include (a) any available process of appeal or review under the applicable rules or law, and (b) any available provision for the correction of the award or for an additional award.[9]

10.08 As to the first requirement, certain rules of arbitration and certain arbitration agreements provide for appeals to 'second-tier' tribunals. Subject to the applicable rules, it is usually the award of that superior tribunal, and not any earlier award, that is final and binding upon the parties.

10.09 As to the second requirement, it is usual for rules of arbitration, as well as national legislation, to provide some mechanism for the correction of awards by the arbitral tribunal itself. For example, the ICC Arbitration Rules provide, at Article 35(1), that the arbitral tribunal, on its own initiative or at the request

---

and enforcement if the enforcing court so concludes. France is one of the more liberal jurisdictions in this regard, famously granting recognition to a Swiss-seated award that had been set aside by Swiss courts: *Hilmarton I*, Cour de Cassation, 1ère Civ., 23 Mar. 1994, [1994] Rev Arb 437. See also *PT Putrabali Adyamulia v Rena Holdings*, Cour de Cassation, Ch. Civ. 1ere, 29 June 2007, in which a French court enforced an award that had been set aside at the seat in England. Similarly, the District Court for the District of Columbia in *Chromalloy Aeroservices v Arab Republic of Egypt* 939 F.Supp. 907, 909 (DDC 1996) enforced an award that had been annulled at its seat in Egypt. In *Corporacion Mexicana de Mantenimiento Integral, S. de R.L. de C.V. v PEMEX-Exploracion y Produccion*, No 10 Civ 206 (AKH) 2013 WL 4517225 (SDNY, August 27, 2013), the US courts enforced an ICC award set aside in Mexico where denying enforcement would be fundamentally unfair and violate basic notions of justice. However, much will depend on the particular award and the enforcing court will still give great weight to the courts of the seat: see, e.g., *TermoRio SA ESP v Electranta SP* 487 F.3d 928 (DC Cir. 2007) (refusing to enforce an award annulled by the courts of the seat in Colombia). For further discussion of this concept, see Chapter 11.

[7] New York Convention, Art. V.1(e); Model Law, Art. 36(1)(a)(v).
[8] See paragraphs 10.21*ff*.
[9] See, e.g., the English Arbitration Act 1996, s. 70(2), which states that an application or appeal may not be brought if the applicant or appellant has not first exhausted (a) any available arbitral process of appeal or review, and (b) any available recourse under s. 57 (correction of award or additional award).

of a party, may correct 'a clerical, computational or typographical error, or any errors of similar nature contained in an Award'. At Article 35(2), the ICC Rules also provide that, at the request of a party, the arbitral tribunal may issue an 'interpretation' of the award.[10] The UNCITRAL Arbitration Rules contain not only an interpretation rule and a 'slip rule',[11] but also a rule that permits either party to ask the arbitral tribunal to make an additional award 'as to claims presented in the arbitral proceedings but omitted from the award'.[12] The rule goes on to state that the arbitral tribunal may do this if it considers the request to be justified and 'considers that the omission can be rectified without any further hearings or evidence.'[13]

(c) Time limits for challenge

10.10 Time limits for applying to correct or amend an arbitral award, or to challenge an award by an application to the relevant national court, are likely to be short and strictly enforced.[14] The position in each case will depend upon the relevant rules or legislation, but by way of example:

- under the UNCITRAL Arbitration Rules, requests for interpretation or correction of an award, or for an additional award, must be made within thirty days after receipt of the award;[15]
- under the Model Law, an application for setting aside an award must be made within three months of receiving the award or, if a request for an interpretation, correction, or additional award has been made, within three months of that request being disposed of by the arbitral tribunal.

---

[10] Article 35 of the 2012 ICC Rules is based on Art. 29 of the 1998 ICC Rules. For a comprehensive analysis of the latter, see Daly, 'Correction and interpretation of arbitral awards under the ICC Rules of Arbitration' (2002) 13 ICC International Court of Arbitration Bulletin 61.

[11] UNCITRAL Rules, Arts 37 and 38.

[12] UNCITRAL Rules, Art. 39.

[13] UNCITRAL Rules, Art. 39. The Model Law also permits the arbitral tribunal, at the request of either party, to issue an additional award: Model Law, Art. 33. The English Arbitration Act 1996 also provides for this possibility under s. 57, and this possibility must be exhausted before any application or appeal to the court against an arbitral award may be made (s. 70(2)).

[14] See, e.g., *Terna Bahrain v Bin Kamil* [2012] EWHC 3283, in which the applicant tried to challenge an award under the English Arbitration Act 1996 for procedural irregularity, but the court refused to hear the challenge because the application was made after the twenty-eight-day period for doing so had expired. See also *Glaser v Legg*, Case No. 12-cv-00805, 2013 WL 870382 (DDC, 11 March 2013), in which a petition to vacate award was untimely, because it was filed more than three months after award was issued; *Companhia do Metropolitano de São Paolo—Metrô v Consórcio Via Amarela*, Apelação 0177130-22.2010.8.26.0100, 3 December 2012, holding that the Brazilian statutory period of five days for challenging an award did not run during the thirty-day period for the correction and interpretation of award provided for by the ICC Rules, but finding the request for annulment to be nonetheless untimely, because the party failed to comply with the ICC Rules in making its second request for clarification of the award.

[15] UNCITRAL Rules, Arts 37–39.

B. Methods of Challenge

10.11 The relevant arbitration rules sometimes provide for 'internal' challenges to an award. This form of challenge is considered first. The correction and interpretation of awards is then considered, before the challenge of awards by application to national courts.

(a) Internal challenge

10.12 The rules under which an arbitration was conducted may provide for review of the award. This is frequently the case with maritime and commodity arbitrations, and other forms of arbitration established by trade associations.[16]

10.13 The most commonly used provision for the challenge of arbitral awards by means of an internal review procedure is that of the Arbitration Rules of the International Centre for the Settlement of Investment Disputes (ICSID). A party who is dissatisfied with the award of an ICSID arbitral tribunal may apply for the interpretation, revision, or annulment of the award.[17] The grounds for so doing include that the tribunal 'was not properly constituted',[18] that the tribunal has 'manifestly exceeded its powers',[19] that there 'was corruption on the part of a member of the tribunal',[20] that there has been 'a serious departure from a fundamental rule of procedure',[21] or that the award has 'failed to state the reasons on which it is based'.[22] These grounds are very similar to the grounds contained in national arbitral systems for the judicial challenge of arbitral awards. This is not surprising. As discussed in Chapter 8, the ICSID system is a self-contained system governed by the ICSID Convention, which does not permit judicial challenge of awards. The internal review mechanism therefore effectively replaces the system of judicial challenge.

---

[16] See, e.g., the Arbitration Rules of the Grain and Feed Trade Association (GAFTA), effective 1 July 2007, and the Arbitration Rules of the Chambre Arbitral Maritime de Paris of 2007. Similarly, r. 47 of the 2013 Arbitration Rules for the Court of Arbitration for Sport (CAS) provides for an internal appeal procedure within CAS, so long as the relevant sports federation or body has expressly provided for such an appeal in its rules. See also Arbitration Rules of the European Court of Arbitration, Arts 23(12) and 28, under which the parties are deemed to have waived any right to challenge, except by appeal to an appellate tribunal consisting of three arbitrators. To appeal, the losing party must deposit the amount of original award with the court, and if it loses the appeal, the award is automatically paid to the prevailing party.

[17] For a thorough review of the ICSID annulment process, see Bishop and Marchilli, *Annulment under the ICSID Convention* (Oxford University Press, 2012). See also Paulsson, Reed, and Blackaby, *Guide to ICSID Arbitration* (2nd edn, Kluwer Law International, 2010), pp. 159*ff*.

[18] ICSID Convention, Art. 52(1)(a).
[19] Ibid., Art. 52(1)(b).
[20] Ibid., Art. 52(1)(c).
[21] Ibid., Art. 52(1)(d).
[22] Ibid., Art. 52(1)(e).

10.14 If the application is for annulment of the award, then ICSID constitutes an ad hoc committee of three members to determine the application.[23] If the award is annulled, in whole or in part, either party may ask for the dispute to be submitted to a new tribunal, which hears the dispute again and then delivers a new award.[24]

10.15 Annulment proceedings under ICSID have proliferated and the resulting case law has revealed much about the parameters of the grounds of annulment. Historically, it was extremely rare for an ICSID annulment committee to annul an award: tribunals generally would not 'second-guess' an award and would annul only for extreme injustices, such as where the tribunal manifestly exceeded its powers (such as by failing to apply the applicable law) or seriously departed from a fundamental rule of procedure. However, several ad hoc committees have annulled awards over less egregious flaws. In a 2010 decision to annul the award in *Fraport v Philippines*,[25] the ad hoc committee considered the tribunal's admission of evidence after the close of proceedings a 'serious departure from a fundamental rule of procedure', because the claimant was deprived of an adequate opportunity to address that evidence. In two other decisions rendered in that same year, the tribunals annulled the underlying awards for manifest excesses of power because they considered that the original tribunals had, arguably, incorrectly interpreted the applicable law.[26] These decisions sparked much controversy[27] and, in response to a request from the Philippines to the ICSID Administrative Council, the ICSID Secretariat issued a report on annulment to help to clarify the scope of annulment under Article 52 of the Convention.[28]

10.16 Many annulment decisions have confirmed the exceptional nature of the remedy, but this has not deterred losing parties from invoking the mechanism with

---

[23] ICSID Rules, r. 52. Unlike the constitution of the original arbitral tribunal, there are no party appointments of annulment panel members.

[24] Ibid., r. 55. If the original award has been annulled only in part, the new tribunal will not reconsider any portion of the award that has *not* been annulled: ICSID Rules, r. 55(3).

[25] *Fraport AG Frankfurt Airport Services Worldwide v Republic of the Philippines*, Decision on Annulment, ICSID Case No. ARB/03/25, 23 December 2010.

[26] *Sempra Energy International v Argentina*, Decision on Annulment, ICSID Case No. ARB/02/16, 29 June 2010, annulling the award based on the tribunal's manifest excess of powers because it disagreed with the tribunal's interpretation of a provision in the relevant bilateral investment treaty; *Enron Creditors Recovery Corporation v Argentina*, Decision on Annulment, ICSID Case No. ARB/01/3, 30 July 2010, annulling the award based on the tribunal's manifest excess of powers (the committee said that the tribunal had 'failed to apply' the applicable law, because it disagreed with the tribunal's interpretation of that law).

[27] See, e.g., Reed and Mandelli, 'Ad hoc or *ad arbitrium*? An audit of recent ICSID annulment decisions', in Rovine (ed.) *Contemporary Issues in International Arbitration and Mediation: The Fordham Papers 2012* (Martinus Nijhoff, 2012); Caron, 'Framing the work of ICSID annulment committees' (2012) 6 World Arb & Med Rev 173.

[28] ICSID, *Background Report on Annulment by the ICSID Secretariat Provided to State Parties* (12 August 2012), available online at https://icsid.worldbank.org/apps/ICSIDWEB/resources/Documents/Background%20Report%20on%20Annulment_English.pdf.

B. Methods of Challenge

ever-increasing frequency, perhaps as a means of postponing enforcement.[29] In 2014, ICSID received thirteen annulment applications—the most in its history.

(b) Correction and interpretation of awards; additional awards; remission of awards

(i) Correction

10.17 There is usually a provision in the relevant arbitration rules, or in the law governing the arbitration, for the correction of computational, clerical, or similar errors. For example, Article 35 of the ICC Rules permits clerical, computational, typographical, or similar errors to be corrected.[30] While primarily intended to allow correction of 'slips' that are obvious on the face of the award, the Article's precise outer limits are unclear.

(ii) Interpretation

10.18 In the same vein, some arbitral rules permit an arbitral tribunal to issue an 'interpretation' of its award.[31] Whilst dissatisfied parties are sometimes tempted to use this facility to invite an arbitral tribunal to revisit the merits of its decision, it is intended only to resolve any uncertainty as to the precise meaning of an award and therefore the manner in which it is to be performed.

(iii) Additional award

10.19 A further power is given to an arbitral tribunal under some rules to deal with any claims that were presented in the arbitral proceedings, but which the tribunal omitted to address in its award. Since an arbitral award may be challenged under many systems if the arbitral tribunal fails to decide all of the issues that were put to it,[32] this is a sensible solution.

10.20 In addition, certain national laws also provide for tribunals to revisit their awards where evidence is later produced of fraud, forgery, or concealment of evidence. By

---

[29] Upon filing for annulment, an automatic stay of execution enters into force and is usually extended by the annulment committee pending issuance of the annulment decision without necessarily requiring the posting of security. This has created a perverse incentive to seek annulment as a means of postponing enforcement with very little cost (because interest is usually fixed far lower than the relevant state's cost of borrowing).

[30] For example, similar rules include UNCITRAL Rules, Art. 38; ICSID Additional Facility Rules, r. 7(1); LCIA Rules Art. 27(1). The UNCITRAL Rules were modified slightly in 2010 to allow a party to request the tribunal to correct not only 'any error in computation, any clerical or typographical error', but also any erroneous 'omission'; it further requires the tribunal to make any appropriate corrections within forty-five days of receipt of the request. Furthermore, under UNCITRAL Rules, Art. 38, any such corrections shall be deemed to 'form part of the award'.

[31] Daly, 'Correction and Interpretation of arbitral awards under the ICC Rules of Arbitration' (2002) 13 ICC International Court of Arbitration Bulletin 62. For example, in ICC Case No. 10189, the tribunal's addendum amended the text of an award in order to avoid any uncertainty as to the time period of the royalty payments owed by the claimant.

[32] An award that is *infra petita*. See, e.g., English Arbitration Act 1996, s. 68(2)(d).

way of example, subsequently revealed fraud is considered to be a ground for revising an award both under French and Swiss law.[33]

(iv) Remission of award

10.21 Certain national laws further provide the domestic courts with the power to remit, or send back, disputes, requiring the tribunal to revisit some, or all, of its findings. In contrast to requests for correction, interpretation, or additional awards (where a party makes a request of the arbitral tribunal), remissions will occur in the context of a party's application to the courts of the seat of the arbitration, for example during a setting-aside application.

10.22 Powers of remission are derived from national arbitration statutes. For example, section 68(3) of the English Arbitration Act 1996 provides that '[t]he court shall not exercise its power to set aside or to declare an award to be of no effect, in whole or in part, unless it is satisfied that it would be inappropriate to remit the matters to the tribunal for reconsideration'. In the United States, the power has been established by means of case law.[34] The ICC Rules acknowledge the possibility of remission and establish the mechanism applicable to the administration of the arbitration in that eventuality.[35]

10.23 It should be noted that national arbitration laws vary widely regarding the scope of the courts' power of remission. Many take their cue from the UNCITRAL Model Law[36] by linking remission to setting-aside proceedings and thereby limiting the scope of grounds for remission to the narrow grounds available for setting aside.[37]

---

[33] See, e.g., French law (Cour de Cassation in *Fougerolle v Procofrance* [1992] J du Droit Intl 974) and Swiss law (Swiss Federal Supreme Court in *Sovereign Participations International SA v Chadmore Developments Ltd* (2001) XXVI YBCA 299, at 301*ff*). This principle was confirmed in the 2011 French Arbitration Law, art. 1502.

[34] See American Law Institute, Restatement (Third) International Commercial Arbitration, § 4-36, TD No. 2 (April 2012), restating the US case-generated rule as positing that '[a] court may in exceptional circumstances remand a U.S. Convention award to the arbitral tribunal with instructions to complete the award or to clarify its meanings'.

[35] ICC Rules, Art. 35(4):

Where a court remits an award to the arbitral tribunal, the provisions of Articles 31, 33, 34, and this Article 35 shall apply mutatis mutandis to any addendum or award made pursuant to the terms of such remission. The Court may take any steps as may be necessary to enable the arbitral tribunal to comply with the terms of such remission and may fix an advance to cover any additional fees and expenses of the arbitral tribunal and any additional ICC administrative expenses.

[36] Model Law, Art. 34(4).

[37] Model Law, Art. 34(4) provides:

The court, when asked to set aside an award, may, where appropriate and so requested by a party, suspend the setting aside proceedings for a period of time determined by it in order to give the arbitral tribunal an opportunity to resume the arbitral proceedings or to take such other action as in the arbitral tribunal's opinion will eliminate the grounds for setting aside.

B. Methods of Challenge

In these countries, the power to remit is essentially a means to 'cure' awards that might otherwise need to be set aside. By contrast, some national laws afford adopt a more flexible approach—such as the United States, the courts of which do not necessarily limit remission to situations in which the only alternative is to vacate (that is, set aside) the award.[38]

(c) Recourse to the courts

10.24 What is a losing party to do if its grievance is not something that can be put right by correction or interpretation of the award and there is no provision for internal review of the award? There are grounds on which an arbitral award may be challenged before a national court at the place of arbitration (the 'competent court', as it is described in the Model Law).[39] However, there are two preliminary issues that need to be addressed before considering the typical grounds for challenging an award:

(i) Place of challenge

10.25 Any challenge to the validity or effect of an award must be addressed to the designated competent court of the seat of the arbitration.[40] If the arbitration had its seat in Switzerland, for example, the competent court is the Swiss Federal Tribunal (although the parties may agree to the court of the canton in which the arbitration took place).[41] In France, it is the Paris Cour d'Appel.[42] In England, it is the Commercial Court of the Queen's Bench Division in the High Court of Justice. In the United States, it is the district court (the federal first-instance court) of the seat of the arbitration.[43]

---

[38] See *Weinburg v Silber*, 140 F.Supp.2d 712 (ND Tex. 2001), remanding the award to the tribunal to explain how it should be discharged in view of the emergence of certain apparently unforeseen circumstances; *Fisher v General Steel Domestic Sales, LLC*, Slip Copy No. 10-cv-0109-WYD-BNB, 2011 WL 524362 (D. Colo., 31 October 2011), remitting to the tribunal to address a jurisdictional issue left undecided. See also Coe, 'Making remission and other "curative" mechanisms part of the forum shopping conversation: A view from the US with comparative notes', in Ferrari (ed.) *Forum Shopping in the International Commercial Arbitration Context* (Sellier European Law, 2013), pp. 382–383.

[39] Model Law, Art. 6, provides for each state to designate the court, courts, or other authority competent to perform the functions laid down by the Model Law, which include the setting aside of awards under Art. 34.

[40] See the decision of the Mexican Supreme Court in Amparo Directo en Revisión No. 8/2011, which deemed that only judges at the seat of the arbitration are competent to annul an award.

[41] Swiss Private International Law Act 1987 (Swiss PIL), Ch. 12, s. 191, as amended.

[42] While a statute will often explicitly prescribe a particular court, it is not always easy to determine which court within the seat is the appropriate court before which to raise a challenge. The Paris Cour d'Appel struggled with the issue of whether a civil or administrative court must determine a challenge to an arbitral award that touched on both administrative and civil law. Ultimately, the Court determined that a civil court should hear the case *unless* the award involved issues of *mandatory* French administrative law: *INSERM v Fondation F. Saugstad*, Paris Cour d'Appel, 13 November 2008.

[43] US Federal Arbitration Act of 1925 (FAA), § 10(a).

10.26 There is one notable exception to this general rule, although it is probably more theoretical than real: the freedom of the parties to an international arbitration to decide how it should be conducted is generally taken to include freedom to subject the arbitration to the procedural law of a country *other than* that in which the arbitration is held. It seems to be both unnecessary and unhelpful for parties to use their freedom in this way.[44] However, the New York Convention itself acknowledges that recognition and enforcement of an award may be refused on the basis that the award has been 'set aside or suspended by a competent authority of the country in which, *or under the law of which*, that award was made'.[45] Some courts have read the reference to 'the country under whose law the award was made' (which is intended to refer to the substantive law governing the award) as a licence to set aside an award that was not made in their own country, but which was governed by their country's substantive law. Thus, in two decisions dating back to the 1980s and 1990s, the Indian courts set aside awards rendered in other states on the basis that the substance of the disputes was governed by Indian law.[46]

10.27 This issue resurfaced in the 2002 case *Bhatia International v. Bulk Trading SA*,[47] which confirmed the supervisory jurisdiction of the Indian courts in certain circumstances in which the seat was not in India, and was followed by the Indian Supreme Court's 2008 decision in *Venture Global v. Satyam Trading*,[48] in which it set aside an award rendered in England on the basis that Indian law governed the substance of the dispute. Decisions such as these appeared to indicate that the Indian courts were free to intervene in arbitrations that had their seat outside of India wherever Indian law governed the merits of the dispute. The Supreme Court of India has since reversed course in 2012, in its Constitutional Court formation, in *Bharat Aluminium Co. (Balco) v. Kaiser Aluminium Technical Services*,[49]

---

[44] 'Unnecessary', because if the law of a particular country contains procedures that the parties prefer, the parties would do better to adopt those specific procedures rather than to try to adopt a law of procedure that is alien to the *lex arbitri* and which might indeed be in conflict with it. 'Unhelpful', because it means adding another set of legal rules to which the arbitration will be subject, in addition to those agreed by the parties or imposed by the *lex arbitri*. This topic is more fully discussed in Chapter 3.

[45] New York Convention, Art. V(1)(e) (emphasis added). See also *International Electric Corporation v Bridas Sociedad Anonima Petrolera, Industrial y Comercial* 745 F.Supp. 172, 178 (SDNY 1990), in which the court held that the italicised words ('since the *situs* of the arbitration is Mexico, and the governing procedural law that of Mexico, only Mexican courts have jurisdiction under the Convention to vacate the award') referred to the procedural law governing the arbitration and not to the substantive law governing the agreement between the parties.

[46] See *Oil & Natural Gas Commission v Western Co. of North America* (1987) AIR 674 (SC); *National Thermal Power Corporation v Singer Corporation et al.* (1993) XVIII YBCA 403. See also Paulsson, 'The New York Convention's misadventures in India' (1992) 7 Intl Arb 18.

[47] (2002) 4 SCC 105.

[48] *Venture Global Engineering v Satyam Computer Services Ltd and anor*, Civil Appeal No. 309 of 2008, Supreme Court of India (arising out of SLP (C) No. 8491 of 2007).

[49] Civil Appeal No. 7019 of 2005, 6 September 2012 (holding that Indian courts will no longer be able to vacate international arbitral awards not seated in India or issue interim measures concerning ongoing international arbitrations seated abroad).

B. Methods of Challenge

in which it overturned *Venture Global* and confirmed the international practice that the power to set aside is limited to the courts of the seat of the arbitration.

(ii) Exclusion and waiver of challenge

In some jurisdictions, parties to arbitrations may be able to exclude their right to challenge an award.[50] Thus, under the arbitration laws of both Switzerland[51] and Belgium,[52] if all parties to an arbitration are foreign, they may agree to exclude the right to challenge the arbitral award. Under the 2011 French Arbitration Law, this right to waive the right to challenge extends to any party.[53]

10.28

In general, a waiver of a right to challenge must be express; general waivers by incorporation, such as that contained in the ICC Rules,[54] will not usually suffice.[55] The ICC Secretariat has confirmed that Article 34(6) of the ICC Rules '*is unlikely to be deemed sufficient* to constitute a waiver of the right to bring proceedings to set aside an award even in those jurisdictions where such a waiver is possible'.[56]

10.29

Parties are unlikely to succeed on any challenge to an award based on an objection that they have failed to raise during the arbitration.[57] This is because they will usually be deemed to have waived that objection. The possibility of waiver is set out both in some national legislations[58] and in the major arbitration rules.[59] For example, consider an international arbitration in London, in which the respondent is in doubt as to the validity of the arbitration agreement, but nevertheless

10.30

---

[50] See *Sociedad de Inversiones Inmobiliarias Del Puerto SA v Constructora Iberoamericana SA*, Court of Appeals on Commercial Matters, Division D, 7 February 2011, in which the Argentina Court of Appeals on Commercial Matters held that parties may validly waive the right to challenge an arbitral award. However, for a contrary view, see the Swiss Supreme Court's annulment of an award rendered by CAS, in which waivers to challenge awards were held to be invalid: Case No. 4P–172/2006, 22 March 2007.

[51] Swiss PIL, Ch. 12, s. 192.

[52] See Belgian Judicial Code, art. 1718, as amended in 2013.

[53] French Arbitration Law, arts 1520, 1522 CCP (2011).

[54] ICC Rules, Art. 34(6).

[55] General waivers may suffice to waive some rights, such as the right to appeal an arbitral award on points of English law contemplated in the English Arbitration Act 1996, s. 69. See *Lesotho Highlands Development Authority v Impreglio SpA and ors* [2005] UKHL 43, [2005] Arb LR 557, at [3] *per* Lord Steyn, finding that, by submitting to ICC arbitration, Art. 34(6) (then Art. 28(6)) of the ICC Rules sufficed to waive the parties' right to appeal.

[56] Fry, Greenberg, and Mazza, *The Secretariat's Guide to ICC Arbitration* (ICC, 2012), paras 3.1254–3.1255 (emphasis added).

[57] See, e.g., *Thyssen Canada Ltd v Mariana Maritime SA and anr* [2005] EWHC 219, in which it was held that a party who takes part in arbitral proceedings and fails to raise an objection as to a serious irregularity affecting the proceedings will lose the right to object, unless it can show that, at the time that it took part or continued to take part in the proceedings, it did not know and could not with reasonable diligence have discovered the grounds for the objection.

[58] See, e.g., English Arbitration Act 1996, s. 73; Belgian Judicial Code, art. 1704(5); Dutch Code of Civil Procedure, art. 1027.

[59] See, e.g., ICC Rules, Art. 39; UNCITRAL Rules, Art. 32; ICDR Rules, Art. 25; ICSID Rules, r. 27; LCIA, Art. 32(1).

participates in the arbitration. The tribunal makes an award against the respondent, who then seeks to challenge the award on the ground that the tribunal lacked jurisdiction. Such a respondent will find that it is too late to rely on such a ground, since English law requires an objection to jurisdiction to be raised at the earliest possible opportunity[60] and provides that if this is not done, the right to object is lost.[61] Accordingly, the award would be a valid award under the law of England (as the law of the seat of arbitration) and, in principle, enforceable under the New York Convention. The Paris Cour d'Appel has also rejected challenges based on objections that the challenging party failed to raise—and was therefore deemed to have waived—during the arbitration itself.[62] Similar provisions to those of English law, to the effect that a plea as to lack of jurisdiction should be raised at an early stage, are found in the UNCITRAL Rules and the Model Law.[63]

10.31 Case law in the United States also supports the proposition that a party will have 'waived its right to seek judicial relief of the arbitrator's award, having participated in the arbitration process and then failing to object and preserve its objection to the arbitrability of the grievance submitted to the arbitrator'.[64]

10.32 Indeed, most developed arbitral jurisdictions uphold awards in these circumstances and most state parties to the New York Convention are ready to enforce such awards. Put simply, if an objection is to be taken, it should be taken without delay.

---

[60] English Arbitration Act 1996, s. 31.

[61] English Arbitration Act 1996, s. 73. See also *teleMates Pty Ltd v Standard SoftTel Solutions Pvt Ltd* [2011] NSWSC 1365 (11 November 2011), in which the Australian Court refused to consider a party's challenge to an arbitral award because the party had failed to object to the tribunal's jurisdiction within thirty days of the preliminary ruling on jurisdiction, as required by the Model Law.

[62] See, e.g., the Paris Cour d'Appel decision in *SA Caisse Fédérale de Crédit Mutuel du Nord de la France v Banque Delubac et Compagnie* [2001] Rev Arb 918. See also the Paris Cour d'Appel decision in *Exodis c/Ricoh France* [2004] Rev Arb 683; the Rouen Cour d'Appel decision in *Cogecot Cotton Co. c/Marlan's Cotton Industries MCI* [2005] Gaz Palais 118. It is noteworthy that, in *A Rahman Golshani v Iran* [2005] Rev Arb 993, the French Cour de Cassation had, for the first time, specifically referred to and applied the notion of 'estoppel' in an international arbitration case. In this case, the Cour de Cassation held that, for a party who had itself made the request for arbitration and had participated without any reservation for more than nine years in the arbitration proceedings, it was inadmissible on the basis of the rule of estoppel to argue that that tribunal had rendered its decision in the absence of an arbitration agreement, or on the basis of an arbitration agreement that is null and void.

[63] UNCITRAL Rules, Art. 23(2) ('no later than in the statement of defence or, with respect to a counterclaim or a claim for the purpose of a set-off, in the reply to the counterclaim or to the claim for the purpose of set-off'); Model Law, Art. 16(2) ('not later than the submission of the statement of defence').

[64] See *Howard University v Metropolitan Campus Police Officer's Union* 519 F.Supp.2d 27, 35 (DDC 2007). See also *United Industrial Workers v Government of the Virgin Islands* 987 F.2d 162, 168 (3rd Cir. 1993), in which it was held: 'Because arbitrators derive their authority from the contractual agreement of the parties, a party may waive its right to challenge an arbitrator's authority to decide a matter by voluntarily participating in an arbitration and failing to object on the grounds that there was no agreement to arbitrate.'

C. Grounds for Challenge

10.33 Less commonly, courts may refuse to set aside an award where the party challenging the award fails to raise its complaint with sufficient force and clarity during the arbitral proceedings. For example, in rejecting a challenge to an ICC arbitration, the Swiss Supreme Court held that the challenging party had not made 'a sufficiently clear complaint' during the original arbitration, thus waiving its right to challenge.[65]

C. Grounds for Challenge

10.34 Each state has its own concept of what measure of control it wishes to exercise over an arbitral process that takes place in its territory, and, in particular, whether it wishes in this respect to distinguish between 'domestic' and 'international' arbitration. In any given case, it is necessary to consult the law of the state concerned in order to determine the grounds on which a particular award may be challenged.

10.35 It is beyond the scope of this book to review all of these different systems of law. What can be done, however, is to try to discern the areas in which judicial control, or review, is likely to occur, and then to consider each of these areas in turn.

10.36 There are essentially three broad areas on which an arbitral award is likely to be challenged before a national court at the seat of the arbitration. First, an award may be challenged on jurisdictional grounds—that is, the non-existence of a valid and binding arbitration agreement—or other grounds that go to the admissibility of the claim determined by the tribunal. Secondly, an award may be challenged on what may broadly be described as 'procedural' grounds, such as failure to give a party an equal opportunity to be heard. Thirdly, and most rarely, an award may be challenged on substantive grounds, on the basis that the arbitral tribunal made a mistake of law.

10.37 These grounds for challenge are reviewed here mainly by reference to the Model Law,[66] which has now been adopted into, or at the very least has inspired, national laws governing arbitration in almost seventy countries around the world.[67]

---

[65] *X. SE & Y. GmbH v Z. B.V.*, Case No. 4A_407/2012, First Civil Law Court (Switzerland), 20 February 2013, of which an unofficial English translation is available online at http://www.swissarbitrationdecisions.com/sites/default/files/20%20fevrier%202013%204A%20407%202012.pdf. See also Thomas, 'An excess of politeness: Swiss court upholds award', Global Arbitration Review, 24 May 2013.

[66] The full title of the Model Law, as has been seen, is the 'Model Law on *International* Commercial Arbitration' (emphasis added). Some states, however, do not distinguish between 'international' and 'domestic' arbitrations, and have either adopted or adapted the Model Law for both types of arbitration.

[67] Sixty-nine, at the time of writing, according to UNCITRAL, online at http://www.uncitral.org/.

(a) Grounds under the Model Law

10.38 Pursuant to the Model Law, an action for setting aside an award may be brought before the designated courts of the state in which an award was made[68] pursuant only to the grounds exhaustively set out in the Law. These grounds are taken from Article V of the New York Convention. There is a pleasing symmetry here: Article V of the New York Convention sets out the grounds on which recognition and enforcement of an international award may be refused, while Article 34 of the Model Law sets out the same grounds (with only slight differences of language) on which an award may be set aside. These grounds are:

- lack of capacity to conclude an arbitration agreement, or lack of a valid arbitration agreement;
- the aggrieved party was not given proper notice of the appointment of the arbitral tribunal, or the arbitral proceedings, or was otherwise unable to present its case;
- the award deals with matters not contemplated by, or falling within, the arbitration clause or submission agreement, or goes beyond the scope of what was submitted;
- the composition of the arbitral tribunal or the arbitral procedure was not in accordance with the agreement of the parties, or with the mandatory provisions of the Model Law itself;
- the subject matter of the dispute is not capable of settlement by arbitration under the law of the state in which the arbitration takes place; and/or
- the award (or any decision within it) is in conflict with the public policy of the state in which the arbitration takes place.[69]

10.39 An application under the Model Law for setting aside an award must be made within three months from the date on which the aggrieved party receives the award (subject to any extended time limit that may be appropriate where corrections, interpretations, or additional awards have been issued under Article 33).[70] The designated court will establish its own procedure for the application to be made.

10.40 One provision of the Model Law mitigates, to some extent, the 'all or nothing' approach of the Model Law, under which an award is either set aside or left to stand. Where appropriate, upon application by a party, the court may suspend the setting-aside proceedings in order to give the arbitral tribunal an opportunity to resume the arbitral proceedings, or to take such other action as, in the arbitral tribunal's opinion, will eliminate the grounds for setting aside.[71] In effect,

---

[68] Model Law, Art. 1(2). Under Art. 6, a state that enacts the Model Law must designate the court(s) within its territory that will fulfil the various functions entrusted to the courts.
[69] Model Law, Art. 34(2).
[70] Model Law, Art. 34(3).
[71] Model Law, Art. 34(4). For a detailed commentary on this Article, see Holtzmann and Neuhaus, *A Guide to the UNCITRAL Model Law on International Commercial Arbitration* (Kluwer Law International, 1994), p. 967.

C. Grounds for Challenge

this is an equivalent provision to that of remitting the award to the tribunal for reconsideration.

With these words of introduction, the grounds for challenge may be broadly categorised as:

- grounds that relate to the adjudicability of the claim in question (including issues of incapacity, invalid agreements to arbitrate, a tribunal's excess of powers, or the arbitrability of the subject matter of the dispute);
- procedural grounds (including issues relating to the composition of the arbitral tribunal); and
- substantive grounds (including mistakes of law, mistakes of fact, and public policy).

(b) Adjudicability

Although grounds relating to the adjudicability of a dispute go well beyond matters of jurisdiction, that is where a consideration of this category should begin. As already discussed elsewhere in this volume,[72] if an objection to jurisdiction is to be taken, it should be taken without delay. Under the doctrine of 'competence-competence', an arbitral tribunal is empowered to decide for itself whether or not it has jurisdiction over a particular dispute. If its jurisdiction is challenged, the arbitral tribunal may decide the point as a preliminary issue in an interim award or as part of its award on the merits. In either case, however, the decision of the arbitral tribunal is not necessarily the last word on the subject: that rests with the national court. The Model Law, for instance, states that if the arbitral tribunal rules as a preliminary question that it has jurisdiction, this ruling may be referred to the competent court (within thirty days) for the court's decision, which *is* final.[73] If the ruling on jurisdiction is made in an award on the merits, this may likewise be challenged under the Model Law, and the award may be set aside on the basis that the arbitration agreement was not valid, or that it dealt with a dispute that was not within the arbitration agreement, or that it went beyond the scope of that agreement.[74]

(i) Incapacity or invalid agreement to arbitrate

The first ground for challenging an award under Article 34(2)(a)(i) of the Model Law provides that:

(i) a party to the arbitration agreement...was under some incapacity; or the said agreement is not valid under the law to which the parties have subjected it or, failing any indication thereon, under the law of this State;...

---

[72] See Chapter 5 for a detailed discussion of how an arbitral tribunal establishes its jurisdiction.
[73] Model Law, Art. 16(3).
[74] Ibid., Arts 16(3) and 34(2)(i) and (iii).

10.44 This conflates two separate grounds. Both the issue of 'capacity' and the requirements for an enforceable arbitration agreement are discussed in detail in Chapter 2. Claims as to the absence of a valid and binding arbitration agreement, in particular, are not an uncommon ground for challenge.[75]

(ii) An arbitral tribunal's excess of powers

10.45 A further ground for challenge under the Model Law is that the arbitral tribunal has exceeded its powers in the decision that it has rendered. In the words of Article 34(2)(a)(iii):

> (iii) the award deals with a dispute not contemplated by or not falling within the terms of the submission to arbitration, or contains decisions on matters beyond the scope of the submission to arbitration, provided that, if the decisions on matters submitted to arbitration can be separated from those not so submitted, only that part of the award which contains decisions on matters not submitted to arbitration may be set aside;...

10.46 This ground of challenge contemplates a situation in which an award has been made by a tribunal that did have jurisdiction to deal with the dispute, but which exceeded its powers by dealing with matters that had not been submitted to it.[76] By way of example, the Paris Cour d'Appel found that a tribunal exceeded its mission by awarding a party damages in an amount that significantly exceeded the damages claimed.[77]

---

[75] See, e.g., *Arab National Bank v El Sharif Saoud Bin Masoud Bin Haza'a El-Abdali* [2004] EWHC 2381; *Republic of Kazakhstan v Istil Group Inc.* [2004] Eng Comm QBD 579, in which an award was set aside based on the Republic of Kazakhstan failing to become a party to the relevant arbitration agreement. See also *Dallah Real Estate and Tourism Holding Co. v The Ministry of Religious Affairs, Government of Pakistan* [2010] UKSC 46 (on appeal from [2009] EWCA Civ 755), in which, in an ICC arbitration with its seat in Paris, the tribunal determined that it had jurisdiction over a non-signatory to the arbitration agreement. In enforcement proceedings, the English Supreme Court, applying French law, later determined that the tribunal did not have jurisdiction over the non-signatory. Subsequently, the losing party brought an action to set aside the award in France, but the Paris Cour d'Appel refused to set aside the award. See also *Jianlong v Golden Ocean* [2013] EWHC 1063, in which a party challenged the award on the basis that the underlying contracts were illegal under Chinese law, and that therefore the arbitration agreements contained in those contracts were also illegal and unenforceable as a matter of English public policy. The court refused to annul the award.

[76] See Liebscher, *The Healthy Award: Challenge in International Commercial Arbitration* (Kluwer Law International, 2003), ch. V(6).

[77] *Paris Lapeyre v Sauvage* [2001] Rev Arb 806, n. Derains. See also *Thai-Lao Lignite & Hongsa Lignite v Laos*, Oral decision, Malaysian High Court, 27 December 2012, reported in *Global Arbitration Review*, available online at http://globalarbitrationreview.com/news/article/31077/laos-award-set-aside-malaysia/, granting Laos's application to set aside an UNCITRAL award in the claimants' favour, finding that the tribunal had exceeded its jurisdiction under s. 37 of the Malaysian Arbitration Act 2005. The court held that the tribunal had 'lumped together and co-mingled' claims filed by the claimants that arose under two separate contracts, each governed by different laws (New York and Laotian, respectively); because it could not be established which parts of the award related to claims under which agreement, the entire award had to be vacated. But compare *Greek Paper Holdings v Greece*, Case No. 102/2012, Areios Pagos (Supreme Court of Greece), holding that, unless otherwise agreed, the parties are free to raise additional claims or

C. Grounds for Challenge

10.47 In another case, a US appellate court held that an arbitral panel exceeded its authority by finding that a requirement under the United Kingdom–Argentina bilateral investment treaty (BIT) that an investor seek relief in local Argentine courts was not a condition precedent to arbitration.[78] The court determined that an arbitrator's decision on whether a condition precedent for arbitrability needed to be fulfilled was beyond the scope of the arbitrators' powers. However, the US Supreme Court reversed that holding, concluding that 'the arbitrators' jurisdictional determinations [we]re lawful'[79]—that is, that the arbitral panel had the authority to determine the issue of whether the local litigation requirement had been fulfilled (or was required to be fulfilled).

10.48 Where an arbitral tribunal fails to deal with *all* of the issues referred to it for determination, it is usually said that the award should at least be held valid in respect of the issues with which it *does* deal.[80] However, this is perhaps too simplistic. The significance of the issues that were not dealt with must be considered in relation to the award as a whole. For example, it is not difficult to envisage a situation in which the issues that were overlooked were of such importance that, had they been dealt with, the whole balance of the award would have been altered and its effect would have been different.

10.49 In such circumstances, it seems fair that the aggrieved party should have a right of recourse against the entire award. Such a right of recourse is found in many national systems of law,[81] but not in the Model Law.[82] Moreover, whilst it appeared as a ground for refusal of recognition and enforcement of an award under the Geneva Convention of 1927, it is not found in the New York Convention.[83]

---

counterclaims over the course of the arbitration, with the permission of the tribunal, as long as all such claims arise out of the same legal relationship already referred to arbitration. The Court further held that a tribunal may issue a declaratory judgment as regards potential future disputes relating to the same legal relationship, as long as they are sufficiently definite and would fall under the scope of the arbitration—even if the arbitration agreement does not explicitly envision future disputes.

[78] *Republic of Argentina v BG Group PLC* 665 F.3d 1363 (DC Cir. 2012).
[79] *BG Group PLC v Republic of Argentina* 134 S.Ct. 1198 (2014), at [19].
[80] To this effect, see van den Berg, *The New York Arbitration Convention* (Kluwer International Law, 1981), p. 318, who points out that the making of an award that is *infra petita* is no longer a ground for refusal of recognition and enforcement under the New York Convention, as it was under the Geneva Convention of 1927.
[81] See the Netherlands Arbitration Act 1986, s. 1065, for an example of a national system containing such a provision. But note that where the parties have discovered that the arbitral tribunal omitted to decide an issue before it, an additional award must first have been applied for and rejected before there is an admissible ground for setting aside: s. 1065(6).
[82] However, Model Law, Art. 33(3), may provide the answer to this problem, in that, at the request of a party, the arbitral tribunal may make an additional award where claims have not been dealt with in the award.
[83] It has been suggested that the same result can be achieved by applying to set aside the award in its country of origin and then by relying on Art. V(1)(e) of the New York Convention, which provides that recognition and enforcement of the award may be refused if it has been set aside in the country in which it was made: see van den Berg, *The New York Arbitration Convention* (Kluwer International Law, 1981), p. 321.

(iii) Arbitrability

10.50 The concept of 'arbitrability' constitutes another ground to challenge an award that has already been discussed in detail.[84] In the terms of the Model Law, an award can be challenged if 'the subject matter of the dispute is not capable of settlement by arbitration'.[85] In the United States, the issue is confused by the use of two concepts: 'procedural arbitrability', which addresses issues of admissibility of a claim; and 'substantive arbitrability', which refers to the situation addressed here in which the subject matter itself is not arbitrable. It is by reference to the law of the place of arbitration that a decision is made as to whether or not the dispute is 'capable of settlement by arbitration' (that is, 'arbitrable').

10.51 As discussed in Chapter 2, the arbitrability of a dispute is usually linked to the underlying public policy of the state in which the arbitration takes place.[86] For example, many states prohibit the arbitration of disputes that are not suited to the confidential nature of the arbitral process and which need to take effect vis-à-vis the world at large. Typically, these include questions of insolvency, personal status, and certain types of intellectual property dispute (such as the validity of patents). The trend has been towards increasing the scope of arbitrable disputes. For example, historic reticence to permit arbitration of antitrust disputes in the United States has given way to a broad incorporation of arbitration for such disputes.[87]

(c) Procedural grounds

10.52 The second broad category of grounds for challenging arbitral awards relates to deficiencies in the way in which the arbitral tribunal was appointed or the arbitral procedure was conducted. As set out in Article 34(2)(c)(ii) of the Model Law, an award can be challenged when 'the party making the application was not given proper notice of the appointment of an arbitrator or of the arbitral proceedings or was otherwise unable to present his case'.

(i) Lack of due process—procedural irregularity

10.53 Certain minimum procedural standards must be observed in the fair and proper conduct of an international arbitration. These procedural standards are designed

---

[84] See Chapter 2.
[85] Model Law, Art. 34(2)(b)(i). See, e.g., Belgian Arbitration Law 2013, s. 1676(5), providing that certain categories of labour dispute are not arbitrable, and that any arbitration agreement relating to such disputes shall be null and void.
[86] For example, in France, limits to arbitrability are set by French concepts of international public policy. See, e.g., the decision of the Paris Cour d'Appel in *Ganz v Nationale des Chemins de Fer Tunisiens (SNCFT)* [1991] Rev Arb 478, n. Ilot; the decision of the Paris Cour d'Appel in *Macron et IDD c/SCAP* [2003] Rev Arb 177, n. Boursier. In Belgium, arbitrability is subject to the Belgian courts' reference to their own mandatory rules of law, such as the Belgian Distributorship Law: Verbist, 'Arbitrability of exclusive distributorship agreements in Belgium: *Lex fori* (and *lex contractus*)?' (2005) 22 J Intl Arb 427.
[87] See *Mitsubishi Motors Corporation v Soler Chrysler-Plymouth, Inc.* 473 US 614, 632 (1985).

C. Grounds for Challenge

to ensure that the arbitral tribunal is properly constituted, that the arbitral procedure is in accordance with the agreement of the parties (subject to any mandatory provisions of the applicable law), and that the parties are given proper notice of the proceedings, hearings, and awards.[88] In short, the aim is to ensure that the parties are treated with equality and are given a fair hearing, with a proper opportunity to present their respective cases.[89]

Most lawyers with experience of litigation or arbitration should find it relatively easy to agree upon these basic principles. The same body of lawyers, however, might find it more difficult to agree upon a specific set of rules designed to implement them. Some national systems of law, whilst rightly insisting upon the need for each of the parties to an arbitration to be given a fair hearing, have little or no legislation to guide the parties or the arbitral tribunal. In practice, it is left to national courts to determine, from case to case, exactly what is required to constitute a 'fair hearing'. This may require that the parties be heard, be allowed to attend any oral hearings, and be represented or assisted by a representative of their choice. Failure to observe these rules of procedure may be a ground for the challenge of an award,[90] although procedural grounds for challenge are often rightly viewed by many national courts with circumspection, because they are often employed by unsuccessful parties in an opportunistic attempt to avoid compliance with the award.[91]   **10.54**

By way of example, US federal courts have regarded the failure to give the parties an oral hearing where one is requested to be a violation of due process, and they   **10.55**

---

[88] See, e.g., certain court decisions in Spain holding that arbitral awards are equivalent to court decisions and that, as such, arbitral awards should not be considered validly notified if they could not have been properly notified under the procedural rules applying to court decisions: Hamilton and Vasquez, 'Madrid update: Due process in the notification of arbitral awards' (2007) 22 Mealey's Intl Arb Rep 27.

[89] The requirement of equality is a specific requirement of some laws: see, e.g., Swiss PIL, Ch. 12, s. 190.

[90] See, e.g., the kinds of 'serious irregularity' referred to in the English Arbitration Act 1996, s. 68(1)–(3). The English view is that there must be an irregularity of a specified kind and that the court must consider that the irregularity has caused or will cause substantial injustice: Shore and Carey, 'Procedural irregularity: Setting aside or remitting awards under English and Irish law—A comparative assessment' (2005) Intl ALR 58.

[91] See, e.g., Decision of 7 January 2004, Case No 4P_196/2003 (2004) 3 ASA Bulletin 592, in which the Swiss Federal Tribunal held that there was no absolute right for a party to hear a witness orally or to ask questions to witnesses the arbitrators had refused to hear. See also, e.g., Decision of 1 July 2004, Case No. 4P_93/2004 (2005) 1 ASA Bulletin 139, in which the Swiss Federal Tribunal held that the mere violation of a procedural rule was not sufficient to have an award set aside. In England, see, e.g., *Lesotho Highlands Development Authority v Impregilo SpA and ors* [2005] 3 WLR 129, in which the House of Lords confirmed the exceptional nature of the remedy available for serious irregularity under s. 68 of the English Arbitration Act 1996; *World Trade Corporation Ltd v Czarnikow Sugar Ltd* [2004] EWHC 2332, in which the Court rejected the argument that failure by the tribunal to give sufficient weight to evidence could fall under s. 68(2)(d) of the 1996 Act 1996. With respect to Hong Kong, see, e.g., *Grand Pacific Holdings Ltd v Pacific China Holdings Ltd*, CACV 136/2011, 19 February 2013, in which the Court of Final Appeal affirmed the Court of Appeal's decision that the procedural irregularities alleged by the losing party were not 'egregious' enough to warrant annulment.

recognise this as a ground for setting aside an award or for refusing recognition and enforcement under the New York Convention.[92] In civil law systems, the right of the parties to have a full opportunity to present their case—the classic *droit de la defense*—often incorporates the *principe du contradictoire*, which requires that no evidence or argument should serve as a basis for a decision unless it has been subject to the possibility of comment and contradiction by the other parties.[93]

10.56 Thus, when a question arises as to whether or not an arbitration was conducted properly, each national court approaches the question from its own particular national standpoint. This is understandable—indeed, inevitable—but it may lead to difficulties. The arbitration proceedings may have been conducted by lawyers from different legal backgrounds, accustomed to different procedures and professional ethics.[94] The rules of the leading arbitral institutions are themselves vague on the question of what procedure should be followed. This is a deliberate policy, since the rules are intended to be suitable for use in many different countries of the world, with many different systems of trial.[95] However, international arbitration has become sufficiently established and widespread for the development of some common procedures, as discussed in Chapter 6.[96]

---

[92] See *Parsons Whittemore Overseas Co. Inc. v Société Générale de l'Industrie du Papier (RAKTA)* 508 F.2d 969 (2nd Cir. 1974).

[93] See, e.g., the decision of the Paris Cour d'Appel in *Burkinabe des Ciments et Matérieux (CIMAT) v Société des Ciments d'Abidjan (SCA)* [2001] Rev Arb 165, n. Cohen. See also *Guignier v HRA Europe* [2001] Rev Arb 199, n. Pinsolle; the decision of the Paris Cour d'Appel in *Société Fashion Box Group SPA v Société AJ Heelstone LLC* [2006] Rev Arb 857; the decision of the Paris Cour d'Appel in *Société Leng d'or v Société Pavan SPA* [2007] Rev Arb 933; *Gouvernement de la République arage d'Egypte c/société Malicorp Ltd*, Cour de Cassation, Ch. Civ. 1ere, 23 June 2010, [2011] Rev Arb 446, in which the French court set aside the award because it was based on legal grounds not raised with the parties; *F Ltd v M Ltd* [2009] EWHC 275 (TCC), at [55]–[56], in which the English High Court remitted the award back to tribunal on the basis that the tribunal had rendered its award on grounds not raised by parties; cf. *Terna Bahrain Holding Co. v Ali Marzook Ali Bin Kamil Al Shamsi et al.* [2012] EWHC 3283 (Comm), in which the London High Court dismissed a set aside action against an ICC award in favour of a Bahraini construction company, dismissing the challengers' contention that the arbitrator had effected a serious irregularity of procedure under s. 68 of the English Arbitration Act 1996 by deciding the case on a basis allegedly not advanced by a party and which the party thus had no opportunity to address. According to Popplewell J, at [85]: 'Relief under section 68 will only be appropriate where the tribunal has gone so wrong in its conduct of the arbitration, and where its conduct is so far removed from what could reasonably be expected from the arbitral process, that justice calls out for it to be corrected.' The court found that no such situation existed in that case.

[94] For example, in some common law systems, it is usual for lawyers to interview witnesses and take statements from them before the hearing—a practice that may be frowned upon (and, indeed, regarded as a breach of professional ethics) in other countries.

[95] Berger, 'Art. 15 UNCITRAL Arbitration Rules: The eternal conflict between arbitral discretion and the parties' due process rights' (2006) 21 Mealey's Intl Arb Rep 29: 'It will ultimately rest on the arbitrators to reconcile the procedural rules with the mandatory rules of due process in order to ensure the integrity of the award.'

[96] Of particular note, the 1996 UNCITRAL Notes on Organizing Arbitration Proceedings, discussed in Chapter 6, should assist in establishing common and acceptable procedures. The IBA Rules on the Taking of Evidence in International Commercial Arbitration (adopted in June 1999 and revised in May 2010) are also an example of commonly accepted procedures in arbitration: they

C. Grounds for Challenge

In Europe, the concept of 'due process' has found expression in the European Convention on Human Rights (ECHR),[97] Article 6(1) of which provides that: 'In the determination of his civil rights and obligations or of any criminal charge against him, everyone is entitled to a fair and public hearing within a reasonable time by an independent and impartial tribunal established by law.' **10.57**

An agreement to arbitrate constitutes a valid waiver of Article 6 ECHR in that arbitration provides no entitlement to a public hearing and an arbitral tribunal is not, within the meaning of Article 6, considered a 'tribunal established by law'.[98] For these reasons, the Swiss Federal Supreme Court held that Article 6 does not apply in arbitration proceedings.[99] In so doing, however, it also held that the arbitral tribunal must nevertheless respect fundamental rules of due process. This finding was echoed in England following the entry into force of the Human Rights Act 1998, which implemented the ECHR. Thus, in *Mousaka v Golden Seagull Maritime*,[100] the court held that: 'The tentacles of the Human Rights Act 1998 reach into some unexpected places. The Commercial Court, even, when exercising its supervisory rule as regards arbitration, is not immune.' **10.58**

It would be difficult to reach a contrary conclusion. An arbitration agreement may constitute a waiver of the right of access to the courts, but is not intended to be a blanket waiver of the guarantees to a 'fair hearing' contained in Article 6 ECHR.[101] When considering a challenge to an award on grounds of a violation of 'due process', courts in Europe may well therefore have regard to the safeguards contained therein. **10.59**

(ii) Further procedural issues

An award is also at risk of challenge where the composition of the arbitral tribunal and the procedure adopted in the arbitration are not in conformity with the agreement of the parties or, failing such agreement, with the law.[102] By way of **10.60**

---

provide a basic framework for the taking of evidence that reflects an international consensus that borrows from both the common law and civil law procedural traditions.

[97] Convention for the Protection of Human Rights and Fundamental Freedoms (Rome, 4 November 1950) (as amended).

[98] For a comprehensive survey of case law on the relationship between Art. 6 ECHR and arbitration, see Liebscher, *The Healthy Award: Challenge in International Commercial Arbitration* (Kluwer Law International, 2003), pp. 61*ff*.

[99] Swiss Federal Supreme Court, 11 June 2001 [2001] ASA Bulletin 566. See also the Paris Cour d'Appel decision of 15 September 1998 in *Cubic Defence Systems v Chambre de Commerce International* [1999] Rev Arb 103, n. Lalive, and the Cour de Cassation decision in the same case two years later, [2001] Rev Arb 511, n. Clay, in which the French courts found that, as an arbitral institution, the ICC International Court of Arbitration was not a 'judicial body' within the meaning of Art. 6 ECHR.

[100] [2001] 2 Lloyd's Rep 657.

[101] See Petrochilos, *Procedural Law in International Arbitration* (Oxford University Press, 2004), para. 4.51.

[102] See Liebscher, *The Healthy Award: Challenge in International Commercial Arbitration* (Kluwer Law International, 2003), ch. V(5). See also Model Law, Art. 34(2)(a)(iv). But note that the Belgium Arbitration Law of 2013 limits the Model Law's grounds for challenge. Under the Model Law, an

example, a failure to comply with the agreement of the parties as to the appointment of the tribunal could include cases in which an arbitrator does not meet the particular qualifications specified in the arbitration agreement; failure to comply with the required procedure could include the rendering of an award without reasons where such a requirement is imposed by law.

10.61 If there is no specific agreement between the parties as to the composition of the tribunal, there can be no complaint if the arbitrators are selected according to the method prescribed by the applicable rules or law. Similarly, if there is no agreement between the parties as to the arbitral procedure, there can be no complaint if the procedure that is followed is imposed by the arbitral tribunal in accordance with its powers, provided that there is compliance with principles of due process such as a fair hearing. However, if there is an agreement between the parties as to the composition of the arbitral tribunal or as to the procedure to be followed or both, this agreement may be disregarded only if it is in conflict with a mandatory provision of the law of the place of arbitration. In such a case, the tribunal would be well advised to communicate and explain this conflict to the parties in order to allow them to comment before any aspect of the agreement is discarded.

10.62 Not all procedural irregularities are equal or sufficient to set aside an award. The materiality to the outcome will be relevant. In *Chantiers de l'Atlantique SA v Gaztransport & Technigaz SAS*,[103] the Commercial Court in London held that even fraud in the arbitral proceedings would not necessarily justify setting the award aside. The court held that a witness for Gaztransport had deliberately misled the arbitral tribunal. However, despite agreeing with the claimant on the existence of fraud in the proceedings, the court held that the fraudulent testimony did not justify setting the award aside, because 'even if the true position had been disclosed to the tribunal, that would, in all probability, not have affected the result of the arbitration'.[104]

10.63 Finally, it is worth noting that some courts treat procedural irregularities—if serious enough—as amounting to violations of public policy. The Tokyo District Court found that a tribunal's treatment of a disputed fact as undisputed amounted to a sufficiently serious procedural irregularity so as to violate Japanese public policy, thereby warranting annulment.[105]

---

award may be set aside if the procedure deviates from that agreed upon by the parties; under the new Belgian law, the award may be set aside only if that deviation was so significant that it actually affected the outcome.

[103] [2011] EWHC 3383.

[104] Ibid., at [369]. (Section 68 of the English Arbitration Act 1996 allows, but does not require, a court to set aside an award on the grounds of 'serious irregularity', including where an award is 'obtained by fraud'.)

[105] *Heisei 21* (Chu) No. 6, Tokyo District Court (13 June 2011), published in *Hanrei Jiho* No. 2128, at 58. See also the judgment of the Polish Supreme Court in Case No. I CSK 312/11, dated 9 March 2012, available online at http://arbitration-poland.com/case-law, analysing a challenge

C. Grounds for Challenge

(d) Substantive grounds

10.64 Few jurisdictions permit any form of appeal on the law or facts from an arbitral award. If the tribunal has jurisdiction, the correct procedures are followed, and the correct formalities are observed, the award—good, bad, or indifferent—is final and binding on the parties.

10.65 The question, however, arises: is it enough to ensure that the correct procedures have been observed, as the Model Law requires, or is something more needed—ranging from correction of any mistakes of law to a complete review of the dispute—so as to ensure that the arbitral tribunal has reached the correct decision?

(i) Mistake of law

10.66 The argument in favour of reviewing arbitral decisions in order to guard against mistakes of law is not difficult to make. There are obvious risks in having a legal system that leaves arbitral awards entirely free from appeal or judicial review. First, there is the risk of inconsistent decisions as the same or similar points come before different tribunals, each one of which is independent of the other. Such tribunals are generally unaware that the same point of law may already have been decided in a different way by another tribunal (although this is not so in several ICSID cases, in which later tribunals have decided the same point of law differently in full knowledge of the earlier decision). This is likely to be of particular importance where the decision turns upon the correct interpretation of a standard-form clause in a widely used contract—such as the Federation of Consulting Engineers (FIDIC) suite of Model Conditions that are widely used for international construction projects, the standard-form contracts used throughout the worldwide commodity, shipping, insurance, or reinsurance markets, or the basic concepts underpinning the substantive protections of investment treaties. Secondly, there is the risk that the arbitral tribunal may not do its work as competently or as professionally as it should if its awards are not subject to substantive scrutiny, either by an arbitral institution[106] or by a competent court.

10.67 There are nevertheless serious disadvantages in having a system of arbitration that gives an unrestricted right of appeal from arbitral awards. First, the decisions of national judges may be substituted for the decisions of an arbitral tribunal specifically selected by, or on behalf of, the parties. Secondly, a party that agreed to arbitration as a private method of resolving disputes may find itself brought unwillingly before national courts that hold their hearings in public. Thirdly, the appeal process may be used simply to postpone the day on which payment is due, so that one of the

---

based on the parties' right to be heard under the lens of public polic, and acknowledging that 'procedural public policy' exists.

[106] For example, ICC Rules, Art. 33, provides for the scrutiny of an award by the ICC's Court before the award is finalised and issued to the parties. This helps to ensure a measure of 'quality control', but the scrutiny is principally as to form and does not affect the tribunal's liberty of decision.

main purposes of international arbitration—the speedy resolution of disputes—is defeated. It is not easy to strike a balance between the need for finality in the arbitral process and the wider public interest in some measure of judicial control, if only to ensure consistency of decisions and predictability of the operation of the law. Internationally, however, the balance has come down overwhelmingly in favour of finality and against judicial review, except in very limited circumstances. The Model Law sets the tone, as has been seen, when Article 5 proclaims that, '[i]n matters governed by this Law, no court shall intervene except where so provided in this Law'.

10.68 The extent of court intervention permitted by different states may be viewed as a spectrum. At one end of the spectrum are states such as France and Switzerland, which exercise a very limited control over international arbitral awards and permit certain parties to 'contract out' of control by the courts of the seat altogether. In the middle of the scale, a large number of states have adopted (either in full or with some modifications) the limited grounds of recourse laid down in the Model Law, which mirror the grounds for refusal of enforcement under the New York Convention. The United States also exercises a similar level of control over awards in its territory. At the other end of the spectrum are countries such as England, which operate a range of controls, including a limited right of appeal on questions of law, which the parties may agree to waive. The examples that follow illustrate the different approaches, including the systems adopted by some of the major countries selected as seats for international arbitration.

10.69 The admonition in the Model Law *against* intervention by national courts in the process of international arbitration was taken to extremes by Belgium, which, at one time, 'delocalised' international arbitration by eliminating the possibility of setting aside an award made in Belgium when none of the parties was a natural person having Belgian nationality or residence, or a legal person having its main office or a seat of operations in Belgium. However, rather than encouraging parties to select Belgium as a seat, it had the opposite effect: the absence of any control by the courts of the seat, however grave the violation of parties' rights by the arbitral tribunal, appeared to create a 'delocalised' award that could be controlled only upon enforcement. The experiment was abandoned and, in 1998, recourse to the Belgian courts to set aside an award made in Belgium was reinstated, even for foreign nationals or corporations, unless they chose expressly to exclude any such application, either in the arbitration agreement itself or in any subsequent agreement.[107]

10.70 France distinguishes between 'domestic' and 'international' arbitrations, and does not permit appeals on points of law to its courts from an international award.

---

[107] Article 1717.4 of the Law of 19 May 1998, amending the Belgian law on arbitration, reads as follows: 'The parties may, by an express statement in the arbitration agreement or by a subsequent agreement exclude any application to set aside the arbitral award when none of the parties is either an individual of Belgian nationality or residing in Belgium or a legal person having its head office or a branch there.' (Translation by Bernard Hanotiau and Joanne Riches.) This remains the state of affairs under the 2013 Belgian Arbitration Law.

C. Grounds for Challenge

Under the French 2011 Arbitration Law, the grounds for recourse against an international award made in France are more limited than those set out in the Model Law,[108] being

- if the arbitral tribunal wrongly upheld or declined jurisdiction;
- if the arbitral tribunal was not properly constituted;
- if the arbitral tribunal ruled without complying with the mandate conferred upon it;
- if due process has been violated; and/or
- if the recognition or enforcement is contrary to international public policy (*ordre public international*).[109]

10.71 Since 2011, French law has adopted the Belgian approach and permits parties to contract out of court control.[110] Indeed, it has gone further, since it does not limit that power to parties who have no connection with France.

10.72 In Switzerland, an award may be set aside only on grounds that closely reflect the French system.[111] There has to have been a defect in the appointment of the arbitral tribunal, a lack of jurisdiction, a failure to decide a claim,[112] a failure to submit deciding claims to arbitration, a failure to treat the parties equally, or incompatibility with public policy.[113] Setting-aside proceedings may be brought only before the Federal Tribunal.[114] In a reflection of the Belgian position, if none of the parties has its domicile, habitual residence, or business establishment in Switzerland, parties may agree (either in the arbitration agreement or subsequently) to exclude all setting-aside proceedings or to limit such proceedings to one or more of the grounds listed in the Act.[115]

10.73 Under section 10(1) of the US Federal Arbitration Act of 1925 (FAA), a court may set aside (or, in the language of the statute, 'vacate') an award in the following circumstances:

(1) where the award was procured by corruption, fraud, or undue means;
(2) where there was evident partiality or corruption in the arbitrators, or [any] of them;

---

[108] Compare arts 1518*ff* of the French Code of Civil Procedure (incorporating the French 2011 Arbitration Law) with the Model Law, Art. 34.
[109] See French Code of Civil Procedure, art. 1520.
[110] See French Code of Civil Procedure, art. 1522 ('By way of a specific agreement the parties may, at any time, expressly waive their right to bring an action to set aside').
[111] If the arbitration is conducted under the Swiss PIL, Ch. 12, which applies to international arbitrations.
[112] See, however, *LV Finance Group Ltd v IPOC International Growth Fund Ltd (Bermuda)*, Case No. 4P_102 (2006) (1st Div. SFT), in which the Swiss Federal Tribunal held that an ICC tribunal's failure to consider facts that later became available would be a ground to set aside the award. The Federal Tribunal was of the view that the ICC tribunal would have come to a different judgment if those facts had been available in the proceedings; therefore it held that the ICC tribunal committed an error of law and would need to reconsider its decision based on the new facts.
[113] This is a précis of the full text of Swiss PIL, s. 190.
[114] Swiss PIL, Ch. 12, s. 191.
[115] Swiss PIL, Ch. 12, s. 192(1).

(3) where the arbitrators were guilty of misconduct in refusing to postpone the hearing, upon sufficient cause shown, or in refusing to hear evidence pertinent and material to the controversy; or any other misbehavior by which the rights of any party have been prejudiced; or

(4) where the arbitrators exceeded their powers, or so imperfectly executed them that a mutual, final, and definite award upon the subject matter submitted was not made.[116]

10.74 The statute does not provide expressly for any judicial review of an arbitral award on the basis of a mistake of law, and US courts have held that an award may not be set aside on such grounds.[117] Nevertheless, some US courts have followed a dictum in *Wilko v Swan*,[118] which considered that awards could be set aside for 'manifest disregard of the law'. However, the US courts have now mostly taken a very restrictive view on challenging awards based on manifest disregard of law.[119] This is confirmed by the decisions of *Hall Street Associates v Mattel*[120] and *Prime Therapeutics LLC v Omnicare, Inc.*[121] It should be noted, however, that *Hall Street* did not lay the matter to rest definitively, and the US Supreme Court has since declined to address whether manifest disregard of the law can be subsumed under the enumerated grounds for challenge under the FAA—such as excess of powers.[122] Lower level appellate courts have taken divergent approaches regarding the continued vitality of the doctrine. For example, the Fifth Circuit has rejected the doctrine in its entirety.[123] On the other hand, the Second Circuit has held that manifest disregard of the law survives as a valid (though narrow) ground for challenge.[124] Nevertheless, even in the Second Circuit, the court has noted that 'review under the manifest disregard standard,

---

[116] There is a possibility of the award being remitted to the arbitrators, where the time within which the award was to be made has not expired: FAA, § 10(b)(5).

[117] See, e.g., *Baxter International Inc. v Abbott Laboratories*, 315 F.3d 829 (7th Cir. 2003).

[118] 346 US 427, 74 S.Ct 182 (1953). In *Shanghai Foodstuffs Import & Export Corporation v International Chemical, Inc.* Case No. 99 CV 3320, 2004 US Dist. LEXIS 1423 (SDNY, 4 February 2004), it was acknowledged that US courts had the authority to set aside non-domestic awards that were rendered in the United States on the basis of 'manifest disregard of the law'.

[119] Beraudo, 'Egregious error of law as grounds for setting aside an arbitral award' (2006) 23 J Intl Arb 351.

[120] *Hall Street Associates, LLC v Mattel, Inc* 552 US 576 (2008). See also Wilske and Mackay, 'The myth of the "manifest disregard of the law" doctrine: Is this challenge to the finality of arbitral awards confined to US domestic arbitrations or should international arbitration practitioners be concerned?' (2006) 24 ASA Bulletin 216.

[121] *Prime Therapeutics LLC v Omnicare, Inc.* 555 F.Supp.2d 993, 999 (D. Minn. 2008).

[122] *Stolt-Nielsen SA v Animal Feeds International Corporation* 130 S.Ct 1758, 1768 (2010), holding that arbitrators exceeded their powers when they granted class arbitration even though the agreement was silent as to class arbitration and overturning the award on basis of public policy, but expressly declining to decide whether 'manifest disregard' survived *Hall Street*.

[123] *Citigroup Global Markets v Bacon* 562 F.3d 349, 350 (5th Cir. 2009): '*Hall Street* restricts the grounds for vacatur to those set forth in § 10 of the Federal Arbitration Act (FAA), and consequently manifest disregard of the law is no longer an independent ground for vacating arbitral awards.'

[124] See *T.Co Metals, LLC v Dempsey Pipe & Supply, Inc.* 592 F.3d 329, 339–340 (2nd Cir. 2010) ('manifest disregard remains a valid ground for vacating arbitration awards').

C. Grounds for Challenge

however, is highly deferential to the arbitrators, and relief on such a claim is therefore rare'.[125]

This approach can be contrasted with the Model Law, in which there is no possibility for challenging an award on the basis of mistake of law, however narrow. On the other hand, in England, a limited right to seek appeal is preserved by section 69 of the Arbitration Act 1996, but it is not unrestricted. First, the parties may 'contract out' of any right of appeal to the national court before or after the start of arbitration proceedings. Although their agreement to do so must be in writing, the provision contained in standard-form rules of arbitration to the effect that the award shall be final and binding has been held to constitute a valid agreement to waive this right.[126] Secondly, even if the right of appeal has been retained, it is in effect a right of appeal only on questions of *English* law.[127] This is important because, given London's position as a neutral international seat, the law governing the substance of the dispute may well be that of another state.[128] Thirdly, the right of appeal is available only with leave of the court, and then only if the decision of the tribunal on the question of law is 'obviously wrong', the question is one of 'general public importance', or the decision 'is at least open to serious doubt', so that it would be 'just and proper in all the circumstances for the court to determine the question'.[129] As a matter of practice, English courts have taken a restrictive view on allowing challenges on grounds of a mistake of law.[130]

10.75

On an appeal on a point of English law, the English court has power to confirm the award, to vary it, to remit it to the arbitral tribunal, or to set it aside, but the court should not set aside the award, in whole or in part, unless satisfied that

10.76

---

[125] *Goldman Sachs Execution & Clearing v Official Unsecured Creditors Committee of Bayou Group* 491 Fed. Appx 201, 2012 US App. LEXIS 13531, 3–4 (2012). See also *Westminster Securities Corporation v Petrocom Energy*, 456 Fed. Appx 42, US App. LEXIS 1069 (2012) (characterising the appropriate standard of review for challenges of manifest disregard as 'extremely deferential').

[126] See, e.g., *Sanghi Polyesters Ltd v The International Investor (KCFC)* [2001] 1 Lloyd's Rep 480. See also *Lesotho Highlands Development Authority v Impreglio SpA and ors* [2005] UKHL 43, at [3] per Lord Steyn, in which it was held that Art. 28(6) of the ICC Rules (now Art. 34(6) of the 2012 ICC Rules) excluded a right of challenge.

[127] English Arbitration Act 1996, ss 69(1) and 82(1). The underlying policy of the English legislators was related to the long-established tradition of arbitration by non-lawyers in certain commercial sectors, e.g. the construction industry or trading in commodities, and the need for certainty regarding the way in which form clauses were to be interpreted.

[128] See, e.g., *AEK v National Basket Association* [2002] 1 All ER (Comm) 70, in which permission to appeal on a point of law under s. 69 was rejected because it related to the arbitrator's application of Greek law.

[129] English Arbitration Act 1996, s. 69(2) and (3). See, e.g., *MRI Trading v Erdenet Mining* [2013] EWCA 156, in which a London Metal Exchange tribunal held that a sale contract was an unenforceable agreement to agree, whilst ignoring the provision requiring that the contract be construed together with a separate settlement agreement, which was the quid pro quo for the sale contract. The Court of Appeal determined that this was obviously wrong as a matter of English law and annulled the award.

[130] For a comprehensive discussion, see Sutton, Gill, and Gearing (eds) *Russell on Arbitration* (23rd edn, Sweet & Maxwell, 2007), paras 8-119–8-161.

it would be inappropriate to submit the matters in question to the tribunal for reconsideration.[131] No further appeal is possible, unless the court considers the question to be one of general importance or one that, for some special reason, should be considered by the Court of Appeal.

(ii) Mistake of fact

10.77 The principal justification for allowing an appeal from the award of an arbitral tribunal on questions of law is that it is in the public interest that the law should be certain, and that, in particular, there should not be different findings by different tribunals as to the meaning and effect of the same words in different contracts.[132] There can be no such general interest in the findings of fact of a particular tribunal in a particular case. They may be wrong—even badly wrong—but that is likely to be of interest only to the parties. Accordingly, almost all states with developed laws of arbitration refuse to allow appeals from arbitral tribunals on issues of fact.[133]

10.78 The question may then be posed: what if the parties wish to expand, by contract, the scope of the reviewing courts powers? This issue was addressed in the US case *LaPine Technology Corporation v Kyocera Corporation*,[134] in which the arbitration clause, after providing for arbitration in accordance with the ICC Rules and the FAA, went on to say:

> The United States District Court for the Northern District of California may enter judgment upon any award, either by confirming the award or by vacating, modifying or correcting the award. The Court shall vacate, modify or correct any award: (i) based upon any of the grounds referred to in the Federal Arbitration Act, (ii) where the arbitrators' findings of fact are not supported by substantial evidence or (iii) where the arbitrators' conclusions of law are erroneous.

10.79 In the district court, Kyocera applied to modify and vacate the award, on the grounds that there were findings of fact that the evidence did not support and that there were wrong conclusions of law. The US court held that its jurisdiction was determined by the FAA and could not be expanded by a private contract.[135] However, the Ninth Circuit overturned this decision and allowed the appeal. The court confirmed that review would be for errors of fact or law, and held that this agreement should be enforced. Accordingly, the District Court was required to review the award, on issues both of fact and of law. Yet this proved not to be the end of

---

[131] English Arbitration Act 1996, s. 69(7).
[132] Compare the English Arbitration Act 1996, s. 69(3)(c)(ii), which provides that one of the requirements for leave to appeal is that the question of law is 'one of general public importance'.
[133] See, e.g., *Edman Controls, Inc.* 712 F.3d 1021, 1024–1025 (7th Cir. 2013), upholding the district court's judgment that 'neither factual nor legal error is a sufficient ground for vacatur', and adding that the Court 'will not overturn an award because an arbitrator "committed serious error" or the decision is "incorrect or even whacky" ', quoting *Wise v Wachovia* 86 F.3d 96, 100 (7th Cir. 1996).
[134] 130 F.3d 884 (9th Cir. 1997).
[135] *LaPine*, 909 F.Supp. 697 (ND Cal. 1995).

C. Grounds for Challenge

the saga. Applying the broader standards of review laid down by the appellate court, the district court nonetheless confirmed the award. This led Kyocera to appeal again. In an *en banc* ruling that has been referred to as '*LaPine II*',[136] the Ninth Circuit then chose to revisit the issue of whether expanded review clauses are enforceable and, in so doing, overturned its earlier decision, holding that:

> [A] Federal Court may only review an arbitral decision on the grounds set forth in the [FAA]. Private parties have no power to alter or expand those grounds, and any contractual provision purporting to do so is accordingly legally unenforceable.[137]

For some time, there remained a difference of opinion between different US courts as to whether or not parties might expand the scope of review.[138] However, in *Hall Street Associates v Mattel*,[139] the US Supreme Court confirmed that parties could not contractually extend the scope of judicial review of an award,[140] because 'the FAA confine[d] its expedited judicial review to the grounds listed in 9 U. S. C. §§10 and 11'. The US Supreme Court added:

10.80

> Instead of fighting the text, it makes more sense to see the three provisions, sections 9–11, as substantiating a national policy favoring arbitration with just the limited review needed to maintain arbitration's essential virtue of resolving disputes straightaway. Any other reading opens the door to the full-bore legal and evidentiary appeals that can 'rende[r] informal arbitration merely a prelude to a more cumbersome and time-consuming judicial review process,' *Kyocera*, 341 F.3d, at 998; cf. *Ethyl Corp. v. United Steelworkers of America*, 768 F.2d 180, 184 (C.A.7 1985), and bring arbitration theory to grief in the post-arbitration process.[141]

(iii) Public policy

An arbitral award may usually be set aside if a national court of the place of arbitration finds (on its own initiative) that the award is in conflict with the public policy of its own country. This is particularly true for states adopting the Model Law.[142]

10.81

Of course, each state has its own concept of what is required by its 'public policy' (or *ordre public*, in the civil law terminology).[143] It is possible to envisage, for

10.82

---

[136] *Kyocera Corporation v Prudential-Bache Trade Services Inc.* 341 F.3d 987 (9th Cir. 2003).
[137] Ibid., at 988.
[138] See, e.g., *Gateway Tech. Inc. v MCI Telecomms Corporation* 64 F.3d 993 (5th Cir. 1995), enforcing a provision requiring the review of arbitral awards for errors of law; *Bowen v Amoco Pipeline Co.* 254 F.3d 925 (10th Cir. 2001), declining to enforce a provision providing for expanded review. See also Fellas, 'The scope of judicial review of arbitration awards' (2003) 230 New York LJ 1.
[139] *Hall Street Associates, LLC v Mattel, Inc* 552 US 576 (2008), at [19].
[140] Suskin, 'The rejection of contractually expanded judicial review under the Arbitration Act in *Hall Street v Mattel* (06-989)' (2008) 23 Mealey's Intl Arb Rep 1.
[141] *Hall Street*, at 1405.
[142] Model Law, Art. 34(2)(b)(ii).
[143] See, e.g., China's Civil Procedure Rules, according to which the People's Court may refuse enforcement of a foreign-related award where it would 'run counter to the social and public interests of the country': Yeoh and Fu, 'The People's Court and arbitration: A snapshot of recent judicial attitudes on arbitrability and enforcement' (2007) 24 J Intl Arb 635. See also *Abnaa Al-Khalaf Co.*

example, a dispute over the division of gaming profits from a casino. The dispute may be taken to arbitration and an award made. In many states, the underlying transaction that led to the award would be regarded as a normal commercial transaction and the award would be regarded as valid. However, in states that do not tolerate gambling, the award might well be set aside on the basis that it offends public policy by upholding and interpreting an illegal contract.

10.83 Most developed arbitral jurisdictions have similar conceptions of public policy. According to the Swiss Federal Supreme Court, public policy denotes fundamental legal principles, a departure from which would be incompatible with the Swiss legal and economic system.[144] Similarly, German courts have held that an award will violate public policy if it conflicts with fundamental notions of justice, *bonos mores*, or conflicts with principles that are fundamental national or economic values.[145] In similar terms, the Superior Court of Justice of Ontario refused to set aside an award rendered by a North American Free Trade Agreement (NAFTA) tribunal, holding that, for an award to offend public policy, it:

> ...must fundamentally offend the most basic and explicit principles of justice and fairness in Ontario, or evidence intolerable ignorance or corruption on the part of the arbitral Tribunal... The Applicant must establish that the awards are contrary to the essential morality of Ontario.[146]

10.84 Notwithstanding these similarities, there is inevitably a risk that one state may set aside an award that other states would regard as valid. Even though many states take a restrictive approach to the application of public policy,[147] the nebulous nature of

---

et al. v Sayed Aghajaved Raza, Challenge No. 64, Qatari Court of Cassation (2012), setting aside a Qatari award on grounds of public order, owing to its not being issued in the name of His Highness the Emir of the State of Qatar. According to the Court of Cassation, this formal requirement of national court judgments extended to all arbitral awards.

[144] See, e.g., *Özmak Makina Ve Elektrik Anayi AS v Voest Apline Industrieanlagenbau GmBH and anor*, Case No. 4P_143/2001, Decision of the Swiss Federal Supreme Court, 18 September 2001 (2002) 20 ASA Bulletin 311. See also *Francelino da Silva Matuzalem v Fédération Internationale de Football Association (FIFA)*, Case No. 4A_558/2011, Decision of the Swiss Supreme Court, 27 March 2012, in which the Swiss Supreme Court held that the restriction of a person's economic freedom violated public policy. The case involved a FIFA arbitration in which a football player, who had repeatedly violated his FIFA obligations, was banned from participating in any football-related activity until the full amount that he owed the organisation was paid.

[145] See the decision of the Karlsruhe Court of Appeal of 14 September 2001.

[146] *United Mexican States v Marvin Roy Feldman Karpa*, File No. 03-CV-23500, Ontario Superior Court of Justice, 3 December 2003, at [87].

[147] See, e.g., the English courts in *Protech Projects Construction (Pty) Ltd v Al-Kharafi & Sons* [2005] EWHC 2165 (Comm), in which Langley J stressed that s. 68(2)(g) of the English Arbitration Act 1996 would be available only in extreme cases and that the court would not be concerned with the correctness or otherwise of the award: public policy under English law could be invoked only where the alleged conduct is akin to something 'unconscionable or reprehensible' and where the applicant had suffered 'substantial injustice'. See also the French courts in *SNF SAS v Cytec Industries BV (Holland)*, Cour de Cassation, Ch. Civ. 1ere, 4 June 2008, in which the French Court held that it would refuse enforcement of an arbitral award based on public policy only where it showed obvious signs of breaking public policy, saying that the breach should be 'flagrant, actual and concrete'. French courts have found such a violation of public policy to exist

the concept may be used by courts in some jurisdictions as a licence to review the merits of a dispute inappropriately. With this in mind, the concept of 'international public policy' (*ordre public international*) has been developed by some jurists and is embodied in the French Code of Civil Procedure.[148] As such, an international arbitral award may be set aside in France 'if the recognition or enforcement of the award is contrary to *international* public policy'.[149] In this way, French law recognises the existence of two levels of public policy: the national level, which may be affected by purely domestic considerations; and the international level, which is less restrictive in its approach.

10.85 There is nothing new, as far as arbitration is concerned, in differentiating between national and international public policy. Indeed, it is a consistent theme to be found in the legislation and judicial decisions of many countries.[150] On this basis, an international award would not be set aside simply if it were to fail to conform to a domestic requirement. For example, the absence of reasons, which might lead to an award being annulled in a domestic arbitration, has been held not to vitiate an international award.[151] Some guidance may be found in French court decisions that have expounded upon what constitutes 'international public policy'.[152]

10.86 Increasingly important for arbitrations with a seat within the European Union is the notion of 'EU public policy'. The Court of Justice of the European Union (CJEU) has confirmed that EU member states must consider not only their own national public policy, but also EU public policy (in, for example, competition or consumer protection contexts) when reviewing arbitral awards.[153]

---

where, e.g., an award includes punitive damages: *Fontaine Pajot*, Cour de Cassation, Ch. Civ. lere, 1 December 2010. For its part, the Indian Supreme Court held, in *ONGC v Saw Pipes Ltd* (2003) 5 SCC 705, at 727, that arbitral awards could be annulled if they were contrary to the fundamental policy of Indian law and the interests of India, or justice and morality.

[148] French Code of Civil Procedure, art. 1514 (as amended in 2011).
[149] Ibid., art. 1520 (emphasis added).
[150] Portugal has a similar provision at art. 1096(f) of the 1986 Code of Civil Procedure, which refers to the principles of 'Portuguese international public policy'. See also the German Federal Supreme Court Decision of 1 February 2001, (2001) 1 RPS 14, in which it held that the notion of public policy is more restricted when applied to foreign awards, and in which it distinguished between domestic and international public policy.
[151] See Delvolvé, 'Essai sur la motivation des sentences arbitrales' (1989) 2 Rev Arb 149.
[152] See, e.g., *Jean Lion et Compagnie v International Co. for Commercial Exchanges (INCOME)*, Case No. 08-10.281, Cour de Cassation, Ch. Civ. lere, 6 May 2009, in which the French Court denied enforcement of an award, in part, because it would violate 'international public policy' by ordering an insolvent party to satisfy an award out of his *income*, which violated the rule that individual actions against a creditor are suspended when a receivership procedure is opened, and may be resumed only to establish the credit and determine its amount; *Commercial Caribbean Niquel v Societe Overseas Mining Investments Ltd*, Case No. 08/23901, Paris Cour d'Appel, 25 March 2010, setting aside an arbitral award on the grounds that the tribunal denied the parties due process, and thereby defied international public policy, in the arbitration by failing to invite comments from parties in connection with the award of damages.
[153] See, e.g., Case C-40/80 *Asturcom Telecomunicaciones SL v Cristina Rodriguez Nogueira* [2009] ECR I–9579; Bermann, 'Navigating EU law and the law of international arbitration' (2012) 28 Arb Intl 397.

10.87 If a workable definition of 'international public policy' could be found, it would provide an effective way of preventing an award in an international arbitration from being set aside for purely domestic policy considerations. International public policy would not concern itself with matters of form, or of a purely domestic nature; rather, it would look to the broader public interest of honesty and fair dealing. In its interim report on public policy as a bar to the enforcement of international arbitration awards, the Committee on International Commercial Arbitration of the International Law Association (ILA) reviewed the development of the concept of public policy during the latter part of the twentieth century.[154] In so doing, it observed that, beyond purely domestic public policy (*ordre public interne*), the narrower category of international public policy (*ordre public externe*, or *ordre public international*) is confined to the violation of really fundamental conceptions of the legal order in the country concerned. Narrower still, the ILA identified a further category—namely, 'truly international', or 'transnational', public policy—which it found to be of 'universal application—comprising fundamental rules of natural law, principles of universal justice, *jus cogens* in public international law, and the general principles of morality accepted by what are referred to as "civilised nations" '.[155] Such definitions are undoubtedly helpful, yet for now remain to be widely accepted.[156] Even today, the warning note sounded by an English judge almost 200 years ago still resonates:

> [Public policy is] a very unruly horse, and when once you get astride it you never know where it will carry you. It may lead you from sound law. It is never argued at all, but when other points fail.[157]

(iv) Summary

10.88 This brief review demonstrates that most states are broadly content to restrict the challenge of arbitral awards to excess of jurisdiction and lack of due process. These grounds for challenge are either adopted directly from the Model Law or reflect the policy behind those grounds. In general, the parties are expected to abide by the decision of the tribunal, however disappointed they may be by the outcome. Other states are prepared to offer a limited measure of judicial review on questions of law, if this is what the parties wish—but the possibility of the review of an award on issues of fact is truly rare.[158]

---

[154] ILA, *Interim Report on Public Policy as a Bar to Enforcement of International Arbitral Awards* (2000), available online at http://www.ila-hq.org/.

[155] Ibid., pp. 6 and 7.

[156] For example, some commentators have suggested widening the ground for setting aside an award under public policy to a tribunal's 'egregious errors of law': Hwang and Lai, 'Do egregious errors of law amount to a breach of public policy?' (2005) 71 Arbitration; cf. Hwang, 'Do egregious errors of amount to a breach of public policy? Further developments' (2005) 71 Arbitration 364.

[157] *Richardson v Mellish* (1824) 2 Bing 229, at 252, [1824–34] All ER 258, *per* Burrough J.

[158] See, e.g. Dasser, 'International arbitration and setting-aside proceedings in Switzerland: A statistical analysis' (2007) 25 ASA Bulletin 444. In Switzerland, only 5.4 per cent of challenges were eventually successful, mostly on jurisdictional grounds and never on substantive grounds of public

D. Effects of Challenge

The effects of a successful challenge differ depending upon the grounds of the challenge, the relevant law, and the decision of the court that dealt with it. This decision in itself may take several forms. The court may decide to confirm the award, refer the award back to the arbitral tribunal for reconsideration, vary the award, or set the award aside, in whole or in part. **10.89**

When an award is set aside, it is unenforceable in the country in which it was made, and it will usually be unenforceable elsewhere.[159] In this situation, the party who won the arbitration, but lost the challenge, is in an unenviable position. If, for example, the award has been set aside completely on the basis that the arbitration agreement was null and void, a further resort to arbitration (on the basis of the void agreement) would be out of the question. Resort to litigation might be considered, but there could be problems of time limit, to say nothing of more substantive difficulties. **10.90**

If the award has been set aside for procedural defects (for example lack of due process), the party who won the arbitration, but lost the challenge, will have to resubmit the dispute to arbitration and the process will start over again. This is a daunting prospect for even the most resilient claimant. **10.91**

A successful party does not wish to be deprived of victory because of a procedural failure on the part of the arbitral tribunal. As the practice of international arbitration becomes increasingly litigious, a party who expects to be on the losing side may seek, during the course of the proceedings, to lay the basis for a claim that the hearing was not conducted fairly. This point should be kept well in mind by parties to an arbitration (usually the claimants) who consider that the arbitral tribunal is being too generous to their opponents in allowing extensions of time and giving them a full opportunity to state their case. Arbitrators are well advised to obtain a clear statement on the record upon conclusion of the last oral hearing that the parties are satisfied with the conduct of the hearing, in order to protect the eventual **10.92**

---

policy. If one considers only the decisions in which the merits of the challenge were reached, then a challenge had 'about a 7 per cent chance of at least partial success': ibid., at 471. See LeRoy and Feuille, 'Happily never after: When final and binding arbitration has no fairy tale ending' (2008) 13 Harv Negotiation L Rev 167, on cases in which US courts have been found to be more willing to hear challenges, but remain restrictive in their setting aside of awards. See also Woodhouse, 'English Act's anniversary: Statistics Settle the pro- and anti-arbitration debate, once and for all' (2006) 2 Global Arbitration Review 27, in which a review of challenges under the English Arbitration Act 2006 found that only 10 per cent of s. 69 challenges and 30 per cent of s. 68 challenges were successful. But see Paulsson, 'Arbitration-friendliness: Promises of principle and realities of practice' (2007) 23 Arb Intl 477, which reflects on the continuing popularity of challenges despite their low chance of success, particularly in relation to s. 69 appeals.

[159] But see the discussion in Chapter 11 relating to cases in which an award has been set aside at the seat of the arbitration, but has nevertheless been enforced in another country.

award. If a party then declares a concern, there is still time for the tribunal to address it before issuing the final award.

E. State Responsibility for Wrongful Setting Aside

10.93 If an award is set aside, is that the end of the story for the party seeking annulment? Does an award-creditor have any recourse when an award is vacated for parochial or other inappropriate grounds? What happens where, for example, a state's courts set aside an award against a state-owned company or an otherwise well-connected national of that state? Put another way, if setting-aside applications are governed by national law, does a state have carte blanche to determine when and where to annul? Some cases suggest that states may be held responsible for certain egregious actions by their courts in the setting-aside process, as a matter of international law. In some instances, claimants have secured awards in international courts and tribunals, granting them the full amount of their previously annulled commercial arbitral awards.[160]

10.94 In one scenario, a decision to set an award aside may breach a state's obligations under a bilateral or multilateral investment treaty, which may in turn afford the frustrated award-creditor a forum for securing relief via investment arbitration (if the party can satisfy the criteria of an 'investor' under that particular treaty). For example, in the 2009 ICSID case *Saipem v Bangladesh*,[161] the state was held liable to the claimant for actions set aside. In that case, the ICSID tribunal held that the Bangladeshi courts had unlawfully interfered with, and ultimately vacated, an ICC award seated in Bangladesh by retroactively revoking a tribunal's authority based on certain procedural decisions that it made concerning the admission of evidence. The ICSID tribunal concluded that the ICC tribunal had acted perfectly within its jurisdiction in determining the admissibility of the evidence and found that the Bangladeshi courts had abused their supervisory jurisdiction over the arbitral process. Bangladesh was thus responsible for an illegal judicial expropriation of Saipem's ICC award, which it called a 'crystallization' of Saipem's original investment in Bangladesh.[162] Similarly, the 2011 UNCITRAL case *White Industries v India*[163] concerned the Indian courts' treatment of a setting-aside action against a

---

[160] King and Moloo, 'Enforcement after the arbitration: Strategic considerations and forum choice', in Ferrari (ed.) *Forum Shopping in the International Commercial Arbitration Context* (Sellier European Law, 2013), pp. 411–412, at 493.

[161] *Saipem SpA v People's Republic of Bangladesh*, Award, ICSID Case No. ARB/05/07, 30 June 2009) (finding Bangladesh liable for its illegal judicial expropriation of Saipem's rights, as crystallised in its award).

[162] Ibid., at [127] (finding that '[t]he ICC Award crystallized the parties' rights and obligations under the original contract', thereby constituting an investment for the purposes of both the Italy–Bangladesh BIT and the ICSID Convention).

[163] *White Industries Australia Ltd v Republic of India*, Final Award, UNCITRAL, 30 November 2011 (denying White's claim of denial of justice under fair and equitable treatment).

E. State Responsibility for Wrongful Setting Aside

Paris-seated ICC arbitral award (and allied stay of enforcement). As noted earlier, until its *Balco* decision in 2012, India had been willing to set aside foreign-seated awards under certain conditions.[164] Although the Indian courts never set aside the ICC award, the state's challenge against the award remained on the courts' docket through various appeals and delays for over the course of nine years. The ICSID tribunal found that such treatment did not amount to a denial of justice, but nevertheless constituted a violation of the obligation to provide investors an 'effective means' with which to challenge decisions of the state.[165] In both *Saipem* and *White Industries*, the investor–state tribunals awarded the claimant the full value of their annulled (or delayed) ICC awards, now payable by the state of the interfering courts.

10.95 In a second scenario, certain inappropriate judicial actions in setting-aside proceedings, or orders of set aside, may breach a state's obligations under international human rights treaties. Most notably, the European Convention on Human Rights (ECHR) affords individuals a means of suing the signatory states directly before the European Court of Human Rights (ECtHR) for violations of their Convention rights. While the ECtHR has yet to directly assess a state's responsibility for vacating an award, several cases indicate that a frustrated award-creditor may find relief on the grounds of the right to a fair trial (Article 6 ECHR) or the right to property (ECHR Protocol No. 1, Article 1).[166]

---

[164] See paragraph 10.27.
[165] *White Industries*, at [11.4.18]–[11.4.19] (finding India in violation of an obligation to afford White 'an effective means of asserting claims and enforcing rights'). The requirement to provide an investor with 'effective means' to challenge decisions of the state was imported from the India–Kuwait BIT by means of the applicable BIT's 'most favoured nation' (MFN) clause.
[166] *Stran Greek Refineries & Stratis Andreadis v Greece*, App. No. 13427/87 [1994] ECHR 48, in which Greece was found to be in violation of both ECHR Protocol No. 1, Art. 1, and Art. 6 ECHR for the concerted action of its legislature and judiciary in annulling a domestic arbitral award, along with the underlying contract and arbitration agreement, as part of a policy of cancelling concessions granted during the pre-revolution military dictatorship. The Court awarded the applicant the full amount of the underlying award, plus interest, to be paid by Greece. See also *Regent Co. v Ukraine*, App. No. 773/03, Judgment of 3 April 2008, ECtHR, in which Ukraine was found to be in violation of both ECHR Protocol No. 1, Art. 1, and Art. 6 ECHR as a result of an undue delay of ten years in enforcing a Ukraine-seated international arbitral award, allegedly because of the insolvency of the award debtor—a state-owned company. The Court awarded the applicant the full amount of the underlying award plus interest, to be paid by the Ukraine. In *Kin-Stib & Majić v Serbia*, App. No. 12312/05, Judgment of 20 April 2010, ECtHR, Serbia was found liable to the applicants under ECHR Protocol No. 1, Art. 1, for refusing to enforce the specific performance part of an international arbitral award of the Yugoslavia Chamber of Commerce in favour of a Congolese company and against a state-owned company. The Court awarded the applicant the value of the specific performance portion of the award plus interest, to be paid by Serbia. See too King and Moloo, 'Enforcement after the arbitration: Strategic considerations and forum choice', in Ferrari (ed.) *Forum Shopping in the International Commercial Arbitration Context* (Sellier European Law, 2013), p. 493, noting that it remains to be seen how the 'ECtHR would view a case in which an arbitral award had been set aside in the country of origin' and suggesting that '[i]f the investment treaty cases are any guide, one might surmise that the Court would require evidence of court malfeasance—or at least misfeasance—before finding a violation of [ECHR Protocol No. 1, Art. 1] in such circumstances'.

11

RECOGNITION AND ENFORCEMENT OF ARBITRAL AWARDS

A.	Background	11.01	D. Enforcement under Regional Conventions	11.131
B.	Enforcement under the New York Convention	11.40	E. Defence of State Immunity	11.141
C.	Enforcement under the ICSID Convention	11.125		

A. Background

(a) Introduction

The successful party in an international commercial arbitration expects the award to be performed without delay. This is a reasonable expectation. The purpose of arbitration, unlike mediation and most other methods of alternative dispute resolution (ADR), is to arrive at a binding decision on the dispute. Once this decision has been made in the form of an award, it is an intrinsic element of every arbitration agreement that the parties will carry it out.[1] To put the point beyond doubt, this is expressly set out in international and institutional rules of arbitration. For example, the Arbitration Rules of the United Nations Commission on International Trade Law (UNCITRAL) state that the award 'shall be final and binding on the parties', and that 'the parties undertake to carry out the award without delay'.[2]

11.01

Such statistics as are available suggest that most arbitral awards are, in fact, carried out voluntarily—that is, without the need for enforcement proceedings in national

11.02

---

[1] See Mustill and Boyd, *Commercial Arbitration* (2nd edn, Butterworths, 1989), p. 47; *Esso/BHP v Plowman* (1995) 11 Arb Intl 282, 283, Expert report of Dr Lew.

[2] UNCITRAL Rules, Art. 34(2). The final and binding nature of the award is further underlined by the optional waiver language contained in the Annex to the UNCITRAL Rules, which states: 'The parties hereby waive their right to any form of recourse against an award to any court or other competent authority, insofar as such waiver can validly be made under the applicable law.'

courts.[3] However, comprehensive and reliable statistics about arbitration are not readily available for two main reasons: first, because arbitration is a private process; and secondly, in any event, there is no particular reason why an arbitral tribunal (or indeed an arbitral institution) should know whether or not an award has been carried out. Unlike a national court, an arbitral tribunal has no role to play in the enforcement of its decision. Once the award has been rendered, the arbitral tribunal usually has nothing more to do with the dispute, unless it is required to make an additional award, or to correct or interpret its award.[4] When an arbitral tribunal has made a final award, its work is usually done and the tribunal is *functus officio*.

11.03 It is sometimes said that the test of a good arbitral award is that it leaves both parties feeling disappointed! Whether or not this is so, it is often true that, in practice, at least one party to an arbitration is dissatisfied with the result. Arbitration is not like conciliation or mediation, in which the process has failed if it does not produce a result acceptable to both parties. In arbitration, there is almost always a 'winner' and a 'loser'.

11.04 What happens if the winner is, in fact, dissatisfied with an award, considering that there were other claims too that should have succeeded? In a national court, an appeal on some aspects of the judgment might be possible. In certain circumstances and under limited conditions, as indicated elsewhere in the volume,[5] an appeal may be possible in arbitration—but the trend is towards the acceptance of arbitral awards, good or bad, unless they can be attacked on grounds of excess jurisdiction, lack of due process, or breach of public policy. A winning party who challenges an award because of dissatisfaction with certain aspects of it risks winning a Pyrrhic victory—that is, there is a risk that if the challenge is successful, the award will be set aside entirely. If this happens, the winner then faces the prospect of being obliged to start, or face, fresh proceedings. This will involve either a new arbitration, or if the reason for setting aside was lack of jurisdiction on the part of the arbitral tribunal, say, a court action.

11.05 The *losing party* generally has more room for manoeuvre. First, such a party may simply carry out the award voluntarily, in accordance with its undertaking so to do. Secondly, the losing party may use the award as a basis for negotiating a settlement. It is perhaps surprising that the successful party to an arbitration might settle for less than the amount awarded, but it might be considered better to accept a lesser payment forthwith than to face further challenge or enforcement proceedings to recover the full amount. Thirdly, and as discussed in Chapter 10, the losing party may challenge the award if this is possible under the rules of arbitration or

---

[3] See Queen Mary University of London, School of International Arbitration, and Pricewaterhouse Coopers LLP, *International Arbitration: Corporate Attitudes and Practices 2008*, available online at http://www.pwc.co.uk/en_UK/uk/assets/pdf/pwc-international-arbitration-2008.pdf, pp. 8 and 10, which suggests that in only 11 per cent of cases did participants need to proceed to enforce an award and, in those cases, in less than 20 per cent did enforcing parties encounter difficulties in enforcement.

[4] See Chapter 10, paragraphs 10.17*ff*.

[5] See Chapter 10, paragraphs 10.64*ff*.

A. Background

the relevant law.[6] Finally, it may resist any attempt by the winning party to obtain recognition or enforcement of the award, in whatever jurisdiction this is sought.

11.06 The purpose of this chapter is to examine the recognition and enforcement of awards. However, it is appropriate to start by discussing the carrying out, or performance, of awards from a wider perspective, so as to place recognition and enforcement in their proper contexts.

(b) Performance of awards

11.07 As already stated, the vast majority of awards are performed voluntarily. However, if the losing party fails to carry out an award, the winning party needs to take steps to enforce performance of it. Effectively, only two steps may be taken. The first is to exert some form of pressure, commercial or otherwise, in order to show the losing party that it is in its interests to perform the award voluntarily. The second is to invoke the powers of the state, exercised through its national courts, in order to obtain a hold on the losing party's assets, or in some other way to compel performance of the award.[7]

(i) Commercial and other pressures

11.08 A successful party may be in a position to exert commercial pressure on a party who fails or refuses to perform an award. For example, if a continuing trade relationship exists between the parties, it may well be in the interests of the loser to perform the award, since failure to do so might entail the loss of further profitable business. If a government or state agency is concerned, other pressures may be brought to bear by the diplomatic services of the successful party. It may be pointed out, for instance, that further development loans depend upon the carrying out of existing awards, or that foreign companies may be discouraged from making further investments if outstanding obligations are not honoured.[8]

11.09 Pressure may also be exerted by the threat of adverse publicity. This method is one that is sometimes adopted by trade associations and which has the effect of discouraging other traders in the market from dealing with the defaulting party. The Arbitration Rules of the Grain and Feed Trade Association (GAFTA), for example, contain the following provision:

> **22. Defaulters**
>
> 22.1 In the event of any party to an arbitration or an appeal held under these Rules neglecting or refusing to carry out or abide by a final award of the tribunal or board of appeal made under these Rules, the Council of GAFTA may post on the GAFTA Notice Board, Web-site, and/or circulate amongst Members in any way

---

[6] As to which, see Chapter 10, paragraphs 10.34*ff*.
[7] For instance, by the winding up of a company.
[8] The establishment of the Iran–United States Claims Tribunal, mentioned in Chapter 1, is an example of state action to protect private investors.

thought fit notification to that effect. The parties to any such arbitration or appeal shall be deemed to have consented to the Council taking such action as aforesaid.[9]

Before 'posting', GAFTA communicates with the defaulter and asks whether there is anything to be said, for example whether there is an outstanding balance due to him or her from the successful party. However, where GAFTA is satisfied that there is a default, its members are informed. This will naturally make them reluctant to deal with the defaulter unless and until the award has been carried out.

11.10 Similarly, but less explicitly, debtor states that end up as losing parties in arbitrations under the International Centre for the Settlement of Investment Disputes (ICSID) may feel (rightly or wrongly) that refusal to perform an award voluntarily may adversely affect their creditworthiness at the World Bank. It may therefore be no coincidence that, to date, the overwhelming majority of ICSID awards have been voluntarily performed.[10]

(ii) Arbitrator's duty to render an enforceable award

11.11 Some rules of arbitration contain an express provision that the arbitrator shall 'make every effort' to ensure that the award is enforceable.[11] This is an obligation to use best endeavours, rather than an obligation to secure a result. It is difficult to see how it could be otherwise. The most conscientious arbitrator in the world cannot guarantee that the tribunal's award will be enforceable in whatever country enforcement may be sought. The most that can be expected is that the tribunal will do its best to ensure that the appropriate procedure is followed and, above all, that each party is given a fair hearing.

(iii) Enforcement by court proceedings

11.12 The ultimate sanction for non-performance of an award is enforcement by proceedings in a national court. This is something that should be borne in mind from the outset of an arbitration.[12] Sometimes, one of the parties (usually the

---

[9] GAFTA Form 125, Arbitration Rules (effective for contracts dated from 1 July 2007 onwards), Art. 22(1).

[10] In recent years, the record of overwhelming voluntary performance has been eroded somewhat. Nevertheless, voluntary performance remains the norm. For a description of the voluntary performance of ICSID awards, see Chapter 8.

[11] See, e.g., International Chamber of Commerce (ICC) Arbitration Rules, Art. 41; London Court of International Arbitration (LCIA) Rules, Art. 32(2); World Intellectual Property Organization (WIPO) Arbitration Rules, Art. 62(e) (providing that the 'Tribunal may consult the Center with regard to matters of form, particularly to ensure the enforceability of the award').

[12] Or even when drafting the arbitration agreement. For example, if any enforcement action is likely to take place in the United States, the arbitration agreement should include an 'entry of judgment' clause. This clause states that judgment may be entered upon the award in any court of competent jurisdiction. The provision seeks to facilitate arbitration, by making it clear that a national court may enforce the arbitration agreement and any award resulting from it. Although the court may well have this power irrespective of the agreement of the parties, an 'entry of judgment' clause will help to avoid a challenge that its omission indicates the parties' intent to exclude any court procedure on the award.

A. Background

claimant) urges the arbitral tribunal to run through the proceedings as quickly as possible, so as to obtain a speedy decision. This is understandable—but it is in the interests of the party that stands to gain most from the arbitration (whether by way of claim or counterclaim) to *ensure* that the proper procedures are followed, in case it should become necessary to apply to a national court for enforcement of the award.

Enforcement usually takes place against assets.[13] This means that, as a first step, it is necessary to trace the assets of the losing party—money in a bank account, an aircraft or a ship, a cargo of oil in transit, or whatever it may be—before applying to the relevant national court for an order against those assets, or, less constructively, for an order that the trade or business of the losing party should be liquidated, if payment of the award continues to be refused.[14]   **11.13**

There are four ways in which a national legal system might provide for the enforcement of arbitral awards. The first arises when the award is deposited, or registered, with a court or other authority,[15] following which it may be enforced as if it is a judgment of that court. The second arises when the laws of the country of enforcement provide that, with the leave of the court, the award of an arbitral tribunal may be enforced *directly* without any need for deposit or registration.[16] The third arises when it is necessary to apply to the court for some form of recognition, or *exequatur*, as a preliminary step to enforcement.[17] The fourth is to sue on the award as evidence of a debt, on the basis that the arbitration agreement constitutes a contractual obligation to perform the award. This last method is cumbersome and frequently leaves it open to the losing party to reopen, by way of defence, the issues already determined by the arbitral tribunal. It is therefore to be avoided, unless no other method is available.   **11.14**

---

[13] Although there might be an award ordering the return of a specific object, such as a valuable painting or, as in *The Temple of Preah-Vihear* case (1962) ICJ 6, at 36–37, the return of artefacts and national treasures. It has been said by some that arbitral tribunals should not, in general, grant orders for specific performance: see Elder, 'The case against arbitral awards of specific performance in transnational commercial disputes' (1997) 13 Arb Intl 1. But, as always, this depends on the scope of the arbitration agreement and the relevant applicable law(s): see Chapter 9.

[14] The successful party may sometimes seek recognition and enforcement of an award in a country in which the losing party may have no assets in order (so to speak) to obtain the *imprimatur* of a respected court upon the award.

[15] As, e.g., under the Swiss Private International Law Act 1987 (Swiss PIL), Ch. 12, s. 193. See also the Egyptian Ministerial Decree, made under s. 47 of the Egyptian Arbitration Law No. 27 of 1994 and published in the Official Gazette, No. 230 of 7 October 2008. Further, see also art. 825 of the Italian Code of Civil Procedure (Book 4, Title VIII, 'Arbitration')—as amended by Legislative Decree No. 40, 2 February 2006.

[16] As, e.g., in England, under the English Arbitration Act 1996, s. 66. See also s. 35(2) of the Australian International Arbitration Act 1974, as amended. Further, see also s. 19 of the Singaporean International Arbitration Act 1994, as amended in 2002.

[17] As, e.g., in France, under art. 1487 of the Code of Civil Procedure, as modified by Decree No. 2011-48 of 13 January 2011. See also art. 66(d) of Law No. 30 of 1999 Concerning Arbitration and Alternative Dispute Resolution. Further, see also art. 518 of the Argentinian National Code of Civil and Commercial Procedure (Further Articles).

11.15 The procedures to be followed in any given case vary from country to country and from court to court. It is not possible to lay down detailed procedural guidelines here nor would it be particularly helpful to do so, since if action has to be taken to enforce an award in a particular jurisdiction, it is necessary to obtain competent advice from experienced lawyers who practise in that jurisdiction.

11.16 What follows, therefore, is a review of the general principles underlying: recognition and enforcement; the choice of the appropriate forum (including 'forum shopping'); the role of the international conventions (in particular the New York and ICSID Conventions) in assisting recognition and enforcement; and the defences that may be raised, including that of state immunity.

(c) General principles governing recognition and enforcement

11.17 The challenge of an arbitral award, discussed in Chapter 10, is concerned with attacking an award at its source, in the hope of having it modified or set aside in whole or in part. Recognition and enforcement, by contrast, are concerned with giving effect to the award, either in the state in which it was made or in some other state(s).

11.18 A distinction may be drawn at the outset between (a) the enforcement of an award in the state that is the 'seat' of the arbitration, and (b) the enforcement of an award that is regarded as a 'foreign', or 'international', award because it was made *outside* the territory of the state in which recognition or enforcement is sought. Enforcement of an award in the country that is the seat of the arbitration is usually a relatively easy process. It generally involves the same processes as are required for the enforcement of an award in a domestic arbitration.[18] Enforcement of an award that is regarded by the place of enforcement as a 'foreign', or 'international', award is a more complex matter. This section is mainly concerned with the recognition and enforcement of such 'foreign' awards.[19]

(d) Difference between recognition and enforcement

11.19 It is necessary to distinguish recognition from enforcement. The terms are sometimes used as though they are always inextricably linked. For example, the New York Convention itself speaks of 'recognition *and* enforcement' of foreign arbitral awards.[20] The terms are, however, distinct. On this point, the 1927 Geneva

---

[18] Enforcement provisions in China, similarly, differentiate between purely domestic awards and those awards that have been made in the People's Republic of China (PRC), but have a foreign element, such as (a) a foreign party, (b) the relevant relationship was formed, changed, or terminated in a foreign country, or (c) the subject matter of the dispute is situated outside the PRC.

[19] The New York Convention, the full title of which is the 'Convention on the Recognition and Enforcement of *Foreign* Arbitral Awards' (emphasis added), also applies to arbitral awards that are 'not considered as domestic awards in the State where their recognition and enforcement is sought' (Art. 1(1)). This may lead to an award made in one state being enforced in that same state under the New York Convention, on the basis that it is not regarded as a domestic award.

[20] In Arts I, IV, and V—but Art. V also speaks of 'recognition *or* enforcement' (emphasis added).

A. Background

Convention was more precise, when it spoke of 'recognition *or* enforcement'.[21] An award may be recognised *without* being enforced.[22] However, if it is enforced, then it is necessarily recognised by the court that orders its enforcement. The precise distinction, in other words, is between 'recognition' and 'recognition and enforcement'.

(i) Recognition

11.20 Recognition on its own is generally a defensive process.[23] It will usually arise when a court is asked to grant a remedy in respect of a dispute that has been the subject of previous arbitral proceedings. The party in whose favour the award was made will object that the dispute has already been determined. To prove this, it will seek to produce the award to the court, and will ask the court to recognise it as valid and binding upon the parties in respect of the issues with which it dealt. The award may have disposed of *all* of the issues raised in the new court proceedings and so put an end to those new proceedings as *res judicata*—that is, as matters in issue between the parties that in fact have already been decided. If the award does not dispose of all of the issues raised in the new proceedings, but only some of them, it will need to be recognised for the purposes of issue estoppel, so as to prevent those issues with which it does deal from being raised again.

11.21 The use of recognition on its own may be illustrated by considering the example of a company that is made a defendant in legal proceedings by a foreign supplier for goods sold and delivered, but allegedly not paid for. Suppose that the dispute between the company and the foreign supplier has already been submitted to arbitration, and that an award has been made, in which the foreign supplier's claim was dismissed. In these circumstances, the company will ask the court to *recognise* the award as a valid defence to the foreign supplier's new claim. If the court is prepared to do this, the claim is dismissed. The legal force and effect of the foreign award will have been recognised, but the award itself has not been enforced.

(ii) Enforcement

11.22 By contrast, where a court is asked to enforce an award, it is asked not merely to recognise the legal force and effect of the award, but also to ensure that it is carried out, by using such legal sanctions as are available. Enforcement goes a step further than recognition. A court that is prepared to grant enforcement of

---

[21] The usage is followed in the English Arbitration Act 1996, which distinguishes between the 'recognition' of a New York Convention award (s. 101(1)) and its 'enforcement' (s. 101(2)). The statute also makes this distinction in other relevant sections.

[22] As happened, e.g., in *Dallal v Bank Mellat* [1986] QB 441, in which the English judge held that an award of the Iran–United States Claims Tribunal was not enforceable under the New York Convention, but should nevertheless be *recognised* as the valid judgment of a competent tribunal. The case is also reported in (1986) XI YBCA 547, at 553.

[23] Although, in some countries, it may be a necessary step along the way to enforcement.

an award will do so because it recognises the award as validly made and binding upon the parties to it, and therefore suitable for enforcement. In this context, the terms 'recognition' and 'enforcement' do run together: one is a necessary part of the other.

(iii) A shield and a sword

11.23 As the example shows, the purpose of recognition on its own is generally to act as a shield. Recognition is used to block any attempt to raise in fresh proceedings issues that have already been decided in the arbitration that gave rise to the award of which recognition is sought.[24] By contrast, the purpose of enforcement is to act as a sword. Enforcement of an award means applying legal sanctions to compel the party against whom the award was made to carry it out. Such legal sanctions may take many forms. When the defaulting party is an individual, sanctions may include seizure of property and other assets, forfeiture of bank accounts, and even, in extreme cases, imprisonment. Where the defaulting party is a corporate body, enforcement is usually directed primarily against the property and other assets of the corporation, such as its stock-in-trade, bank accounts, trading accounts, and so on. In certain situations, however, the directors of the company may be held personally liable (for instance on a guarantee). In such cases, the sanctions may be directed against them personally.

(e) Place of recognition and enforcement

11.24 A party who simply seeks *recognition* of an award will generally do so because he or she needs to rely on the award by way of defence or set-off, or in some other way in court proceedings. For this purpose, the party asks the court concerned to recognise the award as binding on the parties between whom it was made. But the choice of court is not made by the party seeking recognition; it must be a court of the place where the proceedings against him or her are brought—and this fact, of itself, emphasises how important it is that international awards should be accepted as truly 'international' in their validity and effect.

11.25 Where, however, the successful party in an arbitration is seeking to *enforce* an award, the position is different. The first step is to determine in which country, or countries, enforcement is to be sought. To reach this decision, it is necessary to locate the state or states in which the losing party has, or is likely to have, assets available to meet the award. This usually calls for careful (and possibly difficult) investigative work. If enquiries suggest that assets are likely to be available in only one state, the party seeking enforcement of the award has no choice: for better or worse, he or she must seek enforcement in that state. Where there is a choice,

---

[24] As expressed in the English Arbitration Act 1996, s. 101(1), the award is recognised 'as binding on the persons as between whom it was made', so that it may accordingly be used by these persons 'by way of defence, set-off or otherwise' in any legal proceedings in England and Wales or Northern Ireland.

A. Background

the party seeking enforcement is able to proceed in one or more places as seems appropriate.

Court proceedings are necessary to obtain title to a defaulting party's assets or their proceeds of sale, and these proceedings are usually[25] taken in the state or states in which the property or other assets of the losing party are located. However, the party seeking enforcement should always be mindful to consider whether undertaking such a process, which invariably involves further costs, is worthwhile. For example, an order by the French courts for seizure and sale of the defaulting party's goods and chattels in France would not produce any real money if those assets were to prove to be non-existent; nor would an order for the attachment of the defaulting party's bank accounts in England if those accounts were to turn out to be overdrawn.[26] **11.26**

A further factor to be taken into account in selecting a forum for the enforcement of an award is whether, under the New York Convention or some other relevant international convention, the prospective forum recognises and enforces awards rendered at the place of arbitration. Another factor is the attitude of the local courts to requests for recognition and enforcement of foreign awards, and notably whether their outlook is likely to be internationalist or parochial. The attitude that the prospective forum adopts on the question of state immunity[27] is yet another relevant factor if enforcement is being sought against a state or a governmental agency.[28] **11.27**

(i) Forum shopping

The need to locate the place(s) in which a defaulting party has assets is not confined to international arbitration. In domestic court proceedings, it may also be necessary to locate the defaulting party's assets in order to enforce a court's judgment or an arbitral tribunal's award. However, in a domestic dispute, the assets of the losing party are usually situated within the country in which the proceedings take place, since this is normally the country of that party's residence or place of business. In international arbitration, the contrary is likely to be the case. The place of arbitration[29] will usually have been chosen, by or on behalf of the parties, precisely because (inter alia) it is a place with which they have *no* connection. In **11.28**

---

[25] 'Usually', because it may perhaps be thought worthwhile to obtain a court order in a state in which the defendant has no assets, simply to obtain that court's *imprimatur* on the award.

[26] Unfortunately, in practice, all that is generally known is that the defaulting party is a holder of bank accounts in the country concerned. The status of those accounts is not usually known until an order is issued against the bank.

[27] For a discussion of state immunity, see paragraphs 11.141*ff*.

[28] Local law advice is also necessary to establish whether the local courts will have the necessary jurisdiction over the persons and assets against which enforcement is sought.

[29] The chosen place of arbitration is a geographical location, in a given country, or, more usually, in a given town or city. The arbitration agreement generally states, e.g., that any arbitration is to take place in Paris, or that it is to take place in New York, or wherever it may be. But, as has been seen in Chapter 3, once chosen, the physical 'place' of arbitration becomes the juridical 'seat' of the arbitration—an event that may have important legal consequences, depending on the *lex arbitri*.

other words, the place of arbitration has been chosen as a neutral forum. It would be purely fortuitous if the parties were to happen to have assets situated within this neutral country. If the award has to be enforced, it must generally be enforced in a country other than that in which it was made. As will be further explained later in this chapter,[30] this is why it is important that international awards should be recognised and enforced *internationally*, and not merely in the country in which they are made.

11.29 If, as often happens in international commerce, assets are located in different parts of the world, the party seeking enforcement of the award has a choice of country in which to proceed—a chance to go 'forum shopping', as it is sometimes expressed.[31] In looking for the appropriate forum, not merely the location of assets, but also the other factors mentioned (such as the attitude of the local courts, the adherence of the target country to the New York Convention, and so on), must be taken into account.

(f) Methods of recognition and enforcement

11.30 Internationally, it is generally much easier to obtain recognition and enforcement of an international award than of a foreign court judgment. This is because the network of international and regional treaties providing for the recognition and enforcement of international awards is more widespread and better developed than corresponding provisions for the recognition and enforcement of foreign judgments.[32] Indeed, this is one of the principal advantages of arbitration as a method of resolving international commercial disputes.[33]

---

[30] See paragraphs 11.35*ff*.

[31] While the existence of assets within a particular jurisdiction is most commonly used as a basis for enforcement in that jurisdiction, jurisdiction *ratione personae* over a party can sometimes also be used to seize assets outside the jurisdiction in which enforcement is sought. The New York Court of Appeals has held, in *Koehler v Bank of Bermuda Ltd* 12 NY.3d 533 (2009), that assets located outside New York can be ordered to be brought within the jurisdiction for enforcement purposes, as long as a New York court has jurisdiction over the owner or custodian of those assets: see Friedman, 'Enforcement of international arbitration awards in New York: If you take them there, you can collect from anywhere' (2011) 27 Arb Intl 575.

[32] Within the European Union, Council Regulation (EC) No. 44/2001 of 22 December 2000 on jurisdiction and the recognition and enforcement of judgments in civil and commercial matters, which replaced the Brussels Convention of 1968, provides for the enforcement of European national court judgments solely within Europe. In the international arena, The Hague Conference on Private International Law has been struggling in recent years to agree the text of a convention dealing with jurisdiction, and the recognition and enforcement of foreign judgments, in civil and commercial matters. However, this endeavour has been unsuccessful to date. All that the delegates have been able to date to agree is the mutual recognition and enforcement of judgments that were rendered pursuant to exclusive choice of court agreements: the Hague Convention on Choice of Court Agreements of 30 June 2005. In addition, the 2005 Hague Convention has been ratified in only one country, Mexico (and signed, but not yet ratified, by the United States on 19 January 2009 and the European Union, which succeeded on 29 January 2010 to the European Community's signature on 1 April 2009). It therefore contrasts dramatically with the ubiquity of the New York Convention.

[33] See Chapter 1.

A. Background

The method of recognition and enforcement to be adopted in any particular case depends on the place where the award was made (that is, whether it qualifies, for example, as a New York Convention award). It also depends on the relevant provisions of the law at the place of intended enforcement (the 'forum state'). On this aspect, it is usually essential to obtain advice from experienced lawyers in the forum state.[34]

11.31

Local formalities are bound to be involved, whether or not one of the international conventions is applicable. For example, the original or certified copies of the arbitration agreement and award are usually required. The language of the award may well be different from the language of the court of the forum state, so that a translation is required—and it may be necessary for this to be undertaken with considerable formality (for example by consular attestation in the country of origin).

11.32

(g) Time limits

Time limits for the commencement of proceedings for the recognition and enforcement of an arbitral award are usually laid down in national legislation. Careful attention must be paid to such time limits (and to any other time limits contained in the rules of court of the forum state). In this respect, it would be foolhardy not to consult an experienced local practitioner—and this applies as much to the party seeking recognition or enforcement of an award as it does to the party wishing to challenge an award. In the United States, for instance, time limits vary from state to state and, when it comes to recognition or enforcement of an award, the relevant period may be anything from one year to three years.[35]

11.33

(h) Consequences of refusal of recognition or enforcement

The immediate consequence of a refusal to enforce an award is that the winning party fails to get what it wants—namely, seizure of the loser's assets in the place in which enforcement was sought. Although this is a disheartening result for the party seeking enforcement, it should be borne in mind that it may still have an award that can be enforced in another state in which the losing party *has* assets. Much depends upon the reason for which enforcement was refused. If, for example, enforcement was refused for local public policy considerations, it may be possible to find another country in which the same considerations do not apply.

11.34

---

[34] Recognition and enforcement is likely to be easiest to obtain under an international convention where the forum state is bound by such a convention, but other methods of recognition and enforcement may be available, as discussed at paragraphs 11.131*ff*.

[35] See also English Limitation Act 1980, s. 7: 'An action to enforce an award, where the submission is not by an instrument under seal, shall not be brought after the expiration of six years from the date on which the cause of action accrued.' For India, the equivalent period is three years under the Limitation Act 1963, Sch. 1, para. 101. The Canadian Supreme Court has concluded that domestic limitation periods are applicable to enforcing awards under the New York Convention: *Yugraneft Corporation v Rexx Management Corporation* [2010] SCC 19.

However, if enforcement was refused because of a fundamental failure by the arbitral tribunal to give the losing party an opportunity to present its case, it may not be possible to enforce the award elsewhere, since other courts may take the same view.[36] In such an event, the party seeking enforcement may have no option but to recommence arbitral proceedings, assuming that the right to do so has not been lost by lapse of time.

(i) Role of the international conventions

11.35 The dependence of the international arbitral process upon national systems of law is most clearly seen in the context of the recognition and enforcement of international awards. An arbitral tribunal is limited in the powers that it can exercise—and these powers, although usually adequate for resolving a particular dispute, fall short of the coercive powers possessed by national courts. Indeed, a state is generally reluctant to confer on a private arbitral tribunal the sanctioning powers that it confers on the judges in its own courts. The power to enforce an award against a reluctant party by such summary methods as the attachment of bank accounts or the sequestration of assets is a power that forms part of the prerogative of the state. In consequence, the enforcement of awards must take place via the national court at the place of enforcement, operating under its own procedural rules. The detailed procedures adopted in these courts will vary from country to country. However, the effect of the international conventions, culminating in the New York Convention, has been to secure a considerable degree of uniformity in the recognition and enforcement of awards in most of the important trading countries of the world.

11.36 The main international treaties that apply to the recognition and enforcement of international awards are reviewed in the next section. In particular, this chapter includes a discussion of the New York Convention, the ICSID Convention, and a number of regional conventions.

11.37 The New York Convention has the widest scope of application. Subject to two reservations that may restrict its application, the New York Convention facilitates the recognition and enforcement of foreign arbitral awards in the territories of any of its more than 140 signatory states, irrespective of the arbitration rules under which the proceedings were conducted.[37] Enshrining as it does a strong pro-enforcement policy, the New York Convention provides for the recognition and enforcement of foreign arbitral awards by national courts, subject to a handful of procedural and substantive grounds for objecting to enforcement that are intended to be limited in scope.

---

[36] See New York Convention, Art. V(1)(b); Model Law (as amended in 2006), Art. 36(1)(a)(ii).
[37] For example, the ICC Rules, the LCIA Rules, UNCITRAL Rules, or ICSID Additional Facility Rules.

Similarly, the ICSID Convention (sometimes also known as the 'Washington Convention') provides for the enforcement of those arbitral awards that were rendered in proceedings involving a national of one contracting state and another contracting state. Awards falling under the scope of the ICSID Convention are directly enforceable within the territories of all states parties to ICSID.[38] Like the New York Convention, the ICSID Convention has the vast number of more than 140 contracting states.

11.38

In this chapter, we also briefly discuss a number of regional conventions. The application of these regional conventions is far more limited than the application of the New York and ICSID Conventions, not the least because the New York Convention will apply to almost all disputes, thus superseding those regional conventions.

11.39

B. Enforcement under the New York Convention

(a) Introduction

The origins of the New York Convention have already been described in Chapter 1. The New York Convention replaces the 1927 Geneva Convention as between states that are parties to both Conventions,[39] and is a substantial improvement, since it provides for a simpler and more effective method of obtaining recognition and enforcement of foreign awards. The Convention also replaces the earlier 1923 Geneva Protocol as between states that are bound by both,[40] and again constitutes a substantial improvement, because it gives much wider effect to the validity of arbitration agreements than that given under the Protocol. As a result, the New York Convention has been rightly eulogised as 'the single most important pillar on which the edifice of international arbitration rests',[41] and as a convention that 'perhaps could lay claim to be the most effective instance of international legislation in the entire history of commercial law'.[42] It is for this reason that, for now, many remain reluctant to countenance the possible disruption that would accompany the modernisation of the Convention's existing text.[43]

11.40

---

[38] See ICSID Convention, Art. 54.
[39] New York Convention, Art. VII(2).
[40] Ibid.
[41] Wetter, 'The present status of the International Court of Arbitration of the ICC: An appraisal' (1990) 1 Am Rev Intl Arb 91, at 93.
[42] Mustill, 'Arbitration: History and background' (1989) 6 J Intl Arb 43, at 49. See also Schwebel, 'A celebration of the United Nations' New York Convention' (1996) 12 Arb Intl 823.
[43] However, see van den Berg, 'Hypothetical Draft Convention on the International Enforcement of Arbitration Agreements and Awards: Explanatory Note', Paper prepared for the ICCA Conference, Dublin, 2008, available online at http://www.newyorkconvention.org/userfiles/documenten/draft-convention/64_explanatory.pdf.

(i) Enforcing the agreement to arbitrate

11.41 Although the title of the New York Convention refers only to the recognition and enforcement of 'foreign arbitral awards', the Convention also deals with the recognition and enforcement of arbitration agreements. This has already been discussed in Chapter 1. In this chapter, the authors focus only on the recognition and enforcement of 'foreign arbitral awards'.

(ii) Enforcing foreign awards

11.42 In its opening statement, the Convention adopts a strikingly international attitude:

> This Convention shall apply to the recognition and enforcement of arbitral awards made in the territory of a State other than the State where the recognition and enforcement of such awards are sought, and arising out of differences between persons, whether physical or legal. It shall also apply to arbitral awards not considered as domestic awards in the State where their recognition and enforcement are sought.[44]

If this opening Article were to stand without qualification, it would mean that an award made in any state (even if that state were not a party to the New York Convention) would be recognised and enforced by any other state that was a party, as long as the award satisfied the basic conditions set down in the Convention. There is, however, a qualification: Article I(3) of the Convention allows states that adhere to it to make two possible reservations. The first of these is the reciprocity reservation; the second is the commercial reservation, which was also in the 1923 Geneva Protocol.

(iii) First reservation—reciprocity

11.43 Article I(3) of the New York Convention provides that:

> When signing, ratifying or acceding to this Convention, or notifying extension under Article X hereof, any State may on the basis of reciprocity declare that it will apply the Convention to the recognition and enforcement of awards *made only* in the territory of another Contracting State.[45]

To the extent that states take advantage of it, the reciprocity reservation has the effect of narrowing the scope of application of the New York Convention. Instead of applying to all foreign awards, wherever they are made, the scope of the New York Convention may be limited to 'Convention awards'—that is, awards made in a state that is a party to the New York Convention.[46]

---

[44] New York Convention, Art. I(1).
[45] Emphasis added.
[46] At the time of writing, 149 states had acceded to the New York Convention. Of these, seventy-four had done so on the basis of the reciprocity reservation. Some countries that had adopted the reciprocity reservation (such as Germany and Switzerland) have subsequently withdrawn it. See UNCITRAL, 'Status of conventions and model laws', available online at http://www.uncitral.org/uncitral/en/uncitral_texts/arbitration.html.

B. Enforcement under the New York Convention

States that have entered into the New York Convention on the basis of reciprocity have agreed, in effect, that they will recognise and enforce only Convention awards. Accordingly, when seeking a suitable state in which to hold an international commercial arbitration, it is advisable to select a state that *has* adopted the New York Convention, so as to improve the chances of securing recognition and enforcement of the award in other Convention countries.

11.44

Nevertheless, the limiting effect of the first reservation should not be exaggerated. The number of states that make up the international network for the recognition and enforcement of arbitral awards established by the New York Convention grows year by year. The Convention now links the world's major trading nations: Arab, African, Asian, and Latin American, as well as European and North American. As more countries become Convention countries, the reciprocity reservation becomes less significant. The Model Law, for example, in Articles 35 and 36, requires the recognition and enforcement of an arbitral award '*irrespective* of the country in which it was made'.

11.45

(iv) Second reservation—commercial relationships

Article I(3) of the New York Convention contains a further reservation. This entitles a contracting state to declare that it will apply the Convention only to those differences arising out of legal relationships, whether contractual or not, that are 'considered as commercial under the national law of the state making such declaration'.[47]

11.46

The effect of this reservation, like the reservation as to reciprocity, is to narrow the scope of application of the New York Convention,[48] and the fact that each contracting state may determine for itself what relationships it considers to be 'commercial' has created problems in the application of the New York Convention. Relationships that are regarded as 'commercial' by one state are not necessarily so regarded by others—and this does not assist in obtaining a uniform interpretation of the Convention. Indeed, the commercial reservation has led to difficulties of interpretation even within the same state, as is shown by two cases that arose in India. In the first,[49] the High Court of Bombay (now Mumbai) was asked to stay legal proceedings that had been commenced despite the existence of an arbitration agreement. Under the relevant Indian legislation enacting the New York Convention, the court was obliged to grant such a stay, as long as the arbitration

11.47

---

[47] A similar commercial reservation was permitted in the 1923 Geneva Protocol.
[48] Of the 149 states that were parties to the Convention by December 2013, forty-six had taken advantage of the commercial reservation. On 12 March 2001, Serbia and Montenegro confirmed Yugoslavia's declaration of 1982 restricting the application of the Convention to 'economic' disputes. Norway's reservation stated that it would not apply the Convention in any disputes if the subject matter were immovable property in Norway or rights in such property.
[49] *Indian Organic Chemical Ltd v Subsidiary 1 (US), Subsidiary 2 (US), and Chemtex Fibres Inc (Parent Co.) (US)* (1979) IV YBCA 271.

agreement came within the Convention. In ratifying the New York Convention, India had entered the commercial reservation. The court held that whilst the agreement under which the dispute arose was commercial in nature, it could not be considered to be commercial 'under the law in force in India':

> In my opinion, in order to invoke the provisions of [the Convention], it is not enough to establish that an agreement is commercial. It must also be established that it is commercial by virtue of a provision of law or an operative legal principle in force in India.[50]

11.48 This decision has since been disapproved by the High Court of Gujarat. In this second case,[51] the plaintiffs moved for a stay of legal proceedings that, again, had been commenced despite the existence of an arbitration agreement. The court granted this motion. On the argument as to whether or not the contract was commercial in nature, the judge said that the term 'commerce':

> ...is a word of the largest import and takes in its sweep all the business and trade transactions in any of their forms, including the transportation, purchase, sale and exchange of commodities between the citizens of different countries.[52]

The judge added:

> It should be noted that the view of the learned single Judge of the Bombay High Court in *Indian Organic Chemical Ltd's* case has not been approved by the Division Bench of the Bombay High Court. The Division Bench after setting out the view of [the judge] in the aforesaid decision, ultimately disagreed with it...[53]

11.49 This position was confirmed by the Indian Supreme Court in its decision in *RM Investment & Trading Company v Boeing Company*,[54] in which it held that in:

> ...construing the expression 'commercial' in Section 2 of the Act it has to be borne in mind that the 'Act is calculated and designed to subserve the cause of facilitating international trade and promotion thereof by providing for speedy settlement of disputes arising in such trade through arbitration and any expression or phrase occurring [therein] should receive, consistent with its literal and grammatical sense, a liberal construction'... The expression 'commercial' should, therefore, be construed broadly having regard to the manifold activities which are an integral part of international trade today.

11.50 Nevertheless, the point remains that each national state may decide for itself, under the provisions of the New York Convention, what relationships it considers to be 'commercial' for the purposes of the commercial reservation.[55]

---

[50] Ibid., at 273.
[51] *Union of India and ors v Lief Hoegh Co. (Norway)* (1984) IX YBCA 405.
[52] Ibid., at 407.
[53] Ibid., at 408.
[54] 1994 (4) SCC 541, (1997) XXII Ybk Comm Arb 711.
[55] The Tunisian courts, e.g., have construed the commercial reservation so broadly as to exclude enforcement of an award relating to obligations arising under a contract for professional services. See *Société d'Investissement Kal (Tunisia) v Taieb Haddad (Tunisia) and Hans Barrett*

B. Enforcement under the New York Convention

(v) Recognition and enforcement under the New York Convention

11.51 The New York Convention provides for both recognition and enforcement of awards to which the Convention applies. As far as *recognition* is concerned, a state bound by the Convention undertakes to respect the binding effect of awards to which the Convention applies; accordingly, as has been seen, such awards may be relied upon by way of defence or set-off in any legal proceedings. As far as *enforcement* is concerned, a state that is a party to the Convention undertakes to enforce awards to which the Convention applies, in accordance with its local procedural rules. It also undertakes not to impose substantially more onerous conditions, or higher fees or charges, for such enforcement than are imposed in the enforcement of its own domestic awards.[56]

(vi) Formalities

11.52 The formalities required for obtaining recognition and enforcement of awards to which the New York Convention applies are simple.[57] The party seeking such recognition and enforcement is merely required to produce to the relevant court:

[…]

(a) The duly authenticated original award or a duly certified copy thereof; [and]
(b) The original agreement referred to in article II, or a duly certified copy thereof.[58]

11.53 Despite these requirements of Article IV of the Convention, courts in a number of jurisdictions have enforced awards in the absence of an original of the

---

(1998) XXIII YBCA 770. In China, the Supreme People's Court's Circular on Implementing the Convention excludes relationships between 'foreign investors and the host government': Notice of the Supreme People's Court Regarding the Implementation of the Convention on the Recognition and Enforcement of Foreign Arbitral Awards Acceded to by China [1987] *Fa Jing Fa* No. 5, effective from 10 April 1987. On the other end of the spectrum is *Bautista v Star Cruises* 396 F.3d 1289 (11th Cir. 2005), in which a US court denied the application of an exclusion from arbitration under the Federal Arbitration Act of 1925 (FAA) of the 'contracts of employment of seamen, railroad employees or other class of workers engaged in foreign or interstate commerce' to the commercial reservation. Its rationale was that 'to read industry-specific exceptions into the broad language of the Convention Act would be to hinder the Convention's purpose': ibid., at 1299.

[56] New York Convention, Art. III.

[57] Nevertheless, cases in which the application for enforcement fails are reported, from time to time, in the ICCA *Yearbook of Commercial Arbitration* (YBCA), usually because a party has failed to comply with these 'simple' requirements: see, e.g., the decisions of the Italian Court of Cassation in *Lampart Vegypary Gepgyar (Hungary) v Srl Campomarzio Impianti (Italy)* (1999) XXIVa YBCA 699; the Bulgarian Supreme Court's decision in *National Electricity Co. AD (Bulgaria) v ECONBERG Ltd (Croatia)* (2000) XXV YBCA 678. Equally, some jurisdictions take a liberal and pragmatic approach to the fulfilment of formal requirements. By way of example, a Geneva court recognised a Chinese award that had not been translated into French, noting that the spirit of the Convention was to reduce the obligations for the party seeking recognition and enforcement, and that the burden of proof in respect of any questions relating to the authenticity of the arbitration agreement or the award lay on the party opposing recognition: *R SA v A Ltd* (2001) XXVI YBCA 863.

[58] New York Convention, Art. IV. However, see the discussion of the 'writing requirement' in Chapter 2.

arbitration agreement,[59] or indeed without a written arbitration clause at all. By way of example, the Supreme Court of Spain enforced an award of the China International Economic and Trade Arbitration Commission (CIETAC) even though it did not identify the parties thereto, reasoning that the respondent fully participated in the arbitration, thus proving its intention to submit its dispute with the claimant to arbitration.[60]

11.54 If the award and the arbitration agreement are not in the official language of the country in which recognition and enforcement is sought, certified translations are needed.[61] Once the necessary documents have been supplied, the court will grant recognition and enforcement unless one or more of the grounds for refusal, listed in the Convention, are present.

(b) Refusal of recognition and enforcement

11.55 The various grounds for refusal of recognition and enforcement of an arbitration award that are set out in the New York Convention must be discussed in detail. This is not only because of the importance of the Convention itself, but also—and equally crucially—because the provisions of the Model Law governing recognition and enforcement of awards (in Articles 35 and 36) are almost identical to those set out in the Convention.

11.56 First, neither the New York Convention nor the Model Law permit any review on the merits of an award to which the Convention applies.[62]

11.57 Secondly, the grounds for refusal of recognition and enforcement set out in the New York Convention (and in the Model Law) are exhaustive. They are the *only* grounds on which recognition and enforcement may be refused.

11.58 Thirdly, the New York Convention sets out five separate grounds on which recognition and enforcement of a Convention award may be refused at the request of the party against whom it is invoked.[63] It is significant that, under both the Convention and the Model Law (which follows the Convention in this respect), the burden of

---

[59] In *Hewlett-Packard, Inc. v Berg* 867 F.Supp. 1126, 1130, n. 11 (D. Mass. 1994), the court considered Berg's motion to confirm an arbitral award made in his favour. While noting that the submission of uncertified copies of the arbitral award and arbitration agreement fell short of the requirements in Art. VI of the Convention, the court nevertheless felt able to confirm the arbitral award, in part because neither party had contested the validity of the documents submitted.

[60] *Shaanxi Provincial Medical Health Products I/E Corporation v Olpesa, SA*, Tribunal Supremo, Case No. 112/2002, 7 October 2003, (2005) XXX YBCA 617.

[61] New York Convention, Art. IV(2).

[62] This statement, which was made in an earlier edition of this volume, has since been cited with approval by the Supreme Court of India in *Renusagar Power Co. Ltd v General Electric Co.* (1995) XX YBCA 681. The Court added that, in its opinion, 'the scope of enquiry before the court in which the award is sought to be enforced is limited [to the grounds mentioned in the Act] and does not enable a party to the said proceedings to impeach the Award on merits': ibid., at 691.

[63] These grounds are set out in Art. V of the New York Convention.

B. Enforcement under the New York Convention

proof is *not* upon the party seeking recognition and enforcement.[64] The remaining two grounds on which recognition and enforcement may be refused, which relate to the public policy of the place of enforcement, are grounds that may be invoked by the enforcing court on its own motion.[65]

Fourthly, even if grounds for refusal of recognition and enforcement of an award are proved to exist, the enforcing court is *not obliged* to refuse enforcement. The opening lines of Article V(1) and (2) of the Convention say that enforcement 'may' be refused; they do not say that it 'must' be refused. The language is permissive, not mandatory.[66] The same is true of the Model Law.[67] **11.59**

Fifthly, the intention of the New York Convention and of the Model Law is that the grounds for refusing recognition and enforcement of arbitral awards should be applied restrictively. As a leading commentator on the Convention has stated: 'As far as the grounds for refusal for enforcement of the Award as enumerated in Article V are concerned, it means *that they have to be construed narrowly*.'[68] **11.60**

Most national courts have recognised this. There has been approval in the United States, for example, of the 'pro-enforcement bias' of the Convention.[69] However, not all courts follow this internationalist approach. Practitioners of international commercial arbitration are aware, either from their own experience or from the experience of others, of the difficulties that may arise in seeking enforcement of an award under the New York Convention. In particular, the 'public policy' exception[70] enables some states to play the game less fairly than others. Nor is this the only problem.[71] There are states that have ratified the Convention, but have **11.61**

---

[64] This represents a major change from the 1927 Geneva Convention.

[65] New York Convention, Art. V(2).

[66] This interpretation of the relevant provision of the Convention seems to be generally accepted, both in court decisions and by experienced commentators: see, e.g., van den Berg, *The New York Arbitration Convention of 1958* (Kluwer Law International, 1981), p. 265; Delaume, 'Enforcement against a foreign state of an arbitral award annulled in the foreign state' (1997) Revue du Droit International des Affaires 254. For a US decision to this effect, see *Chromalloy Aeroservices Inc. v Arab Republic of Egypt* 939 F.Supp 907, 909 (DDC 1996); for an English decision, see *China Agribusiness Development Corporation v Balli Trading* [1998] 2 Lloyd's Rep 76. The suggestion that the French text of the Convention (in contrast to the equally authentic Chinese, English, Spanish, and Russian texts) is mandatory, rather than permissive, is demolished in Paulsson, 'May or must under the New York Convention: An exercise in syntax and linguistics' (1998) 14 Arb Intl 227.

[67] The same is true for the grounds for refusal under the English Arbitration Act 1996, although it is not based on the Model Law: see, e.g., *Kanoria v Guinness* [2006] EWCA Civ 222, [2006] Arb LR 513.

[68] van den Berg, *The New York Arbitration Convention of 1958* (Kluwer Law International, 1981), pp. 267 and 268 (emphasis added).

[69] *Parsons Whittemore Overseas Co. v Société Générale de L'Industrie de Papier (RAKTA)*, 508 F.2d 969 (2nd Cir. 1974); also reported in (1976) I YBCA 205.

[70] See paragraph 11.34.

[71] For further discussion of these problems, see, e.g., Kerr, 'Concord and conflict in international arbitration' (1996) 13 ASA Bulletin 129, paras 1–157 (also published in (1997) 13 Intl Arb 121); Proceedings of the Fourteenth ICCA Congress, Paris, May 1998. See also Paulsson, 'Why good arbitration cannot compensate for bad courts' (2013) 30 J Intl Arb 345.

either not brought it into effect or have brought it into effect inadequately. There are states in which the local courts or the local bureaucracy are unfamiliar with international arbitration—and perhaps even suspicious of it. There are also oddities of legislation, such as those provisions of a past law in India (now repealed) stating that where the governing law was that of India, the ensuing award was deemed to be a domestic award, even though the seat of the arbitration was in a foreign state.[72]

11.62 Problems of this kind cannot be ignored, but they should not be exaggerated. The New York Convention *has* proved to be a highly effective international instrument for the enforcement of arbitration agreements and, more importantly in the present context, arbitration awards.[73] The Convention is now somewhat dated,[74] and it is by no means applied consistently by all of the states that have adopted it (or which claim to have done so),[75] but it has made the greatest single contribution to the internationalisation of international commercial arbitration. Even though the Model Law may eventually take its place, decisions under the Convention will remain important, since the Model Law's provisions governing recognition and enforcement of arbitral awards are taken directly from the New York Convention.

(c) Grounds for refusal

11.63 Under Article V(1) of the New York Convention, recognition and enforcement of an arbitral award *may* be refused if the opposing party proves that:

[...]

(a) The parties to the arbitration agreement...were, under the law applicable to them, under some incapacity, or the said agreement is not valid under the law

---

[72] Such an award is normally regarded as a foreign (or international) award under the New York Convention. See n. 141.

[73] Indeed, it has been estimated (although statistics about arbitration are notoriously difficult to collect) that 98 per cent of awards in international arbitrations are honoured or successfully enforced, and that enforcement by national courts has been refused in less than 5 per cent of cases: see van den Berg, 'The New York Convention of 1958: Its intended effects, its interpretation, salient problem areas', in Blessing (ed.) *The New York Convention of 1958: A Collection of Reports and Materials Delivered at the ASA Conference Held in Zurich 2 February 1996* (ASA, 1996), p. 25.

[74] For instance, in its definition of an 'agreement in writing' as discussed in Chapters 1 and 2.

[75] See, e.g., Paulsson, 'The New York Convention in international practice: Problems of assimilation', in Blessing (ed.) *The New York Convention of 1958: A Collection of Reports and Materials Delivered at the ASA Conference Held in Zurich 2 February 1996* (ASA, 1996), pp. 100*ff*; Cheng, 'Celebrating the fiftieth anniversary of the New York Convention' (2009) 14 ICCA Congress Series 679. To solve the problem of conflicting interpretations of the New York Convention by various national courts, some commentators have revived Judge Howard Holtzmann's self-named 'impossible dream' of a world court of international arbitral awards with exclusive jurisdiction to determine whether recognition and enforcement of an international arbitration award may be refused for any of the reasons set out in Art. V of the New York Convention: see the discussion in Brower, 'The coming crisis in the global adjudication system' (2003) 19 Arb Intl 415, at 434. For now, the dream remains just that.

B. Enforcement under the New York Convention

to which the parties have subjected it or, failing any indication thereon, under the law of the country where the award was made; or

(b) The party against whom the award is invoked was not given proper notice of the appointment of the arbitrator or of the arbitration proceedings or was otherwise unable to present his [or her] case; or

(c) The award deals with a difference not contemplated by or not falling within the terms of the submission to arbitration, or it contains decisions on matters beyond the scope of the submission to arbitration, provided that, if the decisions on matters submitted to arbitration can be separated from those not so submitted, that part of the award which contains decisions on matters submitted to arbitration may be recognized and enforced; or

(d) The composition of the arbitral authority or the arbitral procedure was not in accordance with the agreement of the parties, or, failing such agreement, was not in accordance with the law of the country where the arbitration took place; or

(e) The award has not yet become binding on the parties, or has been set aside or suspended by a competent authority of the country in which, or under the law of which, the award was made.

Article V(2) provides: **11.64**

Recognition and enforcement…may also be refused if the competent authority in the country where recognition and enforcement is sought finds that:

(a) The subject matter of the difference is not capable of settlement by arbitration under the law of that country; or
(b) The recognition or enforcement of the award would be contrary to the public policy of that country.

These grounds for refusal of recognition and enforcement of foreign arbitral awards are of considerable importance. They represent an internationally accepted standard, not only because of the widespread acceptance of the New York Convention throughout the world, but also because the Model Law adopts the same grounds (although not in precisely the same words) for refusal of recognition and enforcement of an arbitral award, irrespective of the country in which that award was made.[76] In addition, six of these seven grounds for refusal are also set out in the Model Law as grounds for the *setting aside* of an arbitral award by the national court of the place of arbitration.[77]

In an ideal world, the provisions of the New York Convention and of the Model Law would be interpreted in the same way by courts everywhere. Sadly, this does not happen. There are inconsistent decisions under the New York Convention, just as there may be inconsistent decisions within a national system of law (although the latter may be corrected on appeal). Nevertheless, it is useful to consider how national courts in different parts of the world have applied the different grounds for refusal set out in the New York Convention. Whilst these decisions have no binding authority **11.65**

---

[76] Model Law (as amended in 2006), Art. 36.
[77] Model Law, Art. 34. The ground that is omitted, naturally, is that of the award being set aside by a national court of the place of arbitration.

(d) First ground for refusal—incapacity; invalid arbitration agreement

11.66 The first ground for refusal of recognition and enforcement under the New York Convention is set out in Article V(1)(a)[78] as:

> (a) The parties to the agreement...were, under the law applicable to them, under some incapacity, or the said agreement is not valid under the law to which the parties have subjected it or, failing any indication thereon, under the law of the country where the award was made...

The issue of capacity to enter into an arbitration agreement, which may raise particular difficulties in relation to states and state agencies, has already been discussed in Chapter 2, as have issues as to the validity of the arbitration agreement.

11.67 A classic example of a successful defence to enforcement based on invalidity is provided by the decision of the Administrative Tribunal of Damascus in *Fougerolle SA (France) v Ministry of Defence of the Syrian Arab Republic*.[79] The Tribunal, in its decision of 31 March 1988, refused enforcement of two awards under the Arbitration Rules of the International Chamber of Commerce (ICC), holding that they were 'non-existent' because they were rendered 'without the preliminary advice on the referral of the dispute to arbitration, which must be given by the competent Committee of the Council of State'.[80]

11.68 A more recent example of a successful defence to enforcement based on this ground is the decision of the Supreme Court of England and Wales in *Dallah Real Estate v Ministry of Religious Affairs*.[81] In *Dallah*, the enforcement of an ICC award rendered in Paris against the Government of Pakistan was refused on the grounds that the government was not a party to the arbitration agreement. The agreement containing the arbitration clause had been signed by the government-owned Awami Hajj Trust,[82] which subsequently ceased to exist[83] and was held not to be an organ of the state.[84] In so finding, the Supreme Court reversed the arbitral tribunal's own finding on jurisdiction. Lord Mance

---

[78] As already noted, this ground for refusal, and the others that follow, also appear in virtually the same terms in the Model Law (as amended in 2006), Art. 36, as grounds for refusing enforcement of arbitral awards wherever made.
[79] (1990) XV, YBCA 515.
[80] Ibid.
[81] *Dallah Real Estate and Tourism Holding Co. v The Ministry of Religious Affairs, Government of Pakistan* [2010] UKSC 46.
[82] Ibid., at [2].
[83] Ibid., at [8].
[84] Ibid., at [66], [147], [149], [162], and [163].

B. Enforcement under the New York Convention

emphasised that a determination by the arbitral tribunal concerning its own jurisdiction was immaterial to the Court's review:

> The tribunal's own view of its jurisdiction has no legal or evidential value, when the issue is whether the tribunal had any legitimate authority in relation to the Government at all. This is so however full was the evidence before it and however carefully deliberated was its conclusion. It is also so whatever the composition of the tribunal.[85]

11.69 The English Supreme Court's decision is to be contrasted with the outcome of the application for the annulment of the same award before the Paris Cour d'Appel, the Paris court having reached the opposite conclusion on the question as to whether the government was bound by the arbitration agreement as a matter of French law.[86]

11.70 An example that illustrates an unsuccessful attempt to use this defence to enforcement is a decision by the Supreme Court of Austria. In *O Ltd (Hong Kong) v S GmbH (Austria)*,[87] the Court rejected the defendant's argument that a power of attorney to conclude an arbitration agreement must be in writing. In so finding, the Court reasoned that although this formality is required by Austrian law, the New York Convention—which applied to the foreign award at issue—does not.

(e) Second ground—no proper notice of appointment of arbitrator or of the proceedings; lack of due process

11.71 The second ground for refusal of recognition and enforcement of an award under the New York Convention is set out at Article V(1)(b):

> (b) The party against whom the award is invoked was not given proper notice of the appointment of the arbitrator or of the arbitration proceedings or was otherwise unable to present his [or her] case...

This is the most important ground for refusal under the New York Convention (and the Model Law). It is directed at ensuring that the arbitration itself is properly conducted, with proper notice granted to the parties and procedural fairness.

11.72 The point as to notice is a matter of formality, but it is important nonetheless. However, the main thrust of this provision of the Convention is directed at ensuring that the requirements of 'due process' are observed and that the parties are given a fair hearing. If parties from different countries are to have confidence in arbitration as a method of dispute resolution, it is essential that the proceedings should be conducted in a manner that is fair and which is *seen* to be fair. This is

---

[85] Ibid., at [30].
[86] *Gouvernement du Pakistan v Société Dallah Real Estate and Tourism Holding Co.*, Paris Cour d'Appel, 17 February 2011 [2012] Rev Arb 369.
[87] (1997) XXXII YBCA 254.

something that should be borne in mind, by parties and arbitrators alike, from the very outset of the arbitration.

11.73 The court of the forum state will naturally have its own concept of what constitutes a 'fair hearing'. In this sense, as was said in a leading case in the United States, the New York Convention 'essentially sanctions the application of the forum state's standards of due process'.[88] This does not mean, however, that the hearing must be conducted as if it were a hearing before a national court in the forum state. It is generally enough if the court is satisfied that the hearing was conducted with due regard to any agreement between the parties, and in accordance with the principles of equality of treatment and the right of each party to have a reasonable—rather than exhaustive—opportunity to present its case.

11.74 The national court at the place of enforcement thus has a limited role. Its function is *not* to decide whether or not the award is correct, as a matter of fact and law; its function is simply to decide whether there has been a fair hearing. Only a significant and material mistake in the course of the proceedings should be sufficient to lead the court to conclude that there was a denial of 'due process'.

11.75 By way of example, in a case to which reference has already been made,[89] a US corporation, which had been told that there was no need to submit detailed invoices, had its claim rejected by the Iran–United States Claims Tribunal, for failure to submit detailed invoices! The US court—rightly, it is suggested—refused to enforce the award against the US company. In different circumstances, a German court held that an award that was based upon arguments that had not been raised by the parties or the tribunal during the arbitral proceedings, and thus on which the parties had not had an opportunity to comment, violated due process and the right to be heard.[90] In France, in *Overseas Mining Investments*,[91] the successful claimant had not pleaded the grounds on which the arbitral tribunal had found in its favour. In these circumstances, the French Cour de Cassation held that the tribunal's failure to invite both the parties to express their views on the grounds in question violated the *principe de la contradiction*, which was essential for the conduct of a fair hearing. Similarly, in *Kanoria and ors v Guinness*,[92] the English Court of Appeal decided that the respondent had not been afforded the chance to present its case when critical legal arguments were made by the claimant at the hearing, which the respondent could not attend because of serious illness. In the circumstances, the

---

[88] *Parsons Whittemore Overseas Co. Inc. v Société Générale de l'Industrie du Papier (RAKTA)* 508 F.2d 969, 975 (2nd Cir. 1974).
[89] *Iran Aircraft Industries v Avco Corporation* 980 F.2d 141 (2nd Cir. 1992). See Chapter 10.
[90] See the decision of the Stuttgart Court of Appeal, dated 6 October 2001, referred to in Liebscher, *The Healthy Award: Challenge in International Commercial Arbitration* (Kluwer Law International, 2003), p. 406.
[91] *Société Overseas Mining Investments Ltd v Société Commercial Caribbean Nique*, Case No. 08-23901*l*, Paris Cour de Cassation, Ch. 1ere, 25 March 2010.
[92] [2006] EWCA Civ 222, [2006] Arb LR 513.

B. Enforcement under the New York Convention

Court decided that 'this [was] an extreme case of potential injustice' and resolved not to enforce the arbitral award.

11.76 Examples of unsuccessful 'due process' defences to enforcement are, however, more numerous.[93] In *Minmetals Germany v Ferco Steel*,[94] the losing respondent in an arbitration in China opposed enforcement in England on the grounds that the award was founded on evidence that the arbitral tribunal had obtained through its own investigations. An English court rejected this defence, on the basis that the respondent was given an opportunity to ask for the disclosure of evidence at issue and to comment on it, but had declined to do so. The court held that the due process defence to enforcement was not intended to accommodate circumstances in which a party had failed to take advantage of an opportunity duly accorded to it.[95]

11.77 Another example of an unsuccessful attempt to rely on this ground is *Jorf Lafar Energy Co. SCA (Morocco) v AMCI Export Corporation (US)*.[96] The parties were given the opportunity at an early stage of the arbitration to submit witness statements, but AMCI chose not to do so. At a later stage in the proceedings, AMCI requested an oral hearing to present witness evidence. Having been denied the opportunity to do this, AMCI was unsuccessful in its attempt to resist enforcement of the award for violation of due process. The US District Court for the Western District of Pennsylvania held that AMCI had been given an equal and fair opportunity to present its case, and thus had to suffer the consequences of its own failure to present its case when given that opportunity.[97]

(f) Third ground—jurisdictional issues

11.78 The third ground for refusal of recognition and enforcement of an award under the New York Convention is set out at Article V(1)(c):

> (c) The award deals with a difference not contemplated by or not falling within the terms of the submission to arbitration, or it contains decisions on matters beyond the scope of the submission to arbitration, provided that, if the decision on matters submitted to arbitration can be separated from those not so submitted, that part of the award which contains decisions on matters submitted to arbitration may be recognised and enforced...

---

[93] See Liebscher, *The Healthy Award: Challenge in International Commercial Arbitration* (Kluwer Law International, 2003), ch. VIII, paras 2.2 and 2.3.
[94] (1999) XXIV YBCA 739.
[95] Many jurisdictions have taken a similarly restrictive interpretation of the due process defence to enforcement, e.g. German courts have held that a tribunal's refusal to hear evidence can breach the right to be heard only if such evidence is relevant: see Decision of the Bremen Court of Appeal, 30 September 1999, (2001) 4 Intl ALR N-26.
[96] (2007) XXXII YBCA 713.
[97] For a further decision similar to this case, see *Industrie Technofrigo Dell'Orto SpA (Italy) v PS Profil Epitoipari Kereskedelmi SS Szolgatato KFT (Hungary)* (2007) XXXII YBCA 406. The Italian Supreme Court held that Technofrigo had been granted successive time periods within which to present its questions and file observations, and its inability to file an expert report during these periods did not amount to a violation of due process.

It is becoming increasingly common for the issue of jurisdiction to be raised as the first line of defence in a reference to arbitration. The issue may be raised as part of a plea that there was no valid agreement to arbitrate,[98] in which case it would fall under Article V(1)(a) of the New York Convention, or it may be raised under the present heading. Jurisdictional issues as a ground for challenging an award have already been discussed,[99] and it has been noted that the right to raise such an issue may have been lost because of failure to do so at the appropriate time.[100]

11.79 The first part of this ground for refusal of enforcement under the Convention (and under the Model Law) envisages a situation in which the arbitral tribunal is alleged to have acted in excess of its authority—that is, *ultra petita*—and to have dealt with a dispute that was not submitted to it. According to a leading authority on the Convention, the courts almost invariably reject this defence.[101] By way of example, the German courts have rejected *ultra petita* defences raised in complaint of an arbitral tribunal's application of *lex mercatoria*[102] and an arbitral tribunal's award of more interest than was claimed.[103] A further robust rejection of such a defence comes from the US Court of Appeals for the District of Columbia, in a case in which it was pleaded that the arbitral tribunal had awarded a considerable sum of damages for consequential loss when the contract between the parties clearly excluded this head of damage.[104] The Court stated that, without undertaking an in-depth review of the law of contract, it could not state whether a breach of contract would abrogate a clause that excluded consequential damages. However, 'the standard of review of an arbitration award by an American Court is extremely narrow',[105] and (adopting the words of the US Court of Appeals

---

[98] As in the *Pyramids* arbitration: *The Arab Republic of Egypt v Southern Pacific Properties*, Paris Cour d'Appel, 12 July 1984, published in English at (1984) 23 ILM 1048. The award of the ICC tribunal in this case was challenged by the Egyptian government on the basis that it was not a party to the relevant agreement and so was not bound by the arbitration clause. The Paris Cour d'Appel agreed and the award was set aside. For a discussion of the case, see Redfern, 'Jurisdiction denied: The pyramid collapses' (1986) JBL 15. See also (1984) IX YBCA 113 and (1985) X YBCA 487. The claimants then started fresh arbitration proceedings, under the ICSID Convention. For the rest of the story, see Delaume, 'The pyramids stand: The pharaohs can rest in peace' (1993) 8 ICSID Rev—Foreign Investment LJ 231; Paulsson, 'Arbitration without privity' (1995) 10 ICSID Rev—Foreign Investment LJ 232.

[99] See Chapter 10, paragraph 10.42*ff.*

[100] See Chapter 10, paragraph 10.28*ff.*

[101] See van den Berg, 'Court decisions on the New York Convention', in Blessing (ed.) *The New York Convention of 1958: A Collection of Reports and Materials Delivered at the ASA Conference Held in Zurich 2 February 1996* (ASA, 1996), p. 86.

[102] See Decision of the Regional Court of Hamburg, 18 September 1997, (2000) XXV YBCA 710.

[103] See Decision of the Court of Appeal of Hamburg, 30 July 1998, (2000) XXV YBCA 714.

[104] *Libyan American Oil Co. (Liamco) v Socialist People's Libyan Arab Yamahirya, formerly Libyan Arab Republic* (1982) VII YBCA 382.

[105] Ibid., at 388. See also *Telenor Mobile Communications AS v Storm LLC* 584 F.3d 396 (2nd Cir. 2009). In this case, the US Court of Appeals for the Second Circuit rejected Storm's contention that the arbitral tribunal acted in 'manifest disregard of the law' by ignoring a Ukrainian court decision that the arbitration clause in dispute was 'null and void'. The Court noted that there

B. Enforcement under the New York Convention

in the well-known case of *Parsons Whittemore*[106]) the Convention did not sanction 'second-guessing the arbitrators' construction of the parties' agreement', nor would it be proper for the court to 'usurp the arbitrators' role'.[107] Accordingly, enforcement was ordered.

A further example of an unsuccessful attempt to use this ground to resist enforcement is a decision by the US District Court for the Northern District of Illinois, Eastern Division.[108] The respondents argued that the arbitral tribunal had exceeded its authority by giving a preclusive effect to findings of an English court, rather than holding an evidentiary hearing to make its own findings. The US court held that since the parties' arbitration agreement neither stipulated any specific hearing procedure to be followed nor prohibited the tribunal from deciding on issues of preclusion, these were issues to be decided by the arbitral tribunal.[109] **11.80**

The second part of this ground for refusal is concerned with the situation in which it is alleged that the tribunal exceeded its jurisdiction in some respects, but not in others. In such a situation, even if the partial excess of authority is proved, that part of the award which concerns matters properly submitted to arbitration *may* be saved and enforcement ordered. For example, in a case that came before the Italian courts, the court examined the award to determine whether or not the arbitral tribunal had exceeded the limits of its jurisdiction.[110] Having done so, the Italian court granted partial enforcement of the award, to the extent that it dealt with matters within the jurisdiction of the arbitral tribunal. **11.81**

---

is a strong presumption against finding manifest disregard of the law by an arbitral tribunal and upheld the confirmation of the award.

[106] *Parsons Whittemore Overseas Co. Inc. v Société Générale de l'Industrie du Papier (RAKTA)* 508 F.2d 969 (2nd Cir. 1974).

[107] (1982) VII YBCA 382, at 388.

[108] *Sphere Drake Insurance Ltd v Lincoln National Life Insurance Co. et al.* (2007) XXXII YBCA 857.

[109] A further example of where this ground was unsuccessfully relied upon is *Aloe Vera of America, Inc. (US) v Asianic Food (S) Pte Ltd (Singapore) and anor* (2007) XXXII YBCA 489. One of the defendants argued that he was not a party to the arbitration clause and that, by entering an award against him, the arbitrator went beyond the scope of the submission to arbitration. The Supreme Court of Singapore dismissed this argument and held that the issue of whether the defendant was a party to the arbitration clause did not fall properly under this ground. The Court further held that the defendant had brought no evidence to prove that, under Arizona law, the award contained a decision on a matter beyond the scope of the submission to arbitration. In contrast, and as discussed at paragraph 11.68, the Supreme Court of England and Wales adopted a far less deferential approach, and undertook a full examination of the arbitral tribunal's jurisdiction when presented with a potential breach of jurisdictional issues in *Dallah Real Estate and Tourism Holding Co. v Ministry of Religious Affairs, Government of Pakistan* [2010] UKSC 46. The Court also held that while it can have regard to any statements made by the arbitral tribunal on its own jurisdiction, the Court was neither bound nor restricted by such statements.

[110] *General Organization of Commerce and Industrialisation of Cereals of the Arab Republic of Syria v SpA SIMER (Società delle Industrie Meccaniche di Rovereto) (Italy)* (1983) VIII YBCA 386.

(g) Fourth ground—composition of tribunal or procedure not in accordance with arbitration agreement or the relevant law

11.82 The fourth ground for refusal of recognition and enforcement of an award under the New York Convention is set out at Article V(1)(d):

> (d) The composition of the arbitral authority or the arbitral procedure was not in accordance with the agreement of the parties, or, failing such agreement, was not in accordance with the law of the country where the arbitration took place...

The 1927 Geneva Convention provided that enforcement of an award could be refused if the composition of the arbitral tribunal, or the arbitral procedure, was not in accordance both with the agreement of the parties *and* the law of the place of arbitration. This double requirement meant that if an arbitration was not held in strict accordance with the procedural law of the place of arbitration, the consequent award would not be enforced. Under the New York Convention, the double requirement has been dropped and the agreement of the parties comes first. Only if there is no agreement are the arbitration laws of the place of arbitration to be taken into account.

11.83 In a case that came before the Supreme Court of Hong Kong in 1994, it was argued that enforcement of an award made in China should be refused because the composition of the arbitral tribunal was not in accordance with the agreement of the parties.[111] The arbitrators who had been appointed were on the Shenzhen list of arbitrators, but not (as specified in the arbitration agreement) on the Beijing list.

11.84 Giving judgment, Kaplan J said:

> It is clear therefore that the only grounds upon which enforcement can be refused are those specified... and that the burden of proving a ground is upon the defendant. Further, it is clear that even though a ground has been proved, the Court retains a residual discretion.[112]

After considering the facts, the judge said:

> I conclude therefore, somewhat reluctantly, that technically the arbitrators did not have jurisdiction to decide this dispute and that in all the circumstances of this case, the ground specified in the section has been made out. I say technically because the parties did agree to have a CIETAC Arbitration and that is what they got, even though it was held at a place within China not specified in the contract and by arbitrators who apparently were not on the Beijing list.[113]

11.85 Although the ground for refusal of enforcement had been made out, the judge allowed enforcement of the award to go ahead on the basis that the party

---

[111] See *China Nanhai Oil Joint Service Corporation v Gee Tai Holdings Co. Ltd* (1995) XX YBCA 671. Similarly, see *Tongyuan International Trading Group v Uni-Clan* [2001] 4 Intl ALR N-31.
[112] *China Nanhai Oil*, at 672.
[113] *China Nanhai Oil*, at 673.

B. Enforcement under the New York Convention

objecting to enforcement had taken part in the arbitration knowing that, technically, the arbitrators were not selected from the correct list. Having done so, it could not now seek to profit from this error. The judge considered the application of the doctrine of estoppel to other aspects of the New York Convention and said:

> If the doctrine of estoppel can apply to arguments over the written form of the arbitration agreement under Article II(2), then I fail to see why it cannot also apply to the grounds of opposition set out in Article V. It strikes me as quite unfair for a party to appreciate that there might be something wrong with the composition of the tribunal yet not make any formal submission whatsoever to the tribunal about its own jurisdiction, or to the arbitration commission which constituted the tribunal and then to proceed to fight the case on the merits and then two years after the award, attempt to nullify the whole proceedings on the grounds that the arbitrators were chosen from the wrong CIETAC list.[114]

He continued:

> [E]ven if a ground of opposition is proved, there is still a residual discretion left in the enforcing court to enforce nonetheless. This shows that the grounds of opposition are not to be inflexibly applied. The residual discretion enables the enforcing court to achieve a just result in all the circumstances...[115]

11.86 In contrast, *Encyclopaedia Universalis SA (Luxembourg) v Encyclopaedia Britannica Inc. (US)*[116] is an example of the successful reliance on this ground before the US Court of Appeals for the Second Circuit. In their contract, the parties had agreed that (a) the two party-appointed arbitrators must attempt to choose a third arbitrator, and (b), upon the failure of the two party-appointed arbitrators to agree on a third, the English Commercial Court would appoint one. The appellant, Encyclopaedia Universalis SA (Luxembourg), sidestepped the first requirement and prematurely requested the Commercial Court to appoint a third arbitrator. In response to a request by Encyclopaedia Britannica Inc. (US) to refuse enforcement of the award rendered against it, the US Court held that:

> [T]he [English court]'s premature appointment of [the third arbitrator] irremediably spoiled the arbitration process...the issue of how the third arbitrator was to be appointed is more than a trivial matter of form. Article V(1)(d) of the New York Convention itself suggests the importance of arbitral composition...[117]

---

[114] *China Nanhai Oil*, at 677.
[115] Ibid.
[116] (2005) XXX, YBCA 1136.
[117] Ibid., at [8]–[1]0. See also *HSN Capital LLC (US) v Productora y Comercializador de Television, SA de CV (Mexico)* (2007) XXXII YBCA 774, at [3]–[7]. China's Supreme People's Court has more recently gone further still: in *Bunge Agribuss v Guangdong Fengyuan* [2006] *Min Si Ta Zi* No. 41, the designated arbitral institution appointed an arbitrator on behalf of the respondent because of the latter's failure to do so within the permitted time limit. Even though this was entirely consistent with the arbitral rules selected by the parties, the Supreme People's Court held that the failure to consult Fengyuan on the appointment was a valid basis on which to refuse enforcement.

(h) Fifth ground—award suspended, or set aside

11.87 The fifth ground for refusal of recognition and enforcement under the New York Convention is set out at Article V(1)(e):

> (e) The award has not yet become binding on the parties, or has been set aside or suspended by a competent authority of the country in which, or under the law of which, that award was made...

This fifth ground for refusal of recognition and enforcement of an arbitral award (which, like the others, also appears in the Model Law) has given rise to more controversy than any of the previous grounds. First, there is the reference to an award being 'not binding'. In the 1927 Geneva Convention, the word 'final' was used. This was taken by many to mean that the award had to be declared as 'final' by the court of the place of arbitration and this gave rise to the problem of the double *exequatur*. It was intended that the word 'binding' would avoid this problem, particularly since many international and institutional rules of arbitration state in terms that the award of the arbitral tribunal is to be accepted by the parties as final and 'binding' upon them.[118] However, some national courts still consider it necessary to investigate the law applicable to the award to see if it is 'binding' under that law[119]—although the better position appears to be that an award is 'binding' if it is no longer open to an appeal on the merits, either internally (that is, within the relevant rules of arbitration) or by an application to the court.[120]

11.88 There are other problems too, with this fifth ground for refusal, which have led to considerable controversy. At first sight, the proposition that an award *may* be refused recognition and enforcement if it has been set aside or suspended by a court at the place (or seat) of the arbitration seems reasonable enough. If, for example, an award has been set aside in Switzerland, it will be unenforceable in that country—and it might be expected that, if only as a matter of international comity, the courts of other states would regard the award as unenforceable also.

11.89 This is not necessarily so, however. Courts in other countries may take the view (and indeed, as will be described,[121] in some countries they *have* taken the view)

---

[118] See, e.g., UNCITRAL Rules, Art. 34(2).

[119] van den Berg, 'Court decisions on the New York Convention', in Blessing (ed.) *The New York Convention of 1958: A Collection of Reports and Materials Delivered at the ASA Conference Held in Zurich 2 February 1996* (ASA, 1996), pp. 87 and 88.

[120] Ibid., p. 88. If an appeal is pending, the enforcement court may, if it considers it proper, adjourn the decision on enforcement. It may also order the party against whom enforcement is sought to give security: New York Convention, Art. VI. As to the question of which law determines the 'binding' effect of an award, see *Antilles Cement Corporation (Puerto Rico) v Transficem (Spain)* (2006) XXXI YBCA 846, at [9]–[13], in which the Supreme Court of Spain held, at [13], that whether an award is binding 'is not to be examined in accordance with the law of the State where the award is rendered'.

[121] See paragraph 11.94*ff*.

B. Enforcement under the New York Convention

that they will enforce an arbitral award even if it has been set aside by the courts of the seat of the arbitration. This leads to a situation in which an award that has been set aside and so is unenforceable in its country of origin may be refused enforcement under the New York Convention in one country, but granted enforcement in another.

The problem arises because the New York Convention does not in any way restrict the grounds on which an award may be set aside or suspended by the court of the country in which, or under the law of which, that award was made.[122] This is a matter that is left to the domestic law of the country concerned, and this domestic law may impose local requirements (such as the need to initial each page of the award) that judges and lawyers elsewhere would not regard as sufficient to impeach the validity of an *international* arbitral award.

11.90

The allowance for local requirements that is made in the New York Convention has been described by a former secretary-general of the ICC Court as:

11.91

> ...a hitherto rock-solid rampart against the true internationalisation of arbitration, because in the award's country of origin all means of recourse and all grounds of nullity applicable to purely domestic awards may be used to oppose recognition abroad...[123]

Another experienced commentator has referred to the 'anathema of local particularities', which are capable of leading to the setting aside of international awards, and has suggested that 'such local standard annulments' should be given only local effect and should be disregarded internationally.[124]

The argument in favour of the fifth ground is a familiar one. It is the classic argument that the courts of the place of arbitration should have some control over arbitral proceedings conducted on their territory, if only to guard against lack of due process, fraud, corruption, or other improper conduct on the part of the arbitral tribunal. Perhaps the real argument is: how far should this control go? Should it be limited to the first four grounds of the New York Convention,[125] or should it go further? And if so, how much further? The problem is to strike the correct balance between regulation and laissez-faire.

11.92

---

[122] Unlike the Model Law (as amended in 2006), which, in Art. 34, sets out the limited grounds on which an award may be set aside.

[123] Derains, 'Foreword', in ICC (ed.) *Hommage à Frédéric Eisemann* (ICC, 1978), p. 13, translated in Paulsson, 'The case for disregarding local standard annulments under the New York Convention' (1996) 7 Am Rev Intl Arb 99. This is not true of states that have different laws to govern international arbitrations from those that govern domestic arbitrations, but nevertheless the point is a valid one.

[124] See ibid. In a sense, this comes back to the 'delocalisation' debate, which was a source of lively controversy at the time: see, e.g., Paulsson, 'Arbitration unbound: Award detached from the law of its country of origin' (1981) 30 ICLQ 358; Paulsson, 'Delocalisation of international commercial arbitration: When and why it matters' (1983) 32 ICLQ 53. See also the discussion in Chapter 3.

[125] As with the European Convention of 1961.

11.93 Whilst the argument continues, courts in France, Belgium, Austria, and the United States have shown themselves prepared, on occasion, to recognise and enforce arbitral awards even though they have been set aside by the courts at the seat of arbitration.[126] The justification for this is twofold. First, the language of Article V of the New York Convention (as already discussed) is permissive, not mandatory. Specifically, the English language version of the Convention says that the enforcing court *may* refuse recognition and enforcement—not that it *must* do so. Secondly, the New York Convention recognises that there may be more favourable provisions under which an award may be recognised and enforced. The Convention contains the following provision, in Article VII(1):

> The provisions of the present Convention shall not affect the validity of multilateral or bilateral agreements concerning the recognition and enforcement of arbitral awards entered into by the Contracting States nor deprive any interested party of any right he may have to avail himself of the arbitral award in the manner and to the extent allowed by the law or the treaties of the country where such award is sought to be relied upon.

In this way, the New York Convention recognises explicitly that, in any given country, there may be a local law that, whether by treaty or otherwise, is more favourable to the recognition and enforcement of arbitral awards than the Convention itself. The Convention gives its blessing, so to speak, to any party who wishes to take advantage of this more favourable local law.

11.94 The New York Convention has long been regarded as being of fundamental importance to the recognition and enforcement of international arbitral awards. It remains so. However, the possibility of obtaining recognition and enforcement of an award that has been set aside by means of applying a more favourable local law, which does not reflect or rely upon the Convention, should not be overlooked. This approach can be illustrated with some examples emanating from the French and US courts. In the French decision of *Hilmarton*,[127] an award rendered by a tribunal in Switzerland in favour of the respondent was later annulled by the Geneva Court of Appeal. In the meantime, however, the respondent had applied to the French courts to enforce the award and was successful at the first instance. On appeal from the enforcement proceedings in France, the French Cour d'Appel had to decide whether to uphold the lower court's decision to

---

[126] For a comprehensive survey of instances in which national courts have recognised or enforced awards set aside by the courts of the place of arbitration, see Gharavi, *The International Effectiveness of the Annulment of an Arbitral Award* (Kluwer Law International, 2002). Article 1526 of the French Code of Civil Procedure now expressly provides that an application to set aside an arbitral award does not stay the proceedings to enforce the award. For commentary on the rationale behind art. 1526, see Kleiman and Saleh, 'Enforcement of international arbitration awards: Latest developments', available online at http://www.internationallawoffice.com/newsletters/detail.aspx?g=eb1d34c8-92cf-424e-b4c0-4bc8274ea35b.

[127] *Hilmarton Ltd v Omnium de Traitement et de Valorisation (OTV)* (1994) Rev Arb 327; English excerpts in (1995) XX YBCA 663.

B. Enforcement under the New York Convention

enforce the award, even though it had been set aside in the country in which it was made. The Cour d'Appel decided to let the enforcement proceed. This decision was subsequently confirmed by the French Cour de Cassation, which stated that:

> ...the award rendered in Switzerland is an international award which is not integrated in the legal system of that State, so that it remains in existence even if set aside and its recognition in France is not contrary to international public policy.[128]

In *Chromalloy*,[129] the US Federal Court for the District of Columbia enforced an award that had been set aside in Egypt.[130] The Court explicitly contrasted the permissive nature of Article V of the Convention with the mandatory nature of Article VII: **11.95**

> While Article V provides a discretionary standard, Article VII of the Convention requires that, 'The provisions of the present Convention *shall not*...deprive any interested party of any right he may have to avail himself of an arbitral award in the manner and to the extent allowed by the law...of the country where such award is sought to be relied on.'[131]

In *Putrabali*,[132] the French courts enforced an award set aside in England. In so doing, the Cour de Cassation held that: **11.96**

> [A]n international arbitral award, which does not belong to any state legal system, is an international decision of justice and its validity must be examined according to the applicable rules of the country where its recognition and enforcement are sought.[133]

More recently, in a decision of the US District Court for the Southern District of New York in *COMMISA v Pemex*,[134] a Mexican award was enforced under the 1975 Inter-American Convention on International Commercial Arbitration (the

---

[128] Ibid., at 664. When a second award in favour of the claimants was subsequently rendered in Switzerland and enforcement was sought in France, the Cour de Cassation held that the issue was *res judicata* in the French legal order and hence that the award could not be enforced: *Hilmarton Ltd v Omnium de Traitement et de Valorisation (OTV)* (1994) Rev Arb 327; English excerpts in (1997) XXII YBCA 696.

[129] *Chromalloy Aeroservices Inc. v Arab Republic of Egypt* 939 F.Supp 907 (DDC 1996).

[130] See paragraphs 11.78ff.

[131] *Chromalloy*, at 909–910.

[132] *Société PT Putrabali Adyamulia v Société Rena Holding et Société Mnogutia Est Epices* [2007] Rev Arb 507. The first arbitral award was annulled by the High Court of London and a second award with a directly opposite outcome was issued. Both claimant and respondent sought to enforce the awards in France. In the enforcement proceedings of the first award, the losing party argued that the enforcement of the award would be contrary to international public policy, but the Cour de Cassation did not follow that reasoning and enforced the annulled first award. The Cour de Cassation then refused the enforcement of the second award on the basis that *res judicata* attached to the decision enforcing the first award, which was incompatible with the second award.

[133] Ibid.

[134] *Corporación Mexicana de Mantenimiento Integral, S. de R.L. de C.V. v PEMEX-Exploración y Producción*, No 10 Civ 206 (AKH) 2013 WL 4517225 (SDNY, August 27, 2013).

Panama Convention),[135] despite being set aside at the seat. A Mexican court had applied a statute that was not yet in existence at the time the parties entered into the contract, and had set aside the award on the basis that, as a matter of Mexican law, arbitral tribunals lacked the competency to hear and decide cases brought against the Mexican state, or an organ of the state (such as Pemex, Mexico's state-owned oil company). In rejecting the Mexican court's ruling and confirming the award, the US court was careful to explain that it was 'neither deciding, nor reviewing, Mexican law'; rather, its decision was made on the basis that the Mexican court's ruling 'violated basic notions of justice in that it applied a law that was not in existence at the time the parties' contract was formed and left COMMISA without an apparent ability to litigate its claims'.[136]

11.97 Notwithstanding decisions such as *Hilmarton*, *Chromalloy*, *Putrabali*, and *Pemex*, the enforcement of awards that have been set aside by the courts of the place of arbitration remains controversial. With some notable exceptions, courts around the world are more likely than not to decline to enforce annulled awards.[137]

---

[135] As will be explained in paragraph 11.137, the grounds for refusal to enforce foreign arbitral awards under the Panama Convention are similar to those under the New York Convention. In particular, Art. 5(e) of the Panama Convention provides that:

[T]he recognition and execution of the decision may be refused, at the request of the party against which it is made, only if such party is able to prove to the competent authority of the State in which recognition and execution are requested... that the decision is not yet binding on the parties or has been annulled or suspended by a competent authority of the State in which, or according to the law of which, the decision has been made.

[136] *Pemex*, at [14]. See also *Yukos Capital SARL v OJSC Oil Co. Rosneft* [2014] EWHC 2188, in which the English High Court held, as a preliminary issue, that an annulment by the Moscow Arbitrazh Court of arbitral awards rendered in Russia would not prevent the English court from giving effect to the annulled awards (under English common law principles) if it were proven that the annulment offended against basic principles of honesty, natural justice, or English public policy. The awards in question had also previously been enforced by the Amsterdam Appeal Court, despite the local standard annulment in Russia.

[137] See, e.g., *Baker Marine (Nig.) Ltd v Chevron (Nig.) Ltd* 191 F.3d 194 (2nd Cir. 1999), in which, notwithstanding *Chromalloy*, the US Second Circuit refused to enforce an award that had been set aside by the court of the place of arbitration (in this case, Nigeria). See also *Spier v Tecnica* 71 F.Supp.2d 279 (SDNY 1999); *TermoRio SA ESP v Electrificadora Del Atlantico SA ESP* 421 F.Supp.2d 87 (DDC 2006), in which the US court denied the enforcement of a Colombian arbitral award that had been set aside by the Colombian courts on the ground that Colombian law in effect at the date of the agreement did not *expressly* permit the use of ICC procedural rules, which the parties had designated in their arbitration clause. This decision was subsequently upheld by the US appellate court. For a discussion of *Putrabali* and *TermoRio*, see Gaillard, 'Note—29 juin 2007—Cour de Cassation (1re Ch. Civ.)' [2007] Rev Arb 517. In Germany, courts take into account the status of the award in the jurisdiction in which it was rendered. In 1999, the Court of Appeal of Rostock refused to enforce an award rendered by the Moscow Maritime Arbitration Commission that had been set aside in Russia: *Oberlandsgericht Rostock*, 28 October 1999, (2000) XXV YBCA 717, at 719. However, when the Russian Supreme Court overturned the lower courts' decisions setting aside the award, the German Federal Supreme Court similarly reversed the decision of the Court of Appeal of Rostock and deemed it enforceable: *Bundesgerichtshof*, 22 February 2001, (2004) XXIX YBCA 724. A similar approach is taken in Chile: see *EDF Internacional SA v Endesa Internacional SA and YPF SA*, Supreme Court of Chile, 8 September 2011, (2012) 5 Arbitraje: Revista de Arbitraje Comercial

B. Enforcement under the New York Convention

Finally, it should be noted that the only national court that is competent to suspend or set aside an award is the court of the country 'in which, or under the law of which, that award was made'.[138] This court will almost invariably be the national court of the seat of the arbitration. The impracticability of holding an arbitration in country X, but subjecting it to the procedural law of country Y, has already been discussed,[139] and so the prospect of an award being set aside under the procedural law of a state other than that of the seat of arbitration is unlikely. However, an ingenious (but unsuccessful) attempt was made to persuade the US District Court to set aside an award made in Mexico, on the basis that the reference to the law under which that award was made was a reference to the law governing the dispute and not to the procedural law.[140] The US court firmly rejected this argument, stating:

11.98

> Decisions of foreign courts under the Convention uniformly support the view that the clause in question means procedural and not substantive (that is, in most cases, contract law)...
>
> Accordingly, we hold that the contested language in Article V(1)(e) of the Convention...refers exclusively to procedural and not substantive law, and more precisely to the regimen or scheme of arbitral procedural law under which the arbitration was conducted.[141]

The court went on to hold that since the seat of the arbitration was Mexico, only the Mexican court had jurisdiction to set aside the award.[142]

However, courts are not always immune to such creative attempts to resist enforcement. The Indian Supreme Court,[143] for example, has in the past accepted that an award rendered in London that was the object of enforcement proceedings in the United States could be set aside in India simply because the parties had chosen Indian law to govern the substance of their dispute.[144] This type of decision is very

11.99

---

y de Inversiones 915, in which the Court held that an Argentinean award set aside at the place of arbitration could not be enforced in Chile.

[138] New York Convention, Art. V(1)(e).
[139] See Chapter 3.
[140] *International Standard Electric Corporation (US) v Bridas Sociedad Anonima Petrolera (Argentina)* (1992) VII YBCA 639.
[141] Ibid., at 644 and 645.
[142] Ibid., at 645.
[143] *Venture Global Engineering v Satyam Computer Services* [2008] INSC 40.
[144] *Venture Global Engineering v Satyam Computer Services* 233 Fed. Appx 517 (6th Cir. 2007). Similar decisions have been rendered by courts in Indonesia and Russia. In *Karaha Bodas Co. LLC (Cayman Islands) v Persusahaan Pertambangan Minyak Dan Gas Bumi Negara aka Pertamina (Indonesia)*, US District Court, Southern District of Texas, Houston Division, 17 April 2003, (2003) XXVIII YBCA 908, the Central Jakarta District Court annulled a Swiss arbitral award applying Indonesian substantive law in favour of Karaha against Pertamina. In Russia, similar arrogations of authority to annul an award have occasionally emerged: see *OAO Stoilensky GOK v Mabetex Project Engineering SA, et al. and Interconstruction Project Management SA v OAO Stoilensky GOK*, Case No. A08-7941/02-18, Federal Commercial Court of the Central District, 2 September 2003; *Collective Fishing Farm Krasnoye Znamya v White Arctic Marine Resources Ltd*, Case No. A05-4274/2007, Federal Commercial Court of the North-Western District, 25 July 2007, in which Art. IX(1) of the European Convention on International Commercial Arbitration was used as a

much the exception that proves the rule, and the Indian Supreme Court itself has subsequently recognised this. Thus, in its decision in *Bharat Aluminium Co. v Kaiser Aluminum Technical Service, Inc.*,[145] the Indian Supreme Court affirmed that Indian courts have no jurisdiction, in either a supportive or supervisory role, where the seat of arbitration is outside India.

11.100 This completes this review of the five grounds for refusal of recognition and enforcement of an arbitral award laid down in the New York Convention, and the Model Law, and which it is for the party resisting enforcement to prove. As already mentioned, however, there are two other grounds that may be invoked by the enforcement court itself. These concern, first, arbitrability, and secondly, public policy.

(i) Arbitrability

11.101 The New York Convention provides, as does the Model Law, that recognition and enforcement of an arbitral award may be refused:

> ...if the competent authority in the country where recognition and enforcement is sought finds that:
> (a) The subject matter of the difference is not capable of settlement by arbitration under the law of that country...[146]

11.102 Arbitrability has already been discussed in Chapter 2. As indicated, each state has its own concept of what disputes should be reserved for the courts of law and what disputes may be resolved by arbitration. This question may arise both at the beginning of an arbitration ('is this dispute capable of being referred to arbitration?') and at the end ('would this dispute have been capable of settlement by arbitration under the law of the enforcement state?'). The issue of 'arbitrability' under the New York Convention is, of course, an issue for the law of the enforcement state and, being governed largely by questions of public policy, varies from state to state.

11.103 For example, Russian courts have recently interpreted provisions of the Russian Commercial Procedure Code stipulating the exclusive jurisdiction of certain Russian courts over corporate governance disputes as precluding the arbitrability of such disputes. In *Maximov v Novolipetsky Metallurgicheskiy Kombinat*,[147] following the agreement of a contract to purchase shares in a Russian-incorporated company, a dispute arose between the seller and buyer over the purchase price. The seller, who alleged that he had not received the price required under the agreement,

---

basis to set aside awards rendered in Sweden and Norway, respectively, simply because Russian law applied to the substance of the dispute.

[145] Civil Appeal No. 7019 of 2005, Decision of 6 September 2012, given at New Delhi.
[146] New York Convention, Art. V(2)(a). See also the discussion of 'public policy' as a ground to challenge an award at Chapter 10, paragraphs 10.81*ff*.
[147] Case No. N VAS-15384/11, Ruling of the Supreme Commercial Arbitrazh Court, 30 January 2012.

B. Enforcement under the New York Convention

obtained an arbitral award at the Moscow-based International Commercial Arbitration Court (ICAC). However, the Supreme Commercial Arbitrazh Court, upholding the decision of a lower court to set aside the award, held that corporate governance disputes are non-arbitrable under Article 225(1) of the Arbitration Procedural Code.

In another example, the Supreme Court of Singapore ruled that whether a person is the alter ego of a company is an issue that does not have a public interest element, so is within the scope of submission to arbitration and is therefore arbitrable.[148] The defendant had argued that the arbitrator could not hold that he was bound by the arbitration clause based on a finding of an alter ego, since the issue of an alter ego was not arbitrable under Arizona law (the governing law of the contract). The Court dismissed this argument, holding that Arizona law was irrelevant, since the issue of arbitrability in a Singapore court as a ground for refusing enforcement is to be determined under Singapore law.[149]

11.104

(j) Public policy

Recognition and enforcement of an arbitral award may also be refused if it is contrary to the public policy of the enforcement state.[150] It is understandable that a state may wish to have the right to refuse to recognise and enforce an arbitration award that offends its own notions of public policy, and in some jurisdictions an enforcing court is required to examine the possibility of a public policy violation *ex officio*.[151] Yet when reference is made to 'public policy', it is difficult not to recall the sceptical comment of the English judge who said, almost two centuries ago: 'It is never argued at all but where other points fail.'[152]

11.105

Certainly, the national courts in England are reluctant to excuse an award from enforcement on grounds of public policy. At one time, it was said that 'there is no case in which this exception has been applied by an English court'.[153] Inevitably, of course, the exception then arose and was applied in *Soleimany v Soleimany*.[154] In this case, an English court refused to enforce an award giving effect to a contract between a father and son that involved the smuggling of carpets out of Iran, in breach of Iranian revenue laws and export controls. The father and son had agreed to submit their dispute to arbitration by the Beth Din, the Court of the Chief Rabbi in London, which applied Jewish law. As a matter of the applicable Jewish law, the illegal purpose of the contract had no effect on the rights of the parties, and

11.106

---

[148] *Aloe Vera of America, Inc. (US) v Asianic Food (S) Pte Ltd (Singapore) and anor* (2007) XXXII YBCA 489.
[149] Ibid.
[150] New York Convention, Art. V(2)(b).
[151] See Decision of the Geneva Cour de Justice, 11 December 1997, (1998) XXIII YBCA 764.
[152] *Richardson v Mellish* (1824) 2 Bing 229, at 252 *per* Burrough J, [1824–34] All ER 258.
[153] Kerr, 'Concord and conflict in international arbitration' (1997) 13 Arb Intl 121, at 140.
[154] [1999] QB 785.

the Beth Din proceeded to make an award enforcing the contract. In declining to enforce the award, however, the English court held that:

> The Court is in our view concerned to preserve the integrity of its process, and to see that it is not abused. The parties cannot override that concern by private agreement. They cannot by procuring an arbitration conceal that they, or rather one of them, is seeking to enforce an illegal contract. Public policy will not allow it.[155]

11.107 Rare exceptions such as this aside, in most countries the 'pro-enforcement bias' of the New York Convention has been faithfully observed.[156] Indeed, this pro-enforcement bias is itself considered a matter of public policy, as the English courts confirmed in *Westacre Investments Inc. v Jugoimport-SPDR Holding Co. Ltd*.[157] This dispute arose from a 'consultancy' agreement for the procurement of contracts for the sale of military equipment in Kuwait. Westacre commenced arbitration, claiming payment of its 'consulting fee'. Jugoimport defended the claim on the grounds that, in violation of Kuwaiti law and public policy, the contract involved Westacre bribing various Kuwaitis to exert their influence in favour of entering sales contracts with Jugoimport. The agreement between Westacre and Jugoimport was governed by Swiss law, and provided for arbitration in Switzerland. The arbitral tribunal found that there was no evidence of corruption and that lobbying by private enterprises to obtain public contracts was not illegal under Swiss law. The award was first challenged in the Swiss Federal Court, which rejected the challenge on the basis that allegations of corruption had already been dealt with and rejected by the arbitral tribunal. Attempts to enforce the award were subsequently challenged in the English courts, where Jugoimport filed new affidavit evidence in support of its allegation of corruption.

11.108 In decisions that have attracted some critical commentary,[158] the English courts rejected the challenge to enforcement, both at first instance and in the Court of Appeal, on the grounds that: the arbitral tribunal itself had considered the allegations of bribery and found that they had not been substantiated; 'lobbying' was

---

[155] Ibid., at 800.
[156] See the discussion of *Parsons Whittemore Overseas Co. Inc. v Société Générale de l'Industrie du Papier (RAKTA)* 508 F.2d 969 (2nd Cir. 1974) at paragraph 11.61. See also the Second Circuit decision in *MGM Productions Group Inc. v Aeroflot Russian Airlines* WL 234871 (2nd Cir. 2004), in which Aeroflot sought to challenge a Stockholm award because it compensated the claimant for Aeroflot's non-performance of an agreement, the provisions of which allegedly violated the United States–Iran Transactions Regulations adopted pursuant to executive orders issued by the President of the United States under the International Emergency Economic Powers Act of 1977. The Second Circuit rejected the challenge, holding, at [3], that: 'Courts construe the public policy limitation in the Convention very narrowly and apply it only when enforcement would violate the forum state's "most basic notions of morality and justice".' In this case, even if the agreement in operation did violate the Iranian Transactions Regulations, which the arbitral tribunal itself had found was not the case, the award would not contravene public policy, because 'a violation of United States foreign policy does not contravene public policy as contemplated in Art V of the Convention': ibid., at [5].
[157] [1999] 2 Lloyd's Rep 65 (CA).
[158] See Rogers and Kaley, 'The impact of public policy in international commercial arbitration' (1999) 65 J CIArb 4.

B. Enforcement under the New York Convention

not, as such, an illegal activity under the governing law chosen by the parties; and the Court was faced with international arbitration awards that had been upheld by the Swiss Federal Tribunal, and therefore had to balance the public policy of discouraging international commercial corruption against the public policy of sustaining international arbitration awards.

It is clear that the 'public policy' referred to in the New York Convention is the public policy of the enforcement state.[159] The real question is whether that public policy differentiates between international awards and purely domestic awards. **11.109**

The approach of the US courts was summarised by the Federal District Court of Massachusetts in *Sonatrach*.[160] The court stated: **11.110**

> The line of decisions which conclusively tip the judicial scale in favour of arbitration [are] a line of United States Supreme Court opinions which enthusiastically endorse an internationalist approach towards commercial disputes involving foreign entities. These decisions, *The Bremen v Zapata Offshore Co*[161] (forum selection clauses in international commercial contract enforced); *Scherk v Alberto-Culver Co*[162] (international arbitration clause held enforceable when in conflict with federal securities laws); and most recently *Mitsubishi*[163] (international arbitration clause held enforceable when in conflict with Federal Antitrust laws) eschew the parochial tendencies of domestic tribunals in retaining jurisdiction over international commercial disputes. The Supreme Court powerfully advocates the need for international comity in an increasingly interdependent world. Such respect is especially important, in this Court's view, when parties mutually agree to be bound by freely negotiated contracts.[164]

A similar line of reasoning is found in the decision of the New York District Court in the well-known case of *Parsons Whittemore Overseas Co. Inc. v Société Générale de l'Industrie du Papier (RAKTA)*.[165] The court was confronted by an argument that recognition and enforcement of an award should be refused on the grounds that diplomatic relations between Egypt (the respondent's state) and the United States had been severed. The court rejected this argument and referred to the 'general pro-enforcement bias' of the New York Convention.[166] It held that the Convention's **11.111**

---

[159] This is clear from the text of Art. V(2) itself and, accordingly, the Supreme Court of India was right to reject the argument that the references (in the Indian statute that enacted the Convention) to 'public policy', rather than to the 'public policy of India', meant that the words were not restricted to India, but would extend to the laws governing the contract and the place of arbitration: see *Renusagar Power Co. Ltd (India) v General Electric Co. (US)* (1995) XX YBCA 681.

[160] *Sonatrach (Algeria) v Distrigas Corporation (United States District Court) Massachusetts* (1995) XX YBCA 795.

[161] 407 US 1 (1972).

[162] 417 US 506 (1974).

[163] *Mitsubishi Motor Corporation v Soler Chrysler-Plymouth Inc.* 473 US 614, 105 S.Ct 3346, 87 L.Ed.2d 444 (1985).

[164] *Sonatrach (Algeria) v Distrigas Corporation (United States District Court) Massachusetts* 80 BR 606, 612 (1987).

[165] See the discussion of *Parsons Whittemore Overseas Co. Inc. v Société Générale de l'Industrie du Papier (RAKTA)* 508 F.2d 969 (2nd Cir. 1974) at paragraph 11.61.

[166] Ibid., at 973.

'public policy' defence should be construed narrowly, and that enforcement of foreign arbitral awards should be denied on this basis only 'where enforcement would violate the forum state's most basic notions of morality and justice'.[167]

11.112 Courts in other countries have also recognised that, in applying their own public policy to Convention awards, they should give it an international, and not a domestic, dimension. In India, in a case to which reference has already been made,[168] the Supreme Court said:

> This raises the question of whether the narrower concept of public policy as applicable in the field of public international law should be applied or the wider concept of public policy as applicable in the field of municipal law. The Court held that the narrower view should prevail and that enforcement would be refused on the public policy ground if such enforcement would be contrary to (i) fundamental policy of Indian law; or (ii) the interests of India; or (iii) justice or morality.[169]

11.113 French,[170] Swiss,[171] and German[172] courts have made decisions to similar effect.

11.114 These decisions, from courts in different parts of the world, show a readiness to limit—sometimes severely—the public policy defence to enforcement. However, the boundaries of national public policy are not fixed. There are cases, for example, in which the Turkish courts have allowed the public policy defence in circumstances in which, to an outside observer, it seems to be unjustified.[173] Japanese legislation applies the test of 'public policy or good morals' in the enforcement process;[174] Vietnamese legislation requires that the award should not be contrary to the basic principles of Vietnamese law.[175] In the United Arab Emirates (UAE), the concept of 'public policy' has been held to extend to matters of acquisition and termination of ownership rights over property, rendering disputes concerning real estate non-arbitrable.[176]

11.115 Rather than refer to 'public policy', Chinese law refers to the 'social and public interest', which is potentially an even more oblique concept. Chinese courts have recognised an obligation to consider, in every case, whether this 'social and public interest' is violated, even if neither party has raised it.[177] The Supreme People's

---

[167] Ibid., at 974.
[168] *Renusagar Power Co. Ltd (India) v General Electric Co. (US)* (1995) XX YBCA 681.
[169] Ibid., at 702.
[170] See, e.g., *SA Laboratoires Eurosilicone v Société Bez Medizintechnik GmbH* [2004] Rev Arb 133.
[171] (1995) XX YBCA 762.
[172] (1987) XII YBCA 489.
[173] See Kerr, 'Concord and conflict in international arbitration' (1997) 13 Arb Intl 140, at 140 and 141.
[174] Ibid., at 141.
[175] Paulsson, 'The New York Convention in international practice: Problems of assimilation' [1996] ASA Bulletin 101.
[176] *Baiti Real Estate Development v Dynasty Zarooni Inc.*, Petition No. 14 of 2012, Reasons, Dubai Court of Cassation, 16 September 2012, as summarised in Arab, Hammoud, and Lovett, *Summaries of UAE Courts' Decisions on Arbitration* (ICC, 2013), p. 122.
[177] Peerenboom, 'Seek truth from facts: An empirical study of enforcement of arbitral awards in the PRC' (2001) 49 Am J Comp L 39.

B. Enforcement under the New York Convention

Court has issued a statement of how to interpret this 'social and public interest' ground, asking:

> [U]nder what circumstances does the principle of public interest apply? The principle of public interest can apply where there are breaches of fundamental principles of Chinese law, national sovereignty or national security, or breaches of the principles of social ethics and fundamental moral value.[178]

Commentators have summarised this position as meaning that, in China, 'public policy' is broader than 'public morals', and includes 'traditional and societal sentiment'.[179]

Such broad conceptions of public policy may explain decisions such as *Heavy Metal*.[180] In that case, the Supreme People's Court had to decide whether to enforce a foreign-related arbitral award, which directed the respondent to pay compensatory damages to a US heavy metal band, whose performances had been banned by the Chinese Ministry of Culture on the grounds that the artists performed 'outrageous acts' such as drinking, smoking, splashing water, lying on the stage floor while performing, and jumping down from the stage. A CIETAC tribunal awarded damages for the band's lost income. When the band sought enforcement, the Supreme People's Court denied enforcement, on the grounds that the tribunal's findings were in manifest disregard of the underlying facts that the performance of heavy metal music was against 'national sentiments', and accordingly contrary to the social and public interests.[181] Whatever one may think of heavy metal music, it is difficult not to reach the conclusion that this amounted to a troublingly broad interpretation of the public policy exception to the enforcement of arbitral awards. 11.116

The requirement now that lower courts must obtain leave of the Supreme People's Court to refuse recognition or enforcement has certainly helped to reduce the incidence of the use of overly broad interpretations of public policy grounds to deny enforcement of awards in China.[182] According to a 2008 speech by Deputy Chief Justice Wan E'xiang, of the Supreme People's Court, between 2000 and 2008 the Court did not uphold a single decision by the Chinese lower courts that refused to enforce a foreign arbitral award on public policy grounds.[183] Attempts by parties to equate the social and public interest, for example, with a simple violation of 11.117

---

[178] *Explanations on and Answers to Practical Questions in Trial of Foreign-Related Commercial and Maritime Cases (No. 1)*, Issued by the Supreme People's Court on 8 April 2004, art. 43.
[179] Fei, 'Public policy as a bar to enforcement of international arbitral awards: A review of the Chinese approach' (2010) 26 Arb Intl 301, at 311.
[180] *Reply of the Supreme People's Court in the matter regarding the request by Beijing First Intermediary People's Court to Refuse Enforcement of Arbitral Award* [1997] Jing Ta 35 ('*Heavy Metal*').
[181] For further discussion of the topic, see Yeoh, 'Enforcement of dispute outcomes', in Moser (ed.) *Managing Business Disputes in Today's China* (Kluwer Law International, 2007), p. 274.
[182] *Notice Regarding the Local People's Court Handling Foreign-related Arbitral Awards and Foreign Arbitral Awards*, Issued by the Supreme People's Court on 28 August 1995.
[183] Chen and Howes, 'Public policy and the enforcement of foreign arbitration awards in China' (2010) 3 Intl News 14.

Chinese law, or (more worryingly) the interests of state-owned enterprises, have been rejected as falling short of a breach of public policy.[184]

11.118 Russian courts are likewise notorious for expansive interpretations of the notion of public policy. For instance, Russian courts have often declined the enforcement of arbitral awards if the amount of damages awarded under foreign law was 'punitive', or 'disproportionate to the breach', in the eyes of Russian courts.[185]

11.119 In an attempt at harmonisation, the Committee on International Commercial Arbitration of the International Law Association (ILA) has sought to offer definitions of the concepts of 'public policy', 'international public policy', and 'transnational public policy', and recommends that '[t]he finality of awards rendered in the context of international commercial arbitration should be respected save in exceptional circumstances', such exceptional circumstances being the violation of international public policy.[186] The Committee defined 'international public policy' as that 'part of the public policy of a state which, if violated, would prevent a party from invoking a foreign law or foreign judgment or foreign award'.[187]

11.120 The application of competition law raises particular issues of public policy that may become relevant in both annulment and enforcement proceedings. In *Eco Swiss China Time Ltd v Benetton International NV*,[188] the European Court of Justice (ECJ) held that Article 81 of the Treaty Establishing the European Community, or EC Treaty (now Article 101 of the Treaty on the Functioning of the European Union, or TFEU) constituted a matter of public policy within the meaning of the New York Convention and, on this basis, ruled that:

> [A] national court, to which application is made for annulment of an arbitration award must grant that application if it considers that the award in question is in fact contrary to Article 81 EC (ex Article 85), where its domestic rules of procedure require it to grant an application for annulment founded on failure to observe national rules of public policy.[189]

11.121 The French courts (including the French Cour de Cassation) have taken a narrow approach to the impact of EU competition law on the enforceability of awards, setting aside awards on EU competition law grounds only if they show a 'flagrant, specific and concrete breach' of French international public policy.[190] The Swiss

---

[184] Fei, 'Public policy as a bar to enforcement of international arbitral awards: A review of the Chinese approach' (2010) 26 Arb Intl 301, at 305–307.

[185] See Presidium of Supreme Commercial Arbitrazh Court, Information Letter No. 96, 22 December 2005, s. 29; Presidium of Supreme Commercial Arbitrazh Court, Information Letter No. 156, 26 February 2013, s. 6.

[186] ILA, *Final Report of the Committee on International Commercial Arbitration on Public Policy* (2004) 1 TDM.

[187] Ibid. See also *SA Compagnie commercial André v SA Tradigrain France* [2001] Rev Arb 773.

[188] Case C-126/97 [1999] ECR I–3055.

[189] Ibid., at [49].

[190] See *Thales Air Defence BV v GIE Euromissile et al.*, Paris Cour d'Appel, 18 November 2004; also the recent judgment in *SNF SAS v Cytec Industries BV (Holland)*, Cour de Cassation, Ch.

B. Enforcement under the New York Convention

Federal Court has taken an even more restrictive approach. In its decision of 8 March 2006, it held that EU competition law could not be considered to form part of the foundation of all legal orders such as to qualify as a matter of public policy, and, on that ground, simply dismissed the case.[191] For their part, and in contrast, the Dutch and Belgian courts have shown themselves ready to undertake a substantive review of awards from a competition law perspective, and have not refrained from subsequently annulling awards that were found to be in violation of EU competition law (in particular Article 81 EC).[192]

In the United States, too, the interplay between public policy and the enforcement of antitrust arbitral awards has proved significant. The general approach was set by the US Supreme Court in the case of *Mitsubishi v Soler Chrysler-Plymouth*,[193] in which it confirmed the arbitrability of antitrust claims, but emphasised that US national courts would have the opportunity to have a 'second look' at such arbitral awards in the award-enforcement stage to ensure that the legitimate interest in the enforcement of the antitrust laws had been addressed by the arbitral tribunal. In practice, however, US appellate courts have demonstrated different views with respect to their power to review an arbitral award *au fond*. For instance, in 2003, a divided Court of Appeal for the Seventh Circuit, considering the enforcement of a domestic award, quoted *Mitsubishi*, stating that a court should confirm only that the arbitral tribunal 'took cognizance of the antitrust claims and actually decided on them'; no further review of the merits had to be carried out.[194] However, one year later, the US Court of Appeal for the Fifth Circuit did not refrain from a substantive review of the merits of a domestic antitrust arbitral award.[195]

11.122

(k) Other grounds

Although the grounds for refusal of enforcement listed in Article V of the New York Convention are exhaustive, some courts have refused enforcement on grounds derived from other articles of the Convention. Thus, in the US case *Monegasque de Reassurance SAM (Monde Re) v NAK Naftogart of Ukraine and State of Ukraine*,[196] the Second Circuit refused enforcement of a Moscow award on grounds of *forum non conveniens*—a judicial procedural discretion that exists in the common law world, but is unknown in the civil law world. In so doing, it rejected the contention

11.123

Civ. 1ere, 4 June 2008, in which the Cour de Cassation explicitly reiterated the narrow approach to the application of public policy.

[191] See *Tensacciai v Terra Armata*, Swiss Federal Court, 8 March 2006.
[192] See *Marketing Displays International Inc. v VR Van Raalte Reclame BV*, Dutch Court of Appeal, The Hague, 24 March 2005; *SNF v Cytec Industries BV*, Brussels Court of First Instance, 8 March 2007.
[193] See the decision of the US Supreme Court in *Mitsubishi v Soler Chrysler-Plymouth* 473 US 614 (1985).
[194] See *Baxter International v Abbott Laboratories* 315 F.3d 829 (7th Cir. 2003).
[195] See US Court of Appeals for the Fifth Circuit, *American Central Eastern Texas Gas Co. v. Union Pacific Resources Group, Inc.*, 93 Fed. Appx. 1, 2004 WL 136091 (5th Cir. 27 Jan. 2004).
[196] 311 F.3d 488 (2nd Cir. 2002).

that Article V sets forth the only grounds for refusing to enforce a foreign arbitral award, and held that Article III made the enforcement of foreign arbitral awards subject to the rules of procedure of the courts where enforcement is sought, which, so it held, included the rule of *forum non conveniens*.

11.124 More recently, the Second Circuit Court of Appeals in *Figueiredo Ferraz E Engenharia de Projeto Ltda v Republic of Peru*[197] reversed, on grounds of *forum non conveniens*, a lower court's confirmation of a Peruvian arbitral award. Figueiredo had obtained an award against the Peruvian government, which the latter began paying out gradually, in accordance with a subsequently enacted Peruvian statute that limits the amount of money that an agency of the Peruvian government may pay annually to satisfy a judgment to 3 per cent of the agency's annual budget. The Second Circuit held that Peru was a more appropriate forum for the enforcement of the award than New York for a number of reasons, including the Peruvian cap statute. Similarly to the court in *Monde Re*, the Court in *Figueiredo* held that Article III of the New York Convention and its equivalent Article IV of the Panama Convention, providing for the application of local procedural law at the enforcement stage, allow for the application of *forum non conveniens*. However, Judge Lynch, in a powerful dissent, opined that recognising a *forum non conveniens* defence would undermine the enforceability of arbitral awards in general. Indeed, the very idea of *forum non conveniens* is incompatible with the concept of international enforcement of foreign awards, which takes as its starting point that the places of arbitration and principal performance of the obligation are likely to be different, while the resulting award can be enforced internationally subject to limited grounds for refusal. Almost by definition, there is likely to be another jurisdiction with a closer connection to the underlying dispute than the place of enforcement. Nevertheless, the whole point of enforcement under the New York Convention is to internationalise the enforcement of awards rendered elsewhere, not to constrain a party to enforce in the jurisdiction of origin.

C. Enforcement under the ICSID Convention

11.125 The ICSID Convention established ICSID to facilitate the resolution of international investment disputes and thereby to promote foreign investment.[198] This Convention is considered in some detail in Chapter 8. The only point that needs to be emphasised in the present context is that, unless an ICSID award is revised or annulled under ICSID's own internal procedures, each contracting state must recognise an ICSID award as if it were a final judgment of its own national courts and enforce the obligation imposed by that award.[199] To this end, contracting states

---

[197] 663 F.4d 384 (2nd Cir. 2011).
[198] For the meaning of this term, see Chapter 8, paragraphs 8.17*ff*.
[199] ICSID Convention, Art. 54.

C. Enforcement under the ICSID Convention

must designate a competent court or authority, which will deal with any requests for enforcement of an ICSID award.[200]

At the time of writing, the ICSID Convention was in force in some 150 countries.[201] **11.126**

Under Article 53(1) of the ICSID Convention, ICSID awards 'shall be binding on all parties and shall not be subject to any appeal or to any other remedy except those provided for in this Convention'. Article 54(1) of the ICSID Convention requires state parties to 'recognize an award rendered pursuant to [the] Convention as binding and enforce the pecuniary obligations imposed by that award within its territories as if it were a final judgment of a court in that State'. The remedies mentioned in Article 53(1) are restricted to annulment, revision, or interpretation of an award, and they can be obtained only through ICSID. Thus only an ICSID annulment committee may annul the award. Setting aside or any other review of ICSID awards by domestic courts is not available. Article 52(1) contains an exhaustive list of grounds for annulment of ICSID awards, including that (a) the tribunal was not properly constituted,[202] (b) the tribunal has manifestly exceeded its powers,[203] (c) there was corruption on the part of a member of the tribunal, (d) there was a serious departure from a fundamental rule of procedure,[204] or (e) the award failed to state the reasons on which it is based.[205] There was a period in ICSID history during which these grounds were interpreted quite broadly, resulting in *de facto* appeals on points of law and fact.[206] However, in recent years, annulment committees have **11.127**

---

[200] The courts and authorities designated by each contracting state can be found by clicking into each state listed online in the 'Membership' tab, online at https://icsid.worldbank.org/apps/ICSIDWEB/about/Pages/Database-of-Member-States.bak.aspx. See also ICSID Administrative and Financial Regulations, reg. 20(f).

[201] For a list of contracting states and signatories to the ICSID Convention, see online at https://icsid.worldbank.org/apps/ICSIDWEB/about/Pages/Database-of-Member-States.bak.aspx.

[202] This provision is not intended to be an opportunity to challenge members of the tribunal *de novo*; rather, an ad hoc committee would be able to annul an award under Art. 52(1)(a) only if there had been a failure to comply properly with the procedure for challenging members. See *Azurix Corporation v Argentine Republic*, Decision on the Application for Annulment of the Argentine Republic, ICSID Case No. ARB/01/12, 1 September 2009, at [280].

[203] A tribunal can exercise an 'excess of powers' not only in exercising a jurisdiction that it does not have, but also in failing to exercise a jurisdiction that it does possess: see, e.g., *Compañía de Aguas del Aconquija SA and Vivendi Universal (formerly Compagnie Générale des Eaux) v Argentine Republic*, Decision on Annulment, ICSID Case No. ARB/97/3, 3 July 2002, at [86].

[204] Ad hoc committees have restricted annulment on this ground to violations of those principles that are essential to a fair hearing, observing that a violation of a non-fundamental rule, no matter how serious, would not call into question the validity of an award: see, e.g., *Malicorp Ltd v Arab Republic of Egypt*, Decision on Annulment, ICSID Case No. ARB/08/18, 3 July 2013, at [29].

[205] This ground of annulment applies only in a clear case in which there has been a failure by the tribunal to give any reasons for its decision on a particular question, and not in a case in which there has merely been a failure by the tribunal to give correct or convincing reasons: see, e.g., *Enron Creditors Recovery Corporation (formerly Enron Corporation) and Ponderosa Assets, LP v Argentine Republic*, Decision on the Application for Annulment of the Argentine Republic, ICSID Case No. ARB/01/3, 30 July 2010, at [74].

[206] See, e.g., the much-criticised *Patrick Mitchell v Democratic Republic of Congo*, Decision on Annulment, ICSID Case No ARB/99/7, 1 November 2006, in which the ad hoc committee

taken a narrower approach,[207] and annulments of ICSID awards have become rarer. The grounds for annulment are considered in further detail in Chapter 8.

11.128 In the face of multiple ICSID claims, several Latin American countries have withdrawn from the Convention—namely, Bolivia, Ecuador, and Venezuela. The possible effects of these withdrawals on the jurisdiction of arbitral tribunals for claims brought under the ICSID Convention are discussed in Chapter 8.

11.129 In a less dramatic, but nevertheless far-reaching, step, Argentina has reacted to the growing number of ICSID awards against it by arguing that the enforcement of ICSID awards is not automatic. Specifically, Argentina has argued that Article 54 of the Convention requires the claimant party to seek recognition of the award rendered against the respondent state *in that state's national court*. To recall, Article 54 requires each contracting state to enforce 'the pecuniary obligations imposed by that award within its territories as if it were a final judgment of a court in *that* State'. This interpretation has become known as the 'Rosatti doctrine', following its espousal by former Argentine Minister of Justice Dr Horacio Rosatti. However, and perhaps unsurprisingly, it has now been repeatedly rejected by ad hoc annulment committees in *Enron v Argentine Republic*[208] and *Compañia Aguas del Aconquija SA and Vivendi Universal v Argentina*.[209]

11.130 There are a number of regional conventions that may also have a significant bearing on the recognition and enforcement of foreign arbitral awards. The principal conventions are discussed briefly in turn.

D. Enforcement under Regional Conventions

(a) Moscow Convention

11.131 The Moscow Convention was signed on 26 May 1972, the original signatories being those Central and Eastern European states that were grouped together in the Council for Mutual Economic Assistance (CMEA). Now that the German

---

overturned the award on the grounds that the tribunal in the original proceedings had, in its view, incorrectly determined that the claimant held a protected investment within the meaning of the ICSID Convention. The annulment committee deemed that such determination constituted 'manifest excess of powers' under Art. 52(1)(b) of the Convention.

[207] See, e.g., *AES Summit Generation Ltd and AES-Tisza Erömü Kft v Republic of Hungary*, Decision of the Ad Hoc Committee on the Application for Annulment, ICSID Case No. ARB/07/22, 29 June 2012, at [17] ('annulment is an exhaustive, exceptional and narrowly circumscribed remedy and not an appeal').

[208] See *Enron Corporation Ponderosa Assets, LP v Argentine Republic*, Decision on the Argentine Republic's Request for a Continued Stay of Enforcement of the Award, 7 October 2008, at [69], [83], and [85].

[209] See *Aguas del Aconquija SA and Vivendi Universal v Argentine Republic*, Decision on the Argentine Republic's Request for a Continued Stay of Enforcement of the Award Rendered on 20 August 2007, 4 November 2008, at [31]–[37] and [45].

D. Enforcement under Regional Conventions

Democratic Republic has ceased to exist and Poland, the Czech Republic, and Hungary have withdrawn, it applies only to Bulgaria, Cuba, Mongolia, Romania, and Russia, although there is little evidence of current usage.

The Convention regulates the settlement by arbitration of disputes arising from economic, scientific, and technical cooperation within the member countries of CMEA.   **11.132**

The Convention provides that arbitration awards 'shall be final and binding',[210] and they are to be 'voluntarily' enforced by the parties, failing which they may be enforced in the same way as final decisions made in the courts of the country of enforcement.[211] Enforcement proceedings must be brought within two years of the date of the award, and the three grounds of refusal of enforcement closely parallel those in the New York Convention—namely, lack of jurisdiction, denial of a fair hearing, and when the award has been set aside.[212]   **11.133**

(b) Panama Convention

In January 1975, following the Inter-American Conference on Private International Law in Panama, the Panama Convention was signed by twelve South American states.[213] The Convention represents a significant shift away from former hostility toward international arbitration, as reflected in the Calvo doctrine.[214]   **11.134**

The Panama Convention recognises an agreement to submit existing or future disputes to arbitration,[215] and it also provides for the reciprocal enforcement of arbitral awards in member states. This takes place as if the award were a judgment of a court: **11.135**

> An arbitral decision or award that is not appealable under the applicable law or procedural rules shall have the force of a final judicial judgment. Its execution or recognition may be ordered in the same manner as that of decisions handed down by national or foreign ordinary courts, in accordance with the procedural laws of the country where it is to be executed and the provisions of international treaties.[216]

---

[210] Moscow Convention, Art. IV(1).
[211] Moscow Convention, Art. IV(2).
[212] Moscow Convention, Art. V(1).
[213] The text of the Convention appears in (1978) III YBCA 15 and in (1975) 14 ILM 336. See also Blackaby, Lindsey, and Spinillo (eds) *International Arbitration in Latin America* (Kluwer Law International, 2002), pp. 3–6. The Convention came into effect in the United States on 27 October 1990.
[214] At time of writing, nineteen states had ratified this Convention, including the United States: see online at http://www.oas.org/juridico/english/sigs/b-35.html. For a commentary on US participation, see Lowry, 'The United States joins the Inter-American Arbitration Convention' (1990) 7 J Intl Arb 83.
[215] Panama Convention, Art. 1. Unlike the New York Convention, however, it does not deal with the problem of enforcing an arbitration agreement if one of the parties takes court proceedings notwithstanding the agreement to arbitrate.
[216] Panama Convention, Art. 4.

The Convention speaks of 'execution' of an award rather than 'enforcement', but in practice there is no difference. Recognition and execution of an award may be refused, at the request of the party against which it is made, only if that party is able to prove to the competent authority of the state in which recognition and execution is sought that one of the five grounds for refusal laid down in Article 5 of the Panama Convention applies.[217] Under Article 5(2) of the Panama Convention,[218] recognition and execution of an award may also be refused if the competent authority of the state in which recognition and execution is sought, finds:

(a) That the subject matter of the dispute cannot be settled by arbitration under the law of that State; or
(b) That recognition or execution of the decision would be contrary to the public policy ('*ordre public*') of that State.

11.136 Where an application has been made to annul or suspend the award, the authority before which recognition and execution is sought may,[219] under the Panama Convention, postpone its decision; at the request of the party seeking execution, it may also instruct the other party to provide appropriate guarantees.[220]

11.137 It is clear that the Panama Convention was strongly influenced by the provisions of the New York Convention. Indeed, many of the provisions of the former have been copied more or less word for word from the latter. According to one informed commentator, the Panama Convention 'has a tremendous and vital significance'.[221] Certainly, whether because of the Convention or because of other influences—such as the Model Law—arbitration is becoming a more acceptable way of settling disputes in Latin America.

(c) Middle Eastern and North African Conventions

11.138 The Riyadh Arab Agreement on Judicial Cooperation, known as the 'Riyadh Convention', entered into force in 1985,[222] and is one of the most commonly used conventions in the Middle East for the recognition and enforcement of arbitral awards. Importantly, however, and unlike the New York Convention, the Riyadh Convention requires that, to enforce an award made in another Arab country, leave to enforce must be obtained in the country in which the award was made.[223] In the same way, the Agreement on the Execution of Rulings, Requests of Legal

---

[217] These five grounds of refusal closely follow the five grounds set out in the New York Convention, Art. V(1).
[218] Which provision follows the New York Convention, Art. V(2).
[219] Panama Convention, Art. 6.
[220] This provision follows the New York Convention, Art. V(I).
[221] Norberg, 'General introduction to inter-American commercial arbitration' (1978) *III* YBCA 1, at 13.
[222] The following countries are signatories to the Riyadh Convention: Algeria, Bahrain, Djibouti, Iraq, Jordan, Kuwait, Lebanon, Libya, Mauritania, Morocco, Oman, Palestine, Qatar, Saudi Arabia, Somalia, Sudan, Syria, Tunisia, UAE, and Yemen.
[223] See Riyadh Convention, Art. 37.

E. Defence of State Immunity

Assistance and Judicial Notices, entered into by the Gulf Co-operation Council in 1995 and thus known as the 'GCC Convention',[224] has the same requirement, and while it does not specifically refer to arbitral awards, it is considered applicable to them.[225]

States in this region have also entered into regional investment agreements— notably, the Agreement for Promotion, Protection and Guarantee of Investments, entered into by the Organisation of Islamic Cooperation member states and thus known as the 'OIC Agreement',[226] and the Unified Agreement for the Investment of Arab Capital in the Arab States, entered into by the member states of the Arab League (hence the 'Arab League Investment Agreement').[227] These agreements provide for the settlement of investor–state disputes by international arbitration. If an arbitral award rendered under the Arab League Investment Agreement is not implemented, or if the parties fail to resort to arbitration, or the tribunal fails to render an award within a prescribed period of time, the dispute shall be heard by a permanent Arab Investment Court. The decisions of arbitral tribunals under the OIC Agreement and of the Arab Investment Court under the Arab League Agreement are, like ICSID awards, enforceable as though they were final and enforceable decisions of national courts of the state in which enforcement is sought.[228]

11.139

(d) Other regional conventions

This review of various regional conventions is not intended to be exhaustive. Parties or lawyers who are concerned with the recognition and enforcement of arbitration agreements or arbitral awards would be well advised to consider whether there are any regional conventions that may be both relevant and helpful.

11.140

E. Defence of State Immunity

The defences to recognition and enforcement of an international arbitral award, which are laid down in the New York Convention and the Model Law, have been

11.141

---

[224] The following countries are party to the GCC Convention: Bahrain, Kuwait, Oman, Qatar, Saudi Arabia, and UAE.
[225] GCC Convention, Art. 7.
[226] The following countries have ratified the OIC Agreement: Afghanistan, Albania, Bangladesh, Cameroon, Côte d'Ivoire, Djibouti, Gambia, Guinea, Guinea-Bissau, Indonesia, Iran, Jordan, Kuwait, Lebanon, Libya, Malaysia, Morocco, Nigeria, Oman, Pakistan, Palestine, Qatar, Saudi Arabia, Senegal, Somalia, Sudan, Syria, Tajikstan, Tunisia, Turkey, UAE, Uganda, and Yemen.
[227] The following countries are party to the Arab League Agreement: Algeria, Bahrain, Comoros, Djibouti, Egypt, Iraq, Jordan, Kuwait, Lebanon, Libya, Mauritania, Morocco, Oman, Palestine, Qatar, Saudi Arabia, Somalia, Sudan, Syria (temporarily suspended at the time of writing), Tunisia, UAE, and Yemen.
[228] OIC Agreement, Art. 17(d); Arab League Agreement, Art. 34(3).

considered.[229] There is one standard form of defence, however, that is not mentioned in the Convention or the Model Law, but which may be encountered in practice, where the unsuccessful party is either a sovereign state or a state agency: the defence of state immunity, or 'sovereign immunity' as it is often known. This defence, in essence, means that a sovereign state cannot be compelled to submit to the jurisdiction of another state:

> The sovereign was a definable person, to whom allegiance was due. As an integral part of this mystique, the sovereign could not be made subject to the judicial processes of his country. Accordingly, it was only fitting that he could not be sued in foreign courts. The idea of the personal sovereign would undoubtedly have been undermined had courts been able to exercise jurisdiction over foreign sovereigns. This personalisation was gradually replaced by the abstract concept of state sovereignty, but the basic mystique remained. In addition, the independence and equality of states made it philosophically as well as practically difficult to permit municipal courts of one country to manifest their power over foreign sovereign states, without their consent.[230]

11.142 State immunity does not prevent a state or state agency from agreeing to submit to the authority of an arbitral tribunal. It is a well-established principle of international law that a sovereign is bound by an agreement to arbitrate contractual disputes,[231] and the ability so to submit may itself be seen as an incident or attribute of sovereignty.

11.143 State immunity exists at two levels: first, at the level of jurisdiction; and secondly, at the level of execution. Accordingly, there may be both immunity from jurisdiction and immunity from execution, and in considering state immunity, a distinction may need to be made between acts of a state taking place in its capacity as a state (acts *jure imperii*) and those taking place in its commercial capacity (acts *jure gestionis*). As a distinguished Swiss commentator has written, this distinction is clear in theory, but difficult to apply in practice.[232] The distinction is important because some states claim absolute immunity—that is, immunity for all acts carried out by or on behalf of the state—whilst others claim restricted immunity—that is, immunity only for acts *jure imperii*.[233] In *La Générale des*

---

[229] See paragraphs 11.63*ff*.
[230] Shaw, *International Law* (6th edn, Cambridge University Press, 2008), p. 698. See also Lauterpacht, 'The problem of jurisdictional immunities of foreign states' (1951) 28 BYIL 220; Higgins, 'Certain unresolved aspects of the law of state immunity' (1982) 29 NILR 265.
[231] This principle of international law is highlighted in the award of 12 April 1977 of Mahmassani, sole arbitrator in *Libyan American Oil Co. (Liamco) v Government of the Libyan Arab Republic* (1982) 62 ILR 140, at 178. It was noted that even UN General Assembly Resolution No. 1803, dated 21 December 1962, which proclaims permanent sovereignty over natural resources, confirms the obligation of states to respect arbitration agreements.
[232] Lalive, 'Quelques observations sur l'immunité d'exécution des états et l'arbitrage international', in Dinstein (ed.) *International Law at a Time of Perplexity* (Brill, 1989), p. 370.
[233] The United Nations Convention on Jurisdictional Immunities of States and their Property attempts to harmonise the approach taken by states. Adopted by the UN General Assembly in December 2004, it will only come into force once thirty states have ratified it. At time of writing,

E. Defence of State Immunity

Carrières et des Mines,[234] the Privy Council of England and Wales considered whether a mining company owned by the Democratic Republic of Congo represented the state in its capacity as a state or in its commercial capacity. In holding to the latter view, the Privy Council observed that where a separate juridical entity is formed by the state for commercial or industrial purposes with its own management and budget, subject to 'quite extreme' circumstances to the contrary, the separate legal personality should be respected.[235]

(a) Jurisdictional immunity

During the course of arbitration proceedings to which a state is a party, the distinction between absolute and restricted immunity should be of no relevance. The arbitration can proceed validly only on the basis that the state concerned has agreed to arbitrate, and such an agreement is generally held to be a waiver of immunity. This is also taken to extend to the jurisdiction of the relevant court at the seat of the arbitration to supervise the arbitration taking place in its territory. 11.144

The restricted theory of sovereign immunity has been adopted by national courts in many countries,[236] and in some countries the position has been established by legislation. Indeed, it is possible now to state that a majority of states adhere to the doctrine of restricted immunity, although with notable exceptions, such as China, Hong Kong, Brazil, and other Latin American countries.[237] In the United Kingdom, for example, the State Immunity Act 1978 provides that where a state has agreed in writing to submit existing or future disputes to arbitration, the state is not immune in respect of proceedings in the courts of the United Kingdom that relate to the arbitration.[238] Once again, however, the precise position adopted by a given country can be established only by reference to the law and practice of that country. In the United States, for example, it was not clear under the Foreign 11.145

---

only eighteen states had done so (while twenty-eight states have signed the Convention): see online at http://treaties.un.org/Pages/ViewDetails.aspx?src=IND&mtdsg_no=III-13&chapter=3&lang=en.

[234] *La Générale des Carrières et des Mines v FG Hemisphere Associates LLC* [2012] UKPC 27.

[235] Notwithstanding the robust position on sovereign immunity taken by English courts, the British Parliament introduced another obstacle to the enforcement of awards against developing sovereigns, styled 'heavily indebted poor countries' (HIPCs), in the form of the Debt Relief (Developing Countries) Act 2010, which aims to diminish debt in the world's poorest economies, including Africa and Asia. The Act seeks to complement the HIPC initiative and prohibits private creditors from pursuing in English courts any claims against such countries above a limited amount, set by the HIPC Initiative formula: Barratt and Michael, 'Degrees of immunity: A lesson from the Privy Council', in *The European, Middle Eastern and African Arbitration Review* (GAR, 2013), pp. 6–7.

[236] Whilst this position has evolved from case law in some countries, reference must be had also to those countries that have given effect to the 1972 European Convention on State Immunity.

[237] Barratt and Michael, 'Degrees of immunity: A lesson from the Privy Council', in *The European, Middle Eastern and African Arbitration Review* (GAR, 2013), p. 4.

[238] English State Immunity Act 1978, s. 9. See *Svenska Petroleum Exploration AB v Government of the Republic of Lithuania (No. 2)* [2006] EWCA Civ 1529. See also UN Convention on Jurisdictional Immunities of States and their Property 2004, Art. 17, which provides:

> [I]f a State enters into an agreement in writing with a foreign natural or juridical person to submit to arbitration differences relating to a commercial transaction, that State

Sovereign Immunities Act of 1976,[239] as enacted, whether a foreign state's agreement to arbitrate could be regarded as a waiver of immunity from the jurisdiction of a US court. Following the *Liamco* case,[240] in which an award made against the Libyan state was recognised, an amendment to the 1976 Act[241] made it clear that the US courts have jurisdiction, inter alia, to confirm an arbitration award made under an agreement to arbitrate where the arbitration takes place, or is authorised to take place, in the United States, or where the award is governed by a treaty to which the United States is a party.[242]

(b) Immunity from execution

11.146 Problems are most likely to arise when a winning party attempts to enforce and execute its award against a state or state entity. If the state concerned wishes to evade its obligations,[243] it may do so by claiming immunity from execution.[244] It may be thought inappropriate that a state or state entity can escape its legal obligations in this way, but this is the logical result of conferring immunity upon states. Moreover, whilst the existence of an arbitration agreement is usually held to be a waiver of immunity from jurisdiction, such a waiver is generally not held to extend to immunity from execution. By way of example, statute in England[245] requires separate waivers in respect of execution and jurisdiction.

11.147 Thus, under the ICSID Convention, an ICSID award must be treated by a contracting state as if it were a final judgment of a court of that state. However, this provision for the automatic recognition of such an award does *not* mean that

---

cannot invoke immunity from jurisdiction before a court of another State which is otherwise competent in a proceeding which relates to:
(a) the validity, interpretation or application of the arbitration agreement;
(b) the arbitration procedure; or
(c) the confirmation or the setting aside of the award,
unless the arbitration agreement otherwise provides.

[239] Foreign Sovereign Immunities Act of 1976, Title 28, US Code, § 1605(a)(1). See Kahale, 'New legislation facilitates enforcement of arbitral agreements and awards' (1989) 6 J Intl Arb 57.
[240] *Libyan American Oil Co. (Liamco) v Libyan Arab Republic* (1981) 20 ILM 1.
[241] Section 1605(a)(6), as amended 16 November 1988. For commentary, see Delaume, 'Recognition and enforcement of state contract awards in the United States: A restatement' (1997) 91 Am J Intl L 476.
[242] See, e.g., *Chevron Corporation v Republic of Ecuador* 2013 WL 2449172 (DDC 2013), in which the US District Court for the District of Columbia held that the arbitration exception to sovereign immunity under the Foreign Sovereign Immunities Act of 1976 applied in the case of enforcement of an award under a bilateral investment treaty (BIT), which was being enforced under the New York Convention.
[243] If it did not, presumably the question of enforcement would not arise, since it would carry out the award voluntarily.
[244] For further discussion of this topic, see van den Berg, 'The enforcement of arbitral awards against a state: The problem of immunity from execution', in Lew (ed.) *Contemporary Problems in International Arbitration* (CCLS/Kluwer, 1986), p. 359.
[245] State Immunity Act 1978, s. 13(3).

it will be treated as overriding any immunity from *execution* that exists in the contracting state. Indeed, Article 55 of the ICSID Convention states that immunity from execution is a matter of national law. It is surprising that, in a convention that was intended to encourage investment, the state parties did not agree to waive their immunity from execution. It seems, however, that 'abandonment of immunity of execution was mentioned by only one representative and his statement found no echo whatsoever'.[246]

11.148 However, courts in some instances have found ways of circumventing this obstacle to the efficacy of the arbitral process. The decision of the French Cour de Cassation in *Creighton v Qatar* is a notable example.[247] In 1982, Creighton Ltd, a Cayman Islands corporation with offices in the United States, contracted with the Government of Qatar to build a women's hospital in Doha. After obtaining the necessary authorisations, Creighton entered into a contract with the Qatari Ministry of Municipal Affairs and Agriculture on 19 June 1982. In November 1986, Creighton was expelled from the project by the Government of Qatar; in 1987, pursuant to the arbitration clause in the agreement, Creighton commenced ICC arbitration in Paris. In October 1993, final awards were rendered against Qatar.

11.149 After a failed Qatari attempt to challenge the award in France, Creighton sought to enforce the awards against, inter alia, bank accounts held in France by the Qatari ministry. Following Creighton's seizure of those accounts, Qatar initiated proceedings before the Paris Tribunal de Grande Instance to have those seizures lifted, on the grounds of Qatar's immunity from execution. In January 1997, the Paris Tribunal ordered the lifting of the seizures and concluded that the subject matter of the agreement prevented any waiver of Qatar's immunity from execution. Specifically, it held that the construction of a hospital was an activity of a public nature, and therefore subject to state immunity.

---

[246] See Broches, 'Awards rendered pursuant to the ICSID Convention: Binding force, finality, recognition, enforcement, execution' (1987) 2 ICSID Rev—Foreign Investment LJ 287, at 332. See, e.g., Decision 5A_681/2011 of the Swiss Federal Supreme Court, 23 November 2011, which, in considering the enforcement of an ICSID award rendered against Kyrgyzstan, held that the assets of Kyrgyzaeronavigatsia (a Kyrgyz government agency in charge of aerospace control) were protected by sovereign immunity, since they were used for the exercise of sovereign authority. For a view that the problem of immunity from execution of an ICSID award is more theoretical than real, by reason, inter alia, of the obligation in ICSID Convention, Art. 53, to comply with the award, see Delaume, 'Sovereign immunity and transnational arbitration' (1987) 3 Arb Intl 28, at 43.

[247] *Creighton Ltd (Cayman Islands) v Minister of Finance and Minister of Internal Affairs and Agriculture of the Government of the State of Qatar*, Cour de Cassation, 6 July 2000, (2000) XXV YBCA 458 and [2001] Rev Arb 114; cf. *Yugoslavia v SEEE*, Paris Tribunal de Grande Instance, 6 July 1970, (1970) 65 ILR 47, at 49 ('waiver of jurisdictional immunity does not in any way involve waiver of immunity from execution'); Paris Cour d'Appel, 21 April 1982, [1983] J du Droit Intl 145.

11.150 In June 1998, the Paris Cour d'Appel confirmed that there was no waiver of immunity from execution. Creighton appealed again, and on 6 July 2000 the Cour de Cassation overturned the Paris Cour d'Appel's decision. Relying on Article 24 of the then applicable ICC Rules (now reflected in Article 34(6) of the 2012 ICC Rules), by which the parties are 'deemed to have undertaken to carry out the resulting award without delay and to have waived their right to any form of appeal insofar as such waiver can validly be made', the Cour de Cassation found that, in agreeing to ICC arbitration, a state waives not only its immunity from jurisdiction, but also its immunity from execution.[248] Following *Creighton*, the French courts maintained the position that once a state had waived its immunity from execution, it had opened itself to enforcement against its commercial assets. However, in three simultaneous decisions involving the enforcement of interim measures ordered by a foreign court, the Cour de Cassation applied a more exacting test to the waiver of sovereign immunity from execution.[249] All three cases dealt with attachments made by NML Capital on debts owed to Argentina by each of BNP Paribas, Air France, and Total Austral. The Cour de Cassation held that waivers can be effective only if made in an express and specific manner, such that the assets or the category of assets over which the waiver is granted are specifically identified.

11.151 As to the assets over which the immunity from execution can be waived, the position varies. The successful party to an arbitration against a state or state entity is in a better position where the forum state allows execution against the *commercial* assets of a foreign sovereign. This is the position, for example, in countries such as Austria, England, France, Germany, Sweden, and the United States, amongst others. Execution is allowed against funds held by the defaulting state or state entity *for commercial purposes*. Care must be taken to ascertain whether all commercial property of the foreign state is subject to execution (such as in England), or merely that property which is (or was) used for the commercial activity upon which the claim is based.[250]

11.152 However, even where execution against state assets is allowed, national legislation and national courts have traditionally tended to show considerable respect for foreign states. In the United Kingdom, for example, the State Immunity Act 1978 provides that a certificate from the head of a state's diplomatic mission that certain

---

[248] See Meyer-Fabre, 'Enforcement of arbitral awards against sovereign states: A new milestone' (2000) 15 Mealey's Intl Arb Rep 9, at 48–52. See also Carrier, 'France: Shrinking of immunity from execution and discovery of diplomatic immunity from execution' (2003) 18 Mealey's Intl Arb Rep 1, at 46–50, in which Carrier suggests that the wording of ICC Rules, Art. 24 (now 2012 ICC Rules, Art. 34(6)) is not clear enough to deduce such a waiver.

[249] Cour de Cassation, Ch. Civ. 1ere, Arrêt No. 395 du 28 mars 2013 (11-10.450), Arrêt No. 395 du 28 mars 2013 (11-10.450), and Arrêt No. 396 du 28 mars 2013 (11-13.323). See Kleiman and Spinelli, '*NML v Argentina*: Supreme Court tightens waiver of sovereign immunity test', available online at http://www.internationallawoffice.com/newsletters/

[250] See Paulsson, 'Sovereign immunity from jurisdiction: French case law revisited' (1985) 19 Intl Lawyer 277.

E. Defence of State Immunity

property is not used for commercial purposes is sufficient evidence of that fact unless the contrary is proved.[251] Consequently, in 1984, the highest appellate court in England decided that a declaration by the ambassador of a foreign state that its account with a London bank was *not* held for commercial purposes should be accepted as sufficient evidence of this fact, unless the contrary could be proved by showing that the account *was* used almost exclusively for commercial purposes.[252] In reaching this decision, the court was strongly influenced by a decision of the Constitutional Court of the Federal Republic of Germany in the *Philippine Republic* case,[253] in which a similar dispute was decided according to principles of public international law. In recent years, however, courts in some jurisdictions have broadened the scope of government assets that are considered commercial.[254]

Other important targets in the execution of awards against states are assets held by foreign central banks or monetary authorities. The English State Immunity Act 1978, for example, affords those assets complete immunity irrespective of the purposes for which they are used.[255] 11.153

In the United States, the Liberian Eastern Timber Company (Letco), a company registered in France, failed in its attempt to enforce an ICSID award[256] against those assets of the Government of Liberia that were in the United States. There were a series of proceedings in the courts and Letco was permitted to enter judgment against the Liberian government. However, because of state immunity, Letco was refused leave to execute this judgment, first against shipping fees due to the Liberian government, and secondly (and more predictably), against Liberian embassy bank accounts.[257] 11.154

---

[251] State Immunity Act 1978, s. 13(5).
[252] *Alcom Ltd v Republic of Colombia* [1984] AC 580 (HL). See also *SerVaas Incorporated v Rafidain Bank & Republic of Iraq and ors* [2012] UKSC 40, in which a certificate issued by the Iraqi head of mission was held sufficient to prove that the funds in question were earmarked for the restructuring of Iraq's sovereign debt and, as such, protected by sovereign immunity.
[253] (1977) BVerfGE 342.
[254] See, e.g., *Orascom Telecom Holding SAE v Republic of Chad and anor* [2008] 2 Lloyd's Rep 396, at [23], in which enforcement of an ICC award was allowed against Chad's Citibank account, which was set up and operated so as 'to receive the proceeds of a contract for the supply of goods or services, and/or to be part of a system specifically established for the purposes of repayment of the loans by the World Bank etc to Chad'. See also *Russian Federation v Franz J. Sedelmayer*, Case No. ö 170-10, Swedish Supreme Court, 1 July 2011, in which the Court held that an arbitral award could be enforced against a block of flats in Stockholm owned by the Russian government, which was partially used by the Russian Federation to house diplomats, partly for non-commercial (but non-official) purposes and partly for commercial purposes.
[255] State Immunity Act 1978, s. 14(4); *AIG Capital Partners Inc. v Kazakhstan* [2005] App LR 10/20. See also the US Foreign Sovereign Immunities Act of 1976, § 1611(b)(1), which also provides that the immunity of central banks or monetary authorities can be waived: see *LNC Investments Inc. v Republic of Nicaragua* 115 F.Supp.2d 358 (SDNY 2000) for a restrictive approach to waivers of immunity.
[256] One of the original authors was a member of the tribunal.
[257] *Liberian Eastern Timber Co. (Letco) v Government of the Republic of Liberia* 650 F.Supp. 73 (SDNY 1986), 659 F.Supp. 606 (DDC 1987) (embassy bank accounts). For a commentary, see

11.155 More recently, in France, the Compagnie NOGA d'Importation et d'Exportation SA, a Swiss company, was frustrated in its attempt to enforce an ICC award rendered in Stockholm against assets of the Russian Federation. In March 2000, the Paris Tribunal de Grande Instance granted *exequatur* of the award; in May 2000, NOGA proceeded, inter alia, to seize bank accounts opened in the names of the embassy of the Russian Federation in France, the commercial delegation of the Russian Federation, and the permanent delegation of the Russian Federation at the United Nations Educational, Scientific and Cultural Organization (UNESCO). Following Russia's failed attempt to have the seizures lifted by the Paris Tribunal, Russia appealed to the Paris Cour d'Appel. Notwithstanding explicit contractual waivers of immunity from execution in the underlying agreements, the Cour d'Appel held that Russia had not waived its diplomatic immunity, which is governed by the distinct regime of the 1961 Vienna Convention on Diplomatic Relations. A general waiver of immunity from execution therefore did not extend to diplomatic assets.[258] The Paris Cour d'Appel based its decision on Articles 22(3) and 25 of the Vienna Convention, and concluded that all of the accounts that had been seized by NOGA were held by Russian diplomatic bodies and, as such, could not be part of Russia's waiver of immunity from execution.[259] Following failed attempts to enforce its Stockholm award in France against a Russian ship in the port of Brest and Russian Mig fighter jets participating in an air show outside of Paris, NOGA sought to enforce the award in Switzerland, inter alia, against bank accounts of the Russian central bank.[260] However, the Swiss Federal Supreme Court went on to refuse NOGA's attempt to block an award subsequently rendered in Paris in the Russian Federation's favour, which declared that the claim underlying the debt collection proceedings did not exist.[261]

Broches, 'Awards rendered pursuant to the ICSID Convention: Binding force, finality, recognition, enforcement, execution' (1987) 2 ICSID Rev—Foreign Investment LJ 287.

[258] *Ambassade de la Fédération de Russie en France v Compagnie NOGA d'Importation et d'Exportation SA*, Paris Cour d'Appel, Ch. 1ere A, 10 August 2000, [2001] Rev Arb 114; for excerpts in English, see also (2001) XXVI YBCA 273. Although the Cour de Cassation subsequently overturned the Cour d'Appel's decision on 12 May 2004, it did not impugn the Cour d'Appel's reasoning on the relationship between a waiver of immunity from execution and diplomatic immunity. See also Gaillard, 'La jurisprudence de la Cour de Cassation en matiere d'arbitrage international' (2007) 4 Rev Arb 697, at 716–720.

[259] Separately, in February 2000, the Brussels Cour d'Appel followed the decision of the Paris Cour d'Appel in *NOGA* (whilst basing its reasoning solely on Art. 25 of the Vienna Convention) and found the Embassy of Iraq's bank accounts to be immune from execution.

[260] See, e.g., *Fédération de Russie v BNP Paribas (Suisse) SA Compagnie NOGA d'Importation et d'Exportation SA*, Decision 5A_618/2007, Swiss Federal Supreme Court, 10 January 2008.

[261] Decision 4A_403/2008, Federal Supreme Court of Switzerland, 9 December 2008.

INDEX

Note: please see under entries for individual countries for specific topics relating to that country

Abs-Shawcross Draft Convention on Investments
    Abroad 1959 8.08
accommodation
    administration 4.177–4.181
    arbitral institutions, accommodation provided
        by 4.179–4.180
    arbitration centres 4.179–4.180
    breakout rooms 4.178, 6.160
    costs 1.123, 6.187, 9.89
    deliberations, room for 4.178
    fees and expenses 1.123–1.101, 4.202, 9.89
    hearings 4.178, 6.160, 6.187
    hotels 4.181
    ICC Hearing Centre 4.180
    ICSID, accommodation provided by 4.179
    International Centre for Dispute Resolution
        (ICDR) 4.180
    London Court of International Arbitration
        (LCIA) 4.180
    Permanent Court of Arbitration (PCA) 4.179
    security 4.178
ad hoc arbitrations 1.140–1.145
    advantages 1.143–1.144
    applicable law 4.11–4.12
    appointment of arbitrators 4.35, 4.37, 4.46
    arbitration agreements 2.71, 2.79–2.81
    challenges to arbitrators 4.96, 4.105, 4.106
    commencement of an arbitration 4.11–4.12
    conduct of an arbitration 6.06
    definition 1.141
    delocalisation or denationalisation 3.79
    disadvantages 1.145
    equality 1.140
    fees and expenses 4.203, 6.44, 6.46
    flexibility 1.143
    governing law 3.41
    inspection of subject matter 6.152–6.154
    institutional arbitrations 1.143, 1.145, 1.154
    model arbitration clauses 2.79–2.81, 2.99–2.100
    notice 1.66–1.68
    oil concession agreements 1.143
    partial and interim awards 9.22
    Permanent Court of Arbitration (PCA) 1.190
    preliminary meetings 6.44, 6.46
    refusal to participate 1.145
    rules of procedure 1.140–1.145
    states or state entities, involvement of 1.144
    submission agreements 1.142
    time limits 4.11–4.12

    truncated tribunals 4.156, 4.160
    UNCITRAL Rules 1.141, 1.144
adaptation of contracts and filling gaps 9.65–9.71
    awards 9.65–9.71
    civil law countries 9.67
    commercial context 9.67
    fairness 9.68
    hardship clauses 9.69
    hydrocarbon contracts 9.68–9.69
    ICC 9.69
    implied term device 9.66–9.67, 9.71
    intention 9.65–9.67
    interpretation 9.65, 9.70
    long-term contracts 9.68–9.69, 9.71
    rebus sic stantibus 9.71
    standard forms 9.69
    unambiguous terms 9.68–9.70
    UNCITRAL Rules 9.70
    UNIDROIT Principles of International
        Commercial Contracts 9.69
adjudicability
    arbitrability 10.50–10.51
    arbitration agreements 10.43–10.44
    challenges to awards 10.42–10.51
    enforcement of awards 10.47
    excess of powers 10.41, 10.45–10.49
    Geneva Convention 1927 10.47
    incapacity 10.43–10.44
    invalid agreements to arbitrate 10.43–10.44
    jurisdiction 10.42
    UNCITRAL Model Law 10.45–10.46
administration 4.177–4.200 *see also*
    UNCITRAL Notes on Organizing
    Arbitral Proceedings
    accommodation, finding 4.177–4.181
    administrative secretaries 4.169,
        4.192–4.200, 6.158
    arbitration centres 4.179
    arbitrators 4.15
    electronic aids 4.177
    facilities 4.177
    fees and expenses 4.197–4.198, 4.221–4.222
    hearing hours 4.186–4.188
    hearings 4.186–4.187, 6.158–6.159
    institutional arbitrations 1.151
    interpreters 4.182, 4.193
    presiding arbitrators 4.190–4.191, 6.158
    relationship between parties and tribunals 4.189
    secretaries 4.169, 4.192–4.201, 6.158

Index

administration (cont.)
  sole arbitrators 6.158
  staff 1.151
  transcripts 4.193
  venue, fixing the 4.177
  verbatim records 4.184–4.185
administrative secretaries
  administration 4.169, 4.192–4.199, 6.158
  costs and expenses 4.200–4.201
  debates over role 4.195
  fees and expenses 4.197–4.198
  hearings 4.193, 6.158
  institutional arbitrations 4.196–4.197
  interpreters 4.193
  role 4.192–4.199
  transcripts 4.193–4.194
  who to appoint 4.198–4.199
  witnesses 4.194
admissibility of evidence
  civil law countries 6.81–6.83
  common law countries 6.81–6.83
  expert evidence 6.142
  witnesses 6.127–6.129
ADR see alternative dispute resolution (ADR)
advantages of arbitration 1.94–1.107, 1.129 see also disadvantages of arbitration
  ad hoc arbitrations 1.143–1.144
  confidentiality 1.105, 2.161
  enforcement of awards 1.97–1.98, 1.101–1.102
  flexibility 1.104
  ICC arbitration 1.149–1.153
  institutional arbitrations 1.149–1.153
  multiparty arbitrations 2.212
  neutrality 1.97–1.101, 1.132–1.134
  privacy 1.105
  sole arbitrators 4.25
adverse inferences 3.226, 5.18, 5.20, 6.112–6.115, 6.132
adverse publicity 1.105, 11.09
advice
  confidentiality 2.191
  professional advisers 5.48–5.49
  WIPO Rules 2.191
African Conventions 11.138–11.139
agreed terms, awards made on 5.82, 5.85, 9.34–9.39
agreements see arbitration agreements
Aida Reinsurance and Insurance Arbitration Society (ARIAS) Arbitration Rules 3.16–3.22
alter ego principle 2.51, 11.104
alternative dispute resolution (ADR) 1.135–1.139
  amiable compositeurs 1.139
  arbitration as ADR 1.131
  definition 1.137–1.138
  equity clauses 1.139
  ex aequo et bono decisions 1.139
  good faith 1.135–1.136
  mediation 1.138
  mediation/arbitration (med/arb) 1.138
  multi-tier clauses 2.88–2.93
  non-binding ADR 1.138
  objectivity 1.136

American Arbitration Association (AAA)
  class or representative arbitrations 2.230
  Code of Ethics 5.79
  independence and impartiality of arbitrators 4.75
  inspection of subject matter 6.152
  International Centre for Dispute Resolution (ICDR) (Ireland) 1.167
  rules 1.02, 2.230, 6.152
  Supplementary Rules for Class Actions 2.230
  truncated tribunals 4.156, 4.157
amiable compositeurs 1.139, 3.190, 3.192, 3.194–3.196, 9.177
anti-suit injunctions 3.17–3.18, 5.134–5.135
antitrust see competition/antitrust law
appeals
  challenges to awards 4.93, 10.01–10.07, 10.75–10.76
  dissenting opinions 9.188
  enforcement of awards 11.04
  mistake of fact 10.77
  mistake of law 10.66–10.68, 10.75
applicable laws 3.01–3.231 see also choice of law; governing law; *lex arbitri*; substance, law applicable to the
  ad hoc arbitrations 4.11–4.12
  arbitrability 2.130
  arbitral proceedings 1.07
  arbitrators
    challenges 4.92, 4.106
    judicially, arbitrators' duty to act 5.72
    power to determine law 5.16
    qualities 4.52
  bilateral investment treaties (BITs) 8.62–8.77
  capacity 2.34
  complex interaction of laws 3.07–3.08
  conflict of laws 3.198–3.220
  consent 9.50
  dualism 3.04
  enforcement of awards 1.07
  equity and good conscience 3.192–3.197
  ethical rules 3.221–3.228
  European Convention 1961 3.215
  fact, issues of 3.02
  guidelines 3.229–3.231
  interest 9.73, 9.79, 9.83
  interim measures 5.32
  international trade law 1.07
  judicially, arbitrators' duty to act 5.72
  lex arbitri 1.07, 3.07–3.08
  lex mercatoria 1.07
  model arbitration clauses 2.100
  national courts, intervention by 3.05
  national laws 1.07
  non-national law 3.188
  partial and interim awards 9.20, 9.25
  place or seat of arbitration, law of 3.05
  proper law 1.07
  public international law 1.07
  recognition of awards 1.07
  Shari'ah 3.185–3.187, 3.190, 4.52
  transnational law 1.07

Index

vacuum, arbitrations not existing in a
  legal 3.03–3.06
Vienna Convention on the Law of
  Treaties 8.64
appointment of arbitrators 4.33–4.48 *see also*
  vacancies, filling
  2 arbitrators 4.28
  3 arbitrators 4.29–4.31, 4.34, 4.36, 4.39–4.40
  4 or more arbitrators 4.32
  ad hoc arbitrations 4.35, 4.37, 4.46
  agreement of parties 1.71, 4.34–4.36, 4.40
  appointing authorities 4.46–4.48
  arbitral institutions, by 4.36–4.39, 4.41
  arbitration clauses 4.43–4.44
  availability of arbitrators 1.127, 4.60
  chair by co-arbitrators, appointment of 4.40
  choice of arbitrator 1.71–1.76, 4.34–4.36, 4.40
  class or representative arbitrations 2.226–2.227
  commencement of arbitrations 1.71–1.76
  concurrent hearings 2.236–2.237
  culture 4.14, 4.30, 4.76
  defective clauses 4.44
  delay 1.126, 4.02, 4.44
  due process 11.71–11.72
  emergency arbitrators 1.177, 4.03, 4.17–4.21
  equality of treatment 2.214
  expedited formation of tribunals, rules for 1.186
  experts 5.23–5.25, 6.134, 6.135
  failure to nominate arbitrators 4.02
  fair hearings 4.14
  'Grand Old Men' 1.76
  ICC arbitration 1.147–1.148, 1.177, 4.36
  ICSID arbitration 4.37
  independence and impartiality 4.75–4.76
  jurisdiction 4.43–4.44
  language 1.73, 4.14
  lawyers, appointment of qualified 4.50, 4.52, 4.54–4.57, 4.67
  legal backgrounds, as having different 1.72–1.73, 9.102–9.103
  lex arbitri 4.35
  list system 4.38–4.39, 4.41
  litigation, arbitration distinguished from 1.71
  'Managers' 1.76
  methods 4.34–4.48
  multiparty arbitrations 2.214–2.217, 4.22–4.27
  national courts, by 4.35, 4.37, 4.42–4.45
  nationality 1.72, 4.50, 4.61–4.67, 4.99
  nomination by parties 1.71–1.72, 1.100, 4.34–4.36, 4.40, 4.75–4.76, 4.81–4.83, 9.114–9.115
  notice 11.63, 11.71–11.72
  number of arbitrators 1.73, 1.100, 4.22–4.27, 4.34–4.36, 4.40
  Permanent Court of Arbitration (PCA) 1.190, 4.46–4.48
  presiding arbitrator, appointment by co-arbitrators of 4.40
  professional institutions, appointment by 4.41
  qualifications 1.76, 4.15–4.16, 4.54–4.57, 4.68
  qualities 1.71–1.76, 4.49–4.74
  refusal to appoint arbitrators 4.35
  repeat appointments and conflicts of interest 4.124–4.126
  restrictions 4.16
  selection of a tribunal 1.100, 1.104, 1.159–1.161, 4.13–4.16
  sole arbitrators 4.22–4.27, 4.36
  'Technocrats' 1.76
  timetable 4.14
  UNCITRAL Model Law 1.190
  UNCITRAL Rules 4.39, 4.46–4.47
Arab Investment Court 11.139
Arab League Investment Agreement 11.139
Arab states 2.127, 11.138–11.139
arbitrability 2.124–2.160
  adjudicability 10.50–10.51
  agency 2.130
  alter egos of companies 11.104
  applicable law 2.130
  Arab states 2.127
  arbitration agreements 2.124–2.155
  bribery and corruption 2.146–2.153
  'capable of settlement by arbitration', disputes which are 1.64–1.65, 2.25, 2.124–2.127, 10.50
  capacity 2.40–2.41
  categories of disputes 2.131–2.159
  challenges to awards 10.50–10.51
  companies 2.117, 2.157–2.159, 11.104
  competition and antitrust law 2.133–2.138, 10.51
  consent awards or agreed terms awards 9.36
  consumer contracts 2.127
  copyright 2.131
  corporate governance 2.157–2.159, 11.103
  corruption 2.147–2.153
  criminal matters 2.130
  dispute requirement 1.64–1.65
  economic interests, claims involving 2.125
  fraud 2.154
  governing law 2.127–2.128
  insolvency 2.141–2.146
  lex arbitri 3.47
  monopolies or cartels 2.132–2.133
  national courts 2.126–2.127, 7.02
  national laws 2.127–2.128, 2.120
  natural resources 2.155–2.156
  New York Convention 1958 2.29, 2.124, 11.101–11.104
  patents 2.131–2.132, 2.134
  public interest 2.127
  public policy 2.129–2.130, 2.137–2.139, 10.51
  refusal of recognition and enforcement 11.101–11.104
  restraint of trade 2.134
  securities transactions 2.139–2.140
  state and state agencies 2.40–2.41
  subjective arbitrability 2.40–2.41
  trade marks 2.130–2.131
  trade secrets 2.131
  UNCITRAL Model Law 2.29, 2.124, 10.50, 11.99

Index

arbitral institutions, rules of *see also* particular rules (eg ICC Rules)
  arbitration agreements 1.149
  arbitrators 4.50, 4.92–4.101, 4.106, 5.46
  awards 9.01, 9.191–9.194
    challenges 10.01–10.02, 10.09–10.17, 10.30
    clarification 9.191–9.194
    contents 9.152
    enforcement 11.01
  bargaining process 9.117–9.118
  books of rules 1.50, 1.148–1.150
  challenges to arbitrators 4.92–4.101, 4.106
  challenges to awards 10.01–10.02, 10.07–10.17, 10.30
  commencement of an arbitration 4.08–4.12
  competence/competence 5.105–5.109
  conduct of an arbitration 6.01, 6.06, 6.19–6.21
  confidentiality 2.160, 2.190
  conflict of laws 3.213–3.217
  consolidation 2.245–2.247
  costs 9.97
  delay 5.69
  design 1.79
  dissenting opinions 9.132–9.134
  emergency arbitrators 4.17–4.20, 6.28
  enforcement of awards 11.01
  fast track arbitration 6.32–6.40
  flexibility 1.79
  form of awards, validity and 9.143–9.145, 9.149
  hearings 6.157
  immunity 5.66
  incorporation of rules 9.152
  inspection of subject matter 5.22, 6.146–6.154
  institutional arbitration 1.147–1.150, 1.162
  interest 9.73
  joinder and intervention 2.60–2.62, 2.245–2.247
  jurisdiction 5.105
  lex arbitri 3.51–3.52
  majority voting 9.119–9.124
  notification of awards 9.169
  preliminary meetings 6.42, 6.46
  reviews 1.162
  revision 1.149, 1.162, 2.190–2.195
  separability or autonomy of arbitration clauses 2.104
  simplified procedures 6.32–6.33
  time limits 4.08–4.13
arbitral proceedings *see* conduct of an arbitration; hearings
arbitral secretaries *see* administrative secretaries
arbitral tribunals 4.01–4.222 *see also* arbitral institutions, rules of; arbitrators; institutional arbitrations; specific institutions (eg London Court of International Arbitration LCIA))
  administrative fees 1.123–1.124, 9.89
  assembling the tribunal 6.23
  commencement of an arbitration 4.04–4.13
  composition 10.60
  control of process 5.113–5.114, 6.04–6.06
  decision-making 9.100–9.138
  decisions of the tribunal 9.100–9.138
  emergency arbitrators 4.17–4.21
  establishment 2.78, 2.116, 4.01–4.222, 7.11
  failure or refusal to act 2.83, 2.116
  flexibility 1.104
  functus officio, tribunal as 4.220, 11.02
  interim measures 4.03, 7.14–7.61
  jurisdiction 5.91–5.137
  model arbitration clauses 2.78, 2.82, 2.116
  national courts, comparison with 4.01
  organisation 4.01–4.222
  parties, relationship with 4.189
  partnership between national courts and tribunals 7.01, 7.03, 7.07
  powers and duties 1.58, 5.01–5.137
  rules or laws governing tribunal 1.09
  truncated tribunals 4.139, 4.154–4.161
  urgent measures 4.03
  visits to other countries by tribunals 3.60
arbitrary or discriminatory measures 8.118–8.123
arbitration agreements 1.40–1.59, 2.01–2.247 *see also* enforcement of arbitration agreements; submission agreements; validity of arbitration agreements
  ad hoc arbitrations 2.71, 2.79–2.81
  agents, arbitration agreements concluded by 2.56–2.57
  alter ego principle 2.51
  amiable compositeurs, arbitrators as 1.139, 3.194–3.196, 9.177
  analysis of agreement 2.63–2.123
  applicable law 3.91–3.92
  arbitrability 2.124–2.155
  arbitration clauses 1.41, 2.02–2.03
  arbitrators
    number of 1.58, 1.100, 2.77, 4.22
    powers of 5.13–5.14
    sole arbitrators 1.100
    vacancies, filling 2.82
  'arising out of' 2.69
  assignment 2.54–2.55
  autonomy of parties 1.51, 2.01
  basic elements 2.71–2.100
  bilateral investment treaties (BITs) 1.43, 1.217
  breach 7.23
  Brussels I Regulation 5.128–5.137
  'capable of settlement by arbitration', disputes which are 2.29–2.30
  capacity 2.31–2.41
  categories 1.41, 2.02–2.05
  challenges to agreements 5.99
  challenges to awards 10.43–10.44, 10.58
  'claims', 'differences' and 'disputes' 2.68
  class or representative arbitrations 2.224–2.235
  close connection 2.64
  confidentiality 2.161–2.196
  consent 1.53–1.54, 1.115, 2.01, 2.21, 2.42
  consolidation 2.238–2.247
  contents of awards 9.152
  contractual claims 2.64–2.65
  corporations 2.35–2.36
  damages for breach 1.55, 9.45, 9.50

Index

default clauses 2.85
defective clauses 2.197–2.203
devices and facades 2.51
drafting 2.65–2.100, 2.244, 3.10, 3.87, 4.22
electronic communications 1.45, 1.46–1.48, 2.13, 2.16, 2.18–2.23
estoppel 2.53
European Convention 1961 1.29
formalities 2.13–2.23, 9.142–9.145
forms of wording 2.65–2.70
France 2.22, 2.71
Geneva Convention 1927 2.06
Geneva Protocol 1923 2.06
governing law 2.54, 2.66–2.67, 2.84, 3.09–3.36
group of companies doctrine 2.42–2.51
implied consent 2.21
'in connection with', 'in relation to', 'in respect of' 2.69
institutional arbitrations 1.149, 2.79–2.81
interim measures 7.23–7.27
international standards 2.09–2.12
interpretation 2.28, 2.67–2.69
joinder and intervention 2.59–2.62
language 2.86
multiparty arbitrations 2.212–2.247
multi-tier clauses 2.88–2.93
national laws 1.53, 2.01, 2.10
natural persons 2.34
New York Convention 1958 1.44–1.45, 2.06–2.07, 2.14, 2.16
  arbitration clauses 1.44–1.45
  assignment 2.55
  electronic communications 1.45
  recognition of arbitration agreements 2.11
  third parties 1.45
non-signatories 1.114–1.115
novation 2.58
number of arbitrators 1.58, 1.100, 2.77, 4.22
oral agreements 1.48, 2.21
Panama Convention 1975 2.08
parties 2.31–2.62
piercing the corporate veil 2.51
place of arbitration 2.83
privity of contract 2.52–2.53
procedure 2.99–2.100
proof of agreements 2.17–2.18
recognition of awards, refusal of 2.63, 11.63, 11.66–11.67
record of agreements in any form 2.16, 2.18–2.23
refusal of enforcement or recognition 1.40, 2.63, 11.63, 11.66–11.70, 11.82–11.86
Revised UNCITRAL Model Law 1.48, 2.16–2.18
scope 2.63–2.70
separability 2.101–2.113
signatures 2.15
sole option/unilateral option clauses 2.94–2.98
specific performance 1.55
standard forms 2.71, 2.73
standards 2.09–2.12

state agencies 2.37–2.41
statutory claims 2.64–2.65
substance over form 2.21
submission agreements 1.42, 1.51–1.52, 2.02
succession 2.58
third parties 1.45, 1.114–1.115, 2.42–2.62
tort claims 2.64–2.65
treaties and conventions 2.06–2.13
types 1.41–1.43, 2.02–2.05
UNCITRAL Model Law 1.46, 1.48, 2.13, 2.16–2.17
UNCITRAL Rules 2.71
'under this contract' 2.69
vacancies, filling 2.82, 4.149
waiver of right to arbitrate 2.204–2.212
wording, forms of 2.65–2.70
writing 1.44–1.48, 2.13–2.23
arbitration awards *see* **awards**
arbitration clauses *see also* **defective arbitration clauses; model arbitration clauses**
appointment of arbitrators 4.43–4.44
arbitration agreements 1.43, 2.02–2.03
challenges 5.100
clause compromissoire 1.49
contracts 2.113
drafting 1.49, 2.73–2.100, 3.113, 4.22
future disputes 1.41, 1.53, 2.02
governing law 3.09, 3.12–3.13, 3.34
ICC arbitration 1.50, 1.147–1.148
institutional arbitrations 1.147–1.148
jurisdiction 5.100–5.111
midnight clauses 2.04
New York Convention 1958 1.44–1.45
separability or autonomy 2.89–2.100, 3.12–3.13, 3.34, 5.100–5.111
standard form contracts 1.52
time limits 9.165–9.166
UNCITRAL Model Rules 1.50, 2.73
validity 1.52
arbitration, definition of 1.04–1.05
arbitrators *see also* **appointment of arbitrators; challenges to arbitrators; duty of care of arbitrators; independence and impartiality of arbitrators; number of arbitrators; presiding arbitrators; sole arbitrators**
amiable compositeurs 1.139, 3.190, 3.193, 3.195–3.197, 9.177
applicable law
  power to determine 5.16
  restrictions imposed by 4.52
arbitration agreements, powers under 1.58, 5.13–5.14
availability 1.127, 4.50, 4.60, 4.72
awards, duty to render enforceable 11.11
background, differences in 1.70
balance of power, shift in 5.07
codes of conduct 5.79
contempt of court 5.42
contract, restrictions imposed by 4.50–4.51
control of proceedings 6.61–6.63
death or incapacity 4.167–4.168

Index

arbitrators (*cont.*)
  definition of arbitration 1.04
  delay 1.127, 4.02, 4.44, 4.90, 4.107, 4.151,
    5.66–5.68, 5.80
  deliberation 9.100–9.112
  deontology of arbitrators 5.79
  different backgrounds of arbitrators 9.102–9.103
  disqualification 4.79–4.88
  documents, production of 5.18–5.19
  duties 5.03–5.05, 5.43–5.90
    law, imposed by 5.47–5.78
    parties, imposed by the 5.44–5.46
  duty of care 5.39–5.66
  education and training 4.68–4.71
  ethical duties 5.60, 5.79–5.90
  exchange of views 4.192, 9.106, 9.109–9.110
  exclusion of arbitrator from deliberations 9.107
  experience 1.232, 1.238, 4.14, 4.49–4.50, 4.54,
    4.59, 4.68, 4.72, 9.17
  experts 5.23–5.27, 6.137
  fees and expenses 1.123–1.124, 9.88–9.89
  governing law 5.14
  hearings, attendance of young
    practitioners at 4.71
  ICC Rules 4.64, 4.67, 4.69, 5.46
  ICDR Rules 4.65, 4.69
  ICSID arbitration 4.67
  immunity 5.01, 5.68
  incapacity 4.167–4.168
  institutional arbitrations 4.50, 4.69–4.70, 5.46
  insuring against vacancies on
    tribunals 4.167–4.168
  interim measures 5.27–5.34
  interpreters 4.58
  interviews 4.72–4.74
  judicially, duty to act 1.118, 5.69–5.78
  language 4.50, 4.58, 5.17
  LCIA Rules 1.174
  lex arbitri 5.14, 5.16
  limits on powers 1.104, 5.13
  medical examinations 4.168
  national courts 5.41–5.42, 7.14–7.61
  nationality 4.50, 4.61–4.67
  neutrality 1.100, 4.61–4.65
  oaths, admission of 5.13, 5.21
  outlook 4.59
  personal liability 5.61, 5.78
  powers 5.03–5.42
    additional powers 1.106
    arbitration agreements 1.58
    common powers 5.15–5.37
    conferred by parties 5.08–5.09
    direct conferment 5.09
    extensions 5.13–5.14
    governing law 5.14
    indirect conferment 5.09
    lex arbitri 5.14, 5.16
    operation of law, by 5.11–5.14
    restrictions 1.104, 4.50–4.52, 5.22
    sources of power 5.08–5.14
  practical considerations 5.03–5.05
  procedure, establishment of 5.15
  professional qualifications 4.50, 4.53–4.57
  promptly, duty to act 5.67–5.68
  psychology of tribunals 9.113–9.116
  refusal to participate in arbitration 4.154–4.155
  removal 2.83, 5.72
  replacement 4.152–4.168
  resignation 2.122–2.123, 4.150–4.151, 4.155
  restrictions 1.104, 4.50–4.52, 5.22
  seat, power to determine 5.16
  security for costs 5.35–5.37
  selection 1.71–1.76
  Shari'ah, knowledge of 4.52
  site inspections 5.45
  sole arbitrators, qualities of 4.54
  sources of power 5.08–5.14
  standard forms 4.50
  state, delegation of powers of 1.104
  subject matter of dispute, inspection of 5.22
  subpoenas 5.19–5.20
  supporting powers of court 5.41
  time and attention to case, inability to
    give 5.43, 5.79
  time limits 5.67
  training 4.68–4.71, 9.17
  translators 4.58
  truncated tribunals 4.154–4.155
  vacancies, falling 4.152–4.168
  witnesses 1.104, 5.20–5.21
  young practitioners' groups 4.70

Argentina
  arbitrary or discriminatory measures affecting
    investments 8.122
  bribery and corruption 2.149–2.150
  Chile, BIT with 8.132
  expropriation 8.79, 8.162
  failure to perform duty, arbitrator's liability
    for 5.53
  France, BIT with 8.26
  ICSID arbitration 4.136, 8.52–8.54, 11.129
  insolvency 2.145
  interim measures 7.16
  national courts, access to 8.49, 10.47
  Netherlands, BIT with 8.22, 8.33
  New York Convention 1958 1.211
  Rosatti doctrine 11.129
  Spain, BIT with 8.52–8.53
  stay of proceedings 7.60
  United Kingdom, BIT with 5.127, 7.60,
    8.62, 10.47
  United States, BIT with 8.15, 8.79, 8.96, 8.134

**ASEAN Comprehensive Investment
  Agreement** 8.11

assignment 2.42, 2.54–2.55

attachment of bank accounts 11.35

Australia
  ADR 2.92
  confidentiality 2.170, 2.172, 2.183
  immunity 5.55, 5.78
  interest 9.74, 9.76
  waiver 2.207–2.208

Index

Austria
  agency 2.57
  appointment of arbitrators 5.52
  choice of law 3.25
  Federal Economic Chamber, status of International Arbitral Centre of 7.41–7.43
  immunity 11.151
  liability of arbitrators 5.52
  New York Convention 1958 11.70
  recognition and enforcement of awards 11.70, 11.93
  uncertainty 2.199
autonomy of arbitration clauses *see* **separability or autonomy of arbitration clauses**
autonomy of the parties 3.97–3.110
  applicable law 3.97–3.110
  arbitral institutions, rules of 6.16
  arbitration agreements 1.51, 2.01
  choice of law 3.97–3.110
  conduct of an arbitration 1.08, 6.07–6.18
  equal treatment 6.10–6.12, 6.16
  experts 6.18
  Geneva Protocol 1923 6.07
  hearings 6.18
  ICC Rules 3.100, 6.08
  ICSID arbitration 6.08
  independence and impartiality 4.149
  international practice 6.19–6.21
  LCIA Rules 6.08
  limitations 6.07–6.18
  mandatory rules 6.15–6.18
  national courts 7.05
  national laws 3.97–3.99
  New York Convention 1958 6.07, 6.10
  procedure 6.07–6.25
  public policy 3.105, 6.13–6.15
  restrictions 3.105–3.106
  Rome I Regulation 3.98, 3.103
  third parties 6.17–6.18
  time of choice 3.101–3.103
  treaties and conventions, recognition by 3.100
  UNCITRAL Model Law 6.07, 6.10, 6.16
  UNCITRAL Rules 3.100, 6.16
availability of arbitrators 1.127, 4.50, 4.60, 4.72
awards 9.01–9.202 *see also* **challenges to awards; dissenting opinions; enforcement of awards; partial and interim awards; recognition of awards; setting aside awards; validity of awards**
  adaptation of contracts 9.65–9.71
  additional awards 9.33
  annulment 5.111, 5.113, 8.77, 11.127
  arbitral institutions, rules of 9.01, 9.152, 9.191–9.194
  bargaining process 9.117–9.118
  binding awards 1.04, 1.81–1.82, 1.92–1.93, 5.117, 11.87
  categories 9.18–9.39
  clarification of awards 9.186–9.194
  clerical or typographical errors 9.33, 9.188, 9.192

confidentiality 2.177–2.182, 2.190, 9.108
conflicting awards 1.116–1.117, 2.221, 11.65
consent awards or agreed terms awards 9.34–9.39
content of awards 9.151–9.160
correction of awards 9.188–9.189, 9.192, 9.194
decision-making 9.100–9.138
decisions 9.100–9.138
default awards 2.85, 6.196, 9.03, 9.30–9.32
definition 9.05–9.13
delay 1.126–1.127, 11.01
deliberations 9.100–9.138
deposit of awards 9.171–9.172
dispositive, awards must be 9.154
draft awards, review of 1.152, 1.166
drafting 4.184–4.185, 6.188, 9.111
due process 1.204
effective determination of issues 9.154–9.156
errors, correction of 9.188–9.189, 9.192, 9.194
ex parte hearings 6.192, 6.194, 6.196
final awards 1.04, 1.101, 5.57, 9.02–9.04, 9.13, 11.01
  definition 9.04
  functus officio, tribunal as 9.18, 9.23, 9.186, 9.190
  Geneva Convention 1927 11.87
  immunity 5.57
  interpretation 9.187
  public policy 11.119
'floating' awards 3.76
foreign and domestic awards, distinction between 9.29, 11.109
form of awards 9.143–9.151
functus officio, tribunal as 9.18, 9.23, 9.186, 9.190
gap-filling 9.65–9.71
Geneva Convention 1927 11.87
governing law 3.69–3.72
hearings, awards without 6.157
ICC arbitration 1.152, 1.166, 9.195–9.197
ICSID arbitration 9.194
illegality 9.156
imperative tone, awards must be in 9.154
incorporation of rules 9.152
informal discussions 9.105–9.106
institutional arbitrations 1.152
Internet, publication on the 9.200
interpretation of awards 9.187, 9.191–9.194
introductory sections 9.147
judicial procedure, decision-making as 1.75
jurisdiction 5.113, 5.116–5.117, 9.02, 9.162
lex arbitri 3.71
local annulments 11.82, 11.89–11.98
majority voting 9.117–9.127, 9.137
national laws 5.110, 9.188–9.189
New York Convention 1958 9.05
notification of awards 9.169–9.170
opportunity to make representations 9.188
orders/rulings which have status of awards 9.09–9.13
partial and interim awards 5.113, 5.116–5.117, 7.20, 9.06, 9.19–9.28
performance 11.08–11.20

Index

awards (cont.)
  procedural orders and directions
    distinguished 9.08
  psychology of tribunal 9.113–9.116
  public, making 2.177–2.180, 2.189
  public policy 9.156, 11.119
  publication 2.179, 2.189, 9.199–9.201
  reaching decisions, method of 1.83
  reasons 9.159–9.160, 9.157–9.161
  registration 9.171–9.172
  remission 10.21–10.23
  review of awards 9.195–9.199
  SCC Rules 9.191
  separate and concurring opinions 9.128, 9.134
  settlements 1.80–1.82, 1.93, 9.198, 11.05
  sole arbitrators 1.83
  status of awards, rulings/orders which
    have the 9.09–9.13
    finality 9.13
    France 9.09–9.11
    partial awards 9.10
    United States 9.09, 9.12–9.13
  subject matter 1.30
  suspension of awards 11.98
  time limits 9.192
  training and experience of arbitrators 9.17
  treaties and conventions 5.111
  unambiguous, awards must be 9.153
  UNCITRAL Model Law 1.30, 6.199, 9.06
  UNCITRAL Rules 1.80, 9.01–9.02, 9.37, 9.70,
    9.192, 10.09, 10.30
  writing 9.01

bank accounts 4.222, 11.35
bargaining process 9.117–9.118
Belgium
  arbitrability 3.26
  capacity 2.37
  challenges to awards 10.28, 10.72
  competition law 11.121
  delocalisation or denationalisation 3.81,
    3.83, 3.88
  lex arbitri 3.26
  mistake of law 10.69
  national courts 7.05, 10.69
  public policy 11.121
  recognition and enforcement of awards, 11.93
  res judicata 9.174
  review of awards 11.121
  waiver of challenge 10.28
best endeavours 2.153, 11.11
best evidence rule 6.84, 6.90
bias *see* independence and impartiality of
  arbitrators
bilateral investment treaties (BITs) *see also* bilateral
  investment treaties (BITs) and jurisdictional
  issues; expropriation
  access, consent and conditions to 8.45–8.53
  additional requirements 8.21
  amicable settlement period 8.48
  applicable law 8.62–8.68
  arbitrary or discriminatory measures, no 8.86,
    8.103, 8.118–8.123
  arbitration agreements 1.43, 1.217
  attorneys' fees 8.168–8.169
  breach 8.45–8.53, 8.78, 8.69–8.72
    consent and conditions to access 8.45–8.53
    remedies 8.45, 8.49
  challenges to awards 10.47
  commercial contracts 8.44
  compensation 8.141–8.163
  conflict of laws 8.74
  consent and conditions to access 8.45–8.53
  consultation periods 8.45–8.47, 8.50
  contractual dispute resolution clauses 8.54–8.56
  cooling off 8.45, 8.47, 8.50
  corruption 8.36
  costs 8.168–8.169
  currency control 8.130–8.132
  customary international law 8.67, 8.141
  damages 8.163, 8.164–8.165
  diagonal clauses 8.08
  diplomatic protection 8.08–8.09
  direct recourse, right of 8.09
  discriminatory measures, no 8.86, 8.103,
    8.118–8.123
  due diligence 8.115
  European Union, accession to 8.74–8.75
  fair and equitable treatment 8.96–8.112,
    8.159–8.163
  fair market value standards of
    compensation 8.146–8.148, 8.162
  fraud 8.36
  free trade agreements 8.11
  free transfer of funds relating to
    investments 8.129–8.133
  friendship, commerce and navigation (FCN)
    treaties 1.216, 8.08
  full protection and security 8.113–8.117
  good faith 8.36
  ICSID arbitration 1.187, 8.65, 8.68, 8.76, 8.78
  increase in number of BITs 8.10–8.11
  indirect investments 8.31–8.33
  interest 8.166–8.167
  international law 8.70
  international minimum standard 8.96–8.112
  Internet circulation of awards 9.200
  interpretation 8.21–8.23, 8.28–8.46, 8.55,
    8.64–8.75, 8.98, 8.107–8.123, 8.135–8.140
  investment, definition of 8.28–8.44, 8.70, 8.75
  investor, definition of 8.21–8.22
  legal entities 8.20–8.27
  legal stability requirement 8.102
  legitimate expectations 8.99–8.102
  merits of dispute 8.78–8.139
  moral damages 8.164–8.165
  most favoured nation (MFN) clauses 8.50–8.53,
    8.124–8.132
  multilateral economic cooperation treaties 8.11
  national laws 8.72

Index

national treatment 8.50–8.53, 8.124–8.132
nationality discrimination 8.103
notification of disputes 8.45–8.46
portfolio investments 8.44
precedent 8.76
privity, arbitration without 1.217
property, protection of 8.113–8.117
public policy 8.36
publication of awards 9.200–9.201
remedies 8.45
restitution 8.163
Salini test 8.39–8.41, 8.44
standards 8.96–8.112
standing offers 1.217
state responsibility 8.66
states, disputes involving 1.217
substance of dispute, law applicable to 8.62–8.70
umbrella clauses or observation of undertakings 8.56, 8.134–8.139
UNCITRAL Rules 5.127
undertakings, observance of specific investment 8.134–8.140
Vienna Convention on the Law of Treaties 5.127

bilateral investment treaties (BITs) and jurisdictional issues 8.14–8.77
annulment of awards 8.77
applicable law 8.62–8.77
companies 8.27
consultation periods 8.47, 8.50
contractual, claims which are purely 8.56, 8.59–8.60
definition of investment 8.28–8.43
domicile 8.18
dual nationality 8.19
duration 8.15
effective date 8.15
embassy or government, contacting relevant 8.14
exclusive jurisdiction clauses 8.54–8.56
existence of applicable treaty 8.14–8.16
'fork in the road' provisions 8.57–8.58, 8.61
ICSID Convention 8.26–8.28, 8.63
ICSID Tribunal 8.54–8.55
interpretation 8.137–8.139
jurisdiction clauses 8.54–8.56
legal entities 8.20–8.27
local courts, parallel claims before 8.57–8.61
merits of the dispute 8.78–8.95
most favoured nation clauses 8.125–8.132
national treatment 8.125–8.132
nationality 8.16–8.19
natural persons 8.18–8.19
parallel claims before local courts 8.57–8.61
prior to date of coming into effect, protection 8.15
protected investments 8.28–8.44
protected investors 8.17–8.27
residence 8.18
retrospectivity 8.15

substance of dispute, law applicable to 8.62–8.77
termination or expiry, legal status of investments prior to 8.16
UNCITRAL Arbitration Rules 8.63
undertakings, observance of specific investment 8.134–8.139

bi-polar arbitrations 2.153
BITs *see* bilateral investment treaties (BITs)
Bolivia 8.12, 8.23, 11.128
boycotts 5.119, 5.120, 6.192
Brazil
anti-suit injunctions 3.17
arbitrability 2.125, 2.145
bankruptcy 2.145
commencement of arbitration 4.12
due process 5.72
governing law, 3.16–3.17, 3.21–3.22
jurisdictional immunity 11.145
state and state agencies 2.37

break out rooms 4.178, 6.160
bribery and corruption
arbitrability 2.146–2.153
bilateral investment treaties (BITs) 8.36
Criminal Law Convention on Corruption, Additional Protocol to 5.88
criminal purposes, use of arbitration to further 5.87–5.90
ICC arbitration 2.148–2.150
International Law Association (ILA) 2.126
public policy 2.126
separability 2.151
UNCITRAL Rules 2.152

briefs *see also* written submissions or pleadings
conduct of an arbitration 6.201–6.202
post-hearing briefs 6.201–6.202
research, time needed for 6.202
submission of post-hearing briefs 6.201–6.202

Brussels I Regulation 5.128–5.137
anti-suit injunctions 5.134–5.135
arbitration agreements 5.128–5.137
concurrent proceedings 5.131
domicile 5.128
exclusion of arbitration 5.128–5.137
exclusive jurisdiction 5.136
Green Paper 5.137
Heidelberg Report 5.137
interim measures 5.130–5.131
jurisdiction 5.128–5.137
Recast Regulation 5.137
sole option/unilateral option clauses 2.98
validity of arbitration agreements 5.128–5.129

bundles 6.116, 6.164
burden of proof
investment arbitration 8.25
last word, which party has 6.190
national courts 5.112
oral evidence 6.198
recognition and enforcement of awards 11.58
standard of proof 6.89
UNCITRAL Rules 6.84

Index

Calvo doctrine 8.02–8.03, 11.134
Canada *see also* North American Free Trade Agreement (NAFTA)
   consolidation 2.238
   interest 9.76
   negligence 5.55
   Panama, free trade agreement with 8.11
   waiver 2.209, 4.146
'capable of settlement by arbitration', disputes which are 1.64–1.65, 2.29–2.30, 2.124–2.126, 10.50
capacity
   adjudicability 10.43–10.44
   agents, arbitration agreements concluded by 2.56
   applicable law 2.34
   arbitrability 2.40–2.41
   arbitral tribunals 2.82
   arbitration agreements 2.31–2.41
   arbitrators, replacement of 4.167–4.168
   challenges to awards 10.43–10.44
   contract law 2.31, 2.33–2.34
   corporations 2.35–2.37
   death or incapacity 4.89, 4.167–4.168
   directors 2.35
   enforcement of awards, refusal of 2.32, 11.66
   European Convention 1961 2.39
   national laws 2.34
   natural and legal persons 2.31, 2.34
   New York Convention 1958 2.32, 2.34, 11.66
   parties 2.32–2.41
   recognition of awards, refusal of 2.32, 11.66
   Rome I Regulation 2.34
   state and state agencies 2.37–2.41
   state immunity 2.39
   ultra vires 2.35
   UNCITRAL Model Law 2.32, 2.34
cartels 2.132–2.133
case management 1.235, 6.45, 6.50
case review conferences 6.64, 6.103
cause of action estoppel 9.174
Central Transnational Law Database 3.168
centres of arbitration 1.189, 4.179–4.180
certainty
   choice of law 3.112, 3.202
   defective arbitration clauses 2.197, 2.199–2.201
   fees and expenses 1.164
   national courts 4.35
   negotiate, agreements to 2.90
chair (presiding arbitrators) 4.40, 4.141, 4.190–4.191, 6.158, 9.119–9.120, 9.123–9.134
challenges *see* challenges to arbitrators; challenges to awards; challenges to jurisdiction
challenges to arbitrators 4.89–4.151
   ad hoc arbitrations 4.92, 4.102, 4.106
   appeals 4.107
   applicable law 4.92, 4.106
   arbitral institutions, rules of 4.92–4.101, 4.106
   civil law countries 4.159
   common law countries 4.146
   confidentiality of challenge decisions 4.91
   conflicts of interest 4.96, 4.104, 4.120–4.135
   connection with one of parties 4.120–4.123
   counsel, connection with 4.124–4.131
   delay 4.90, 4.107, 4.147, 4.151, 5.80
   disclose conflict of interest, failure to 4.96, 4.104
   efficiency of process, risk to 4.89
   grounds 4.92–4.104, 4.109
   ICC Rules 4.96, 4.109–4.111
   ICSID arbitration 4.98–4.100, 4.115–4.117, 4.120–4.123, 4.144
   independence and impartiality 4.79, 4.93–4.102, 4.121–4.150
   issue conflict 4.132–4.135
   LCIA Rules 4.97, 4.112–4.113
   legitimacy of process, risk to 4.89
   national laws 4.102–4.107
   nationality 4.99
   pre-judgment of issue 4.138–4.142
   presiding arbitrators 4.90, 4.141
   principal base 4.118–4.140
   procedure 4.106–4.117
   proximity 4.121
   publication of decisions 4.113
   qualities required, lack of 4.98–4.101
   reasons 4.110–4.112
   removal 4.96
   resignation 4.150–4.151
   statistics 4.89
   tactics 4.89–4.90, 4.151, 5.80
   time limits 4.114
   transparency 4.91, 4.110, 4.113
   UNCITRAL Model Law 4.107
   UNCITRAL Rules 4.94–4.95, 4.114, 4.138
   waiver 4.143–4.147
challenge to awards 10.01–10.95
   additional awards 10.19–10.20
   adjudicability 10.42–10.52
   annulment of awards 10.06, 10.14–10.16
   appeals 9.43, 10.01–10.07, 10.75–10.76
   arbitrability 10.50–10.51
   arbitral institutions, rules of 10.01–10.02, 10.07–10.17, 10.30
   arbitration agreements 10.43–10.44, 10.58
   bilateral investment treaties (BITs) 10.47
   clerical or typographical errors 10.09, 10.17
   commodity arbitrations 10.12
   confirmation of awards 10.89
   correction of awards 10.09, 10.17
   currency of awards 9.18, 9.41–9.43
   dissenting opinions 1.85
   due process 10.53–10.59
   effects of successful challenges 10.89–10.92
   enforcement of awards 9.141, 10.03–10.05, 10.47, 10.89–10.92
   EU law 10.86
   excess of powers 9.43, 10.45–10.49
   exclusions 10.28–10.33
   fair hearing, right to a 10.57–10.59, 10.95
   fraud 10.62
   Geneva Convention 1927 10.47, 10.49

Index

grounds 10.13, 10.30, 10.34–10.88, 10.89–10.92
Human Rights Act 1998 10.58
ICC Rules 10.09, 10.17, 10.29, 10.94
ICSID arbitration 10.13–10.17
incapacity 10.43–10.44
independent and impartial tribunals 10.04, 10.57
internal challenges 10.11–10.16
interpretation of awards 10.09, 10.13, 10.18
jurisdiction 5.124, 10.30, 10.36, 10.42
lex arbitri 10.02, 10.04
maritime arbitrations 10.12
methods of challenge 10.11–10.33
mistakes of fact 10.77–10.80
mistakes of law 10.36, 10.66–10.76
national courts 9.141, 10.06, 10.25, 10.36
national laws 3.110–3.127, 10.20, 10.34–10.38
New York Convention 1958 10.03, 10.05, 10.30, 10.32, 10.39
objections, failure to raise 10.30–10.32
peaceful enjoyment of possessions 10.95
place of challenge 10.25–10.27
preconditions 10.07–10.09
procedural grounds 10.36, 10.52–10.63, 10.89–10.92
procedural irregularities 10.53–10.59
pro-enforcement bias 10.03
public hearings 10.57–10.58
public policy 10.63, 10.81–10.87
purpose of challenge 10.06
recourse to courts 10.24–10.33
referral back to tribunals 10.34, 10.89
remedies, exhaustion of available 10.07
remission of awards 10.21–10.23
setting aside awards 10.05–10.06, 10.33
  grounds 10.38–10.39, 10.55, 10.62, 10.69
  remission 10.21–10.23
  state responsibility 10.93–10.95
  time limits 10.10
slip rule 10.09
state responsibility for wrongful setting aside 10.93–10.95
substantive grounds 10.36, 10.64–10.88
time limits 9.07, 10.10, 10.39
trade associations 10.11
UNCITRAL Model Law 10.03, 10.10, 10.30, 10.38–10.41, 10.45–10.46, 10.65, 10.88
UNCITRAL Rules 10.09, 10.30
validity of arbitration agreements 10.43–10.44
validity of awards 10.25
variation 10.89
waiver of challenges 10.28–10.33
challenges to jurisdiction 5.92–5.99, 7.12
  awards, challenging 5.124
  choices open to tribunal 5.115–5.117
  combined approach 5.125
  concurrent control 5.113
  grounds 5.99
  national courts 5.122–5.123, 7.12
  partial challenges 5.92–5.97
  procedural aspects 5.118
  respondents, options open to 5.119–5.126

separability or autonomy of arbitration clauses 5.103–5.106
time limit for raising challenges 5.118
UNCITRAL Model Law 7.12
changes in law 3.95, 3.120–3.127, 3.136–3.137
Channel Tunnel project 3.149–3.153, 7.46–7.50
characteristic performance, place of 3.203
Chile 8.11, 8.28, 8.52–8.53
China *see also* **CIETAC (China International Economic and Trade Arbitration Commission) Rules; Hong Kong**
  composition of tribunal 11.83
  due process 11.76
  enforcement of awards 11.83, 11.117
  illegality 2.112
  jurisdiction, objections to 2.209
  Peru, BIT with 8.32
  sovereign immunity 11.145
  UNIDROIT Principles 3.180
choice of forum 3.205–3.207, 11.26–11.31
choice of law 3.97–3.127 *see also* **Rome I Regulation on the Law Applicable to Contractual Obligations**
  arbitral tribunals 3.204, 3.211–3.220
  autonomous system of law 3.110
  certainty 3.112, 3.202
  changes in law 3.117–3.118
  Channel Tunnel project 3.149–3.150
  characteristic performance, place of 3.203
  choice of forum as choice of law 3.205–3.207
  clauses 2.84, 3.107–3.108, 3.113, 3.116, 3.141–3.155, 3.207
  close connection 3.203, 3.209–3.210
  conflict rules 3.198–3.220
  connecting factors 3.203, 3.208–3.210
  direct choice method 3.213
  drafting 3.113, 3.116
  entrenchment of clauses precluding unfair treatment 3.119
  European Convention 1961 3.215
  express choice 3.18–3.20, 3.216
  force majeure clauses 3.119
  general principles of law 3.134–3.135
  governing law 2.84
  Guiliano and Lagarde Report 3.202
  hardship clauses 3.119
  ICC Rules 3.191
  ICSID Convention 3.124
  implied or tacit choice 3.23, 3.201–3.204, 3.208, 3.216
  intention 3.202
  Jewish law 3.106
  lex arbitri 3.84–3.85
  lex fori 3.211–3.213
  lex mercatoria 3.175–3.176
  Libyan oil nationalisation arbitrations 3.140–3.155
  mandatory provisions 3.127–3.130
  model arbitration clauses 2.84
  national law 3.109–3.127, 3.140–3.155
  non-national law 3.140–3.191

choice of law (*cont.*)
  performance characteristic of contract 3.210
  place of arbitration, choice of 3.217–3.219
  procedural law, choice of foreign 3.65–3.68
  public international law 3.132–3.135, 3.140–3.155
  public policy 3.105
  revision clauses 3.119
  rules of law, choice of 3.214–3.220
  stabilisation clauses 3.120–3.127
  states or state entities, parties to contracts with 3.214
  substance, law applicable to the 3.91–3.220
  suitability 3.115–3.116
  systems of national law 3.113–3.118
  tronc commun doctrine 3.146–3.154
  UNCITRAL Model Law 3.216

CIETAC (China International Economic and Trade Arbitration Commission) Rules
  appointment of arbitrators 4.36, 4.66
  confidentiality 2.163
  establishment 1.168
  inspection of the subject matter 6.152
  internationality 1.168
  nationality 4.66
  New York Convention 1958 11.53, 11.84–11.85
  nomination of arbitrators 4.36, 4.66
  public policy 11.116
  recognition and enforcement of judgments 11.53, 11.84–11.85

civil law countries
  adaption of contracts 9.67
  arbitration clauses 1.49
  challenges to arbitrators 4.159
  clause compromissoire 1.49
  commercial, meaning of 1.35
  compromis or *compromisso* 1.51
  damages 9.45
  dissenting opinions 9.135
  documentary evidence 6.94
  due process 10.55
  duty of care of arbitrators 5.52, 5.63
  electronic documents, production of 6.105
  estoppel 9.174
  evidence 6.77–6.84
  gaps, filling 9.67
  hearings 6.169
  informal discussions 9.106
  interest 9.77
  judicially, arbitrators' duty to act 5.75
  punitive damages 9.45
  res judicata 9.174
  rectification 9.63
  specific performance 9.52
  witnesses 6.125

claims commissions and international tribunals 1.196 *see also* **Iran-US Claims Tribunal**

clarification of awards 9.186–9.194
  arbitral institutions, rules of 9.191–9.194
  clerical or typographical errors 9.188, 9.192
  ICSID arbitration 9.194
  interpretation of awards 9.191–9.194
  national laws 9.188–9.191
  opportunity to make representations 9.188
  proceedings after awards 9.186–9.199
  SCC Rules 9.191
  time limits 9.192
  UNCITRAL Rules 9.192–9.193

class or representative arbitrations 2.133, 2.135–2.137, 2.224–2.235, 10.51, 11.122

clause compromissoire 1.49

clerical or typographical errors 9.188–9.189, 9.192
  arbitration agreements 2.64
  challenges to awards 10.09, 10.17
  ICC Rules 9.33

closing submissions 6.187–6.190

collective redress 2.235

commencement of an arbitration 4.04–4.10
  ad hoc arbitrations 4.11–4.12
  appointment of arbitrators 1.71–1.76
  arbitral institutions, rules of 4.08–4.10
  ICC Rules 4.08–4.09
  ICSID arbitration 4.09
  national courts 7.09–7.12
  notice of arbitration 1.66–1.68, 4.11
  time limits 4.05–4.10
  UNCITRAL Rules 1.66–1.68

commercial contracts 8.44

commercial, meaning of 1.35–1.38
  civil law countries 1.35
  commercial reservation 1.37, 11.46–11.50
  Geneva Protocol 1923 1.36
  New York Convention 1958 1.37
  treaties and conventions 1.240
  UNCITRAL Model Law 1.38

commercial pressures on enforcement 11.08–11.10

commercial relationships reservation 1.37, 11.42, 11.46–11.50

commodity arbitrations *see also* **oil**
  challenges to awards 10.12
  inspection 6.146
  review of awards 9.195
  umpires or referees 2.77

common law countries
  challenges to arbitrators 4.146
  dispute requirement 1.63
  dissenting opinions 9.131, 9.135–9.136
  duty of care of arbitrators 5.54–5.55, 5.64
  electronic documents, production of 6.106
  estoppel 9.174
  evidence 6.77–6.80
  existing and future disputes 1.63
  experts 6.144
  hearings 6.169, 6.190
  interest 9.76
  judges 6.77
  res judicata 9.174
  restitution 9.53
  specific performance 9.52
  witnesses 6.176

Index

companies
  alter egos 2.44, 11.104
  arbitrability 2.117, 2.157–2.159, 11.104
  arbitration agreements 2.35–2.36
  bilateral investment treaties (BITs), jurisdictional issues and 8.26
  capacity 2.35–2.37
  corporate document retention policy, destruction in line with 6.115
  corporate governance 2.157–2.159, 3.129, 11.103
  directors 2.32, 2.35, 4.120–4.122, 9.185, 11.23
  enforcement of awards 11.23
  group of companies doctrine 1.115, 2.42–2.51
  international arbitration, characteristics of 1.22
  succession 2.58
  ultra vires 2.35
  unfair prejudice claims in shareholder claims 2.159
  veil, piercing the corporate 1.115, 2.51
compensation *see also* damages
  bilateral investment treaties (BITs) 8.79–8.96, 8.141–8.163
  causation 8.143–8.144, 8.159
  currency 9.41–9.43
  customary international law 8.141, 8.157
  expropriation 8.79–8.96, 8.146–8.158, 8.162
    characterisation, purpose of measures not affecting 8.93–8.95
    customary international law 8.157
    direct expropriation 8.81
    Hull formula 8.146
    indirect expropriation 8.82–8.86
    lawful expropriation 8.156–8.158
    prompt, adequate, and effective compensation 8.79–8.80
    undertakings and assurances, acts contrary to 8.87–8.92
    unlawful expropriation 8.156–8.158
  fair and equitable treatment 8.159–8.162
  fair market value 8.146, 8.162
  Hull formula 8.146
  Libyan oil nationalisation arbitrations 3.120, 3.140
  measure of compensation 8.146–8.162
  prompt, adequate, and effective compensation 8.79–8.80
  restitution 9.54–9.57
competence/competence 5.105–5.109
competition/antitrust law
  arbitrability 2.133–2.138, 10.51
  Commission 2.133
  EU law 2.133, 2.137–2.138, 11.120–11.121
  mandatory provisions 3.128–3.130
  monopolies and cartels 2.132–2.133
  national laws 2.133
  public policy 2.137–2.138, 3.130, 11.120–11.122
  restraint of trade 2.134
compound interest 9.76–9.89
compromis or *compromisso* 1.51
compromises *see* settlements
conciliation 1.138

concurrent hearings 2.236–2.237, 2.241–2.242
concurring and separate opinions 9.128, 9.134
conduct of an arbitration 1.06–1.12, 6.01–6.204 *see also* evidence; hearings
  ad hoc arbitrations, rules of 6.06
  after hearings, procedure 6.200–6.204
  agreements on procedure 6.04
  applicable law 1.10
  arbitral institutions, rules of 6.06, 6.19–6.21
  arbitral tribunal, assembling the 6.23
  arbitration agreements 2.99–2.100
  autonomy of parties 1.08, 6.07–6.18
  awards, procedural grounds for challenging 10.52
  briefs, submission of post-hearing 6.201–6.202
  challenges to awards 10.53–10.59
  consent 6.06
  control of process 1.06–1.08, 6.04–6.06
  costs 6.23
  expedited procedures 6.26–6.40
  experienced arbitrators and counsel, practices of 6.19
  fast track arbitration 1.07, 6.32–6.40
  flexibility 1.79, 6.01
  freedom of parties 6.02, 6.07
  ICC Rules 1.78
  institutional arbitration 1.147–1.150, 1.162, 1.165
  international law 1.08, 1.12
  international practice 6.19–6.21
  irregularities 10.53–10.59
  lex arbitri 1.09–1.10, 1.78, 3.49
  litigation, arbitration distinguished from 6.22
  meetings 6.41–6.50
  national laws 1.08–1.10, 1.12
  parties
    autonomy 1.08, 6.07–6.18
    control of process 1.06–1.08, 6.04–6.06
    masters of proceedings, as 1.58
  post-hearing briefs 6.201–6.202
  preliminary steps 6.41–6.63
  Procedural Order No 1 6.06, 6.52
  rules of procedure 6.01, 6.06
  simplified procedures 6.32–6.33, 9.165
  structure of an arbitration 6.22–6.25
  tactics 9.96
  treaties and conventions 1.225, 6.19–6.21
  UNCITRAL Model Law 3.45, 6.20–6.21
  UNCITRAL Notes on Organizing Arbitral Proceedings 3.230, 6.51, 6.179, App 1
  UNCITRAL Rules 1.78
  written submissions or pleadings 6.65–6.74
conferencing
  experts 6.181–6.186
  hearings 6.181–6.186
  pre-hearing conferences 6.163–6.165
  video conferencing, by 6.41
  witnesses 6.180
confidentiality 2.161–2.196
  advantages of arbitration 1.105, 2.161
  adverse publicity 1.105
  advisors 2.194
  agreements 2.158, 2.196

673

Index

confidentiality (*cont.*)
   arbitral institutions, rules of 2.163, 2.190–2.195
   arbitration agreements 2.161–2.196
   awards 2.177–2.182, 2.190, 9.108
   challenges to arbitrators 4.91
   class arbitration 2.232
   classical position 2.165–2.169
   confidentiality agreements 2.161, 2.196
   current trend 2.170–2.176
   definition 2.191
   deliberation 9.108
   disclosure, standards of 2.166–2.169
   dissenting opinions 9.108
   hearings 2.160
   ICC Rules 2.160, 2.163, 2.192
   ICSID Rules 2.184–2.185, 2.188, 2.190
   implied duty 2.162–2.167, 2.175, 2.168–2.169
   International Centre for Dispute Resolution (ICDR) Rules 2.179
   investor-state arbitrations 2.183–2.189
   LCIA arbitration 2.191
   NAFTA (North American Free Trade Agreement) 2.183, 2.185–2.190
   privacy 1.105, 2.163–2.164, 2.166
   public interest 2.165, 2.168, 2.170, 2.183, 2.190
   publication of awards 2.179, 2.190, 9.199, 9.201
   revision to tribunal rules 2.190–2.195
   trade secrets 1.105, 2.131, 2.191–2.193
   transparency 2.188–2.189
   UNCITRAL Rules 2.164
   WIPO Arbitration Rules 2.193–2.195
conflict of interests
   challenges to arbitrators 4.96, 4.104, 4.120–4.135
   connection with one of parties 4.120–4.123
   counsel, arbitrators' connection with 4.124–4.131
   disclosure 4.96, 4.104
   ethical duties of arbitrators 5.80
   IBA Guidelines 4.82, 4.84–4.88, 4.148, 5.80, App K
   independence and impartiality of arbitrators 4.82, 4.84–4.88, 4.121–4.137, 4.148
   waiver of objections 4.148
conflict of laws 3.198–3.220
   applicable law 3.198–3.220
   arbitral institutions, rules of 3.214–3.217
   bilateral investment treaties (BITs) 8.74
   choice of law 3.198–3.220
   connecting factors 3.208–3.210
   European Convention 1961 3.215
   governing law 3.33
   lex fori 3.211–3.213
   national laws 3.214–3.220
   Rome I Regulation 3.210
   stabilisation clauses 3.124
   time limits 4.07
   treaties and conventions 3.214–3.217
   UNCITRAL Model Law 3.216
conflicting awards 1.116–1.117, 2.221, 11.61, 11.99
connecting factors
   choice of law 3.203, 3.209–3.210
   close connection 2.64, 2.84, 3.19, 3.24, 3.203, 3.209–3.210
   conflict of laws 3.208–3.210
connection of arbitrators with one of parties
   challenges to arbitrators 4.120–4.123
   independence and impartiality 4.121–4.122
   materiality 4.121
   proximity 4.121
consent
   amiable compositeurs, arbitrators as 3.196
   arbitration agreements 1.53–1.54, 1.115, 2.01, 2.21, 2.42
   bilateral investment treaties (BITs) 8.45–8.53
   class arbitration 2.232
   conduct of an arbitration 6.06
   consent awards or agreed terms awards 9.34–9.37
   consolidation 2.221, 2.242–2.247
   deemed or assumed consent 1.115
   disadvantages of arbitration 1.108
   equity and good conscience 3.196
   group of companies doctrine 1.115, 2.46, 2.50
   ICSID arbitration 8.08
   implied consent 1.59, 2.21
   joinder and intervention 2.59
   multiparty arbitrations 1.113
   non-signatories to arbitration agreements 1.115
   publication of awards 9.199
   states, of 8.08
   third parties 2.42
   trustees in bankruptcy, consent of 2.146
   validity of arbitration agreements 1.53
   veil, piercing the corporate 1.115
consent awards or agreed terms awards 9.34–9.39
   arbitrability 9.36
   criminal purposes, use of arbitration to further 5.82, 5.85
   fees and expenses 9.37
   ICC Rules 9.37
   national law 9.37
   settlement agreements 9.34–9.38
   signatures 9.35
   UNCITRAL Model Law 9.37
conservatory measures *see* **interim measures**
Consolato des Mare 3.157–3.158
consolidation
   arbitral institutions, rules of 2.245–2.247
   arbitration agreements 2.238–2.247
   arbitration clauses 2.243–2.244
   concurrent hearings 2.241–2.242
   consent 2.221, 2.242–2.247
   consistent decisions 2.240
   court-order consolidation 2.238–2.242
   Departmental Advisory Committee 2.241–2.242
   disadvantages of arbitration 1.111
   enforcement of awards 2.240, 2.247
   ICC arbitration 2.245
   ICC Commission on International Arbitration 2.243–2.244
   LMAA Rules 2.242
   multiparty arbitrations 2.221, 2.238–2.247

Index

New York Convention 1958 2.240
recognition of awards 2.240, 2.247
Swiss Rules 2.246
UNCITRAL Model Law 2.239, 2.245
UNCITRAL Rules 2.245
consortia 2.214
construction contracts
   applicable law 3.93
   experts 6.133
   inspection 3.59–3.60, 6.146
   multiparty arbitrations 2.218–2.222
   seat theory (*locus arbitri*) 3.59–3.60
consumer contracts 2.127
consumer protection 1.22, 3.43
contempt of court 5.42
contents of awards
   arbitral institutions, incorporation of rules of 9.152
   arbitration agreements 9.152
   dispositive, awards must be 9.154
   effective determination of issues 9.154–9.156
   illegality 9.156
   imperative tone, awards must be in 9.154
   incorporation of rules 9.152
   public policy 9.156
   reasons 9.159–9.160
   unambiguous, awards must be 9.153
contract law
   defined legal relationship requirement 2.25–2.27
   duty of care of arbitrators 5.50–5.52, 5.63
   governing law 3.12–3.14
   Principles of European Contract Law (PECL) 3.168
   substantive law of contract 3.39
   time limits 4.05–4.06
   UNIDROIT Principles 3.160, 3.168, 3.171–3.173, 3.178–3.184
contracts and filling gaps, adaptation of *see* adaptation of contracts and filling gaps
control of process
   arbitral tribunal, shift to 5.113–5.114, 6.04–6.06
   arbitrators 6.61–6.63
   conduct of an arbitration 6.04–6.06
   court control 5.112–5.117, 7.62
   jurisdiction 5.113–5.114
   parties 5.113–5.114, 6.04–6.06
   state participation 1.202–1.203
conventions *see* treaties and conventions
cooling off 8.45, 8.47, 8.50
copyright 2.132
core bundles 6.116
corporate governance
   arbitrability 2.157–2.159, 11.103
   mandatory law 3.129
   unfair prejudice claims in shareholder claims 2.159
corporations *see* companies
correction of awards
   challenges to awards 10.09, 10.17–10.24
   clarification of awards 9.188–9.189, 9.192, 9.194
   time limits 10.10

corruption *see* bribery and corruption
costs
   accommodation 1.123, 6.187, 9.89
   administrative fees of arbitral institutions 1.123–1.124, 9.87, 9.88–9.89
   administrative secretaries 4.200–4.201
   arbitral institutions, rules of 9.97
   arbitration, costs of the 9.87, 9.89
   assessment of costs 9.93–9.98
   bilateral investment treaties (BITs) 8.168–8.169
   conduct of an arbitration 6.23
   costs of arbitration 9.88–9.89
   criteria 9.96–9.98
   defective arbitration clauses 2.203
   deposits 9.89
   disadvantages of arbitration 1.122–1.125
   discretion 9.99
   evidence 6.203–6.204
   experts 9.90
   fees and expenses 1.123–1.124, 1.154, 1.159, 9.87, 9.88–9.92, 9.97
   fixed fees 1.154
   hearings 6.23, 6.160, 6.187
   hidden costs 9.91–9.93
   hourly rates 9.94, 9.97
   ICC Rules 9.87, 9.93
   ICDR Rules 9.87
   ICSID 8.169
   indirect costs 9.91–9.92
   institutional arbitrations 1.154, 1.159, 1.181, 9.86–9.95
   Iran-US Claims Tribunal 9.98
   LCIA Rules 1.175, 9.87, 9.93
   legal costs 9.87, 9.90–9.93, 9.96–9.97
   lex arbitri 9.99–9.100
   litigation, compared with 1.124–1.125
   losing parties 9.96, 9.137
   management and executive time 9.91
   national laws 9.99–9.100
   one-stop shopping 1.125
   partial awards 9.95
   parties, costs of 9.87, 9.90–9.98
   preparation of case 9.90
   procedural tactics 9.96
   reasonableness 9.97
   rooms for meetings and hearings, hire of 1.123
   sanctions 1.175, 1.181
   SCC Rules 9.87
   security for costs 5.35–5.37
   SIAC Rules 9.87
   time spent, records of 9.97
   transcripts 9.89
   travel expenses 9.87, 9.88, 9.90, 9.92
   tribunal, costs of the 9.87, 9.88
   UNCITRAL Rules 8.169, 9.87, 9.89, 9.92–9.93, 9.98
   witnesses 9.87, 9.88, 9.90, 9.92
Council for Mutual Economic Assistance (CMEA) 11.131–11.132
counsel *see* counsel, connection with; lawyers

counsel, connection with 4.124–4.131
　chambers, members of same 4.128–4.130
　conflicts of interest 4.124–4.131
　disclosure 4.124–4.125
　divided legal profession in England 4.127–4.130
　financial relationships 4.124
　independence and impartiality 4.124–4.131
　International Bar Association (IBA)
　　independence and impartiality 4.129–4.131
　　Rules of Party Representation 4.131
　repeat appointments 4.124–4.126
counterclaims
　compound interest 9.76
　default claims 2.85
　fees and expenses 4.205
　jurisdiction 5.92–5.95, 5.118
　LCIA Rules 6.67
　pre-hearing conferences 6.166
　waiver 2.209
　written pleadings 6.70
crime
　arbitrability 2.130, 2.147–2.154
　bribery and corruption 2.147–2.154, 5.87–5.90
　Criminal Law Convention on Corruption,
　　Additional Protocol to 5.88
　fraud 2.154, 8.36, 10.62
　money laundering 5.82–5.85
　use of arbitration to further criminal
　　purposes 5.82–5.91
cross-examination
　experts 6.134, 6.138, 6.185
　witnesses 6.129, 6.177–6.178
culture
　adverse inferences 6.113
　appointment of arbitrators 4.14, 4.30, 4.76
　disclosure 4.85, 5.81, 6.93
　judicially, duty to act 5.75
　preliminary meetings 6.41
　witnesses 6.123, 6.125
currency
　bilateral investment treaties (BITs) 8.130–8.132
　challenges to awards 9.18, 9.41–9.43
　compensation 9.41–9.43
　control 3.178, 8.130–8.133
　expropriation 8.146
　fees and expenses 2.203
　free flow of currency 3.116
　interest 9.74
customary law
　applicable law 3.200
　bilateral investment treaties (BITs) 8.67, 8.141
　breach 8.01
　codification 3.165
　compensation 8.141
　dissenting opinions 9.131
　expropriation 8.67, 8.157
　fair and equitable treatment 8.106, 8.109–8.111
　ILC Draft Articles on State Responsibility 8.167
　investment arbitration 1.195, 8.01, 8.67,
　　8.109–8.112, 8.141, 8.157, 8.167
　language 2.86

　law of the sea 3.158
　lex mercatoria 3.164–3.165
　sources of public international law 3.134
　standard form contracts 3.184
　uniform rules 3.184

damages 9.44–9.51 *see also* **compensation**
　applicable law 9.50
　arbitration agreements 1.55, 9.45, 9.50
　bilateral investment treaties (BITs) 8.163,
　　8.164–8.165
　civil law countries 9.45
　declaratory relief 9.60–9.62
　delay 5.68
　duty of care of arbitrators 5.53
　enforcement 9.49–9.51
　lex arbitri 9.50
　moral damages 8.164–8.165
　New York Convention 1958 9.49
　punitive damages 9.44–9.51
　quantum and liability, bifurcation of 6.54–6.59,
　　9.26–9.27
　submission agreements 9.48
death or incapacity of arbitrators 4.89, 4.167–4.168
decision-making and decisions by tribunals
　awards 9.100–9.138
　bargaining process 9.117–9.118
　deliberation 9.100–9.112
　dissenting opinions 1.84–1.86, 9.108, 9.129–9.138
　exchange of views 9.109–9.110
　majority voting 9.117–9.127
　mediation and conciliation, arbitration
　　distinguished from 1.82
　number of arbitrators 1.84
　psychology of tribunal 9.113–9.116
　reaching decisions, method of 1.83
　rogue decisions or errors 4.26
　separate and concurring opinions 9.128, 9.134
　settlements 1.80–1.82, 1.93
　sole arbitrators 1.83
　UNCITRAL Rules 1.80
declaratory relief 5.122, 9.60–9.62
default awards 2.85, 6.196, 9.03, 9.30–9.32
default hearings 6.191–6.199
defective arbitration clauses 2.76, 2.85,
　2.197–2.203
　appointment of arbitrators 4.44
　costs 2.203
　delay 2.211
　exchange control 2.203
　ICC arbitration 2.199–2.201
　inconsistency 2.197, 2.198
　inoperability 2.197, 2.202–2.203
　model arbitration clauses 2.66
　New York Convention 1958 2.202
　pathological arbitration clauses 2.201
　payments, lack of ability to make 2.203
　stay of proceedings 2.197
　Stockholm Chamber of Commerce 2.199
　striking out 2.204
　uncertainty 2.197, 2.199–2.201

Index

want of prosecution 2.205
waiver 2.204–2.211
defined legal relationship requirement 2.25–2.28
definition of arbitration 1.04–1.05
delay
  appointment of arbitrators 4.02, 4.44
  arbitral tribunal, constitution of 1.126
  arbitrators 1.127, 4.02, 4.44, 4.90, 4.107, 4.147, 4.151, 5.66–5.68, 5.80
  availability, confirmation of arbitrator's 1.127, 4.60
  awards 1.126–1.127, 11.01
  challenges to arbitrators 4.90, 4.107, 4.147, 4.151, 5.80
  damages 5.68
  defective arbitration clauses 2.211
  disadvantages of arbitration 1.126–1.127
  evidence 6.203
  ex parte hearings 6.194
  expedited hearings 6.27, 6.40
  ICC arbitration 1.156, 5.69
  inordinate and inexcusable delay 2.211
  institutional arbitrations 1.155–1.156
  International Bar Association (IBA) 5.81
  interpreters 4.183
  jurisdiction 5.114
  national courts 5.114
  partial and interim awards 9.24
  refusal to participate 6.194
  removal of arbitrators 5.67
  rules 5.69
  sanctions 5.67–5.68
  UNCITRAL Model Law 5.67
  waiver 2.211
  written submissions or pleadings 6.73
deliberation
  awards 9.100–9.112
  decision-making 9.100–9.112
  different backgrounds of arbitrators 9.102–9.103
  dissenting opinions 9.129–9.138
  exchange of views 4.192, 9.106, 9.109–9.110
  exclusion of arbitrator 9.107
  ICSID arbitration 9.109
  Iran-US Claims Tribunal 9.103, 9.108, 9.113, 9.134
  judicial decision-making 9.101–9.102
  secrecy or confidentiality 9.108
delict or tort 2.25–2.27, 2.64–2.65 *see also* **duty of care of arbitrators**
delocalisation or denationalisation
  ad hoc arbitrations 3.79
  arbitral institutions, rules of 3.79
  arbitration agreements 1.53, 2.01
  definition 3.76
  enforcement of awards, place of 3.81
  'floating' arbitrations 3.76
  'floating' awards 3.76
  governing law 3.73–3.83
  ICSID arbitration 1.188
  injunctions 3.90
  lex arbitri 3.73–3.82, 3.88–3.90
  mistake of law 10.69

  national laws 1.51
  New York Convention 1958 3.81
  procedural directions 3.79
  UNCITRAL Model Law 3.74, 3.81
  universal *lex arbitri* 3.73–3.74
denationalisation *see* **delocalisation or denationalisation**
deposit of awards 9.171–9.172
deposits 4.221–4.222, 6.66, 9.89
devices and facades 2.51
diplomatic immunity 11.155
diplomatic protection 1.186, 8.04–8.09
diplomatic services 11.08, 11.152
directions and orders, awards distinguished from 9.08
directors 2.35, 4.120–4.122, 9.185, 11.23
disadvantages of arbitration 1.108–1.134 *see also* **advantages of arbitration**
  ad hoc arbitrations 1.145
  arbitrators, limits on powers of 1.104
  conflicting awards 1.116–1.117
  consent 1.108
  consolidation 1.111
  costs 1.122–1.125
  delay 1.126–1.127
  institutional arbitrations 1.154–1.156
  judicialisation 1.118–1.122
  multiparty arbitrations, joinder, and consolidation 1.109–1.113
  non-signatories to arbitration agreements, problem of 1.114–1.115
  third parties 1.114–1.115
disclosure 7.39–7.44
  confidentiality 2.171–2.174
  conflicts of interests 4.96, 4.104
  continuing duty 4.80
  counsel, connection with 4.124–4.125
  culture 4.85, 5.81, 6.93
  dispensing, with 1.07
  disqualification, grounds for 4.79–4.88
  experienced arbitrators and counsel, practice of 1.238
  IBA Evidence Rules 1.238
  IBA Guidelines on Conflicts of Interest 4.82, 4.84–4.88
  independence and impartiality of arbitrators 4.79–4.88, 4.105
  judicialisation 1.119–1.120
  standards 2.166–2.174
  third parties 7.22–7.23
discovery 1.119–1.120, 6.94, 7.39–7.40, 7.43–7.44
discrimination 4.62, 8.86, 8.103, 8.118–8.123
dispute requirement
  arbitrability 1.64–1.65
  common law countries 1.63
  documentary evidence 6.99–6.102, 6.118
  existing and future disputes 1.62–1.63, 2.05
  Geneva Protocol 1923 1.62
  New York Convention 1958 1.61–1.62
  open and shut cases 1.60–1.61
  summary judgments 1.60–1.61

Index

disqualification of arbitrators, disclosure of
  grounds for 4.79–4.88
disruption 4.151, 6.195, 9.93
dissenting opinions 9.107–9.108, 9.111, 9.129–9.138
  advantages 1.85
  appeals 9.136
  challenges to awards, as platform for 1.85
  civil law countries 9.135
  common law countries 9.131, 9.135–9.136
  confidentiality 9.163
  decision-making 1.84–1.86, 9.129–9.138
  deliberations 9.129–9.138
  enforcement of awards 9.137
  freedom of expression 1.85
  ICC Rules 9.133
  ICSID arbitration 9.132
  independence and impartiality 1.86, 9.138
  investment arbitration 1.86
  Iran-US Claims Tribunal 9.134
  LCIA Rules 9.132
  majority voting 9.137
  national laws 9.131
  Netherlands 9.131
  precedent 9.136
  sign awards, refusal to 9.130
  states, arbitration between 9.129
  validity of awards 9.137
  when and how opinions should be
    given 9.135–9.138
documentary evidence 6.89–6.119
  adverse inferences 6.112–6.115
  'agreed', use of word 6.117
  arbitrators, powers of 5.18–5.19
  authenticity 6.118
  best evidence rule 6.92
  civil law countries 6.94
  core bundle 6.116
  corporate document retention policy, destruction
    in line with 6.115
  destroyed documents 6.115
  discovery 6.94
  disputes 6.99–6.102, 6.118
  documents on which parties rely 6.92
  early stage, production of documents at
    an 6.92, 6.97
  electronic documents, production of 6.104–6.110
  ex parte hearings 6.198
  experts 6.118
  forensic experts 6.118
  IBA Evidence Rules 6.95–6.103, 6.113
  language 6.119
  limitations 6.97–6.99
  meetings 6.100–6.102
  numbering 6.116
  objections 6.112
  presentation 6.116–6.118
  Redfern Schedule 1.238, 1.243, 6.100–6.102
  relevance and materiality 6.97–6.98
  subpoenas 5.19
  third parties, documents in possession
    of 6.111–6.112

time line flow chart 6.92
translations 6.119
unfavourable documents 6.94–6.95
witnesses 6.111–6.115
written submissions, production after delivery
    of 6.92
documents only arbitration 4.172, 6.155
domestic arbitration
  consumer protection 1.22
  documents only arbitration 6.155
  enforcement of awards 11.18, 11.51, 11.122
  ethics 5.79
  foreign and domestic awards, distinction
    between 9.29, 11.109
  independence and impartiality 4.75
  international arbitration, characteristics
    of 1.19–1.26, 3.44
  lex arbitri 3.44
  national courts 1.130
  private individuals 1.22
domestic courts *see* national courts
domestic law *see* national laws
Dominican Republic and Central America-United
    States Free Trade Agreement
    (DR-CAFTA) 8.11
double exequatur 9.171, 11.87
drafting
  appointment of arbitrators 4.22
  arbitration agreements 2.65–2.100, 2.244, 3.10,
    3.87, 4.22
  arbitration clauses 1.49, 2.73–2.100, 3.113, 4.22
  awards 4.184–4.185, 6.188, 9.111
  choice of law 3.113, 3.116
  jurisdiction 2.65–2.70
  model arbitration clauses 2.03, 2.73–2.100
  seat theory 3.87
  stabilisation clauses 3.124
  submission agreements 2.120–2.123
  UNCITRAL Model Law 1.228
Dubai International Arbitration Centre
    (DIAC) 6.31
due diligence 5.51, 5.67, 8.115
due process *see also* fair hearings
  appointment of arbitrators, proper notice
    of 11.63, 11.71–11.72
  awards 1.204, 10.53–10.59, 10.88
  challenges to awards 10.53–10.56, 10.88
  civil law countries 10.55
  equality of treatment 10.53
  minimum standards 10.53–10.54
  national courts 10.56
  national laws 10.54–10.55
  procedural irregularity 10.53–10.56
  refusal of recognition and
    enforcement 11.71–11.76
duty of care of arbitrators 5.48–5.66
  arbitral institution, liability of 5.62–5.63
  civil law countries 5.52, 5.63
  common law countries 5.54–5.55, 5.64
  contract law 5.50–5.52, 5.63
  damages 5.53

Index

exclusion of liability 5.55, 5.66
IBA Rules of Ethics 5.60
ICC Rules 5.55, 5.63
immunity 5.50, 5.54–5.66
indemnities for personal liability 5.61
LCIA Rules 5.55
negligence 5.48, 5.53, 5.55
personal liability 5.61
professional advisors 5.48–5.49
professional liability insurance 5.61
skill and care 5.48
uniformity 5.59

early or summary determinations 6.38–6.40
EC law *see* **EU law**
economic equilibrium clauses 3.124–3.127
Ecuador
bilateral investment treaties (BITs) 8.12, 8.46, 8.118, 8.129–8.130
ICSID Convention 8.12, 11.128
interim measures 9.58
pre-judgment 4.142
United States, BIT with 8.118, 8.129–8.130
education and training of arbitrators 4.68–4.71
Egypt-UK BIT 8.124
electronic aids 4.177
electronic communications
applicable law 3.96
arbitration agreements 1.45, 1.46–1.48, 2.13, 2.16, 2.18–2.23
definition 1.222
domain name disputes 1.189
Internet, publication of awards on 2.190, 9.200
LCIA Rules 1.173
New York Convention 1958 1.45
publication of awards 9.200
Revised UNCITRAL Model Law 1.222
writing 1.47, 1.222, 2.13, 2.16, 2.18–2.23
electronic documents, production of 6.104–6.110
civil law countries 6.105
common law countries 6.101
discretion of tribunal 6.108
documentary evidence 6.104–6.111
electronically stored information (ESI) 6.104–6.105, 6.109
IBA Evidence Rules 6.109
litigation 6.104–6.106
relevance and materiality 6.110
rules 6.109
Sedona Principles 6.107
emergencies *see* **emergency arbitrators; urgent action**
emergency arbitrators 4.17–4.21
appointment 1.177, 4.03, 4.17–4.21
arbitral institutions, rules of 4.17–4.20
ex parte hearings 6.28
ex parte relief 4.19
expedited procedure 6.28
ICC Rules 1.177, 4.17, 4.20–4.21
ICDR Rules 4.17
interim relief 4.19, 4.21, 7.17, 7.28–7.29

LCIA Rules 1.177, 4.17
SCC Rules 4.17
SIAC Rules 4.17
Swiss Rules 4.17
Energy Charter Treaty (ECT) 8.11, 8.21, 8.75
enforcement of arbitration agreements 1.55–1.57
Geneva Protocol 1923 1.57
history 1.17
indirect enforcement 1.56
international effect 1.57
jurisdiction 5.122
national courts 1.56, 7.10
national laws 1.08
New York Convention 1958 1.57, 2.07, 7.10
treaties and conventions 1.205
UNCITRAL Model Law 7.10
validity of arbitration agreements 2.23–2.24
writing 2.23
enforcement of awards *see also* **New York Convention on Recognition and Enforcement of Foreign Arbitral Awards 1958, enforcement under; refusal of recognition and enforcement of awards**
advantages of arbitration 1.97–1.98, 1.101–1.102
appeals 11.04
Arab League Investment Agreement 11.139
arbitral institutions, rules of 11.01
arbitration agreements 1.40
arbitrators' duty to render enforceable awards 11.11
assets 11.13, 11.24–11.29, 11.34
attachment of bank accounts 11.35
best endeavours 2.153
bi-polar arbitrations 2.153
challenges 9.141, 10.03–10.05, 10.47, 10.89–10.92
choice of forum 11.24–11.29
CIETAC Rules 11.53
commercial and other pressures 11.08–11.10
companies 11.23
confidentiality 2.177
consolidation 2.240
court proceedings, by 11.12–11.16
delay 11.01
delocalisation or denationalisation 3.76
domestic awards 1.31
ex parte hearings 6.192
finality of awards 1.101, 11.01
foreign or international awards 11.18
form of awards 9.139–9.140
forum shopping 11.16, 11.28–11.29
functus officio, tribunal as 11.02
general principles 11.17–11.18
Geneva Convention 1927 1.210
Geneva Protocol 1923 1.208–1.209
Gulf Co-operation Council (GCC) Convention 11.138
ICC Rules 1.88, 9.14
implied terms 11.01
interest 9.80–9.84
investment agreements 11.139
jurisdiction 9.15

679

enforcement of awards (*cont.*)
  language 9.150, 11.32, 11.54
  lex mercatoria 3.175–3.176
  local formalities 11.32
  losing parties 1.89, 11.05
  methods of enforcement 11.30–11.32
  Middle Eastern conventions 11.138–11.139
  Montevideo Convention 1899 1.207
  Moscow Convention 1972 11.121–11.133
  national courts 1.91–1.93, 1.201, 11.35, 11.37
  national laws 1.198, 11.35
  North African Conventions 11.138–11.139
  Organization of Islamic Cooperation (OIC) Agreement 11.139
  Panama Convention 1975 11.134–11.137
  performance of awards 11.07–11.16
  place of enforcement 11.24–11.29
  pro-enforcement bias 10.03
  public policy 9.16, 11.34–11.35, 11.61, 11.64, 11.105–11.122
  recognition, difference between enforcement and 11.19–11.23
  refusal, consequences of 11.34
  regional conventions 11.36, 11.39, 11.130–11.140
  regional investment agreements 11.139
  rendering internationally enforceable awards 9.14
  Riyadh Arab Agreement on Judicial Cooperation 11.138
  sanctions 11.22–11.23
  seat of arbitrations, enforcement in 11.18
  sequestration 11.35
  setting aside awards 10.89–10.92
  settlements 11.05
  shield and sword 11.23
  state immunity 11.27, 11.141–11.155
  statistics 11.02
  time limits 11.33
  title to assets, getting 11.25–11.29, 11.34
  treaties and conventions 1.91, 1.205, 11.30, 11.35–11.140
  validity of arbitration agreements 1.40
  writing 1.44
equality of treatment
  ad hoc arbitrations 1.140
  arbitrators, powers of 5.15
  autonomy of the parties 6.10–6.12, 6.16
  bilateral investment treaties (BITs), fair and equitable treatment under 8.96–8.103
  due process 10.53
  inspection 6.149
  judicially, arbitrators' duty to act 5.71
  lex arbitri 1.140, 3.48
  multiparty arbitrations 2.214
  New York Convention 1958 6.10, 11.73
  refusal of recognition and enforcement 11.73
  UNCITRAL Model Law 6.10, 6.16
  UNCITRAL Rules 6.16
equity and good conscience 3.192–3.197
  amiable compositeurs, arbitrators deciding as 3.192, 3.194–3.196

  applicable law 3.192–3.197
  choice of law 3.109
  consent of parties 3.195
  equity clauses 3.192–3.197
  interpretation 3.192–3.193
  merits, deciding cases on the 3.193
  non-national law 3.192–3.197
  rules of law, application of relevant 3.193
errors *see also* **mistake of fact; mistake of law**
  clarification of awards 9.188–9.189, 9.192, 9.194
  clerical or typographical errors 2.64, 9.53, 9.188–9.189, 9.192, 10.09, 10.17
  correction of awards 9.188–9.189, 9.192, 9.194
  number of arbitrators 4.26, 4.31
  rectification 9.63–9.64
  rogue decisions or errors 4.26
  sole arbitrators 4.26
Estisna form, financial transactions in 3.186
estoppel
  arbitration agreements 2.53
  cause of action estoppel 9.174
  issue estoppel 9.174, 9.180, 9.185, 11.20
  refusal of enforcement or recognition 11.83, 11.85
  third parties 2.36, 2.53
ethical duties 5.79–5.90 *see also* **independence and impartiality of arbitrators**
  applicable duties 3.221–3.228
  arbitrators, duties of 5.56–5.90
  codes of conduct 5.79
  deontology of arbitrators 5.79
  International Bar Association (IBA) Guidelines on Conflicts of Interest 5.80
  Rules of Ethics 5.60, 5.80
  lawyers 3.221–3.228, 5.79–5.80, 6.124
  time and attention to case, inability to give 5.79
  witnesses 6.123–6.124
EU law
  bilateral investment treaties (BITs) 8.74–8.75
  Brussels I Regulation 5.128–5.137
  challenges to awards 10.86
  class arbitration 2.235
  collective redress, consultation on 2.235
  competition law 2.133, 2.137–2.138
  Energy Charter Treaty (ECT) 8.75
  Insolvency Regulation 2.143
  money laundering 5.83–5.84
  public policy 10.86
  supremacy of EU law 8.75
European Convention 1961
  applicable law 3.215
  arbitration agreements 1.29
  capacity 2.36
  choice of law 3.216
  nationality 1.29
  reasons 9.160
  states, capacity of 2.39
European Convention on Human Rights *see* **particular rights (eg fair hearings)**
European Union *see* **EU law**

evidence 6.75–6.154 *see also* documentary evidence; experts; witnesses
  admissibility 6.81–6.83
  assistance with evidence 7.06
  best evidence rule 6.92
  burden of proof 6.84, 6.89
  case review conferences 6.103
  categories of evidence 6.89–6.90
  civil law countries 6.77–6.83
  collection of evidence 6.75–6.154
  common law countries 6.77–6.83
  costs 6.203–6.204
  delay 6.203
  destruction of evidence 7.37
  ex parte hearings 6.196, 6.198
  fact-finding 6.75–6.76
  freezing orders 7.38
  fresh evidence 6.203–6.204
  gathering evidence 6.75–6.155
  hearsay 6.129
  'hybrid' tribunals 6.83
  injunctions 7.38
  inspection of subject matter of disputes 6.146–6.154
  interim measures 7.33, 7.37–7.38
  judges 6.77
  jury trials 6.81, 6.85
  law, issues of 6.75
  national courts 7.06, 7.33, 7.37–7.38
  new evidence, introduction of 6.203–6.204
  preservation of evidence 7.37–7.38
  seat, taking evidence outside the 6.130–6.133
  standard of proof 6.85–6.88
  statistics 6.75
  trade usages 3.183
  urgent action 7.38
  weight of evidence 6.90
  written submissions 6.91
ex aequo et bono decisions 1.139, 3.190, 3.196
ex parte hearings 6.193–6.199
  awards
    challenges 6.192, 6.194
    default judgments, akin to 6.196
    enforcement 6.192
    issue of 6.192
    UNCITRAL Model Law 6.199
  default judgments, awards akin to 6.196
  delay, creation of unreasonable 6.194
  disruption of hearings 6.195
  documentary evidence 6.198
  emergency arbitrator procedures 6.28
  enforcement of awards 6.192
  evidence 6.196, 6.198
  Libyan oil nationalisation cases 6.193
  procedure 6.196–6.199
  refusal to participate 6.193–6.194
  UNCITRAL Model Law 6.199
  written submissions 6.196, 6.198
excess of powers 5.08, 9.43, 10.41, 10.45–10.49
exchange of views between arbitrators 4.192, 9.106, 9.109–9.110

exclusion of liability 3.181, 5.55, 5.66
exclusive jurisdiction clauses 3.16, 8.54–8.56
expedited procedure 6.26–6.40 *see also* fast-track procedures
  delay 6.27, 6.40
  Dubai International Arbitration Centre (DIAC) 6.31
  early or summary determinations 6.38–6.40
  emergency arbitrator procedures 6.28
  expedited formation 6.28–6.31
  formation of tribunal 6.28–6.31
  LCIA Rules 6.29–6.30
  Swiss Rules of Arbitration 1.07
  time limits 9.165
expenses *see* fees and expenses
experienced arbitrators and counsel, practice of
  advocacy, demise of old-fashioned 1.238
  availability 4.60
  awards 9.17
  conduct of an arbitration 6.19
  disclosure, limits on 1.238
  IBA Rules of Evidence 1.238
  soft law, as 1.232
experts 6.133–6.145
  admissibility 6.142
  agreement on experts 6.137
  appointment by tribunal 5.23–5.27, 6.135–6.137
  arbitrators, powers of 5.23–5.27, 6.137
  autonomy of the parties 6.18
  categories of experts 6.143
  choice of experts 6.137
  common law systems 6.144
  conferencing 6.181–6.186
  conflicting evidence 6.138–6.139, 6.142, 6.181
  construction disputes 6.133
  costs 9.90
  cross-examination 6.134, 6.138, 6.185
  delegation 5.26, 6.136
  documentary evidence 6.118
  fees and expenses 9.90
  foreign law 6.144–6.145
  forensic document examiners 6.118
  IBA Evidence Rules 5.23, 6.141–6.142
  Iran-US Claims Tribunal 6.137
  negotiations 1.95
  neutral experts, assistance from 5.23–5.25
  oral evidence 6.134, 6.138
  parties, presented by the 5.23–5.25, 6.134, 6.138–6.141
  reports 5.23–5.26, 6.137, 6.141, 6.143, 6.184
  role 6.133–6.134, 6.183
  shipping disputes 6.133
  transcripts 6.186
expropriation 8.79–8.94
  acquired rights for investors 8.88
  breach of contract by state 8.91
  characterisation, purpose of measures not affecting 8.93–8.95
  compensation 8.79–8.96, 8.146–8.158, 8.162
  characterisation, purpose of measures not affecting 8.93–8.95

expropriation (*cont.*)
  compensation (*cont.*)
    customary international law 8.157
    direct expropriation 8.81
    Hull formula 8.146
    indirect expropriation 8.82–8.86
    lawful expropriation 8.156–8.158
    prompt, adequate, and effective
      compensation 8.79–8.80
    undertakings and assurances, acts
      contrary to 8.87–8.92
    unlawful expropriation 8.156–8.158
  control and interference by state 8.85
  customary international law 8.67, 8.157
  DCF (discounted cash flow) 8.148, 8.150, 8.154
  de facto or creeping expropriation 8.82–8.83, 8.95
  direct expropriation 8.81
  discrimination 8.86
  economic impact of measures 8.85
  fair market value 8.148, 8.147–8.155
  Hull standard of compensation 8.146
  ILC Articles on State Responsibility 8.167
  indirect compensation 8.82–8.83, 8.86
  interest 8.166–8.167
  international law 8.82
  interpretation 8.67
  measure of compensation 8.146–8.154, 8.162
  prompt, adequate and effective
    compensation 8.79–8.94
  purpose of measures 8.91–8.93
  restitution 9.58
  stock market value 8.151
  taxation 8.86
  undertakings and assurances, actions
    contrary to 8.87–8.92

facades and devices 2.51
facilities 4.177, 6.160 *see also* **accommodation**
fact, issues of
  applicable law 3.02, 3.93
  evidence 6.75–6.76
  quantum and liability, bifurcation of 6.58
  witnesses 6.120–6.132, 6.177
fair and equitable treatment under
  BITs 8.96–8.112, 8.159–8.163
fair hearings 10.53–10.54
  appointment of arbitrators 4.14
  challenges to awards 10.57–10.59, 10.95
  national courts 11.73–11.74
  refusal of recognition and
    enforcement 11.72–11.74
  waiver 10.58
fast track arbitration 6.32–6.40
  arbitral institutions, rules of 6.32–6.37
  conduct of an arbitration 1.07, 6.32–6.40
  early, or summary, determinations 6.38–6.40
  Formula One (F1) case 6.34–6.37
  ICC arbitration 6.34–6.37
  simplified procedures 6.32–6.33
  Swiss Rules of Arbitration 1.07, 6.33

time limits, abridgment of 6.32
urgent action 6.32–6.40
fees and expenses 4.202–4.222
  accommodation 4.202
  ad hoc arbitrations 4.203, 6.44, 6.46
  ad valorem method 1.154, 4.204–4.206
  administration 1.123–1.124, 4.197–4.198,
    4.221–4.222, 9.89
  administrative secretaries or
    registrars 4.197–4.201
  assessment
    ad valorem method 4.204–4.206
    fixed fees 4.204, 4.209
    methods of 4.204–4.209
    time spent method 4.204, 4.207–4.208
  bank accounts for deposits 4.222
  certainty 1.164
  commitment or cancellation fees 4.212–4.214
  consent awards or agreed terms awards 9.37
  costs 1.123–1.124, 1.154, 1.159, 9.88–9.92
  deposits 4.221–4.222
  estimates 1.164
  experts 9.90
  fixed fees 1.154, 4.204, 4.209
  fixing fees 4.203
  functus officio 4.220
  ICC Rules 4.205, 4.217
  ICSID arbitration 4.218–4.219
  informality 4.202
  institutional arbitrations 1.154, 1.159,
    1.164, 4.203
  invoices, monitoring 4.208
  lawyers 9.90
  LCIA Rules 1.164
  negotiations 4.210–4.211
  New York Convention 1958 11.51
  per diem rate 4.217, 4.219
  preliminary meetings 6.44, 6.46
  procedural rules, guidelines and
    recommendations 4.191
  professionals 9.90
  reasonableness 1.164
  records 4.208
  reimbursement method 4.215
  securing payment 4.220–4.222
  security 4.220
  sole arbitrators 4.25
  subsistence expenses 4.215–4.217
  time spent method 4.204, 4.207–4.208
  travel expenses 4.215, 9.87, 9.88, 9.90, 9.92
  UNCITRAL Rules 4.208
finality
  awards 1.04, 1.101, 5.57, 9.02–9.04, 9.13, 11.01
  definition 9.04
  enforcement of awards 1.101, 11.01
  functus officio, tribunal as 9.18, 9.23,
    9.186, 9.190
  Geneva Convention 1927 11.87
  immunity 5.57
  interpretation 9.187

Index

partial and interim awards 9.23
public policy 11.119
status of awards, rulings which have 9.13
financial relationships with arbitrators 4.124
fixing dates for hearings 4.173–4.176
flexibility
  ad hoc arbitrations 1.143
  advantages of arbitration 1.104
  arbitral tribunal, choice of 1.104
  conduct of an arbitration 6.01
  electronic documents, production of 6.108
  fees and expenses 4.202
  hard law 1.243
  Iran-US Claims Tribunal 1.196
  rules 1.79
  seat theory (*locus arbitri*) 3.59
  soft law 1.243
'floating' arbitration 3.76, 3.84
'floating' awards 3.76
force majeure 3.119, 3.124
foreign law
  choice of foreign procedural law 3.65–3.68
  experts 6.138–6.145
forensic experts 6.118
'fork in the road' provisions 8.57–8.58, 8.61
formalism 3.193, 8.23, 9.12, 9.106
formalities *see also* **writing requirement**
  arbitration agreements 2.13–2.23, 9.142–9.145
  conduct of an arbitration 1.06–1.07
  governing law 9.146
  ICC Rules 9.149
  ICSID arbitration 9.144
  introductory sections of awards 9.147
  language 9.150
  LCIA Rules 9.149
  local formalities 11.32
  New York Convention 1958 9.140, 11.51–11.54
  recognition of awards 11.32
  signatures 9.148–9.149
  substance over form 2.21
  translations 9.150
  UNCITRAL Model Law 9.143
  validity of awards 9.142–9.150
  written submissions or pleadings 6.72–6.73
forum non conveniens 11.123–11.124
forum shopping 3.47, 3.86, 11.16, 11.28–11.29
France
  adaption of contracts 9.67
  applicable law 3.35
  arbitrability 2.125, 2.134
  arbitration agreements 2.22, 2.71
  Argentina, BIT with 8.26
  capacity 2.37
  challenges to awards 10.71–10.72
  choice of law 3.217
  competition law 2.134, 2.138
  conflict of laws 3.216
  counsel, connection with 4.125
  court control, contracting out of 10.71
  damages 9.45

deliberation 9.109
delocalisation 3.77
disclosure 4.105
equity and good conscience 3.194
gaps, filling 9.68
governing law 3.34
group of companies doctrine 2.45–2.50
ICC Rules 1.28
immunity 5.65, 11.148–11.150, 11.155
independence or impartiality 4.105
informal discussions 9.106
international, definition of 1.28
lex arbitri 3.44
mistake of law 10.68, 10.70
multiparty arbitrations 1.111
public policy 10.84, 11.121
refusal of recognition and enforcement 11.75, 11.94–11.95
separability 2.106
sole option/unilateral option clauses 2.98
state immunity 11.148–11.150, 11.155
states or state entities 2.37
status of awards, rulings which have 9.09–9.11
third parties 2.53
fraud 2.154, 8.36, 10.62
free trade agreements (FTAs) 8.11 *see also* **North American Free Trade Agreement (NAFTA)**
free transfer of funds relating to investments 8.129–8.132
freedom of expression 1.85
freezing clauses 3.120, 3.124–3.126
freezing orders 3.80, 5.42, 7.38
friendship, commerce and navigation (FCN) treaties 1.216, 8.03, 8.08
full protection and security principle 8.113–8.117
functus officio, tribunal as 4.220, 9.18, 9.23, 9.186, 9.190, 11.02

GAFTA Rules 11.09
gap filling *see* **adaptation of contracts and filling gaps**
general principles of law 3.134–3.135, 3.144, 3.161
Geneva Convention 1927 1.18, 1.210 *see also* **Geneva Protocol 1923**
  adjudicability 10.47
  arbitration agreements 2.06
  challenges to awards 10.47, 10.49
  enforcement of awards 1.210, 5.124, 11.19–11.23, 11.87
  New York Convention 1958 1.212, 5.124, 11.40
  recognition of awards 1.208, 11.19–11.23, 11.87
Geneva Protocol 1923 1.207–1.209
  arbitration agreements 1.57, 2.06
  autonomy of the parties 6.07
  commercial, meaning of 1.36
  commercial reservation 1.37
  dispute requirement 1.62
  enforcement of arbitration clauses 1.208
  enforcement of awards in territory of state where awards made 1.208–1.209

683

Index

Geneva Protocol 1923 (*cont.*)
  existing and future disputes 1.62
  New York Convention 1958 1.213, 11.40, 11.42
  objectives 1.208–1.209
  seat theory (*locus arbitri*) 3.53
Germany
  agents 2.57
  arbitrability 2.140, 2.144
  assignment 2.55
  bankruptcy 2.144
  choice of law 3.65–3.66
  enforcement and recognition of awards 11.75, 11.79, 11.113, 11.151–11.152
  immunity 11.151
  interest 9.73
  lex arbitrii 3.62
  public policy 9.49, 10.83
  punitive damages 9.45, 9.49
  res judicata 9.174
  securities transactions 2.140
  several parties in one contract 2.214
  uncertainty 2.199
globalisation 1.01
good conscience *see* **equity and good conscience**
good faith 1.135–1.136, 2.92, 3.178, 8.36
governing law 3.37–3.90 *see also* **applicable laws; choice of law**
  ad hoc arbitrations 3.41
  arbitrability 2.127–2.128
  arbitral tribunal and proceedings, different law governing 1.11
  arbitration agreements 2.54, 2.66–2.67, 2.84, 3.09–3.36
  arbitration clauses 3.09, 3.12–3.13, 3.34
  arbitration, law governing the 3.37–3.90
  arbitrators, powers of 5.14
  assignment 2.54
  awards are made, place where 3.69–3.72
  choice of law clauses 2.84
  close connection 2.64, 2.84, 3.19, 3.24, 3.203, 3.209–3.210
  combining approaches 3.36
  common intention of parties 3.33–3.35
  conflict of laws 3.33
  contract, law of the 3.12–3.14
  delocalisation 3.73–3.83
  form of awards, validity and 9.149
  harmonisation 1.205, 1.218
  ICC Rules 3.40, 3.70
  institutional arbitrations 3.41
  lex arbitri 1.10, 3.15–3.32, 3.37–3.53, 3.62–3.64, 3.80, 3.84–3.90
  lex mercatoria 3.175
  model arbitration clauses 2.84, 2.100, 2.115
  national laws 3.12–3.32
  neutral forums 3.37, 3.39
  New York Convention 1958 3.14
  preliminary meetings 6.46
  procedural law, choice of a foreign 3.65–3.68
  seat, choice of 2.84
  seat theory (*locus arbitri*) 3.53–3.62, 3.84–3.90

  signatures 9.149
  submission agreements 3.09, 3.13
  substantive issues 3.10, 3.39
  UNCITRAL Model Law 3.40, 3.70, 3.216
  validity of agreements 3.14
  Vienna Convention on the Law of Treaties 8.64
group of companies doctrine 1.115, 2.42–2.51
  common intention 2.46–2.49
  consent 2.46, 2.50
  piercing the corporate veil 2.51
  third parties 2.42–2.50
guidelines
  applicable law 3.229–3.231
  non-national law 3.221–3.231
  vacancies, falling 4.153
Guiliano and Lagarde Report 3.202
Gulf Co-operation Council (GCC) Convention 11.138
gunboat diplomacy 8.01, 8.04

Hague Convention on Taking of Evidence Abroad 6.131
Hague Peace Conventions 1899 and 1907 1.189, 1.193, 8.04
hardship 3.119, 3.124, 9.69
harmonisation
  governing law 1.205, 1.218
  institutions 1.02
  language 1.01
  lawyers 3.221–3.228
  national laws 1.205, 1.239, 2.10
  professional bar rules 3.224–3.228
  UNCITRAL Model Law 1.205, 1.218
heard, right to be 5.33
hearing hours 4.186–4.188
hearings 6.155–6.199 *see also* **fair hearings**
  accommodation 4.178, 6.160, 6.187
  administration 4.193, 6.158–6.159
  after hearing, procedure 6.200–6.204
  arbitral institutions, rules of 6.157
  attendance of young practitioners 4.71
  autonomy of the parties 6.18
  break out rooms 6.160
  burden of proof 6.190
  civil law countries 6.169
  closing submissions 6.187–6.190
  common law countries 6.169, 6.190
  concurrent hearings 2.236–2.237, 2.241–2.243
  conferencing 6.181–6.186
  confidentiality 2.171–2.174
  costs 6.23, 6.160, 6.187
  default hearings 6.191–6.199
  dispensing with hearings 1.07
  due process 6.190
  duration 4.176, 6.168
  ex parte hearings 6.192–6.199
  expert conferencing 6.181–6.186
  facilities 6.160
  fixing dates 4.173–4.176
  holiday periods 4.175
  interpreters 4.183, 4.193

Index

language 4.193
last word, who has the 6.190
length of hearings 4.176, 4.183, 6.168
location 3.149–3.153, 4.172, 6.162
observers 4.71
opening statements 6.172
organisation 4.170–4.176, 6.158–6.167
post-hearing briefs 6.201–6.202
pre-hearing conferences 6.163–6.167
preliminary hearings 6.43–6.44
presence of parties 4.171–4.172
procedure 6.168–6.190
public hearings 10.57–10.58
time limits 6.172
transcripts 4.193, 6.160, 6.187–6.188
UNCITRAL Notes on Organizing Arbitral Proceedings 6.170
verbatim records 6.160
witnesses
    conferencing 6.180–6.186
    examination 6.173–6.179
    presence of 4.172
history 1.13–1.17
    dispute resolution 1.13–1.17
    enforcement of arbitration agreements and awards 1.17
    jurisdiction 1.16
    merchants, disputes between 1.13, 1.15
    national regulation 1.15–1.16
    national laws 1.16–1.17
    private justice, localised system of 1.15–1.17
    reputation 1.13
    states, disputes between 1.191–1.196
    treaties and conventions 1.17, 1.18
holiday periods 4.175
Holocaust Tribunals 1.196
Hong Kong
    consolidation 2.239
    emergency arbitrators 4.17, 7.17
    enforcement of awards 11.83
    HKIAC Rules 2.61, 4.17
    interest 9.73–9.74, 9.76
    joinder and intervention 2.61
    regional arbitration centre, creation of 1.168
    sovereign immunity 11.145
hotels 4.181
human rights *see also* particular rights (eg fair hearings)
    challenges to awards 10.58
    Human Rights Act 1998 10.58
    setting aside awards 10.95
Hungary 8.75, 11.131
hydrocarbon contracts 9.68–9.69

IBA Rules on Taking of Evidence 6.95–6.103
    adverse inferences 6.113
    disclosure, limits on 1.238
    documentary evidence 6.95–6.97, 6.99, 6.113
    electronic documents, production of 6.109
    experienced arbitrators and counsel, practice of 1.238
    experts 5.23, 6.141–6.142
    inspection 6.146
    lex arbitri 3.52
    soft law, as 1.235–1.236
    text App J
    witnesses 6.121, 6.124, 6.175
ICC Rules
    2012 Rules, text of App F
    additional awards 9.33
    appointment of arbitrators 4.36
    arbitral proceedings 1.78
    arbitration clauses 1.50
    arbitrators 4.23, 4.64, 4.67, 4.69, 4.166, 5.46
    autonomy of the parties 3.100, 6.08
    availability of arbitrators 4.60
    awards 9.133, 10.09, 10.17, 10.22, 10.29, 10.94
    Challenge Procedure 4.109–4.111
    challenges to arbitrators 4.109–4.111
    challenges to awards 10.09, 10.17
    clerical or typographical errors 9.33
    commencement of an arbitration 4.08–4.09
    confidentiality 2.160, 2.163, 2.192
    consent awards or agreed terms awards 9.37
    costs 9.87, 9.93
    delay 5.69
    dissenting opinions 9.133
    duty of care of arbitrators 5.55, 5.63
    emergency arbitrators 1.177, 4.17, 4.20–4.21
    enforcement of awards 1.88, 9.14
    fast track arbitration 6.34–6.37
    fees and expenses 4.205, 4.215
    governing law 3.40, 3.70
    inspection 6.152
    interest 9.77
    interim measures 1.177, 5.27–5.28, 7.14, 7.17, 7.19, 7.20, 7.24
    joinder and intervention 2.61
    jurisdiction 5.107–5.108
    language 2.86
    lawyers 1.237, 3.227
    majority voting 9.123–9.124
    multiparty arbitrations 1.111, 2.214
    national committees 4.69
    nationality 4.64, 4.67
    non-national law 3.190
    notification of awards 9.169
    parallel proceedings 7.56–7.58
    partial and interim awards 9.21
    privacy 2.160
    reasons 9.157, 9.159
    refusal of enforcement or recognition 11.67–11.69
    remission of awards 10.22
    removal of arbitrators 4.96
    requests for arbitration 4.08
    revision of Rules 1.177
    scrutiny 9.133
    seat theory (*locus arbitri*) 3.57
    soft law 1.235, 4.23, 4.36
    sole arbitrators 4.23, 4.36, 4.64
    state immunity 11.150

Index

ICC Rules (*cont.*)
  text App F
  time limits 4.08–4.09, 9.167–9.168
  truncated tribunals 4.156, 4.158–4.159
  vacancies, falling 4.167
  validity of agreements 5.106–5.107
ICDR *see* ICDR Rules; International Centre for Dispute Resolution (ICDR) (Ireland)
ICDR Rules 1.146, 2.71, 4.17, 4.180, 7.17
  arbitrators 4.24, 4.65, 4.69, 4.166
  conduct of an arbitration 6.21
  confidentiality 2.180
  costs 9.87
  emergency arbitrators 4.17
  interim measures 7.17
  list of arbitrators 4.69
  nationality 4.65
  publication of awards 9.199
  sole arbitrators 4.24
  statements of claim and defence 6.68
  text App G
  truncated tribunals 4.156
  vacancies, falling 4.166
  written submissions or pleadings 6.68
ICSID Rules
  Additional Facility Rules 2.185
  autonomy of the parties 6.08
  confidentiality 2.184–2.185, 2.188, 2.190
  default awards 9.32
  dissenting opinions 9.132
  early or summary determinations 6.39
  form of awards, validity and 9.144
  interim measures 5.29–5.31
  jurisdiction 5.113
  nationality 4.67
  procedural orders 2.185
  transparency 2.188
  text App E
ILC Draft Articles on State Responsibility 8.66, 8.167, 9.77, 9.79
illegality 2.112, 2.151, 9.156, 11.107 *see also* crime
immunity *see also* state immunity
  arbitral institutions, rules of 5.66
  arbitrators 5.01, 5.50, 5.54–5.66, 5.68, 5.78
  diplomatic immunity 11.155
  duty of care of arbitrators 5.50, 5.54–5.66
  judicially, arbitrators' duty to act 5.78
  personal liability 5.61
  public policy 5.56, 5.58–5.59
implied or tacit choice of law 3.201–3.204, 3.208
implied term device 9.66–9.67, 9.71
incapacity *see* capacity
INCOTERMS 3.177, 3.183
indemnities for personal liability 5.61
independence and impartiality of
    arbitrators 4.75–4.88, 5.46
  AAA/ABA Code of Ethics 4.75
  appointment of arbitrators 4.75–4.76
  challenges to arbitrators 4.79, 4.93–4.102, 4.121–4.150
  challenges to awards 10.04, 10.57
  conflicts of interest 4.82, 4.84–4.88, 4.121–4.137, 4.148
  connection of arbitrators with one of parties 4.121–4.122
  counsel, arbitrators' connection with 4.124–4.131
  declarations 5.46
  disclosure 4.79–4.88, 4.105
  disqualification, disclosure of grounds for 4.79–4.88
  dissenting opinions 1.86, 9.138
  financial relationships 4.124
  ICSID arbitration 4.98–4.100, 4.136
  impartiality, definition of 4.78
  independence, definition of 4.77
  International Bar Association (IBA) Guidelines on Conflicts of Interest 4.82, 4.84–4.88, 4.136, 4.148–4.149
    waiver 4.148–4.149
  International Council of Arbitration for Sport (ICAS) 4.137
  judicially, arbitrators' duty to act 5.76
  LCIA Rules 4.97
  national courts 7.04–7.06
  nationality 4.65, 4.99
  objective test 4.77, 4.139
  party autonomy 4.149
  party-nominated arbitrators 4.75–4.76, 4.81–4.83
  pre-judgment of issue 4.138–4.142
  psychology of tribunals 9.114–9.115
  single arbitrators 1.100
  subjective test 4.78
  UNCITRAL Rules 4.94
  waiver 4.79, 4.143–4.149
    advance waivers 4.148
    IBA Guidelines 4.148–4.149
    objections to arbitrators 4.79, 4.143–4.147
    party autonomy 4.149
India
  challenges to awards 10.27, 10.94
  defective arbitration clauses 2.183
  exchange control 2.183
  foreign and domestic awards, distinction between 9.29
  ICC Rules 10.94
  New York Convention 1958 11.47–11.49, 11.61, 11.99
  public policy 11.112
  refusal of recognition and enforcement 11.61, 11.99
  setting aside awards 10.94
  time limits 9.163
informal discussions 9.105–9.106
injunctions
  anti-arbitration injunctions 7.51–7.59
  anti-suit injunctions 3.17–3.18, 5.134–5.135
  Brussels I Regulation 5.134–5.135
  delocalisation or denationalisation 3.90
  evidence 7.38
  final injunctions 9.59
  freezing orders 3.80, 5.42, 7.38

Index

interim injunctions 9.59
jurisdiction 5.122
seat theory 3.90
status quo, measures aimed at
  preservation of 7.48–7.50
third parties 9.59
inquisitorial approach 2.153, 6.09
insolvency 2.141–2.145, 10.51
inspection of subject matter of dispute 6.146–6.154
  AAA Rules 6.152
  ad hoc tribunals 6.152–6.154
  commodity arbitrations 6.146
  construction contracts 3.58–3.60, 6.146
  discretion 6.149
  equality of treatment 6.149
  evidence 6.146–6.154
  IBA Evidence Rules 6.146
  ICC Rules 6.152
  ICSID arbitration 6.153
  LCIA Rules 6.152
  presence of parties 6.149–6.150, 6.153
  procedure 6.149–6.151
  rules 5.22, 6.152–6.154
  site inspections 6.146–6.153
  transcripts 6.150
  UNCITRAL Rules 6.152
  visits to other countries by tribunals 3.60
  WIPO Rules 6.152, 6.154
institutional arbitrations 1.140, 1.146–1.189
  see also **arbitral institutions, rules of; arbitral tribunals; specific institutions (eg London Court of International Arbitration (LCIA))**
  administration 1.151, 4.196–4.197
  advantages 1.149–1.153
  appointment of arbitrators 4.36–4.39, 4.41
  arbitration agreements 1.149, 2.79–2.81
  arbitration clauses 1.147–1.148
  arbitrators 4.50, 4.69–4.70, 5.46
  assistance to parties 1.153, 1.163
  awards, review of draft 1.152
  centres of arbitration 4.179–4.180
  chambers of commerce 1.146
  choice of law 3.204, 3.211–3.220
  costs 1.154, 1.159, 1.181, 9.95–9.96
  definition 1.146
  delay 1.155–1.156
  disadvantages 1.154–1.156
  duty of care of arbitrators 5.62–5.63
  existence, institutions no longer in 1.160–1.161
  extensions of time 1.156
  fees and expenses 1.154, 1.159, 1.164, 4.203
  harmonisation 1.02
  interim relief 1.176–1.177
  internships 4.70
  leading institutions 1.165–1.181
  lex fori 3.211–3.213
  list of institutions 1.146
  model arbitration clauses 2.79–2.81
  notice 1.69–1.70
  permanency 1.160–1.161
  quality control 1.152

reasons for selection 1.159–1.164
regional institutions 1.146
rules of procedure 1.147–1.150, 1.162, 1.165
sanctions 1.181
staff 1.151, 1.163, 1.165
time limits 1.155–1.156
trades or industries 1.157
training 4.69
types of disputes 1.157
institutions *see* **arbitral institutions, rules of; institutional arbitrations; specific institutions (eg London Court of International Arbitration (LCIA))**
insurance
  Aida Reinsurance and Insurance Arbitration
    Society (ARIAS) Arbitration
    Rules 3.16–3.22
  vacancies on tribunals, against 4.167–4.168
intellectual property *see* **World Intellectual Property Organisation (WIPO) and WIPO Rules**
interchange of views between arbitrators 4.192, 9.106, 9.109–9.110
interest
  applicable law 9.73, 9.79, 9.83
  arbitral institutions, rules of 9.73
  bilateral investment treaties (BITs) 8.166–8.167
  civil law countries 9.77
  common law countries 9.76
  compound interest 1.106, 9.76–9.79
  enforcement of awards 9.80–9.84
  expropriation 8.166–8.167
  ICC Rules 9.77
  ILC Draft Articles on State
    Responsibility 9.77, 9.79
  lex arbitri 9.81
  national laws 9.80–9.81
  post-award interest 9.83–9.84
  prohibition 9.80–9.81
  rate 9.74–9.75, 9.83–9.84
  remedies 9.77–9.84
  UNCITRAL Model Law 9.76
interim awards *see* **partial and interim awards**
interim measures 7.14–7.61
  applicable law 5.32
  arbitral institutions 7.14–7.61
    applications to 7.26–7.31
    inability to act prior to formation 7.17
    no power, where institution has 7.16
    powers of 5.33, 7.14–7.61
    rules 5.31
  arbitration agreements, breach of 7.23
  arbitrators 5.27–5.34
  awards, labelled as 7.20
  balance of convenience test 5.32
  Brussels I Regulation 5.130–5.131
  classification 7.31
  competent court, powers of 7.22–7.31
  discretion 5.31
  documentary disclosure 7.39–7.44
  emergency arbitrators 4.19, 4.21, 7.17, 7.28–7.29

Index

interim measures *(cont.)*
  enforcement 7.19–7.20, 7.22, 7.29–7.30
  evidence, preservation of 7.33, 7.37–7.38
  ex parte measures 1.223, 5.33–5.34, 7.21
  exceptional circumstances 5.33
  heard, right to be 5.33
  guidance 5.31–5.32
  ICC Rules 1.177, 5.27–5.28, 7.14, 7.17, 7.19, 7.20, 7.24
  ICSID Rules 5.29–5.31
  inability to act prior to formation of tribunal 7.17–7.19
  institutional arbitration 1.176–1.177
  International Centre for Dispute Resolution (ICDR) 7.17
  LCIA Rules 7.17
  national courts 4.03, 7.05, 7.13–7.61
  Netherlands Arbitration Institute (NAI) Rules 7.17
  New York Convention 1958 7.19
  parallel proceedings 7.51–7.61
  parties to arbitration, effect only on 7.18
  preliminary orders 5.34
  Singapore International Arbitration Centre (SIAC) 7.17
  status quo, measures aimed at preservation of 7.45–7.50
  Stockholm Chamber of Commerce (SCC) 7.17
  terminology 7.14
  third parties 7.20, 7.22
  UNCITRAL Model Law 5.27–5.28, 5.32, 5.34, 7.14, 7.18, 7.21, 7.24, 7.26
  UNCITRAL Rules 5.27, 7.24
  urgent action 5.34, 7.17–7.18, 7.22, 7.27–7.28
  witnesses, attendance of 7.32–7.36

international arbitration, characteristics of
  conduct of an arbitration 6.19–6.21
  consumer protection 1.22
  corporations 1.22
  domestic disputes 1.19–1.26, 3.44
  international, meaning of 1.26–1.34
  internationality requirement 1.31–1.34
  national laws 1.19–1.20, 1.34
  nationality of parties 1.26, 1.29–1.30, 1.34
  nature of disputes, international 1.26–1.34
  neutral countries, selection of 1.21
  New York Convention 1.57, 7.19, 11.91, 11.62, 11.110, 11.124
  place of arbitration, law of 1.21
  states or state entities 1.22, 1.25
  transnational arbitration 1.19
  UNCITRAL Model Law 1.26

International Bar Association (IBA) *see also* **IBA Rules on Taking of Evidence**
  code of conduct, formulation of 1.237
  conflicts of interest, guidelines on App J
  connection with one of parties 4.119
  delay 5.81
  counsel, connection with 4.129–4.131
  Guidelines on Conflicts of Interest 4.82, 4.84–4.88, 5.80

  connection with one of parties 4.119
  counsel, connection with 4.129–4.131
  delay 5.81
  independence and impartiality of arbitrators 4.82, 4.84–4.88, 4.136, 4.148–4.149
  Revised Guidelines 4.85
  text App K
  waiver 4.148–4.149
  immunity 5.60
  independence and impartiality of arbitrators 4.82, 4.84–4.88
  party representatives, guidelines on 1.179–1.180, 3.225–3.226
  Rules of Ethics 5.60, 5.80
  Rules of Party Representation 4.131
  Taskforce Guidelines Monitoring Committee 4.85
  waiver 4.148–4.149

International Centre for Dispute Resolution (ICDR) (Ireland) 1.146, 2.71, 4.17, 4.180, 6.21, 7.17 *see also* **ICDR Rules**

International Chamber of Commerce (ICC) arbitration 1.02 *see also* **ICC Rules**
  accommodation 4.180
  adaptation of contracts 9.69
  advantages 1.149–1.153
  arbitration clauses 1.147–1.148, 2.199–2.201
  awards
    draft awards, review of 1.152, 1.166
    reviews 9.195–9.197
  bribery and corruption, arbitrability and 2.151–2.153
  case management 1.235
  code of conduct for counsel, formulation of 1.237
  Commission on International Arbitration 2.212, 2.243–2.244
  consolidation 2.245
  defective arbitration clauses 2.199–2.201
  delay 1.156
  extensions of time 1.156
  failure to appear 1.150
  fraud 2.154
  gaps, filling 9.69
  ICC Hearing Centre 4.180
  legal representation 1.237
  multiparty arbitrations 2.212, 2.223
  role 1.166
  Secretariat 1.166
  Shari'ah 3.186
  soft law 1.235
  terms of reference 1.166, 2.245
  time limits 1.156

International Centre for the Settlement of Investment Disputes (ICSID) arbitration *see also* **ICSID Rules**
  accommodation 4.179
  annulment of awards 8.77, 11.127
  appointment of arbitrators 4.37

Index

arbitrators 4.37, 4.67, 4.98–4.100, 4.115–4.123, 4.144
bilateral investment treaties (BITs) 1.187, 8.10–8.11, 8.26–8.28
Challenge Procedure 4.116–4.117
challenges to arbitrators 4.98–4.100, 4.115–4.123, 4.144
challenges to awards 10.13–10.17
clarification of awards 9.194
commencement of an arbitration 4.09
connection of arbitrators with one of parties 4.120–4.123
consent of state 8.08
costs 8.169
deliberation 9.109
delocalisation or denationalisation 1.188
diplomatic protection 1.186
fees and expenses 4.218–4.219
increase in number of arbitrations 1.188
independence and impartiality 4.98–4.100
inspection 6.153
interpretation of awards 9.194
judicially, arbitrators' duty to act 5.71
jurisdiction 8.26–8.28, 8.54–8.55, 8.63
Libyan oil nationalisation arbitrations 3.143
location 1.186
majority voting 9.125–9.126
memorial and counter-memorial 6.69
mistake of law 10.67
North American Free Trade Agreement (NAFTA) 1.187
performance 11.10
pre-judgment of issues 4.141
public international law 3.131
res judicata 9.177
setting aside awards 10.94
state, consent of 8.08
states, arbitration involving 1.186–1.187
time limits 4.09
World Bank 1.186
written submissions or pleadings 6.69
International Council of Arbitration for Sport (ICAS) 4.137
International Court of Justice (ICJ) 1.194–1.195
international law *see* **conflict of laws; public international law**
International Law Association (ILA)
applicable law 3.200
lex mercatoria 3.176
public policy 10.87, 11.119
res judicata 9.175, 9.178, 9.181
transnational law 3.160
International Law Commission (ILC) 8.66, 8.167, 9.77, 9.79
international trade law 1.10
international treaties and conventions *see* **treaties and conventions**
international tribunal, proposal for 1.117
internationality requirement 1.31–1.34
Internet, publication of awards on 2.190, 9.200

internship schemes 4.70
interpretation
adaptation of contracts 9.65, 9.70
arbitration agreements 2.28, 2.67–2.69
awards 9.187, 9.191–9.194
bilateral investment treaties (BITs) 8.21–8.23, 8.28–8.46, 8.55, 8.64–8.75, 8.98, 8.107–8.123, 8.135–8.140
challenges to awards 10.09, 10.13, 10.17–10.24
clarification of awards 9.191–9.194
defined legal relationship requirement 2.28
equity and good conscience 3.193
expropriation 8.67
gaps, filling 9.65, 9.70
ICSID arbitration 1.186, 9.194
New York Convention 1958 1.214, 11.47–11.48, 11.65
refusal of recognition and enforcement 11.65
res judicata 9.175
Russian Commercial Procedure Code 11.103
SCC Rules 9.191
standard form contracts 3.184
UNCITRAL Rules 9.192
UNIDROIT Principles of International Commercial Contracts 3.179
interpreters 4.58, 4.169, 4.177, 4.182–4.183, 4.193, 9.87
intervention *see* **joinder and intervention**
interviews
arbitrators 4.72–4.74
witnesses 6.121, 6.124
investment *see* **International Centre for the Settlement of Investment Disputes (ICSID) arbitration; ICSID Rules; investment treaties, arbitration under**
investment treaties, arbitration under 8.01–8.169
see also **bilateral investment treaties (BITs); expropriation**
Abu-Shawcross Draft Convention on Investments Abroad 1959 8.08
Arab Investment Court 11.139
Arab League Investment Agreement 11.139
ASEAN Comprehensive Investment Agreement 8.11
Calvo doctrine 8.02–8.03
complaints about investment system 8.12
confidentiality 2.183–2.189
diplomatic protection 8.04–8.09
dissenting opinions 1.86
Dominican Republic and Central America-United States Free Trade Agreement (DR-CAFTA) 8.11
Energy Charter Treaty (ECT) 8.11, 8.21
enforcement of awards 11.139
free transfer of funds relating to investments 8.129–8.133
friendship, commerce and navigation (FCN) treaty 1.216, 8.03, 8.08
Hague Peace Convention 1907 8.04
investment, definition of 8.28–8.44

investment treaties, arbitration under (*cont.*)
  legitimacy 8.12
  multilateral economic cooperation
    treaties 8.11
  national courts 7.43
  North American Free Trade Agreement
    (NAFTA) 8.11
  OECD Draft Convention on the Protection of
    Foreign Property 1967 8.08
  Organization of Islamic Cooperation (OIC)
    Agreement 11.139
  regional agreements 11.139
  setting aside awards 10.94
  stabilisation clauses 3.122–3.123, 3.126–3.127
  transparency 2.189
Iran 3.106, 3.118, 3.147, 9.108 *see also* **Iran-US Claims Tribunal**
Iran-US Claims Tribunal
  costs 9.96, 9.98
  deliberations and decisions 9.103, 9.108,
    9.113, 9.134
  dissenting opinions 9.134
  due process 11.75
  experts 6.137
  expropriation 8.153
  independence and impartiality 9.108
  pre-hearing conferences 6.165
  public international law 3.132
  publication of awards 9.199
  refusal of enforcement or recognition 11.75
  tribunal psychology 9.113
  UNCITRAL Rules 1.196
Ireland
  interest 9.76
  International Centre for Dispute Resolution
    (ICDR) 1.146, 1.167, 2.71, 4.17, 4.180,
    6.21, 7.17
  negligence 5.55
Islam *see* **Shari'ah law**
issue estoppel 9.174, 9.180, 9.185, 11.20
Italy
  agents 2.57
  enforcement and recognition of awards 11.81
  friendship, commerce and navigation (FCN)
    treaties 8.03
  national courts 5.132–5.134
  res judicata 9.174
  third parties 2.53

Japan 9.77, 10.63, 11.114
Jay Treaty 1794 1.191
Jewish law
  choice of law 3.106
  lex arbitri 3.85
  non-national law 3.64, 3.106, 3.190
  public policy 11.106
joinder and intervention 1.109–1.113
  arbitration agreements 2.59–2.62
  HKIAC Rules 2.61
  ICC Rules 2.60
  rules of arbitral tribunals 2.60–2.62

  Swiss Rules of Arbitration 2.61
  third parties 1.109–1.113, 2.59–2.62
joint ventures 2.214
judges
  common law countries 6.77
  control of proceedings 7.62
  evidence 6.77
  judicial assistance 3.46, 6.131, 7.32–7.36
judgments
  default judgments 6.196
  summary judgments 1.60–1.61
judicial review 9.24, 10.78–10.80
judicialisation 1.118–1.122
judicially, arbitrators' duty to act 5.70–5.78
  applicable law 5.72
  civil law jurisdictions 5.75
  decision-making 9.101–9.102
  equality 5.71, 5.73
  fair opportunity to present case 5.70
  ICSID arbitration 5.71
  immunity 5.78
  independent and impartially, duty to act 5.74
  judicialisation of arbitration 1.118
  juris novit curia 5.73
  LCIA Rules 5.71, 5.74
  personal liability of arbitrators 5.78
  recovery of loss 5.78
  removal of arbitrators 5.72
  UNCITRAL Rules 5.71
jurisdiction *see also* **bilateral investment treaties
    (BITs), jurisdictional issues and; challenges
    to jurisdiction**
  appointment of arbitrators 4.43–4.44
  arbitral tribunals 5.91–5.137
  arbitration agreements 2.65–2.70, 5.99,
    5.110, 5.122
  arbitration clauses, autonomy or separability
    of 2.110, 2.113, 5.100–5.111
  boycotting arbitrations 5.119, 5.120
  Brussels I Regulation 5.128–5.137
  challenges to awards 5.124, 10.30, 10.36,
    10.42, 10.88
  combined approach 5.125
  competence/competence 5.105–5.109
  concurrent control 5.113–5.114
  court control 5.112–5.117
  declarations 5.122
  default awards 9.32
  delay 5.114
  drafting 2.65–2.70
  enforcement of awards 5.124, 9.15
  exceeding jurisdiction 5.92–5.99, 11.79, 11.81
  history 1.16
  ICC Rules 5.107–5.108
  ICSID arbitration 5.113
  inherent powers 5.105
  injunctions 5.122
  interim awards 5.113, 5.116
  intervention 2.59, 5.126
  Libyan oil nationalisation cases 5.120
  limitations 5.110

690

Index

national courts 5.112–5.117, 5.122–5.123,
    5.126, 7.12
  challenges to jurisdiction 5.122–5.123
  court control 5.112–5.117
  intervention, form of court 5.126
  New York Convention 1958 5.122
national laws 5.96, 5.108, 5.111
New York Convention 1958 5.09, 5.111, 5.117,
    5.122, 11.78–11.81
objections 5.94, 5.121
own jurisdiction, tribunal's power to
    decide 5.105–5.109, 5.110
partial and interim awards 9.19, 9.24
procedural aspects 5.118
refusal of recognition and
    enforcement 11.82–11.85
respondents to challenge, options open
    to 5.119–5.126
severability 1.54
sources 1.59
state immunity 11.141–11.145, 11.150
submission agreements 5.98
time for raising challenges 5.118
time limits 9.162
treaties and conventions 5.99, 5.111,
    5.128–5.137
UNCITRAL Model Law 5.108–5.110,
    5.117, 7.12
UNCITRAL Rules 5.108, 5.121
United States 5.126, 11.79–11.80
jury trials 6.81, 6.85
jus gentium 3.162

language
  appointment of arbitrators 1.73, 4.14
  arbitration agreements 2.86
  arbitrators 4.50, 4.58, 5.17
  documentary evidence 6.119
  enforcement of awards 9.150, 11.32, 11.54
  form of awards, validity and 9.150
  harmonisation 1.01
  hearings 4.193
  ICC Rules 2.86
  interpreters 4.58, 4.169, 4.177, 4.182–4.183,
    4.193, 9.87
  model arbitration clauses 2.86–2.87
  neutrality 1.100
  New York Convention 1958 11.52
  recognition of awards 11.33
  translations 2.87, 4.58, 6.119, 9.150, 11.52
lawyers *see also* **IBA Rules on Taking of Evidence;**
    International Bar Association (IBA)
  administrative secretaries or registrars,
    appointment as 4.198
  arbitrators
    appointment as 4.50, 4.52, 4.54–4.57, 4.67
    connection with lawyers 4.124–4.131
  chambers, members of same 4.128–4.130
  code of conduct 1.237
  conflicts of interest 4.124–4.131
  costs 3.226–3.227, 9.90

  ethical rules 3.219–3.228
  experienced arbitrators and counsel,
    practice of 1.238
  harmonisation 3.219–3.228
  ICC Rules 1.237, 3.227
  LCIA Rules 1.178–1.180, 3.228
  professional bar rules when acting in arbitrations
    abroad 3.219–3.228
  professional misconduct rules 6.124
  regulation 3.227
  soft law, conduct as 1.236
  specialisation within legal profession 3.156
  young practitioners' groups 4.70
LCIA Rules
  Annex 1.179–1.180
  appointment of arbitrators 2.216, 4.60
  arbitrators, requirements on 1.174
  autonomy of the parties 6.08
  availability of arbitrators 4.60
  Challenge Procedure 4.112–4.113
  challenges to arbitrators 4.97, 4.112–4.113
  confidentiality 2.191
  costs 1.175, 9.87, 9.93
  dissenting opinions 9.132
  duty of care of arbitrators 5.55
  electronic communications 1.173
  emergency arbitrator,
    appointment of 1.177, 4.17
  expedited procedure 1.174, 6.29–6.30
  false statements or evidence, warnings on 1.180
  form of awards and validity 9.149
  harmonisation 1.02
  independence and impartiality 4.97
  inspection 6.152
  interim measures 7.17
  judicially, arbitrators' duty to act 5.71, 5.76
  lawyers 1.178–1.180, 3.228
  lex arbitri 3.15
  multiparty arbitrations 1.111, 2.216
  notice 1.69
  partial and interim awards 9.21
  parties, duties of 1.175
  rectification 9.64
  revised Rules 1.172–1.173
  seat theory (*locus arbitri*) 3.58
  security for costs 5.37, 5.40
  separability or autonomy of arbitration
    clauses 2.105
  signatures 9.149
  sole arbitrators 4.23
  staff 1.171
  Statement of Case 6.67
  Statement of Defence 6.67
  Statement of Reply 6.67
  text app H
  time limits 6.30
  trade secrets 2.191
  truncated tribunals 4.158
  vacancies, falling 4.166
  witnesses 6.124
  written submissions or pleadings 6.67

Index

legal profession *see* lawyers
legitimate expectations 8.99–8.102
length of hearings 4.176, 4.183, 6.168
lex arbitri 1.10, 3.07–3.08
   Aida Reinsurance and Insurance Arbitration Society (ARIAS) Arbitration Rules 3.16–3.22
   anti-suit injunctions 3.17–3.18
   appointment of arbitrators 4.35
   arbitrability 3.47
   arbitral institutions, rules of 3.51–3.52
   arbitral proceedings 1.09–1.10
   arbitrators, powers of 5.14, 5.16
   awards are made, where 3.71
   challenges to awards 10.02, 10.04
   choice of law 3.84–3.85
   closest and most real connection 3.24
   codes of law 3.44, 3.62
   conduct of arbitration 1.09–1.10, 3.49
   consumer protection 3.43
   content 3.43–3.47
   costs 9.99
   damages 9.50
   definition 1.09, 3.05, 3.37–3.38, 3.42
   delocalisation or denationalisation 3.73–3.82, 3.88–3.90
   domestic arbitration 3.44
   equality of treatment 1.140, 3.48
   exclusive jurisdiction clauses 3.16
   express choice of law 3.18–3.20
   forum shopping 3.47, 3.86
   governing law 1.10, 3.15–3.22, 3.37–3.53, 3.62–3.64, 3.80, 3.84–3.90
   IBA Evidence Rules 3.52
   ICSID arbitration 3.52
      implied choice of law 3.23
      interaction of laws 3.07–3.08
   interest 9.81
   interim measures 3.52
   Jewish law 3.85
   judicial assistance 3.46
   LCIA 3.15
   mandatory provisions 1.78, 1.140, 3.64, 3.86
   national laws 1.09
   New York Convention 1958 1.225, 3.26, 3.28, 3.46–3.47
   procedural law, as 3.62–3.64
   procedural rules 3.48–3.52, 3.62–3.64
   public policy 3.64
   seat theory (*locus arbitri*) 3.53–3.61, 3.84–3.90
   separability 3.15
   state monopolies over certain types of disputes 3.47
   substantive issues 1.09, 3.39
   truncated tribunals 4.160
   UNCITRAL Model Law 3.45–3.46, 3.84
   UNCITRAL Rules 3.51
   universal *lex arbitri* 3.73–3.74
   validity of arbitration agreements 3.25
   witness statements 3.49

lex fori (law of country where action brought) 3.208, 3.211–3.213
lex mercatoria (law merchant)
   advantages 3.163
   applicable law 1.10, 3.161–3.177
   Central Transnational Law Database 3.168
   choice of law 3.175–3.176
   codification 3.165, 3.168, 3.171–3.173, 3.177
   creeping codification 3.168
   customary law 3.164–3.165
   enforcement of awards 3.175–3.176
   functional approach 3.169–3.176
   general principles of law 3.161
   governing law 3.74
   INCOTERMS 3.178
   International Law Association (ILA) 3.176
   jus gentium 3.162
   list method 3.168
   new *lex mercatoria* 3.162, 3.166–3.177
   Principles of European Contract Law (PECL) 3.168
   public international law 3.161
   stare decisis 3.173
   UNIDROIT Principles 3.161, 3.168, 3.171–3.173
   Uniform Customs and Practice (UCP) for Documentary Credits 3.176
   uniformity 3.163
liability and quantum, bifurcation of 6.54–6.59, 9.26–9.27
Libyan oil nationalisation arbitrations
   applicable law 3.140–3.155
   choice of law clauses 3.140–3.155
   compensation 3.121, 3.142
   concurrent law clauses 3.143, 3.145
   ex parte hearings 6.193
   ICSID arbitration 3.143
   jurisdiction 5.122
   national law 3.140–3.155
   neutrality 3.146
   public international law 3.140–3.155
   restitution 3.120, 9.55
   stabilisation clauses 3.120–3.121
   state parties 3.145–3.147
   transnational law, choice of 3.142
limitation of liability 3.181, 6.57–6.58, 9.28
limitation periods *see* time limits
limits of arbitrators' powers 1.104, 4.50–4.52, 5.22
Lithuania-Ukraine BIT 8.22
Livenote 4.185
LMAA (Lloyd's Maritime Arbitration Association) Rules 2.242, 6.155
location of hearings 3.149–3.153, 4.172, 6.162
locus arbitri see seat theory (*locus arbitri*)
London Court of International Arbitration (LCIA) 1.170–1.175 *see also* LCIA Rules
   accommodation 4.180
   fees and expenses 1.164
   London Chamber of Arbitration 1.170
   non-cooperation 1.177
   staff 1.171
long-term contracts 9.68–9.69, 9.71

Index

majority voting
  arbitral institutions, rules of 9.119–9.124
  awards 9.117–9.127, 9.137
  bargaining process 9.117–9.118
  decision-making 9.119–9.127, 9.137
  dissenting opinions 9.137
  ICC Rules 9.123–9.124
  ICSID arbitration 9.125–9.126
  non liquet, findings of 9.125
  presiding arbitrators 9.119–9.120, 9.123–9.124
  procedure, questions of 9.119–9.120
  UNCITRAL Model Law 9.122
  UNCITRAL Rules 9.119–9.120
mandatory provisions
  applicable law 3.127–3.130
  autonomy of the parties 6.15–6.18
  choice of law 3.127–3.130
  competition or anti-trust law 3.129–3.130
  lex arbitri 3.64, 3.65
  public policy 3.130
  time limits 9.165–9.166
maritime arbitration
  challenges to awards 10.12
  consolidation 2.242
  documents only arbitration 6.155
  experts 6.133
  LMAA Rules 2.242, 6.75
materiality of evidence 6.97–6.98, 6.110
mediation 1.138
mediation/arbitration (Med/Arb) 1.138
medical examinations of arbitrators 4.168
meetings *see also* **preliminary meetings**
  accommodation 4.179
  documentary evidence 6.100–6.102
  informal meetings 4.189
  location 3.57–3.61, 4.170–4.171
  preliminary steps 6.41–6.50
  presence of parties 4.171–4.172
  Redfern Schedule 1.238, 1.243, 6.100–6.102
memorials 6.69, 6.73
merchants, disputes between 1.13, 1.16 *see also lex mercatoria* (law merchant)
Middle Eastern conventions 11.138–11.139
midnight clauses 2.04
mistake *see* **errors; mistake of fact; mistake of law**
mistake of fact 10.77–10.80
  appeals 10.77
  challenges to awards 10.36, 10.77–10.80
  judicial review 10.78–10.80
  public interest 10.77
mistake of law 10.66–10.75
  appeals 10.66–10.68, 10.75
  challenges to awards 10.36, 10.66–10.76
  delocalisation 10.69
  ICSID arbitration 10.67
  national courts, intervention by 10.68–10.75
  standard form contracts 10.66
  UNCITRAL Model Law 10.69–10.75
mixed commissions 1.196

model arbitration clauses 2.03, 2.73–2.100 *see also* **standard form contracts**
  ad hoc arbitrations 2.79–2.81, 2.99–2.100
  amicable settlements 2.88–2.89
  applicable law 2.100
  arbitration tribunal
    establishment of 2.78, 2.117
    failure or refusal to act 2.83, 2.117
    incapacity 2.82
    removal 2.83
    vacancies, filling 2.82, 2.117
  choice of law clauses 2.84
  contents 2.73–2.100
  default clauses 2.85
  defective clauses 2.76
  different methods of resolving disputes, recourse to 2.118
  drafting 2.03, 2.73–2.100
  governing law 2.84, 2.100, 2.116
  incorporation 2.114
  institutional arbitrations 2.78–2.81
  language 2.86–2.87
  multi-tier clauses 2.88–2.93
  national courts 2.115
  number of arbitrators 2.77, 2.117
  other procedural matters 2.99–2.100
  place of arbitration 2.83, 2.100, 2.117
  remedies 2.100
  security 2.100
  settlements 2.88–2.89
  submission to arbitration 2.117
  UNCITRAL Model Law 2.73, 2.99, 2.114
  vacancies, filling 2.82, 2.117
  validity of arbitration agreements 2.76
money laundering 5.82–5.85
monopolies or cartels 2.132–2.133
Montevideo Convention 1899 1.207
moral damages 8.164–8.165
Moscow Convention 1972 11.131–11.133
  Council for Mutual Economic Assistance (CMEA) 11.131–11.132
  enforcement of awards 11.131–11.133
  refusal of enforcement, grounds for 11.133
  signatories 11.131
most favoured nation (MFN) clauses 8.50–8.53, 8.124–8.132
multilateral economic cooperation treaties 8.11
multiparty arbitrations, joinder, and consolidation 1.109–1.113
  advantages 2.212
  appointment of arbitrators 2.213–2.217, 4.22–4.27
  arbitral institutions, rule of 2.245–2.247
  arbitration agreements 2.212–2.247
  class arbitration 2.224–2.235
  concurrent hearings 2.236–2.237
  conflicting awards 2.221
  consent of parties 1.113
  consolidation 2.221, 2.238–2.247
    consent, by 2.243–2.244
    court-ordered 2.238–2.242
    institutional rules, under 2.245–2.247

693

Index

multiparty arbitrations, joinder, and consolidation (*cont.*)
consortiums 2.213
construction projects 2.218–2.222
disadvantages of arbitration 1.109–1.113
enforcement of awards 2.216–2.217
equality 2.213
ICC arbitration 2.223
ICC Commission on International Arbitration 2.212, 2.243–2.245
ICC Rules 1.111, 2.214
joint ventures 2.213
LCIA Rules 1.111, 2.216
New York Convention 1958 2.216–2.217
recognition of awards 2.216–2.217
several contracts with different parties 2.213, 2.218–2.223
several parties to one contract 2.213–2.217
UNCITRAL Model Law 2.217
multi-tier clauses 2.88–2.93
ADR 2.88–2.93
advantage 2.89
agreements to agree 2.92
amicable settlement 2.88–2.90
arbitration agreements 2.88
certainty threshold 2.90–2.91
definition 2.88
drafting 2.92
good faith 2.92
negotiate, agreements to 2.90–2.93

NAFTA *see* **North American Free Trade Agreement (NAFTA)**
national courts 7.01–7.64
appointment of arbitrators 4.35, 4.37, 4.42–4.45
arbitrability 2.126–2.127, 7.02
arbitral proceedings, comparison with 4.01
arbitral tribunals, establishment of 7.11
arbitration agreements 1.56, 2.66–2.67, 7.10
arbitrators, powers of 5.41–5.42, 7.14–7.61
assistance 5.41–5.42
awards
 challenges 9.141, 10.06, 10.25, 10.36
 enforcement of awards 1.91–1.93, 1.201, 11.12–11.16, 11.35–11.37, 11.151–11.159
 judicial control of 7.62
beginning of arbitration, involvement in 7.09–7.12
bilateral investment treaties (BITs) 8.57–8.61
challenges to awards 9.141, 10.06, 10.25, 10.36
challenges to jurisdiction 5.122–5.123, 7.12
choice of law 7.04
competent court 7.06, 7.22–7.31
control 5.112–5.116, 7.62
defective arbitration clauses 2.197–2.204
delay 5.114
documentary disclosure 7.39–7.44
due process 10.56
during the arbitral proceedings, involvement 7.13–7.64
emergency arbitrators 7.17, 7.28–7.29, 7.37

end of the arbitration, involvement at the 7.64
enforcement of agreements 7.10, 11.64, 11.73–11.76, 11.87–11.100
enforcement of awards 1.91–1.93, 1.201, 11.12–11.16, 11.35–11.37, 11.151–11.159
establishment of tribunal 7.11
evidence 7.06, 7.33, 7.37–7.38
exclusion of involvement of courts 7.06
fair hearings 11.73–11.74
ICSID Convention 11.129
independence and impartiality of arbitrators 7.11
independence of arbitration 7.04–7.06
interim measures 4.03, 7.05, 7.14–7.61
international disputes 1.131
internationalisation 7.64
intervention 7.13
investment disputes 7.43
involvement in proceedings 7.01–7.64
judicial control of proceedings 7.62
jurisdiction 5.112–5.117, 5.122–5.123, 5.126, 7.12
limits on arbitration 7.02
mistake of law 10.68–10.75
model arbitration clauses 2.125
New York Convention 1958 5.122
parallel proceedings, interim relief in respect of 7.51–7.61
partnership relationship with tribunals 7.01, 7.03, 7.07
party autonomy 7.05
performance 11.12–11.16
public interest 2.127
public policy 7.02, 11.106–11.116
recognition of awards 1.201, 11.64, 11.73–11.74, 11.87–11.100
'relay race' comparison 7.07–7.08
role in proceedings 7.01–7.64
state entities as parties 1.131
state participation in arbitral process 1.202–1.205
status quo, preservation of the 7.45–7.50
stay of proceedings 1.56
suspension or setting aside awards 11.99
third parties 6.18
UNCITRAL Model Law 7.06
urgent action 4.03, 7.17
waiver 2.204–2.211
witness attendance 7.32–7.36
national laws
agents, arbitration agreements concluded by 2.57
applicable law 1.10, 3.111–3.127
arbitrability 2.127–2.128, 2.133
arbitration agreements 1.09, 1.53, 2.01, 2.10
arbitration friendly legislation, adoption of 1.228
arbitrators, challenges to 4.102–4.107
autonomy of the parties 3.96–3.99
awards
 challenges 1.201, 10.20, 10.34–10.38
 clarification 9.188–9.189
 enforcement 1.198, 11.35
 jurisdiction 5.111
 recognition 1.198, 11.82, 11.87–11.100
 remission 10.22–10.23

694

Index

bilateral investment treaties (BITs) 8.72
'capable of settlement by arbitration', disputes which are 2.30
capacity 2.34
challenges to arbitrators 4.102–4.107
challenges to awards 10.20, 10.34–10.38
choice of law 3.109–3.127, 3.140–3.155
clarification of awards 9.188–9.189
competition law 2.133
conduct of an arbitration 1.08–1.10, 1.12
conflict of laws 3.214–3.220
consent awards or agreed terms awards 9.37
costs 9.99
delocalisation or denationalisation 1.51
due process 10.54–10.55
enforcement of arbitration agreements 1.09
enforcement of awards 1.198, 11.35
governing law 3.12–3.32
harmonisation 1.205, 1.239, 2.10
history 1.16–1.17
interest 9.80–9.81
international arbitration, characteristics of 1.19–1.20, 1.34
international law 1.10
jurisdiction 5.96, 5.108, 5.111
lex arbitri 1.09
Libyan oil nationalisation arbitrations 3.140–3.155
New York Convention 1958 11.82, 11.87–11.100
recognition of arbitration agreements 1.09
recognition of awards 1.198, 11.82, 11.87–11.100
refusal of recognition and enforcement 11.82, 11.87–11.100
regulation of international arbitration 1.198–1.205
separability or autonomy of arbitration clauses 2.108, 5.102
state immunity 11.145, 11.147
systems of law, other 1.241
time limits 4.07, 9.163, 11.33
treaties and conventions 1.08, 1.17, 1.92, 1.206, 1.239–1.240
tronc commun doctrine 3.146–3.147, 3.155
UNCITRAL Model Law 1.08, 1.227–1.228
national treatment 8.50–8.53, 8.124–8.132
nationalisation *see* Libyan oil nationalisation arbitrations
nationality
  arbitrators 1.72, 4.50, 4.61–4.67, 4.99
  bilateral investment treaties (BITs), jurisdictional issues and 8.16–8.19
  challenges to arbitrators 4.99
  CIETAC Rules 4.66
  discrimination 4.62, 8.103
  European Convention 1961 1.29
  ICC Rules 4.64, 4.67
  ICDR Rules 4.65
  ICSID arbitration 4.67
  independence and impartiality 4.65, 4.99
  international arbitration, characteristics of 1.26, 1.29–1.34
  international, meaning of 1.26, 1.29–1.34
  neutrality 4.61–4.65
  New York Convention 1958 1.30
  objective test 4.139
  organisation of arbitration 4.169
  sole arbitrators 4.61–4.63
  UNCITRAL Model Law 1.26, 1.34
natural persons 2.34
natural resources 2.155–2.156
negligence 5.48, 5.53, 5.55
negotiations
  agreements to negotiate 2.90–2.93
  expert negotiators 1.95
  fees and expenses 4.210–4.211
  good faith 1.136
Netherlands
  Argentina, BIT with 8.22, 8.33
  bilateral investment treaties (BITs) and jurisdictional issues 8.31
  challenges to arbitrators 4.102
  competition 11.121
  conflict of laws 3.217
  consolidation 2.238
  corporate governance 2.157
  Czech Republic, BIT with 8.103
  dissenting opinions 9.131
  duty of care of arbitrators 5.53
  governing law 3.37
  interest 9.77
  national courts 5.130
  Netherlands Arbitration Institute (NAI) 4.39, 7.17
  place where award is made 3.70
  public policy 11.121
  res judicata 9.174
  Slovakia, BIT with 8.74, 8.103
  trade usages 3.182
  Venezuela, BIT with 8.34
  writing 2.19
neutrality
  advantages of arbitration 1.97–1.101, 1.132–1.133
  arbitrators 1.100, 4.61–4.65
  experts 5.23–5.27
  governing law 3.37, 3.39
  international arbitration, characteristics of 1.21
  interpreters 4.183
  language 1.99
  nationality 4.61–4.65
New York Convention 1958, enforcement under *see also* refusal of recognition and enforcement under New York Convention 1958
  arbitrability 2.29, 11.101–11.104
  arbitration agreements 1.44–1.45, 1.212–1.213, 2.06, 2.11, 2.63, 7.10, 11.41
  assignment 2.55
  validity 1.40, 2.07, 3.14
  writing 2.14, 2.16
  arbitration clauses 1.44–1.45, 2.193
  autonomy of the parties 6.07, 6.10
  'capable of settlement by arbitration', disputes which are 2.29

695

Index

New York Convention 1958, enforcement under (*cont.*)
  capacity 2.32, 2.34
  challenges to awards 10.03, 10.05, 10.30, 10.32, 10.39
  commercial, meaning of 1.37
  commercial relationships reservation 1.37, 11.42, 11.46–11.50
  consolidation 2.240
  damages 9.49
  defective arbitration clauses 2.182
  defined legal relationship requirement 2.25
  definition of arbitration 1.04
  delocalisation or denationalisation 3.81
  dispute requirement 1.61–1.62
  electronic communications 1.45, 2.16
  enforcement of arbitration agreements 2.07, 7.10, 11.41
  equality of treatment 6.12
  existing and future disputes 1.62
  fees and charges 11.51
  foreign awards, definition of 1.31
  formalities 9.140, 11.52–11.54
  general principles 1.225
  Geneva Convention 1927 1.212, 11.40
  Geneva Protocol 1923 1.213, 11.40, 11.42
  governing law 3.14
  harmonisation 1.205
  importance 1.212, 1.215, 2.11
  India 11.47–11.49
  inoperability 2.182
  interim measures 7.19
  international effect 1.57, 7.19, 11.62, 11.91, 11.110, 11.124
  interpretation 1.214, 11.47–11.48
  jurisdiction 5.91, 5.111, 5.117, 5.122
  language 11.52
  lex arbitri 1.225, 3.26, 3.28, 3.46–3.47
  multiparty arbitrations 2.216–2.217
  national courts 5.122
  nationality 1.30
  Panama Convention 1975 11.137
  parties, number of 1.211
  pro-enforcement bias 11.107, 11.111
  public policy 11.107, 11.111
  reciprocity reservations 11.42–11.45
  recognition of arbitration agreements 1.91, 2.07, 2.11
  recognition of awards 2.11, 11.42–11.52
  reservations 11.40–11.50
  revision 1.218
  scope 11.36–11.37, 11.45, 11.47
  seat theory (*locus arbitri*) 3.53–3.54
  text of Convention App B
  standards 2.11
  third parties 1.45
  time limits 9.07
  translations 11.52
  UNCITRAL Model Law 1.218
  validity of arbitration agreements 1.40, 2.07, 3.14
  writing 1.44–1.45, 2.16

New Zealand 5.78, 7.20, 9.76
nomination of arbitrators by parties
  agreement of parties 1.100, 4.34–4.36
  co-arbitrators 4.40
  dissenting opinions 1.86
  independence and impartiality 1.100, 4.75–4.76, 4.81–4.83
  multiparty arbitrations, 1.111
  psychology of tribunals 9.114–9.116
  submission agreements 1.42
non liquet, findings of 9.125
non-national law *see also lex mercatoria*; public international law; transnational law
  applicable law 3.188–3.191
  authority to apply 3.188–3.191
  choice of law 3.190–3.191
  concurrent laws 3.136–3.139
  equity and good conscience 3.192–3.197
  general principles of law 3.134–3.135, 3.144, 3.161
  guidelines and rules, selection of other 3.219–3.231
  ICC Rules 3.191
  ICSID Convention 3.189
  Jewish law 3.85, 3.106, 3.190
  rules of law agreed by parties 3.189–3.191
  Shari'ah 3.185–3.188, 3.190
  trade usages 3.182–3.183
  tronc commun doctrine 3.146–3.155
  UNCITRAL Model Law 3.190
  UNIDROIT Principles 3.161, 3.168, 3.171–3.173, 3.178–3.184
non-signatories to arbitration agreements 1.114–1.115
North African Conventions 11.138–11.139
North American Free Trade Agreement (NAFTA)
  bilateral investment treaties (BITs) 8.103
  confidentiality 2.183, 2.185–2.190
  fair and equitable treatment 8.103
  ICSID arbitration 1.187
  investment chapter 8.11
  public policy 10.83
  restitution 9.57
notice of arbitration
  ad hoc arbitrations 1.66–1.68
  appointment of arbitrators 11.61, 11.71–11.72
  commencement of an arbitration 4.11
  ICC Rules 1.69
  institutional arbitrations 1.69–1.70
  LCIA Rules 1.70
  SCC Rules 1.70
  SIAC Rules 1.70
  sole arbitrators 1.68
  starting arbitrations 1.66–1.68
  time limits 4.11
  UNCITRAL Rules 1.66–1.68
notification of awards
  arbitral institutions, rules of 9.169
  ICC Rules 9.169
  time limits 9.169–9.170
  UNCITRAL Rules 9.169
  validity of awards 9.169–9.170

Index

novation 2.58
number of arbitrators 4.22–4.36, 4.54–4.57 *see also* **sole arbitrators**
 2 arbitrators 4.28
 3 arbitrators 4.29–4.31, 4.34, 4.36, 4.39–4.40
 4 or more arbitrators 4.32
 appointment of arbitrators 1.73, 1.100, 4.22–4.36, 4.39–4.40
 arbitration agreements 1.58, 1.100, 2.77, 4.22
 challenges to awards 10.14
 errors, risk of 4.26, 4.31
 model arbitration clauses 2.77, 2.116
 nomination by parties 1.100
 qualities of three arbitrators 4.55–4.58
 states, arbitrations between 4.22
 umpires or referees 2.77, 4.22, 4.28
 UNCITRAL Model Law 4.27
 UNCITRAL Rules 4.27
 uneven number 2.77, 4.22, 4.29–4.32

oaths, admission of 5.13, 5.21, 6.126
OECD Draft Convention on the Protection of Foreign Property 1967 8.08
oil *see also* **Libyan oil nationalisation arbitrations**
 ad hoc arbitrations 1.143
 concession agreements 1.143, 3.120
 hydrocarbon contracts 9.68–9.69
 Oil Gas Energy Mining Infrastructure Dispute Management (OGEMID) 9.200–9.201
one-stop arbitration 1.125, 2.66
opening statements 6.172
opinions 9.128, 9.134 *see also* **dissenting opinions**
opportunity to present case
 autonomy of the parties 6.16
 default awards 9.31
 judicially, arbitrators' duty to act 5.71
 refusal of recognition and enforcement 11.73–11.74
 time limits 9.165
 witnesses 6.130–6.132
oral agreements 1.48, 2.21
orders and directions, awards distinguished from 9.08
organisation of arbitral tribunals 4.101–4.222 *see also* **UNCITRAL Notes on Organizing Arbitral Proceedings**
 administration 4.169, 4.178–4.200
 administrative secretaries or registrars 4.192–4.200
 hearings 4.170–4.177, 6.158–6.165
 meetings 4.170–4.172
 nationality of arbitrators 4.169
Organization of Islamic Cooperation (OIC) Agreement 11.139

pacta sunt servanda 3.159
Panama Convention (Inter-American Convention on International Commercial Arbitration) 1975
 arbitration agreements 2.08
 Calvo Doctrine 11.134
 enforcement of awards 11.134–11.137
 New York Convention 1958 11.137
 postponement of decisions 11.136
 public policy 11.134
 refusal of enforcement of awards, grounds for 11.135
 Venezuela 11.137
parallel proceedings
 anti-arbitration injunctions 7.51–7.59
 ICC Rules 7.56–7.58
 injunctions 7.51–7.59
 interim measures 7.51–7.61
 states or state entities 7.51–7.55, 7.60
 stay of foreign proceedings 7.60
 UNCITRAL Rules 7.52–7.54, 7.60
partial and interim awards 9.19–9.28
 ad hoc arbitrations 9.22
 applicable law 9.20, 9.25
 arbitral institutions, rules of 9.20
 arbitration agreements 9.20
 challenges 10.25–10.27
 costs 9.95
 definition of awards 9.06
 delay 9.24
 disadvantages 9.24
 ICC Rules 9.21
 judicial review 9.24
 jurisdiction 5.113, 5.116, 9.19, 9.24
 LCIA Rules 9.21
 liability and quantum, separation of 9.26–9.27
 limitation clauses 9.28
 money awards 9.02
 powers of tribunals 9.20–9.23
 status of awards, rulings which have 9.10
 UNCITRAL Model Law 9.23, 9.24
 UNCITRAL Rules 9.02, 9.20
parties *see also* **autonomy of the parties**
 absence of parties 11.75
 appointment of arbitrators 1.71–1.76, 4.34–4.36, 4.40, 9.114–9.116
 arbitral proceedings 1.58
 arbitral tribunals, relationships with 4.189
 arbitration agreements 2.31–2.62
 arbitrators, duties of 5.03–5.04
 capacity 2.31–2.42
 control of process 5.113–5.114, 6.04–6.06
 costs 9.87, 9.90–9.98
 experts 5.23–5.25, 6.134, 6.138–6.141
 hearings, presence at 4.171–4.172
 independence and impartiality of party-nominated arbitrators 4.75–4.76, 4.81–4.83
 joinder and intervention 2.59–2.62
 LCIA Rules 1.175
 third parties 2.42–2.58
 UNCITRAL Model Law 1.46
 witnesses, as 6.125–6.126, 6.129
patents 2.130–2.131, 2.134
pathological arbitration clauses 2.181
peaceful enjoyment of possessions 10.95

697

Index

performance of awards 11.07–11.16
  adverse publicity 11.09
  assets, performance against 11.13
  best endeavours 11.11
  commercial and other pressures 11.08–11.10
  diplomatic services 11.08
  enforceable awards, arbitrators' duty to render 11.11
  GAFTA Rules 11.09
  ICSID arbitration 11.10
  national courts, proceedings in 11.12–11.16
  time limits 11.18
  trade associations 11.09
Permanent Court of Arbitration (PCA)
  ad hoc arbitrations 1.190
  appointment of arbitrators 1.190, 4.46–4.48
  Hague Convention 1899 1.189
  Hague Convention 1907 1.189
  private parties, administration of arbitration between 1.190
  Secretary-General, appointment of arbitrators by 4.46–4.48
  states, arbitrations involving 1.183
  UNCITRAL Model Law 1.190
Permanent Court of Justice, establishment of 1.194
personal liability of arbitrators 5.61, 5.78
Peru 3.68, 8.32, 11.124
piercing the corporate veil
  alter ego principle 2.51
  arbitration agreements 2.51
  consent 1.115
  group of companies doctrine 2.51
  objectives 2.43
  third parties 2.51
  trade usages 2.45
place of arbitration, law of the *see* **lex arbitri**
pleadings *see* **written submissions or pleadings**
points of claim 6.72
post-hearing briefs 6.201–6.202
precedent 1.116, 3.173, 8.76, 9.55–9.56, 9.136, 9.199
pre-hearing conferences 6.163–6.167
  agenda items 6.164
  Iran-US Tribunal 6.165
  large and complex cases 6.163
  oral hearings 6.167
  timing 6.163
pre-judgment of issues 4.138–4.142
preliminary issues
  case review conferences 6.64
  conduct of an arbitration 6.41–6.63
  hearings 6.43–6.44
  jurisdiction 5.118
  liability and quantum, bifurcation of 6.54–6.59
  Procedural Order No 1 6.52
  separation of issues 6.60–6.64
preliminary meetings 6.41–6.51
  ad hoc arbitrations 6.44, 6.46
  adjournments 6.48–6.51
  agents, nomination of 6.45
  arbitral institutions, rules of 6.42, 6.46
  case management 6.50
  cultural differences 6.41
  fees and expenses 6.44, 6.46
  governing law 6.46
  items to be covered 6.46–6.47
  manner and timing for presenting key elements of case 6.46
  private meetings 6.43–6.44
  representation 6.45
  rulings, reluctance to make 6.49–6.50
  stages 6.43
  telephone, by 6.41
  'time out' 6.48–6.50
  video conferencing, by 6.41
preliminary steps 6.41–6.63
  meetings 6.41–6.50
  preliminary issues 6.53–6.63
  Procedural Order No 1 6.52
  UNCITRAL Notes on Organizing Arbitral Proceedings 6.51
presiding arbitrator, appointment of 4.40
Principles of European Contract Law (PECL) 3.168
privacy
  advantages of arbitration 1.105
  class arbitration 2.232
  confidentiality 1.105, 2.160–2.161, 2.163
  ICC Rules 2.160
  UNCITRAL Rules 2.161
privity of contract 2.52–2.53
procedural irregularity 10.53–10.59
Procedural Order No 1 6.06, 6.52
procedural orders and directions distinguished 9.08
procedural rules, guidelines and recommendations 3.229–3.231
  examples 3.230
  fees 4.191
  Procedural Order No 1 6.06, 6.52
  terminology 4.191
  soft law 3.230
  UNCITRAL Notes on Organizing Arbitral Proceedings 3.230
procedure *see* **conduct of an arbitration; hearings**
professions *see also* **lawyers**
  advisors 5.48–5.49
  fees and expenses 9.90
  professional advisors 5.48–5.49
  professional liability insurance 5.61
  professional qualifications of arbitrators 4.50–4.57
  transcripts, professional writers of 4.185
  transnational law 3.157
proof *see* **burden of proof; standard of proof**
proper law 1.10
property, protection of 8.08, 8.113–8.117
provisional measures *see* **interim measures**
psychology of tribunals
  3 member tribunals 9.113
  awards 9.113–9.116
  decision-making 9.113–9.116
  independence and impartiality 9.114–9.115

698

Index

party-nominated arbitrators 9.114–9.116
unanimity 9.113
public effect of arbitration 1.92
public hearings 10.57–10.58
public interest
  arbitrability 2.127
  confidentiality 2.165, 2.168, 2.170, 2.183, 2.190
  mistake of fact 10.77
  national courts 2.127
public international law 3.131–3.135
  applicable law 1.10, 3.131–3.135
  bilateral investment treaties (BITs) 8.70
  choice of law 3.132–3.135, 3.140–3.155
  conduct of an arbitration 1.08, 1.12
  expropriation without compensation 8.82
  general principles of law 3.134–3.135, 3.144
  ICSID arbitration 3.132
  Iran-US Claims Tribunal 3.132
  lex mercatoria 3.161
  national laws 1.10
  pacta sunt servanda 3.159
  participants 3.131–3.132
  sources 3.134
  states 1.182, 3.131–3.132, 3.135
public policy
  arbitrability 2.129–2.130, 2.137–2.139, 2.147, 10.51
  autonomy of the parties 3.105, 6.15–6.16
  bilateral investment treaties (BITs) 8.36
  bribery and corruption, arbitrability and 2.147
  challenges to awards 10.63, 10.81–10.87
  choice of law 3.105
  CIETAC Rules 11.116–11.117
  competition law 2.137–2.138, 3.130, 11.120–11.122
  content of awards 9.156
  damages 9.47
  enforcement of awards 9.16, 11.34–11.35, 11.61, 11.64, 11.105–11.122
  EU law 10.86
  finality of awards 11.119
  immunity 5.56, 5.58–5.59
  insolvency 2.141
  International Law Association (ILA) Committee 10.87, 11.119
  international public policy 10.84–10.87, 11.109–11.114, 11.119
  Jewish law 11.106
  lex arbitri 3.64
  mandatory provisions 3.130
  national courts 7.02, 11.106–11.116
  national public policy 10.84–10.87, 11.109–11.114
  New York Convention 1958 11.61, 11.64, 11.105–11.122
  North American Free Trade Agreement (NAFTA) 10.83
  Panama Convention 1975 11.135
  punitive damages 9.47
  refusal of recognition and enforcement 11.61, 11.64, 11.105–11.122
  setting aside awards 10.81–10.87
  states or state entities, involvement of 1.144
  transnational public policy 11.119
  treaties and conventions 1.240
  UNCITRAL Model Law 10.81
publication of awards 9.199–9.201
  adverse publicity 1.105, 11.09
  bilateral investment treaties (BITs) 9.200–9.201
  challenges to arbitrators 4.113
  confidentiality 2.179, 2.190, 9.199, 9.201
  consent 9.199
  ICDR Rules 9.199
  Internet, circulation by 9.200
  Iran-US Claims Tribunal 9.199
  Oil Gas Energy Mining Infrastructure Dispute Management (OGEMID) 9.200–9.201
  precedent 9.199
  transparency 9.201
punitive damages 9.44–9.51

qualifications of arbitrators 1.76, 4.15–4.16, 4.50–4.57, 4.68
qualities of arbitrators 4.49–4.74 *see also* **independence and impartiality of arbitrators**
  applicable law, restrictions imposed by 4.52
  challenges to arbitrators 4.98–4.101
  choice of arbitrator 1.71–1.76
  contract, restrictions imposed by 4.50–4.51
  education and training 4.68–4.71
  English language 4.58
  experience 4.14, 4.49–4.50, 4.54, 4.59, 4.68, 4.72
  hearings, attendance of young practitioners at 4.71
  ICC Rules 4.64, 4.67, 4.69
  ICDR Rules 4.65, 4.69
  ICSID arbitration 4.67
  interpreters 4.58
  interviews 4.72–4.74
  language 4.50, 4.58
  lawyers, appointment of qualified 4.50, 4.52, 4.54–4.57, 4.67
  nationality 4.50, 4.61–4.67
  neutrality 4.61–4.65
  number 4.54–4.57
  outlook 4.59
  professional qualifications 4.53–4.57
  qualifications 1.76, 4.15–4.16, 4.50–4.57, 4.68
  Shari'ah, knowledge of 4.52
  sole arbitrators 4.61–4.64, 4.74
  time and attention to case, ability to give 5.43, 5.79
quantum and liability, bifurcation of 6.54–6.59, 9.26–9.27

reasons
  awards 9.159–9.160, 9.157–9.161
  challenges to arbitrators 4.96
  contents of awards 9.157–9.161
  European Convention 1961 9.160
  ICC Rules 9.157, 9.159
  intelligible decisions, need for 9.161
  UNCITRAL Rules 9.159
  Washington Convention 9.159

rebus sic stantibus 9.71
recognition of arbitration agreements
   applicable law 1.10
   national laws 1.09
   New York Convention 1958 1.91, 2.07, 2.11
   treaties and conventions 1.91
recognition of awards
   consolidation 2.240
   defensive process, as 11.20–11.21, 11.24
   enforcement of awards distinguished from recognition 11.19–11.23
   formalities 11.52
   general principles 11.17–11.18
   Geneva Convention 1927 1.208
   ICSID Convention 1.91, 11.36, 11.38–11.39, 11.125, 11.130
   issue estoppel 11.20
   language 11.32
   local formalities 11.32
   methods of enforcement 11.30–11.32
   Montevideo Convention 1899 1.207
   multiparty arbitrations 2.216–2.217
   national courts 1.201
   national laws 1.198
   New York Convention 1958 11.37, 11.42–11.45
   place of recognition 11.24–11.29
   reciprocity reservations 11.42, 11.45
   registration or deposit of awards 9.171
   res judicata 11.20
   set-off 11.24
   shield and a sword 11.23
   time limits 11.33
   treaties and conventions 11.30, 11.35–11.39
   validity of arbitration agreements 1.40
   writing 1.44
recommendations 3.229–3.231
rectification 9.63–9.64
Redfern Schedule 1.238, 1.243, 6.100–6.102
referees *see* **umpires or referees**
refusal of recognition and enforcement of awards
   see also **refusal of recognition and enforcement under New York Convention 1958**
   consequences 11.34
   Geneva Convention of 1927 10.49
   Moscow Convention 1972 11.133
   multiparty arbitrations 2.217
   Panama Convention 1975 11.135
   public policy 11.34
   UNCITRAL Model Law 1.40, 10.49
refusal of recognition and enforcement under New York Convention 1958 11.55–11.101
   absence of parties 11.75
   appointment of arbitrators, proper notice of 11.63, 11.71–11.72
   arbitrability 11.101–11.104
   arbitration agreements 1.40, 2.63
      composition of tribunal not in accordance with 11.82–11.86
      invalidity of 11.63, 11.66–11.70
   binding award 11.87
   capacity 2.32, 11.66
   CIETAC Rules 11.85, 11.116–11.117
   composition of tribunal not in accordance with agreement or relevant law 11.82–11.85
   due process 11.71–11.76
   equality of treatment 11.73
   estoppel 11.83, 11.85
   fair hearings 11.72–11.74
   forum non conveniens 11.123–11.124
   Geneva Convention 1927 11.82, 11.87
   grounds 11.55–11.102, 11.123–11.125
   ICC Rules 11.67–11.69
   incapacity 11.66
   inconsistent decisions 11.65
   interpretation 11.65
   Iran-US Claims Tribunal 11.75
   jurisdiction 11.78–11.81
   local annulments 11.89–11.98
   merits, prohibition of review on 11.56
   multiparty arbitrations 2.217
   national courts 11.64, 11.73–11.74, 11.87–11.100
   national laws 11.82, 11.87–11.100
   non-binding awards 11.87–11.100
   opportunity to be heard 11.73–11.74
   Peru 11.124
   pro-enforcement bias 11.61
   public policy 11.61, 11.64, 11.105–11.122
   Russian Commercial Procedure Code, interpretation of 11.103
      arbitrability 11.103
      International Commercial Arbitration Court (ICAC) 11.103
   setting aside of awards by national courts 11.64, 11.87–11.100
   standards 11.64
   subject matter not capable of settlement by arbitration 11.64
   suspended awards 11.87–11.100
   UNCITRAL Model Law 11.55–11.61, 11.64–11.65
   validity of arbitration agreements 11.63, 11.66–11.70
   validity of awards 11.90
   writing 11.70
refusal or failure to participate in arbitrations
   ad hoc arbitrations 1.145
   arbitrators' refusal 4.154–4.155
   boycotts 5.119, 5.120
   default awards 9.30–9.31
   delay 6.194
   disruption 6.194
   ex parte hearings 6.193–6.195
   jurisdiction 5.120
   truncated tribunals 4.153–4.155
regional conventions
   enforcement of awards 11.36, 11.39, 11.131–11.140
   institutional arbitration 1.146
   investments 11.139
   Panama Convention 2.08, 11.134–11.137
registrars *see* **administrative secretaries or registrars**
registration or deposit of awards 9.171–9.172

Index

regulation of international arbitration 1.197–1.238
  arbitrators and counsel, practice of experienced 1.238
  assistance, applications to court for 1.200
  enforcement of awards 1.198
  national laws 1.198–1.205
  practice of international arbitration 1.224–1.238, 1.242–1.243
  recognition of awards 1.198
  Revised UNCITRAL Model Law 1.221–1.223
  seat of arbitration, law of 1.198
  treaties and conventions, role of 1.206–1.217, 1.228
  UNCITRAL Model Law 1.218–1.219, 1.225–1.227
rejoinders 6.70, 6.77
'relay race' comparison 7.07–7.08
relevance of evidence 6.97–6.98, 6.110
remedies 9.40–9.99 *see also* **compensation; damages; injunctions**
  bilateral investment treaties (BITs) 8.45, 8.49
  challenges to awards 10.07
  contracts and filling gaps, adaptation of 9.63, 9.65–9.71
  costs 9.88–9.99
  declaratory relief 9.60–9.62
  interest 9.73–9.84
  model arbitration clauses 2.100
  rectification 9.63–9.64
  restitution 9.53–9.58
  specific performance 1.55, 9.52
remission of awards
  Arbitration Act 1996 10.22
  challenges to awards 10.21–10.23
  ICC Rules 10.22
  national laws 10.22–10.23
  setting aside awards 10.21–10.22
  UNCITRAL Model Law 10.23
removal of arbitrators 2.83, 5.72
replies 6.70
representation 1.179–1.180, 2.236, 6.45 *see also* **lawyers**
representative or class arbitrations 2.133, 2.135–2.137, 2.224–2.235, 10.51, 11.122
res judicata
  amiable compositeurs, arbitrators as 9.177
  awards 9.173–9.185
  cause of action estoppel 9.174
  civil law countries 9.174
  collateral estoppel 9.180
  common law countries 9.174
  definition 9.173
  estoppel 9.174, 9.180, 9.185
  existing disputes 9.177–9.178
  ICSID arbitration 9.177
  International Law Commission (ILA) Committee 9.175, 9.178, 9.181
  interpretation 9.175
  issue estoppel 9.174, 9.180, 9.185
  recognition of awards 11.20
  single economic entity analysis 9.185
  subsequent disputes 9.179–9.181
  third parties 9.182–9.185
  triple identity test 9.178
resignation of arbitrators 4.150–4.151, 4.155
restitution
  bilateral investment treaties (BITs) 8.163
  common law countries 9.52
  compensation 9.54–9.57
  enforcement 9.56
  expropriation 9.58
  Libyan oil nationalisation case 3.120, 9.55
  North American Free Trade Agreement (NAFTA) 9.57
  stabilisation clauses 3.120
restraint of trade 2.134
review of awards 9.195–9.199, 10.20
  ICC arbitrations 9.195–9.197
  settlements 9.198
  standards of review 9.195
Revised UNCITRAL Model Law 1.18, 1.221–1.223
  arbitration agreements 1.48, 2.16–2.17
  electronic communications 1.46, 1.222
  interim measures, *ex parte* applications for 1.223
  oral agreements 1.48
  proof of agreement 2.17
  record of agreements in any form 2.16
  Working Group 1.221–1.223
  writing 1.48, 1.222, 2.16–2.18
revision clauses 3.119
Rhodian Sea Law 3.157
Riyadh Arab Agreement on Judicial Cooperation 11.138
Rome I Regulation on the Law relating to Contractual Obligations
  autonomy of the parties 3.98, 3.103
  capacity 2.34
  choice of law 3.103, 3.202
  close connection 3.210
  conflict of laws 3.210
  express choice 3.202
  Guiliano and Lagarde Report 3.202
  mandatory rules 3.105
rules 1.229–1.235 *see also* **arbitral institutions, rules of; specific rules (eg UNCITRAL Rules)**
  ad hoc arbitrations 1.141–1.145
  conduct of arbitration 6.01, 6.06
  established rules 1.229–1.132
  general provisions 1.229–1.232
  guidance 1.235
  hard law 1.233–1.234
  ICSID Convention 1.226
  rule books 1.149–1.150
  soft law 1.232, 1.235–1.236
rules of law 3.193, 3.218–3.220
Russia
  arbitrability 11.103
  Commercial Procedure Code, interpretation of 11.103
  corporate governance 2.158, 3.129, 11.103
  Energy Charter Treaty (ECT) 8.21
  enforcement of awards 11.118, 11.131, 11.155

Russia (*cont.*)
  LCIA 1.171
  legal entities 8.21
  Moscow Convention 1972 11.131
  national courts 11.118
  Permanent Court of Arbitration (PCA) 1.189
  public policy 11.118
  punitive damages 11.118
  refusal of enforcement or recognition 11.103
  sole option/unilateral option clauses 2.97

salvage agreements 8.41
Saudi Arabia 1.211, 3.187, 4.52, 9.72, 9.81, 9.195
SCC *see* **Stockholm Chamber of Commerce (SCC) Rules**
seat theory (*locus arbitri*)
  applicable law 3.05
  choice of law 3.208–3.209
  construction disputes, inspections in 3.59–3.60
  definition of seat of arbitration 3.55
  flexibility 3.59
  floating arbitration 3.84
  Geneva Protocol 1923 3.53
  governing law 3.53–3.62, 3.84–3.90
  ICC Rules 3.57
  injunctions 3.90
  inspections 3.59–3.60
  international arbitration, characteristics of 1.21
  LCIA Rules 3.58
  lex arbitri 3.53–3.61, 3.84–3.90
  model arbitration clauses 2.83, 2.100, 2.117
  New York Convention 1958 3.53–3.54
  territorial link 3.54, 3.56
  treaties and conventions 3.53
  UNCITRAL Model Law 3.59
  visits to other countries by tribunals 3.60
secrecy *see* **confidentiality**
secretaries *see* **administrative secretaries**
securities transactions 2.139–2.140
security for costs 5.35–5.40
Sedona Principles 6.107
selection of arbitral tribunals 1.71–1.74, 1.100, 4.13–4.16
separability or autonomy of arbitration clauses 2.101–2.113
  arbitrability 2.134
  arbitral institutions, rules of 2.104
  arbitration agreements 2.101–2.113
  bribery and corruption, arbitrability and 2.138
  challenges to clauses 5.100
  competence 5.110–5.111
  competence/competence 5.105–5.109
  definition 1.54, 2.101
  France 2.106
  lex arbitri 3.15
  manifestly void, where agreements are 2.112
  national laws 2.108, 5.102
  secondary contracts 2.102
  UNCITRAL Model Law 2.105
  UNCITRAL Rules 2.104

  validity of arbitration agreements 1.54
  validity of clauses 5.100–5.102, 5.110–5.111
separate and concurring opinions 9.128, 9.134
separation of issues 6.60–6.64
sequestration 11.35
set-off 11.24
setting aside awards
  challenges to awards 10.05–10.06, 10.33
  grounds 10.38–10.39, 10.55, 10.62, 10.69
  remission 10.21–10.23
  state responsibility 10.93–10.95
  time limits 10.10
  competition law 11.121
  fraud 10.62
  ICSID arbitration 11.121
  judicially, arbitrator's duty to act 5.74
  oral hearings 10.55
  rectification 9.64
  remission 10.21–10.23
  state responsibility 10.93–10.95
  UNCITRAL Model Law 5.117, 10.10, 10.23, 10.38–10.39, 10.69
settlements
  amicable settlements 2.88–2.90
  awards 1.80–1.82, 1.93, 9.198, 11.05
  bilateral investment treaties (BITs) 8.48
  consent awards or agreed terms awards 9.34–9.38
  continuity of role 1.107
  enforcement of awards 11.05
  model arbitration clauses 2.88–2.89
  multi-tier clauses 2.88–2.90
Shari'ah law
  applicable law 3.185–3.187, 3.190, 4.52
  arbitrators with knowledge of Shari'ah law 4.52
  ICC arbitration 3.186
  Estisna form, financial transactions in 3.186
  general principles 3.185
  non-national law 3.185–3.187
  Qur'an 3.185
signatures
  arbitral institutions, rules of 9.149
  arbitration agreements 2.15, 2.42
  consent awards or agreed terms awards 9.35
  dissenting opinions 9.130
  form of awards, validity and 9.148–9.149
  ICC Rules 9.149
  LCIA Rules 9.149
  refusal to sign awards 9.130
  writing requirement 2.15
simplified procedures 6.32–6.33, 9.165
Singapore *see also* **Singapore International Arbitration Centre (SIAC)**
  alter egos 11.104
  confidentiality 2.169
  interest 9.74
  internationality 1.24
  Maxwell Chamber 4.180
  mediate, agreements to 2.92
  uncertainty 2.199

Index

Singapore International Arbitration Centre (SIAC)
commencement of arbitration 1.70
costs 9.87
emergency arbitrators 4.17
establishment 1.169
inability to act prior to formation 7.17
interim measures 7.17
Model Law 1.169
Rules 1.70, 1.169, 4.17
witnesses, preparation of 6.124
site inspections 5.45, 6.146–6.153
Slovakia-Netherlands BIT 8.74, 8.103
small claims 6.155
soft law 1.232, 1.235–1.236, 3.230
sole arbitrators 4.23–4.27, 4.36
administration 6.119
advantages 4.25
arbitration agreements 1.100
awards 1.83
decision-making 1.83
experiences and practice, as 1.232
fees and expenses 4.25
IBA Evidence Rules 1.235–1.236
ICC arbitration 1.235, 4.23, 4.36
ICDR Rules 4.24
interviews 4.74
lawyers, conduct of 1.236
LCIA Rules 4.23
nationality 4.61–4.63
number of arbitrators 1.100, 4.23–4.27
professional qualifications 4.54
qualities 4.54
sole option/unilateral option clauses 2.94–2.98
arbitration agreements 2.94–2.98
Brussels I Regulation 2.98
definition 2.94
enforcement 2.95–2.98
independence and impartiality 1.100
validity 2.95–2.98
Spain
Argentina, BIT with 8.52
Chile, BIT with 8.52–8.53
enforcement of awards 11.53
most favoured nation (MFN) clause 8.52–8.53
qualifications 4.52
specialisation within legal profession 3.156
specialised staff 1.163
specific performance 1.55, 9.52
sport 4.137
Sri Lanka 8.08, 8.65, 8.114
stabilisation clauses
change of laws 3.120–3.127
choice of law 3.120–3.127
compensation 3.121, 3.127
conflict of laws 3.125
economic equilibrium clauses 3.124–3.127
force majeure clauses 3.124
freezing clauses 3.124–3.125
hardship clauses 3.124
investments 3.122–3.123, 3.126–3.127

Libyan oil nationalisations
arbitrations 3.120–3.121
oil concession agreements 3.120
regulatory chill 3.123
restitution 3.120
risk allocation 3.127
traditional clauses 3.124, 3.125
staff 1.151, 1.163, 1.171
standard form contracts *see also* model arbitration clauses
adaptation of contracts 9.69
arbitration agreements 2.71, 2.73
arbitration clauses 1.52
arbitrators 4.50
class or representative arbitrations 2.226, 2.230–2.231
customary law 3.184
gaps, filling 9.69
interpretation, uniform rules for 3.184
mistake of law 10.66
rectification 9.64
UNIDROIT Principles of International Commercial Contracts 3.184
standard of proof 6.85–6.88
standards
arbitration agreements 2.09–2.12
bilateral investment treaties (BITs) 8.96–8.112
disclosure 2.166–2.174
due process 10.53–10.54
expropriation 8.146–8.148, 8.162
refusal of enforcement and recognition 11.64
review of awards 9.195
state or state entities 1.204
treaties and conventions 2.09–2.12
UNIDROIT Principles of International Commercial Contracts 3.179, 3.183
start of arbitrations *see* commencement of an arbitration
state agencies 2.37–2.41
state immunity
absolute immunity 11.143–11.144
capacity 2.39
commercial acts (acts *jure gestionis*) 11.143
commercial assets, execution against 11.151–11.155
diplomatic immunity 11.155
enforcement of awards 11.27, 11.141–11.155
ICC Rules 11.150
ICSID Convention 11.147
jurisdiction 11.141–11.145, 11.150
national laws 11.145, 11.147
restricted immunity 11.143–11.144
sovereign dignity 1.184
state acts (acts *jure imperii*) 11.143
State Immunity Act 1978 11.145, 11.152–11.153
submission to jurisdiction 11.142, 11.145
waiver 11.144–11.146, 11.150–11.151, 11.155
state responsibility
bilateral investment treaties (BITs) 8.66
human rights treaties 10.95
ICSID arbitration 10.94

Index

state responsibility (*cont.*)
  investment treaties 8.66, 10.94
  setting aside of awards, wrongful 10.93–10.95
statements of claim 6.68
states or state entities *see also* state immunity
  ad hoc arbitrations 1.144
  Alabama Claims arbitration 1.192
  approval requirement 2.37–2.38
  arbitrability 2.40–2.41
  arbitration agreements 1.25
  arbitrations involving states or state entities 1.182–1.190
  assistance to parties 1.202
  bilateral investment treaties (BITs) 1.217
  capacity 2.37–2.41
  choice of law 3.213
  claims commissions or tribunals 1.196
  commissioners 1.191, 1.196
  consent of states 8.08
  control over process 1.202–1.203
  disputes between states 1.191–1.196
  dissenting opinions 9.129
  due process 1.204
  economic considerations 1.183
  European Convention 1961 2.39
  Hague Peace Conventions 1899 and 1907 1.193
  history 1.191–1.196
  ICSID arbitration 1.186–1.187, 8.08
  ILC Draft Articles on State Responsibility 9.77, 9.79
  in absentia, awards granted in 1.183
  injunctions 7.51–7.55
  international arbitration, characteristics of 1.19, 1.21
  International Court of Justice (ICJ) 1.194–1.195
  international law 7.56
  international transactions only, agreements permitting 1.25
  Jay Treaty 1794 between United States and UK 1.191
  Libyan oil nationalisation arbitrations 3.145–3.147
  minimum standards 1.204
  mixed commissions 1.196
  national courts 1.131
  national prestige, questions of 1.184
  neutral process, submission to 1.182
  number of arbitrators 4.22
  parallel proceedings 7.51–7.55, 7.60
  participation in arbitral process 1.202–1.205
  Permanent Court of Arbitration (PCA) 1.189–1.190, 1.194
  Permanent Court of Justice, establishment of 1.194
  political considerations 1.183
  public international law 1.182, 3.131–3.132, 3.135
  public policy 1.144
  sovereignty 2.155
  standards 1.204
  state immunity 1.184, 2.39

stay of proceedings 7.60
tronc commun doctrine 3.146–3.147, 3.155
status quo, measures aimed at preservation of 7.45–7.50
stay of proceedings
  appointment of arbitrators 4.44
  defective arbitration clauses 2.214
  enforcement of arbitration agreements 1.56
  parallel proceedings 7.60
  states or state entities 7.60
  waiver 2.206
Stockholm Chamber of Commerce (SCC) Rules
  commencement of an arbitration 1.70
  confidentiality 3.25
  costs 9.87
  emergency arbitrators 4.17
  interim measures 7.17
  uncertainty 2.199
  UNIDROIT Principles 3.180
striking out 2.184, 2.206
'subject matter capable of settlement by arbitration' requirement 1.64–1.65, 2.29–2.30, 2.124–2.126, 10.50
subject matter of dispute, examination of *see* inspections
submission agreements 1.51–1.52, 2.02, 2.119–2.123
  ad hoc arbitrations 1.142
  arbitrators, resignation of 2.122–2.123
  contents 1.51, 2.03, 2.120–2.123
  damages 9.48
  definition 1.42
  drafting 2.120–2.123
  existing agreements 1.51, 2.02–2.03
  future disputes 1.52
  governing law 3.09, 3.13
  jurisdiction 5.98
  procedural arrangements 2.121
  punitive damages 9.48
  resignation of arbitrators 2.122–2.123
  scope 2.03
  time limits 9.165–9.166
  vacancies, filling 2.66
submissions *see* written submissions or pleadings
subpoenas
  arbitrators, powers of 5.19–5.20
  documents, production of 5.19
  third parties 6.111
  witnesses 6.130, 7.34–7.36
subsistence expenses 4.215–4.217
substance, law applicable to the 3.91–3.197
  arbitral tribunal, decisions by 3.200
  arbitration agreements 3.91–3.92
  autonomy of the parties 3.96–3.110
  bilateral investment treaties (BITs) 8.62–8.70
  changes in law 3.95, 3.136–3.139
  choice of law 3.91–3.219
  combined laws 3.136–3.155
  concurrent laws 3.136–3.155
  construction contracts 3.92
  contract law 3.39
  documents, examination of 3.91

electronic communications 3.96
equity and good conscience 3.192–3.197
facts, establishment of the 3.91
frontiers, crossing 3.95–3.96
general principles of law 3.131–3.135
ICSID Convention 3.138
International Law Association (ILA)
  report 3.200
lex arbitri 1.09, 3.39
lex mercatoria 3.161–3.177
Libyan oil nationalisation
  arbitrations 3.140–3.155
mandatory law 3.127–3.130
national frontiers, crossing 3.95–3.96
national laws 3.111–3.127
nationalisation 3.139–3.155
non-national law, authority to apply 3.188–3.191
public international law 3.131–3.135
Shar'iah law 3.185–3.188
stabilisation clauses 3.120–3.127
trade usages 3.182–3.184
transnational law 3.156–3.191
tronc commun doctrine 3.146–3.155
unfair treatment, precluding 3.119
UNIDROIT Principles 3.178–3.180
uniformity and consistency 3.200
witnesses 3.91
substantive grounds for challenging awards 10.64–10.88
  mistake of fact 10.77–10.80
  mistake of law 10.66–10.75
  public policy 10.81–10.88
  UNCITRAL Model Law 10.61
succession 2.42, 2.58
summary or early determinations 6.38–6.40
summary judgments 1.60–1.61
Sweden *see also* **Stockholm Chamber of Commerce (SCC) Rules**
  assignment 2.55
  clarification of awards 9.191
  confidentiality 2.176, 2.181–2.183
  defective arbitration clauses 2.199
  deliberation 9.107–9.108
  dissenting opinions 9.107
  interpretation of awards 9.191
  lex arbitri 3.25, 3.43
  notice of arbitration 1.70
Switzerland
  agents, arbitration agreements concluded by 2.57
  amiable compositeurs 3.190
  applicable law 1.10, 3.36, 3.37, 3.55–3.56
  arbitrability 2.134, 2.144, 2.152
  bilateral investment treaties (BITs) and jurisdictional issues 8.17
  bribery and corruption and arbitrability 2.152
  challenges to arbitrators 4.102, 4.147
  challenges to awards 10.25, 10.28, 10.72, 11.88
  commencement of arbitration 4.12
  competition law 2.134, 11.121
  conflict of laws 2.246
  consolidation 2.246

dissenting opinions 9.131
electronic communications 1.47
emergency arbitrators 4.17
enforcement of awards 11.155
European Convention on Human Rights 10.57
evidence 1.47
expedited procedure 1.07
ex aequo et bono 3.190
fast track arbitration 1.07
form of awards, validity and 9.146
governing law 3.36, 3.80, 9.146
group of companies doctrine 2.45
Holocaust Tribunals 1.196
illegality 2.151, 11.107
immunity 11.155
independence or impartiality 4.102
insolvency 2.144
institutional arbitration 1.146
interim measures 7.26
internationality 1.24, 1.30
interpretation 2.66
joinder and intervention 2.61
judicially, arbitrators' duty to act 5.75
lex arbitri 1.10, 3.44, 3.55–3.56
majority voting 9.123
mistake of fact 10.77
mistake of law 10.66–10.76
multi-tier clauses 2.91
nationality 1.30
non-national law 3.190
oaths 5.14
Pakistan, BIT with 8.17
Philippines, BIT with 8.138
procedural law, choice of 3.65–3.66
provisional or conservatory measures 7.14, 7.26
public policy 10.83, 11.107–11.108, 11.113, 11.121
res judicata 9.174
review of awards 9.196, 10.20
rules of law 3.190
setting aside awards 11.88
Sri Lanka, BIT with 8.08
state and state agencies 2.39
substantive law 1.10
Swiss Rules of Arbitration 1.07, 2.61, 2.246, 4.17, 6.124, 9.123
third parties 2.45
time limits 4.12
validity of agreements 2.107
waiver 4.147
witnesses 5.20, 7.33
writing 1.47, 2.19
written submissions 6.68

tacit or implied choice of law 3.201–3.204, 3.208
telephone, meetings by 6.41
third parties
  agency 2.42
  arbitration agreements 1.45, 1.114–1.116, 2.42–2.62
  autonomy of the parties 6.17–6.18
  consent 2.42

Index

third parties (*cont.*)
  Contracts (Rights of Third Parties) Act 1930 2.52
  disclosure 7.39–7.40
  documentary evidence 6.111–6.112
  estoppel 2.36, 2.53
  group of companies doctrine 2.42–2.53
  injunctions 9.59
  interim measures 7.18, 7.22
  joinder and intervention 1.109–1.113, 2.59–2.62
  national courts 6.18
  New York Convention 1958 1.45
  privity 2.52–2.53
  res judicata 9.182–9.185
  signatures 2.42
  succession 2.42, 2.58
  veil, piercing the corporate 2.51
  witness *subpoenas* 6.111, 6.130, 7.36
  writing 2.42
time and attention to case, arbitrators' ability to give 5.43, 5.79
time limits
  abridgment 6.32
  ad hoc arbitrations 4.11–4.12
  appointment of arbitrators 4.14
  arbitral institutions, rules of 4.08–4.10
  arbitration clauses 9.165–9.166
  arbitrators 4.114
  cause of action, accrual of 4.05
  challenges to arbitrators 4.114
  challenges to awards 9.07, 10.10, 10.39
  clarification of awards 9.192
  commencement of an arbitration 4.05–4.10
  conflict of laws 4.07
  contract law 4.05–4.06
  correction of awards 10.10
  disadvantages of mandatory limits 9.165–9.166
  enforcement of awards 11.33
  expedited or simplified procedures 9.165
  extensions of time 1.156, 6.73, 9.164
  fast track arbitration 6.32
  frustrating proceedings 9.164
  hearings 6.172
  ICC arbitration 1.156, 4.08–4.09, 9.167–9.168
  ICSID arbitration 4.09
  institutional arbitrations 1.155–1.156
  jurisdiction to make awards 9.162
  LCIA Rules 6.30
  litigation 4.05
  national laws 4.07, 9.163, 11.33
  New York Convention 1958 9.07
  non-mandatory provisions 9.167–9.168
  notice of arbitration 4.11
  notification of awards 9.169–9.170
  opportunity to present case 9.165
  performance 11.18
  procedure, as matter of 4.07
  recognition of awards 11.33
  registration or deposit of awards 9.172
  submission agreements 9.165–9.166
  substance, as matter of 4.07
  validity of awards 9.162–9.168
  written submissions or pleadings 6.73–6.74
'time out' of meetings 6.48–6.50
timetables 4.186–4.188
tort claims 2.25–2.27, 2.64–2.65 *see also* duty of care of arbitrators
trade 1.10, 8.11
trade associations 4.28, 10.12, 11.09
trade marks 2.130–2.131
trade secrets 1.105, 2.131, 2.191–2.193
trade usages 2.45, 3.182–3.184
training of arbitrators 4.68–4.71, 9.17
transcripts
  administrative secretaries 4.193–4.194
  costs 9.89
  experts 6.186
  hearings 4.196–4.197, 6.160, 6.187–6.188
  Livenote 4.185
  professional writers 4.185
  vacancies, falling 4.163
  verbatim records 4.184–4.185, 6.160
translations 2.87, 4.58, 6.119, 9.150, 11.52
transnational law 3.156–3.191 *see also lex mercatoria* (law merchant)
  applicable law 1.10, 3.156–3.191
  Central Transnational Law Database 3.168
  Consolato des Mare 3.157–3.158
  customary laws of sea 3.157
  international arbitration, characteristics of 1.19
  International Law Association (ILA) 3.160
  Libyan oil nationalisation arbitrations 3.140
  non-national law, authority to apply 3.188–3.191
  pacta sunt servanda 3.159
  professionals, development of special rules by 3.157
  Rhodian Sea Law 3.157
  Shari'ah law 3.185–3.187
  specialisation within legal profession 3.156
  specific rules of law 3.156
  trade usages 3.182–3.184
  UNIDROIT Principles 3.177–3.180
transparency 2.188–2.189
travel expenses 4.215, 9.87, 9.88, 9.90, 9.92
treaties and conventions *see also* bilateral investment treaties (BITs); investment treaties, arbitration under; particular treaties (eg Geneva Convention 1927); regional conventions
  arbitration agreements 1.91, 2.06–2.13
  autonomy of the parties 3.100
  commercial disputes 1.240
  conduct of arbitrations 1.225, 6.19–6.21
  conflict of laws 3.214–3.217
  enforcement of arbitration agreements 1.205
  enforcement of awards 1.205
  friendship, commerce and navigation (FCN) treaties 8.03, 8.08
  history 1.17, 1.18, 8.08
  jurisdiction 5.99, 5.111, 5.128–5.137
  list of important treaties 1.18
  multilateral economic cooperation treaties 8.11

Index

national laws 1.08, 1.17, 1.92, 1.206, 1.239–1.240
public policy 1.240
recognition of arbitration agreements 1.91
recognition of awards 11.30
regulation 1.206–1.217, 1.229–1.232
reservations 1.240
seat theory (*locus arbitri*) 3.53
standards 2.09–2.12
unification 1.240
validity of arbitration agreements 2.09–2.10
Vienna Convention on the Law of Treaties 5.127, 8.64
writing requirement 2.13
tribunals *see* **arbitral institutions, rules of; arbitral tribunals; institutional arbitrations; specific institutions (eg London Court of International Arbitration (LCIA))**
tronc commun doctrine 3.146–3.155
   Channel Tunnel project 3.147–3.153
   choice of law 3.146–3.154
   combined laws 3.146–3.155
   national law 3.146–3.156
   state parties 3.146–3.147, 3.155
truncated tribunals 4.154–4.161
   AAA International Arbitration Rues 4.156, 4.157
   ad hoc arbitrations 4.156, 4.160
   ICC Rules 4.156, 4.158–4.159
   ICDR Rules 4.156
   LCIA Rules 4.158
   lex arbitri 4.160
   refusal to participate, arbitrators' 4.154–4.155
   resignations 4.155
   UNCITRAL Model Law 4.156
   UNCITRAL Rules 4.160
   vacancies, filling 4.139, 4.154–4.161
trustees in bankruptcy, consent of 2.146
Turkey 11.114
types of arbitration 1.140–1.190
   ad hoc arbitrations 1.140–1.145
   institutional arbitrations 1.140, 1.146–1.189
   lex arbitri, mandatory rules of 1.140
   state, arbitrations involving a 1.182–1.190

Ukraine-Lithuania BIT 8.22
ultra vires 2.35
umbrella clauses or observation of undertakings 8.134–8.140
umpires or referees
   commodity arbitrations 2.77
   number of arbitrators 2.77, 4.22, 4.28
   trade associations 4.28
unambiguous terms 9.68–9.70
unanimity 9.112–9.113, 9.118, 9.127, 9.130
UNCITRAL (United Nations Commission on International Trade Law)
   List of Matters for Possible Consideration in Organizing Arbitral Proceedings App I
   Notes on Organizing Arbitral Proceedings 3.230, 6.51, 6.179, App I
   Rules on Transparency in Treaty-based Investor-State Arbitration 2.189

UNCITRAL Model Law 1.02, 1.18 *see also* **Revised UNCITRAL Model Law**
adjudicability 10.45–10.46
adoption 1.219
amiable compositeurs 1.139
appointment of arbitrators 1.190
arbitrability 2.29
arbitration agreements 1.40, 1.46, 2.13, 2.16–2.17, 7.10
arbitration clauses 1.50, 2.73, 2.105
arbitration friendly, as being 1.227
autonomy of the parties 6.07, 6.10, 6.16
awards
   challenges 10.03, 10.10, 10.30, 10.37–10.41, 10.45–10.46, 10.52, 10.65, 10.88
   decisions 1.80
   definition of 9.06
   enforcement 1.40, 10.49
   ex parte hearings 6.199
   form of awards, validity and 9.143
   remission 10.23
'capable of settlement by arbitration', disputes which are 2.29
capacity 2.32, 2.34
challenges to arbitrators 4.107
challenges to awards 10.10, 10.30, 10.37–10.41, 10.45–10.46, 10.88
choice of law 3.216
commercial, meaning of 1.38
conduct of an arbitration 3.45, 6.20–6.21
conflict of laws 3.215
consent awards or agreed terms awards 9.37
consolidation 2.239, 2.245
defined legal relationship requirement 2.25
delay 5.67
delocalisation or denationalisation 3.74, 3.81
electronic communications 2.16
enforcement of awards, refusal of 1.40, 10.49, 11.55–11.62, 11.64–11.65
equality of treatment 6.10, 6.16
evidence abroad, taking 6.132
ex parte hearings 6.199
form of awards and validity 9.143
general principles 1.227
governing law 3.40, 3.70, 3.216
harmonisation 1.205, 1.218
interest 9.76
interim measures 5.27–5.28, 5.32, 5.34, 7.14, 7.18, 7.21, 7.24, 7.26
international arbitration, characteristics of 1.22
international, meaning of 1.31–1.34
internationality requirement 1.31–1.34
jurisdiction 5.108–5.110, 5.117, 7.12
lex arbitri 3.45–3.46, 3.84
majority voting 9.122
mistake of law 10.69–10.76
model arbitration clauses 2.73, 2.99, 2.113
multiparty arbitrations 2.217
national courts 7.06
national laws 1.08, 1.227–1.228
nationality 1.26, 1.34

Index

UNCITRAL Model Law (*cont.*)
  New York Convention 1958, revision of 1.218
  non-national law 3.190
  number of arbitrators 4.27
  partial and interim awards 9.23, 9.24
  parties to contracts 1.46
  Permanent Court of Arbitration (PCA) 1.190
  public policy 10.81
  recognition of awards, refusal of 1.40, 11.55–11.62, 11.64–11.65
  regulation of international arbitration 1.218–1.219, 1.225–1.227
  seat theory (*locus arbitri*) 3.59
  subject matter of arbitration awards 1.30
  success of Model law 1.219–1.220
  text App A
  trade usages 3.18
  truncated tribunals 4.156
  validity of arbitration agreements 1.40
  waiver 2.205
  witnesses 6.132, 7.32–7.34
  writing 1.46, 2.13, 2.16–2.17
UNCITRAL Notes on Organizing Arbitral Proceedings 3.230, 6.51, 6.179
  contents 6.51
  hearings 6.179
  preliminary steps 6.51
  procedural rules, guidelines and recommendations 3.230
  text App I
UNCITRAL Rules
  ad hoc arbitrations 1.141, 1.144
  adaptation of contracts 9.70
  amiable compositeurs 3.196
  appointment of arbitrators 4.39, 4.46–4.47
  arbitration agreements 2.71
  autonomy of the parties 3.100, 6.13, 6.16
  awards 1.80, 9.01–9.02, 9.37, 9.70, 9.192, 10.09, 10.30
  bilateral investment treaties (BITs) 5.127, 8.63
  bribery and corruption, arbitrability and 2.152
  Challenge Procedure 4.114
  challenges to arbitrators 4.94–4.95, 4.114, 4.138
  challenges to awards 10.09, 10.30
  clarification of awards 9.189
  commencement of arbitration 1.66–1.68
  confidentiality 2.164
  consolidation 2.245
  costs 8.169, 9.87, 9.88, 9.90, 9.92
  default clauses 2.85
  equality of treatment 6.16
  ex aequo et bono 3.196
  fairness 3.196
  fees and expenses 4.208
  gaps, filling 9.69
  independence and impartiality 4.94
  injunctions 7.51–7.54
  inspection 6.152
  interim measures 5.27, 7.24
  interpretation of awards 9.192
  Iran-US Claims Tribunal 1.196

  judicially, arbitrators' duty to act 5.69
  jurisdiction 5.121
  lex arbitri 3.51
  litigation 6.84
  majority voting 9.119–9.122
  notice 1.66–1.68
  notice of arbitration 1.66–1.68
  notification of awards 9.169
  number of arbitrators 4.27
  parallel proceedings 7.52–7.54, 7.60
  partial and interim awards 9.02, 9.20
  pre-judgment of issue 4.138
  privacy 2.154
  procedure 1.78
  reasons 9.159
  separability or autonomy of arbitration clauses 2.105
  text App D
  truncated tribunals 4.160
  vacancies, falling 4.165
  witnesses 6.128
  writing 9.01
UNIDROIT Principles of International Commercial Contracts 3.177–3.181
  applicable law 3.178–3.181
  exclusion or limitation of liability 3.181
  good faith and fair dealing 3.178
  interpretation, aid to 3.179
  lex mercatoria 3.161, 3.168, 3.171–3.173
  non-national law 3.161, 3.168, 3.171–3.173, 3.178–3.184
  scope 3.178
  standard form contracts 3.184
  standards, as 3.179, 3.183
  Uniform Customs and Practice (UCP) for Documentary Credits 3.183
Uniform Customs and Practice (UCP) for Documentary Credits 3.176, 3.183
United States *see also* American Arbitration Association (AAA); Iran-US Claims Tribunal; North American Free Trade Agreement (NAFTA)
  arbitrability 2.127, 2.133–2.137, 2.142, 10.50, 11.101
  Arbitration Fairness Act 2007 2.127
  Argentina, BIT with 8.134
  bankruptcy 2.133, 2.142
  bilateral investment treaties (BITs) 8.118, 8.129–8.130, 8.134
  capacity 2.36
  challenges to awards 10.32, 10.47, 10.73–10.74
  Chile, free trade agreement with 8.11
  clarification of awards 9.189
  class arbitrations 2.225–2.231, 2.233–2.235, 3.31
  companies 2.36
  competition 2.133, 2.135–2.137, 10.51, 11.122
  confidentiality 2.173–2.175
  consolidation 2.239
  consumer contracts 2.127
  damages 9.45–9.49
  disclosure 2.174, 7.39–7.40, 7.43–7.44

Index

discovery 1.119–1.120, 6.85, 7.39–7.40, 7.43–7.44
documentary evidence 6.95
Dominican Republic and Central
  America-United States Free Trade
  Agreement (DR-CAFTA) 8.11
due process 10.55, 11.74, 11.76
duty of care of arbitrators 5.55
Ecuador, BIT with 8.118, 8.129–8.130
enforcement of awards 10.03
estoppel 2.53, 9.180, 9.185
ethical duties of arbitrators 5.79
expropriation without compensation 8.79
immunity 5.55, 5.65, 11.145, 11.154
interest 9.76
interim measures 7.26
issue estoppel 9.185
Jay Treaty 1794 1.191
jurisdiction 5.126, 11.79–11.80
lex arbitri 3.28–3.32
mistake of fact 10.78–10.80
pre-emption 3.31–3.32
pre-trial depositions 1.119
public policy 11.110, 11.122
punitive damages 9.45
refusal of enforcement or recognition 11.74, 11.76, 11.79–11.80, 11.86, 11.95, 11.123
res judicata 9.177, 9.180, 9.185
securities transactions 2.139
separability or autonomy of arbitration
  clauses 2.107
setting aside awards 10.55
state immunity 11.145, 11.154
status of awards, rulings which have 9.09, 9.12–9.13
subpoenas 5.19–5.20, 6.111
third parties 2.53
time limits 9.163–9.164, 11.33
truncated tribunals 4.156–4.158
waiver 2.210
witnesses 1.119, 6.111, 7.34–7.35
urgent action *see also* **emergency arbitrators**
  appointment of arbitrators 4.03
  evidence 7.38
  fast track arbitration 6.32–6.40
  interim measures 5.34, 7.17–7.18, 7.22, 7.27–7.28
  national courts 4.03, 7.17–7.19

vacancies, filling 4.152–4.168
  3 person tribunals 4.139
  ad hoc arbitrations 4.153
  arbitration agreements 2.82, 4.149
  assent to replacement to pleadings and
    documents 4.162
  challenges 4.139
  death or incapacity 4.167–4.168
  ICC Rules 4.166
  ICDR Rules 4.166
  insuring against a vacancy 4.167–4.168
  LCIA Rules 4.166
  medical examinations 4.168
  model arbitration clauses 2.82, 2.117

oral proceedings, before and after start
  of 4.162–4.165
procedure 4.139
retracing steps 4.162–4.165
transcripts, reading of 4.163
truncated tribunals 4.139, 4.154–4.161
UNCITRAL Rules 4.165
WIPO Rules 4.165
validity *see* **validity of arbitration agreements;**
  validity of awards
validity of arbitration agreements 2.13–2.30
  adjudicability 10.43–10.44
  capacity 11.66–11.67
  challenges to awards 10.43–10.44
  consent 1.53
  defective clauses 2.76
  Brussels I Regulation 5.128–5.129
  enforcement of arbitration agreements 2.23–2.24
  enforcement of awards 1.40
  existing disputes 2.05
  formal validity 2.13–2.24
  future disputes 2.05
  governing law 3.14
  ICC Rules 5.106–5.107
  lex arbitri 3.25
  model arbitration clauses 2.76
  New York Convention 1958 1.40, 3.14
  recognition of awards 1.40, 11.63, 11.66–11.70
  refusal of recognition and enforcement 11.63, 11.66–11.70
  relationships, requirement for defined 2.25–2.28
  severability 1.54
  subject matter capable of settlement by
    arbitration 2.29
  treaties and conventions 2.09–2.10
  UNCITRAL Model Law 1.40
  writing 2.13–2.24, 11.70
validity of awards
  arbitral institutions, rules of 9.143–9.145, 9.149
  arbitration agreements 9.142–9.145
  challenges 10.25
  contents of awards 9.151–9.161
  dissenting opinions 9.137
  form of awards 9.142–9.150
  governing law 9.146
  ICC Rules 9.149
  ICSID arbitration 9.144
  introductory sections of awards 9.147
  language 9.150
  LCIA Rules 9.149
  notification of awards 9.169–9.170
  refusal of recognition and enforcement 11.90
  registration or deposit of awards 9.171–9.172
  signatures 9.148–9.149
  time limits 9.162–9.168
  translations 9.150
  UNCITRAL Model Law 9.143
veil, piercing the corporate *see* **piercing the**
  corporate veil
Venezuela 8.12, 11.128, 11.137
venue, fixing the 4.177

Index

verbatim records 4.184–4.185, 6.160
video conferencing 6.41
Vienna Convention on the Law of Treaties 5.127, 8.64
Vietnam 11.114
visits to other countries by tribunals 3.60
voting *see* majority voting

waiver of right to arbitrate 2.204–2.211
  arbitration agreements 2.204–2.211
  class arbitration 2.234
  delay 2.211
  national courts 2.204–2.211
  stay of proceedings 2.206
  striking out 2.206, 2.211
  UNCITRAL Model Law 2.205
WIPO *see* World Intellectual Property Organisation (WIPO)/WIPO Rules
without notice *see ex parte* hearings
witnesses *see also* experts
  administrative secretaries 4.194
  admissibility 6.127–6.129
  affidavits 6.122
  applicable law 3.93
  arbitrators 1.104, 1.238, 5.20–5.21
  assistance of courts 6.131, 7.32–7.36
  attendance 4.172, 6.122, 6.130, 7.32–7.36
  breaks 6.179
  civil law countries 6.125
  coaching 6.179
  common law countries 6.176
  compellability 1.104, 5.20, 6.111
  conferencing 6.180–6.186
  corroboration 6.129
  costs 9.87, 9.88, 9.90, 9.92
  credibility 6.124, 6.173
  cross-examination 6.129, 6.177–6.178
  cultural differences 6.123, 6.125
  dispensing with witnesses 1.07
  documentary evidence 6.111–6.115
  ethics 6.123–6.124
  examination 6.173–6.179
  experienced arbitrators and counsel, practice of 1.238
  fact witness evidence 6.120–6.132, 6.177
  Hague Convention on Taking of Evidence Abroad 6.131
  hearing hours 4.188
  IBA Evidence Rules 6.121, 6.124, 6.175
  interim measures 7.32–7.36
  interpreters 4.182
  interviews 6.121, 6.124
  judicial assistance 6.131, 7.32–7.36
  LCIA Rules 6.124
  leading or closed questions 6.178
  national courts 7.32–7.36
  oaths 5.21, 6.122
  objections to questions 6.178
  overseas, taking evidence 6.130–6.132
  parties as witnesses 6.125–6.126, 6.129

  preparation 6.123–6.124
  presence after giving evidence 4.172
  presentation of witness evidence 6.122
  professional misconduct by lawyers 6.124
  re-examination 6.177
  reliability 6.120, 6.124
  requests for assistance 6.131
  rules of evidence 6.176
  seat, taking evidence outside the 6.130–6.132
  sequestration 6.179
  statements 3.49
  subpoenas 6.111, 6.130, 7.34–7.36
  taking evidence overseas 6.130–6.132
  third parties, *subpoenas of* 6.130, 7.38
  UNCITRAL Model Law 6.132, 7.32–7.34
  UNCITRAL Rules 6.128
  weight 6.127–6.129
  written evidence 3.49
wording of arbitration agreements, forms of 2.65–2.70
World Bank
  Guidelines on compensation for expropriation 8.146
  ICSID arbitration 1.186
World Court (International Court of Justice) 1.194–1.195
World Intellectual Property Organisation (WIPO)/WIPO Rules
  advisors 2.194
  appointment of arbitrators 1.189
  Arbitration Centre 1.189
  confidentiality 2.193–2.195
  inspection 6.152, 6.154
  trade secrets 2.193
  vacancies, falling 4.152, 4.165
writing requirement *see also* **written submissions or pleadings**
  agents, arbitration agreements concluded by 2.57
  arbitration agreements 1.44–1.48, 2.13–2.24
  awards 9.01
  definition 1.44–1.46, 1.222, 2.14–2.16
  electronic communications 1.45, 1.46–1.48, 2.16, 2.18–2.23
  enforcement of arbitration agreements 2.23
  enforcement of awards 1.44, 11.70
  New York Convention 1958 1.44–1.45, 2.14, 2.16
  oral agreements 2.21
  proof of agreements 2.17–2.18
  recognition of awards 1.44, 11.70
  record of agreements in any form 2.16, 2.18–2.23
  relaxation of rule 2.13, 2.16
  Revised UNCITRAL Model Law 1.222, 2.16–2.18
  signatures 2.15
  substance over form 2.21
  treaties and conventions 2.13
  UNCITRAL Model Law 1.46, 2.13, 2.16–2.17
  UNCITRAL Rules 9.01
  validity of agreements 2.13–2.24, 11.70

Index

written submissions or pleadings 6.65–6.74
  ad hoc arbitrations 6.65
  arbitral institutions, rules of 6.67–6.69
  conduct of an arbitration 6.65–6.74
  counterclaims 6.70
  delay 6.73
  deposit, amount of 6.66
  documentary evidence 6.92
  evidence-gathering 6.91
  ex parte hearings 6.196, 6.198
  extensions of time 6.73
  form 6.72–6.73
  further pleadings 6.204
  ICDR Rules 6.68
  ICSID arbitration 6.69
  LCIA Rules 6.67
  memorials 6.69, 6.73
  points of claim 6.72
  rejoinders 6.70
  replies 6.70
  sequential and simultaneous exchanges 6.69
  simultaneous exchange 6.69
  statements of case 6.67, 6.73
  statements of claim 6.66
  terminology 6.71–6.72
  time and length limits 6.73–6.74
  vacancies, falling 4.162

young practitioners' groups 4.70

Zimbabwe, expropriation in 8.81